PSYCHOLOGY LIBRARY EDITIONS:
PERCEPTION

Volume 27

PERCEIVING, ACTING AND KNOWING

PERCEIVING, ACTING AND KNOWING

Toward an Ecological Psychology

Edited by
ROBERT SHAW AND JOHN BRANSFORD

Routledge
Taylor & Francis Group
LONDON AND NEW YORK

First published in 1977 by Lawrence Erlbaum Associates, Inc.

This edition first published in 2017
by Routledge
2 Park Square, Milton Park, Abingdon, Oxon OX14 4RN

and by Routledge
711 Third Avenue, New York, NY 10017

Routledge is an imprint of the Taylor & Francis Group, an informa business

British Library Cataloguing in Publication Data
A catalogue record for this book is available from the British Library

ISBN: 978-1-138-68824-7 (Set)
ISBN: 978-1-315-22895-2 (Set) (ebk)
ISBN: 978-1-138-20386-0 (Volume 27) (hbk)
ISBN: 978-1-138-20505-5 (Volume 27) (pbk)
ISBN: 978-1-315-46793-1 (Volume 27) (ebk)

Publisher's Note
The publisher has gone to great lengths to ensure the quality of this reprint but points out that some imperfections in the original copies may be apparent.

Disclaimer
The publisher has made every effort to trace copyright holders and would welcome correspondence from those they have been unable to trace.

PERCEIVING, ACTING, AND KNOWING

Toward an Ecological Psychology

EDITED BY
ROBERT SHAW
JOHN BRANSFORD

LAWRENCE ERLBAUM ASSOCIATES, PUBLISHERS
1977 Hillsdale, New Jersey

DISTRIBUTED BY THE HALSTED PRESS DIVISION OF
JOHN WILEY & SONS
New York Toronto London Sydney

Lawrence Erlbaum Associates, Inc., Publishers
62 Maria Drive
Hillsdale, New Jersey 07642

Distributed solely by Halsted Press Division
John Wiley & Sons, Inc., New York

Library of Congress Cataloging in Publication Data

Main entry under title:

Perceiving, acting, and knowing.

"The chapters in this volume derive from a conference . . . held by the Center for Research in Human Learning at the University of Minnesota, July 23–August 17, 1973."

1. Cognition–Congresses. 2. Perception–Congresses. I. Shaw, Robert E. II. Bransford, John. III. Minnesota. University. Center for Research in Human Learning.
BF311.P347 153.7 76–47481
ISBN 0-470-99014-7
ISBN 978-1-1382-0505-5

Contents

Preface

This volume is neither just for the specialist nor just for the novice. Rather, it should appeal to anyone sufficiently interested in psychology to have obtained a sense of its current history. This book is not simply a "state of the art" book on recent psychological research, although a wide range of fundamental research topics is carefully discussed—such topics as perception, action, memory, development, esthetics, language, and speech. Nor do the essays contained in this volume merely reflect a "business as usual" attitude about contemporary psychological theory. Through these essays the authors express a collective attitude that a careful scrutiny of the fundamental tenets of contemporary psychology may be needed. In some essays specific faults in the foundations of an area are discussed, and suggestions are made for remedying them. In other essays the authors flirt with more radical solutions, namely, beginning from new foundations altogether.

Although the authors do not present a monolithic viewpoint, a careful reading of all their essays under one cover reveals a glimpse of a new framework by which theory and research may be guided. Hence, the subtitle of the book, *Toward an Ecological Psychology,* distills the essence of their tacit agreement, namely, a deeply felt commitment that a full appreciation of what the animal's or human's world is like provides an indispensable context of constraint for understanding how information about such a world may be processed. Here a consensus obtains that justifies the book as it did the holding of the conference from which the book was engendered. The success of our joint efforts represented by this volume may well be likened to the proverbial blind men who attempt to ascertain the nature of a large and complicated animal from multifarious and necessarily limited viewpoints: There is no argument as to the existence of the beast but only over what form it might ultimately assume.

The chapters in this volume derive from a conference on Perceiving, Acting, and Knowing held by the Center for Research in Human Learning at the University of Minnesota, July 23–August 17, 1973. In order to better understand reasons for including the present chapters, however, it is necessary to consider happenings whose history extends even farther back in time.

In one way or another, most of the contributors to this volume have been associated with the Center for Research in Human Learning at the University of Minnesota. Many contributors were graduate students at the center (Bransford, Franks, Mace, McCarrell, Pittenger, Strange, Verbrugge, Weimer); others were postdoctoral associates (Pufall, Shankweiler, Shaw). Still others had been visiting professors or lecturers whose ideas played important roles in directing thinking at the center (Cunningham, Gibson, Pribram). Three contributors were faculty members of the center (Jenkins, Maratsos, Shaw) and one contributor (Nitsch) was a student (and frequently a teacher) of previous center students. Only Hester, Loftus, and Turvey remain. Hester was a graduate school colleague of Shaw at Vanderbilt, so we became aware of his interest in art and perception. The conference provided an excellent opportunity to hear his ideas. Loftus was one of the pioneers in the newly budding field of semantic memory research, and the conference provided an ideal vehicle for hearing her. Turvey's work on action and perception was extremely relevant, so it seemed almost inconceivable to hold the conference without him.

The spark that initiated the Minnesota conference was the Pennsylvania State University Conference on Cognition and the Symbolic Processes (see Weimer & Palermo, 1974). Participants at that conference explored some highly exciting ideas and the many participants expressed the desire to explore them in greater detail. The present editors therefore proposed the Minnesota Conference and view it as an outgrowth of the Pennsylvania State University Conference. Both conferences were oriented toward the development of an Ecological Psychology, a theme that is further explored in the introductory chapter to this volume.

We are indebted to many people for their contributions to the conference and the present volume. Our primary debt is to the faculty and staff at the Center for Research in Human Learning for helping the conference run so smoothly. Kathy Casey deserves a special note of thanks in this regard. The funds for the conference was provided by NICHD Grant HD-00098, and we are extremely grateful for this.

Jerry Wald did a great deal of the editing. We cannot thank him enough for his outstanding work. Bill Mace also contributed his highly skilled expertise to the editing process, and we are extremely grateful to him. Thanks are also due to Lawrence Erlbaum and his staff for their skillful and enthusiastic support while preparing this book.

Much of the editing was done while Robert Shaw was a fellow at the Center for Advanced Study in the Behavioral Sciences at Stanford. This support is most gratefully acknowledged. John Bransford is also grateful for support from the National Institute of Education (NE-6-00-3-0026) while working on the book.

Our greatest thanks extends to James J. Jenkins for his leadership during the first ten years of the Center for Research in Human Learning. Through his guidance and enthusiasm, the center became an exciting environment for exploring new directions and approaches. We are extremely pleased to dedicate this volume to him.

1

Introduction: Psychological Approaches to the Problem of Knowledge

Robert Shaw
University of Connecticut

John Bransford
Vanderbilt University

The major issue addressed by the authors of this volume concerns the problem of how we obtain and act upon knowledge about the world. Obviously, no single nor simple answer to such a complex problem can be given. Yet the problem of knowledge has been the central focus of psychological theories since the inception of the field as an experimental science over a century ago. Act psychology, structuralism, functionalism, radical behaviorism, Gestalt psychology, neobehaviorism, and, finally, information-processing theories have all attempted answers to this problem—with relative degrees of success.

The authors in the present volume offer hypotheses, speculations and tentative solutions to aspects of the problem of knowledge. Since they present a diversity of ideas, it seems helpful to read the various chapters with some guiding questions in mind. The purpose of this chapter is to provide a few such questions that the reader might add to his or her own.

Among the many significant questions raised in this volume there is one of paramount concern to us all, namely, whether the traditional approach to psychological theory and research which emphasizes the *how* of psychological processing might not need supplementation by an alternative approach that emphasizes the *what* of psychological processing. If we conceive of humans and animals as information processing systems, then perhaps it would be wise to ask not only how such information is processed but also what the nature of such information might be. One answer, and the one we wish to examine in this chapter, runs like a thread throughout the fabric of this volume, tying together the variety of ideas into a coordinated patchwork: What is the nature of the epistemic process by which people know their world and the nature of the world that it might be known?

We call the common thread of interest in this question the *ecological* attitude—an attitude toward theory and research that fully appreciates the world as the source of information by which animals and humans perceive events, comprehend circumstances, and act successfully in the service of biological, psychological, and social needs. To the extent, however, that there exists dissension among the authors of the subsequent chapters as to what constitutes an adequate answer to the what-question posed by the ecological approach, to that extent the issues separating traditional information-processing approaches from the ecological approach are sharply dramatized. To aid the reader in an appreciation of these issues we turn now to a discussion of the assumptions of each approach.

PART ONE: THE ECOLOGICAL APPROACH TO PSYCHOLOGY

The Need for a New Approach

In the attempt to develop new approaches to old problems, inevitably questions arise regarding the unanalyzed and, therefore, unchallenged presuppositions tacitly or explicitly accepted by the field. To establish a new brand of psychological theory necessarily requires that several fundamental tenets of traditional, contemporary psychology be challenged and, if possible, overthrown to make way for the new approach. However, before presenting the tenets of the ecological approach to the problem of knowledge, it will be useful to consider some of the major assumptions and hypotheses that underlie current cognitive psychology, since this is the area of psychology which has assumed responsibility for solving the problem of knowledge.

The man–machine analogy. Current cognitive theory may best be characterized as the information-processing approach—an approach that feeds upon the man–machine, or brain–computer, analogy. This analogy has been the staple of most psychological theorists' diets for the last decade or so.

The information-processing approach, more than any previous one, seems to recognize the need for precision when characterizing psychological processes. In their search for ways to construct models that explain how knowledge might be represented, stored, and retrieved from memory, it was natural for psychologists to turn for help to the fast developing field of computer science, once the promise of behaviorism was seen to be overblown. After all, what seemed to be analogical problems were being explicitly addressed by computer scientists in their attempts to understand complex information-processing devices. How natural it was to extend the concept of computer to include the psychological machinery of humans in order to see if analogs of the information-processing solutions might not be found to hold there as well. Thus, there is no great mystery in explaining how current cognitive theory came to rely so heavily on computer science concepts and its modeling techniques. For many cognitive theorists their prayers for precision seemed to have been answered.

There should be little quarrel with the contention that this metaphor has in many ways served our field well, for it has helped to free many psychologists from the excessive restrictions of radical behaviorism. Similarly, this mechanistic metaphor has reinstated a serious and worthwhile concern for understanding how knowledge is represented and organized within humans and animals as self-organizing, knowledge-gathering systems. Moreover, the acceptance of the analogy of cognitive structures to computational structures (for example, networks, hierarchies, or heterarchies of control functions) has the additional virtue of fostering an appreciation for exactitude in theory that ultimately demands mathematically rigorous models (Cunningham, this volume). All this is surely an improvement over the simplistic serial processing models offered by stimulus-response theory over the preceding decades.

Yet we psychologists can not be content to rest on our theoretical laurels, especially when garnered so easily from the successes of another field. It would be both unfair and unwise to expect the solutions given by computer scientists to their problems to also qualify mutatis mutandi as solutions to our own problems, since serious questions can be raised whether or not the two sets of problems are even abstractly the same (Shaw & McIntyre, 1974).

It is wise to remember that computer scientists' systems are artificially contrived while ours are naturally evolved; their systems are passive while ours are active; their systems are purposeless (except in a second-hand way) while ours pursue primary goals of self-survival and adaptation; their systems, as complex as they are, are still astronomically simpler than those psychologists must understand. And what of the role of emotional, personality, and social factors in determining the questions appropriate to humans but as yet undefined for artificial systems? Indeed, to be realistic, we should ask who should be the tutor and who the tutored? Consequently, it is not unreasonable to suggest that at this juncture in the history of these two young sciences the most relevant concepts computer science may offer psychology are still in the offing. Thus, not pessimism but prudence counsels psychologists to assume a wait-and-see attitude before pronouncing sentence upon the man–machine analogy. Indeed, the profound question of what constitutes a machine hangs in the balance over and against the question of what is a human. The answer may surprise us all.

On the other hand, there is the danger that premature application of the man–machine analogy to psychology, to the exclusion of other approaches, may unnecessarily restrict our thinking about problems whose solutions demand greater theoretical flexibility than strict adherence to the analogy allows. For instance, as psychologists, there is a natural and understandable tendency to ignore certain complications of our phenomena for the sake of expediency in either doing experiments or constructing models. Rarely do we clearly enunciate any method by which theoretical principles designed to explain animal and human behavior in the laboratory might be generalized back to the natural contexts in which the behaviors originated. We tend to forget that humans and animals are active, investigatory creatures driven by definite intents through a complex, changing environment replete with meaning at a variety of levels of analysis.

Thus we feel no tinge of theoretical compunction in blithely comparing such active, knowledge-seeking beings with unconscious, static machines that lack a wit of natural motivation. Unlike humans and animals, who perceptually mine the world for information on a need-to-know basis, artificial systems can only soak up information passively by being spoon-fed batches of alpha-numeric characters that have been conceptually predigested by human programmers. In sharp contrast to natural information, such symbolic information is devoid of any natural meaning for the machine and, therefore, can play no role in either its adaptation or survival in a relatively dust-free, humidity controlled, air-conditioned environment. In such a sterile model for man, perceiving becomes a passive process and knowing a purposeless one, and as for action (that is, purposive behavior), it remains nonexistent.

Of course, it would be grossly unfair to criticize the computer science area for the rather myopic view many psychologists have taken of such problems, since too often the best concepts that computer science offers are much better than what psychologists elect to borrow. The theory of locomoting, special-purpose computers (robots), as well as current attempts by cyberneticists to devise prosthetic devices based on computer components (for example, artificial limbs and helmets with video inputs to the tactile system to aid the blind) are among the avant garde projects which may inspire new life in the nearly dead man–machine metaphor, and thereby open fresh vistas for psychological theorists. Again it is wiser to counsel patience than pessimism regarding the ultimate worth of the metaphorical extension of the techniques of either field to the province of the other. Rather let us critically scrutinize the current coinage of the metaphor so as to assay what pragmatists would call its "cash value" as a working hypothesis.

Some light might be shed on the nature of the quest for alternatives to the man–machine analogy if a sharp line of delineation is drawn around those epistemological questions explicitly asked, or tacitly assumed by the field, and those equally significant questions given short shrift. Typically, the questions given short shrift are those concerning the nature and origins of the information processed; how ecologically significant information is selected; and how its value to the animal or human might be determined. The latter questions focus on *what* is processed whereas current theory focuses on the *how* of processing. Attempts to reduce questions regarding *what* is processed to questions regarding *how* what is processed *is* processed are doomed to failure because the two questions fail to address the same issue.

More specifically, the man–machine analogy is overdrawn when human perception is likened to the decoding process by which computers compile data, and human knowledge to the concept of retrieval of information from storage. The man–machine analogy becomes a hindrance rather than an aid to psychological theory when it derails our thinking about how living creatures gather and act upon knowledge in dynamic natural contexts. Such questions can in no way be reduced to questions of how information is represented, stored, or retrieved from storage by static devices in artificially controlled environments. Rather the question should be how information "stored" in the world can be perceptually extracted by active, investigative creatures in their relatively successful effort to survive calamity and achieve well-being.

If the ecological approach merits any serious consideration as an alternative approach to psychological theory, then it might best be revealed by contrasting this approach with the more popular one of information processing psychology. In fairness, however, it should be remembered that although the ecological approach may at this time be only programmatic, in the sense that it offers embryonic theory sketches in the place of fully adequate theories of the knowledge-gathering activities of humans and animals, the information-processing approach is no less programmatic. So far it too has failed to offer adequate solutions to any of the major problems of psychology (for example, perception, memory, attention, action, language, motivation, emotion, personality). The timetable for success of any approach cannot be predicted, although the probability of success might be, if we but consider which of the approaches poses the significant questions most sensibly. The judicious allocation of the resources of our field demands that we avoid, if we can, the vain pursuit of will-o-the-wisp questions.

Let us not, however, delude ourselves: Our field is much too young, our theories too sketchy, the mettle of our techniques too untried, to condemn with certitude any approach without fair trial. Consequently, the purpose of this introductory chapter (and the whole book for that matter) is not to reject out of hand any existing program of research, but to make way for an alternative program—the ecological approach.

In the next sections of this chapter, we address several fundamental issues of psychological theory from the vantage point of the ecological approach, questions such as: What is the nature of knowing? Is perception direct or mediated? What is the role of inference and memory in perceiving the true properties of the world? And, finally, what are the recalcitrant issues that most sharply distinguish current information processing approaches to psychological theory from the alternative ecological approach adopted by many of the authors (although not all) of this volume. Since the last question is the guiding thread of this essay, it will be discussed most fully.

The Ecological and Information-Processing Approaches Compared

A wise adage asserts that *man proposes but nature disposes!* This aphorism elegantly expresses the fundamental tenet of the ecological approach—that the nature of humans is inextricably intertwined with the nature of a world in which they live, move, and have their being. In short, the ecological attitude is founded on the fundamental belief that man is indeed the mirror of nature. This view does not suggest, however, that psychological phenomena may be reduced to physical ones, but that physical phenomena be interpreted in the light of their relevance to psychological phenomena—an attempt, if you will, to "ecologize" physics so as to understand better how the world provides a habitat for humans as knowing-agents, and not just as physical or biological objects. Thus the ecological attitude germinates in the minds of theorists who come to the stark realization that humans, as must all living things that survive, depend upon their natural and cultural environments for knowledge as well as victuals. For such theorists it is impossible to accept any longer models for man whose only virtue is that they were contrived to function efficiently in artificial contexts.

The environment in which animals and humans have evolved, and upon which they depend for their well-being can be construed from both the material and functional viewpoints: The *material* environment of a species provides resources in the form of "hard" goods, such as air, water, food, shelter, mates and tools, while the *functional* environment provides resources in the form of "soft" goods, such as the requisite knowledge-gathering experiences for planning and executing adaptive actions. By *adaptive* actions we mean, rather redundantly, those perceptual and behavioral activities by which the hard or soft goods needed for survival and well-being are secured. Taken together, the sum total of the material and functional aspects of the general environment required by a particular species in order to achieve optimal adaptation, that is, the requisite hard and soft goods, defines an ecological *niche* for that species. Hence the ecological niche for an animal is not *where* it lives (its *habitat*) but *how* it lives. (See Gibson, this volume.)

The ecological approach calls for nothing less than a complete understanding of the complex and everchanging relationship of person-as-knower to the environment-as-known. Hence a complete understanding of the informational aspects of the ecological niche, as well as the behavioral consequences of such information, is of paramount concern to the ecological approach, regardless of the animal under study—humans not excluded. But, as we shall see, the concept of ecologically significant information (Mace, this volume; Shaw, McIntyre, & Mace, 1974) is as radically different from the concept of information used in communication theory, computer science, or some psychological theories currently in vogue, as the concept of ecologically significant action patterns is radically different from the behaviorists' concept of unintentional animal movements (Turvey, Weimer, this volume).

It is natural, however, when attempting to clarify a new approach to problems in an area, that the old way of asking the questions come under fire. The subtitle of the next chapter by William Mace is a dramatic case in point: *Ask not what's inside your head but what your head is inside of.* This way of putting the issue of how best to represent knowledge speaks boldly in favor of the ecological attitude, namely, that as theorists we not lose sight of our major phenomenon: people and animals are knowing-agents who live and learn within a broader context of epistemic constraints than subjective theories of knowledge would have us believe. (It is ironic, given our behaviorist heritage, that the pendulum has swung so far back in the other direction that most contemporary cognitive theories tend to be subjective in just this way.)

Mace's restatement reminds one of Ryle's (1949) wise admonition, too often unheeded by psychologists, to beware of careless usage of spatial metaphors when addressing the question of how knowledge accrues. Perception, even analogically speaking, is not a process by which the senses, like some *itinerant* mailman, collects coded messages about world facts and tosses them into the mailbox of the mind to be deciphered, sorted, and stored in memorial pigeon-holes by some mysterious little postal clerk and perused by him at some later time.

Such a view needlessly dichotomizes the act of perceiving from the act of knowing just as it does the act of knowing from the act of remembering. One might ask, if we glibly treat these processes as separate, as many information-processing theories tend to do, if there is any real hope of getting our Humpty Dumpty theory back together again. (Bransford, McCarrell, Franks & Nitsch, Jenkins; this volume).

Even worse, by positing a functional sequence of information-processing stages that suggest a spatial and temporal arrangement (for example, iconic store, short-term memory, long-term memory), such theories become unavoidably muddled when asked to indicate the stage at which, or by which, a percept is experienced, a memory recalled, a concept understood, language comprehended, a problem solved, or an action planned. (See Jenkins, Jiménez-Pabón, Shaw, & Sefer, 1974, for an alternative approach.) Notice the problems the sequential stage model is heir to: Who does the experiencing in this model? Must we posit some little man who views the output of the final stage of the processing sequence? If we do, what is to prevent us from asking for still another theory to explain his experience? Would we not then be forced to posit within his tiny head a more miniscule sequence of processing stages complete with its own tiny observer to witness its final output? And then, within the cranium of this Lilliputian observer, are we not forced to posit still a more miniscule sequence with its diminutive observer, ad infinitum?

How do we stop passing the seat of the experience, like the proverbial buck, from the highest level of processing ever inward through a potentially infinite set of nested sequences of processing stages? Once begun, by what principle might the regress be terminated? No one has yet suggested a cogent way of getting such theories off the slippery slide of a regress through an infinite phalanx of homunculi, once the chaining and nesting of processing stages has been assumed. However, since the homunculus hypothesis seems to enjoy an atavistic claim on each generation of theorizing, let us pause to consider it in more detail.

The homunculus hypothesis. Both Attneave (1961) and Bullock (1961) freely endorse a hierarchical notion of the homunculus hypothesis which they believe to be nonregressive and nonghostly. However, neither view offers a coherent theory of how such homunculi concepts can be entertained without first solving the semantic categories problem, that is, the problem of providing a finite representation of the potentially infinite set of behaviors and perceptions available to animals and humans. In short, it is the problem of how to provide descriptions of what is perceived, or what constitutes acts, that is sufficiently accurate to be empirically true and sufficiently economical to be theoretically manageable.

Bullock (1961) quite simply identifies the experiences underlying our knowledge of perceptions and actions with the converging firing patterns of neurons. Thus, he unequivocally endorses a strong version of what philosophers call the *identity solution* to the mind–body question. Although he believes this hierarchical model avoids the infinite regress problem for homunculi, since the number of neural levels posited is finite, it opens up a regress of a different sort—a regress due to the unrestricted differentiation of semantic categories. Since Bullock's hierarchical approach is a very popular one in contemporary psychology, let us see where such theories go astray.

Bullock suggests that for any given behavior there must ultimately be at least one neuron that "decides" whether to initiate the behavior or not. Since rational behaviors are nearly always decided on the basis of current perceptual experiences, we must assume that this ultimate neuron (or, at least the collection of "cardinal" neurons feeding it) is also the seat of such experiences. Consequently, there must be as many neural homunculi of this sort as there are coherent perceptions or behaviors. The crucial question that must be resolved if this theoretical scheme is going to work at all is what counts as a coherent pattern of experience. If the potential number of such experiences is left unrestricted, in principle, then, in violation of Occam's wise admonition, the theory sinks into the mire of speculation carried under by the weight of too many imponderables.

But surely the speaking, writing, or reading of sentences qualifies as a coherent experience, as does the recognizing of objects and events, or the solving of problems—a myriad of which confront us day-by-day. Moreover, since the collection of such sets of experiences is astronomically large, with each set comprised of a potentially infinite membership, it is difficult to see how pandemonium-like, hierarchical schemes help at all.

By postulating neural homunculi that correspond in a one-to-one fashion with such experiences, Bullock does not avoid a regress into a potentially infinite hierarchy of conscious entities. The fallacy is in believing that the finite number of candidate neurons, which *materially* restrict the number of causal supports for experiences, in any way *functionally* restricts the variety of experiences possible. What is needed for such theoretic schemes to be useful is a principled restriction on the categories of experiences available—a careful delimitation of *what* is known.

Clearly, as Bullock himself argues, there seems to exist considerable redundancy in the neural support for experience; the mapping of categories of experience onto neural functions as demanded by the mind–body indentity hypothesis might just as likely be one-to-many as many-to-one. Therefore, if one-to-many, that is, if there are more potential neural firing patterns than meaningful experiences, given the finiteness and mortality of man, then the problem is how the vast inventory of such functional supports for experiences might be realistically restricted. Thus, theories like Bullocks do not suffer from being too weak but from being too powerful—an embarrassment of riches rather than a paucity of concepts.

The crucial question then is how the taxonomy of significant experiences can be realistically restricted, rather than how such experiences might be functionally supported once they are clearly defined. The ecological approach to psychology, with its concept of ecologically significant information, purports to offer a methodological tool for trimming the fat from such theories of *how* processing occurs. (Gibson, Mace, this volume.)

Attneave (1961) offers a more unitary view of the homunculus hypothesis, but like Bullock's pluralistic view also fails to avoid the semantic regress, that is, entailing an unrestricted set of categories of experience. He argues that the homunculus is really just an "organism-within-an-organism" which possesses its own receptor surface nested within the receptor surface of the organism. "It is supposed," he asserts, "that each receptor at the surface of H [the homunculus] is sensitive to a class of objects or events; for example, that the homunculus has a receptor for dogs, another for pianos, another for automobiles, and so on [p. 778]."

Although Attneave means the above classes of experiences to be treated as variables, and hence to be to some extent abstract, he fails to explain how the number of variables might be kept below the maximum possible. Since this maximum is clearly a potentially infinite set, again a set of principled restrictions is required if his theory is to avoid the regress of infinitely differentiating semantic categories.

To be fair, it should be pointed out that this semantic regress is not the one Attneave or Bullock were trying to avoid in their theory sketches, but it is one that is just as damning for a theory of knowledge as the sequential stage regress entailed by other information-processing theories. Indeed, it is the semantic regress which has all but brought to a halt the psycholinguistic revolution of the 1960s that was inaugurated by Chomsky's transformational theory of English syntax.

To the extent that our theories cannot avoid violation of Occam's wise admonition not to multiply theoretical entities beyond necessity, the regressive fallacy will be a thwart to cogent theory construction in psychology. It matters little whether such regresses are potentially infinite in principle or of just theoretically unmanageable finite lengths, the outcome is the same—unacceptable theory.

Thus, we must conclude that where sequential stage models offer no true solution to the problem of psychological experience but only a corridor of mirrors to endlessly reflect ourselves, so hierarchical theories like the above offer only a way of endlessly reflecting inwardly the infinite facets of the world. If the ecological approach can avoid either form of the regressive fallacy, it will have to be considered a front runner in the scientific sweepstakes.

Hence, given the desire to avoid the regresses arising from the use of vague spatiotemporal metaphors or the assumption of unrestricted categories of experience, it is wise to avoid altogether certain insidious forms of theoretic questions that entail these problems. We now see that such questions as, Where does the last stage of perceptual processing occur? or, Where in the sequence of stages can we fit the knowing-agent? are philosophical red herrings which lead our theories astray. In contrast, we shall argue that the ecological approach provides at least one sensible response to such questions. From the ecological viewpoint the knowing-agent is not some final stage in the epistemic process, some caboose at the end of a train of ideas, nor even a missing link in a cause-and-effect chain; rather the knowing-agent is the *totalité* of the process itself. Knowing is itself the process which resides neither wholely within the subject as a punctiform effect or response, nor wholely within the world as a cause or stimulus; rather, as an ecological concept; it stands like the mythical Colossus of Rhodes, astride the physical and psychological domains, one foot planted firmly on either shore. (More will be said about this in Part Two.)

The ecological approach, unlike information-processing theories, denies also that nature, in any sense, communicates messages to us written in a kind of sensory shorthand which, to be comprehended, must be translated by a phalanx of cognitive homunculi into a more readable longhand for perusal by whom no one can say. Rather, it seems more parsimonious to assume that evolution has rendered such busy work unnecessary by designing perceptual systems, naturally selected over eons of practical use, to extract meaning directly from the structured energy propagations without benefit of any other stage of epistemic mediation.

Hence, when asked where the buck of knowledge ceases to be passed, or where the epistemic regress ends, the ecological psychologist responds: At the beginning of the process; it stops with perception, the process upon which the intrinsic meaning of man's relationship to his world is founded. It is the perceiver who knows and the knower who perceives, just as it is the world that is both perceived and known. Neither memory, nor inference, nor any other epistemic process than perception intervenes between the knowing-agent and the world it knows, for knowing is a direct rather than an indirect process.

PART TWO: DIRECT VERSUS INDIRECT THEORIES OF KNOWING

> But do I hear a shout indirectly, when I hear the echo? If I touch you with a barge-pole, do I touch you indirectly? Or if you offer me a pig in a poke, might I feel the pig indirectly—*through* the poke?
>
> [J. L. Austin, 1962, p. 16]

It is sometimes argued that we do not perceive the world and its contents directly, rather we perceive something else in its place from which we then infer the world. Candidates for this "something else" have traditionally been such things as sense-data (for example, pointillistic patches of color, spots of texture, or margins of light contrast), or our own retinal images, or even states of our central nervous systems. Thus, from the standpoint of these hypotheses, we do not experience the world per se when engaged in the act conventionally known as "perceiving," rather we infer the world's objective existence from experience with the surrogate phantasms that it somehow gives rise to.

The ecological approach disagrees with the hypotheses that perception is indirect whereas most information-processing theories agree with it. However, there are several points of agreement between the two approaches that must be discussed before their differences can be fully appreciate. These points of agreement revolve around classic philosophical positions regarding the relations of a knower to his world.

Realism versus Nominalism and Phenomenalism

Traditionally, the hypothesis of *realism,* in opposition to nominalism, asserts that abstract concepts or ideas may refer to properties, relations, objects, classes, etc., that have a real objective existence, that is, that their existence does not depend on their being perceived or thought about.

By contrast *nominalism* asserts that abstract things, such as classes and relations, do not exist but may be denoted by words as useful fictions. From the standpoint of this doctrine such fictions must be constructed by the mind from the elementaristic aspects of objects as they might appear in isolation from other elementaristic aspects. (Later we will see how the doctrine of indirect realism, the version of realism championed by most information-processing approaches smacks of nominalism and how direct realism, the version of realism championed by the ecological approach, attempts to explain the direct apprehension of abstract entities, invariances, without recourse to cognitive construction.)

For our purposes, the reading we would like to give to the hypothesis of realism is as follows: *An external and objective world truly exists with real properties, abstract or otherwise, that may be experienced by virtue of perception rather than experienced as fictitious constructions by virtue of intellective, mnemonic or imaginative processes.* In short, it is the belief that perceptual knowledge of a world that exists apart from ourselves is truly possible.

This view is also opposed to *phenomenalism* which asserts that all that truly exist are the phenomena we experience. Radical adherence to this view would deny what realists believe to be important distinctions between subjective and objective aspects of knowledge. To our knowledge, no living psychologist currently embraces the doctrine of phenomenalism. Therefore, whatever distinguishes the ecological approach from the information-processing approach, one can be sure that it is not the issue separating realism and phenomenalism.

What does distinguish the two approaches, however, is the brand of realism adhered to. Let us consider the various versions of the realist hypothesis which may or may not be relevant to distinguishing between the two approaches to psychological theory.

The Varieties of Realism

Direct versus indirect realisms. Theories of knowledge, and the perceptual theories entailed by them, come in two basic varieties: direct and indirect.[1] Theorists who proceed on the assumption that we actually perceive the world, its properties, and contents directly instead of some surrogate for the world accept the hypothesis of *direct* realism. By contrast, realist theories that deny direct experience of the world but assume we experience the world secondhand, through the mediation of a representation or imagistic construct, accept the hypothesis of *indirect* realism. The difference between these two types of realism is not that one is perceptual while the other is nonperceptual, say, cognitive or intellectual; rather they differ with respect to what is believed to be perceived, the world or some world substitute.

Put differently: The indirect realist rejects the idea that the world as such is the *proximal* cause of our perceptual experience, what we experience is believed to be one of the links in the cause-and-effect chain that binds the perceiver to the distal cause of his percept in the world.

The sequence of causal links presumably consists of (a) the object or event, (b) the ambient energy modulated by it and propagated to the point of pickup in the receptor organ, (c) the receptor system itself including neural tracts and brain processes, and, finally, (d) the occurrence of the perceptual experience as part of the agent's state of phenomenological awareness.

Science has taught us that a break anywhere in this causal chain from object to percept prevents the phenomenological experience from occurring. For instance, without light no object is seen; without an intact eyeball, properly functioning optic nerve tract or brain processes, the perceiver is functionally blind. Thus, the items (a)–(d) are all a necessary part of the causal *support* of the percept.

When fleshed out in appropriate detail, the above story is called the *causal theory of perception* (Russell, 1927), a story so widely accepted among contemporary scientists that to deny it immediately places one's credibility as a theorist in jeopardy. We do not mention this familiar story of how percepts are presumably "caused" in order to contest it, but to remind ourselves and the reader that it is only a hypothesis. As the proverbial saying goes, sequential arguments

[1] Later we will have reason to question seriously the usefulness of the indirect/direct realism distinction when applied to perception. For the time being, however, we will explore the distinction in a manner unprejudiced by this anticipation until it proves too problematic to continue to do so.

are only as strong as their weakest links. It is prudent, therefore, to recognize that the causal chain endorsed by this theory may have several weak links; moreover, which of the links presumed weakest is usually symptomatic of the version of realism held. Let us now explore each of the links for possible fractures.

The mind–body problem. The perennial obstacle to a successful causal theory of perception is the so-called "mind–body" problem. Often it is argued that the linkage between world and percept is not properly homogeneous, since unlike the physical and biological links, the connection of final brain state to percept is problematic. How can a physical causal process give rise to a nonphysical (mental) experience? How can something so immaterial be the effect of a causal sequence that is quite material? Now is not the time, however, to attempt to resolve this problem, but it is worth noting that the problem of the relation of mind to body is not resolved by the causal theory of perception and, therefore, can play no role in its popular acceptance.

A second weak link in the causal theory of perception supposed by many indirect realists is in the world-to-receptor hookup, a problem to which we now turn.

Adumbrative Theories

Some indirect theorists believe that the world is itself the weak link in the causal argument, that it fails to structure the energy distributions at the receptor organ in a manner sufficiently rich or precise to allow perception alone to be the source of our knowledge. Consequently, they argue that some constructive process must intervene to enrich, or adumbrate, the anemic perceptual information. The constructive process putatively required to enrich the available perceptual information, usually believed to be manifested in retinal images or brain states, is sometimes thought to be intellectual (inferential) (Helmholtz, 1925; Brunswik, 1956) or anamnesic (memorial) (Gregory, 1970) or both. Recently, in nonscientific circles, it has even become popular to speculate that the constructive process, in keeping with certain Eastern philosophies, may be imaginative (Pearce, 1971).

The constructivist version of indirect perceptual theory, however, should not be confused with nonconstructivist versions of that theory which believe that although the retinal image or brain state is what is perceived, these constructs nevertheless provide unimpoverished, reasonable facsimiles of the world. In this case they are not viewed as intellectually enriched constructs but as high fidelity cross-sections of the flow of information from the world. More will be said about such nonconstructive versions of the indirect realists' hypothesis later.

Two versions of adumbrative or constructive theories deserve mention, those that partake of a priorism and those that partake of a weaker form of nativism.

The former is completely at odds with the ecological approach while some versions of the latter are much less so.

A priorism and constructive theory. To adumbrate literally means "to give faint shadow or resemblance of; to outline or sketch; or to foreshadow or prefigure." Consequently, the epithet *adumbrative* should be applied to all theories that claim information about the world must be restored to the retinal image, or cerebral states, in order to account for the observed richness of perceptual experiences and their close fit to things they represent. Merely, to call such theories "constructive" fails to capture the fact that the intervening construct is not just a haphazard or spontaneous arrangement of properties which, by sheer luck, happens to reflect the structure of the world in an appropriate fashion. Rather, the constructively augmented experience is presumed to be constrained somehow to fit a faint memory of what is perceived, or is in some other remarkable way prefigured by inferential processes to correspond to the perceived object.

The constructive theorist, therefore, to make this theory work, must explain how the constructive process becomes constrained by, and attuned to, physical reality in just such a way as to adumbrate, or sketch in, the ambiguous or missing portions of the retinal image, or cerebral state, so as to provide a true picture of reality. Without such an explanation, the constructive process becomes utter imagination and, thereby, violates the basic tenet of realism which initiated its birth.

Immanual Kant offered the most thorough attempt to face up to the problem of how raw experience (or what he called *sensible intuition*) is appropriately adumbrated by intellect in conformity with a real world that is itself inadequately experienced. In Kant's theory of knowledge, concepts such as number, substance and relation (the categories of pure reason) are assumed to apply to a world from which they were never learned. He called these *synthetic* a priori concepts. Their a priori character follows necessarily from the putative character of *the* world: although real rather than merely phenomenal, the world is also unknowable in itself (what is called *noumenal*). Consequently, the only positive fact about the properties of the real world that can be counted as necessary is that the a priori categories of mind do apply. Without this assumption, Kant argued, knowledge of the world would be impossible. On the truth of this fundamental presupposition relies the possibility of there being a principle to guide the adumbrative powers of mind.

Although many contemporary constructive realists (for example, Piaget, Pribram, Fodor, and most information-processing theorists) might balk at certain specifics contained in Kant's proposal, they must nevertheless accept, as a logical primitive of their own position as indirect realists, something comparable to Kant's synthetic a priori.

The cognitive capacity to adumbrate perceptual experience properly so as to allow one to parlay meager perceptual wagers into true knowledge of the world, not only must be present at birth, since such a power cannot be perceptually learned, but must also be present from the dawn of human intelligence.

Unlike Kant, current indirect theorists, who believe that adumbration of perceptual experience is required, have Darwin to fall back on to explain the emergence of an externally controlled, constructive capacity of mind. Thus, we turn now to the evolutionist's alternative to a priori realism.

Evolutionism. We now see that a bone of contention between indirect realists of the constructive variety and direct realists is captured in the phrase, *perceptual knowledge is impossible without proper adumbration by cognition.* This is a recalcitrant difference when the adumbration process is assumed to be truly a priori; however, when other interpretations of the above thesis are invoked the waters become muddied again.

It is a mistake to see the difference between constructive and direct realism as merely another instance of the classic confrontation between nativism and empiricism. This issue is more complicated today than in earlier centuries before Darwin, given the restricted forms of nativism offered by evolutionary principles. Ideas believed innate to an individual need not be believed innate to a species. Thus the issue as to what constitutes a priori knowledge is no longer as clear-cut as before, for what is a priori to an individual member of a species may not be a priori for the species. In this way evolutionism has taken the sting out of nativism; one need not be a radical rationalist in order to be a nativist of some sort.

Consequently, the implied nativism of constructive theorists may even find its way, in a more temperate form to be sure, into the arsenal of ideas of the ecological theorist. Direct realists of this persuasion (for example, Gibson, Mace, Turvey, the authors of this chapter) do not forsake the proposition that the perceptual systems not only become tuned to the world by experience, but are genetically preattuned by the evolutionary experience of the species. Indeed, given current evidence, it would be foolish to believe otherwise (see Gibson, this volume; Shaw & McIntyre, 1974).

Similarly, given the empiricist flavor of behaviorist learning theories of the 1950s that has leached over into cognitive theories of the 1960s and 1970s, most information-processing theorists would feel uncomfortable being classified with radical nativists who avow a priorism. Moreover, it is not totally inaccurate to classify many contemporary psychologist who give lip service to the cognitive approach as cryptoneoempiricists. Neither, however, should we overlook the contemporary cognitive theorists (for example, Chomsky, Piaget, Pribram) who might reject the label of a priorist if this were interpreted as cynicism regarding a programmatic solution to the problem of innate ideas promised by evolutionists.

The upshot of the above discussion is that both ecological psychologists and information-processing ones, as proponents of direct and indirect realism, respectively, emphatically disavow the thesis of radical empiricism—namely, that the mind of man at birth is a blank tablet such that all psychological abilities are traceable to the individual's particular learning experiences. Instead the issue separating the two approaches reduces to the interpretation of how evolutionary attunement plays a role in the adumbration of perceptual experiences—that it does somehow and to some extent is not in question.

For the ecological theorist, evolution plays an indispensable role in perception by designing the perceptual systems of individuals to be especially attuned to the most significant dimensions (not specific contents!) of information required for adaptive functioning within the ecological niche provided their species by nature. Perception, however, is no less direct for having been genetically preattuned (an adumbrative process), for what is perceptually experienced *is* solely the information presented to the senses by the world. All that genetic preattunement accomplishes is greater facility for the perceptual systems differentiating the information made available by the environment so as to extract perceptual invariants that embody the ecologically significant properties of the perceiver's world. Knowing the world truly, if not completely, is inevitable given the direct nature of perception and the sufficiency of the information made available to both species and its individual members.

Therefore, no enrichment of perceptual information by nonperceptual processes is needed, since the phenomenological experience that results from the proper pickup of that information provides a sufficient basis for knowing how to survive, maintain health, and achieve reasonable success in other endeavors.

The Possibility of Error

Under normal circumstances our perceptual systems are quite capable of picking up information that provides true specification of most significant properties of the world. On occasion, however, when certain necessary conditions on observation are not met, the available information may be deficient or perceptual sampling so restricted that errors in judgment ensue. For instance, if the biological support for perception is withdrawn, say, by some physical or chemical trauma to the central nervous system, proper modulation of the available information may become impossible. These insults to the perceptual systems may lead to distortions of the information picked up or even to hallucinatory experiences. Of course the possibility of detecting such problems in perception logically presupposes the ultimate availability of sufficient information to specify what is true.

Another source of faulty judgment about the nature of what is perceived might arise from deficient information—that is, from the physical support of perception being withdrawn, say, because of contingent restrictions on perceptual sampling. A person who is unable to see an object from the proper distance, from the proper perspective, or under proper illumination, may judge the nature of his experience incorrectly because he elects to go beyond the information given. Again it follows from the fact that such situations can ultimately be corrected, on the basis of further perceptual sampling, that true perceptual experience is possible.

The fundamental assumption of the ecological approach is simply that contingently deficient perceptual information may be rendered sufficient for correct judgment by allowing the perceiving agent more time to sample and/or more space in which to maneuver (Gibson, 1966). For instance, one may believe the facade on a movie set to be a real castle—an error in judgment, until one takes the time to notice its papier maché quality or to walk around behind it. Gibson (1966) defines perception as the pickup of information over time—a sufficient amount of time, that is, for extracting the significant information available over space to correctly judge the nature of ecologically relevant phenomena. Thus, the point to be emphasized is that cognitive judgments are parasitic on perceptual experiences; they are logically posterior to perception rather than either anterior to it or part of it.

Furthermore, the ecological position assumes that the majority of judgments relevant to the survival, health and welfare of a person can, in principle, be validated or invalidated on the basis of perceptual evidence alone. Hence adumbration of perceptual experiences by nonperceptual processes is rendered unnecessary by evolution since by natural selection the perceptual systems may become optimally attuned by their biological design to pick up certain forms of information and not others. For instance, the frog will perceive a small object in motion (for example, a flying insect) and flick it from the air with its sticky tongue while ignoring the same small object when static in its field of vision. Thus the specialization of the sense, through evolution, to pick up ecologically relevant information in an optimal fashion, constitutes a direct adumbrative process, a process that guides perceptual differentiation through the welter of available information without recourse to indirect adumbrative processes of a nonperceptual origin. To assume otherwise that evolution attuned the perceptual systems to function erroneously, to pick up misleading information, is to assume that evolution is a fundamentally maladaptive process—an assumption that undercuts its theoretical value as a scientific hypothesis. Consequently, one must be careful not to confuse the sometimes unreliable functioning of the perceptual systems as physiological processes with evidence that they are always fundamentally in error. Error, like success, is a relative term to be measured against the degree of adaptive behavior exhibited by people and animals day by day in coping with their worlds—an accomplishment that is by no means perfect, but far from being random or negatively correlated with success as the sheer number of people populating our planet now attests.

Thus, it would be a fundamental mistake to argue that because the necessary conditions for perception can on occasion be violated, then perception is an unreliable source of knowledge about the world. The laws governing perception are no different from other natural laws in this respect—true knowledge about the world is only yielded if certain conditions on their application are observed, what is sometimes called their initial and boundary conditions.

Thus, the fundamental claim of the ecological approach, as a version of direct realism, is in no way infirmed by the admission of the possibility of error in perceptual judgment, since this in no way gives carte blanche to the charge that perception is unlawful and, hence, incapable of yielding reliable knowledge about the world. Rather it is only to admit what must be true of any lawful process, namely, that whenever the ceteris paribus clause is satisfied and the senses function reliably, then perceptual information specifies true propositions about the world.

Naive versus critical realism. Sometimes it is claimed, and quite unfairly, that direct realism necessarily entails naive realism (Maxwell, 1970, pp. 3–34). *Naive realism* is the view that what is known about the world is both unadulterated and unexpurgated with respect to even its most subtle details, as such, the view roundly denies Kant's pessimistic claim that the world is noumenal or essentially unknowable in itself.

Perceptual theories based on naive realism are the most optimistic of all theories, since they claim that the information needed to specify all the properties of the world is readily available to the senses. Hence the world is exactly as it seems (Russell, 1940, p. 14).

For all practical purposes naive realism becomes indistinguishable from phenomenalism, since whatever is deemed known is also deemed perceivable; thus perceptual phenomena comprise all that is real. But direct realism purports to reject phenomenalism just as assuredly as does indirect realism; must we conclude then that direct realists are deluded when believing themselves to be realists, since in fact, they are de facto nominalists? Or, perhaps, the claim that direct realism entails naive realism may well be false. Indeed this criticism can be shown to be false by carefully considering several dimensions of knowledge on which various types of realisms may be compared.

Consider a scale on which we rate the degree of completeness of our knowledge of reality. Imagine, say, an eleven point scale ranging from 0, or *no* knowledge, on one end to 10, or *total* knowledge, on the other. The most optimistic of all theorists, the naive realist, would provide an anchor point on the upper end of the scale, with a score of 10 points, indicating a belief that our knowledge of the world is perfect. Holding down the anchor point on the lower end of the scale, and receiving a score of 0, would be the most pessimistic of all theorists, the cynical realist. Such a theorist, as a realist, still believes in the existence of an external world but denies that we can know anything whatever about it.

On this end of the scale, for instance, we might place Kant in his most pessimistic moments, say, before he became convinced that the categories of pure reason necessarily apply to the noumenal world. However, immediately after formulating the argument that we must be capable of knowing at least one fact about the world, namely, that the *synthetic* a priori categories apply, Kant might deserve a small positive score on the scale, say, a 1.0.

Where should we place those believers in direct and indirect realism so as to express their opposition to one another? If this scale of completeness of knowledge is truly the dimension on which the two versions of realism may be compared, then they should occupy polar positions on the scale. Furthermore, if direct realism necessarily entails naive realism then the two should fall together on the upper end of the scale. On the other hand, if neither of the above claims holds, then the positions on the scale held by direct and indirect realists should prove uncorrelated.

It only takes a moment's consideration to see that this latter statement holds, for neither direct or indirect realists believe knowledge of reality to be total. The issue that separates the two is not *how much* can be known but *by what means* whatever is known is known. Hence, in sharp disagreement with naive realists, direct realists no less than indirect realists may agree with Kant that we know little about the world itself. In this case, the proper qualifier for the realism adhered to would be *critical.*[2]

Thus, it is quite possible for a person to be either a direct realist, or indirect realist, while at the same time being a *critical* realist—one who believes our knowledge of the world to be something less than perfect. Unlike the naive realist, who believes things appear exactly as they are, the critical realist realizes that one's judgment may be led astray if the information sampled is accidentally impoverished, or if the perceiver's ability to sample the information is artificially restricted. (Recall the earlier example of the paper maché castle; also see Gibson's 1966 theory of illusions.)

The characterization of Gibson's form of realism is clearly critical, as Mary Henle (1974) correctly observes (although she seems to see an inconsistency in

[2] Historically speaking, *critical* realism is the name primarily attributed to two groups of American philosophers which include such thinkers as Durant Drake, A. K. Rogers, George Santayana, and C. A. Strong on the one hand, and A. O. Lovejoy, J. B. Pratt, and R. W. Sellars on the other. Both groups agreed that what we are directly aware of in perception are not actually properties of external objects but are "character-complexes . . . irresistibly *taken,* in the moment of perception to be the characters of existing outer objects [Drake, 1920, p. 20]." The usage, however, that we are giving to the term is broader than their more narrow connotation. In contrast to their view which was dualistic, we do not mean to imply either dualism or monism. Rather what we see as the issue among critical realists of various persuasions (for example, direct versus indirect realists) devolves upon the theoretical interpretation of "character-complexes" and their relation to the objects they specify (that is, is the relation direct or indirect). We can see no purpose served by arbitrarily restricting the doctrine of critical realism to the narrower interpretation that accident gives historical precedent.

one professing both a direct and critical realism, presumably because she mistakenly equates direct realism with naive realism).[3] Thus, on the scale denoting completeness of knowledge, critical realists would populate all those regions lying between naive realism and cynical realism, with their exact position being determined by the degree of pessimism or optimism held.

But notice, the issue between naive realists and critical realists, in general, is not one of the veridicality of perceptual knowledge but of its completeness (although one might wish to puzzle over the ways incomplete knowledge may lead one to false judgments).

The obvious scale on which direct and indirect theories of perception may be contrasted is *degree of proximity* of the object of perceptual experience to the information source in the world which determines it. In other words, assuming the causal theory of perception, one might rate the distance separating the proximal cause of the percept from its distal material cause in the world. Consequently, by definition, direct realists would receive a minimal score of 0, since they believe the proximal and distal cause of perception to be the same.

Indirect realists, on the other hand, receive positive distance scores, depending on the link in the causal chain believed to be the proximal cause of the percept (for example, retinal image or brain state). By contrast, naive realists could be assigned any score whatever, since any link in the causal chain, from world, energy propagation, receptor state, to brain state, may be presumed to provide a complete specification of the world as it stands, indirect though that specification may be. All that is required for naive realism to hold is that the causal stage experienced be a source of complete knowledge of the world.

If the stage experienced is not the world itself, then that stage provides *epistemic mediation* for the person's knowledge of the world. It is important to realize that whatever link in the causal chain is presumed to be the proximal cause of perceptual experience, that link is directly perceived. To assume otherwise would lead to a regress of endlessly interpolating epistemic mediators between the knowing-agent and the object known with nothing ever qualifying as a true proximal cause of perceptual experience.

Naive realism requires only that the epistemic mediator be perfect, but in no way mandates the link to be experienced. The naive realist who believes the world itself to be the object of experience is also a direct realist. But this is not the general case, for other naive realists may believe some other stage in the causal sequence to effect epistemic mediation with the world; thus they would be indirect realists. Any view, direct or otherwise, which believes epistemic mediation to be perfect is by that belief a naive realism. Therefore, the claim that direct realism necessarily entails naive realism seems quite certainly false.

[3] Or, perhaps, she believes that critical realism entails dualism while direct realism does not. This would be in keeping with the traditional interpretation of critical realism as discussed in the preceding footnote.

The goal of this section was to show that although direct and indirect theories of perception partake of different forms of realism, neither can be rejected out of hand for being unscientific, that is, for being obviously naive, uncritical or in violation of the basic precept of causal explanation, a precept believed by many to be essential to any completely adequate scientific explanation. However the two types of theories are to be distinguished, the difference must lie elsewhere.

To discover the basis of their distinction, it would be wise to look more carefully at the concept of epistemic mediation. If this concept is found to apply validly to perception, then a case for indirect perception might be made (as many theorists already believe). On the other hand, if this concept proves to be theoretically vacuous, to serve no real explanatory purpose, then a case in support of direct perception will be made (as a few of us believe can be).

In Part Three, we question whether there is any logical necessity at all for believing perception to be indirect, indeed whether the term itself has any clear meaning when applied to perception.

PART THREE: THE "DIRECT" PERCEPTION OF INVARIANT INFORMATION

> Philosophers, it is said, "are not, for the most part, prepared to admit that such objects as pens or cigarettes are ever directly perceived." Now of course what brings us up short here is the word "directly"—a great favorite among philosophers, but actually one of the less conspicuous snakes in the linguistic grass . . . it is essential to realize that here the notion of perceiving *in*directly wears the trousers—"directly" takes whatever sense it has from the contrast with its opposite. . . .
>
> [J. L. Austin, 1962, p. 15, commenting on A. J. Ayer, 1940, pp. 1–2].

Taking Stock

Before returning to the crux of the issue separating direct and indirect realists, let us take stock of those issues that do *not* necessarily divide them. The above discussion, if correct, suggests a broader base of common agreement than might first have been apparent.

1. *The rejection of phenomenalism.* It goes without saying that, as realisms, both views by definition oppose phenomenalism in their common belief that there is more to the world than perceptual phenomena. Moreover, they concur with the popular viewpoint of contemporary physics, namely, that some properties and entities may be unobservables and yet be known through rational inference. For instance the track in a hydrogen bubble chamber or Wilson cloud chamber may provide perceptual evidence for the postulation of inferred entities given one's acceptance of certain physical laws and theoretical assumptions

provided by quantum mechanics. Indeed, both views may even agree that there exist some types of subatomic particles which are in principle not visible (for example, quarks).

This concession in no way jeopardizes the consistency of the direct realists' belief that perception, one mode of knowing, is direct, while inference, another mode of knowing, is indirect; for inferring is not perceiving and it would be a grievous mistake to treat them equivalently. In perceiving, according to direct realism, the object known is experienced, while in inferring, the object known is not experienced. (For instance, one *perceives* the bubble track of a particle but *infers* the particle). Hence perception and inference are not, epistemically speaking, processes of the same type. This distinction allows for agreement on a second proposition.

2. *The possibility of error in knowledge.* Since inference and perception are epistemically distinct one might lead to error while the other might not. Both views wish to account for error, since neither believes knowledge to be perfect. The indirect realist is willing to entertain the possibility that our senses may somehow "lie" to us–but this is surely metaphorical, for our senses are dumb, they do not *tell* us anything. It is the person, not the senses, who judges by inferring conclusions, just or no, from perceptual experiences. Thus, for the direct realist, perception merely *is what it is,* it is in principle neither true nor false; rather, it is the judgment inferred from premises believed applicable to the percept that may sometimes go astray. To think otherwise is to commit what Ryle (1949) called a *category mistake,* mistaking an entity of one type with that of another, such as confusing a word with the object it takes.

3. *Evolutionism.* It is unfair for either view to suggest that the other *necessarily* takes a radical position with respect to either rationalism or empiricism. Given the option of evolutionism as a reasonable compromise between the extreme positions of radical nativism (a priorism) or radical empiricism (behaviorism), either theorist is free to accept the scientifically popular, neo-Darwinian compromise without fear of fundamental inconsistency. The direct realist is perfectly willing to accept the possibility that the perceptual systems have been genetically preattuned to differentiate environmental information in a selective manner. Thus, the adumbrative process need not have a nonperceptual origin. If one assumes it does, as some constructuve theorists do, then there is truly the danger of sliding into a priorism.

4. *The acceptance of critical realism.* One of the least thoughtful, and yet most persistent complaints levied by indirect realists at direct realism is the claim that it either (a) necessarily entails naive realism or (b) is identical with naive realism. Both claims can be countered by showing that direct realism, no less than indirect realism, may assume knowledge of the world is less than perfect, that given the information available over some restricted temporal or spatial period, how the world *seems* may not be how it truly is. Thus, when rating the two views on a scale of completeness of knowledge about the world we find that

either direct or indirect realism may vary from naive realism (a score of perfect) to cynical realism (a score of zero).

5. *The ultimate criticism.* There is one final charge that might be raised against direct realism and the theory of direct perception entailed by such. Admitting that the theory of direct perception is no less scientific than theories of indirect perception, one might conclude that for all practical purposes the two types of theories are the same, one serving no better as a guide to research than the other. Perhaps, one might even go so far as to argue that, to the extent that the theory of direct perception is concocted to be reasonable, it conflates onto some version of the theory of indirect perception. This criticism is not so farfetched as might first be thought.

Unfortunately, it is indeed sometimes the case that sympathetic interpreters of Gibson's theory of direct perception equivocate when asked if one perceives the world or just the information made available by the world. For instance, the critic might point out that Gibson himself defines perception as the pickup of information over time. Therefore, if the world makes the information available, does not information stand as an epistemic mediator between the perceiver and its world? Hence, we should legitimately conclude then that, by positing information as a mediating construct, Gibson's own theory of perception can properly be dubbed "indirect."

If we assume, however, that the causal theory of perception holds, the critic might concede, for sake of detente, that Gibson's theory may truly be considered *less* indirect than other theories because it assumes the proximal cause of perception to be a more distal link in the causal chain than that assumed by other indirect theories–say, by retinal image or brain state theories. In other words, Gibson's theory assumes the perceptual experience to be of information carried by energy distributions in the environment lying outside the perceiver's body rather than being an experience of retinal images or brain states lying quite inside the perceiver's body.

Although this interpretation allows Gibson's theory of perception to be less indirect than others, it would nevertheless be indirect–differing from retinal image theory or brain state theory only quantitatively rather than qualitatively. From here the issue between the ecological approach and other types of information-processing theories becomes, as Pribram (this volume) suggests, merely one of determining experimentally whether perception is the detection of information instantiated in the ambient energy arrays of the physical environment or the detection of information instantiated in physiological constructs, say, in the dynamic states of receptor or cerebral processes.

As fair as this compromise may seem, it is too slick, for it shoots right past the real issue, namely, the claim by direct realism that knowledge of the world is possible only because we do perceive the world and not merely some phantom surrogate of the world. Moreover, what is at stake between theories of direct and indirect perception is the practical issue of where our field should focus its resources in an attempt to characterize *what* is most directly responsible for perceptual knowledge.

Should our research efforts be directed at experimental manipulation of retinal or cerebral variables and the development of corresponding dependent measures, or should our research efforts attempt to "ecologize" physics in the hope of discovering the direct source of perceptual knowledge and corresponding ways of charactering it? Thus, the resolution of the issue of whether perception is direct or indirect is not merely of academic concern but has practical implications for research and how researchers should be trained.

Given the above concerns, it becomes crucial that we resolve this last issue of whether direct perception can be treated de facto as a disguised form of indirect perception. We turn now to a resolution of this problem.

The Meaning of Being Direct

To fully appreciate why the above claim is invalid—why direct perception can in no sense be reduced to a version of indirect perception—it is helpful to consider the meaning of the two terms. Austin (1962) makes several interesting observations regarding their relationship as polar concepts.

In the passage quoted at the beginning of Part Three, Austin suggests that the term "direct" is "one of the less conspicuous snakes in the linguistic grass"; its sense may remain obscure until placed in sharp contrast to some precise usage of the term "indirect." As he so elegantly puts it: It is the latter term which clearly "wears the trousers"—that is, which takes priority in setting usage in linguistic contexts. To see why this is so, let us consider an analogous case where the meaning of one member of a contrastive pair of terms, the dominant one, determines which of several possible connotations the second member is to take.

To understand what "colored" means we must first understand what "uncolored" means. Since the normal circumstance for humans is to be able to perceive the multicolored facets of the world, to draw our attention to this property dimension, it clearly helps to contrast it with its opposite—"uncolored." However, the meaning of the latter term is ambiguous. One sense of being *uncolored* is to be colorless such as pure air, water, or glass. Here "uncolored" means *colorless or transparent.* But another sense of "uncolored" means *to be without hue,* as in the case of neutral gray pigments or white pigments, where there is a careful balance of all hues. Thus, if someone were to say "I saw a colored object today," we would not know immediately what was meant. The sense that "colored" takes depends by contrast upon which sense of "uncolored" was intended.

For instance, if the linguistic contrast intended was between "colored" and "uncolored," in the sense of colorless or transparent, then "colored" would be synonymous with "opaque." On the other hand, if the intended linguistic contrast is between "colored" and "uncolored," in the sense of neutral gray, then "colored" would be synonymous with "tinted" (by some hue). Here we find that the sense of "colored" is less conspicuous than that of "uncolored"; hence, it is the latter term which (like "indirect") "wears the trousers" in the contrastive relationship and, therefore, whose sense must be clarified first. (Terms such as "uncolored" are sometimes said to be semantically marked.) Consequently, we should not be surprised that the technical use of the terms "direct" and "indirect" can be equally problematic.

An important suggestion, however, emerges from the above argument that one member of a linguistic contrast may be dominant in setting the sense of the other (that is, semantically marked); it is in theories which adopt the term "indirect" as a key concept that technical language is most likely to go astray. Thus, contrary to what is sometimes claimed, the burden of clarification naturally falls on indirect realists rather than on direct realists since it is their half of the contrast that is semantically marked.

To see why this is so, contrast the claim that *one can perceive objects indirectly* with the claim that *one can see unreal objects.* Austin (1962) suggests the following scenario for a conversation revolving around the latter claim: "I can see an unreal duck"—"What on earth do you mean?"—"It's a decoy duck"—"Ah, I see! Why didn't you say so at once? [p. 18]." Here we understand specifically what "unreal" means (that is, artificial) so that if someone then remarked, "Oh, but next to the decoy is a *real* duck," we would then know exactly the sense intended (that is, a living, flesh and blood duck).

In a similar vein, to grasp what is intended by the assertion that we perceive the world *directly* requires that we first determine what it would mean to perceive the world *indirectly.* However, if the latter semantically marked term turns out to have no useful interpretation, then the former contrastive but unmarked term becomes vestigial and can be dropped from usage. In such a case, the assertion that *we perceive the world directly* could then be shortened, without loss of meaning, back to its original, commonsense form of simply *we perceive the world*—something few people would question until tutored in certain brands of philosophy.

If the above argument is correct, and "direct" is the semantically unmarked term in the linguistic contrast, then this may account for the difficulty encountered by so-called *direct* realists (for example, J. J. Gibson) in making their positions clear, when asked to do so outside of the countercontext provided by a well articulated indirect theory. Hence the obstacles which block the path to a clear understanding of how perception may in principle be indirect, a fortiori block the path to a clear understanding of how perception may in principle be direct. Let us consider some of these obstacles.

The Meaning of Perception Being Indirect

The chief obstacle to the acceptance of theories that knowledge is indirect is the simple fact that people are very good at noticing the world and its properties but terribly inept at noticing the properties of constructs hypothesized to mediate perception. When we dodge a baseball, we do not seem to notice that the retinal image projected from the oncoming missile through the lens of the eye must be upside down and backward. People and cars down the block do not appear smallish or to change size upon approach and recession as their retinal images must; rather they are experienced as possessing the stature and substance we know them to have. Similarly, when biting into an apple, we experience the juicy, red object as existing in our hands and not in our brains or eyeballs.

Thus, it is indirect theorists rather than direct theorists who must defend their theoretical circumlocutions since they have been concocted to disallow our speaking of the objects of perception as being what they seem. This is only fair, for whenever a theory goes against the natural grain of experiences common to all people, the burden of motivating unnatural expressions or surprising conclusions must fall to the offending party. Again, to follow Austin's line of illustration for this point consider the following:

If someone reports to you, during a time of war, that a sighting of enemy ships is indirect, then it should merely provoke the question of what exactly is meant. If, however, that person goes on to explain that what actually was seen were blips on a radar screen and not the ships themselves, then the natural reply should be, "Well, why didn't you say so in the first place!"

Clearly, in the light of what might be meant by the claim that a sighting of enemy ships is *indirect,* (that is, their blips were seen on radar), it is now possible to interpret a counterclaim that a sighting of enemy ships might thereby be *direct,* say, as a sighting by telescope from the crows nest of a ship. However, the more radical claim by an indirect realist that even a sighting of enemy ships through a telescope is also really indirect suggests that only a sighting by the naked eye would constitute a direct perception of the enemy ships. But the recalcitrant indirect realist must not let go of his argument at this point, but must push on with the surprising claim that even a sighting of enemy ships by the naked eye is actually indirect–in some extraordinary sense to be sure.

What ultimate meaning for the term "direct" does this latter claim imply–that *direct* perception of something must be accomplished without the lens of the eye since it too casts images to the eyeless homunculus? And since we might consider the cortical projections from the eye to be images, (at least in the mathematical sense), must a direct perceiver be excised of his visual cortex as well?

This interpretation of "indirect" perception thus leads to an absurd interpretation of "direct" perception. Moreover, such a radical interpretation of indirect becomes hoisted on its own petard, for if no clear meaning can be attributed to one half of a linguistic contrast, none can be attributed to the other either. Again we find that it is the indirect theorist who ultimately must explain his concept first before the direct theorist can know what to say in response.

All that the direct perceptual theorist can offer is the boring repetition of his first premise; namely, that the perception of X is indeed what it seems–the perception of X rather than Y. If all the indirect theorist can do is persist in inexplicably claiming that the direct theorist's claim is absurd on prima facie grounds—that the perception of *X* is *really* the perception of *Y*—an impasse to further reasonable argument must be recognized.

Or, perhaps, the linguistic problem of attributing a clear meaning to "in-direct," since it is the dominant or semantically marked half of the indirect/direct perception contrast, is sympotomatic of a deeper philosophical confusion. To dramatize this possible confusion and to illustrate some of its practical implications for perceptual theory, let us again paint a scenario of a possible confrontation between the two opposing theorists. Bear in mind, also, that the core of the disagreement may be as much one of attitude as it is of substance.

If you were to tell a friend that he did not really see his wife when looking straight into her uncovered face while awake, sober, and attentive, then he would be quite astounded. His next question should be to ask if you had played a trick on him by substituting in the place of his wife someone who looked remarkably like her, say an actress with clever makeup or an unsuspected identical twin sister. Furthermore, on denial by you that either was the case, he would be quite perplexed regarding what you meant.

You might explain that what you meant to say was that he did not see her directly as supposed but *indirectly*. However, on touching her warm, animate, three-dimensional body instead of the coolor, flat surface of a mirror, your friend would feel quite justified in vociferously denying your claim.

You may then continue, if your patience persists, to explain that you did not mean to claim that he saw her image reflected in a mirror, but her image as reflected in the eye. At this your friend should reply that he never thought otherwise, but express perplexity that you should call this an *indirect* view of his wife.

Perhaps, with a creeping feeling of futility, you might try one final sally to put over the subtlety of your point! "Look, my good man, what I really mean to say is that all you, or anyone else for that matter, have ever seen or will ever see—*all*, mind you, are but little phantasms of the world in the eye—flattish, smallish, images of objects on the back of the eyeball!"—"Oh, God!" your friend might then gasp in complete befuddlement, unable to continue.

Most likely the argument would end here with you thinking your friend quite dense and possessing no head for science, and with him quite convinced that you are more than just a little mad. In a less jocular vein, however, it should be pointed out that the above dialogue dramatizes the extreme difficulty direct and indirect realists have traditionally faced when trying to convey their respective positions to one another. The difference is indeed as much one of attitude as of substance. We should, therefore, take great care to consider fairly the merits of each position and avoid, so far as possible, engaging in the easy polemics that arise from either attitude. It helps to remember that neither view, as argued before, is inherently unscientific, although one may be better science than the other.

The chief obstacle to clarifying the indirect view, we now see, devolves upon the simple fact that people are very good at noticing the world but terribly inept at noticing the properties of the mediating constructs postulated as way stations for perception. Indeed, only after years of practice do artists even approach the skill of attending to objects by *reduced* vision—the ability to disregard the effects of the constancies of size, shape, color, and brightness (Arnheim, 1964; Hester, this volume.)

Furthermore, the fact that people can develop the ability to attend to the properties of the retinal image provides a source of evidence that runs counter to the indirect realist's hypothesis, since the perceived properties of the retinal image are not at all like the properties of the real objects. The former exhibits none of the constancies that characterize the latter and hence are readily distinguishable from them. How then can retinal images be the basis of our perceptual experience of objects? Perhaps, a better guess is that retinal images (or other sensory icons) are but epiphenomenal spill-over from the perceptual process by which we experience the world.

In the final section of this chapter, we explore the suggestion that, when properly construed, direct realism provides an acceptable scientific framework within which theories of perception might be constructed. However, our tactic will be to question the fruitfulness of the direct/indirect dichotomy for perception, not because no clear theory of direct perception is possible, but because no valid theory of indirect perception is available with which it might be contrasted. Without such a contrast, the epithet "direct" serves no real purpose.

Of course, we do not mean to deny the obvious fact that traditionally a contrast between the two types of theories has been verbally drawn; rather we will try to show that such a contrast is, at best, trivially true where the term "indirect" may be validly applied to perception, and, at worst, misleading when the term "indirect" is misapplied to perception.

Perceiving is not inferring. The key question which motivates the theoretical position that perception is indirect might be phrased as follows: If all we are capable of experiencing are our retinal images or brain states, as often claimed, then why should we ever suppose that our experience even indirectly refers to a real world? If all that we experience is "within" our own heads, then how did we ever come to the realist's conclusion that anything exists completely and independently outside ourselves? In other words, how can indirect realism avoid falling into phenomenalism?

The indirect realist typically answers this charge by claiming that we infer that some of the properties of our experience are true of the world. But, unfortunately for this view, we are not aware that we are merely inferring the fit of such properties to the world; rather we feel an irresistible compulsion to attribute such properties to the world while in the act of experiencing them. At least such a one-step inferential process, if that is what it is, seems to be *direct.*

To claim, however, that our experience of the world is really an experience of such a direct inference, is merely to regress the original question rather than to answer it; for now we must ask why an experience of an inference should ever be taken to be a perceptual experience of the real properties of the world—the very question with which we began.

Furthermore, it will not do simply to assume that inferences somehow may, willynilly, be taken for perceptions. Rather, how such a mistake can occur requires a cogent theory to explain the nature of the confusion—a theory which must be supplied by its claimant, the indirect theorist, and not by the direct theorist. Consider an absurd implication of such a claim: When we infer that "Socrates is mortal" is a true statement from the proverbial syllogism, in no sense are we compelled to believe that the man Socrates, who we are told lived more than 2000 years ago, is part of our perceptual experience of the current world. Indeed, if we should experience whatever we infer, then it would be more accurate to call such experiences hallucinations rather than perceptions.

Moreover, by this line of reasoning we might suppose that logicians and lawyers, who presumably do more inferential work than most of us, should show signs of hallucinating much of the time, while schizophrenics, who presumably do not reason well at all, should yield the least evidence of hallucinating, with ordinary people falling somewhere in between. Thus, the claim that inferential experience can be phenomenologically as rich as perception, must be false, or at best only metaphorically true. Unfortunately, such a metaphor seems difficult to comprehend. Perception is not inferential and no verbal sleight of hand can equate the two.

Perception is not memory. An equally silly claim is that perceptual experience is somehow based on memory. If we take the claim literally, then we must ask why we do not hallucinate whatever we remember, say our deceased grandmothers, when recalling them to mind. The British Empiricists' claim that memories may be distinguished from percepts because they are less "vivid" does not really work at all, for it leaves unanswered the question of how things are perceived in the first place. When experiencing novel objects or events, since there are no memories to draw upon, memory can play no role at all in primary perceptual processes.

If perception as such is neither memory nor inference, then what might we ask is the proper interpretation of the claim that perception is indirect? The indirect realist, as suggested earlier, has one option left open to him; he may assume that although neither memory nor inference can epistemically mediate or adumbrate perception, some psychological correlate of the retinal image or a brain state, say the sensory icon, may succeeed in doing so.

Let us try, one last time, to give a precise meaning to the hypothesis that perception is indirect rather than direct. The scheme that the theoretical contrast must satisfy can be minimally given as follows: *Perception of X (for example, the world, an apple, an enemy ship, a person's face) is not direct as it seems but is really indirect—that is, when looking at, listening to, or feeling for X we do not experience the properties of X but the properties of Y instead—where*

Y is some physiological correlate (for example, a brain state) or physical correlate (for example, a retinal image) of X.

By contrast, the direct theory of perception can now be made quite explicit; it simply denies the validity of the above proposition by asserting that *to perceive X is to experience the properties of X rather than the properties of something else.*

The crux of the issue comes down to whether or not either party can give a cogent argument as to which set of properties is experienced. For the indirect theorist, it must be shown that our experience of the properties of *X* is somehow indirect vis à vis the properties of *Y* which are distinct from those of *X;* while for the direct theorist, it must be shown that our experience of the properties of *X* are indeed an experience of the properties of *X* with no other properties not belonging to *X* being experienced in their stead—that is, with no other ones acting as epistemic mediators.

Perception: A Process Transparent to the Properties of the World

The first thing to notice is that there is no serious proposition for the direct realist to challenge if all that the indirect realist means by the above hypothesis is that the properties of the mediating construct *Y are* the properties of *X*. In other words, the two views are only trivially different if the theory of indirect perception asserts that we see the world somehow *through* a retinal image or brain state in the sense that perceptual information about the world "flows" through them. Such a view, in essence, agrees with the direct realist's hypothesis that the central nervous system, no less than air, the lens system of a telescope, or the lens or humors of the eye, is essentially *transparent* to the properties of the world as conveyed by perceptual information.

The stick used to probe the shape and depth of a hole, or to feel the roughness or solidity of a terrain, is perceptually transparent to the shape, depth, and texture information picked up at the other end. Similarly, if you are offered a pig in a poke (a sack) to feel and you succeed in identifying its contents, then the poke provides a functionally transparent medium to the pig. In such a case we might say that the pig-in-the-poke situation affords pickup of pig-invariant, haptic information.

Obviously, if the two views of realism are not to be just trivially different, then the properties of the perceptual referent must differ significantly from the properties exhibited by the hypothesized mediating construct. Otherwise, as William James suggests, a difference that makes no difference is no difference at all. On the other hand, s serious puzzle is posed for indirect realism if the properties exhibited by the construct should depart too radically from those exhibited by the object presumed known. Consequently, a necessary condition for knowledge of the world—that is, for any kind of realism—is that the physical and physiological processes which support the act of perception must somehow be functionally transparent to the properties of the world. Let us explore this necessary requirement in more detail.

Insofar as the properties of the construct itself are perceived, then the construct offers no information about its world-referent but only information about its own properties as an epiphenomenon of the causal process supporting perception. Hence, under such circumstances the construct, although a causal mediator, is not an epistemic mediator—that is to say, it plays no contributory role in perception but only a supportive one.

Thus, we must recognize that an egregious error is committed whenever one asks whether or not the epistemic act of perceiving the world is causally supported—causally supported, yes, but no sense can be attached to the former question. To avoid this problem of slipping unaware between levels of discourse—that is, between talk about causation and talk about knowledge—let us agree to distinguish two popular but equivocal uses of the term "perception": perception as a causally supported, time-dependent process must be distinguished from perception as an immediate, epistemic act.

Perception—An epistemic act or causal process? The time has arrived to make good on the promissory note offered earlier and supply a rebuttal of the criticism that the direct perception of information is but another form of epistemic mediation since it stands between the perceiver and his world. The only proper response a direct realist can give to this charge is to assert unequivocally that the pickup and differentiation of available information brings the knowing-agent into direct contact with *some* of the significant properties of the world, namely, with those properties that are of considerable ecological significance. Such contact, however, is epistemic rather than mechanical or causal in nature.

For instance, a mechanical or causal contrivance, say a telephone or phonograph, can put us in direct epistemic contact with another person's voice over distances of space or time, respectively, that are too great to allow direct mechanical contact betwen our bodies. If the person is a friend and the transmission signal is of sufficiently high fidelity, we will recognize the voice as familiar and, perhaps, even correctly identify its unique source. Thus, the transmission of the acoustic signal, as modulated originally by our friend's vocal tract, provides the causal support needed to convey sufficient information for correctly identifying the voice heard. It is the identification which is the epistemic act, not the process of transmission as such.

Indeed, it would be a category mistake to confuse the properties of the transmission process not directly assignable to our friend's voice quality with those that are. Clearly, the ownership of the familiar vocal qualities left invariant by the transmission process is our friend's rather than the electrical process as such.

Similarly, we directly experience the structure of a Beethoven piano concerto when we hear it over the radio. The perception of the concerto is the experience of the information specifying its acoustic structure as left invariant by the vibratory action of air molecules set in motion by the piano and likewise as preserved by the radio transmission process which eventuates in the speaker pulsations by which we hear the concerto over our radios. We should no more count the properties of these electromechanical media as an intrinsic part of the perception of the music than we should count the vibratory activities of our cochlear or neural transmissions. For, in hearing the music, we come into epistemic contact with the structure of the music rather than with the structure, or activities, of those processes furnishing the causal support of the music.

In general, then, *perception is the act of apprehending the properties of the message conveyed rather than the properties of the medium by which they are conveyed.* In fact, we a fortiori do not experience the message when we experience the supporting media. Thus, we must guard against reifying the information experienced in perception. Information is parasitic on its source. Unlike the medium which causally supports the pickup of the information, by definition, information has no structure that does not belong to the world referent which is its source. Any properties of the causal process which supports the information not assignable directly to the environmental source are by definition not information but *noise*—that is, properties of activities or structures that are uncorrelated with the source.

The so-called "directness" of perception as an epistemic act rests on the fundamental thesis that the tissue media of the human body, no less than the physical media of the environment, provide only causal support for information about the world and, as such, are essentially transparent to most of those properties of the world required by organisms in order to maintain a sufficient level of adaptive functioning. It seems quite reasonable to assume that evolution, after so long a time, should have tailored the perceptual systems to be sensitive to the ecologically significant properties of the world rather than to the abberations produced by dysfunctional properties of the eyeball, inner ear, neural tracts, or brain states. Can even a prima facie case be given for the adaptive significance of organisms having sensations of their organs of reception?

No. It seems more likely that nature would have designed the perceptual systems of animals and humans so as to render the various media functionally transparent to the ecologically significant properties of the world upon which the survival, health, and happiness of all animals sorely depend. We might even expect that the sensory physiology of humans and animals, if it does any transforming of incoming information at all, should act to enhance rather than destroy the fidelity of such information. Eyeglasses, hearing-aids, and other prosthetic sensory devices are based on rather simple principles by which specific dimensions of useful information can be focused and amplified.

Should we expect nature to be so slack in selection of evolutionary laws as to overlook similar ways of enhancing information that plays such an obvious and important role in the survival of the species? Ample evidence suggests that the perceptual systems are highly specialized; but to what end if not to accomplish the successful transmission of important information about the world?

Perception as process versus perception as act. To clarify the above proposition requires that a careful distinction be drawn between *perception*$_1$ as a causal process, wherein causal mediation is logically possible, and *perception*$_2$ as an epistemic act, wherein no epistemic mediation is logically possible. Consider, first, what is meant by epistemic mediation.

The thesis of *epistemic mediation,* as discussed earlier, suggests that one must know X before one can experience Y. Here X would be the epistemic mediator of the experience Y. For instance, we must learn the rules of chess before we can play chess. Here *the learning of the rules* mediates the *experience of playing chess.*

Similarly, we must learn how to hold a nail against a suitable material (for example, wood), to grasp the proper end of a hammer, and how to swing it, before we can experience the act of hammering. Thus, learning to coordinate the proper materials, tools, and activities is epistemically necessary if we are to experience the desired end result. The means–end analysis of problems and tasks, in general, constitutes true epistemic mediation of the experienced goal state.

But notice, it is not the rule book, chess pieces, or chess board which epistemically mediate the experience of playing chess, nor even the moving of the pieces around the board in proper response to an opponent's moving of a piece. All these aspects of the game provide what Aristotle called the *material* cause (for example, board and pieces, two players), *formal* cause (for example, the rules and strategies), and *efficient* cause (for example, the moving of the pieces) of the game. These necessary components of the game of chess, along with the *final* cause, perhaps (for example, the desire to win), constitute the *causal support* of the game. In no sense, however, do they constitute epistemic mediators of the experience of playing the game.

Likewise, in no sense does the physics of the energy propagated (for example, light, sound) from object to receptor system, nor the physiology of the neural transmission from receptor to cortex, constitute processes which epistemically mediate perception$_2$—the act of perceiving. At best such processes only constitute causal support for perception$_2$ while constituting everything that we mean by perception$_1$—the process of perception. Let us unpack this distinction further.

Constitutive versus preparatory experiences. To continue the analogy: Neither do the experiences of seeing the board, pieces, and moves made by the opponent, nor the experiences of planning and executing one's own moves in accordance with the rules, qualify as epistemic mediators of the experience of playing the game of chess. For these experiences are *constitutive* of the game experience, that is part of its content, rather than *preparatory* to it. Epistemic mediation is always preparatory to accomplishing an act but never constitutive of the experience of the act.

To confuse the experiences which are constitutive of an act with the experiences only preparatory to it, is to be guilty of a category mistake—the mistaking of one type of thing for a thing of a different type. More precisely, it would be to confuse that which is directly contributory to our knowledge of the act with that which is only ancillary[4] to it.

Consider still another example: To eat a meal we must first prepare the meal; but the experience of eating the meal is not the same as the experience of preparing the meal. The former experience is directly contributory to (or constitutive of) our knowledge of the meal while the latter is only ancillary (or preparatory) to that knowledge (although the latter experience is constitutive of our knowledge of preparing the meal!)

Thus we must ask the indirect realist if the experience of the retinal image, or brain state, as causally determined by an object, is constitutive of our knowledge of the object or only preparatory to that knowledge. If, as we have supposed throughout, the indirect realist means the experience of such constructs to be an epistemic mediator of our knowledge of the object, that is preparatory to such knowledge, then there is no quarrel with the direct realism, for such a view would not preclude the possibility that we also directly experience the object. It would not preclude it, just as preparation of a meal does not preclude our consuming it. We would, however, be quite perplexed if they thought it should.

On the other hand, if the indirect realist meant instead that our experience of the retinal image (or other construct), as causally determined by the object, were constitutive of our knowledge of it, then we would be perplexed as to how experience of one object (for example, the retinal image) could be tantamount to experiencing another unless, of course, the objects were in some fundamental sense the same object. Then we would feel justified in concluding that whatever their presumed difference it would be in no significant way a difference which made a difference. Thus it should be quite accurate to say that the so-called "mediating" construct is, indeed, functionally transparent to the properties of its world-referent. Again there should be little to quarrel about since there would not be a nickel's difference between the two views.

There is, however, a third possibility that the indirect realist may have in mind; one which we feel is actually the source of the current confusion regarding whether or not perception is direct or indirect. This is the claim that the

[4] It is interesting to note that the Latin root of the word "ancillary" is ancillari(us), as relating to maidservants (ancilla). The experiences that epistemically mediate are like the work done by servants in preparing the food to be eaten, while the experiences of chewing, swallowing, etc., are constitutive of the act of eating. Thus, it is a mistake to consider the component experiences that are integral to a complex perceptual act as epistemic mediators of that perception.

experience of the retinal image, or brain state, is both preparatory to *and* constitutive of our knowledge of the world-referent which causally determines it. Let us explore this claim carefully, since it is here that a category error is most likely to occur.

How might the indirect realist rationalize the claim that the experience of a construct is both preparatory and constitutive of our perceptual knowledge of the world? He might argue, as suggested earlier, that experience of the given construct "mediates" our knowledge of its world referent by preparing us either to recall previous information about it, or to make inferences as to its probable nature (Brunswik, 1956; Gregory, 1970; Bransford *et al.*, this volume). Unfortunately this suggestion does not help, as the following illustration shows.

Suppose that a round, red, fruity smelling, object is placed before us. We perceive these properties and recall that such properties typically specify a sweet, juicy, edible object called an *apple*. Consequently, we infer from the available information that the present object is also an apple and, therefore, quite edible. But upon biting into the object, we discover, much to our surprise, that it is not a *real* apple at all but an inedible, waxy substance that had been impregnated with a fruity perfume. Hence our mistake was not perceptual but judgmental. It is our cognitive induction which is at fault, not our perception of the object's true properties.

The moral of the above example is that memorial or inferential information is not necessarily adequate for distinguishing experiences, say, the edibility of real apples from the inedibility of wax apples—the only information that necessarily suffices must be perceptual in nature. A fundamental principle of epistemology is indicated here, namely, the principle that *the information needed to differentiate among experiences of a certain type (for example, perceptions) must be constitutive of those experiences rather than merely ancillary or preparatory to them (for example, memorial or inferential).*

To experience the edibility of an apple as an adult there is good reason to believe that we must have certain general preparatory experiences as a child: We must learn how to grasp objects with the size, weight, shape, and surface texture as apples, how to bring them to the mouth, and how to bite, chew, and swallow them. We might call this the *memorial* or historical preparation for the perceptual experience in question.

Similarly, when perceiving the subset of properties (for example, shape, color, size, texture, and odor) shared by the wax object and real apples, we are prepared on the basis of our memory to infer inductively the edibility of the object in front of us. However, it is only upon perceiving the information actually made available by our biting into and chewing the object that we realize our error. This is because only information constitutive of an experience (for example, the perceived edibility of an apple) is necessarily adequate for distinguishing it from other experiences (for example, the perceived inedibility of wax applies). Preparatory knowledge, as provided by memory or inference, can bring us to the threshold of perceptual experience, may even bid us enter, but can in no way participate in the knowledge drived from such experiences.

Thus, we must conclude that, insofar as we are able to distinguish perceptual experiences, then we must do so on the basis of the knowledge accruing directly from them, and never from knowledge accruing indirectly from other types of experiences (for example, inference or memory). Such cases where inference or memory do save us from error are just such cases where they adequately prepare us to expect what we subsequently experience. Error in judgment arises when they do not adequately prepare us for what follows.

But notice, it is necessarily the ensuing perceptual experience which is the final arbiter of our knowledge, since ultimately what properties are true constituents of the world-referent must also be true constituents of our perceptions—else the world is but an inferential mirage, and any form of knowledge about it, without any real foundation.

Elementarism versus holism in perception. But, perhaps, there is still a way the indirect realist might accept the above argument and yet remain unconvinced that perception is an epistemically pure act—that perceptual experience is uncontaminated by memorial or inferential constituents. The indirect realist might argue as follows: It is reasonable to assume that some perceptions are more complex than others. Consider, for instance, the difference in perceiving a musical note, a melodic phrase, a movement, or the whole concerto. Or, to give another example, consider what is involved in perceiving a chess piece, a move of the piece, an opening strategy, or the whole chess game. Must we not assume, the indirect realist might press, that the lesser constituents of a whole situation are necessarily perceived prior to the perception of the whole? If so, then the perception of the whole requires time—a time during which the previous experiences of the lesser ingredients must be held in memory until they can all be accumulated and integrated into the experience of the whole. Thus the resulting perception, as an integration of memories, can properly be said to be epistemically mediated by memory while at the same time being comprised of memories. In this sense is not memory, contrary to the earlier argument, indeed both preparatory to perception of the whole (for example, the concerto) *and* constitutive of it (for example, memory of the notes, melodic phrases, movements)?

The answer is no, because to draw such a conclusion is again to be guilty of a category error—the mistaking of experiences preparatory to a perceptual act with the knowledge gained from experiences constitutive of the act. Or as Ryle (1949) put it, such a category mistake is like that committed by a young child who, upon seeing the marching soldiers, hearing the band, and witnessing the passing of the horse drawn canons, remarks with great puzzlement to his father that he thought he was going to see a parade—as if the parade were something substantively different that what was already experienced.

The act of perceiving the whole parade consists precisely in perceiving, not something different from the components of the parade, as viewed in isolation, but something more—the interrelationship among the components which perceptually welds them into a single event. That the successive ordering of each component must be remembered if the complete character of the parade is to be appreciated, is not at all in question—but to assume that such memories play a constitutive role in perception is to commit a category error.

The perceptual act is nothing more or less than apprehension of the configurational properties of the event—the network of adjacent and successive relationships in which the individual components of the event mutually participate. Thus, perception is the act of experiencing that mutual participation rather than the memory of their successiveness.

Indeed, insofar as their successiveness and independence are remembered as isolated events, to that extent they are not perceived as participating in the same superordinate event. Hence memory and perception are complementary and act in contrary directions with respect to experiencing wholeness. For the child who was only capable of experiencing the horse drawn canons, the soldiers, or band in isolation, there is no parade. We might say of such a child, if the condition proved chronic, that he was a victim of parade "agnosia"—the inability to recognize certain configurational properties of series. But notice, we would not, however, say that such a child were amnesic, since there would be no evidence of loss of memory for specific contents.

The failure to make this distinction is such a popular source of error that it may be well to illustrate in several ways the complementary nature of memory and perception: Tasting the individual ingredients before they are combined into the cake batter is not to taste the finished cake. Whether or not there is accurate memory of each ingredient that goes into a recipe is irrelevant to the experience of the final product—although memory for what was done may, of course, help guide the preparation. However, the only knowledge constitutive of the experience of the whole accrues at the moment of experiencing the whole. Nothing that precedes that experience of the final combination of ingredients can even in principle be constitutive of the knowledge accruing from it.

Thus, memory of the ingredients as successively experienced is not necessarily sufficient to explain, or to determine, the perception of their combined presentation. Moreover, the combining is accomplished in the act of perceiving, not in the act of remembering. Memory can only bring successive parts closer together in time; it can not integrate them into a presentation to be experienced whole.[5] What we have called *perception*$_1$ is the name of the process by which the requisite act of integration is achieved. By contrast, the experiencing of this act is what we have called *perception*$_2$.

Perception$_1$ can be likened to an election process—a sequence of preparatory steps that consumate in the installation in office of a duly elected official. Perceptual experience (perception$_2$), as an epistemic act, is analogous to the

[5] My thanks to Michael Turvey for this observation.

consummatory aspect of such a process. Consider: The preparatory steps to an election involve many distinct but complex ingredients–nomination of candidates, campaigning, registering and polling of the electorate, counting the votes, public posting of the results, as well as a final inauguration ceremony and installation into office. None of these components of the election process counts as an election in and of itself, although they are all preparatory to its successful realization. What constitutes the experience of an election is both more subtle and more general than the experience of any of these. What constitutes an experience of an election is the act of realization that all the preparatory steps have been successfully (legally) consummated.

Perception is itself such a consummatory act. By their very nature, such acts are directly experienced and thereby sufficient unto themselves as a valid source of knowledge. We should not say for certain that the election of an official had been successfully achieved unless we believed each step in the election process had been legally executed. Similarly, we should not experience the perception of a complex event unless the preparatory stages of processing had been properly satisfied. In the former case, a failure to satisfy the necessary antecedent conditions would render the election a fraud and, in the latter case, the perception a hallucination.

Conclusions

If the above arguments are valid, then there is no cogency to the argument that perception is *indirect.* Indeed, sufficient problems are encountered in attempting to clarify the meaning of such a claim that it seems wise to abandon the term altogether. However, in the wake of such problems of interpretation, it may be equally wise to avoid the use of the contrastive term "direct" when addressing perceptual issues.

The recalcitrant issue, in any case, is not whether or not perception is "direct" or "indirect" but how to keep clear the distinction between perception as a causal process (perception_1) and perception as an epistemic act (perception_2). The former concept retains all that is viable in the notion that perception somehow depends upon necessary physical and physiological factors (causal support), while the latter concept retains all that is viable in the notion that perceptual experiences may in some cases be mediated–those cases being where previous knowledge prepares one for further knowledge.

Regarding the possible role of memory or inference in perception: any form of epistemic mediation to which they may contribute serves perception but does not contribute directly to its nature. Although there is no denying the necessary role of causal process as support for the act of perceiving the world, there is considerable reason for denying that any stage of the causal process–neither retinal image, neural transmission nor cerebral state–can serve as an epistemic mediator of perceptual experience.

In the final analysis, the most important thing we can say about the nature of perception is this: We perceive the world, perhaps, as through a glass darkly—but we *do* perceive the world. As scientists, we may attempt to infer how we might do so, but as perceivers no inference is involved in the doing.

ACKNOWLEDGMENTS

Preparation of this chapter was supported in part by Haskins Laboratories, New Haven, Connecticut, and by the Department of Psychology, Unversity of Connecticut. We wish to thank William Mace for critical suggestions.

REFERENCES

Arnheim, R. *Visual thinking.* Berkeley, California: University of California Press, 1964.

Attneave, F. In defense of homunculi. In W. A. Rosenblith (Ed.), *Sensory communication.* Published jointly at Cambridge, Massachusetts: MIT Press, and New York: Wiley, 1961. Pp. 777–781.

Austin, J. L. *Sense and sensibilia.* London: Oxford University Press, 1962.

Ayer, A. J. *The foundations of empirical knowledge.* New York: Macmillan, 1940.

Brunswik, C. *Perception and the representative design of psychological experiments.* Berkeley, California: University of California Press, 1956.

Bullock, T. H. The problem of recognition in an analyzer made of neurons. In W. A. Rosenblith (Ed.), *Sensory communication.* Published jointly at Cambridge, Massachusetts: MIT Press, and New York: Wiley, 1961. Pp. 717–724.

Drake, D., *et al. Essays in critical realism: A comparative study of the problem of knowledge.* London: Macmillan, 1920.

Gibson, J. J. *The senses considered as perceptual systems.* Boston: Houghton-Mifflin, 1966.

Gregory, R. L. *The intelligent eye.* New York: McGraw-Hill, 1970.

Helmholtz, H. von. *Treatise on physiological optics* (Translated by J. C. P. Southall). Rochester, New York: Optical Society of America, 1925.

Henle, M. On naive realism. In R. B. MacLeod & H. L. Pick (Eds.), *Perception: Essays in honor of James J. Gibson.* New York: Cornell University Press, 1974. Pp. 40–56.

Jenkins, J., Jiménez-Pabón, E., Shaw, R., & Sefer, J. *Schuell's aphasia in adults.* New York: Harper & Row, 1974.

Maxwell, G. Theories, perception, and structural realism. In R. G. Colodny (Ed.), *The nature and function of scientific theories.* Pittsburgh: University of Pittsburg Press, 1970. Pp. 3–34.

Pearce, J. C. *The crack in the cosmic egg.* New York: Julian Press, 1971.

Russell, B. *The analysis of matter.* London: George Allen and Unwin, 1927.

Russell, B. *An inquiry into meaning and truth.* New York: Norton, 1940. P. 14.

Ryle, G. *The concept of mind.* London: Hutchinson, 1949.

Shaw, R., & McIntyre, M. Algoristic foundations for cognitive psychology. In W. Weimer & D. Palermo (Eds.), *Cognition and the symbolic processes.* Hillsdale, New Jersey: Lawrence Erlbaum Associates, 1974.

Shaw, R., McIntyre, M., & Mace, W. The role of symmetry in event perception. In R. B. MacLeod & H. Pick (Eds.), *Perception: Essays in honor of James J. Gibson.* New York: Cornell University Press, 1974.

Part I

PERCEPTION, ACTION, AND DEVELOPMENT

SECTION A

Perceiving Our World

2

James J. Gibson's Strategy for Perceiving: Ask Not What's Inside Your Head, but What Your Head's Inside of

William M. Mace

Trinity College

INTRODUCTION

For many years James Gibson has been impressed with the precision of visually guided behavior. In 1938 he published a study of automobile driving (Gibson & Crooks, 1938); during World War II he studied visual components of aviation, particularly the activity of landing airplanes. The priority that these studies reflect, and which seems to have been developing with increasing explicitness as Gibson's ideas have developed, is to treat perception as a biologically adaptive activity first and as a study of "interesting phenomena" much later–if at all. On Gibson's view, even though it is surely true that all perceptual phenomena, and particularly curiosities such as illusions, can tell us something important about how visual systems work, curiosities are probably the last things we want to worry about in our theories. First, theories should do justice to the everyday perceptual accomplishments that contribute to the survival of the species. The problem of guiding ourselves (cf. Gibson, 1958; Turvey, this volume), as well as cars and airplanes is primarily a problem of veridical perception. These are cases where perception seems to be in close touch with the environment. Yet the traditional theories of space perception available to Gibson when he was faced with the practical problem of understanding airplane landings and visually guided locomotion had little to say about such cases. Therefore he gradually struck out on his own.

THE FIRST VERSION OF GIBSON'S PROGRAM: PERCEPTUAL PSYCHOPHYSICS

New Conceptions of the Stimulus

By 1950 Gibson thought that the need was for what Troland called a psychophysics of perception (cf. Lombardo, 1973, for an extensive discussion of the history and development of Gibson's ideas, including his relation to Troland). It was believed at the time that the "givens" in the light to the eye could not support perceptual phenomena, but only elementary experiences such as sensations. Organized percepts were thought to be constructed by adding order and meaning to the sensations which elementary stimuli were capable of evoking directly. Gibson reopened the case for thinking of perception as being a function of stimulation by offering new conceptions of the stimulus. Even though it seemed clear that perception could not be a direct function of the variables of stimulation such as frequency and intensity of light (those variables ordinarily controlled in psychophysical experiments), there was no reason to believe that perceptual experiences could not be supported by any of a wide variety of other patterns of variation in light. The best known candidates for being alternative, "higher order," variables of stimulation relevant to perception were the gradients of texture and texture flow that Gibson discussed in *The Perception of the Visual World* (1950). These were shown to specify surface extent and surface slant (Purdy, 1958) as well as the path traveled by a moving observer (Gibson, Olum, & Rosenblatt, 1955).

The new insight Gibson provided in these examples was that the stimulus for perception is just as much a problem for research and theory as are the mechanisms of perception. In fact once the appropriate description of stimulation becomes a scientific problem, one might well presume that it is logically and strategically prior to any detailed proposals about processing (Mace, 1975). That is certainly the major thrust of current linguistics and psycholinguistics (Chomsky, 1972). By specifying the accomplishments of a system first, one can gradually limit the class of plausible mechanisms for perception to those that satisfy the job description. For example, Gibson has argued that just as units of structure can be sought at many levels of analysis in the light, so perceptual mechanisms functioning as units might be analyzed at corresponding levels of analysis. Thus, as he has often argued, even though light may be a stimulus for a rod or a cone, patterns like gradients are stimuli for organs such as eye-brain systems. He has never worked out a detailed theory of the detection of a particular variable of stimulation, but he has not been mute on the matter of processing either. His suggestion that the functional organization of perceptual systems must be analyzed with respect to corresponding levels of stimulus patterning is a serious constraint that more detailed theories must consider (Gibson, 1966). Surely imposing constraints to be satisfied by possible mechanisms is a key part of any effort to understand what mechanisms are actually at work.

Environmental Constraints on Stimuli Surfaces

The perceptual psychophysics that Gibson proposed was actually more than merely an attempt to specify constraints on processing models. In addition to arguing for perception as a function of stimulation he argued that much stimulation is a function of the environment—and, therefore, that it is possible to view perception as a function of the environment. Theories built within a program like this would not slight the facts of biological adaptation and useful perceptual activity. By considering the environment and its structure as part of perceptual theory the scientific task of understanding perception does not necessarily become easier, but the task looks more like the investigation of natural law and less like the contemplation of miracles.

Surprisingly it is not uncommon for perceptual psychologists to ignore or downplay the important role that environment-dependent stimulus mapping relations play in Gibson's theory, applauding him only for recognizing the role of "higher order" variables in stimulation (Garner, 1970; Hochberg, 1974). Apparently researchers who are willing to investigate stimulus structure do not recognize a need for principled limitations on the stimulus variables sought. The psychophysical task *is* simplified inasmuch as one would limit the patterns used in experiments to those which might correspond to selected environmental properties. Otherwise Gibson's insight that "higher-order" variables of stimulation could function as stimuli for perception would have opened a Pandora's box of possibilities. Researchers could wander aimlessly through long lists of patterns searching for those to which observers responded in experiments constrained only by their imaginations and the existing body of literature, possessing a selection strategy based solely on luck and tenacity.

The environmental features that have occupied Gibson most are surfaces, especially the ground. He has maintained that what organisms see when perceiving the arrangement of the world is never "space" per se as presented in traditional theories, but surfaces and their interrelations. To say that one sees a vast expanse of space, or depth, receding far into the distance is wrong to Gibson. The experience should really be described in terms of the extended surface seen, since a person can only see an expanse of distance when presented an appropriate texture gradient indicating a ground surface extending to a horizon. By contrast, Gibson has pointed out that a person looking at patterns which ought to be specific to pure space, such as a *Ganzfeld,* give rise to little if any experience of space. He said,

> Spaces are determined by their surfaces. . . . A space *is* a surface; at least an environmental space always has a floor or a ground. . . . In general, a space is an unbounded surface. . . . The biggest space we are capable of seeing is the surface of the terrain. . . .

The sky, paradoxically, presents scarcely any stimulation for space perception although it is what psychologists have been tempted to call space [Gibson, 1959, p. 478].

The transitive relation of the physically extended ground to optical texture gradients to the *perceived* extended ground was the paradigmatic instance of stimulation as a function of the environment and perception as a function of stimulation, hence perception as a function of the environment.

Through the 1950s, Gibson held to the idea that his "ground" theory of perception could be considered a basically psychophysical program. Since that time, however, Gibson has discovered his system developing beyond anything that could properly be called psychophysics. His is now a radical position in the literal sense of proposing to reformulate drastically the foundations of perceptual theory.

THE REVISED VERSION OF GIBSON'S PROGRAM: AN ECOLOGICAL APPROACH TO PERCEPTION

Gibson's psychophysical approach to perception marked a significant departure from mainstream thinking on how to frame and answer questions about perception. Few others had entertained the possibility of studying stimulus structure with the aim of finding correspondences between stimulus and percept, and of concentrating on biologically significant percepts. However, there was much in Gibson's early vision which was far more traditional than the ecological approach he is now developing. Succinctly put, the psychophysical program was basically a stimulus–response psychology. It was new in that it took the stimulus as well as stimulus–response relations as objects of investigation, but traditional in considering perception to be a set of responses to presented stimuli (albeit "higher order" stimuli).

What is important to realize now is that Gibson does not presently hold a stimulus–response view in any commonly understood sense, even though he continues to maintain that perception of the environment is direct as opposed to being mediated by nonpercpetual stages of psychological processing (e.g., memory, inference, or imagination). To do this is what requires his current approach to be so radical—radical in the sense that he claims that a direct theory of perception is both plausible and necessary.

His current approach is also radical in the sense that, first, it requires developing a theory of what there is to be perceived as an integral part of a theory of how perceptual processing could possibly occur and, secondly, it requires a theory of how processing actually does occur. Gibson makes it clear in his current theory that one can only have direct perception if the environmental and organismic components of perceptual theory are compatible. Presumably they will be compatible only if one develops each component of the theory with an eye to the other. For Gibson, one cannot realistically expect to synthesize a general theory of perception from patching together a theory of the physical world constructed by physicists who are primarily interested in the imperceptible microstructure of matter with a theory of optics developed for lens makers, astronomers, and microscopists with a theory of image recording developed for painters and geometers with a theory of neural functioning developed for communication engineers so as to yield a unified theory of adaptive perception for ecologically minded psychologists.

Thus Gibson himself has done a great deal of work on the question of what there is to be perceived in the environment and in energy structures (for example, an optical array where vision is under discussion) as well as sketching out new ideas of how to catalogue perceptual systems in ways that mesh with his analyses of what there is to be perceived. Each of these components, the *what* and the *how,* must be considered an integral part of the same perceptual theory for Gibson. (For a detailed discussion of this point see Shaw & McIntyre, 1974.) If they do not fit together, then the structure falls and direct perception becomes untenable.

Over the last 10–15 years Gibson has tried to develop enough theory in each of these realms to demonstrate that direct perception is indeed plausible even if hordes of difficult details remain to be worked out. The research and theory that form the content of Gibson's program such as his analysis of the optic array, stimulus information, and the functional organization of perceptual systems are what Gibson most often points to as radical features of his work. These will be treated soon.

The remainder of this chapter will first describe the key concepts currently holding the system together and then will examine the multiple underpinnings which make direct perception plausible by discussing five different ways one could hold an indirect theory of perception.

MOTION PERSPECTIVE AS A CASE AGAINST PERCEPTUAL PSYCHOPHYSICS

The concepts that Gibson developed which decisively distinguish his ecological approach from his psychophysical approach may be illustrated by referring to his paper on motion perspective (Gibson *et al.,* 1955). This paper presents a formalization of principles Gibson had discovered from his work on aircraft landing, the full implications of which, however, were not pursued until after this paper.

Essentially the Gibson *et al.* (1955) analysis of what they called motion perspective was a generalization of earlier analyses of motion parallax by Helmholtz. In motion parallax the rate of optical flow of points in a stable environment relative to a moving point of observation is inversely proportional to the distance of the environmental points from the observer. The farther away the points, the slower they translate in the visual field. However, this is an analysis of that portion of the visual field parallel to the path of locomotion. Gibson noted that there is, in fact, texture flow all around the moving point of observation. Gibson *et al.* (1955) formalized the case of rectilinear motion over an extended surface showing that motion parallax was a special case of their motion perspective.

There are three items of special interest in their analysis. The first is the observation that the equations for texture "motion" not only specify relative distances of stable environment points, but that the path of locomotion of the moving point is reciprocally specified. That is, the same global transformation of texture can be decomposed into parts that are specific to the environment and to the path of whatever is moving in that environment:

> The fundamental visual perception is that of *approach to a surface.* This percept always has a subjective component as well as an objective component, i.e., it specifies *O*'s position, movement, and direction as much as it specifies the location, slant, and shape of the surface [Gibson *et al.*, 1955, p. 383].

A second important feature is that significant parameter values such as the angle of inclination of the approach to the surface and the point of imminent contact remain the same as long as the motion is uniform and the environment stable. They are invariant properties of the optical flow. The third fact to note is that the moving point of observation generates a specific texture flow with its characteristic invariants defined relationally among many samples of points. This suggested to Gibson that the path of locomotion was probably specified everywhere in the flowing texture–which would in turn imply that any eye sensitive to the crucial variables of stimulation could register these variables at different places in the array. On this analysis one could theoretically take various *samples* of the flowing texture and get the same surface and path information.

What all this has in common with the psychophysical program (within which this particular analysis was carried out) is a concern for correspondence between optical texture and environmental conditions with special attention to the optical texture generated by surfaces. What makes it hard to fit into a psychophysics is that none of the traditional interpretations of the concept of a stimulus seem to be involved (see Gibson, 1960, for a survey and discussion of these meanings). Ordinarily the notion of stimulus has indicated something that could be applied or presented to an animal followed by an observable response. But each of the three points mentioned above makes it difficult to view the optical flow as a stimulus that could be presented in the ordinary psychophysical experiment.

First, if one were to test the sensitivity of an organism to the world events potentially available, there are at least two major judgments to be made instead of one—the path of locomotion and the layout of the environment. To say that one stimulus could cause two simultaneous, complementary responses (that is, what Gestaltists have called a "scission" effect) is unlike psychophysics as traditionally practiced. More importantly, such dual specification contained in the changing stimulation to a moving point of observation (that is, a locomoting observer) indicates that a very special kind of analysis is needed to explain how such perceptual processing might occur. Presumably, such an analysis will be in terms of acts of perceptual differentiation into orthogonal components of information—one component specifying invariant environmental properties, another specifying the observer's place in that environment as a creature with a history.

Traditional psychophysics, on the other hand, has typically been rationalized as the study of automatic responses to stimuli (rather than acts) which serve as building blocks for perception. From this viewpoint, however, the observer is but a passive receiver. Under such a view, Gibson argues, a perceiver would not be able to differentiate stimulation into its most useful dimensions. Thus, traditional psychophysics encounters serious difficulty in attempting to explain why the optical motions of an image over the retina is not intrinsically ambiguous with respect to whether the source of the optical motion is due to observer movement or environmental motion. Under this view it is not at all clear that one can explain how passive registration of a stimulation flux will allow the observer to extract the perceptual invariants specifying the stable layout of the world.

Second, Gibson *et al.* (1955) point out that crucial features of both the environment and the path of locomotion are specified by relations which remain invariant in the optical flow of texture. But how might one present an invariant in a psychophysical experiment? One can certainly present displays in which invariant relations are defined, but to regard an invariant relation as a stimulus, in the sense of being a "goad" which elicits behavior (Gibson, 1960), is incompatible with the view that the perceptual system actively separates invariant information from variant information.

The above two points are really the same, in that perceptual processing must decompose the information detected into subjective–objective components as well as variant–invariant components. If one accepts the view that important optical structure is to be found in the decomposition of a total structure such as a flow gradient, then the idea that there can be isolated stimuli which give rise to isolated responses that somehow become percepts (and this must be assumed by psychophysics if it is to be regarded as relevant to perception at all) has to be rejected.

Finally, the idea that texture flow can contain structure without reference to a retinal projection creates a psychophysical puzzle. Ordinarily one would think that an observer who is sampling different segments of an optic array over a long while would be getting different stimuli. Although this is certainly true in some sense, such a view ignores the possibility that the information specifying the path of locomotion and much of the environmental layout (ground plane, horizon, etc.) remain invariant as long as the organism is sampling within the same transforming array.

Major features of the ecological approach information and the optic array. Since the geometry provided by Gibson *et al.* (1955) specifies a great deal about the environmental events generating it, one would think that such "variables of stimulation" would play an important role in perceptual theory. Yet, as the above discussion shows, it is difficult to see what role they might play in traditional views. Over the years, Gibson solved this dilemma by rejecting the notion of stimulus in favor of stimulus *information.* This latter notion captures all the important aspects of the foregoing example. Because many connotations of the term "stimulus" are misleading from Gibson's point of view (Gibson, 1960), he now prefers to avoid all use of the term. Thus "stimulus information" is replaced with phrases such as "information contained in . . ." some specified type of array. This idea of information is a particularly central concept, and thus will be used to organize the full discussion of Gibson's ecological approach.

Whenever environmental events structure light (or any other vehicle of structure if not discussing vision) in a specific fashion, Gibson asserts that the light contains *information* for those events. This use of the term information to indicate structure specific to its sources is a special one. It is not the same as the Shannon and Weaver concept of information as a measure of uncertainty more commonly found in perceptual psychology. By using this term instead of "stimulus," Gibson hoped to avoid the muddles he pointed out in his review of the stimulus concept (Gibson, 1960) and retain the possibilities of direct perception expressed in his psychophysical program. *Information* was also meant to capture the insights illustrated in Gibson, Olum, and Rosenblatt (1955) along with their extensions. Hence, for the reasons already mentioned, perceiving based on the detection of variables of stimulation (information) such as were shown in that analysis could not be thought of as simple responding to physical stimuli.

Information (for vision) is a geometric concept defined over a transforming optic array, the 360° solid angle of variations in ambient light intensity converging on a point of observation from all directions. Animals or humans do not enter the picture except as a scale factor for selecting appropriate environmental features to analyze. Thus Gibson can speak of available information in an optic array. Whether or not a particular observer can detect such information is a logically distinct question, though of course a necessary question for the psychologist.

The optic array is taken as structure *surrounding* a point of observation. The point of observation in the geometric analysis (for which the nodal point of an observer's eye may be substituted in applications) is taken to be *immersed* in this array structured by environmental events. To replace the traditional image of the "stimulus" for vision as a picture that can be presented to an observer by the ambient optic array has a number of consequences. First the structured ambient array is always present and cannot be turned on and off the way stimuli in psychological experiments can be. It makes far more sense to characterize the basic contact of organisms with such an array as one of exploration than as a response. Furthermore it makes no sense to think of an organism's responding to isolated bits of such an array as if they existed in hermetically sealed packages. Rather one would be more likely to view the perceiver's problem as one of decomposition. That is, if a point is immersed in a richly nested structure of optical events, which of these can a particular perceiver separate out to respond to? Finally, the particular optic array of the terrestrial environment which is light above and dark below, in correspondence to sky and earth, provides the foundation for an absolute frame of reference within which all other event structure can be nested. Gibson now argues that this fundamental invariant is perhaps the best place to emphasize that his approach deals with real environmental space, which does have an intrinsic polarity, and not with abstract geometric space, which does not. In doing so he hopes to avoid the regresses and hopeless relativism that are implied in discussions of frames of reference in much perceptual literature.

Since *information* refers to variables that are specific to environmental features, Gibson must determine what these correspondences are. Where there are persistent features of the environment such as the substantiality and rigidity of surfaces to be specified, Gibson would want to find correspondingly persistent features of the ambient array (invariant information). Where there are changes in the environment such as motions, there should be changes in array structure (variant information). One should note carefully that specificity and not intuitive similarity is the basis for correspondence. Gibson does not expect the information for motion to be motion or the information for shape to be forms. Rather, in cases where persistent environmental properties are specified, he says that the information is contained in "timeless and formless invariants." Structures defined in terms of adjacent and successive orders of units are the types of things he has in mind here. Interestingly enough, this all follows from the assumption that the ambient optic array has a nested structure. If the point of observation is surrounded by densely packed structured light, then there are no units to move or to form the basis of shape perception. Every change in the array, whether induced by movements of an observer, by motions of objects, by changes in material composition, or by changes in shape must be regarded as a transformation of the *whole* array. To say that an object in the array moves, in the example of motion, would be to presuppose the appropriate decomposition of the array (in terms of figure ground, phenomenal identity, and so forth) which is, of course, the problem to begin with.

Information for self and the world. A central feature intrinsic to Gibson's sense of information that has already been discussed somewhat is that the same transforming optic array not only can specify change and nonchange generally, but also specifies the movements and postures of the observer and the arrangement and rearrangements of the environment simultaneously. Gibson asserts that *all* information has two poles of specification, a "subjective" aspect and an "objective" aspect, as illustrated in Gibson *et al.* (1955) in particular and more generally in all cases of locomotion through a basically stable environment (Gibson, 1958; Lee, 1974). In such cases he has often suggested that the variants in the array specify subjective movement and the invariants specify the persisting environment, although this is a simplification meant more to stimulate thinking than to provide closure. Gibson calls the structure specific to environmental events exterospecific (as opposed to "exteroceptive" which is associated with specialized receptors) and the structure specific to the organism or point of observation propriospecific. These are aspects into which information can be decomposed regardless of its manifest form (although the focus of this discussion has primarily been on information available in optical form). Gibson maintains that information carried in any manner can contain both propriospecific and exterospecific information. Therefore, he sees no need for classifying sensory organs into those specializing in detecting states of the self and those specializing in detecting states of the world. To dramatize the argument against specialized receptors Gibson discusses "visual kinesthesis" as an example of obtaining propriospecific information from light (1958) and a variety of examples of haptic shape perception to illustrate obtaining exterospecific information from the skin-joint system (e.g., Gibson, 1962).

Generalizing the array concept. Throughout this chapter I am following Gibson's practice of concentrating on examples from light and vision. Nevertheless the principles of Gibson's approach require that the full story of perception be told in more than light and sight. The terrestrial world filled with a variety of events contains many different embodiments of patterned energy. What each of these can specify must be investigated just as carefully as light. Thus one could analyze the specifying potential of vibrations in the air (ecological acoustics), of the gases dissolved in air (ecological olfaction and gustation), or of patterns of deformation of the skin and articular stresses (ecological haptics). One should recognize that these are each quite different embodiments of event structures. Various combinations of them co-occur. Each embodiment has its own strengths and weaknesses in terms of the events it can specify. For instance, chemicals in the air do not seem capable of maintaining the kind of persistent detail that reverberating volumes of light patterns do. Opaque surfaces have somewhat different consequences for structuring acoustic vibrations and light. The same world of events should be regarded as simultaneously structuring each of the possible embodiments of information in a specific fashion, but the different capacities of the patterning media themselves constrain the aspects of the world that can be specified in them.

Facts such as these should in turn have consequences for the possible evolutionary design of perceptual systems by nature and their analysis by researchers. That is, no one perceptual system (that is, sense modality) should be regarded as a privileged purveyor of truth in the Bishop Berkeley tradition. Each should be considered as having access to information about the same set of events simultaneously. But each should also be recognized as potentially having special capabilities, strictly as a consequence of what can be specified in light, sound, smell, and so forth. Possessing multiple channels of sensitivity allows observers to differentiate more available information than they could otherwise. In cases where two or more perceptual systems happen to overlap in the information they are obtaining, one should regard this as redundant information and not as a case of enrichment or integration (where the integration implies combining units that were not previously integrated). Thus a cube which is seen and felt at the same time and is identifiable as a cube through either system, is a cube specified in two ways at the same time on Gibson's view. The invariant information specifying the cube is presumed to be sufficiently abstract so as to be identical for both touch and vision. Some properties, however, may be modality specific. For instance, the temperature of the cube is more likely to be available to touch than to vision, whereas the color of the cube is more likely to be available to vision than to touch.

Thus there is no claim that there are not important distinctions. Yet to the extent that the information of interest is that specifying geometrical shape Gibson would assert that it is the same across modalities. In this way the observer, whether animal or human, was designed to conform with the identities and differences that exist in the world of events rather than as an assemblage of message channels which have no meaning apart from the way they are combined (say, as implied in Bishop Berkeley's idea that vision derives its meaning from touch).

The environment. The actual investigations which fall into the area of perceptual research that Gibson designates as ecological optics have one basic goal in common; they have all sought to characterize the geometric structure underlying the most important properties of the world, such properties as rigidity, nonrigidity, occluding edges, shape and size. It is important to realize that finding variables of an array which are specific to environmental structures depends as much on selecting the appropriate environmental structures as it does on finding the correct "higher order" geometric variables. Gibson's stress on the nature of surfaces played this role in his earlier work. Thus an equally important problem for Gibson's general approach is the attempt to formulate a description of the environment that is compatible with theories of every array (optic array, acoustic array, haptic array, etc.) which can contain information about the environment.

From 1966 on, Gibson has begun his account of perception with a description of environments, where by environment he means a description of the physical world which is relevant to the time and space scale of organisms. His careful environmental description is intended to capture the qualities of the physical world which have made the origin and maintenance of life possible. It is also meant to show that the composition and arrangement of substances, media, and the surfaces of their interfaces structure light (and acoustic vibrations, etc.) in specific ways. Thus a substance that is rigid should interact with light in ways that are different from substances that are nonrigid, and these differences may be specific. If an environment specifically structures an array, it is clear that an organism capable of processing this array's structure would be in contact with that environment.

Ecological optics: The current status of research. It is very important to have the overall coherent view such as Gibson is developing, but no matter how plausible or promising it appears, there is no substitute for detailed investigations. Much of the research conducted by Gibson and his followers has been devoted to working out detailed examples of information. For the most part these emphasize geometric analyses of ecologically significant situations intended to discover possible environmentally structured array specificities. They have not emphasized research on characterization of the environment itself. In this respect this aspect of the overall enterprise which Gibson calls *ecological optics* is a continuation of the program begun as perceptual psychophysics and pursued primarily in the search for "higher order variables of stimulation." The overall approach to perception in terms of ecology that Gibson takes is probably best thought of as a metatheory rather than a theory in the sense of offering specific, falsifiable hypotheses. The overall approach and its subcomponents such as ecological optics should be evaluated in terms of their fruitfulness. No one will ever be able to claim truth or falsity for it. However, the work conducted within a subspecialty such as ecological optics is full of testable and tested hypotheses. Some of the key steps have been taken by the following investigators: Gibson *et al.* (1955) whose work has already been discussed; Purdy (1958), who worked out an analysis of the correspondence between gradients of texture and surface slant; Hay (1966), who showed that the changing pattern or the shadow of an arbitrarily moving rigid plane surface was specific to the shape and slant of that surface; Farber (1972), who extended Hay's work by investigating a special case where the magnified projection of a rigidly rotating plane specified a nonrigid motion; Sedgwick (1973), who showed the power of the terrestrial horizon to specify the size of objects seen against it; Kaplan (1969), who investigated the role of the progressive appearance and disappearance of texture in specifying the occlusion of one *opaque* surface by another; Mace and Shaw (1974), who investigated the role of translatory symmetry in specifying the perception of one surface through another (transparent "depth"); Lee (1974), who provides a mathematical description of the optical flow pattern afforded a moving observer showing the existence of both exterospecific and propriospecific information; John Pittenger who, with Robert Shaw (this volume), showed that the perceived age of faces can be explained in terms of a "remodeling" transformation belonging to a special geometry for nonrigid shapes. Only when specific proposals such as those in these studies can be made is it possible to construct and control stimulus conditions for perceptual experiments to see if particular organisms actually use the available information or not. The studies conducted with the information defined in the above work have generally shown excellent results, but none have established open-and-shut cases. They should be seen as decisive groundbreaking operations opening the way for a great deal of constructive work on many fronts in the future.

FIVE WAYS TO HAVE A THEORY OF INDIRECT PERCEPTION

Throughout most of his career a tenet of Gibson's has been that perception must be *direct* rather than mediated by memory, inference or any other psychological process. It has seemed apparent to him that only a theory of direct perception can do justice to the facts of evolution and adaptive behavior. Yet the construction of such a theory cannot proceed by fiat. As I have tried to show, a coherent theory of direct perception must have a broader scope than merely trying to model the mechanisms of perception. It must recognize that a theory of environments and a theory of the patterns of energy created by environments are just as much a part of a complete theory of perception as are theories of what organisms do. Once it is explicitly recognized that these are all mutually dependent components of perceptual theory, then they can be developed in compatible ways. Only as they are developed in compatible ways can direct perception make sense. I suspect that much of the consistent criticism Gibson has received for holding a direct theory of perception (e.g., Gregory, 1972; Gyr, 1972; Johansson, 1970) stems from not recognizing how thoroughly comprehensive such a theory must be. To further clarify the multiple foundations of Gibson's direct perception, let us examine what theorists seem to have meant by indirect perception. Contrary to the dichotomy implied in the direct–indirect contrast, there seem to be at least five common grounds used to support the claim that perception is indirect. Holding any one of them would be sufficient to make a person an indirect theorist. Consequently, to hold a direct position such as Gibson's requires an alternative to each one.

What Structures Can Count as Stimuli?

Any theory of perception presupposes some set of structures that are detected by the perceptual processes rather than constructed. Early theorists claimed that perception was based on point sensations in a frozen moment of time. Currently more complex entities such as oriented lines are being proposed as directly detectable structures. Since perception results in the experience of events that are spatially unified and exist continuously over time, a theory whose basic structures of stimulation do not have these qualities must interpose compounding or constructive mechanisms to build unified percepts. This integration of substructures is an intervening process thought to be different from the end result of perceiving. Such an approach represents one way that a theory of perception can be indirect. Helmholtz (1925) was quite explicit on this point: "*A direct image* of a portion of space of three dimensions is *not* afforded either by the eye or by the hand. It is only by comparing the images of the two eyes, or by moving the body with respect to the hand, that the idea of solid bodies is obtained [p. 23; italics added]."

Gibson, on the other hand, holds that such a "piecing-together" description of stimulus processing is not necessary because structure in the stimulation itself consists of spatial and temporal relationships. For him, structure is patterned discontinuity in an array. Thus a pattern of regularly appearing or disappearing texture relative to some point in the environment can be thought of as an instance of structure in the optic array defined over time. Such regularities or invariants which are defined only over change are common in mathematics, being at least as old as the derivative, and should not be ignored in descriptions of stimuli available for perception. It is important to realize that Gibson's definition of structure is sufficiently abstract to apply to media other than light, indeed, any medium that can preserve any pattern of discontinuities over time. Since order and change of order are not modality-specific characteristics, Gibson's definition makes it possible to say that the same stimulus structure is equally available to several senses. For example, the adjacent order of the vertices of a cube are an obvious aspect of its physical structure. This physical adjacent order will produce corresponding adjacent orders both in the pressure patterns to a hand that grasps the cube and in the light patterns to an eye that looks at it.

From the viewpoint of Gibson's dynamic approach to stimulus analysis, the observation that organisms perceive events structured over time no longer provides sufficient reason to conclude that perception is an indirect, constructive process which adds a dimension of temporal integration not to be found in raw impinging stimuli. Since dynamic structures may count as stimuli, perceptual processes using them may be referred to as *direct detection processes,* which occur over time because the stimuli being processed are defined over time. Thus, Gibson has overcome one obstacle to a direct theory of perception, or the notion that givens or data are momentary slices in time, by changing what can count as structural givens in stimulation to include regularities of change.

A consideration of current single cell "detector" mechanisms may help to dispel the notion that Gibson's ideas about direct response to complex relationships are abstract speculations that cannot be physically realized.[1] The perceptual apparatus of amphibians and mammals is somehow constructed so that certain central cells respond to relationships that are defined in terms of space (line detectors) and in terms of space–time (motion detectors). Their existence is thoroughly documented. Recently, Gross, Rocha-Miranda, and Bender (1972) have reported "monkey paw" detectors in the inferotemporal cortex of *Macaca mulatta.* None of the investigators in these areas seems to have felt a need to explain the action of such cells by referring to comparisons of current input with stored images or integrating momentary images over time with constructive operations. Detector cells should be considered to be examples of physical systems which are organized ("tuned" in Gibson's terminology) to give specific responses to specific relations in light. These detectors do not, of course, prove the existence of mechanisms that respond directly to the more complex relations that Gibson discusses. However, the single cell work does provide an analogue to Gibson's notion of direct perception of structured events, which in turn makes the idea plausible and shows that it cannot be dismissed on a priori grounds.

Does Information Exist?

As already discussed, stimulation is said to contain information if its structure is specific to the environmental sources of that structure. Only if stimulation contains such specific structure could it specify its sources, and only if it specified its sources could the detection of such structure be said to be direct perception of these sources. The possibility of direct contact with an environment thus depends heavily on the existence of information in Gibson's sense. Indeed, ecological optics, the theoretical and empirical investigation of the information available in light has occupied most of the time of Gibson and his students. If information in Gibson's sense did not exist, then intervening steps in perceptual processing such as hypothesis constructing and testing are necessary. Assuming the idea that the structure of stimulation does not specifically

[1] The observations in this paragraph are primarily those of John B. Pittenger, Department of Psychology, University of Arkansas at Little Rock.

correspond to any of its sources, then, requires that perception be indirect. Gibson has avoided this lure into mediation by developing his concept of information.

The Senses Considered as Perceptual Systems

Traditionally the "senses" have been regarded as separate input channels funneling messages to a central processor which must compare the inputs coming in from each in order to make unitary decisions about the current state of the world. To the extent that perception is a product of putting together these messages from separate channels, perception must be regarded as indirect or constructive. Richard Gregory (1969) has suggested that perception of visual patterns is indirect because "what matters is whether the object is useful, a threat, or food. It is non-optical properties that are important [p. 245]." And later he asserts: "To build a seeing machine, we must provide more than an 'eye' and a computer. It must have limbs, or the equivalent, to discover non-optical properties of objects for its eyes' images to take on significance in terms of objects and not merely patterns [p. 246]." In other words, our skin and body have certain privileges not enjoyed by the visual system—namely that patterns of deformation of the skin created by objects and patterns of muscle movements created, say, by walking toward an object are directly meaningful.

This view goes back at least to Bishop Berkeley and is apparently forced by the assumption of meaningless punctate stimulation for vision. Interestingly enough it is not supported by a shred of empirical evidence or coherent theory. For instance, if one arranges conflicts of information available to various modes of attention, the conflicts are always resolved in favor of vision (e.g., Pick, 1970). Or imagine some of Gibson's favorite key cases, a fish swimming upstream or a bird flying against the wind. How could nonvisual criteria such as effort expended or muscles recruited have any effectiveness for guidance in these cases? Could it really be very convincing to try to account for these kinds of phenomena by saying that somehow organisms learned to trust vision gradually after first not trusting it? How could this work? It is really quite difficult to see why the pupil would always outstrip its teacher in perceptual conflict situations. What would guide such a shift of control?

For Gibson, the difference between meaningful and meaningless stimulation has nothing to do with whether or not stimulation across modalities is integrated. As described above, there is information differentially available to the various sense modalities. Hearing is better than seeing when one is interested in events taking place behind a nearby opaque surface; though seeing is certainly better than hearing in determining the opacity or shape of a surface. Touch is clearly better at perceiving temperature differences. And so it goes. Rather than having these be isolated systems to correlate, however, Gibson would have each of these modes of attention (each of which has the motor resources of the body available to it) sampling the same structured world. When they are sampling the same events, there would rarely be contradictory information—though the information could be richer as suggested in the examples immediately above.

In summary, for Gibson, the senses operating as perceptual systems are all sensitive to information about the entire environment. Each mode of attention has its own special capacity for detecting information but these specialties reflect the nature of the embodiment of world structure as well as the nature of the detecting system.

Affordances

Gibson's concept of affordances, that is, information specifying the adaptive value of objects or events for organisms, is an important result of considering the senses to operate as perceptual systems rather than uncoordinated sensory channels. (See Gibson, this volume.) As indicated above, Gregory and others often seem to give special status to nonoptical stimuli. From Gibson's viewpoint these arguments are seen to rest upon a very narrow set of examples that ignore the important role of visual perception in survival and adaptation. Although it is true that no organism has ever been killed or maimed by a purely optical event, say by just seeing a club swung, successful avoidance of harm may require seeing it swung in time to dodge. Try hiding in a glass phone booth to avoid being seen by a mugger or using a cellophane fig leaf to avoid public embarrassment. Consider the indispensable role of optical information for transparency (e.g., in seeking water), opacity (e.g., in avoiding bumping into objects), coloration (e.g., in selecting ripened fruit) and patterns (e.g., in using camouflage to avoid predators) before accepting Gregory's or Bishop Berkeley's exclusive appeal to nonoptical properties of stimulation in order to give meaning to visual information. Indeed the felt effects of being caressed, kissed, clubbed or burned derive as much meaning from seeing the initiating source as the proper interpretation of the source depends upon its felt effects. Full meaning of such events arises from the systematic coordination of all sense modalities. This coordination is made possible by the fact that the spectra of energy forms appropriate to each sense modality have a source (the object or event) which possesses a unitary structure as von Hornbostel (1927) so well knew.

Gibson's notion of affordance not only allows one to describe the environment from a point of observation, but does so with respect to a particular observer, taking into account the observer's size, form, and capabilities. Affordances constitute a partitioning of an environment with an organism in mind instead of, say, the more neutral partitioning of the environment of energy flux into observer–independent properties by classical physics.

Some typical examples of affordance descriptions of environmental properties are walk-on-ability, grasp-ability, injury, collision and nutrition. One says that environmental properties *afford* the above activities; for example, a coffee cup at room temperature affords grasping by humans. Although defined relative to an organism, affordance relations exist independent of conscious experience or any subjective states of an organism. A persistent surface which is strong enough to hold the weight of an animal can be said to afford support for it whether the animal is in a state of realizing it or not.

Without this concept one could say that even if Gibson's position on the previous three points were accepted, perception of the world could nevertheless be indirect because an organism detecting Gibson's higher order invariants would still have to make a connection between those invariants and properties of the world which were useful to him. Not only would there be this step, but there might also be a step from a property to what the organism could do with it. For example the animal might have to connect the invariant structure of a perceived pattern with a property such as "hardness" or "opacity" and then from these infer what activities it can perform. The concept of affordance makes the last step unnecessary. It says that "hard" and "opaque" are no longer the descriptions of any properties whose invariants we're seeking. Rather we are seeking optical structure (where vision is concerned) that corresponds to what can be seen through, hidden behind, hammered with, and the like. An affordance partitioning of the world would be very different from one based on "properties" defined with respect to events that do not involve organisms directly.

A full appreciation of what is entailed in an affordance analysis also removes the need for talking about the other "step" in perception, that from computing the input structure to finding the environmental property to which it corresponds—even where the environmental property is expressed in affordance terms. This is the step in Gibson's direct perception theory which is hardest to comprehend and even harder to accept. Johansson (1970) expresses typical reservations. He argues that there must be some kind of code allowing the organism to infer the nature of the world around him from the structure in the light which he detects. A more internal threat to the coherence of the theory of direct perception which I will deal with sneaks in through Gibson's typical examples of affordances. Take "graspability." To say that an organism sees the graspability of an object could imply that it had to make a cross-modal correlation à la Gregory and lead right back to a version of constructive theory.

Both of these possible Trojan horses can be dealt with through a more careful consideration of what a thorough affordance description of an environment would look like. Instead of "senses" Gibson speaks of modes of attention. Let us examine vision as a mode of attention relative to which affordances can be described. By sticking to one mode of attention I hope to avoid raising the issue of cross-modal correlation for at least a little while, since it is something of a red herring.

Imagine an organism in an open field looking to the horizon. The optic array consists of a light upper portion and a darker lower portion, the sky above and the earth below. The gradient of the earth's texture can be thought of as specifying what optical transformations are afforded in this particular optic array for this particular organism with its size, shape, and exploratory capacities. In such a case, all optic array transformations obtainable by displacement would be specified. Suppose there was an indistinct object near the major light–dark transition in the array (the horizon). How might the visual system magnify part of its optic array so as to clarify the indistinctness and to identify the relative permanence in the overall structure? By using its legs, of course!

This type of description can be used to illuminate what Gibson means by perceptual systems as well as affordance structure. For him, vision is a system capable of actively exploring the environment precisely because it is a subsystem of a more complex system, the human body; as a subsystem evolution has attuned vision to work in a well integrated fashion with other subsystems (for example, the motor system). In this sense it is the whole organism which "sees" and thus which can use its legs to carry out visual investigations of the environment. The whole body can be mobilized in the interests of visual exploration and, for Gibson, counts just as much as a part of the visual system (when being used for visual exploratory purposes) as the eyeball itself. From this point of view, it is to be expected that so-called motor sections of the nervous system should be involved in perceiving. It should also be expected that careful consideration of the motor nervous system would ultimately equivocate on the very existence of a firm distinction between the motor and sensory aspects of the nervous system when considered with respect to perceiving. (See Turvey, Chapter 9, this volume.)

When Gregory said it was nonoptical properties of the world that really mattered, he did not consider whether or not there might be specific optical correlates for the events he had in mind. Expanding stimulus patterns which specify looming objects, for example, could again be considered from the optical viewpoint as well as from the point of view of mechanical contact with the skin. Thus one could say with justification equal to Gregory's that a symmetrically expanding pattern which fills the entire visual field is one to be avoided. Surely it makes at least as much sense to say that the *optical* event which specifies collision should be avoided as to say that the *tactile* events corresponding to collision are what the organism is avoiding (in the cases where it actually does avoid the potentially injurious event). Indeed, there is evidence that animals will attempt to avoid optical looming, as if experiencing the imminence of an impending collision, although no tactile stimulation is possible (Schiff, Caviness, & Gibson, 1962). Information for occluding surfaces, supporting surfaces and open vistas is information for possible paths open to the visual system for clarifying the optical structure of the environment. Thus, a very rich partitioning of the whole environment can be referred to an affordance analysis of vision alone (or any other mode of attention).

Second-Hand Perceiving

A fifth sense of indirect perception is a literal one which Gibson himself has often discussed—seeing at second hand, as in pictures. When one looks at a photograph or a representational painting or a movie, one is looking at a segment of someone else's optic array. Though sharing some similarities with a natural optic array, these displays are not the same as a full optic array, and, therefore, cannot be explored in the same ways. They do not contain all of the same information and, consequently, should be analyzed separately. This is not to say Gibson is not interested in such forms of indirect perception. In fact he has written often about the problem of perceiving pictures (e.g., Gibson, 1971) and certainly has no prejudice against the study of indirect perception when it is construed as the perception of someone else's view. Obviously interest in this problem in no way compromises his belief in the notion of direct perception.

On the other hand, the belief that the retinal image is the stimulus for vision would indeed make perception indirect. If what is really perceived were the retinal image projected from the world rather than aspects of the world itself, then perception would be second hand, and hence indirect; moreover, under this view seeing a picture would be an account of how one normally sees the world instead of being just an account of a very special case of seeing, as Gibson would have it. Gibson's objections to the idea that we see the world by means of retinal images are numerous. Here are five:

1. An observer for the image is implied and this observer's perception must be explained. Such homunculus explanations lead to infinite regresses.

2. No theory is provided to explain what aspects in the organization of the image are sufficient to account for visual perception. All an image can account for is the fact that some organization from the world is faithfully mapped on to physiological structures. Since this organization, whatever it might be, must be further mapped throughout the nervous system, all that is asserted is a causal chain. There seems to be no compelling reason to claim that the "ultimate perceiver" of the nervous system is in any more direct contact with the retinal image than with the patterns in the environment. Thus, the so-called "mind–body" problem raises its ugly head.

3. One gets into hopeless muddles with respect to problems of orientation. The image is often referred to as upside down or left-right reversed. But such judgments must be made with respect to some frame of reference. The ultimate frame of reference of earth and sky cannot change in normal perceiving. They cannot be upside down. Yet when considered as a picture in the head which is upright in the world the image is upside down. Many theorists have taken this to indicate that the world should be perceived as upside down. That is part of the retinal image-as-stimulus assumption. However it assumes that the observer is well-oriented in order to notice that the image is inverted. Although Gibson does not claim to have a fully articulated theory of what happens in optical inversion experiments, he is nevertheless quite sure that reference to the retinal image is not helpful (compare Gibson, 1964, for a discussion of Kohler's prism studies).

4. There are organisms such as the horseshoe crab which functionally perceive and appear to be sensitive to much the same information that is detected

by other organisms (Schiff *et al.*, 1962), but they have no retinal images because they have no retinas.

5. One never supposes that there are auditory or haptic images which are the real objects of perception. One does not say that the skin is in indirect contact with substances it touches. Gibson sees no reason why variant and invariant information and their detection should not be thought of as examples of the same types of decomposition process in each mode of attention. (An excellent philosophical argument against claims that images are the direct objects of perception may be found in Austin, 1962.)

Above are five different ways that an indirect theory of perception might be held. There are surely more. However, these points illustrate that Gibson's view that perception is direct apprehension of many important aspects of the environment is a reasonable alternative to the indirect view which is fraught with logical weaknesses. On the other hand a proponent of any of the indirect positions bears the considerably heavier burden of showing how such a view is compatible with both evolution and adaptive behavior.

CONCLUSIONS

In my opinion, the fruitfulness of Gibson's research project is well established. Insofar as it has been based upon a direct theory of perception this provides a strong argument that such a theory is both logically consistent and empirically sound. However, though thoroughly sketched now, the approach is far from complete. It should be recognized that what Gibson said of his psychophysical theory in 1959 is also true of his current ecological theory:

> The theory offered is immature in the sense that the program of investigations called for has only begun. It is also immature in that its potential scope seems to be wider than the scope of the problems to which it has been applied.
>
> . . . The theory has been extraordinarily fruitful in suggesting to the author hypotheses for experiments and in opening up new ways of experimenting on old problems. The important question is whether it will serve the same function for others [Gibson, 1959, p. 499].

A full appreciation of Gibson's theory requires a careful review of over a quarter of a century of work. Nothing less suffices to give a clear picture of the breadth and depth of his thinking about the most difficult problems in the theory of knowledge that psychology must face. His work is truly a significant exercise in experimental epistemology. There can be no doubt, however, that many of his views are quite radical, strikingly so if we look at Koffka's statement of the problems of perception. He asked "Why do things look as they do?" After rejecting as utterly ridiculous the answer "because they are what they are," and as reasonable but wrong "because the proximal stimuli are what they are,"

Koffka settled on an answer appealing to organized brain processes set up by proximal stimuli. In his psychophysical program, Gibson showed that by reconceiving the stimulus structure one could make a good case for the second of Koffka's answers. One might say "things look as they do because the proximal stimuli are what they are—we just looked at the wrong proximal stimuli." But now, with his ecological program, reconceptualizing the physical environment as well as the stimulus, Gibson is suggesting that what was utterly ridiculous might be true. We may be able to change Koffka's question to the stronger "why do things look as they *are*?" and seriously answer "because they are what they are."

REFERENCES

Austin, J. L. *Sense and sensibilia.* New York: Oxford University Press, 1962.

Chomsky, N. *Language and mind.* (2nd ed.) New York: Harcourt Brace Jovanovich, 1972.

Farber, J. M. The effects of angular magnification on the perception of rigid motion. (Doctoral dissertation, Cornell University, 1972). *Dissertation Abstracts International,* 1972–1973, **33**, 450B. (University Microfilms No. 73-7134.)

Garner, W. The stimulus in information processing. *American Psychologist,* 1970, **25**, 350–358.

Gibson, J. J. *The perception of the visual world.* Boston: Houghton-Mifflin, 1950.

Gibson, J. J. Visually controlled locomotion and visual orientation in animals. *British Journal of Psychology,* 1958, **49**, 182–194.

Gibson, J. J. Perception as a function of stimulation. In S. Koch (Ed.), *Psychology: A study of a science.* Vol. 1. New York: McGraw-Hill, 1959.

Gibson, J. J. The concept of the stimulus in psychology. *American psychologist,* 1960, **15**, 694–703.

Gibson, J. J. Observations on active touch. *Psychological review,* 1962, **69**, 477–491.

Gibson, J. J. Introduction. In I. Kohler. The formation and transformation of the perceptual world. *Psychological issues.* Vol. 12. New York: International Universities Press, 1964.

Gibson, J. J. *The senses considered as perceptual systems.* Boston: Houghton-Mifflin, 1966.

Gibson, J. J. The information available in pictures. *Leonardo,* 1971, **4**, 27–35.

Gibson, J. J., & Crooks, L. E. A theoretical field analysis of automobile driving. *American Journal of Psychology,* 1938, **51**, 453–471.

Gibson, J. J., Olum, P., & Rosenblatt, F. Parallax and perspective during aircraft landings. *American Journal of Psychology,* 1955, **68**, 372–385.

Gregory, R. L. On how so little information can control so much. In C. H. Waddington (Ed.), *Toward a theoretical biology.* Vol. 2. Chicago: Aldine-Atherton, 1969.

Gregory, R. L. Seeing as thinking: An active theory of perception. *The Times Literary Supplement,* June 23, 1972, 707–708.

Gross, C. G., Rocha-Miranda, C. E., & Bender, D. B. Visual properties of neurons in inferotemporal cortex of the Macaque. *Journal of Neurophysiology,* 1972, **35**, 96–111.

Gyr, J. W. Is a theory of direct visual perception adequate? *Psychological Bulletin,* 1972, **77**, 246–261.

Hay, J. C. Optical motions and space perception: An extension of Gibson's analysis. *Psychological Review,* 1966, **73**, 550–565.

Helmholtz, H. von. In J. P. C. Southall (Ed.), *Physiological optics.* Vol. 3. New York: Dover, 1925.

Hochberg, J. Higher-order stimuli and interresponse coupling in the perception of the visual world. In R. B. MacLeod & H. L. Pick, Jr. (Eds.), *Perception: Essays in honor of James J. Gibson.* Ithaca, New York: Cornell University Press, 1974.

Johansson, G. On theories for visual space perception. A letter to Gibson. *Scandinavian Journal of Psychology,* 1970, **11**, 67–79.

Kaplan, G. Kinetic disruption of optical texture: the perception of depth at an edge. *Perception & Psychophysics,* 1969, **6**, 193–198.

Lee, D. N. Visual information during locomotion. In R. B. MacLeod & H. L. Pick (Eds.), *Perception essays in honor of James J. Gibson.* Ithaca, New York: Cornell University Press, 1974. Pp. 250–67.

Lombardo, T. J. J. Gibson's ecological approach to visual perception: Its historical context and development. Doctoral dissertation, University of Minnesota, 1973. *Dissertation Abstracts International,* 1973–1974, **34**, 3534–3535B. (University Microfilms No. 74–721.)

Mace, W. M. Ecologically stimulating cognitive psychology: Gibsonian perspectives. In W. Weimer & D. Palermo (Eds.), *Cognition and the symbolic processes.* Hillsdale, New Jersey: Lawrence Erlbaum Assoc., 1974.

Mace, W. M., & Shaw, R. E. Simple kinetic information for transparent depth. *Perception and Psychophysics,* 1974, **15**, 201–209.

Pick, H. L., Jr. Systems of perceptual and perceptual–motor development. In J. P. Hill (Ed.), *Minnesota symposia on child psychology.* Vol. 4. Minneapolis: University of Minnesota Press, 1970.

Purdy, W. C. The hypothesis of psychophysical correspondence in space perception. Doctoral dissertation, Cornell University, 1958. *Dissertation Abstracts International,* 1958, **19**, 1454–1455. (University Microfilms No. 58-5594.) (Reproduced in part as Rep. R60ELC57 of the General Electrical Technical Information Series.)

Schiff, W., Caviness, J. A., & Gibson, J. J. Persistent fear responses in Rhesus monkeys to the optical stimulus of "looming." *Science,* 1962, **136**, 982–983.

Sedgwick, H. The visible horizon: A potential source of visual information for the perception of size and distance. Doctoral dissertation, Cornell University, 1973. *Dissertation Abstracts International,* 1973–1974, **34**, 1301–1302B. (University Microfilms No. 73–22, 530.)

Shaw, R. E., & McIntyre, M. Algoristic foundations to cognitive psychology. In W. B. Weimer & D. S. Palermo (Eds.), *Cognition and the symbolic processes.* Hillsdale, New Jersey: Lawrence Erlbaum Associates, 1974.

Shaw, R. E., McIntyre, M., & Mace, W. M. The role of symmetry in event perception. In R. B. MacLeod & H. L. Pick, Jr. (Eds.), *Perception: essays in honor of James J. Gibson.* Ithaca, New York: Cornell University Press, 1974.

von Hornbostel, E. M. The unity of the senses. *Psyche,* 1927, 7, 83–89. Reprinted in W. D. Ellis, *A source book of Gestalt psychology.* New York: Harcourt Brace, 1938.

3
The Theory of Affordances[1]

James J. Gibson
Cornell University

A description of what the environment *affords* the animal can be given in terms of a list beginning with simple and ending with complex things. Such a list includes features of the terrain, shelters, water, fire, objects, tools, other animals, and human displays. In addition, the information that is available in ambient light for the perception of substances, their surfaces, and the layout of these surfaces must also be described. An attempt should also be made to connect the two, to show that the variables of substances and layout combine to make affordances for animals and to demonstrate that the optical information for perceiving the variables combines to yield information for perceiving the affordances. What is being attempted is an explanation of how the "values" or "meanings" of things in the environment could be directly perceived.

What is meant by *an affordance?* A definition is in order, especially since the word is not to be found in any dictionary. Subject to revision, I suggest that *the affordance of anything is a specific combination of the properties of its substance and its surfaces taken with reference to an animal.* The reference may be to an animal in general as distinguished from a plant or to a particular species of animal as distinguished from other species. Note that the properties of substance and surface are physical properties but that they are not described in classical physics, only in ecological physics. The combination of properties is uniquely related to the animal or species being considered. It is assumed that if the properties of substance and surface are given in light the combination is given, and hence that if the properties are perceivable the special set of properties will be perceivable. In fact we can entertain the hypothesis that the affordance may be more easily perceived by an animal than the properties in isolation, for the

[1] This is a preliminary version of a chapter from a forthcoming book entitled *An Ecological Approach to Visual Perception* to be published by Houghton-Mifflin Co.

invariant combination of properties is "meaningful" whereas any single property is not.

The affordances of the environment are what it offers animals, what it provides or furnishes, for good or ill. Let us consider two examples, the first being an affordance for terrestrial animals in general and the second being an affordance for man in particular.

If a substance is fairly rigid instead of fluid; if its surface is nearly horizontal instead of slanted; if the latter is relatively flat instead of convex or concave; and if it is sufficiently extended, that is, large enough, then it affords support. More particularly it affords support to large animals who would sink into a surface of water, or in a swamp. It is a surface of support, and we call it a substratum, ground, or floor. It is stand-on-able, permitting an upright posture for quadrupeds and even for bipeds. Thus it may also be walk-on-able. If there is optical information for the four properties listed, rigidity, levelness, flatness, and extendedness then the affordance can be perceived if the information is detected.

The next example is more particular. If an object that rests on the ground has a surface that is itself sufficiently rigid, level, flat, and extended, *and if this surface is raised approximately at the height of the knees of the human biped,* then it affords *sitting-on.* We call the object a seat, stool, bench, or chair. It affords support for the rump, whether or not it affords support for the back. If these five properties coexist the object is in fact sit-on-able; they combine to yield a higher-order property for the human observer. The object may then be perceived as sit-on-able without much attention being paid to the five properties in isolation. Note that knee-high for a child is not the same as knee-high for an adult so that sit-on-ability must be taken with reference to a subclass of the human species. The surface layout may be a natural seat like a log or a ledge or an artificial seat like a chair or a couch; the affordance is the same. Note that some properties like the color and texture of the surface are irrelevant to the fact of being a seat, and that other properties only determine what kind or subclass of seat it is, stool, bench, chair, etc.

Now just as surfaces are stand-on-able and sit-on-able so also are they bump-into-able or get-underneath-able, or climb-on-able, or fall-off-able. Different layouts afford different kinds of behavior and different sorts of encounters, some beneficial and some harmful. I tried to classify these offerings and opportunities of the layout but the classification should now be enlarged upon.

Moreover the objects of the environment afford activities like manipulation and tool using. The substances of the environment, some of them, afford eating and drinking. The events of the environment afford being frozen, as in a blizzard, or burned, as in a forest fire. The other animals of the environment afford, above all, a rich and complex set of interactions, sexual, predatory, nurturing, fighting, play, cooperating, and communicating. What other persons afford, for man, comprise the whole realm of social significance. We pay the closest attention to the optical information that specifies what the other person is, what he invites, what he threatens, and what he does. For each of these kinds of affordance the question we must ask is, how is it perceived? First, what is the stimulus information to specify it and, second, how is the information picked up?

THE NICHES OF THE ENVIRONMENT AND THE REALITY OF AFFORDANCES

Environmental scientists, ecologists, make use of the concept of a *niche.* A given species of animal is said to utilize a certain niche in the environment. It is not the same as the *habitat* of the species, that is, where it lives, but rather how it lives. I suggest that a niche is a set of affordances. The natural environment offers many ways of life and a way of life is a set of affordances that are utilized.

The reciprocity of animal and environment is implied by this theory for the niche implies a certain kind of animal and the species implies a special niche. But the independent existence of an unlimited environment is also implied, for the niches must be available before animals can begin to exploit them. The affording of life by the environment is presumably of unlimited richness and complexity. The physical, chemical, meteorological, geological and geographical conditions of the surface of the earth, and the preexistence of plant life, are what make possible animal life. They have to be invariant or persisting for animals to evolve.

The environment affords many different kinds of food and many different ways of getting food. It affords various sorts of preexisting shelters or places to hide; in holes, crevices, and caves, and various materials for the making of shelters such as mounds, nests, and huts. It affords various kinds of posture like floating, clinging, resting, and standing, and various kinds of locomotion like swimming, crawling, walking, climbing, and flying. These offerings have all been taken advantage of, which is to say that the niches have been occupied. But, for all we know, there may be many offerings of the environment that have not been taken advantage of, that is, niches not yet occupied.

Architecturally speaking, a niche is a place that is suitable for a piece of statuary, that is, a place into which the object fits. The metaphor is interesting. Ecologically speaking, a niche, although not literally a place, is a setting of environmental features that are suitable for the animal, and into which it fits metaphorically.

The concept of the niche emphasizes an important fact about affordances, namely that they are real. Although an affordance consists of physical properties taken with reference to a certain animal it does not depend on that animal. In this respect an affordance is not like a value which is usually supposed to depend on the observer nor is it like a meaning which is almost always supposed to depend on the observer. An affordance is not what we call a "subjective" quality of a thing. But neither is it what we call an "objective" property of a thing if by that we mean that a physical object has no reference to any animal. An affordance cuts across the dichotomy of subjective–objective and helps us to understand its inadequacy. The affordances of the environment are facts of the environment, not appearances. But they are not, on the other hand, facts at the level of physics concerned only with matter and energy with animals left out.

The *niche* for a certain species should not be confused with what some animal psychologists have called the *phenomenal environment* of the species. This can be taken erroneously to be the "private world" in which it is supposed to live, the "subjective world," or the world of "consciousness." I will argue that the behavior of an observer depends on his perception of the environment, surely enough, but that this does not at all mean that his behavior depends on a so-called private, or subjective, or conscious environment. The organism depends on its environment for its life but the environment does not depend on the organism for its existence.

MAN'S ALTERATION OF THE NATURAL ENVIRONMENT

In the last few thousand years, as everybody now realizes, the very face of the earth has been modified by man. This means that the layout of surfaces has been changed, by cutting, clearing, leveling, paving, and building. There are still natural deserts and mountains, swamps and rivers, forests and plains, but they are being encroached upon and reshaped by man-made layouts. Moreover the *substances* of the environment have been partly converted from the natural materials of the earth into various kinds of artificial materials like bronze, iron, concrete, and bread. Even the *medium* of the environment—the air for us and the water for fish—is becoming slowly altered despite the restorative cycles that yielded a steady state for millions of years prior to man.

Why has man changed the shapes and substances of his environment? So as to change what it affords him. He has made more available what benefits him and less pressing what injures him. In making life easier for himself, of course, he has made life harder for most of the other animals. Over the millenia he has made it easier for himself to get food, easier to keep warm, easier to see at night, easier to get about, and easier to train his offspring.

This is not a new environment, an artificial environment, distinct from the natural environment, but the same old environment modified by man. It is a mistake to separate the natural from the artificial as if there were two environments. Artifacts have to be manufactured from natural substances. It is also a mistake to separate the cultural environment from the natural environment, as if there were a world of mental products distinct from the world of material products. There is only one world, however diverse, and all animals live in it, although we human animals have altered it to suit ourselves.

The fundamentals of the environment, the substances, the medium, and the surfaces are the same for all animals. No matter how powerful men become we are not going to alter the fact of earth, air, and water, the lithosphere, the atmosphere, and the hydrosphere, together with the interfaces that separate them. For terrestrial animals like us the earth and the sky are a basic structure on which all lesser structures depend. We cannot change it. We all fit into the substructures of the environment in our various ways for we were all, in fact, formed by them. We were created by the world we live in.

FURTHER EXAMPLES OF AFFORDANCES

The theory is that, although the environment consists of substances, surfaces, and the medium at one level, it consists at another level of affordances for animals. The substantial properties and the shape properties combine to make properties of higher order. The latter are not as easily analyzed by chemistry and geometry as substance and shape are but they are just as real. Let us consider some additional examples.

What Do Substances Afford?

Recall the formula that air, water, and earth or, more generally, the gaseous, liquid, and solid state, are increasingly *substantial.* Then note that air, although insubstantial, affords breathing because of its oxygen. It also affords unimpeded locomotion. When the air is illuminated it affords visual perception, being transparent. Water, more substantial than air, affords drinking. But for us it does not afford breathing but drowning. Being a solvent it affords bathing and washing. Being fluid it affords pouring from one vessel to another. A *surface* of water will be considered later; only note now that it does not afford support for heavy animals—only for waterbugs.

Solid substances, being still more substantial, afford all sorts of physiological and behavioral activities. Certain of them afford eating, more exactly ingestion, and of those that afford ingestion some afford nutrition as against others that do not. Some few in fact afford the opposite of nutrition, poisoning. (Note that I say nothing here about what affords *pleasure* in eating; that is another matter entirely.) Whether or not a vegetable substance affords nutrition depends upon the biochemical state we call *ripeness,* and this often is specified by the color of its surface. Solids also afford various kinds of manipulation or manufacture depending on the kind of solid state. Some, like flint, can be chipped; others, like clay, can be molded; still others recover their original shape after deformation; and some resist deformation strongly unless smelted by fire. Manipulation and manufacture are forms of behavior that are mostly but not exclusively characteristic of primates—not exclusively, since wasps and birds manufacture nests.

What Do Surfaces and their Layouts Afford?

Passing from the substances of the environment to their surfaces, consider what the "shapes" of surfaces afford, by which is meant the solid geometrical shapes, or what I have called their *layout.* I said that a solid, level, flat, extended surface affords support and constitutes a ground for a terrestrial animal. He can stand on it and maintain equilibrium, or come to rest on it and maintain a fixed posture with respect to gravity, gravity being a force perpendicular to the ground. He does not fall or slide as he would on a cliff or a steep hillside. Note that equilibrium and a stable posture are prerequisites to other forms of behavior such as locomotion and manipulation. The ground is literally a basis for behavior, and also a sort of basis for visual perception, as I maintained in what I once called the "ground theory of space perception" (Gibson, 1950). If this is true the physical–geometrical features of the ground and its affording of support to a terrestrial animal do not belong to separate realms of discourse; they are one and the same. Geometry, in the last analysis, is connected with life.

If the ground is lie-on-able and stand-on-able it is also walk-on-able and run-over-able. It affords locomotion. For an animal with feet, it affords what we call "footing" although this depends on the absence of foot-sized obstacles like loose rocks, and the absence of slipperiness caused by the presence of banana-peels or smooth ice. Hikers need to pay attention to the footing.

The terrestrial earth, of course, is seldom solid, level, flat, and extended all the way out to the horizon. It is "cluttered." Usually there are features of the terrain with which the flat earth is furnished. Deferring consideration of relatively small detached objects for the moment, let us list the terrain features that do not afford pedestrian locomotion but require other kinds. They seem to be surfaces of water or of watery earth, slopes upward of varying steepness to the maximum of a cliff wall, slopes downward of varying steepness to the maximum of a cliff brink, and finally simple obstacles.

A surface of water like a stream or a pond affords only special sorts of locomotion, swimming or wading, for which the animal may or may not be equipped. The same is true of a swamp. A slope upward begins to require climbing when steep, and a wall may be unclimable although a small wall, a "step," is negotiable. Similarly a slope downward begins to afford falling when steep, and the brink of the cliff is dangerous—a falling-off place. Men have altered the layout of such slopes by building stairways so as to facilitate the behavior of ascending and descending. The steps of a stairway are of such size as afford stepping up or down, given the size of the legs of a man.

In short for the ordinary environment, there are barriers to locomotion in some directions. If there are barriers to locomotion in all directions the observer is "imprisoned" as in the case of a complete enclosure, or cell. The situation of the saint who lived on top of a high pillar was also that of a prison, be it noted, although he was surrounded by brinks instead of walls. But ordinarily there are openings, that is to say paths, between barriers and then the special kind of locomotion that we call *roundabout* is afforded. A special kind of barrier, smaller than a wall or fence, is a simple *obstacle.* Like a wall, an obstacle affords collision but, being of animal size, it can be avoided without roundabout locomotion.

The progress of locomotion, we can now observe, is visually guided, and it depends on the avoidance of obstacles, barriers, brinks, and surfaces of deep water. The steering of locomotion, the control of it, depends on the progressive perceiving of these features of the environment, their negative affordances. There will be more about the control of locomotion later, but it is worth recalling now that optical information is available in ambient light for the perceiving of these features of the layout as well as for the perceiving of locomotion itself. The features I have listed above are relevant to pedestrian locomotion but a modified list could be drawn up for the locomotion of birds, and for fish.

The imminence of collision with an obstacle or barrier is optically specified for any kind of locomotion: walking, flying, or swimming. There are at least some general laws that hold for perception in all animals. The information for imminence of collision is a high rate of symmetrical outflow of part of the ambient optic array, the approach to the maximum possible visual solid angle which specifies zero distance. This can be described as "looming," (Schiff, 1965). The larger the silhouette the closer to contact or collision.

The Affording of Concealment

This is the place to describe an interesting kind of social behavior that is afforded by a cluttered environment of opaque surfaces. I mean the act of hiding, both the hiding of an object from other observers and the hiding of oneself from other observers. Concealing or screening one's body is something that many animals do, both the hunted and the hunter, both prey and predator, and even human children at play.

One of the rules of ecological optics is that at any fixed point of observation some parts of the environment are projected or revealed and the remaining parts are unprojected or concealed. The reciprocal of this rule is that the observer himself, his body, is revealed at some points of observation and concealed at the remaining points. An observer thus perceives not only that other observers are unhidden or hidden from him but also that he is unhidden or hidden from other observers. The practicing of this kind of perception is what babies do in playing "peek-a-boo" and what children do when they play "hide and seek." The act of hiding is to position one's body at a point of observation that is concealed at the point of observation of another or other observers—to go to a *hiding place.* I omit the optics of peepholes; the reader can work it out for himself.

All this depends on the perception of occluding edges in the layout. The reciprocity of the observer and the environment is once more emphasized. The greatest degree of concealment is afforded by an enclosure (as defined earlier) and complete concealment is afforded by a complete enclosure. What we call "privacy" in the design of housing is the providing of opaque enclosures. Note that the screening of perception is not the same as the barring of locomotion; a screen and a barrier may be different. An opaque and rigid sheet does both, but an opaque and flexible sheet like a cloth curtain affords locomotion without perception whereas a transparent and rigid sheet like a glass window affords perception without locomotion. And a translucent sheet affords illumination but not perception, as I pointed out in formulating ecological optics. I omit the complexities of one-way screens for vision but they can be worked out from the principles that govern semitransparency.

Besides hiding himself an observer can hide portable objects from other observers. These are usually objects of *value,* so called. Both animals and men perform this sort of social behavior. Food objects, utensils, and money can be buried in the earth or concealed in a chest or put away in a drawer. All of us, the higher animals, look for good hiding places, both for ourselves and for our treasures.

What Do Detached Objects Afford?

A movable object affords an astonishing variety of behaviors, especially if it is small relative to the size of the animal under consideration. If so, it is portable, that is, it affords lifting and carrying. For an animal with hands, a primate, the object may (or may not) afford grasping. To be graspable, an object must have opposite surfaces separated by less distance than the span of the hand. It must have an appropriate width, and the width can be perceived visually.

Of course an attached or immovable object may also be grasped but then it is not portable. Instead it affords support, as a tree branch supports a monkey. The rung of a ladder and the hand-hold of a mountain climber on a cliff face are graspable in this special sense.

In general graspable detached objects afford *manipulation.* There are so many kinds of manipulation and so many kinds of manipulated objects to accompany them that we can only sample the set. In "a new terminology for surface layout," I described sheets, sticks, fibers, and containers in geometrical terms, and I mentioned tools and clothing, but that was a bare beginning. Here are a few examples:

1. An elongated object of moderate size and weight affords *wielding.* If used to hit or strike it is a *club* or *hammer.* If used by a chimpanzee behind bars to

pull in a banana beyond his reach it is a sort of *rake*. In either case it is an extension of the arm. A rigid staff also affords leverage and in that use is a *lever*. A pointed elongated object affords piercing; if large it is a *spear*, if small a *needle* or *awl*.

2. A rigid object with a sharp dihedral angle, an edge, affords cutting and scraping. It is a *knife*. It may be designed for both striking and cutting and then it is an *axe*.

3. A graspable rigid object of moderate size and weight affords throwing. It may be a *missile* or only an object for play, a *ball*. The launching of missiles by supplementary tools other than the hands alone, the sling, the bow, the catapult, the gun, and so on is one of the behaviors that makes man a nasty dangerous species.

4. An elongated elastic object like a fiber, thread, thong, or rope affords knotting, binding, lashing, knitting, and weaving. These are kinds of behavior where manipulation leads to manufacture.

5. A hand-held tool of enormous importance is one that, when applied to a surface, leaves traces and thus affords *trace making*. It may be a stylus, brush, crayon, pen, or pencil but if it marks the surface it can be used to depict and to write, to represent scenes and to specify words.

We have thousands of names for such objects and we classify them in many ways, tools like pliers and wrenches, utensils like pots and pans, weapons like swords and pistols. All of these objects have properties or qualities: color, texture, composition, size, shape, and features of shape, not to mention mass, elasticity, rigidity, and the like. Nevertheless I suggest that what we perceive when we look at them are their affordances, not their qualities. We can, of course, discriminate these dimensional qualities if required to compare them as objects. But the unique combination of qualities that specifies what the object affords us is what we normally pay attention to.

If this is true for the adult, what about the young child? There is now a great deal of evidence to show that the infant does not begin by first discriminating the qualities of objects and then learning the combinations of qualities that specify the objects themselves. Phenomenal objects are not built up of qualities. It is quite the other way around. Objects, more exactly the affordances of objects, are what the infant begins by noticing. The meanings are observed before the substances and surfaces are. Affordances are invariant combinations of variables. And it is only reasonable to suppose that it is easier to perceive an invariant combination than it is to perceive all the variables separately.

What Do Other Animals and Other People Afford?

The richest and most elaborate affordances of the environment are provided by other animals and, for us, other people. These are, of course, detached objects with topologically closed surfaces but they change the shape of their surfaces while yet retaining the same fundamental shape. They move from place to place, changing the postures of their bodies, ingesting and emitting certain substances, and doing all this spontaneously, initiating their own movements, which is to say that their movements are *animate.* These bodies are subject to the laws of mechanics and yet not subject to the laws of mechanics. They are so different from ordinary objects that infants learn almost immediately to distinguish them from plants and nonliving things. When touched they touch back, when struck they strike back, in short they *interact* with the observer and with one another. Behavior affords behavior, and the whole subject matter of psychology and of the social sciences can be thought of as an elaboration of this basic fact. Sexual behavior, nurturing behavior, fighting behavior, cooperative behavior, economic behavior, political behavior—all depend on the perceiving of what another person or other persons afford—or sometimes on the misperceiving of it.

What the male affords the female is reciprocal to what the female affords the male; what the infant affords the mother is reciprocal to what the mother affords the infant; what the prey affords the predator goes along with what the predator affords the prey; what the buyer affords the seller cannot be separated from what the seller affords the buyer, and so on. The perceiving of these mutual affordances is enormously complex but it is nonetheless lawful, and it is based on the pickup of the information in touch, sound, odor, taste, and ambient light. It is just as much based on stimulus information as is the simpler perception of the support that is offered by the ground under one's feet. For other animals and other persons can only give off information about themselves insofar as they are tangible, audible, odorous, tastable, or visible.

The other person, the generalized *other,* the *alter* as opposed to *ego,* is an ecological object with a skin, even if clothed. It is an object although it is not merely an object, and we do right to speak of *you* and *he* instead of *it.* But he has a surface that reflects light and the information to specify what he is, what he invites, promises, or threatens, and what he does, can be found in the light.

Summary: Positive and Negative Affordances

The foregoing examples of the affordances of the environment are enough to show how general and powerful the concept is. Substances have biochemical offerings, and afford manufacture. Surfaces afford posture, locomotion, collision, manipulation, and in general behavior. Special forms of layout afford shelter and concealment. Fires afford being warmed and being burned. Detached objects, tools, utensils, weapons, afford special types of behavior to primates and men. The other animal and the other person provide mutual and reciprocal affordances at extremely high levels of behavioral complexity. At the highest level, when vocalization becomes speech and manufactured displays become images, pictures, and writing, the affordances of human behavior are staggering. No more of that will be considered at this stage except to point out that speech, pictures, and writing still have to be perceived.

At all these levels, from matter to men, we can now observe that some offerings of the environment are beneficial and some are injurious. These are slippery terms which should only be used with great care, but if their meanings are pinned down to biological and behavioral facts the danger of confusion can be minimized. First, consider substances that afford ingestion. Some afford nutrition for a given animal, some afford poisoning, and some are neutral. As I pointed out before, these facts are quite distinct from the affording of pleasure and displeasure in eating, for the experiences do not necessarily correlate with the biological effects. Second, consider the brink of a cliff. On the one side it affords walking-along, locomotion, whereas on the other it affords falling-off, injury. Third, consider a detached object with a sharp edge, a knife. It affords cutting if manipulated in one manner but it affords being cut if manipulated in another manner. Similarly, but at a different level of complexity, an ordinary metallic object affords grasping but if charged with current it affords electric shock. And fourth, consider the other person. The animate object can give you caresses or blows, contact comfort or contact injury, reward or punishment, and it is not always easy to perceive which will be provided. Note that all these benefits and injuries, these safeties and dangers, these positive and negative affordances are properties of things taken with reference to an observer but not properties of the experiences of the observer exclusive of the things. They are not subjective values; they are not feelings of pleasure or pain added to neutral perceptions.

There has been endless debate among philosophers and psychologists as to whether values were physical or phenomenal, in the world of matter or only in the world of mind. For affordances as distinguished from values the debate does not apply. They are neither in the one world or the other inasmuch as the theory of two worlds is rejected. There is only one environment, although it contains many observers with limitless opportunities for them to live in it.

THE ORIGIN OF THE CONCEPT OF AFFORDANCES

The Gestalt psychologists recognized that the meaning or value of a thing seems to be perceived just as immediately as its color. The value is clear on the face of it, as we say, and thus it has a *physiognomic* quality in the way that the emotions of a man appear *on his face.* To quote from the *Principles of Gestalt Psychology* (Koffka, 1935): "Each things says what it is . . . a fruit says 'Eat me'; water says 'Drink me'; thunder says 'Fear me'; and woman says 'Love me' [p. 7]." These values are a vivid and essential feature of the experience itself. Koffka did not believe that a meaning of this sort could be explained as a pale context of memory images or an unconscious set of response tendencies. The postbox "invites" the mailing of a letter, the handle "wants to be grasped," and things "tell us what to do with them [p. 353]." Hence they had what Koffka called "demand character."

Kurt Lewin had coined the term *Aufforderungscharakter* which had been translated as *invitation-character* (by J. F. Brown in 1929) and as *valence* (by D. K. Adams in 1931). The latter term came into general use. *Valences* for Lewin had corresponding *vectors,* which could be represented as arrows pushing the observer toward or away from the object. What explanation could be given for these valences, the characters of objects that invited or demanded behavior? No one, not even the Gestalt theorists, could think of them as physical and, indeed, they do not fall within the province of ordinary physics. They must therefore be phenomenal, given the assumption of dualism. If there were two objects, and if the valence could not belong to the physical object it must belong to the phenomenal object–to what Koffka called the "behavioral" object but not to the "geographical" object. The valence of an object was bestowed upon it in experience, and bestowed by a need of the observer. Thus Koffka argued that the postbox has a demand character only where the observer needs to mail a letter. He is attracted to it when he has a letter to post, not otherwise. The value of something was assumed to change as the need of the observer changed.

The concept of affordance is somewhat related to these concepts of valence, invitation, and demand but with a crucial difference. The affordance of something does not change as the need of the observer changes. Whether or not the affordance is perceived or attended to will change as the need of the observer changes but, being invariant, it is always there to be perceived. An affordance is not bestowed upon an object by a need of an observer and by his act of perceiving it. The object offers what it does because it is what it is. To be sure, we define what it is in terms of ecological physics instead of physical physics, and it therefore possesses meaning and value to begin with. But this is meaning and value of a new sort.

For Koffka it was the *phenomenal* postbox that invited letter mailing, not the physical postbox. But this duality is pernicious. I prefer to say that the real postbox (the only one) affords letter-mailing to a letter-writing human in a community with a postal system. This fact is perceived when the postbox is identified as such, and it is apprehended whether the postbox is in sight or out of sight. To feel a special attraction to it when one has a letter to mail is not surprising but the main fact is that it is perceived as part of the environment–as an item of the neighborhood in which we live. Everyone above the age of six knows what it is for and where the nearest one is. The perception of its affordance should therefore not be confused with the temporary special attraction it may have.

The Gestalt psychologists explained the directness and immediacy of the experience of valences by postulating that the ego is an object in experience and that a "tension" may arise between a phenomenal object and the phenomenal ego. When the object is in "a dynamic relation with the ego" said Koffka, it has a demand character. Note that the "tension," the "relation," or the "vector" must arise in the "field" that is, in the field of phenomenal experience. Although many psychologists find this theory intelligible, I do not. There is an easier way of explaining why the values of things seems to be perceived immediately and directly. It is because the affordances of things for an observer are specified in stimulus information. They seem to be perceived directly because they are perceived directly.

The accepted theories of perception, to which the Gestalt theorists were objecting, implied that no experiences were direct except sensations, and that sensations mediated all other kinds of experience. Bare sensations had to be clothed with meaning. The seeming directness of meaningful perception was therefore an embarrassment to the orthodox theories and the Gestaltists did right to emphasize it. They began to undermine the sensation-based theories. But their own explanations of why it is that a fruit says "Eat me" and woman says "Love me" is a bit strained. The Gestalt psychologists objected to the accepted theories of perception but they never managed to go beyond them.

THE PROCESS OF PERCEIVING AFFORDANCES

The definition of an affordance can now be elaborated by saying that it is a combination of physical properties of the environment that is uniquely suited to a given animal—to his nutritive system or his action system or his locomotor system. A substance is chemically valuable relative to a given nutritive system, herbivorous or carnivorous. An object is valuable relative to a given action system, one with claws or another with hands. A surface layout has locomotor value relative to the kind of legs and feet the animal possesses.

If there is information in ambient light to specify substances, solid objects, and surface layouts there is information to specify their affordances for eating, for manipulation, and for locomotion, that is, for behavior. When an observer perceives edibility he perceives it in relation to his mouth and teeth and digestive system; when he perceives manipulability he perceives it in relation to his hands, to which the object or tool is suited; when he perceives the possibility of locomotion he perceives it in relation to what his locomotor system is capable of in walking or climbing, the slopes it can descend or the ditches it can jump over. This is only to reemphasize that perception of the environment is inseparable from proprioception of one's own body—that egoreception and exteroception are reciprocal. A man can bite into an apple but not a rock; he can get a grip on a handle but not on a wall; he can jump over a gap commensurate with his size and strength but he will fall into a crevasse that is too wide to jump. He measures these features of the environment by the standard of his body. And this is just as true for a mouse as it is for a man.

Many of the chemical, physical, and geometrical properties of the natural environment are specified in ambient light, as I tried to show in my discussion of ecological optics. The hypothesis I proposed in *The Senses Considered as*

Perceptual Systems (Gibson, 1966) is that the visual system of a mature observer can *pick up* this information or else can be altered by perceptual learning so that it is picked up. I now want to extend this proposal to cover the perception of affordances. These unique *combinations* of chemical, physical, and geometrical properties are also specified in ambient light. A compound invariant of optical structure is just another invariant. And a genuinely invariant compound can presumably be detected as a unit, without any need to associate the components. In classical terminology, several "stimuli" that always go together constitute one "stimulus." If these unique optical compounds are meaningful in the sense that they specify benefits and dangers for the given observer they should be easier to detect, that is, picked up with less learning, than other combinations of optical information that are not ego-related. The properties of things as such are less important to an observer than the affordances for him.

For example, the meaning of an arbitrary combination of properties invented by an experimenter in a laboratory should be harder to detect than the meaning of a natural invariant compound. An ape can learn that a one-inch flat blue triangle on the panel of a discrimination apparatus specifies a piece of banana behind the panel. But he should learn more easily that a 6-inch long rounded yellow surface specifies a banana behind its skin. The solid yellow object says "Eat me," in Koffka's words, more directly than does the flat blue form. The panel of the apparatus may come to say "Push me," but only that.

If this is true, some compound invariants specify their affordances directly and we say that the object or surface looks like what it is. Other compound invariants do not specify their affordances so directly and then we are apt to say that the object or surface does not look like what it is. The fact that a small piece of metal in a complex household gadget affords electric shock may be a hidden fact; to perceive it entails the apprehension of a set of concealed connections. Learning to apprehend electrical connections is rather difficult, and even the electrician sometimes makes mistakes.

The Misperceiving of Affordances

The brink of a cliff affords falling off; it is in fact dangerous and it looks dangerous to us. It seems to look dangerous to many other terrestrial animals besides ourselves, including infant animals. Experimental studies have been made of this fact. If a sturdy sheet of plate glass is extended out over the edge it no longer affords falling and in fact is not dangerous, but it may still look dangerous. The optical information to specify depth-downward-at-an-edge is still present in the ambient light; for this reason the device was called a "visual cliff" by Gibson and Walk (1960). Haptic information was available to specify an adequate surface of support but this was contradictory to the optical information. When human infants at the crawling stage of locomotion were tested with this apparatus many of them would pat the glass with their hands but would not venture out on the surface. The babies misperceived the affordance of a transparent surface for support, and this result is not surprising.

Similarly, a man can misperceive the affordance of a sheet of glass by mistaking a closed glass door for an open doorway and attempting to walk through it. He then crashes into the barrier and is injured. The affordance of collision was not specified by the outflow of optical texture in the array, or insufficiently specified. He mistook glass for air. The occluding edges of the doorway were specified and the empty visual solid angle opened up symmetrically in the normal manner as he approached, so his behavior was properly controlled, but the imminence of collision was not noticed. A little dirt on the surface, or highlights, would have saved him.

These two cases are instructive. In the first a true affordance of support went unexploited because a false negative affordance of falling opposed it. In the second a negative affordance of collision went unnoticed and a positive affordance of exiting (going out) was mistakenly registered. A failure to perceive what is present in the environment and a perceiving of something not present in the environment are both cases of misperception. Usually they go together. To see what is there implies not seeing what is not there.

The very possibility of perceiving entails, of course, the possibility of misperceiving. The problem for the psychology of perception is to discover the conditions that govern both. For a theory of visual perception based on the pickup of available information, a theory of direct perception not mediated by subjective sensations, misperception can be explained in two general ways: either the available information is inadequate or, if not, the process of information pickup is deficient. On the one hand, visual perception fails in the dark because of the absence of stimulation, and it fails in a fog-filled medium because of the absence of structure in ambient light even with the presence of stimulation. Information is not available. It may also fail because the available optical information is equivocal or contradictory, or even sometimes because it is discrepant with the information given to touch, although this is rare. On the other hand invariants may fail to be picked up because the eyes are closed, or because the lens of the eye is opaque, or because the retina is diseased or dazzled, or because the optic nerve is severed. At the level of the whole visual system information may not be registered because the retina-nerve-brain-eye system is immature, or because the observer has not yet learned to extract the specifying invariants, or simply because the observer fails to look around him, or fails to look at the fine details. I have described the possible reasons for misperceiving in Chapter 14 of *The Senses Considered as Perceptual Systems* (Gibson, 1966).

No wonder, then, that quicksand is sometimes mistaken for sand, that a pitfall can be mistaken for solid ground, that poison ivy is sometimes mistaken for ivy, and that acid can be taken for water. A wildcat is not easy to distinguish from a cat, and a thief may look like an honest man. When Koffka asserted that "each thing says what it is" he neglected to mention that it may lie. The affordances of danger are sometimes hidden, like the electric shock in the radio cabinet and the shark under the calm water.

Nevertheless, however true all this may be, the basic affordances of the terrestrial environment are perceivable, and are usually perceivable directly, without an excessive amount of learning. The reason is that the basic properties of the environment that combine to make an affordance are specified in the structure of ambient light and that hence the affordance itself is specified in ambient light. And, moreover, an invariant variable that is commensurate with the body of the observer himself is more easily picked up than one not commensurate with his body.

REFERENCES

Adams, D. K. A restatement of the problem of learning. *British Journal of Psychology* (General Section), 1931, **22**, 150–178.

Brown, J. F. The method of Kurt Lewin in the psychology of action and affection. *Psychological Review*, 1929, **36**, 200–221.

Gibson, E. J. and Walk, R. D. The "visual cliff." *Scientific American*, 1960, **202**, 64–71.

Gibson, J. J. *The perception of the visual world*. Boston: Houghton Mifflin, 1950.

Gibson, J. J. *The senses considered as perceptual systems*. Boston: Houghton Mifflin, 1966.

Koffka, K. *Principles of Gestalt psychology*. New York: Harcourt, Brace, & World, Inc., 1935.

Lewin, K., Vorsatz, Wille, und Bedurfnis. *Psychologische Forschung*, 1926, 7, 294–385. Reprinted as: Will and needs in W. D. Ellis (Ed.), *A sourcebook of Gestalt psychology*. London: Routledge & Kegan Paul, 1938.

Schiff, W. Perception of impending collision: A study of visually directed avoidant behavior. *Psychological Monographs*, 1965, **79**, 604.

4

Some Comments on the Nature of the Perceived Universe

Karl H. Pribram

Stanford University

INTRODUCTION

The 1960s saw a burst of new approaches to persistent problems in psychology. For me these approaches were heralded in the concepts of Image and Plan (Pribram, 1960). In a series of papers and books, often with the help of colleagues, I attempted to portray the power of these conceptions. At the neurological level, a two-process mechanism was detailed to show how Images and Plans were, in fact, generated (Pribram, 1971). At the behavioral level the concept Plan originated early on in observed similarities in the organization of serial actions and the organization of computer programs (Pribram, 1960). The concept Image took somewhat longer to ground in a model that allowed specific hypotheses to be generated. But by the mid-1960s it became clear that optical information processing systems could provide this model, especially in the construction of holographically produced Images (Pribram, 1972). These rather sketchy proposals have gradually been filled out with the accumulation of data from several laboratories, including my own. *Languages of the Brain* (Pribram, 1971) spells out the relevance of these data to the theory and more recent additions are to be found in two papers: "The Holographic Hypothesis of Memory Structure in Brain Function and Perception" (Pribram, Nuwer, & Baron, 1974) and "How Is It that Perceiving So Much We Can Do So Little?" (Pribram, 1974a).

Rather than detail once again the supports for the concepts of Image and Plan, I want here to address a set of specific issues that derive from the theories as they have been developed and to show that the computer theory of Plans and the holographic theory of Images are not mutually exclusive but stand in relation to each other much as other fundamental scientific theories (specifically theories in theoretical physics) do today.

My interest in these issues has several roots. The tap root concerns the two-process mechanism of brain function involving discrete nerve impulses and the pre- and postsynaptic depolarizations and hyperpolarizations that constitute a dynamic slow potential microstructure best described by continuous wave equations. This led me to inquire of my son, Professor John K. Pribram, a physicist, some details on the conceptual aspects of the parallel problem in quantum physics. The results of this inquiry are described below.

A second major root stems from discussions with Professor Daniel Pollen on the nature of the Fourier or Fourier-like process in the visual system. We repeatedly puzzled on the nature of the reality imaged by the process. The cortical mechanism which we thought to be holographic stems from transformations of a series of retinal images. These images themselves were constructed by the optics of the eye. Could it be that the retinal image was a special case (similar to a photographic image) in a series of reversible transformations that include other more holographic-like stages? Do we need a cortical imaging process at all?

It finally occurred to me that the questions critical to these issues related to the nature of the external "reality" that was being transformed by the organism's perceptual mechanisms. In this respect, therefore, I had come to the same point of inquiry as James Gibson in the formulation of his elegant program of research. And it also led directly (on recommendation from J. K. Pribram) to interaction with theoretical physics in the person of David Bohm who in his own way came to Gibson's position (Bohm, 1965, Appendix). Some of the early fruits of these inquiries and interactions are described below.

THE HOLONOMIC THEORY

Holograms provide a powerful mechanism for storing the image construction properties of optical information processing systems. What called attention to holograms is their distributed information state which makes them like the brain, highly resistant to damage. In addition, the holographic state allows a fantastic memory storage capacity: some hundred million bits of retrievable information have been stored in a cubic centimeter of holographic memory. This is accomplished by separately storing modulations of one or another spatial or temporal frequency. It is somewhat as if there were myriads of FM (frequency modulation) radios compressed into a tiny space. The short wave length of light (as compared to sound) makes such capabilities possible. In the brain, the short wave lengths characterizing the slow potential microstructure can be assumed to serve in a similar fashion.

There are other properties (e.g., associative recall; translational, i.e., positional, and size invariance) of holograms that make the analogy with brain function in perception and memory attractive. These have been presented in another paper

(Pribram, Nuwer, & Baron, 1974). Here I want to emphasize that testable hypotheses can be formulated and models of actual brain function can be proposed within the domain of what can loosely be called the holographic properties of optical information processing systems. We have reviewed the evidence for image construction by the brain. What assemblies of neurons (and their processes), if any, function as true Fourier holograms? Which brain structures function more like Fresnel holograms? Which mimic a Fourier process by convolving, integrating neighboring neural events and those at successive stages? These questions are being asked and experiments are being performed to provide answers.

As might be expected, such experiments have already encountered one serious obstacle in drawing too close a parallel between optical information processes and image construction by the brain. This obstacle concerns the size of the receptive fields recorded for cells in the primary visual projection system. For example, the projection from the macular portion of the retina, the foveal receptive fields, is extremely small—some 3–5° of visual angle as a maximum. A hologram of this size will hardly account for the fact that information becomes distributed across the entire visual system as indicated by the evidence from resections and from electrophysiological recordings.

A search has therefore been made for larger receptive fields that integrate the input from the smaller fields of the primary projection cortex. Such larger fields have been found in the cortex that surrounds the primary projection areas. It would be simple if one could assume that here, rather than in the primary projection cortex, the true holographic process takes place.

But this simple assumption runs contrary to other evidence. First, it would not account, by itself, for the distribution of information within the projection cortex. Second, complete resection of this *peri* projection cortex (where the larger receptive fields are found) produces no permanent damage to image construction as far as one can tell from animal experiments (Pribram, Spinelli, & Reitz, 1969).

Beyond these visual areas of the brain cortex, however, there is another, lying on the inferior surface of the temporal lobe which, when it is resected, leaves monkeys markedly and permanently impaired in their ability to make visual discriminations (Pribram, 1954, 1960, 1969). This impairment is limited to the visual mode (H. Pribram & Barry, 1956; M. Wilson, 1957). Only visual performances demanding a choice are impaired; other visual functions, such as tracking a signal, remain intact (Pribram, 1971, Chapter 17). The difficulty involves the ability to selectively attend to visual input (Gerbrandt, Spinelli, & Pribram, 1970; Rothblat & Pribram, 1972; Gross, 1972).

Much to everyone's surprise, this visual "association" area (as the area with comparable function is known in man (Milner, 1958) appears to function remarkedly well when all known visual input to it is destroyed. As already noted, removal of the perivisual cortex has little permanent effect; destruction of the thalamic input (from the pulvinar) to the inferior temporal cortex has no effect whatsoever (Mishkin, 1972; Ungerleiter, personal communication). Even combined lesions of perivisual and thalamic inputs do not permanently disrupt visual discriminations.

These data make plausible the hypothesis that the inferior temporal cortex exerts its effect on vision via an output to the primary visual projection system (Pribram, 1958). Evidence in support of this hypothesis has accrued over the past 15 years: the configuration and size of visual receptive fields can be altered by electrical stimulation of the inferior temporal cortex (Spinelli & Pribram, 1967); recovery cycles in the visual projection systems are shortened by such stimulation (Spinelli & Pribram, 1966); the pathways from the inferior temporal cortex have been traced (Whitlock & Nauta, 1956; Reitz & Pribram, 1969).

Thus, another, more specific hypothesis can be entertained, namely, the suggestion that the inferior temporal cortex helps to program the functions of the primary visual projection systems. Specifically, such programming, as well as programming by input from sensory receptors, could "get together" the distributed store of information from the various loci of restricted receptive field size. If the relevant loci were addressed in unison they would, in fact, function like a hologram.

The difference, therefore, between brain function and the function of optical information processing systems is the one set out at the beginning of this chapter. Brain is *both* an image construction and a programming device. Optical systems construct only images.

The thesis presented here, therefore, suggests that the holographic-like store of distributed information in the primary visual projection system is akin to the distributed memory bank of a computer. The computer's memory is organized more or less randomly; the brain's memory has been stored along holographic principles. Both must be addressed by programs which access the appropriate "bits" of information. The computer does this serially; the brain, to a large extent, simultaneously, by pathways that allow signals to be transmitted in parallel. Such simultaneity in function produces momentary brain states that are akin to the holographic patterns that can be stored on film.

Because of these differences between brain and optical systems, it may be better to talk about brain function as holonomic rather than just holographic or hologrammic. The term holonomic is used in engineering whever the systems, in an interactive set of such systems, are reasonably linear in their function. Linearity allows the computation of the functions of each system and therefore an estimate of the amount of their interaction–the "degrees of freedom" that characterize the interactive set. The interactions are known as the holonomic constraints on the system. In the context of the model of brain function in vision suggested here, the neural systems that determine any momentary visual state would have to be shown to be linear; then the amount of interaction among the systems in producing the holographic visual state would appear as the degrees of freedom characterizing that state.

Evidence is available to show that the visual system, despite local non-linearities, acts linearly overall above threshold (e.g., Ratliff, 1965). This is the case in other neural systems, notably the motor system (Granit, 1970). It is thus reasonable to propose that the holonomic model applies to brain functions other than visual. Support for such a proposal comes from work on the auditory (von Békésy, 1960), somatosensory (von Békésy, 1959) and even gustatory (von Békésy, 1967; Pfaffmann, 1960) and olfactory systems (Gesteland, Lettvin, Pitts, & Chung, 1968).

Briefly summarizing, the holonomic model of brain function proposed that the brain partakes of both computer and optical information processes. The brain is like a computer in that information is processed in steps by an organized and organizing set of rules. It differs from current computers in that each step is more extended in space—brain has considerably more parallel processing capability than today's computers.

This parallel processing aspect of brain function leads to another difference. The rules of parallel processing are more akin to those that apply to optical information processes than they are to those used in current serial computers. Thus the momentary states set up by the programming activity are considerably like those of image constructing devices, that is, holographic. Thus memory storage is also holographic rather than random as in today's computers. This does not deny, however, that storage of rules also takes place—as it does in machine peripherals (e.g., tapes for minicomputers). What the model requires is that the "deep structure" of the memory store is holographic.

Since the holographic state is composed by programs and since the distributed store must be got together by the actions of and interactions among programs, the holographic brain state can be analyzed according to the systems that produces it. Thus the holonomic constraints or degrees of freedom that characterize the holographic state can be determined. The holonomic model of brain function is therefore mathematically precise, and its assumptions (such as overall linearity of component programming systems) and consequences (the distributed nature of the deep structure of the memory store) are, at least in principle, testable.

IS PERCEPTION DIRECT OR CONSTRUCTIONAL?

I want now to address some consequences to psychology (and perhaps to philosophy) of the holonomic theory of brain function. The theory, as we have seen, (1) stems from the metaphors of machine and optical information processing systems; (2) has developed by analogy to those systems, spelling out some similarities and some differences; until (3) a testable holonomic model of brain function could be proposed. One way of understanding the model better is to compare it to another and to observe its relative explanatory power.

An apparent alternative to the "holonomic" model is presented by James Gibson's (1966) comprehensive "ecological" model of perception. Gibson's model proposes that the "information" perceived is inherent in the physical universe and that the perceiver is sensitive to whatever information remains invariant across transformations produced by changes in the environment, by organism-environment displacements, and by the organism's processing apparatus. The key concept in the ecological theory is "direct perception"—the environment as an ecological niche is directly apprehended by the perceiver.

By contrast, the holonomic theory is constructional. Images are constructed when input from inferior temporal cortex (or its analog in other perceptual systems—see Pribram, 1974) activates, organizes the distributed holographic store. Images are produced and are therefore as much a *product of* the "information residing in" the organism, as they are of "information" contained in the environment. Philosophically speaking, the holonomic model is Kantian and Piagetian; the ecological model partakes of a critical realism.

Clinical neurological experience wholly supports the holonomic view. Patients are seen who complain of macropsia and micropsia and other bizarre distortions of visual space. For instance, I once had a patient who, after a blow on the head, experienced episodes of vertigo during which the visual world went spinning. His major complaint was that every so often, when his perceptions again stabilized, they left him with the world upside down until the next vertigo which might right things once again. He had developed a sense of humor about these experiences, which were becoming less frequent and of shorter duration: his major annoyance he stated to be the fact that girls' skirts stayed up despite the upside-down position!

Further "clinical" evidence in support of the holonomic model comes from the experimental laboratory. Resections of the primate inferior temporal cortex markedly impair size constancy—the transformations across various distances over which environmental information must remain invariant in order to be "directly" perceived as of the same size.

Yet Gibson (1966, 1968) and others who share his views (e.g., Johannson, 1973; and more recently Hebb, in press), make a good case that in normal adult humans, perception is direct. A series of ingenious experiments has shown that by appropriate manipulations of "information," illusions indistinguishable from the "real" can be created on a screen. The demonstrations are convincing and make it implausible to maintain a solopsistic or purely idealistic position with respect to the physical universe—that nothing but a buzzing blooming confusion characterizes external reality. With respect to the experiments he has devised, Gibson is correct.

Furthermore, if perception is direct, a dilemma for the holonomic theory would be resolved. When an optical hologram produces an image, a human observer is there to see it. When a neural hologram constructs an image, who is the observer? Where is the "little man" who views the "little man"? Direct perception needs no little men inside the head. Gibson (1966), in fact, deplores the term image because it calls up the indirectness of the representational process. However, if what we "directly perceive" is a constructed *image* and not the true organization of the external world–and we mistake this perception as veridical–perception would be both direct and constructional.

The question to be answered therefore is by what mechanism can perception be both direct and constructional? A clue to the resolution of this dilemma comes from the Gibson (and Johansson) experiments themselves. Their displays produce the *illusion* of reality. When we know the entire experiment we can label the percept as an illusion, even though we directly experience it. In a similar fashion, the sound coming from the speakers of a stereophonic system is experienced directly. When we manipulate the dials of the system (changing the phase of the interacting, interfering sound waves) so that an equal part of the sound comes from each of the two speakers, we say that an illusion has been produced–the sound has been projected to the space between the speakers. Perception continues to be direct, but considerable computation is involved in determining the conditions over which the "information" contained in the sound remains invariant. We do not naively assume that the fireplace generates the sound. Despite the directness of the perception, it can be superficially misleading as to the actual characteristics of the physical universe.

The issues appear to be these. Gibson abhors the concept "image." As already noted, he emphasizes the "information" which the environment "affords" the organism. As an ecological theorist, however, Gibson recognizes the importance of the organism in determining what is afforded. He details especially the role of movement and the temporal organization of the organism–environment relationship that results. Still, that organization does not consist of the construction of percepts from their elements; rather the process is one of responding to the invariances in that relationship. Thus perceptual learning involves progressive differentiation of such invariances, not the association of sensory elements.

The problem for me has been that I agree with all of the positive contributions to conceptualization which Gibson has made, yet find myself in disagreement with his negative views (such as on "images") and his ultimate philosophical position. If indeed the organism plays such a major role in the theory of ecological perception, does not this entail a constructional position? Gibson's answer is no, but perhaps this is due to the fact that he (in company with so many other psychologists) is basically uninterested in what goes on inside the organism.

What then does go on in the perceptual systems that is relevant to this argument? I believe that to answer this question we need to analyze what is ordinarily meant by "image." Different disciplines have very different definitions of this term.

The situation is similar to that which obtained in neurology for almost a century with regard to the representation we call "motor." In that instance the issue was stated in terms of whether the representation in the motor cortex was punctile or whether in fact movements were represented. A great number of experiments were done. Many of them using anatomical and discrete electrical stimulation techniques showed an exquisitely detailed anatomical mapping between cortical points and muscles and even parts of muscles (Chang, Ruch, & Ward, 1947). The well-known homunculus issued from such studies on man (Penfield & Boldrey, 1937).

But other, more physiologically oriented experiments provided different results. In these it was shown that the same electrical stimulation at the same cortical locus would produce *different* movements depending on such other factors as position of the limb, the density of stimulation, the state of the organism (his respiratory rate, etc.). For the most part, one could conceptualize the results as showing that the cortical representation consisted of movements centered on one or another joint (e.g., Phillips, 1965). The controversy was thus engaged—proponents of punctate muscle representation vis-à-vis the proponents of the representation of movement.

I decided to repeat some of the classical experiments in order to see for myself which view to espouse (reviewed in Pribram, 1971, Chapters 12 and 13). Among the experiments performed was one in which the motor cortex was removed (unilaterally and bilaterally) in monkeys who had been trained to open a rather complex latch box to obtain a peanut reward (Pribram, Kruger, Robinson, & Berman, 1955–1956). My results in this experiment were, as in all others, the replication of the findings of my predecessors. The latch box was opened, but with considerable clumsiness, thus prolonging the time taken some two- to threefold.

But the interesting part of the study consisted in taking cinematographic pictures of the monkeys' hands while performing the latch-box task and in their daily movements about the cage. Showing these films in slow motion we were able to establish to our satisfaction that no movement or even sequence of movements was specifically impaired by the motor cortex resections! The deficit appeared to be *task* specific, not muscle or movement specific.

My conclusion was therefore that, depending on the *level of analysis,* one could speak of the motor representation in the cortex in three ways. Anatomically, the representation was punctate and of *muscles.* Physiologically, the representation consisted of mapping the muscle representation into *movements,* most likely around joints as anchor points. But behavioral analysis showed that these views of the representation were incomplete. No muscles were paralyzed, no movements precluded by total resection of the representation. *Action,* defined as the environmental consequence of movements, was what suffered when motor cortex was removed.

The realization that acts, not just movements or muscles, were represented in the motor systems of the brain accounted for the persistent puzzle of motor equivalences. We all know that we can, though perhaps clumsily, write with our left hands, our teeth, or, if necessary, our toes. These muscle systems may never have been exercised to perform such tasks, yet immediately and without practice can accomplish at least the rudiment required. In a similar fashion, birds will build nests from a variety of materials, and the resulting structure is always a habitable facsimile of a nest.

The problem immediately arose of course as to the precise nature of a representation of an act. Obviously there is no "image" of an action to be found in the brain if by "image" one means specific words or the recognizable configuration of nests. Yet some sort of representation appears to be engaged that allows the generation of words and nests—an image of what is to be achieved, as it were.

The precise composition of images-of-achievement remained a puzzle for many years. The resolution of the problem came from experiments by Bernstein (1967) who made cinematographic records of people hammering nails and performing similar more or less repetitive acts. The films were taken against black backgrounds with the subjects dressed in black leotards. Only joints were made visible by placing white dots over them.

The resulting record was a continuous wave form. Bernstein performed a Fourier analysis on these wave forms and was invariably able to predict within a few centimeters the amplitude of the next in the series of movements.

The suggestion from Bernstein's analysis is that a Fourier analysis of the invariant components of motor patterns (and their change over time) is computable and that an image-of-achievement may consist of such computation. Electrophysiological data from unit recordings obtained from the motor cortex have provided preliminary evidence that, in fact, such computations are performed (Evarts, 1967, 1968).

By "motor image" therefore we mean a punctate muscle–brain connectivity that is mapped into movements over joints in order to process environmental invariants generated by or resulting from those movements. This three-level definition of the motor representation can be helpful in resolving the problems that have become associated with the term "image" in perceptual systems.

In vision, audition, and somesthesis (and perhaps to some extent in the chemical senses as well) there is a punctate connectivity between receptor surface and cortical representation. This anatomical relationship serves as an *array* over which sensory signals are relayed. At a physiological level of analysis, however, a mapping of the punctate elements of the array into functions occurs. This is accomplished in part by convergences and divergences of pathways but even more powerfully by networks of lateral interconnectivities, most of which operate by way of slow graded dendritic potentials rather than by nerve impulses propagated in long axons. Thus in the retina, for instance, no nerve impulses can be recorded from receptors, bipolar or horizontal cells. It is only in the ganglion cell layer, the last stage of retinal processing, that nerve impulses are generated to be conducted in the optic nerve to the brain (reviewed by Pribram, 1971, Chapters 1, 6, and 8). These lateral networks of neurons operating by means of slow graded potentials thus map the punctate receptor–brain connectivities into functional *ambiences*.

By analogy to the motor system, this characterization of the perceptual process is incomplete. Behavioral analysis discerns perceptual constancies just as this level had to account for motor equivalences. In short, *invariances* are processed over time and these invariances constitute the behaviorally derived aspects of the representation (e.g., Pribram, 1974b). Ordinarily, an organism's representational processes are called *images* and there is no good reason not to use this term. But it must be clearly kept in mind that the perceptual image, just as the motor image, is more akin to a computation than to a photograph.

We have already presented the evidence that for the visual system at least, this computation (just as in the motor system) is most readily accomplished in the Fourier or some similar domain. The evidence that pattern perception depends on the processing of spatial frequencies has been reviewed. It is, after all, this evidence more than any other that has suggested the holonomic hypothesis of perception.

The perceptual image, so defined, is therefore a representation, a mechanism based on the precise anatomical punctate receptor–cortical connectivity that composes an *array*. This array is operated upon by lateral interconnections that provide the *ambiences* which process the *invariances* in the organism's input. The cortical representation of the percepts go therefore beyond the anatomical representations of the receptor surfaces just as the cortical representation of actions goes beyond the mere anatomical representations of muscles.

It is, of course, a well-known tenet of Gestalt psychology that the percept is not equivalent of the retinal (or other receptor) image. This tenet is based on the facts of constancy (e.g., size) and the observations of illusions. Neurophysiologists, however, have only recently begun to seriously investigate this problem. Thus Horn (Horn, Stechler, & Hill, 1972) showed that certain cells in the brainstem (superior colliculus) maintained their firing pattern to an environmental stimulus despite changes in body orientation; and in my laboratory Spinelli (1970) and also Bridgeman (1972) using somewhat different techniques demonstrated constancy in the firing pattern of cortical neurons over a range of body and environmental manipulations. Further, neurobehavioral studies have shown that size constancy is impaired when perivisual and inferior temporal cortex is removed (Humphrey & Weiskrantz, 1969; Ungerleider, 1975).

The fact that the cortex becomes tuned to environmental invariances rather than just to the retinal image is borne out dramatically by a hitherto unexplained discrepancy in the results of two experiments. In both experiments a successful attempt was made to modify the orientation selectivity of the cortical neurons of cats by raising them from birth in environments restricted to either horizontal or vertical stripes. In one experiment (Blakemore, 1974) the kittens were raised in a large cylinder appropriately striped. A collar prevented the animals from seeing parts of their bodies–so they were exposed to only the stripes. However, and this turns out to be critical, the kittens could observe the stripes from a variety of head and eye positions. In contrast, in the other experiment, which was performed in my laboratory (Hirsch & Spinelli, 1970), head and eye turning was prevented from influencing the experiment by tightly fitting goggles onto which the stripes were painted. In both experiments cortical neurons were found to be predominantly tuned to the horizontal or vertical depending on the kittens' environment, although the tuning in Blakemore's experiments appeared to be somewhat more effective. The discrepancy arose when behavioral testing was instituted. Blakemore's kittens were consistently and completely deficient in their ability to follow a bar moving perpendicular to the orientation of the horizontally or vertically striped environment in which they had been raised. In our experiment Hirsch, despite years of effort using a great number of quantitative tests, could never demonstrate any change in visual behavior! The tuning of the cortical cells to the environmental situation which remained invariant across transformations of head and eye turning was behaviorally effective; the tuning of cortical cells to consistent retinal stimulation had no behavioral consequences.

These results are consonant with others obtained in other sensory modes and also help to provide some understanding of how brain processing achieves our perception of an objective world separated from the receptor surfaces which interface the organism with his environment.

Von Békésy (1967) has performed a large series of experiments on both auditory and somatosensory perceptions to clarify the conditions that produce projection and other perceptual effects. For example, he has shown that a series of vibrators placed on the forearm produce a point perception when the phases of the vibrations are appropriately adjusted. Once again, in our laboratory we found that the cortical response to the type of somatosensory stimulation used by von Békésy was consonant with the perception, not with the pattern of physical stimulation of the receptor surface (Dewson, 1964; Lynch, 1971). Further, von Békésy showed that when such vibrators are applied to both forearms, and the subject wears them for awhile, the point perception suddenly leaps into the space between the arms.

Other evidence for projection comes from the clinic. An amputated leg can still be perceived as a phantom for years after it has been severed and pickled in a pathologist's jar. A more ordinary experience comes daily to artisans and surgeons who "feel" the environment at the ends of their tools and instruments.

When validation is lacking or incomplete, we tend to call the perception an illusion and pursue a search for what physical events may be responsible for the illusion. Gibson and his followers are correct, perception is direct. They are wrong if and when they think that this means that a constructional brain process is ruled out or that the percept invariably and directly gives evidence of the physical organization that gives rise to perception.

As noted, there is altogether too much evidence in support of a brain constructional theory of perception. The holonomic model, because of its inclusion of parallel processing and wave interference characteristics readily handles the data of projection and illusion that make up the evidence for direct perception. The holonomic model also accounts for the "directness" of the perception; holographic images are not located at the holographic plane, but in front or beyond it, away from the constructional apparatus and more into the apparently "real," consensually validatable external world.

STRUCTURE AND PROBABILITY

In the concluding part of this chapter, I want, therefore, to explore some questions as to the organization of this external "real" physical world. Unless we know something of consensually validatable "information" that remains invariant across transformations of the input to the brain—and, as we have seen, we cannot rely only on the directness of our perceptual experience for this knowledge—how can we think clearly about what is being perceived? Questions as to the nature of the physical universe lie in the domain of the theoretical physicist. The science of physics has enjoyed unprecedented success not only in this century, but in the several preceding ones. Physicists ought to know something, therefore, about the universe we perceive; and, of course, they do. However, as we shall shortly see, the structure–distribution problem is as pervasive here as it is in brain function.

The special theory of relativity made it clear that physical laws as conceived in classical mechanics hold only in certain circumscribed contexts. Perceptions of the Brownian "random" movements of small suspended particles, or of the paths of light coming from distances beyond the solar system, strained the classical conceptions to the point where additional concepts applying to a wider range of contexts had to be brought in. As in the case of direct perception, the laws of physics must take into account not only what is perceived, but the more extended domain in which the perception occurs. The apparent flatness of the earth we now know as an illusion.

The limitations of classical physics were underscored by research into the microcosm of the atom. The very instruments of perception and even scientific observation itself became suspect as providing only limited, situation-related information. Discrepancies appeared, such as an electron being in two places (orbits) at once or at best moving from one place to another faster than the speed of light—the agreed-upon maximum velocity for any event. And within the nucleus of the atom matters are worse–a nuclear particle appears to arrive in one location before it has left another. Most of these discrepancies result from the assumption that these particles occupy only a point in space–thus when the equations that relate location to mass or velocity are solved, they lead to infinities. Furthermore, in the atomic universe, happenings take place in jumps–they appear to be quantized, that is, particulate. Yet when a small particle, such as an electron, or a photon of light, passes through a grating and another particle passes through a neighboring grating, the two particles appear to interact as if they were waves, since interference patterns can be recorded on the far side of the gratings. It all depends on the situation in which measurements are made whether the "wavicle" shows its particle or its wave characteristics.

Several approaches to this dilemma of situational specificity have been forwarded. The most popular, known as the Copenhagen solution, suggests that the wave equations (e.g., those of Schrödinger, 1935, and de Broglie, 1964) describe the average probabilities of chance occurrences of particulate events. An earlier solution by Niels Bohr (the "father" of the Copenhagen group, 1966) suggested that particle and wave were irreconcilable complimentary aspects of the whole. Heisenberg (1959) extended this suggestion by pointing out that the whole cannot in fact be known because our knowledge is always dependent on the experimental situation in which the observations are made. Von Neumann (1932) added, that given a positivistic operational framework, the whole reality becomes therefore not only unknown but unknowable. Thus the whole becomes indeterminable because we cannot in any specific situation be certain that what we are observing and measuring reflects "reality." In this sense, as well as from the viewpoint of brain processes, we are always constructing physical reality. The arguments of the quantum physicist and those of the neurophysiologist and psychologist of perception are in this respect identical.

But several theoretical physicists are not satisfied with these solutions or lack of solutions. Feynman, Leighton, and Sands (1965), for instances, note that though we have available most precise and quantitative mathematical descriptions in quantum mechanics, we lack good images of what is taking place. (His own famous diagrams show time flowing backwards in some segments!) De Broglie (1964), who first proposed wavelike characteristics for the electron fails to find solace in a probabalistic explanation of the experimental results that led him to make the proposal. And de Broglie is joined by Schrödinger (1935), who formulated the wave equation in question and especially by Einstein, whose insights led him to remain unconvinced that an unknowable universe, macro and micro, was built on the principle of the roulette wheel or the throw of dice.

I share this discomfort with attributing too much to chance because of an experience of my own. In the Museum of Science and Industry in Chicago, there is a display which demonstrates the composition of a Gaussian probability distribution. Large lead balls are let fall from a tube into an open maze made of a lattice of shelves. The written and auditory explanations of the display emphasize the indeterminate nature of the path of each of the falling balls and provide an excellent introduction to elementary statistics. However, nowhere is mention made of the symmetrical maze through which the balls must fall in order to achieve their probabilistic ending. Having just completed *Plans and the Structure of Behavior* (Miller, Galanter, & Pribram, 1960), I was struck by the omission. In fact, students of biology routinely use statistics to discover the orderliness in the processes they are studying. For example, when a measurable entity shows a Gaussian distribution in a population, we immediately look for its heritability. Perhaps the gas laws from which statistics emerged have misled us. A Gaussian distribution reflects symmetrical *structure* and not just the random banging about of particles. Again, the physical reality behind the direct perception may contain surprises.

Moreover, when we obtain a probabilistic curve, we often refer to a distribution of events across a population of such events—that is, a Gaussian distribution. Could it be that for the physical universe, just as in the case of brain function, structure and distribution mutually interact? After all, the brain is a part of the physical universe. For brain function, we found structure to be in the form of program and distribution in the form of holograms. Is the rest of the physical universe built along these lines as well?

THE STRUCTURAL AND HOLONOMIC ASPECTS OF ORGANIZATION

David Bohm (1957), initially working with Einstein, has among others, made some substantial contributions to theoretical physics compatible with this line of reasoning. Bohm points out, as noted above, that the oddities of quantum mechanics derive almost exclusively from the assumption that the particles in question occupy only a point in space. He assumed instead that the "wavicle" occupies a finite space which is structured by subquantal forces akin to electromagnetic and gravitational interactions. These interacting forces display fuctuations—some are linear and account for the wave form characteristics of the space or field. Other interactions are nonlinear (similar to turbulence in fluid systems) and on occasion produce quantal events. In biology, Thom (1972) has developed a mathematics to deal with such occurrences in the morphogenetic field and this mathematics has been applied to perception by Bruter (1974). Thom calls the emergence of quasi-quantal structures from turbulant processes "catastrophes." In physics, the quantal structures that result from such catastrophic processes may, therefore, be only partially stable. Thus, they can disappear and reappear nearby in a seemingly random fashion, which, on the average, however, are subject to the more regular oscillations of the forces. In biology, observations pertaining to the entrainment of oscillatory processes by clocks or temporary dominant foci parallel these concepts. Bohm goes on to point out where in the subquantal domain these events will become manifest: the interactions of high-frequency and high-energy particles in nuclear reactions, in black bodies, etc. An article in a recent issue of *Scientific American* reviews the contemporary scene in these attempts at a Unified Field Theory in the subquantal domain (Weinberg, 1974).

More recently, Bohm (1971, 1973) has reviewed the conceptual development of physics from Aristotelian through Gallilean and Newtonian times to modern developments in the quantum mechanics. He points out how much of our image of the physical universe results from the fact that, since Gallileo, the opening of new worlds of inquiry in physics has depended on the use of lenses. Lenses have shaped our images and lenses objectify. Thus we tend to assess external space in terms of objects, things and particulars.

Bohm goes on to suggest that image formation is only one result of optical information processing and proposes that we seriously consider the hologram as providing an additional model for viewing the organization of physical processes. He and his group are now engaged in detailed application of this basic insight to see whether in fact a holographic approach can be helpful in solving the problems of high-energy nuclear physics. Initial· developments have shown promise.

As noted above, the subquantal domain shows striking similarities to holographic organization. Just as in the case of brain processes presented here, Bohm's theoretical formulations retain classical and quantum processes as well as adding the holographic. The holographic state described by wave equations and the particle state described quantally, are part of a more encompassing whole. The parallel holds because the holographic models describe only the deeper levels of the theory which is thus holonomic, rather than holographic, as we found it to be for the special case of brain function (where the deeper level is constituted of pre- and postsynaptic and dendritic potentials and the quantal level, of the nerve impulses generated by these slow potentials).

Bohm relates structural and holographic processes by specifying the differences in their organization. He terms classical and particle organization explicate and holographic organization implicate. Elsewhere (Pribram, 1971), I have made a parallel distinction for perceptual processes: following Bertrand Russell (1959), I proposed that scientific analysis as we practice it today, begets knowledge of the extrinsic properties (the rules, structures, etc.) of the physical world. My proposal departs from Russell's, however, in suggesting that intrinsic properties (e.g., which he defines as the stoneness of stones) are also knowable—that in fact they are the 'ground' in which the extrinsic properties are embedded in order to become realized. Thus artists, artisans, and engineers spend most of their time realizing the extrinsic programs, laws and rules of the arts and sciences by grounding them in an appropriate medium. For example, a Brahms symphony can be realized by an orchestra, on sheet music, on a long-playing record, or on tape. Each of these realizations come about after long hours of development of the medium in which the realization occurs. Russell was almost correct in his view that the intrinsic properties of the physical world are unknowable—they have apparently little to do with the more enduring extrinsic properties, show no resemblances among themselves, and demand considerable know*how* to replicate.

The sum of these ideas leads to the proposal that the intrinsic properties of the physical universe, their implicate organization, the field, ground or medium in which explicit organizations, extrinsic properties, become realized, are multiform. In the extreme, the intrinsic properties, the implicate organization, is holographic. As extrinsic properties become realized, they make the implicate organization become more explicit.

The consequence for this view is a reevaluation of what we mean by probabilistic. Until now, the image, the model of statistics, has been indeterminacy. If the above line of reasoning is correct, an alternate view would hold that a random distribution is based on holographic principles and is therefore determined. The uncertainty of occurrence of events is only superficial and is the result of holographic "blurring" which reflects underlying symmetries (much as does the Gaussian distribution in our earlier example) and not just haphazard occurrences. This relation between appearance and reality in the subquantal domain of nuclear physics and its dependence on underlying symmetries (spin) is detailed in the review article in *Scientific American* already referred to (Weinberg, 1974).

A preliminary answer to the question posed at the outset of this section—what is it that we perceive?—is therefore that we perceive a physical universe not much different in basic organization from that of the brain. This is comforting since the brain is part of the physical universe as well as the organ of perception. It is also comforting to find that the theoretical physicist working from his end and with his tools and data has come to the identical problem (which is, in Gibson's terms, the nature of the information which remains invariant across situations) faced by the neurophysiologist and psychologist interested in perception (Bohm, 1965, Appendix). Though surprising, the fact that at least one renowned theoretical physicist has made a proposal that addresses this common problem in terms similar to those set forth on the basis of an analysis of brain function is most encouraging. For science is of a piece, and full understanding cannot be restricted to the developments made possible by one discipline alone. This is especially true for perception—where perceiver meets the perceived and the perceived meets the perceiver.

ACKNOWLEDGMENTS

This work was supported by NIMH Grant No. MH12970-08 and NIMH Career Award No. MH15214-13 to the author.

REFERENCES

Bernstein, N. *The Co-ordination and regulation of movements.* New York: Pergamon Press, 1967.

Blakemore, C. Developmental factors in the formation of feature extracting neurons. In F. O. Schmitt & F. G. Worden (Eds.), *The neurosciences third study program.* Cambridge, Massachusetts: MIT Press, 1974. Pp. 105–113.

Bohm, D. *Causality and chance in modern physics.* Philadelphia: University of Pennsylvania Press, 1957.

Bohm, D. *The special theory of relativity.* New York: W. A. Benjamin, 1965.

Bohm, D. Quantum theory as an indication of a new order in physics. Part A. The development of new orders as shown through the history of physics. *Foundations of Physics,* **1**(4), 359–381, 1971.

Bohm, D. Quantum theory as an indication of a new order in physics. Part B. Implicate and explicate order in physical law. *Foundations of Physics,* **3**(2), 139–168, 1973.

Bohr, N. *Atomic physics and human knowledge.* New York: Vintage Press, 1966.

Bridgeman, B. Visual receptive fields sensitive to absolute and relative motion during tracking. *Science,* **178**, 1106–1108, 1972.

Bruter, C. P. *Topologie et perception.* Paris: Doin-Maloine S. A., 1974.

de Broglie, L. *The current interpretation of wave mechanisms: A critical study.* Amsterdam: Elsevier, 1964.

Chang, H. T., Ruch, T. C., & Ward, A. A., Jr. Topographical representation of muscles in motor cortex in monkeys. *Journal of Neurophysiology,* **10**, 39–56, 1947.

Dewson, J. H. III. Cortical responses to patterns of two-point cutaneous stimulation. *Journal of Comparative Physiological Psychology,* **58**, 387–389, 1964.

Feynman, R. P., Leighton, R. B., & Sands, M. (Eds.), *The Feynman lectures on physics. Quantum mechanics, Vol. III.* Reading, Massachusetts: Addison-Wesley, 1965.

Evarts, E. V. Representation of movements and muscles by pyramidal tract neurons of the precentral motor cortex. In M. D. Yahr & D. P. Purpura (Eds.), *Neurophysiological basis of normal and abnormal motor activities.* New York: Raven Press, 1967. Pp. 215–254.

Evarts, E. V. Relation of pyramidal tract activity to force exerted during voluntary movement. *Journal of Neurophysiology,* **31**, 14–27, 1968.

Gerbrandt, L. K., Spinelli, D. N., & Pribram, K. H. The interaction of visual attention and temporal cortex stimulation on electrical activity evoked in the striate cortex. *Electroencephalography and Clinical Neurophysiology,* **29**, 146–155, 1970.

Gesteland, R. C., Lettvin, J. Y., Pitts, W. H., & Chung, S. H. A code in the nose. In H. L. Oestreicher & D. R. Moore (Eds.), *Cybernetic problems in bionics.* New York: Gordon & Breach. Pp. 313–322, 1968.

Gibson, J. J. *The senses considered as perceptual systems.* Boston: Houghton-Mifflin, 1966.

Gibson, J. J. What gives rise to the perception of motion? *Psychological Review,* **75**(4), 335–346, 1968.

Granit, Ragnar. *The basis of motor control.* New York: Academic Press, 1970.

Gregory, R. L. *Eye and brain.* New York: McGraw-Hill, 1966.

Gross, C. G. Visual Functions of inferotemporal cortex. In R. Jung (Ed.), *Handbook of sensory physiology.* Vol. 7, Part 3B. Berlin: Springer-Verlag, 1972.

Hebb, D. O. To know your own mind. In *Images, perception and knowledge symposium: The University of Western Ontario* (to be published).

Heisenberg, W. *Physics and philosophy.* London: Allen & Unwin, 1959.

Hirsch, H., & Spinelli, D. N. Distribution of receptive field orientation: Modification contingent on conditions of visual experience. *Science,* **168**, 869–871, 1970.

Horn, G., Stechler, G., and Hill, R. M. Receptive fields of units in the visual cortex of the cat in the presence and absence of bodily tilt. *Experimental Brain Research*, **15**, 113–132, 1972.

Humphrey, N. K., & Weiskrantz, L. Size constancy in monkeys with inferotemporal lesions. *Quarterly Journal of Experimental Psychology*, **21**, 225–238, 1969.

Johansson, G. Visual perception of biological motion and a model for its analysis. *Perception and Psychophysics*, **14**, 201–211, 1973.

Lynch, J. C. A single unit analysis of contour enhancement in the somesthetic system of the cat. Unpublished doctoral dissertation, Stanford University, Neurological Sciences, 1971.

Miller, G. A., Galanter, E. H., & Pribram, K. H. *Plans and the structure of behavior*. New York: Henry Holt and Co., 1960.

Milner, B. Psychological defects produced by temporal lobe excision. In H. C. Solomon, S. Cobb, & W. Penfield (Eds.), *The brain and human behavior* (Proceedings of the Association for Research in Nervous and Mental Disease). Baltimore: Williams & Wilkins, 36, 244–257, 1958.

Mishkin, M. Cortical visual areas and their interaction. In A. G. Karczmar & J. C. Eccles (Eds.), *The brain and human behavior*. Berlin: Springer-Verlag, 1972.

Penfield, W., & Boldrey, E. Somatic motor and sensory representation in the cerebral cortex of man as studied by electrical stimulation. *Brain*, **60**, 389–443, 1937.

Pfaffmann, C. C. The pleasures of sensation. *Psychological Review*, **67**, 253–268, 1960.

Phillips, C. G. Changing concepts of the precentral motor area. In J. C. Eccles (Ed.), *Brain and conscious experience*. Berlin and New York: Springer-Verlag, 1965. Pp. 389–421.

Pribram, H., & Barry, J. Further behavioral analysis of the parieto-temporo-preoccipital cortex. *Journal of Neurophysiology*, **19**, 99–106, 1956.

Pribram, K. H. Toward a science of neuropsychology: (Method and data). In R. A. Patton (Ed.), *Current trends in psychology and the behavioral sciences*. Pittsburgh: University of Pittsburgh Press, 1954. Pp. 115–142.

Pribram, K. H. Neocortical function in behavior. In H. F. Harlow and C. N. Woolsey (Eds.), *Biological and biochemical bases of behavior*. Madison, Wisconsin: University of Wisconsin Press, 1958. Pp. 151–172.

Pribram, K. H. A review of theory in physiological psychology. In *Annual Review of Psychology*, **2**, 1–40. Palo Alto, California: Annual Reviews, 1960.

Pribram, K. H. The amnestic syndromes: disturbances in coding? In G. A. Talland & N. C. Waugh (Eds.), *Pathology of memory*. New York: Academic Press, 1969. Pp. 127–157.

Pribram, K. H. *Languages of the brain: Experimental paradoxes and principles in neuropsychology*. Englewood Cliffs, New Jersey: Prentice-Hall, 1971.

Pribram, K. H. Some dimensions of remembering: Steps toward a neuropsychological model of memory. In J. Gaito (Ed.), *Macromolecules and behavior*. Chpt. 17. New York: Appleton-Century-Crofts, 1972.

Pribram, K. H. How is it that sensing so much we can do so little? In *The Neurosciences Study Program, III*. Cambridge, Massachusetts: MIT Press, 1974. Pp. 249–261. (a)

Pribram, K. H. The isocortex. In D. A. Hamburg & H. K. H. Brodie (Eds.), *American handbook of psychiatry*, Volume 6. New York: Basic Books 1974. (b)

Pribram, K. H., Kruger, L., Robinson, R., & Berman, A. J. The effects of precentral lesions on the behavior of monkeys. *Yale Journal of Biology and Medicine*, **28**, 428–443, 1955–1956.

Pribram, K. H., Nuwer, M., & Baron, R. The holographic hypothesis of memory structure in brain function and perception. In R. C. Atkinson, D. H. Krantz, R. C. Luce, & P. Suppes (Eds.), *Contemporary developments in mathematical psychology*. San Francisco: Freeman, 1974.

Pribram, K. H., Spinelli, D. N. & Reitz, S. L. Effects of radical disconnextion of occipital and temporal cortex on visual behavior of monkeys. *Brain,* **92,** 301–312, 1969.

Ratliff, F. *Mach bands: Quantitative studies in neural networks in the retina.* San Francisco: Holden-Day, 1965.

Reitz, S. L., & Pribram, K. H. Some subcortical connections of the inferotemporal gyrus of monkey. *Experimental Neurology,* **25,** 632–645, 1969.

Rothblat, L., & Pribram, K. H. Selective attention: Input filter or response selection? *Brain Research,* **39,** 427–436, 1972.

Russell, B. *My philosophical development.* New York: Simon & Schuster, 1959.

Schrödinger, E. Discussion of probability relations between separated systems. *Proceedings of the Cambridge Philosophical Society,* **31,** 555–563, 1935.

Spinelli, D. N. Recognition of visual patterns. In *Perception and its disorders.* Research publication of the Association for Research in Nervous and Mental Disease, Vol. 48, 1970. Pp. 139–149.

Spinelli, D. N., & Pribram, K. H. Changes in visual recovery functions produced by temporal lobe stimulation in monkeys. *Electroencephalography and Clinical Neurophysiology,* 20, 44–49, 1966.

Spinelli, D. N., & Pribram, K. H. Changes in visual recovery function and unit activity produced by frontal cortex stimulation. *Electroencephalography and Clinical Neurophysiology,* **22,** 143–149, 1967.

Thom, R. *Stabilite structurelle et morphogenese.* Reading, Massachusetts: W. A. Benjamin, 1972.

Ungerleider, L. Deficits in size constancy discrimination: Further evidence for dissociation between monkeys with inferotemporal and prestriate lesions. Paper presented at the Eastern Psychological Association Convention, April, 1975.

von Békésy, G. Synchronism of neural discharges and their demultiplication in pitch perception on the skin and in hearing. *Journal of the Acoustical Society of America,* **31**(3), 338–349, 1959.

von Békésy, G. *Experiments in hearing.* New York: McGraw-Hill, 1960.

von Békésy, G. *Sensory inhibition.* Princeton, New Jersey: Princeton University Press, 1967.

von Neumann, J. *Mathematische Grundlagen der Quantenmechanik.* Berlin: Springer-Verlag, 1932.

Weinberg, S. Unified theories of elementary-particle interaction. *Scientific American,* **231**(1), 50–59, 1974.

Whitlock, D. G., & Nauta, W. J. Subcortical projections from the temporal neocortex in *Macaca mulatta. Journal of Comparative Neurology,* **106,** 183–212, 1956.

Wilson, M. Effects of circumscribed cortical lesions upon somesthetic and visual discrimination in the monkey. *Journal of Comparative and Physiological Psychology,* **50,** 630–635, 1957.

5

Perceiving the Face of Change in Changing Faces: Implications for a Theory of Object Perception

Robert Shaw

Center for Advanced Study in the Behavioral Sciences

John Pittenger

University of Arkansas at Little Rock

PART I: THEORETICAL MOTIVATION

The Problem of Object Perception

Typically, objects are best recognized by their shape. For this reason philosophers have considered shape to be a primary quality of objects while color has been deemed a secondary quality. But what is the shape of an object by which it might be recognized? Traditionally, theorists have identified the shape of objects with their spatial forms given in terms of their metric Euclidean description. In order for these spatial measurements to be useful, it is further assumed that the object must be rigid; in other words, that its shape does not change when displaced. For if shape were not invariant under displacement, no object would look the same when moved to a new place or even when reoriented in its old place.

Following in this tradition many psychologists have assumed that the perceptual information by which objects are recognized is identical with the optical information specifying its rigidity. Perhaps this is why nearly all experiments in the area of visual perception have used rigid objects as their stimuli, thereby tacitly endorsing the view that object perception is tantamount to the perception of the rigid shape of objects. Such theorists hold that the perceptual information by which objects can be identified is isomorphic to the exact physical measurements of the object. This view has been termed the "constancy" hypothesis (Hochberg, 1964) (not to be confused with the phenomenon of perceptual constancies). Unfortunately, this hypothesis is false. However, faith in the validity of the constancy hypothesis, as part of the heritage of naive realism, is so wide spread that it is worth reviewing some of the evidence against it.

Specifically, the constancy hypothesis is inconsistent with several well-known phenomena. For instance, the so-called "geometric" illusions, such as the Müller–Lyer, Ponzo, Poggendorf, Wundt, and Herring illusions all provide counter evidence to the claim that perceptual information is isomorphic with the exact physical description of objects. Physically straight lines may appear bent, parallel lines may appear nonparallel, objects of equal size may appear larger or smaller than one another, and well-aligned objects may appear misaligned.

To put the matter a little differently, there is abundant evidence that the geometry of perceptual space is not in perfect agreement with the classical geometry of physical space. This, of course, does not imply that objects are not recognized primarily in terms of their shape, but rather that we need a more adequate theory of what is meant by the shape of an object. In our opinion, the uncritical acceptance of the metric Euclidean ideal for shape and the classical view of perceptual space has thwarted attempts by most theorists to explain object perception, or as it is sometimes called, "form" or "pattern" perception. It is our contention that a less restrictive view of the nature of perceptual space is needed; one that construes the concept of shape more broadly. It is our hypothesis that a more adequate concept of shape and, consequently, a better understanding of object perception might emerge from studies which use stimulus materials other than simple, static, rigid objects. The studies reported in Part II of this chapter satisfy these guidelines.

Toward a More Adequate Conception of Shape

The constancy hypothesis was designed to explain perception of the physical world. Much to the chagrin of the naive realist, however, the very existence of geometric illusions indicates the utter failure of the hypothesis to even explain the perception of rigid geometric figures. To make matters still worse for the hypothesis, the natural world, as normally perceived, is replete with many identifiable shapes that are not rigid. Obviously, the constancy hypothesis is even less adequate for explaining the perception of these shapes. Consider the fact that natural objects which grow do not retain their rigid geometric forms but may still be recognized as the same object at different stages of growth. For example, we are often quite able to recognize persons who we have not seen for a long while, in spite of the fact that they may have grown to maturity, grown fatter or slimmer. Similarly, we are able to identify the species of plants and animals at different stages of growth. The incredible property of growth transformations, unlike simple displacements, is that they radically alter the Euclidean shapes of objects in a nonrigid fashion and yet do not destroy their structural identity. Thus, in spite of their somewhat elastic nature, growing faces somehow still preserve sufficient information in their nonrigid shapes to specify their species, race, sex, and individual identify.

When an artist caricatures a face, he applies nonrigid transformations to it. Not only do such transformations not destroy the perceived identity of the face, they frequently serve to enhance it. Ryan and Schwartz (1956) demonstrated that caricatures of objects are often more easily recognized than either photographs or veridical line drawings of the objects. Gardner and Wallach (1965) similarly were able to show that profile silhouettes of babies and adults could be transformed so as to be judged more "babyish" or adult-like than normative representations. They likened these idealizations to what ethologists have called "supernormal" stimuli. Ethologists have shown in a variety of species that highly caricatured representations of natural prey, predators, rivals, mates, etc. are sometimes more likely to release inherited fixed-action patterns of behavior than the real object.

In all these cases, nonrigid transformations preserve or even enhance the perceptual recognition of objects. This implies that the equivalence classes of psychologically effective stimuli cannot be captured in the traditional Euclidean theories of perceptual space. In the next section we sketch the theoretical and methodological considerations that have guided our research into the problem of object perception.

The Nature of Perceptual Space

If classical metric Euclidean geometry fails to provide a suitable theory of perceptual space, then what geometry might? Before this question can be properly addressed it would be useful to consider what properties such a theory of perceptual space must possess. Our first consideration will be to provide a conceptualization of a space in general that is different from the traditional conception taught us by classical Euclidean geometry. Secondly, we will not assume a priori that there necessarily exists only a single geometry for perceptual space, that is, we will allow for the possibility that the structure of perceptual space may at any given time conform to the geometry of the stimuli being perceived.

Although this is surely a radical hypothesis, it seems to us still more conservative than the postulation of a unique structure to perceptual space regardless of what is being perceived as traditionally has been done. By assuming that perceptual space may be flexible we make the determination of its geometry on any particular occasion an empirical task. Whether we can ultimately discover a single unified theory of perceptual processing is both a theoretical as well as an empirical challenge that cannot be adequately dealt with by simplistic assumptions regarding the possible nature of perceptual space. A few background remarks about revolutionary revisions in the concept of physical space developed in this century will provide the requisite context for understanding what we believe might be the nature of perceptual space.

A *geometry* can be thought of as a theory of *a* space and, conversely, for each possible concept of space there must be a geometry. Newton's space for classical physics was absolute in the sense that it was a *locus in which* rigid objects could be placed. Einstein rejected this notion of physical space in favor of one proposed a half century earlier by Riemann. Riemann's concept of space was not absolute, not merely "a locus in which . . . ," but, rather, he considered space relative in the following sense: Space itself has a structure. Its structure is induced from the "stuff" it contains. Change the material in the space and you change the structure of the space itself. For example, the amount of mass in a region of space determines the degree of curvature of space in that region. Strictly speaking, in such a space there is but one object, namely, the space structure as a whole. What are individual objects *in* space for Newton become local aspects *of* the structure of Riemann's space—a field notion (Bell, 1949).

We can now state the hypotheses regarding shape which will guide our research on the nature of object perception: (a) *the perceived shape of an object is due to the structure of the space to which it belongs;* and (b) *the structure of perceptual space is dependent upon the structure of the objects perceived as well as upon the structure of the perceptual systems.*

As unusual as these hypotheses might seem, there is considerable evidence to support them. For instance, regarding the first hypothesis, it appears that geometric illusions can be explained by the fact that the objects (lines) in the space induce a structure on the whole space. Consider a pair of parallel lines ruled on white paper. They look parallel until a fan pattern of radial lines is drawn around them (Herring's or Wundt's illusion); two circles appear equal in size until two converging lines are drawn around them (Ponzo illusion); or two lines appear of equal length until oppositely directed pairs of fins are added to each (Müller–Lyer illusion). Hence, changing the contents of a region of space changes its structure. In all such cases, the difference between the physical objects and the perceived objects argues that perceptual space is nonrigid and resilient, possessing an overall structure with field properties analogous to what Einstein argued for physical space.

Support for the second hypothesis, that perceptual space is structured by the objects perceived, can be found in two lines of research. Moore and Parker (1972), for instance, have programmed a pattern processing model which "sees" geometric illusions apparently as people do. When given, say, the Müller–Lyer figures as input instead of computing the exact physical measurements showing the equal figures to be equal, it computes a discrepancy in length of the same magnitude as shown in the judgment of people. In a Master's thesis under the direction of the principal author, Johnson (1973) was able to show that this effect arises because the model samples the continuous line drawings in a discrete manner by means of a parallel processor not unlike the retinal mosaic of the vertebrate eye. The hypothesis that the discretization of visual inputs by the nervous system of organisms causes such errors in perceptual processing suggests that illusions should be seen by nonhumans as well. Indeed, Révész (1934) found that chicks were susceptible to the Jastrow illusion. If this hypothesis is valid, then the existence of geometric illusions provides evidence that perceptual space can be structured by intrinsic properties of the central nervous system (e.g., its discrete functioning).

Furthermore research by Piaget and Inhelder (1956) and others (Laurendeau & Pinard, 1970; Pufall & Shaw, 1973) on the ontogenesis of perceptual space in the child demonstrates that experience can indeed alter the structure of perceptual space. Piaget argues that the child progresses from a concrete "action" space to a representational one as the symbolic function of intelligence develops. Borrowing the notion of a hierarchy of geometries from Klein, Piaget maintains that from roughly 2 to 12 years of age the child's concept of perceptual space progressively develops from topology to Euclidean geometry. Therefore, the view that seems best supported is that perceptual space for the child, no less than for the adult, is a family of spaces with no single geometry. Perhaps this is why no significant progress has been made as yet in relating the areas of object perception and space perception. Indeed, the proposed view of perceptual space, in following Riemann's concept of space, collapses both areas into a single one, where object perception is but the study of local regions of a more general spatial structure.

Thus, while there is good reason to agree with the Gestaltists' claim that the classical view of perceptual space as an inert, absolute space is woefully inadequate and must be rejected, we need not revert to their view of perceptual space as a field of mysterious forces in the cortex where isomorphic representation of physical objects act upon each other. On the other hand, James J. Gibson's (1966) theory of information pickup offers the basis from which we might propose a better alternative. Let us assume with Gibson that perceptual experiences belong to an *information* space, rather than to a field of mysterious cerebral forces as the Gestaltists did. Consequently, it seems likely that through evolution the perceptual systems have become intrinsically structured so that animals and humans are preattuned at birth to pickup just those dimensions of physical stimulation that convey ecologically significant invariants of information. Furthermore, there is ample evidence that the senses are not only genetically preattuned but become more sensitively calibrated to pickup those exigencies of the environment that bear directly on the survival, success and well-being of the perceiver—what has sometimes been called the "education of attention."

In addition to the intrinsic source of structualization of perceptual space by evolution and experience, there are extrinsic sources, namely, those properties of the environment and its contents which structure the energy distributions picked up. Before attempting to characterize more precisely how perceptual space becomes structured, let us explain the conundrum that the geometrical approach avoids.

Perceptual Theory as Ecological Rather Than Empirical or Phenomenological

Traditionally, no perceptual theory has successfully explained the relation of things experienced to things merely described. The first has to do with the phenomenology of perception while the second has to do with physicalistic or behavioristic descriptions of the conditions underwhich perceptions arise. Since our main goal in science has been to provide descriptions of phenomena capable of public corroboration, we have elected to eschew the more private or subjective aspects of experience in favor of a phenomenology-free language—at least so far as possible. The difference between an empirical science and a phenomenological one is that the former describes the conditions under which an observation or measurement might be successfully carried out *ceteris paribus* while the latter attempts to describe the experience of observing per se. Herein lies the fundamental difficulty of perceptual theory because such a theory, unlike physics, chemistry or biology, has as its raison d'être the scientific explanation of the relationships between the percept directly experienced (and hence phenomenological) and the object described from observation (and hence empirical). By our tacit attempts to pattern psychology after classical physics, we have saddled ourselves with a theoretical language which by design is inappropriate to our task. An empirically biased theoretical language which can describe only the antecedent conditions for perceiving but never the experience itself. Hence the meaningfulness of percepts from the first person perspective is lost.

Psychology is the juncture between science and epistemology; for it is here that the issue concerning what is known by description makes contact with the issue concerning what is known by acquaintance. Whatever else the so-called "mind–body" problem might be, it is surely perpetuated by this bifurcation in language whereby talk about the phenomenological consequents of perception belong to a separate mode of discourse than talk about the empirical antecedents of perception. This is why, as psychologists, we are much better able to provide a scientific description of the conditions under which a percept is likely to be experienced than we are a description of the perceptual experience itself, witness the failure of introspective psychology.

The modern forms of the causal theory of perception which have been adopted by consensus by both psychologists and philosophers fails to address the problem of perceptual experience at all, but merely postulates an identity between states of the brain and concomitant perceptual experiences. The recalcitrant mystery of this correspondence is apt to be swept under the rug. The language of perceptual theory tends to become "squishy" at this juncture where experience and the causal support for experience are semantically amalgamated.

Our aim, however, is not to rehash this old chestnut but to suggest that as psychologists we give it a decent burial. With respect to the attempt to resolve the mind–body dilemma by seizing it by either horn, you are damned if you do and damned if you don't. Therefore, let us choose the third way of resolving it and pass between the horns if we can; let us be no more phenomenologists than we are physicalists or behaviorists. Rather we need a third mode of discourse for perceptual theory which subsumes both of the other perspectives under a common rubric, and treats the object of perception and the perceptual experience inter se.

The distance separating the object to be perceived from the percept of the object is not truly spatial and, therefore, can not be bridged by causal sequences which unite physical objects with their nonphysical counterparts, the perceptual experiences, through the action of energy propagations on neural signals. The theory of the causal chain is science of the impersonal pronoun; science done in the third person, for example, "*It* causes *it* to be transformed to *its* new state from which *it* gives rise to *its* new effect." The impersonal pronoun *it* is used as subject of a verb that expresses a condition or action when no reference to an agent is to be made. No wonder that perceptual experiences, which by their very nature can not be impersonalized but must belong to some agent, are emasculated of all meaning when science is carried out in this mode of discourse. On the other hand, phenomenology is theory carried out in the first person singular, for example, "I experienced *X* when perceiving under such and such conditions."

To go from one mode of discourse to the other in order to provide a spurious causal analysis of perception is an egregious error, for it implies that the agentive mode of discourse in the first person singular is logically equivalent to the nonagentive mode of discourse in the impersonal third person. No amount of hand-waving can equate *it* with *I*. (For a fuller discussion of the need of agent-like constructs in psychology, see Shaw & McIntyre, 1975.)

What psychology needs is a theoretical language that somehow incorporates both the objectivity provided by physicalistic science and the person orientation of phenomenology. Such a language, ideally, would be *ecological* in the sense that it would be publically confirmable and yet would retain concepts that are meaningful with reference to agents. Following the above argument, an ecologically based theoretical language would be in the first person plural mode of discourse. For example, "If *we* agents, with the same attunements, pickup information made available by such and such a physical display, then *we* will typically have the same experience *X*." Such a theoretical language is well suited to explaining social agreement in perceptual experiences—the data foundation upon which the field rests.

Consequently, we propose as a candidate a geometric language wherein the relationship between percepts and objects perceivable are denoted as primitive terms. Such dyads are sufficient to provide the variables over which all knowledge relations might be constructed. In such a language perceptual space is an ecological information space since by a percept we no longer mean just a subjective experience nor a chain of states in a biological "it." Rather a percept refers to the state of an agent who is in the act of picking up information made available by events in the environment that specifies the potential value (affordances) those events have for the satisfaction of present or future actions.

In short, the concept of the affordance value of perceptual information, as proposed by Gibson (see his chapter, this volume), is the *tertium quid* needed to solve the problem of perception. Consequently, the problem to be addressed by perceptual theory is three fold: First, *what* is the nature of the information abstracted from physical displays (e.g. objects, events) in the world. Secondly, *how* is the abstraction process carried out? And, finally, for *whom* is the information intended? Is it intended for a hungry person, a person who wishes to stand, a bored person, a person who intends to hit a bullseye with an arrow, etc.

By construing the problem of perception (and action) in the first person plural we automatically include the reference criteron "we" to whom public conformation of all theoretical claims must ultimately be addressed. Hence, the ecological approach has the same built-in social objectivity of an empirical approach. But more importantly, given our recent flirtation with behaviorism, the "we" of the ecological approach retains its phenomenological reference so that the relative value of perceptual information is measured against the needs and intentions of the perceiving agent.

Under this view, the fact that information has an emotional appeal or an affective color is retained as an indispensable datum for experimental psychology. Moreover, so far as agents are comparably attuned and the perceptual situation analogous, then the meaning and value of the information for these agents can be objectively determined.

The Geometric Approach to Perceptual Theory

Currently, no single perceptual theory exists which encompasses both the intrinsic factors of perception arising from the design and attunement of the perceptual systems as well as the extrinsic factors contributed by the objects and events perceived. A significant reduction in the scope of the problem and considerable more precision might be achieved by a "geometrization" of the dual factors involved. Likewise, this approach may be used to raise the concept of perceptual information to the level of meaningful information which is both knowable directly by acquaintance and not just describable in abstract, valueless terms. What is required is a means of relating the experience of percepts to the information liberated from objects and events in the world by an active, investigative, perceiving creature.

In an attempt to cut the Gordian knot of the mind–body conundrum, we offer the following postulate for perceptual theory:

The act of picking up perceptual information is *the act of experiencing it; the information abstracted from the objects, object complexes and events of the world are intrinsically valuable to the perceiving agent since, by definition, such information specifies the nature of its source and the active relationships the animal or human perceiver might enter into with respect to that source.*

This is, of course, just a restatement of Gibson's claim that the information made available by the world is information that specifies what that world affords a given observer for good or ill. This is what it means to base perceptual theory on an ecological physics, that is, a physics described in terms selective of the attributes of the terrestrial environment that are most relevant to the successful existence of a perceiving animal or human. (Economics, political science, sociology, and anthropology are already ecologically relevant disciplines in this sense.)

By analogy to Newton's classical problem in physics regarding the action-at-a-distance achieved by one object on another through gravitational attraction, we have in psychology the action at a distance of objects and events in the physical environment on the psychological states of a person or animal. Using mathematical techniques developed by Minkowski, Einstein was able to rid physics of mysterious forces acting over empty distances that separate objects. He accomplished this feat by replacing the empty distance between objects with the structure of space itself in the manner suggested by Riemann's global approach to geometry. Thus, the mass of one body was now to be thought of as penetrating the mass of another body as ripples of a distant disturbance on the surface of a pond might interpenetrate and affect one another. Like the pond, space itself provides the support for the disturbing effects of bodies placed in close proximity as well as for the warping of orbits of planets awash with the motions of large masses as they run their distant courses.

A geometrization of perceptual theory might prove similarly beneficial in our efforts to clarify the perceptual effect of environmental bodies on conscious, sentient beings. Without the precision of geometric characterization, like Newton's gravitational attraction, perceptual information remains a mysterious force by which changes are effected across the distances that separate perceiver from that perceived. True, the physical distance that separates the body of the knowing-agent from object-known is filled with a flux of energy (light, sound, odors, etc.), but in what sense is it "filled" with information?

The space of perceptual information is no more the space of physics than it is the subjective space of phenomenological experience. Both such spaces are constructs abstracted from the more complex space of relationships that bind a knowing agent to the objects known. This abstraction is all the physicists or the phenomenologist knows and what the psychologist must dutifully acknowledge. Where the two complementary disciplines arise from denial of another half of the dyadic epistemic relation, psychology must begin with a more balanced view. As psychologists, we do not abstract solely from either term—the physical space or phenomenological space—rather we abstract from the relations defined by the product of the two spaces. The space of perceptual information is this new product space—an amalgamated spatial continuum not unlike the Einstein–Minkowski amalgamation of the three dimensions of physical space with the independent dimension of time.

The invariants of perceptual information thus become the invariants of the higher dimensional continuum and the primitive correspondence upon which knowledge rests. In this sense, the geometrization of perceptual theory achieves a mergence of psychology with epistemology.

In Part II we attempt to illustrate this geometric approach to the problem of perceiving faces as a special case of perceiving objects which are not rigidly inert in shape but undergo dynamic change due to growth. Our tactic is to discover the relevant invariants of perceptual information that specify aging, a significant ecological dimension of change, by discovering a geometry for growth defined in terms of transformations on structures that are potentially perceivable. We then carry out experiments to show that the postulated geometry of growth space does indeed specify the perceived changes in objects placed in that space, that is, the objects appear to age.

Thus, the geometry of growth space that we attempt to give is not just one that captures biological aspects of change but, more importantly for our purposes, it is one that captures the perceptual information that humans (and, perhaps, even animals) experience. The ecological validity of the tasks performed by our subjects in these experiments seems to us well indicated by the ease and naturalness with which they were performed.

PART II: THE GEOMETRY OF GROWTH— A THEORY OF PERCEPTUAL INFORMATION FOR AGING FACES

Introduction

A geometry is a set (usually a group) of transformations which leave certain properties of the structure of a space invariant. In fact, under the Riemannian view of space, what we mean by a geometric object is just such a set of properties left invariant by the transformations. For instance, in metric-Euclidean geometry, the geometry taught us in secondary school, shape is equivalent to the property of *rigidity* belonging to all geometric objects. By a rigid object (or shape) we mean one such that the distance between any pair of points on its surface remains unchanged when the object is transformed by displacement or reflection. A transformation that leaves a property (for example, rigidity) invariant is called a *symmetry* operation or *transformational invariant* of the space (for example, rotation). The full set (or group) of transformations which constitute symmetry operations for rigid objects (that is, leaves their shape unchanged) is exactly what we mean by Euclidean geometry. Rotation, translation, and reflection are the transformational invariants of Euclidean space (sometimes called the Euclidean group). The properties which remain invariant under the geometric transformations are usually called the *symmetries* or *structural invariants* of the space. For instance, rigidity is a symmetry or structural invariant of Euclidean space. Hence when you know the transformational invariants (symmetry operations) and the structural invariants (symmetries) of a given space, then you know all there is to know about that space, that is to say, you have a geometry or theory of the space.

The important point to be underlined from the above discussion is that the concept of invariant has two meanings: On the one hand, it can mean a symmetry operation (transformational invariant) while on the other it can mean a symmetry of the space (structural invariant). To anticipate what is to come; it is our intention to show how Gibson's intuitive concept of invariant perceptual information can be rigorously characterized in terms of these two symmetry concepts. By doing so we will achieve nothing less than a theory of perceptual information. Or to put the matter differently, such a theory will qualify as a geometry of perceptual space. Consequently, to illustrate this approach we will concentrate on the development of a theory for the perception of objects.

Toward a Revised Concept of Shape

As pointed out above, the concept of shape corresponds to just those properties left invariant under the transformations associated with the geometry. As we relax these properties by introducing symmetry-breaking operations into the geometry, we weaken the concept of geometric shape (structural invariants) by reducing the number of symmetries of the space. In this way a hierarchy of geometries (or spaces) can be defined which range from the most restrictive, metric Euclidean geometry, to the least restrictive, topology. Moreover, the concept of shape by which objects in each of these geometries may be distinguished or recognized as belonging to the same equivalence class, is relative to those properties of the space left invariant under the transformations defining the given geometry. Let us briefly survey what becomes of the concept of shape as we descend from the highest to lower geometries on this hierarchy.

For metric Euclidean geometry, the shape of an object is identical to the property of rigidity. You will recall from the earlier discussion, that this symmetry of Euclidean space simply means that the distance between any pair of points, $x_1 - x_2 = d$, where x_i refers to the abscissa of the point, remains invariant under the symmetry operations on the space (e.g. rotation, translation, or reflection). Surely, this concept of shape is very useful and a salient recourse for identifying objects. But it is by no means adequate for recognizing the structural equivalence of objects when they have been nonrigidly transformed, say by a change in their size (similar objects). Consider, for instance, the fact that a toy car is still recognized as a car in spite of its diminished size, just as giant's cap would still be recognized as belonging to the class of objects found in your local haberdashery. Thus, size invariance does not seem to be a necessary condition for our recognition of objects. Technically speaking, a rigid object can not change size since this requires a stretching or compressing simultaneously in all directions. Such a size transformation that leaves the shape of the transformed object similar to that of its original form is called a *radial transformation, homethetic transformation* or, simply, a *transformation of similitude.* By augmenting the Euclidean group of transformations with this size transformation a new geometry is created by violating or breaking a symmetry of the space. This, in turn, defines a space in which the congruence of rigid objects is but a special case of objects whose shapes are similar. Objects in such a space are said to have similar shapes if a *ratio of similitude* exists which maps one object into another, that is, if $x'_1 - x'_2 = k(x_1 - x_2)$ holds for *every* point on each object, where x'_i refers to the abscissa value of the point corresponding to x_i on the original object that has been transformed by a positive integral value k.

Hence, the ratio of similitude is the structural invariant corresponding to the concept of the shape of an object in similarity space. Let us proceed to relax the symmetry properties of the space even further by introducing still more symmetry-breaking operations into the original set of Euclidean transformations.

A table remains the same table if a leaf is inserted so as to extend its length. A man on stilts is still recognizable as the same person in spite of his elongated height. A cube of clay is still the same mass if compressed or stretched into a rectangular shape. All of these transformations in the shape of an object, whether accompanied by size transformations or not, do not destroy completely the aspects of shape by which they may be recognized as a transformed object rather than a new object.

The geometry which results from a *strain* operation that linearly stretches or compresses an object in but one direction at a time is called *affine* geometry. Examples of other objects with *affine*-equivalent shapes are squares and rectangles, on the one hand, and circles and ellipses on the other. A second affine transformation is a *shear* which takes the angles of an object into new angles. Shearing the angles of a square transforms it into a rhombus or shearing the angles of a rectangle transform it into a parallelogram. Such affine-equivalent shapes are not similar since the distances among points in all directions do not remain proportional. Rather a shape invariant is created; one that must satisfy a *ratio of division,* that is, where the relationship

$$\frac{x_1 - x_2}{x_2 - x_3} = \frac{x'_1 - x'_2}{x'_2 - x'_3}$$

holds among three collinear points on the original object and three collinear points on its transform. The flattening out of shapes in photographs made with a high-power telescopic lens is an example of a affine transformation. Still we find buildings and people photographed under such conditions readily recognizable. Consequently, information specifying shape must be still more abstract than that proposed by either simple Euclidean or similarity geometry. But can some semblence of the intuitive concept of the shape of an object be retained in still weaker geometries? Let us proceed to consider the even less restrictive notion of projectively equivalent shapes.

In projective geometry little is preserved to count as "shape" except those properties, such as linearity, which are not lost under central or parallel projection. Consider, for instance, the shapes of various shadows of objects: a trapezoidal shadow can be cast from a square object that is tilted with respect to the wall or screen used as the projective plane; similarly, a trapezoidal shape can be tilted so as to cast a square or rectangular shadow.

Thus, square, rectangular, and trapezoidal shapes are said to be projectively equivalent. Whereas affine transformations never destroy the parallelism of sides of an object, projective transformations may. The shape invariant preserved by projective transformation is called an *anharmonic ratio* or, simply, a *cross-ratio.* The cross-ratio relationship that must be satisfied by projectively equivalent shapes can be expressed as follows:

$$\frac{(x_1 - x_4)(x_3 - x_2)}{(x_1 - x_3)(x_3 - x_4)} = \frac{(x'_1 - x'_4)(x'_3 - x'_2)}{(x'_1 - x'_3)(x'_3 - x'_4)}$$

where the x_i's refer to four distinct collinear points and the primed symbols refer to points lying on the projectively transformed object.

Before venturing further down the hierarchy of geometries to discover the weakest conception of shape information possible, let us pause to recognize an interesting trend in the nature of the shape invariant for each successively weaker geometry. The geometric invariants by which equivalent shapes are defined becomes increasingly more complex and abstract as we descend from higher to lower geometries. By casting the shape invariant for each of the geometries discussed above in the same form this trend becomes quite apparent:

(1) Euclidean space:

$$x_1 - x_2, \quad \text{a distance invariant.}$$

(2) Similarty space:

$$k(x_1 - x_2), \quad \text{a ratio of similitude.}$$

(3) Affine space:

$$\frac{x_1 - x_2}{x_2 - x_3}, \quad \text{a ratio of division.}$$

(4) Projective space:

$$\frac{(x_1 - x_4)(x_3 - x_2)}{(x_1 - x_3)(x_3 - x_4)}, \quad \text{a cross ratio.}$$

Thus, we can see that the concept of equivalent shapes becomes more complex because the equation specifying the shape invariant involves an increasing number of terms to be evaluated as well as operations to be performed. Even more interesting for perception, however, is the fact that in each subsequently weaker space the information specifying the shape invariant becomes considerably more abstract in the technical sense that fewer and more subtle properties of the space remain invariant. This is obvious from the fact discussed earlier, namely, that to construct weaker geometries you augment the Euclidean group of transformations with an ever increasing number of symmetry-breaking or invariant-destroying operations. It must be the case, then, that the most liberal concept of shape should reside in the weakest geometry of all which lies at the lowest point of the hierarchy–in a topology.

We will not attempt to survey all the geometries that can be defined by the proposed relaxation method of introducing new symmetry-breaking operations into Euclidean space. Our aim is not to be exhaustive, but to demonstrate that the natural ambiguities that inhere in our intuitive concept of shape can be expressed rigorously in terms of geometric symmetry theory.

In the next section we explore the topological conception of shape that seems to capture best what is meant by the shape invariant preserved under the viscal-elastic change produced by the biological process of growth.

Toward a Geometry of Growth Space

The final question that must be answered is whether or not a perceptually significant shape invariant exists in the weakest of all geometries–a topology. A topology consists of a set of transformations that map the set of points S of one object into a set of points S' such that it is $1 - 1$, continuous, and has a continuous inverse. The shape invariant for a topology is specified by a homeomorphism. Homeomorphisms preserve connectivity, endlessness of a curve, the property of being a closed curve, incidence relations, linear order, and cyclic order.

The relevant question for perceptual theory, is whether there exist ecologically significant objects for which changes occur that are homeomorphic, that is, are specified by a topological shape invariant. Unlike projective transformations which preserve linearity, topological transformations take curved lines into straight lines and vice versa. Thus, if we can find an example of homeomorphically equivalent forms that are perceptually equivalent shapes, then we will have evidence that a topological shape invariant is ecologically valid. The human face seems to be such a case. Consider the following description of the remodeling transformation imposed upon the face as it grows:

The human face, like any living object, is radically changed by growth. Enlow (1968) describes growth as a "remodeling" process which not only changes the size of the object (a transformation of similitude) but its shape as well (a nonrigid transformation). For instance, at first the neonatal human head exhibits an exaggerated cranium and a diminutive face. Over time, the facial complex grows more rapidly than the skull so that the overall dimensions of the head and face become disproportionately altered. The most important fact of growth is that craniofacial growth, no less than that of other parts of the body, does not take place merely by enlarging or even by depostion of interpolated tissue layers. Hard bone, unlike soft tissue, is not capable of interstitial growth since these involve expansive changes of existing tissue. Consequently, growth follows a "remodeling" process by which new bone tissue successively forces relocation of all other parts of the craniofacial complex. Growth, then, can be defined as a global remodeling process which induces a "viscal-elastic" change over the craniofacial complex resulting in a change in both its shape and size.

If growth is indeed a remodeling transformation, then it not only changes the size of the face over time but, more importantly, modifies the shape of the face. In spite of such gross changes, older faces are still readily recognized as being transforms of younger ones seen earlier rather than being new faces never before seen. Indeed, most adults have had the experience of recognizing people that they have not seen for a decade or so, in spite of the gross changes that may have occurred to their faces due to growth or weight change. It is also quite common to recognize the common species of plants or animals in spite of the fact that they may be at different stages of growth. And, of course, we find it quite easy to recognize the sex and race of people never seen before.

Although it is quite popular in current perceptual theory to claim that the shape equivalence of such objects may be due to the pickup of common features that are easily isolatable from the space in which they occur (i.e., that they are context-free features), we will try to show that this is an inadequate theory of object perception. The recognition of faces, animal or plants that have aged, or the identification of the species, race, or sex of people, animals, or plants requires the pickup of a shape invariant that is a symmetry of a topological space.

After several years of both theoretical and empirical work we have finally discovered what may prove to be the most appropriate topological transformation to model growth. We call this topological transformation a *cardioidal strain.* The best way to understand what it does and why it is a transformational invariant of topological space rather than some more symmetrical space is to review the way in which it was discovered. (Later we will provide empirical evidence that it is also an informational invariant that is perceptually real.)

The structural invariant for the growth of dicotyledenous structures. A common observation is that most plants follow a growth policy that is surprisingly symmetrical. Monocotyledenous or bladed plants grow symmetrically from opposing sides of a stem such as do grass and weeds. However, a more interesting growth pattern is that followed by dicotyledenous vegetables or flowers, for example, the kidney bean, pumpkins, apples, turnips, etc. These plants tend to grow symmetrically around a nodal point at the end of a stem rather than from the sides of the stem itself.

What makes the growth of dicotyledons interesting is the fact that the human head grows in a similar fashion. From the embryonic stage to adulthood the profile of the human head, (ignoring facial detail and the mandible), is decidedly dicotyledenous in shape, possessing an approximate bilateral symmetry similar to that of an inverted valentine heart. Geometrically speaking, the technical term for an inverted heart-shaped figure (with a rounded top) is *cardioid.*

An experimental test. Using three skull profiles, a 1-year old, a 10-year old and a 25-year old, we were able to show that a strain transformation (to be defined later) would map one skull continuously into another. That is to say, the strain transformation used was at least homeomorphic. We were able to achieve a nearly perfect fit of a cardioid when transformed by strain and shear to each skull profile for approximately two-thirds of its perimeter, omitting the facial mask (Shaw, McIntyre, & Mace, 1974).

The importance of this finding for understanding the nature of growth proved serendipitously inestimable, for from this we were able to infer that the structual invariant of growth space might be a cardioidal shape invariant. Just as distance is the shape invariant for Euclidean space, the ratio of similitude is for similarity space, etc., so we suspected, but did not know at first how to prove, that the shape invariant for growth space might be cardioidal. Many years passed from this speculation (about 1971) until we were to show that the transformational invariant (the homeomorphic strain operation) was indeed a symmetry operation of a very special topological space. (Of course, at the time, we did not yet know to apply the geometrization approach suggested by Riemann to our problem.)

Although the next section is rather technical, and may be skipped without losing the thread of our argument, it is important to prove that the cardioidal strain transformation, which we believe to provide an accurate geometry for growth space, is indeed topological rather than Euclidean, similitudinal, affine, or projective. For if we know it is a topological shape invariant, then we have a good idea of how abstract and formally complex perceptual information for the age level of faces might be. And more generally, we obtain some idea of how abstract and thus featureless, in the concrete sense, that perceptual information for shape might be.

Growth as cardioidal strain. D'Arcy Thompson (1917), the great British naturalist, suggested three candidates for the nonrigid component of the growth transformation: *strain, shear,* or *radial* (similarity) transformations. As we will try to show later, only the strain transformation is a likely candidate for the shape invariant perceived when judging the relative age level of human faces.

Strain derives from an analysis of the interaction of forces on various types of tissues during growth. The strain imposed upon bony tissue by the stresses caused by the growth of the highly elastic soft integuments is as Thompson argued, "a direct stimulus to growth itself." Therefore, the growth of the skull strains its shape along lines of least resistance dictated by the stress forces imposed by the growth of the brain, change in fluid pressures from within the cranial cavity, as well as the viscal constraints imposed by epithelia, muscle, cartilage, gravitational attraction, and atmospheric pressure from without. For all these reasons, strain seems appropriate as a geometry of the growth process which remodels the head in accordance with the stress imposed by the biological and physical forces mentioned above. Furthermore, by treating these forces geometrically, in the manner of Riemann's global approach, their resultant effect can be expressed as a symmetry of growth space. For example, the middle row of Fig. 2 (page 121) (where shear level equals zero), illustrates how an arbitrarily selected face (the one at zero shear and zero strain) can be homeomorphically transformed into other facial profiles at different relative age levels. By inspection, it is easy to see that the seven facial transforms depicted in that row are not Euclidean equivalent or even similar shapes. To prove, however, that they may not be either affine or projectively equivalent forms is not so obvious from inspection alone. Consequently, we offer the two following proofs to demonstrate this fact.

Proof 1. A geometrical transformation is merely a function that relates geometric objects. Such a relation, $y = f(x)$ or $T(x) \rightarrow y$, means there exists two sets of objects (points, lines, circles, facial profiles, etc.) such that to each object x in one set there corresponds a definite object y in the other. The geometric objects that play the role of independent variables are called *originals* and those that play the role of dependent variables are called *images* for example, $T(\text{face}_1)$

→ $face_2$, where $face_1$ might be a younger vision of $face_2$; hence, $face_1$ is the *original* and $face_2$ the *image*. Let us also assume that the transformation T stands for the growth process by which $face_1$ is remodeled into $face_2$. (See Fig. 1.)

We refer to T as a cardioidal strain because when applied to a circle expressed in rectangular coordinates it maps the circle through a family of limacons which ultimately terminate in a cardioid, (that is, an epicycloid of one loop). Figure 1, (row where shear equals zero), indicates part of this series. Beginning with the spatial grid at zero strain and zero shear and moving in either direction along the row, notice how the cardioidal strain deforms this standard rectangular grid continuously into the grids with nonlinear lines. Consequently, a circle expressed in the standard grid, under this type of strain transformation, would become limacons of various degrees of deformation. Moreover, if the series were extended sufficiently far in either direction, then the hypothetical circle would ultimately be transformed into a cardioid.

It is especially important to note that the transformation is applied to the whole structure of the two-dimensional space (that is, the standard grid in Fig. 1), following the global approach suggested by Riemann, rather than being

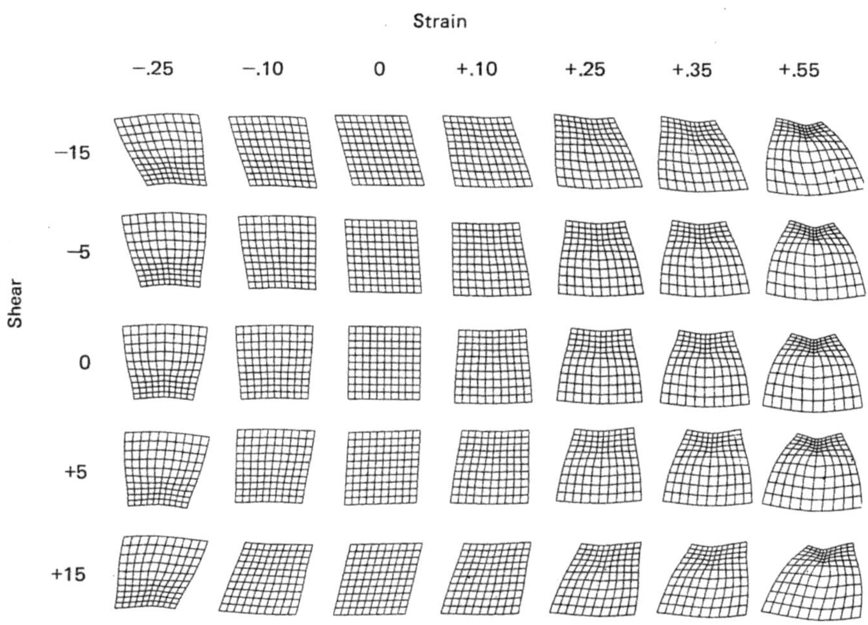

FIG. 1 Transformations of a two-dimensional Euclidean space by an affine shear transformation and a topological (cardioidal) strain transformation (standard grid is at shear = 0, strain = 0).

applied just to the circle itself as an object in that space. The circle, or any other object for that matter, placed in the space to which the cardioidal strain is applied, will be deformed to the same degree that the whole space is. Consequently, the facial profiles in Fig. 2 (which were used as stimuli in the experiments to be reported) were produced in just this manner; namely, the prototypical face (located at the zero-strain and zero-shear position in the array depicted in Fig. 2) was transformed (by a computer) into all the other facial profiles by applying the two global transformations, strain and shear, to the standard space. (More will be said about the role of shear in a later section.)

Since cardioidal strain is our postulated geometry for growth, it is important to see how this transformation works. A simple, one-dimensional affine strain has the form of a linear transformation,

$$x' = x, \quad y = ky \qquad \text{or} \qquad x' = kx, \quad y' = y$$

where x', y' are the new coordinates of the transformed point (x, y) (i.e., any point in the standard Cartesian space) and k is a positive integer. However, if we

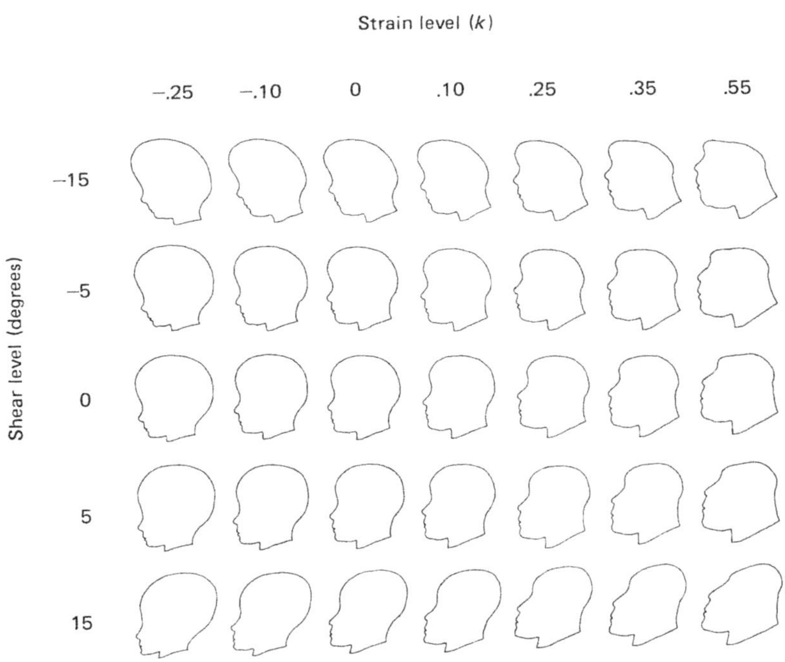

FIG. 2 Transformations of a facial profile by shear and strain (untransformed profile is at shear = 0, strain = 0).

allow the coefficient of strain to be some value other than a positive integer, say a trignometric function, then the strain transformation defined is nonaffine. Moreover, if the strain coefficient defines a nonlinear change that deforms arcs of curves into lines and vice versa, then the resulting transformation is also nonprojective. Consequently, we show in what follows that the cardioidal strain is neither affine nor projective, but rather must belong to some special form of topology.

The cardioidal strain transformation used in our studies can be stated most elegantly in polar coordinates as

(1)
$$r' = r'(1 - k \sin \theta), \quad \theta' = \theta$$

By restating Eq. (1) in rectangular coordinates, we see that this is not an affine strain, since a given affine strain must act linearly in but one direction, that is it is one-dimensional. The translation from polar to rectangular coordinates can be made by the equations

$$x = r \cos \theta, \quad y = r \sin \theta,$$

then new coordinates achieved by transforming x and y would be

$$x' = r' \cos \theta, \quad y' = r' \sin \theta.$$

Now substituting the value of r' from Eq. (1) yields

$$x' = r(1 - k \sin \theta) \cos \theta',$$

or

$$x' = (1 - k \sin \theta)\, r \cos \theta';$$

but since $\theta = \theta$ and $x = r \cos \theta$, then the above equation finally yields

$$x' = (1 - k \sin \theta)x.$$

By a similar argument we solve for y' and get $y' = (1 - k \sin \theta)y$. Now let $(1 - k \sin \theta) = k'$, where k is the coefficient of cardioidal strain. We now have

$$x' = k'x, \quad y' = k'y,$$

which means that the cardioidal strain is neither affine (linear) nor projective. The transformation is neither simple nor affine: it is not simple (one-dimensional) because the coefficient of strain k' applies to both x and y coordinate dimensions; it is not affine since k' is a trignometric function rather being a positive integer.

Proof 2. To prove that the cardioidal strain is not projective, we need only show that it does not preserve collinearity of points but rather takes straight lines into curved ones. Although inspection of Fig. 1 is sufficient to show that the cardioidal strain does just that, it would be useful to state this fact formally: If we take the equation for a cardioid in polar form, that is, $r = a(1 - \sin \theta)$, and let x or y equal a and add our coefficient of strain k, then this yields the equation of a family of limacons, that is, $r = a(1 - \mathrm{k} \sin \theta)$. When $k = 1$ the equation yields a cardioid, when $1 > k > 1$ yields a family of limacons, and when $k = 0$ the equation yields the special case of the circle. This means that the cardioidal strain is a strain transformation belonging to a topology rather than to affine or projective space. We can now give our final argument regarding the nature of the shape invariant preserved by growth.

Any figure which can be homeomorphically transformed into a circle is called a *simple closed curve.* We have shown that the cardioid is a simple, closed curve of best fit for a large portion of the perimeter of a human skull. Although we have only worked with the data points of three skull profiles, it was possible to transform a normal cardioid to fit each and to strain each of these cardioids into one another (Shaw, McIntyre, & Mace, 1974). In our efforts to find the curve of best fit for human skull profiles, we serendipitously discovered the mathematical formulation for the remodeling of the head profile due to growth, the cardioidal strain.

Using the global geometric approach developed by Riemann, we next showed that the cardioidal strain homeomorphically transforms cardioids into circles. Thus, to the extent that the cardioid fits the curve of the head's profile, these figures tend to be transformed into circles also by the cardioidal strain. It is a theorem of topology that figures that are homeomorphic to a circle are topologically equivalent figures (Gans, 1969, p. 198). Thus, to a significant extent (roughly 240°) the profiles of humans of different ages are topologically equivalent under the cardioidal strain transformation, that is, they are topologically equivalent shapes.

Hence the cardioidal curve of the human head profile is a symmetry of this special topological space, and thus constitutes a shape invariant for our theory of growth space. Notice also (Fig. 2) that the facial features approximated by the cardioid are also preserved to some extent by the cardioidal strain. These, then are also part of the shape invariant for this topology of growth space.

A strain transformation that was stronger (i.e., preserved fewer symmetries) than cardioidal strain might be too elastic and destroy all structural properties of the facial profile, say as a sculptor might deform a clay bust of a person into a formless lump. Indeed, the weakness of this particular strain transformation is its strength as a possible geometry for growth.

Every growth process has a "viscal" component as well as an "elastic" one; the viscal component of the transformation preserves the structural invariants that specify the species, race, sex, and individual identity while the elastic component expresses the transformational invariant by which the style of change due to growth can be distinguished from other types of change (displacements, size changes, etc.). Possessing both of these necessary qualities, the cardioidal strain transformation is a prime candidate for a geometry of the growth space of human faces as seen in profile.

Evidence for the Proposed Geometry of Growth: Perceiving the Age Level of Faces

Recently we began a series of experiments to test the adequacy of the cardioidal strain as a model for the transformational invariant of growth space (Pittenger & Shaw, 1975a, b). In addition to the strain transformation, a careful study of the remodeling of facial profiles due to growth suggests that an affine transformation may also play a significant role, namely, shear. A shear transformation modifies the angle of the facial profile (the so-called "Camper" angle) making the chin more or less jutting (prognathic) while at the same time controlling the slope of the forehead. Clearly, the profile of the human face is sheared as it grows, for recall that the mandible grows disproportionately faster than the cranial dome (see Fig. 2, column under zero strain). This accounts for the fact that adults, as compared to babies, typically do not have such diminutive faces nor exaggerated craniums.

Consequently, we felt it important to determine to what extent the perception of the relative age level of faces might be due to shear as well as to strain. If degree of affine shear accounted for the perceptual information specifying age level, then it rather than the cardioidal strain would be the better geometric model for the growth process, at least in so far as the space of human facial profiles is concerned. Moreover, if such proved to be the case, then the structural invariant of this growth space, by which the recognizable shape of faces is determined, would be a symmetry of affine space rather than a symmetry of topological space. The following experiments were run to test this possibility as well as the adequacy of cardioidal strain in general as a model for growth.

Comparing strain with shear. It was assumed that a psychological correlate of the growth of the human face is its perceived change in relative age level. By the use of a computer program, a single facial profile was transformed over seven levels of strain and five levels of shear (Fig. 2) in the global manner discussed earlier. Since the product of these two transformations is not commutative, shear was always applied first. Hence, for example, the profile in the upper left-hand corner of Fig. 2 is derived from the profile at (0, 0) by shearing the y axis of the two-dimensional coordinate space away from the x axis in a counterclockwise direction by 15° and then by straining (that is, stretching) the units along the y axis by a coefficient of $k = -.25$ (where $y' = k'y$ for $k' = [1 - k$

sin θ]). In this way, the stimuli to be used in the proposed experiment were generated by the coordinate transformation method suggested by Thompson (1917) in a manner consistent with the Riemannian concept of space as a structure rather than an empty vessel.

Twenty subjects were then presented with 35 slides of the transformed profiles depicted in Fig. 2 and asked to estimate their relative age levels. They did this by choosing an arbitrary number to represent the age level of the first profile presented and assigning other numbers to represent the age level of the succeeding profiles that were proportional to the age level estimate of the first. The subjects were run in four groups of five subjects each, with each group receiving a different random order of presentation.

Using a Monte Carlo technique of analysis with five thousand runs to estimate the distribution we found that 91% of the relative age judgments made by subjects agreed with the hypothesis that the strain transformation produced monotonic perceived age changes in the standard profile. On the other hand, using the shear transformation to predict their judgments produced only 65% agreement. Thus, we found as expected that the topological strain transformation was by far the stronger of the two variables of age-change and, thereby, was the best candidate to represent the remodeling aspect of growth.

Perceptual sensitivity to strain. A second experiment was designed as a preliminary test of the following hypothesis: perceptual information specifying the relative age level of individuals plays a major role in the determination of certain dominance relationships in both animal and human societies (so-called "pecking" orders). Such information is probably also a factor in the selection of mates and in helping parents determine the appropriate time to wean offspring and encourage their independence. For instance, the length of the beaks of young birds apparently provides the stimulus which prompts the mother bird to encourage her offspring to leave the nest (Lorenz, 1943). Assuming that perceptual information for age level also plays a significant role in human society, then one should expect humans to exhibit a perceptual sensitivity to very small changes along this dimension. Moreover, if strain produces changes in faces resembling growth, then subjects should also exhibit sensitivity to changes produced along this naturally salient dimension.

Consequently, sensitivity to the shape changes produced by the strain transformation was assessed in the second experiment by presenting pairs of profiles produced by different levels of the transformation and requiring subjects to choose the older profile in each pair. A series of profiles was produced by applying strain transformations ranging from $k = -.25$ to $+.55$ to a single profile, where k is the coefficient of strain used in the equation controlling the computer plots. Eighteen pairs of profiles were chosen; three for each of six levels of difference in degree of strain. The pairs were presented twice to four groups of 10 subjects. Different random orders were used for each presentation and each group. Subjects were informed that the study concerned the ability to make fine discriminations of age and that for each pair they were to choose the profile which appeared to be older. During the experiment they were not informed whether or not their responses were correct. By correct response we mean the choice of the profile with the larger degree of strain as the older.

Several results were found: First, an analysis of variance on percentage of errors as a function of difference in strain showed a typical psychophysical result—a decline in accuracy with smaller physical differences and an increase in sensitivity with experience in the task. However, two other aspects of the results are more important for the question at hand. First, subjects do not merely discriminate the pairs consistently but choose the profile with the larger strain as the older profile with greater than chance frequency; in the first presentation the larger strain was selected on 83.2% of the trials and in the second, on 89.2% of the trials. In each presentation, each of the 40 subjects selected the profile with the larger k as older or more than 50% of the trials. In other words, the predicted effect was obtained in every subject. A sign test showed the chance probability of this last result to be far less than .001. Thus the conclusion of the first experiment is confirmed in a different experimental task.

A second finding was that sensitivity to the variable proved to be surprisingly fine. Although no scale yet exists by which perceptual sensitivity to strain can be calibrated to absolute age estimates, the results of this experiment suggests that such a scale will have to be adjusted to very fine tolerances indeed. Subjects in this experiment demonstrated an ability to discriminate shape differences between pairs of adjacent profiles produced by strain that were only a few times greater than the absolute limit determined for visual acuity in resolving spatially adjacent lines (Shlaer, 1937). This is surprising since the figures to be discriminated were never seen superimposed but always on different halves of the screen. Figure 3 provides a dramatic example of how extremely small these differences in degree of strain can be and still be reliably discriminated (especially note the right-hand figure).

Perceiving individual identity. Finally, a third experiment was designed to investigate the following hypothesis: In spite of the radical remodeling faces undergo when they grow, sufficient structural invariants are preserved to permit their perceptual identification at different age levels. Consequently, a crucial test of strain as a model of the transformational invariant of growth space would be to show that it also preserves identity. As a preliminary test of this hypothesis, profile views of the external portions of the brain cases of six different skulls were traced from x-ray photographs and subjected to five levels of strain. Five pairs of transformed profiles were selected from each individual sequence; the degree of strain for members of three pairs differed by .30 and those of the other two pairs by .45 values of k. A profile of a different skull was assigned to

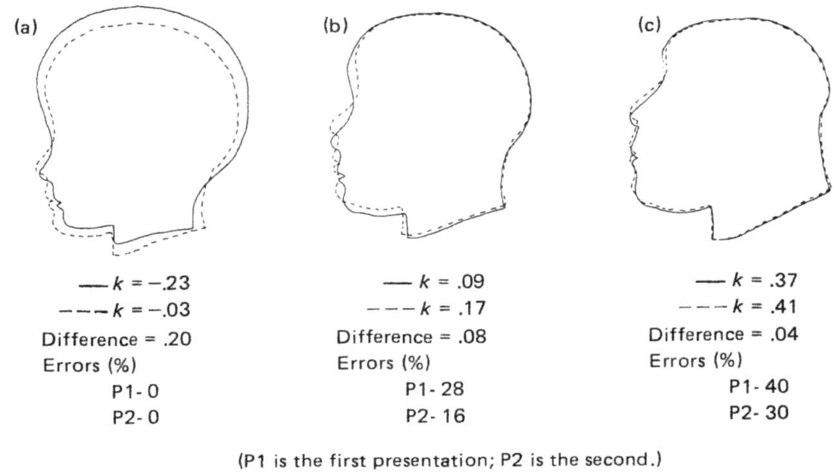

FIG. 3 Sample profile pairs, Experiment 2: (a) errors in presentation 1 = 0%, errors in presentation 2 = 0%; (b) errors in presentation 2 = 28%, errors in presentation 2 = 16%; (c) errors in presentation 1 = 40%, errors in presentation 2 = 30%.

each of the above pairs which had the same degree of strain as one of the members of the pair. Slides were constructed of the profile triples such that the two profiles from distinct skulls which had the same level of strain appeared in random positions at the bottom. Thirty subjects were presented the slides and asked to select which of the two profiles at the bottom of the slide that appeared most similar to the profile at the top (Fig. 4). The overall percentage of errors was low. For the 30 sets of stimuli presented to 30 subjects, the mean error was less than 17%, with no subject making more than 33% errors. Since no subject made 50% or more errors, a sign test on the hypothesis of chance responding (binomial distribution) by each subject yields a probability of far less than .001. Indeed, this finding was corroborated in another set of studies where Pittenger and Shaw (in press) also found that people are quite able to rank order by age photographs of people taken over nearly a decade of growth from pre- to postpuberty years.

The results of these studies provide support for two important hypotheses: The strain transformation, due presumably to growth, not only provides the major source of the relevant perceptual information for age level, but also leaves invariant sufficient perceptual information for the specification of the individual identity of the person by the shape of the head alone. An additional implication of these findings is that the information for perceived aging or growth may be very abstract indeed. In the next section, we discuss a set of experiments

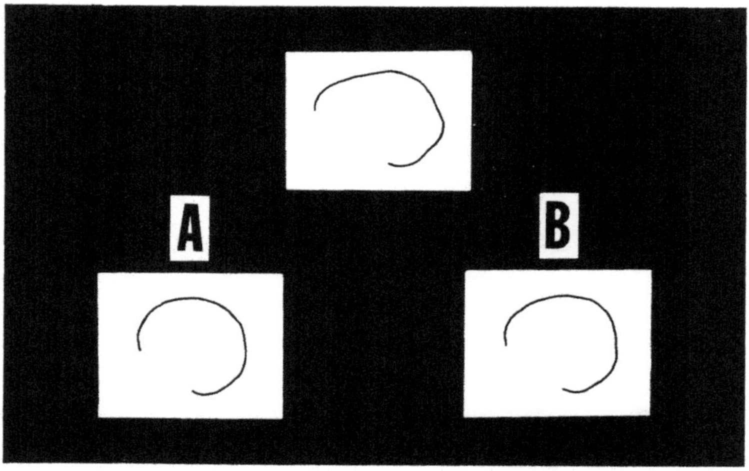

FIG. 4 Sample stimulus Experiment 3. The upper profile, $k = .30$, is the same individual as B, $k = -.15$, whereas A, $k = -.15$, is the profile of a different individual.

designed to help us determine exactly how abstract our model of perceptual growth space must be.

Perceived Aging as the Pickup of Abstract Invariants of Growth Space

Assuming people perceive relative age level by detecting the invariant aspects of difference relations between structural states of the face at different stages of growth leads to the prediction that the precise nature of the facial features supporting the difference relation should prove of little consequence to age perception. This is exactly what one finds to be the case. In the experiment mentioned above using photographs of faces, we found that adult subjects have no trouble at all providing rank-order age judgments of photographs of different individuals who are all unfamiliar to the subject (Pittenger & Shaw, 1975a). Here since no person's face appeared twice, there is no possibility that the perceived difference relation is between topographical states of the same face. Therefore, the information for relative age level must be quite abstract, at least as much so as the difference relation people learn to perceive who succeed at the so-called "oddity" problem (Gibson, 1969).

But exactly how abstract is the perceptual information for the relative age level of faces? We suspect it is so abstract as to be essentially independent of the absolute features of a single face viewed over time, or of those features common to all faces, or even of those features common to all animate objects that grow. This assumption suggests the following hypothesis: *perceptual information for age level is both abstract and global, inhering in the effects that the proposed strain transformation has on any object to which it can be applied.* In the sense discussed earlier, the strain transformation, when applied to a coordinate framework, provides an abstract model for a dynamic "growth" space. Any object, human, animate or otherwise, represented within this growth space will be globally remodeled in a manner proportional to the degree of strain applied to the total spatial structure (as shown in the first experiment).

A dramatic test of this hypothesis would be to show that objects other than human facial profiles, when subjected to the same experimental treatment as the stimuli used in the first experiment, will nevertheless elicit identical rank-order age judgments. Indeed, this is exactly what was found in two independent studies using computer-generated drawings of dog profiles and Volkswagen cars. Following the exact procedure used for generating the human facial profiles in the first experiment, it was found that adult subjects had no trouble rank-ordering by age these sets of transformed nonhuman profiles and automobile drawings. The pattern of results were highly significant and their analysis paralleled precisely that reported in the first experiment.

Although, our subjects may have experienced seeing dogs at different age levels, it is not possible that they could have seen automobiles grow as viscal-elastic events. Therefore, it seems reasonable to conclude that the subjects were able to rank-order the inanimate stimuli because the difference relations perceived to hold between them specifies a naturally salient style of change, namely, growth.

The combined results of the above experiments testify to the explanatory power and empirical fruitfulness of the geometric approach to perceptual phenomena. Furthermore, this approach offers a plausible interpretation of J. J. Gibson's (1966) claim that perception is not based upon the discrimination of elementary stimuli (that is, features) but upon the perception of higher order forms of invariant information picked up over time.

CONCLUSIONS

The arguments and research reviewed above, clearly suggest the need to construe the concept of the shape of an object more broadly than traditionally done. A large variety of ways exists by which equivalence classes of objects might be defined ranging from rigid objects with the same Euclidean shape, such as rocks, cross sections of steel beams, houses, cars, to plants and animals of various sizes and stages of growth, whose semielastic shapes still retain sufficient, topological structure to allow classification into the same species, race, sex, family or identity category. For these reasons, it seems wiser and more useful for perceptual theory to hold a liberal view of the concept of shape, since under different circumstances objects may be judged perceptually equivalent depending upon whether they share congruent shapes, similar shapes, affine-equivalent shapes, projectively–equivalent shapes, or topologically equivalent shapes.

Furthermore, it should be noted that this list of differential geometric shapes is by no means complete; the perceptual information by which subjects may judge other collections of objects to be perceptually equivalent may require discovery of the appropriate shape invariant as defined in still some other geometry than those surveyed here, say in equiaffine or conformal geometries where areas or angles are preserved, respectively. Of course, exactly which geometric definition of shape is most appropriate to a given class of experimental stimuli is not an a priori affair, but must be discovered empirically, much in the same way that the best distance metric must be discovered for scaling various kinds of data. There is an important difference which should be emphasized, however, namely, that the concepts of the shape invariant provided by affine geometry on down on the hierarchy of geometries (for example, projective geometry or the topologies) are *nonmetric* in character. This means that, roughly speaking, the concept of shape as specified in these weaker geometries are based on qualitative rather than quantitative properties of objects.

The most important implication of the reported studies for perceptual theory is the following: The degree of abstractness manifested by the topologically equivalent shapes produced by growth suggests that the relevant perceptual information by which they are judged equivalent must be equally as abstract. Moreover, recall that a geometry is nothing less than a theory of the structure (symmetries) of the space, or class, of shape-equivalent objects; this suggests that, in order for the perceptual judgments to be made, the perceptual space of subjects across such a wide range of tasks must be sufficiently flexible to take on the structural properties of the space of the shape-equivalent objects used as stimuli, otherwise no interjudge reliability would be found to exist across subjects. Recall that in the tasks reported above, the effect was found to exist, not just in the group, but within each subject who participated.

For all the above reasons, there does indeed seem to be some justification for holding onto the working hypothesis posed earlier; namely that not only is the perceived shape of an object due to the structure of the space (equivalence class) to which it belongs, but that the very structure of perceptual space itself is malleable, being dependent upon the structure of the objects perceived. If so, then not only does the proposed geometric approach coalesce the problems of object perception and layout ("space" or "depth") perception so that they might be treated in a unified way, but it also suggests how adaptation effects might be explained under the same geometric theory of perceptual space.

ACKNOWLEDGMENTS

Preparation of this paper was supported in part by a Career Development Award to Robert E. Shaw from the National Institute of Child Health and Human Development (1 K04-HD24010) and by grants to the University of Minnesota, Center for Research in Human Learning, from the National Science Foundation (GB-35703X), the National Institute of Child Health and Human Development (HD-01136 and HD-00098), and the Graduate School of the University of Minnesota. Thanks are also due the Center for Advanced Study in the Behavioral Sciences for the support given Robert Shaw during the writing of this chapter.

REFERENCES

Bell, E. T. *Development of mathematics.* (2nd ed.) New York: McGraw-Hill, 1949. Pp. 420–468.

Enlow, D. *The human face, an account of the postnatal growth and development of the craniofacial skeleton.* New York: Hoeber Medical Division, Harper & Row, 1968.

Gans, D. *Transformations and geometries.* New York: Appleton-Century-Crofts, 1969.

Gardner, B. T., & Wallach, L. Shapes of figures identified as a baby's head. *Perceptual and Motor Skills,* 1965, **20,** 135–142.

Gibson, E. J. *Principles of perceptual learning and development.* New York: Appleton-Century-Crofts, 1969.

Gibson, J. J. *The senses considered as perceptual systems.* Boston: Houghton Mifflin, 1966.

Hochberg, J. E. *Perception,* Englewood Cliffs, New Jersey: Prentice-Hall, 1964. P. 34.

Johnson, K. L. An explanation and implementation of a theory of form based on a chordal analysis of discrete patterns. Masters thesis, Department of Computer Science, University of Minnesota, September, 1973.

Laurendeau, M., & Pinard, A. *The development of the concept of space in the child.* New York: International Universities Press, 1970.

Lorenz, K. Die angeborenen formen möglicher vererbung. *Zeitschrift für Tierpsychologie,* 1943, **5,** 235–409.

Moore, D. J. H., & Parker, D. J. Machine perception. *Australian Telecommunications Research,* 1972, **6**(1), 3–11.

Piaget, J. & Inhelder, B. *The child's conception of space.* London: Routledge & Kegan Paul, 1956.

Pittenger, J., & Shaw, R. E. Perception of relative and absolute age in facial photographs. *Perception and Psychophysics,* 1975, **18,** 137–143. (a)

Pittenger, J., & Shaw, R. E. Aging faces as viscal-elastic events: implications for a theory of non-rigid shape perception. *Journal of Experimental Psychology: Human perception and performance.* 1975, **1,** 374–382. (b)

Pufall, P., & Shaw, R. E. An analysis of the development of children's spatial reference system. *Journal of Cognitive Psychology,* 1973, **5,** 151–175.

Révész, G. System der optischen und haptischen Raumtauschungen. *Zeitschrift für Psychologie,* 1934, **131**, 296–375.

Ryan, T. A., & Schwartz, C. B. Speed of perception as a function of mode of representations. *American Journal of Psychology,* 1956, **69**, 60–69.

Shaw, R., & McIntyre, M. Algoristic foundations for cognitive psychology. In D. Palermo & W. Weimer, (Eds.), *Cognition and symbolic processes.* Hillsdale, New Jersey: Lawrence Erlbaum Assoc., 1975. Pp. 305–363.

Shaw, R., McIntyre, M., & Mace, W. The role of symmetry in event perception. In R. MacLeod & H. Pick, Jr., (Eds.), *Studies in Perception: Essays in honor of J. J. Gibson.* Ithaca, New York: Cornell University Press, 1974.

Shlaer, S. The relation between visual acuity and illumination. *Journal of General Psychology,* 1937, **21**, 165–188.

Thompson, D. A. W. *On growth and form.* (2nd ed.) Cambridge, England: Cambridge University Press, 1942. (Original edition, 1917.)

SECTION B
Developing Knowledge

6
Visual Attention and Sensibility

Marcus Hester

Wake Forest University

The study of visual and optical qualities of paintings, especially abstract paintings, is a subject of major interest to the perennial attempt to provide a scientific basis for art criticism. What needs to be shown is that the effects of paintings are causal in nature. If so, then we might expect significant relations to hold between factual knowledge about vision and art criticism. Further, we might also expect critical explanations and characterizations of such effects to be verifiable where most critical claims are not. Hopefully, we might shed some light on the subject of justification of a limited type of critical claim, a claim about the effects of a painting. The two questions to be explored then are, first, the question of justification of critical explanations or characterizations of the effects of abstract paintings and, second, the question of the relevance of factual knowledge about vision to these claims.

As a sample characterization of an effect of an abstract painting, we might take the following: "The shallow, stage-like space in Jackson Pollock's 'Autumn Rhythm' is reminiscent of late cubism." In contrast, as a sample explanation of the same effect, we might take: "The spatial effect is due to the fact that the black skeins become figural with respect to the warm background. The skeins tend to assume a position in front of the picture plane. Further, the ground has a somewhat atmospheric quality and thus tends to recede as do objects enveloped in haze, mist, and other atmospheric phenomena. Finally, the texture of the black skeins tends to advance over the less textured warm ground." As we shall see, the study of perception has discovered many facts and principles relevant to the critical evaluation of such claims about the effects of paintings.

With respect to the above questions, I will defend two theses and attempt to develop a theory of *sensibility*, that is, a theory of how people develop that mode of visual attention required to sense various effects available in a painting. The first thesis asserts that *specific critical claims should not be considered apart from generalizable acts of sensing*, such as the act of sensing direction, mass or balance in a painting. Thus, a critical claim about a painting, a characterization or explanation of an effect, cannot be understood in isolation from a developed sensibility to the mode of perceptual information addressed by the critical claim.

At first sight, this thesis regarding the role of sensibility does not seem different from a traditional concept of aesthetic taste. However, this thesis is new in emphasizing that sensibility is in part due to the refinement of *perceptual abilities* (perceptual refinements). In this respect it is not at all like a traditional concept of taste. Moreover, as we shall see, the role of sensibility in the philosophy of mind is considerably different from that usually attributed to a mental faculty required for aesthetic judgment.

The second major thesis of the chapter is that *factual knowledge plays no necessary role in the confirmation of specific critical claims*; rather it is more relevant to the question of whether general acts of sensing have any foundation in ordinary perceptual abilities (or what we shall call *normalcy*). For example, knowledge of correlations, such as "the effects of space due to overlapping forms, texture gradients, color and atmospheric quality," can not be used to substatiate or refute a specific claim, such as "that painting by Pollock has great depth."

Factual knowledge, such as knowing what perceptual cues correlate with what effects, is relevant to understanding how people develop the ability to sense such effects in a class of paintings. This is analogous to the case where a natural law can be used to explain the occurrence of a class of events but cannot be demonstrated with certainty to apply in any specific case. In a similar vein, a psychologist may demonstrate that an organism has a habitual pattern of behavior but can not claim with certitude that a given response is due to the existing habit. Consequently, what is needed to support the two theses is a theory of how sensibilities to certain classes of effects may be developed.

MEANING OF EFFECTS OF ABSTRACT PAINTINGS

Effects, Suggestions, and Evocations

Effects of abstract paintings can be distinguished from their suggestions and evocations. What an abstract painting *suggests* is whatever ideas it calls to mind. This is more ideational than what the painting *evokes*, which refers to the emotive tones of the work. *Effects*, on the other hand, refer to the visual and optical qualities of a painting, such as space, light, motion, and its dynamic aspect.

A complete analysis of the content of the abstract expressionistic paintings discussed cannot be fully understood without distinguishing their suggestions and evocations from their effects. This is often difficult in practice. For instance, the same blob of paint that suggests blood may be a cue to space. Thus, it is often the case that a thing may both specify space and lend an emotive tone to that space.

For the above reasons, when analyzing paintings it is absolutely necessary that effects should be distinguished from their suggestions and evocations. Consequently, in this chapter I shall develop a theory of sensibility only to effects. Thus, it must be regarded as only a partial theory of sensibility since a full theory would discuss sensibility to suggestions and evocations as well.

Because I distinguish effects from recognizable images, a primary motivation for picking pure abstracts, rather than representational paintings, is to examine the visual qualities such works can create without involving acts of identification and recognition. For instance, Holbein's "Erasmus of Rotterdam" hardly just gives an effect of Erasmus but involves the viewer in recognizing and identifying many familiar forms as well.

Four Kinds of Effects

At least four major types of effects can be noted: First, and the most clearly causal effects typically exploited in abstract paintings, are those which work solely for physiological reasons, (color contrast induced by complements being an example). A second, and very different range of effects are those arising from *composition*. Compositional effects can guide vision, such as when colors capture the eye or lines lead the eye. Notice that these effects describe what happens to the eye in viewing rather than a phenomenal experience of the viewer (space, for example). Thus, a shift in idioms is required from "gives the effects of ____" to "has the effect of ____." Both learned scanning habits and Gestalt laws of grouping are presumably relevant to compositional effects.

A third type of effect paintings may have on viewers is due to *cross-sensory effects*. These arise when a visual cue excites an effect that is not purely visual as in "the forms give the impression of being massive" or "the slanting of top-heavy shapes give the impression of impending collapse." (Space, of course, is also a cross-sensory effect).

A final important kind of effect are the many cues sufficient to create an experience of three-dimensional space. For instance, figure-ground relations create an experience of space even when the figures are extremely abstract and unfamiliar. Similarly, a depth effect can be created by the fact that "cool" colors (blue and green) tend to recede in paintings while "warm" colors (red and yellow) tend to come forward. Moreover, a depth effect can be created by atmosphere, that is, the fact that distant objects appear cooler in color than nearer ones, loss of focusable detail with distance, etc., or by the overlapping of forms (occlusion) or the overlapping of colors (transparency).

Such cues as these are so basic to visual perception as to constitute information for the form or structure of the visual world per se and not just for its content. Indeed, space seems to constitute a general category of vision. For this reason, perceptual cues specifying three dimensionality are more basic to visual perception than to any particular aspect of the world or to any specific type of object.

The claim therefore to be explored in subsequent sections of the chapter can be stated as follows: *abstract paintings create phenomenal effects by setting into operation the categorical aspects of vision rather than by merely eliciting our knowlege of specific particulars and types.* In other words, abstract paintings succeed because they exploit what Kant referred to as the "forms of sensible intuition."

These four kinds of effects, physiological reactions, composition, cross-sensory effects, and spatial cues, have only briefly been considered since they are so well-known and may be readily reviewed in detail in many books on perception (e.g., Gibson, 1966), or on the psychology of art (e.g., Arnheim, 1954). It should be emphasized, however, that there are many *kinds* of factors involved in these effects. There are the *nature* of the eye, *habits* of scanning, the *disposition and nature* of the eye as seeing figure and ground, *general knowledge* of atmosphere and texture in space, and *general knowledge* of cross-sensory correlations. Various combinations of these factors are set in operation by visual causes in the abstract and create phenomenal effects. By "visual cause" I mean any stimulus in a context (such as overlapping or placing a color on another) which creates a phenomenal effect. "Phenomenal effect" covers the full range of qualities such as space, light, and motion. "Causal correlation" means the correlation, based on the nature of seeing, between visual causes and effects. This concept is important to the problem discussed next.

The Problem of Contextualism

A major problem that arises in viewing art is that of contextualism. Even though the causal correlations cited are well-known and work in decontextualized illusion illustrations (figures with no context), the same correlations might not work in a rich context. Suppose the Müller–Lyer illusion had parallel lines drawn close to and at right angles to the illusory lengths. At certain distances from the illusory lengths, the parallel lines would clearly tend to cancel the effect because they would act as conflicting cues to length. Contextualism in painting is somewhat analogous, there being both reinforcement and conflict among various cues. Suppose, for example, there is a conflict between the plane a color tends to assume and overlapping of planes as in many abstract paintings by Hans Hofmann. The richness of context destroys the agreement we can get from contrived examples on psychological tests. The complexity of contextualism becomes even richer when it includes qualities (some of which are not effects), suggestions, and evocations. For example, the emotive tone of color schemes may affect the relative depth of the planes to which they are applied.

If an ideal subject viewed a given painting, presumably all these variables would sort themselves out into dominant and subordinate effects. But with an actual subject, even with the most powerful devices to draw attention, there is still considerable variability in the manner of viewing. Viewer distance and the order in which an eye will "read" parts of the painting cannot be well controlled for paintings whereas such factors can be controlled in psychological experiments with illusory figures.

Finally, there are at least two very different kinds of contextualism, a contextualism of effects consists of a lumping together of suggestions, elusive qualities, and evocations in a hierarchy of dominant and subordinate effects; however, there remains a second kind of contextualism—the contextualism of purposes. Dominant effect is not the same as the main purpose. The subordination of means to ends is a different kind of ordering from the relation of dominant and subordinate effects. A sensitivity to the main purpose of a work is different from a sensitivity to its dominant effect, though sensing of dominant effects is usually a means to a purpose and sometimes the main purpose itself.

In my opinion, however, contextualism even in these rich painting contexts is overdone, and there are two important kinds of qualificiations. First, there is reason to believe that there is a hierarchy of effects which can be established experimentally due to unequal weighting of factors in the background of normalcy required for ordinary perception. In the example mentioned, overlapping will usually override the more subtle indication of space by color. Form perception therefore will usually override a more subtle spatial cue. Of course, a large enough area of color with a very strong spatial tendency might override even Gestalt indications and tendencies. I suspect one could even determine experimentally how much area tended to override a more basic factor such as overlapping. At present, however, only the second answer to contextualism will be developed.

The answer (or a new form of contextualism if you prefer) is that attention is a process which inherently decontextualizes and recontextualizes by selecting certain features of paintings while ignoring others. For this reason, certain learned modes of attention and sensibility clearly eliminate much of the problem of variability mentioned earlier and, thereby, aid the painting in realizing its phenomenal fullness.

The same kind of factors which operate in normal vision and are demonstrable in illustrations of illusions also operate in painting contexts. For example, the appearance of known correlations (such as texture gradients creating space) in critical explanations of what the effect of space is due to, offers some support for this claim. However, a scientific explanation of vision is not relevant to criticism at the level of specific disputes over whether or not a painting gives a certain effect; but rather it is relevant at the level of characterizing a kind of sensibility to general visual categories.

If analytical attention to visual causes, in certain modes, is not to be a fraud, then it must be based upon an understanding of normal vision. Scientific exploration justifies general acts of sensing effects over classes of paintings, at least in the sense of providing a characterization of real visual possibilities. Looking at a painting in terms of texture, overlapping, color planes, and atmospheres will give a sense of space; moreover, the causes of such effects can be theoretically determined.

Factual knowledge of causal relations is relevant at the level of potentialities of the medium as viewed, not at the level of justifying some claim about a particular painting effect. One wonders however if there is not enough historical knowledge of art to tell us about known correlations, and that no causal theories are needed. Does art history tell us all we need to know about the potentialities of the medium? Perhaps not, for art history tells us about purported effects, but not whether purported effects have any foundation in normalcy. There remains the question of whether a painting works visually.

I will return to the subject of causal correlations and contextualism towards the end of the chapter after developing the necessary theoretical background to deal with this thorny problem. We will now take what appears to be a large digression into the subject of attention and sensibility. An adequate theory of sensibility, however, is absolutely necessary before the problem posed by traditional contextualism can be solved.

ACTS OF VISUAL ATTENTION

Introduction

Visual attention will be understood here to mean a *channeling of visual awareness mostly, but not entirely, by verbal means, in which the object of attention through characterizations or descriptions induces an "uptake" in acts of noticing.* I will try to show that visual attention to something like color, when skilled and complete, is a redundant complex of verbal categories, spatial reference aids, techniques, and devices for focusing attention, and techniques for controlling the eyes. These redundant elements of visual attention can be ordered into objectside, intermediate, and eyeside elements of attention. "Objectside" refers to the particular physical object, specifically an abstract painting, as described or characterized, the verbal description or characterization being essential to define the object of attention. Attention to an object thus will always be conditioned by certain circumstances, though it must be recognized that attention can be channeled by nonverbal means, as in animals. Nonverbal means of directing attention, say by pointing, constitute what is meant by the intermediate element of attention. However, attention to a very complex visual object such as the effects given by an abstract painting is certainly learned by verbal means, with aid from nonverbal devices and techniques. In the section called "Sensibility and Noticing," I shall show that the actual physical object provides various sorts of uptake within the channels of attention, and thus, in a sense, the actual object of attention itself fills in the final gap between the verbal description or characterization and the actual seeing of the object in those terms. For now, "objectside" means the particular aspect of a painting as characterized or described. On the eyeside are actual eye directions such as "blur the eyes to observe color." "Eyeside" refers to eye directions such as focus, scan, blur, or squint the eyes. Also "eyeside" is used loosely to cover headside or bodyside directions such as "if you want to look just at the color scheme, then blur your eyes or stand back so far that you cannot recognize the objects." For convenience I shall refer to *objectside, intermediate*, and *eyeside* aspects of visual skills such as attending to color.

By "*acts* of visual attention" I mean that some modes of seeing are deliberately learned, often involving practiced eye techniques, devices, types of attention, eventuating in a visual skill in a fairly literal sense. During the process of learning the lessons may be assimilated into a smooth and practiced visual act, like other skilled acts, with the subsequent development of what I call perceptual refinement abilities—abilities such as discrimination, sensitivity, and acuity.[1] To clarify what is meant by perceptual refinement abilities consider the following case: The astronomer practices averted vision, the holding of the fovea several degrees off of the object of attention, so as to select the rod-laden portion of the retina that is more sensitive to light. One's sensitivity can often be extended by more than a magnitude by this eye technique, and it is amazing how much more detail of dim celestial objects an astronomer can see as compared to an untrained observer of the same visual ability. Analogously, one can practice modes of attention appropriate to abstract paintings, and with practice the act becomes smooth and efficient with the development of perceptual refinement abilities which I will call sensibility.

Of course, there are also important differences between a visual skill like averted vision and sensitively perceiving an abstract painting. These differences can be emphasized by pointing out that one does not look at aspects and features of nature in the same ways as at the elements of art; one does not look at color in the same ways as at a color scheme. Nonetheless, there is full

[1] "We can now suppose that the perceptual systems develop perceptual skills, with some analogy to the way in which the behavioral systems develop performatory skills" (Gibson, 1968).

justification for calling sensitive perception an act of vision in the full sense of an intentional and purposive activity for sensing impressions and effects of paintings. Consequently, sensitive perception is a deliberately cultivated act.

Also "acts of visual attention" means a visual act of some generality. There are no skills of perceptual refinement abilities uniquely derived from nor applicable to just one painting but only for a class of paintings considered in a certain way. This is just to say, as emphasized below, that with respect to sensibility the object of attention is an element of art, and elements of art must be embodied in at least several works. Critical characterizations and explanations often suggest a general mode of sensing. (There are exceptions, as when a critic characterizes or explains the peculiarities of an anomalous work.) The critic usually means, and the context will show when this is so, that the terms of the explanation or characterization can be applied to a class of works of some extension—say other works by the painter in the same period, the whole corpus of works by a painter, works of the same school, works of the same period, etc.

Sensibilities, then, are visual acts of *kinds* or *types* in the sense of being about a class of some extension and in being specified in terms of elements of the works of this class. Emphasis on this sort of generality is necessary in order to emphasize acts of sensing, acts so general as to permit use of the concepts of skill, habits, practices of viewing. Consequently, all my remarks are about visual acts of some generality, though the visual acts may involve odd and hyphenated modes of attention such as color-scheme-considered-from-an-expressionistic point of view. By "acts of attention" then is meant habitual attention in certain terms to an element of art in a class of some extension.

Viewing particular paintings. Given that the perceptual refinement abilities upon which sensibility rests must be developed from viewings of a wide class of paintings, the problem of how we attain a stable viewing of a particular painting remains. Although acts of attention have the generality noted above, strictly speaking, an act of attention is a complete act only when there is an uptake of noticing within the terms of what is being attended to. Consequently, the generality of the visual act is the terms in which one sees, while the uptake of noticing is a particular realization within those terms. Thus, attention when completed by a successful uptake, (i.e., a "Eureka!" experience), is like any act in being a particular occurrence; it either happens or it does not.

Our particular viewings without a developed sensibility have no more stability and intelligibility than would our particular acts without the stabilities of character traits, habits, moods, etc. The complex activities involved when viewing a particular painting includes many things—habitual modes of attention, memories, images of other paintings, verbal descriptions, titles; moreover, for a given person these categories are more or less stable. When less stable, every viewing is different from other viewings. When these stabilize with practice they provide a consistent basis in terms of which one views paintings, though of course every viewing is also a unique realization of uptake. There may be many kinds of occurrences or kinds of uptake. A painting may appear to be definite or unique (style) or of a particular type; an effect may appear to result from a certain cause, or an image may appear to be animated with some suggestion or evocation. On a particular viewing a Pollock painting can have a very definite space, say that of late cubism, look as though the space were due to overlapping strands, look as though the drip gestures are intense. (Kinds of uptake are further discussed below.) We can notice all these things on an occasion, given visual skills and sensibilities. There are no doubt many things that affect a particular viewing other than sensibility, but sensibility is the stabilizing center. The situation is analogous to interpreting a person's acts, which, as particular occurrences, can only be understood in terms of taking place in a background of more stable things such as habits, dispositions, character traits, moods, and specific intentions.

To anticipate a later argument, our "verification" of the critic's explanations and characterizations should not be isolated from our own sensibility and the state of our perceptual refinement abilities with regard to the relevant mode of sensing a particular painting. Our confidence in the correctness or incorrectness of a critical claim should be directly proportional to our awareness of our own sensibility in the relevant mode of attention. Before we have the relevant sensibility we cannot distinguish between a projection of the explanation or characterization onto the painting from the sensing of the painting as explained or described.

Objectside (Verbal) Aspects of Attention

Generally attention is related to ostensive defining. Many techniques such as pointing or directing one's glance can also be used to draw or direct attention. But knowing what someone means is not simply attending to that which they refer. The same sort of category mastery required to understand ostensive defining is also necessary to understand attention. Attention, however, may use additional means, even devices and techniques, because it places emphasis on perceiving the object in certain terms, that is in some specific way rather than just arbitrarily.

The most relevant similarity between referring and attending is pointed out by Wittgenstein in his well-known arguments about ostensive defining. A child does not learn words by ostensive defining (though ostensive teaching can be involved) because such defining already presupposes mastery of basic categories and behavioral aspects of such pointing. If I say "that is sepia" the "that" can mean an indefinite number of things. Only if the learner knows the category of color can we ostensively define, for we can then say "sepia is a color, and that is sepia." Before a child knows the basic categories necessary to understand ostensive defining, we use only trial and error (ostensive teaching), with only the teacher knowing the categories. Ostensive defining requires a vast amount of stage-setting or category mastery.

Analogously, attention, at least attention to anything at all complex, involves channeling of perceptual awareness by verbal categories. To reiterate: Attention is always in certain terms. Once the verbal lessons have been learned, attention has its autonomy, and certainly we often attend without consciously using verbal categories. We can honestly say "yes, I noticed the color" without meaning we thought about the color.

Mastery of the concept of color requires, of course, more than just the use of the word "color." A full understanding of how to attend to color can manifest itself in other verbal and nonverbal devices, in behavioral gestures, in techniques, and even in what one does with his eyes. Since attention to color is a matter of visual attention, there is more involved in mastery of attention to color than just referring or ostensively defining color, as noted above. Attention to color is a visual skill, which can clearly be refined to increase discriminative ability. The verbal and nonverbal devices, behavioral gestures, techniques, and eye directions go beyond what is necessary to ostensively define color, though it will be seen there is some overlap. For example, a child must master several verbal devices if he (or she) is to use concepts such as color; these devices we call *part–whole reference aids*. Such aids consist of verbal expressions or characterizations which draw the viewer's attention to parts of wholes or to the wholes themselves. "Part" is a covering term for any number of spatial units–figments, fragments, parts, pieces, segments, areas, planes, regions, blended areas, brushstrokes, blobs, drips, etc. These combine into very different kinds of wholes. Of course, we usually combine part–whole reference with aspection, that is, we look at areas of color, sections of line, rays of light where each of the supplemental reference aids (area, section, ray) indicate the kind of part unit appropriate to the aspect. In fact, aspects are just certain kinds of part–wholes. Color is one kind of part–whole, texture another. In general, a child who constantly referred to a piece of color, or who did not show he knew that a line occurred in sections and sweeps, would not be said to understand the concept of color or line, respectively.

Intermediate Aspects of Attention

Pointing is one kind of intermediate and nonverbal aid to attention involved in the mastery of concepts such as color. Some kinds of pointing are even relevant to aspect terms and reference aids. For instance, a generalized gesture to a vaguely bounded area is appropriate to an area of color, while a sweeping gesture pointing to a sweep of line can capture behaviorally the nature and tempo of the sweep of line. A good museum lecturer does not point to color, line or texture in the same way. One does not point to pieces, sections and areas in the same way. A child who referred to a piece of color would possibly also make inappropriate gestures in ostensively defining color for others. There is of course redundancy in spatial reference aids and gestures. Also intermediate are techniques such as cupping one's hands so as to isolate a color from its context and from aspects such as shape or outline. Of course, there is redundancy between cupping one's hands, spatial aids such as "area," behavioral gestures and aspection terms such as "color." Also cupping one's hands is a good illustration of the difference between reference and ostensive defining and visual attention, for cupping one's hands goes beyond the requirements for clear reference and clearly is a part of the visual skill of attending to color. Another example of an intermediate element in mastery of the skill of looking at color are devices such as a piece of paper with a hole in it. Such devices, of course, do something very similar, sometimes with some advantages, to cupping one's hands.

Eyeside Aspects of Attention

Completely on the eyeside are such techniques as blurring one's eyes or standing back so far one cannot recognize the subject matter. Both are good eyeside techniques, often advised by critics and artists, for looking at areas of color in color schemes. In summary, from the objectside to the eyeside there is redundant and overlapping verbal equipment, behavioral gestures, techniques, devices and eye techniques which are employed in skilled attention to color. Any one element in this visual skill can be omitted or even not known since they are redundant, whereas lack of many of them lessens the visual skill and makes one more reluctant to claim mastery of the skill of attending to color. There are analogous redundancies in ordinary reference and ostensive defining.

Color viewing. Mastery of attention to the category of color involves viewing techniques ranging from the eyeside to the objectside such as blurring the eyes, using devices which emphasize color, using proper reference aids such as "area" or "region," looking in correct part–whole terms, attending to the color of the object of attention. A person may develop differential sensitivity by these various techniques. Thus, some methods of attending to color differ radically from those used to attend to texture, shape, or outline. This is due to the fact that color is an aspect of objects which is visually pervasive in ways that texture, shape and outline are not. To see what this means, select a painting, first, blur the eyes so as to destroy visual texture then mask the outline with a funnel of paper, finally, step back too far to recognize the subject matter. Clearly, each of these techniques possesses subtleties of its own and thus makes it quite different from the others as a method of attending to color.

Thus, there is a cluster of such techniques from the eyeside to the objectside. These techniques range from manipulation of the eyes or their augmentation by devices, through nonverbal reference aids, such as hand gestures, to verbal suggestions indicating where one should look in a painting in order to notice certain significant aspects. It is important to notice that the use of the aspect term "color" exhibits a category consistency, in that it refers to what remains perceptually invariant across all the viewing techniques mentioned, from objectside to eyeside.

Attention to abstract paintings sometimes requires category abnormalities such as looking at the shape of holes in some of DuBuffet's paintings and Moore's sculptures. Very often, in fact, painters want to change our reference equipment or at least refine it. Notice Ben Shahn's (1967) book entitled *The Shape of Content*. Such category changes or crossings affect attention on the eyeside and objectside.

The direct approach of characterizing the object in the painting world, the one used by most critics, seems much less artificial than emphasizing eyeside modes of attention. One can, of course, usually derive the modes of attention from the characterization of the object, though not conversely. This sort of free shifting and interchangeability of modes of attention and objects meant is typical of ordinary reference too. Even though critics do not usually give eyeside directions, one can usually derive the eyeside modes of attention from the characterization of objects as given. In addition one can also often derive further details about analytical techniques of looking and sensing. Sometimes these remedial lessons are necessary to develop our sensing. "Blur the eyes" is sometimes a help in looking at color schemes. Also, explaining what an effect is due to is remedial, but sometimes indispensable. In sum, attention is a complex visual skill involving eyeside techniques appropriate to objectside categories.

Attention to Abstract Paintings

Attention to abstract paintings has certain perculiarities due to the object's phenomenal nature and to the nature of eyeside modes of attention. Because one often encounters entirely new types of wholes in abstract painting, ordinary aspection and part–whole reference sometimes prove inadequate. From the discussion of contextualism there seems to be two kinds of wholes: *natural phenomenal wholes* (Gestalts) involving principles of groupings, factors from the background of normalcy (hierarchy of effects), as opposed to *purposive wholes* where that aspect of the painting results from the artist's successful fulfillment of some goal. In the latter case, the proper unit of analysis is the "means–end" strategy. For example, the artist may wish to convey a certain mood in order to dramatize a social message inherent in the content of the painting. To do so he may utilize the contrast effect of certain complementary colors. However, the part–whole relationship of the colors to the total color scheme used is not an appropriate unit for a means–end analysis of the artist's intention. Correctly selecting and executing a color scheme, like composition, is an element of painting technique which is itself a subart that must be mastered by the artist. The desired end, therefore, is often achieved via some set of phenomenal effects.

Another way of stating how ordinary aspection, part–whole reference and elements of painting differ is to say color schemes are not the same as color, nor line the same as outline or natural shape. "Look at the color scheme" involves a different kind of looking from "look at the color." "Notice the drawing" has a distinct visual feel, a sort of overall looking at contours of line edges, and no ordinary looking is like it (differences we shall return to shortly). Sensibility has to be to the elements of painting, and elements often include phenomenal effects. In sum, ordinary visual attention is in terms of space–time and aspection reference. Eliminating time, looking at paintings is roughly looking at spatial parts and wholes and aspecting (e.g., denoting values of colors, shade, texture, etc.). Ordinary aspecting and ordinary part–whole are not completely adequate, however, for we must learn to see in terms of the elements of painting, in terms of color schemes instead of just areas of color. The contrast between elements of art and ordinary aspection will be the basic difference between sensibility and a visual act such as averted vision.

Peculiarities of the object of attention when viewing abstracts. Peculiarities in the object of attention when it is an effect of an abstract painting quickly become obvious. These peculiarities revolve around the fact that we attend to visual causes *in order to* sense effects such as space. Ordinarily, we learn visual techniques to discount misleading visual cues. For example, the skilled judge of distance on a golf course learns to discount valleys and emphasize texture and size constancy of the flag on the green. We attend so as to overcome misleading cues.

In abstract painting, the converse is in a sense true. We emphasize the cues and allow them to create a full world of phenomenal effects. Our knowledge of causal correlations is, in fact, an important part of our aesthetic education, and the particular ones cited here have been known at least since Leonardo. The nature of our viewing is simply the viewer counterpart to the fact that space and other effects have long been a part of the painter's purposes. We must then learn to *decontextualize* and *recontextualize* along entirely different lines than in ordinary vision. The good judge of distance decontextualizes from valleys and recenters on textures. In a painting, we decontextualize from a flat wall and from surface texture of paint, and recontextualize on cues that give an illusion of space. We know that painters often exploit cues to create phenomenal worlds, and we use our knowledge of causal correlations to center on these cues in order to savor the size, scale, nature of, say, picture space. Of course, our recontextualizing, though in a sense odd, is itself based in normalcy in recentering on visual cues which cause effects because of normalcy.

Another way of putting the same oddity of the object of attention when it is effects is to say the object of attention is a merely phenomenal world. (Of course, we also attend to literal qualities such as paint texture.) Both the structure of the painting world spatially and the qualities of the "things" within the world are purely phenomenal. One cannot get into these worlds to explore around. Space, motion, and tactile–kinesthetic qualities are in a painting only visually, phenomenally, and they can never be checked cross modally. This means that ordinary sensibilities (such as a sense of distance, sense of mass, senses of various tactile–kinesthetic qualities) are activated, but cut off from usual pedestrian modes of confirmation. (For suggestiveness and evocation we employ still other ordinary sensibilities such as a sense of danger, sensing a threat, sensing a mood. These probably involve sensing subtle features of behavior and gesture.) Ordinary sensibilities are confirmed and developed by ordinary mundane and nonintuitive procedures. Using ordinary vision to gather tactile–kinesthetic information such as how something would feel, how stable kinesthetically it is, can be checked. The apparent distance, depth and scale of space can be checked. But one cannot explore around in the painting world. It is there only visually, in fact, even more tenuously, it is there only to our sensibility. Not only can we check if our ordinary sensing is accurate, but we can cast our attention to a wider context in places we know we are likely to be fooled, and we learn which sort of sensing to practice to override misleading cues. A good judge of distance has to learn to discount and emphasize, just as does a good judge of weight or mass.

A way of generalizing this point about oddities of the object of attention when the object is an effect is to say that qualities in a painting become special sensibles of vision even when those qualities are not ordinarily special sensibles. Space and motion are not ordinarily special sensibles, for other senses can confirm them. But a painting only looks spatial (in the volumetric sense), and if it looks spatial then it is phenomenally spatial so far as critics and viewers go. In fact, we must say somewhat more weakly that a painting only gives a sense or impression of space. The space exists only to our sensibility, thus I prefer the idioms "gives a sense of" and "gives an impression of" to concepts with such ordinary epistemological baggage as "looks," "appears," and "seems."

Ordinarily we are interested in going from how things look to how they really are. In a painting, we are interested in how paintings really look, or more accurately what effects and impressions they give to trained sensibility. Thus there is much greater dependence on descriptions of others, though of course we want eventually to develop integrity in our own sensibility. Critics, of course, freely use "looks," "appears," and "seems" in discussing effects and impressions, but they assume that the context will make clear an implicit qualification "looks spatial in the way paintings look spatial." They assume we will take their remarks as being about sensibles that are special to vision.

Eyeside peculiarities. If we switch from the objectside (phenomenal world of painting) to the eyeside matter of modes of attention, we discover some distinctive modes of attention, or at least we discover some ordinary modes being strangely employed. In this section, it is necessary that I be somewhat autobiographical in trying to discuss the phenomenological qualities of my own looking at abstracts. "Look at the color scheme" calls for a mode of vision which I call *nonfocused field looking.* One can blur his eyes or stand back some distance and try to see the whole field at once. We look at areas and regions, but not in a focused manner as we do with textures. One does not look at outlines or volumes. "Look at the texture" can take at least two modes of viewing. There is *foveal scanning* where acute vision is employed on areas or regions of texture. Further, there is *nonfoveal field viewing* where one tries to have acute vision of a field. A base runner at second base practices nonfoveal field looking in trying to watch the shortstop and pitcher at once. A more common example of nonfoveal field looking is when driving one is, say, trying to watch a car in the left lane, a car at an intersection and a bicyclist all at once. This sort of looking is like trying to attend to all the textures of an expanse at once. Of course, the angular size of the field is very important in this kind of looking, and that is one reason distance from a painting is often important.

A related mode of vision, though it is *nonfoveal spot* or *area looking* instead of field looking, is the astronomer practicing averted vision in order to see a dim galaxy. "Look at line drawing" is different from the above. Here one does not look at areas, or even at fields, but one's eye will often sweep the line, especially with regard to fine calligraphy. One looks at how sections or sweeps lead into and create rhythmical variations on other sections and sweeps. "Look at spatial composition" is nonfoveal and field, but now it is not in terms of areas of color or texture, but in terms of masses and qualities of equilibrium. Balance and proportionality are important. "Look at dynamic qualities" can be field, in terms of masses, but now the orientation of the masses is basic. Dynamic qualities also can mean linear rhythms.

Nonfocused field looking, various kinds of nonfoveal field and foveal scanning is only a suggestive beginning of a list of modes of attention. The typical objects of attention in a painting (color schemes, drawing, composition, etc.) are applicable to specific abstract paintings. One looks for the tensions in Hofmann's planes of color by a sort of nonfoveal, limited or narrow area field, with keen awareness of the edges of the planes, trying to sense the position they tend to assume. It is not like looking at color schemes, nor like the edges of fine calligraphy. One's eye butts against the edges of Hofmann's plane, it does not sweep these edges. The best description is perhaps just that we look at a plane of color, an outlined geometrical unit in space. Pollock's "all-over" composition lends itself to many modes of attention. One can practice nonfoveal field looking from a distance to sense the location in front of the picture plane of the strands of black. One can move closer and practice foveal scanning, savoring the equal distribution of energy and interest.

Perhaps, in fact, Pollock's all-over composition is one of the best forms of composition for the inherently variable nature of attention to paintings. The extreme variability of visual attention does not disturb his painting as it does traditional compositions which try to maintain special centers of interest, special places the eye is lead or drawn. Similarly, Barnett Newman intended for his works to be viewed from a distance such that they flooded the field of vision with subtly modulated colors. One cannot take them in at once, and, except for the bands, there is no place the eye rests. Thus, one falls into nonfocused scanning. Mark Rothko, in his very atmospheric works, also intended for the eye to wander in a void of color field and atmosphere, while at the same time the strong blended verticalities and horizontals of framing color areas emphasize the picture plane.

The modes of attention could be indefinitely expanded. In fact, a subtle phenomenology of viewing would show peculiarities of viewing for each painter, and even sometimes for each painting. I have tried to show that visual attention is a complex of redundancies from eyeside to objectside, and to suggest some peculiarities of attention on both the eyeside and objectside where one attends to purely phenomenal qualities such as space. A characterization of these peculiar visual skills will be given shortly.

Decontextualizing and Recontextualizing

Every visual act of attention inherently involves some decontextualizing and some recontextualizing. Decontextualizing involves discounting certain space–time and aspection modes of attention, where recontextualizing involves emphasizing certain part–whole and aspects, thus forming a new kind of whole, so to speak. In ordinary vision one decontextualizes and recontextualizes to avoid illusions. In judging and sensing distance on a golf course, one decontextualizes or discounts valleys and recontextualizes on texture and size constancy of the flag and green. One discounts cues one knows to be misleading and emphasizes cues one knows to be more reliable. If we decontextualize and recontextualize in certain ways we can certainly prevent the painting from working. We decontextualize from, say, surface texture in order for the spatial effects to work. Such decontextualizing and recontextualizing might well be noticed in changes from foveal and focused vision to nonfoveal field vision. We even decontextualize in our most synoptic modes of attention.

One never just looks for or at a dominant effect, but at or for a dominant effect of some kind. As an example we might take some visual acts of attention with regard to a painting by Hans Hofmann. We do not look at the work simply as areas of color such as we might find on a test palette. We do not attend excessively to the texture of paint, though the picture plane is certainly important in Hofmann. (In fact, the texture is an important element in setting up the tensions Hofmann desired. The tensions come from alternating modes of vision.) These decontextualizings make inoperative irrelevant modes of attention. Then we recontextualize. We do a nonfoveal field looking with a heightened awareness of the edges of the planes of color. We attend to areas or regions which include several planes of color. And we try to sense where the planes extend to, which ones tend to recede and which ones tend to advance.

This is recontextualizing along lines that are relevant to allowing the painting to do what it is meant to do, a mode of attention which aids the cues which have a foundation in the background of normalcy. "Look at the color scheme" decontextualizes from textures, shapes, volumes and recontextualizes on areas, regions or fields of color viewed simultaneously. Areas or regions have vague boundaries, and thus the eyeside directions of blurred vision or distant viewing. Part–whole and aspects may fall into one kind of grouping before instructions on visual attention than after. Early in our experience of abstracts we may look for fragments, pieces and figments of ordinary objects. But in pure abstracts with all over painting there must be different elements and part–wholes. These are ways of decontextualizing and recontextualizing.

Another way of stating these points is this: The thing is dissolved in abstract paintings, dissolved at least into figments and fragments. The thing was beginning to be dissolved by traditional composition and color schemes where the purposes of art overrode considerations of representational fidelity. When the dominant consideration becomes the elements of art, the painter can still have as much or as little relation to nature and human nature as he wishes, and he does this by exploiting or limiting factors in the background of normalcy. At the extreme of elements, where the thing is completely dissolved because of considerations of art, remember that we are still looking at the results of *acts* of painting, and these tie in richly with normal acts. Although some acts are not gesture-like, as in choosing, placing, arranging colors in paintings by Piet Mondrian, with regard to Pollock, however, the lines are acts of gesture. They constitute a celebration of the creative act, and we sense a painting by Pollock much more kinesthetically than we do one by Mondrain. Some modes of attention are peculiar in that they demonstrate the dominance of artistic technique over the realism of what is depicted; thus, they emphasize the elements of art rather than the content of the painting. For example, cross-category modes of attention requiring one to notice the shape of a hole in a Dubuffet exhibit what we mean by decontextualizing and recontextualizing.

Since all visual acts involve decontextualizing and recontextualizing, there is nothing odd about contextualism in painting. Thus some of the bite is taken out of the objection that causal correlations, though operative in abstract painting, are rendered useless as generalizations because of contextualism. A form of this objection occurs below, however, in saying that knowledge of causal correlations will not refute or verify a specific critical explanation or characterization of effects, but that such knowledge is relevant at the level of analytically learning a general visual act. One looks at many paintings in terms of the knowledge expressed in the proposition that "texture creates space," and with practice one learns to sense space in these terms. But the deduction: "Texture creates space. There is texture in Pollock. Therefore there is pictorial space in Pollock" will not do. However, having assimilated the generalization that texture creates space into a practiced visual act does increase our sensibility, and we do decide on the basis of our sensibility whether Pollock creates space or not. The confidence in our judgment rises with the practice of our visual act of sensing space due to texture.

Synoptic and analytic modes of attention. Decontextualizing and recontextualizing of various sorts can be stated in terms of the distinction of visual causes and effects. For the more analytical type of attention, one attends to the visual cause and expects the effect to follow. For example, one attends to texture with the expectation that a sense of space will follow. Our knowledge of causal correlations, thus, is assimilated into this sort of analytical attention. Instead, we often practice a more synoptic mode of attention, doing something like attending to the space without being aware of what causes the sense of space. Even though in synoptic attention we may not notice texture as a cue to space, we no doubt see, in some weaker sense than explicit visual noticing, the texture, for texture can cause us to sense space even when we do not explicitly notice it. No doubt when we sense phenomenal qualities in a painting there is a cause for our sensing just as there is a cause of the Müller–Lyer illusion even though we cannot cite the cues causing the illusion. Illusions need causal explanation. Often critics just characterize the kind of space, and we simply agree or disagree on the characterization so far as our sensibility goes. Obviously both kinds of attention decontextualize and recontextualize on cues such that, given a background of normalcy, the painting gives a sense of space. Synoptic and analytical modes of attention are further examined below.

SENSIBILITY

Attention with any degree of complexity is like any learned skill. At first it is clumsy, stiff, academic and unresponsive. Later it can become smooth and there is a noticeable increase in perceptual refinement abilities. Attention is learning to see in certain terms. *Sensibility just means the development of perceptual refinement abilities subsequent upon practice of certain modes of attention.* Perceptual refinement abilities most literally are specifiable in terms such as discrimination, acuity, and sensitivity. But with regard to skilled acts like averted vision, such terms do not fully describe the skill. Averted vision requires motor skill in order to resist foveating the object of attention. Further, it requires ability to attend to a nonfoveal region. Thus even though averted vision increases sensitivity, sensitivity alone is not a sufficient description of the act. Unidimensional concepts such as sensitivity, discrimination or acuity are not sufficient specifications of any visual skill. Analogously, increase in literal perceptual refinement abilities such as discrimination and sensitivity are relevant to increases in sensibility, though not of course definitive of sensibility. Perhaps it does not need arguing that habitual attention to color increases one's discriminative ability, and that such discrimination is relevant to sensibility to color schemes. A critic who could only discriminate a few colors would hardly be taken seriously as an analyst of color schemes. Excellent discrimination is a necessary condition for any high degree of sensibility to color schemes. Of course, discrimination alone is not sufficient; a fuller characterization of various forms of sensibility will take us into various peculiarities of these kinds of visual acts, into differences alluded to earlier as the distinction between ordinary aspects and elements of art.

It will perhaps be helpful to state more exactly what kinds of perceptual refinement abilities are appropriate to abstract paintings. This is especially imperative since even more literal visual skills such as averted vision cannot be characterized in terms of discrimination, acuity, or sensitivity alone. An answer to this question has already been given in the discussion of eyeside and objectside techniques and categories for perceiving abstract paintings. There are a number of eyeside techniques such as blurred vision and various kinds of field looking. Objectside there are matters such as sensing the position of planes of color and sensing tactile–kinesthetic qualities. In a sense the only way of specifying the perceptual refinement abilities is to go through a series of abstract paintings and comment on different abilities needed for each. This has already been done in the section just mentioned (eyeside and objectside factors in attention), and now it remains only to reemphasize the plurality and open-endedness of the perceptual refinement abilities needed for abstract paintings.

Defining the perceptual refinement abilities in terms of the object of attention is not so circular as it may seem. We now think of emotions as being constituted by the object of emotion and not, as in dualism, as being merely contingently related to the object (see Kenny, 1964). Analogously, one cannot specify the kind of attention apart from the object of attention. Painting effects are somewhat peculiar and unique even though they exploit visual normalcy for their very existence, and this also has been indicated in the comments on painting effects as special sensibles. Thus it seems permissible to express perceptual refinement abilities as increased ability to sense complex and hyphenated effects such as the position-colors-tend-to-assume-spatially or the tactile–kinesthetic-qualities-of-forms. No skills can be specified in terms of isolated abilities. Skills are specified in terms of their typical activity even though isolated aspects of the skill may be common to many activities. The structure of each activity recombines isolated skills from other activities. Sensibilities of various kinds are related to other visual acts, but the distinctness of sensing effects as elements of art recombines ordinary skills in unique ways. Good critics have highly developed perceptual refinement abilities to effects and impressions of paintings which is part of what is meant by saying they have sensibility.

Sensibility and Noticing

Attention is distinguished from noticing. One can pay attention but still not notice something. Attention is a preparation for acts of seeing, sensing, and noticing. "Notice" as a command form does mean to pay attention, but paying attention does not guarantee one will notice in the success sense. Attention is related to the general state of being attentive, being observant, being alert. One can even notice without being attentive, as in "my attention was aroused," "I inadvertantly saw," "something caught my eye," or "my eye was drawn." But even though ordinary noticing can take place without attention, involuntarily, noticing a subtlety can hardly take place without preparation, thus the oddity of an unexperienced person saying, "I suddenly noticed the cubistic space of a Pollock." Since noticing subtle effects of paintings requires sensibility, such noticing could not be a form of noticing without having cultivated certain visual skills. We can inadvertently or accidentally notice only those things we can see with ordinary perceptual skills. One does not inadvertently notice the details of a dim galaxy or the spatial structure of a Pollock.

Noticing involes a sort of uptake on the part of the object of attention. In a purposive activity like looking at or for something, there is a give and take of vision. We practice space–time reference, aspection and modes of attention visually, and often the object rewards, so to speak, our looking at or for. Sometimes the uptake on the part of the object is very minimal as in "notice the red" said of a very ordinary red; however, this sort of noticing is really *noting*. Moreover, this sort of noticing is close to ordinary referring. The only kind of attention referred to here is that which occurs in aesthetic contexts. Here the object requires considerable perceptual subtlety, and, therefore, there is room for more uptake than in ordinary aspection. "Notice the blue" uttered in front of a painting by Newman means "Notice the elusive, unique, peculiar, atmospheric blue!" In fact, if in an art museum I say "notice the blue" and you simply see an ordinary blue you will likely say something like "I don't see what you mean. It looks like a very ordinary blue to me." Likewise, if you do see what I mean when I say "notice Newman's blue" you will have a more dramatic uptake than in ordinary attention and you will say "I see what you mean" as a sign that the painting has rewarded your attention.

There exists a variety of uptakes bridging, so to speak, the final gap between the verbal channels of attention and the particular visual object actually seen. The nature of the verbal act and the verbal context tell us what kind of uptake is expected. The object of attention is a particular as characterized or described. Some of the kinds of uptake which the particular provides within the channels of trained attention are these: In characterizing a spatial effect the critic is often trying to articulate the uniqueness, the *je ne sais quoi* of the painting space. In characterizing one tries to express that which we could see before the characterization but could not say. Characterization in articulating subtle effects achieves Isenberg's ideal of criticism in bringing about communication at the level of the senses (see Isenberg, 1949).[2] One sort of uptake then is savoring uniqueness, and "I see what you mean" can mean "I grasp the elusive visual quality of just this work." The uptake could be very different if we are to see the painting as belonging to a school or type. "Notice the late cubistic space in Pollock" gets a very different sort of uptake from "Notice the unique and peculiar space of Pollock." "Notice that Pollock's space is due to overlapping strands of paint" gets a third sort of uptake, for here we get an abstractable schemata by which we can look at other paintings. Here we notice what the space is due to and not the uniqueness of the space or the type of space. "Notice the intensity of Pollock's paint gestures" is different still. Uptakes then can include seeing uniqueness, typing, explaining, and characterizing the emotive tone.

In summary, critics practice many verbal acts (describing, analyzing, characterizing, interpreting, explaining) in many contexts for which there are a wide variety of uptakes.

Sensibility and Perception

A basic difference between sensibility and averted vision is that sensibility includes sensing phenomenal effects. But even sensibility to effects is *perceptual* attention. To notice a given effect one must attend in the proper visual mode. Indeed, the logic of sensing as defined here entails perceiving. I would deny that one was sensing an effect of an abstract painting unless one was perceiving the visual cause of that effect. But this is also true of ordinary visual sensibilities. Consider for example one's sense of distance, balance, direction, mass, etc. These are not internal senses, rather each is a mode of perceptual awareness that is exercised in specific activities with respect to specific objects. In other words, they are object and activity specified. For example, a sense of direction may involve perceptual skills such as perceiving sun and star positions, feeling prevailing winds, recognizing familiar landscapes from many angles, possessing an accurate visual memory, etc.

Sensibility is a mode of visual attention in that it implies an ability to use the eyes in a skillful way so as to sense the effects and impressions of paintings.

[2] See also Wittgenstein's (1953) comments on the contrast between the color known to everyone and the particular impression of a color I am now getting. "I don't turn the same kind of attention on the colour in the two cases. When I mean the colour impression that (as I should like to say) belongs to me alone I immerse myself in the colour—rather like when I 'cannot get my fill of a colour' [p. 277]."

These effects and impressions, however, cannot be specified or defined apart from their visual causes.

Further, sensing is a mode of perceptual attention in the sense that the effects are achieved by exciting the background of perceptual normalcy. This is a key difference between sensibility and various forms of projection. Seeing the Müller–Lyer illusion is perceiving. One does not perceive the illusory lengths in the full success sense of "perceive," but one of the lines certainly looks longer than the other.

There is no one relation between seeing and sensing, though all types of sensing are modes of perception. The richness of their relationship has been hinted at several times before. Some of the differences are indicated by appearance concepts. Complements really look more intense when near each other, but paintings do not really look spatial. Several factors may be operating here. Perhaps we are more reluctant to attribute "really looks" to an effect which is not a special sensible of vision. Also relevant is what we might call the phenomenological quality of the look of the object. Giving a sense of space does not have the same feel visually as color complements appearing more intense. Further, giving a sense of space is not like really looking spatial in the sense that we might confuse picture space with real space. Matters such as these provide reason for preferring the idioms "gives a sense of" or "gives an impression of" to concepts which carry a lot of ordinary epistemological baggage such as "looks," "seems," and "appears." Finally, as emphasized at the outset, "causal correlation" is used as a covering concept. There are important differences, not explored here, between kinds of visual causes, kinds of effects, and even kinds of relationship between visual causes and effects. Very different qualities such as color intensification, a sense of space, a sense of motion, a sense of light, etc., could not all be expected to have the same sort of relationship to visual causes. There is no single relation existing between seeing and sensing, rather all the causal correlations mentioned are activated in modes of *visual* attention that are based in visual normalcy. The modes of visual attention in sensibility are unusual in that one is not trying to discount the illusionistic tendencies as in ordinary vision (going from looks to how things really are), but one is trying to sense the uniqueness of the phenomenal world of this painting. A definite or distinct visual impression is the goal of this sort of seeing, but it is a mode of seeing.

The uptake to be expected from these kinds of visual acts is quite different from identifying types or recognizing particulars. Averted vision, however, does concern recognizing and identifying. There are clearly visual acts which specifically have to do with the categories of vision, the spatial "jelling" of the visual world, without which no animal could see at all. Seeing is less oriented to type and more oriented to a general category like seeing three dimensional objects in space. My dog can see a tennis ball but not identify it in the full sense of type identification; moreover his seeing consists in knowing the ball is a solid bouncy object, and acting as though he knows this. He does not know the ball is for playing tennis. Another way of putting this is that sensing space effects induces the very structure of the visual world of the painting, and ordinary spatial cues induces the very structure of the ordinary visual world. The falling into place of the structure of the visual world, its perceptual "jelling," is a different visual act from recognizing and identifying particulars or types of ordinary objects within the spatial world.

Orientation in space is also categorical. The parallel here to Kant is deliberate. Space, orientation of objects in space, the essence of a three dimensional object are more like forms of intuition than like particulars and types. Abstract paintings activate these very general categorical aspects of vision. The emotive tones also are attached to such "spaces" and "things." Thus their generality, but vagueness.

There are also acts on "objects" within picture space more analogous to recognizing and identifying. Shapes and their orientation sometimes tend to express tactile qualities. But here again there is something more universal than identifying a type or particular, namely, a bare seeing in more abstract and universal categories. Because abstract painters excite the more universal aspects of vision such as texture, overlapping and atmosphere to create space, these determine the very form of seeing, and not just the content of seeing a particular or type.

The full force of pure abstracts, that is those lacking recognizable objects, is now evident: In this domain the primary visual acts of recognition and identification do not operate. At best the "things" in abstract paintings are what Austin (1962) called "odd things" such as planes, areas, and atmospheres. However, since abstracts operate on the level of "odd" things rather than ordinary objects, there is no way to evaluate the perceptual "jelling" that occurs when the painting succeeds. Thus, the phenomenal world of abstract paintings is fundamentally odd and subject to much imprecision in judgment.

In summary, there are structuring acts such as jelling whereby the painting sets up its basic spatial structure when correctly perceived. There are also visual acts within the picture space having to do with "recognition" or "identification" of "things" such as blobs, atmospheres, planes, or lines. Identifying and recognizing have to be put in quotes because they are not ordinary type and particular identification. Instead they have to do with very general schemata of things, schemata such as shapes, forms, planes, and lines in picture space. The "identification" and "recognition" of things in abstract paintings thus sets into operation our general knowledge of categories of things instead of setting into operation, as genuine identification and recognition do, our knowledge of actual particulars and types. Thus, one can recognize that abstract forms, shapes, lines, colors, etc. sometimes are abstracted from nature, and when so they retain only the most general categories of things. Of course, a painter can maximize or minimize the relation of his abstract elements to nature, but it is important to emphasize that paintings without recognizable objects or identifiable types can set in motion our abstract schema of things. As Kandinsky noted, it is more difficult to expurge nature from painting than it is to imitate her (Kandinsky, 1947). Basic visual categories function with the least visual cues. Further the points are explicitly relevant to understanding the relation of seeing and sensing: Both the structuring acts such as jelling of the basic painting space and more limited acts such as "recognition" or "identification" are visual acts. With regard to picture space, one does perceive visual causes such as texture, overlapping, and atmosphere and sense the space so set up. The visual act of structuring even with regard to effects and impressions of space (in contrast to actual space) is a visual act, in a certain mode, and with visual skills. The visual acts which are close to ordinary visual acts of recognizing and identification are visual acts in the genuine sense because one does perceive shapes, forms, orientations of shapes and forms, etc., in a picture space. Other acts of sensing such as the sensing of natural groupings (based perhaps on Gestaltist principles of grouping) are also genuine visual acts. Of course, as with ordinary vision, there is a rich interplay between structuring acts such as sensing space due to texture and specific acts of "identification." There is much redundancy and mutual reinforcing which is visually sorted into a coherent "hypothesis" or "reading" of space. Sensibility to these sorts of things is a perceptual refinement ability. Thus sensing is essentially related to seeing.

Sensibility to the Elements of Art

It should be emphasized that modes of attention, and thus sensibilities, are developed in terms of aesthetic positions such as purism, expressionism and abstract naturalism; thus sensitive vision is developed at least as much by experience with works of art as by ordinary visual acts. The elements of art cannot be considered, as has been done thus far, as abstractions such as color schemes and drawing divorced from aesthetic positions. No critic just looks at a color scheme, but looks at color schemes from a particular point of view such as purism, expressionism, or abstract naturalism. Moreover, these various aesthetic positions differentially structure the complex ordinary abilities carried over into an aesthetic context. Different kinds of sensibility do not have the same structure. For instance, a purist looks at color schemes in terms of harmonies, rhythms, color qualities such as luminosity, spatial positions of color planes, relations of color schemes to other pure painting elements such as shapes, and various tensions and reinforcing of all these levels of color schemes. The expressionist discusses sensibility and attention in many of the same terms, but with further emphasis on emotive tones, moods, expressive power or impact, suggestiveness, mythological–archetypical meanings, depth psychology and symbolisms of color schemes. The abstract naturalist also shares many terms of attention with the purist, but there is further attention to various sorts of resonances of abstract elements with nature, including suggestions, hints in the color schemes to colors of things in nature and whole relational resonances between the painting considered as a microcosm or metaphor to nature. Each of the three positions mentioned thus calls for a complex and hyphenated mode of attention and sensibility. Subsequent to the exercise of trained sensibilities of various kinds are pleasures peculiar to each, purism giving a pleasure in sensing subtleties of painting elements considered in themselves, expressionism giving a pleasure perhaps like catharsis, abstract naturalism giving a pleasure in metaphysical insight. It is further evident that the kinds of sensing abilities called for in these aesthetic positions are very different. The continuities and differences between kinds of sensibilities and ordinary visual skills are also very different. The purist might emphasize sensitivities which have some continuity with ordinary sensibilities to harmony, balance, and rhythm. The expressionist connects sensibilities to ordinary sensibilities to moods and emotive tones of color, gestures, etc.

We can make these further remarks about the relation of the natural eye and the cultural eye both of which are of course idealizations. We can very roughly divide the things which come to pervade and constitute attention into verbal and nonverbal matters, and both verbal and nonverbal matters structure ordinary and cultural vision.

In the ordinary visual world, we see objects which have all sorts of other qualities due to our expectancies of what these objects do in our activities. We see unstable forms and shapes at angles which tend to collapse. We see objects and expect tactile kinaesthetic experiences from the way they look. We see odd things such as clouds and blood, and these have wider meaning. These are nonverbal matters pervading ordinary visual attention. Also pervading ordinary attention are aspection terms such as "color," "texture," "mass," etc. Both sorts of matters can come to animate the abstract and odd "things," the very schematized and categorical "things" in abstracts. A form may be animated with tactile kinaesthetic qualities. A drop of red may come to be animated with visual images of blood and with the meaning of blood. Attention to color schemes is pervaded by the ordinary meanings of "color." Put differently, from acting and talking in the visual world, visual images and meanings are stored in all levels and kinds of memory, which can be deliberately activated by cues employed by the painter, although in the case of abstracts there is a deliberate limitation on the range of cues since no ordinary recognizable objects are present.

The structure of the abstract and the "things" in the abstract almost inevitably activate the more generalizable and categorical aspects of ordinary visual objects. Since our experience of paintings comes to be stored in all levels and kinds of memory, then Pollock's backgrounds may remind us of atmospheres in nature and thus come to be animated by images of atmosphere. On the other hand, Pollock's spaces may remind us of late cubism and thus come to be animated by images stored from viewing cubistic works. From our visual experience of paintings and our knowledge of the process of painting, the image may come to be animated with constructionists qualities. Unlike natural objects, a painting is a constructed and made object. Pollock's drip gestures may come to be animated with what it would feel like to make those gestures, with constructionists ideas of this painting. Further, not only do these sorts of nonverbal matters from the history of painting come to animate our present viewing of Pollock, but verbal matters do too, as in titles and specific declarations of intention given by Pollock. Specific verbal declarations of intention raise the very complex problem of the intentional fallacy (if it is a fallacy), and I shall return to this problem shortly. What "background of normalcy" must now mean is not just a subject with normalcy due to ordinary visual acts, but a normalcy that includes various kinds of memory derived from skills and practice on paradigm art works.

There are many levels of memory operating in the natural eye and cultural eye, and some of these levels are more easily put out of gear than others. Visual habits are very hard to put out of gear, while recognizable objects can be eliminated. Other levels of natural visual memory are not put out of operation by abstract paintings, and perhaps these levels are better exploited than ignored. They are of course very greatly exploited in the plastic qualities in abstract expressionism, in the creation of spaces by using cues from normalcy. The painting image is bound to be animated by some forms of memory from normalcy. When we go into an art museum, we can consciously employ certain levels of cultural memory, like images from members of a related school, but there are no doubt levels of the natural eye which are less controllable and will operate willy-nilly.

It is a common experience that the order of seeing a series of paintings determines striking similarities or differences. The way a painting looks depends on which paintings one has just seen. Probably this is true of what we have just seen in the normal world. Seeing an ice cream sundae makes us see some Oldenburgs differently. *Every viewing is an occasion or occurrence*, and our active memory and less consciously aware levels of memory no doubt all operate. What we will say at any one time depends on our active vocabulary at that time, and analogously how the painting will appear depends on active elements in our visual memories on many levels. There are concepts, verbal statements of intent, visual images, memory on many levels—all operating to form the painting I now see and the impressions, effects, suggestions, and evocations which come to animate this particular viewing depend on active memory, both cultural and natural, at the time of viewing. This need not be hopelessly subjective, for given an ideal of the natural eye, cultural eye, extent and relation of them, we can prune away extraneous elements in our active memory and heighten others.

The line between the cultural eye and natural eye is obviously fluid, some viewers having normal ordinary visual experiences but almost no training of the eye on paintings and others having a great deal of training on how to view paintings. Further, some aesthetic positions and painters deliberately exploit the natural eye by activating normalcy, and others deliberately limit the influence of normal seeing. Some more investigation of the relation of the cultural eye and natural eye is called for, but these few remarks can be made here. Obviously for most viewers, the natural eye has considerable advantage in terms of amount of exposure, and thus we would expect the cultural eye to be rather pervaded with habits, knowledge and kinds of attention from the ordinary visual world, pervaded as a second language often is by one's native tongue. Presumably, with sufficiently radical changes in our visual environment (given some liberties with the nature of the eye also), we could learn to sense genuinely the purported effects of any abstract painting, for we could devise an environment in which the background of "normalcy" would be contrived to make the painting work.

Obviously this is never done except in the very limited sense that the enthusiasts of a certain painter might get so much visual exposure to his work as to make the purported effects actually work, at least in the eye of a narrow coterie or clique. For the more ordinary viewer the relation of the cultural eye and natural eye is more like this: For the nonverbal aspects of attention to a painting, we would expect these to be heavily pervaded by the nonverbal aspects of the natural eye. But we need to specify how pervasive the influence is by making a further distinction in types of nonverbal matters in normalcy:

1. What has been called a background of normalcy consists of extremely basic things like scanning habits, general knowledge of correlation of looks and tactile kinaesthetic qualities. Here there obviously has to be a very great dependence of the cultural eye on the natural eye, *for the very creation of effects depends on painting cues selectively activating the background of normalcy in order to create effects.*
2. With regard to modes and centers of attention in normalcy, things which draw, stop or lead our eye, and the relation of modes and centers of attention learned from looking at paintings, there is a much looser relationship.

Normalcy in attention does not exert such influence over the cultural eye's attention and center of attention for the background of normalcy concerning attention is not presupposed and exploited to create effects. The following speculation on the relation of these two modes of attention is offered. When the element of art to which we have learned to attend is significantly like an aspect of nature to which we ordinarily attend, there is no doubt considerable influence of the natural eye on the cultural eye. For example, color-in-space-considered-puristically is significantly similar to the color aspect, and thus we can expect that matters which draw our attention to color will also operate in attention to color schemes, that is, attention to an aspect of nature will somewhat pervade attention to an element of art.

But color schemes also have autonomy, for we look at color schemes by a sort of nonfocused field viewing technique in an attempt to see the relation of color areas to each other. These differences in attention to color and color schemes are of course reflected in the pleasures of savoring colors versus the pleasures of sensing a color scheme. For an element of art such as line, which is intrinsically connected to the art of drawing, there is perhaps even more independence of the cultural eye's attention from that of the natural eye. Line drawing is not the natural aspect of outline, especially in abstract paintings. When there is a significant similarity between the visual cause of some effect and those factors attracting normal attention, we can expect natural attention to be exploited in order to cause us naturally to notice an element of art. Principles governing normal vision, such as Gestalt formation and other factors that play a role in structuring and focusing normal attention, no doubt function in the painting context.

These remarks can now be related to the above comments on visual causes and contextualism. Contextualism is lessened when our attention is naturally drawn, by genuine sensing, to modes and centers of attention by which painting effects are created. It is true, however, that subtle effects do not demand attention in ways which we would describe as striking or compelling, and thus we have to learn to sense these effects. Further, our attention is often attracted to an element of art because of our sense of craft to that element of art, and this sense of craft, as analyzed below, is developed in a cultural and not a natural context. These speculations need to be carried further.

With regard to verbal matters affecting the relation of the natural eye and the cultural eye, a different set of continuities and differences exist. We can apply verbal directions regarding how to look at a painting with great ease and flexibility; in fact, appreciation may be no more than verbal knowledge of a painting's purpose and looking at it in those terms. But, alas, we cannot see and sense paintings with such flexibility for sensibility as perceptual refinement ability is a set of skills, and like all skills it has the status of ingrained habits which are practiced in, and respond to, the context of their usual employment. Eyeside matters such as types of techniques and other matters in seeing such as scanning habits and general knowledge which works very directly and immediately in structuring the spatial world cannot be changed as easily as verbal directions on how to appreciate a painting. Thus we have the problem of the relation of appreciation and sensibility.

This very elastic postpuristic concept of sensibility is not even aesthetic. No position on purism, expressionism or abstract naturalism is assumed. Further, no claim is being made about the limits of sensibility, for the subject of suggestions and evocations of abstract paintings have not been dealt with, nor have we discussed the degree to which natural and conventional meanings can truly be sensed. Many modern critics and painters agree that one must not bring *knowledge* of symbolism, purposes and factual matters known about nature to a painting, but must be able to sense a painting's wider qualities. I have simply tried to show what sensibility is at the level of philosophy of mind. It consists of various kinds of perceptual refinement abilities; thus I have tried to clarify what we mean when we say a painting "gives a sense of ____" or "gives an impression of ____" or "has the effect of ____." If investigation of vision shows that abstract paintings really cannot carry, at the level of sensibility, the rich sort of metaphysical and expressionistic content purported for these paintings, we shall have to say that these paintings do not truly *give a sense of* many of the purported suggestions and evocations.

Sensibility and Appreciation

At the verbal level, appreciation could be as extensive as art, for we can easily shift verbal instructions. Thus we can appreciate the whole history of western art as in a book like Gombrich's (1972) *The Story of Art.* There is, however, a retarding stability in our vision. The nature of the eye, scanning habits, basic factors of orientation, general cues to the structure of the visual world, general knowledge of abstract and odd things, these all have a considerable inertia of their own. Modes of sensing cannot be put on with the same ease and frequency as appreciation, for each mode of sensing requires specializing in certain skills that may be incompatible with those of other modes of sensing. We can no more simply decide at this moment to sense a painting in its relevant mode than we can decide suddenly to be a skillful astronomical observer or biological microscopist. We can decide to seek the kind of sensibility required, but we cannot achieve sensibilities as easily as we can appreciation.

It is, of course, often surprising to discover how fruitful it is to see and sense a painting in a mode foreign to that intended by its creator; on the other hand, there are clearly times when a mode of sensing works against the work of art. Every serious painter can ask that we appreciate his point of view, but the form of sensibility we develop must respond to other considerations as well. At the level of appreciation we can have both maximum sympathy and maximum distribution with regard to other paintings, but it is doubtful whether we can have this at the level of sensibility. Here some hard choices arise, for our sensing is simply the viewer counterpart of the question of what art should be.

The distinction between sensibility and appreciation, however, can be somewhat overdrawn. A consideration of what can be called synoptic and analytic modes of attention will help soften this distinction, for in the more synoptic modes of attention there is considerable overlap of appreciation and sensibility. In fact, appreciation is essentially related to sensing, for sensing is assimilation at the level of actually seeing what were perhaps merely verbal formulations of purpose at the level of appreciation.

Where analytic modes of attention may become more appropriate to extended viewing of a painting, since it has to do with actually sensing the cause of effects present, synoptic modes of attention are usually more appropriate in the initial stages of viewing. Up to this point we have dealt primarily with the nature of analytic modes; we now need to consider synoptic modes.

Synoptic modes involve preliminary sampling of what the painter attended to most carefully, where and on what he or she expended most effort, and the nature of his or her primary purpose. This kind of sensing does not rely just upon perceptual refinement abilities, but can be increased by knowledge of the history of art and a feeling for crafts of various sorts. The purely natural eye certainly would not be drawn to the main purposes in a painting by the same cues which ordinarily attract attention or draw attention or stop attention. The non-purely visual sensing of what a painter intends requires a flexible entertainment of purposes, a part of which is a sense of various sorts of craft or accomplishment. One would hardly notice the quality of a color scheme or drawing without having experience with quality of drawing or color schemes in other works. One gets to know what quality looks like. One entertains various elements of art from various points of view until one senses some quality in the value and craft sense. There is even a sort of uptake here, the painting answers, so to speak, to some mode of sensibility (purism, expressionism, or abstract naturalism). The uptake is not purely visual as in "notice the uniqueness of Pollock's space" but is an uptake in the sense of the painting seeming richer and fuller from some aesthetic point of view. Originally, we may have expected a more innocent eye with regard to painting than we have in ordinary life, however, we must now admit that training in appreciation helps to develop sensibility to the elements of art in a way analogous to how practical experience helps develop part–whole and aspection skills.

Sensing dominant effects or impressions is an unspecialized intermediate form of sensing, a kind of sensing of fields of force, places to which attention is drawn, aspects or elements which draw attention. Dominant effect denotes the main and dominant emergent effect on a whole series of subordinated effects. Thus synoptic attention involves a true visual sensing of dominant effects and a sensing of main purposes conditioned by knowledge of the history of art. No doubt sensing dominant effects is not only a matter of causal field sensitivity based on normalcy but is conditioned by appreciation, that is by recognizing that the context of the painting is another element of art. Knowing to entertain a rich range of elements of art helps one sense the real dominant effect for one is less likely to be blind to some overriding consideration in that particular painting context. If one knows how to sense space in terms of texture, overlapping, atmospheres and color planes he is less likely to ignore the context than one who senses space only in terms of overlapping.

Synoptic attention involves feeling out the basic nature of the painting world, while specialized perceptual refinement abilities are for only certain painting worlds. I do not make synoptic and initial attention entirely a matter of perceptual sensing of effects. Synoptic attention then involves sensing main purposes, which does not involve perceptual refinement alone but is more developed by appreciation, and sensing dominant effects used as means to main purposes. The latter is a perceptual sensing of a highly contextual kind, involving sensing natural Gestalting and aspection. It is more like field looking for subtle tendencies and counter tendencies visually. The perceptual refinement abilities developed with regard to dominant effects and impressions do not involve matters such as discrimination, sensitivity and acuity. Rather they are perceptual refinement abilities to emergent effects in what are sometimes elaborate hierarchies of effects. Sensing dominant effects is obviously very basic in dealing with the problem of contextualism.

Presumably, sensing dominant effects would never develop without knowledge of typical purposes of painters, but this does not mean that one cannot, with practice, develop ability to sense dominant effects or impressions, and thus the form of synoptic sensing becomes a mode of true perceptual sensing. Many modes of attention, as well as many other skills, would be almost impossible to learn without verbal teaching, but attention and sensibility can develop integrity of their own and become skilled sensing. Averted vision is seeing, though one would never naturally notice dim galaxies. Likewise sensing dominant effects is a highly contextual sensing, though one would never naturally notice them, and thus a dominant effect is rarely a striking or compelling effect as the Müller–Lyer illusion is a striking or compelling illusion. To merely notice some subtle visual effects takes training.

Correlated to visual acts of synoptic *versus* analytical types, are critical verbal acts of synoptic (characterizing) *versus* analytical types (explaining effects). Of course, just as there is no unique level of critical verbal act, some critics doing a lot of characterizing of effects and little explaining, there is no unique level of visual act, whether synoptic or analytical. We largely learn the visual acts from the verbal acts of various sorts. This is the significance of relating attention to ostensive defining. We quite literally, as argued earlier, learn to *see in certain terms.* We assimilate "categories" in a unified eyeside–objectside act of vision. We can now add that we learn to *see at certain levels* from analytical attention to a detail or part to synoptic attention to wholes which make up elements of art.

Sensing what is important in a painting is not being visually sensitive so much as being perceptive in a wider sense. Perceptiveness includes discovering how to talk about a painting, possessing or developing a sensitivity to its purpose, while sensitivity to visual effects may be phenomenal, visual or even optical. Having great perceptiveness to a painting is not the same as merely seeing how the painting really looks. "Really looks" is a claim about visual functioning, and many perceptive remarks are not of this sort. Perceptiveness involves something other than sensibility, sometimes it involves saying things which after being said are obvious and important, such as "painter x always shows his subjects frontally" or "after period x, the painter used only analogue colors." "Hofmann's color schemes are never moody, but show a jocund and cheerful personality" is a perceptive remark, but not one requiring *visual* sensitivity. This kind of perceptiveness is very important for describing main purposes of a painter. It goes with sensitivity to purpose and to style.

Another kind of perceptiveness is to the quality of work. One's attention might be drawn to the quality of drawing because of knowledge of the state of the art, but this is not like noticing an effect. One can see quality when one's eye has art historical training and exposure. A critic needs this sort of perceptiveness, but it is different from being sensitive in some specific visual regard. There are many kinds of factors in what we might call a standard of performance. One might see quality because of familiarity with the usual level of skill in that kind of material. Departure from a standard of performance might well cause one familiar with it to notice important things about a painter, a noticing which would be perceptive but not visually sensitive. Often stating what the painter obviously did involves entertaining a wide range of what could have been done and what was not done. What is left out is important, especially if it pervades, so to speak, what was chosen. Often a choice is made polemically against other choices. Choices are made meaningful by knowing the possibilities or alternatives considered. Certainly fairness involves sensing what the painter emphasized. Knowledge of art history, books like Gombrich's (1972) *Story of Art,* certainly expand the number of purposes one considers when viewing a painting, and certain kinds of perceptiveness are obviously increased by consideration of a wide and flexible range of possibilities. Perhaps with respect to modern art being literate is not required, but what is required is almost a technical knowledge of painting. Acts of vision may be even more important than in traditional painting where much value depended on subject matter. Very sophisticated modes of attention are required, and these require knowledge of a wide range of possibilities.

Sensibility and Philosophy of Mind

It is very difficult to specify what sensibility is because none of the well-developed categories in philosophy of mind, so far as I know, describe it. It is neither an emotion, sensation, perceptual faculty, nor character trait (habits), but possesses some similarities to them all. It is like dispositions, such as habits in that habitual employment of certain terms of attention becomes ingrained, and relevant sensitivites are heightened. This is the truth in saying sensibility is a skill. It is like seeing in that it involves modes of sensory attention in contrast to imagining, projecting into, or even seeing as. Full sensibility, in contrast to the limited form of sensibility to effects, is related to emotions, moods and emotive tones in that it is sensitivity to suggestions and evocations of the painting. Sensibility is related to ordinary sensibilities expressed in such idioms as "a sense of balance," "sense of rightness," "intuition," "instinct," "sense of distance," "sense of danger," "sense of space," "sense of mass," etc., etc. Sensibility is a covering term which can be best characterized as a group of refined perceptual abilities, though this is rather vacuous until the object to which one is sensitive is specified. Ordinary life equips us with and develops a wide range of sensibilities.

Of course, the nature and proficiency of a specific sensibility varies according to the kinds of habitual activities. In ordinary contexts also it is essential to note that the sensibilities come to verifying tests unlike those in the pure phenomenal world of painting. I have divorced sensibility from what was traditionally meant by taste, and have drawn sensibility closer to sensitive perception. This certainly can affect the way we think of critical judgments. I have tried to show that learning to see abstracts is not a metaphor, but is in some ways analogous to learning to see galaxies, though there are important differences. My theory places the critic's judgments much more in the area of art historical statements of importance due to exploiting the medium, and the medium is now seen to include important parts of our background of normalcy.

CONCLUSION

The problem of contextualism, the problem of the intentional fallacy, and the problem of distinguishing projecting from sensing, that is, of distinguishing the projection of descriptions, characterizations, explanations, etc. into a painting from sensing what is actually present, are all problems of the same kind. Contextualism with regard, for example, to explaining a spatial effect is the problem of whether a known correlation in fact operates in a particular painting, whether something like texture is a cue to space in that painting. The intentional fallacy, as a version of the same problem, is expressed by statements by a painter who says "I intended to create an effect of space by the use of texture." A further version of the same problem is a critic's explanation "the space is due to the use of texture." Appreciation is seeing a painting in certain terms. Sensibility, however, is a different matter, and we cannot evaluate with any confidence a characterization or explanation of a painting effect until we have developed our sensibility as a refined perceptual ability in the mode relevant to the verbal characterization or explanation. Once we are practiced at looking at texture as creating space, once we start to see and sense definite spaces (a gradual and difficult process of learning), we can with some confidence evaluate various verbal acts such as characterizations or explanations of painting effects.

We can have no confidence in the nature, or even the existence of, Pollock's space without being practiced in a visual act of some generality. The generality can be limited or extensive. We can sense his space in terms of other works of the same period, the corpus of Pollock's works, works of other abstract expressionists, works of late cubism, works of Cézanne and those influenced by Cézanne, etc. Sensibility must, however, be a visual act of some generality. Sensibility as perceptual refinement abilities, as skills and habits of seeing and sensing, cannot be one time occurrences. Every act of viewing when attention is completed by the uptake of noticing is an occurrence, as noted above, but sensibility is the stable core of acts of viewing, and it is this stable core of a visual act of some generality by which we evaluate any characterization, explanation, etc. We should no more expect to evaluate verbal acts apart from sensibility than we should expect to be able to evaluate actions apart from more stable elements such as character traits, habits, moods, etc. Sensibility is the stable and developing core of specific acts of viewing. Analogously, we cannot characterize, describe, or even see details of a dim galaxy the first time we practice the act of averted vision. It is only by practice that we develop the relevant sort of perceptual refinement abilities. This completes the summary of my arguments for the first thesis mentioned in the introduction, namely, that we should not and cannot evaluate a critic's or painter's explanation, characterization, etc., except in the context of a developed sensibility.

The second thesis can also be dealt with rather summarily, for the problem of factual information about vision as related to critical acts of characterizing or explaining is a part of the same problem of distinguishing sensing from projecting a description, explanation, characterization, etc., of a painting effect. Factual knowledge is relevant at the level of general acts of sensing, not at the level of a specific viewing, for the same reasons given above. However, we can make these further significant, though limited, claims about the fruitfulness of the relation between investigations of vision and criticism. I expect that the most direct relevance between factual knowledge about vision and criticism will be at the level of critical *explanations* of effects, for we can reasonably expect that explanations of the form "space in Pollock is due to texture" will be both increasingly defined and, perhaps, even changed by increased knowledge about vision. One might counter by saying that all the visual causes of effects a painter and critic need to know have already been discovered in the history of painting, and there is no doubt that painters in experimenting have discovered how to create a wide range of effects. However, even so simple and well known illusions as the Müller–Lyer illusion is not definitely understood in terms of its visual causes. There is no reason to doubt that when a definitive explanation of this illusion is forthcoming, it will have phenomenological relevance in articulating and even changing the cues we thought were causing the illusion. We will be able to articulate the cues we are now only seeing which cause the effect. A causal correlation can work without our being able to say what the cause is, though no doubt we are seeing something which is consistently causing the illusion. Eventually, we shall be able to say exactly what the cue is which is causing the illusion, and this will increase our phenomenological awareness of exactly what we are seeing when we sense the illusion.

I expect the same sort of increase in phenomenological awareness in criticism. There is reason to believe that facts about vision will increasingly enter the critic's explanatory repetoire and that explanations such as "texture tends to create space" will be refined and even changed. This is not to say that science will replace criticism, for acts of sensibility are directed towards and developed by the history of painting, and the generation of effects in the painting context do not respond to the same interests or cut the same way as illusion illustrations in psychological experiments. Acts of sensibility are queer on both the eyeside and objectside. However, I see no reason to doubt that knowledge about vision will articulate and even change what we thought were the visual causes of distinct effects in painting context. There are no doubt many visual causes of definite effects we can see but can not articulate. For all these reasons, one expects critical explanations will be especially enriched by factual knowledge about visual effects.

REFERENCES

Arnheim, R. *Art and visual perception.* Berkeley and Los Angeles: University of California Press, 1954.

Austin, J. L. *Sense and sensibilia* (reconstructed from the manuscript notes by G. J. Warnock). Oxford: Clarendon Press, 1962.

Gibson, J. J. *The senses considered as perceptual systems.* Boston: Houghton Mifflin, 1968.

Gombrich, E. H. *Story of art.* (12th ed., enlarged and redesigned) London: Phaidon (distributed by Praeger, N.Y.), 1972.

Isenberg, A. "Critical Communication," *The Philosophical Review,* (July, 1949), 330–344. Reprinted in Joseph Margolis, *Philosophy looks at the arts: Contemporary readings in aesthetics.* New York: Charles Scribner's Sons, 1962.

Kandinsky, W. *Concerning the spiritual in art.* (Trans. Michael Sadleir, Francis Golffing, Michael Harrison, and Ferdinand Ostertag.) New York: George Wittenborn, Inc., 1947. P. 71n.

Kenny, A. *Action, emotion and will.* London: Routledge & Kegan Paul, 1964.

Shahn, B. *The shape of content.* Cambridge, Massachusetts: Harvard University Press, 1967.

Wittgenstein, L. *Philosophical investigations.* (Trans. G.E.M. Anscombe.) New York: Macmillan, 1953.

7

The Development of Thought: On Perceiving and Knowing

Peter B. Pufall

Smith College

Piaget's (1970b) thesis that "To know is to transform reality in order to understand how a certain state is brought about [p. 15]" seems straightforward. Yet the apparent simplicity of this statement quickly slips away as one attempts to examine the structure and function of these cognitive activities; moreover, it becomes particularly complex when one tries to reconstruct the genetic history of thought. For Piaget (1970a), knowing and its development are intimately linked to action. He presumes that thought is a biologically derived function, which not only structures the objects on which it acts but also restructures itself through its own activity. To draw out the biological analogy, any such structuring activity consists of two functions: *assimilation,* a function by which the object is incorporated into existing structures (that is, analogous to the digestive process by which food is assimilated into the blood stream) and *accommodation,* the function by which the existing structures are modified in accordance with the object to be known (that is, analogous to the change in composition of the blood as it accommodates the digested nutrients).

One consequence of this action–based theory of cognition is the denial that perception is the efficient cause of knowing. Rather Piaget views perception as a process by which only figurative aspects of objects (color, shape, texture, etc.) are known. Thus, perception is specific, referring to concrete aspects of objects, rather than to general, abstract systems of activities by which symbolic representations of objects can be constructed, transformed or related to one another. The abstract system of logical and mathematical operations by which this is accomplished is characteristic of the highest level of conceptual activity, namely, operational knowing.

Three implication arise from Piaget's treatment of perception as a form of figurative rather than operative knowing: (1) since perception is an aspect of figurative knowing it develops only insofar as developmental changes in operative functioning are reflected in figurative knowing; (2) as an aspect of figurative knowing it is incomplete, dealing with static figural states not invariants; and (3) it does not provide the basis of operative development and, in fact, if emphasized over structured transformations can yield distorted information. These implications become clearer in the preoperatory child's understanding of quantitative invariance. He infers a relation from figural states (2) which distort the underlying quantitative relation (3). However, the choice of one dimension over another as an index of what "more" or "less" means is not given in the figural state but rather is an intuition reflecting operative functioning even at the preoperatory level (1).

The distinctiveness of operative and figurative knowing is also exemplified in the development of the child's ability to perceive and reconstruct geometric forms.

Preschool children, about age 3, can discriminate among geometric forms but cannot reproduce them; all closed figures, circular or angular, are reproduced as closed circular figures. Thus, there is a developmental lag between perception and performance (Maccoby, 1968; Maccoby & Bee, 1965; Olson, 1970). The lag indicates that to perceive similarities and differences is not to know directly how they are reconstructed. The latter knowledge depends on the development of operative structures marked by the reversible relation of analysis and synthesis. These operative activities emerge slowly and are gradually elaborated into more comprehensive systems. Not until around age 4 does the child accurately copy a square, and this same square rotated 45° to look like a diamond cannot be drawn for one or two years after that. The relations intrinsic to the square do not change. The relation of that object to its field and to the child are changed, and, as a consequence, the particular action systems which have to be engaged to reproduce it are altered. That is, new operative structures have to be developed. (The recent work of Goodnow & Levine, 1973, on the grammar of action provides some provocative insights into the particulars of this developmental sequence.)

Piaget's analysis of the problem of graphic representation is often confused because of his use of the term *schema,* which is sometimes interpreted to mean image or icon (Gibson, 1966), and also because he stated that an image is an internalized activity (Piaget & Inhelder, 1969) which is often confused with a motor-copy position on perception. This confusion results from the fact that activity is often equated with movement per se, that is, the morphological pattern, and not understood as an abstract structure or scheme (Piaget, 1970a), which is generalizable and not particular.

The same type of criticism arizes when memory is involved because Piaget holds that memory implies the organization information into schemes. These schemes themselves are not learned or memorized in the restricted sense used by psychogolists but rather they exist and develop by their very functioning. He explains memory in the restricted sense as "simply the figurative aspect of the conservation of schemata (to be understood as schemes)" (Piaget, 1971, p. 187; author's own brackets).[1]

If operational knowing does not have its genesis in perception or figurative knowing in general, then how does Piaget explain the genesis of knowledge? Piaget (1967) puts it succinctly". . . every structure presupposes a construction. All these constructions originate from prior structures . . . [p. 150]." His position is stated more forcefully in the following passage:

> . . . each period of his (her) development partly explains the periods that follow. This is particularly clear in the case of the period where language is still absent. We call it the "sensorimotor" period because the infant lacks the symbolic function; that is, he does not have representations by which he can evoke persons or objects in their absence. In spite of this lack, mental development during the first eighteen months is particularly important, for it is during this time that the child constructs all the cognitive substructures that will serve as a point of departure for his later perceptive and intellectual development . . . [Piaget & Inhelder, 1969, p. 31].

In short then every structure (act of knowing) generates from another structure. This position has been interpreted as implying either some form of preformationism or a subjectivism. The former position is rejected on the grounds that operative structures develop only gradually and the latter on the grounds that structures emerge in a systematic fashion across individuals. Piaget does not deny that there is an obligatory relation between the environment and the construction of thought. Every environmental intrusion precipitates a compensating or equilibrating activity on the part of the knower. Each equilibrating activity involves both an assimilative activity (a conserving function in thought) and an accommodative activity (a nonconserving function in thought). These reciprocal functions guarantee the balance between stability and openness to new information necessary for adaptive progress.

A novel aspect of Piaget's theory is that cognitive structures not only equilibrate to environmental intrusions but are also self-regulatory. By mere virtue of the fact that the structures function they become internally modified so as to form a more coherent system. They reconstruct themselves so as to achieve a new, higher level of equilibrium and thereby become increasingly more able to compensate for environmental intrusions. As will be noted, to achieve this higher level of equilibrium, the cognitive structures become relatively independent of particular content and, thus, more abstract.

That cognitive structures function in a stable fasion fits comfortably into our understanding of homeostatic mechanisms. Consequently, each level of cognitive

[1] This explanation seems to avoid the criticism leveled by Gibson. The mind is not characterized as a collection of images which mediate perception or memory. However, to the author's knowledge there is no clear explanation of how a specific experience can be imagined or remembered. That is, if to imagine or remember is to reconstruct from operatory structures which are general there seems no way to decide what specific characteristics should be remembered, or how they are processed in the act of remembering.

development can be characterized as a set of homeostatic structures. This fact can be illustrated with respect to the preoperative period of thought where two sets of objects are equal in number if set in one-to-one correspondence. When the elements are displaced so as to destroy the perceptual correspondence, the two sets are judged to be unequal and the longer row to be numerically larger. At this level of development the homeostatic structure conserves quantity in terms of length relation. Conserving this structure does not, of course, conserve number at the level of thought. While at another level the child might judge in terms of length if the two sets differ dramatically in terms of length, he will now judge in terms of density if the lengths are comparable (Pufall & Shaw, 1972). This suggests two homeostatic functions which conserve themselves on the basis of different information. Finally, at the operative level the child judges that two sets remain equivalent even though perceptually different, indicating that the transformations and the perceptual variations they yield are compensated in thought. Thus, the developmental course seems to be marked first by a single structure which is equilibrated, followed by a transitional state of disequilibrium in which substructures are differentiated but not yet integrated. And, finally, a new state of equilibrium emerges in which these substructures are integrated. Hence, in this way, homeostasis is ultimately achieved at a higher level.

Homeostatic functioning is conservative, in the sense that it tends to maintain the child at a given level of development. Consequently, since it accounts for functioning at a given level, it cannot account for changes in level of functioning as the child moves from one period to another. At best, the above analysis in terms of homeostatic processes only provides a descriptively adequate understanding of development. But development itself implies a violation of homeostasis. Hence, to explain the transition between levels of development requires an augmentation of the homeostatic process by another process to account for change. Piaget (1971) calls this additional process, *homeorhesis.* Here the homeostatic process accounts for the continuities of development within single periods; the hemeorhetic process is needed to account for discontinuities in development exhibited between periods. Consequently, equilibration does not specify the ordered course of development; it only specifies that a structure will function and that it will respond to the object or event to be known. To supplement this mechanism, Piaget (1970a, 1971) proposes *abstraction* as a regulative mechanism of change.

For Piaget there are two forms of abstraction, each of which is action based, but which differ in terms of the focus of abstraction. *Abstraction* from *objects per se* or *physical abstraction* is the discovery of properties of objects, whereas *reflective abstraction* is the discovery of structure within the *actions per se*. It is obvious that the latter abstractions yield logical–mathematical structures while the former yields an understanding of physical properties of objects. These physical properties vary in their degree of abstractness depending on the level at which they are known, that is, sensory–motor or operatory. It is also true, then, that the nature of these abstract properties is going to reflect the functioning of logical–mathematical reasoning. Physical abstractions are physical not because they are directly perceived or known but because their reality is imputed to the object and not to actions on that object. Perhaps some examples reflecting the functioning of these forms of abstraction will make them clear.

A sensory–motor understanding of ball might include an appreciation that it can be grasped, lifted, bounced, etc. While this knowledge is clearly action-based it is also obvious that it refers to properties of objects. They have a size to which the hand can accommodate or not, a weight which is within the child's limits of strength or not, and a quality which makes it return when thrown against a hard surface. At the operational level of knowing these same properties might be known in a more abstract manner. Balls can vary in terms of their volume, mass, or elasticity. These higher level properties are discovered or abstracted through the child's own actions; however, in this case the actions are operational. That is the actions are structured so that both observed and impled transformations are considered.

A set of balls can also be logically structured, for example, transitively related. We know that if ball *A* is bigger than *B*, which in turn is bigger than *C*, then *A* is bigger than *C*. The transitive structure which makes this conclusion logically necessary is not absrtacted from these balls nor is the the structure imputed to be a property of that or any set of balls. Moreover, the transitive structure is abstracted from the child's own actions of ordering but reflected to the level of operational reasoning by virtue of the fact that action is no longer sequential (*A* is followed by *B* which is followed by *C*) but is reversible (*B* can both be larger than *C* and smaller than *A*).

Piaget's position on cognitive development has been challenged. Some have argued that cognitive development is genetically based in perceptual processes. Others have argued that cognitive development is based in action but they have interpreted Piaget to mean that development is an internalization of particular movements not the abstraction from actions. Briefly, let me take each of these in turn.

The provocative findings of Bryant (1974; Bryant & Trabasso, 1971) challenge not only when operatory schemes develop, but more significantly challenge the hypothesis that operatory schemes are abstracted from actions. Bryant (1974) proposed that young children can make transitive inferences based on perceptual information specified by an external framework. The implication of his position is that these frameworks are detected directly and that the inference is passive in the sense that the structuring framework does not have to be constructed by the child. Thus, given the appropriate perceptual conditions and minimizing the role of performance factors such as memory, inference is a necessary outcome.

There are serious questions about these conclusions given the facts of the experiment. Why is the route to success so tortuous if the inference is based on information specified in the perceptual context? While memory for the contrasting pairs seems to be implicated in the answer to this question, it seems to beg the question. Why is it such a difficult problem for the very young child to remember the relations within a pair? Perhaps the difficulties exist because the child does not have the available structures for organizing the information and, consequently, the sequence of relations is understood as arbitrary rather than necessary. There also seems to be good reason to question the perceptual nature of the inference. In one experiment the child never saw the lenths of the sticks but only saw the tops of the sticks. Yet they performed as well as those who had seen the sticks. Therefore, it seems implausible that the child necessarily "... compares different objects which he sees at different times through their own common relation to a constant background [p. 57]." Indeed, if this were the case children in the latter condition would be compelled to infer that all elements were equivalent.

While there seems to be ample reason to doubt Bryant's conclusions, there remains the need to explain the findings and, particularly, to see whether they are consistent with respect to Piaget's position. Youniss and Furth (1973) suggest that the behavior of the children in Bryant's studies does not necessarily implicate transitive inference. In an unpublished study they have shown that young children will impute a "transitive" relation to a sequence of events even though there is no logical reason to do so. By contrast, older children do not because they understand transitive logic. It seems reasonable to argue that younger children do not have an overgeneralized understanding of transitive logic but, instead, they are capable of ordering events into a sequence. Perhaps this ordering is similar to ordering a set of actions when making a plan. Once ordered one can make "inferences" about what subactivity comes before another subactivity but certainly that "inference" should not be confused with a cognitive activity implying a logical necessity.

This argument is consistent with Piaget's theory in two critical respects. One: it holds that even the pseudotransitivity behavior of young children is based in the active organization of information. Two: it suggests that logical transitivity is not at first passive nor based in figural knowing or perception.

This is not to claim that operational transitivity in particular and logical–mathematical thought in general develop out of overlearned habitual systems such as that studied by Bryant. Nor is it to be taken as a validation of neobehavioristic positions such as that of Berlyne (1954). Berlyne's interpretation, or better his transcription of Piaget's theory into behavioristic terms, attempted to capture cognitive development not as a process of abstraction but of internalization of action. He proposed that objective transformations expressed in the child's own manipulations or in his observations of other's manipulations are internalized as transformational mediating reponses. Such a mediator, presumably, is acquired in the same way as other mediating events—through the internalization of motor activities. Internalization, in mediational theories, implies an isomorphic relation between the activities which are originally overt but become covert at some later point in time. This mediational account, however, encounters several serious problems in explaining how the internalization process is initiated. Only if some executive function were imputed could internalization in the typical mediational sense be considered seriously. Then, of course, there is the attendent problem of explaining the development of the executive function and the development of its coordination with these action systems.

It seems unlikely that Piaget intends that action-based knowing should be reduced to specific motor movements. The actual movements only serve an instrumental purpose by establishing correspondences, ordering, etc.,—in other words altering the figurative aspects of knowing (Furth, 1969; Piaget, 1969). Both reflective abstraction and physical abstraction imply the construction of structures with properties that are not contained in the motor actions themselves. Moreover, abstraction implies the structuring of mental activities which go beyond those particular experiences from which the abstractions are derived. In a recent study (Pufall, 1973b), children could not predict the outcome of rotating a sequence through 180 and 360° were given experience with rotation through 135° and back again so that they could track the displacement of the objects. On subsequent testing, they correctly predicted the orderings after the 180° and 360° rotation. Clearly the children had abstracted a conceptual system which assimilated rotational transformations beyond those immediately experienced in training.

Before leaving this section and the question of mechanisms of development, it seems appropriate to reconsider abstraction in the light of the distinction between figurative and operative knowing. Operative structures are abstracted but figurative knowing participate in the process of abstraction insofar as it is the emperical link between abstract knowledge and the object to be known. The notion of elasticity is constrained by our figurative experience of a bouncing ball. Although numeric equivalence is abstracted actions of correspondence it is clear that establishing the figurative correspondence is a necessary experience if the operational scheme is to develop (Piaget, 1952; Pufall, Shaw, & Syrdal-Lasky, 1973). Moreover, it is from activities of setting up correspondences that the child discovers that figurative properties vary systematically with number. Thus, the child not only constructs an operational understanding (if nothing is added or subtracted number is conserved) but also this knowledge reflects back on figurative knowing in that the child recognizes the logical necessity of the numeric relation between two rows given their length–density relations.

Conservation in Thought

The compensatory property of thought which sets off preoperatory activity from operatory thought is its reversibility. Actions are structured as operations when one mental activity implies a reverse activity. For example, *inversion* or negation is an aspect of reversibility and is manifest in rationalizations of conservation predicated on the fact that a transformation can be reversed so as to reproduce the original perceptual relations; and *reciprocity* is manifest in the child's arguments from compensation of perceptual parameters, for example, length and density in the case of numeric equivalence.

However, Piaget, (1967) refers to compensation in another way when discussing equilibration. The more equilibrated thought becomes, the more able it is to compensate, in the sense of assimilation, information provided by an event as well as transformations relating events. This aspect of equilibration then is the shift of the knowing activity from its dependence on direct experience with the figurative object of knowing and its physical transformations to a knowing activity which assimilates an event to an equilibrated structure.

In a recent study (Pufall, Shaw, & Butcher, in preparation), we provide a demonstration of this developmental trade-off between figuratively specified transformations and operative thought. We tested 4-, 5-, and 6-year-old children on a set of number tasks. On some of the tasks the transformation conserved the original equivalence (conservation task) while another set of transformations did not (nonconservation). Half of the children could observe the transformations and half could not. On the conservation task, the youngest children did not judge the sets to be equivalent even if a conserving transformation was observed; and, while there was improvement with increasing age, only one-third of the oldest children judged that the two sets were equal if they could not observe the transformation. On nonconservation tasks, the youngest children did not judge the numeric relation correctly, but the five year old children did judge that the sets were unequal after observing the transformation, even though in some cases length was equivalent. Hence, all of the older children (5- and 6-year-olds) can assimilate a transformation relating states and do not reason exclusively from the figurative properties which result from the transformation.

This evidence makes it clear that even though late preoperatory thought reflects an understanding of transformations which change the relation from equivalence to nonequivalence, it is just as clear that thought is not completely structured so that as yet the child does not reflect on that knowledge. Consider, for example, that the child acknowledges the fact that in the case of nonconservation problems addition and subtraction changes the numeric relation, and yet does not go on to reason in the case of conservation problems that *because* nothing has been added or subtracted the sets remain equivalent. The child's understanding of transformation is restricted to the direct observation of it and does not involve, at that level, the reversible organization of transformational activities and the implication of this structuring for quantitative relations. Finally, only after about age 6 years does the child reason through the various relations among length, density, and number when presented with a figurative instance but no transformational history. At that level, operative structures are equilibrated and follow laws of logical necessity, that is, the structures of thought are conserved in that they are completely reversible.

Developmental Dependencies in Thought

One of the implications of Piaget's genetic theory of though is that we should be able to identify the forerunners of thought in the child's actions at an earlier level; and, moreover, these actions or schemata should hold some structural relation to subsequent thought. Two methods have been used to analyze this implication—or, perhaps, to attack the theory. The first tries to induce change through principles of learning, for example, reinforcement or discrimination learning sets, while restricting cognitive experiences which specify transformations or induce conceptual conflict. From this method it is reasoned that if change is induced then the theory of action based thought is incorrect and, moreover, that conceptual development follows extablished laws of learning. The second approach examines the theory by testing the predicted sequential dependencies among cognitive structures.

Those adopting the first approach have offered various interpretations of "what" is discriminated when the child learns to conserve. For example, Braine and Shanks (1965) proposed that the child learns to discriminate "apparent" from "real" differences. This argument not only begs the question of what constitutes an understanding of the distinction between "apparent" from "real" but it is also inconsistent with some developmental facts. For example, some conservations are understood before the child understands the "real–apparent" distinction (Langer & Strauss, 1972). Another variation on the theme of discrimination learning is that conservation occurs when the child learns to attend to the "relevant" and to disregard the "irrelevant" dimension (among others, Gelman, 1969; Kingsley & Hall, 1967; Wallach, Wall, & Anderson, 1967). This orientation in turn holds that the concept, for example, numeric equivalence, is a figural property as are relations such as length and density. Therefore learning involves only learning to discriminate and attend to the appropriate figural property (number) in the appropriate context, that is, in response to verbal questions asking whether quantities are equal or not. Obviously this perspective is diametrically opposed to an action-based theory of cognition.

The success of the training procedures used in all of the above mentioned studies would seem to provide support for their theoretical position. While it is difficult to argue with success (or data) the approach seems in many cases tangential to Piaget's theory and, perhaps, without any clear direction as to what is being studied.

Consider the concept of number equivalence and the implication of equating it with length and density as properties directly available in the figurative display of two linear sets. One implication is that it is a preformed concept which the child does not demonstrate in the typical conservation experiment because of performance factors. For example, there might be semantic confusion due to the ambiguous comparative phrase "same as," or there might be a memory problem as the child tries to integrate information over time. Through systematic discriminative training the child learns under what conditions he is to attend to number and under what conditions he is not being asked to attend to number. However, this approach does not explain why the cue for number is so difficult to access. Another implication is that through the education of attention number is detected as a distinctive property of any array composed of discrete elements (Odom, 1972). But again this approach does not specify the structure of the attended property, that is, what is number? It is this epistomological question that Piaget attempts to answer. Number is not to be reduced to a figural property, but is to be recognized as an abstraction. As a consequence, the perceptual properties of a set are not irrelevant but are compensated in thought. Because the perceptual properties are compensated, it becomes a logical necessity that if rows are equal in length but not in density then they are not equal numerically. If no element is added or taken away from each of two equal sets, then the sets remain equal; and a phenomenal index of this logical necessity is reflected in the look of incredulity expressed on the face of the operational child when asked if the sets remain equal.

The second approach in which sequential dependencies are examined has yielded confusing results. One set of studies found ordered relations among cognitive activities (Bower & Wishart, 1972; Brainerd & Brainerd, 1972; Inhelder & Sinclair, 1969; Moynahan & Glick, 1972; Murray & Youniss, 1968; Schlossberg & Pufall, 1974; Youniss & Murray, 1970); a second set of studies found the reverse relation (Gelman & Weinberg, 1972); while still a third set found no relation at all (Dodwell, 1962; Schlossberg & Pufall, 1974). Although all of these studies seem to tap different cognitive activities, there is no apparent trend in any of the three sets of studies to explain why some predictions hold and others do not. In spite of this confusion this attack seems the most valid and fruitful approach to our investigations of the developmental hierarchies of thought and their developmental relations.

It might be especially fruitful to combine this approach with one that includes training experiences. Inhelder and Sinclair (1969) point out that some conceptual areas are precursors of areas yet to emerge. The psychological dependency can be tested by first identifying children expressing or not expressing the precursors and then giving them training. While negative results would not necessarily refute the dependency being examined, positive results would take us beyond the descriptive level. Some very exciting experimentation on the stage sequence in object concept (Bower & Wishart, 1972) and compensation reasoning in conservation (Curcio, Kattef, Levine, & Robbins, 1972) has been done. Moreover, such a procedure combining training with sequential dependencies analysis might help clarify ambiguities in the results. Schlossberg and Pufall

(1974) identified a number of children who succeeded on one type of length task but did not conserve number while others conserved number but did not succeed on any length tasks. This observation suggests no sequential relation among these conceptual areas. However, after training on length and number tasks the former children no longer succeeded on the length task while the latter group learned to conserve number but did not improve on the length tasks. Apparently rather than no relation, we discovered an even more complicated pattern of development of cognitive structures.

THE CONSTRUCTION OF THOUGHT

In the first part of this chapter I have attempted to outline the self-regulated aspects of intellectual growth and at the same time indicate the functional relation between figurative thought which is constrained by the structure of information in the world and operative thought which is governed by laws of logical necessity. In the following section the thesis that thought constructs reality will be examined.

Construction of Object Permanency

Piaget's (1954) masterful work on the child's understanding of an objects permanency has been replicated in whole or in part by numerous researchers (Gratch & Landers, 1971; Landers, 1971). Even Bower (1967, 1971), whose early work seemed to challenge the facts of object permanency, has in recent publications validated the stages of development (Bower & Paterson, 1972; Bower & Wishart, 1972). Yet Piaget's interpretation of these findings continues to be criticized, especially by Gibson (1966). Piaget contends that an object's continued existence, is specified by the structure of intellectual activities; hence, that it is conserved in thought. However, Gibson (Gibson, Kaplan, Reynolds, & Wheeler, 1969) points out that the occluding transformation which Piaget employs in the object permanence task does not specify its destruction but only its occlusion and, therefore, the continued existence of an object. In contrast to Piaget, Gibson contends that the invariance of the object is specified in the information available in the transformations in the optic array; hence, its conservation does not depend on intellectual activity but rather on the nature of information in the world.

A final resolution of differences between Gibson and Piaget seems a goal too ambitious for this chapter. What can be accomplished is a clarification of each theorist's position with respect to the phenomenon of object permanence. Both agree that information processing is active. For Piaget this processing involves the activity of assimilating information to intellectual structures, while for Gibson it involves a perceptual activity by which environmental information is differentiated. However, both agree that information is not derived from sensations nor characterized as a system of internal registries which contain images or copies of sensory events.

They differ in terms of what constitutes perception. For Piaget (1969) perception is descrete, while for Gibson (1966) it takes place over time. A consequence of Piaget's position is that it carries with it the conclusion that perceptions are not accurate reflections of the world, that perception is subject to distortions which must be compensated for by intellectual activities. This position receives its empirical support from experiments which manipulate expectations or sets, from perceptual experiments where the quality of information is poor or the time "to act" upon it is restricted, and from studies of perceptual illusions (Piaget, 1969).

Piaget also attributes the failure to conserve quantity to the unreliability of perceptual or figurative information. However, the unreliability of information in this latter case does not relate to whether or not the child perceives the level of water as it really is in a liquid quantity conservation problem or to whether the child fails to discriminate between the acts of pouring which add or subtract something from a quantity. Piaget does not suggest that there is enhancement or filling-in of information. He proposes that the knowledge that one can have about the world is more than a mere perception of invariance.

According to Piaget intellectual activities structure these perceptions, while according to Gibson the world is structured and, therefore, intellectual mediating activities are not required. However, for Piaget, to construct this reality is to reconstruct it at the level of knowing. For the preoperatory child this reconstruction is reflected in his practical organizing of displacements of objects in space, and eventually in his symbolic representations of space. For the formal operational person this reconstruction might be a psychological theory of reality, for example, ecological optics.

In sum, while an occluding transformation specifies the continued existence of the occluded object, the child has to reconstitute that information in the act of knowing before he can practically deal with this perceptual invariant (Piaget, 1969). The reality constructed, moreover, is always constrained by the structure of the world reflected in figurative thought. As noted previously, it seems that this constraint is imperative to the construction of a structured system of thought. It probably should go without saying, but, if this constraint were not available, then the structure of knowing would either be completely subjective or perhaps nonexistent.

Construction of Spatial Reference Systems

The development of object permanence allows the child to deal with spatial organization at the level of practical knowing. Yet to develop is the capacity to represent spatial organization. This latter capacity has been investigated by examining children's map-reading skills (Pick, 1972), perspective taking (Flavell, Botkin, Fry, Wright, & Jarvis, 1968; Laurendeau & Pinard, 1970; Piaget & Inhelder, 1969; Pufall & Shaw, 1973; Shantz & Watson, 1970, 1971), and mental manipulation of spatial arrays (Huttenlocher & Presson, 1973) among others. In general, these abilities imply the operation of a reference system, that is, an abstract system within which aspects of space can be organized and by which transformations yielding new perspectives can be coordinated. Piaget and his co-workers (Piaget & Inhelder, 1956; Piaget, Inhelder, & Szeminska, 1960) have documented the development of reference systems vis-à-vis geometric systems, finding that the child's first representations of space preserve *topological* properties but do not conserve either *projective* relations or *Euclidean* values. Not until the onset of operational thought in early grade school do the latter two referential systems begin to manifest themselves in the child's spatial thinking. This developmental sequence has been replicated by other researchers (Laurendeau & Pinard, 1970, and Pufall & Shaw, 1973). A recent study by Coie, Costanzio, and Farnhill (1973) has explored the development of specific aspects of projective relations.

Piaget and Inhelder (1956) also offer another scheme within which to understand the development of reference systems. They reason that the evolution of any reference system is predicated on the functioning of infralogical[2] structures, primarily the multiplication of spatial relations, which assimilate the above referential systems. The change in cognitive structures around the first year of grade school is marked by a shift from thought which conserves binary relations to thought which conserves relations in a multiplicative scheme (Laurendeau & Pinard, 1970; Piaget & Inhelder, 1956; Pufall & Shaw, 1973).

The above analyses of spatial thinking capture the formal characteristics of knowing space, that is, the operative structures. They do not analyze the content of our spatial knowledge. The content can be specified at two levels. First, there is the *frame of reference*, which determines the nature of the axes coordinated in thought (Attneave & Reid, 1968; Rock, 1956; Rock & Heimer, 1957). One frame of reference is *egocentric* and defines the axes as near–far, left–right, and headward–footward. Another is defined in terms of axes intrinsic to the *physical* space, such as horizontals and verticals, as well as projections running at right angles to these two axes. A third is specified as the *gravitational* frame of reference specified by the force of gravity, detected by the proprioceptive systems, and the horizon. While each of these reference frames is phenomenally available (Attneave, & Reid, 1968), it is more likely that the adult will opt to organize space within a physical reference frame (Rock, 1956; and Rock &

[2] Piaget and Inhelder (1956) make a distinction between logic operations and infralogical operations. At a formal level they have equivalent properties; however, infralogical operations conserve the object of knowing through symbolic representations, for example, images, while logical operations conserve collections in terms of classes and numerical sets which are known independent of their figurative quality.

Heimer, 1957). This preference for a physical frame of reference appears to develop and has been explained within organismic theory as the outcome of the increasing tendency to differentiate self from world (Glick, 1964; Glick & Wagner, 1966; MacFarland, Wagner, & Werner, 1962).

At a second level of analysis, content refers to *perceptual features* of any space. These features range from surface qualities of color, form and texture to more abstract relational features, such as edge and corner, and relational properties, such as central versus peripheral, medial versus lateral. The surface features probably function as perceptual anchors for reference systems even during the preschool years; when the child conserves the proximity between a position and a distinctive feature he probably differentiates among the positions about that feature in terms of an egocentric system, such as "the ball is to the left of the box" (Pufall & Shaw, 1973.) The problem is that at this level the child cannot coordinate objects within a complete system nor can he coordinate objects independent of self. The more abstract properties undoubtedly have to be learned, perhaps through a process of differentiation (Gibson, 1966), and some appear to emerge as functional properties after the child has already acquired infralogical operations to coordinate spatial content of at least a two-dimensional space (Pufall, 1973b).

Spatial thinking intimately involves operative knowing in the form of infralogical structures and figurative knowing insofar as what is known always refers back to an act of perception, that is, image. Moreover, between these poles of preoperational thought is the self as the center of functional activity (Piaget, 1970a). Numerous studies indicate the continued functioning of egocentricity in spatial thinking as adults (Huttenlocher & Presson, 1973; Pufall & Shaw, 1973). This is due to the simple fact that our knowing of space at any moment is coordinated through a single perspective. This fact in turn suggests that the genesis of operational reference systems is in the actions of self in the perceptual world.

Even as young as two years of age, children understand that another person can perceive an object even though they cannot see it directly (Masanghay, McCluskey, Sims-Knight, & Flavell, mimeo); and Shantz and Watson (1970, 1971) have shown that three-year-old children expect the projective relations to self to have changed if they assume a new perspective. The child's spatial thinking is not dominated by egocentrism if he changes perspective through movement or if directed to acknowledge that a person can have a perspective different than his own. However, this same child does not possess a reference system within which he can transform perspectives and, therefore, represent accurately the other person's perspective.

These facts alone then do not provide an insight into the development of reference systems. A study by Pufall, Megaw, and Aschkenasy (1974) examined the ability of four-year-old children to locate an object in space after they had altered their perspective on that space by walking around it. Their performance on this type of task was compared to their performance on a duplicating location task in which the identical spaces were set side by side but differing in orientation. In both conditions the child had to relate what was seen from one perspective to that of another; in the case of the walk-around task the child had to remember the location as perspective was changed, while no memory factor was involved in the second condition. Four-year-old children made significantly fewer errors and no egocentric errors when perspective change was contingent on their own activity.

Huttenlocher and Presson (1973) advance the hypothesis that perspective change contingent on one's own activity might be easier because the relation of all or part of the space to self is tracked directly or symbolically (imaginally) as one moves about the space. Although the data are only in preliminary stages of analysis, Jane Megaw's thesis work using a covered space weakens the argument for an hypothetical mechanism which tracks a directly perceived space; and it seems unlikely that children as young as four years of age are tracking a representation of space. That is, it seems doubeful that the child imagines a space and then tracks his change in perspective as he moves about that space.

Perhaps the ease of conserving spatial relations when one moves through space is explained best by Gibson's (1966) conjecture that perspectives are "contained" in the act of perceiving; hence, as one moves through space the primary fact of perception is that space is rigid which implies that the projective relations among objects populating the space are constant. At the same time it is a fact that the projective relations to self are variant. It seems reasonable to postulate that it is this variance that is due to the activity of the perceiver which would motivate "exploratory activities" in search of higher-order invariances (Gibson, 1966).

This analysis can be recast in Piagetian terms. As we move through the world our activity generates changes with respect to what content is to the left or right, or near or far. However, our physical frame of reference remains invariant. At the preoperatory level, the conflict between the two might motivate abstracting a reference system by which each of these frames of reference can be transcribed into the other. Such a reference system would coordinate perspectives so that an egocentric perspective would be understood to be relative but, perhaps more importantly, would eventually allow us to differentiate exhaustively those spatial relations specified within an egocentric frame of reference from those specified within a physical frame of reference.

Our investigations of spatial thinking help to clarify the developmental relations among egocentrism, operative thought, and figurative aspects of space. The basic technique has been to present the child with two identical spaces set side by side. These spaces can either be oriented the same way or one can be rotated, usually 180°. If the child is organizing space egocentrically, then it should lead to predictable errors in the rotated condition when she tries to place an animal on her space, which duplicates the experimenter's placement on the other space.

The first study was not developmental; only kindergarteners were tested (Pufall, 1975). As was expected theses children made a high percentage of errors when the child's space was rotated 180°, the vast majority of these were egocentric. However, when the child's space was rotated 90° she made fewer errors and almost no egocentric errors. The reduction in egocentrism does not seem to be related to the degree of rotation per se as much as to the effects of the two rotations. The spaces were simulated farm scenes with a road running through the middle near to far and a stream running through the middle left to right. When one is rotated 180° these aspects are realigned with each other and with the child's egocentric system. When one is rotated 90°, the stream of one is in the same axial orientation as the road in the other. As a consequence an egocentric attitude would change the feature next to which the object was placed. Additionally, the animal's orientation would have to be shifted from parallel to a right angle to a feature. A more recent study (Pufall, Megaw, & Aschkenasy, 1974) yields results consistent with these assumptions. The spaces were circular and the objects on them were inside an isosceles triangle. Rotation did not produce any figurative congruence between spaces nor did it produce similarities with respect to an egocentric frame of reference. Although errors were high, the percentage that were egocentric never reached the same magnitude as those found with rectangular space.

Apparently, if the two spaces are figuratively similar, then the children organize space egocentrically but not when they are dissimilar. Perhaps in both cases they approach the spaces egocentrically and alter that attitude only if the placement yields perceptual discrepancies. When these discrepancies are detected the child shifts to a "world" orientation; and while not always correct in their placements, they infrequently function egocentrically.

In another set of studies we presented children, 6 and 10 years of age, with space divided into quadrants with pegs in each corner of each quadrant. Some children had colored pegs and performed very well, essentially making no errors of location (Pufall & Shaw, 1973). Other children had white pegs in the corners of each quadrant (Pufall, 1973b). In the latter condition, the younger children, in contrast to the older children, made many errors, and the majority of them were egocentric. They appeared to organize the contents of quadrants egocentrically. For instance, if the experimenter's animal was located on the near side of the far right hand peg, the child would put hers on the near side of the far-right peg, irrespective of quadrant. Even in making their errors the 6-year-old children indicated that they were structuring space, logically multiplying the dimensions of near–far and left–right. Their intellectual functioning reflects concrete operational reasoning. As long as there is perceptually distinct information to be organized, they can do and organize it. But in its absence they resort to an egocentric orientation.

Our final experimental condition has yielded interesting information about the child's capacity to imagine the rotation of planar spaces. We showed the children two completely symmetrical spaces which when rotated looked the same as before rotation. Then we placed an animal on our space and asked the child to imagine what it would look like when rotated 180° and to indicate his answer on his display. Those children who had experienced the spaces with colored pegs in each quadrant (Pufall & Shaw, 1973) made numerous errors, the older children being more likely to make egocentric errors than the younger children. From their behavior, turning head and trunk and pointing their finger so as to describe a circle, it appeared that they were processing the transformation in a way similar to the adults in Shepard and Metzler's (1971) study. They seemed to be imagining a unit; for the 10-year-old children the unit appeared to be the content of the quadrant moving through space which they did not relate to the whole space. This led to some odd placements as the child would change a location from the center to an outside corner. Those 10-year-old children who had been previously tested with white pegs did not show many errors. Although their activities were not systematically recorded, they seemed to be less likely to try to twist and turn to achieve a new perspective. Rather, they seemed to be using another type of transformation, that is, inverting the relations such as near–far while at the same time maintaining the correct relation of the object to abstract features of the space, such as the midline vertical. The older children might not differ from the younger in terms of operative structures, such as logical multiplication, as much as they differ from them in terms of the abstract relations organized within these structuring activities.

A Model of Spatial Thought

A model might serve the purpose of summarizing the data and speculation about children's spatial thought. The model consists of three assumptions about the relation of self to world:

1. The primary reference frame is *self* and has to be so by virtue of the act of knowing and preceiving.
2. The world is assumed to be invariant, that is, rigid.
3. We shift from an egocentric frame of reference to a physical frame if the egocentric frame of reference generated relations substantially inconsistent with the physical frame. The model also consists of three assumptions about development.
4. The development of cognitive reference structures is due to activities, on relations intrinsic to the world, perceptual activities a la Piaget and Inhelder (1956) or exploratory activities a la Gibson (1966).
5. These are enhanced by self-world discrepancies.
6. Even after the child has developed abstract referencing systems, development occurs in terms of detecting abstract geometric invariants.

REFERENCES

Attneave, F., & Reid, K. Voluntary control of frame of reference and slope equivalence under head rotation. *Journal of Experimental Psychology,* 1968, *78,* 153–159.

Berlyne, D. C. Knowledge and stimulus–response psychology. *Psychological Review,* 1954, **61,** 245–254.

Bower, T. G. R. The development of object permanence: Some studies of existence constancy. *Perception and Psychophysics,* 1967, **2,** 411–418.

Bower, T. G. R. The object in the world of the infant. *Scientific American,* 1971, **225,** 30–38.

Bower, T. G. R., & Paterson, J. G. Stages in the development of the object concept. *Cognition,* 1972, **1,** 47–55.

Bower, T. G. R., & Wishart, J. G. The effects of motor skill in object permanence. *Cognition,* 1972, **1,** 165–172.

Braine, M. D. S., & Shanks, B. L. The development of conservation of size. *Journal of Verbal Learning and Verbal Behavior,* 1965, **4,** 227–242.

Brainerd, C. J., & Brainerd, S. H. Order of acquisition of number and quantity conservation. *Child Development,* 1972, **43,** 1401–1406.

Bryant, P. *Perception and understanding in young children.* London: Methuen, 1974.

Bryant, P. E., & Trabasso, T. Transitive inferences and memory in young children. *Nature,* 1971, **232,** (5311), 456–458.

Coie, J. D., Costanzo, P. R., & Farnhill, D. Specific transitions in the development of spatial perspective-taking ability. *Developmental Psychology,* 1973, **9,** 167–177.

Curcio, F., Kattef, E., Levine, D., & Robbins, O. Compensation and susceptibility to conservation training. *Developmental Psychology,* 1972, **7,** 259–265.

Dodwell, P. C. Relation between the understanding of the logic of classes and of cardinal numbers in children. *The Canadian Journal of Psychology,* 1962, **16,** 152–160.

Flavell, J. H., Botkin, P. T., Fry, C. L., Wright, J. W., & Jarvis, P. E. *The development of role-taking and communication skills in children.* New York: Wiley, 1968.

Furth, H. G. *Piaget and knowledge: Theoretical foundations.* Englewood Cliffs, New Jersey: Prentice-Hall, 1969.

Gelman, R. Conservation acquisition: a problem of learning to attend to relevant attributes. *Journal of Experimental Child Psychology,* 1969, **7,** 167–187.

Gelman, R., & Weinberg, D. H. The relationship between liquid conservation and compensation. *Child Development,* 1972, **43,** 371–385.

Gibson, J. J. *The senses considered as perceptual systems.* Boston: Houghton Mifflin Company, 1966.

Gibson, J. J., Kaplan, G. A., Reynolds, H., & Wheeler, K. The change from visible to invisible: A study of optical transitions. *Perception & Psychophysics,* 1969, **5,** 113–116.

Glick, J. A. An experimental analyses of subject-object relationships in perception. (Doctoral dissertion, Clark University.) Ann Arbor: University Microfilms, 1964.

Glick, J. A., & Wagner, S. Effect of variation on distance between subject and object on space localization. *Perceptual and Motor Skills,* 1966, **23,** 438.

Goodnow, J. J., & Levine, R. A. "The grammar of action": Sequence and syntax in children's copying. *Cognitive Psychology,* 1973, **4,** 82–98.

Gratch, G., & Landers, W. F. Stage IV of Piaget's theory of infants' object concepts: A longitudinal study. *Child Development,* 1971, **42,** 359–372.

Huttenlocher, J., & Presson, C. C. Mental rotation and the perspective problem. *Cognitive Psychology,* 1973, **4,** 277–299.

Inhelder, B., & Sinclair, H. Learning cognitive structures. In P. H. Mussen, J. Langer, & M.

Covington (Eds.), *Trends and issues in developmental psychology*. New York: Holt, Rinehart, & Winston, 1969. Pp. 2–21.

Kingsley, R. C., & Hall, V. C. Training conservation through the use of learning sets. *Child Development,* 1967, **38,** 1111–1126.

Landers, W. F. Effect of differential experience in infants' performance in a Piagetian Stage IV object-concept task. *Developmental Psychology,* 1971, **5,** 48–54.

Langer, J., & Strauss, S. Appearance, reality and identity. *Cognition,* 1972, **1,** 105–128.

Laurendeau, M., & Pinard, A. *The development of the concept of space in the child.* New York: International Universities Press, 1970.

Maccoby, E. E. What copying requires. *Ontario Journal of Educational Research,* 1968, **10,** 163–169.

Maccoby, E. E., & Bee, H. L. Some speculation concerning the lag between perceiving and performing. *Child Development,* 1965, **36,** 365–377.

MacFarland, J. H. Wagner, S., & Werner, H. Relation between perceived location of objects and perceived location of one's own body. *Perceptual and Motor Skills,* 1962, **15,** 322.

Masanghay, Z. S., McCluskey, K. A., Sims-Knight, J., & Flavell, J. H. The development of inference about the visual percepts of others. mimeo.

Moynahan, E., & Glick, J. Relation between identity conservation and equivalence conservation within four conceptual domains. *Developmental Psychology,* 1972, **6,** 247–251.

Murray, J. P., & Youniss, J. Achievement of inferential transitivity and its relation to serial ordering. *Child Development,* 1968, 1271–1268.

Odom, R. Effects of perceptual salience on the recall of relevant and incidental dimensional values: A developmental study. *Journal of Experimental Psychology,* 1972, **92,** 285–291.

Olson, D. R. *Cognitive development: The child's acquisition of diagonality.* New York: Academic Press, 1970.

Piaget, J. *The child's conception of number.* London: Routledge & Kegan Paul, 1952.

Piaget, J. *The child's construction of reality.* New York: Basic Books, 1954.

Piaget, J. *Six psychological studies.* New York Random House, 1967.

Piaget, J. *The mechanisms of perception.* New York:Basic Books, 1969.

Piaget, J. *The child and reality: Problems of genetic psychology.* New York: Grossman Publ., 1970. (a)

Piaget, J. *Genetic epistomology.* New York: Columbia University Press, 1970. (b)

Piaget, J. *Biology and knowledge.* Edinburgh: Edinburgh University Press, 1971.

Piaget J., & Inhelder, B. *The child's conception of space.* London: Routledge & Kegan Paul, 1956.

Piaget, J., & Inhelder, B. *The psychology of the child.* New York: Basic Books, 1969.

Piaget, J., Inhelder, B., & Szeminska, A. *The child's conception of geometry.* New York: Harper Torchbooks, 1960.

Pick, H. Mapping children–mapping space. Paper presented at the meeting of the American Psychological Association, Honolulu, Hawaii, 1972.

Pufall, P. B. Egocentrism in spatial thinking: It depends on your point of view. *Developmental Psychology,* 1975, **11,** 297–303.

Pufall, P. B. Developmental relations between egocentric and coordinate reference systems. Symposium paper at the 1973 meeting of The Society for Research in Child Development, Philadelphia, Pennsylvania, 1973. (a)

Pufall, P. B. Induction of linear-order concepts: A comparison of three training techniques. *Child Development,* 1973, **44,** 642–645. (b)

Pufall, P. B., Megaw, J. S., & Aschkenasy, J. Developmental changes in perspective taking: Differences between looking and acting. Paper presented at the meeting of the Eastern Psychological Association, Philadelphia, Pennsylvania, 1974.

Pufall, P. B., & Shaw, R. E. Precocious thoughts on number: The long and short of it. *Developmental Psychology,* 1972, **7,** 62–69.

Pufall, P. B., & Shaw, R. E. Analysis of the development of children's spatial reference systems. *Cognitive Psychology,* 1973, **5**, 151–175.
Pufall, P. B., Shaw, R. E., & Butcher, M. The development of number: A study of figural and transformational properties in number judgements, in preparation.
Pufall, P. B., Shaw, R. E., & Syrdal-Lasky, A. Development of number conservation: An examination of some predictions from Piaget's stage analysis and equilibration model. *Child Development,* 1973, **44**, 21–27.
Rock, I. Orientation of form on the retina and in the environment. *American Journal of Psychology,* 1956, **69**, 513–528.
Rock, I., & Heimer, W. The effect of retinal and phenomenal orientation on the perception of form. *American Journal of Psychology,* 1957, **70**, 493–511.
Schlossberg, B., & Pufall, P. B. An examination of the developmental relations among seriation, number, and length. Paper presented at the meeting of the Eastern Psychological Association. Philadelphia, Pennsylvania, 1974.
Shantz, C., & Watson, J. S. Assessment of spatial egocentrism through expectancy violation. *Psychonomic Science,* 1970, **18**, 93–94.
Shantz, C., & Watson, J. S. Spatial ability egocentrism in the young child. *Child Development,* 1971, **42**, 171–181.
Shepard, R. N., & Metzler, J. Mental rotation of three dimensional objects. *Science,* 1971, **171**(3972), 701–703.
Wallach, L., Wall, A. J., & Anderson, L. Number conservation: The roles of reversibility, addition-subtraction, and misleading perceptual cues. *Child Development,* 1967, **39**, 425–442.
Youniss, J., & Furth, H. G. Reasoning and Piaget. *Nature,* 1973, **244**, 314–315.
Youniss, J., & Murray, J. P. Transitive inference with nontransitive solutions controlled. *Developmental Psychology,* 1970, **2**, 169–175.

8

The Mechanics of Growth and Adaptive Change

Michael Cunningham

University of California, Santa Cruz

INTRODUCTION: WHY PSYCHOLOGY MUST USE MECHANICAL MODELS OF THE MIND

It is impossible to be *absolutely* certain that a theory of any sort is ever true. For example, one theory that many of us believe strongly is that no one is capable of moving objects just by thinking about them (psychokinesis). However one is sure of this theory, there is still the barest logical possibility that everyone but myself is capable of psychokinesis but for reasons unknown have formed a global conspiracy to hide this fact from me. Indeed, the only thing one can "know" for sure are the theories or fantasies one chooses to believe on the basis of evidence deemed both appropriate and secure. Thus, scientific skepticism is merely a healthy confession that we are all vulnerable to error and, therefore, should remain open to all reasonable arguments.

Consequently, in this chapter I wish to share with you my beliefs and theories regarding the nature of cognitive growth and change. Two major points will be made: First, all such theories should be publicly expressible in the clearest and most concise form possible. Second, the best possible form such theories can take to meet the first requirement is to be *mechanistic.*

But must psychology ultimately rely upon mechanistic theories of mind, that is, theories expressed in terms of explicit functions for which there exist procedures by which the value of such functions may be precisely computed. One obvious reason for an affirmative answer is that by their very nature such mechanistic theories can be shared publicly since they are formally precise rather than just intuitive. Let us explore this argument for a moment.

Two kinds of theories are possible: mechanistic (formal) ones which can always be made public and intuitive ones which usually cannot be and hence necessarily remain private beliefs. Mechanistic theories, unlike intuitive ones, can be reliably communicated to other people because there exists a convention by which definite conclusions can be drawn from the theory by anyone appropriately tutored. Such theories can be reduced to finite descriptions of mechanical procedures for calculating the answers to the various questions that might be posed. Furthermore, these theories are so simple and mechanical that one can safely communicate them to even the most naive and obstinate colleagues. On the other hand, private theories cannot so communicate although one may value them highly. From such intuitive theories, however, one may fashion public theories that can be safely broadcast without fear of futile argument over misunderstandings and without fear of embarrassment from friends who profess to accept them but cannot agree about their implications.

Thus, a mechanical view of the mind (and the universe) is imposed on us by the social desire to confirm our ideas with others. Even if something is perfectly understood, in a nonmechanical way, say by intuition or revelation, and all answers to all questions could be given correctly, one would still be unhappy with the theory until it could be understood by others. It is at this point that mechanism is essential.

With this understanding of the reasons for using mechanisms (e.g., algorithms, computations) for scientific theories or models, I would like to proceed to a discussion of three classes of mechanism that people have been able to use.

THREE CLASSES OF MECHANISM OR PUBLIC THEORY: TABLE, STATE, AND GROWING MACHINES

Class I: Table Machines

The simplest kind of theory that can be transmitted to someone is an exhaustive list of all possible conditions (or perhaps all questions that might be posed for the theory) together with a description of what happens as a result of each condition. Abstractly the set of conditions about which the theory has something to say might be represented as an input alphabet. For each symbol in the input alphabet there is one output symbol. The correspondence of an output symbol for each input symbol is simply memorized or listed in a table. A table theory or machine might be schematized as shown in Fig. 1. This machine would operate by receiving an input symbol and emitting an output symbol as directed by its table of input–output pairs. Such a theory, to my mind, is about as predictable, rigid, and mechanical as you can get, and still be capable of producing psychologically nontrivial behavior.

To be communicated to other people, the description of a table machine must be finite. A complete description would define an alphabet of the symbols used and an operation or a list of all input–output pairs in the machine's table. Of course the alphabet of symbols might be very large and the operation performed

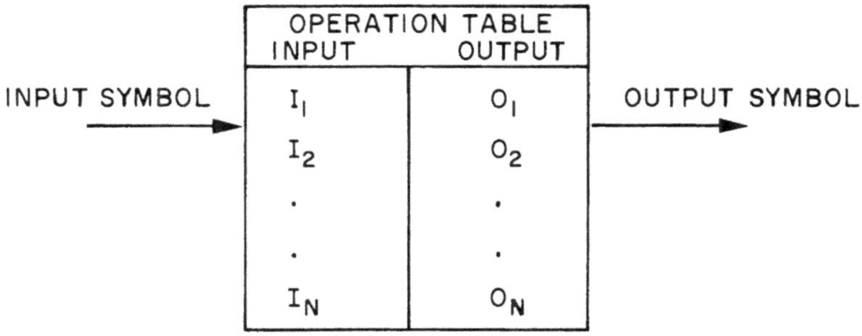

FIG. 1. A table machine, the simplest kind of public theory or raw data.

may be very complex (a different output for each input). A table theory could be very big and sophisticated if only humans were patient enough to use and communicate it. For example, we might let each word in the English language be a different symbol in the alphabet. Or we might let each pair of words be a single symbol. With an alphabet having a separate symbol for each string of 500 or less English words, we could construct a table theory that described with an output of "yes" or "no" all grammatical sentences of interest to almost anybody. There is absolutely nothing wrong with such a theory of grammar except that humans cannot deal with it. The number of symbols and the table it uses are too big. For the same reason, table theories are inadequate for describing organisms that grow or learn or change their behavior with time. Since a table does not change, it will always give the same output each time it receives the same input. If we want a theory for something which has input–output behavior that may change in time, then the time must be included as part of the input symbol so that different parts of the table will be used for different times. Even worse, an organism's behavior depends not only on its input and the time, but on the whole past history of the organism, so the organism's history must be part of the input symbol for a table theory. Fortunately there are other classes of mechanism that deal more satisfactorily (economically) with time changes of input–output behavior.

Class II: State Machines

A table machine can be made into a state machine by adding a variable which is used to save at least part of the most recent output symbol and then using this stored output as part of the next input symbol as suggested in Fig. 2. State machines are usually defined so as to have a set of internal state symbols. In such a case the input to the operation table is assumed to be a pair of symbols; one from the environment (the real input symbol) and one from the machine itself (the feedback state symbol). Similarly on the output side of the operation table there are pairs of symbols; one is output to the environment and the other is

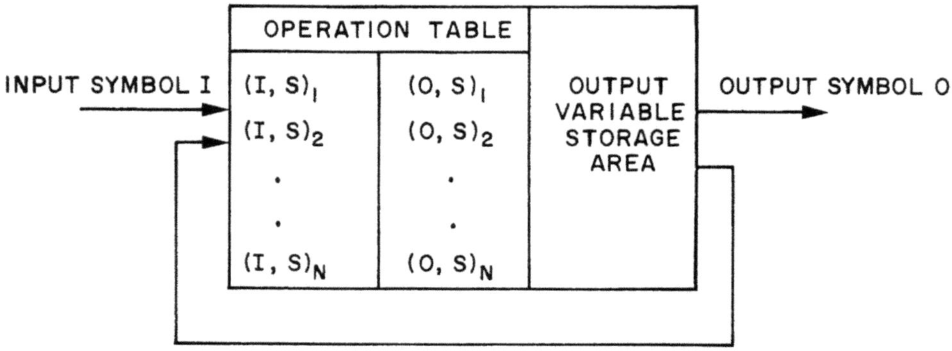

FIG. 2. A state machine, a more powerful and common kind of public theory.

sent back (or retained) in the machine. Just as we were willing to let two words be represented by a single symbol, we now might let an input and state symbol pair be represented by a single symbol or at least a single entry in the one operation table.

On the other hand it is often more convenient to break the state machine into parts. For example a separate table might be given for the real output symbols and another table for the internal state symbols as in Fig. 3. This decomposition into two pieces results in more tables, but the tables might be simpler. For example if there were *S* different internal states and *O* different outputs, then there might be as many as *S* times *O* different pairs in the right-hand side of the table in Fig. 2. But the total number of different symbols appearing in the right-hand side of both tables in Fig. 3 would be at most *S* plus *O*, which is less. There would be repeats of the same symbol on the right in Fig. 3. Because of these repeats it may be possible to eliminate some of them and shorten the table to gain some descriptive economy. For example, if for a particular state symbol appearing on the left-hand side of a table, no matter what input symbol it was paired with, we read off the same thing on the right side of the table, then we would replace all such entries with a single entry in the table. This entry might have a blank where the input symbol on the left would have been, to indicate that no matter what input, this entry is used. Even further, it may be possible to decompose the machine more by using several state variables instead of one. Eventually we might end up with a large number of variables, each with its own relatively small operation tables as suggested in Fig. 4.

Machine decompositon (which might also be applied to table machines) is a complex problem. For a simple example, I remember that it has something to do with the reason a hundred numbers can be easily represented with only ten symbols and two decimal place variables. Even more, it has to do with decimal arithmetic being easy because the one's place is relatively independent of the ten's place. Machine decomposition consists of discovering or inventing a representation of a machine where the variables are relatively independent of each other.

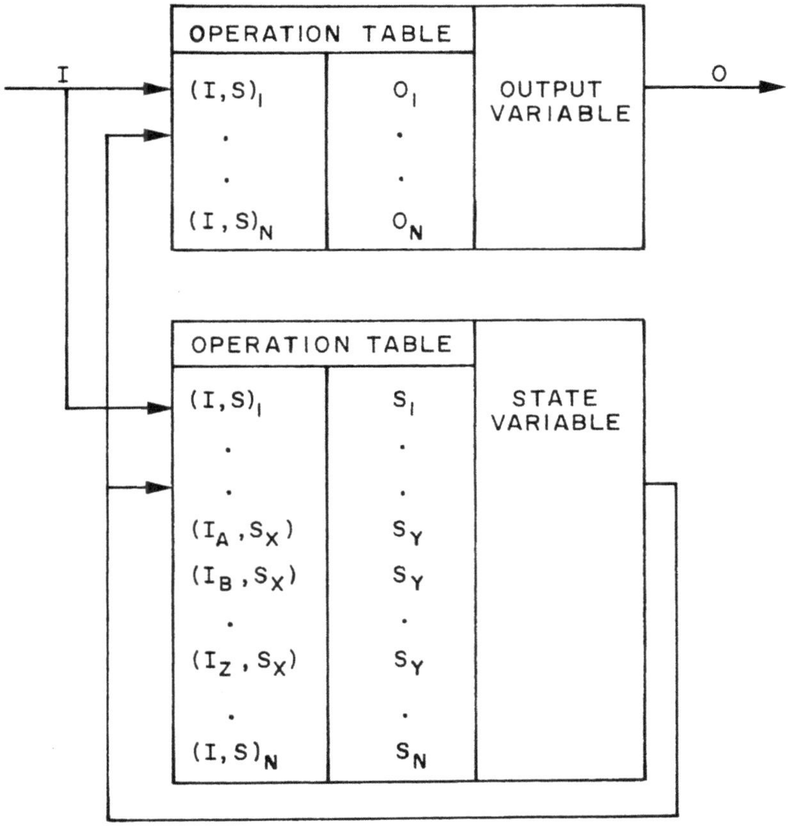

FIG. 3. A partly decomposed state machine with the entries in the operation table for the state variable showing some cases where the state does not depend on the input.

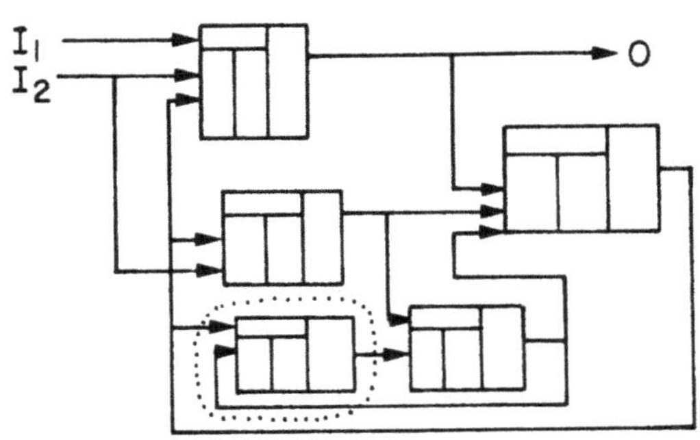

FIG. 4. A thoroughly decomposed state machine.

It is this relative independence that allows descriptive economy. Also, relative to one variable, another may seem invariant; such a relative invariant in a large table may also be described as a symmetry. The discovery of these relative invariances is a form of induction.

A few points should be stressed. First, every decomposed machine, as in Fig. 4, still behaves exactly the same as some single table machines, as in Fig. 2. It is not true that a larger number of variables and a more complex structure of interconnections make possible the expression of a theory that couldn't have been expressed by a single variable. All the structure and interdependence that is made explicit in a decomposition was implicit in some one large operation table. Still, we might prefer the more complex looking decomposition because it makes the structure more apparent, and further because it may afford an economy of description and communcation. Not only might it be a shorter description, but it may also be that the colleague to whom the description is being given, already knows some of the tables from other theories.

Relative to a table machine, the chief advantage of a state machine is its capacity for storing some internal information or resetting internal conditions so that it can respond differently to the same input depending on its internal state. For example an organism may respond to a stimulus and then change the value of some internal association strength so that it later responds differently to the same stimulus. Further, the internal settings may depend on a long sequence of past events, and not just on the most recent input.

The chief disadvantage of a state machine is that it must be initially set up to handle not only what an organism learns, but also everything it might have learned but did not. For example, a state machine to describe the human acquisition of a language must have all the states and all the operating tables that describe how the states change for every language a person might learn and for every possible order in which each language might be acquired. Describing the acquisition of language may seem much too much to expect from any theory, public or private. But even for very simple things, state machines are inadequate. For example, it is not possible to set up a state machine that can be used as a theory of such a simple language as arithmetic. This is because arithmetic has indefinitely large numbers, so no finite communicable state (or table) machine can even list all the numbers. In our every day lives we get around this limitation by memorizing some finite tables for multiplication and addition of the ten digits, and then using these tables on indefinitely large numbers which we construct by tacking on more decimal places. We let our numbers grow by adding on a new variable in a certain place, as needed.

Class III: Growing Machines

A state machine can be made into a growing machine simply by having some rule for adding a new variable to the network of already existing variables. (In an equivalent undecomposed machine this would be the same as creating new symbols and enlarging the operation table.) Such a new variable is suggested by the circled unit in Fig. 4. Rather than simply changing the value of some variables, a growth process actually changes a state machine into a different state machine.

There are three important things to be said in favor of growing machines. First, they can do things that no table or state machine can do, simply by virtue of their ability to grow larger than any one state machine. For example a growing machine can at least count as high as anyone wants, just by growing a string of decimal-place variables. Second, growing machines provide for two different kinds of change. One is the change in the value of the variables as described by operations and the other is the change in structure described by the growth process. Thus there is a real qualitative difference in functioning and growth. Too often our theories of growth (and learning) have merely been theories of adaptation where a few variables only change value more gradually than others. Growing machines provide a way to separate growth and adpatation conceptually. Third, growing machines are superior because they offer new forms of descriptive and communicative economy. Describing growth as the addition of a variable to a decomposed machine (instead of the addition of symbols and the expansion of the operation table) allows the machine to grow very fast. Adding one variable that takes on ten values is equivalent to *multiplying* the size of the operation table and the alphabet of symbols by a factor of ten. Also, instead of having to describe first off a very large state machine, it may be possible to describe only a very small one together with a simple rule or growth process for gradually enlarging it.

How simply can the growth process be described? We need only specify three things which are; when the new variable is added, what the new variable's operation table is, and how the new variable is linked to the old ones. This might easily be done by saying that the new variable is to be added whenever a certain old variable takes on a certain value, that the new variable always has a certain specified operation table, and that the new variable is linked to old variables that at the time have taken on certain values. (Some care must be taken that the old variables can be made to depend on the new one, there must be so to speak unused sockets on their left sides for the new variable to plug into.)

A well-known result by A. N. Turing and others indicates that it is possible to specify very simple growing machines that are powerful enough for one of them to be able to imitate any other machine of any sort whatsoever that anyone has been able to think of (Arbib, 1969; Minsky, 1967). Put another way, the fundamental nonresult of twentieth century logic has been that every attempt to come up with a new class of machines (or a new method of computation) has ended up being a particular variation of growing machines and equivalent in capacities to one of Turing's Universal Tape Machines. For much further detail, I refer the reader to a text on automata theory (the ones by Minsky, 1967, or Arbib, 1969, are good). I only want to make two points here. First, it seems very likely that growing machines of one sort or another are the most powerful and comprehensive kind of public theory we can have—although no one has been able to prove this, it just turns out again and again. And second, the kinds of growing machines that have been developed so far have been designed primarily to make it easy to prove certain things about what they can do. As a result their growth processes and the interconnections of their variables are kept very simple, so while it is possible to prove that they can do just about anything, it is clear that it takes a lot of specifying to get them to do any particular thing. The problem I would pose is; what kind of growing machine is complex enough and powerful enough to serve with descriptive economy as a convenient public theory for psychology?

Recapitulation

By way of recapitulation I will set out a little mnemonic I use to remember the important concepts involved in a growing machine. A growing machine consists of a set of constructs:

$$\langle V, A, L, O, G \rangle$$

where V is a finite set of *variables* which at any one time are assigned certain values or symbols; A is a finite *alphabet* or set of symbols which are assigned to (or stored in) the variables; L is a finite set of *links* or interconnections that define how the variables depend on each other (this is the structure of the machine); O is a finite set of *operations* or tables of finite size which define how the variables change from one symbol to another (this is the functioning of the machine); G is a finite set of *growth processes* which describe exactly when new variables are added, how they are linked to old ones, and what their operation tables must be.

Of course, to be a public theory a growing machine must have a fairly *small* and *complete* description, and further a description which is so *simple* and *explicit* that even my most obstinate and simple minded colleague (a computer?) can agree to understand it.

What I have described here is obviously not itself a public theory. I have not been able to come up with a general method for precisely defining growing machines that satisfies me. The trouble has been that different ways of describing a growing machine make it easy to do or understand different things. What I am looking for is a general way of describing them that will make it easy to construct machines that will stand as public theories or models of human intelligence. That is no simple task so I am unembarrassed to admit failure. Should I come up with something interesting, rest assured I'll let people know.

In the next section, I will describe some of the causes of the difficulties typically encountered. These difficulties arise because there are certain things which it seems obvious one should try to do in a public theory. Some of these things may not be as relevant to the description of human intelligence as they appear, and in fact by making them easy to do, we may be making our real task more difficult.

SOME THINGS WE SHOULD STOP WORRYING ABOUT

Mechanical Mind

First, as argued earlier, we should stop worrying whether or not the mind is mechanical and simply decide that public theories *should* be mechanical. Mechanism has to do with the communicability of theories, not with what the theories are about. If we accept this concept then we can turn our attention to a search for powerful, economical ways of describing mechanical theories in general.

Closed Systems

Once we decide to use public theories that can be given finite, mechanical description, we often outdo ourselves by also deciding that theories should only be about finite things; we set up permanently closed, self-contained systems (mechanisms). It is appropriately modest to agree that we will not try to have one mechanical model for the whole universe, but by strictly fixing the outer boundaries, it becomes difficult to talk about the interaction between the thing a mechanical theory is about and the rest of the environment or universe. In modern quantum mechanics for example it is difficult to write out the equations for a set of particles without assuming first that there is absoutely nothing else in the universe that can ever interact with them. If is difficult to add complications as they are encountered. More generally, mathematicians develop some solutions to systems of equations in which variables change values, but they have great difficulty when the equations themselves change or when new variables and equations are allowed to be added—even in a lawful manner.

Growing machines force our attention to the environment, encouraging us to consider seriously where the new variables come from. A growing machine that is being simulated on a computer grows by appropriating from the host computer new unused memory locations. Turing's machines grow by having an attendant in the environment who patches on new lengths of computing tape whenever the machine needs more. And one carries out large computations by appropriating scraps of paper from the environment that nobody else is using, and writing on them. At another level molecules in the blood stream help to restructure brain cells.

So, instead of talking only about closed fixed systems, we could begin by talking about very large, incompletely described systems which will represent an environment. The environment could be partially described as a set of variables, alphabets, links, operations, and binding processes. In the environment new variables are not grown, but rather old ones are reconnected by changing their links; a variable depends at one time on one variable and then again on another. Now a completely specified subsection of the environment can be described as a growing machine whose growth process is simply an environmental binding process viewed locally. Some of the growing machine's variables will be linked to variables outside in the environment and these variables will serve as the input–output interface with the environment as suggested in Fig. 5.

Now within this larger open system we can address ourselves to some interesting questions. One is, how are environmental variables incorporated into the growing machine; how do my brain cells restructure themselves using nutrients from their environment, and what does this do to the variables of electrical activity in my brain (at another level of discourse). Another interesting question is, how does the structure of the environmental variables working through the input–output interface change the values and structures of the growing machine variables and vice versa; how do we use bits of paper in our computations and more generally interact with the environment behaviorally? It is in serious preparation for answering this last question (or even asking it intelligently) that the ecological approach to psychology insists on a more careful investigation of the environmental variables themselves.

Prediction before the Fact

Prediction seems bound up with a whole host of mathematical concepts such as proof, convergence, stability, and the halting problem for Turing machines.

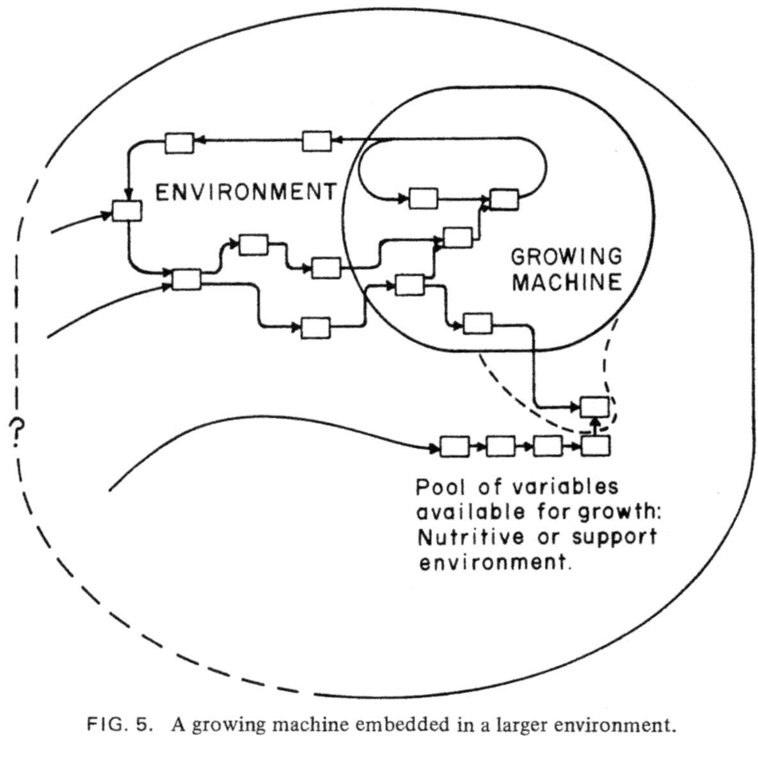

FIG. 5. A growing machine embedded in a larger environment.

However, an excessive concern for these things is inappropriate for a public theory of human intelligence. The plain fact of the matter is that human beings are not always predictable, or stable, their behavior does not generally converge, and there is only one way to halt them. When a child learns something new, its behavior does not converge or settle down or stabilize, but rather its behavior moves into new modes of exploration and interaction with the environment that never occurred before.

It turns out that growing machines too are generally unpredictable and unstable, their behavior does not always converge, and they halt only if carefully supervised. Most investigators of growing machines consider all these as highly undersirable properties, and they devote much effort to avoiding them. It seems to me these properties make growing machines very attractive possibilities for modeling and understanding human behavior. But let me focus on the single property of predictability and try to explain why it is unreasonable to expect any public theory to predict human behavior (or generally the behavior of things which grow).

First let us consider Class I or Class II public theories. Suppose Mr. Philosopher Knowitall approached Mr. Human Perverse and says:

KNOWITALL: I have a completely successful theory for predicting human behavior.

PERVERSE: I don't believe it. Prove it to me.

KNOWITALL: O.K. Propose any situation you like. I'll write on a piece of paper my prediction of what you will do in that situation. Then we'll put you in the situation, see what you do, and compare the results with my prediction. Of course you cannot see my prediction until you've done your thing.

Mr. Perverse agrees and after dozens of trials in which Mr. Knowitall unerringly predicts his behavior, our transcript resumes:

PERVERSE: I don't understand. Even when I acted as I normally wouldn't, you still knew what I was going to do.

KNOWITALL: Yes. My theory takes into account that you may know I am watching and playing the prediction game with you.

PERVERSE: (admiringly) That's quite a theory. Could you possibly teach it to me?

KNOWITALL: (unwittingly) Why yes, of course. It's a public theory. Here's how you figure out what you'll do. . . .

At this point in this kind of argument there is always a gap where the alleged theory is supposedly described. After his instruction Mr. Perverse proposes:

PERVERSE: (slyly) Let's test your theory again on me . . .

There is little more than literary exercise in recording Mr. Knowitall's disappointment when his theory turns out to be 100% wrong now. Since Knowitall's public theory was at best a state machine, Mr. Perverse was able to compute in advance its prediction and so do exactly the opposite. In fact Knowitall's theory couldn't have worked all the time in the first place if one of the test situations led to Perverse learning or guessing the theory. This argument, however, is unsatisfying because it all depends on Mr. Perverse finding out about the theory. Except at that one particular point, it still might be possible that his behavior was predictable. In practice we know that no one can predictably manipulate a human's behavior for long before the human finds out or suspects and reacts perversely. To be predictable is sooner or later to be too simple.

Let us suppose now that Mr. Perverse approaches Mr. Philosopher Knowbetter who has a Class III (growing machine) theory of human behavior.

PERVERSE: Tell me, do you have any good theories about human behavior?
KNOWBETTER: As a matter of fact I do.
PERVERSE: (with exaggerated interest) Please do tell me about them.
KNOWBETTER: Certainly. . . .

Here too the curtain of the unknown occludes our view. The transcript resumes with:

PERVERSE: Well now, I suggest a little test of your theory's predictive powers OK? I'll propose a situation and you write down your theory's prediction of what I'll do in that situation. Then I'll do whatever I do in that situation and we'll see if you were right.

KNOWBETTER: (smiling) OK. But you needn't even tell me what the situation is.

PERVERSE: (shaken) What!?

KNOWBETTER: (whips out a piece of paper) As a matter of fact I already have my prediction written down here.

PERVERSE: But there is nothing written on that paper!

KNOWBETTER: I know. My theory has nothing to say about how you will act. My theory only sets up a working model of a purely hypothetical person.

PERVERSE: But can't you at least predict what your hypothetical person would do?

KNOWBETTER: Well, yes, but calculating that prediction is exactly equivalent to setting up the model and letting it run. So by the time I have the prediction, my hypothetical person has already done it. In my theory, description, prediction and simulation are all the same thing.

PERVERSE: What if I told your theory *about* a hypothetical person *to* that hypothetical person?

KNOWBETTER: Well, then your educated hypothetical person would be quite a different person from my original one.

PERVERSE: Ah. I see. The predictions my educated person could make using your theory would only apply to your original hypothetical person but not necessarily to my educated one. I don't suppose it would do any good to describe to my educated hypothetical person all about educated hypothetical persons? Or maybe I could let him use your theory to work that out for himself?

KNOWBETTER: No, I'm afraid not. The description would never catch up to the person using it.

PERVERSE: Don't you have anything to say about real persons?

KNOWBETTER: Not much. Except that they behave rather like my hypothetical ones. I'm better at making up hypotheses than I am at finding out all the facts anyway.

PERVERSE: Aren't you interested in the facts at all; don't you want to make any predications about the real world? Like, how about setting up a hypothetical me?

KNOWBETTER: No. I'm only human. I'd rather decide how things could be than find out. Besides, in the process of setting up a good model of you I would have to find out a lot about you. Just in the process of asking you questions about yourself, I'd be changing you into a different person. I'd never keep up with you. And it's too much work anyway. I'd rather set up seomthing simple and let it do the work of growing into something complex. Even if I cannot predict your behavior, if I could only make something that behaved like you, I would be content to rest. I learned quite a bit trying to play that prediction game. It's made a new person out of me.

THE GROWTH OF HUMAN INTELLIGENCE

Many people have been building growing machines (that is, theories) for some time now, particularly in the fields of logic and computation. In fact there are thoroughly mechanical theories about such an advanced human endeavor as the process of mathematical proof. Mechanical procedures have been described (Robinson, 1965, but see Nilsson, 1971) which will always construct a proof for a theorem provided only that the theorem turns out to be true. The only trouble is these proofs may take a very long time to construct, which is to say, they may not be very elegant. I think this may be due to the fact that we are very timid about the growth processes we give to these theories. If we let these things grow too fast, we may not be sure they will ever stop growing, converge, stabilize, or come to a halt and give an answer. In fact the best mechanisms we have now for logic may never halt if given what turns out to be a false theorem. Excessive growth is a very real and practical problem for mechanical theorem provers, and the logicians, to achieve their goals, must do something to keep their theory under control.

However, the valid concerns of the logicians are not so relevant for a theory of human behavior. In particular, for a growing machine simulation of human behavior, it is not so important that the thing come to a halt (representing death?), or that it converge (doesn't a healthy human's behavior diverge into more and more varied forms) or that it stabilize (do humans ever make up their minds irreversibly?). So, the growth processes used in growing machines so far may not do what a psychologist would like. In the remainder of this section I propose to tell everything I think I know about the growth process of human intelligence. (It is unbearable resisting the temptation to end this section here.)

Human Theorem Proving

Let me begin with the people I have been talking about. What is it that logicians are able to do in their proofs that their mechanical theory does not? I think it is this: Often a logician will introduce a new symbol, give it precise definition in terms of the old symbols, and then using this new symbol, speed on with the proof. (More generally, a mathematician will say "Suppose we had a certain (function, set, matrix, . . .), call it λ, such that . . .") So far, a growing machine can do the same. The new symbol and the clumping together of old symbols in a certain relation represents intellectual growth for the logician. The new symbol is not merely an abbreviation that simply shortens the proof, rather it serves to focus the logician's attention and to restructure his thought. In terms of a growing machine, the logician's linking up of a new variable, or the expansion of an operation table by adding a new symbol, may make possible new, more economical decompositions. The resulting enlarged system may thus end up being more easily communicated, and, in view of the limits on our processing capacity (Miller, 1956), more easily used.

So, human intelligence grows by creating a new variable, or new values an old variable may assume, such that the global complexity of the whole system increases, but the local complexity of the problem being solved is reduced. The real problem is how to know (mechanically) what will reduce local complexity. For now my suggestion is simply that growing machines and decompositon may give us a formal handle on the problem, and further, a careful psychological investigation might give us some content to cast into that form. A few examples may help to clarify this conclusion.

Hierarchies of Theories

Again and again I see complex theoretical systems constituting themselves in a hierarchical structure of levels of discourse as characterized in Fig. 6 (see Simon, 1969). This structure seems to me likely to have something to do with the way human intelligence grows. Take the mathematics-to-psychology hierarchy for example. Of course it is too late to watch its growth, and the real history is very complex, but evidence of how people developed these theories remains. Specifically, the particle of physics is theoretically a clumping of interrelated states, operators, equations of motion and mathematical properties. The atom or

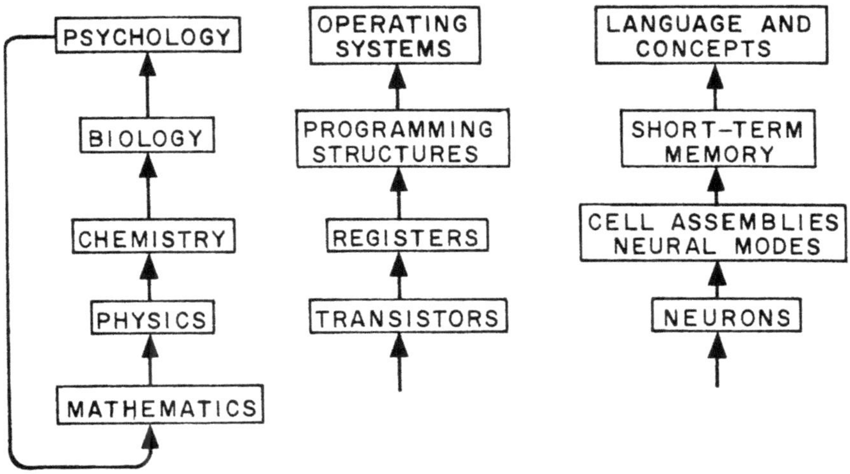

FIG. 6. Hierarchies of theories where a number of constructs at a lower go together to make a unit in a higher theory.

molecule of chemistry is a clumping of closely related particles in physics. The living cell of biology is a clumping of molecules in chemistry. Psychobiology is a special clump of cells, and psychology is this clump of cells interacting with clumps in the environment. And a mathematical concept should be a clump of some sort in psychology so the system closes on itself in a circle (which is better than dribbling on forever, or mysteriously terminating in unquestioned axioms).

The transistor-to-operating-systems hierarchy represents the levels of discourse for talking about a computer. No one tries to describe a computer as a wiring diagram of its transistors, rather the transistors are clumped into modules and registers. A discussion of more complex functions treats as units, whole clumps of memory registers called routines, programs, or data structures. And a really serious discussion talks about operating systems of interacting programs and data structures. One nice thing about the computer example is that its development is recent and proceeded in fact from bottom (with vacuum tubes or relays for transistors) to top.

In my own work I took the step from cell assembly to short-term memory in the third hierarchy of Fig. 6. Arguing with Hebb (1949) that a discussion of behavior in terms of individual neurons would be too complex, I postulated patterns of neural activity as the basic unit that seemed reasonably definable in terms of assemblages of large numbers of neurons throughout the brain. But rather than making that definition, I started with cell assembly as a basic simple unit, postulated how they would interact and grow, and used this higher-level theory to model the development of sensorimotor intelligence described by Piaget. Then when I was done, it became clear that my clumps organized themselves into larger clumps (or at least I began seeing them that way) that could act as short-term memory for the goal directed behavior that emerges towards the end of Piaget's sensorimotor period (Cunningham, 1972). Quickly regrouping, I pushed along towards language, but as Quillian (1972) suggests, it is now essential to give a simple mechanical definition of the behavior and formation of these larger clumps and use them to describe the yet higher functions.

So, again and again we see humans complicating their problems by inventing new terms, ideas, concepts and clumps and ending up with a whole nest of complexly interrelated theories instead of just one. But by increasing the global complexity we simplify a particular local discussion.

Piaget's Objectification

Another example of this complex-simplification process of intellectual growth is Piaget's theory of sensorimotor intelligence. Piaget writes of the coordination of basic sensorimotor schemata which could in a growing machine be represented as the creation of a new variable with links to the two previously independent sets of variables that might represent the schema of the hand and of the eye. Piaget asserts that the child attributes objective reality to something grasped and seen only after such coordinations have been constructed or learned. Here it seems that the coordinating variables are themselves the child's internal representation of an object. In a sense the coordinating variables are the child's hypothesis that there are objects that exist independently of any one of his sensorimotor schemata. Such new variables at once complicate matters (since anything seen may now be reached for, and anything sensed with the hand may now be looked for) but also simplify matters by allowing the two schemata (of hand and eye) to function together in a coordinated fashion with objects in the environment. There is only one object rather than disparate sights and tactile stimulation.

ARTIFACTS OF INTELLIGENCE

Presumably, we cannot know with certainty anything except what it is for the moment that we choose to believe. So, too, we do not know that anything at all is mechanical—except for the mechanical theories we can construct and use in our heads. If ecological psychology has a concern for the environmental structures that are immediately available to the senses, then the other side of that coin must be a concern for the structures that the mind imposes on its environment. These complexly structured theories, mechanisms and languages are artifacts molded by the mind and I can think of no better data from which we might get an impression of the mind than from the things that are solely of its creation. Computers and programming languages provide a particularly good example as Papert (1971) suggests.

Mechanism theorists tell us that it seems every mechanism, algorithm, computation or public theory can be expressed as some kind of growing machine. The puzzle I would propose is this: What is the psychological reality behind such things as symbols and variables, linked structures and operations, and growth or binding processes? And if there is any, why is it we evolved to think this way?

REFERENCES

Arbib, M., *Theories of abstract automata.* Englewood Cliffs, New Jersey: Prentice-Hall, 1969.

Cunningham, M., *Intelligence; Its organization and development.* New York: Academic Press, 1972.

Hebb, D. O., *Organization of behavior.* New York: Wiley, 1949.

Miller, G., The magical number seven plus or minus two, *Psych. Rev.,* **63,** 81–97, 1956.

Minsky, M., *Computation: Finite and infinite machines.* Englewood Cliffs, New Jersey: Prentice-Hall, 1967.

Nilsson, N., *Problem-solving methods.* New York: McGraw-Hill, 1971.

Papert, S., in his public lectures and with Minsky in *Project MAC Progress Report,* MIT, 1971.

Piaget, J., *Origins of intelligence in children.* New York: Norton, 1963.

Quillian, M. R., review of *Intelligence, Science* **178,** 971–972, 1972.

Robinson, J. A., A machine oriented logic based on the reolution principle, *Journal of the Association for Computing Machinery,* 1965, **12,** 23–41.

Simon, H., *The sciences of the artificial.* Cambridge, Massachusetts: MIT Press, 1969.

SECTION C
Acting and Perceiving

9

Preliminaries to a Theory of Action with Reference to Vision

M. T. Turvey

University of Connecticut
and
Haskins Laboratories

Of the distinction which his own efforts had done much to foster, Magendie commented in 1824:

> The organs which concur in muscular contraction are the brain, the nerves, and the muscles. We have no means of distinguishing in the brain those parts which are employed exclusively in sensibility, and in intelligence, from those that are employed alone in muscular contraction. The separation of the nerves into nerves of feeling and nerves of motion is of no use: this distinction is quite arbitrary [cited in Evarts, Bizzi, Burke, Delong, & Thach, 1971, 111–112].

More recently this viewpoint has been expressed in a different but closely cognate fashion by Trevarthen (1968): "Visual perception and the plans for voluntary action are so intimately bound together that they may be considered products of one cerebral function [p. 391]."

In the light of such remarks, it is curious that theories of perception are rarely, if ever, constructed with reference to action. And, while theories of perception abound, theories of action are conspicuous by their absence. But it must necessarily be the case that, like warp and woof, perception and action are interwoven, and we are likely to lose perspective if we attend to one and neglect the other; for it is in the manner of their union that the properties of each are rationalized. After all, there would be no point in perceiving if one could not act, and one could hardly act if one could not perceive.

Of course, history has not been remiss in comments on the relation between perceiving and acting. From the time of Aristotle it has been taught that the motor system is the chattel of the sensory system. Nourished by the senses the motor system obediently expresses in automaton and relatively uninteresting fashion the cleverly contrived ideas of the higher mental processes, themselves offshoots of the sensory mechanisms. In this view, action is interpretive of the sensory mind and thus, in principle, problems of coordinated activity are secondary to and (if we assume an associative link between sensory and motor) independent of problems of perception. It has also been taught, usually with less fervor, that perception is a disposition to act: to perceive an event is to be disposed to respond in a certain way. Modification of this view leads to a constructive theory of mind in which it is argued that higher mental processes in addition to perception are skilled acts that reflect the operating principles of the motor system. In short, experience is constructed in a fashion intimately related to the construction of coordinated patterns of movement. So far as action assumes primary importance in this approach to mind, we would expect its proponents to put great store by the analysis of coordinated motions. However, where motor-theoretic interpretations have been forwarded to account for perception and the like, statements of how acts are actually produced have been either absent or trivial (e.g., Bartlett, 1964; Festinger, Burnham, Ono & Bamber, 1967; Liberman, Cooper, Shankweiler, & Studdert-Kennedy, 1967; Sperry, 1952). Curiously, action-based theories of perception and of mind in general have been advanced on a nonexistent theory of action.

Thus, it seems that the theory of action deserves more attention than it has received and that the interlacing of the processes of perceiving and acting is a problem we can perhaps no longer afford to ignore. This chapter is a preliminary and speculative response to these reproofs. Its purpose is twofold: first, to identify a set of basic principles to characterize the style of the action system in the production of coordinated activity; second, to describe, in a rough and approximate way, how the contents of vision may relate to the processes of action. To a significant degree, the ideas expressed in this chapter derive, on the one hand, from the work of Nicolai Bernstein (1967) and Russian investigators who have followed his intuitions, and on the other hand, from the analysis and amplification of the Russian views by Peter Greene (1971a, b). We begin our inquiry by illustrating an equivalence between problems of action and problems of perception and cognition (cf. Turvey, 1974).

THE CONSTANCY FUNCTION IN ACTION, AND ACTION AS CONSEQUENCE

A visually presented capital letter A can occur in various sizes and orientations and in a staggering variety of individual scripts. Yet in the face of all this variation, the identification of the letter remains, for all intents and purposes, unaffected.

This phenomenon of constancy is not limited to the domain of perception, but is equally characteristic of action. Thus, the letter A may be written without moving any muscles or joints other than those of the fingers. Or, it may be written through large movements of the whole arm with the muscles of the fingers serving only to grasp the writing instrument. Or, more radically, one can write the character without involving the muscles and joints of either arms or fingers, by clenching the writing instrument between one's teeth or toes. It is evident that a required result can be attained by an indefinitely large class of movement patterns.

On examination of the phenomenon of constancy in action we might raise the query: How can these indefinitely large classes of possible movement patterns be stored in memory? The answer is that they are not. Clearly, I do not have on record in memory all possible temporal sequences of all possible configurations of muscle motions that write A; indeed, I have yet to perform them and by all accounts I never will. The essential question about our A-writing task, therefore, can be stated more fundamentally: How can I produce the indefinitely various instantiations of A without previous experience of them?

In response to this question let us turn our attention to linguistic theory. A departure point for transformational grammar is that our competency in language is such that we can produce and understand a virtually infinite number of sentences. As Weimer (1973) has pointed out, there are echoes of Plato's paradoxes in Chomsky's (1965) claim that our competence in language vastly outstrips our experience with it. Chomsky's claim is motivated by the observation that experience with a limited sample of the set of linguistic utterances yields an understanding of any sentence that meets the grammatical form of the language. To explain this competency is, for Chomsky (1966), a central problem in the theory of language. But, given the points advanced above, the constancy function in action is likewise indicative of a competency that exceeds prior learning. The child, we may note, learns to write A under conditions that restrict her to a small subset of the very large set of A-writing movements. But she is able subsequently to write A with practically any movement pattern she chooses, that is, she can write A in novel ways. A writing is creative in the sense that language is creative.

The search for a workable account of the creativity manifest in language has led transformational grammarians to what can be aptly described as "the explanatory primacy of abstract entities" (Hayek, 1969). The idea is that the speak–listener has at his disposal an abstract system of rules or principles, referred to as the deep structure, that allows him to generate and to understand an indefinitely large set of sentences, referred to as the surface structure. This distinction, drawn in linguistic theory, between deep and surface structure will prove relevant to our analysis of action in two important respects. The first is the idea that deep structure is far removed from surface structure; grammarians argue that although the deep structure determines the surface structure, it is not manifested in the surface structure. The second is that the child must come to determine the nature of the underlying deep structure from a limited experience with surface structures. Chomsky and his colleagues assume that the child essentially "looks through" the utterances she hears to the abstract form behind those utterances. The child is said, therefore, to construct a theory of the regularities of her linguistic experience. Similarly, our hypothetical child learning to write the letter A must determine from her limited experience with the set of A-writing movements a theory of how to write A. Thus, we may conclude that the ability to write A in indefinitely various ways is based on procedures that are abstract and generative, like the grammar Chomsky has in mind for language. Others have sought similar parallels between action and grammar (e.g., Lenneberg, 1967).

There is an interesting upshot to this discussion of action constancy. We generally say that an abstract representation, a concept, underlies our ability to recognize indefinitely various As. Let us call this the perception concept of A. Now clearly we may propose that there is an action concept of A underlying our ability to write A in indefinitely various ways. So in general are there two different kinds of structures, two different classes of concepts—one specific to perceptual events, the other specific to action events? In short, is the constancy function in perception achieved in ways fundamentally different from the constancy function in action? If it is, then the construction of theories of how we identify events (see Neisser, 1967)—theories of the perception concept—can proceed virtually independent of the construction of theories of the action concept. On the other hand, if the constancy function is treated in the same way in both perception and action, that is, if there is only one class of appropriate structures or only one class of appropriate procedures for achieving constancy, then the theory of identification and the theory of production ought not to be considered separately. In this view, which I suspect is the more viable, any account of constancy in perception must also be an account of constancy in production—a perceptual account of constancy must be potentially translatable into an action account of constancy. If such a translation is in principle implausible then we may suppose that the account is incorrect.

The reader's attention is drawn in this preamble to one other important aspect of action—its relation to "consequence." An act modulates environmental events, but philosophers have found that they cannot conceptually distinguish between occurrences that are actions and occurrences that are consequences (see Care & Landesman, 1968). A typical argument from language usage might go like this: George kicks the football (of the round kind) and scores the goal that wins the championship. Now we could say that George kicked the football and that a consequence of his action was that a goal was scored. Or we could say, just as appropriately, that George scored a goal with championship-winning consequences. "Scored the goal," therefore, can be viewed either as consequence or as action. We may wish for criteria to determine which occurrences should receive an action label, and which occurrences should receive a consequence label. Unfortunately, the criteria that have been advanced have not met with any degree of universal approval.

The failure to distinguish conceptually between action and consequence is understandable from the viewpoint of Bernstein (1967). He comments:

> Whatever forms of motor activity of higher organisms we consider . . . analysis suggests no other guiding constant than the form and sense of the motor problem and the dominance of the required result of its solution, which determines, from step to step, now the fixation and now the reconstruction of the course of the program as well as the realization of the sensory correction [p. 133].

The implication is that an action plan as a statement of consequences is not a static structure but a structure that is by virtue of processes we will discuss below, continually becoming. Yet in all of its phases of change, phases that constitute a tailoring of the plan to the current kinematic and environmental contingencies, the essential character of the action plan remains invariant. What is to be achieved, what is to be consequence of the evolving pattern of motions, persists from the conception of an act through its evolution to its completion.

The arbitrariness of distinguishing between action and consequences parallels the arbitrariness of distinguishing between perception and memory. As William James (1890) observed and as other concur (e.g., Gibson, 1966a), the traveling moment of present time is not a razor's edge and no one can identify when perception ends and memory begins. The distinction between action and consequence is as much a will-o'-the-wisp as the distinction between perception and memory.

THE DOMAIN OF ACTION CONCEPTS

For present purposes we will entrust ourselves to the view of concepts as functions (Cassirer, 1957). Thus, we may represent an action concept such as that for A writing as $A(x)$ and explore the nature of the variable x that enters into this function. We perform this exercise in order to identify some fundamental characteristics of the action system. Let us assume that the elements entering into $A(x)$ are a proper subset of the set of elements that enter into any rule for coordinated activity. And, in addition, that coordinated activity is under the management of an "executive system" and that the character of the elements entering into $A(x)$ and any other action function are mirrored in the character of (or constraints on) this system.

One view of the executive is that expressed in the traditional piano or push-button metaphor. In this metaphor muscles are represented cortically in keyboard fashion, one muscle per key, and central impulses to the muscles are held to be unequivocally related to movement. The essence of the view is that the executive instructs each muscle individually. At the outset we may question the worth of this metaphor simply on the ubiquity of reciprocal innervation: The intricate and extensive interrelation among muscles makes it both arduous and wasteful to instruct them singly. But more importantly, we can argue (as did Bernstein, 1967) that there cannot be an invariant relation between innervational impulses and the movements they evoke.

Consider the movement of a single limb segment in relation to a fixed partner and under the influence of a single muscle. The differential equation describing this situation is of the form

$$I\, d^2\alpha/dt^2 = f(E, \alpha, d\alpha/dt) + g(\alpha),$$

where I is the inertia of the limb segment, α is the angle of articulation, E the innervational level of the muscle, and f and g are the functions determining respectively, the muscle force and gravitational force acting on the limb segment.

If we take $E = E(\alpha, d\alpha/dt)$, that is, independent of time and simply a function of position and velocity, then the equation reduces to that for a movement of a limb indifferent to central influences; in brief, an instance of central paralysis. If, for contrast, we assume that the excitation of a muscle is solely a function of a centrally predetermined sequence and independent of the peripheral variables of position and velocity, that is, $E = E(t)$, then the equation is that of a system insensitive to, or ignorant of, changes in local conditions. Obviously, it is more judicious to argue that $E = E(t, \alpha, d\alpha/dt)$, in which case the fundamental equation can be written

$$I\, d^2\alpha/dt^2 = f\,[E(t, \alpha, d\alpha/dt), \alpha, d\alpha/dt] + g(\alpha).$$

Solutions to equations of this kind depend on the initial conditions of integration. The implication, therefore, is that in order to obtain the same movement for various values of α and $d\alpha/dt$, different innervational states E will be needed. In a word, the relationship existing between impulses to the muscle and the movement of the single limb segment is equivocal: same impulses may produce different movements and different impulses the same movement.

We continue Bernstein's argument by noting that in the temporal course of moving a limb segment changes occur in the force of gravity (which is related by a function $g(\alpha)$ to the angle of articulation) and in other external forces operating on the limb and that these changes affect E. Now suppose that the limb segment traces out a rhythmical motion. This rhythmical motion can be identified with a function relating the required forces at the joint to time. However, another function can be identified relating forces at a joint to time, and the forces in this case correspond to the changes in the external force field. As a result, the sequence of impulses to the muscle can be interpreted as determining a mapping of the function generated by the variations in the external field over time to the desired function. Now suppose that the same rhythmical motion is traced out with the hand holding on separate occasions (a) a hammer, (b) a baton, and (c) a can of beer. The function relating the changes in the external force field to time will differ in each instance even though the pattern of the rhythmical movement is unchanged. In each of the three instances a different mapping would be required from the function generated by the external force field to the desired function specifying the rhythmical pattern. The import of this, as Bernstein (1967, pp. 20–21) points out, is that the sequence of impulses to the muscle "cannot maintain even a remote correspondence" to the factual form of the movement.

A third criticism of the push-button metaphor is that if the executive behaved in the fashion suggested, instructing each muscle individually, then it would be called upon to manage the enormous number of degrees of freedom that the motor apparatus attains

> . . . both in respect to the kinematics of the multiple linkages of its freely jointed kinematic chains, and to the elasticity due to the resilience of their connections–the muscles. Because of this there is no direct relationship between the degree of activity of muscles, their tensions, their lengths, or the speed of change in length [Bernstein, 1967, p. 125].

Herein lies a fundamental principle which simply states that the number of degrees of freedom of the system controlling action is much less than the number of mechanical degrees of freedom of the controlled system (Kots, Krinsky, Naydin, & Shik, 1971). A homely example illustrates the point: try writing a letter, for example, *W*, while simultaneously making circular motions with a foot. An experimental illustration is provided by Gunkel (1962): when one makes movements of different rhythms simultaneously with the two hands, the amplitude of the movements performed by one of the hands is modulated by the frequency of the movements performed by the other. Thus, it is not difficult to demonstrate that the number of degrees of freedom of the executive is very small; on the push-button metaphor it would have to be very large. We can conclude, therefore, on three counts, that the executive does not, or indeed cannot, control individually each motor unit or even each muscle participating in a complex act.

One consequence of the conclusion that in the course of performing a coordinated pattern of movements the executive system does not control muscles singly is that it need not be apprised of peripheral details, since such information would be irrelevant. In this light let us take another look at the equation for the movement of a single-limb segment. In that equation the innervational impulse is expressed as a function of time, angle of articulation (muscle length), and velocity, that is, $E = E(t, \alpha, \mathrm{d}\alpha/\mathrm{d}t)$. But if the executive is stripped of the responsibility for instructing individual muscles and if it is ignorant of the current, precise details of the external force field then clearly executive instructions are not written in the form relevant to that field, that is, in the form $E(t, \alpha, \mathrm{d}\alpha/\mathrm{d}t)$.

Moving a single-limb segment rhythmically requires an action plan and we may suppose that executive instructions spell out that plan (in the sense of defining the contours and timing of the movement) through a sequence of impulses of the form $E(t)$. The action plan and impulses of the form $E(t)$ must correspond, or so it would seem, to the factual form of the movement, in contrast to impulses of the form $E(t, \alpha, d\alpha/dt)$, which on the above account bear no such relationship to the movement. Thus, we see that the action plan (the deep structure) is dissimilar to the innervational signals issued to the muscles (the surface structure) and these signals in turn are dissimilar to the movement that evolves: ". . . it is as if an order sent by the higher center is coded before its transmission to the periphery so that it is completely unrecognizable and is then again automatically deciphered" (Bernstein, 1967, p. 41). In general, if impulses of the form $E(t)$ are close to the action plan and hence close to the actual form of the movement, then those impulses of the form $E(t, \alpha, d\alpha/dt)$ are close to the muscles and to the actual forces operating at the joint complexes. On this view, the mapping of $E(t)$ to $E(t, \alpha, d\alpha/dt)$ identifies the evolution of an act; in particular, it identifies the adaptation of an action plan to the prevailing field of external forces.

But if the executive does not control individual muscles, then what does it control? In response to this question, students of action (e.g., Bernstein, 1967; Gelfand, Gurfinkel, Tsetlin, & Shik, 1971) propose that the executive charge is to control the modes of interaction of lower centers. These, it is argued, are capable, through the systems that they govern, of producing a coordinated movement pattern in a relatively autonomous fashion.

Consider a commonplace, coordinated activity such as running. There are lower centers that control individual limbs, with each center asserting particular relations among the components of the limb that it controls. Thus, the interaction between these centers determines the coordinate motion of the limbs, and the problem of coordination in running becomes for the executive a problem of intercenter coordination (Shik & Orlovskii, 1965). Let us pursue this example in more detail because it is representative of a mode of organization that we will entertain as characteristic of the action system.

We have evidence that mechanisms inherent in the segmental apparatus of the mammalian spinal cord can initiate and maintain flexion–extension or stepping movements of the limbs in the absence of afferent participation (Eldred, 1960). Apparently, these segmental pattern generators determine the fundamental form of flexion–extension activity, but they do not specify in detail the actual spatial and temporal characteristics of the motion (Engberg & Lundberg, 1969). It is the role of afferent information, enumerated through autonomous (reflex) structures (and of tuning influences from above, as we shall see later) to supply the requisite spatial and temporal details and thus to tailor the basic pattern to the field of external forces. A small leap now takes us to the assertion that walking and running can be attributed to a relatively simply executive instruction which sets into charcteristic motion the entire segmental apparatus and which, in itself, is deficient in information about the actual strategic order of necessary muscle contractions (cf. Evarts *et al.*, 1971).

This mode of organizing action achieves the following. First, it resolves the degrees of freedom problem noted above by apportioning relatively few degrees to the executive level but relatively many to the subsystems whose activities the executive regulates. (Since it is the subsystems that must deal with the vagaries of kinematic linkages and muscles). Second, and related, it reduces the detail required of the executive instructions, for with autonomous lower centers those instructions do not have to be coded for the individual muscle contractions that will ultimately occur.

In overview, what has emerged is the understanding that the element entering into the design of an act is typically not an individual muscle but a group of muscles functioning cooperatively together. We have good reason to speculate that the reflexes may well comprise the "basis" of the set of all such functional groupings and hence of the infinitely large set of all acts (Easton, 1972a). A "basis" is a mathematical structure found in the theory of vector spaces. It is defined as a linearly independent (nonredundant) set of vectors that under the operations of addition and scalar multiplication spans the vector space. Essentially, a "basis" contains the minimum number of elements that are required to generate all members of the set.

We have several reasons for identifying the set of reflexes as the "basis" for action. First, reflex systems are not independent entities that function in isolation. On the contrary, there are a multiplicity of functional relations among reflexes and other structures. Second, virtually every reflex observed experimentally and clinically is an instance of a reasonably complex configuration of motions often elicitable by a single stimulation. Third, reflex systems are under very effective and often complex control by supraspinal structures (cf. Eccles & Lundberg, 1959; Evarts *et al.*, 1971; Kuno & Perl, 1960). And fourth, reflexes are obviously purposeful and adaptive, and they may be organized and modulated flexibly by means of the operations of ordering, summing, fragmentation, and through their "local sign" properties (Easton, 1972a). Collectively, these characteristics of reflexes suggest that

> . . . the neuronal mechanisms which have been studied as reflex arcs can be utilized in a variety of ways by virtue of the interaction between reflex pathways and by the action of control systems that are present, even at the level of the spinal cord segment. The dichotomy between reflex control and central-patterning control of movement may in this sense be artificial [Evarts *et al.*, 1971, p. 62].

Through the provision of reflexes, evolution has supplied a partial answer to the degrees of freedom problem. We might now suppose that a further reduction in the burden of control is achieved ontogenetically through the gathering together of reflexes into larger functional units (cf. Gelfand *et al.*, 1971; Paillard, 1960; Pal'tsev, 1967b). We will refer to reflexes and functional combinations of reflexes as "coordinative structures" (a term borrowed from Easton (1972a) but used here with greater latitude).[1] Of cardinal importance to this chapter is the assumption that a closely knit functional combination of reflexes performs as a relatively autonomous unit; by this assumption, relative autonomy is a fundamental property of coordinative structures, at any level of complexity.[2]

In sum, we have seen that the executive does not construct acts from individual muscle contractions. What we now infer is that acts are synthesized from a set of coordinative structures for which the reflexes constitute a basis.

We return now to the question of the variable entering into action concepts of the form $A(x)$. The executive does not deal in muscles, so muscle properties (length, tension) can be ruled out. The executive does deal in coordinative structures (at least so we may argue), but these similarly cannot be the elements we seek. An action concept such as that supporting A writing is indifferent to functional groupings of muscles in the same way that it is indifferent to individual muscles. However, the analogy drawn above between the set of reflexes and a "basis" in vector space theory provides a clue to the answer. To reiterate: A basis is a subset of a set of elements which when acted upon by suitable operations generates the entire set of elements. We assume, therefore, a repertoire of operations that modify and relate the coordinative structures so as to produce any and all acts. Thus, we may conjecture that the elements entering into an action concept are the operations defined over the set of coordinative structures. In this sense an action concept is analogous to a mathematical operator, a function whose domain is a set of functions, of which differentiation is a classical example.

[1] One motivation for bringing reflexes and functional combinations of reflexes under the single heading "coordinative structures" is the assumption that for the activation of either a single reflex or a single functional combination of reflexes, one degree of freedom of the control system is enough (see Kots *et al.*, 1971). In regard to functional combinations it is important to recognize that new tasks may often require the discovery of new combinations and their establishment as single functional units. In very large part acquiring a skill is, as Bernstein (1967) would have expressed it, a problem of reducing the degrees of freedom in the action structures being regulated (see Kots & Syrovegin, 1966).

[2] Consider insect flight. The evidence suggests that it is not due to a built-in structural system of simple segmental reflex loops nor to any flight center, yet identified. Rather, it seems that there is a functional system of distributed oscillators–autonomous pattern generators–which on receipt of the appropriate *nonphasic* input are coupled together as a unit which then operates autonomously in a preset fashion (Weiss-Fogh, 1964). Walking may use some of the very same oscillatory structures as flying, but for locomotion on the ground they would be mutually coupled in a different way (cf. Wilson, 1962) to form a different autonomous unit.

THE ORGANIZATION OF THE ACTION SYSTEM

The foregoing account identifies two particularly important properties of the action system. First, acts are produced by fitting together structures each of which deals relatively autonomously with a limited aspect of the problem. Second, the action plan is stated crudely "in three-dimensional kinematic language" (Gelfand *et al.,* 1971), yet the actual pattern of motions is precise in displacement, speed, and time of occurrence. To achieve this measured performance the differentiation of an action plan must proceed through multiple stages of computation in which needed details emerge gradually. Patently, a computation of details over time is inelegant and inefficient for a system that has a limited repertoire of skills, but it is preferred for a system called upon to solve novel action problems posed by ever-varying kinematic and environmental conditions.

We commonly classify a system that behaves in this fashion as hierarchic, a classification that is certainly suggested by the unqualified use of the term "executive" in the preceding discussion. By a hierarchy we understand that an executive at the highest level of a decision tree makes the important decisions and spells out the fundamental goals. Decisions on the details are left to the immediately subordinate structures which in turn leave decisions that they cannot make, for whatever reason, to even lower structures. This general strategy is repeated until the final remaining decisions are made by the lowest structures in the decision tree.

The crucial property of a substructure in a hierarchy is that in the perspective of a higher level it is a dependent part, but in the perspective of a lower level it is an autonomous whole. Koestler's (1969) term "holon" expresses this whole–part personality of hierarchic substructures; a holon is defined as "a system of relations which is represented on the next higher level as a unit, that is, a relatum" (Koestler, 1969, p. 200). We may question, however, the notion explicit in the concept of a hierarchy that the *direction* of the whole–part personality of substructures is immutable. Certainly from the viewpoint of the "geometry" of anatomical arrangements certain structures may appear as dependent parts of other structures, and a compelling argument may well be made for the immutability of this relation in the peripheral reaches of the neural mechanisms supporting action and perception. Yet from a computational viewpoint in which we emphasize "knowledge" structures rather than anatomical structures the relation between any two structures need not be fixed; either may treat the other as a relatum, or subprocedure, depending on the problem to be solved at a given moment. This commutability of "subordinate" and "executive" roles, of "lower" and "higher," is expressed in the related interpretations of biological systems as "coalitions" (Reaves, 1973; Shaw, 1971; von Foerster, 1960) or "heterarchies" (Minsky & Papert, 1972). In these interpretations, management of the action system would not be the prerogative of any one structure; many structures would function cooperatively in the framing of action plans and desired consequences, although not all structures need participate in all decisions (Reaves, 1973). Furthermore, while it is certainly the case that the action system has very definite and nonarbitrary (anatomical/computational) structures, in these interpretations the partitioning of these structures into agents and instruments and the specification of relations among them is arbitrary. Any inventory of basic constituent elements and relations is equivocal (Reaves, 1973). Decentralization of control and arbitrariness of partitionings are not alien notions to students of action theory (e.g., Berstein, 1967; Greene, 1971b) as evident from Greene's apologia:

> The 'executive' and 'the low-level systems' will occur frequently . . . These terms are simply abbreviations for what I really mean: any two subsystems, one of which, at the moment, in respect to the task under consideration, is behaving like an executive relative to the other. The systems are not unique, and their relation is not immutable: a 'lower' part of the nervous system might, for instance, at some time behave like an executive relative to some higher part [Greene, 1971b, pp. 2–3].

ACTION AS HETERARCHIC

Perception and action contrast in that the tasks of the former are to digest, abstract, and generalize, while the tasks of the latter are to spell, concretize, and particularize (Koestler, 1969). One is the mirror image of the other. For the sake of argument and to facilitate comparisons with perception, let us say that the "input" to the action system is an intention (e.g., to pick up a cup, to write one's name). (We respectfully ignore the problem of how an intention is determined and in addition we give due recognition to the likelihood that some of the structures responsible for determining an intention may also be responsible for its translation into an action plan and for the plan's subsequent differentiation). Therefore, an intention is an "event" for the action system in the way that, say, a scene is an event for the visual, perceptual system.

Taking a leaf from artificial intelligence research on visual perception, we may say that action involves knowledge domains or abstract representations—where a representation is defined as a set of entities, a description of the relations among them, and a description of their attributes (Minsky & Papert, 1972; Sutherland, 1973). Thus, for the perception of scenes portrayed in two dimensions we may identify, as examples, (1) a Lines Domain in which "bars, picture-edge, vertex, end, midpoint" are the entities; "join, intersect, collinear, parallel" are the relations; and "brightness, length, width, orientation" are the attributes; and (2) a more abstract Surfaces Domain where "surface, corner, edge, shadow" are the entities; "convex, concave, behind, connected" are the relations; and "shape, tilt, albedo" are the attributes (see Sutherland, 1973). From a hierarchical view we might think of perception as an ordered sequence of unidirectional mappings from less abstract to more abstract representations and the differentiation of an intention as the successive mappings of the intention onto a series of progressively *less* abstract representations. But the argument from the coalitional/heterarchical interpretations of organization is that the conversation between abstract representations (domains, knowledge structures) is not one way. A fundamental result in artificial intelligence research on scene analysis is that while it is necessary to construct descriptions in many different domains, a procedure that exploits only unidirectional mapping from a lower domain to the next and higher domain is significantly limited in its capability to interpret a scene successfully (Sutherland, 1973). Success in scene interpretation is greatly enhanced by allowing a more flexible strategy in which processing in lower domains can use, as subprocedures, hypotheses generated about structures in higher domains (e.g., Falk, 1972).

Let us comment briefly on entities that in theory could be gathered together to form domains in action. On the basis of what has already been said it would be logical for us to identify the entities in a representation with coordinative structures. In this regard it is important that reflexes can be arranged on a scale from complex and wide-ranging to simple and local. The organization of reflexes reveals "parallel hierarchies of complexity whose regularity and order leave little to be desired: local spinal reflexes, such as the flexion reflex, appear to be subsumed by reflexes requiring an intact spinal cord such as the scratch and long spinal reflexes, and these in turn are subsumed by pontine and medullary reflexes, such as the tonic neck and labyrinthine reflexes, and, at still higher levels, by locomotion and righting" (Easton, 1972a, p. 593). This suggests that we might equate the entities in *each* abstract representation of an act with coordinative structures, remarking that in higher domains an action plan is represented by functions defined over a relatively small number of large and complex coordinative structures and in lower domains by functions over a relatively large number of small and simple coordinative structures. We are thus provided with the following description of the evolving act: *an act evolves as the mapping by a coalitionally/heterarchically organized system of an intention onto successively larger collections of increasingly smaller and less complex coordinative structures, with each representation approximating more closely the desired action.*

There are many other ways we might conceivably characterize the entities of a representation in the building of a theory of action, but I hope the arguments that follow will pinpoint the special advantages conferred on a system in which the entities at all levels of representation are relatively autonomous structures. At all events, let us simply note at this juncture two contrasts between action as hierarchy and action as coalition/heterarchy. In one, the contrast is between the hierarchic strategy of a detached higher level dictatorially commanding lower levels and the heterarchic strategy of procedures constructing a representation in a higher domain entering into "negotiations" with lower domains in order to determine how the higher representation should be stated. In the other, the contrast is between the hierarchic principle of low-level structures unquestioningly responding to high-level instructions and the heterarchical principle of procedures establishing a representation in a lower domain reprocessing higher representations from the perspective of the special kinds of knowledge available to the lower domain.

The anatomical and neural structure of mechanisms related to movement suggests quite strongly that the fluidity called for by coalitional/heterarchical organization, the constant shuttling back and forth between domains, is not without basis. Consider, for example, the notion of internal feedback. Most generally the idea of feedback in behaving organisms is identified in two senses. In one sense, it is information that arises from the muscles as a direct consequence of their being active; in the other sense, it is information originating outside the organism as an indirect consequence of muscular contraction. The latter is often dubbed "knowledge of results." These senses of the concept of feedback are not exclusive, for they omit the afferent information that arises from structures within the nervous system in the course of an act's emergence. We refer to this feedback from the nervous system to itself as internal (Evarts *et al.*, 1971) and it plays a central role in the evolution of coordinated activity.

In reference to internal feedback from spinal centers, Oscarsson (1970) has remarked on the fact that a number of ascending pathways (at least six spinocerebellar tracts) are not especially well equipped to provide information about muscle contraction. Rather, the organization of these ascending paths suggests that they monitor activity in spinal motor centers, which in turn provide an abstracted account of the relation between themselves and other lower centers. This property of ascending paths fits the character of descending paths: most descending fibers terminate in interneuronal pools rather than passing directly to motor neurons. The basis for this arrangement may lie in the fact that the coordination of movement rests on the patterning of groups of motor neurons rather than on instructions to individual units, and the mapping between domains consists of predictions of how functional groupings of muscles (coordinative structures) will behave (cf. Arbib, 1972). Spinal centers thus provide a means for checking predictions against the current status of lower centers. Therefore, interneuronal pools may function as "correlation centers" (Arbib, 1972) reporting the degree to which an action plan is evolving as desired or indeed capable of evolving in the desired manner from a particular representation. At all events, there are probably many such internal feedback loops broadcasting the state of each level of the actor from executive to muscle (Taub & Berman, 1968), a highly desirable state of affairs from the perspective of a strategy in which executive procedures draw rough sketches and low-level procedures furnish needed details.

Our appreciation of the flexible relations between neuroanatomical structures supporting action is fostered further by recognition of the fact that signals from above can bias the abstracted accounts supplied by spinal centers. Many supraspinal mechanisms exert influences on the first synapse in ascending systems, that is, the synapse between the peripheral afferent neuron and the second order neuron which crosses the spinal cord to the tracts projecting to the brain (Ruch, 1965a). These influences from above are exerted mainly by motor areas and motor tracts, including the classically defined principal motor tract, the pyramidal (corticospinal) tract.

Current deliberations on the interrelations among the motor cortex, basal ganglia, and cerebellum may well be resolved on the acceptance of the coalitional formulation (see Kornhuber, 1974). We know that before the first signs of muscle innervation relevant to a particular movement significant changes occur in the activities of the cerebellum and basal ganglia, in addition to the motor cortex (Evarts, 1973; Evarts *et al.,* 1971). This contrasts sharply with more traditional interpretations of basal ganglia–cerebellar processes operating as movement control and error-correcting devices coming into play only after the innervation of muscles. Rather, it would seem that these mechanisms gang together in the constructing and differentiating of action plans—they incorporate different procedures, each using the others as subprocedures as the situation demands. The structure of the cerebellum and its relations with other structures exemplifies the flexibility of neural computation in action. The cerebellum receives inputs from the entire cerebral cortex, projects to the motor cortex. (Evarts & Thach, 1969), and is in two-way communication with the segmental apparatus of the spinal cord and thus with the structures that will actually execute the intended configuration of motions.

Thus the cerebellum can operate as a comparator, relating information about cerebral events to information about spinal events. The argument has been made that the cerebellum carries out a speeded-up differentiation of representations of the action plan, thereby providing a projection of their outcome and a basis for their modification. On this argument the cerebellum plays a significant role in tailoring action plans to prevailing environmental and kinematic conditions prior to their realization as muscle events and thus prior to feedback from muscle contraction (see Eccles, 1969; Kornhuber, 1974).

EXECUTIVE IGNORANCE: EQUIVALENCE CLASSES AS INSTRUCTIONAL UNITS

Clearly, coalitional/heterarchical organization is far more flexible than hierarchical organization. Yet this flexibility is constrained in important ways. For example, in action there would be limits on the depth to which procedures constructing a representation on a higher domain may go in search of useful hypotheses. For any given higher abstract representation of an intention the utility of knowledge about any lower domain would be inversely related to the degree of abstraction separating the two domains. Hypotheses about individual alpha–gamma links (the smallest coordinative structures) regulating muscle contraction, for example, would not be useful to the determination of relevant large coordinative structures and related functions. And this, of course, is no more than a restatement of the degrees of freedom problem noted above. It then follows that while a representation of an intention in a higher domain is mapped into an immediately lower domain, the particular form that the representation will actually take in the lower domain cannot be known in advance, for the procedures operating in the lower domain have access to knowledge that is immaterial, in principle, to the procedures in the higher domain.

This form of "ignorance" has been duly recognized by students of action. We recall the earlier comment that the role of the executive (which is understood to be not a single neuroanatomical structure but a set of procedures engaging a number of neuroanatomical structures) is to modify the mode of interaction among elements at a lower level (Bernstein, 1967; Gelfand *et al.,* 1971). As a general rule, however, it is argued that the executive does not have advance knowledge of which particular state, out of a set of possible states, a lower level will arrive at after a mode of interaction has been specified (Greene, 1971b; Pyatetskii-Shapiro & Shik, 1964). In this perspective Greene (1971a) asks: "Can there be units of information that behave deterministically, even though the executive can rarely specify control functions more narrowly than to place them within broad classes of possible realizations? [p. 22]." Consider a situation in which the executive specifies a function transferring a given system into a "model" state. Now we may say that the "model" state serves not as a binding decree to be followed dogmatically by the system but rather as the identifier of a "ballpark," that is, an equivalence class of states convertible into the "model" state. For the system two states are defined as equivalent if they differ by a transformation that is realizable by the system. To Greene's (1971a, b) way of thinking the interconverting of states or functions is characteristic of low-level systems, so that a state or function specified by the executive (or for that matter any higher domain) may be substituted for by one from the same equivalence class but one which is more attuned to the current conditions operating within and around the system and to the system's privileged knowledge of the capabilities of other low-level structures. Similarly, executively specified functions determining the switching from one structure to another form another "ballpark," and low-level systems may autonomously interconvert transition functions of the same equivalence class as the need arises. By this reasoning the units of information that behave deterministically are not functions but equivalence classes of functions. (The reader should refer to Greene, 1971a, b, for a more detailed and formal account of the various kinds of possible equivalence classes.)

In both of the above instances (specification of model states and transition functions) the executive instructions would be judged as satisfactory by the executive even though the instructions (functions) specified were not those actually carried out by the instructed systems. However, executive ignorance about which functions or states actually arise in the lower levels, implies a high degree of uncertainty in executive commands, since for any given system the executive is specifying an unknown member of a family of possible functions or states. "This uncertainty introduces ambiguities and errors in an executive system's memory, commands, and communications to other executive systems" (Greene, 1971b, pp. 4–11). And we must expect these ambiguities and errors to be propagated through the action system during an act's evolution. The question arises, therefore, of how a configuration of motions is coordinated with precision and finesse? Indeed, in the face of this apparent chaos we should ask how coordination can be achieved at all? We can only assume that the action system is so constructed and its procedures so related that these ambiguities and errors are immaterial to the differentiation of an action plan (cf. Pyatetskii-Shapiro & Shik, 1964).

For Greene (1971a, b) the answer lies in the relations among the various equivalence classes: even though errors induced in one class may lead to erroneous specification in another, that specification would still be confined within the equivalence class of the desired function. Thus the equivalence classes as invariant units of information provide a means for specifying instructions in terms that are reliable and intelligible, even though an executive system is ignorant of the desultory character of low-level systems. We may summarize with Greene (1971a):

> Roughly speaking the equivalence classes serve as ballparks into which it is sufficient for the executive to transfer the state: once the state enters the ballpark it will be automatically brought to the correct position without further attention–although ambiguities inevitably lead to erroneous signals, these signals will never be moved outside their correct ballparks or equivalence classes. Hence the equivalence classes seem to be systematically behaving units of information in situations in which the individual elements themselves will behave in haphazard fashion [pp. 24–25].[3]

THE ACTION PLAN AND THE ENVIRONMENT

Taking stock of our analysis thus far, we may draw a rough sketch of how an action plan is represented in the highest domain, namely, as the specification of a subset of large coordinative structures that almost fits what is intended, and a set of functions on that subset (identifying the necessary equivalence classes) that

[3] From what has already been said, it is evident that the derivation of a pattern of motions from its underlying representation is the cumulative result of the application of a long series of "rules." We should suppose, therefore, that there are regularities in the representation of an act in the highest domain that are obscured at the movement level by the application of these rules. In part, Greene's (1971a) equivalence classes are an attempt to recover the regularities, and the rules of the action system are defined by the conditions underlying the change in identity of functions and states, that is, interconverting of elements within a class. Obviously the enterprise undertaken by Greene has much in common with current approaches to problems in linguistics.

will relate its elements both adjecently and successivly in a particular way. Thus, the serial nature of an act is said to arise not from the extemporaneous linking of component motions but rather from the differentiation of an already formed plan (cf. Bernstein, 1967; Evarts *et al.,* 1971; Lashley, 1951; Pribram, 1971). We have not, however, made any comment on the relation between the action plan and perception. To rectify this omission we return once again to the nature of an action concept, more precisley, $A(x)$. We do so on the following rationale: If some common ground between the action *concept* $A(x)$ and its perceptual counterpart can be identified, then perhaps we can gain some perspective on the relation between the action *plan* and the perceived environment in which the action plan is to unfold.

Consider, much as we did before, a sample of As written by the same individual using different muscle combinations, that is, one A may have been written by small motions of the fingers, another by large motions of a leg with the writing instrument grasped between the toes. Members of the sample will differ metrically: They will probably be of different sizes, of varying orientations, and of differing degrees of linearity, that is, some will be written in curved strokes, while others will be virtually straight. And supposedly all members of the set will differ spatially in that they will occupy different locations on the page. On inspection we would probably have little difficulty identifying each members as an instance of capital A. But in what sense are they equivalent? In geometry, figures are defined as equivalent with respect to a group of transformations. We say that two figures are equivalent if and only if the group contains a transformation that maps one figure onto the other. The group of transformations relevant to this discussion, that is, relevant to our sample of As, is clearly nonmetrical and, by elimination, must be topological. It is nonmetrical properties rather than metrical properties (which would be left undisturbed by the metric groups: the group of motions, the similarity group, and the equiareal group) that are of significance to the perceptual determination of membership in the class of capital A.

But the same token, the action concept supporting A writing is determined by nonmetrical properties rather than metrical properties. After all, the sample of As we are considering was the product of an actor, and the sample, as we have noted, is indifferent to metrics. Since this is no more than a paraphrase of an argument by Bernstein (1967) we should let Bernstein draw the relevant conclusion concerning the action concept of A:

> The almost equal facility and accuracy with which all these variations can be performed is evidence for the fact that they are ultimately determined by one and the same higher directional engram in relation to which dimensions and position play a secondary role . . . the higher engram, which may be called the engram of a given topological class, is already structurally extremely far removed . . . from any resemblance whatsoever to the joint muscle schemata; it is extremely geometrical, representing a very abstract motor image of space [p. 49].

In short, the action concept of writing A and the perception concept for identifying A share common ground in their dependence on nonmetrical properties, and it is not difficult to imagine an isomorphic relation (of some degree) between them (Turvey, 1974). But this is a very special case and we may ask: Does the action plan in general relate in similar fashion to the perceived environment? Bernstein (1967) hazards the guess that it does. For him the high-level abstract representation of an action plan may be construed as a projection of the environment relevant to the intention, where this projection relates to the environment topologically but not metrically.

Owing to the vagueness of this argument we may feel that we have not really acquired any new insights (after all, what does it mean to talk about an isomorphism between action plans and environmental events?) Yet honoring our eccentricities for the present we may acknowledge that we have reinforced our respect for the action plan and the action coalition/heterarchy. In earlier arguments we established the fact that the high-level abstract representation of an action plan was not a projection of muscles and joints. In the current argument we maintain that an action plan may be usefully construed as a projection of the environment. Therefore, we view the task of the action coalition/heterarchy as that of translating an abstract projection of the environment into joint–muscle schemata.

Some research by Evarts (1967) is of special relevance to these speculations. Evarts showed that when a monkey makes a movement of the wrist to counteract an opposing force (in a task in which the direction of force and the direction of displacement are varied orthogonally) recordings from unit cells in the motor cortex are related to the amount of force needed rather than to the degree of displacement. Moreover, this activity in the motor cortex is manifest prior to evidence of muscular contraction. As Pribram (1971) points out, Evarts' observation suggests that the representation at the motor cortex is a mirror image of the field of external forces. But by our account this "image" must represent the action plan at a fairly late stage in its differentiation and, in terms of the earlier analogy with linguistic theory, is more closely related to the surface structure of art than to the deep structure. Indeed, Evarts (1973) has claimed recently that the representation of movement at the motor cortex, rather than identifying the highest level of motor integration (a classical point of view), is, on the contrary, much closer to the muscles and hence much lower in the organization of the action system than representations in other (traditionally lower) anatomical systems such as the cerebellum and the basal ganglia.

Accepting the proximity of this motor cortical representation to the act's surface structure we can see that by this level the action heterarchy has transformed a projection of topological properties of the environment into a projection of environmental contingencies (e.g., forces). According to Bates (cited by Evarts, 1973) force is the logical output for the motor cortex; velocity is the single integral of this quantity and displacement is the double integral, and both of these quantities are theoretically more difficult to specify than force itself. Yet ultimately acts call for accurate displacements, and accurate displacements, in turn, call for a projection of metrical properties of the environment. We are led, therefore, by this reasoning to another description of the evolving act, namely, that *the action plan unfolds as a series of progessively less abstract projections of the environment.*

THE PROBLEM OF PRECISION AND THE CONCEPT OF TUNING

The realization of an action plan as a coordinated pattern of motions requires its translation from the crude language of coordinative structures to the precise language of muscles. Commerce between animal and environment reduces ultimately to the regulation of pairs of antagonistic muscle groups coupled together at joints. In the translation from abstract action plan to mechanical response the alphamotorneuron stands as the penultimate component. The central question now is how can alphamotorneurons specify to muscles the needed lengths and tensions when these terms, length and tension, are not in the lexicons of higher domains and hence, by definition, cannot be ingredients in an action recipe. In short, we seek to understand more fully the mechanisms through which the action system generates precise commands to muscles from crude commands to coordinative structures.

An instructive portrayal of the problem in limited form follows from the concluding comments of the preceding section—that a suitable output for the motor cortex is force. Suppose that subsequent processes, metaphorically speaking, integrate this quantity. Then, as already noted, the single integral will yield velocity and the double integral will yield displacement. But the particular velocity and the particular displacement obtained for any given force will depend on the end-points or limits of integration. Thus, specification of force alone is insufficient for the achievement of a desired velocity or displacement—the limits of integration must also be identified. How such "end points" might be supplied in the relating of action to environment is the kernel of our problem.

We now proceed to consider and illustrate properties of the spinal cord that will aid our inquiry. Earlier we remarked that the role of higher levels of the nervous system is to pattern the interactions within and among coordinative structures. Let us now recognize that, in the main, coordinative structures have their origins in the spatially divided and relatively autonomous sybsystems of the spinal cord. And let us modify our terms slightly to read: the role of the higher levels of the nervous system is to modulate interactions within and among neural mechanisms at the spinal level (cf. Gelfand *et al.*, 1971; Obituary: Tsetlin, 1966).[4]

[4]This viewpoint is also expressed by students of motor control in insects (e.g., Rowell, 1964; Weiss-Fogh, 1964; Wiersma, 1962).

The segmental apparatus of the spinal cord is a functional entity well suited to the organization of coordinated activity. Its component structures are richly interconnected by a variety of horizontal and vertical linkages, providing an intrinsic system of complex interactions which is no less essential for the evolving act than supraspinal influences. The spinal cord is an active apparatus that does not passively reproduce instructions from above (Gurfinkel, Kots, Krinskiy, Pal'tsev, Fel'dman, Tsetlin, & Shik, 1971) and, indeed, may regulate its degree of subordination to supraspinal mechanisms (Sverdlov & Maksimova, 1965; Verber, Rodionov, & Shik, 1965). Several properties of spinal cord architecture and dynamics provide the basis for this interpretation. We take note of some of them here. First, of the great many interneurons in the spinal cord relatively few are afferent neurons. Second, interneurons rather than motor neurons are the terminal points for the majority of descending fibers from the brain. Third, the majority of synapses in the spinal cord are formed by connections between spinal neurons, and relatively few are formed from axons coming from the brain and spinal ganglia. And fourth, reciprocal facilitiation and inhibition, and myotatic reflex action are all processes at the segmental level (see Gurfinkel *et al.,* 1971).

The integrity of the spinal cord rests on the fundamental servoprocess manifest in the alpha–gamma link regulating muscle contraction. Upon this servoprocess are built the intra- and intersegmental reflexes. We suppose that the modus operandi for integrating reflexes (the basis of the set of coordinative structures) in coordinated action exploits rather than disrupts the fundamental servomechanism. Indeed, this will prove to be the key notion for unraveling the problem of how precise instructions are formulated at the level of alphamotorneuron activity.

But before examining the evidence for this view we observe that in the unfolding of the action plan on the segmental apparatus the responsibility for demarcating coordinative structures and for the parsing of those structures may devolve on separate neuroanatomical systems. Greene (1971b) cites a series of experiments by Goldberger in which the corticospinal and brainstem spinal paths in monkey were interrupted. With corticospinal interruption the animal can no longer inhibit unwanted components of a coordinative structure such as the group of muscle contractions that extend joints of the same limb. Thus, for example, when presented with food that he must stretch for the monkey reaches out with extended limb but cannot then close his fingers to grasp the food. If with the joints flexed the animal grasps food placed close to him and raises it to his mouth he cannot then let go. In contrast, brain-stem spinal interruption appears to impede the animal's ability to restrict the evoked coordinative structures to those relevant to the task. When extending an arm to reach for food at a distance the group of contractions that rotate the limb, or those that raise the limb, may come into play in addition to the task-relevant group of limb extensors.

In short we see that the delimiting of coordinative structures and the manner of their decomposition are effected in the segmental apparatus by instructions from separate mechanisms. But now we must pass from this gross differentiation of the action plan at the segmental level to the finer differentiation afforded by the fundamental servomechanism (or, more aptly, the fundamental coordinative structure).

The main body of a muscle consists of extrafusal fibers that on contraction alter the relative positions of the bones to which they are attached. The innervation of extrafusal fibers is supplied by alphamotorneurons. Within the main body of the muscle are intrafusal fibers which are wrapped around the middle by the terminals of sensory fibers. These sensory fibers and the intrafusal muscle fibers to which they attach are referred to collectively as a muscle spindle. Muscle spindles connect to the extrafusal fibers at one end and to a tendon at the other and are therefore "in parallel" with the extrafusal fibers. Two functionally distinct spindle components can be identified: a static component that is sensitive to the instantaneous muscle length and a dynamic component that is sensitive to the rate of change of muscle length (Matthews, 1964). On contraction of the intrafusal fibers, the spindle receptors register the difference in length and the difference in rate of change of length between the intrafusal and extrafusal fibers. The induced receptor excitation is communicated to the linked alphamotorneurons which respond by recruiting more extrafusal fibers until the discrepencies in length and velocity have been annulled. Thus, in a situation in which a load is applied to a muscle extending it beyond its resting length, the spindle feedback provides an autonomous means of tailoring the muscle response to the new conditions. This negative feedback system identifies the fundamental servomechanism; it is now incumbent upon us to show that this servomechanism is biasable in ways of considerable importance to the theory of action.

Intrafusal fibers, like extrafusal fibers, have a source of innervation, the gammamotorneurons. These motorneurons fall into two relatively independent classes, the gammastatic and the gammadynamic, regulating respectively the static and dynamic components of muscle spindles (Matthews, 1964). Again, gammamotorneurons, like alphamotorneurons, are under high-level control but the motor nerves that project from brain to gammamotorneurons and those that project from brain to alphamotorneurons are largely separate and thus it is optional whether the spindles and the main body of a muscle contract and relax together. "The spindles could therefore be activated while the main muscle remained passive, and vice versa" (Merton, 1973, p. 37).

We see therefore that the gamma system allows for the modulation of the fundamental servomechanism. The gamma-static motorneurons can control the equilibrium state of the servomechanisms while the gamma-dynamic motorneurons can control the "damping" of the servomechanism, that is, the rate at which it achieves equilibrium. Thus, the servomechanism is not only informed of what it has done, but more importantly it can be informed of what it must do.

This completes the elementary description of the biasable nature of the fundamental servomechanism; but one or two points remain to be considered.

In addition to the biasable feedback loop signaling length and velocity through spindle receptors, there is another which signals muscular force through tendon organs. The signals conveying force feedback coverge on interneurons on their way to alphamotorneurons. As before, interneurons can be manipulated by higher-level instructions so that the inhibitory effects of force feedback on alphamotorneuron activity can be modulated. The biasable feedback loops conveying length, velocity, and force are inextricably linked in the regulation of the servomechanism. So we may expand on our comments above. While higher level control signals to alphamotorneurons set the servomechanism going, the higher level control signals to the gamma system and to the interneurons transmitting force information from the tendon organs function less as instigators of movement than as modulators of the gain of the feedback loops, that is to say, they serve to adjust the ratios of the outputs of feedback loops to their inputs. This principle of higher-level modulation of spinal reflexes is generalized to the segmental mechanism of reciprocal inhibition by which we understand that spindle activity not only impinges upon an alphamotorneuron of its own muscle but also via inhibitory motorneurons upon an alphamotorneuron of the antagonist muscle. Spindle output contributes both to agonist contraction and to antagonist relaxation in the regulation of pairs of muscles controlling a joint. Clearly, from all that has been said the reflex interplay between agonist and antagonist is biasable.

We are now in a position to identify the property of the spinal cord that is central to our current concerns (and for which we will shortly provide evidence), namely, that the system of segmental interactions is biasable and as a general strategy the activating of coordinative structures occurs against a background of spinal mechanisms already prejudiced toward executive intentions. Thus, it may be argued that the control of movement is in many respects the reorganization or *tuning* of the system of segmental interactions and that this attunement precedes the transmission of activating instructions to coordinative structures (Gelfand *et al.*, 1971; Gurfinkel *et al.*, 1971).

Before we pass from this elementary discussion of tuning to take up the topic in earnest let us glance at two examples of how alpha–gamma linkage might embellish a relatively simple instruction. For the first, consider the previously discussed action of stepping, recognizing the fact that a double joint flexor of the hip also produces extension at the knee. The high-level representation of stepping can be said to specify crudely a general "flexor plan" for the limb (Lundberg, 1969). The knee flexors innervated on this plan are strong enough in the early phases of the movement to prevent extension but as flexion proceeds the double-joint muscle will become stretched inducing an intense discharge of spindle activity. The spindle feedback will impinge upon hip-flexor alphamotorneurons and also produce reciprocal inhibition of the motor units belonging to knee flexors. Thus during the swing the knee flexors originally innervated on the flexor plan will suffer inhibition from the spindle activity of the double-joint muscle. The upshot of this interplay is the differentiation of the broadly stated flexor plan into coordinate stepping (Lundberg, 1969).

For the second example, consider a sudden change in the loading on an outstretched arm: a heavy object is placed into the hand, in a task where the arm's inclination to the ground is to be kept constant. We may suppose that instructions to the appropriate coordinative structures quickly bring the arm back into a close approximation to the desired position, with spindle feedback coming into play to finely tune the terminal point of the trajectory (cf. Arbib, 1972; Navas & Stark, 1968) and to maintain the arm in its desired position under the new conditions. In this sense we construe the alpha and gamma systems as participating in a "mixed ballistic-tracking strategy" (Arbib, 1972, p. 134) with the alpha system determining the ballistic component which gets the limb quickly into the right ballpark and the gamma system determining the superimposed tracking component which supplies the needed refinements.

From what has been said about the segmental apparatus and its pretuning we understand that the alpha–gamma processes of the two examples cited above do not take place in a vacuum. Rather, they occur against a backdrop suitably colored by supraspinal influences. It can be demonstrated that in the final 30 msec or so preceding a movement there is a pronounced enhancement of the effect of reciprocal inhibitation on the future antagonist of that movement (Kots & Zhukov, 1971, see below). What this suggests is that a motion like stepping or raising the arm is anticipated through the supraspinal tuning of the segmental mechanisms of reciprocal inhibition. We should also recognize that the backdrop for a voluntary act is not limited to adjustments in spinal reflexes. Thus, for example, when an arm is raised voluntarily by a person standing upright it is possible to observe in the period immediately prior to the first signs of arm muscle activity, anticipatory activity in a number of muscles of the lower limb and trunk (Belen'kii, Gurfinkel, & Pal'tsev, 1967). Figuratively speaking, when one moves an arm in a standing position one first performs "movements" with the legs and the trunk and only then with the arm.

In summary, we have considered in preliminary but sufficient fashion the kinds of mechanisms that effect significant variation in the behavior of low-level holons without infringing upon their autonomy. These mechanisms suitably controlled from higher domains allow for the precise regulation of muscular contraction. The gist of the whole matter is given in a short paragraph by Pribram (1971):

> When reflexes become integrated by central nervous system activity into more complex movements, integration cannot be effected by sending patterns of signals directly and exclusively to contractile muscles, playing on them as if they were a keyboard. Such signals would only disrupt the servoprocess. In order to prevent disruption, patterns of signals must be transmitted to the muscle receptors, either exclusively or in concert with those reaching muscle fibers directly. Integrated movement is thus largely dependent on changing the bias, the setting of muscle receptors [p. 225].

To this we need only add that the modulation of interneuronal pools must also play a significant part in the biasing of servomechanisms.

MOVEMENT-RELATED SEGMENTAL PRETUNING

Our task now is to view evidence for segmental pretuning in voluntary movements. But before we do so we must acknowledge that the available evidence comes from experiments in which the performers on cue are required to flex a knee, bend an elbow, extend a foot, and in general to execute movements whose trajectories, velocities, degrees of displacement, etc., are indifferent to the environment. To my knowledge there are no experiments on segmental pretuning for acts that depend on the detection of environmental properties for their performance. As a precautionary measure, therefore, we will distinguish between movement-related and environment-related pretuning. The former will refer to the changes in the segmental apparatus preceding the execution of a simple voluntary motion that is unrelated to the environment, in the sense that neither the actor's position with respect to the environment nor the position or orientation of objects with respect to each other and to the actor are altered by the motion. The latter, environment-related pretuning, will refer to segmental changes that precede actions or, more precisely, components of actions which are environmentally projected, in that their purpose is to displace the actor with respect to the environment or to displace (or rotate, or reflect) objects with respect to the actor, or both.

The goal we are approaching slowly is that of understanding, in a rough and approximate way, how seeing enters into doing. To this end we will need to extrapolate from movement-related pretuning to a general picture of how environmental properties control action. At all events, our immediate concern is with movement-related pretuning and we begin with some general comments.

The methodology for investigating movement-related pretuning has much in common with the methodology that characterizes the information-processing approach to visual perception (cf. Haber, 1969) which seeks to determine how visual "information" is modified in the course of its flow in the nervous system. Thus, techniques of masking, delayed partial-sampling, and reaction time are used to assess the correlation between stimulus and response at varying delays after visual stimulation.

In a similar if less sophisticated vein the tuning experiments that we will consider in this section judiciously apply the principle of probing the nervous system, in particular the spinal cord, in the interval elapsing between a warning signal and a cue to respond, or (more especially) between a cue to respond and the first signs of activity in the agonists executing the motion. The probes are simple reflexes elicited during the interval, with the latency and amplitude of the reflexes (recorded by the electrical response of the corresponding muscles) taken as indicants of the state of the segmental apparatus prior to the movement. The reflexes used for this purpose have generally been tendon reflexes elicited by a tap and the Hoffman or H reflex, which is a monosynaptic reflex in the gastrocnemius–soleus muscle group and elicited by electrical stimulation of the tibial nerve in the popliteal fossa (Hoffman, 1922).

As an introduction to the procedure and to the observations that will be of interest to us we consider two exemplary experiments. In the first (Gurfinkel *et al.*, 1971) the participant is seated with legs flexed and on command extends one leg, the responding leg remaining constant throughout the experiment. Surface electromyographic (EMG) recording of activity in the quadriceps femoris muscle reveals that the tibia extension occurs at a latency of 160–180 msec. If the patellar reflex is evoked in the same leg within 100 msec or so of the cue to respond the amplitude of the reflex is unaffected (compared to the control condition in which no command to extend is given). However, if the patellar reflex is elicited beyond this period then its amplitude is enhanced the closer to the command that it is elicited. We infer, therefore, that the state of the segmental apparatus has been altered prior to activation of the muscle group extending the knee. In the second example (Gottlieb, Agarwal, & Stark, 1970), the participant is again seated normally but with the right leg extended, knee slightly flexed, and the foot firmly strapped to a plate to which he transmits an isometric force through either plantar flexion or dorsiflexion. The task of the participant is to match the level of his foot torque with a target level specified by the experimenter in what is, essentially, a continuous tracking task in which the varying target level of torque and the level of the participant's matching torque are displayed on a scope viewed by the participant. The H reflex is elicited at different delays subsequent to the target adopting a new level, and both the H reflex and the activity in the gastrocnemius-soleus muscle group (agonist in plantar flexion) and the anterior tibial muscle (agonist in dorsiflexion) are measured. Summarized briefly, the results are that the amplitude of the H reflex is distinctly augmented if elicited in the period 60 msec prior to the initial signs of voluntary motor unit activation in plantar flexion and is generally inhibited in approximately the same interval before the first signs of voluntary dorsiflexion. Again we infer that there are changes in the spinal cord that precede agonist activation.

How specific is segmental pretuning? Consider initially some further experiments reported by Gurfinkel *et al.* (1971). In one, two movements are executed by the subject on separate occasions: flexing the leg at the hip joint and extending the knee. Measures are taken of the tendon reflex of the rectus head of the quadriceps femoris muscle, which spans two joints, and of the lateral head of the same muscle, which spans only one joint. When the hip is flexed a premovement increase is observed only in the amplitude of the tendon reflex elicited by stimulation of the rectus head. But it is important to note here that while the rectus head of the quadriceps femoris is involved in hip flexion the lateral head is not. By contrast, when extension of the knee is called for, a movement that involves both heads of the quadriceps femoris, both reflexes are significantly increased in amplitude prior to signs of voluntary motor neuron activity. In another experiment Gurfinkel *et al.* (1971) observed that in the 70–80 msec prior to flexing the leg at the knee the patellar reflex is amplified, but they also observed that the patellar reflex is amplified (although not to the same degree) prior to flexing the elbow of the arm ipsilateral to the leg in which the patellar reflex is elicited. We may conclude therefore that both specific *and* nonspecific changes in the segmental apparatus of the spinal cord precede voluntary motor unit activation.

This conclusion is buttressed by some other experiments that examine the changes in the spinal cord during the period intervening between a warning signal and the signal to execute a given movement. We take, as examples, experiments reported by Requin and Paillard (1971) and by Requin, Bonnet, and Granjon, (1968). In these experiments the movement is extension of the foot (plantar flexion), and both tendon and H reflexes are recorded from both the participating leg and the nonparticipating leg. Following the warning signal there is evidence of an increase in the amplitude of the reflexes measured in both legs, an increase which persists for the reflexes of the nonparticipating leg but is progressively depressed in the participating leg with greater proximity to the cue to respond. In short, these experiments provide evidence that after a warning signal and before a signal to execute a movement there occur both a nonspecific change in spinal sensitivity and a specific change related to the motorneuron pool—the servomechanisms—about to be involved in the forthcoming movement. In the view of Requin and his colleagues the depression of the reflex amplitude in the participating leg is due, under the conditions of the warning signal procedure, to central (supraspinal) influences that selectively "protect" the direct participants in the movement from irrelevant influences exerted upon them prior to their activation.

Evidently in the premovement period specific changes occur in the feedback loops related directly to agonist regulation. But can we demonstrate similar effects in the more extended feedback loop relating the state of an agonist to its antagonist? Two experiments by Kots (Kots, 1969; Kots & Zhukov, 1971) provide an answer.

Kots (1969a) wanted to know whether the enhancement in the H-reflex excitability of the motor neurons of the gastrocnemius evidenced in the latent period of a voluntary movement depended on the role the gastrocnemius was to play in the forthcoming movement. To this end the H-reflex amplitude was measured in the gastrocnemius when it was the future agonist of the movement, that is, in plantar flexion, and when it was the future antagonist of the movement, that is, in dorsiflexion. It was observed that following a command to move, the amplitude of the H reflex was significantly enhanced in the period beginning 60 msec prior to the first signs of voluntary motor unit activation only when the gastrocnemius was future agonist. When the antagonist role was assumed, the H reflex was neither enhanced nor depressed in the latent period but was found to decline sharply immediately following the first myogram signs of motor unit activity in the agonist muscle, the anterior tibial.

It would appear, therefore, that the effect of tuning was specific to agonistic activity and that the failure to detect a depression in the H reflex when the gastrocnemius was the antagonist suggests that the "positive" priming of agonist centers is not paralleled by a "negative" priming of antagonist centers. The absence of antagonist depression in Kots' (1969a) experiment contrasts with the evidence of such depression in the experiment of Gottlieb *et al.* (1970), described above. While not stating it explicitly, the report of the latter experiment implies that plantar flexion and dorsiflexion were mixed randomly in the course of an experimental session; in Kots' experiment the two response modes were examined separately and this difference in procedure may account for the difference in results. At all events, taken together, the two investigations suggest that depressing the motor neurons of antagonistic muscles in the latent period of voluntary movement is not a necessary concommitant of tuning agonists. However, as we shall see in the second experiment of Kots (Kots & Zhukov, 1971), there is indeed an adjustment made in the inhibitory influences on the antagonists of a movement during the latent period that is not manifest as a depression in motor neuron excitability.

The Kots and Zhukov (1971) experiment made use of paired stimulation, a procedure that is comparable to the forward masking procedure commonly used in visual information-processing experiments (e.g., Turvey, 1973); essentially, a leading stimulus is used to impede the response to a lagging stimulus. For Kots and Zhukov the leading member of the stimulus pair was electrical stimulation of the peroneal nerve and the lagging member was electrical stimulation of the tibial nerve. Peroneal nerve stimulation elicits a direct response (the M response) in the motor neurons of the anterior tibial muscle without accompanying M and H responses in the gastrocnemius–soleus muscle group. Tibial nerve stimulation, as we have already seen, elicits the monosynaptic H reflex of the gastrocnemius–soleus group. The H response in the gastrocnemius–soleus group is significantly depressed when elicited very shortly after peroneal stimulation, say 2–4 msec. The brief latency of this effect implies that it is realized by the "spinal apparatus of reciprocal inhibition" (Kots & Zhukov, 1971). We can therefore exploit this paired-stimulation procedure to monitor the state of reciprocal inhibition mechanisms during the latent period of a voluntary movement. Thus, Kots and Zhukov sought to determine whether the impairment in the H reflex induced by prior peroneal stimulation was intensified in the latent period of voluntary dorsiflexion. In more general terms, they sought to determine whether there is pretuning of the mechanisms of reciprocal inhibition. During dorsiflexion, reciprocal inhibition would protect the anterior tibial muscle from the antagonistic response of the gastrocnemius–soleus muscles; Kots and Zhukov looked to see if this mechanism was primed for its task before voluntary activation of the anterior tibial motor neurons. The experiment showed that in the final 30 msec prior to dorsiflexion the paired-stimulation effect was significantly enhanced and, moreover, that this enhancement could not be due to a reduction in excitability of the motor neurons of the gastrocnemius–soleus group, since the H response in the absence of preceding peroneal stimulation was unaltered during the latent period. Of course, this is what Kots (1969a) had found before.

Collectively, the experiments we have discussed suggest that a profound reorganization of the spinal cord precedes movement.[5] There are both nonspecific and specific components of this reorganization, and the latter have been shown to include the mechanisms of reciprocal inhibition in addition to the servomechanisms regulating agonist activity. Moreover, the reorganization of the interaction among neural mechanisms at the spinal level follows the pattern of initially diffuse becoming more localized the closer in time to the manifestation of the desired movement (Gelfand *et al.*, 1971). It is evident, therefore, that in the differentiation of an action plan the realization of instructions to coordinative structures is determined by the state of these structures on receipt of the instructions (cf. Gurfinkel & Pal'tsev, 1965).[6] Since the argument is that coordinative structures when activated perform in a relatively autonomous fashion, it follows that the details of their performance are very much determined by the state of the segmental apparatus at the time of activation.

TUNING AS PARAMETER SPECIFICATION

The elegance of tuning as a control process is that it permits the regulation of an autonomous system without disrupting the system's autonomy. So far we have illustrated this principle only in the control of servomechanisms at the level of muscle contractions. But this should not blind us to the likelihood of tuning as a general principle fundamental to all domains of the action heterarchy. We recall the comment that actions are produced by fitting together substructures, each of

[5] While we have chosen to discuss only experiments using simple, single movements we should note that other experiments have examined patterns of segmental pretuning in the performance of sequential and rhythmic movements (e.g., Kots, 1969b; Surguladze, 1972). Thus, Kots (1969b) showed that in the sequential performance of two movements opposite in direction in the ankle joint the segmental organization for the second movement is realized during the execution of the first.

[6] To demonstrate this point Gurfinkel and Pal'tsev (1965) examined the effect of eliciting a tendon reflex subsequent to a cue for voluntary movement (extension of the knee) on the latency of the voluntary movement. They found that the latent period of voluntary extension was linearly dependent on the time at which the reflex was elicited. In addition they showed that this effect held even when the reflex was elicited in the leg contralateral to that executing the voluntary leg extension. It is assumed that the reflex induces a change in the segmental apparatus and that the realization of commands for leg extension is therefore dependent on the prevailing state of the system of spinal relations.

which deals relatively autonomously with a limited aspect of the action problem. In addition, we recall that each domain may be construed as a representation in which relations are defined on a set of autonomous structures with the size of these structures becoming progressively smaller and their number progressively larger as the action plan is mapped into progressively less abstract representations. We now hypothesize that into each representation tuning functions may enter as modulators of coordinative structures.

Miller, Galanter, and Pribram (1960), discussing the acquisition of typing, suggest that the student typist learns to put feedback loops around larger and larger segments of her behavior. We might well suppose that this notion applies beyond typing to skilled acts in general, and with internal feedback loops in addition to the more commonly understood forms of feedback. We can imagine tuning functions of a more abstract kind related to the modulation of feedback between action segments that collectively behave as relatively autonomous units in the performance of any given skilled behavior. Again tuning would permit appropriate variation without disrupting, in these instances, the *acquired* self-regulating procedures.

To extend our usage of tuning, we will adopt a most important and provocative hypothesis, namely, that tunings parameterize the equivalence classes of functions specified by executive procedures. This follows from Greene's (1971a, b) contention that the smallest units of information available to an executive are probably not functions but families of functions parameterized by possible tunings.

Although we are here attempting to pass beyond the idea of tuning limited to the fundamental servomechanism we may profitably exploit our earlier discussion of that mechanism to illustrate the notion of tuning as parameter specification. We take as our departure point the experimental and mathematical analysis supplied by Asatryan and Fel'dman (1965) and Fel'dman (1966a, b) of the maintenance of joint posture and of the simple voluntary movement needed to achieve a desired angle of joint articulation. Consider a simple mass-spring system defined by the equation $F = -S_0(l - \lambda_0)$ where F is the force, S_0 is the stiffness of the spring, l is the length of the spring and λ_0 is the steady-state length of the spring, that is, the length at which the force developed by the spring is zero. This simple mass-spring system is controllable to the degree that the parameters S_0 and λ_0 are adjustable. Changing λ_0 with S_0 constant generates a set of nonintersecting characteristic functions, $F(l) = -S_0(l - \lambda)$, and changing both parameters generates a set of functions $F(l) = -S(l - \lambda)$ that will pass through all points in the plane defined by the cartesian product $F \times l$.

Let us now suppose that a joint–muscle system is analogous to our simple mass-spring system, in which case we can argue that the problem of controlling a joint-muscle system reduces to that of fixing certain characteristics of the system, that is, of setting mechanical parameters of the muscles, or more precisely, of setting biases on the fundamental servomechanisms. In the analogy the characteristic functions of a joint–muscle system are of the form $M(\phi)$ where M is the total muscular moment and ϕ is the joint angle. And each $M(\phi)$, therefore, is determined by the mechanical parameters of the muscles regulating the joint:

$$\lambda = (\lambda_1, \lambda_2, \ldots, \lambda_n), \qquad S = (S_1, S_2, \ldots, S_n),$$

where n is the number of muscles.

Given the foregoing comments let us now consider experiments using the technique of partial unloading—a technique (which we will shortly describe) that would assay the characteristic properties of an ordinary spring. These experiments (Asatryan & Fel'dman, 1965) sought to demonstrate that for a given situation the variations of muscular moment as a function of joint angle (or vice versa) are defined by an initial setting of the parameters, that is, by a characteristic function. For purposes of analysis we will refer to the state of the joint–muscle system as α, where α is defined by the vector (M, ϕ). When M and ϕ are constant for some period of time then α is a steady state of the system.

The experimental methodology may be described briefly. The participant's forearm is fixed on a horizontal platform whose axis of rotation coincides with the axis of flexion and extension of the forearm. The horizontal platform is attached to a simple pulley system supporting a set of weights which can be selectively unloaded. At the outset of a trial the participant establishes a steady state, α_s, of the joint–muscle system: given a specified angle of articulation the participant must establish a muscular moment to compensate for the effect of the moment of external forces—determined by the weights and their direction of pull on the horizontal platform—opposing flexion (or extension) of the joint. Thus for a standard initial opposing force, different steady states, α_s, can be established for different joint angles, ϕ_s. Once the steady state is established at a given ϕ_s the participant is then asked to close his eyes and the weight is unloaded, with the amount of unloading varying across trials. The new angle of articulation—the new steady-state α_s'—to which the arm briefly moves following unloading (and before the participant can make compensatory adjustments) is recorded. From a series of experiments such as the one we have described Asatryan and Fel'dman (1965) demonstrated that for all possible initial states α_s of the joint–muscle system a set of *nonintersecting functions,* $M_s(\phi)$ (or $\phi_s(M)$), are generated relating muscular moments to the new steady-state angles of the joint. Moreover they showed that the form of the function $M_s(\phi)$ does not depend on the external moments but is determined unambiguously by the parameters of the initial state of the system. (This was demonstrated by using a set of external moments that were rising functions of joint angles, and a set that were diminishing functions of joint angles.) So we conclude that the function $M_s(\phi)$ for each α_s is an invariant characteristic of the joint–muscle system: If the system is perturbed it will follow a trajectory of states leading to a new state of equilibrium, where both the trajectory and the equilibrium state are defined by the parameters fixed in the initial steady-state α_s. And since the curves are nonintersecting, the transition from one $M(\phi)$ to another requires changing λ_i with little, but preferably no change, in S_i (Asatryan & Fel'dman, 1965). It would seem, therefore, that a joint–muscle system does behave like a spring, that is, like a vibratory system, and that the action structures can choose parameters for this "spring" in accordance with the prevailing conditions. For a brief period of time following perturbation, until new parameters of the spring can be specified, the joint–muscle system behaves in the way that we would expect the chosen "spring" to behave.

We now proceed to develop this theme through the experiments of Fel'dman (1966b). These were conducted with a slight variation on the apparatus described above. The pulley-weight system was replaced by a detachable spring that opposes flexion of the joint but is insufficiently taut to prevent flexion. At rest the joint is flexed at an angle ϕ_0, and on the occurrence of an auditory cue the participant must establish as rapidly as possible and without the aid of vision the steady angle ϕ_1. (The participant is given a practice session so that he can achieve ϕ_1 with a minimum of error). During a series of trials the spring is occasionally detached within the period subsequent to the auditory cue and prior to movement. Now suppose that at the outset of a trial a fixed invariant characteristic $M(\phi)$ has been determined for the attainment of a steady-state α_1, corresponding to the desired angle ϕ_1. In the steady-state α_1, $\phi = \phi_1$ and $M = M_e$, where M_e is the moment of force provided by the spring attached to the platform. But when the spring is detached, a new steady-state $\alpha_1{}' = (0, \phi_1)$ is required to achieve the same angle of articulation ϕ_1, which means, of course, that a new invariant characteristic $M'(\phi)$ is needed. The question is: Can the transition from one invariant characteristic to another be effected during the execution of the movement? If it cannot, then when the spring is detached the joint will move to the angle ϕ_2 determined by the characteristic function $M(\phi)$. In the space (M, ϕ), ϕ_2 will be at the intersection of $M(\phi)$ with $M = 0$ (since $M_e = 0$). The results of the experiment reveal that during the rapid establishment of a desired steady angle in the joint, correction of the invariant characteristics of the joint–muscle system (correction of the parameters defining the projected steady state) does not occur. The correction is made only after the achievement of the new steady state (corresponding to ϕ_2) when the error becomes obvious.

Now we wish to prove that the joint–muscle system truly behaves in this situation like a mass-spring system; although the movement of such a system as a whole is determined by the initial conditions, the equilibrium position does not depend on them and is determined only by the parameters of the spring and the size of the load. Using the paradigm described above we attach a pulley-weight system opposing extension such that release of the weight induces passive extension in the joint. Thus there are two external moments operating on the limb: a spring-opposing flexion and a weight-opposing extension. The participant becomes acquainted with the situation in which the spring is detached in the latent period before movement to the intended angle ϕ_1, bringing about passive flexion of the joint. But on some occasions the weight is also detached, leading additionally to passive extension before the voluntary movement. The results show that these rather radical and unpredictable changes in the initial conditions do not alter the behavior of the joint–muscle system: The trajectory of the system is still determined by the initial setting of parameters, that is, it moves to the state defined by the characteristic function $M(\phi)$ established at the outset of the trial. In brief, the equilibrium position is independent of the initial conditions (Fel'dman, 1966b).

In further analyses, this time of rhythmic movements of the joints, Fel'dman (1966b) was able to demonstrate that there is an independent parameter setting for the dynamics of the joint–muscle system. We may, therefore, envisage the set of fundamental servomechanisms (the alpha–gamma links together with the tendon feedback loops) regulating joint flexion and extension as collected together into a single vibratory system for which "static" and "dynamic" parameters can be specified. Choice of static parameters for the system determines the aim of a movement (the final steady state) independently of initial conditions; choice of the dynamic parameters determines (to a large extent) the rate and acceleration of the movement and also its form (aperiodic, oscillatory, etc.) (Fel'dman, 1966b).

This analogy between systems controlling action and vibratory systems suggests that *we may usefully conceive of coordinative structures in general as biasable, self-regulating vibratory systems.* In their simplest forms such systems might be modeled by the following second-order homogeneous linear differential equation with constant coefficients:

$$mX''(t) + kX'(t) + sX(t) = 0,$$

where $X(t)$ is the function relating the displacement of the system from a steady state to time.[7] In such a system the setting of the parameter s defines the "stiffness" of the system and thus its equilibrium state, and the setting of the parameter k defines the friction or damping constant which determines the rate at which the system achieves equilibrium and the form of its behavior, that is, whether it oscillates or not. By way of summary, we have seen that the functional tuning of the segmental apparatus of the spinal cord may be likened to the specification of the parameters s and k for vibratory systems. On the

[7] This simple linear differential equation is given only to illustrate a principle. It is not meant to model (although it might) an actual coordinative structure. If we were to make the illustration more realistic and more general we would need to consider forced vibration in addition to free vibration, and to concern ourselves with equations in which the applied force varied with time or acted in an arbitrarily short interval.

assumption that all coordinative structures behave as vibratory systems, then tuning as parameter specification emerges as a viable procedure for adjusting the behavior of selected coordinative structures at all levels of abstraction of the action heterarchy. Thus, while some coordinative structures coordinate autonomously a greater number of pieces of the action apparatus than other coordinative structures (compare, for example, two classes of basic coordinative structures, the long spinal reflexes and the flexion reflexes), the manner of their attunement is fundamentally the same.

We now address the important question of whether the tuning and activation of autonomous systems are governed by the same mechanisms. Again, we will proceed on the assumption that the regulatory principles for large systems follow very much the pattern of small systems. This permits us the latitude of extrapolating from the tuning of small systems, that is, the fundamental servomechanism, about which we know something, to large systems, about which we know very little. The evidence of segmental pretuning suggests, among other things, that the nervous system has available a means of selectively raising and lowering the gain of spindle and tendon organ feedback loops. Indeed, the comment was made earlier that the control of the alpha and gamma systems is largely separate so that it is optional whether the two systems be concurrently active. But in the experiments we have taken as evidence for segmental pretuning, can a case be made for the selective modulation of servoprocesses independent of instructions sent specifically to activate alphamotorneurons, either directly or indirectly through gammamotorneurons? In experiments exploiting the H reflex and plantar flexion, such as those of Gottlieb *et al.* (1970), we might suppose that changes in the reflex during the latent period reflect nothing more than the increasing excitability of gastrocnemius–soleus motor units brought about by direct supraspinal signals to the alphamotorneurons. Or, in a similar vein, the increase in the H reflex represents the increased excitability in the alphamotorneuron pool of the gastrocnemius–soleus group in response to stimulation from the gamma system, which is in turn responding to directions from above. In these accounts the variation in the reflex is not an independent event but an epiphenomenon of alpha system innervation; that is to say, the voluntary EMG and the H-wave variations are manifestations of the same controlling input. Against this argument, however, Gottlieb *et al.* (1970) point out that changes in the wave form and amplitude of the H reflex are not correlated with changes in the agonist or antagonist EMG and, in addition, that the time courses of the recordings are clearly different. From their point of view it is much simpler to propose that for their particular form of voluntary movement there is a means for modulating the H reflex (and by inference, the fundamental servomechanism) that is separate from the means for activating alphamotorneurons. In more general terms we may conjecture that the mechanisms of tuning and activating coordinative structures are largely separate.

THE RELATIONSHIP BETWEEN THE EXECUTIVE AND TUNING

Let us summarize briefly our thinking thus far. The executively specified action plan identifies the relevant subset of coordinative structures and a set of functions on that subset (identifying the necessary equivalence classes) that will modulate its elements and relate them in a certain fashion. In the course of spelling out the action plan through successive procedures within the action heterarchy the functions identified by the executive may be substituted for by functions more suited to the current low-level conditions of the system. The interconverting of functions, however, leaves the equivalence classes invariant. Of these interconversions and of the low-level realization of the details of the action plan, the executive remains virtually ignorant.

The eventual activation of coordinative structures takes place against a background of prearranged interactions within the segmental apparatus of the spinal cord. We say that the segmental apparatus has been pretuned, or simply, tuned, and that the detailed performance of coordinative structures is determined by the extent interactive state of the segmental apparatus. The tuning of coordinative structures and the activation of coordinative structures appear to be governed by separate mechanisms.

We now ask: If it is the case that the activation and tuning of coordinative structures are separately controlled events, at what level is the separation first evident? More precisely, we are keenly interested in the issue of whether tuning is the responsibility of the executive, and thus part of the initial representation of the act, or whether this responsibility lies outside the executive's domain.

For a given movement such as plantar flexion we may suppose that the executive specifies a tuning function to the servomechanisms for the (possibly) separate alpha and gamma instructions to follow. The independence of movement-related tuning would arise, on this account, because the tuning function is effected by substructures different from those responsible for motor neuron activation, much along the lines that the delimiting of coordinative structures and their decomposition are controlled separately. In this view the family of possible tunings defines just another equivalence class, another invariant unit of information for the executive specification of solutions to action problems.

Alternatively, we may propose that *segmental tuning is not specified in the action plan but is determined by other structures on acknowledgment of the executive's intention* (cf. Greene 1971a, b). There would be special advantages accruing to a devolution of responsibility for specifying action plans and segmental tuning, advantages that would be especially pronounced when actions are related to environmental events. For example, it would mean that the executive could develop a repertoire of plans appropriate to frequently occurring classes of environmental events, so that when confronted with an event of a certain class the executive issues a standard set of instructions and leaves to relatively independent tuning systems the responsibility for achieving the appropriate variant. Indeed, the largely invariant species-specific behavior of animals documented in the now celebrated works of ethologists (e.g., Tinbergen, 1951) strongly suggests that evolution has thoroughly exploited the principle of separating action-plan specification from tuning. The instinctive rituals are released by stimulation of a simple kind—the red belly of the stickleback, the spot under the herring gull's beak—but the unfolding stereotypic behavior is flexible: it relates to the lie of the land, to the contingencies of the local environment. We should suppose that these species-specific action plans are adjusted by the pickup of information about the environment, that is to say, their tuning is environment related.

Visual Control of Locomotion

Locomotion provides an instructive example of this viewpoint, for although locomotion propels an animal through its cluttered, textured environment, the basic locomotion pattern generator is independent of local conditions (Evarts *et al.*, 1971). The necessary adaptive modifications are effected by feedback from the peripheral motor apparatus (the muscles and the joints), from changes in tactual motion, from the basic orienting system (Gibson, 1966b), and most significantly, from the perceptual pickup of information about surfaces and objects, about the relations among them and the moving animal. Visually detected information about the environment plays a fundamental role in permitting anticipatory changes in the basic locomotion pattern through "feed forward"; appropriate changes in coordination may be induced before the animal confronts a certain kind of surface irregularity or a certain kind of object. To manipulate the locomotion plan by touch or kinesthetic feedback alone would be unsatisfactory, since this form of regulation would often occur after an ill-adjusted movement and thus would specify compensatory changes for states that are no longer current. It is far better to have the low-level realization of the plan adjusted beforehand through patterns of feed forward related to properties of the optic array and to leave to touch and joint–muscle feedback the task of achieving small, final adjustments. At all events, the locomotion illustration raises the important issue in the present context of how the visual detection of environmental properties relating to the modification and control of locomotion is realized in the language of the action system.

With this issue in mind let us proceed to examine in some detail the problem of how an animal moves about in a stable environment. We take as our orientation J. J. Gibson's (1958) analysis of locomotion and its control by vision. First, we recognize, following Gibson, two fundamental assertions: (1) the control of locomotion relative to the total environment is governed by transformations of the total optic array to a moving point; (2) the control of locomotion relative to an object in the environment is governed by transformations of a smaller bounded cone of the optic array—a closed contour with internal texture in the animal's visual field. Second, and again respecting Gibson, we recognize the following as aspects of locomotion requiring our attention: (1) beginning locomotion in a forward direction; (2) terminating locomotion; (3) locomoting in reverse; (4) steering toward a specific location or object; (5) approaching without collision; (6) avoiding obstacles; (7) pursuing and avoiding a moving object. Additionally, we recognize that locomotion must be adjusted to the physical properties of the surface—its convexities and concavities, its slants and slopes, its edges.

For each of the aspects of locomotion we can identify correspondences in the flow patterns of the optic array. Thus, to initiate locomotion in a forward direction is to activate and relate the coordinative structures that comprise the locomotor synergism (Gelfand *et al.,* 1971) in such a fashion as to make the forward optic array flow outward; to cease locomotion is to terminate the optic flow; and to locomote in reverse is to pattern the locomotor synergism in a manner that makes the optic array flow inward. To move faster or slower is to make the rate of flow increase and decrease respectively. As Gibson (1958) remarks: "An animal who is behaving in these ways is optically stimulated in the corresponding ways, or, equally, an animal who so acts to obtain these kinds of optical stimulation is behaving in the corresponding ways [p. 187] ." Now during forward movement the center of the flow pattern is the direction in which the animal is moving, that is to say, the part of the array from which the optic flow pattern radiates corresponds to that part of the solid environment to which the animal is locomoting. If the animal changes direction then naturally the center of flow shifts across the array. Thus we can say that to maintain locomotion in the direction of an object is to keep the center of flow of the optic array as near as possible to that part of the structure of the optic array which the object projects.

In moving about a stable environment an animal will approach solid surfaces that it will need to contact or avoid as situation and history demand. Objects are specified in the optic array by contours with internal texture. Areas between objects are specified either by untextured homogeneous regions (that is, sky) or by densely textured regions (that is, sand, grass). In approaching an object the closed contour in the array corresponding to the boundaries of the object expands with the rate of expansion for a uniform approach speed, accelerating in inverse proportion to the animal's proximity to the object. If the animal is on a collision course with the object, then a symmetrically expanding radial flow field will be kinetically defined over the texture bounded by the object's contours. On the other hand, if the expansion is skewed, that is, if the pattern of texture flow is asymmetrical then this specifies to the animal that it is on a noncollision course. A translation of the center of the flow pattern laterally to the animal's right or to the animal's left specifies that the animal will bypass the object on, respectively, its right or left. In Gibson's (1958) account the guiding principle for approaching an object without collision is to move so as to cancel the forward and relatively symmetrically expanding flow of the optic array corresponding to the object at the instant when "the contour of the object on the texture of the surface reaches that angular magnification at which contact is made [p. 188]."[8] And to avoid objects, to steer successfully around them, the animal needs to keep the center of the centrifugal flow of the optical array outside the contours with internal texture and inside the homogeneous or densely textured surface areas.

Suppose now that the object to which movement is being directed is a moving object, as in the case of one animal pursuing another. We can again identify corresponding properties of the optic array. A prey fleeing a predator is specified by the fact that for the predator the overall optic array flows from a center, but a contour with internal texture within the overall flow pattern is not expanding; absolute expansion of the contour means that our predator is making good ground on its prey, contraction of the contour may mean that our prey will live to run another day. The principle of pursuit is summed up lightheartedly by Gibson (1958), ". . . the rule by which a big fish can catch a small fish is simple: maximize its optical size in the field of view [p. 188]."

We see, in short, that controlling locomotion calls for the detection of change, detection of rates of change, and detection of rates of rates of change in the flowing optic array. It also calls for the detection of changes in parts of the structure of the optic array with respect to the optic array as a whole. We assume that animals are sensitive to all of these properties of stimulation that vary over time and that they do indeed detect them (Gibson, 1966b; Ingle, 1968). We should also note that modulating the optic array through movement and modulating movement through changes in the optic array go hand in hand; thus the cybernetical loop of afference, efference, reafference is virtually continuous.

But we must now face up to a point that has been neglected thus far. In directing its locomotion to one object and weaving its way among others, and in pursuing one moving object and fleeing another the animal exhibits its capacity to make discriminative responses. But these responses must be based upon different properties of stimulation from those that determine the control of locomotion: they are responses that are specific to those properties of the optic array which do not change as opposed to those which do; importantly, they are properties of stimulation that do not result from the animal's locomotion. The animal must be able to detect permanent properties of its environment: it must be able to detect whether a surface affords locomotion and whether a contour with internal texture affords collision; it must be able to detect whether a moving textured contour affords eating or whether it affords being eaten.

[8] For an interesting experiment in insect behavior that is of some relevance to these comments and to the general theory of perception–action relations see Goggshall (1972).

In respect to the surface supporting locomotion the terrestrial animal must detect the gradients of optical texture specifying slant and slope, the topological shearing of texture specifying edge, and the changes of texture gradient specifying convexities and concavities. As it moves rapidly across a rough terrain, it must adjust its footfall pattern, temporally and spatially; it must adjust its gait to the wrinkled surface. It must detect surface protuberances and surface breaks that require leaping over as opposed to those that require going round or avoiding; it will often need to make transitions between running and leaping. With respect to the permanent properties of the environment we concur with Gibson (1966b) that the animal can detect in the changing optical flux those mathematically invariant properties that correspond to the physically constant object or surface and which afford for the organism possibilities for action.

We are led, therefore, to a distinction between those properties of stimulation which afford approach, avoidance, pursuit, flight, changes in the footfall pattern of a gait, and transitions from running to leaping, and those properties of stimulation which control locomotion in each of these respects. It would seem that the former are those properties which do not vary over time while the latter are those properties which do. And the pickup of change and nonchange are concurrent perceptual activities.

Tuning Reflexes and Environment-Related Tuning

At this stage of our inquiry as to how vision enters into locomotion (and into action in general) we turn our attention to the concept of tuning reflexes. In addition to those reflexes that resemble parts of acts, such as the flexion and crossed extension reflexes, or are themselves simple yet self-sufficient acts such as the righting reflex and the scratch reflex, we can identify a further class of reflexes whose task it appears is to impose biases upon the action system. We can distinguish, therefore, between "elemental" reflexes and "tuning" reflexes (Greene, 1969). As illustrations of tuning reflexes we can take classically defined postural or attitudinal (Magnus, 1925) reflexes such as the tonic neck reflex, which biases the motor apparatus for movement in the direction of gaze, and the labyrinthine reflexes, which bias the musculature to resist motion on an incline or to resist rotation (Roberts, 1967). Quite recently evidence has been forwarded of low-level tuning resulting from movements of the eyes (Easton, 1971, 1972a). In the cat, stretching the horizontal eye muscles facilitates a turning of the neck and head from the direction of gaze and stretch of the vertical eye muscles influences the forelimbs. Indeed, it appears that the eyes looking upward might foster forelimb flexion and the eyes looking downward might foster forelimb extension (Easton, 1972a).

The principal function of tuning reflexes seems to be that of altering the intrinsic system of segmental relations rather than that of initiating configurations of motions in components of the motor machinery.[9] The impression is that tuning reflexes adjust the bias in the fundamental servomechanisms (cf. Gernandt, 1967). In general it may be argued that the main advantage of tuning reflexes, whether induced by prior motion or induced more directly, is a reduction in the detail required of high-level instructions (Easton, 1972a). Thus when a cat turns its head to gaze at a passing mouse, the angle of tilt of the head and the degree of flexion and torsion in the neck will elicit a reflex modulation of the segmental apparatus such that a broadly stated executive instruction to "jump" will be realized as a jump in the right direction (Magnus, 1925; Ruch, 1965b). Clearly, such modulation must precede the innervation of muscles or the cat would constantly miss its target; obviously the cat in flight cannot rely on corrective feedback.

How do tuning reflexes relate to the visual control of locomotion? Analysis of the biomechanics of walking and running in animals (e.g., Arshavskii, Kots, Orlovskii, Rodionov, & Shik, 1965; Shik & Orlovskii, 1965; Shik, Orlovskii, & Severin, 1966) reveals that with change in speed or gait the majority of kinematic parameters is kept constant, suggesting that adjustments in the locomotion plan require a relatively minimal change in coordination. The action problem posed by the need to change speed of running or gait may be solved in most instances by a change in only two parameters. May we suppose, therefore, that a change in a small set of parameters is all that is needed to control locmotion through a "wrinkled" and object-cluttered terrain? Movement in a forward direction calls for a particular organization of the basic coordinative structures. If an animal so moving detects an invariant specifying an object or surface in its path that is to be avoided, then it must alter the organization of the relevant coordinative structures in order to change direction. But change in direction need not actually require direct executive intervention in the low-level organization of the locomotion plan; a shift in the direction of gaze may be all that is needed. In theory at least the tonic neck reflexes and related tuning reflexes could effect the necessary reorganization of the segmental apparatus. Similarly, if the contoured texture in the optic array afforded

[9] The potential range of changes in the segmental system induced by postural changes, and their implications for the behavior of coordinative structures is suggested in the following paragraph from an address delivered by Magnus almost fifty years ago:

> Every change in attitude, with its different positions of all parts of the body, changes the reflex excitability of these parts and in some cases changes also the sense of the reflex evoked, excitations being converted into inhibitions, reflex extensions into flexions and so on. One and the same stimulus applied to one and the same place on the body may give rise to very different reactions in consequence of different attitudes which have been imposed to the body before the stimulus is applied [Magnus, 1925, p. 346].

For further intriguing and provocative comments on tuning reflexes see Jones (1965) and Fukuda (1957).

jumping on, then the act of directing the eyes or eyes and head upward would facilitate the transition in segmental organization from that of running to that of jumping.

These examples suggest the following: in the course of locomotion the detection of invariants affording specific changes in locomotion may serve to activate singularly simple action plans such as a change in the direction in which the head and/or eyes are pointing. Often these adjustments in orientation—owing to the functional tuning link between head and eye movements and the segmental apparatus—are sufficient to produce the needed parameters for the segmental realization of change in locomotion.

As we have noted, the optical stimulation for a moving animal has components of both change and nonchange (Gibson, 1966b). If the components of nonchange, specifying the permanent entities in the animal's environment, relate to action plans and their activation, to what do the changing components of stimulation relate? We must suppose that they relate to the mechanisms of tuning; but how is this relation effected? The following considerations may help us to move toward an answer to this question.

To leap from object to object is to project the body in particular trajectories, with each trajectory requiring different horizontal and vertical vectors of extension thrust. Variations in force could be achieved either through variations in the degree of activation of coordinative structures or parts of coordinative structures as might be permitted by the local sign properties of reflexes (the dependency of reflex patterns on the origin of stimulation) or through direct facilitation of motor neuron activity, or both (cf. Easton, 1972a). In theory, both of these sources of force variation are plausible instances of tuning. We can say therefore that each leap calls for the specification of parameters to the intrinsic system of segmental relations where these parameters relate to the desired trajectory. Now we might ask whether trajectory-related parameters could be determined through tuning reflexes. But cursory analysis would suggest that mechanical modulation—spinal tuning elicited reflexively by a prior motion such as directing the eye–head system toward an object—is inadequate for the task. Consider a cat perched on a particular platform. At a distance of X feet from its perch is another, higher platform. Directing its gaze to the top surface of the higher platform yields, say, a particular angle of neck extension and hence a particular tuning of the segmental apparatus. Yet we observe that we could arrange any number of higher platforms of different heights at any number of reasonable distances either more or less than X feet from the cat's perch that would correspond to the same inclination of the neck and hence to the same tuning parameters and hence, supposedly, to the same degree of thrust if the cat chose to jump. In brief, reflex tuning induced by any particular orientation of the eye–head system is ambiguous with respect to distance. Mechanically induced tuning, therefore, cannot supply the tuning parameters relevant to a given trajectory. How then are they supplied? We are forced to conclude that they are supplied by the properties of the optic array that specify relative distance and height in the cat's normal cluttered and textured environment, and that these optical properties are realizable as segmental tunings without the intervention of executive procedures and without mechanical mediation.

With this conclusion in mind consider what we might now say about the scenario that unfolds when a scampering mouse appears at a leapable distance from an interested cat. In the cat's field of vision the mouse is projected as changing patterns in the optic array. Concurrently, there is a pickup by the cat's visual system of those properties of stimulation that change over time and those properties that do not. The former specify how far away the mouse is, in what direction it is moving, at what rate it is moving, and where it will be in a following instant relative to the cat; the latter specify the mouse's identity as something that affords catching and eating. Orienting in the direction of the mouse adjusts the segmental apparatus through the tuning reflexes for a movement in that direction; as the direction of gaze shifts according to changes in the mouse's location the mechanically induced segmental tuning likewise adjusts appropos the new direction. On activation of the action plan to pounce, the tuning parameters for the needed trajectory specified by the transformations in the optic array are given to the segmental system of interactions. The activation of coordinative structures then takes place against a backdrop of segmental relations appropriately adjusted for the generation of a precise, on-target leap.

In this cat-and-mouse story there are two main themes: one is that the activation of crudely stated action plans and environment-related tuning are based on different properties of stimulation; the other is that the properties of visual stimulation that control movement and the family of possible tunings that effect the control are tightly linked. In Gibson's view, perception is direct. He has also remarked that: "The distinction between an S–R theory of control reactions and and S–R theory of identifying reactions is important for behavior theory" (Gibson, 1958, p. 190). On this distinction we might now comment that in control reactions the relation is between changing properties of stimulation and patterns of tuning, and in identifying reactions it is between nonchanging properties of stimulation and action plans.

Mittelstaedt (1957) describes a similar story about prey capture in the mantis. A mantis strikes its prey with pinpoint accuracy within a latency of 10–30 msec, a period too brief to allow for adjustments during the course of the strike trajectory. The problem is to account for how this accuracy is achieved when the prey appears at a strikable distance either to the left or to the right of the body axis at some variable angle; and when the head is oriented at some (different) angle to the prothorax with which the forelegs—the striking instrument—are articulated. Mittelstaedt's modeling of this sutuation implies that the visual and proprioceptive information specifying the relevant relations is conveyed not to the executive issuing the strike signal but to the segmental machinery of the forelegs. On our account we would say that the higher-order invariant specifying "prey" triggers the strike command (the strike action plan) but the properties of optical stimulation specifying the coordinates of the prey with respect to the body axis, and its rate and direction of movement, do not enter into the executive decision, for most assuredly that would introduce undesirable delays. Rather, these properties are realized as segmental tuning parameters effecting needed adjustments in the centers controlling foreleg extension. We may say of the mantis' prey catching that the prey determines the ballistic component while the prey's location and movement determine the tuning component in a mixed ballistic-tuning strategy. Moreover, we recognize what might indeed be a general principle, namely, that different properties of stimulation enter into the unfolding act at different levels.

In respect to this last point let us make one final comment on the topic of locomotion, which began this particular phase of our inquiry. We have argued that environment-related tuning is relatively independent of executive procedures. For locomotion we can say that tuning is coupled to the pickup of information conveyed by continuous transformations in the optic array. While the detection of higher-order invariants (affordances) may inject gross adjustments in locomotor activity, the fine control of locomotion in an object-cluttered and wrinkled terrain is through environment-related tuning which adapts the activity to the conditions by modulating a relatively small set of parameters, and does so without involving the higher domains of the action coalition/heterarchy.

Pal'tsev (1967a, b) advanced a theory that is of special relevance to this account of locomotor regulation. First, Pal'tsev (1967a) recognizes that in respect to uniform movements an argument can be made that in addition to movement-related segmental pretuning there is another type of reorganization of the segmental relations that is brought about *during* the execution of the movements. This latter form of tuning is due in Pal'tsev's (1967a) view to the fact that to a very large extent the interactions among different structures of the spinal cord are reorganized by processes that are inherently spinal. The segmental apparatus tunes itself, as it were, in harmony with the main supraspinal influence. By comparing experimental results on the effects spinal reflexes induce in neighboring spinal reflexes with the general picture of locomotion Pal'tsev (1967b) is led to the supposition that following the first few locomotor cycles the strategic ordering of muscle events in locomotion can be determined solely by the segmental system of relations. As he sees it, the supraspinal patterns of feedforward serve only to identify and to "trigger" the particular locomotion plan: the continuation of the plan, the subsequent locomotor cycles in walking or running, is then the responsibility of spinal processes. Which is to say that control of locomotion is simply and elegantly transferred from supraspinal structures to spinal structures. Thus, locomotion exhibited in the pursuit by a predator of its prey could proceed with insignificant involvement of the highest sectors of the action system. If such is the case, then it would be propitious for the nervous system to exploit the principle of conveying visually specified adjustments in locomotion relatively directly to the segmental apparatus in which locomotion control is invested. This conclusion is consonant with the often expressed point of view that the spinal cord is a system that during action serves to integrate different supraspinal influences (cf. Pal'tsev & El'ner, 1967).

Two Kinds of Vision

In some respects the ideas just expressed are reminiscent of the claim that there are two separate but interdependent visual systems related to action (Trevarthan, 1968). It appears that a distinction is drawn in the neuroanatomy of the brain "between vision of relationships in an extensive space and visual identification of things" (Trevarthan, 1968, p. 301). In its simplest form the distinction is demonstrated most straightforwardly by the experiments of Schneider (1969): a hamster with intact superior colliculus but no visual cortex can orient to objects but cannot distinguish between them; conversely, with intact visual cortex and no superior colliculus the hamster can successfully distinguish objects but cannot locate them and orient to them except through trial-and-error. In very general terms it appears that there is a functional differentiation between two kinds of vision that relates in part to forebrain–midbrain differences.

Let us remark briefly on the vertebrate midbrain. Suppose that we drew a map of the projections from the eyes to the midbrain tectum and suppose that we did so for two dissimilar vertebrates, the goldfish and the cat. The eyes of the goldfish are aligned roughly perpendicular to the body axis, while those of the cat are aligned parallel to the body axis. If one drew maps in the optical coordinates of the eye, one would find that for the two vertebrates the projection from the eyes to the midbrain differed considerably. But if the maps were drawn in the coordinates of the behavioral field, that is, with respect to the symmetry of the body, one would observe that the two maps were virtually identical. Indeed, if one went on to obtain such maps for other vertebrates, one would find that the mapping from eyes to tectum in the coordinates of the behavioral field is relatively invariant, and thus indifferent to the variation in alignment between eyes and body axis (see Trevarthan, 1968). One might conjecture that body-centered visual space is represented by a precise topographical mapping in the midbrain in very much the same way in all vertebrates.

This map of visual loci also maps a topography of points of entry into the action system. Stimulating points on the tectum produces orienting movements of eyes, head, and trunk to the corresponding visual location (cf. Apter, 1946; Ewert, 1974; Hyde & Eliasson, 1957). A singularly important feature of the midbrain is that in respect to the symmetry of the body it provides a precise topographical map of points in visual space and a virtually identical map of orienting movements to those points (Apter, 1946). Because of this feature the midbrain serves to map object locations onto the set of movement-induced tunings. But there is reason to suppose that the capabilities of the midbrain extend beyond this and are concerned in a more general way with the control of locomotion.

Let us say that the two kinds of vision relating to forebrain–midbrain differences relate in turn to different kinds of acts performed in the animal's behavioral space. Discussing primates, Trevarthan (1968) conveys the tenor of this viewpoint as follows:

> Orientations of the head, postural adjustments, locomotor displacements change the relationship between the body and spatial configurations of contours, surfaces, events, and objects. These movements occur in what I shall call *ambient vision*. In contrast praxic actions on the environment to use pieces of it in specific ways are performed with the motor apparatus of the body and the visual receptors oriented together so that both vision and the acts inflicted on the environment occur in one part of the behavioral space. The vision applied to one place and a specific kind of object, or deployed in a field of identified objects, I shall call *focal vision* [p. 302]."

Trevarthan builds his case upon facts found in the effects of surgically separating the cerebral hemispheres. This separation exhibits many instructive and curious phenomena, including that of central concern to Trevarthan's thesis—the capability of the split-brain primate to double perceive and learn for some types of visual stimulation but not for others and correspondingly to perform some aspects of visually defined acts chaotically and yet to perform others with no evident impairment. We note that the separated cortices may learn, independently and simultaneously, conflicting solutions to a visual discrimination problem when the stimuli are clearly of different identities, as in the example of cross versus circle, but not when the stimuli differ on a single dimension such as bright versus dim. In the former case, that of an identity difference, what is learned by one hemisphere is available to the other only if it in turn has the opportunity to learn the same thing; in the latter case, what is learned by one hemisphere is without practice available to the other. The inference is that differences in degree may be apprehended by visual mechanisms of the midbrain, while the apprehension of differences in identity is the responsibility of cortical visual mechanisms (Trevarthan, 1968). And Trevarthan emphasizes that it is the transformations relating the to-be-distinguished stimuli rather than the ease of distinguishing between them that is important to the dissociation.

Paralleling this dissociation in split-brain vision is a dissociation in split-brain action. If an object such as a peanut is presented to the commisurectomized primate both hands may reach forward with precision to grasp it; however, the activities of the two hands appear indifferent to each other, resulting often in collision. Given an object to manipulate and explore, the split-brain displays an inability to relate the activities of the two hands. The needed collaboration is replaced by redundant and conflicting movements.

In sharp contrast to these anomalies of voluntary movements of the hands in the field of focal vision, no such schism is witnessed in locomotion in which the hands play an important role. Locomotion-related movements of the arms and hands are properly coordinated to each other and to the motions of the hind limbs; and in terms of displacement, velocity and timing are finely attuned to the environmental structures supporting the action (Trevarthan, 1968).

While there are many more questions to be asked of these dissociations in vision and action and of the relation between them we can with some reasonable certitude draw the following conclusions. First, low-level sections of the visual system can effect the pickup of transformations in the optic array corresponding to changes in gross environmental properties such as texture and contour and to the detection of simple invariants such as solidity—in short, those properties of the optic array relevant to the control of locomotion. And in this regard it is of some import to note that electrical stimulation of the midbrain can bring about parameter changes in the segmental functions governing locomotion (Shik, Severin, & Orlovskii, 1966). Second, the higher-level sections of the visual system detect higher-order invariants specifying identity and more complex transformation that would be relevant to and indeed result from the skilled manipulation of objects. For it is evident that separating the hemispheres gives rise to two separate visual frames for the regulation of manipulative behavior and to a consequent breakdown in coordination between the two hands, but leaves intact the visual frame for the regulation of locomotion.

RELATING THE CONTENTS OF VISION TO ACTION: A SUMMING UP

We come now to a general summary of these speculations on how vision enters into action. We have provided two rather different descriptions of the unfolding act, and it will be helpful to collect them together at this time. In one we envisaged the act as evolving through the establishment of progressively less abstract representations, from the specification of relations among and within a few relatively large coordinative structures to the specification of relations among and within many relatively small coordinative structures, the fundamental servomechanisms. In the other we saw the action plan unfolding as ordered successions of progressively less abstract projections of the environment. What we must now attempt is a reconciliation of these separate views.

The kernel notion is this essay has been the idea of building acts through the fitting together of relatively autonomous units. This principle of operation reflects the fundamental argument that there are far too many degrees of freedom in coordinated activity for it to be controlled by a single procedure in a single instant. One consequence of this viewpoint is that the initial representation of an act in the highest domain must necessarily be crude in comparison to its ultimate representation in terms of instructions to muscles.

Similarly we saw that in view of the degrees of freedom problem the representation in the highest domain could not be constructed in respect to the details of skeletal space; the perception of the disposition of the limbs and branches of the body at any moment can only enter into the representation in the most general way as an abstracted account of the body's "pose" at that instant. Using very much the same rationale we are led to believe that in interactions with the environment not all the contents of vision can be involved in the determination of the initial representation of an act. Again we suppose that the executive procedure uses only the perceptual description that it can handle; the description cannot be detailed and by necessity must be fairly abstract. Earlier, following Bernstein (1967), we used the term "topological properties" to identify the description of the environment to which the initial representation of the action plan related. We may now regard these properties as invariants of a higher order, for example, those which specify the identities of objects and their possibilities of transformation. In any event, the manifestation of the action plan as motions finely attuned to the nuances of the environment's structure tells us quite plainly that the detailed contents of vision must be interjected into the act during its evolution. We have argued that tuning of coordinative structures is probably the mechanism through which the interjection of environmental details is brought about.

If these speculations are not too far off the mark, then we might further conjecture as follows. The determination of an act as an orderly pattern of motions is distributed across many structures. In the coalitional/heterarchical language used above, we say that it is distributed across different domains. But where the differentiation of an action plan requires information about the environment, we should suppose that the procedures operating at each domain incorporate optically specified environmental properties. It seems unlikely however that the entry of environmental properties into the various representations of an unfolding act is a haphazard affair. Rather, we hypothesize that the properties of the optic array interlace with the representation of an action plan in a systematic fashion: different properties map into different representations. We have, of course, already implied that this might be the case in arguing that the specification of action plans and the tuning of structures correspond to different properties of stimulation. But now suppose that the properties of stimulation relevant to the control of action may themselves be arranged from more complex to more simple; then perhaps we can imagine a natural mapping of these properties onto the unfolding act, a mapping that preserves their order. Of the properties of optical stimulation relevant to the control of action, those of a higher order are realized as tunings in higher domains and those of a lower order are realized as tunings in lower domains of the action heterarchy.

We conclude with some final thoughts on the general characterization of the perception–action relation. With respect to the representation of the action plan in the highest domain, it is not so much that the specification of a subset of large coordinative structures and functions defined on them relates to higher-order properties of the optic array but rather that the description of the plan in action terms and the description of the plan in perceptual terms are dual statements about the same thing. Earlier we described the action concept for A writing as an operator defined over a set of functions relevant to the manipulation of coordinative structures; but we have also referred to the action concept for A writing in geometrical terms consonant with the points of view expressed by Bernstein (1967) and Lashley (1951), and further suggested that the two descriptions were isomorphic. Similarly, with respect to tuning, we have implied that there is a relatively direct mapping of the properties of optical stimulation relevant to the control of action onto the set of tunings. To draw these concepts together, we can say that "detection of control-relevant optical properties" and "specification of environment-related tuning parameters" are descriptions of the same event: one is the dual of the other.

Perhaps we can gain a purchase on the duality of perception and action events by considering a problem drawn from a rather special domain of the perception-action relation—communication between members of the same species. For a variety of reasons it has been suggested that the perception of sounds of speech is achieved by reference to the mechanisms of articulation (see Galunov & Chistovich, 1966; Liberman *et al.*, 1967; Zinkin, 1968). One version of this action-based theory of speech perception suggests that the listener seeks to determine (tacitly and unconsciously of course) which phoneme articulation plans could produce the acoustic pattern; the listener uses the inconstant sound to recover the articulatory gestures that produced it and thereby arrives at the speaker's intent (Liberman *et al.*, 1967). Other students of speech, however, have argued against the articulatory matching explanation of the perception of speech sounds and have suggested that the explanation be sought in the sensitivity of the nervous system to higher-order properties of acoustic stimulation (e.g., Fant, 1967, Abbs & Sussman, 1971). There is growing evidence for neural mechanisms that selectively respond to complex acoustic invariants (e.g., Roeder & Treat, 1961, Frishkopf & Goldstein, 1963; Capranica, 1965), and it is becoming increasingly less venturesome to propose that the perception of phonological attributes of speech is direct rather than mediated (cf. Abbs & Sussman, 1971). However, viable descriptions of invariants in speech stimulation have been elusive.

Commendable as a direct perception interpretation is, we still must account for the evidently tight coupling between structures detecting speech sounds and structures producing speech sounds (see Chistovich, 1961; Chistovich, Fant, deSerpa-Leitaõ, & Tjernlund, 1966). Suppose, as Gibson (1966b) suggests, that vibratory patterns specify their source. Then we can say that a listener perceives articulation because the invariants of virbration correspond to the invariants of articulation: the phonemes are present in the neural activity and vocal tract activity of the speaker and in the air between the speaker and the listener. Thus the linguistically relevant invariants on the input side are the same as the linguistically relevant invariants on the output side, and it is in this sense that perceiving and producing speech correspond (cf. Halwes & Wire, 1974). Now suppose that we were to describe an articulatory action plan as a set of relations defined over a collection of coordinative structures, then we would argue that our description is also a description of the relevant relations in the acoustic pattern. An appropriate analogy is the group concept in mathematics: given two different sets of elements, with a group structure defined on each, we might find that although the elements differ (even radically) in the two instances, their manner of inner interlocking is the same, in which case we say that they represent the same abstract group. Our hypothesis, therefore, is this: the structure that affords perception of a speech sound also affords its production; speech perception and speech production are related by abstract structures that are common to both but indigenous to neither (cf. Turvey, 1974). There is some evidence, though slight, that structures with this dual property may have been exploited in the evolution of intraspecies communication. For example, the calling song of male crickets is composed of stereotyped rhythmic pulse intervals. Cross breeding of two species of crickets with marked differences in the rhythmic structure of their songs produces hybrids whose calling song is distinctly different from either parental song. It has been shown that genetic differences that cause song change in males also alter song reception in the females: hybrid females prefer the song of hybrid males (Hoy & Paul, 1973). What intrigues is the speculation that the action plan for song generation in the male and the female's selective sensitivity to the male's song are coupled through a common set of genes (Hoy & Paul, 1973). Thus, at some level of abstraction the same structure may underlie song production in the male and song reception in the female.

Whether a stronger and more general case can be made for the dual representation notion remains to be seen. There is the possibility, of course, that the principle we have tried to describe has meaning, if at all, only in the communication mode: speaking and perceiving speech, reading and writing, and the primitive instantiations of signaling in animal and insect communication. On the other hand, when one considers the failure of schemes in which sensory input is routed through a central network into motor responses, the growing uneasiness over the application of the terms "sensory, motor, associative" to higher neural structures, the increasing usage of the bimodal term "sensorimotor" (see Evarts *et al.*, 1971, for comments on each of these points), and the arbitrariness of action-based theories of perception, then the notion of perceiving and acting as dual representations of common neural events may be a reasonable alternative to the sensory and motor views of mind.

ACKNOWLEDGMENTS

The preparation of this paper was supported by a Guggenheim Fellowship awarded to the author for the period 1973-1974. I thank N. S. Sutherland for kindly providing facilities and assistance at the Laboratory of Experimental Psychology, University of Sussex, Brighton, England.

REFERENCES

Abbs, J. H., & Sussman, H. M. Neurophysiological feature detectors and speech perception: A discussion of theoretical implications. *Journal of Speech and Hearing Research,* 1971, **14,** 23–36.

Apter, J. T. Eye movements following strychninization of the superior colliculus of cats. *Journal of Neurophysiology,* 1946, **9,** 73–86.

Arbib, M. A. *The metaphorical brain: An introduction to cybernetics as artificial intelligence and brain theory.* New York: Wiley, 1972.

Arshavskii, Yu. I., Kots, Ya. M., Orlovskii, G. N. Rodionov, I. M., & Shik, M. L. Investigation of the biomechanics of running by the dog. *Biophysics,* 1965, **10,** 737–746.

Asatryan, D. G., & Fel'dman, A. G. Functional tuning of the nervous system with control of movement or maintenance of a steady posture–1. Mechanographic analysis of the work on the joint on execution of a postural task. *Biophysics,* 1965, **10,** 925–935.

Bartlett, F. C. *Remembering.* Cambridge, England: Cambridge University Press, 1964.

Belen'kii, V. Yi., Gurfinkel, V. S., & Pal'tsev, Ye. I. Elements of control of voluntary movements. *Biophysics,* 1967, **12,** 154–161.

Bernstein, N. *The coordination and regulation of movements.* London: Pergamon Press, 1967.

Capranica, R. R. The evoked vocal response of the bullfrog: a study of communication by sound. *Research Monographs,* No. 33. Cambridge, Massachusetts: MIT Press, 1965.

Care, N. S., & Landesman, C. *Readings in the theory of action.* Scarborough, Ontario, Canada: Fitzhenry and Whiteside, 1968.

Cassirer, E. *The philosophy of symbolic forms.* Vol. 3. *The phenomenology of knowledge.* New Haven, Connecticut: Yale University Press, 1957.

Chistovich, L. A. Classification of rapidly repeated speech sounds. *Soviet Physics-Acoustics,* 1961, **6,** 393–398.

Chistovich, L., Fant, G., deSerpa-Leitaõ, A., & Tjernlund, P. *Mimicking of synthetic vowels.* (STL-QPSR 2/1966) Stockholm, Sweden: Royal Institute of Technology, 1966.

Chomsky, N. *Aspects of the theory of syntax.* Cambridge, Massachusetts: MIT Press, 1965.

Chomsky, N. *Topics in the theory of generative grammar.* The Hague: Mouton, 1966.

Easton, T. A. Patterned inhibition from horizontal eye movement in the cat. *Experimental Neurology,* 1971, **31,** 419–430.

Easton, T. A. On the normal use of reflexes. *American Scientist,* 1972, **60,** 591–599. (a)

Easton, T. A. Patterned inhibition from single eye muscle stretch in the cat. *Experimental Neurology,* 1972, **34,** 497–510. (b)

Eccles, J. C. The dynamic loop hypothesis of motor control. In K. N. Leibovic (Ed.), *Information processing in the nervous system.* Berlin and New York: Springer-Verlag, 1969.

Eccles, R. M., & Lundberg, A. Supraspinal control of interneurones mediating-spinal reflexes. *Journal of Physiology,* 1959, **147,** 565–584.

Eldred, E. Posture and locomotion. In H. W. Magoun (Ed.) *Handbook of physiology: Neurophysiology,* Vol. II. Washington, D.C.: American Physiological Society, 1960.

Engberg, I., & Lundberg, A. An electromyographic analysis of muscular activity in the hindlimb of the cat during unrestrained locomotion. *Acta Physiologica Scandinavia,* 1969, **75**, 614–630.

Evarts, E. V. Representation of movements and muscles by pyramidal tract neurons of the precentral motor cortex. In M. D. Yahr & D. P. Purpura (Eds.), *Neurophysiological basis of normal and abnormal motor activities.* New York: Raven Press, 1967.

Evarts, E. V. Brain mechanisms in movement. *Scientific American,* 1973, **229**, 96–103.

Evarts, E. V., and Thach, W. T., Motor mechanisms of the CNS; Cerebrocerebellar interrelations. *Annual Review of Physiology,* 1969, **31**, 451–489.

Evarts, E. V., Bizzi, E., Burke, E. E., Delong, M., & Thach, W. T. Central control of movement. *Neurosciences Research Program Bulletin,* 1971, **9**, No. 3.

Ewert, J-P. The neural basis of visually guided behavior. *Scientific American,* 1974, **230**(3), 34–42.

Falk, G. Interpretation of imperfect line data as a three dimenstional scene. *Artificial Intelligence,* 1972, **3**, 101–144.

Fant, G. Auditory patterns of speech. In W. Wathen-Dunn (Ed.), *Models for the perception of speech and visual form.* Cambridge, Massachusetts: MIT Press, 1967.

Fel'dman, A. G. Functional tuning of the nervous system with control of movement or maintenance of a steady posture–II. Controllable parameters of the muscles. *Biophysics,* 1966, **11**, 565–578. (a)

Fel'dman, A. G. Functional tuning of the nervous system with control of movement or maintenance of a steady posture–III. Mechanographic analysis of the execution by man of the simplest motor tasks. *Biophysics,* 1966, **11**, 766–775. (b)

Festinger, L., Burnham, C. A., Ono, H., & Bamber, D. Efference and the conscious experience of perception. *Journal of Experimental Psychology Monograph,* 1967, **74**(4, Pt. 2).

Frishkopf, L., and Goldstein, M. Responses to acoustic stimuli from single units in the eighth nerve of the bullfrog. *Journal of the Acoustical Society of America,* 1963, **35**, 1219–1228.

Fukuda, T. *Stato-kinetic reflexes in equilibrium and movement.* Tokyo: Igaku Shoin, 1957.

Galunov, V. I., & Chistovich, L. A. Relationship of motor theory to the general problem of speech recognition (review). *Soviet Physics-Acoustics,* 1966, **11**, 357–365.

Gelfand, I. M., Gurfinkel, V. S., Tsetlin, M. L., & Shik, M. L. Some problems in the analysis of movements. In I. M. Gelfand, V. S. Gurfinkel, S. V. Fomin, & M. L. Tsetlin (Eds.), *Models of the structural-functional organization of certain biological systems.* Cambridge, Massachusetts: MIT Press, 1971.

Gernandt, B. E. Vestibular influence upon spinal reflex activity. In *Myotatic, kinesthetic and vestibular mechanisms: Ciba Foundation Symposium,* London: Churchill, 1967.

Gibson, J. J. Visually controlled locomotion and visual orientation in animals. *British Journal of Psychology,* 1958, **49**, 182–194.

Gibson, J. J. The problem of temporal order in stimulation and perception. *Journal of Psychology,* 1966, **62**, 141–149. (a).

Gibson, J. J. *The senses considered as perceptual systems.* Boston: Houghton Mifflin, 1966. (b).

Goggshall, J. C. The landing response and visual processing in the milkweed bug, *Oncopeltus fasciatus. Journal of Experimental Biology,* 1972, **57**, 401–414.

Gottlieb, G. L., Agarwal, G. C., & Stark, L. Interaction between voluntary and postural mechanisms of the human motor system. *Journal of Neurophysiology,* 1970, **33**, 365–381.

Greene, P. H. Seeking mathematical models for skilled actions. In D. Bootzin & H. C. Muffley (Eds.), *Biomechanics.* New York: Plenum Press, 1969.

Greene, P. H. Introduction in I. M. Gelfand, V. S. Gurfinkel, S. V. Fomin, & M. L Tsetlin (Eds.), *Models of the structural-functional organization of certain biological systems.* Cambridge, Massachusetts: MIT Press, 1971. (a)

Greene, P. H. Problems of organization of motor systems. *Quarterly Report No. 29, Institute for Computer Research,* University of Chicago, 1971. (b)

Gunkel, M. Über relative koordination bei willkürlichen menschlichen Gliedbewegungen. *Pflügers Archiv für die gesamte Physiologia,* 1962, **215,** 472–477.

Gurfinkel, V. S., Kots, Ya. M., Krinskiy, V. I., Pal'tsev, Ye. I., Fel'dman, A. G., Tsetlin, M. L., & Shik, M. L. Concerning tuning before movement. In I. M. Gelfand, V. S. Gurfinkel, S. V. Fomin, & M. L. Tsetlin (Eds.), *Models of the structural–functional organization of certain biological systems.* Cambridge, Massachusetts: MIT Press, 1971.

Gurfinkel, V. S., & Pal'tsev, Ye. I. Effect of the state of the segmental apparatus of the spinal cord on the execution of a simple motor reaction. *Biophysics,* 1965, **10,** 944–951.

Haber, R. N. Information processing analyses of visual perception: An introduction. In R. N. Haber (Ed.), *Information processing approaches to visual perception.* New York: Holt, Rinehart, & Winston, 1969.

Halwes, T., and Wire, B. A possible solution to the pattern recognition problem in the speech modality. In W. Weimer & D. Palermo (Eds.), *Cognition and the symbolic processes.* Hillsdale, New Jersey: Lawrence Erlbaum Assoc., 1974.

Hayek, F. A. The primacy of the abstract. In A. Koestler & J. R. Smythies (Eds.), *Beyond reductionism (The Alpbach Symposium).* Boston: Beacon Press, 1969.

Hoffman, P. *Untersuchungen über die Eigenreflexe (sehnreflexe) menschlicher Muskeln.* Berlin: Springer-Verlag, 1922.

Hoy, R. R. and Paul, R. C. Genetic control of song specificity in Crickets. *Science,* 1973, **180,** 82–83.

Hyde, J. E., & Eliasson, S. G. Brainstem induced eye movements in cats. *Journal of Comparative Neurology,* 1957, **108,** 139–172.

Ingle, D. Spatial dimensions of vision in fish. In D. Ingle (Ed.), *The central nervous system and fish behavior.* Chicago: University of Chicago Press, 1968.

James, W. *The principles of psychology.* New York: Holt, 1890.

Jones, F. P. Method for changing stereotyped response patterns by the inhibition of certain postural sets. *Psychological Review,* 1965, **72,** 196–214.

Koestler, A. Beyond atomism and holism–the concept of the holon. In A. Koestler & J. R. Smythies (Eds.), *Beyond reductionism (The Alpbach Symposium).* Boston: Beacon Press, 1969.

Kornhuber, H. H. Cerebral cortex, cerebellum, and basal ganglia: An introduction to their motor functions. In F. O. Schmitt & F. G. Worden (Eds.), *The neurosciences third study program.* Cambridge, Massachusetts: MIT Press, 1974.

Kots, Ya. M. Supraspinal control of the segmental centres of muscle antagonists in man–I Reflex excitability of the motor neurones of muscle antagonists in the period of organization of voluntary movement. *Biophysics,* 1969, **14,** 176–183. (a)

Kots, Ya. M. Supraspinal control of the segmental centres of muscle antagonists in man–II Reflex excitability of the motor neurones of muscle antagonists on orgnization of sequential activity. *Biophysics,* 1969, **14,** 1146–1154. (b)

Kots, Ya. M., Krinskiy, V. I., Naydin, V. L., & Shik, M. L. The control of movements of the joints and kinesthetic afferentation. In I. M. Gelfand, V. S. Gurfinkel, S. V. Fomin, & M. L. Tsetlin (Eds.), *Models of the structural–functional organization of certain biological systems.* Cambridge, Massachusetts: MIT Press, 1971.

Kots, Ya. M., & Syrovegin, A. V. Fixed set of variants of interactions of the muscles of two joints in the execution of simple voluntary movements. *Biophysics,* 1966, **11**, 1212–1219.

Kots, Ya. M., & Zhukov, V. I. Supraspinal control of the segmental centres of muscle antagonists in man–III "Tuning" of the spinal apparatus of reciprocal inhibition in the period of organization of voluntary movement. *Biophysics,* 1971, **16**, 1129–1136.

Kuno, M., & Perl, E. R. Alteration of spinal reflexes by interaction with suprasegmental and dorsal root activity. *Journal of Physiology,* 1960, **151**, 103–123.

Lashley, K. S. The problem of serial order in behavior. In L. A. Jeffress (Ed.), *Cerebral mechanisms in behavior (The Hixon Symposium).* New York: Wiley, 1951.

Lenneberg, E. *Biological foundations of language.* New York: Wiley & Sons, 1967.

Liberman, A. M., Cooper, F. S., Shankweiler, D. P., & Studdert-Kennedy, M. Perception of the speech code. *Psychological Review,* 1967, **74**, 431–461.

Lundberg, A. Reflex control of stepping. *Proceedings of Norwegian Academy of Science and Letters.* Oslo: Universitetsforlaget, 1969.

Magnus, R. Animal posture. *Proceedings of the Royal Society of London,* 1925, **98** (Ser. B), 339–353.

Matthews, P. B. C. Muscles spindles and their motor control. *Physiological Reviews,* 1964, **44**, 219–288.

Merton, P. A. How we control the contraction of our muscles. *Scientific American,* 1973, **288**, 30–37.

Miller, G. A., Galanter, E., & Pribram, K. H. *Plans and the structure of behavior.* New York: Henry Holt & Co., 1960.

Minsky, M., & Papert, S. Artificial Intelligence. *Artificial Intelligence Memo, 252.* Artificial Intelligence Laboratory, M.I.T., Cambridge, Massachusetts, 1972.

Mittelstaedt, H. Prey capture in mantids. In B. T. Scheer (Ed.), *Recent advances in invertebrate physiology.* Eugene, Oregon: University of Oregon Press, 1957.

Navas, F., & Stark, L. Sampling or intermittency in hand control system dynamics. *Biophysical Journal,* 1968, **8**, 252–302.

Neisser, U. *Cognitive psychology.* New York: Appleton-Century-Crofts, 1967.

Obituary: M. L. Tsetlin, *Biophysics,* 1966, **11**, 1080.

Oscarsson, O. Functional organization of spinocerebellar paths. In A. Iggo (Ed.), *Handbook of sensory physiology,* Vol. II *Somato-sensory system.* Berlin: Springer-Verlag, 1970.

Paillard, J. The patterning of skilled movements. In J. Field, H. W. Magoun, & V. E. Hall (Eds.), Handbook of physiology: *Neurophysiology. Vol. 3.* Washington, D.C.: American Physiological Society, 1960.

Pal'tsev, Ye. I. Functional reorganization of the interaction of the spinal structure in connexion with the execution of voluntary movement. *Biophysics,* 1967, **12**, 313–322. (a)

Pal'tsev, Ye. I. Interactions of the tendon reflex areas in the lower limbs in man as a reflexion of locomotor synergism. *Biophysics,* 1967, **12**, 1048–1059. (b)

Pal'tsev, Ye. I., & El'ner, A. M. Change in the functional state of the segmental apparatus of the spinal cord under the influence of sound stimuli and its role in voluntary movement. *Biophysics,* 1967, **12**, 1219–1226.

Pribram, K. H. *Languages of the brain: Experimental paradoxes and principles in neuropsychology.* Englewood Cliffs, New Jersey: Prentice-Hall, 1971.

Pyatetskii-Shapiro, I. I., & Shik, M. L. Spinal regulation of movement. *Biophysics,* 1964, **9**, 525–530.

Reaves, J. M. The "coalition": A reaction to the machine metatheory in cognitive psychology. Unpublished manuscript, Center for Research in Human Learning, University of Minnesota, 1973.

Requin, J., Bonnet, M., & Granjon, M. Evolution du niveau d'excitabilité Médullaire chez l'homme au cours de la periode préparatoire au temps de réaction. *Journal de Physiologie,* 1968, **1**, 293–294.

Requin, J., and Paillard, J. Depression of spinal monosynaptic reflexes as a specific aspect of preparatory motor set in visual reaction time. In *Visual information processing and control of motor activity.* Sofia: Bulgarian Academy of Sciences, 1971. Pp. 391–396.

Roberts, T. D. M. *Neurophysiology of postural mechanisms.* London: Butterworths, 1967.

Roeder, K., & Treat, A. The reception of bat cries by the tympanic organ of Noctuid moths. In W. A. Rosenblith (Ed.) *Sensory communications.* Cambridge, Massachusetts: MIT Press, 1961.

Rowell, C. H. F. Central control of an insect segmental reflex. I. Inhibition by different parts of the central nervous system. *Journal of Experimental Biology,* 1964, **41**, 559–572.

Ruch, T. C. Transection of the human spinal cord: The nature of higher control. In T. C. Ruch & H. D. Patton (Eds.) *Physiology and biophysics.* Philadelphia: W. B. Saunders, 1965. (a)

Ruch, T. C. Pontobulbar control of posture and orientation in space. In T. C. Ruch & H. D. Patton (Eds.), *Physiology and biophysics.* Philadelphia: Saunders, 1965. (b)

Schneider, G. E. Two visual systems. *Science,* 1969, **163**, 895–902.

Shaw, R. E. Cognition, simulation and the problem of complexity. *Journal of Structural Learning,* 1971, **2**, 31–44.

Shik, M. L., & Orlovskii, G. N. Coordination of the limbs during running of the dog. *Biophysics,* 1965, **10**, 1148–1159.

Shik, M. L., Orlovskii, G. N., & Severin, F. V. Organization of locomotor synergism. *Biophysics,* 1966, **11**, 1011–1019.

Shik, M. L., Severin, F. V., & Orlovskii, G. N. Control of walking and running by means of electrical stimulation of the mid-brain. *Biophysics,* 1966, **11**, 756–765.

Sperry, R. W. Neurology and the mind-brain problem. *American Scientist,* 1952, **XL**, 291–312.

Surguladze, T. D. Functional changes in the segmental apparatus of the spinal cord on execution by man of rhythmic movements. *Biophysics,* 1972, **17**, 141–145.

Sutherland, N. S. Intelligent picture processing. Paper presented at Conference on the Evolution of the Nervous System and Behavior, Florida State University, Tallahassee, 1973.

Sverdlov, S. M., & Maksimova, Ye. V. Inhibitory influences of efferent pulses on the motor effect of pyramidal stimulation. *Biophysics,* 1965, **10**, 177–179.

Taub, E., & Berman, A. J. Movement and learning in the absence of sensory feedback. In S. J. Freedman (Ed.), *The neurophysiology of spatially oriented behavior.* Homewood, Ill: Dorsey Press, 1968.

Tinbergen, N. *The study of instinct.* Oxford: Clarendon Press, 1951.

Trevarthen, C. B. Two mechanisms of vision in primates. *Psychologische Forschung,* 1968, **31**, 299–337.

Turvey, M. T. On peripheral and central processes in vision: Inferences from an information-processing analysis of masking with patterned stimuli. *Psychological Review,* 1973, **80**, 1–52. (b).

Turvey, M. T. A note on the relation between action and perception. In M. Wade & R. Martens (Eds.) *Psychology of motor behavior and sports.* Urbana, Illinois: Human Kinetics, 1974.

Veber, H. V., Rodionov, I. M., & Shik, M. L. "Escape" of the spinal cord from supraspinal influences. *Biophysics,* 1965, **10**, 368–370.

von Foerster, H. On self-organizing systems and their environments. In M. C. Yovits & S. Cameron (Eds.), *Self-organizing systems.* New York: Pergamon Press, 1960.

Weimer, W. B. Psycholinguistics and Plato's paradoxes of the *Meno. American Psychologist,* 1973, **28,** 15–33.
Weiss-Fogh, T. Control of basic movements in flying insects. In *Homeostasis and feedback mechanisms: Symposia of the Society for Experimental Biology.* No. XVIII. Cambridge, England: Cambridge University Press, 1964.
Wiersma, C. A. The organization of the arthropod central nervous system. *American Zoologist,* 1962, **2,** 67–68.
Wilson, D. M. Bifunctional muscles in the thorax of grasshoppers. *Journal of Experimental Biology,* 1962, **39,** 669–677.
Zinkin, N. I. *Mechanisms of speech.* The Hague: Mouton, 1968.

10

A Conceptual Framework for Cognitive Psychology: Motor Theories of the Mind[1]

Walter B. Weimer

The Pennsylvania State University

The recent trend away from the behavioristic paradigm has become all but a stampede, as the resurgence of cognitive psychology illustrates. Yet as has often happened in the history of science, there is a danger that this paradigm (in Kuhn's, 1970, sociological and exemplary senses of the term) will be abandoned before the real reasons for its inadequacy are fully understood by the domain's practitioners. Such paradigm clashes tend to obscure important things, such as that the successor paradigm, to all intents a totally contradictory position, will often share the most important mistakes of its predecessor. This is especially true at the metatheoretical level, and a "new look" theory will often have limitations within itself that its protagonists will have cited as reasons for rejecting its predecessor. Much of cognitive psychology, as the "revolutionary" successor to behaviorism, seems to have made exactly this mistake with regard to its conception of mind and its functioning.

This chapter argues that much contemporary 'cognitive psychology'[2] is neither cognitive nor adequate as a psychology, because it shares an inadequate metatheoretical conceptual framework with its predecessors (such as behaviorism).

[1] This chapter is adapted from Chapter 10 of my forthcoming *Structural Analysis and the Future of Psychology*. Some of its major themes were presented at the Conference on Perception, Action, and Comprehension held at the Center for Research on Human Learning, University of Minnesota, August, 1973.

[2] Throughout the customary philosopher's distinction separates single from double quotation marks. Double quotation marks indicate direct citation or the use of a word or phrase in its traditional connotation; single or scare quotes indicate that the traditional connotation does not apply.

Despite its claims to be revolutionary, and its affiliation (through psycholinguistics) with the revolution in linguistics occasioned by Chomsky, current cognitive theory and research is little better than work done within behaviorism. I wish to argue that the major advances, such as denial of the sufficiency of associationism, and of the utility of the "principles" of reinforcement and learning (conditioning), readmittance of mentalistic entities and theoretical formulations, and even the adoption of a constructive approach to cognition, are not enough. A 'cognitive' psychology that makes these changes *without repudiating the conceptual framework underlying behaviorism* (and its predecessors) is no more adequate than behaviorism. Where theory and research within such a cognitive framework have managed to contribute to our understanding of mind, it has been in spite of that framework rather than because of it.

Such a sweeping claim needs to be given specific formulation. My argument is wholly metatheoretical. The implicit (occasionally explicit) conceptual framework behind such cognitive theories is inadequate. Both cognitive psychology and behavioristic psychology fail because they embrace a *sensory* conception of mind. Conversely, an adequate and truly cognitive psychology must adopt a different metatheoretical framework and explore theories consonant with what can be called a *motor* conception of mind. This chapter attempts to characterize both sensory and motor conceptions of mind (and the theories consonant with them) (Note 1) and argues for the indispensability of motor theories for any adequate psychology.

1 THE SENSORY METATHEORY OF MIND

Psychology, with its long past and short history, has modern formulations stemming from ancient roots. Since the time of Aristotle the mind has been regarded as intrinsically sensory in nature, as a passive black box or window that is (somehow) sensibly impressed by input from the environment. A root metaphor of mind has evolved from the common-sense, everyday experience of looking at the world. Vision, conceived as the passive reception of information that both exists and possesses an intrinsic psychological character *independently* of the organism, became the paradigm exemplar of mental processing. At the same time, behavior, or motor activity, became divorced from mental activity and was seen as a *consequence,* or by-product following from genuine (or sensory) mental events.

This "common-sense" reasoning, although a refreshing and bold conjecture to the ancient Greeks, has now become a literally truistic and trivial common-place. To argue against this root metaphor of the sensory conception seems at first inconceivable. Arguments in favor of the motor conception are often rejected out of hand by theorists who reason that "everybody knows that *x, y,* and *z*" where these variables range over essential tenets of the sensory metatheory. This chapter argues that what everybody knows, the common sense of contemporary psychology, is not only dead wrong both conceptually and empirically, but also retarding the development of an adequate psychology. It argues against a position whose familiarity has made it credible and acceptable, in support of an alternative which is (initially, at least) seemingly incredible, and therefore, unacceptable. We shall proceed by examining some aspects of the sensory metatheory per se (this in itself is a significant task, since the transparency and obviousness of the position guarantee that it is rarely scrutinized—it has become conceptually *invisible*), by providing scanty documentation of the position in contemporary literature, and then by arguing that on the basis of considerable highly corroborated data and theory, it is actually the sensory metatheory that is incredible and to be rejected.

1.1 Some Basic Sensory Tenets

Metatheories are like perspectives or vantage points: they provide a point of view from which a domain may be scrutinized. In providing such conceptual underpinning to a domain of inquiry a metatheory is in itself all but invisible: one "sees" the domain through the conceptual glasses that constitute the metatheory, but one does not see the metatheory itself. Thus, a metatheory is characterized only indirectly, by pointing out those of its aspects that structure and constrain the domain addressed. Taking the sensory metatheory in its simplest abstraction, as the view that everything that is properly mental (for the philosopher) or cognitive (for the psychologist) involves the sensory (specifically, what has classically been called the sensory component of the nervous system), let us look briefly at how it has colored three main approaches to cognitive psychology.

Consider the following statement from a text rightly regarded as having reintroduced cognitive psychology to America, after five decades of behaviorism:

> The term "cognition" refers to all the processes by which the sensory input is transformed, reduced, elaborated, stored, recovered, and used. It is concerned with these processes even when they operate in the absence of relevant stimulation, as in images and hallucinations. Such terms as *sensation, perception, imagery, retention, recall, problem-solving,* and *thinking,* among many others, refer to hypothetical stages or aspects of cognition. . . . The organization of this book follows a sequence which is logically implied by the [above] definition. . . . It follows stimulus information "inward" from the organs of sense, through many transformations and reconstructions, through to eventual use in memory and thought [Neisser, 1967, pp. 4, VII].

This approach makes cognitive psychology, which Neisser is at pains to point out is an approach to the entire psychological field, a matter of "Stimulus Information and its Vicissitudes [p. 4]." Not surprisingly, there are no chapters on motor functions, such as skilled behavior or coordination and control, to be found in this book. Neisser's contribution, as evidenced by his own evaluations, has been to reintroduce a constructive approach to cognition, and to argue for the active nature of the processor who cognizes (especially in viewing memory as reconstruction rather than storage; see the "Utilization Hypothesis" in Chapter 11) (Note 2). In gross oversimplification then, cognitive psychology for this text is the application of constructive formulations to the entire realm of information (stimulus) processing.

An entire generation of researchers has grown up trained on Neisser's book, and it is typical to find in the literature echoes such as this, written as uncontroversial statement of fact in a book review by a theorist in the information-processing camp:

> When stimulation is first presented to the mind, it is automatically acted upon by the system in a series of stages. At each stage features are abstracted and used for subsequent stages of abstraction. Thus, a word presented visually may be encoded in features first representing areas of dark and light, then lines, angles, shapes, and so on, then letters, then letter groups, then words coded linguistically and semantically, then synonyms and associates, then the overall context or situation in which the word appears. . . . The features that are abstracted are placed in the short-term memory store, where they may be used by the subject. . . . Eventually some portion of this information in short-term memory is transferred to, and stored in, long-term memory and the coding process is complete [Shiffrin, 1973, p. 400].

Similar comments appear in the revival of the psychology of consciousness that is an indispensible component of Ornstein's (1972) attempt at a synthesis of traditional and esoteric traditions:

> It is the function of sensory systems, then, by their physiological design to reduce the amount of "useless and irrelevant" information reaching us and to serve as selection systems. The information input through the senses seems to be gathered for the primary purpose of biological survival [p. 23]. . . . We first *select* modalities of personal consciousness from the mass of information reaching us. This is done by a multilevel process of filtration, for the most part sorting out survival-related stimuli. We are then able to *construct* a stable consciousness from the filtered input [p.17].

Common to these positions is an implicit notion that cognition is to be understood "from the outside inward," that it is a matter of the structuring and restructuring of sensory information by intrinsically sensory systems, and that the products of cognition must somehow subsequently be married (in a peculiar sort of shotgun wedding) to action. Thus, cognition has a puzzling, dualistic character for sensory theorists: "Many complex memory representations appear to have a dual character. On the one hand, they can be brought to consciousness and inspected like an image. On the other, they can produce a particular behavior [Posner, 1973, p. 8]." And in all, constructive theorizing is not an issue: even Skinner (though he would never admit it) is a constructivist when dealing with cognition.

1.2 The Communalities of Sensory Psychology

Since the recent abandonment of passive, empty organism stimulus–response formulations in favor of active, constructive approaches is usually taken as a hallmark of the cognitive revolution, this last point may occasion surprise. Thus, it may be helpful to detour through some problems (and their tentative solutions) that have occupied the sensory metatheory. We can see some of the communality in opposing views by looking at such seminal issues as what is learned in perception, what is stored in memory, and the genesis of action.

1.2.1 Perception and the informational basis of behavior. Behaviorism proclaimed its scientific status by decreeing that the stimulus must be physically specifiable. Having done so it replaced "perception" by "disposition to respond," claiming that the problem of perception is to specify the particular stimuli that result, via learning, in particular behaviors. The retreat from classic behaviorism acknowledged the abstract nature of the stimulus, and the distinction between functional and physical stimuli arose. It got to the point that the 'stimulus' in, for example, concept learning became a relational concept (Bourne, 1966). With this admission the behaviorist became a cognitive psychologist who, for better or worse, clings to an old "habit" of classifying everything as either a stimulus, response, or reinforcement. Where is the revolutionary difference between the cognitive and behavioral theorist if both acknowledge that the informational basis of perception (and hence, learning) is intrinsically abstract?

1.2.2 Memory and the utilization of "stored" information. For classic behaviorism, as Neisser points out in discussing the Reappearance Hypothesis, what was learned and what was remembered (habits or associations) were enduring entities that could be somehow retrieved from a storage compartment deep within the organism. The "revolution" has been to abandon storage of surface elements in favor of the 'storage' of deep structure rules for the generation of elements. Note 2 has quoted how Skinnerian behaviorism has claimed exactly this position as its own. Let us quote Skinner (1974) again:

> The metaphor of storage in memory . . . has caused a great deal of trouble. The computer is a bad model. . . . (It is not the behaviorist incidentally, but the cognitive psychologist, with his computer-model of the mind, who represents man as a machine.) [p. 110]

All that is wrong with this quotation is that Skinner has misperceived a monolithic opposition, and fails to distinguish storage theorists within the cognitive camp (e.g., Melton & Martin, 1972; Miller, 1974) from those who do not utilize computer metaphors (e.g., Gibson, 1966; Neisser, 1967). So both behaviorism and cognitive psychology do and do not utilize storage concepts to account for memory. Where are the revolutionary differences? What principled distinctions remain when a behaviorist such as Paivio (1971) can call himself a cognitive psychologist simply for studying images?

1.2.3 Action and the initiation of behavior. How is action generated? If we grant any analysis of the input or stimulus information whatsoever, how is it connected to behavior? Naive behaviorism (of the Watsonian genre) believed the myth that all behavior is reflexive, and that output was tied to input by chains of reflexes. No one believes that today, and with historical hindsight everyone cites Lashley's (1951) paper on serial order to support the claim. But what mechanisms are available? The behaviorist faces theoretical bankruptcy here, for reflexes and associations just won't work. There just is no behaviorist account of the genesis of action worth criticizing. Does this mean victory for the cognitive theorist? Hardly. The revolution here has been negative in effect: pointing out the inadequacy of extant formulations is no substitute for a viable theory of action. And the classic cognitive theorists have no theory at all. Neisser does not even discuss the topic, and for that matter, neither does anyone else (except certain neurophysiological psychologists: see Section 2).

1.3 Toward a Conceptually Adequate Psychology

The fact that enterprising behaviorists can make their views consonant with what is typically taken to be representative cognitive formulations is not surprising—they are indeed an enterprising lot. Nor does it mean that there are not thoroughly convincing arguments against behaviorism that make this tiresome game of catching up far too costly to play for those who are intellectually honest (see Weimer, 1974, and the references therein cited). What it does mean is that much so-called cognitive psychology is totally inadequate to the task of characterizing the human higher mental processes and their relation to behavior. It is time to explicitly adopt, in addition to the philosophical and methodological arguments against behaviorism, an adequate conceptual framework for cognitive theorizing. In order to effect a principled separation of theoretical cognitive psychology from positions such as behaviorism one must abandon the sensory metatheory in favor of the motor framework. Such a move will have numerous consequences, including providing answers for the problems discussed in Section 1.2, answers that successfully integrate acting and perceiving, something that has never before been done by either behaviorism or cognitive psychology. What the motor metatheory asserts is that there is no sharp separation between sensory and motor components of the nervous system which can be made on functional grounds, and that the mental or cognitive realm is intrinsically motoric, like all the nervous system. The mind is intrinsically a motor system, and the sensory order by which we are acquainted with external objects as well as ourselves, the higher mental processes which construct our common sense and scientific knowledge, indeed everything mental, is a product of what are, correctly interpreted, constructive motor skills. Let us indicate why this must be so by overviewing the physiological basis of action.

2 PHYSIOLOGICAL PSYCHOLOGY AND THE ACTIVE MIND

Recent research in neuropsychology has led to the abandonment of sensory and associationist conceptions of mind. By recapping the progressive refutation of building block, reflexive conceptions of neural functioning, and the input–output chaining models of cortical control, we can see why sensory theories of mind must be abandoned.

Neuropsychology originally accepted reflexology as its theoretical model of neural functioning. Pioneered by Sechenov in *Reflexes of the Brain* (1863), it was popularized by Sherrington (1906) and taken as established scientific fact into behaviorism from the writings (as they were misunderstood by John B. Watson) of Pavlov (1927). In this framework all behavior is the result of input–output connections between the sensory and motor components of the central nervous system (CNS). The motor cortex of the brain was regarded variously as a "switchbox" or "piano keyboard" that activated muscular (and hence, behavioral) output. The motor cortex was the keyboard upon which the sensory mind played to produce behavior. The only question concerned whether the keys encoded a representation of individual muscles or represented more complex movements and combinations. But more recent research, overviewed by Eccles (1973) and Pribram (1971a, b), has devastated this simplistic conception. Let us overview the motor control of action, and then look at symbolic activity as an instance of brain functioning, to see how this leads to a generative, motoric conception of mind.

2.1 The Motor Control of Action

The first problem for the discrete input–output reflexological approach came with the discovery of the γ efferent system. The motoneurons of the pyramidal tract are composed of large (α) and small (γ) fibers. The α fibers exclusively innervate extrafusal (contractile) muscle fibers while the γ fibers innervate muscle spindles lying in parallel to the extrafusal muscle. When γ fibers are electrically stimulated, a change in the afferent signals going to the spinal cord from the muscle receptors results. One-third of the fibers leaving the spinal cord for muscle tissue are γ fibers and do not result in muscle contraction, but rather influence muscle receptors *independently* of any changes produced in the muscle. Thus, signals from muscle receptors to the brain do not accurately reflect the state of contraction of the muscle, but are instead part of a servomechanism or servo control loop (Eccles, 1973, p. 115). The action of the loop can be biased by the motor cortex over a wide range by discharge of the γ fibers, and γ fiber activity "presents" muscle contraction much as does the bias knob on a thermostat. It is now known that voluntary movements are initiated by α contraction, which results in coactivation of the γ loop fibers, which in turn gives automatic adjustment to a load (at the spinal level of control).

When knowledge of the action of the γ feedback loop is combined with the realization that the motor cortex is informed by sensory nerves from skin and muscle through pathways as direct as those by which such signals reach the sensory cortex (Pribram, 1971a), whose primary function appears to be to signal the cortex the progress of the movement it has just programmed, the reflex conception is seen to be untenable.

But if not by simple reflexes how does the cortex control action? Granting that its mechanism is motoric, a servo-loop control system rather than a reflexive one, how does the 'keyboard' operate? Pribram discovered that ablation of motor cortex has little effect on muscle function in particular movements, but greatly disrupted skilled action:

> My interpretation of this finding was that behavioral acts, not muscles or movements, were encoded in the motor cortex. An act was defined as an achievement in the environment that could be accomplished by a variety of movements which became equivalent with respect to the achievement. Thus, a problem box could be opened by use of a right or left hand; amputees have learned to write with their toes. Encoded in the motor cortex are the determinants of problem solution and of writing—not the particular movements involved in the performance [Pribram, 1971b, p. 14].

But what determinants of action are encoded in the motor cortex? Evarts (1967; Evarts & Thach, 1969) found that the motor cortex cells that fired when a monkey pushed a lever to and fro were responding not as a function of length of movement or stretch of muscle, but rather as a function of the force needed to perform the task. The motor cortex represents the field of forces necessary to achieve a functionally specified action:

> The brain's motor mechanism can encode the set points, the information necessary to achieve certain acts. The brain need not keep track of the rhythms of contraction and relaxation of individual muscles necessary to achieve an act any more than the thermostat needs to keep track of the turnings on and off of the furnace. The encoding problem is immensely simplified—only end states need to be specified [Pribram, 1971b, pp. 16–17].

These results, along with the classic study of Bernstein (1967) and current research (e.g., Greene, 1971) reviewed by Turvey in this volume, are devastating to both the reflex model of neural functioning and the sharp distinction of sensory and motor components of the mind. Reflexology is ruled out because of the feedback loop control of muscle contraction at the periphery, and because the keyboard in the cortex controls abstract, functionally specified actions rather than particular muscle movements. The cerebellum is also intimately concerned with the skilled control of functionally specified movements (Note 3). But equally important, it becomes obvious that the classic sharp separation of sensory and motor components is untenable. The feedback loop is a motor component performing a sensory function, and some 'sensory' fibers project directly to motor rather than sensory cortex. Further, the information coded in the 'motor' cortex is quite 'sensory' in nature, being concerned with, as Pribram puts it, the image of achievement of abstract actions specified in terms of their functional consequences. This stretches Aristotelian conceptions of mind to the breaking point, and forces a return to the active epistemologist's conception of mind as a generator of not only its output but also its input (Note 4).

2.2 Sign and Symbol as Motoric Skill

One may grant the motor theory of mind for behavioral action, but what of the higher, symbolic functions characteristic of man's mental functioning? Can the use of signs and symbols really be understood upon the model of actions? Following Pribram, I wish to argue that not only can they be so interpreted, but that there simply is no alternative to doing so.

Let us begin by defining signs and symbols. A sign is a token of a context-free code. A symbol is a token of a context-sensitive (restricted) code. A code is a pattern of repetition. Signs and symbols are representations, tokens that "stand for" something else. Symbols are signs that derive their meaning from a particular context. Letters on a page are signs, but the meanings that they convey to a reader when part of a written natural language are symbolic. The question we must consider is: How does the brain control its input (and output) in determining signs and symbols?

As we know from overviewing the metatheory, the traditional sensory answer postulates a series of linearly chained processing steps, in which progressively more abstract features are extracted (recall the quotation from Shiffrin in Section 1.1). The simpler features are supposed to be abstracted (via the subtractive theory of abstraction: see Cassirer, 1953) at the receptors themselves, then more abstract features at the intermediate way stations and "primary projection areas" of the cortex. The very complex information necessary to utilize signs (say in discrimination learning or delayed response tasks) was assumed to involve "association" areas of the cortex immediately after the projection areas, according to the sequence in Fig. 1. If this linear processing model were correct, then destruction of connecting tissue separating the primary projection areas from the relevant "association" areas should impair signing ability. Considerable evidence (reviewed in Pribram, 1971a) indicates that this is not the case, and that the classic picture is incorrect. Cortico–cortical relays are not the mechanism of signing and symbolizing (at least in nonhuman primates).

The evidence available indicates that information from the cortex is transmitted "downstream" to subcortical structures for preprocessing, and then relayed to the primary sensory and motor cortex. Instead of the classic view that perception occurs in the primary sensory cortex and that "what is learned" is then *added* by the association of input from the association cortex, in the case of vision, for example, "the inferior temporal cortex influences visual processes

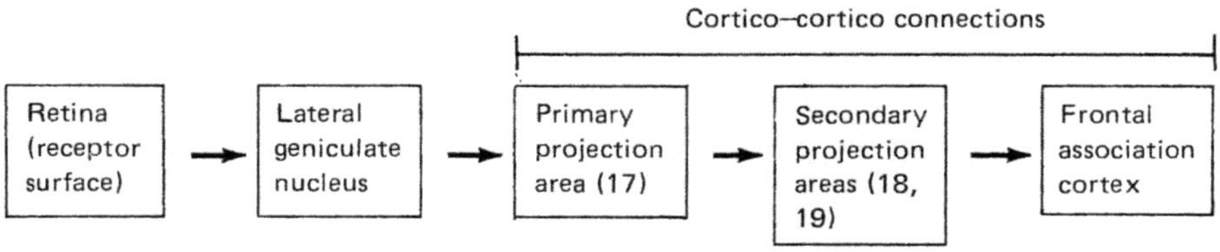

FIG. 1 Diagram of classic conception of (visual) perceptual abstraction and integration. "Higher" perceptual abilities were assumed to involve successive abstraction of information from preceding areas, such that, for example, pattern perception involved cortico–cortico connections.

not so much because it *receives* visual information *from* the primary cortex, but because it *operates* through corticofugal connections *on* visual processes occurring *in* the subcortical structures [Pribram, 1971a, p. 318]." Motor involvement indispensibly enters at this point: "Sign and symbol manipulation thus involves the same brain structures that are used by the organism in the construction of acts. The suggestion that derives from these anatomical facts is that signifying and symbolizing are acts, albeit acts of a special sort [Pribram, 1971a, p. 22]."

The structures implicated in signification and symbolization are anatomically and functionally somewhat distinct, which results in reasonably specific postulations concerning their motoric nature and involvement (Note 5). But for our purposes, the point remains: not only are higher, symbolic activities intrinsically motoric, but they can be conceived as actions, skilled activities of the CNS, analogously to the way in which skilled movement is conceived. [They are acts of a *special* sort (as in the quotation above) only in that they are mental and symbolic.]

Signification and symbolic activity, which involve the creation of meaning, appear to occur when cortico–subcortical connections are activated, and these connections relay in brain stem structures implicated in motoric function (see Fig. 3 in Note 5). Thus Pribram proposes a "motor theory" underlying meaning:

> Man makes meaning through signs, symbols, propositions and reasoning by way of corticofugal-subcortical connections that importantly involve the motor mechanisms of the brain. I propose that man's thrust toward meaning derives from the fact that his brain's motor mechanisms are better developed than those of animals [Pribram, 1971b, p. 30].

We shall have more to say about meaning in Section 8. But to repeat the point here, the motor mechanism of the brain cannot be narrowly identified with the control of muscle tissue. Although the distinction between sensory systems and muscle effector systems can be made on well-motivated taxonomic grounds, this distinction cannot be made at the functional, neurophysiological level. Instead, the evidence just sketched indicates that *both* classic sensory systems *and* muscle effector systems are intrinsically motoric in nature. If this is so, there is simply no alternative presently available to the generic motor theory of mind. Everything man can perform, perceive, and conceive results from his CNS being a generator, a creator, of both its sensory input and all its behavioral and conceptual output. The motor theory conceptual framework thus postulates that sensation, feeling and emotion, perception, conception, and action are motor functions, and that everything that is properly called mind falls into one or more of these categories.

3 COGNITION AS SKILLED ACTION

Granting the generic framework, the problem of specifying motor theories of particular cognitive processes remains. A review of theoretical formulations of specific cognitive domains will indicate how the metatheory relates to specific psychological and philosophical theories. This section looks in cursory fashion at topics recurring throughout this book, that is, at thought, concept formation, memory, and knowledge itself (both tacit and explicit) to see what motor theories of these domains propose; in Section 4 the problems of perception will be considered; the sensory order occupies Section 5; Section 6 examines the nature of consciousness, and Section 7 the problem of motivation; finally Section 8 focuses on the problem of meaning.

3.1 Thought as Skilled 'Behavior'

On one point, cognitive and behavioristic formulations agree: thinking is to be understood as behavior. Although classic behaviorist formulations attempted to reduce thought to 'overt' behavior by modeling it upon the peripheral musculature (Note 6), it was always deemed the epitome of skilled performance. Cognitive analyses are in complete agreement on this latter point:

> When we say, . . . that thinking is an advanced form of skilled behavior, what we mean is that it has grown out of earlier established forms of flexible adaptation to the environment and that the characteristics which it possesses and the conditions to which it submits can best be studied as they are related to those of its own earlier forms [Bartlett, 1958, p. 199].

Bartlett's book was a beginning attempt to study thinking, particularly as it is exemplified in problem solving, from this point of view. But man the thinking, cultural creature that Cassirer aptly called *Homo symbolicus* is not merely a smart animal. Rather he is qualitatively different in that the fantastic power of thought (to be creative or productive and to transcend time) has enabled man to achieve emancipation from the various bodily skills. As Bartlett emphasized, thinking is an adaptive skill, but it is qualitatively advanced beyond bodily skills:

> The skills of the body are attached to the demands of the world of the moment, but thinking can meet those far away in any direction and even those which have no time or place. And because, now, body movement is supplemented by signs and symbols—all the varied media of its expression which thinking can employ—the thinker is in a position to attain a vast increase in the range and delicacy of his adaptability [Bartlett, 1958, p. 200].

But little if any effort has been devoted to following up Bartlett's lead: it is time for psychology to transcend the behaviorist attempt to reduce thinking to bodily skill, to see just how it is similar and how it is different from other skills, and in which directions the uniqueness of man lies (Note 7).

3.2 Concept Formation and Creativity

Problems of learning, specifically the issues of what is learned and under what conditions, have dominated theoretical psychology since the days of Watsonian behaviorism. Traditionally the answers proffered have been particular behavior patterns (responses or concept identifications, and so on) as a result of reinforced experience with particular stimulus instances. Thus it was confidently asserted that the child learned what triangularity means by playing with different triangles (and less confidently but equally explicitly assumed that the adult did likewise with notions such as freedom and dignity), and that what was involved in all such instances were the same principles already well known from basic animal learning studies. Learning was a matter of identifying (really, subtracting out) the relevant dimensions of stimulus configurations and then attaching a response to them.

But the resurgence of cognitive psychology uncovered a fact, known to all but psychologists since the time of Plato, that destroyed this account by showing that the mechanism involved could not be either subtractive or an association (in any technically precise sense) of particular stimuli and responses; that is, it was rediscovered that all concept formation is creative or productive. The number of experienced particulars required to learn even the simplest concept (e.g., that Δ instantiates triangularity) is indefinitely large. To know a concept is to be able to apply it appropriately to a totally novel instance, one that need not ever have occurred before in the organism's history, or indeed the history of the world (Weimer, 1973). The problem of productivity, which destroyed the structuralist approach in linguistics, is equally devastating to any associationist or behaviorist psychology which does not make a mockery of the meaning of those terms.

But how can organisms come to recognize, on the basis of *no* prior exposure, all potential instances as instances of the *same* concept? The theories currently being developed in psychology are modeled upon the structure of theories in linguistics that account for the productivity of sentences. Such grammars make indispensible use of fundamentally abstract entities (which are nowhere found in the experienced or surface structures of sentences) in their rules of determination of the construction of sentences, and allow indefinite recursion in their derivation of surface instances from underlying or "deep" conceptual structures. All generic concepts appear to be the same as an underlying deep structure in that they can be characterized only by the abstract rules of determination which are their grammar.

What is learned in concept formation is thus never purely perceptual nor particular; it is instead the rules of determination that constitute the invariant relations in a group (in the mathematical sense). Our "perceptual" knowledge is based upon "rules of seeing" that determine the invariant aspects of our environment and the group theoretic transformations applicable to them. But no sensory experience alone is identical with any concept: what the knowledge or concept is consists of both the underlying rules of determination and the surface representation that is experienced.

Thus concept formation, since it is creative, must be abstract, generative, and nonperceptual. In these attributes concept formation exemplifies motor theoretic principles in direct opposition to sensory formulations, which have postulated that concept formation is concrete, associative, and perceptual. The realization that concepts embody motor theoretic principles of determination has more often occurred to philosophers than psychologists. Psychologists should study the writings of Cassirer (1953) to see that a thorough treatment of the abstract nature of conceptual determination was available in 1910, Hanson (1970) to see a beautiful portrayal of the nonperceptual nature of concept formation in science, and Kuhn (1974) to see the generative nature of learning from exemplars. We have dealt with these aspects of conceptual abstraction more fully in the philosophical context of the problems of induction (Weimer, 1975), and that discussion should amplify this brief section.

3.3 Memory and Comprehension within Constructive Theory

Similar conclusions apply to memory as to concept formation. The theory of memory developed by Bransford and his associates (e.g., Bransford & Franks, 1971; Bransford & Johnson, 1972; Bransford & McCarrell, 1974), emphasizing the mind's ability to utilize the information with which it is presented by generating contextual understanding rather than storing particulars, is a paradigmatic motor theory. Within this framework "memory" is a matter of the active, ongoing modulation of information rather than the retrieval of stored items or particular "bits." This approach claims that human understanding is a matter of the mind's ability to generate structural patterns of information which are meaningful and meaning-filled conceptual gestalts to which new information can be assimilated. Indeed, the very act of assimilation, what we often simply call "thinking," is a motoric skill, and that *is* understanding or comprehending:

> Our approach to comprehension focuses on the comprehender's ability to use his general knowledge to create situations that permit the relations specified in input sentences to be realized, or to postulate situations (e.g., instigating forces) that allow perceptual events to be understood. In short, the ability to create some level of semantic content sufficient to achieve a click of comprehension depends upon the comprehender's ability to think (Bransford & McCarrell, 1974, p. 220).

3.4 Knowledge and Genetic Epistemology

These remarks on cognition make it clear that the processes underlying human knowledge are (pace Bartlett) skilled actions. But what of knowledge per se? Piaget's approach to the acquisition of knowledge, what he calls genetic epistemology, is one example of a motor theoretic approach to knowledge (Note 8). Piaget holds that the child comes to know the world and remember its objects in terms of actions upon that world, rather than in terms of passively noticing relations among objects per se. Indeed, the relations between objects (which is all that the sensory metatheory acknowledges as knowledge) can only become objects-of-knowledge through active participation and dynamic interchange with those objects. The only relations among objects that can be known are those resulting from the way in which we behave with respect to those objects. And all behavior, as Piaget emphasizes, is a matter of (biological) adaptation, comprised equally and indispensibly of assimilation and accommodation. Knowing (within this framework) is adapting, and adapting is actively behaving: to know is to do.

3.5 Tacit Knowledge and the Unconscious Mind

Although conceptions of the unconscious have a long history in psychological speculation (e.g., Leibniz, Hartley, and Helmholtz all made the notion indispensible to their systems well prior to Freud), such notions are really highly problematic within the sensory metatheory. That the 'unconscious mind' must be literally a contradiction in terms for sensory theorists becomes obvious when the identification of mind with the alleged sensory component is acknowledged. In that framework unconscious mental processes are unsensed sensory processes, and they can occur, by definition, only below the cortical "level" of control. Thus, classic conceptions have identified the *un*conscious with the *sub*conscious, which in turn was identified with the subcortical. The popular connotations of the Freudian id demonstrate this progression nicely, with the additional twist that rationality was identified with the conscious-cortical level and irrationality with all that goes on "below." But the point remains: "sensory" conceptions of the unconscious sharply divide "higher" cortical processes from "lower" processes and relegate all unconscious phenomena to the lower processes, and they do so in order to avoid glaring contradiction.

But as is well known today, tacit or unconscious processes are inextricably involved in all our affairs, whether sensory or motor, conscious or otherwise (Polanyi, 1966; Turvey, 1974; Weimer, 1973, 1974, 1976). For an example in a traditional sensory domain, consider the problem of perceptual thing–kind identification: How does one know a face, say, to be an instance of a face? In traditional motor terms, the process of writing a sentence is a mundane, although far from insignificant, example. No explicit knowledge or ability is sufficient to account for even these 'trivial' instances of tacit awareness and skill, and all the fundamental problems of psychology (knowledge, action, perception, conception, conation, and all the rest) are manifestations of such tacit processes. Perhaps the most that one can presently say is that the problems of tacit knowledge (thus construed) are the problems of meaning (see Section 8).

We have no theories, even on the farthest horizon, that account for the problems of the unconscious represented in tacit awareness and skill. But we need not be saddled with a conceptual framework that renders no solutions possible. From the motor theory framework one can at least attempt to assay what is involved without running into contradiction and inherent confusion. Indeed, from this perspective the long delay in recognizing that unconscious or tacit processing precedes all conscious or explicit behavior is solely a product of the sensory metatheory: the shock wave caused by Polanyi (e.g., 1966) in philosophy and, for example, by Turvey (1974) in psychology results largely from a realization of the existence of pervasive problems that were literally not acknowledged to exist by sensory theorists. The problem for the future psychology of knowledge and action appears somewhat paradoxical: we require a theory of tacit knowing and doing that will also account for the "little bit" of conscious or explicit phenomena that we sometimes exhibit.

Is the appearance of paradox genuine or spurious? Granting the motor metatheory and the physiological evidence sketched in Section 2, it is not the least surprising that no sharp break can be maintained between either conscious-unconscious or cortical-subcortical. The CNS is an integrated entity, a coalition in Shaw's terms (Shaw & McIntyre, 1974), and from the functional rather than anatomical perspective it is an integrated unit. Even the extreme localization of consciousness within the language (dominant) hemisphere discussed in Section 6.2 *requires* that the vast majority of neural events be tacit. And if consciousness is dependent upon involvement within a train of neural impulses in one hemisphere, then it is obvious that all other neural activity, including the vast majority involved in even the 'highest' mental processes, will remain tacit. Therefore, our paradoxical statement, although a severe shock to the conscious ego, is actually to be expected.

4 PERCEPTION AS A MOTOR SYSTEM

We must turn now from overviews to more substantive theoretical formulations in order to give both evidential flesh and specific theoretical bones to motor theories. Consider first the domain of perception. The conscious experience of perception does not at first seem to lend itself to interpretation within the motor theory. Once again we wish to argue not only that it is susceptible to such interpretation, but that the motor theory provides the only framework capable of accounting for perception. The senses, considered as perceptual systems, are motor systems through and through.

This section considers the *conscious* experience of perception; the problem of modality, which concerns why we have experience at all, is treated in Section 5. What we require for perceptual experience is a theory of the representation of information within the given modal systems; that is, the major problem for a theory of perceptual experience is to account for how information within a modal system is utilized by the organism to create the experience that it has. Since we can only infer but not directly assess experience in other animals, the data for this section must come from human perceptual experience. Specifically, we shall examine the perception of speech and visual form to see how motor theories developed for these areas are representative of accounts that can handle all perception. In a nutshell, the motor theory of perception holds that experience within a modality results from the involvement of the same structural and functional neurophysiological apparatus as is involved in producing (as a sender of information rather than a receiver) that information. The account has face validity for the 'near' senses such as touch, and the perception of speech; once it has been developed for the latter domain we must see if it can be stretched to encompass the distance senses of vision and audition.

4.1 A Motor Theory of Phonological Experience

The phonological–articulatory mode of constructing experience has been studied intensively for the last two decades. Largely as a result of the Haskins Laboratories researches, it has become clear that this mode of experience is fundamentally different from audition, and deserves to be recognized as a separate speech mode (Liberman, 1959; Liberman, Cooper, Shankweiler, & Studdert-Kennedy, 1967; Liberman, Mattingly, & Turvey, 1972). The motor theory of speech begins by assuming (on the basis of considerable research) that: "*Underlying the experience of language at the phonological level, in every form of language use, are processes which are basically identical to the motor coordination processes involved in speaking, with the motor commands being in some way inhibited in all cases but that of overt speech* [Halwes & Wire, 1974, p. 386; italics theirs]." What the theory proposes is that our understanding of speech *as such* requires the hearer to utilize the same central neural machinery that would be involved in speaking: "The assumption is that at some level or levels of the production process there exist neural signals standing in one-to-one correspondence with the various segments of the language—phoneme, word, phrase, etc. Perception consists in somehow running the process backward . . . [Liberman *et al.*, 1967, p. 454]." Thus in both perception and production we construct or generate the conscious experience of speech.

It is worth noting that the motor theory of speech perception has nothing to do with so-called analysis by synthesis. Such routines propose to understand the operation of a "black box" (such as a speaker-hearer) by constructing a model that "outputs" what a priori analysis of the black box specifies as its output; that is, analysis by synthesis performs an analysis and then synthesizes the output determined by the analysis. The motor theory does not say that speech perception is a matter of analysis by synthesis; to propose so would be to assert that the perception of speech involved a totally redundant operation (of synthesis). Rather, the motor theory proposes that the process of analysis (which *is* speech perception) is actually synthesis; that is, a constructive motoric process. The evidence in favor of this conception, which is extensive, is indicated in Halwes and Wire (1974).

This general account can be directly extended to explain how we perceive any skilled action that we ourselves can perform. Therefore, touch, taste, the experienced aspects of locomotion through the environment, and so on, presumably involve the motor command systems that are utilized in producing the movements of touching, tasting, and locomoting; that is, these perceptual systems are in fact motor skills production systems: this is the motor theory in its essential form and in its strongest claim. In these cases it is easy to construe the systems involved as intrinsically production systems; but the case of vision, for example, requires more comment (see Section 4.3). But in all cases, to say that the classic 'sensory' systems are actually 'motor' systems is to assert that sensing is an activity involving neural structures traditionally assumed to be inherently motoric in function. Therefore the representation of information in the sensory systems, which *is* perception, is a productive motor function.

4.2 Pattern Recognition and the Höffding Step

The heart of the problem of perception is easily stated: granted the sophisticated analysis of input information that occurs when nonmetal objects (either "external" objects or our own physical bodies) produce patterns of firing in 'sensory' channels, how do we get from such coding of input information to perceptual understanding? How do we get from patterns of neural impulses in the sensory orders to recognition of objects? This, of course, is the problem of thing–kind identification, which concerns the recognition of an *X as such* on the basis of the neural impulses causally resulting from *X*. Granting the causal theory of perception, how do we get from mediate causal linkages (sensory impulses in the CNS) to the ultimate result of the causal chain, perceptual understanding?

Harald Höffding (1891) called attention to this problem in arguing against associationist chaining theories. His analysis shows clearly that the linkage between two "associated" elements, say physical object *A* and perceptual understanding (naming) *B*, is never direct or linear, as associationism proposed. Rather, the linkage is always of the form shown in Fig. 2. The letter "a" represents analysis of the input in terms of thing–kind categories, and "b" the corresponding "proper part" neural component of understanding that must occur before the response "B" (either overtly or covertly naming the object) can occur. The problem of perceptual understanding is the problem of the Höffding step: How do we get from "a" to "B"? How do we achieve meaning in perception?

No motor theory yet discussed (or for that matter, any psychological theory ever imagined) makes explicit what is involved in the Höffding step; that is, how the motor involvement in perception is to accomplish the jump from sensation to perception, from analyzed information coded in neural impulses to meaning and recognition, has not been specified.

But if the perceptual systems can plausibly be interpreted as motor production systems, it is possible that this problem does not arise. Consider the case of speech perception if the account sketched in Section 4.1 is correct:

> Assume that the auditory system extracts certain structures from the input acoustic signal, which are just those structures it has been evolutionarily "designed" to extract in order to permit the recognition of speech. Now, on Pribram's analysis of the nature of the motor cortex, it is at least possible that the Höffding step problem simply disappears. Presumably those invariant structures which are linguistically relevant on the input side are the same structures as those which are linguistically relevant on the output side, in the coordination of the articulatory muscles, for there is a strict isomorphism between the linguistically relevant aspects of the acoustic signal and the linguistically relevant aspects of the articulatory gestures, the former being produced directly by the latter. Moreover, the neural machinery for processing the acoustic signal evolved together with the neural machinery for controlling articulation. So the recoding problem, the problem of getting from acoustic signal to articulation, dissolves and we are left with the relatively simple task of moving the information specifying the input structures into the motor cortex [Halwes & Wire, 1974, pp. 387–388].

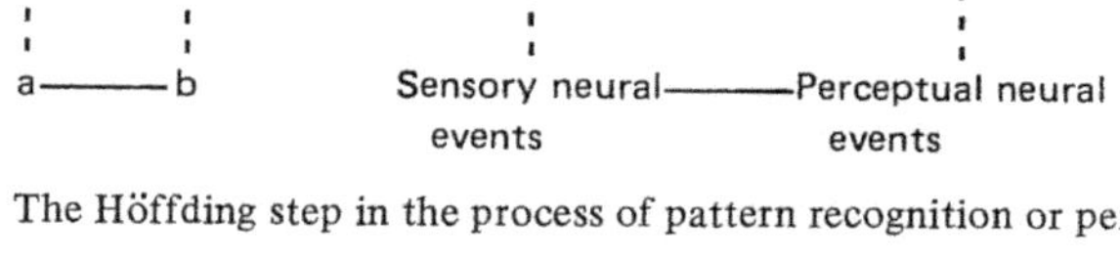

FIG. 2 The Höffding step in the process of pattern recognition or perception.

This line of reasoning solves the problem of recognition in *perception* by assimilating it to the problem of meaning in *production.* Thus the traditional *coding* problem, the problem of the Höffding step, vanishes as a pseudoproblem. But the problem of meaning or understanding does not vanish in this manner: it is only relocated in (if this approach is correct) its actual position. This approach tells us how meaning is manifested (in terms of motor involvement), but it does not tell us what meaning is.

This discussion has one benefit in any case: it forces a clear distinction between two different kinds of questions that may be asked in perception. One question, the only one pursued by the majority of cognitive psychologists, has to do with the "How" of perception, and concentrates upon the constructive processes which achieve our perceptual experience. But the question of how we perceive can only be addressed by presupposing knowledge of a second question, concerning the "What" of perception. Gibson (1950, 1966) and his associates have devoted much attention to specifying what the information is that is perceived, and have elaborated a position that does not emphasize constructive processes, at least in visual perception. Gibson's approach, Ecological optics, argues that all the information necessary to account for perception is present in the ambient optic array, and that when the "What" is correctly specified, there is no need for any coding such as the Höffding step. There is no need, for instance, to involve memory or reconstructive processes in perception if the information specifying perceptual experience is present in the stimulus. The problem instead is to explain how the senses, considered as perceptual systems, modulate information. But the modulation of information that Gibson envisages is a transduction of incoming energy rather than a translation (or encoding), and this has led some theorists to propose that constructive theory, which apparently does deal with coding, be limited to linguistic systems (Note 9).

But as the Halwes and Wire reasoning makes clear, there is no need for the Höffding step in the constructive domain of language either. The opposition between the Gibsonian and constructive positions is, we believe, based on misconceptions on both sides. The constructivist must realize that no construction can occur in any mental realm unless there is information available upon which constructive processes operate. The slogan "Everything is a construction" is a contradiction in terms: unless there is an informational basis available, no construction can occur. Similarly, the Gibsonian must realize that pointing out that the information necessary to account for perception is specified in the optic array (or the speech signal, etc.) says nothing about how we perceive. An adequate theory of perception must include not only a specification of what is perceived but also an account of how it occurs. Further, if it is to be a theory of organismic perception, it must be consonant with a specification of "Who" perceives, that is, a theory of the 'algoristic basis' (as Shaw calls it; see Shaw & McIntyre, 1974).

Rather than pursue a conflict of misunderstandings, let us examine visual perception from the point of view of a motor theory. We can agree with both Gibson that the "what" of perception is specified by information in the stimulus array, and with the constructivist that the problem is to specify how the mind turns that information into perceptual experience.

4.3 Vision as a Motor System

Vision is prima facie problematic for a motor theory because it is a distance sense in which no obvious motor productions are involved. Unlike speech, we do not 'produce' vision the way we produce, as well as perceive, speech, body postures, and so on (an exception is imagery: see Section 4.4). Therefore, the conscious experience of visual phenomena requires our attention. Both Sperry (1952) and Festinger (Festinger, Burnham, Ono, & Bamber, 1967) have proposed motor theories of vision; we shall overview the latter account, which places efference, or motor commands, at the center of visual form perception.

If discussion were confined to perception of motor movements, there would be no problem in specifying a motor theory of perception. But efferent instructions issued by the CNS to the eye seem to play no role in visual perception. For instance, we do not have to "follow" a contour with eye movements to perceive the contour. Therefore we must retreat one step and speak of "readiness" to issue motor commands to the eye as being involved in conscious perceptual experience. Sperry suggests the following:

> If there be any objectively demonstrable fact about perception . . . it is the following: Insofar as an organism perceives a given object, it is prepared to respond with reference to it. This preparation-to-respond is absent in an organism that has failed to perceive. . . . The presence or absence of adaptive reaction potentialities of this sort, ready to discharge into motor patterns, makes the difference between perceiving and not perceiving [Sperry, 1952, p. 301].

But how, experimentally, could one assay anything as tenuous as a "readiness to respond"? Festinger provided the answer: "If, without changing anything about the pattern of retinal stimulation, one could alter the particular preprogrammed sets of efferent instructions that were activated and held in readiness for immediate use, one would expect to produce a change in visual perception [Festinger *et al.,* 1967, p. 14]." These investigators performed a series of experiments with prism spectacles and contact lenses to test an "efferent readiness" theory of visual form (contour) perception which they state as "this theory, . . . holds that visual perception of contour is determined by the particular sets of preprogrammed efferent instructions that are activated by the visual input into a state of readiness for immediate use [Festinger *et al.,* 1967, p. 34]."

It is crucial to note that this is a theory of the *conscious* experience of perception. Visual input per se is acknowledged, but not given the primary role in determining experience. Rather, the theory states that experience results from the motor commands activated into a state of readiness by the CNS upon receipt of the incoming visual information. It is thus a constructive theory of visual experience, since the contour is not "seen" in terms of the input at all, but rather in terms of the efferent commands issued in response to that input: perceptual experience could not occur without input to the visual system (and as Gibson states, that information is sufficient for perception), but that input is not the determinant of the ensuing perceptual experience.

The data support Festinger's efferent readiness theory in the four experimental paradigms he examined. Perhaps the most interesting case involved mounting a distorting prism directly on the eye via a contact lens. In this case, the subjects' objective eye movements must conform to the contour to maintain fixation. In this instance:

> The old well-learned efference for an eye movement to fixate that is activated by visual input will result in a loss of fixation. To move the eye and maintain fixation along the contour, *S* wearing the contact lens must learn a new set of efferent instructions to issue in response to the visual input. If the conscious experience of visual perception of contour is, indeed, determined by efferent readiness activated by the visual input, then to the extent that *S* learns a new afferent–efferent association and, hence, a different efferent readiness is activated by the visual input, he will have a different visual perception of the contour.
>
> In accordance with these theoretical expectations all three *S*s showed appreciable change in the visual perception of curvature as a consequence of simply scanning the line while wearing the contact lens. This occurred whether *S* viewed an apparently straight line or an apparently curved line. Further evidence suggests that there is appreciable, perhaps complete, interocular transfer of this change in perception of contour. The data also provide a hint that, if the eye movement involved is a smooth tracking movement, there is less change in visual perception than if the eye movements are saccadic [Festinger *et al.*, 1967, p. 35].

Subjects in this condition did experience changed perception of the contour, regardless of whether they were viewing an apparently straight or an apparently curved line.

Thus, there is evidence that even such a prima facie unlikely instance as visual form perception is susceptible to interpretation by a motor theory. (Presumably a similar account can be detailed to handle the phenomena of auditory perception, although none has yet been worked out.) Indeed, since no other (sensory) theory yet proposed can address data such as Festinger's, it appears that the motor theory approach is virtually without rivals in the domain of perception, at least with regard to the "how" questions involved.

4.4 Imagery and Hallucination as Motor Constructions

Further evidence for the motoric nature of perception comes from the constructive processes underlying imagery and hallucination (rather, processes which *are* images and hallucinations). Despite Gibson's correct insistence that the information specifying perception is available in the stimulus array, this specification of what is involved does not address the processes by which perception occurs. The "what" question is being dealt with beautifully by Gibson and his associates, but the "how" question remains. Constructive theory in cognitive psychology developed as an attempt to deal with this latter question. Let us examine the constructive account of imagery, to see the motoric nature of such processes, and to see that constructive theory does not make perception an illusory process.

The motor theory of perception has often been criticized in this manner:

> Such views maintain that perception per se is more a reflection of the response patterns instigated in the brain by an input than it is a resultant of the input patterns. This appears an extreme view–taken to its logical and absurd conclusion it would mean that we would perceive every woman on the street as Aphrodite (and in whatever state of dress or undress we are set to see her at the moment) and every man as Adonis. There is, of course, some truth to this–"beauty" is to a large extent in the eye of the beholder. Yet the distortions of perception that are ordinarily possible are limited. When they go beyond these limits we speak of them as illusions and hallucinations. And though any account of the perceptual process must take into consideration the possibility of the production of illusions and hallucinations, the account need not make illusions and hallucination the perceptual way of life [Pribram, 1971a, pp. 91–92].

Such criticism is fundamentally misguided, because the motor theory asserts that *the processes underlying perception are identical to those underlying hallucination and imagination, but it does not assert that perception is always illusory.* The problem of the veridicality of perception, its degree of adequacy of representation of, or correspondence to, the nonmental realm is orthogonal to the problem of explaining the nature of perception. In this latter regard, perception and hallucination are on a par. We can equally speak of "hallucinating what is really there" and "perceiving what isn't there." What we require is a theory of the constructive processes underlying perception that accounts for the *fact* that perception and hallucination are different areas of a continuum, rather than antagonistic or unrelated processes. (The problem of truth, and the adequacy of representation provided by perceptual construction, is a 'philosophical' issue quite different from the nature of such construction.)

Motor theories have predominated in the field of imagery since the beginning of academic psychology. Alexander Bain (1855) proposed an explicit motor theory of imagery, as well as a motor theory of thought. William James did likewise in the *Principles* in 1890. Wundt, the founder of psychology, abolished the distinction between sensation and image: "There is absolutely no reason why a sensation–blue, green, yellow, or what not–should be one thing when it is accompanied simply by an excitation in the 'visual center' of the cortex, and another and quite different thing when this excitation is itself set up by an operation of some external stimulus [Wundt, 1912, p. 14]." Two lines of research have shown Wundt's reasoning to be correct. The first, and most familiar, shows 'perception' in the absence of external stimulus input, that is, shows that we construct images we are unaware to be images. The tachistoscope, with a blank stimulus card and instructions to "tell me what you see" is the usual vehicle for such studies (Eriksen, 1958; Goldiamond & Hawkins, 1958; Neisser, 1967), although Warren (1970) shows the same effect in speech perception when a subject 'hears,' for example, "to" in "go to the store," when nothing but white noise is actually present. The second line of research stems from Perky (1910), a student of Titchner's, and shows that we can equally easily mistake perception for images. The "Perky effect" is the confusion of perception with imagination. If a subject is told to fixate a spot and imagine, say, a banana, he will believe that a picture of a banana projected on the spot is his image, despite its orientation, color, and so on being different from his initial "image." The data indicate therefore that there is no difference in kind between the experience of perception and imagination (Segal, 1971). Experientially it makes no difference whether we perceive or hallucinate. This is all but unintelligible unless both processes are constructive, motoric actions in which experience is determined by central neural commands or expectations rather than the actual sensory input.

There is also evidence to indicate that the same 'motor' is involved in both perception and hallucination. Studies of eye movements during dreaming, auditory imagery during reading, emg recording during imagined action, and so on, all show action patterns virtually indistinguishable from their overt correlates. Brooks (1968) shows that engaging imagery in a modality delays overt responding in that mode, but not in another, suggesting that imagery and responding occupy common neural channels. Segal and Fusella (1970) show that visual imagery decreases the ability to detect visual signals, suggesting that imagery and perception also occupy common channels.

All this research, in combination with enormous amounts of data indicating the constructive nature of perception (Gregory, 1966; Lindsay & Norman, 1972; Neisser, 1967), can easily be made sense of by construing perception, imagination, and hallucination as constructive processes within the motor theory framework. No other theory has yet successfully reconciled the indistinguishability of these processes, or been able to address data such as that of Festinger and his co-workers, or of Penfield (Penfield & Roberts, 1959) which shows imagery to result from direct stimulation of certain areas of the cortex.

5 THE SENSORY ORDER AND THE PROBLEM OF MODALITY

Psychologists rarely deal with what must be the most obvious and fundamental problem posed by perception: the fact that our phenomenal experience has the qualitative dimensions that it does. Hayek (1952) stated the problem that we face with unparalleled clarity:

> What psychology has to explain is not something known solely through that special technique known as "introspection," but something which we experience whenever we

> learn anything about the external world and through which indeed we know about the external world; and which yet has no place in our scientific picture of the external world and is in no way explained by the sciences dealing with the external world: Qualities. Whenever we study qualitative differences between experiences, we are studying mental and not physical events, and much that we believe to know about the external world is, in fact, knowledge about ourselves.
>
> It is thus the existence of an order of sensory qualities and not a reproduction of qualities existing outside the perceiving mind which is the basic problem raised by all mental events. Psychology must concern itself, in other words, with those aspects of what we naively regard as the external world which find no place in the account of that world which the physical sciences give us [Hayek, 1952, pp. 6–7].*

This is the problem of modality: Why should sights be sights, sounds be sounds, speech be speech, and so on? Within a given sensory order the same issue arises: Why should red, say, be what we occurrently know as red? The problem, in short, is the philosophical one of "raw feels": to account for the qualitative dimensions of perception that we know by acquaintance in human experience. How and why are the sensory orders what they in fact are?

Why the sensory orders have the particular qualities that they do is beyond the limits of human inquiry; but how the modalities are functionally differentiated can be sketched with a fair degree of confidence. When elaborated, the account reinforces the motor theory of mind by dealing with an area that is perhaps the least obvious domain to which it could apply.

In order to tackle this problem at all it is necessary to point out once again that the 'absolute' nature of sensory qualities cannot be a problem for theoretical inquiry. The problems we can formulate are immediately cast in the language of description rather than acquaintance. All that can be *communicated* are the differences between sensory qualities, and such differences do not enable us to assert that the qualities different people experience are similar in any "absolute" sense. All we can discuss is whether different sensory qualities differ in the same way for different individuals. The intrinsic nature of raw feels is simply not a proper subject matter for conceptual thought, and therefore is beyond the bounds of both science *and* common sense. As Hayek put it:

> There are no questions which we can intelligibly ask about sensory qualities which could not also conceivably become a problem to a person who has not himself experienced the particular qualities but knows them only from the descriptions given to him by others. . . . Nothing can become a problem about sensory qualities which cannot in principle also be described in words; and such description in words will always have to be description in terms of the relation of the quality in question to other sensory qualities [Hayek, 1952, p. 31] (Note 10).

With this proviso restated, let us trace the historical development of thought on the sensory order. We may begin with the extremely influential position of Johannes Müller, presented in the 5th volume of his *Handbook of Physiology* in

*From F. Hayek, *The Sensory Order.* Chicago: University of Chicago Press, 1952 Copyright © 1952 by the University of Chicago Press.

the 1830s. Müller propounded the doctrine of the specific energies of nerve substances: "Sensation consists in the sensorium's receiving . . . a knowledge of certain qualities . . . of the nerves of sense themselves; and these qualities of the nerves of sense are in all different, the nerve of each having its own particular quality or energy [quoted in Boring, 1950, p. 84]." This doctrine, which merely codified prevalent thought among physiologists, attributes the qualities of the sensory modalities to the characteristics of the nerves that compose those modalities: "The nerve of each sense seems to be capable of one determinate kind of sensation only, and not of those proper to the other organs of sense; hence, one nerve of sense cannot take the place and perform the function of the nerve of another sense [quoted in Boring, 1950, p. 84]."

Müller's pupil, Helmholtz, studying audition, extended the theory to account for differences within each modality by proposing (what Boring calls) the theory of specific *fiber* energies: each nerve fiber within a sensory order was assumed to have a characteristic quality. But in his place theory of hearing, Helmholtz added another idea current at the time: that quality depends equally upon the place in the nervous system. Helmholtz focused attention upon places in the receptor, for example, by looking for "resonators" on the basilar membrane. Other investigators looked for places in the termination of sensory fibers, that is, in the brain. In 1870 Fritsch and Hitzig, working within a long tradition of brain localization of function, discovered by electrical stimulation the motor area of the precentral gyrus. Subsequent investigators tended to attribute sensory qualities to the central termination of the fibers on the basis of extensive stimulation studies.

By the turn of the century Müller's doctrine had been abandoned, and it was assumed that sensory qualities resulted from a combination of localizations—both the place in the receptor from which the impulse originated, and the cortical termination at which it arrived. Knowledge of the neural impulse, culminating in Bernstein's theory that the impulse is a wave of electrical depolarization, precluded any specific qualities for individual nerves. But it did not take long for the combined localization views to be refuted. Lashley (1929) showed that the cortical terminations of sensory messages were not indispensible to discrimination, and proposed the thesis of equipotentiality in place of localization of function. Lashley's mass action thesis admits localization, but holds that no particular localization is necessary for any particular cerebral functining. Since the proponents of localization had themselves shown that the receptors were not crucial (by producing sensory qualia by stimulating the cortex directly), there is not much left of the localization view, at least at the level of specific sensory qualities.

But if sensory qualities are not due to the character of individual nerves and do not depend essentially upon either the receptors from which they originate or the central neural termini to which they transmit, to what can they be attributed? By abandoning anatomical localization for functional localization in terms of relations among patterns of neural impulses, Hayek provided the only alternative that is compatible with known CNS functioning. The sensory order can only be understood as a system of connections of impulses within the active CNS. As Hayek noted, the nervous system is fundamentally an instrument of classification, and the sensory order receives the properties it possesses in virtue of the patterns of impulses that create it. To repeat Hayek's point:

> The sensory order (or other mental) qualities are not in some manner originally attached to, or an original attribute of, the individual physiological impulses, but . . . the whole of these qualities is determined by the system of connexions by which the impulses can be transmitted. . . . It is thus the position of the individual impulse or group of impulses in the whole system of such connexions which gives it its distinctive quality [Hayek, 1952, p. 53].

To put the point another way, Hayek's generic theory of mind is sufficiently rich that it encompasses the sensory order as a special case without in any way changing that generic theory. And as should be obvious, Hayek's theory of mind is a motor theory: the mental realm exists only in virtue of the generation of impulses within the nervous system. This activity, which is inherently classificatory in nature, creates both the traditional 'sensory' and 'motor' aspects of behavior. Not only does the nervous system generate behavior, but it also generates the order of events within the organism which *is* mind. Since the mind is, in the last analysis, the pattern of events that make it up, it is obvious that all its attributes depend upon patterns. Pattern talk is equally as indispensible for the understanding of theories and conceptual frameworks (see Hanson, 1970) as it is for sensory experience, and for precisely the same reasons in both cases (Note 11).

6 THE NATURE OF CONSCIOUSNESS

Perception, as conscious experience, is one thing; but what of the nature of consciousness per se? What theoretical accounts of consciousness are available? So far as I am aware, there is only one hypothesis as to the nature of consciousness in the literature which deserves to be labeled 'theoretical': the proposal of Roger Sperry (1952, 1966, 1968, 1969, 1976). All other accounts are merely paraphrastic, defining consciousness in terms of attention and awareness, and self-consciousness in terms of self-awareness.

In essence, Sperry proposes that consciousness is our knowledge by acquaintance of what we know by description as the motor production command system of cortical activity involved in thinking and attending. As such, consciousness is an emergent property of cerebral activity having to do with the functional organization of the active brain. Further, since we are aware of our own consciousness, it follows that the brain must be able to detect and to react to the pattern properties of its own activity. Self-consciousness simply is the functional brain's detection of its patterns of activity.

Two points that are integral to this conception of consciousness are worthy of separate mention. The first concerns the role of consciousness in the causation of human affairs, the second locates consciousness within the brain. Both have profound effects upon classic positions on the mind–body problems.

6.1 The Causal Efficacy of Consciousness

Concomitant with this picture of consciousness is an admission of its causal efficacy. On this point, Sperry (1952, 1969, 1976), Eccles (1973), and Pribram (1971a) agree: consciousness plays a directive role in the flow of cerebral impulses, and thus is essential to voluntary action. Consciousness *supervenes* (as Sperry puts it) in the generation of behavior in virtue of its position at the top of the organizational hierarchy which *is* the human mind. Neural impulses "are simply carried along or shunted this way and that by the prevailing overall dynamics of the whole active process [Sperry, 1969, p. 534]" (Note 12).

This puts experience, our knowledge by acquaintance, right back in the heart of the problems facing scientific psychology. As Sperry notes:

> Perceived colors and sounds, etc., exist within the brain not as epiphenomena, but as real properties of the brain process. When the brain adjusts to these perceived colors and sounds, the adjustment is made not merely to an array of neural excitations correlated with the colors and sounds but rather to the colors and sounds themselves [Sperry, 1969, pp. 535–536].

Thus *epistemically* the only tenable mind–body position is an emergent interactionism (see Weimer, 1976).

6.2 The Localization of Consciousness

Although a slight digression from the motor theory of consciousness, it is worth remarking that Sperry's work with commissurotomized patients has enabled an anatomic localization of consciousness within the brain undreamed of even a decade ago. The remarkable finding that results from callosal sectioning is that all the actions programmed from the minor hemisphere (98% of the time the right hemisphere) are not recognized by the conscious subject as being actions of his own initiation. Conscious awareness of the initiation of actions is restricted entirely to the dominant, speech-localized hemisphere. Actions initiated by the right or minor hemisphere are unconscious, or tacit. Voluntary awareness therefore resides in the major hemisphere, presumably in the anatomically specialized areas for speech comprehension—largely Wernike's area (Geschwind, 1972). Only the dominant hemisphere has access to language, and when the minor hemisphere is cut off from it, the conscious being, the self, can no longer verbalize the proceedings of the minor hemisphere. Sectioning of the callosum reveals what has always been the case with consciousness: that the minor hemisphere is unconscious, and that linkage through the corpus callosum is necessary for it to either give or receive information from the conscious "self" (Note 13).

Two points need to be mentioned in this regard. First, since the areas of the major hemisphere that are implicated as underlying consciousness are concerned with speech perception, the motor theories of these two domains become linked. The motor theory of consciousness now becomes prima facie as plausible as the motor theory of speech perception, and vice versa. Second, certain simplistic mind–body positions are empirically refuted (Eccles, 1973). Specifically, the classic neural identity theory as propounded by Feigl (1967) is refuted, for it is not the case that the conscious mind is coextensive with the entire brain, as that identity theory holds. Further, double knowledge theories that assume we know all the brain by description and experience by acquaintance are wrong, because we know by acquaintance only a tiny part of the activity of the brain. The problem for the mind–body relationship is to explain why and how only this particular part of the brain is involved in conscious experience and "selfhood." Tacit knowledge is a severe problem for the various forms of the identity theory yet proposed (Weimer, 1976).

7 THE PROBLEM OF MOTIVATION

Classically, the problems of motivation center around the activation, energization, and direction of behavior. In sensory conceptions of mind, motivation is either *extrinsic* to the organism or at best concerned with its information-processing capabilities; that is, *motivation is external to the CNS,* arising from such classic sources as strong and painful external stimuli, internal bodily and homeostatic states such as hunger and thirst, and sex (if sex is not considered in the previous category). Drive theory was the classic approach to motivation in stimulus–response psychology, and Dollard and Miller's (1950) statement that drives are "strong stimuli which impel action [p. 30]" received universal assent: the quarrels concerned whether such stimuli arose from physiological need states, whether their reduction was reinforcing, how they led to choice of goals, and affected learning, and so on. In such passive conceptions of mind, a motivational variable was required to arouse the organism from a quiescent state, to make it behave *ab initio*. Indeed, Woodworth (1918) introduced the concept of drive into psychology from the analogy of the drive train in an automobile, without which a car cannot move or "behave." This conception of the nature and role of motivation was sufficiently strong to lead some theorists to account for evidence refuting it (such as observations of exploration, play, curiosity, etc., even in rats) by postulating a "boredom drive" whose reduction, and hence reinforcement, was attainment of a state of stimulation after a lack of input. Stimulus deprivation thus became the ultimate drive in the absence of other identifiable sources, and the passive organism could be goaded into action by either the presence or absence of stimulation (see, e.g., Fowler, 1965).

From a stimulus–response–reinforcement point of view, no other way of treating motivation seemed feasible. But if that framework, and the passive conception of the organism, are abandoned, the problem of motivation is entirely different. Indeed, part of the problem for cognitive theory is that the old problems of motivation just don't arise when considering the higher mental processes. Proliferating new drives, such as a drive to communicate, or to reduce semantic "dials" in a "cognitive mixer" (Osgood, 1971) to "explain" why we speak, and so on, is simply absurd. To say that any classic source of motivation underlies thought, reasoning, imagery, creativity, perceiving, testing a scientific theory, and so on, no longer makes sense. But the problems of the domain of motivation remain: How can we understand what, for example, motivates our quest for knowledge?

Without denying the utility of a restricted, nondispositional theory of extrinsic motivation, especially for intense 'stimulus' inputs, it seems clear that such accounts must be supplemented by a theory of the motivation intrinsic to the higher mental processes. What is required is a mechanism of motivation inherent in the active CNS, dealing with information processing and action. Psychology must unpack the promissory note found in "acknowledging an intrinsic motivation or a motivation inherent in the organism's informational interaction with circumstances through the distance receptors and in its intentional, goal-anticipated actions [Hunt, 1965, p. 197]." We must acknowledge that *motivation is intrinsic to the operation of the CNS,* and that the extrinsic sources of motivation that can be retained from classic motivation theory have their 'source' in the intrinsic motivation of nervous systems; that is, cognitive psychology must develop a "motor theory" of motivation.

But no such theory exists, although there are faint hints at what is involved (Hunt, 1965; Pribram, 1971a). In the meantime the field of motivation is changing in two directions at once. On one hand, there is a proliferation of "new looks" toward old problems (growth motivation, personal causation à la DeCharms, 1968, etc.), attempting to replace the drive theory framework without entirely abandoning what the sensory conception construes as motivation. On the other hand, cognitive psychology is dealing with motivational problems and issues (such as the issues stated in the title of this volume), but not developing a specific theory of motivation. This second approach uses motivation without mentioning it, and treats the problems of motivation in the process of addressing other issues. Implicit in this approach is the idea that an adequate motivational theory will be a by-product of a completed cognitive psychology, but that motivation, as a separate domain, may not have any counterpart in the cognitive framework. If this is indeed the choice we face, between trying to translate the old motivational system into the cognitive paradigm and abandoning the field as a separate entity, it is clear which way to go.

8 THE MANIFESTATION AND REPRESENTATION OF MEANING

The focal problem of philosophy and psychology is meaning: both disciplines have as an essential task the explanation of its nature and functioning. This section overviews the nature of major problems and their relation to the motor theory framework. Section 8.1 proposes an identity of the problems of meaning and tacit knowledge; Section 8.2 proposes that the motor involvement in the manifestations of meaning be modeled upon craftsmanship; Section 8.3 explores a conceptual framework for understanding the context relativity of comprehension; and Section 8.4 considers holography as the neurological "motor" underlying the representation of meaningful information.

8.1 Meaning as the Problem Underlying Tacit Knowledge

I have made this argument in a number of locations; a succinct presentation occurs in Weimer (1974), which I can do little better than repeat:

> I would like to argue that the entire problem of tacit knowledge is nothing more, nothing less, than the problem of meaning. In this sense, there is only one problem that has ever existed in psychology, and everything the field has investigated is merely a manifestation of that problem, a different aspect of the same elephant, an elephant that we have grasped at since the dawn of reflective thought without ever reaching at all.
>
>> This problem has many names. In the language of behaviorism, it is a matter of stimulus generalization or of stimulus equivalence. In the terminology of Gestalt psychology, it is the problem of contact between perceptual processes and memory trace: the so-called "Höffding step." Among philosophers, the question is usually formulated in terms of "universals" and of "abstraction from particulars." For Bruner and his associates, it is the problem of categorization. In computer technology, it is called "character recognition" when only letters and numbers are to be identified, or more generally "pattern recognition" [Neisser, 1967, p. 47].
>
> The problem, "When are stimuli equivalent?", *is* the problem of stimulus recognition, which *is* the problem of concept formation, *ad infinitum,* all of which together constitute the problems of meaning. Stimuli are equivalent, in the final analysis, only because they mean the same thing. No matter where one goes in psychology there comes a point at which one runs straight into an insurmountable wall that is, conceptually speaking, infinitely high and wide. All we can do is look up and see that written on that wall are all the problems of the manifestations of meaning [Weimer, 1974, pp. 427–429].

8.2 Craftsmanship and Skill in the Manifestation of Meaning

The motor theory of mind yields a very informative analogy or model of the manifestation of meaning in all cognition and action: if meaning is action, then its exhibition is a matter of *craftsmanship.* The motor involvement (recall Section 2) in the creation of meaning is an instance of skill, and the most fruitful metaphor for the understanding of skill is still Plato's conception of the soul as a craftsman, or artificer, who constructs the entire realm of human participation in the universe. The motor theory asserts that the manifestation of meaning is a product of the skill of the CNS, and thus that the way to study meaning is to study the ways in which the CNS is skilled. Craftsmanship thus becomes the root metaphor of mind, instanced in every 'act' of either the reception of information or the production of behavior. Meaning becomes the underlying interrelationship of all 'higher' mental processes, manifested in each such process but not identifiable with any one of them. Thus meaning is always context dependent: dependent upon the framework that relates all 'higher' mental processes (rather than upon any one such process).

8.3 The Contractual Nature of Understanding

No long ago it was thought that an adequate psychology could be context free—that the rules of determination for the assimilation of information and the production of action could be written in a grammar that utilized no context-dependent constraints. The abandonment of this program in linguistics has now ramified throughout psychology and one of the most prevalent effects of the 'cognitive revolution' has been the realization of the necessity for context-sensitive rules for both comprehension and production. The phenomenon of ambiguity, especially in its deep structural form, has been perhaps the most significant substantive importation into psychology from transformational linguistics.

Comprehension, the ability to render incoming information meaningful, is basically the skill of resolving ambiguity. Most research in comprehension that has occasioned recent interest, such as that of Bransford and his collaborators, consists in little more than demonstrations of the now "obvious" fact that if a subject is given an appropriate context he can understand virtually any input whatsoever (or conversely, that seemingly easily understandable input can be rendered incomprehensible by supplying the "wrong" context). Thus "context" is now the key word in the experimental study of comprehension (e.g., see Jenkins', 1974, overenthusiastic extension of Pepper's, 1942, metaphor of contextualism).

However, context per se may or may not be the determining factor in comprehension: there are higher order constraints that determine when a given context will or will not produce certain effects. Following Proffitt (1976) I call these higher order constraints *contracts.* The determining factor in comprehension that specifies when contextual sensitivity will or will not be evidenced then becomes contractual obligation. Contractual obligation is a matter of the subject's coming to treat incoming information as bound up within the terms of a contract, a contract that specifies what contexts are appropriate to use for the assimilation of subsequent information.

The theatrical metaphor is a good vehicle for understanding the nature of a contract. How one interprets, say, a play depends upon the manner in which one comes to treat the happenings upon a stage. We are perfectly willing to admit that, say, a poorly hung curtain is "really" a wall between two rooms in the context of a play, but moments later that same curtain is just a stage prop. Or consider the performance of a good magician (one whose "magic" is concerned with the wonder of the world, rather than a clever, but always ego-involved, perpetrator of mere tricks). His performance induces awe, amazement, profound respect, and in a very important sense, belief; but not so a carnival "trickster." Are such effects just due to context? Certainly not. The context remains the same (or can be identical), but the contract one employs to interpret the context changes. One *participates* in the play or magic show in a very different way from what one does in just being in a theater or sitting in an audience. It is as if there is a prior agreement between the playwright (or magician) and ourselves that we will accept subsequent information only within certain contexts and not in others. It is as if we are contractually obligated to utilize certain contexts and to ignore others that are, a priori, equally capable of being imposed upon the events in question. We present incoming information to ourselves through contracts that define the way events *ought to be,* and hence establish given contexts at the expense of others.

The concept of contractual obligation allows a novel interpretation of the phenomenon of learning: instead of being a "meaningless" matter of reinforced practice, as standard textbooks assert, it is a matter of contractual change. What is learned, that is, that which allows the organism to respond appropriately in novel contexts, is a changed contract. Learning is thus a restructuring of the meanings of events through contractual change. Therefore when contracts and contexts compete, it is the contract that determines what one will see (Proffitt, 1976). We learn to render the world meaningful in terms of contracts which specify permissible contexts, not in terms of contexts alone.

8.4 The Representation of Meaning

The old problem of storage, of how the nervous system makes available representations of input, has largely given way to a new problem which concerns what it takes to recreate a perspective. The problem of memory (in all cases except sheer rote learning) no longer revolves around the storage of input, but now concerns the utilization of meaningful information. But where is that information if not stored away within the nervous system? How can one utilize information that isn't always there?

Until recently, no one could have answered this question. But with the development of optical holography, we at least have a model of how the nervous system could recreate a perspective without utilizing any traditional concept of 'storage.' Transferring the hologram from its initial optical conception into neurological functioning requires acknowledgment that the nervous system does not function solely by discrete neural impulses. Instead one must take account, as Pribram (1971a) has constantly emphasized, of the role of the junctional microstructure and the continuously graded slow potential activities of neuronal aggregates. When acknowledgment is made of this second mode of activity of neural functioning, the way is clear for conceptual and empirical advances of the order of magnitude of those made when the reflex arc conception was abandoned. We can now understand how the brain could, as a functional neural hologram, make available to itself virtually immediately a continuous series of perspectives from which to render perceptions intelligible and to serve as the basis for actions. The representation of meaning can thus be modeled upon the holographic metaphor, and this "motor" for the generation of meaning by 'memory' clears up conceptual confusions that simply debilitated the sensory metatheory.

9 SUMMARY

Traditional identifications of sensory and motor, from the neural level of analysis to the behavioral, have been based upon the "passive" reception of incoming information and the muscle involvement in behavior, respectively. As should be obvious by now, both these interpretations, couched as they are in purely surface structure terms, must be abandoned in favor of a deep structural account of (broadly speaking) perceiving and acting. When one penetrates to the deep conceptual level underlying these disparate surface phenomena it becomes clear that the abstract structure underlying them, although common to both, cannot be identified with either. Thus the question of how to interpret 'the mind' (construed as that abstract, underlying structure) arises. The sensory metatheory of mind arose as an initially plausible attempt to make 'the mental' intrinsically sensory, by the simple expedient of stretching the surface meaning of sensory and abandoning action (to the status of a consequence of mental processing). This chapter has argued instead for a motor metatheory of mind which, abandoning both traditional interpretations of sensory and motor, attempts to characterize the communality of acting, perceiving, and comprehending.

Any viable psychological theory must encompass the fundamental fact of productivity or creativity in all perception, cognition, language, and action. It is the productive nature of all organismic activity which simultaneously rules out any as yet proposed alternative to the motor metatheory and which also provides its strongest support. The revolution in cognitive psychology, to the extent that it has as yet occurred, consists mainly in recognizing the pervasive presence of problems of productivity. This chapter attempts to aid that revolution by making the problems explicit in domains that have not as yet received sufficient examination, and by proposing the extension to all domains of the class of theory most capable of encompassing productivity. The result is a conceptual framework which, for the first time, allows both the incorporation of the basic insights of the transformational revolution in linguistics into psychology and also unites the information-processing capabilities of the psychological subject with his potentialities for action.

CHAPTER NOTES

Note 1. It must be emphasized that this chapter argues against a sensory *conception* of mind and in favor of a motor *conception,* but that it makes this metatheoretical argument by discussing theories that fit these conceptual frameworks. Thus "the sensory theory" and "the motor theory" are (possibly misleading) short-hand formulations employed to save space and function as labels. There is indeed no general motor theory of mind, nor any general sensory theory; there are only substantive theoretical formulations which stem from one or the other metatheoretical framework.

Note 2. Such an approach lands Neisser with strange bedfellows indeed. One can hardly imagine a more characteristic constructive slogan than "seeing does not imply something seen," yet this is a battle cry not only of the traditional cognitive theorist but also of the most extreme radical behaviorist:

> A man need not copy the stimulating environment in order to perceive it, and he need not make a copy in order to perceive it in the future. When an organism exposed to a set of contingencies of reinforcement is modified by them and as a result behaves in a different way in the future, we do not need to say that it stores the contingencies. What is "stored" is a modified organism, not a record of the modifying variables [Skinner, 1969, p. 274].

Skinner (1974) has even contradicted his earlier empty organism, passive conception of man by admitting the controlling influence of covert events (e.g., p. 223) in a formulation that comes very close to being "mediational." The point to remember, however, is that Skinner cannot dismiss all of cognitive psychology on this point, but only the "computer modelers" and "information processors" (such as Shiffrin in the subsequent quotation in the text). And unfortunately for Skinner, he is also quite inconsistent: when it comes to his "explanation" (which is to say, paraphrase) of rule-governed behavior, Skinner relies very explicitly on the storage of symbolic contingencies (see Mahoney, 1974, especially Chapter 9).

All of this serves to emphasize a crucial point: seemingly disparate theoretical formulations, especially when the theorists involved *want* to separate themselves from the opposition, may nonetheless be identical or very similar on crucial points because they are variants of the same metatheory. Since Skinner and Neisser are both "sensory" theorists, it is not at all surprising that essentail aspects of their positions overlap.

Note 3. The cerebellum has grown commensurately with the neocortex throughout vertebrate evolution, and the immense superiority of man's skills is due to this coordination of development. Man's superiority is a matter of his skills, both motor skills in the traditional sense and such "higher" skills as language, thought, and culture. By performing an enormous number of computations, the cerebellum acts as a comparative computer to control skilled movements. There is immediate input to the cerebellum from the motor cortex, and the cerebrum cannot initiate any action without informing the cerebellum. J. C. Eccles has exhaustively investigated the cerebellum in the last decade, and this is his summary statement of its functioning:

> What you do with ordinary movements is to give a general command–such as "place finger on nose," or "write signature," or "pick up glass"–and the whole motor performance goes automatically. For example, you don't have to spell out your name letter by letter when you're writing your signature–if you did, the bank manager would not recognize it! You just give the general command from the cerebrum and let the cerebellum take over in order to give the fine characteristic details.
>
> Normally our most complex muscle movements are carried out subconsciously and with consummate skill. The more subconscious you are in a golf stroke, the better it is, and the same with tennis, skiing, skating, or any other skill. In all these performances we do not have any appreciation of the complexity of muscle contractions and joint movements. All that we are voluntarily conscious of is a general directive given by what we may call our voluntary system. All the finesse and skill seems naturally and automatically to flow from that. It is my thesis that the cerebellum is concerned in all this enormously complex organization and control of movement, and that throughout life, particularly in the earlier years, we are engaged in an incessant teaching program for the cerebellum. As a consequence, it can carry out all of these remarkable tasks that we set it to do in the whole repertoire of our skilled movements in games, in techniques, in musical performance, in speech, dance, song, and so on [Eccles, 1973, pp. 122–123].

Man can perform skilled behaviors such as threading a needle or building a miniaturized transistor circuit that are far beyond the control limits of movement of even the highest primates, and his ability to perform such delicate operations is due to the interaction of the cerebellum with the cerebrum. The exhibition of intelligence in skilled performance could not take place without the coalitional control of the cerebellum (see Note 13).

Note 4. Historical alternatives to sensory theories of mind extend at least as far back as Plato, for the *Timaeus* develops a prototypic motor theory of mind. As a sidelight to developing Plato's cosmology and ethics, the *Timaeus* develops a conception of the World Soul as an *artificer* or *craftsman* who shapes the universe according to divine plans or templates. This Divine Craftsman not only shapes and animates the cosmos, he is also the model for living things such as man. The essence of man is thus craftsmanship, and our creativity and productivity is due to this generative capacity that we share with the divine artificer. Regardless of how fanciful the account seems, it is clear that Plato had an active epistemology and a motor theory of mind that made craftsmanship and creativity the prime metaphors for understanding the uniqueness of man (his soul).

Plato also proposed more specific motoric theories of the higher mental processes. Not long ago the writer listened to an introductory lecture on perception which pointed out (to the instructor's wry amusement and the students' utter bewilderment) that Plato had been so "unscientific" as to propose that vision involved the eye "spitting out" particles which struck the objects seen. This sensory theorist then pointed out how the first True Scientist (Aristotle) had proposed today's common-sense view that vision involves the eye passively registering information. Although ridiculed by sensory theorists then and now, Plato's notion embodies a motor theory of vision quite consonant with current views (such as those outlined in Section 4 below).

Plato's alternatives to Aristotelian conceptions were virtually ignored throughout history, although the active epistemologists such as Leibniz and Kant kept alive some of his views. I have suggested that the Platonic epistemology is far more tenable than its Aristotelian alternative (Weimer, 1973), and this entire chapter argues as forcefully as possible that Plato's motor theory, at least in its emphasis, is the only viable conception that we have.

Note 5. Pribram locates signification in pathways related to so-called primary sensory systems. Signs are thus constructed when actions operate upon perceptual images: "Discrimination learning, pattern recognition, selective attention, all involve neural choice mechanisms, choices that beget actions which in turn modify what is Imaged [Pribram, 1971a, p. 312]." Anatomically these functions seem to involve structures posterior to the central sulcus, such as the prestriate cortex and portions of the temporal lobe.

The connections important to symbolic processes seem to involve frontal lobes and certain limbic structures. Pribram argues that the limbic system is anatomically suited to symbolic behaviors because context sensitivity requires that "a set of contexts must become internalized (i.e., become brain states) before the appropriate response can be made. Building sets of contexts depends on a memory mechanism that embodies self-referral, rehearsal, or, technically speaking, the operation of sets of recursive functions. . . . The closed loop connectivity of the limbic systems has always been its anatomical hallmark and makes an ideal candidate as a mechanism for context dependency [Pribram, 1971b, pp. 24–15]."

This corticofugal conception can be compared with the classic cortico–cortico relay conception by studying Fig. 3.

Note 6. The motor theory is not the muscle theory. A very telling joke about John B. Watson's rabid antimentalism states that Watson made up his windpipe that he didn't have a mind. Thinking, for Watson, was merely the activity of the peripheral musculature involved in speech. With this peripheralism and "muscular" emphasis Watson had a *muscle* theory of the mind, but not a motor theory as we are using the term. Watson's mind was passivist, empiricist, and associationist, and his nervous system was a switchboard with discrete sensory and motor components. In contrast a motor theory requires an active epistemology, postulation of rich innate structuring, emphasizes the inherently 'motor' nature of the sensory–perceptual systems, and is incompatible with associationism as

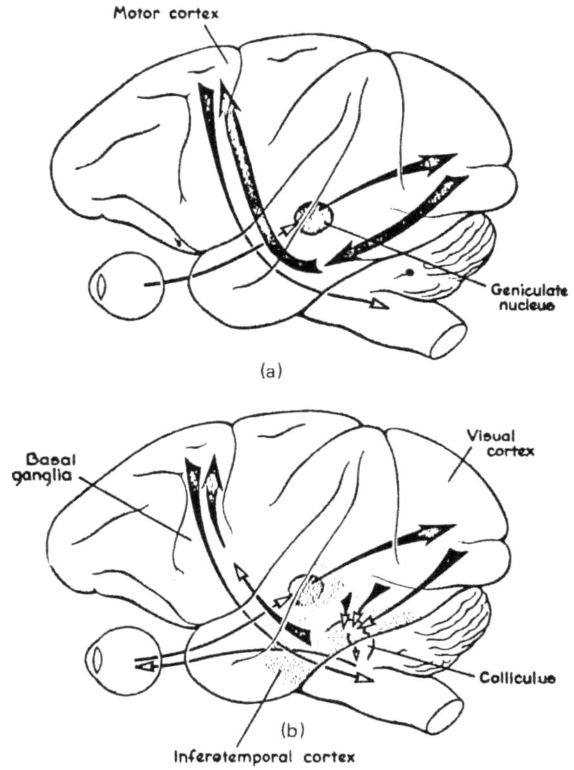

FIG. 3 Comparison of the classical (a) and Pribram's proposed (b) mechanism of cortical involvement in perception and cognition. Classic mechanism involved cortico–cortico connections from "primary" sensory areas to frontal association areas to motor cortex. Pribram's proposal involves cortico–subcortico connections of "association" areas with basal ganglia and other subcortical motor areas. (From Pribram, 1971a, p. 368.)

the only principle of mental functioning. But most importantly, the motor metatheory is a theory about the *central* nervous system only, and it makes no identification of higher mental functioning with either the peripheral nervous system or behavioral responding. To do the latter, as Watson did in identifying thinking with the activity of the larynx, is to commit the *operationalist's fallacy* of confusing the evidence with that which is evidenced.

Note 7. Thinking is not unique among human skills in its hierarchical organization and productivity. Students of motor skills have long recognized the commonality between language and skills, and the inadequacy of stimulus–response models to account for the complexity of skilled behavior. For example, Fitts (1964) defined skilled responses as those in which receptor–effector–feedback processes are both spatially and temporally highly organized, and took the goal of skills-learning study to be the explanation of how such organization or patterning comes about. He argued this way well before the revolution in psycholinguistics had made itself felt to the remainder of psychology: "Rather than viewing perceptual–motor behavior as a series of motor responses made to reach some goal, it is possible, and I believe considerably more profitable, to view such behavior as an information processing activity guided by some general plan or program [Fitts, 1964, p. 248]." Later, speaking of learning as an adaptive process, Fitts noted that "Basic to the adaptive system is the existence of hierarchical processes [p. 250]." He noted that as long ago as 1899 R. S. Woodworth had concluded polyphasic (two-phase) motor units (which he took to be basic components of skills) were patterned in advance of their initiation, and remain uninfluenced by sensory inputs during their execution. Woodworth also argued that rapid polyphasic reponses, such as tapping successive targets, involve the preformation and emission as a unit of more than one polyphasic unit.

Since this high degree of sophistication and awareness of the issues has characterized the area of skills learning for at least three quarters of a century, one may wonder why this area did not lead the revolt against behaviorism. Two factors are especially relevant: First, the area has always been viewed for its practical and applied utility rather than its theoretical import; second, the "theories" that were developed have been paraphrastic redescriptions of the data to be explained. Woodworth's descriptive conclusions, for example, are as correct today as 75 years ago, but descriptions are not explanations. It remained for other theorists (e.g., Bartlett, Chomsky) to look to language for theoretical concepts (deep structure, schemata, etc.) which, with present-day hindsight, the motor skills data were just waiting to suggest.

But regardless, the point remains: thinking is representative of all skills in its coalitional organization and patterning, and its productivity. And in this regard, skill learning is part of the domain of cognitive psychology.

Note 8. Piaget remains a biologist looking at psychological development: development and evolution within the individual are intrinsic to biological adaptation. Adaptation is always an organism–environment interaction, and adaptation so construed is the biological basis of knowledge. Piaget is therefore a biological constructive theorist. As Furth (1969) puts it, "knowledge is neither solely in the subject, nor in a supposedly independent object, but is constructed by the subject as an indissociable subject–object relation [p. 19]." Since the term "knowledge" in traditional usage implies static or fixed objects that are stored away by the organism, Piaget rarely speaks of knowledge, but rather of the processes of adaptation and the exhibition of intelligence:

> Piaget . . . employs the assimilation-accommodation paradigm throughout all the manifestations of knowing activities. With increasing adaptation in mental development the undifferentiated matrix of organism-in-environment becomes structured into organism-

> knows-environment. The structure that is thus built up is intelligence, considered as the general framework within which we know the world [Furth, 1969, p. 181].

This means that sensation or stimulation alone cannot constitute knowledge. Further, unless there is a structure within the organism (a scheme or schemata) prepared to assimilate or accommodate to stimulation, it will not even lead to knowledge. Compare this to Shiffrin's position quoted in Section 1.1.

Note 9. The clash between Gibsonian and constructivist accounts of perception is well brought out in several contributions and discussion sections in Weimer and Palermo (1974). By concentrating on the question of what is perceived, and emphasizing the modulation of information present in the stimulus array, the Gibsonian need not speak of constructive processes when dealing with the elementary aspects of perception of the properties of the visual array. The information specifying surfaces, texture gradients, presumably even depth, is given directly in the stimulus array. In contrast, information specifying the meaning of speech sounds is not directly present in the acoustic signal, and requires processing of an apparently constructive sort. Thus Turvey (1974) postulates two modes of perception, one of which is constructive and restricted to linguistic materials, the other tacit and nonconstructive.

But against this view it can be maintained that all perception is constructed because what we experience in perception, our knowledge by acquaintance, is not a reflection of the objects that cause our experience, but rather of our processing structure (see Section 5). One can argue with Gibson that the *information* is directly there in the stimulus array, but it is clear that our *experience* is not. All perceptual experience must be a construction, even of the elementary properties such as surface, texture, and depth. Insofar as perception involves meaning, there must be construction and inference. It will not do to say that we perceive the way a radio receiver merely modulates, or transduces, the information present in radio waves. A radio doesn't perceive the information it transduces. We, as percipient beings, do more than modulate that information, we perceive it and (try to) understand it. If the radio could perceive, it would do more than modulate. That "more" would involve constructing a perceptual experience.

Note 10. The contention that all the attributes of sensory and other mental qualities are relations to other qualities, and that the totality of such relations exhausts what we can know by description of the mind, does not deny the occurrence of knowledge by acquaintance. A congenitally deaf scientist who studies music will never know its experienced qualities, to be sure; but "What we are denying is not that sensory qualities may possess attributes which those who cannot hear cannot learn about, but that whatever incommunicable attributes sensory qualities may possess can even raise a scientific problem [Hayek, 1952, p. 34]." Likewise, phenomenal experience is always richer than our knowledge by description can capture: "The congenitally blind or deaf can never learn *all* that which the seeing or hearing person owes to the direct experience of the sensory qualities in question, because no description can exhaust all the distinctions which are experienced [Hayek, 1952. p. 35]."

Note 11. It is instructive in this regard to compare Hanson's treatment of patterns in the epistemic context of understanding the nature of theories with Bransford's treatment of patterns in comprehension. In both instances, what is emphasized is that seeing entities as patterned, as conceptually specified gestalts, occasions understanding. In the philosophical context that understanding is "theoretical explanation," while Bransford refers to it somewhat more generically as comprehension. Hanson (1970) states the following:

> That patterns affect the significance of lines, dots, shapes, and patches—which might have been in perceptual turbulance otherwise—is our fundamental datum. It has profound epistemological consequences. Knowledge is a function of how our experiences cohere. Observations made before the perceptual pattern is appreciated are epistemically distinct from the observations (and their descriptions) made after that pattern has cast them into intelligible constellations. . . . Just as perceptual pattern recognition at once gives significance to elements perceived and yet differs from any perception of dots, shapes, and lines, so also *conceptual* pattern recognition at once gives significance to the observational elements within a theory and yet differs from any awareness of those elements vis-à-vis their primary relationship to events and objects [pp. 236–237].

As Bransford and McCarrell (1974) put it: "We have argued that one's knowledge of his environment is considerably richer than knowledge of the perceptual characteristics of isolated objects, and that perceptually derived knowledge entails knowledge of *relations* rather than things [p. 200]."

Both positions are extensions to different levels of analysis of the fundamental point that Hayek made concerning the organization of the nervous system.

Note 12. The problem plaguing a theory that attributes causal efficacy to consciousness is to explain how *part* of the system of neural impulses could control the occurrence of other neural impulses. Since there is no difference among the impulses per se, it is hard to see how organizational direction could come from some and not others. Neither active firing nor active inhibition seems adequate, for these processes are too tied to anatomic localization to deal with a functionally specified system. How then can we explain Sperry's "prevailing overall dynamics of the whole active process" as the mechanism of causal control?

One possible answer is provided by the concept of *mutual entrainment* (see Dewan, 1969, 1976). As an empirical phenomenon, mutual entrainment refers to the emergence of regulation in a system composed of a large number of subsystems, due to the mutual interactive effects of those subsystems. For example, AC generators in the United States (except Texas) are entrained. They all lock in step and stabilize their output by virtue of being connected to a common transmission system. This self-organization in which a system of oscillators functions as a single unit is easily explained:

> If one generator leads the others in phase, i.e., if it is slightly faster, then its energy will be *absorbed,* not only by the load, but also by all generators which lag behind it. This will increase the load on the generator, forcing it to slow down a bit so that it won't "get out of step." If by chance it *lags* in phase, the other generators pump energy *into* it so that it catches up. Thus, generators which go a bit too fast are slowed down while those that lag are speeded up. They *pull together in frequency* . . . The stability and accuracy of a *system* of generators is far greater than any single unit. This mutual entrainment is a splendid example of *self-organization,* . . . an *emergent property of the entire system* which goes far beyond what any single unit can accomplish in accuracy and power [Dewan, 1976, p. 185].

Consciousness could, via mutual entrainment of neural impulses, thus exert a controlling influence. What we require now is a theory of generalized control of mutually entrained systems to understand how consciousness could act, and to derive testable predictions about changes in output with changes in the relevant entrainment relations. This will lead to theories of adaptive control systems providing additional, self-regulating control for more basic feedback systems. Consciousness, as a coping system, would be such an adaptive or perhaps a *super*adaptive control system (Dewan, 1976). It would also, as argued in Note 13, be a *coalitional* control system.

Note 13. Sperry's contention that each hemisphere is autonomously conscious is prima facie support for a position developed by Robert Shaw to deal with the enormous complexity of the organized system that is the totality of human higher mental processes. Shaw argues that the concept of hierarchical control systems, although an enormous improvement over linear or chaining control systems, is still incapable of dealing with the higher mental processes as a whole. When attention is confined to any single process, such as language, perception, or skills, a hierarchical control model may be adequate to model the system. But a hierarchical model cannot account for the autonomy of functioning that all the higher mental processes exhibit within a single person. When dealing with the person as a whole, there is no single locus of control that is always in command of the entire system, as is required by the logic of hierarchies. Instead, the person as a whole seems to be a *coalition* of hierarchical structures, somehow allied together but with no single locus of control. There is cooperation, but not determinate control, among the various mental systems. There is also a lack of determinate specification of boundaries between systems. Clearly perception is not skilled locomotion, yet one cannot separate the systems in any determinate manner—the boundaries are intrinsically "fuzzy." Further, persons are super-additively complex entities: they are more than just the sum of the systems making them up, which is another property of coalitional structures (see Shaw & McIntyre, 1974; Von Foerster, 1962).

One can see the coalitional nature of the mind by considering the effects of removing or suppressing a higher mode in hierarchical control systems. Were this to occur in a hierarchy, functioning would be disrupted, and the overall organization of the system would deteriorate. But precisely this does not occur in a coalitional structure: functioning may change, but it is not disrupted or disintegrated. Sperry's account of the relationship between the major and minor hemispheres indicates precisely the decentralization of control, fuzziness of boundaries, resistance to disruption, and so on, that is characteristic of coalitions. But the concept of coalitional structure allows us to understand both the unity of the person (as a singular subject of conceptual activity, as the "self," etc.) and also the welter of diverse systems that "go together" to make him up. The person 'goes together' exactly as a coalitional structure "goes together." Such an account reconciles 'unity in diversity' far better than a hierarchical model can allow, and makes explicit the persistent historical theme (familiar in the esoteric traditions such as Yoga) that the higher mental processes are 'tools' of the 'I' or self. Indeed, if the mind were a hierarchy, it would be nonsense to say that the higher mental processes were its tools—for how could something be a tool of itself? But if the mental processes are understood as hierarchical systems within a superadditive coalitional structure, then not only Sperry's observations, but clinical observations of "divided selves," and the esoteric conception of the mind as a tool of the 'I,' make sense.

REFERENCES

Bain, A. *The senses and the intellect.* London: Parker, 1855.

Bartlett, F. C. *Thinking.* New York: Basic Books, 1958.

Bernstein, N. *The co-ordination and regulation of movements.* Oxford: Pergamon Press, 1967.

Boring, E. G. *A history of experimental psychology.* New York: Appleton-Century-Crofts, 1950.

Bourne, L. *Human conceptual behavior.* Boston: Allyn and Bacon, 1966.

Bransford, J. D., & Franks, J. J. The abstraction of linguistic ideas. *Cognitive Psychology,* 1971, **2**, 331–350.

Bransford, J. D., & Johnson, M. K. Contextual prerequisites for understanding: Some investigations of comprehension and recall. *Journal of Verbal Learning and Verbal Behavior.* 1972, **11**, 717–726.

Bransford, J. D., & McCarrell, N. S. A sketch of a cognitive approach to comprehension: Some thoughts about understanding what it means to comprehend. In W. B. Weimer & D. S. Palermo (Eds.), *Cognition and the symbolic processes.* Hillsdale, New Jersey: Lawrence Erlbaum Associates, 1974. Pp. 189–229.

Brooks, L. Spatial and verbal components of the act of recall. *Canadian Journal of Psychology,* 1968, **22**, 349–368.

Cassirer, E. *Substance and function and Einstein's theory of relativity.* New York: Dover, 1953.

DeCharms, R. *Personal causation.* New York: Academic Press, 1968.

Dewan, E. M. Cybernetics and attention. In C. R. Evans & T. B. Mulholland (Eds.), *Attention in neurophysiology.* London: Butterworth, 1969, 323–343.

Dewan, E. M. Consciousness as an emergent causal agent in the context of control system theory. In G. G. Globus, I. Savodnik, & G. Maxwell (Eds.), *Consciousness and the brain: A scientific and philosophical inquiry.* New York: Plenum Press, 1976. Pp. 181–198.

Dollard, J., & Miller, N. E. *Personality and psychotherapy.* New York: McGraw-Hill, 1950.

Eccles, J. C. *The understanding of the brain.* New York: McGraw-Hill, 1973.

Eriksen, C. W. Unconscious processes. In M. R. Jones (Ed.), *Nebraska Symposium on Motivation.* Vol. VI. Lincoln: University of Nebraska Press, 1958, Pp. 169–227.

Evarts, E. V. Representation of movements and muscles by pyramidal tract neurons of the precentral motor cortex. In M. D. Yahr & D. D. Purpura (Eds.), *Neurophysiological basis of normal and abnormal motor activities.* Hewlett, New York: Raven Press, 1967, Pp. 215–254.

Evarts, E. V., & Thach, W. T. Motor mechanisms of the CNS, cerebro-cerebellar interrelations. *Annual Review of Physiology,* 1969, **31**, 451–498.

Feigl, H. *The mental and the physical.* Minneapolis: University of Minnesota Press, 1967.

Festinger, L., Burnham, C. A., Ono, H., & Bamber, D. Efference and the conscious experience of perception. *Journal of Experimental Psychology,* 1967, **74**, 1–36. (Monograph supplement.)

Fitts, P. Perceptual–motor skills learning. In A. W. Melton (Ed.), *Categories of human learning.* New York: Academic Press, 1964, Pp. 243–285.

Fowler, H. *Curiosity and exploratory behavior.* New York: Macmillan, 1965.

Fritsch, G., & Hitzig, E. Uber die elektrische Erreglearkeit des Grosshirns. *Archiv für Anatomie and Physiologie,* 1870, 300–332.

Furth, H. *Piaget and knowledge.* Englewood Cliffs, New Jersey: Prentice-Hall, 1969.

Geschwind, N. Language and the brain. *Scientific American,* 1972, **226**, 76–83.

Gibson, J. J. *The perception of the visual world.* Boston: Houghton Mifflin, 1950.

Gibson, J. J. *The senses considered as perceptual systems.* Boston: Houghton Mifflin, 1966.

Greene, P. H. Problems of organization of motor systems. *Quarterly Report No. 29,* Institute for Computer Research, University of Chicago, 1971.

Goldiamond, I., & Hawkins, W. F. Vexierversuch: The log relationship between word-frequency and recognition obtained in the absence of stimulus words. *Journal of Experimental Psychology,* 1958, **56**, 457–463.

Gregory, R. L. *Eye and brain: The psychology of seeing.* New York: McGraw-Hill, 1966.

Halwes, T., & Wire, B. A possible solution to the pattern recognition problem in the speech modality. In W. B. Weimer & D. S. Palermo (Eds.), *Cognition and the symbolic processes.* Hillsdale, New Jersey: Lawrence Erlbaum Associates, 1974, pp. 385–388.

Hanson, N. R. A picture theory of theory meaning. In R. Colodny (Ed.), *The nature and function of scientific theories.* Pittsburgh: University of Pittsburgh Press, 1970. Pp. 233–274.

Hayek, F. *The sensory order.* Chicago: University of Chicago Press, 1952.

Höffding, H. *Outlines of psychology.* New York: Macmillan, 1891.

Hunt, J. McV. Intrinsic motivation and its role in psychological development. In P. Levine (Ed.), *Nebraska Symposium on Motivation.* Vol. XIII. Lincoln: University of Nebraska Press, 1965. Pp. 189–282.

James, W. *The principles of psychology.* New York: Holt, 1890.

Jenkins, J. J. Remember that old theory of memory? Well, forget it! *American Psychologist*, 1974, **29**, 785–795.

Kuhn, T. S. *The structure of scientific revolutions* (2nd ed.). Chicago: University of Chicago Press, 1970.

Kuhn, T. S. Second thoughts on paradigms. In F. Suppe (Ed.), *The structure of scientific theories.* Urbana: University of Illinois Press, 1974. Pp. 459–482.

Lashley, K. S. *Brain mechanisms and intelligence.* Chicago: University of Chicago Press, 1929.

Lashley, K. S. The problem of serial order in behavior. In L. A. Jeffress (Ed.), *Cerebral mechanisms in behavior: The Hixton symposium.* New York: Wiley, 1951. Pp. 112–146.

Liberman, A. M. Some results of research on speech perception. *Journal of the Acoustical Society of America,* 1959, **29**, 117–123.

Liberman, A. M., Cooper, F. S., Shankweiler, D. P., & Studdert-Kennedy, M. Perception of the speech code. *Psychological Review,* 1967, **74**, 431–461.

Liberman, A. M., Mattingly, I. G., & Turvey, M. T. Language codes and memory codes. In A. W. Melton & E. Martin (Eds.), *Coding processes in human memory.* Washington: Winston, 1972.

Lindsay, P. H., & Norman, D. A. *Human information processing.* New York: Academic Press, 1972.

Mahoney, M. *Cognition and behavior modification.* Cambridge, Mass.: Ballinger, 1974.

Melton, A. W., & Martin, E. (Eds.) *Coding processes in human memory.* Washington: Winston, 1972.

Miller, G. A. Toward a third metaphor for psycholinguistics. In W. B. Weimer & D. S. Palermo (Eds.), *Cognition and the symbolic processes.* Hillsdale, New Jersey: Lawrence Erlbaum Associates, 1974. Pp. 397–413.

Neisser, U. R. *Cognitive psychology.* New York: Appleton-Century-Crofts, 1967.

Ornstein, R. E. *The psychology of consciousness.* San Francisco: Freeman and Company, 1972.

Osgood, C. E. Where do sentences come form? In D. D. Steinberg & L. A. Jakobovits (Eds.), *Semantics: An interdisciplinary reader in philosophy linguistics and psychology.* Cambridge: Cambridge University Press, 1971. Pp. 497–529.

Paivio, A. *Imagery and verbal processes.* New York: Holt, Rinehart, and Winston, 1971.

Pavlov, I. P. *Conditioned reflexes* (V. Anrep, translator). Oxford: Clarendon Press, 1927.

Penfield, W., & Roberts, L. *Speech and brain mechanisms.* Princeton, New Jersey: Princeton University Press, 1959.

Pepper, S. C. *World hypotheses.* Berkeley: University of California Press, 1942.

Perky, C. W. An experimental study of imagination. *American Journal of Psychology,* 1910, **21**, 422–452.

Polanyi, M. *The tacit dimension.* Garden City, New York: Doubleday, 1966.

Posner, M. *Cognition: An introduction.* Glenview, Illinois: Scott, Foresman, 1973.

Pribram, K. H. *Languages of the brain.* Englewood Cliffs, New Jersey: Prentice-Hall, 1971. (a)

Pribram, K. H. *What makes man human?* New York: The American Museum of Natural History, 1971. (b)

Proffitt, D. R. Demonstrations to investigate the meaning of everyday experience. Unpublished doctoral dissertation, Pennsylvania State University, 1976.

Sechenov, I. M. The reflexes of the brain (A. A. Subkov, translator). In *I. M. Sechenov, Selected works.* Moscow & Leningrad: State publishing house for biological and medical literature, 1935. (Originally published, 1863.)

Segal, S. J. (Ed.) *Imagery: Current cognitive approaches.* New York: Academic Press, 1971.

Segal, S. J., & Fusella, V. Influence of imaged pictures and sounds on detection of visual and auditory signals. *Journal of Experimental Psychology,* 1970, **83,** 458–464.

Shaw, R., & McIntyre, M. Algoristic foundations to cognitive psychology. In W. B. Weimer & D. S. Palermo (Eds.), *Cognition and the symbolic processes.* Hillsdale, New Jersey: Lawrence Erlbaum Associates, 1974. Pp. 305–362.

Sherrington, C. S. *The integrative action of the nervous system.* New Haven: Yale University Press, 1906.

Shiffrin, R. M. Information processing (Review of *Coding processes in human memory,* A. W. Melton & E. Martin, Eds.) *Science,* 1973, **180,** 440.

Skinner, B. F. *Contingencies of reinforcement.* New York: Appleton-Century-Crofts, 1969.

Skinner, B. F. *About behaviorism.* New York: Knopf, 1974.

Sperry, R. W. Neurology and the mind-brain problem. *American Scientist,* 1952, **40,** 291–312.

Sperry, R. W. Mind, brain, and humanist values. *Bulletin of Atomic Science,* 1966, **22,** 2–6.

Sperry, R. W. Hemisphere deconnection and unity in conscious awareness. *American Psychologist,* 1968, **23,** 723–733.

Sperry, R. W. A modified concept of consciousness. *Psychological Review,* 1969, **76,** 532–536.

Sperry, R. W. Mental phenomena as causal determinants in brain function. In G. G. Globus, I. Savodnik, & G. Maxwell (Eds.), *Consciousness and the brain: A scientific and philosophical inquiry.* New York: Plenum Press, 1976. Pp. 163–178.

Turvey, M. T. Constructive theory, perceptual systems, and tacit knowledge. In W. B. Weimer & D. S. Palermo (Eds.), *Cognition and the symbolic processes.* Hillsdale, New Jersey: Lawrence Erlbaum Associates, 1974. Pp. 165–180.

Von Foerster, H. Biologic. In E. E. Bernard & M. R. Care (Eds.), *Biological prototypes and synthetic systems* (Vol. 1). New York: Plenum Press, 1962.

Warren, R. M. Perceptual restoration of missing speech sounds. *Science,* 1970, **167,** 392–393.

Weimer, W. B. Psycholinguistics and Plato's paradoxes of the *Meno. American Psychologist,* 1973, **28,** 15–33.

Weimer, W. B. Overview of a cognitive conspiracy: Reflections on the volume. In W. B. Weimer & D. S. Palermo (Eds.), *Cognition and the symbolic processes.* Hillsdale, New Jersey: Lawrence Erlbaum Associates, 1974. Pp. 415–442.

Weimer, W. B. The psychology of inference and expectation: Some preliminary remarks. In G. Maxwell & R. M. Anderson, Jr. (Eds.), *Induction, probability, and confirmation.* Minnesota Studies in the Philosophy of Science, Vol. VI. Minneapolis: University of Minnesota Press, 1975. Pp. 430–486.

Weimer, W. B. Manifestations of mind: Some conceptual and empirical issues. In G. G. Globus, I. Savodnik, & G. Maxwell (Eds.), *Consciousness and the brain: A scientific and philosophical inquiry.* New York: Plenum Press, 1976. Pp. 5–31.

Weimer, W. B., & D. S. Palermo (Eds.) *Cognition and the symbolic processes.* Hillsdale, New Jersey: Lawrence Erlbaum Associates, 1974.

Woodworth, R. S. *Dynamic psychology.* New York: Columbia University Press, 1918.

Wundt, W. *An introduction to psychology* (R. Pitner, translator). New York: Macmillan, 1912.

Part II

LANGUAGE AND KNOWING

SECTION A

Knowing through Language

11

Speech and the Problem of Perceptual Constancy

Donald Shankweiler

University of Connecticut
and
Haskins Laboratories

Winifred Strange
Robert Verbrugge[1]

University of Minnesota

Speech perception is not ordinarily included in the body of phenomena and theory that convention defines as the psychology of perception. Yet the problem of how the perceptual categories of speech are specified in the acoustic signal is a primary example of the problem of perceptual constancy. In spite of its neglect by psychology, speech and its signal have been intensively studied by members of other disciplines. We think that some of the results and puzzles generated by this research are relevant to the concerns of our colleagues whose primary interests are in other facets of human cognition.

Speech perception at any level involves classification. The classificatory step is assumed whenever we move beyond a purely physical (acoustic) description of speech to a psychophysical description in terms of perceptual units. Unlike certain problems in traditional psychophysics in which the choice of units may be arbitrary, there is wide consensus about what the units of perception are in the case of speech. This consensus is the product of centuries of linguistic investigation, during which many attempts have been made to isolate the various levels and units that constitute our perception of speech. Viewed in terms of structure, speech is a hierarchical system that manifests what Hockett (1958) called a "duality of patterning": it employs both meaningful and meaningless

[1] Now at the University of Connecticut and Haskins Laboratories.

units. Morphemes (or, roughly speaking, words) are the smallest of the meaningful units. In all languages, morphemes have an internal structure composed of smaller meaningless segments, the phonemes (Bloomfield, 1933). Since the communication of meanings ultimately rests on a foundation of phonemic structure, a basic part of the task of understanding how speech is perceived is to discover the conditions for the perception of phonemic categories.[2] For present purposes, we will ignore meaning and concern ourselves only with the phonemic message—that is, with the perception of syllables and their phoneme segments, familiar to us as the consonants and vowels.

In speech, as in handwriting, no two "signatures" are alike. In generating the "same" phoneme, different speakers do not produce sounds that are acoustically the same. Indeed, the same signal is never exactly repeated by the same speaker. In perceiving speech, as in identifying objects, we ordinarily regard only those distinctions that are critical, ignoring those that are merely incidental. While no one would deny that speech signals are intrinsically variable for many reasons, the implications of this variability for perception have not been widely appreciated. In brief, they constitute a major problem in *perceptual constancy*.

THE PERCEIVING MACHINE AND THE ONE-TO-ONE PROBLEM

Although our concern is with how the human perceptual system works, it may help us to bring this problem into focus if we consider how a machine might proceed in recovering a string of phonemic segments. Consider, for example, the problems to be solved in designing a voice-operated typewriter. The goal of such an automatic speech recognition device is to type out the appropriate string of phonemic symbols (or perhaps standard orthographic symbols) in response to any speech input. In the simplest case, the only information available to the device will be the acoustic waveform itself. A human listener, of course, can usually take advantage of other sources of information, including both the linguistic and the situational context of the utterance.[3] While acknowledging the

[2] The phoneme is the minimal unit by which perceivers differentiate utterances. For example, the word *bad* has three phonemic segments, /b/, /æ/, and /d/, that differentiate it from such words as *dad, bed,* and *bat.* In different utterances, a phoneme may be realized acoustically in different ways; linguists call these variants "phones." For example, the final /t/ in *bat* might be either released (acoustically, a pause followed by a burst) or unreleased (no burst). The class of phones is potentially infinite, and it is arguable whether phones (however defined) are natural perceptual units. Our emphasis in this paper is on how the identity of a phoneme is perceived despite variations in its acoustic form.

[3] The importance of context to human listeners has been elegantly demonstrated by Miller, Heise, and Lichten (1951), who found a remarkably predictable relationship between the amount of acoustic distortion that yields a given level of intelligibility and the informational redundancy of the message. For a given signal-to-noise ratio, intelligibility was greater for words heard in sentence context than for words heard in isolation.

importance of context, we should not overlook the fact that listeners can identify arbitrarily chosen words and nonsense syllables with high accuracy when listening conditions are favorable. In other words, we are not posing an unrealistic problem for our hypothetical device; human listeners can do remarkably well when little contextual information is available.

Many attempts have been made in recent decades to design a voice-operated typewriter, but the problem has thus far proved elusive. Despite a degree of success with severely restricted vocabularies when words are spoken by one of a few trained talkers, a generally useful speech recognizer continues to be unattainable. As Hyde (1972) notes, "there are still no devices which can perform even moderately well on normal (conversational) speech in normal (noisy) environments by a normal range of talkers [p. 399]."

It is worth considering for a moment how the operation of a speech recognition system has typically been conceived. As in many other automatic pattern recognition devices, the procedure involves two stages. In the first stage, the basic units or segments are located. For example, in automatic reading of print, this would correspond to isolating individual letters. In the second stage, each segment is identified as an instance of one of a fixed set of objects. In the case of print reading, this would correspond to identifying a segment as a particular letter of the alphabet. Thus a successful voice-operated typewriter would have to be able to perform two operations on the acoustic waveform of any speech signal. First, it would have to divide the waveform into acoustic segments that have a one-to-one correspondence through time with the sequence of phonemes in the utterance. Second, it would have to detect the presence or absence of acoustic features that are critical for identifying particular phonemes. This second stage is often conceived of as requiring a set of filters, each filter being tuned to a critical acoustic property (defined along dimensions such as frequency, intensity, and duration).

This strategy implies certain widespread assumptions that only in recent years have been successfully challenged. For example, we find that in the standard accounts of speech acquisition, it is tacitly assumed that speech consists of a collection of elementary sounds "transparent" to the infant, such that he or she automatically recognizes a parent's utterance of /d/ as "the same sound" as his or her own utterance of /d/ (Watson, 1924; Allport, 1924). Similarly, taxonomic linguists working in the tradition of Bloomfield (1933) supposed that all languages are sampled from a common inventory of sounds (phones). Working from phonetic transcription of a large number of utterances as a base, these linguists developed highly successful procedures for determining which sound contrasts played a role in any particular language. It was believed that the great practical success of transcription as a tool for language description rested on a narrow physical base, and that, in principle, an acoustic definition could be given for each phone. In this view, speech was conceived as a kind of sound alphabet, in which each phone is conveyed by a discrete package of sound with a characteristic spectral composition. The pervasiveness of this assumption has been noted by Denes (1963):

> The basic premise of (most speech-recognition) work has always been that a one-to-one relationship existed between the acoustic event and the phoneme. Although it was recognized that the sound waves associated with the same phoneme would change according to circumstances, there was a deep-seated belief that if only the right way of examining the acoustic signal was found, then the much sought-after one-to-one relationship would come to light [p. 892].

In fact, the perceptual skills that underlie phonetic transcription have never been explained well enough that an algorithm could be written to permit a machine to do the job. From our present perspective it is clear why no one has been able to develop a voice-operated typewriter based on the strategy outlined above. First, there are no clearly bounded segments in the acoustic waveform of roughly phonemic size; that is, there are no acoustic units available for setting up a correspondence with phonemes. Second, even if boundaries are arbitrarily imposed on the continuous signal, the segments corresponding to a particular phoneme often vary considerably in their acoustic composition. Moreover, any one of those acoustic segments, transferred to a different phonemic environment, might be heard as a different phoneme altogether. Not only do the physical attributes specifying a particular phoneme vary markedly, but the same physical attribute can specify different phonemes depending on the context.

THE CONTINUOUS SIGNAL DOES NOT REVEAL THE SEGMENTATION OF THE PHONEMIC MESSAGE

The conclusions stated above are the results of three lines of investigation begun in the mid 1940s and continuing to the present. We turn now to review briefly the nature of the evidence.

Of special importance from our standpoint are a series of tape-cutting and tape-splicing experiments that had the effect of shaking the general confidence that phonemes are conveyed by isolable bits of sound. These experiments failed to find any way to divide the signal on the time axis to yield segments of phoneme size. For example, given a consonant–vowel syllable such as *go,* there is no way to cut the piece of magnetic tape so as to produce the consonant /g/ alone. Some vowel quality always remains. Moreover, if a consonant–vowel syllable is cut at some point, the consonantal portion may not be heard as the same phoneme when spliced to a recording of a different vowel. Schatz (1954), for example, found that the consonantal portion of an utterance of /pi/ was heard as /k/ when it was joined to the vowel /a/. Harris (1953) and Peterson, Wang, and Sivertsen (1958) independently concluded that assembled speech made by splicing together prerecorded segments is not generally intelligible when the units are smaller than roughly a half syllable.[4] Some investigators (e.g., Cole & Scott, 1974a, b) continue to argue that speech perception may be based in large part on the detection of acoustic invariants for phonemes. They have claimed that a one-to-one correspondence *can* often be found, that spliced segments *can* preserve their identity when transferred to new phonemic contexts. However, much of this apparent "invariance" disappears when one is careful to cut the initial segment sufficiently short so that no trace of the subsequent vowel remains (cf. Kuhl, 1974).

A second important development is the study of spectrographic displays of speech. This work was made possible by the invention of the sound spectrograph (Koenig, Dunn, & Lacey, 1946) during World War II and by the general availability of such devices for research during the postwar years. The spectrograph displays, in graphical form, the time variations of the spectrum of the speech wave. This representation of the sound patterns of speech is valuable for the information it gives about articulation. The energy in speech sounds is concentrated in a small number of frequency regions that appear on a spectrogram as horizontal bands (called "formants"). The location of the formants on the frequency scale reflects the primary resonances of a talker's vocal tract (Fant, 1960). Since the shape of the vocal cavity changes at the joining of successive consonants and vowels, the formant frequencies may be seen to modulate up and down as one scans a spectrogram along the time axis. However, efforts to locate discrete information-bearing units along the time axis have met with repeated failure. The phonemic and syllabic segments, which are so clear perceptually, have no obvious correlates in a spectrogram, as evidenced by the fact that spectrograms are very difficult to read, even after much experience (Fant, 1962; but see also Kuhn & McGuire, 1975).[5]

Figure 1 shows spectrograms of two syllables, *bib* and *bub*. Note that the formant frequencies are nonoverlapping for the entire duration of the syllables, not just in the middle portion. Although the syllables differ phonemically (i.e., perceptually) in one segment (the medial vowel), acoustically they differ throughout.

Failure to find obvious acoustic cues in spectrograms led to a third line of investigation: a variety of experiments with synthetic speech, produced by devices that place acoustic parameters under the experimenter's direct control. Early work by researchers at Haskins Laboratories made use of hand-painted

It does not follow from this result that the minimal perceptual unit is larger than the phoneme. The inference we would draw is that decisions about phoneme identity are made with regard to information distributed over the whole syllable (and sometimes, perhaps, over a number of syllables).

[5] In remarking on the difficulty of reading spectrograms our point is not that the spectrogram does not represent the relevant phonemic information, but rather that the ear has readier access to the brain's phonemic decoder than the eye.

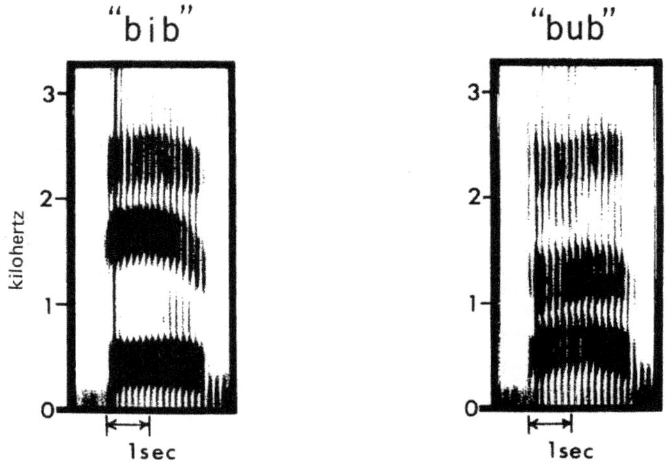

FIG. 1. Spectrograms of tokens of two syllables that differ in the vowel. Note that the formant pattern of "bib" does not coincide with that of "bub" in any portion.

patterns resembling spectrograms that were converted into sound by a photoelectric device, the Pattern Playback (Cooper, Liberman, & Borst, 1951). The Pattern Playback and subsequent computer-controlled electronic synthesizers have made it possible to do analytic studies in which one parameter is varied at a time, to determine which parameters were critical for particular phonemes. Only through systematic psychophysical experimentation of this sort has it been possible to locate the linguistically relevant information in the speech spectrum (Cooper, Delattre, Liberman, Borst, & Gerstman, 1952; Liberman, 1957; Liberman, Cooper, Shankweiler, & Studdert-Kennedy, 1967; Liberman, Harris, Hoffman, & Griffith, 1957). A major conclusion of this research is that, in general, there is no simple one-to-one correspondence between perceptual units and the acoustic structure of the signal. To be successful, synthetic speech must encode the information for phonemes into acoustic patterns at least a half syllable or full syllable in length.

These findings make it possible to understand why the design of a voice-operated typewriter proved so difficult. Phonemes are not merely joined acoustically; they overlap so that two or more are represented simultaneously on the same stretch of sound. Conversely, segmentation is impossible because information for one phoneme is usually spread over wide stretches of the signal. Even if segmentation were attempted, the cues isolated would be radically different in another phonemic environment. As shown in Fig. 1, all four segments corresponding to /b/ would differ markedly in slope and formant frequency range.

In sum, the radically context-dependent structure of speech dooms to failure the kind of pattern recognition procedure outlined above. A procedure that combines a prior stage of segmentation with an analysis of segments by a set of tuned-filter "detectors," operating independently and in parallel, will be insufficient as a job description of an automatic recognition machine (and insufficient as a model of human speech perception as well). One contemporary approach to the recognition problem (Mermelstein, 1974) is explicit on this point, acknowledging that a speech recognizer would have to extract information about component phonemes over longer stretches of the signal than a syllable and would have to incorporate rules about how that information is distributed. The system described by Mermelstein does *not* assume that the segmentation and labeling problems are independent.

SYLLABLE NUCLEI AS TARGETS

A commonly suggested strategy for speech recognition (Fant, 1970) is to classify first those phonemes that are most "transparent" in the signal, and then to use that information as a basis for determining what the more contextually variable phonemes are. For example, the research described earlier found that the acoustic form of many consonants is heavily dependent on the coarticulated vowel. If the vowel were easily detected in speech signals, then it could be identified first and used as a basis for disambiguating the neighboring consonant.

There are several reasons for supposing that vowels could be extracted readily by a routine based on a filter bank, though it would not be possible, in general, for consonants. In productions of sustained vowels, the positions of the formants on the frequency axis serve roughly to distinguish the vowels of a particular talker. For a high front vowel such as /i/, the first and second formants are spaced far apart (on the frequency axis) while the second and third formants are spaced close together. For a high back vowel /u/, the pattern is just reversed. These patterns can be synthesized with a combination of steady-state resonances which simulate the formants found in spectrograms of natural vowels. Synthetic stimuli are readily labeled as vowels by listeners, and it is possible to generate the full complement of English vowels with two or three formants (Delattre, Liberman, Cooper, & Gerstman, 1952).

This acoustic characterization of vowels as steady-state entities is reinforced by articulatory considerations. The flow of speech is marked by a rhythmic pattern of syllables; each syllable contains a vowel "nucleus" that is usually coarticulated with one or more consonants. It is usual to think of consonants as the dynamic component of speech, since they are generally produced by movement of the articulators, and to regard vowels as the static component, since they may be produced with a stationary vocal tract configuration and sustained indefinitely.

This contrast is emphasized by the concept of an idealized vowel as a prolonged, static entity defined (acoustically) by the frequencies of the first two or three formants, that is, by the primary resonances of the stationary vocal tract. At least for individual talkers, then, there should be a distinctive set of frequency values associated with each vowel, in contrast to the variable values associated with the talker's consonants. In that case, vowels should be retrievable by a simple two-stage recognition procedure: it would be a straightforward matter to detect the presence of steady states electronically (thereby isolating vowel segments for analysis), and a filter bank could then determine which set of critical frequencies the vowel sound best fits.

Unfortunately for this approach, the apparent simplicity of vowels is largely an illusion. Vowels in natural continuous speech, unlike the artificially prolonged vowels of the phonetics laboratory, are not generally specified by steady states at all. Let us see why this is so.

First, as a result of coarticulation, vowels are encoded into the structure of a full syllable. The imprint of the vowel is not localized but is smeared throughout the entire temporal course of the syllable. Thus, information about a vowel is available in the transitions as well as in the steady-state portion (if, indeed, a steady state is even attained). This was clear in the earlier example of the syllables *bib* and *bub;* in both cases, the vowel affected the spectral pattern of the entire syllable. Moreover, the acoustic properties of the vowel nucleus may be affected by coarticulated consonants. Measurements by House and Fairbanks (1953) and Stevens and House (1963), for example, indicated consistent changes in the duration, fundamental frequency, and formant frequencies and intensities of vowels, depending on consonantal context. It should also be noted that consonants can affect the structure of neighboring vowels if (by the phonological rules of the dialect) a distinction between two consonants is actually manifested by a difference in the neighboring vowels. For example, the /d/ in *rider* is distinguished from the /t/ in *writer* by the increased duration of the vowel that precedes it. Similarly, in some dialects of English, a nasal phoneme, such as the /n/ in *pants,* is realized by a nasalization of the preceding vowel; thus the spectral structure of the vowel /æ/ will vary markedly depending on whether *pats* or *pants* is spoken. Because the coarticulation effects between consonants and vowels do not operate in one direction alone, but are two-way effects, there is no obvious acoustic invariant that characterizes a vowel in all consonantal contexts.

A second major source of variance in the acoustic structure of vowels is the tempo of articulation. During rapid rates of speech, steady-state configurations may never be attained at all. Acoustic analysis of rapid speech supports the hypothesis of articulatory "undershoot," since syllable nuclei often do not reach the steady-state formant frequency values characteristic of vowels in slowly articulated syllables (Lindblom, 1963; Stevens & House, 1963). Lindblom and Studdert-Kennedy (1967) found that listeners showed a shift in the acoustic criteria that they adopted for vowels (i.e., there was a shift in the phoneme boundary between them) as a function of perceived rate of utterance. Apparently, human listeners compensated for this simulated articulatory undershoot by perceptual overshoot. These data show that formant transitions, which are generally understood to carry consonantal information, may also aid in specifying the vowel. Thus, in ordinary speech, vowels, like consonants, are dynamic entities that are scaled by the pace of speaking.

A third source of acoustic variation in vowels is associated with the individual characteristics of the talker. We perceive this variation directly when we identify *persons* on the basis of voice quality. On the other hand, such individual variation is irrelevant and becomes "noise" when our intent is to recover the linguistic message. Inasmuch as formant frequencies reflect vocal tract dimensions, it is obvious that the absolute positions of the formants will not be the same for a child as they are for an adult. The extent of the problem is suggested by Joos (1948):

> The acoustic discrepancies which an adult has to adjust for when listening to a child speaker are nothing short of enormous—they commonly are as much as seven semitones or a frequency ratio of 3 to 2, about the distance from /ɛ / to /U/ [p. 64].

Somehow, in spite of this, we manage to understand small children's speech reasonably well and they ours. This is especially remarkable given that the difference between children and adults cannot be described by a simple scale factor. The vocal tract not only increases in size but changes in shape, and the consequent changes in the acoustic output are correspondingly complicated. Indeed, Fant (1966) has argued that the assumption of an invariant relation between formants one and two for a given vowel is just as untenable as the assumption that the *absolute* formant frequencies of the vowel are invariant for all talkers. Thus, the relation between utterances of a syllable by an adult and a small child is not the multiplicative relation that obtains between versions of a melody played in different keys.

Having discussed variation based on physical differences in the sound-production apparatus, we should also mention differences that are social in origin, reflecting local variations of dialect within the larger language community. These variations are associated, of course, with geographical region, ethnic group, and socioeconomic class. Additional sources of talker-related variation are idiosyncratic speech mannerisms, emotional state, and fatigue. These sources, in addition to those we have discussed above, pose enormous difficulties to the design of an automatic recognition device.[6]

No one, to our knowledge, has seriously considered how an automatic speech recognition routine would adjust its criteria to compensate for the variations associated with coarticulation, tempo, and talker. When we consider the magnitude and variety of variations that we take in our stride as perceivers, we begin to realize something of the complexity of the relations between the signal and

[6] Reflect, too, on the variety of transformations of the signal that might be produced by the commonplace feats of talking with food in the mouth, with a cigar between the lips, or with teeth firmly clamped on a pencil (cf. Nooteboom & Slis, 1970).

the phonemic message. The difficulties encountered by the task of machine recognition command a new respect for the subtlety and versatility of the human perceptual apparatus and lead us to a new appreciation of the abstract nature of speech perception.

WHAT SPECIFIES A VOWEL?

The idea that vowels can be defined as fixed sets of steady-state values is an oversimplification that bears little relation to the structure of natural speech. We have found it necessary to reopen the question of what specifies a vowel, and we wish to introduce some recent findings as a case study in the problem of perceptual constancy.

Vowels, as we noted earlier, are traditionally defined by formants. Vowel quality is associated with concentrations of acoustic energy in a few relatively narrow portions of the frequency spectrum; energy in the regions between these bands is generally weak and has little perceptible effect on vowel quality. In distinguishing among vowels, the lowest two formants are traditionally thought to be the most significant; the contribution to perception of the third and higher formants is problematical. For this reason, vowels are customarily represented as points located in a two-dimensional space defined by the first and second formants. As a result of variations among talkers, the points in this acoustic vowel space are actually regions. A critical question for perceptual theory is: How much or how little do these regions overlap?

A thorough assessment of this question was made by Peterson and his colleagues (Peterson, 1951; Peterson & Barney, 1952), who obtained spectrographic measurements of tokens of ten American English vowels produced by 76 talkers (including men, women, and children). Figure 2 (page 337), which is redrawn from Peterson and Barney (1952), shows the vowel space defined by measurements of formants one and two (F_1 and F_2). We note that there is considerable overlap in some regions. In running speech we might expect a comparable analysis to show still more overlap. The findings showed not only lack of invariance in the position of the formants in children and adults, but also considerable average differences between men and women and considerable variation among talkers of the same age group and sex.

In his pioneering monograph on acoustic phonetics, Joos (1948) had discussed earlier the dilemma that such variation poses for theories of speech perception. If different spectra are heard by listeners as the same vowel, on what does the judgment of sameness depend? It cannot, he concludes, be due to any evidence in the sound:

> Therefore the identification is based on outside evidence. . . . If this outside evidence were merely the memory of what the same phoneme sounded like a little earlier in the conversation, the task of interpreting rapid speech would presumably be vastly more

difficult than it is. What seems to happen, rather, is this. On first meeting a person, the listener hears a few vowel phones and on the basis of this small but apparently sufficient evidence he swiftly constructs a fairly complete vowel pattern to serve as background (coordinate system) upon which he correctly locates new phones as fast as he hears them . . . [Joos, 1948, p. 61].

Thus, in Joos' view, the listener calibrates the talker's vowel space on the basis of a small subset of sample utterances. The listener needs some reference points to define the range and distribution of the talker's vowels. These reference signals, Joos suggests, could be supplied by extreme articulations (in terms of tongue height and point of tongue contact). Thus, Joos (1948) leaves no doubt that the coordinate system he has in mind is based at least in part on a model of the vocal tract:

The process of correctly identifying heard vowel colors doubtless in some way involves articulation. A person who is listening to the sounds of a language that he can speak is not restricted to merely acoustic evidence for the interpretation of what he hears, but can and probably does profit from everything he "knows," including of course his own way of articulating the same phones [Joos, 1948, p. 61].

Since the publication of Joos' work, a normalization step in speech perception has been assumed by virtually everyone who has written on the subject, whether or not the writer accepted Joos' version of the motor theory of speech perception (or, indeed, any other version of motor theory). The idea that a listener makes use of reference vowels for calibration of a talker's vowel space has also persisted. Gerstman (1968) and Lieberman (1973), whose contributions we will discuss presently, each have taken up the reference vowel idea and defended it. What is surprising, given this overwhelming consensus, is how few attempts have been made to measure the ambiguity in perception of vowels that is directly attributable to talker variation.

Joos' (1948) statement of the constancy problem implies that, for an unknown talker, isolated syllables should be highly ambiguous from the standpoint of the perceiver. It is perplexing, then, that two experiments that directly measured the perceptual ambiguity of natural speech found little support for this prediction. Peterson and Barney (1952), to whom we are indebted for systematic acoustic measurements of individual differences in vowel formants, also attempted to assess the perceptual consequences of the variation they discovered in production. The same recorded utterances used in making the spectrographic measurements were also assembled into listening tests. Listeners had to identify tokens of ten vowels in /h–d/ consonantal environment; the set consisted of *heed, hid, head, had, hod, hawed, hood, who'd, hud,* and *heard.* Syllables produced by groups of 10 talkers (men, women, and children) were randomly mixed on each listening test, insuring that opportunities for normalization would be slight. Although plots of the first two formants show that the regions occupied by these vowels overlap considerably, perceptual judgments were remarkably accurate, with 94% of the words perceived correctly. A similarly low error rate for perception of a larger set of vowels, which included diphthongs, was reported by Abramson and Cooper (1959).

These perceptual data do not support the notion that a single syllable, spoken in isolation, is necessarily ambiguous. Apparently, the information contained within a single syllable is usually sufficient to allow whatever adjustment for individual talker characteristics might be required. However, the history of the research following Peterson and Barney's (1952) study shows that this conclusion was not generally drawn.

The work of Ladefoged and Broadbent (1957) and Ladefoged (1967) is widely cited as evidence that the listener has relative criteria for vowel identification and that the identity of a vowel depends upon the relationship between the formant frequencies for that vowel and the formant frequencies of other vowels produced by the same talker. As a result, vowel space must presumably be rescaled for each voice a listener encounters. The Ladefoged and Broadbent (1957) study was designed to find out whether subjects could be influenced in their identifications of a test word by variations in an introductory sentence preceding it. Synthetic speech was used in order to gain precise control over the acoustic parameters. A set of test syllables of the form *b*–vowel–*t* was prepared on the synthesizer. Listening tests were made up in which the test words were presented following a standard sentence: *Please say what this word is.* Variants of this sentence were produced by shifting the frequencies of the first or second formants up or down. Each was intelligible despite wide acoustic differences. The results showed that the same test word was identified as *bit* when preceded by one version of the test sentence (i.e., one "voice") and as *bet* when preceded by a second version (another "voice") in which the first formant varied over a lower range. The authors conclude from perceptual shifts such as this that the identification of a vowel is determined by its relation to a prior sample of the talker's speech (provided here by the test sentence).

Ladefoged (1967) interprets these findings within the framework of Helson's (1948) adaptation level theory. This theory attempts to account for the extraordinary efficiency of the compensatory mechanisms that achieve constancies, such as color constancy under changing illumination, by supposing that the perceiver scales his responses not to the absolute properties of each stimulus, but according to the weighted mean of a set of stimuli distributed over time. The introductory sentence, in the Ladefoged and Broadbent experiment (1957), is understood as providing the standard or anchor, thus creating an internal adaptation level to which the test words are referred. We shall return to the adaptation level hypothesis presently, after we have introduced some relevant findings of our own.

If it is true that a listener needs a sample of speech in order to fix the coordinates of a talker's vowel system, we need to know how large a sample is required and whether particular vowels are more effective than others as "anchors." As we noted earlier, Joos (1948) believed that the best reference signal would be one that allows the listener to determine the major dimensions of the talker's vocal tract. We therefore suggested that the "point vowels" /i/, /ɑ/, and /u/ might be the primary calibrators of vowel space, since they are the vowels associated with the extremes of articulation. Lieberman and colleagues (Lieberman, Crelin, & Klatt, 1972; Lieberman, 1973) agree that these vowels probably play an important role in disambiguating syllables produced by a novel talker. They note that the point vowels are exceptional in several ways: they represent extremes in acoustic and articulatory vowel space, they are acoustically stable for small changes in articulation (Stevens, 1972), and they are the only vowels in which an acoustic pattern can be related to a unique vocal tract area function (Lindblom & Sundberg, 1969; Stevens, 1972).

Gerstman (1968) has made one of the few direct attempts to test the idea that a subset of vowels can serve to calibrate a talker's vowel space and reduce errors in recognition of subsequently occurring vowels. Gerstman developed a computer algorithm that correctly classified an average of 97% of the vowels in the syllables produced by the Peterson and Barney panel of 76 talkers. For each talker's set of ten utterances, the program rescaled the first and second formant frequency values of each medial vowel, taking the extreme values in the set as the endpoints. Since these extreme formant values are typically associated with /i/, /ɑ/, and /u/, the procedure corresponds to a normalization of each talker's vowel space with reference to his own utterances of the point vowels. The classification system was essentially a filter bank that classified the vowels according to the *scaled* values for the first two formants, and the sums and differences of these values. By inserting the normalization stage between segmentation and classification, Gerstman's program succeeded in reducing by half the errors in classification made by human perceivers (recall that Peterson & Barney's, 1952, listeners made 6% errors). We must keep in mind, however, that a successful algorithm is not a perceptual strategy, but only a possible strategy. Although it is of interest that such an algorithm can, in principle, serve as the basis for categorization of the signals, we are aware of no evidence that the human perceptual apparatus functions analogously. For example, it would be necessary to demonstrate that humans scale individual formants and calculate sums and differences between them.

It seemed to us that speculation had far outstripped the data bearing on the vowel constancy problem. In fact, the few studies of perceivers' recognition of *natural* (as distinguished from *synthetic*) speech indicated that isolated syllables spoken by novel talkers are remarkably intelligible. Therefore, it seemed important to verify Ladefoged and Broadbent's (1957) demonstration with natural speech in which all the potential sources of information that are ordinarily available to perceivers are present in the signal. Similarly, Gerstman's (1968) success in machine recognition using the three point vowels as calibrating signals needed to be evaluated against the performance of human listeners. Accordingly, we designed experiments to determine the size of the perceptual problem posed for the listener when the speaker is unknown. This involved a comparison of perceptual errors, under matched conditions, when the test words were spoken by many talkers and when all were produced by only one talker. We also sought to discover whether certain vowels (e.g., the point vowels) have a special role in specifying the coordinates of a given talker's vowel space.

HOW DOES A LISTENER MAP A TALKER'S VOWEL SPACE? AN EXPERIMENT TO DETERMINE THE SIZE OF THE PROBLEM

We (Verbrugge, Strange, & Shankweiler, 1974) first attempted to measure the degree of ambiguity in vowel perception attributable to lack of congruence of the vowel spaces of different talkers. To measure this, we presented listeners with unrelated words or nonsense syllables, so that broad linguistic context would make no contribution to the act of identification. Our studies of this problem were fashioned after Peterson and Barney (1952). We presented nine vowels in the consonantal environment /p–p/; thus, the set consisted of /pip/, /pɪp/, /pɛp/, /pæp/, /pɑp/, /pɔp/, /pʊp/, /pʌp/, and /pup/. In one listening test, the listeners heard tokens spoken by 15 different voices (five men, five women, five children), arranged in random order. To determine what proportion of perceptual error is due to uncertainty about the talker, as opposed to other sources, a second listening test was employed in which a single talker uttered all the tokens on a given test. The talkers were given no special training. They were urged to recite the syllables briskly in order to bring about some undershoot of steady-state targets. Our objective was to achieve conditions as similar as possible to normal conversational speech.

Listeners misidentified[7] an average of 17% of the vowels when spoken by the panel of 15 talkers, and 9% when each of three tests was spoken by a single individual (a representative man, woman, and child from their respective groups). The difference between these two averages, 8%, is a measure of the error attributable to talker variation. Although this is a statistically significant difference [$t(50\ df) = 5.14$, $p < .01$], its absolute magnitude is surprisingly small. Less than half the total number of errors obtained in the variable-talker condition can be attributed to talker variation.

[7]We have taken the intended vowel of the talker as the criterion of correct identification. That is, we have defined an identification error as a response by the listener that does not correspond to the phonemic category intended by the talker. It might be the case that errors so defined are as much due to mispronunciation as to misperception. No correction was given to talkers during recording other than to clarify orthographic confusions in a few instances. In the case of the youngest children, some coaching was required before they pronounced the nonsense syllables. However, no adult models were provided immediately prior to utterances that were included in the tests.

Listeners can identify vowels in consonant–vowel–consonant (CVC) syllables with considerable accuracy even when they are spoken by an assortment of talkers deliberately chosen for vocal diversity. The intended vowel was identified on 83% of the tokens in a test designed to maximize ambiguity contributed by vocal tract variation.[8] In a second study, listeners were asked to identify 15 vowels (monophthongs and diphthongs) spoken /h–d/ context by 30 talkers. Here, the rate of identification errors was 13% overall and 17% for the nine monophthongs alone. The results of both studies are in essential agreement with earlier perceptual data reported by Peterson and Barney (1952) and Abramson and Cooper (1959), although the error rates obtained by these investigators were even lower than those we obtained.[9]

These findings do not bear out the common assumption of a critical need for extended prior exposure to a talker's speech. The information contained within a single syllable appears to be sufficient in most cases to permit recognition of the intended vowel; familiarity with a voice seems to play a rather small role in the identification process.

ARE THE POINT VOWELS USED BY LISTENERS AS AIDS TO NORMALIZATION?

We (Verbrugge, Strange, & Shankweiler, 1974) next examined the possibility that an introductory set of syllables increased the likelihood that a succeeding vowel produced by the same talker was correctly recognized. Because we wished to test a specific hypothesis about the stimulus information required for normalization, we did not employ an introductory sentence as Ladefoged and Broadbent (1957) had done. Instead, we introduced each target syllable by three precursor syllables; this provided three samples of the talker's vowels and little else. In one condition of the experiment, the precursors were /hi/, /hɑ/, and /hu/; these syllables contain examples of the talker's point vowels. For a second condition, we chose /hɪ, hæ, hʌ/, a set of nonpoint vowels that (like the point

[8] Each of the 15 talkers spoke only three tokens containing different vowels. These tokens were separated in the test by no fewer than eight intervening tokens spoken by different talkers. Listeners were unable to judge how many talkers were included on a test.

[9] We suspect that these studies made somewhat less severe demands on listeners' perceptual capacities than our own. In the Peterson and Barney (1952) study, listeners heard only 10 different talkers on a particular test. Each talker spoke 2 tokens of each of 10 /h–d/ syllables. The study yielded an overall error rate of 6%. The Abramson and Cooper (1959) study employed eight talkers, each of whom spoke one token of 15 /h–d/ syllables. The overall error rate in that study ranged from 4 to 6%. An additional source of perceptual difficulty in our tests is the fact that /ɑ/ and /ɔ/ are homophonous in the dialect of most of our talkers.

vowels) are quite widely separated in the space defined by the first and second formants.

Neither set of precursor syllables brought about a systematic reduction of perceptual errors in identifying the target vowels. The errors in each precursor condition averaged 15% (compared to 17% in the earlier condition without precursors), but in neither case does this difference approach significance.[10] The principal effect of the /hi/, /hɑ/, /hu/ precursors was to shift the pattern of responses somewhat, some vowels showing improved identification, others showing poorer identification.

The idea that normalization is specifically aided by the point vowels, as suggested by Joos (1948), Gerstman (1968), and Lieberman (1973) is not supported by these data. In fact, *no* precursor syllables that we tried were found to have a systematic effect. A single, isolated syllable is usually sufficient to specify a vowel; prior exposure to specific subsets of vowels could not be shown to supply additional information. It would seem unnecessary to invoke a psychophysical weighting function in order to establish an internal adaptation level (cf. Ladefoged, 1967). We may surmise that the isolated syllable is not so ambiguous an entity as is sometimes implied.

Because of the repetitive and stereotyped manner in which the precursors were presented, some readers might be inclined to doubt whether listeners made full use of the phonetic information potentially available and therefore to question whether these experiments are adequate to test the hypothesis. We can reply to this objection indirectly by referring to a further experiment in which the same precursor syllables did produce a measurable effect on perception of a subsequent target syllable. This experiment involved the same 15 talkers as the earlier experiment, but differed in that the test syllables were produced in a fixed sentence frame: *The little /p–p/'s chair is red.* Each talker was instructed to produce the sentence rapidly, placing heavy stress on the word *chair.* The destressed, rapidly articulated /p–p/ syllables were excised from the taperecording and assembled into the two new listening tests. In one condition, the /p–p/ targets were prefaced by the same tokens of the /hi, hɑ, hu/ precursors employed in the previous experiment. On this test, listeners made an average of 29% errors in identifying the vowels in the target syllables. In the other condition, no precursors were present. On this test, listeners misidentified 24% of the same vowels. Thus, misperception of target vowels occurred with significantly *greater* frequency when they were preceded by precursors [$t(35\ df) = 2.88, p < .01$]. We may suppose that the precursors impaired recognition of succeeding vowels in this instance because they specified a speaking rate slower than that at which the

[10] This result was confirmed in a separate study of 15 vowels in /h–d/ context. When no precursors were present, errors averaged 13%. When each /h–d/ syllable was preceded by the syllables, /kip/, /kɑp/, /kup/, 12% of the responses were errors. The difference was not significant.

/p–p/ syllables were actually produced. Thus, whereas we failed to find evidence for effects of precursors on normalization of vocal-tract differences, we do find evidence for adjustment to a talker's tempo (as hypothesized by Lindblom & Studdert-Kennedy, 1967), on the basis of preceding segments of speech.

THE ROLE OF FORMANT TRANSITIONS IN VOWEL PERCEPTION

Our results suggest that the identity of a vowel in a syllable spoken by a new talker is likely to be specified by information within the syllable itself. The phonetic context supplied by preceding syllables apparently serves a function other than that of adjustment for a new set of vocal tract parameters: it may enable the perceptual system to gauge the tempo of incoming speech and to set its criteria accordingly. We were encouraged by these preliminary findings to look for the sources of information that specify the vowel within the syllable, and to explore how that information is used by the perceiver in the process of vowel perception.

As we noted earlier, the formant transitions in a syllable vary systematically as a function of both the consonant and the vowel. Therefore, we might expect that the listener utilizes information contained in the transitions in recovering the identity of the medial vowel. Research on the identification of isolated steady-state vowels (i.e., vowels that are *not* coarticulated with consonants) indirectly supports this expectation. Perception of isolated vowels is notably unreliable. Fairbanks and Grubb (1961) presented nine isolated vowels produced by seven phonetically trained talkers to eight experienced listeners. The overall identification rate was only 74%; rates for individual vowels ranged from 53% to 92%. Slightly better identification of isolated vowels was obtained by Lehiste and Meltzer (1973) for three talkers, where, again, talkers and listeners were phonetically skilled. Fujimura and Ochiai (1963) directly compared the identifiability of vowels in consonantal context and in isolation. They found that the center portions of vowels, which had been gated out of CVC syllables, were less intelligible in isolation than in syllabic context.

Research bearing on this question has also been done with synthetic speech. Millar and Ainsworth (1972) reported that synthetically generated vowels were more reliably identified when embedded in an /h–d/ environment than when acoustically identical steady-state target values were presented in isolation. Finally, Lindblom and Studdert-Kennedy (1967) noted that listeners used different acoustic criteria to distinguish pairs of vowels depending on whether judgments were made on isolated vowels or on the same vowel targets embedded within a CVC environment.

There are at least two ways that the transitional portions of the acoustic signal might provide information for vowel identity. One possibility is that transitions play a role in specifying talker characteristics. Since the loci of formant transitions for a particular consonant vary with differences in vocal-tract dimensions (Fourcin, 1968; Rand, 1971), transitions might serve as calibration signals for normalization. Particularly when the phonemic identity of the consonants is fixed and known to the listener, the transitions might serve to reduce the ambiguity of the vowel by providing information about vocal-tract characteristics of the talker who produced the syllable.

We may also envision a second possibility that is at once more general and more parsimonious: the acoustic specification of vowels, like consonants, is carried in the dynamic configuration of the syllable. In other words, the syllable *as a whole* cospecifies both consonants and vowel. In this view, transitions may be regarded as belonging to the vowel no less than to the consonants. If this were true, we would expect that the perception of medial vowels would be aided by the presence of consonantal transitions regardless of whether the perceiver encounters many talkers on successive tokens or only one.

To make an experimental test of these possibilities, we (Strange, Verbrugge, & Shankweiler, 1974) constructed a new set of listening tests that contained a series of isolated vowels. In one condition the vowels were spoken by the same panel of 15 talkers described above. In a second condition, a single talker produced the full series of vowels. Together with the earlier tests with /p–p/ syllables, these materials allowed us to compare the relative effects on vowel identifiability of two major variables: presence or absence of consonantal environment and presence or absence of talker variation within a test. This also placed us in a position to evaluate the alternative hypotheses about how consonantal environment contributes to vowel perception.

According to either hypothesis, we would expect that the perception of isolated vowels would be less accurate than the perception of medial vowels on a listening test in which the tokens are produced by different talkers. However, the two alternative hypotheses generate different expectations concerning the error rate on isolated vowels and medial vowels when the talker does not vary within a test. If the advantage of consonantal environment is due to use of transition cues for normalization, we could expect to obtain no difference between performance on these two conditions, because in neither case is there a need for repeated calibration. Therefore, we would expect that vowel recognition would be as accurate for the isolated vowels as for the medial vowels. If, on the other hand, the consonantal environment provides critical information for the vowel independent of talker-related variation, we would expect a difference in consonantal environment to affect performance whether or not talkers vary within a test. Thus, we would expect identification of isolated vowels to be less accurate than medial vowels even for tests in which the talker did not vary.

The results for the isolated vowel tests support the latter hypothesis. The average error in the variable-talker condition was 42% (compared to 17% errors on the comparable test in which vowels were spoken in /p–p/ environment). This increase in errors is consistent with either hypothesis. However, the results for the single-talker condition *also* showed a large increase in errors when there was no consonantal environment. The average error in the single-talker condition was 31% for the isolated vowels (compared to 9% errors on medial vowels). Moreover, a vowel-by-vowel comparison showed that for every vowel in both talker conditions, the error rate on the isolated vowel was greater than on the corresponding medial vowel. Both major variables (Consonants Present versus Absent and Talker Variation Present versus Absent) were shown to produce significant differences in overall errors [$F(1, 94\ df) = 125.17$ and 21.18, respectively, $p < .01$]. The decrease in accuracy of vowel recognition due to the absence of consonantal environment was approximately the same whether talkers varied or not (i.e., the analysis showed no significant interaction between variables). We may surmise, therefore, that consonantal transitions do not aid in specifying a vowel by providing information for a normalization stage. On the contrary, these results indicate that the presence or absence of transitions is much more critical for accurate recognition than the degree of experience with a talker's vocal-tract parameters. Whereas the presence of within-test talker variation impairs recognition by only about 8%, the absence of a consonantal environment impairs performance by more than 20%.

The possibility cannot be overlooked, however, that the relatively poor perception of isolated vowels is attributable primarily to the talkers' inability to produce them reliably. Since isolated vowels do not occur in natural speech (with a few exceptions), talkers may produce them in peculiar ways, with formant frequencies uncharacteristic of the values found in natural syllables. Also, the characteristic relative durations of the vowels (Peterson & Lehiste, 1960) might not be preserved by talkers in their productions of isolated vowels.

To investigate these possibilities we undertook spectrographic analysis of the tokens of isolated vowels and medial vowels used in our listening tests. Center frequencies of the first three formants and vowel duration were measured for all the tokens in the variable-talker tests, as well as for tokens of all nine vowels spoken in isolation by each of the 15 talkers. The data provided no evidence that the isolated vowels were produced in an aberrant manner. Average formant frequencies for men, women, and children correspond quite closely to those reported by Peterson and Barney (1952) (for vowels in /h–d/ environment), with the exception of /ɔ/.[11] When the formant frequencies of each talker's isolated and medial vowels are compared, the values are found to be highly similar. Measurements of vowel duration also fail to account for the increased error rate for isolated vowels. Although the durations of these were for the most part longer than the vowels in /p–p/ environment, the relative durations of the nine isolated vowels are much the same as the relative durations of vowels in consonantal environment. We may suppose, therefore, that the higher error rate

[11] This deviation is due to a dialect difference between our group of talkers (predominantly natives of the upper Midwest) and Peterson and Barney's group.

for isolated vowels compared to that for vowels in a fixed consonantal environment cannot be explained on the grounds that isolated vowels tend to be produced in an aberrant manner.

The message of these perceptual data is clear: Isolated, sustained vowels, although they correspond well to the phonetician's idealized conception of a vowel, are poorly specified targets from the standpoint of the listener.[12] Lehiste and Peterson (1959) found that many hours of practice were needed by untrained listeners before they could identify isolated vowels accurately, even when the tokens were painstakingly produced by a single phonetically trained talker. The ability to identify these "ideal" vowels may be a highly specific skill with little relevance to the identification of vowels in natural speaking situations.

At this point the objection might still be raised that the tests used to measure the perceptual difficulty of medial vowels are unrepresentative of natural conditions. One possibility is that there may be an advantage associated with consonantal context of the context is known beforehand (/p–p/ in this case), but that this advantage would be largely eliminated if the identity of neighboring consonants were unknown (as is often the case in natural speech). To test this possibility, we constructed a listening test in which the target vowels were enclosed by a variable consonantal environment. A panel of 12 talkers (a subset of the original 15) spoke a series of consonant–vowel–consonant syllables. In each syllable, one of the six stop consonants (/b, d, g, p, t, k/) appeared before the vowel and one of the six appeared after the vowel; consonants were selected so that each occurred equally often in each position. One group of listeners was asked to identify only the vowel in each test token; a second group was asked to identify the two consonants as well as the vowel. The average error in identifying the vowels was 22% for the first group and 29% for the second. Both error rates are well below the 42% error rate obtained on the variable-talker test with isolated vowels. In other words, even when listeners do not know the identity of either the consonants or the vowel, recognition is significantly more accurate for medial vowels than for isolated vowels.

A second possible objection to the earlier tests with medial vowels might be that syllables spoken in isolation (in "citation form") are unrepresentative of the syllables found in rapid, connected speech. The medial vowels in rapidly spoken syllables might be at least as difficult to identify as isolated vowels, since the vocalic portions of such syllables often fail to reach the steady-state values characteristic of syllables spoken in citation form. The study reported earlier in this chapter bears directly on this question. When /p–p/ syllables spoken in destressed position were excised from a carrier sentence and assembled into a

[12] The formant space is less compressed for isolated vowels than for medial vowels. Thus, if the values of static first and second formants were the primary carriers of vowel quality, isolated vowels should be better perceived because their acoustic values are more widely separated.

listening test, listeners made an average of 24% errors in perceiving the medial vowels. This is not much greater than the 17% error rate for perception of /p–p/ syllables read from a list, but is substantially less than the 42% error rate for isolated vowels. One might have guessed that the brevity of the short /p–p/ syllables and their failure to reach steady-state values would make them more difficult to identify than isolated vowels, which are longer in duration and more stable acoustically. Apparently, the presence of a consonantal environment more than compensates for these difficulties.

CONCLUDING REMARKS ON THE PROBLEM OF VOWEL CONSTANCY

Let us consider what we have learned about how the perceiver might achieve constancy of vowel quality. In our studies of vowel perception the objective was to isolate sources of vocalic information in the natural speech signal. We employed signals that presented as many characteristics as possible of normal conversational speech, including a representative range of signal variations that result from physical differences among talkers.

Each way of conceptualizing the vowel contains an implied solution to the problem of perceptual constancy. We first considered the assumption that the vowel can be characterized by a steady-state output of the vocal tract, and that, to a first approximation, fixed formant loci are associated with each vowel quality of all speakers. To the extent that this assumption is correct, the constancy problem is trivial. Only minor adjustments for variation would be required.

We saw that this conception of the vowel as a simple acoustic event, segmented in time and in spectral frequency composition, was widely shared among students of speech, including those who initiated earlier attempts at automatic speech recognition. We have reviewed a number of findings that are incompatible with this view. First, steady states are the exception, not the rule, in continuous natural speech. As a result of coarticulation of vowels with preceding and following consonants, the syllable is not discretely partitioned, and the information for the vowel is smeared throughout the syllable. Moreover, the variability occasioned by the phonemic environment of a vowel is compounded by the changes that accompany different speaking rates and different vocal tract sizes. In retrospect, it is easy to see why attempts to design a generally useful speech recognition machine have so far failed.

A more sophisticated conception of the vowel acknowledges the problem of variability but continues to assume that vowels, even in running speech, can be perceived with reference to a single set of acoustic values. This view proposes that tokens of the "same" vowel fall on a line in vowel space defined by the first and second formants. The formant frequencies of two talkers' vowels would then be constant multiples of one another. We noted that this relationship could not literally hold, because vocal tracts differ in shape as well as in size. This rules out an analogy to a melody played in a different key, or to a magnetic tape recording played back at a different speed. The failure of these analogies is revealed by Peterson and Barney's (1952) measurements of first and second formant frequencies in men, women, and children. The results of the measurements (displayed in Fig. 2) showed wide disperson of formant values for different speakers with considerable overlap of formants for neighboring vowels. Even when one considers only those tokens on which perfect agreement was obtained by listeners, much scatter among formant values is observed (cf. Peterson & Barney's, 1952, Fig. 9).

Failing to find the invariant relation preserved by linear scaling, investigators have sought a transformation that might yield a closer approximation. For example, it has become an accepted practice to plot units of frequency (Hz) on a scale of *mels* (Peterson, 1961; Ladefoged, 1967).[13] Transformation of formant frequencies to mels might be defended on the grounds that this unit reflects the response of the auditory system to frequency. However, we are skeptical that the constancy problem can be illuminated by a search for the right scale factor. Ladefoged (1967), who attempted to reduce variability by employing phoneticians as talkers, concluded that separation of all vowels cannot be attained by scaling the first- and second-formant frequencies, whether in linear fashion or nonlinearly, as on a scale of mels.

Although no one has succeeded in demonstrating a generally applicable scaling (normalizing) function, it is widely assumed that perceivers must apply such a function to each new talker they encounter. There has been speculation about the minimal stretch of speech required for calibration. Ladefoged's (1967) application of adaptation-level theory to the problem of speaker normalization reflects the common assumption that some extended sample of a new talker's utterances is required for determining the weights that enable the normalizing adjustments to be made. As we noted, Joos (1948) and Lieberman (1973) proposed that ambiguity of a new talker's utterances can be resolved by reference vowels that permit the perceiver to construct a model of the talker's vowel space, scaling the input according to parameters derived from these calibration vowels.

Listeners can apparently adjust their criteria for perception of synthetic vowels according to the formant ranges specified by a precursor sentence (Ladefoged & Broadbent, 1957). The successful performance of Gerstman's (1968) normalizing algorithm indicates that frequencies of the first and second formants could, in principle, suffice for this purpose. However, we doubt, as does Ladefoged (1967) himself, that first and second formant frequencies exhaust the

[13] A *mel* is a psychophysical unit reflecting equal sense distances of pitch and bearing an approximately logarithmic relation to frequency for frequencies above 1000 Hz (Stevens & Volkmann, 1940).

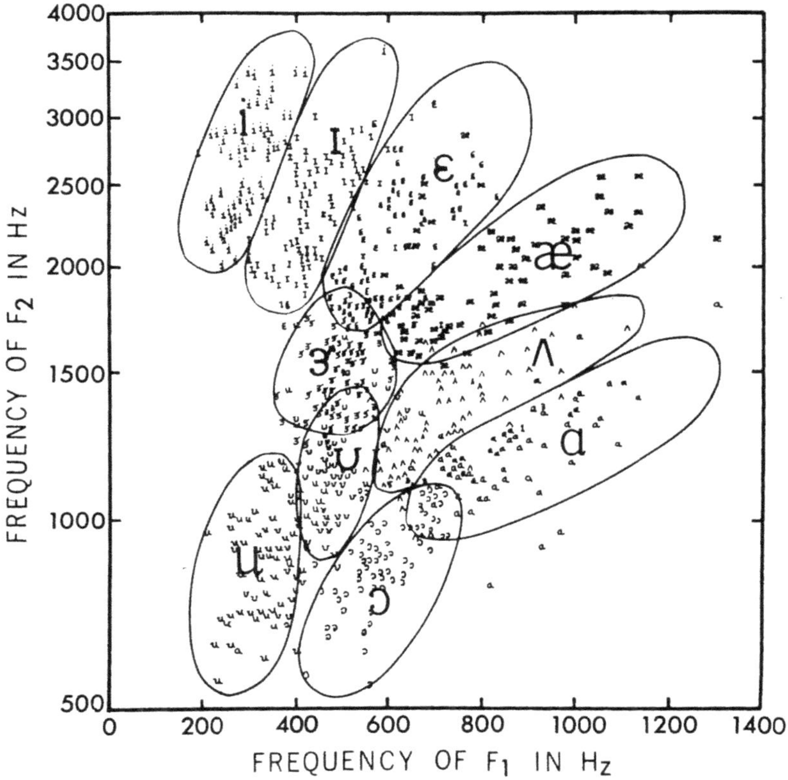

FIG. 2. First- and second-formant frequencies of American-English vowels for a sample of 76 adult men, adult women, and children. The closed loops enclose 90% of the data points for each vowel category. (Redrawn from Peterson & Barney, 1952.)

sources of information that specify a vowel *in a natural speech signal.*[14] Moreover, the fact that listeners can perceive randomly ordered syllables accurately indicates that there is little need for a mechanism that requires a sample of several syllables in order to construct a normalization schema. Finally, in our own experiments with natural speech, we failed to find that point vowel precursors, or another set of widely spaced vowels, brought about a systematic improvement in recognition of the following vowel.

Our results do not, therefore, support the view that vowels are relational values in a metric space that must be scaled according to other vowels produced by the same talker. If that theory were correct, it is difficult to see how precursors could fail to improve recognition of an immediately following medial vowel. The

[14] This is also Peterson's (1961) conclusion, based upon studies of filtering.

presence of coarticulated consonants within the syllable proved far more useful for categorizing natural vowels than prior experience with a talker's utterance. In sum, our studies failed to provide supporting evidence for current conceptions of the normalization process. They force us to consider whether there is justification for a separate and preliminary normalization stage in speech perception.[15]

A major difficulty with all the proposals stated above is that they view the invariance problem in terms of the relation among formant frequencies of relatively sustained vowels. Even if such efforts to discover an algorithm were successful, they would not be sufficient to explain perception of vowels in natural conversational speech because in such utterances a region of steady-state energy is rarely present in the signal. The presence of sustained acoustic energy at certain "target" frequencies is not essential for identification of a vowel under natural listening conditions. On the contrary, there is evidence that changing spectral patterns are much superior to sustained values as carriers of vowel quality. We cited earlier reports that isolated steady-state vowels are poorly perceived, even after listeners were given substantial training and when the target vowels were spoken by phonetically trained talkers (Fairbanks & Grubb, 1961; Lehiste & Meltzer, 1973). The results of our perceptual studies definitely confirm the perceptual difficulty of isolated vowels. Listeners misidentified 31% even when all items within a given test list were produced by the same talker. Moreover, vowels coarticulated with surrounding consonants, as is normal in running speech, were considerably more intelligible than isolated vowels spoken by the same talkers (e.g., 9% of vowels in /p–p/ environment were misidentified). It seems unlikely, therefore, that the perceptual system operates by throwing away information contained in formant transitions. Indeed, Lindblom and Studdert-Kennedy (1967), in studies with synthetic speech, demonstrated that listeners use this information directly in their placement of vowel phoneme boundaries. Vowel identifications varied with direction and rate of transitions even when the formant frequency values at the syllable centers were held constant. In short, it is futile to seek a solution to the constancy problem by analysis of any acoustic cross section taken at a single instant in time, and we must conclude that the vowel in natural speech is inescapably a dynamic entity.

Heuristic procedures for automatic recognition of consonants often begin by guessing the identity of the coarticulated vowel, since it is known that the specific shapes of the formant transitions are conditioned by the vowel. The vowel is assumed to be a stable reference point against which the identity of the consonant may be determined. But this, of course, presupposes that the vowel is more directly available than the consonant. We have now examined a number of indications that the problem of perceptual constancy may be no less abstract for

[15] But see Summerfield and Haggard (1973). These investigators measured an increase in reaction time to synthetic syllables from different (simulated) vocal tracts which they interpret as reflecting extra processing time required for a normalization stage.

the vowel than for the consonant. We found that isolated steady-state vowels provided especially poor perceptual targets. Moreover, there were not substantially more errors in identifying the medial vowels of rapidly spoken syllables (where steady states were presumably not attained), compared to errors on medial vowels in syllables read from a list. It is clear that we can no longer think of defining vowels in terms of acoustic energy at characteristic target frequencies. A recognition device based on filters tuned to specific frequencies is as unworkable for vowels as it is for consonants. If the idea of the vowel target is to be retained, it must take account of the dynamic character of the syllable.

Lindblom's (1963) conception has this virtue. Formant contours are characterized as exponential functions that tend toward asymptotic "target" values associated with the vowel nucleus. Thus, a target can be defined acoustically even though it corresponds to no spectral cross section through the syllable. Our perceptual data presented here are compatible with this view that vowels are specified by contours of moving formants with certain invariant properties over stretches of approximately the length of a syllable.[16]

We may find a parallel to this conclusion in studies of speech production. Investigation of the manner in which phonemes are joined in the syllable reveals context-dependent relationships similar to those we have noted in the acoustic signal. Lindblom's (1963) dynamic theory of vowel articulation is, in fact, an attempt to explain how contextual influences on the acoustic and phonetic properties of vowels are produced. According to this view, undershoot in running speech is brought about by inertia in the response of the articulators to motor excitations occurring in rapid temporal succession. Invariant neural events corresponding to vowel targets thus fail to bring articulators to the positions they assume when the vowel is produced in a sustained manner.

Lindblom's (1963) inference of articulatory undershoot during rapid speech has been confirmed by cinefluorographic data (Gay, 1974). His account of the mechanism of undershoot has not gone unchallenged, however. MacNeilage (1970) presented a different view of the inherent variability of speech production. Basing his conclusions on extensive electromyographic studies of context effects in articulation, he argued that variability of muscle contraction is not to be understood merely as an unfortunate consequence of mechanical constraints

[16] Our understanding of the vowel has been influenced by Gibson's (1966) approach to the problems of event constancy in visual perception, which is to seek regularities in the stimulus pattern that can only be defined over time. A similar approach is taken by Shaw, McIntyre, and Mace (1974), and by Shaw and Pittenger (this volume). We tend to agree with these authors that the dynamic invariants specifying an event may be perceived *directly* by perceptual systems that are appropriately tuned. While Lindblom (1963) and Lindblom and Studdert-Kennedy (1967) offer a dynamic characterization of vowels, they apparently made the usual assumption that only temporal cross sections can be directly perceived, and they supposed that vowel perception is *mediated* by a process of analysis-by-synthesis in which the dynamic invariants are used to compute possible input patterns.

on articulator motion, but as necessarily built into the system in order to permit attainment of relatively invariant target shapes. Gay (1974) cited his cinefluorographic findings in support of MacNeilage's hypothesis that variability of gesture must be regarded as a design characteristic. However, unlike MacNeilage, he concluded that there was variability not only of gesture, but of spatial target, since he failed to find invariance of vocal-tract shape for a central vowel /*a*/ that held across speaking rates and consonantal environments. The same conclusion was drawn by Nooteboom (1970), who argued that the kinds of reorganization that occur in talking with the teeth clenched make it difficult to retain the idea of invariant spatial targets. Just as the attainment of a specific acoustic target value is not necessary for the successful perception of a vowel, it is probably the case that the attainment of a specific target shape is not necessary for its effective production. Thus, in production as in perception, it has become increasingly difficult to entertain the notion of an invariant target for each vowel, as long as the meaning of invariance is restricted to a specific vocal tract shape and its resonances. It is likely that the units of production, like the units of perception, cannot be defined independently of the temporal dimension. Speech, viewed either as motor gesture or as acoustic signal, is not a succession of static states. Invariance in vowel production, then, can be discovered only in the context of the dynamic configuration of the syllable.

The reader might wonder at this point whether the various productions and acoustic forms of a vowel are so heterogeneous that no coherent physical definition (however abstract) could be found that embraces them all. Perhaps the required invariance is not to be found in the acoustic signal at all. If it is not, a radical solution to the constancy problem is to suppose that the variants of a phoneme are physically unrelated, and to assume that the brain stores separately a prototype of each vowel and consonant for every phonemic environment. If we can extend to speech perception an argument made by Wickelgren (1969) concerning its production, then Wickelgren's hypothesis of "context-sensitive allophones" is such a proposal. However, the proposal has little to recommend it. Halwes and Jenkins (1971) find a number of flaws, two of which are critical. First, the proposal fails to capture the phonological relations that are known to be important in understanding both the production and perception of speech. Second, it ignores the "creativity" inherent in the production of speech that permits the reorganization of articulatory movements to maintain intelligibility even when normal speech movements are blocked, as when talking with the teeth clenched or with food in the mouth, or when under the influence of oral anesthesia.

In light of the evidence we have surveyed, it is obvious that attempts to understand the psychophysical constancy relations in speech have failed to discover transparent isomorphisms between signal and perception. This failure has led many to doubt whether a psychophysics of speech could ever illuminate the constancy problem. But certainly, it does not follow from the complexity of the psychophysical relation that the signal fails to specify the phonemic message uniquely.[17] The emphasis that current theories place upon the relational nature of the vowel is misleading because it underestimates the richness of the signal in natural speech, a richness that is attested by the great tolerance of the perceptual system for a degraded speech signal (as in noisy environments or after filtering). To abandon the search for acoustic invariants because the psychophysical relations are complex would surely be a backward step. It should be appreciated, however, that commitment to the principle of invariance does not bind us to a literal isomorphism between signal and percept. The weight of evidence conclusively opposes a one-to-one mapping of perceptual segments and their dimensions upon physical segments and their dimensions. In the case of vowels, we have argued that the invariants cannot be found in a temporal cross section but can only be specified over time.[18] For vowels, as for other phonologic segments, a major goal of research is to discover the appropriate time domains over which invariance might be found.

ACKNOWLEDGMENTS

The authors' research reported in this paper was begun during the academic year 1972–1973, while D. Shankweiler was a guest investigator at the Center for Research in Human Learning, University of Minnesota, Minneapolis. The early portion of the work was supported in part by a grant from the National Institute of Child Health and Human

[17] We doubt that a "distinctive feature" description of speech would allow a simpler psychophysical relation to be stated. Phonemes are often characterized by a set of component features that are the basis for contrastive phoneme pairs. For example, /b/ and /d/ contrast in *place of articulation,* whereas /d/ and /t/ contrast in *voicing.* There is substantial evidence that such features are integral to the perceptual analysis of speech. We believe that the same arguments apply to the detection of distinctive features as apply to the perception of phonemes–namely, they are specified abstractly over stretches of speech of varying length. Thus a recognition model that includes feature recognition as an early stage must meet the same tests that we have outlined for phoneme recognition in general.

[18] A derived invariant, defined in terms of relations, has been described for the voicing distinction in consonants. In spectrographic analyses of voicing in stop consonants in many languages, Lisker and Abramson (1971) discovered a unity among the apparently diverse and unrelated acoustic features that are correlates of the voiced–voiceless distinction. Their work suggests that aspiration, explosion energy accompanying stop release, and first formant intensity may all be understood in terms of control of the time relations between stop-closure release and the onset of laryngeal vibration. The derived cue, voice-onset time, is a relatively invariant property of the signal for a given overall speaking rate. However, voice-onset time is not a simple property in that it is definable only in terms of a temporal relation between two events occuring within the syllable. See Lisker (1975) and MacNeilage (1972) for discussions bearing on the importance of timing in speech.

Development (NICHD) to the Center, and in part by grants awarded to Shankweiler and to J. J. Jenkins by the National Institute of Mental Health. The later portion of the research and the preparation of this paper was supported by grants from NICHD to the Center and to Haskins Laboratories, New Haven, Connecticut.

We are grateful to T. Edman for his substantial assistance with all phases of the experimental work, and to J. J. Jenkins for advice and encouragement from the project's inception. Other colleagues who commented on earlier drafts of this paper are: G. M. Kuhn, T. Nearey, and M. Studdert-Kennedy. It is a pleasure to acknowledge their help.

REFERENCES

Abramson, A. S., & Cooper, F. S. Perception of American English vowels in terms of a reference system. (Quarterly Progress Report, 1959, QPR 32, Appendix 1) New Haven, Haskins Laboratories.

Allport, F. H. *Social psychology.* Boston: Houghton Mifflin, 1924.

Bloomfield, L. *Language.* New York: Henry Holt, 1933.

Cole, R. A., & Scott, B. The phantom in the phoneme: Invariant cues for stop consonants. *Perception and Psychophysics,* 1974, **15,** 101–107. (a)

Cole, R. A., & Scott, B. Toward a theory of speech perception. *Psychological Review,* 1974, **81,** 348–374. (b)

Cooper, F. S., Delattre, P. C., Liberman, A. M., Borst, J. M., & Gerstman, L. J. Some experiments on the perception of synthetic speech sounds. *Journal of the Acoustical Society of America,* 1952, **24,** 597–606.

Cooper, F. S., Liberman, A. M., & Borst, J. M. The interconversion of audible and visible patterns as a basis for research in the perception of speech. *Proceedings of the National Academy of Sciences,* 1951, **37,** 318–328.

Delattre, P. C., Liberman, A. M., Cooper, F. S., & Gerstman, L. J. An experimental study of the acoustic determinants of vowel color: Observations on one- and two-formant vowels synthesized from spectrographic patterns. *Word,* 1952, **8,** 195–210.

Denes, P. B. On the statistics of spoken English. *Journal of the Acoustical Society of America,* 1963, **35,** 892–904.

Fairbanks, G., & Grubb, P. A. A psychophysical investigation of vowel formants. *Journal of Speech and Hearing Research,* 1961, **4,** 203–219.

Fant, C. G. M. *Acoustic theory of speech production.* The Hague: Mouton, 1960.

Fant, C. G. M. Descriptive analysis of the acoustic aspects of speech. *Logos,* 1962, **5,** 3–17.

Fant, C. G. M. A note on vocal-tract size factors and nonuniform F-pattern scalings. *Quarterly Progress and Status Report,* 1966, No. **1,** 22–30, Stockholm, Sweden, Speech Transmission Laboratory, Royal Institute of Technology.

Fant, C. G. M. Automatic recognition and speech research. *Quarterly Progress and Status Report,* 1970, No. **1,** 16–31, Stockholm, Sweden: Speech Transmission Laboratory, Royal Institute of Technology.

Fourcin, A. J. Speech source inference. *IEEE Transactions on Audio- and Electroacoustics,* 1968, **AU-16,** 65–67.

Fujimura, O., & Ochiai, K. Vowel identification and phonetic contexts. *Journal of the Acoustical Society of America,* 1963, **35,** 1889 (Abstract).

Gay, T. A cinefluorographic study of vowel production. *Journal of Phonetics,* 1974, **2,** 255–266.

Gerstman, L. J. Classification of self-normalized vowels. *IEEE Transactions on Audio- and Electroacoustics,* 1968, **AU-16,** 78–80.

Gibson, J. J. *The senses considered as perceptual systems.* Boston: Houghton-Mifflin Co., 1966.

Halwes, T., & Jenkins, J. J. Problem of serial order in behavior is not resolved by context-sensitive associative memory models. *Psychological Review,* 1971, **78,** 122–129.

Harris, C. M. A study of the building blocks in speech. *Journal of the Acoustical Society of America,* 1953, **25,** 962–969.

Helson, H. Adaptation level as a basis for a quantitative theory of frames of reference. *Psychological Review,* 1948, **55,** 297–313.

Hockett, C. F. *A course in modern linguistics.* New York: Macmillan, 1958.

House, A. S., & Fairbanks, G. The influence of consonant environment upon the secondary acoustical characteristics of vowels. *Journal of the Acoustical Society of America,* 1953, **25,** 105–113.

Hyde, S. R. Automatic speech recognition: A critical survey and discussion of the literature. In E. E. David, Jr., & P. B. Denes (Eds.), *Human communication: A unified view.* New York: McGraw-Hill, 1972.

Joos, M. A. Acoustic phonetics. *Language,* Supplement, 1948, **24,** 1–136.

Koenig, W. H., Dunn, H. K., & Lacey, L. Y. The sound spectrograph. *Journal of the Acoustical Society of America,* 1946, **18,** 19–49.

Kuhl, P. Acoustic invariance for stop consonants. *Journal of the Acoustical Society of America,* Supplement, 1974, **55,** 55. (Abstract.)

Kuhn, G. M., & McGuire, R. McI. Results of a spectrogram reading experiment. *Status Report on Speech Research,* 1975, *SR-39/40,* New Haven, Haskins Laboratories.

Ladefoged, P. *Three areas of experimental phonetics.* London and New York: Oxford University Press, 1967.

Ladefoged, P., & Broadbent, D. E. Information conveyed by vowels. *Journal of the Acoustical Society of America,* 1957, **29,** 98–104.

Lehiste, I., & Meltzer, D. Vowel and speaker identification in natural and synthetic speech. *Language and Speech,* 1973, **16,** 356–364.

Lehiste, I., & Peterson, G. E. The identification of filtered vowels. *Phonetica,* 1959, **4,** 161–177.

Liberman, A. M. Some results of research on speech perception. *Journal of the Acoustical Society of America,* 1957, **29,** 117–123.

Liberman, A. M., Cooper, F. S., Shankweiler, D., & Studdert-Kennedy, M. Perception of the speech code. *Psychological Review,* 1967, **74,** 431–461.

Liberman, A. M., Harris, K. S., Hoffman, H. S., & Griffith, B. C. The discrimination of speech sounds within and across phoneme boundaries. *Journal of Experimental Psychology,* 1957, **54,** 358–368.

Lieberman, P. On the evolution of language: A unified view. *Cognition,* 1973, **2,** 59–94.

Lieberman, P., Crelin, E. S., & Klatt, D. H. Phonetic ability and related anatomy of the newborn, adult human, Neanderthal man, and the chimpanzee. *American Anthropologist,* 1972, **74,** 287–307.

Lindblom, B. E. F. Spectrographic study of vowel reduction. *Journal of the Acoustical Society of America,* 1963, **35,** 1773–1781.

Lindblom, B. E. F., & Studdert-Kennedy, M. On the role of formant transitions in vowel recognition. *Journal of the Acoustical Society of America,* 1967, **42,** 830–843.

Lindblom, B. E. F., & Sundberg, J. A quantitative model of vowel production and the distinctive features of Swedish vowels. *Quarterly Progress and Status Report,* 1969, **No. 1,** 14–32, Stockholm, Sweden, Speech Transmission Laboratory, Royal Institute of Technology.

Lisker, L. On time and timing in speech. In T. A. Sebeok (Ed.), *Current trends in linguistics.* Vol. 12. The Hague: Mouton, 1975.

Lisker, L., & Abramson, A. S. Distinctive features and laryngeal control. *Language,* 1971, **47,** 767–785.

MacNeilage, P. F. Motor control of serial ordering of speech. *Psychological Review,* 1970, **77,** 182–196.

MacNeilage, P. F. Speech physiology. In J. H. Gilbert (Ed.), *Speech and cortical functioning.* New York: Academic Press, 1972.

Mermelstein, P. A phonetic-context controlled strategy for segmentation and phonetic labeling of speech. *Status Report on Speech Research,* 1974, *SR-37/38,* 191–197, New Haven, Haskins Laboratories.

Millar, J. B., & Ainsworth, W. A. Identification of synthetic isolated vowels and vowels in h–d context. *Acustica,* 1972, **27,** 278–282.

Miller, G. A., Heise, G. A., & Lichten, W. The intelligibility of speech as a function of the context of the test materials. *Journal of the Acoustical Society of America,* 1951, **41,** 329–335.

Nooteboom, S. G. The target theory of speech production. (IPO Annual Progress Report No. 5, 1970, 51–55.) Eindhoven, Holland: Institute for Perceptual Research.

Nooteboom, S. G., & Slis, I. A note on the degree of opening and the duration of vowels in normal and "pipe" speech. (IPO Annual Progress Report No. 5, 1970, 55–58.) Eindhoven, Holland: Institute for Perceptual Research.

Peterson, G. E. The phonetic value of vowels. *Language,* 1951, **27,** 541–553.

Peterson, G. E. Parameters of vowel quality. *Journal of Speech and Hearing Research,* 1961, **4,** 10–29.

Peterson, G. E., & Barney, H. L. Control methods used in a study of the vowels. *Journal of the Acoustical Society of America,* 1952, **24,** 175–184.

Peterson, G. E., & Lehiste, I. Duration of syllabic nuclei in English. *Journal of the Acoustical Society of America,* 1960, **32,** 693–703.

Peterson, G. E., Wang, W. S. T., & Sivertsen, E. Segmentation techniques in speech synthesis. *Journal of the Acoustical Society of America,* 1958, **30,** 739–742.

Rand, T. C. Vocal tract size normalization in the perception of stop consonants. *Status Report on Speech Research,* 1971, *SR-25/26,* 141–146, New Haven, Haskins Laboratories.

Schatz, C. The role of context in the perception of stops. *Language,* 1954, **30,** 47–56.

Shaw, R., McIntyre, M., & Mace, W. The role of symmetry in event perception. In R. B. MacLeod and H. L. Pick (Eds.), *Perception: Essays in honor of J. J. Gibson.* Ithaca, New York: Cornell University Press, 1974.

Stevens, K. N. The quantal nature of speech: Evidence from articulatory-acoustic data. In E. E. David, Jr. & P. B. Denes (Eds.), *Human communication: A unified view.* New York: McGraw-Hill, 1972.

Stevens, K. N., & House, A. S. Perturbation of vowel articulations by consonantal context: An acoustical study. *Journal of Speech and Hearing Research,* 1963, **6,** 111–128.

Stevens, S. S., & Volkmann, J. The relation of pitch to frequency—a revised scale. *American Journal of Psychology,* 1940, **53,** 329–353.

Strange, W., Verbrugge, R., & Shankweiler, D. Consonant environment specifies vowel identity. *Status Report on Speech Research,* 1974, *SR-37/38,* 209–216, New Haven, Haskins Laboratories.

Summerfield, A. Q., & Haggard, M. P. Vocal tract normalization as demonstrated by reaction times. *Speech Perception,* 1973, Series 2, No. 2, 1–14. Department of Psychology, The Queen's University of Belfast.

Verbrugge, R., Strange, W., & Shankweiler, D. What information enables a listener to map a talker's vowel space? *Status Report on Speech Research,* 1974, *SR-37/38,* 199–208, New Haven, Haskins Laboratories.

Watson, J. B. *Behaviorism.* New York: Norton, 1924.

Wickelgren, W. A. Context-sensitive coding, associative memory, and serial order in (speech) behavior. *Psychological Review,* 1969, **76**, 1–15.

12

Disorganization in Thought and Word

Michael P. Maratsos

University of Minnesota

As psychologists we have an evident and reasonable preoccupation with trying to bring about order in our description of how human beings think and in our descriptions of their cognitive organizations. There is indeed much order and coherence to be described and analyzed; but I think that it is a simple fact that much of adult thinking, concept organization, reasoning, and arguing is at best partially coherent. Concepts are often fuzzy, reasoning is frequently faulty, and arguments frequently end in impasses or proceed in wrong-headed ways that are hard to make sense of.

This chapter addresses the problem of disorganization—or perhaps rather partial organization. Much of it has clear ancestry in some of the outstanding work of the twentieth century in the fields of word meaning and thinking, particularly philosophical linguistic analysis by the figures Wittgenstein and Austin, and developmental analysis by men such as Vygotsky, Piaget, and Werner. All these figures were concerned with this problem, though the latter three tended to regard it as a problem almost completely confined to children (Piaget), or to children, savages, and the insane (Vygotsky; Werner also includes the lower classes); a conclusion which I think both Wittgenstein and Austin would rightly find much too generous to civilized adults. The chapter begins with a discussion of the organization of word meanings, both synchronically (as in use at one time) and developmentally (as they change in the course of a language history or in the course of acquisition). In the succeeding section the discussion turns to similar topics in human classification, concept formation and argumentation. The thesis shall be that indeed similar problems arise in both areas of discussion, and for noncoincidental reasons; in particular the problems will be traced to problems in human judgments of partial and complete similarity between two situations or problems. We begin with a discussion of the partial disorder to be found in the structure of word meanings.

WORD MEANINGS

Synchronic Organization

By synchronic organization is meant the organization of the meaning of a word at a single time in the language. It has long plagued philosophers and linguists alike that the meaning of a word often does not appear to be constant across uses. Nevertheless, the notion that a given word has a meaning which is constant if one could only ferret it out has been a common one, as noted in Austin (1963) and Wittgenstein (1953). Both of these writers argued, and convincingly so, that words do not commonly have such a single meaning. What makes it seem so is that often the various meanings of a word may persistently share something of meaning or connotation so that the ensemble seems unified. Instead, the meanings of words have various kinds of resemblances among each other which I shall try to outline below.[1]

One kind of resemblance, noted by Aristotle, was called by him a paronymous organization. To illustrate such an organization we may consider the meanings and uses of the words *healthy, sad,* and *happy.* In all three cases there seems to be a nuclear meaning which is found in the phrases *healthy person, sad person,* and *happy person.* The words refer to states of a person. Now, for the case of *healthy,* consider the following uses: "His complexion is healthy"–*healthy complexion;* "That exercise is healthy"–*healthy exercise.* In the former case, healthy seems to mean "symptomatic of a state of health in a person," and in the latter "causative of a state of health." Similarly for *sad face* or *happy face* versus *sad book* or *happy book.* Our uses of the terms are also bound by real-world suppositions. The phrase *sad complexion* sounds peculiar because we do not usually think of complexions as indicating sadness, though they may indicate health.

Such structures are found readily in other words, though not as often as might be expected.[2] The word *earn*, for example, means to "acquire by labor, merit, or performance," or "deserve by labor, merit, performance." We may even say sarcastically of someone that he earns, say, $20,000 a year as a professor, but he hardly earns any of it, pointing out that he acquires the salary but does not

[1] Nida (1958), endeavoring to show that the meanings of a word may have no relation at all, cites the case of *charge,* which may mean, among other things, what the Light Brigade did and what a merchant does for his goods. Such cases are commonly called *homonyms,* two separate words which happen to have the same phonological realization, and are completely irrelevant to the point.

[2] Such cases occasionally fail to generalize in surprising ways. For example, one does not use the expression *jealous face,* to mean a face which seems to express jealously (compare to *sad face, happy face, healthy complexion*), or at least the usage is a strained one. And there seems to be no use of *jealous* to mean "causative of" (as in *healthy,* in *healthy exercise*), although such usages are easy to conceive.

merit it. Meanings may revolve around a central meaning in other ways. Bronfenbrenner (1960) pointed out that Freud used the term *identification* to mean both the process of identifying with someone and the outcome of the process. The central concept may be restricted to various extents among meanings as well. The term *family* revolves around a notion of kinship through bloodlines, but obviously differs in meaning in the following uses: "What position do you hold in your family?" "Is your family concentrated in one geographical area, or do they live all over the country?" "When did your family first come to America?" In the first case the reference is usually taken to be to the nuclear family: father, mother (husband, wife), and children. The second question can refer to the living members of the known wider family—cousins, uncles, and so on. In the third question, *family* clearly means a group of people united by a line of descent which may go back generations. A word such as *day* shows similar variation around a central notion of light–dark shift. It may refer to the 24-hr period which contains both day and night, or to just the light portion, or even to the working portion of a day, as in "how was your day?"

A word may also contain meanings which seem to spread further and further apart around various central meanings. The word *command,* as a verb, has a set of complexly related meanings. It may mean to issue an order from a position of authority, as in "he commanded the troops to leave." It may also mean having something at one's bidding or disposal, as in "he commands many resources." In the last meaning an element of clear success is added that is lacking in "he commanded the troops to leave," but the notion of directly issuing an order is lost. The word may also mean to have control, as in one who commands a situation; to have a competence as in having command of a language, and so on. The various meanings seem to cluster around a notion of secure position or authority, with clear links among the terms; but successive meanings grow further away. Such relations are common. Consider *heavy* in "This thing is heavy (to carry)," "This atom is heavy (for an atom)," "This meal is heavy (hard to digest, dense, rich food)," "His features are heavy (massive)."

In some cases it no longer seems that the meanings of the word necessarily share a common element of meaning. Rather there are a number of elements which keep cropping up among the words, no one of which perhaps appears in all. Wittgenstein called such word meanings family resemblances, noting how in families various facial features reappeared in different members, but often no one feature appeared in all. The result in such cases is a feeling of overall resemblance and unity without any unique unifying element. Vygotsky called such structures *chain complexes.* He noted that word meaning *A* might have something in common with word meaning *B,* and meaning *B* with meaning *C,* and *C* with *D,* but different members of the chain might have almost nothing in common; for example, *D* and *A* might share almost nothing in common. Wittgenstein wittily pointed to just such a case in the German word *spiel* (which is translated into English as both *play* and *game*): it can mean what actors do on the stage, what athletic players do, strategies and tricks people may indulge in socially and emotionally, and so on. Very commonly used terms in a language display such links endemically; the dictionary definitions of a word such as *run*, or *in*, abound in such interconnections.

An interesting characteristic of such shared, linking meanings is that they need not be what would normally be considered part of the 'essential' meaning of both terms, taking 'essential' to be those aspects of the original referent of a term without which it appears the term cannot be applied. For example, "having shape" is an essential part of the term "hexagonal;" or similarly, "shapeless" can only be applied to things which have some shape (as opposed to totally nonconcrete things such as gravity). In contrast, friendliness is not a necessary part of the referent of *dog*, but many dogs are friendly and faithful, and for many speakers, dog connotes friendliness. Many links among meanings appear to be by such "nonessential" meaning links. For example, *heavy* in *heavy features* probably shares a link with normally heavy objects through the frequent massiveness of the latter. A particularly good example of such links can be found in slang terms such as *screw*. The most noncolloquial meaning of the verb is "to drive or tighten a screw; to fasten, tighten, or attach by or as if by means of a screw" (American Heritage Dictionary, 1969). By some resemblance of the actions involved, perhaps, *screw* has evolved to also stand for sexual intercourse (the noncolloquial meaning originated as a French importation into English, and so was probably earlier). Most likely because of traditional sex-role considerations, *screw* in the sexual sense has a strong contextual connotation of one person taking advantage of the other, which seems to provide a link to another meaning of *screw*, to take advantage of someone or cheat them.

Such links by common characteristic situational overtone or empirical correlate, as discussed above for *screw* and *heavy*, characterize nearly any commonly used verb or adjective, and many nouns. Metaphor commonly plays on such characteristic qualities of words and situations. For example, for someone to "light someone else's (spiritual) way" means to make it possible for them to comprehend things. *Light* in general is associated with making it possible to see, and so forms many characteristic metaphorical links. People may also use connotation and context in everyday speech, in speaking of things such as a "true son" whereby they mean a son who characteristically does what sons at their best should do.

Developmental and Diachronic Data

Data from children's semantic acquisition is at yet not widely available, but even so instances exist that are of interest. Labov (1973), in intensive observation of his own infant's early language development, found that the initial organization of her first two words, *cat* and *mama*, indeed has a complexive nature. The child used *mama* to refer to any member of her family, and also to refer to visitors who stayed long enough at the house to become friendly. That the concept had a stronger core of meaning revolving around her actual mother, however, was demonstrated by the fact that when asked where *mama* was, the child always pointed to her actual mother. The word *cat* was also used most frequently and vociferously of actual cats, particularly to the one at home. But the infant also applied the word to objects which shared aspects with true cats, such as furry objects, statues of animals, and so forth.[3] Schulte, cited in Preyer (1890) similarly cites the case of a child who first used the word *ass* to refer to a goat with rough hide that stood on wheels. The word was then used to refer to moving things, and then extended to include things with a rough surface. The infant seems to have formed an initial concept of the disjunction of two elements (that is, "moves" or "rough surface"). Maratsos (1974) has found that older preschool children (more so than younger ones) employ the environmentally correlated element of the height of an object (distance from its top to a common floor) in their definitions of the words *big* and *tall.* If a taller object was compared with a clearly shorter one which was raised to a higher point, children would often pick the higher object as the tall one; under some conditions a small rabbit toy lifted above a much larger elephant was judged to be the "big one" of the pair, although under normal conditions gross size defined the meaning of *big.*

Aside from basically synchronic data like that cited above, the developmental literature also shows children extending the meaning of a term in a complex-like fashion at times. In the study by Maratsos cited above, the tendency to incorporate the element of highness grew with age in preschool children. Chain-complex-like word meaning changes may be found in diary accounts of infant semantic development. Piaget (1962) observed one of his children developing the following meanings in turn for *no more;* anything going away; anything overturned; anything at a distance; said as the child held something for an adult to throw; said when the child wanted an object someone was holding; said to mean "begin again." Another of Piaget's children applied *bow-wow* first to dogs, then to a dog seen from their balcony, then eventually to anything (e.g., prams, neighbors, hens, dogs, horses) seen from the balcony. A child studied by Pavlovitch (1920, cited in Clark, 1973) first used the word *bébé* to refer to her own reflection in a mirror. The word was subsequently applied in new uses to a photograph of herself, all photographs, all pictures; all books with pictures, and finally to all books. Romanes (1888, cited in Clark, 1973, and in Vygotsky, 1962) reports an infant who first used *quah* to refer to a duck in water. She then used it to refer to her milk in a bottle (liquid), to birds (ducks are birds), a coin with an eagle on it, and finally for a while to all coins.

[3] Labov, in systematic cross-sectional work, also demonstrates a similar (though less scattered) organization of adults' meaning for the word *cup.* The perceptual appearance of an object carries the greatest weight—something that looks just like a coffee cup is judged to be a cup no matter what its use. As the appearance approaches that of a bowl (by lengthening one edge more so that it looks more like a lip) the use to which the object is put becomes more important in speaker's judgments. Something between a cup and bowl in appearance will be judged to be a cup if it holds coffee, but a bowl if it holds vegetables.

Extensive documentation also exists in diachronic linguistics (historical changes in languages) of meaning shifts of a complexive nature. The shift may occur through a shared core of meaning. The Latin verb *pilare* in archaic Latin meant "to be covered with hair." By the imperial period it had come to mean "to depilate, to pull out the hair." Often meanings have branched off from older ones by becoming first more specific: such a case is that of *true,* which originally meant "faithful, loyal," as in "true to one's word," "true to one's family." With time it has also come to mean accurate, conformable to fact.

Quite frequently newer meanings are related to older ones, as in synchronic organization, by a link of emotional overtone or more general, nonessential meaning. The German word *Elend* once meant (as *Ellent*) "foreign land." Perhaps from contexts such as "banished into foreign lands," it acquired the meaning of "exile," and subsequently because of the emotional overtones of exile, its present meaning of "misery." The German word *ungefahr,* employing both links of essential meaning and of contextual connotation, has changed successively from an original meaning of "without danger" to mean "without bad intent," "without intent," "incidentally," and finally "approximately about."[4] It is quite likely that present synchronic word organizations have resulted by the accretion of such new meanings without the loss of older ones, as in the case of *true* above.

On the whole, then, there seem to be ample similarities among the synchronic links among word meanings, children's semantic organizations, and the change of word meaning both in children's acquisitions and in new word usages in language histories. In the following section we shall try to develop the thesis that similar kinds of organizations may be found in concept formation tasks and reasoning tasks in both children and in adults. We shall then attempt to elaborate the hypothesis that some of the similarities of organization among word structure, word change, and conceptual thinking are not coincidental (although some probably are), and analyze more fully the underlying cognitive basis for these problems.

COGNITIVE ORGANIZATION

The first task of this section is to document the presence of complexive structures in human concept formation and reasoning. A major part of the support is to be found in work with children's concepts and concept elucidation.

[4] Word changes may take even more surprising courses. Vygotsky (1962) cites the case of the Russian word *sutki,* which once simply meant "seam." It came with time to mean "twilight," the juncture of day and night. With more time it came to mean the twenty-four hour period *between* twilights, and now means the equivalent of the English *day* as a twenty-four hour period of time. Similarly, the word *shambles* changed from "table" to "butcher table" to "scene after a very bloody battle" to "scene after a very messy battle" to its present meaning.

Both Piaget (Inhelder & Piaget, 1969) and Vygotsky, employing slightly different methods, have found that children frequently classify shapes in complexive manners. Vygotsky (1962) essentially employed a nonsense-word concept formation task. His subjects were presented with an array of objects of different shapes–rectangles, squares, cylinders; different sizes–large, small; and different colors. On the bottom of each block was a nonsense syllable, such as *yiv*. Classes of objects predetermined by the experimenter had different names: *Yiv* might be placed at the bottom of all of the large triangles. At the beginning of the study, the experimenter would hold up one such shape and read off its name. He then suggested that the subject try to put together other shapes of the same name. Adults typically make a well-organized guess and stick to it. If a large yellow triangle had been held up, an adult might guess that *yiv* referred to all of the yellow shapes, and collect them together. When the subject was finished, the experimenter would then hold up one of the collected objects and read its name. For example, since *yiv* referred to large triangles, "yellow" as a guess would be incorrect, as would be shown by holding up a yellow square labeled *bik*. The subject could then try again.

The interest lay not so much in how accurate the subject was as in what kinds of piles of objects he assembled. Adults, as mentioned above, typically made a systematic initial guess and persisted on that basis. Children behaved differently, in a number of ways. Early on, they might simply put together any pleasing array of shapes, based on momentary whims. A more advanced grouping was what Vygotsky (and we after him) called a chain complex. The child might, beginning with a small yellow triangle, next select a pair of yellow objects, a circle and a square. Next, however, he might change his apparent criterion for *yiv* and select a red square, which shared the characteristic of squareness with the previous object but no longer was yellow. Through similar chained sequences the child would arrive at a collection with many links among the objects but with no overall unifying principle.

A still more advanced form of grouping was called an *associative complex* by Vygotsky. Given a small yellow triangle, the child would leave it in the center of the objects perhaps, and append to it triangles, yellow objects, or small objects, objects which each shared a characteristic with the initial object, but which themselves formed a complex. Such a structure is clearly analogous to the kind of word organization called *paronymous* (e.g., *sad* person, *sad* face, *sad* book).

Inhelder and Piaget (1969), employing a task with less resemblance to a verbal concept formation task, obtained quite similar results. Their subjects received shapes of varied form and color and were asked to put the ones together that belonged together. Some subjects were shown hierarchically organized classifications by adults as examples of what was meant. Nevertheless, they also obtained both associative and chain complexive structures. They also obtained, as a fairly common result, an early behavior consisting of arranging the shapes into wholistic forms such as a house. In free classification of this type children performed more adequately at an earlier age, arriving at unified hierarchical classification schemes by the ages of six or so, as compared to Vygotsky's finding that in his task, complexive organizations only ceased by adolescence. But the kinds of behaviors obtained led to quite similar structures.

Children's reasoning and explication also seem to employ complexive organization. The case *par excellance* is snycretic reasoning, discussed by both Piaget (1962, 1955) and Werner (1954). The basic problem of syncretic reasoning is the following:

Situation *A*	Situation *B*
Characteristics *a, b*	Characteristic *a*
	Therefore *b*

Because of partial similarity of one situation to another, children may assume further similarities of one to another in an unjustified manner. Piaget (1962) has recorded instances of such reasoning in his younger daughter Jacqueline. At 2 years 10 months of age Jacqueline had a temperature and desired oranges to eat. It was, however, too early in the season for oranges to be obtained. It was explained to her that they were still green rather than orange. She seemed to accept the facts. But a moment later, as she was drinking her (orange) camomile tea, Jacqueline exclaimed "Camomile isn't green, it's yellow already . . . give me some oranges!" Similarly, Jacqueline had a friend who was a little hunchbacked boy, whom she sometimes went to see. At one time he was ill with influenza, and so she could not see him. She said "poor boy, he's ill, he has a hump." Later, on a walk, she asked whether the boy was still ill in bed. On being told that he was not, she said "good, he hasn't a big hump now."

In the above, in what is also called tranductive reasoning, the child seems to reason from similarity of particulars to new similarities. For example, the similarity of tea and oranges in having colors and being ingestible leads to the conclusion that oranges are ripe because the tea is orange. Piaget (1955) also carried out work with older children. In this study they were given a list of sayings (e.g., "Filing can turn a stake into a needle.") and a list of explications (e.g., "As we grow older we grow better."). Children who occasionally made correct matches between sayings and explications also displayed many uses of syncretic reasoning in explaining the appropriateness of incorrect choices. It is impossible here to sample adequately from the rich store of examples Piaget gives. One example is given below:

> Mat (10; 0) connects the proverb "So often goes the jug to water that in the end it breaks" with the sentence "As we grow older we grow better." Now the proverb has been understood verbally (i.e., literally). For Mat it means: "*You go to the water so often that the jug cracks; you go back once again and it breaks.*" The corresponding sentence is explained as follows: "*The older you get the better you get and the more obedient you become.*" Why do these two sentences mean the same thing (question of experimenter)? "*Because the jug is not so hard because it is getting old, because the bigger you grow, the better you are and you grow old*" [Piaget, 1969, p. 150].

In their explications the children often made matches because of the possibility of finding some aspect of similarity between the proverb and the chosen explication; having found one similarity (or even participation in a common scheme) between the two, they picture the rest as similar as well.

We will not discuss here related results from Werner (1954) or Bruner, Oliver, and Greenfield (1966), who also found that children would unite word meanings (Werner & Kaplan 1952) or concepts (Bruner) on the basis of various kinds of partial similarity and justify their unity in syncretic ways. In all these cases, there is an overattribution of further similarity of outcome or attribute on the basis of partial and often complexlike links. Adults, although the case is perhaps less systematically documented, clearly also employ complexive concepts and syncretic reasoning. Their difficulties are generally less easy to analyze because the concepts with which they deal are themselves more complex and abstract. As a result it becomes difficult to both keep in mind the concepts being reasoned about and their true relations and to do this well enough to see their complexive links. But I think that careful analysis can show entirely comparable problems in adult cognition. A perfectly common and applicable case is reasoning by analogy, to which many of us are unduly wont. The dialogues of Plato (1928) in particular are marked by continual use of reasoning and proof by analogical means. In one sequence from the dialogue *Euthyphro,* Plato (through Socrates) considers the question"How should men serve the gods?" Trying to reason an answer to the question by beginning with clear cases, he considers a question he seemingly holds to be equivalent, "How do horses serve men?" The answer to this last question is then employed to answer the first one in an unconvincing manner. The problem, of course, is that the service of horses to men has some similarity with men's service to the gods (and for idiomatic reasons, even the same verbal expressions can be used), but the similarity is clearly not enough to motivate the eventual conclusion of how men should serve the gods. The reasoning may be schematized:

Situation *A*:	Situation *B*:
Horses serve men.	Men serve the gods.
X(horses) serve *Y*(men).	*X*(men) serve *Y*(gods).
X serves *Y* in manner *Z*.	Therefore, as in *A*, *X* should serve *Y* in manner *Z*.

Another general instance is found in an endemic form of argumentation. In such arguments, the point is whether two situations are the "same" (share enough important characteristics in common for a conclusion or outcome in one to be generalized to the other) or "different" (differ in so many important characteristics that no transfer is possible). To take a hypothetical example, Person 1 may argue "The United States now is just like the Roman Empire was when it began its fall. We have an originally energetic wealthy class, which is soft now. The Roman Empire fell, and the United States will fall." Person 2 may then argue that the two cases are not the same at all, because "No, it's completely different. Rome had no organized financial system which the United States does; and besides, Rome fell to the pressure of encroaching barbarians, and there are no encroaching barbarians now." I think everyone has heard and participated in arguments like these. The first party piles up what seem to him important (often important for emotional reasons) similarities between two situations or people, claims they are "the same," and so what was true of the first situation or person is true of the second. The second party brings up dissimilarities, claims the cases are different, and so denies the extension of similarity. The piling up of similarities and differences often seems to depend more on the psychological conspicuousness of certain aspects than on their relation to the main argument.

A particularly strong characteristic of such discussions and arguments (and other lines of reasoning) is the insistence that two situations are either "the same" or "different." Analytically it is clear that nearly any two objects or situations have some degree of difference. If we take *same* to mean "absolutely the same," then nothing is the same as anything. We could hardly say anyone was the same person they were in any infinitesimal instant of time before, because of organic and psychological changes. In fact, when we say two things are *the same,* we simply mean they are the same in what seem to us important respects. But in many processes of conscious reasoning and argument, we act as though *same* meant "completely the same," so that once it is shown that two situations are *the same* by similarity of important respects, then they are automatically *the same* in any other important respect. The same arguments apply to the predicate and concept *different;* the dissimilarity of a few (conspicuous) aspects may lead people to view two situations as *different,* hence "completely different."

Analytically, one can make valid inferences about characteristics shared by two situations only under the following conditions: if Situations X and Y share Characteristic a (or Characteristics a, b, c), and a (or a, b, c) can be shown to entail Characteristic z on logical or unimpeachable empirical grounds, then X and Y will both share z. Instead, people typically overattribute similarity of difference on what are essentially correlational grounds. They seem to believe that there is a magical condition of "sameness" or "differentness" which can be automatically decided on the basis of number or importance of similarities. (Of course, it is quite reasonable to guess, hypothesize, or suggest that if X and Y share Characteristic a (or a, b, c) in common, and X has z, then Y will also have z. If in the past only X has had both a (or a, b, c) and z, so that the association is previously unique, then it becomes even more reasonable to guess that Y also has z.)

Adults assuredly think, argue, and prove—they believe—things in this manner. Moving from the above general kinds of examples, I shall try to now give more specific examples that seem to be exemplary cases of adults reasoning about difficult subjects.

Case 1: Psychologist K. is a well-known psychologist who in lecture developed the following line of reasoning. Wishing to show that motives are concepts, he proceeded as follows:

1. Concepts are clearly cognitions.
2. A line of argument was given to demonstrate that motives are also cognitions.
3. Therefore, motives are concepts.

A perfectly parallel argument may be found in noting that cats are animals, dogs are animals, therefore cats are dogs. The similarity of motives and concepts in being cognitions led K. to believe that it followed that they shared enough further similarities to claim that motives are concepts.

Case 2: Charles Rosen, a musicologist, has written an excellent book called *The Classical Style* (1972) about the musical style of the classical composers Haydn, Mozart, and Beethoven. He describes sonata form as a combination of rhythmic, harmonic, cadential, and structural elements. Discussing a section from Haydn's *Creation*, he notes that it shares many of the attributes of sonata form, and concludes:

> For Haydn, the "sonata" is not a form at all, but an integral part of the musical language, and even a necessary minimum for any large statement that can be made within that language. The themes here are reduced to very small fragments, as are the musical paragraphs, but the proportions of a sonata movement without an isolated development section but with articulated expositon and symmetrical recapitulation . . . is as present as ever [Rosen, 1972, p. 370].

Rosen's procedure in this passage was to claim that since the musical organization of the discussed section employed some elements of what is called a sonata form, the piece is a sonata form. The presence of some elements of sonata form justifies uniting the section with other examples of sonata form, and attributing further similarities as a consequence. It is a matter of little difficulty to imagine the objection of another musicologist that given the elements of sonata form that are missing or severely transformed, the section is hardly in sonata form at all.

Within my own field (developmental psychology) there seems to me to exist examples of syncretic reasoning. One example, I think, is Piaget's claim that thinking and cognition consists of mental actions. This idea has, I think, profound influence yet insufficient basis in his work. Piaget's general strategy has been to demonstrate that the mind is "active" in rearranging and transforming elements for all cognitive operations. Therefore cognition is a series of actions. In cases in which the claim seems particularly dubious he generally points to some element of activity in the situation and concludes that the generalization holds. For example, considering the case of seriation of objects of different sizes (such as the arrangement of sticks of different lengths into a series starting with the shortest and ending with the longest), he points out a possible objection: does not the essential operation seem to be a perceptual comparison of heights that itself involves little activity? But, Piaget (1965) argues, when the child performs the task, he performs actively in moving the sticks together for comparison, arranging them, and the like, so clearly seriation is an action. Similarly, he has argued that even seeing involves active *elements* such as moving the eyes about to trace the outline of the object, so it also is an action. The general resemblance of such reasoning to syncretic thought seems clear. Nor is the problem simply a terminological one, a slight definitional extension of the word *action,* as those familiar with Piaget's work can attest (though they might disagree with points in the above very briefly made analysis). Piaget argues that the bases of cognition must lie in the sensorimotor activities of infancy. For conceptual activities have active elements like those of infancy. If cognitions are actions, then they clearly take their origin in similar overt *actions.* Furth (1969), in his work *Piaget and Knowledge,* has in effect noted that there are indeed similarities between the organizations of early sensorimotor activities and later conceptual activities, but not identity enough for the former entirely to motivate the latter. He emphasizes Piaget's concept of *reflective abstraction,* which seems to consist of the filtering from overt motor activities to internal cognitive operations of common, but not necessarily motoric, organization and principles. Such emphasis involves, I think, a considerable weakening of Piaget's original claims. Piaget's reasoning often appears to be clearly syncretic. His arguments that cognitions are actions comprise a clear case where such reasoning has profound effects upon his general thought, the necessary hastiness of the analysis offered here notwithstanding.

CONCLUSIONS

The cases discussed above—child and adult reasoning—provide ample (analogical)[5] similarities to the descriptions of the different types of word structures and developments discussed earilier. For clearly the verbal cases involve extending the usage of a word (call this the additional characteristic) by means of a

[5] Of course at this point I am employing one of the characteristic strategies of syncretic thought. It is being suggested from the similarity among the kinds of structures formed in the different areas of discussion that a further similarity obtains in the manner of their ontogenesis. There is nothing intrinsically misleading in such a procedure. As long as the natural tendency to attribute further similarities on the basis of existing ones does not become a claim of proof, the method is a fertile source of suggestions, guesses, hypotheses, and insights. Many human activities depend on this kind of thought in a positive way: activities in language such as poetry and the use of metaphor, and activities in cognition such as hypothesis formation. Evolutionarily, in fact, the use of continued attribution of similarity provides clear advantages. The basis of generalization is essentially to treat different situations in a similar fashion on the basis of what seem to the organism like criterially similar attributes among contexts. The strategy is bound to lead to false conclusions and unrewarding behaviors, but without it, little activity is possible that is not bound to particular situations.

partial overlap of similarity of a new possible context of usage with an old one in which use of the word was appropriate. For example, if the basic meaning of the word *sad* is that one uses it to describe the state of a person who is sad, extending it to refer to a situation or referent which is symptomatic of someone in the state of sadness (*sad face*) is to extend the use of the word on the basis of an overlapping linkage, the state of someone who is sad. In more extreme cases, if *Elend,* which originally meant "foreign land," became overextended to mean "exile," it was probably by means of the linkages between "foreign land," and "exile." The two are not equivalent, but may have been *enough so* for extension of the verbal usage from one situation to the other. A similar situation holds for the more connotationally-bound extension of *Elend* as "exile" to *Elend* as "misery," in which the link is not one of essential meaning, but of conspicuous overlap of connotation. The claim, then, is that it is possible that people will extend an old word to a new situation on the basis of some link, a link which by the general rules of linguistic usage should not be sufficient (if we take this rule to be that a word should be used only in situations which fulfill exactly all the previous essential criteria for its use).

At the same time, even if one person extends his use of a term, others must assimilate the new usage for it to become a part of the language. Here the fact that the formation of complexive structures characterizes thought extensively may be important in people's judging others' new usages "equivalent enough" to extend to the novel situation, and in their ability to adequately store the new use. There is little reason to doubt that people do indeed become confused and inaccurate over what counts as "equivalent enough." It would have been impossible otherwise to believe they sensed unified, constant meanings in terms which in fact had meanings united only by family resemblances. Especially when faced with situations which require thinking of a slightly new type, people easily confuse one type of similarity or equivalence for another–for example, confuse the linkage characteristic of family resemblances for the linkage characteristic of a truly unified, single determined concept or meaning such as is occasionally found in scientific concepts or even in a few ordinary language concepts. People could thus easily accept new usages which had some relation to the old as equivalent enough for lexical usage, particularly if the linkage were through a very conspicuous element in the situation. (Quite similarly they may also be confused or wrongly convinced by syncretic arguments.)

Of course, the proposals here, largely ones that seek to extend and make clear the analyses implied in earlier work, are only tentative ones. In various cases, such as that of language change, processes other than that of complexive growth as described above could result in similar outcomes. One widely suspected means of linguistic change is the practice of euphemistic reference–referring to an unpleasant situation with terms appropriate for a neutral or pleasant one. *Imbecile,* for example, at one time simply meant "weak". It was apparently applied euphemistically to persons of "weak mind," and with time its true contextual meaning came to predominate (Robertson & Cassidy, 1954). *Wanton* similarly once meant "untaught." Speakers do not seem confused or to overestimate similarity when they refer euphemistically; the misuse is initially purposeful, though the change of normal meaning may not be. Another possible source of noncomplexive change may be found in simple misunderstanding between generations. In most of the above cases it has been assumed that the person(s) who overextended a word use correctly apprehended the original meaning of the term. But new permanent meanings for a word may also have arisen from a misunderstanding on the part of someone who previously had no understanding of the older meaning. For example, if after a while *imbecile* was mostly used of imbeciles, a speaker growing up and hearing the word used mostly in that context could easily understand it as having only the meaning proper to its more modern use without ever apprehending the older. Thus a younger generation's understanding of the word use of the older generation may also be a source of meaning change.

The existence of such alternate hypotheses can be taken as cautions that we cannot directly infer causal relations from the similarities among change and organization in thought to those in word meanings.[6] To extend this work it remains to obtain more information from naturalistic observations of language change and acquisition and experimental demonstrations (Werner & Kaplan, 1952, have provided us with one study of this kind already). On the whole, nevertheless, the parallels between complexive and syncretic thought and the types of word change and organization discussed in this chapter are too clear for dismissal. Too many findings and observations already available stem more reasonably from the hypothesis of complexive thought as a causal factor for alternative hypotheses to be satisfactory, complete substitutes.[7]

[6] Few chapters of this length can discuss an entire area and this is no exception. Many interesting problems in word meaning and word change have been completely passed over. Among them stand such interesting tendencies as that of people to make reference to someone or something by a part (*Redbeard, Bluebeard* as names; *Redcoats* to refer to British soldiers in the American Revolutionary War) or even by some closely associated object (*The Crown* for the English monarch and his authority; *Pharoah,* which originally referred not to the Egyptian ruler but only to the great house in which he dwelt—with time it was used to refer directly to the ruler himself; our own *White House,* which is becoming more animate with time, in such sentences as *The White House today declared its intentions of co-operating fully with communist authorities in the Mideast*). It seems likely that such a means of reference stems from a natural tendency of the human mind to tag or refer to fuller experiences by conspicuous or associated parts; an image which is itself incapable of representing the fullness of a remembered situation may nevertheless help in the memory of it or in keeping it in mind (Bartlett, 1932).

[7] A child whose language development is being studied by the author and others has, for example, been observed to use the word *horn* (the meaning of which was previously quite clear to him) to mean the action of touching someone or something else with a horn, a quite novel meaning. He seems to have abstracted from noun–verb pairs like *hammer-to hammer, shovel-to shovel* the overly broad hypothesis (rarely applied even by him) that one can say *to X* to mean "to do something with *X*." Such a hypothesis would be impossible if complexive thinking were not a natural process. Werner (1954) cites similar cases from a German-speaking child.

More positively, I should like to conclude this discussion by noting an important and perhaps not obvious theoretical premise of most of the exposition in this paper, namely, that people may "know" something at one level of functioning, such as the true relations among situations, or the proper equivalences necessary to satisfy word use, but be confused or lax about relations at another level, such as word usage in a situation that is somewhat novel, or about judging whether a new word use is consonant with old ones enough to be extended, or about judging whether a word has a unified meaning. The problem of knowledge at one level of something known at another, I should like to suggest in passing, seems to me indeed a crucial one. We have often assumed in the past, I think, that something is known in just one way, so that any procedure tapping that knowledge is equivalent to any other, since all procedures tap the same thing. So for example, it has been claimed (Menyuk, 1971) that young children define words in terms of the functions of their referents, since when they are asked, for example, what a bottle is, they are likely to say "It's something that you put stuff in." Similarly, since children at five or six give word associations like the verb *bark* to *dog,* rather than another noun such as *cat,* they do not functionally use word classes like noun or verb, or organize words in that fashion. But there is no reason to accept such results at face value. Five- and six-year old children are now known to use words syntactically depending on their word class with great discrimination and accuracy. Using word classes to organize responses in word association tasks is a different problem. The general matter is probably best illustrated in a study of Piaget's. He asked children if various *words* were strong or not—for example, "Is the word *daddy* strong?" Children at five or six generally answered in terms of the referent of the word, rather than answering that words themselves are not strong or weak, but simply refer. So one child answered that the word *daddy* is strong because daddies are strong, while umbrellas are weak. Some children were traditional—they knew better, but kept forgetting and slipping back, as the following passage shows:

> Aud (8; 8): "Are words strong? - *No, words are nothing at all. They aren't strong, you can't put anything on them.*—Tell me a word.—*'Curtains.' It isn't strong because if you put anyting on it, it tears. A word isn't strong because you can't build up anything on it.*— . . . Are there any words that are strong?—*No.*—Tell me another word.—*'Umbrella-stand.' It is strong because you can put umbrellas in it* . . . [Piaget, 1969, p. 58].

Such work, and other work, has been widely cited to show children cannot disentangle a word from its referent. Badly stated, the proposition is of course nonsense. When children hear the word *fire* they do not form blisters on their skin or even flinch back as though from heat. In normal use children do not confuse words with their referents. But at the level of functioning required by being asked to consciously consider problems such as Piaget's, they do indeed. There is no single, unified knowledge of word-referent relations; rather there are different levels of functioning at which the relation may be known. Similarly, the fact that six-year olds may define words in terms of function is interesting, but does not display their "meaning of the word." I have asked people, for example, whether the meaning of the word *convince,* as in "*X* convinced *Y* to do something," means that *Y* necessarily carries out the action. They generally say "yes" when the question is proposed. But in fact *convince* does not entail such a definition, and people know it does not. When asked if one could say that *"Mary convinced John to leave, but he didn't after all because he changed his mind,"* they agree there is nothing at all odd about such a usage, which shows that *convince* does not entail, by meaning, the performance of the infinitival action. (Compare to *force,* as in *Mary forced John to leave,* in which case it is anomalous then to state that John did not leave.) Their conscious inspection of their meaning for *convince* probably involves inspection of its normal use, in which the infinitival action is generally performed; but their conscious inspections provide no direct route to the meaning they actually have stored for use of the term.

So it seems reasonable to propose that someone, whether child or adult, might truly understand a concept or lexical item, and even generally work on the basis of strict equivalence of essential elements, and yet overextend the use of a word (or concept) in a novel use, and accept new uses as being ones that fit the old, or accept complexive structures as unified ones. The general problem of judging at one cognitive level the relations of similarity and equivalence at another is clearly one that deserves attention. The resulting complexive thought seems characteristically a source of human hypotheses, guesses, judgments, concepts; it seems unlikely that it is not also a characteristic source of much of the instability in our use, organization, and intuitions of the structure of words (see Footnote 7).

ACKNOWLEDGMENTS

The original talk from which this paper is taken was written while the author was being supported by grants HD-01136 and National Science Foundation Grant GB35703X.

REFERENCES

The American Heritage Dictionary. Boston: Houghton-Mifflin, 1969.

Austin, J. L. The meaning of a word. In Charles Canton (Ed.), *Philosophy and ordinary language.* Urbana, Illinois: University of Illinois Press, 1963.

Bartlett, F. *Remembering.* Cambridge, England: Cambridge University Press, 1932.

Bronfenbrenner, U. Freudian theories of identity & their derivatives. *Child Development,* 1960, **31**, 15–40.

Bruner, J., Olver, R., & Greenfield, P. *Studies in cognitive growth.* New York: Wiley, 1966.

Clark, E. V. What's in a word. On the child's acquisition of semantics in his first language. In T. E. Moore (Ed.), *Cognitive development and the acquisition of language.* New York: Academic Press, 1973, 65–110.

Furth, H. *Piaget and knowledge.* Englewood Cliffs, New Jersey: Prentice-Hall, 1969.

Inhelder, B., & Piaget, J. *The early growth of logic in the child.* New York: Norton, 1969.

Labov, W. A child's meaning for *cat* and *mama.* Colloquium delivered at the University of Minnesota, 1973.

Maratsos, M. When is a high thing the big one? *Developmental Psychology,* 1974, **10**, 466–475.

Menyuk, P. *The acquisition and development of language.* Englewood Cliffs, New Jersey: Prentice-Hall, 1971.

Nida, E. A. Analysis of meaning and dictionary making. *International Journal of American Linguistics,* 1958, **24**, 279–292.

Pavlovitch, M. *Le langage enfantin: Acquisition du serbe et du francais par un enfant serba.* Paris: Champion, 1920.

Piaget, J. *The language and thought of the child.* Cleveland: World Publ., 1955.

Piaget, J. *Play, dreams, and imitation.* New York: Norton, 1962.

Piaget, J. *The child's conception of number.* New York: Norton, 1965.

Piaget, J. *The child's conception of world.* Totowa, New Jersey: Littlefield, Adams, 1969.

Plato (no first initial). *The works of Plato.* Selected and edited by Irwin Edman. New York: The Modern Library, 1928.

Preyer, W. *The mind of the child.* New York: Appleton, 1890.

Robertson, S., & Cassidy, F. G. *The development of modern English.* (2nd ed.) Englewood Cliffs, New Jersey: Prentice-Hall, 1954.

Rosen, C. *The classical style: Haydn, Mozart, Beethoven.* New York: W.W. Norton, & Co. Inc. 1972.

Romanes, G. J. *Mental evolution in man.* London, 1888.

Vygotsky, K. *Thought and Language.* Cambridge, Massachusetts: MIT Press, 1962.

Werner, H. Change of meaning: A study of semantic processes through the experimental method. *The Journal of General Psychology,* 1954, **50**, 181–208.

Werner, H., & Kaplan, E. The acquisition of word meanings: A developmental study. *Monographs of the Society for Research in Child Development,* 1952, **51**.

Wittgenstein, L. *Philosophische Untersuchungen* (translated by D. E. M. Anscombe). Oxford: Blackwell Press, 1953.

13
Resemblances in Language and Perception

Robert R. Verbrugge

University of Connecticut

> This is one thing that cannot be learned from anyone else, and it is the mark of great natural ability, for the ability to use metaphor well implies a perception of resemblances. (Aristotle, *Poetics;* cited in Hawkes, 1972)

Accounting for the perception of resemblances has been one of the most important and obstinate problems facing experimental psychology. How do we recognize the similarity of an event to one experienced before, in spite of differences in detail? It is a problem of describing both what it is that we learn about a type of event and how it is that we detect and later recognize its characteristics. The interest in these questions is attested to by a huge literature on concept formation and identification, stimulus and response generalization, perception (including the perception of speech sounds and linguistic forms), recognition memory, learning set, and so on.

Until recently, there has been surprisingly little research on how we apprehend events through the medium of linguistic forms. In particular, there has been almost no psycholinguistic research on the ways language is used to draw attention to resemblances. Analogies appear in many different forms: *similes* ("the swinging putters left behind a wake like the shining weave of a flying fish"–TV sports commentator), *metaphors* ("we live in a time when meaning falls in splinters from our lives"–popular song), *symbols* ("he believes in Mother and apple pie"), *proverbs* ("look before you leap"), and *models* ("imagine that these two atoms are billiard balls on a pool table . . . "). Beyond these there are parables, fables, poems, plays, scientific theories, and other works of fiction. The frequency with which we use and encounter these linguistic forms makes it puzzling why there has been so little study of how we comprehend them—especially given the central role of the perception of resemblances in human cognition.

The neglect of metaphor by contemporary psychology is probably due to the field's origins in a philosophical and rhetorical tradition which had little place for such uses of language. For example, Aristotle argued that the primary function of language is the accurate description of reality, and that the closer the correspondence between words and the classes of natural things, the better this function will be fulfilled. Poetic language is "imitative," not descriptive, and thus is distinct from the languages of rhetoric and logic, whose goals are persuasion and clarity:

> All such arts are fanciful and meant to charm the hearer. Nobody uses fine language when teaching geometry (*Rhetoric* III; cited by Hawkes, 1972).

The Aristotelian position might be summarized (and caricatured) as follows. There is a set of primitive properties by which we may classify all objects and events. Words refer to specific classes (concepts) defined in terms of those properties: hence the proper use of words may be defined in objective, physical, measurable ways. The meaningfulness of strings of words (sentences) may be evaluated as if they were selfcontained logical propositions about the properties of things. If different parts of a sentence entail incompatible properties, then the proposition is illogical and meaningless. Thus metaphoric sentences are strictly illogical. Their vividness and novelty may prove useful, in passing, to make a drab speech more eye-catching, but the meaning conveyed by the speaker is independent of them.

The impact of this tradition is still being felt. Many twentieth century schools of thought (logical positivism, behaviorism, taxonomic and transformational linguistics) have maintained much of the Aristotelian view of language, and thus have shared a discomfort with metaphor and other subjective manifestations. Two underlying assumptions seem most critical. One is a positivistic attitude that structure can be discerned and defined in publicly available ways, that is, that structure is independent of the observer. The second is what Pepper (1942) has called "immanent formism," the belief (in part) that the structure of things is manifested directly in their physical form ("on the surface"), that the natural world can be classified by these overt physical properties.

These attitudes have had a crippling effect on psychological study of the processes by which we perceive resemblances, both in the comprehension of analogic language and in the direct perception of shared structure. The goal of this chapter is to show that these two modes of apprehending commonalities are intimately related, perhaps identical in some respects. The approach to be developed will replace positivism with an interactive and perspectivist view of meaning, in which the interpretive and selective activities of the perceiver are critical; and it will reject immanent formism in favor of the view that the perceived structure of things is best defined in terms of abstract, "formless" relations. Taken together, these views provide an exciting basis for studies of metaphor, analogic thought, and imaginative processes in general.

THE PROBLEM OF LINGUISTIC DEVIANCE

The study of language structure took a giant step during the "linguistic revolution" of the last twenty years (e.g., Chomsky, 1957, 1965). It was a shift, in Pepper's (1942) terms, from an "immanent formism" to a "transcendent formism." Taxonomic linguists assumed that the segmentation of strings of phonemes and morphemes posed no problem since the identity of the structural elements was apparent ("immanent") in the surface form. Transformational linguists, to the contrary, asserted that there were deeper identities than were manifested on the surface, in at least two senses. First, there were grammatical relations which might not be apparent in the "surface structure"; for example, Sentences (1) and (2) are superficially more similar than (1) and (3):

(1) Joan is easy to help.
(2) Joan is willing to help.
(3) It is easy to help Joan.

But Sentences (1) and (3) are structurally equivalent at a deeper level, and different in that respect from (2), since (4) is not equivalent to (2):

(4) It is willing to help Joan.

A second sense in which sentences bear a deep identity is that utterances of a sentence may show variability due to grammatical errors, phonetic substitutions, hesitations, dialect differences, etc. In spite of these surface deviations from grammatical and phonological norms, we are able to recognize the underlying sentence which a speaker intended. This is similar to our ability to classify a particular tree as an oak, in spite of any deformities it may have due to local environmental conditions.[1] The concept of an oak tree, or a grammatical sentence, or a perfect gas, transcends any particular manifestation.

This shift to a transcendent formism has been productive for linguistics and it has forced psychologists to think about how an organism might perceive structural relations which are inherently abstract. Even so, the transformationalists have maintained many of the traditional assumptions: that sentences may be described in isolation, that sentences may be treated as self-contained propositions in a logical calculus, that the meaning of sentences is assembled from

[1] Pepper ascribes this example to Aristotle-as-transcendent-formist. An extensive study of the "growth policies" underlying the appearance of natural forms has been made by Thompson (1942).

meanings associated with words, and that meanings are properties in a classificational scheme not unlike the Aristotelian theory of types. The following arguments are an attempt to demonstrate that this residue of positivism and immanent formism makes certain linguistic theories inadequate as a basis for a psychology of comprehension. The inadequacies will be particularly obvious in the case of understanding metaphoric language.

The boldest semantic theory, in the context of Chomsky's (1965) transformational grammar, is that proposed by Katz and his colleagues (e.g., Katz, 1971, 1972; Katz & Fodor, 1963). Katz has the virtue of being relatively explicit, so the psychological implications of his position may be more clearly stated. Katz's (1971) goal is to account for the semantic properties and relations of sentences—synonymy, antonymy, contradiction, meaningfulness, entailment, etc. Very crudely his position is as follows. The underlying deep structure of a sentence is the best place to define semantic as well as syntactic relations. Lexical items may be substituted for the nonterminal symbols at the deep structure level and thus will be labeled according to their role in the phrase structure (noun, verb, auxiliary, etc.). This disambiguates the senses of the "same" word used as different parts of speech (e.g., "play" may be a noun or verb). Associated with each potential use of a lexical item is a set of *semantic markers* (e.g., one feature of "shadow" is –Physical Object) and *selection restrictions* (e.g., one restriction of "waterproof" is that it can only be used to predicate on a +Physical Object). Thus the sentence

(5) Shadows are waterproof.

will have incompatible semantic markers, and Katz's system will brand it "meaningless." The meaning of a sentence is a composite of the meanings of its parts, and the total proposition is meaningful only if it contains no logical inconsistencies.

This is really the old Aristotelian system in a new disguise. What is lost is the naive view that sentence structure directly reflects the reality being described; Katz wisely asserts that language's surface form is a partial and ambiguous reflection of an "underlying reality." But what remains is (a) a classificational scheme which has a reassuringly substantive and immanent feel about it; (b) a basis for meaning which is asserted to be independent of people's cognitions ("Ideas, thoughts, cognitions, etc., like utterances, are performance phenomena, while meanings, like phonological features and syntactic categories, are abstractions that form part of competence"; Katz, 1971, p. 121); and (c) a logical system which labels metaphor as inexplicit and meaningless (Katz does not discuss metaphor directly, but his attitude is exemplified in such phrases as "unexplicated and highly metaphorical relation" and "metaphorical and loose notions").

The immediate problem at this point is that we can make sensible interpretations of sentences which Katz's system would brand as meaningless. For example, we could interpret Sentence (5) to mean that we can throw as much water at a shadow as we like, but the shadow will go unharmed. Such interpretations (which we readily give to metaphors in context) are bound to pose a problem for those who leave the processes of human imagination out of their account of meaning. Psychologists, who have tended to borrow on the linguists' concepts and terminology, typically express a mixture of fascination and helplessness over accounting for "deviant" uses of language. For example, Slobin (1971) writes: "You are also able to interpret deviant sentences. . . . In fact, much of the understanding of certain kinds of poetry is based on this ability to find interpretations for grammatically unusual constructions—an activity which can be especially pleasurable [pp. 4–5]." Chomsky (1965), too, recognized the need to account for interpretations given to expressions (not sentences!) which violated his intuitive selection restrictions, and expressed the hope that such interpretations could be made by adding a (totally unexplicated) process called "analogy":

> [Expressions such as "sincerity may admire the boy"] deviate in some manner . . . from the rules of English. If interpretable at all, they are surely not interpretable in the manner of the corresponding sentences [e.g., "the boy may admire sincerity"]. Rather, it seems that interpretations are imposed on them by virtue of analogies that they bear to nondeviant sentences [Chomsky, 1965, p. 76].

Note the persistent dichotomy between deviant and well-formed, poetic and ordinary, figurative and literal, etc., in these accounts, along with the admission that users of the language are able to interpret both kinds of sentences. Is there any psychological justification for calling one form of comprehension typical and the other special, or for supposing that the processes of comprehension in the two cases are different at all?

Consider the following sentence:

(6) My aunt is a butcher.

It is typical to describe two alternative interpretations for such a sentence: one literal, the other figurative. For example, I might be saying (a) that my aunt is a member of the profession that slaughters animals for market, or (b) that my aunt is *like* such a person in some unspecified way (which would have to be inferred in context). But where are the boundaries between sharing some, many, most, or all of the properties of "a slaughterer of animals for market"? Dictionaries list several figurative (now *standard*) uses of "a butcher" which carry only part of the sense of "slaughterer of animals for market" or carry a sense which overlaps only partially with it: a dealer in meats, one guilty of needless bloodshed, a candy vendor on trains, a bungler. The boundary between standard and novel uses is difficult to define and changes continually. Dictionaries are jammed with metaphors, both dead and dying, and more are arriving every day.

Does it make sense to say that we comprehend Sentence (6) by first trying the standard predicating potentials of "butcher," only seeking a figurative sense if the first effort leads to logical inconsistencies, or a contradiction of some prior knowledge (for example, that my aunt is a plumber by trade)? The fact that we seldom notice the potential ambiguity of such sentences is a prima facie, although not necessarily compelling, argument against such a two-stage model. It is also unparsimonious to assume that some interpretations (the literal) proceed like the self-contained "semantic reading" of the linguist, while other interpretations (the figurative) must invoke special cognitive, inferential processes which have no formal role in linguistic theory. It appears more reasonable to assume that a *complete* account of semantic relations must include psychological variables and must include them in the interpretation of *all* sentence forms.

THE COMPREHENSION OF METAPHORIC SENTENCES

In recent years more and more attention has been devoted to the integral role of a listener's cognitive activity in defining the semantic content of words and sentences. One important component of this activity is a listener's inferences about a speaker's intentions, expectations, and beliefs. These variables are part of the structure of "speech acts," the utterances of requests, threats, assertions, promises, etc., in social contexts (cf. Austin, 1962; Lakoff, 1972; Searle, 1969).

There have been several attempts recently to define figurative and literal language as two types of speech act which happen to use a common form, for example, "an *X* is a *Y*" (Gordon & Lakoff, 1971; Mack, 1973; Steinmann, 1975). The potential ambiguity of a sentence like (6) is resolved by intuiting the speaker's intention. For example, Steinmann (1975) has argued, in the case of sentences like (6), that the "predicating potential" of "is a butcher" is realized if the speaker intends the literal meaning, but is abandoned if he intends it to be interpreted figuratively. Steinmann defines literal usage by the equivalence of "intended meaning" and "sentence meaning," while a figurative use of language expresses an intended meaning different from what the sentence itself means. In the latter case, the "propositional-act potential" of another sentence is realized (for example, "my aunt is cruel"), but which other sentence(s) are intended by the speaker must be "inferred" by the hearer "with some guidance from the verbal and situational context." This is the same awkward dualism assumed by Katz and Chomsky: the interpretation of literal sentences is straightforward and analytic, while a special process must be invoked for interpreting deviant forms. The speech act approach is less extreme than the earlier linguistic views since there is no pretense that literal "interpretation" is a process independent of real speakers and hearers. We intend to speak literally and infer (or perceive) such intents in others.

Even so, the rigid dichotomy between literal and figurative meanings is troublesome. In some senses all language use is figurative, since the contexts in which linguistic forms are used are always novel. The situations in which use of a term is "appropriate" show gradations of similarity; there is no abrupt shift from "standard" situations (defined by a fixed set of criterial properties) to "deviant" situations. (Recall the difficulty in bounding the standard uses of "is a butcher.") Our experience with word use does give us a strong sense of what contexts are most typical, and we can exploit this knowledge in interpreting the sentences we hear. But the acceptable manifestations of these constraints cannot be sharply bounded: expressing novel semantic intentions through familiar forms is an integral part of language use.

Thus it is questionable whether there is an independent level of "sentence meaning" which is available to all users. Note that if we refuse to posit such a level of meaning, the speech act dichotomy between literal and figurative usage disappears, and with it the dual process model. This may be the most sensible and parsimonious move from the standpoint of modelling the processes by which language is used and comprehended, though it would still be necessary to explicate our fuzzy intuitions about "literal" usage. One possible basis for such intuitions would be the perception of a strong similarity between a particular context of word use and our experience of previous contexts, coupled with a tendency to treat concepts as if they had object permanence.

The processes by which listeners infer the sense of a novel sentence have been receiving more and more attention from experimental psychologists (cf. Bransford & McCarrell, 1974, for a representative summary of this research). Most of the experiments to date have been designed to demonstrate the presence of inferential processes, that is, to show that subjects comprehend more from a sentence or passage than is explicitly provided. In particular, it is possible to demonstrate that the process of understanding a sentence can involve more than the criteria for literal use of its component words (that is, more than a set of normatively-defined semantic features). This is especially important if all language use is to some extent a figurative extension of previous uses.

Verbrugge and McCarrell (1973) have reported a study of the role of extralinguistic inferences in the comprehension of *metaphoric* sentences. Metaphors are a natural candidate for the study of such processes, since they typically set up an equivalence between a *topic* and a *vehicle* (what the topic is being compared to), but leave the *ground* (the nature of the equivalence) unspecified. Verbrugge and McCarrell reasoned that if this ground is inferred when a metaphor is heard, then a statement of the ground should be an excellent prompt for the recall of all or part of the original sentence. In one experiment they presented subjects with a series of sentences like (7) and (8), or their topics alone (Sentence 9). (The related grounds are presented in parentheses.)

(7) Tree trunks are straws for thirsty leaves and branches. (are tubes which conduct water to where it is needed)

(8) Tree trunks are pillars for a roof of leaves and branches. (provide support for something above them)

(9) Tree trunks

In a prompted recall task, subjects were given a set of phrases and were asked to recall the topic most related to each one. When the phrase was a ground relevant to the sentence heard, recall was high; when the phrase was the ground appropriate to another metaphor involving the same topic, recall was poor. When subjects had heard only the topics, either ground produced intermediate recall. This suggests that a metaphor leads us to infer a particular predication on a topic. For example, the properties attributed to tree trunks in the above metaphors are not the sort of thing one would store as semantic markers in a lexicon (as criterial features for word use). The properties are part of our tacit knowledge of the structure and physiology of trees, and they rely for their activation on what we also know about the vehicle. In fact, in many cases the vehicle may lead us to understand something *new* about the topic, to note a property we were unaware of before. Thus the sense of a metaphor is not contained in the sentence itself, nor is such a sentence illogical and meaningless. Its meaning is a result of our inferring a basis for an equivalence which the sentence merely asserts.

This research leads naturally to the following generalizations about the apprehension of meaning through language:

1. It is not the elementary linguistic forms which determine meaning, but the role they play in a larger relation. (This opposes the assumptions of immanent formism.) Thus the meaning of the phrase "tree trunks" in Sentences (7) and (8) is not a fixed set of properties, but is defined by the perceived role of tree trunks in a context suggested by a particular sentence predicate.

2. Meaning is intrinsically a *psychological* relation. (This opposes the positivistic assumption that meaning can be characterized independent of a comprehender.) Words and sentences take on determinate meaning only when embedded in a *psychological* relation. Meaning is a product of our interaction with words, it is what we apprehend about the world through the medium of words.

3. Since only part of the import of a sentence is specified directly, language may be viewed as a set of abstract instructions to perform certain kinds of inferential and problem-solving procedures depending on the context (cf. Bransford & McCarrell, 1974, for a development of this position). For example, in Metaphors (7) and (8), the copula "are" directs the comprehender to justify an equivalence relation at whatever level it is possible and useful to do so. A sentence is like a piano score: a rough specification of what is to be performed, but abstract and incomplete enough to demand a lot of elaboration. A score constrains the pianist's interpretation, but hardly determines it. Similarly, the interpretation of meaning is a cognitive performance guided by sentences:

> It seems that there are *certain definite* mental processes bound up with the working of language, processes of understanding and meaning. The signs of our language seem dead without these mental processes; and it might seem that the only function of the signs is to induce such processes; and that these are the things we ought really to be interested in [Wittgenstein, 1958, p. 3; italics in original].

THE PERCEPTION OF EVENTS

What activities are involved in the inference or extraction of the ground of a metaphor? Aristotle relates metaphor to the "perception of resemblances." Is this itself a metaphor, comparing two separate sets of processes, one linguistic, the other perceptual? Or are the processes identical in certain ways? It is worth turning for a moment to the traditional domains of perception to see what account they give of our detection of similarities among events.

Classes of events that we perceive as similar or to which we respond similarly have usually been characterized by psychologists as "concepts" or "equivalence classes." The concept or class is typically defined in terms of the physical properties shared by its members, that is, in terms of their common elements or attributes. The properties are particular values along dimensions such as color, shape, size, orientation, intensity, frequency, etc. The implicit claim is that all classes of objects can be characterized exhaustively by a list of their distinctive visual features, auditory features, tactile features, etc. These features are presumably *irreducible* components of our environment and provide a sufficient basis for constructing our concepts of dynamic events as well as of the objects involved in them. Thus a system of "attributive concepts" is essentially the Aristotelian theory of types in a new guise, and it is remarkably similar to Katz's system for classifying the word objects which are assembled into sentence events.

Some of the problems with this approach to perception are a product of its immanent formism. Three problems are especially relevant to the question of perceiving resemblances through language:

1. The first problem is one pointed out long ago by the Gestaltists: we can perceive the similarity of *patterns* of physical variables, in spite of changes in their specific physical composition. A pattern has an integrity which cannot be broken down into the attributes of its component parts. For example, a melody may be heard as the same in spite of changes in key, tempo, ornamentation, etc. The identity of the melody is determined by a particular ordering of its component notes; the *relations among* the frequencies and durations of the notes are what is critical.

2. What seem to be categorical features of our environment may actually rely on complex relations among physical variables for their specification. This is certainly true of the acoustic basis for the perception of phonemic categories (cf. Studdert-Kennedy, 1974), and it is no doubt true of the optical basis for perceiving putative visual features (hues, shapes, sizes, etc.; cf. Gibson, 1950, 1966). In other words, when psychologists label certain categories as "features" they presuppose (or ignore) a process of categorization which is intrinsically relational. We are able to recognize novel instances of a pattern just as we recognize novel uses of a term. This is possible in each case because our concepts

do not depend on the specific attributes of elements at the lowest level (physical parameters, semantic features, etc.; cf. Shaw & Wilson, 1976, for a more complete critique of this problem).

3. The common elements approach implies a "subtractive" process in conceptual abstraction, that is, generalizations are made by retaining only the properties shared by all instances, and by discarding all particulars which are not shared (cf. Cassirer, 1923). The concept of "metal," for example, becomes almost vacuous because the various instances of metals (gold, copper, silver, tin, etc.) have almost no physical features in common. Most of what we understand about metals involves structural relations among their components and their interactions with other substances. Such relational similarities will never be found in a search for common features if features are defined by local physical parameters.

Cassirer's alternative to the common elements approach is to see concepts as abstract with respect to any particular manifestation. Elements are not discarded, but given an abstract place in a structure, like a variable in a mathematical equation. Thus a concept is richer than any particular set of instances, because it can "generate" all of them and more by assuming one value after another in each of its variables.

While the faith in local sensations and common properties has continued to dominate work in perception and concept learning, interest in abstract relations has not been entirely dormant. Michotte (1963), for example, has studied the abstract relations that provide the basis for our perception of physical causation. In his experiments, one perceives two "segregated" patterns (call them objects, if you will) which interact according to certain definite temporal and spatial relations. Those relations determine the quality of the event.

Gibson (e.g., 1950, 1966, 1971) has also devoted considerable attention to the abstract character of the physical "invariants" which specify depth, motion, the separation of surfaces, types of events, etc. For example, it is the relation *among* texture elements, often over time, which specifies many such properties: a density gradient of texture elements may specify depth, the displacement of some texture elements and the deletion of others may define a moving edge, and so on. Gibson asserts that the form of events is specified by "formless invariants"—the specific nature of the optical or acoustic energy supporting a relation is not important. So, for example, he might describe the events in Fig. 1 as two examples of a nonreversible "wiping" transformation, defined by a complex spatiotemporal relation between the displacement of one set of texture units (the rectangle or semicircle) and the disappearance or breakage of texture units "underneath" them. Painting and dusting are examples of this class of transformations. Clearly the identity of the materials involved (circles, squares, patterned wallpaper, dust) is not the critical factor.

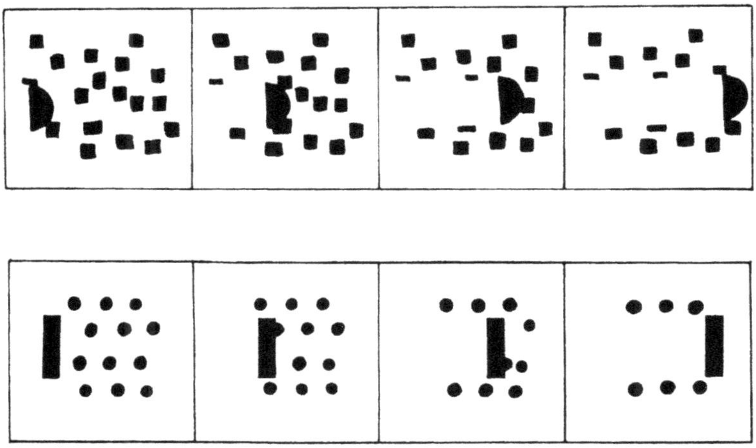

FIG. 1

The approach taken by Michotte and Gibson represents an attack on the immanent formism which has dominated theories of perception: the world we perceive is *not* built up out of "concrete" bits of substance, but is composed of relations in which elements are embedded. There is a striking resemblance between their arguments in the domain of perception and the arguments made above against concepts of sentence meaning in the domain of linguistic semantics. The perceived quality of an event, like the meaning of a sentence, cannot be defined solely by the properties of its constituent elements.

In addition to its immanent formism, there was a second problem with the traditional view of language: the idea that the information in sentences could be defined in isolation from a particular reader or hearer. The analogous problem in perception is whether there is an objective means of defining the physical basis for our percepts.

The Gestaltists, with their fondness for illusions and nonveridical perceptions, tended to minimize the role of physical information in determining our percepts. Gibson has been wary of their approach, because of its subjective quality and because it abandons too quickly the effort to find a level of physical description at which perception is veridical. Thus, he has recently proposed the development of an "ecological physics" which would substitute abstract relations among physical variables for the simpler variables of traditional psychophysics. These relations would characterize the basis for our perceptions of environmental "affordances" such as graspable, impenetrable, "walk-on-able," slippery, etc. (cf. Gibson, Chapter 3, this volume). A critical problem is whether this move to an ecological description of physical information can be accomplished *without* reference to any particular organism or class of organisms. What might it mean, for example, to assert that the information is "available" for detection, but that other factors determine whether it is actually "picked up" by an organism? Such an approach sounds dangerously similar to Katz's view that the linguist describes available semantic information, while the psychologist studies our actual interpretation of it.

There are several reasons why the notion of information available "in isolation" cannot be rigidly adhered to, any more than in semantic theory:

1. The physical structure of a class of organisms plays an implicit role in defining what is walk-on-able, swim-through-able, dangle-from-able. What is graspable by a monkey is not necessarily graspable by a rhinoceros. The information available to two eyes with overlapping visual fields (e.g., disparity) is not available when these is no overlap.
2. The affordance of a physical object, considered in isolation, is ambiguous to a single species as well. For example, a culvert under a road could afford a cat a tunnel to escape through, a dark place to hide, or an opening through which to watch something beyond. The momentary motivational state of the cat actualizes a particular affordance; potential affordances can only be defined with reference to such potential organismic states.
3. The information available to an organism (in a pragmatic sense) will depend on its maturational level and the degree to which it has learned to attend to various relations (cf. E. J. Gibson, 1969). A basketball affords different things to a child and an adult, and a painting affords different things to an art historian and a novice.
4. An organism's *activity* is critical in determining what it experiences. Moving around a motionless object defines it in a way that a single glance cannot. Orienting toward an event behind us, bringing it up close to increase resolution, backing off from it to foveate all at once, manipulating it in our hands, etc.: all of these involve adjusting to the constraints on our perceptual systems in order to pick up information which would otherwise be unavailable.

Not all of these arguments have a *direct* bearing on the question of defining perceptual information in isolation; some of the arguments involve the *processes* by which organisms apprehend structure (actualize a potential affordance). The reason for detailing them is not to deny the importance of a physical level of support for perception, or the importance of defining that support in terms of higher-order relations. Rather it is to argue against the specific claim that there is an organism-*independent* level of description which will be of any use to a psychologist. An event's "affordance" (like a sentence's "meaning") is intrinsically a psychological relation. The capacities, motivational state, training, and activity of the perceiving individual are essential variables in determining the nature of that relation. What we experience is the product of our perceptual skills and the physical energies in which we are immersed.

FIGURAL THOUGHTS AND FIGURATIVE SYMBOLS

By this point, it is clear that there are some striking resemblances between apprehending events through language and by direct perception. Two important ones are these: (a) apprehending events is not a function of the specificities of elementary forms, but of the abstract relation in which those forms are embedded; and (b) the apprehended meaning of an event cannot be defined in terms of the properties (even abstract ones) of the composition considered in isolation, but is a psychological relation between an active, knowing agent and the physical compositions it encounters.

But there is also a striking dissimilarity between these two modes of cognition. The physical composition of an utterance has almost no direct relation to the physical composition of the events it may be intended to describe. The relation is essentially arbitrary, or "symbolic." On the other hand, abstract relations are *directly* specified when we attend to them with our perceptual systems, that is, the relations are directly and "naturally" instantiated in the relationship holding between the observer and the physical composition. Direct perception does not require an arbitrary translation step to get from the physics of an event to our perception of it. (This is the essence of Gibson's, 1966, 1971, arguments against the need to speak of "cues" and "inference" in perception, and "conventions" in pictorial perception.)

However, a rigid dichotomy between arbitrary and direct specification is difficult to maintain. One problem is that there are intermediate cases. The sequences in Fig. 1 only specify a dynamic event if one understands the conventions of comic strips and interprets the layout accordingly. A similar spatial translation of time is found in a piano score, where the order of notes in successive lines represents an unbroken continuity in time. Similarly, maps, diagrams, and blueprints directly specify certain spatial relations, but their interpretation *also* demands some conventional assignments of what is a gravel road, an electrical wire, or a water pipe. Some writers argue for a continuum between the conventional and the direct, with written language or mathematical notation at one extreme and natural events at the other (e.g., Hanson, 1970), while others maintain the traditional distinction between "symbols" and "sign." It is not at all clear what difference it would make whether a particular act of comprehension involved a mixture of two *types* of specification, or a mixture of different values along a continuum.

Jenkins, Jiménez-Pabón, Shaw, and Sefer (1974) have recently elaborated the distinction between "symbolic" (arbitrary) and "figural" (direct) modes of cognition in developing a model for aphasia. However, their scission of cognition into two modes is only partial. They argue that our understandings and intentions vis-à-vis the world are abstract with respect to *either* mode of expression, and that what the aphasic has lost is the ability to apprehend and express propositions by *symbolic* means. The aphasic has *not* lost the ability to perceive events or communicate intentions by figural means. The case of the composer Ravel provides a striking example (Alajouanine, 1948; Bogen, 1969). Ravel became aphasic at the height of his career and lost not only his capacity for speech, but his ability to read and write musical notation as well. However, he was still able to sing, play a tune by ear, and *compose*. Thus his "musical thinking" was intact—what he had lost was his ability to interpret arbitrary specifications of musical relations.

The analogy between sentences and musical scores introduced earlier in the chapter now takes on more substance. First, it suggests that there may be an *identity* between an abstract relation as specified by physical energy (for example, a melody as a dynamic pattern of acoustic energy) and as specified by symbolic forms (for example, a melody on a musical score). Moreover, the figural specification (the sound pattern) seems to be the basis for the abstract relation. When we interpret a score we translate from the arbitrary figural properties of the printed page into the figural patterns of sound (whether we play on a piano or our vocal cords). This is reminiscent of Russell's claim that our "knowledge by description" is based on our "knowledge by acquaintance" (cf. Jenkins *et al.*, 1974). Understanding of music as an acoustic pattern must be a prerequisite to learning to use musical notation successfully. As Ravel's case indicates, understanding of musical relations can continue to function in the absence of notational skills, but it is difficult to conceive of the opposite being true.

A second possibility raised by the sentence-musical score analogy is that one can speak of "figural thinking" which operates not in symbolic terms, but in the medium of the abstract relations of direct perception and action. (Recall that Ravel could not think in notational terms, but could think creatively (compose) in the medium of musical relations.) These processes of figural thought can be placed under the control of a symbolic specification (as in sight reading music or listening to a story), but hardly depend on it for their existence. Finally, these figural processes may be the same ones involved in our imaginative elaborations on what we see and hear.[2]

These possibilities have some fascinating implications for the understanding of

[2] Throughout this chapter the term "inference" has been used fairly loosely. The reason for this can now be summarized. It may be that many of our novel expectations and insights are the product of *figural* thought. Thus it is not necessary to assume that all novel but appropriate cognitions are the product of symbolic propositions. Inferential activities in other animals (e.g., chimpanzees, Köhler, 1931; rats, Tolman, 1932) may be viewed as examples of a kind of figural thinking which is basic to human cognition as well. (Cf. Arnheim, 1969; Bogen, 1969; Gibson, 1971.) Finally, the inclusion of figural thinking may make it possible to ascribe much of what appears "inferential" to the direct perception of structure at a higher level.

metaphoric sentences, and for the "perceptual" bases of sentence comprehension in general.

ANALOGIES AND THE IMAGINATION

Consider the following analogy:

(10) An empty prison cell is like a Venus flytrap, waiting for its next victim to enter.

The sentence asserts a resemblance between two things, but what *is* the resemblance and what *are* the two things? Clearly the fragments "an empty prison cell" and "a Venus flytrap, waiting for its next victim to enter" share little in terms of their physical composition. There are no words in common, nor are there any words (besides "a" and "an") which might even be construed as synonyms. At the grammatical level we note that each is a noun phrase, but that only reflects the very abstract fact that we are comparing two things or events. If we consider the two objects, a prison cell and a Venus flytrap, again there is little physical resemblance to be found. A clue is provided by the final clause: "waiting for its next victim to enter." This leads us to elaborate an event given what we know about the behavior of a Venus flytrap when something "enters" it: if a fly happens to land inside, the plant will quickly close to trap the fly, and then begin slowly to consume it.

At this point we will still be frustrated if we search for common elements, because the addition of a hapless fly to the flytrap does not make it resemble a prison cell (in terms of superficial form) any more than it did before. But the entry of the fly does bring a dynamic relation to our attention: the flytrap is a cavity which can shut to form an enclosure. Now we have our first resemblance: a prison cell is also a cavity which may be sealed by shutting and locking the door. The fly's activity makes a second dynamic relation available: the closure of the cavity follows the entry of a smaller object. Again our knowledge of prisons allows us to complete the resemblance on the other side: a new prisoner passes through the open door of a cell and is locked inside. If we wish to go on we can seek even further resemblances. Consider the fly's fate, which we might abstractly call an example of progressive destruction of integrity. With little effort we can instantiate this dynamic relation in the case of the prisoner: his health, or personality, or "spirit" may deteriorate over time. In general, what we are doing is creating a more and more elaborate event beyond the tiny fragment "a prison cell," a process guided interactively by our understanding of both prisons and Venus flytraps.

Several aspects of this process of discovering resemblances are worth making explicit.

First, note that the resemblances have nothing directly to do with the shape of the words, their associations and synonyms, the grammatical structure of the sentence, or the objects explicitly referred to.[3] The resemblances are *abstract* relations (mainly dynamic ones) shared by two complex events. That is, the resemblances are essentially figural—they could potentially be specified by a worldly event as easily as by the events we imagine at the bidding of the sentence. For example, anyone who has mastered the conventions for scanning comic strips will perceive in each sequence of Fig. 2 most of the dynamic relations we discovered in Sentence (10). A movie would project these relations even more naturally and directly. Best of all, of course, would be watching a flytrap as it snares a victim.

Without a description of abstract relations based in figural pattern perception, one would be hard put to explain the resemblance between Sentence (10) and Fig. 2, or between Sentences (10) and (11):

(11) An enemy fortress is like the open mouth of a killer whale, when a fish accidentally swims in.

Clearly the mode of specification is not critical, nor are the elements which manifest the relation, in themselves, important. If we searched for the common elements of prison cells, circles, Venus flytraps, fortresses, semicircles, and killer whales, our cognitive cupboards would surely be bare.

Second, note that the analogy in Sentence (10) guided our attention to certain characteristics of an empty prison cell by comparing it to an event in which those characteristics were fairly salient. Compare our understanding of "an empty prison cell" in Sentence (10) with what we understand from another analogy involving the same topic:

(12) An empty prison cell is like seeing a room through Venetian blinds.

When we seek an interpretation for this sentence, the resemblance we discover will be something like "a small enclosure seen (by someone) through a striped pattern which alternately allows and obstructs vision." In this case we have embedded the prison cell in quite a different event than the first time. In effect, Sentence (12) asks us to imagine someone (preferably *ourselves*) standing outside a prison cell and looking in through the bars.

But consider what this imaginative act entails. Not only are we "attending" to a very different kind of relation in this case, but we are "orienting" in ways that remind us of an organism's activity in an environment. Sentence (12) asks us to perform operations similar to those we perform when perceiving an event

[3]Thus, there are obvious limitations on the usefulness of approaches to metaphor based on word associates, word clusters, or implicit meaning-unit responses (e.g., Brown, Leiter, & Hildum, 1957; Koen, 1965; Osgood, Suci, & Tannenbaum, 1957), or approaches based on the contents of images (e.g., Paivio, 1971).

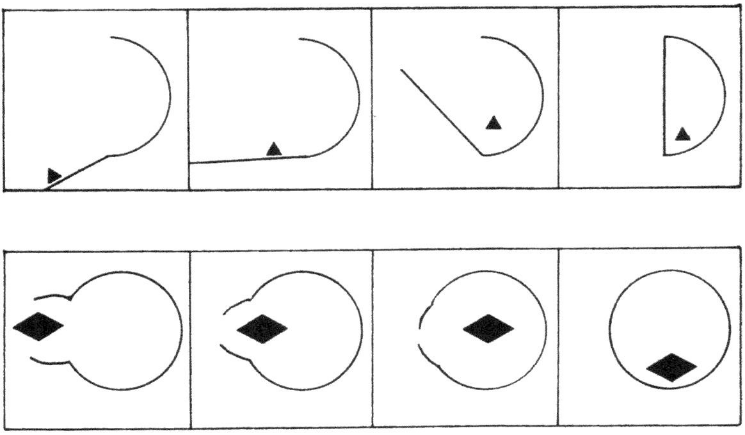

FIG. 2

directly: it asks us to adopt a station-point just outside a prison cell, to orient toward the cell, and to look into it, beyond the bars themselves. Thus, our orientation to the event is more critical to the sense of the metaphor than the orientation of the bars on an empty prison cell or the slats on Venetian blinds (in fact they are vertical in one case and horizontal in another). Recall that these activities of moving about the environment, orienting toward things, and looking are exactly what Gibson considers integral to normal perception. This implies that the basis in perception for the understanding of symbolic analogies may involve more than an identity of abstract, figurally-based relations (as so far defined). If perception is more than the passive apprehension of structure, then we can expect that analogies will also activate the relations underlying our actions in the world. Seeing anything in a room by looking through Venetian blinds requires that we be as close to the window imaginatively as we would have to be in real life. If this is true, we will need a broader conception of "figurally-based" relations which incorporates both our perceptual activity and the dynamics of events.

A third aspect of our comprehension of a sentence like (10) is that we fill in events which are only crudely or incompletely specified in the sentence. That the "victim" was a fly in one event and a prisoner in the other had to be supplied from our knowledge about the things that were specified. We also had to supply information about flytraps' behavior, prison cell doors, the fate of flies captured by flytraps, etc. Once a relation was perceived in one domain, it was like a mathematical equation which could be used to generate events in the second domain by supplying appropriate particulars for its variables. Where this was possible, we accepted the relations as part of the sense of the analogy. But if, for example, we sought an instantiation of horizontal stripes in the context of a prison cell, Sentence (12), we would probably fail and thus be forced to seek a sense for that analogy which was abstract with respect to orientation. Finally, note that the generation of elements in the second domain relied on the abstractness of our concepts. The process would be very awkward to explain by a common elements approach.

The processes of intermingling two domains are clearly related to the use of models and analogies in scientific theories. Hesse (1966), for example, describes "theoretical explanation as [a] metaphoric redescription of the domain of the explanandum" (that which is to be explained). In part, this amounts to using familiar relations in the domain of the vehicle to isolate and describe properties of the domain under investigation. As we have seen, the power of this approach is that once some part of the structure of the vehicle is seen to be shared by the events under study, we may fill out our understanding of the topic domain by imagining entities and generating predictions consistent with that structure. The relations supplied by the vehicle are indispensible in this process. Thus scientific theories are a form of "knowledge by description": creating and understanding scientific assertions depends on our "knowledge by acquaintance" and is therefore rooted in our understanding of figurally based relations. In fact, it is likely that most of what we learn through language is a result of analogic references to the relations made available by our earlier experience.

SOME EXPERIMENTS ON ANALOGIC SENTENCES

A recent series of studies by the author (Verbrugge, 1974) demonstrated many of these phenomena with sets of analogies in simile form. In some of the experiments, subjects heard either (a) a list of analogies which predicated a set of topics with one set of vehicles, e.g., Sentence (10), (b) a list of analogies predicating the same topics with different vehicles, e.g., Sentence (12), or (c) a list of the topics alone, e.g., "an empty prison cell." As in the Verbrugge and McCarrell (1973) study, subjects' recall for the sentences was prompted with a set of cues. In these experiments, however, the prompts were a second set of *analogies* (each specifying the same relations as a target sentence), rather than verbal descriptions of the shared relations. Both symbolic and figural analogies were used as prompts to explore whether subjects inferred relations which were abstract with respect to the mode of specification. For example, recall of Sentence (10) was prompted with either Sentence (11) (a symbolic analogy) or Fig. 2 (a figural analogy); both of these prompt analogies were designed to specify essentially the same relation as that specified by the acquisition sentence.

When subjects were given a set of the symbolic prompts in a paced prompted recall task, they were able to recall an average of 69% of the target sentences when the prompts specified relevant relations. This was close to the maximum degree of correct pairing to be expected under any conditions (82%, estimated by an unpaced matching task) and was significantly greater than the number of sentences subjects were able to produce in free recall (47%). The effectiveness of the symbolic analogies as prompts is remarkable, since there were no lexical, referential, or syntactic similarities to guide recall. The only available basis was the similarity of an abstract relation among the objects referred to in the sentences. In neither the acquisition sentences nor the prompt sentences was this relation made explicit; it was only available if subjects elaborated the topical domain (from a perspective suggested by the vehicle) and discovered the appropriate resemblance. This distinctive inferred relation was apparently more central to subjects' experience (and memory) of a sentence than the presence of distinctive "immanent forms": symbolic analogies which specified relevant relations were significantly better as prompts than distinctive content words chosen at random from each of the target sentences.

When subjects' recall was prompted with figural analogies, the effectiveness of the prompts varied depending on the subjects' task during acquisition. When subjects wrote verbal descriptions of the shared relations or simply listened to the sentences, prompted recall was relatively poor (38% and 30%, respectively). However, when subjects drew sketches of the relations (the kinds of patterns and events described in the sentences), they later recalled an average of 62% of the sentences. This is close to the number of sentences subjects were able to pair with the figural analogies in an unpaced matching task (69%). As with symbolic analogy prompts, the effectiveness of the figural analogies can only be ascribed to their specification of relevant relations *among* the objects depicted. Recall could not be ascribed to thinking directly of the original objects themselves, since subjects who viewed the figural analogies *without* having heard the acquisition sentences very seldom thought of the objects mentioned in the related sentences. For example, only 9% of subjects viewing Fig. 2 thought of Venus flytraps and 2% thought of prison cells.

The power of a vehicle in guiding the discovery or activation of relations was also demonstrated with both types of prompts. When subjects had heard irrelevant predications on a topic or just the topic alone, the prompts produced only about 10% recall even though they specified relations which were true of the topic.[4] For example, Sentence (11) and Fig. 2 were poor prompts for "a prison cell" when subjects' attention had been drawn to the (abstract) affordances of barred apertures by Sentence (12).

[4] In contrast to the Verbrugge and McCarrell (1973) study, prompted recall of the topics alone was not intermediate between recall of relevant and irrelevant sentences. The reason for this is probably that the grounds of the earlier study tended to be more salient as properties of the topics (considered in isolation) than the grounds in the analogies of the present study. Thus subjects in the earlier study would be more likely to think of the relevant relations during their acquisition experiences and (on average) be better prepared to recognize the relations in the related prompts.

Overall, figural specifications of relations were found to be as effective as symbolic specifications in prompting recall of abstractly similar events. The most parsimonious explanation is that the *same* relation can be specified by both modes, and that the prompting of recall need not be mediated exclusively by either mode. In particular, it is highly unlikely that the recall with either mode of prompts was mediated by verbal associates or shared linguistic features. In fact, articulating the ground of an analogy in a sketch (a figural activity) was superior to articulating it in words (a verbal or symbolic activity). (This superiority was found for free recall as well as for figural prompted recall.) If anything, the processes which mediate recall seem to have a more natural affinity with the *figural* mode. It is difficult to avoid the conclusion that the comprehension of analogic sentences involves imagining events in a medium of abstract, figurally-based relations.

Support for this conclusion was found in a set of experiments on "mixed-mode analogies," that is, analogies with *verbal* topics and *figural* predicates. For example, subjects saw the topic "an empty prison cell is like . . ." displayed on a projection screen, followed by a short animated cartoon of a schematic event like one of those in Fig. 2. The expectation guiding these experiments was the following: if it is true that the verbal predicates of analogic sentences guide attention to certain figurally-based resemblances, then figural predicates should be at least as effective in guiding attention to the relevant relations. This expectation was confirmed; in fact the relevant symbolic and figural analogy prompts were *more* effective in producing recall of the topics than they had been when subjects listened to analogic sentences (74% with symbolic prompts, 89% with figural prompts). The figural predicates probably focus subjects' attention more sharply on the relations specified by the prompts, while the symbolic predicates tend to be less constraining. However, the difference between the two modes of predication was minor compared to the difference between relevant and irrelevant predications. Irrelevant prompts produced recall of only 14% of mixed-mode analogies' topics. Thus figural predicates can affect a comprehender's access to certain relations as powerfully as symbolic predicates. The perception of resemblances seems to be independent of the particular mode of instantiation as well as of the particular objects supporting the shared relation.

METAPHOR: THE QUICK AND THE DEAD

How does the vehicle exert its influence on our understanding of a topic? In the research just reported this influence was unmistakable, but the design did not allow a test of *how* subjects inferred or abstracted the shared relations. The process might be thought of in terms of one of two perceptual metaphors: either as a back-and-forth scanning of two juxtaposed events, or as a kind of fusion of the two domains into a single event. Though this suggestion is certainly speculative, the distinction has considerable intuitive appeal and has many analogues in literary criticism and the philosophy of science.[5]

The first approach is that assumed in the earlier analysis of sentence (10): the events are elaborated separately and a relation found in one is sought in the other. It is a process similar to looking back and forth at two pictures or cartoon sequences set side by side (e.g., Figs. 1 and 2), scanning for resemblances. This is the kind of thinking encouraged by similes, especially those which are essentially equalities between two events requiring no further elaboration; for example,

(13) A snowflake is like an asterisk.

Since juxtaposition leaves the topic uncontaminated by the vehicle, such analogies are best fitted to the Aristotelian view that metaphor merely decorates meaning.

The second approach is more difficult to describe, but is probably more important. It involves a fusion of both events, and thus a transformation or warping of each domain according to the particular constraints of the other. In the case of Sentence (10), for example, we may imagine the prison cell transformed into the shape of a Venus flytrap, but on its side, since a prison door opens that way. The cell may have an animate quality to it: it is "waiting"; you can almost hear its mouth watering. (This suggests there is a second vehicle beyond the first: a hostile animal, like a wolf–in fact the Venus flytrap is a fascinating plant because it is so "animate.") A fly enters the cell in the guise of a prisoner, the door folds shut, and the prisoner-fly begins to dissolve on the floor.

This interpretation is exaggerated and bizarre, but it is not an uncommon kind of thing to do, especially in response to metaphors which assert an *identity* between two things. For example, the sentence

(14) Skyscrapers are the giraffes of a city.

asserts that skyscrapers *are* giraffes; in fact, the response of many people to it is to visualize a huge giraffe in the middle of a city skyline, its neck extending far above the "other" buildings. What this process seems to entail is that each domain is operated on in parallel, and the more they are found to share the more they will fuse. Metaphors in which little is shared (especially mixed metaphors) are likely to lead to awkward and motley fusions.

It is not immediately obvious which of these processes is intrinsically more powerful in guiding our perception of resemblances. Fusion seems to involve a more imaginative transformation than simple juxtaposition, yet it can also

[5] For example, Coleridge made a distinction between Fancy, "a power of assembly or collocation, involving simply the mechanical noting of resemblances," and Imagination, "a unifying 'esemplastic' power" (Hawkes, 1972, p. 47).

produce bizarre and distracting hybrids. The juxtaposition view seems most compatible with those philosophers of science who view an analogy as a kind of temporary instrument, discovered in an unaccountable flash of insight, exploited for its use in generating and testing hypotheses, and then discarded when the theory has been formalized in its own right. The acceptance of a theory, and the discovery of facts which confirm or disconfirm it, are public processes in which private metaphors and fantasies play no part. If Rutherford prefers to visualize atoms as tiny red billiard balls, it may be of anecdotal interest, but it is irrelevant to the symbolic equations which represent the nature of particle interactions.

An alternative view, closely related to the fusion process, is that the vehicle is integrally related to the origin, understanding, use, and acceptance of a scientific theory. People who have defended this view have labelled the domain of the vehicle in various ways: a "root metaphor" (Pepper, 1942), a "paradigm" (Kuhn, 1970), a "metaphoric redescription" (Hesse, 1966), a "world view," and so on. The approach is inevitably "perspectivistic." Facts are an illusion fostered by the positivists and immanent formists. Our understanding of an event is guided by our prevailing metaphor. Like the prison cell, the domain we wish to understand is *transformed* according to the properties of the metaphoric vehicle. Thus the perspectivist claims that a symbolic formalization of a theory never exhausts its meaning–symbols only take on meaning and explanatory power when *interpreted* (by a someone). In fact, a long debate has raged in the philosophy of science over whether different theories with common formalizations are equivalent and whether the "surplus meaning" associated with formal entities in theories can be excluded when the theories are evaluated (e.g., Carnap, 1956; Hanson, 1966; MacCorquodale & Meehl, 1948).

In part, this debate involves the question of whether a word or theory maintains its power of specification when its metaphoric basis is no longer active. Metaphors may be ignored, may die, may fade away. For example, we now speak of "chair legs" without activating the original metaphoric domain (people's legs), but the metaphor was very much alive to the Victorians who insisted that, in all modesty, chair legs ought to be covered by "skirts" which extended to the floor. When a metaphor is alive, it is rich with potential for novel inferences. When it has died, the old vehicle is left with only a narrow power of specification (as in the case of chairs' legs), or it becomes altogether meaningless in the present context (as in the case of "phlogiston" or "animal spirits"). As Pepper (1942) writes:

> Concepts which have lost contact with their root metaphors are empty abstractions. When a world theory grows old and stiff . . . , men begin to take its categories and subcategories for granted and presently forget where in fact these come from, and assume that these have some intrinsic and ultimate cosmic value in themselves [p. 113].

Thus the fate of metaphor in a general language community must be the same in a scientific community as well. Due to excessive formalization or to a paradigm shift, the metaphoric domain of a theory may no longer be activated by its users.

The relations previously discovered may continue to generate research, but without the transforming potential of the vehicle, they ossify and cannot in themselves be productive of *new* understanding. A formalization, in itself, is lifeless–like the words in a sentence or the notes in a piano score. It cannot encapsulate meaning. A theory requires interpretation, and thus is open to *changes* in interpretation.

All too often the formalist attitude leads us to believe that theories may be made completely explicit, or that the meanings of terms may be publicly codified into dictionaries. In the growth of a science, of a community, or of a person, metaphoric understanding is a dynamic process, which makes continual access to prior, figurally based experience. It is a fallacy to think that a symbolic description can capture the essence of this understanding. And if understanding is a process of change, then it is no more helpful to consider meaning as a closed system of standard senses than it is to look at a single snapshot of a dynamic event:

> A dictionary is a frozen pantomime. Our problem is only beginning when we consider the pale flowers of the 'nosegay of faded metaphors' that it presses between its pages. A semantic theory must account for the *process* of metaphorical invention–all the more so, a theory that stems from generative grammar with its emphasis on creativity . . . It is characteristic of natural language that no word is ever limited to its enumerable senses, but carries within it the qualification of 'something like' [Bolinger, 1965, p. 567].

To date, psychology has devoted little attention to analogical processes, perhaps out of a feeling that they are "deviant" or "subjective." This is more than unfortunate: there may be no more important human skill than perceiving the "something like" through language.

ACKNOWLEDGMENTS

Preparation of this paper was supported in part by grants to the University of Minnesota, Center for Research in Human Learning, from the National Science Foundation (GB-3570X), the National Institute of Child Health and Human Development (HD-01136), and the Graduate School of the University of Minnesota. The author would like to thank John Bransford, James Jenkins, Robert Shaw, and Gary Stahl for their helpful comments and criticism during the preparation of the paper.

The author is currently an Assistant Professor at the University of Connecticut. Correspondence should be addressed c/o Department of Psychology, University of Connecticut, Storrs, Connecticut, 06268.

REFERENCES

Alajouanine, T. Aphasia and artistic realization. *Brain,* 1948, **71**, 229–241.

Arnheim, R. *Visual thinking.* Berkeley: University of California Press, 1969.

Austin, J. L. *How to do things with words.* Cambridge, Massachusetts: Harvard University Press, 1962.

Bogen, J. E. The other side of the brain II: An appositional mind. *Bulletin of the Los Angeles Neurological Societies,* 1969, **34**, 135–162.

Bolinger, D. The atomization of meaning. *Language,* 1965, **41**, 555–573.

Bransford, J. D., & McCarrell, N. S. A sketch of a cognitive approach to comprehension: Some thoughts about understanding what it means to comprehend. In W. B. Weimer & D. S. Palermo (Eds.), *Cognition and the symbolic processes.* Hillsdale, New Jersey: Lawrence Erlbaum Assoc., 1974.

Brown, R. W., Leiter, R. A., & Hildum, D. C. Metaphors from music criticism. *Journal of Abnormal and Social Psychology,* 1957, **54**, 347–352.

Carnap, R. The methodological character of theoretical concepts. In H. Feigl & M. Scriven (Eds.), *Minnesota studies in the philosophy of science.* Vol. 1. Minneapolis: University of Minnesota Press, 1956.

Cassirer, E. *Substance and function.* New York: Dover Publications, 1923.

Chomsky, N. *Syntactic structures.* The Hague: Mouton, 1957.

Chomsky, N. *Aspects of the theory of syntax.* Cambridge, Massachusetts: MIT Press, 1965.

Gibson, E. J. *Principles of perceptual learning and development.* New York: Appleton-Century-Crofts, 1969.

Gibson, J. J. *The perception of the visual world.* Boston: Houghton Mifflin, 1950.

Gibson, J. J. *The senses considered as perceptual systems.* Boston: Houghton Mifflin, 1966.

Gibson, J. J. The information available in pictures. *Leonardo,* 1971, **4**, 27–35.

Gordon, D., & Lakoff, G. Conversational postulates. In *Papers from the 7th Regional Meeting,* Chicago Linguistic Society, 1971.

Hanson, N. R. Equivalence: The paradox of theoretical analysis. In P. K. Feyerabend & G. Maxwell (Eds.), *Mind, matter, and method: Essays in philosophy and science in honor of Herbert Feigl.* Minneapolis: University of Minnesota Press, 1966.

Hanson, N. R. A picture theory of theory meaning. In R. G. Colodny (Ed.), *The nature and function of scientific theories.* Pittsburgh: University of Pittsburgh Press, 1970.

Hawkes, T. *Metaphor.* London: Methuen, 1972.

Hesse, M. B. *Models and analogies in science.* South Bend, Indiana: University of Notre Dame Press, 1966.

Jenkins, J. J., Jiménez-Pabón, E., Shaw, R. E., & Sefer, J. W. *Schuell's Aphasia in adults.* (2nd ed.) New York: Harper & Row, 1974.

Katz, J. J. *The underlying reality of language and its philosophical import.* New York: Harper & Row, 1971.

Katz, J. J. *Semantic theory.* New York: Harper & Row, 1972.

Katz, J. J., & Fodor, J. A. The structure of a semantic theory. *Language,* 1963, **39**, 170–210.

Koen, F. An intraverbal explication of the nature of metaphor. *Journal of Verbal Learning and Verbal Behavior,* 1965, **4**, 129–133.

Köhler, W. *The mentality of apes.* New York: Harcourt Brace, 1931.

Kuhn, T. S. *The structure of scientific revolutions.* (2nd ed.) Chicago: University of Chicago Press, 1970.

Lakoff, R. Language in context. *Language,* 1972, **48**, 907–927.

MacCorquodale, K., & Meehl, P. E. On a distinction between hypothetical constructs and intervening variables. *Psychological Review,* 1948, **55**, 95–107.

Mack, D. Metaphorical ambiguities. In D. L. F. Nilson (Ed.), *Meaning: A common ground of linguistics and literature.* Proceedings of a conference in honor of Norman C. Stageberg, University of Northern Iowa, Cedar Falls, April, 1973.

Michotte, A. The perception of causality. London: Methuen, 1963.

Osgood, C. E., Suci, G., & Tannenbaum, P. *The measurement of meaning.* Urbana, Illinois: University of Illinois Press, 1957.

Paivio, A. *Imagery and verbal processes.* New York: Holt, Rinehart, & Winston, 1971.
Pepper, S. C. *World hypotheses.* Berkeley: University of California Press, 1942.
Searle, J. R. *Speech acts: An essay in the philosophy of language.* Cambridge, England: Cambridge University Press, 1969.
Shaw, R. E. & Wilson, B. E. Abstract conceptual knowledge: How we know what we know. In D. Klahr (Ed.), *Cognition and instruction.* Hillsdale, New Jersey: Lawrence Erlbaum Assoc., 1976.
Slobin, D. I. *Psycholinguistics.* Glenview, Illinois: Scott, Foresman, 1971.
Steinmann, M. Figurative language and the two-code hypothesis. In R. W. Fasold & R. W. Shuy (Eds.), *Analyzing variation in language.* Washington, D. C.: Georgetown University Press, 1975.
Studdert-Kennedy, M. The perception of speech. In T. A. Sebeok (Ed.), *Current trends in linguistics.* The Hague: Mouton, 1974.
Thompson, E. *On growth and form.* (2nd ed.) Cambridge, England: Cambridge University Press, 1942. 2 vols.
Tolman, E. C. *Purposive behavior in animals and men.* New York: Century Co., 1932.
Verbrugge, R. R. The comprehension of analogy. Unpublished doctoral dissertation, University of Minnesota, 1974.
Verbrugge, R. R., & McCarrell, N. S. The role of inference in the comprehension of metaphor. Paper presented at the meeting of the Midwestern Psychological Association, Chicago, May 1973.
Wittgenstein, L. *The blue book.* Oxford: Basil Blackwell & Mott, 1958.

SECTION B
Accessing Knowledge

14

How to Catch a Zebra in Semantic Memory

Elizabeth F. Loftus

University of Washington

When Class D baseball was in the midst of its waning days, the team from Fulton, Tennessee rather suddenly changed its nickname from Railroaders to Lookouts. It wasn't that anybody was particularly unhappy with the name Railroaders. What happened is that the uniforms of the Fulton team were rapidly fraying at the seams, and the slightly more affluent "Lookouts" from Chattanooga graciously gave away some of their used uniforms. Since "Lookouts" was lettered on the hand-me-downs, the owners of the Fulton team either had to change the lettering or change the team name. It was apparently easier to change the name of the team. The fact that the "Lookouts" were named after the famous mountain overlooking Chattanooga, while the city of Fulton looked out upon an absolutely flat area, was something that the owners of the Fulton team saw fit to completely ignore.

Clearly names are arbitrary things. If I and a few friends decide to call "milk" by some other name, we can do so, and we do not change the quality of the object to which we refer. In fact, we might actually move to France and call it "du lait" or move to Spain and call it "leche"; either way we are still referring to that "opaque white fluid secreted by female mammals for nourishment of their young (Fowler & Fowler, 1964). Attributes, on the other hand, are not arbitrary. Milk is white, no matter what we call it. If we try to change its color by, say, adding chocolate syrup, we now have "chocolate milk." We have changed the quality of the object. Both the names and the attributes of objects that we know are stored in semantic memory. In this chapter, I will argue that the retrieval of these two types of information involve different strategies. Before presenting this argument, and a resultant model for semantic memory retrieval, a brief discussion of some "history" is appropriate.

SEMANTIC MEMORY: SOME RECENT RESEARCH

Although the area of semantic memory has been the focus of a great deal of recent research activity, it is still far too early to provide exact details about the mechanism by which we retrieve semantic information. One earlier effort was aimed at determining the extent to which the retrieval mechanism involves successive as opposed to simultaneous consultation of the memory store. The successive-simultaneous distinction was thought to be a basic distinction with many important consequences: one of them concerns the effect of size of the array to be searched on searching time. To the extent that the retrieval process involves successive consultation of the memory store, retrieval time should be a function of the number of items in the array to be searched. Conversely, to the extent that simultaneous consultation (or "parallel processing") is involved, retrieval time should be relatively unaffected by the number of items in the array.

In an attempt to shed light on this issue, a number of experiments were performed in which array or category size was a major independent variable. Many experiments shows that it takes longer to decide that a word is a member of a large category than to decide it is a member of a small category (Atkinson & Juola, 1971; Landaver & Freedman, 1968; Juola, Fischler, Wood, & Atkinson, 1971; Meyer, 1970; Tzeng, 1972; Wilkins, 1971) but some did not (Rips, Shoben, & Smith, 1973; Smith, Haviland, Buckley, & Sack, 1972). Even when an effect of category size was observed, a strictly sequential processing model was not usually proposed. Landauer and Freedman (1968) concluded that the reaction time (RT) differences observed for scanning large versus small categories was too small to be interpreted as evidence for the existence of a successive scanning process. Landauer and Meyer (1972) proposed a "category-search" model, but made no specific assumptions about the order or manner of search, that is, whether it was serial or not. Tzeng's (1972) retrieval mechanism incorporates both parallel and successive processes–successive draws and parallel scanning within the items of each draw. Collins and Quillian (1969) proposed a complex network model.

Freedman and Loftus (1971) departed from the previous work that had studied identification time and instead measured the speed with which a subject could actually produce a word himself. Instead of giving the subject a stimulus and asking him to decide whether it was a member of a category, he was given a category and asked to produce a word that belonged in it. For example, a subject who was asked to name a *fruit* beginning with the letter *P* might say *peach, pear,* or *plum,* among other possibilities. Because category size had no effect on RT, a sequential scanning process seemed unlikely, and instead a hierarchical network model, fashioned after that of Collins & Quillian (1969), was proposed. Since that time, other network models of human memory have appeared (Anderson, 1972; Crothers, 1970; Rumelhart, Lindsay, & Norman, 1972) indicating the popularity of the approach. In network models, human memory is conceived as a giant network of interconnected nodes. The nodes usually correspond to individual concepts, ideas, or events in the system. The links or connections between the nodes specify particular relations that hold between the concepts. To illustrate, the system might have the concepts DOG and ANIMAL which would be represented as distinct nodes with a connection between them specifying that a DOG is a member of or a subset of ANIMAL.

In the next three sections, I will discuss (1) the original model proposed by Freedman & Loftus (1971), (2) some evidence for the model and some problems with it, and (3) the modifications of the model which resulted in a new model–the Dictionary–Network Model.

THE FREEDMAN–LOFTUS MODEL

No serious investigator of human memory believes that retrieval involves a sequential scan through the entire contents of memory. As Tomkins (1970, p. 63) has noted, such a mechanism would result in a 50-year old man requiring somewhere on the order of 400 years to answer the question "What is your name?" Similarily the process of finding a particular category member does not appear to involve a strictly sequential scan. If the retrieval process does not involve successive scanning, of what does it consist? The original model proposed by Freedman and Loftus (1971) assumed a *hierarchical* organization, meaning a system that is divided into a number of interconnected subsystems, each of the latter being hierarchical itself. Specifically, the basic conception was that of a memory store organized into a complex hierarchy composed of categories (e.g., animals) with subsets of each (e.g., birds, dogs) and supersets (e.g., living things). Within each category, a variety of subsets exist. Some are noun categories that are specialized members of the larger set (e.g., birds and dogs are subsets of animals). Some are clusters of words that are highly associated for any of a number of reasons. They may have qualities in common (e.g., all begin with the letter "S" or all have long names or all rhyme). They may be associated with each other in the individual's experience (e.g., all be animals in the Pooh books). These clusters are probably more idiosyncratic than the main noun categories, but are somewhat consistent across individuals. And finally, under each category is an undifferentiated enumeration of exemplars. Within all subsets, clusters, and enumerations, the instances will be listed in a more or less constant order, according to their frequency in the language or dominance in the category.

How does a person retrieve a category member; for example, how does he find a "yellow fruit"? Freedman and Loftus assumed that the process involved two major steps: (1) entering the appropriate category–"fruits" and (2) finding an appropriate member of that category–"lemon" (plus, of course, the time required to produce that response verbally). Thus, the subject first enters the category "fruits," then he enters a cluster of yellow fruits, and reads out the first entry. If instead he was looking for a fruit beginning with P, the category "fruits" would be entered directly, the subset "fruits beginning with P" would be found, and the first entry read out. In both cases, retrieval consists of finding a main set and a subset, rather than serially searching through an array of instances. The Freedman and Loftus (1971) reaction time experiment is not only consistent with the general model, including the assumption that the memory store is organized primarily into noun categories, but it also provides an estimate of the duration of the first step of the retireval process.

Every stimulus pair (e.g., fruit–yellow, fruit–P) was presented with the noun category either first or second with a short interval between the noun and restrictor. When the noun comes second, the total retrieval process begins only after its presentation. When the noun comes first, the first step of the process (category entry) can be begun before the second half of the pair is presented. Since reaction times are measured from the presentation of the second half of the pair, any difference due to order can be assumed to be caused by that part of the process that is completed before the second half is shown. Thus, the difference between noun first and noun second is an indication of the existence of step one and of its duration. The evidence is as follows: when nouns are presented first, the mean reaction time is 1.87 sec; with nouns second, it is 2.12 sec. This difference of .25 is quite stable across somewhat different conditions, supporting the idea that step 1 consists of entering the noun category, and suggesting that the duration of Step 1 is approximately .25 sec.

To summarize, Freedman and Loftus presented a hierarchical storage model, and proposed that retrieval from semantic memory consists of two distinct steps (entering the appropriate category, and then finding an appropriate member of that category). The general model is consistent with the lack of relationship between category size and RT, and is given some support by the difference in RTs when the noun is presented first and second. That difference of .25 sec also serves as an indication of the duration of Step 1 of the retrieval process.

THE FREEDMAN LOFTUS MODEL: THE CASE FOR AND AGAINST

Support for the Model

Evidence on various aspects of the model can be found in several recent publications. For example, Loftus (1972) provides evidence that the semantic memory store is organized primarily into noun categories. In her experiment, 200 subjects were presented with 20 nouns and 20 adjectives. If the stimulus word was a noun category, subjects were told to write any item that belonged in that category (e.g., seafood–oyster, clam, fish). For adjectives, the subjects were told to write any item which had the inherent quality of that adjective (hard–

brick, rock, wood, etc.). The mean number of responses given to noun stimuli was greater than the mean number of responses given to adjective stimuli. More detailed analyses of the response protocols indicated that when the stimulus was a noun almost all of the subjects' responses were instances of that noun category. There was some tendency to group together category members which have qualities in common. For example, Sweden, Norway, and Finland (all Scandinavian countries) often occurred together in the response protocols for "country." It appears that within many categories, a variety of subsets often exist—subsets whose members are highly associated perhaps as a result of the fact that they have these qualities in common. In contrast, when the stimulus was an adjective, subjects tended to name a number of items from one noun category, shift to another category and name a number of items from that noun category, shift to another category and name a number of items from that category, shift again, and so on. An actual sample protocol for the stimulus "small" best illustrates this point: "Fly, bee, ant, eye, ear, toe, finger, grape, cherry, strawberry." The subject named three insects, four body parts, and three fruits. Apparently the reason the subjects name fewer items in the case of adjectives is that they used time shifting from one category to another. In the case of nouns, any "shifting" which may occur is confined within the main noun category itself.

There exist additional empirical and theoretical arguments for noun priority. For instance, Marshall and Newcombe (1966) observed a dyslexic patient who had great difficulty reading verbs, adjectives, and prepositions, but could read nouns quite well. Miller's (1969) data is also relevant. He asked judges to sort words on the basis of similarity of meaning. Results indicated that judges sorted first on the basis of part of speech (nouns with nouns, verbs with verbs, etc.), then within each syntactic category they proceeded to sort on some other basis. Nouns were sorted on the basis of their class terms (for example, knight and mother are both persons). The real point of interest if that people put verbs together, not on the basis of their meanings, but on the basis of nouns that could be used with them. Adjectives, too were frequently classified on the basis of the nouns they could modify. At a theoretical level, the work of Chomsky (1965) also suggests some priority for nouns. When substituting words into phrase markers, nouns are selected independently and verbs are selected in terms of those nouns. Chomsky shows that serious complications in grammar would arise were one to first insert verbs by means of context-free rules, and then select nouns in terms of the verbs.

All of this evidence suggests strongly that nouns have some sort of priority, that they are somewhat more accessible than other types of lexical items. The assumption that the semantic memory store is organized primarily into noun categories therefore seems reasonable. Having made the assumption, other types of memory phenomena fall into place. Category clustering is a case in point. If a person is asked to recall a list of instances of various categories such as "dog, turnip, horse, carrot . . . " in any order he wishes, his recall will be clustered by categories. The order "dog, horse, turnip, carrot . . . " would quite probably be observed (Bousfield, 1953). If a subject first entered an area of memory which contained a particular category, then searched the category for recently observed items, then switched to another category, etc., clustering is exactly what would be expected.

Without going into great detail, it is worth noting that other aspects of the model have been empirically supported. Loftus, Freedman, and Loftus (1970) have provided additional evidence that each category in the hierarchy can be entered directly, whereas Loftus and Freedman (1972) further support the notion that the retrieval process consists of category entry as the first major step.

Problems with the Model

Despite the supporting evidence, there are several difficulties with the model. First, the notion that so many clusters exist—that every category contains separate clusters for each letter— seems implausible. It is true that when asked to name fruits beginning with the letter P, the subjects have little difficulty in rapidly producing many correct responses. That is, they generally do not say "peach," pause and then say "pear," pause and then say "plum." Further, the typical pattern we have found in informal testing is a spurt of several responses, perhaps followed by a pause and then several more responses, etc. While this might suggest that these words are clustered in some sort of functional relationship, there are other examples where this "clustering" or rapid responding does not occur. Subjects who are asked, for example, to name articles of furniture that begin with the letter C do typically say "chair," pause and then say "chest," pause and then say "couch."

A second reason for modifying the model was alluded to in the opening paragraphs of this chapter regarding the distinction between names and attributes. The model, as it stands, assumes that the process of retrieving an "edible bird" is functionally equivalent to the process of retrieving a "bird beginning with the letter C." To find an edible bird, according to the model, the category "birds" is entered, the subset "edible birds" is entered, and the first entry is read out. Analogously, to find a bird beginning with the letter C, "birds" is again entered, the subset "birds beginning with C" is entered and the first entry is read out. In both cases retrieval consists of finding a main set and a subset. Nowhere in the model is a distinction made between a stimulus which restricts the type of object (the bird must be edible) and a stimulus which restricts the name of the object (the bird's name must begin with the letter C). "Edible" is an attribute of some birds "beginning with the letter C" is a characteristic of the names of some birds. Searching for an attribute may not involve the same process as searching for a name. For years philosophers have emphasized the distinction between attributes and names (see for example, Quine, 1960), and more recently pilot data collected in our laboratory suggest that different strategies are involved in the search for an attribute versus the search for a name.

The pilot data in question resulted from an experiment in which subjects were shown a noun category paired with either an adjective or a letter, and asked to produce a word that fit the restrictions imposed by the two. In one condition adjective and letter trials were randomly intermixed (the "mixed" condition); this condition serves as a replication of Freedman & Loftus (1971). There were also two "blocked" conditions. In one, subjects saw only noun categories paired with adjectives (i.e., only adjective trials), while in the other blocked condition subjects saw only noun categories paired with letters (that is, only letter trials).

We found that the time to respond on an adjective trial was independent of whether the subject knew he would be seeing an adjective, that is, the RT on adjective trials was equal in mixed and blocked conditions. However, a subject's responses on letter trials were dramatically affected by his expectations; he responded significantly faster in the blocked than in the mixed condition.

Without making additional assumptions, the original model has difficulty handling these results. In addition, the results argue strongly for the point we have been making: There is a difference between an adjective and a letter trial, between a question which restricts the type of object and one which restricts the name of the object. Two types of strategies appear to be possible: The strategy for adjective trials is not influenced by advance warning that an adjective is coming, whereas the strategy for letter trials is so influenced. Clearly, a model of retrieval should reflect these differences.

THE DICTIONARY–NETWORK MODEL

We shall consider here a new model which has a somewhat changed conception of the memory structure and an elaborated conception of the retrieval mechanism. The new model incorporates the fact that when a word is stored in semantic memory, at least three kinds of information about that word are included: semantic, phonemic, and orthographic information. This is a desirable feature since we know that subjects use these three kinds of information in attempting to search their semantic memories to find a particular word (Brown & McNeill, 1966).

The major structural change includes the addition of a "dictionary," which is simply a listing of the lexical items of the language (see Fig. 1.) As to the question of what constitutes a lexical item, we realize that it could be a word, a morpheme, an idiom, or some other unit, but we do not attempt to decide that issue here. As to the question of whether the listing is ordered (it could be ordered alphabetically, or according to frequency of usage, or age of acquisition

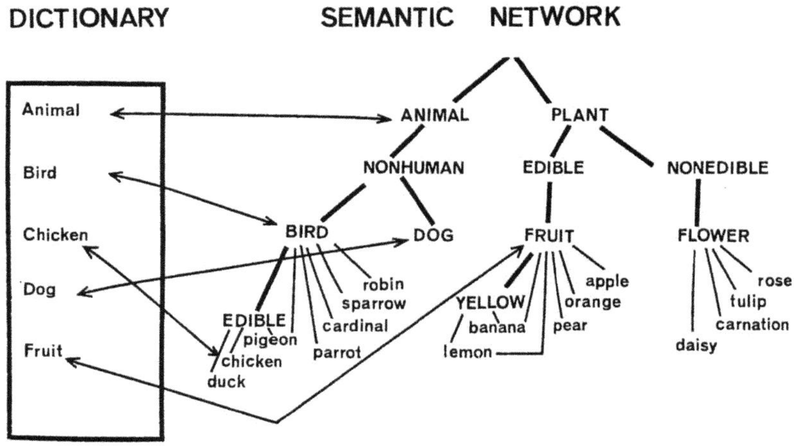

FIG. 1. The dictionary network model.

or in some other way) we do not attempt to decide that issue here. This dictionary is of a very special kind: it includes both phonemic and orthographic information about each of its entries,[1] and in addition, each entry serves as an address telling where semantic information can be found. Thus, the system is content addressible; each entry provides direct access to the portion of semantic memory that represents the meaning of that entry. Our assumptions about the organization of semantic information are similar to our earlier formulations. We retain the notion of a hierarchical organization composed of categories (e.g., animals) with subsets of each (e.g., birds, dogs) and supersets (e.g., living things). We retain the idea that within each category there are clusters of items that have qualities in common (e.g., large animals, yellow birds). We no longer assume the existence of clusters of items that have phonemic attributes in common (e.g., all animals beginning with the letter B). Information about the sounds and spelling of items is contained in the phonetic–orthographic dictionary.

To illustrate, the word *animal* might receive an entry in the dictionary as diagrammed schematically in Fig. 1. Since the dictionary itself contains phonemic and orthographic information about the word *animal*, we can use this information to answer questions like "what letter does the word *animal* begin with?" or "How is the last syllable of the word *animal* pronounced?" To answer a question about the meaning of a word, it is necessary to consult that part of the semantic store which contains this information. Figure 1 presents a fragment

[1] To accompany a dictionary, one additional component is needed, namely a set of rules for governing its use. These rules would allow us to know what is likely to be listed in the dictionary and what is not. For the moment we will not be concerned with these rules, since in our experiments all inputs are "allowable."

of a hierarchy that might be encountered as part of someone's semantic memory structure. We can use the information in the semantic network to answer questions like "Is a bird an animal?" or "What is the name of an edible bird?"

Using this as a general model, we can begin to describe how a subject manages to find an answer to the kinds of questions he is asked in our experiments. How does he find (1) a category member to which a particular adjective is applicable (e.g., edible birds); and (2) a category member beginning with a particular letter (e.g., an animal beginning with "D").

Consider case (1) in which the subject must name an edible bird. We now assume that the retreival process has at least three major steps. In keeping with our earlier view, the first step consists of entering the appropriate category (e.g., "birds.") The next step consists of finding an appropriate cluster of items and picking a member of it. Once this member is found, the third step involves looking up the "name" of the item by reentering the dictionary via a pathway from that member to its name. Thus, the subject finds that the edible bird he has picked is called a "chicken." At first glance, the notion that one could find a member without knowing the "name" of that member may seem awkward. But, on second glance, there is no reason why a particular type of category member, or any other concept for that matter, must necessarily have available a single "name" for it. Clearly there can be concepts without names. For example, one can comprehend the concept of a "navigational instrument used in measuring angular distances, especially the altitude of sun, moon, and stars at sea," without the name "sextant" being accessible (Brown & McNeill, 1966). One can surely comprehend the meaning of "damp, soft snow" without being a Laplander and having a single name for it. The Dictionary-Network Model is a reasonable system that allows access of conceptual meaning via the lexical entry in the dictionary as well as permitting use of the meaning as a direct guide to the lexical entry.[2]

Consider Case 2 in which a subject must name an animal beginning with the letter D. Again, the subject begins by entering the "animal" category, which is accomplished by looking up "animal" in the dictionary, and going directly to the portion of memory that contains information of the meaning of "animal." The next step is somewhat different for questions of this type. Here we assume that the subject systematically proceeds along pathways leading from animal instances to the dictionary representations of the names of those instances. This

[2] This view is in agreement with Broadbent (1971). He argues that words do more than simply stand for the objects they represent. They function to "select certain stored information [p. 469]." If a word simply stood for the object it represented, a paradox would result; a sentence such as "Richard Nixon is President of the United States" is informative, yet the two names in it both refer to the same entity. Broadbent argues that the sentence should be viewed as a transfer of information in memory between two previously labeled regions of memory.

quasiparallel simultaneous search proceeds towards the dictionary from all possible members (though a less dominant member may start off more slowly or slightly later). The dictionary is used to determine whether a given animal instance is one that begins with the letter D, and the search terminates when one is found.

THE CASE FOR THE DICTIONARY–NETWORK MODEL

Now that we have outlined a general model for the structure of semantic memory and have outlined a specific process model, we tie the general scheme to some experimental data. Since the attribute versus name distinction is central to the dictionary–network model, the experiments described are concerned with further exploration of the difference between searching for an attribute and searching for a name.

The "Adjective versus Letter" Experiment

Grober and Loftus (1974) completed an experiment that was similar in many respects to the pilot study discussed earlier. Subjects were shown nouns paired with adjectives or letters which were presented in blocked and mixed conditions. In the mixed condition, adjective trials (MA) and letter trials (ML) were randomly mixed together. In the blocked condition, subjects saw only adjective trials (BA) or only letter trials (BL). Across subjects, specific noun–letter and noun–adjective stimuli occurred equally often in the mixed and blocked conditions. Thus, for example, half of the subjects saw "Fruit–P" in a mixed condition and half saw it in a blocked condition. Every subject received all four conditions and the order of the conditions was counterbalanced across subjects. An important addition to this experiment involved the inclusion of an interval between the presentation of the noun and restrictor: on half the trials the interval was short (.5 sec) while on the remaing trials it was long (2.5 sec). Reaction time was measured from the onset of the restrictor.

Our predictions in terms of the Dictionary–Network Model are as follows: on adjective trials, the first step of the process is to enter the category. The next step involves finding the appropriate cluster to enter, and cannot begin until the subject knows what cluster he is to enter. The subject must wait until the adjective is presented before he can begin this next step. Knowing that an adjective is coming, or having a long interval of time, should be of no help; therefore, there should be no effect of blocking or of interval duration.

A different situation is assumed for letter trials. Here, the first step of the process is entering the category. The next step is a quasi-parallel simultaneous search towards the Dictionary. That is, the subject traces some number of pathways leading from category instances to the Dictionary representations of those instances. This step can be started during the interval between the presentation of the category name and the restricting letter *if* the subject knows a letter is coming; BL trials should therefore be faster than ML trials. Furthermore, if more searches can be completed (i.e., paths can be traced) in a longer interval of time, then having a long interval should help on BL trials.

First consider the results shown in Fig. 2, which illustrates reaction time in mixed and blocked conditions for adjective and letter trials. The most important finding was the significant interaction between the type of trial and whether it occurred in a mixed or a blocked condition. As predicted, a subject's response time is fastest if he knows a letter is forthcoming.

To assess the effects of interval duration, we looked at mixed and blocked trials separately. For mixed trials, interval duration had no effect. This replicated the lack of effect reported by Freedman and Loftus (1971). For blocked trials, however, interval duration had a dramatic effect: RTs for letter trials presented with a long interval were considerably faster than those in any of the other conditions.

An alternative interpretation of these data is possible. Perhaps on blocks of trials involving letter cues, the subject simply sets his mouth to say a word

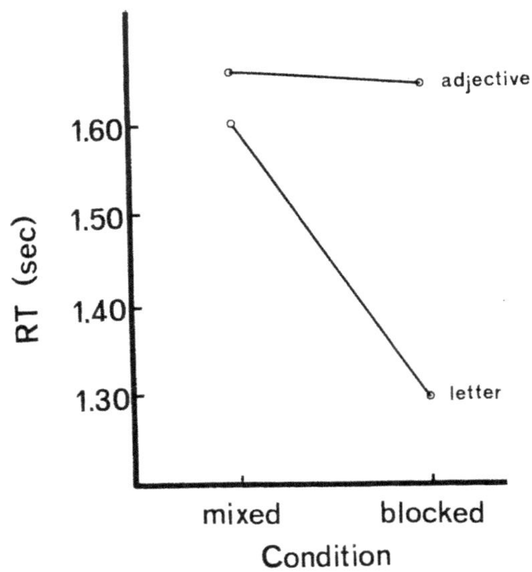

FIG. 2. Reaction time for noun–adjective and noun–letter stimuli in mixed and blocked conditions.

beginning with the cued letter before (or even simultaneously with) the search through memory for an appropriate category member. Having one's mouth set might speed RT by reducing the response execution component. For adjective trials, a subject could not use such a response set strategy, and for mixed letter trials he might not. To settle this issue, ten subjects participated in an experiment identical to the "adjective versus letter" experiment except for the fact that no interval occurred between presentation of noun and restrictor. If the alternative interpresentation is correct, the advantage of the BL condition should remain since a subject should still be able to set his mouth to say a word beginning with the letter while he is searching for a member. The results indicated, however, that without an interval the advantage of the BL condition disappeared.

The "Adjective plus Letter" Experiment

In this experiment subjects were presented with stimuli consisting of a noun category plus an adjective and a letter (e.g., animal–small–M) and had to produce a member of the category that satisfied the two restrictions. That is, the response had had to be a member of the category that began with the given letter and to which the adjective was applicable (e.g., "mouse" for the above example.). The subjects saw the category first, but the order in which the adjective and letter restrictors were presented was varied: on half the trials the adjective came .5 sec. before the letter (e.g., animal–small–M), while on the remaining trials the letter came first (e.g., animal–M–small). Reaction time was taken from the onset of the last restrictor.

The model predicts that a subject should be faster when the adjective is presented first. The reasoning is as follows: In either case, the first step of the process is to enter the noun category. When the adjective appears first, the subject can then enter an appropriate cluster of items. At this point he systematically proceeds along pathways leading from instances that are within that cluster to the dictionary representations of the names of those instances. The dictionary is used to determine whether any of the instances begin with the appropriate letter, and the search terminates when one is found. As before, this quasiparallel simultaneous search can be started during the interval before the restricting letter appears, since the subject knows a letter is coming.

When the letter appears first, however, the picture is somewhat complicated. The subject may do one of two things. First, after entering the category, he may begin to trace pathways towards the dictionary attempting to find a member that begins with the given letter. Once he finds the member, he must go back to the semantic network to see if the adjective applies to it. This strategy requires an extra "trip" between the dictionary and the network. Alternatively, to save the trouble of this extra trip, the subject might simply wait until the adjective arrives, essentially converting a "letter–adjective" trial into an "adjective–letter" trial. Either way the prediction is a slower RT when the letter appears first.[3]

We might mention that our prediction for the "adjective plus letter" experiment is not obvious: other quite reasonable models would not make this prediction. For example, one type of set-theoretic model assumes that once a category is entered, its members are sequentially searched in a relatively fixed order and that the search is terminated when an appropriate instance is located (e.g., Heider, 1973). To the extent that retrieval involves such a successive consultation of the memory store, the speed of retrieval should not be a function of the order of presentation of adjective and letter. If each instance is successively examined to see if it meets both specifications, and the search terminates when such an instance is found, there is no reason to expect that presentation order will affect retrieval time.

A slightly different serial model assumes that subjects enter a subcategory defined by the category name and the first restrictor, and begin searching in a fixed order for an instance which satisfies the second restrictions. This model would predict that RT is faster when the letter is presented first. The reasoning is as follows: when the letter is presented first, a very small subcategory is usually defined, and finding an instance that fits the adjective restrictor should be a very easy matter. For example, if given animal–M–small, searching the category "animals beginning with M" should result in rapid production of a small animal beginning with M since roughly half of the members of that subcategory could conceivably (depending on the subject's criterion) be considered small. When the adjective is presented first, the subcategory defined by the noun and the adjective is searched to find an instance that fits the letter restrictor. Since the standard of acceptability is much higher now (the instance must begin with a particular letter), the expected length of search for an instance meeting this standard is longer. In other words, a serial search for an instance meeting the letter restriction would involve consultation of many more items.

The results of the above-mentioned study are shown in Fig. 3, and are in accord with the predictions from the dictionary–network model: when the adjective comes first, the average reaction time is 1.00 sec, whereas when the adjective comes second, it is 1.45 sec.

[3]One could argue that the reason that "adjective–letter" trials would be faster than "letter–adjective" trials is because in the former case you have to read only one letter, while in the latter case you have to read an entire word. (Recall that RT was taken from the onset of the second restrictor). In answer to this argument, I report some data on the reading response to printed letters and words. In an experiment by Cattell (reported in Woodworth & Schlosberg, 1954, p. 57), the subjects were shown letters and words and responded by reading them aloud. Cattell obtained the following average reaction times from his two trained subjects: reading single letters, 409 msec; short words, 388 msec; long words, 431 msec.

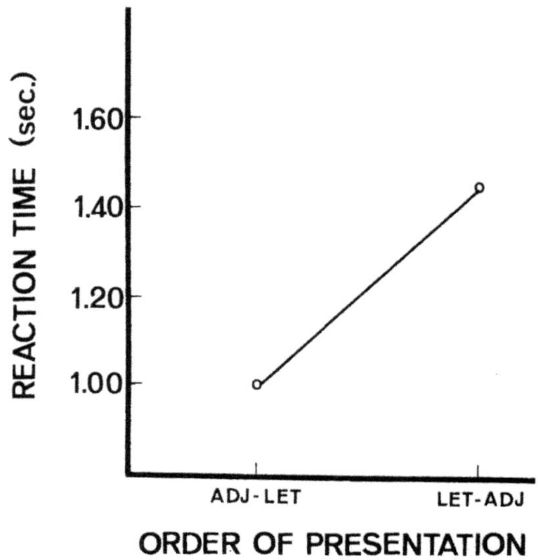

FIG. 3. Reaction time as a function of order of presentation of adjective and letter restrictors.

Differential Organization in Output: A Demonstration

One observable consequence of the Dictionary–Network Model concerns the number and organizations of words that a subject produces in a given amount of time under various conditions. If we present a subject with an adjective (such as "small") and ask him to write down as many items as he can that have the inherent quality of the adjective, his output is organized with regard to semantic properties (Loftus 1972). When given a letter stimulus, however, and asked to name words that begin with that letter, subjects should do something very different: they should be able to produce more items, and these items should not necessarily be organized with regard to semantic properties. The reasons for these expectations are as follows. When given a letter, the subject enters the dictionary at the proper phonetic region, generates an item, tests to see if the item is a word, and then outputs the word. The semantic network need not enter into the process. When given an adjective, however, the subject must, in addition, make use of the semantic network to test whether the particular item at hand does, in fact, have the quality of the adjective. Thus, when presented with an adjective, fewer items should be produced when the amount of time given is limited.

The experiment that tested this prediction was quite straightforward. Subjects were given a notebook with a stimulus written on the top of each page. They were told that if the stimulus was an adjective, they should write down as many items as they can that have the quality of the adjective. If the stimulus was a letter, they were to write down words beginning with that letter. They were given one minute to respond to each stimulus.

The average number of words produced given an adjective was 9, whereas given a letter, subjects produced over 14 items. The output given an adjective stimulus was more often than not organized according to semantic properties (as described by Loftus, 1972); the output after a letter stimulus was not so organized. To illustrate, when asked to produce words beginning with the letter G, one subject began by writing "glue, glib, glide, gloat, gleam. . . ." This protocol is typical of what is observed: organization is clearly orthographic or phonemic, but not, in general, semantic.

As a point of interest, we also observed the "S versus Z" effect: in the course of one minute, subjects produced about 16 words beginning with S, whereas they produced only 6 words beginning with Z. To explain this effect is relatively easy: suppose that the process of naming words beginning with any letter involves (1) entering the dictionary, (2) generating an item, and (3) testing to see if the item is a word. Words are then output while nonwords are rejected. The reason more S words than Z words are produced hinges on the fact that there simply are more words beginning with S than words beginning with Z. (Count the S and Z pages in a regular dictionary or the number of Ss and Zs in a Scrabble game for quick proof.) Since less phonetic variety exists for Z words, it is likely that, while generating items beginning with Z, more nonwords are generated. These must be rejected, and each rejection, of course, takes time.

THE FUTURE

The theoretical ideas the experimental studies being conducted in the area of semantic memory can be of tremendous benefit to education. For example, we will have a much better idea of what and how to teach to the extent that we can characterize the memory structures people build and the retrieval mechanisms people use.

A second benefit to education is that the techniques being used to determine the structure and retrieval of well learned information can be applied to information that is in the process of being learned. One attempt to do this (Loftus & Loftus, 1974) began in a situation in which natural learning of categories was taking place. The situation was a graduate school in psychology where students were learning, among other things, the names of psychologists. They learn that any given psychologist may be associated with one or more subfields of psychology (perception, memory, social, etc.), which is tantamount to learning to categorize psychologists with respect to these areas. A question of interest is whether different structures and retrieval strategies might be evident in people who are in different stages of graduate school. Will the retrieval strategies of the advanced student show any similarity to the retrieval of well learned information such as animals, fruits, etc.?

To answer this question, an experiment was designed which asked graduate students to produce the names of psychologists. On any given trial, the psychologist named had to satisfy two restrictions: both (1) an area of psychology and (2) a letter of the alphabet were shown (e.g., "Learning–B") and the subject had to produce the name of a psychologist that began with the given letter and who was associated in the subject's mind with the given area. For example, a subject who was presented with the stimulus "Learning–B" might say "Bower," "Bourne," or "Blodgett," among other possibilities. On half the trials, a subject saw the area first (e.g., "Learning–B") while on the remaining trials he saw the letter first (e.g., "B–Learning"). Reaction time was taken from the onset of the last restrictor. As may be clear without further mention, this "area plus letter" experiment is extremely similar to the "adjective plus letter" experiment in which subjects had to name, for example, an animal that was small beginning with M. In the latter experiment, RT was much faster when the adjective preceded the letter. If memory for psychologists is as efficient, one might expect the same advantage in RT to obtain when the area precedes the letter.

The results, shown in Fig. 4, indicate that advanced students were faster when the area was presented first, while the beginning students favored the condition in which the letter occurred first. This finding makes a great deal of sense when you consider what a student of psychology knows. The advanced student is aware that the "category" of psychologists is subdivided into areas such as learning and perception, just as his category of animals is subdivided. When given the area before the letter, this student can restrict himself to the area-defined subclass, and then search for a psychologist whose name begins with the particular letter requested. The beginning student, however, does not have psychology so well organized; the field is not yet neatly subdivided. This student knows a few important names; he probably knows Freud, Skinner, Piaget, and possibly some others. When the letter is given before the area, the beginning student probably begins scanning his "list" for a name beginning with the particular letter requested, and then produces that name almost irrespective of which area is presented. If the student stretches it, Piaget and Skinner could both "fit" into quite a few different areas of psychology.

Regardless of the exact storage or the exact retrieval mechanisms that these two types of students are using, two things are clear: the retrieval patterns observed in the present study are related to how much instruction a person had completed, and (2) the more experience a student has had with the field of psychology, the more his retrieval of this information seems to mirror the retrieval of material that we know is well organized and learned. It is tempting to speculate that reaction time measures can be used to assess—in much more subtle

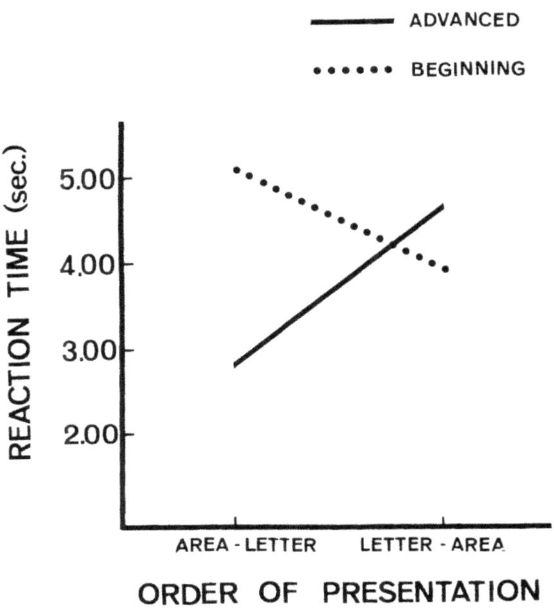

FIG. 4. Reaction time as a function of order of presentation of area and letter for beginning and advanced students.

ways than we now do—a student's progress in learning new material. Ultimately these measures will tell us a great deal about the process of acquiring new material.

CONCLUSION

In this Chapter I have presented some theoretical ideas and related empirical facts concerning semantic memory. A major theme has been the distinction between the name of an object and the attributes of that object. The theoretical ideas are embodied in a Dictionary-Network Model; the facts accounted for deal with a specific type of retrieval. While the Model is not the only possible explanation for the data, it has considerable value as a framework for (1) discussing particular semantic memory experiments and (2) viewing other kinds of memory phenomena—category clustering, word-classification findings, the TOT phenomenon, and cognitive acquisition, to name a few.

ACKNOWLEDGMENTS

This research and the preparation of the manuscript was supported by a grant from the National Institute of Mental Health.

REFERENCES

Anderson, J. R. Fran: A simulation model of free recall. In G. Bower & J. Spence (Eds.), *Psychology of learning and motivation.* New York: Academic Press, 1972.

Atkinson, R. C., & Juola, J. F. Factors influencing speed and accuracy of word recognition. Technical Report No. 77. Institute for Mathematical Studies in the Social Sciences. Stanford University, Stanford, California, 1971.

Bousfield, W. A. The occurrence of clustering in the recall of randomly arranged associates. *Journal of General Psychology,* 1953, **49**, 229–240.

Broadbent, D. E. *Decision and stress.* New York: Academic Press, 1971.

Brown, R., & McNeill, D. The "tip of the tongue" phenomenon. *Journal of Verbal Learning and Verbal Behavior,* 1966, **5**, 325–337.

Chomsky, N. A. *Aspects of the theory of syntax.* Cambridge, Massachusetts: MIT Press, 1965.

Collins, A. M., & Quillian, M. R. Retrieval time from semantic memory. *Journal of Verbal Learning and Verbal Behavior,* 1969, **8**, 240–247.

Crothers, E. J. The psycholinguistic structure of knowledge. In studies in Mathematical Psychology and Psycholinguistics. Technical Report, Quantitative Psychology, University of Colorado, Boulder, Nov. 1970, 1–93.

Fowler, H. W., & Fowler, F. G. (Eds.) *The Concise Oxford Dictionary.* London: Oxford University Press, 1964.

Freedman, J. L., & Loftus, E. F. Retrieval of words from long-term memory. *Journal of Verbal Learning and Verbal Behavior,* 1971, **10**, 107–115.

Grober, E. H., & Loftus, E. F. Semantic memory: searching for attributes versus searching for names. *Memory & Cognition,* 1974, **2**, 413–416.

Heider, E. R. On the internal structure of perceptual and semantic categories. In T. M. Moore (Ed.), *Cognitive development and the acquisition of language.* New York: Academic Press, 1973.

Juola, J. F., Fischler, I., Wood, C. T., & Atkinston, R. C. Recognition time for information stored in long-term memory. *Perception & Psychophysics,* 1971, **10**, 8–14.

Kintsch, W. Notes on the structure of semantic memory. In E. Tulving & W. Donaldson (Eds.), *Organization of memory.* New York: Academic Press, 1972.

Landauer, T. K., & Freedman, J. L. Information retrieval from long-term memory: category size and recognition time. *Journal of Verbal Learning and Verbal Behavior,* 1968, **7**, 291–295.

Landauer, T. K., & Meyer, D. E. Category size and semantic-memory retrieval. *Journal of Verbal Learning and Verbal Behavior,* 1972, **11**, 539–549.

Loftus, E. F. Nouns, Adjectives, and Semantic Memory. *Journal of Experimental Psychology,* 1972, **96**, 213–215.

Loftus, E. F., & Freedman, J. L. Effect of category-name frequency on the speed of naming an instance of the category. *Journal of Verbal Learning and Verbal Behavior,* 1972, **11**, 343–347.

Loftus, E. F., Freedman, J. L., & Loftus, G. R. Retrieval of words from subordinate categories in semantic hierarchies, *Psychonomic Science,* 1970, **21**, 235–236.

Loftus, E. F., & Loftus, G. R. Changes in memory structure and retrieval over the course of instruction, *Journal of Educational Psychology,* 1974, **66**, 315–318.

Marshall, J. C., & Newcombe, F. Syntactic and semantic error in paralexia. *Neuropsychologia,* 1966, **4**, 169–176.

Meyer, D. E. On the representation and retrieval of stored semantic information. *Cognitive Psychology,* 1970, **21**, 242–300.

Miller, G. A. A psychological method to investigate value concepts. *Journal of mathematical psychology,* 1969, **6**, 169–191.

Quine, W. V. *Word and object.* Cambridge, Massachusetts: MIT Press, 1960.
Rips, L., Shoben, E., & Smith, E. E. Semantic distance and the verification of semantic relations. *Journal of Verbal Learning and Verbal Behavior,* 1973, **12,** 1–20.
Rumelhart, D. E., Lindsay, P. H., & Norman, D. A. A process model of long-term memory. In E. Tulving & W. Donaldson (Eds.), *Organization of memory.* New York: Academic Press, 1972.
Smith, E. E., Haviland, S. E., Buckley, P. B., & Sack, M. Retrieval of artificial facts from long-term memory. *Journal of Verbal Learning and Verbal Behavior,* 1972, **11,** 583–593.
Tomkins, S. S. A theory of memory. In J. S. Antrobus (Ed.), *Cognition and affect.* New York: Little, Brown, & Company, 1970.
Tzeng, O. J. L. A triggering system for scanning processes in long-term memory. *Journal of Verbal Learning and Verbal Behavior,* 1972, **11,** 662–670.
Wilkins, A. J. Conjoint frequency, category size, and categorization time. *Journal of Verbal Learning and Verbal Behavior,* 1971, **10,** 383–385.
Woodworth, R. S., & Schlosberg, H. *Experimental Psychology.* New York: Holt, Rinehart, & Winston, 1954.

15

Remember That Old Theory of Memory? Well, Forget It![1]

James J. Jenkins

University of Minnesota

From the early 1950s till the early 1960s, Wallace Russell and I directed a project aimed at examining the role of language in behavior. While that project involved most of the staff of the psychology department at Minnesota at one time or another, and concerned itself with everything from clinical protocols to nonsense syllables, the long-term, persisting core of the project turned out to be the studies that Russell and I performed with word associations. Here we examined the effects of established associations on learning, recall, recognition, perception, and problem solving. Everywhere we looked we seemed to find powerful relationships. Then we proceeded to establish associations *de novo* and repeated these studies with materials constructed entirely in the laboratory so we could control the histories of the associations that we were dealing with. (An account of these studies is given in Jenkins, 1963, and Jenkins, 1970.)

Those were very exciting days for us. When the research program began, there was virtually no experimental evidence for mediation theory, although such theory was widely applied in the analysis of higher-mental processes (e.g., Osgood, 1953). By the time the program was over, mediational phenomena were well established, due in part to our efforts. When the program began, experimentalists (with a few exceptions like Cofer & Foley, 1942) regarded association norms as something belonging in the clinical domain. By the time the program was over, experimentalists were using norms for all kinds of materials as important ingredients in their investigations. But, on the other hand, when the research program began, we were hopeful that we could proceed directly from our experimental work to a general account of language itself. By the time the

[1] Presented as Presidential Address, Division 3, American Psychological Association, Montreal, 1973.

program was over, we were convinced that that particular journey was not possible.

So, in spite of the fact that the theory we espoused was gaining in popularity and in spite of the fact that we had produced a very large number of successful experiments (Russell and I had done about 120 studies and David S. Palermo and I had done about 40 or 50), we abandoned that line of research. The trouble was that we became convinced that the "higher mental processes" were not the kinds of things that we had originally believed them to be. In spite of the fact that we were moving rapidly, we were not going where we wanted to go.

As we struggled with this problem, I became convinced that I was caught in a metatheoretical trap, a trap that I had built for myself without ever realizing it. My friends and I were carrying about with us common sets of unexamined beliefs and attitudes that both directed and limited our research and theory in many ways. I will leave it to others to examine their own presuppositions; the following are the ones that I now see as dominant in my thinking in the 1950s.

1. *Units.* I believed that words were the fundamental units of language. To me this was natural and obvious.
2. *Relations.* I believed that there was one kind of relation between words, associative linkage. Words became linked to each other through use together or use in the same "frames."
3. *Structures.* I believed that mental structures (if there really were any such) were assemblies of links, essentially chains of the fundamental units in their fundamental relation. Hierarchies, like Hull's "habit family hierarchies," were simply lists of chains varying in strength, so that one was employed first, then another.
4. *Complex behaviors.* I believed that complex behaviors were built of simple subassemblies; that things got more complicated but not different "in kind." (This belief justified concern with simple units and relations and sanctioned experiments on such units in the faith that they would eventually add up to the complex behaviors of language.)
5. *Mechanistic explanation.* I believed that explanation ultimately rested on a description of the machinery that produced the behavior. I believed that a description of the machinery plus the history of the organism and its present circumstances inevitably predicted its behavior. There are two correlaries of this belief. First, I thought that the action of the machinery must necessarily be automatic. And, second, I could see that most of the interesting behaviors had to be explained by extensive reliance on learning and memory.

While these particular expressions of belief are probably unique to me, it is easy to see that they embrace the usual metatheoretical presuppositions that we identify with associationism. The associationist believes in some kind or kinds of basic units. (The number is not important.) He believes in some kind or kinds of relations between units. He holds that the more complex behaviors are the same "in kind" as simple behaviors. He believes that explanation consists of an explication of mechanism. He believes that behavior is automatic and for any kind of complex behavior, he relies on memory.

This view is so pervasive in American psychology that it is almost coextensive with being an experimentalist. Indeed, I think many of us confuse the dicta of associationism with the grounds of empirical science itself. But associationism is only one view; it is not a necessary view.

In this chapter, I would like to sketch for you an alternative position and present some experiments that convince me that there is exciting and productive work to do when we approach our field from another perspective. I will argue that this position alters the way we interpret phenomena, emphasizes the importance of natural problems and realistic methodology and changes what counts as an explanation.

The domain I have chosen is memory. Associationism is most dominant and clearly revealed in this area and, as I have pointed out, a general associationist account of almost anything leans heavily on memory.

In place of the traditional analysis, I suggest a contextualist approach. This means not only that the analysis of memory must deal with contextual variables but also that what memory is depends on context. This view clashes with the associative view but I hope that I can convince you that the contextual approach is closer to the truth in the simple sense that it is in better correspondence with experimental data than the usual associative theory.

A CONTEXTUALIST FORMULATION

The term contextualism is not highly familiar to American psychologists, but it is an American philosophical position that has been intimately intertwined with American psychology for three-quarters of a century.[2] Another name for it is *pragmatism* and it has its roots in William James, C. S. Peirce, and John Dewey. Unfortunately, to most of us the term *pragmatism* refers to only one aspect of the total philosophy, namely the use of practical criteria for judging "truth." That aspect is not the one I want to emphasize here, nor is it the aspect that bears most directly on conceptions of memory. Hence, I have chosen the less familiar, but more descriptive name, *contextualism.*

Contextualism holds that experience consists of *events.* Events have a *quality* as a whole. By quality is meant the total meaning of the event. The quality of

[2] For an introduction to contextualism and its contrast with mechanism the reader is referred to S. C. Pepper, *World Hypotheses,* Berkeley: University California Press, 1942. (Paperback, 1970.)

the event is the resultant of the interaction of the experiencer and the world, that is, the interaction of the organism and the physical relations that provide support for the experience. The relations can be thought of and analyzed into *textures.* A texture in turn consists of *strands* lying in a *context.*

Consider as an example of an *event,* a listener hearing a sentence. The total meaning of the sentence in that context is the quality of the event. We might note that the event persists in time over some period but that all of it at once forms a single, unified, psychological moment. This is the "specious present" of William James–the span of dimensionalized time is psychologically unified in experiencing the quality of the event. The textures that support the quality of the event are those of the hearer and those of the world. If our concern is with the qualities of the utterance, we can turn our attention to its *texture,* which consists of the words and grammatical relations between them in that context. Within that texture we can easily make out strands that make up the phrases. We can also see that some of the strands extend across the context of the phrases, that a word in one phrase depends on or determines a word elsewhere. We can become aware of the choices and presuppositions that the analyzed strands refer to. Some words and phrases can be shown to acquire their exact meaning in that event, from their relations to more far-flung aspects of the context; a gesture, a reference, a topic previously spoken of, an event known to both the speaker and the hearer to be in the future, presumed common knowledge and so on.

In this fashion, the analysis of the utterance will proceed far beyond the immediate physical context of the sentence and far beyond the physical stimuli immediately present. For the contextualist, no analysis is "the complete analysis." *All* analyses eventually "sheer away" from the event into more extensive contexts. This argues that there is no one analysis, no final set of units, no one set of relations, no claim to reducibility, in short, no single and unified account of anything. What makes an analysis good or bad for us is its appropriateness for our research and science and its utility in our pursuit of understanding and application.

This is a crucial difference between associationism and contextualism. Associationism asserts that there is some one correct and final analysis of any psychological event in terms of a set of basic units and their basic relations. When you have reduced an event to these terms, you are through; the job is done once and for all. The contextualist takes the much less comfortable position that a "complete" or "final" analysis is a myth; that analyses mean something only in terms of their utilities for some purposes. This means that being a psychologist is going to be much more difficult than we used to think it to be. And it means that the domain of experimentation and experimental methodology will have to be criticized more intently than we thought necessary before.

Before I can persuade you to join in these discomforts, I am sure that I must offer you something better than exhortations. Let us see if this view contributes to the generation and understanding of experiments.

EXPERIMENTAL EXAMPLES

I want to put before you three types of experiments that we have been performing in our laboratories at Minnesota in the last few years. I think each type illustrates some important aspect of the contextualist's position. The free recall studies that we will consider first, showed us the importance of "comprehension" in determining the quality of an event. The experiments on the recognition of events, that we will consider next, showed us the *un*importance of contiguity in time and taught us some novel things about the activity involved in the recognition of related and unrelated items. Finally, the studies of the integration of information, that we will consider last, brought both of these together and showed us that the subject's orientation toward comprehension changed the nature of what was remembered in such a way as to produce radical changes in recall and recognition.

Free Recall

The free recall experiments started innocently enough in pursuit of a simple question: If we could get subjects to attend to the meaning of words, would they show more associative clustering in recall than subjects who attended to other aspects of the words?

Associative clustering is an old phenomenon (Jenkins & Russell, 1952). If one presents stimuli and responses from a word association test in random order and asks subjects to recall the words, the subjects cluster the associates together in recall. For example, if the list of words contains *table, king,* and *salt* early in the list, and words like *chair, queen,* and *pepper* later in the list, the subjects will recall the words out of order; that is, they tend to recall *table* and *chair* together, *king* and *queen* together and *salt* and *pepper* together. In the late 1950s we assumed that this effect was an automatic consequence of associative strength, but in the 1960s we thought we had better take another look at it. Tom Hyde and I (Hyde & Jenkins, 1969) decided to see whether what the subject was doing when he heard the words had an effect on the recall phenomena.

For a task that would require *comprehension* of the stimulus words, we asked the subjects to rate whether the words were pleasant or unpleasant. For non-comprehension tasks we decided to focus the subjects on the *form* of the words; we asked them to indicate whether the words they heard would be spelled with an "e," or we asked them to estimate the number of letters in each word. We called these *formal* tasks. All subjects heard the same word list in the same order via tape recorder.

The results were very interesting. When subjects performed the task that required that they comprehend the words, their recall was excellent and they showed a high degree of associative clustering. They were as proficient in recall and clustering as a control group of intentional learners who performed no orienting task at all! On the other hand, the subjects who performed the formal tasks recalled only half as many words and showed little associative clustering. (As the literature suggests, whether the learning was incidental or intentional had no appreciable effect on recall for any of the groups doing orienting tasks.) It was impressively clear that the most important determiner of recall was the nature of the event the subjects experienced, when their task brought them into contact with the stimulus words. It suggests that subjects recall the quality of the events they have experienced, not stimuli to which they have been exposed. And in spite of the fact that we often think of comprehension as automatic for skilled readers and listeners (such as our subjects) a radical difference appears in recall between subjects who were required to comprehend the words and those who were not.

As contextualists we must say that the occurrence of the word on the audio tape is no quarantee of any particular experience for any auditor. The quality of his experience is determined by the interaction that he has with the physical texture presented. That texture can provide support for many different kinds of experience. In this simple case, the quality of the experience is governed largely by the task instructions that we have given the subject insofar as they affect his comprehension of the words.

But the associationist is not easily upset by this experiment. He draws our attention to explanations that do not have recourse to terms like *comprehension* and *quality of events.* And he objects that the phenomenon is limited. Let us look at some of these arguments and objections briefly.

"Maybe," say the critics, "the results are due to the number of units each group has to consider. The comprehension groups deal with words; the formal groups deal with letters. The formal groups are penalized because they have to think about a lot of units and the recall is in terms of the kinds of units the comprehension group is using." Fair enough. Let us change tasks and see if this possible explanation holds up.

Carroll Johnston and I (Johnston & Jenkins, 1971) selected *rhyming* as our formal orienting task, and we selected *appropriate modifiers* (giving adjectives for nouns and nouns for adjectives) for our comprehension orienting task. Thus, all subjects listened to words and wrote other words in response. The results duplicated the first experiment. The subjects doing the formal task (making rhymes) showed poor recall and little clustering. The subjects performing the task that required comprehension showed recall and clustering essentially like that of the intentional learning group which had no orienting task to perform. Exit the first counter hypothesis.

It was suggested that the effect relied entirely on the organization made possible by the associates in the list and that the tasks did not really affect recall of individual words. This notion was quickly refuted by running comparable experiments with both related and unrelated words (Hyde & Jenkins, 1973).

Tasks requiring comprehension resulted in twice as much recall as formal tasks that did not require comprehension, even including formal tasks like assigning part of speech to the words.

The third and fourth alternative explanations usually arose together—although they are contradictory. We call them the "time hypothesis" and the "effort hypothesis." The arguments are as follows:

1. *The time hypothesis:* The tasks requiring comprehension must be easy. The subjects do them rapidly and have the remaining time for rehearsal. The formal tasks take more time and, thus, these subjects have little opportunity to rehearse. The differences you find are due to differential opportunities for rehearsal.
2. *The effort hypothesis:* The comprehension tasks are difficult. These subjects must pay more attention and devote more effort to the task in "processing" words. Thus, they remember more readily. The formal tasks do not require much attention or effort and thus are not remembered.

David Walsh and I (Walsh & Jenkins, 1973) tackled these "mirror twin" hypotheses in an unorthodox kind of study that Walsh invented. Take a list of words. Determine their recall level with a good comprehension task. Determine the recall level with a formal task. Now, using the same time intervals for presentation, ask new subjects to do two tasks in the interval for each word. If the time hypothesis is correct, recall on any combination of tasks should be poorer than recall on either task alone. If the effort hypothesis is correct, recall on any combination of tasks should be better than recall on either task alone. However, if the quality of the experience is the important factor (as we supposed) then comprehension tasks should produce good recall whether they are performed alone or in combination with some other task. On the other hand, formal tasks should result in poor recall alone and in combination with each other. But when they are combined with a comprehension task, they should not detract from it.

This reasoning presents a nice experiment. If the time hypothesis is correct, all combinations of tasks will yield poor recall. If the effort hypothesis is correct, all combinations will result in improved recall. If the contextualist position is correct, those combinations containing a comprehension task will result in good recall and those combinations that involve only formal tasks will result in poor recall.

In an extensive series of experiments with many different kinds of formal tasks, the outcome was clearly in favor of the qualitative contextualist position. Both the time and the effort hypotheses were defeated. Comprehension tasks, alone or in combination with anything else, resulted in recall as good as that of an intentional learning group which performed no orienting task. Combinations of two formal tasks resulted in poor recall. (See Hyde, 1973, for an independent replication.)

The last candidate for an alternative explanation was related to the feeling that something about the experiment was artifactual. Perhaps, our colleagues suggested, the general "set" of the subjects was affected in some way by the comprehension instructions—that it was not the particular task or the fact that it required comprehension but, rather, that the subjects developed a different set which somehow affected the recall. Now, surely overall set has an important influence on the outcome of an experiment, but our particular analysis denied that the effects we were getting depended on such an overall orientation.

To investigate this problem, Robert Till and I (Till & Jenkins, 1973), following a suggestion from Endel Tulving, performed a series of experiments with a within-subject, within-list design. In this experiment each subject performed each kind of task. The subject heard each word followed by a letter, that is, Table—A. The word was the object of his attention as usual. The letter was a cue that told him which task to perform on that particular word. Some tasks required comprehension of the word and some did not. The technique permits the comparison of the recall of words that have been involved in comprehension tasks versus formal tasks for each subject during a single list presentation.

The results are reassuring with respect to the earlier analysis. Subjects recalled twice as many words from the subsets on which they performed comprehension tasks as they did from the subsets on which they performed formal tasks.

These experiments, and many others that we have performed, convince me that the best way to think of this experiment is in the contextualist's framework, taking the event to be the interaction of the subject with the individual word. The quality of this event is radically different in tasks requiring comprehension, from the quality of the event when comprehension is not required. These differences in quality are reflected in the radical differences observed in recall.

How could you further enhance recall of the word list? For the contextualist a reasonable move would be to develop a situation in which context was even more novel and the comprehension had to be developed in some special manner related to that context. Buford Wilson and John Bransford (personal communication), reasoning in just this fashion, created such an experiment. They asked one group of subjects to rate each word as "pleasant or unpleasant to you *if you were on a desert island.*" As they predicted, the recall of words by this group was even better than the recall by the usual "pleasant–unpleasant" rating group.

I must also point out before going on, that the analysis given here applies equally well to other tasks that we know will facilitate the free recall of single words: tasks such as asking subjects to form images, to rate words for vividness of imagery, to sort words into semantic categories, etc. If the task requires comprehension, the quality of the event is such that it is readily recalled.

EVENT RECOGNITION

Let us proceed to another type of experiment that I will call "event recognition" for want of a better name. What I want to illustrate here is that the phenomena we find in recognition depend on the quality of event that the subject constructs from the experimental material during the acquisition phase of the experiment. (In the free recall studies we kept the materials constant and showed the effects of varied tasks; here we will keep the tasks constant and show the effect of varying the materials.)

For our experimental example let us take the exciting and original work of John Bransford and Jeffery Franks on the abstraction of linguistic ideas (Bransford & Franks, 1971). For our purposes the seminal study they invented as graduate students can serve as the key illustration. The material in the study was a set of sentences. The subjects were asked to listen to the sentences, hold them in memory for a few seconds and answer an elliptical question about each one. Although there were no instructions about the nature of the sentences that were used in the experiment, it is apparent to even a casual listener (or reader) that the sentences fall into four interrelated groups. Each group of sentences consists of the "elements" of some overall event, taken one, two or three at a time in various sentence compositions.

A typical set of sentences that a subject might hear in such a study is given in Table 1. The reader who has never participated in such an experiment is invited to read each acquisition sentence, one at a time, count to five, answer the question, then go on to the next sentence, repeat the routine, etc. The reader should then take the recognition test. The best way to understand the experiment is to experience it.

After the acquisition set was read to the subjects, the recognition set of sentences was presented and the subjects were asked to judge whether they had heard each sentence before and to give a confidence rating to the judgment.

The results of the study are just the opposite of what one would expect from an "associative–link" model of memory. In general, the subjects are *certain* (with ratings between plus four and plus five on a scale of five) that they have heard the full, complex sentences that describe the four events. In fact, of course, they have not heard those sentences, nor have they even heard any sentences that long. As the sentences get shorter and shorter (down to "The cat jumped on the table" and "The girl lives next door") the subjects are less certain about whether they heard them or not, although they generally believe that they have.

Whether the sentence *actually* occurred or not in the acquisition set has very little influence on its rating as long as it is one of the *possible* sentences that describes the event. (In the recognition set given in the Table, no "old" sentence is presented, for example, yet subjects will estimate that from 5 to 80% of the sentences were presented earlier.) If, however, the sentences are mixed (for

TABLE 1
Sample Experiment by Bransford and Franks (1971)

Acquisition Sentences: Read each sentence, count to five, answer the question, go on to the next sentence.

The girl broke the window on the porch.	Broke what?
The tree in the front yard shaded the man who was smoking his pipe.	Where?
The hill was steep.	What was?
The cat, running from the barking dog, jumped on the table.	From what?
The tree was tall.	Was what?
The old car climbed the hill.	What did?
The cat running from the dog jumped on the table.	Where?
The girl who lives next door broke the window on the porch.	Lives where?
The car pulled the trailer.	Did what?
The scared cat was running from the barking dog.	What was?
The girl lives next door.	Who does?
The tree shaded the man who was smoking his pipe.	What did?
The scared cat jumped on the table.	What did?
The girl who lives next door broke the large window.	Broke what?
The man was smoking his pipe.	Who was?
The old car climbed the steep hill.	The what?
The large window was on the porch.	Where?
The tall tree was in the front yard.	What was?
The car pulling the trailer climbed the steep hill.	Did what?
The cat jumped on the table.	Where?
The tall tree in the front yard shaded the man.	Did what?
The car pulling the trailer climbed the hill.	Which car?
The dog was barking.	Was what?
The window was large.	What was?

STOP. Cover the preceding sentences.
Now read each sentence below and decide if it is a sentence from the list given above.

Test Set: How many are new?

The car climbed the hill.	(old ___, new ___)
The girl who lives next door broke the window.	(old ___, new ___)
The old man who was smoking his pipe climbed the steep hill.	(old ___, new ___)
The tree was in the front yard.	(old ___, new ___)
The scared cat, running from the barking dog, jumped on the table.	(old ___, new ___)
The window was on the porch.	(old ___, new ___)
The barking dog jumped on the old car in the front yard.	(old ___, new ___)
The tree in the front yard shaded the man.	(old ___, new ___)
The cat was running from the dog.	(old ___, new ___)
The old car pulled the trailer.	(old ___, new ___)
The tall tree in the front yard shaded the old car.	(old ___, new ___)
The tall tree shaded the man who was smoking his pipe.	(old ___, new ___)

(continued)

TABLE 1—*Continued*

The scared cat was running from the dog.	(old ___, new ___)
The old car, pulling the trailer, climbed the hill.	(old ___, new ___)
The girl who lives next door broke the large window on the porch.	(old ___, new ___)
The tall tree shaded the man.	(old ___, new ___)
The cat was running from the barking dog.	(old ___, new ___)
The car was old.	(old ___, new ___)
The girl broke the large window.	(old ___, new ___)
The scared cat ran from the barking dog that jumped on the table.	(old ___, new ___)
The scared cat, running from the dog, jumped on the table.	(old ___, new ___)
The old car pulling the trailer climbed the steep hill.	(old ___, new ___)
The girl broke the large window on the porch.	(old ___, new ___)
The scared cat which broke the window on the porch climbed the tree.	(old ___, new ___)
The tree shaded the man.	(old ___, new ___)
The car climbed the steep hill.	(old ___, new ___)
The girl broke the window.	(old ___, new ___)
The man who lives next door broke the large window on the porch.	(old ___, new ___)
The tall tree in the front yard shaded the man who was smoking his pipe.	(old ___, new ___)
The cat was scared.	(old ___, new ___)

STOP. Count the number of sentences judged "old."

example, "The scared cat running from the barking dog broke the window"), or if a new arbitrary fact is introduced ("The tall girl who lives next door broke the window"), subjects reject the sentence with certainty.

What has happened here is clear to the contextualist. The subjects have used the various strands repeatedly available in the texture of the experiment to construct four events which are completely described by the four long, complex sentences. The quality of each of the events is indeed the total meaning of the complex sentence. Once the fusion of the strands into events has occurred (particularly since the strands are heard over and over again in various combinations), the subject cannot perform an analysis to recover the exact pattern of input that furnished support for the construction that he made.

The analysis here is very much like the contextualist's account of the development of science—pulling together separate strands and seeing the unity of events even though they are not presented contiguously in time or space. The notion of *fusion* is an old one in the contextualist tradition and is often appealed to in explanation of the paucity of analysis available in aesthetic experience or mystical experience. (And I might suggest in passing that in the case where highly fused events arise from strands that are not systematically presented, historical reconstruction as to the sources of the event will as a general rule be unsuccessful.)

Regardless of our particular analysis, it is clear that the phenomena disclosed by these experiments pose formidable problems for storage theories of memory.

Selection and integration of relevant strands and the accompanying phenomena of fusion are stubborn facts that cannot be set lightly aside. But such facts are not easily discussed in the associative framework.

If one wants to "push" the contextual analysis a little, an enlightening experiment is one that keeps the superficial form of the basic experiment above, but changes the quality of the events involved. If one takes away the "contextual glue" of the four themes, the results of the experiment change in dramatic ways. Peterson and McIntyre (1973) presented individual, unrelated sentences of the same length and grammatical structure as in the original experiment. When they examined recognition data for sentences that were actually presented, they found that the recognition confidence curve ran in the opposite direction. With related sentences the subjects were sure that they heard the long, complex sentences and were uncertain about the short, simple ones. With unrelated sentences, subjects were sure about the short, simple sentences, but uncertain about the long ones. Of course, in a study with unrelated sentences, the only events available to the subject are the individual sentences themselves. The shorter and simpler the event, the more likely the subject can satisfy himself that it is really the same; the longer it is, the less likely he is to have integrated the event and the more possibilities there are that something is different.

We must also notice that the phenomena that are apparent here are equally evident in a host of psycholinguistic experiments. The studies by Sachs (1967) on memory for form and content of sentences in stories, illustrate both the salience of quality and the effects of fusion. When her subjects were queried about a sentence that was embedded in the context of a story, the *form* of the sentence was incompletely remembered. The *meaning* of the sentence, however, was readily retained since it was an integrated strand in the texture of the larger event. Violations of meaning or sense were readily detected but form vanished with the specious present.

If we contrast Sachs' study with the psycholinguistic experiments that have used *unrelated* sentences (e.g., Clifton & Odom, 1966), we have another illustration of recognition phenomena changing when the quality of the event changes. In the psycholinguistic experiments, for example, the syntactic form of the sentence is systematically related to false recognition and false recall, but the truth or falsity of the content described by the sentence (the difference between affirmation and negation) is no more important than whether the sentence is active or passive in form. The point is, of course, that there is no context in which the content of the sentence makes any sense or any difference. Hence, affirmation and negation have only syntactic meaning. That is, if each sentence is an unrelated event, then only variables at the level of construction of the sentence are of any importance.

Experiments on miniature linguistic systems reveal similar phenomena. If subjects are trained to label items in a color–form matrix such as that used by Esper (1925), they learn the *system* but ordinarily do not remember which specific instances they were given in the training trials, even though they may have seen the same instances many times. In general, memory is for systems, not for instances. With a small set of examples, subjects may remember particulars. With a liberal set of examples, however, they cannot reliably discriminate the instances on which they were trained from other acceptable instances in the system (Foss, 1968; Keeney, 1969; Segal, 1962).

INTEGRATING INFORMATION

I want to present now a more complex task that requires a good deal of work on the part of the subject. In this experiment the subject must "problem solve" to achieve the complete event that we want him to apprehend. This experiment was developed by J. Richard Barclay (1971) in extending the work of Bransford and Franks. Barclay's experiments show both of the phenomena that we have noted earlier. First, changing the subject's task changes the kind of event that the subject experiences. Second, taking individual sentences as events results in very different recall and recognition behaviors than those observed when the entire experience is integrated into a single event.

In several different experiments Barclay presented subjects with sets of sentences. The sentences gave a piecemeal account of the pairwise relations of a series of five objects that were arrayed on some dimension such as "left–right" or "taller–shorter" or "faster–slower"; for example, there might be five animals standing in a left–right array, five men varying in height, or five cars varying in speed.

The "comprehending" subjects were told that they would hear sentences describing the relations between the five animals (or men, or cars) and that they were to listen carefully to the sentences so that at the end they could properly line up the objects in order. The control subjects were told that they would hear a set of sentences that were about animals (or men or cars) and that they were to try to remember the sentences that they heard. After hearing the sentences several times, the subjects were given a comprehension test and a test of sentence recognition or recall.

The first result of the experiments was the expected finding that 80–100% of the comprehending subjects constructed the correct array of objects. However, only 0–10% of the subjects who were trying to remember the sentences could do so, despite the fact that they heard the same information as subjects in the "comprehension" group. The second result was that the comprehending subjects were excellent in discriminating true sentences from false sentences but could not remember which of the true sentences they had actually heard. All of the true sentences seemed familiar to them, and about equally so, whether they were original sentences, correct paraphrases, or correct inferences from the original sentences.

The group that was specifically told to remember the sentences presented quite a different picture. These subjects were poor at recognizing which of the sentences they had heard and almost equally poor at separating true sentences from false ones. In other words, when subjects considered the sentences as the events of the experiment, they learned very little, their confusions were determined by variables at the sentence construction level, and they showed evidence of massive interference. With the array itself as the event to be constructed, specific sentence memory was essentially nil; but the general constraint of what was an acceptable or "true" sentence was virtually perfect. The same results were obtained in recall experiments. The comprehending subjects recalled no false sentences and "recalled" true sentences independently of whether they had heard them or not.

This experiment is a dramatic example of the principles we have encountered in both of the foregoing types of experiments. First, what the subject was instructed to do with the input was the most important determiner of the nature of what was remembered. Second, when the event itself was well fused, the specific instances from which the event was constructed were not readily discriminated. Finally, the availability of the global event in this case makes it possible for the subject to reject one class of sentences (the false ones) and to accept another class of sentences (the true ones) as likely to have occurred even though he could not discriminate what actually occurred. That is, the event (the representation of the array which is remembered) is related to sentences in such a way that permissible utterances can be generated or recognized with great accuracy even though actual, historical sentences cannot. What is remembered is definitely not verbal and probably not even linguistic, but it plays a key role in determining which linguistic constructions are recognized and recalled.

DISCUSSION

What kinds of lessons can we draw from these experiments? First and foremost, I think it is clear that we should shun any notion that memory consists of a specific system that operates with one set of rules on one kind of unit. What is remembered in a given situation depends on the physical and psychological context in which the event was experienced, the knowledge and skills that the subject brings to the context, the situation in which we ask for evidence for remembering and the relation of what the subject remembers to what the experimenter demands.

Contextualism calls us back to considering what the subject believes and knows when we talk of memory. It simultaneously suggests that we look to the sources of this belief and to the subject's ways of constructing and reconstructing his experience. William James pointed out that the only thing that distinguishes memory from the other higher mental processes is just that belief. He argued that there is nothing unique in the object of memory and no special faculty evident in its manifestations. Apart from the belief that the construction of the mind is attributed to the past, he saw nothing to set memory apart from perception, imagination, comparison and reasoning.

Such a claim is unsettling because it says: *Memory is not a box in a flow diagram.* It is also threatening since it seems to demand an understanding of all "the higher-mental processes" at once. Yet, that is what the data of our experiments suggest. Surely, these studies imply that we cannot deal with memory without dealing with instructions, perception, comprehension, inference, problem solving and all the other processes that contribute to the construction of events. The theoretical contextualist agrees. He argues that there is no other approach. To study memory without studying perception is to invite disaster in one of two ways: on the one hand, failing to understand the inputs to the subject or, on the other hand, pushing all the difficult problems out of memory into the unknown perceptual domain for someone else to study. To study memory without studying inference is to be baffled by the transformations that the subject puts on his experience. To study memory without studying language is to be confounded by paraphrase and the issues of meaning And so on.

The contextualist avoids despair at this point, not by predicting success for a global assault on all higher mental processes simultaneously but by asking again, "What kind of an analysis of memory will be useful to you in the kinds of problems you are facing? What kinds of events concern you?" If you limit the events for some purpose, he will lead you into an analysis of context, textures that support experiences, strands that interrelate aspect of experiences, etc.

You should notice that methodological issues and the choices of experimental paradigms become crucial when you take the contextualist view. It is not true on this view that one can study any part of the "cosmic machine" to just as good an effect as any other part. The important thing is to pick the right kinds of events for your purposes. And it is true on this view that a whole theory of an experiment can be elaborated without contributing in an important way to the science because the situation is artificial and nonrepresentative in just the senses that determine its peculiar phenomena. In short, contextualism stresses relating one's laboratory problems to the ecologically valid problems of everyday life.

CONCLUSIONS

It would be easy to believe from this brief presentation that contextualism is merely eclecticism given a fancy name. It would also be easy to suppose that my plea is for miniature theories that will eventually integrate into a global theory.

And it is easy to imagine that all of us could be contextualists and at the same time continue working in just the same fashion that we always have on associative theories. But none of these beliefs is correct.

Contextualism is historically tolerant of other approaches and is always willing to examine a claim that the cosmic machine is all of one piece. But at rock bottom there is a profound difference in belief between *associationism,* which presupposes fundamental units and relations out of which all else is constructed, and *contextualism,* which presupposes that events are primary and that the quality of events determines what the possibilities are for a host of analyses.

The associationist finds that semantic features (or word associates or images or what have you) are important in predicting recall of individual words. "Fine" says the contextualist, "but do not bet any appreciable amounts of money that those will be important considerations when you combine words in sentences or embed them in different contexts."

The associationist finds that grammatical features are predictive of memory distortions in single sentences and believes that he has a theory of comprehension. "Look out," says the contextualist, "Those are unlikely candidates for relevant variables for understanding sentences in context." And so it goes.

The contextualist does not believe in one order of phenomena that dominates the psychological world. He does not believe that there is a single paradigm of explanation such as mechanism. Explanation for the contextualist consists of explicating for some purpose the quality of an event that we find important or interesting. That entails in turn a description of its spread in time and its degree of fusion. It further calls for a discussion of the textures that support the quality of the event and the strands making up the texture and relating it to relevant aspects of its context. Unlike the associationist explanation, the contextualist explanation is put together from the top down, rather than from the bottom up, and it is oriented toward the event rather than toward the supposed machinery.

I believe that the field of memory research is moving towards contextualism and I, for one, welcome it. I think that an awareness and acceptance of this movement will free us to explore the ecologically valid problems of memory that are of real importance to us. I think it will help us to be alert to the identification of new, emergent phenomena as they are encountered. In short, I think that contextualism provides a real, viable and optimistic alternative to the oldest theory of them all.

ACKNOWLEDGMENTS

Preparation of this paper was supported in part by grants to the University of Minnesota, Center for Research in Human Learning, from the National Science Foundation (GB-35703X), The National Institute of Child Health and Human Development (HD-01136), and the Graduate School of the University of Minnesota.

In addition to the students and colleagues mentioned in the text, I must thank Robert Shaw, Walter Weimer, Robert Verbrugge, Nancy McCarrell, Jerry Wald, and Christine Bremer for assistance. The central theme of the paper, however, was derived from suggestions made by the late Richard M. Jenkins and it is to him that this paper is dedicated.

REFERENCES

Barclay, J. R. The role of comprehension in remembering sentences. Unpublished doctoral dissertation, University of Minnesota, 1971.

Bransford, J. D., & Franks, J. J. The abstraction of linguistic ideas. *Cognitive Psychology,* 1971, **2,** 331–350.

Clifton, C., Jr., & Odom, P. Similarity relations among certain English sentence constructions. *Psychological Monographs,* 1966, **5,** 35.

Cofer, C. N., & Foley, J. P., Jr. Mediated generalization and the interpretation of verbal behavior: I. Prolegomena. *Psychological Review,* 1942, **49,** 513–540.

Esper, E. A. A technique for the experimental investigation of associative interference in artificial linguistic material. *Language Monographs,* **1,** 1925.

Foss, D. J. An analysis of learning in a miniature linguistic system. *Journal of Experimental Psychology,* 1968, **76,** 450–459.

Hyde, T. S. Differential effects of effort and type of orienting task on recall and organization of highly associated words. *Journal of Experimental Psychology,* 1973, **79,** 111–113.

Hyde, T. S., & Jenkins, J. J. Differential effects of incidental tasks on the organization of recall of a list of highly associated words. *Journal of Experimental Psychology,* 1969, **82,** 472–481.

Hyde, T. S., & Jenkins, J. J. Recall for words as a function of semantic, graphic and syntactic orienting tasks. *Journal of Verbal Learning and Verbal Behavior,* 1973, **12,** 471–480.

Jenkins, J. J. Mediated associations: Paradigms and situations. In C. N. Cofer & B. S. Musgrave (Eds.), *Verbal behavior and learning.* New York: McGraw-Hill, 1963.

Jenkins, J. J. The 1952 word association norms. In L. Postman & G. Keppel (Eds.), *Norms of word association.* New York: Academic Press, 1970. Pp. 1–38.

Jenkins, J. J., & Russell, W. A. Associative clustering during recall. *Journal of Abnormal and Social Psychology,* 1952, **47,** 818–821.

Johnston, C. D., & Jenkins, J. J. Two more incidental tasks that differentially affect associative clustering in recall. *Journal of Experimental Psychology,* 1971, **89,** 92–95.

Keeney, T. J. Permutation transformations of phrase structures in letter sequences. *Journal of Experimental Psychology,* 1969, **1,** 28–33.

Osgood, C. E. *Method and theory in experimental psychology.* New York: Oxford University Press, 1953.

Pepper, S. C., *World hypotheses.* Berkeley: University of California Press, 1942.

Peterson, R. G., & McIntyre, C. W. The influence of semantic 'relatedness' on linguistic integration and retention. *American Journal of Psychology,* 1973, **86,** 697–706.

Sachs, J. Recognition memory for syntactic and semantic aspects of connected discouse. *Perception and Psychophysics,* 1967, **2,** 437–442.

Segal, E. Stimulus perception as a function of response set. Unpublished doctoral dissertation, University of Minnesota, 1962.

Till, R. E., & Jenkins, J. J. The effects of cued orienting rasks on the free recall of words. *Journal of Verbal Learning and Verbal Behavior,* 1973, **12,** 489–498.

Walsh, D. A., & Jenkins, J. J. Effects of orienting tasks on free-recall in incidental learning: "Difficulty," "effort" and "process" explanations. *Journal of Verbal Learning and Verbal Behavior,* 1973, **12,** 481–488.

16
Toward Unexplaining Memory

John D. Bransford
Vanderbilt University

Nancy S. McCarrell
George Peabody College for Teachers

Jeffery J. Franks
Kathleen E. Nitsch
Vanderbilt University

> The amount of detailed information which an individual has at his command and his theoretical elaborations of the same are mutually dependent; they grow in and through each other. It is because of the indefinite and little specialized character of our knowledge that the theories concerning the processes of memory, reproduction, and association have been up to the present time of so little value for a proper comprehension of these processes. For example, to express our ideas concerning their physical basis we use different metaphors–stored up ideas, engraved images, well-beaten paths. There is only one thing certain about these figures of speech and that is that they are not suitable [Ebbinghaus, 1885, p. 5].

This chapter argues for the value of attempting to "unexplain" memory. Our purpose is not to deny the importance of *remembering,* nor to deny that past experiences affect organisms' subsequent interactions with the environment. But we question the fruitfulness of assuming that a concept of *memory* underlies these events.

Of course, there are many ways in which one can use the term "memory." If the term is used to mean "whatever is responsible for remembering" or "whatever factors determine the effects of previous experiences on subsequent interactions" then it becomes an essentially circular concept. But is the term "memory" usually used in this way? It seems reasonable to suggest that current uses of the term memory frequently involve tacit or explicit assumptions not too different from those noted by Ebbinghaus: for example, that memory can be broken down into a set of *memories*, that these consist of relatively independent *traces* that are stored in some *location*, that these traces must be *searched for* and *retrieved* in order to produce remembering, and that appropriate traces must be "contacted" in order for past experiences to have their effects on subsequent events. If memory is defined in this way, it becomes important to consider the possibility that the concept of memory (and memories) is simply one of many general hypotheses about the processes underlying remembering and the manner in which previous experiences have their effects on current events. In short, the "searching for traces" conceptualization of memory (hereafter called the *memory metaphor*) may simply be one of many possible metaphors, and it may not be the most fruitful metaphor.

This chapter begins the task of questioning the fruitfulness of the prevailing memory metaphor. To what extent does it lead to new insights? To what extent does it help us understand problems like perceiving, comprehending, learning and transfer? How fruitful is the current metaphor for conceptualizing the problem of *remembering* (which is the problem with which it is most closely allied)? The present chapter simply explores these questions. In effect, it is a working paper written in the hopes that others will be prompted to improve upon the present arguments or to show how they are wrong.

SECTION 1

Memory versus the Processes by Which Past Experiences Affect Subsequent Interactions with the World

Attempts to understand most psychological phenomena lead to a consideration of effects of previous experience on subsequent experiences and interactions with the environment. This appears to provide a prima facie case for a general concern with "memory." However, is it necessarily the case that the effects of past experience are to be accounted for in terms of "memories" represented in the form of stored traces which must be contacted in order to mediate interpretations of subsequent events? We shall begin to examine this question by briefly discussing the problems of learning and perceiving and distinguishing them from the problem of remembering. The phenomena of learning and perceiving are obvious cases involving the effects of past experiences. We briefly discuss views of these phenomena that do not involve memory metaphor assumptions. From these views we shall eventually raise questions designed to prompt search for an alternative to the memory metaphor that may also be applicable to the phenomenon of remembering.

First consider learning; for example, the problem of what it means to learn to play tennis. As Bartlett (1932) noted, one does not learn particular responses, nor connections between responses and stimulus situations (for example, connections between a particular response and the stimulus of a tennis ball coming over the net and bouncing in the right-hand corner of the court). Previous experience allows the creation of more finely tuned "novel but appropriate" acts (e.g., see Bernstein, 1967; Greene, 1971; Turvey, Chapter 9, this volume). But note that questions about tennis playing ability are not equivalent to questions normally asked when *remembering* is studied in the laboratory. The type of question asked in memory experiments is more equivalent to "Try to reproduce those exact strokes that you just made" or "Describe the places where the ball hit during your last volley."

It seems possible that a tennis player, for example, might be relatively accurate at answering the latter questions. And it might be argued that the ability to do so depends on stored "memories" of previous experiences. But even granting (for the moment) this "memory" assumption, one surely would not wish to simply *equate* the ability to play tennis with a list of previous memories of tennis playing experiences. Such an equation seems as implausible as equating one's "knowledge of his native language" with a list of memories of previously experienced sentences or even paraphrases of these sentences (e.g., see Chomsky, 1965). One's ability to remember will undoubtedly be related to the nature of the knowledge acquired through learning, but it would seem strained to equate the problem of *learning* with the problem of how *memories* are stored and retrieved.

A further example of differences between problems of learning and memory stems from J. Gibson's (1966) claim that perception does not depend on memory (see especially his Chapters 12 and 13). The present authors find that reactions to Gibson's claim are frequently adamant, and include exclamations like "That's ridiculous, it is obvious that perceptions depend on previous experiences one has had." But Gibson's statement does not deny that past experiences affect the organism. Instead, it differentiates the problem of learning from the problem of how one forms and stores "memories." Processes by which past experiences influence current perceptions need not involve some mediated contact with previously stored traces. Resistance to Gibson's statement frequently reveals our tacit assumptions that learning necessarily results in "memories," and that these stored memories are responsible for mediating new interactions with the world.

As an alternative to reliance on "memories," Gibson assumes that learning involves the attunement of the system to invariant information. "The development of this attunement, or the education of attention, depends on past experience but not on the *storage* of past experiences" (Gibson, 1966, p. 262). Gibson's theory therefore stands in contrast to those theories of perception which assume that sensations must be *enriched* by contact with previously stored memory traces (and see Gibson & Gibson, 1955). For example, Gregory (1972) argues that ". . . perceptions are constructed by complex brain processes from fleeting fragmentary scraps of data signaled by the senses and drawn from the brain's memory banks . . . [p. 707] ." Gregory makes explicit his assumption that previous experiences result in the formation and storage of memories that must mediate and enrich subsequent interpretations of perceptual events. As Mace (this volume) notes, such "memory enrichments" are assumed to be responsible for determining the *meaning* of sensations. In short, many perceptual theorists relegate the problems of interpretation and meaning to memory and cognitive theorists. Yet many of the latter theorists do just the reverse. For example, Anderson and Bower (1973) state:

> Even the most abstract structures seem capable of being reduced to perceptual data . . . . The language of the mathematic grammarians seems at times to be little more than uninterpreted symbols, mere tiles to be shuffled about according to string formation rules. *But real languages always remain close to their perceptual base in their interpretation* [p. 155; italics ours] .

If one simultaneously holds both a sensation enrichment theory of perception and a position similar to that of Anderson and Bower (and such a combination seems rather typical), it becomes questionable whether, or how, meaning ever gets into the system. Gibson, by rejecting the assumption that stored memories are necessary for perception, avoids such troublesome buck-passing. His alternative of perceptual learning as attunement of the perceptual systems provides a different and possibly more fruitful perspective for examining the effects of previous experience on subsequent experience and performance.

Past Experience as Setting the Stage for the Articulation of New Information

What are the characteristics of learning, perceiving, and comprehending that raise questions about the fruitfulness of the memory metaphor? One such characteristic that seems primary is that these activities all intrinsically involve the articulation of novel information. The problem for the memory metaphor is that storage and retrieval of traces only deals with old, previously articulated information. Memory traces can perhaps provide a basis for dealing with the "sameness" of the present experience with previous experiences, but the memory metaphor has no mechanisms for dealing with novel information. This suggests that a different, more fruitful metaphor might be found.

As a first step toward such an alternative, consider the possibility that a major role of past experience is to provide "boundary constraints" that *set the stage* for articulating the uniqueness as well as sameness of information. And contrast this "stage-setting" metaphor with the assumption that previous experience merely provides an accumulation of memories that are responsible for meaningful interpretations of subsequent events. In our opinion, the stage setting metaphor is both plausible and important. For example, Gibson and Gibson (1955) argue that perceptual learning involves a process of *differentiation* rather than *enrichment* by previously accumulated memories. The ability to differentiate an input from others presupposes that one can detect its uniqueness (relative to a set of alternatives) as well as its sameness (i.e., the invariant information across past and present experiences). Experience with a set of items sets the stage by providing boundary constraints that specify relative invariances with respect to past experience, but the present experience goes beyond these boundaries. Unique aspects of the present situation are articulated as well. In short, the nature of one's present experience *depends upon* previous experiences but cannot be *reduced to* memories of such experiences. Perception is direct *given* the attunement that previous experiences provide. As an example, consider someone who usually drives a pickup truck and then drives a car. The smoothness of the car's ride is very noticeable. Past experience with pickup trucks appears to set the stage for articulating the distinctiveness of a car's movement, but the perception of the latter cannot simply be reduced to previous memories of experiences of driving a truck.

Note that the stage-setting metaphor assumes that meaningful recognition can be direct *given* the appropriate level of organismic attunement (and see Gibson, this volume). It is therefore assumed that meaningful recognition need not be mediated by "contact" with previous memories that were stored. As Gibson (1966) states: "Recognition does not have to be the successful matching of a new percept with the trace of an old one. If it did, novelty would have to be the failure to match a new percept with any trace of an old one after an exhaustive search of the memory store, and this is absurd [p. 278]." It seems useful to note that others (e.g., Norman, 1969) have also pointed toward the absurdity of assuming an exhaustive search of memory in order to know that something is novel (e.g., *X* is a novel word). Yet the "solution" to this problem has frequently been conceptualized within the framework of the memory metaphor; namely that one automatically knows "where to look" for the item and finds that there is nothing stored in that "place." Such a solution may seem adequate for explaining how someone knows that he has no information about something. But how can such an explanation account for the fact that the attuned perceiver can frequently articulate the nature of the new information? Such an act involves something more than the mere realization that one has no information about event *X*. For example, how can the truck driver articulate the uniqueness of a car's ride instead of merely perceiving that the experience is different from anything experienced before? (Assuming, of course, the truck driver never rode in a car before.)

Even if one assumes that an organism can "find" a trace and determine that it is similar but not identical to the new experience, there still remains a problem of accounting for the possibility of recognizing the specific nature of the uniqueness. At some point, the direct perception of novel information seems to be a necessary assumption. The stage-setting metaphor attempts to make this assumption explicit. The role of past experience is viewed as establishing boundary constraints that attune the organism and allow the articulation of unique aspects of a situation. Past experience is not viewed as simply providing memory traces that must be found and matched or compared to inputs. Put another way, meaningful perception is assumed to depend on how an input fits into an abstract framework (e.g., see Bransford & McCarrell, 1974) rather than how an input makes contact with previous memory traces that were stored.

Linguistic Comprehension and the Uniqueness of Understood Meanings

The stage-setting metaphor has implications for conceptualizing questions about linguistic comprehension as well as perception. For example, relatively short-term effects of past experience can be equated with the effects of context on comprehension. Elsewhere (e.g., Bransford, McCarrell, & Nitsch, 1976) it has been argued that the *understood meaning* or *significance* of utterances is uniquely specified as a function of the contextually induced attunement of the listener. The argument is that linguistic comprehension cannot simply be equated with "finding," "selecting," and "amalgamating" previous "meaning elements" that were stored (e.g., see Katz & Fodor, 1963).

Note that finding, selecting, and amalgamating assumptions lie within the domain of the memory metaphor, where the meaning elements are basically stored traces. It is difficult to see how such assumptions imply anything other than the notion that novel understood meanings (significances) are simply due to novel combinations of old "meaning elements" that were stored. A memory metaphor approach to linguistic comprehension neglects the problems discussed in the preceding section. That is, at some point "old" "meaning elements" were "new" or "novel," and the memory metaphor does not provide a basis for articulating new information. The stage-setting metaphor suggests that if one assumes the existence of "meaning elements," then the significances of these individual "elements" also change as a function of organismic attunement. From a stage-setting perspective, the role of past experience is not simply to provide a repertoire of stored meanings (or senses) that can be retrieved and novelly recombined in terms of syntactic rule structures and selection restrictions. Instead the role of past experience is to provide the organism with abstract tools that can be used to articulate novel significances that a speaker or writer intends.

Consider some possible understood meanings or significances of a statement like "I'm going to drive to Minneapolis tonight." If the speaker is in St. Paul, Minnesota, the statement if not surprising. If the speaker is in California, one realizes that the person is in for a long drive. And if the speaker is in Europe, the statement seems strange. Or consider reading a newspaper headline like "Peace finally comes to Europe." What is the significance of this statement? If one is reading an old newspaper, it is a historical fact. If one is reading today's paper, it is understood differently. And what is the significance of a phrase like "today's paper"? The understood significance of this utterance changes every day.

It seems obvious that a listener's knowledge of (or past experience with) his native language plays an extremely important role in determining the significance of statements. Yet the examples immediately above suggest it might be fruitful to regard such linguistic knowledge as tools that can be *used* to understand unique significances as a function of contextual attunement. From this perspective, comprehension cannot simply be equated with the retrieval, selection, and amalgamation of previously stored "meaning units." A "stage-setting" approach to comprehension orients one toward the potential for increasing refinements and changes in understood meanings or significances. And these understood meanings are uniquely specified as a function of the listener's level of contextually induced attunement.

Consider for example, what is involved in helping someone experience an input in a particular manner. Assume that a speaker wants a listener to experience the utterence "go buy some" as being extremely funny. What would the speaker have to do to produce such an effect? Clearly, the speaker would have to create some contextual support that provided a framework for experiencing a certain significance of this utterance. The context or framework provides a level of attunement that sets the stage for the nature of the experience afforded by a linguistic event. Could one ever exhaust the potential significances of an utterance? This seems unlikely. It seems more plausible to assume that a clever speaker could always specify some framework that permitted a unique articulation of information that the listener never considered before. According to the memory metaphor, such unique understanding arises from the novel combination of old meaning elements. The role of context would be to select from among those possible stored meanings in order to find ones that fit the selection restrictions of the linguistic strings (but see Barclay, Bransford, Franks, McCarrell & Nitsch, 1974; Franks, 1974). Of course, further elaborations of specific information might arise from deductive inference. But the nature of one's deductions is a function of how one initially comprehends the input information (e.g., see de Groot, 1965; Katona, 1940; Staudenmayer, 1975); hence, one must still face the problem of accounting for differential interpretations of individual "meaning elements" as a function of the contextually induced level of attunement of the comprehender.

To further highlight the problems involved, consider the selection and amalgamation metaphor in light of a problem of nonverbal comprehension. For example, imagine a gesture of an outstretched hand with all five fingers extended. What might such a gesture mean? When performed in the context of questions like "Who wants to go with me?," "How many children are there in your family?," "How tall is your father?," etc., it has three very different significances. It seems strained to assume that one has stored a set of "meanings" of an outstretched hand and simply selects among these as a function of context.

Information about hands provides constraints on the significances understood by the comprehender, but the understood meaning seems to be a function of the relationship between the hand and the abstract framework generated by context rather than a function of a "match" to a previous meaning that was stored. It seems plausible to suggest that what is called "linguistic meaning" should also be viewed as information that sets constraints on the potential significances of any utterance. But the understood meaning of an utterance cannot simply be reduced to the selection and amalgamation of such linguistic meanings. The basic problem of understanding involves grasping the significances of inputs, and significances are uniquely specified as a function of the *relationship* between a contextually induced framework and the particular input. The stage setting metaphor attempts to emphasize that understanding involves *relationships;* it is an *activity* rather than a *thing.*

Summary of Section 1

To summarize, we have suggested that notions of "memory" underlie usual assumptions about the effects of past experiences on subsequent interactions with the environment. Yet one can assume that past experiences affect subsequent experiences without necessarily assuming that it is the accumulation of stored memories that underlie such effects. One alternative is that past experience "sets the stage" for subsequent experiences. From this perspective, the perceived meaning of experiences is uniquely specified. It depends on past experiences but cannot be reduced to contact with "stored traces" of past experiences. A strength of the stage-setting metaphor is therefore that it emphasizes the human capacity for appreciating unique aspects of information never explicitly articulated before.[1]

Early in the present section, it was also suggested that the problem of how past experiences affect subsequent perceptions is not necessarily equivalent to the problem of *remembering* as it is studied in most laboratory experiments. The key problem with a memory metaphor approach to perceiving and comprehending was its inadequacy for dealing with the novel and unique aspects of experiencing. Remembering appears to be a phenomenon in which novelty and uniqueness are minimized whereas "sameness with" or "repetition" of previously experienced information is maximized. It follows that the memory metaphor may be more applicable to the remembering domain.

It is important to note, however, that the stage setting approach emphasizes that perceiving and comprehending are activities whose function is to articulate the significance of inputs. Significances are assumed to be uniquely specified as a

[1] Our discussion of the stage-setting metaphor is necessarily cursory. We hope to develop it further in subsequent papers. In particular, we hope to contrast it with conceptualizations of "semantic memory." The latter still fall within our definition of the memory metaphor.

function of the *relationship* between an input and some abstract framework or set of boundary conditions. The processes of understanding or "knowing" are therefore viewed as the generation of a particular significance as a function of organismic attunement. Perhaps the act of remembering also involves the generation or creation of a certain experience that has a particular significance (that is, that experience *X* is a "memory"). If so, then it is the attunement constraints on creation that a theory of remembering must attempt to explain. The problem of remembering is the major concern of the remainder of this chapter. The next section explores questions about the fruitfulness of the "storage of memories" metaphor for providing insights into the problem of remembering. We then attempt to look at problems of remembering from a re-creation point of view.

SECTION 2

Remembering and the Memory Metaphor

Most theories of memory are based on studies of *remembering*. And most studies of remembering involve an important constraint on the nature of the questions asked of subjects; namely, the subjects are asked whether certain inputs occurred in the context of a particular memory task. For example, in experiments on recognition memory, subjects are not asked to indicate whether they have ever experienced the test items; they are asked whether certain items were experienced in the context of that experiment.

Within the memory metaphor, such context problems are usually handled by greatly increasing the amount and nature of the information assumed to be stored with each trace. For example, traces are assumed to have "list tags," "time tags," and "experiment tags" attached to them which code the necessary contextual information (e.g., see Anderson & Bower, 1972, 1973). Tagging approaches have been described by Watkins and Tulving (1975):

> According to tagging theory, remembering a word entails attaching an occurrence marker or tag to its representation in a permanent memory system. This representation is frequently conceptualized as a node in a semantic network. Recall entails gaining access to the node and deciding about the presence of an appropriate tag [p. 5].

A tagging approach does not seem fruitful for explaining contextual effects on comprehension (e.g., see Bransford & Johnson, 1973; Bransford & McCarrell, 1974; Bransford, McCarrell, & Nitsch, 1976). For example, the sentence *The haystack was important because the cloth ripped* results in very different experiences depending on whether it occurs in the context of *parachute* versus *house*. It is not the "same experience" distinguished only by a contextual tag. Similarly, an utterance like *Bill has a red car* is innocuous and easily understood in the context of an experiment where it is presented as an example of something to be remembered, rated, or analyzed. But try walking up to someone, simply say "Bill has a red car" and see what happens. Generally the listener will be extremely perplexed. He will know what was *said* but not what was *meant* (e.g., see Bransford, McCarrell, & Nitsch, 1976). Again, the same utterance in different contexts is not "that same utterance" *plus* the mere addition of a context tag.[2]

Of course, arguments about the effects of context on perceiving and understanding need not affect one's assumptions about *memory.* Anderson and Bower (1973), for example, relegate the former problems to HAM's linguistic and perceptual parsers. For HAM, issues in perceiving and understanding are divorced from the problem of memory *per se.* In contrast, other theorists (e.g., Bartlett, 1932; Köhler, 1947) argue that the processes underlying remembering are similar to those underlying activities such as perceiving and thinking. The present chapter attempts to support the latter point of view. As part of the memory metaphor, tagging conceptions imply that remembering depends on first finding an item and then finding a tag that specifies its context of occurrence (for example, that word *X* occurred in a particular experiment). An alternative more congruent with a stage-setting metaphor is that remembering does not involve "finding" stored items plus tags, but instead involves a re-creation of previous experiences. From this perspective, some degree of contextual information for stage setting may be a *prerequisite* for re-creating previous acts. For example, consider once again the task of helping a listener experience the utterance "Go buy some" as being extremely funny. To do so, the speaker would have to create some contextual support that provided a framework for experiencing a certain significance of this utterance. The context or framework would therefore provide a level of attunement that constrains the nature of the experiences afforded by this linguistic event. There may exist similar attunement constraints on reexperiencing (that is, remembering). If so, then contextual information is not something simply appended to stored traces and searched for in order to produce remembering. Instead, some degree of contextual attunement could be a prerequisite for re-creating previous experiences.

In the next section, we will discuss some general attunement constraints on remembering. Our purpose is to raise questions about the adequacy of equating context effects with the storage of tags that are appended to traces. In subsequent sections we more closely question the assumption that prerequisite contextual information merely affects how one comprehends *test* items, and

[2] Anderson and Bower (1973, p. 348) note that a sentence like *The rock crushed the hut* must be stored as something like "In Context C, I studied that 'The rock crushed the hut'." The assumption seems to be that, if spoken in a different context, the utterance would be the same and only the context tag would be different. However, an utterance like *Bill has a red car* is understood very differently when presented in the context of an experiment versus a social context (for example). The information necessary to understand and hence the processes of comprehending differ as a function of context.

that memory per se only deals with the outputs of this comprehension process which are then used to "direct one's search" for *stored* items. Imbedded within the memory metaphor are notions not only of contextual tagging but also *search* for traces and tags. These "search" aspects of the memory metaphor will also be questioned.

Context and Remembering: General Attunement Constraints on Reexperiencing

Consider some simple "experiments" conducted by the present authors. These illustrate some of our concerns with the importance of stage setting, that is, general attunement constraints, on the act of re-creating previous experiences. In the first experiment, the experimenter approached a group of people in a seminar and stated: "This is a recognition experiment. I want you to tell me whether you have heard these words before." Then the experimenter added: "That is, heard them between 1:00 and 1:15 yesterday." And the experimenter immediately began reading the words. Students violently objected to this procedure. A frequent comment was "Wait a minute, I don't know where I was." Such information was considered a prerequisite to making any recognition decisions. Of course, in most experimental situations subjects have no problems specifying the relevant contextual setting. The nature of the task and instructions specify the setting in advance.

Why the violent objections on the part of the subjects? Why did they first have to determine "where they were"? Did they need to know where they were in order to specify the appropriate "context tags" to check for? If so, what would these tags look like? Would they say "experienced at 1:03 on Monday, October 2, 1974"? Would they say "list number 6,405, item number 3" (assuming that there is something equivalent to "list tags" in real world experiencing)? And if they recognized a particular input, could they then "read off" a host of tags indicating other previous experiences with that item? It seems more reasonable to assume that the act of re-creating "where one was" was actually a prerequisite for determining the nature of the experiences afforded by the presentation of the test words.

A second "experiment," a thought experiment, further illustrates the importance of considering the hypothetical process of recreating a perspective or level of attunement (i.e., Bartlett's "attitude") that sets constraints on the nature of the experiences afforded by various probes. Assume that one wishes to study relatively long-term memory; for example, memory after one month. The typical way to conduct such a study would be to bring the subjects into a laboratory, present them with some inputs (e.g., 40 words) and perhaps test them (e.g., on recognition memory). One would then dismiss the subjects without further mention of a later test. After one month, the subjects would be presented with the 40 test words (plus foils) and asked to recognize those heard earlier. Even after one month, the subjects would probably perform better than chance in this type of task. And each recognition decision could probably be made within a relatively short period of time.

Now contrast this condition with another one: The subjects are simply brought into the laboratory, read the same 40 target words, and asked to indicate whether they can re-create a *particular time* that they had experienced each word *any time* during the last month. If one actually attempts to re-create a particular episode where a word was heard (rather than simply guess on the basis of assumed probability of occurrence), this task is very difficult. Intuitively, it takes much longer to make a decision under these latter conditions than it does in the typical memory experiment noted above. But if one assumes that the recognition decisions are based on finding context tags attached to items, it seems strange that the task of finding *any tag* within the last month (Condition 2) is more difficult than finding a *particular tag* that occurred almost 4 weeks earlier (Condition 1). From the present perspective, the subjects in Condition 1 have an advantage. They know they were in an earlier experiment, and that the task is relevant to just that context. Knowledge of their contextual setting therefore provides an abstract level of attunement that constrains the experiences afforded by the nature of the probes. Of course, the presentation of probes should further focus or articulate this general level of attunement. This notion is discussed later in the chapter.

Consider a third "experiment" related to the present discussion. An experimenter and a friend were sitting in the latter's living room. The experimenter pointed to a brass table and said, "Tell me what it makes you think of." The friend's responses were "Brass, India, round, pretty, etc." The experimenter then made up some excuse for the question and the conversation turned to other topics. Somewhat later, the experimenter said, "Try to remember what you did last Christmas." The experimenter then pointed to the brass table and said, "Tell me what it makes you think of." This time the friend's responses were very different. The friend said, "Oh yes, I remember when you were so mysterious in the store where we were Christmas shopping and you wouldn't let me see what you bought. Then I remember opening this large package on Christmas morning and finding the brass table," etc. In short, the table now acted as a prompt to allow the friend to re-create previous, personal experiences. But these experiences weren't re-created every time the friend looked at the brass table. However, given a certain "attitude" (cf. Bartlett) or "level of attunement" (e.g., "What happened last Christmas?"), the table acted as an effective "retrieval" cue.

It is ecologically adaptive that familiar objects do not automatically remind us of previous experiences. If they did, our minds would be deluged with past experiences. Every time we saw our car, or a friend, or our office coffee cup, or heard a recently experienced word, we would reexperience those situations in which those entities have been previously encountered. This would be a cumbersome state of affairs. On the other hand, events do sometimes seem to spontaneously remind one of previous experiences. Certain "memories" seem to appear from "out of the blue." Yet it is not clear that the phrase "out of the blue" is really appropriate. For example, a colleague has remarked that faces of people start to look familiar (that is, remind him of colleagues from around the country) whenever he is anticipating going to a psychological convention and seeing old friends. This hints that stage setting may be behind these memories "out of the blue." In other cases, it often seems that during a conversation certain comments remind one of particular facts or stories. But it is not necessarily the case that these same comments, if spoken in the context of different conversations, would produce the same results. For example, one of us was conversing with a colleague and said: "It's such a beautiful day. I feel like simply sitting on the sidewalk and watching people. Maybe I'll even set up a stand and meet people by selling lemonade." Immediately after this comment the colleague was asked: "Does my choice of words remind you of anything?" The colleague's initial answer was "no." Then, after a relatively long pause, she said: "Do you mean the stimulus trigram used in our studies of recognition memory?" This trigram (that is, *enterprise: sidewalk, lemonade*), in fact, constituted the code name used to refer to these recognition studies. And more than five such studies had recently been conducted. Despite this fact, the words *sidewalk* and *lemonade* had not automatically prompted the recreation of this information given the conversational context that occurred.

The preceding situations seem to exemplify some strong constraints on any adequate theory of remembering. Such a theory must not only explain how internally generated or explicitly presented cues *do* help one recreate previous experiences, but it must explain why potential cues *do not* always prompt one to remember. As Bergson (1911) notes in his *Creative Evolution:* "We trail behind us, unawares, the whole of our past; but our memory pours into the present only the odd recollection or two that in some way complete our present situation [p. 167]." It seems that any adequate characterization of one's "present situation" must ultimately include an account of the global level of "attunement" set by the context of the situation. This level of attunement will affect the nature of the experiences afforded by potential cues. Sometimes, of course, one may recognize that something is merely familiar (for example, a song, a face, a statement). In such cases one may attempt to recreate more information about the situation, for example, *where* or *when* the input was experienced before. In everyday situations we therefore do not always have to recreate the exact context in which an input was originally embedded in order to feel that it was previously experienced. Yet the above discussion suggests that even such feelings of familiarity do not necessarily come from "out of the blue." They appear to depend on the organism's momentary state of "attunement."

To summarize this section, we have argued that some level of "attunement" seems to set the stage for remembering. Attunement is a neglected aspect of remembering for the literature that approaches remembering from the perspective of the memory metaphor. The stage-setting metaphor stresses the importance of further elucidating the nature of this prerequisite attunement. However, mere recognition of the potential importance of prerequisite stage setting for the overall problem of remembering would not constitute critical evidence contrary to the memory metaphor. It is doubtful, for example, that anyone would deny the importance of comprehending *test* items as well as acquisition items in a memory task. One could still remain within the memory metaphor by subscribing to some variation of the tack taken by Anderson and Bower (1973). For them, such stage-setting factors are presumably relegated to initial linguistic and perceptual parsers. Given this assumption, the problem of remembering begins where the parsers stop; that is, with some comprehended or encoded representation of the *test* items. One can remain within the memory metaphor by assuming that it is the test-item-as-comprehended that "directs one's search" for stored traces. The next section examines these search assumptions. Its purpose is to raise questions regarding their fruitfulness for understanding remembering.

Search and the Memory Metaphor: What Is Presupposed?

We have argued that contextual constraints on remembering might be incorporated into the memory metaphor by elaborating the nature of the comprehended test items. The comprehended test item then directs one's search for tagged traces. Attention must therefore be focused on the "search" aspects of the memory metaphor.

Consider how the test-item-as-comprehended affects memory; for example, recognition memory. A number of theorists have shown that test context affects recognition (e.g., Bobrow & Light; cf. Bower, 1972). Light and Carter-Sobell (1970), for example, presented the subjects with acquisition sentences like *She likes strawberry jam.* During recognition, the subjects were presented with phrases such as *blueberry jam* versus *traffic jam* and asked to indicate whether they had heard the last word in each phrase (e.g., *jam*) during the acquisition task. Those subjects presented with the test phrase *blueberry jam* exhibited better recognition performance than subjects presented with *traffic jam.* In short, context affected subjects performance even in a recognition task. Frequently, the account of such results assumes that comprehension involves the "tagging" of a particular *meaning* or *sense* of a lexical item, and that remembering involves a process of "finding" the appropriate *meaning* trace plus tag (e.g., see Reder, Anderson, & Bjork, 1974). For example, the test phrase *traffic jam* may direct one to search for a meaning of *jam* that is different from the meaning heard during acquisition. One therefore "looks" at the wrong meaning and fails to find the appropriate tag. The cue *blueberry jam,* on the other hand, may more probably lead one to the originally expressed meaning of *jam;* hence one is more likely to find the appropriate tag. In short, the context in which a test item is embedded appears to influence one's interpretation of that item, and that interpretation affects where one searches or looks. Put more generally, *knowledge of what one is looking for influences the nature of one's search processes.* This seems to be a basic assumption underlying "search" portions of the memory metaphor. Even if one assumes that "recognition is automatic," often behind this view is the further assumption that one automatically knows what one is looking for and "where to look" for this stored item (or stored meaning) plus tag.

Consider what the notion of search means when instantiated in everyday activities. Assume that someone is looking for a pair of socks. He will obviously have more success if he has a separate place for his underwear, shirts, pants, coats, etc., than if all of his clothes are simply stored in one clump. In the former case, the person can simply restrict his search to the underwear drawer. And if he is searching for a screwdriver rather than a pair of socks, it is unlikely that he will look in his underwear drawer. His search processes will be modified as a function of the likely places in which articles will be stored.

But note that these efficient search strategies *presuppose* knowledge about *where* to search for items and *what* items one is searching for. For example, one must *already know* that his clothes are stored in separate categories in order to avoid searching for socks in the coat closet. And one must *already know* the likely places in which he has stored a screwdriver in order to avoid searching for it in his underwear drawer. Where do such knowledge constraints come from in a memory experiment? For example, how could recognition or retrieval probes direct one's search processes or tell him "where to look?"

In everyday situations, some search problems are handled by special filing systems that tell one where to look for items. A library cataloging system is an example. Some theorists have proposed that human memory works in an analogous manner (e.g., memory is "content addressable"). An obvious problem with this analogy is that the library system only works due to the comprehension processes of its users. Within the memory metaphor, the comparable comprehending homunuculus has been relegated to the initial parsers. If one follows the analogy, the domain of the memory metaphor must therefore be restricted to the cataloging system itself without a comprehending user. Or it must at least be restricted to a user who rather automatically follows some prearranged search strategy without becoming involved in additional comprehension processes along the route that alter the prearranged search. To be cogent, it appears that the memory metaphor must assume that memory search becomes essentially algorithmic once given initial comprehension of the test item. What, however, specifies the search algorithms? Is there one algorithm, or a fixed set of algorithms? Must subjects store search algorithms in addition to memory traces plus tags? Would the account merely replace the question of how one finds a trace with the question of how one finds a search algorithm?

We reiterate that theories of direct access (or automatic recognition) still seem to presuppose that one "finds" a stored trace or memory. Assumptions of direct access do not obviate the need to specify the mechanisms responsible for such feats. However, a number of theorists (e.g., Mohs, Wescourt, & Atkinson, 1975) have argued against notions of direct access. As an alternative, they suggest that inputs are stored within structures, and that it is the organization of these stored structures which determines the effectiveness (in terms of probability correct or speed) of search. For example, a frequent assumption is that items may be stored together, as in a categorical or hierarchical manner. One can then restrict his search to some category or set of categories, and the smaller the set size or category the greater the speed and probability of effective search. In our opinion, such theories still presuppose some notion of "direct access." The access is now to a set, category or conceptual entity rather than the target item. Such theories make the further assumption, however, that once one "finds" the appropriate structure, search is determined by the particular structure that was stored.

It seems useful to raise some questions about hypothesized "stored structures" and about access to items in such structures. For example, if subjects have stored a set of inputs in a particular structure, must they then invariably search through that structure in a particular manner? Is search again algorithmic? If there are *optional* ways to gain access to elements in the structure, then what determines the ease of access? This latter question becomes equivalent to questions about how probes (e.g., as in recognition or cued recall) facilitate remembering. More particularly, the issue concerns *constraints* on the effectiveness of various probes. For example, one constraint seems to be that there are an "optimal number of items" per category or cue (e.g., Mandler, 1967).

Consider a study by Bransford and Nitsch (in preparation). Its purpose was to instantiate some intuitively obvious constraints on remembering. In particular, the study attempted to show that: (1) certain hypothesized structures of storage may "explain" one type of memory performance (e.g., free recall) but fail to explain another type (e.g., cued recall); (2) various cued recall probes permit subjects to "gain access" to different parts of hypothesized stored structures, hence there are variable points of "entry" into such structures; (3) there are definite constraints on cue effectiveness; in particular, constraints on the number of items that can be "associated" with a particular cue. Potential implications of the study are discussed below.

The Bransford–Nitsch study consisted of reading 28 acquisition sentences to three different groups of subjects. All subjects heard the same predicates (*tuning a violin, catching a ball,* etc.). Only the subject nouns were changed. Group 28 heard 28 distinct subject nouns. Group 7 heard seven different subject nouns with four predicates for each subject noun (that is, they heard four sentences about a boy, four about a policeman, four about a truck, etc., and these were blocked during acquisition). For Group 1 all 28 sentences were about a single topic, that is, a boy. All subjects were asked to image each sentence during acquisition (for example, "image a boy tuning a violin"). Following acquisition they were asked to free recall.

Free recall results indicated that Group 7 was superior to Groups 28 and 1. Group 1 exhibited the lowest recall. Such results parallel what would be expected given assumptions about benefits of categorization plus assumptions about the optimal number of items per category. For example, subjects in Group 7 could be expected to have "stored" the sentences in seven different categories and to have searched these categories. And indeed, their recall protocals were clustered in terms of the categories they had heard. But the subjects in Group 1 heard too many members of a single category, hence their ability to recall was limited.

Following free recall, all subjects were given probes to aid them in retrieval. One-half of the subjects in each group received the subject nouns as retrieval cues and the others received the object nouns. Under subject noun cue conditions, the subjects in Group 28 exhibited the best performance. Group 7 subjects were second and Group 1 subjects were the worst. In fact, Group 1 showed no improvement between free and cued recall.[3]

Now consider the results from subjects given the object nouns as retrieval cues. These results (as were those for subject noun cues) were scored only in terms of correct verb recall in order to compensate for the different numbers of subject nouns each group heard. And verbs were picked so as to minimize accurate guesses on the basis of general knowledge. For example, besides *tuning* a violin, one could *play, buy, drop, carry* a violin, etc. The number of incorrect verbs recalled was, in fact, less than 1%. Under object-cueing conditions, all three groups exhibited equivalent performances, and averaged 25 of 28 sentences correctly recalled. These results (especially considering Group 1) indicate that the problem of the optimal number of items per category is not a limitation on *storage*. Could it be a limitation on search?

Assume that the input sentences were stored in different organizational structures for the three different groups of subjects: Group 28 subjects "stored" each sentence individually, those in Group 7 stored them in terms of 7 different categories, and Group 1 subjects stored them all under one category. How did the presentation of retrieval cues help the subjects augment their recall? For example, when the subjects received the object nouns as cues, did they then

[3] Superficially, there is a flaw in the comparison of cued vs. free recall scores for Group 1 subjects. Cued recall should not exceed free recall if, during free recall, all the cues explicitly presented during cued recall were accessible to the subjects. For Group 1 subjects, the explicitly presented cue(s) (that is, boy) were undoubtedly accessible during free recall. Note, however, that the study still permits the conclusion that there is a definite constraint on cue effectiveness. When all sentences are cued by the same cue (Group 1), cued recall is inferior to Groups 7 and 28. There is also a different way to view these data. Suppose one looks at the ease of recalling a particular target sentence (e.g., "a boy tuning a violin") as a function of the list context in which it is embedded. The cue "boy" is much more effective for recreating the target sentence if the subjects have heard only one sentence about a boy (Group 28) than if they heard all sentences about a boy (Group 1). Intralist cue effectiveness is a function of the total set to which an input belongs (Garner, 1974).

have to search through their various stored organizational structures in order to "find" the proposition containing the object noun? If they did, then *why couldn't they simply search and find that proposition under other recall conditions as well?* It was assumed that the subjects in Group 7 stored the sentences in terms of seven categories organized by subject nouns and searched through these in free recall. Did these subjects have to search through these same categories when given the object nouns as cues? This seems highly unlikely given that their recall cued by object nouns was *superior* to recall cued by subject nouns. Why should subjects be able to effectively search for items containing the appropriate object nouns, yet fail to search as effectively for items containing the subject nouns? Similar arguments can be made about the performance of Group 1 subjects: If the subjects had to search to find a proposition containing a particular object noun, why couldn't they search just as well when given the subject noun as a cue?

The above results suggest that the presentation of cues allowed the subjects to somehow "modify their search processes." But it has already been noted that the ability to "know where to look" presupposes some knowledge of "where things are likely to be stored." In addition, if one postulates the existence of certain "stored organizational structures" on the basis of free recall performance then it would appear that the presentation of cues allowed the subjects to somehow "bypass" such structures. Perhaps the notion that inputs are "organized and stored together" is also an unfruitful metaphor. One might alternatively view performance in free recall as depending on the implicit generation of retrieval cues (and see Tulving, 1974). The organization postulated on the basis of free-recall performance would therefore not necessarily reflect the "structure of storage" as much as it reflects the availability of the implicit cues that subjects themselves use.[4]

Of course, the possibility that free recall is essentially an implicit cued-recall task does not solve the problem of how retrieval cues operate. If one doubts the assumption that cues or probes automatically tell one "where to look" for stored traces (plus appropriate tags) then what alternative metaphors are left to pursue? And which metaphors can gracefully incorporate obvious facts like those illustrated in the Bransford and Nitsch study; for example, the fact that a probe like "A boy" is much more effective for helping subjects remember a sentence like *A boy tuning a violin* if the subjects have heard only one rather than 28 sentences about "a boy." Must one postulate a limit on the number of "addresses" (indicating "where to look") that can be "stored" with any potential cue?

[4] We do not mean to suggest that remembering does not depend on initial encoding (for example, on what might be called initial "storage"). Initial encoding obviously influences the effectiveness of retrieval cues.

One theoretical possibility that is consistent with the memory metaphor might be that all propositions about a concept (e.g., about a boy) are attached to the same concept node in a memory network (e.g., see Anderson, 1975; Anderson & Bower, 1973). The more facts one learns about a concept, the harder it should be to retrieve old facts. In addition, "the search for a target proposition is subject to a cut-off time after which searching will cease" (Anderson, 1975, p. 250). This model still assumes content addressability of individual elements (for example, direct access to the "boy" node). It must also assume direct access to the object nouns in order to account for the effectiveness of those items as retrieval cues. In addition, the model postulates a limitation on search. Later, we discuss data that appear to raise doubts about the search limitation explanations of the Anderson and Bower model. First, however, we attempt to recast the problem of remembering into a "re-creation" metaphor rather than a "search for stored traces" metaphor. In the process, we attempt to redefine intuitively important concepts such as "direct access," "retrieval," "search," etc. For example, search processes are assumed to involve a gradual refinement of one's level of attunement in an attempt to re-create a particular experience. Such processes are therefore assumed to be more like those involved in creating a particular action (e.g., see Bernstein, 1967; Greene, 1971; Hayek, 1952, 1969; Turvey, this volume) than they are like a search for some *thing* stored in a particular place.

SECTION 3

Toward a Re-Creation Metaphor of Remembering

Consider Bartlett's (1932) claim that the act of remembering is related to thinking (and see Neisser, 1967). To what extent might it be fruitful to view remembering in this way? In thinking, one may experience a general feeling for the abstract form of some endeavor. One may begin with a vague "feeling of knowing" that some argument is erroneous or that she or he has some potentially fruitful idea. Only gradually does this abstract framework become articulated or focused. Finally it may reach a level sufficient for specifying particular, concrete ideas about what should be done.

In a similar manner, the process of remembering often seems to begin from an abstract "attitude" (cf. Bartlett, 1932) or "level of attunement." But this needs to be *focused* or *articulated* in order to achieve sufficient resolution to create a conscious experience that we call "remembering events." Sometimes, of course, one has a mere feeling of familiarity (e.g., what does that remind me of?) or "feeling of knowing" (e.g., "I'm sure I could recognize it if I heard it"; see Hart,

1965). Given a particular "attitude" or "level of attunement," the presentation of a probe (e.g., a "retrieval cue") can help one achieve further articulations. Phenomenally, the presentation of a probe frequently results in an "aha" experience, especially if one has been trying to recall information and then receives an appropriate probe. What processes underlie these "aha" experiences? More generally, what processes underly our abilities to *re-create* those experiences that we call remembering events?

Consider the possibility of viewing "retrieval" (re-creation) processes from the perspective of direct resonance. The simplest example of resonance is one involving tuning forks. If one strikes a "C" fork, another "C" fork in the vacinity will resonate to the vibrations that the former fork creates. But a resonance theory of remembering must clearly go beyond a mere "tuning fork" analogy. First, resonance must be based on semantic "resemblances" rather than merely on acoustic properties. Second, it seems fruitful to avoid the notion that one simply stores discrete "tuning forks" (that is, traces) that "await" the resonance process. It is obvious that previous experiences will "prime" or "tune" the organism, but the nature of this tuning may necessitate assumptions other than those about relatively independent traces that must be "found" in spatially discrete locations. Indeed, the heart of any resonance theory must involve the notion of *attunement* that *sets constraints* on the resonance processes. Without considerations of attunement, the resonance metaphor would quickly degenerate into a variant of the assumption that probes automatically tell one "where to look" for items that were previously stored.

As an introduction to attunement constraints on resonance, consider the Bransford and Nitsch study discussed earlier. Here it was argued that the presentation of probes seemingly allowed the subjects to "bypass" hypothetical "stored organizational structures." In fact, it was argued that assumptions about the organization of "what was stored" (based on free recall data) may more accurately reflect the accessibility of implicitly generated cues that it reflects the form of "spatially organized storage" per se. In addition, the study documented an intuitively obvious constraint on cue effectiveness: the cue "a boy" was much more effective for helping the subjects re-create previous experiences (for example, re-create an experience of hearing *A boy tuning a violin*) if the subjects had heard only a single sentence about "a boy" rather than 28 sentences about "a boy." What is the nature of this constraint on resonance? Why is there a limit on the optimal number of items per category or cue?

Consider the possibility that a probe must allow one to further *focus* or *articulate* his present level of attunement. As noted earlier, this problem can be seen as analogous to having a general feeling for an idea but needing further information in order to articulate some concrete, conscious experience. A similar process could underlie the problem of re-creating previous experiences; that is, of remembering events. For example, given 28 sentences with *different* subject nouns, a cue like "boy" would be sufficiently unique to allow the necessary degree of resolution to re-create a previous experience. Given 28 sentences beginning with "a boy," however, presentation of the cue "boy" would essentially be ambiguous. It would be analogous to presenting the subjects with a cue like "you heard *something*" when they had heard 28 different subject nouns during the acquisition task.

Assume, therefore, that some degree of focused resolution is a prerequisite for re-creating previous experiences. This would be equivalent to assuming that a probe must specify unique aspects of some experience, or that a probe must allow one to unambiguously differentiate among previous experiences he has had. Of course, aspects of the problem of differentiation are well known (e.g., see E. J. Gibson, 1969; Saltz, 1971). An emphasis on differentiation nevertheless seems especially important when considering factors that influence the effectiveness of retrieval cues.

Consider the problem of differentiation or uniqueness from a slightly different perspective. At Vanderbilt, Barry Stein has conducted a number of retrieval studies using similes as target stimuli. His studies extend previous work on similes that J. G. Nesbitt (1974) began. In Stein's studies, typical similes might be *A pin is like a nail; A bumper is like a statue; A pliers is like a crab,* etc. During acquisition, the subjects in Group 1 were simply asked to indicate the ease with which they could "solve" each of a list of 24 similes. Following acquisition, they were read the subject noun and asked to recall the second member of each pair. Cued recall reached an *overall* level of 59% accuracy. Given that the subjects indicated they had solved a simile, cued recall reached a level of 78% accuracy. For those similes that were impossible to solve during acquisition cued recall was only 35%.

Consider a second group run in Stein's study. These subjects heard the same similes in the same order. During acquisition, however, they were asked to rate each simile on a "soft–hard" dimension rather than an "easy–difficult" (to solve) dimension. That is, they were to rate whether the two items in each simile were relatively the same or different on a hardness–softness scale. Following acquisition, the subjects in Group 2 were given the subject nouns as retrieval cues. The procedure was identical to that used in Group 1. Gor Group 2 subjects, overall cued recall performance dropped to a level of 21% accuracy. Performance reached a level of 36% accuracy given that the subjects had decided that two items were the same on the soft–hard dimension. Acquisition ratings of "different" resulted in a cued-recall rate of 14%. In short, Group 2 subjects performed far below Group 1 subjects. It is instructive to note that in subsequent studies Stein found no differences between Groups 1 and 2 on recognition for individual subject and object nouns. The groups differed slightly in their abilities to recognize appropriate versus inappropriate pairings of previous acquisition items, but the differences were not nearly large enough to account for the magnitude of the differences in cued recall. What might account for this large decrement in Group 2's cued recall?

Note that the "retrieval" problem in Stein's study is not one of "finding" the "stored stimulus item" given a retrieval probe. This is not where group differences occur. Instead the problem is one of being able to "follow the connection" between the first and second member of each pair. And there was only one "connection" attached to each individual subject noun.[5] Does the ability to remember depend on "finding" or "following" connections, or on something else?

Consider the initial experience of Group 1 subjects. For them, each simile was presumably solved in a relatively unique manner. For example, to solve a simile such as *A pin is like a nail,* one must interpret "pin" in a particular manner (e.g., one may focus on the fact that it is long and pointed). Given the probe "a pin," it seems reasonable to assume that subjects must re-create their original experiences (which, for example, would include focusing on a *pin's* pointedness, etc.). This latter information would then uniquely specify another experience involving pointedness (i.e., a *nail*), hence cued recall would be relatively good.[6]

Contrast this situation with that found under Group 2 conditions. Here, the experiences generated by a probe like "a pin" would involve a respecification of its relative hardness. But a host of other items on the list were thought of in terms of their hardness, hence this information would not be sufficient to provide a focused resonance for re-creating the appropriate item from each pair. Viewed from this perspective, Group 2 in the Stein study is functionally equivalent to Group 3 in the Bransford and Nitsch study (where subjects heard all sentences about "a boy" and received "boy" as a retrieval cue). In the Stein study, the subjects have essentially been provided with the same functional cues for a large number of different events.

An analog to Group 2 of the Stein study might be to present a list of animal similes; for example, *A whale is like a rabbit* (because they both breathe), *A horse is like a spider* (because they both move), *A gnat is like a bull* (because they both eat), etc. Intuitively, such a list should be extremely difficult to remember. In fact, we find that given the subject nouns as retrieval cues, the subjects average less than 4 items correct out of 12. But the problem is not simply due to the fact that all "stimulus" and "response" terms are animals. These same animal words can be re-paired so that the cued recall performance will be excellent. For example, consider pairs like *A whale is like an elephant; A*

[5] Because there is only one proposition per subject noun, Stein's results are not easily handled by simply postulating some limit on search due to too many propositions attached to a single noun (e.g., see Anderson, 1975).

[6] Experiments III and IV in Barclay, Bransford, Franks, McCarrell, and Nitsch (1974) document the importance of re-creating one's initial acquisition perspective in order for a retrieval cue to be maximally effective.

horse is like a zebra; A gnat is like a mosquito, etc. Under these pairing conditions, our subjects averaged 11.5 (of 12) items in cued recall. These results are by no means surprising. Given an inspection of the lists, it is obvious that one will be easy to remember and the other extremely hard. But what underlies these "clear intuitions"? Why is one list so easy and the other so hard?

It seems reasonable to assume that there exist some unique resemblances between a whale and an elephant (for example). Both are animals that are relatively large. And we find that similes like "A whale is like a skyscraper" are also recalled excellently given the subject noun; hence the fact that a whale and elephant are both animals does not necessarily play a crucial role. On the other hand, a whale and a rabbit are both animals that exist, breathe, eat, move, etc. But a host of other animals fit this description as well. Such information therefore fails to help one *differentiate among* other acquisition experiences that occurred.

Of course, it is tempting to assume that the subjects in Stein's "soft–hard" condition simply failed to "form" the appropriate "connections" among items. Similarily, it seems intuitively obvious that similes such as *A whale is like a rabbit* and *A gnat is like a bull* are less adequately comprehended than similes such as *A whale is like an elephant; A gnat is like a mosquito,* etc. With respect to the two lists of animal similes, for example, one can literally "feel" the greater degree of comprehension (e.g., see Bransford & McCarrell, 1974) or "depth or processing" (e.g., see Craik & Lockhart, 1972) in the second list as opposed to the first. Put more globally, it seems obvious that "quality of encoding" can affect accuracies in remembering. But what is the nature of the relationship between encoding and remembering? Does quality of encoding affect the "strength" of stored traces and connections among traces? Perhaps an emphasis on re-creation suggests an alternative metaphor. Perhaps the degree to which events, at their original occurance, are differentiated from the rest of one's knowledge affects the ease of re-creating such experiences at a later time.

An additional experimental example may further clarify the "strength of stored connections" versus "re-creation/differentiation" issue. Consider a list of 15 sentences that all include different proper names in the subject and object positions (for example, *John is talking with Sally; Bill is helping Sam; Betty is eating lunch with Ralph*). Following a single acquisition trial, the subjects are provided with the subject nouns (for example, *John, Betty*) and asked to recall the sentence that went with each name. Informal pilot data suggest that the subjects do very poorly in this task. Now contrast this situation with one in which the acquisition sentences contain names of people with whom the subjects are well acquainted. For example, one might use the names (including last names) of professors and fellow students that all the subjects know. Under these latter conditions, our informal pilot data suggest that subjects' performance improves markedly. Furthermore, if one can articulate a *reason* why two people are interacting, the task seems even easier. For example, if *X* is *Y*'s student and one knows that they are working on a particular project together, then a statement like *Y is talking with X* seems to be more "richly" understood and easier to re-create.

The mere "fact" that previous knowledge about the participants in events can affect comprehending and remembering is not really at issue. Instead, the issue seems to be the manner in which one characterizes such "past knowledge" effects. For example, does past knowledge allow one to form "stronger" or a "greater number" of connections between subject and object items? Or does past knowledge set the stage for the articulation of unique events that are therefore more differentiable from other knowledge?

In this context, it is useful to consider Anderson and Bower's (1973) statements about meaningfulness and connectionism. They note that an important characteristic of many mnemonic devices is that ". . . they make the information to be remembered more memorable by adding further information. This addition of further information should mean more elements to associate together, so, on most associationist accounts, such mnemonics should make the task harder rather than easier [p. 57]." Later, they state: "The fact that the best remembered material appears to go against the spirit of associationism is an embarrassment to every existing associationist theory. However, being embarrassed is not the same as being proven false [p.57]."

We agree that HAM can seemingly overcome many of these "embarrassments"—especially by making assumptions about linguistic and perceptual parsers. But we believe it unfruitful to separate problems of remembering from problems of comprehending and perceiving. In addition, by emphasizing differentiation as a crucial process underlying re-creation (i.e., remembering), one is not embarrassed upon finding that meaningful events facilitate remembering. In general, meaningful events are those that are more differentiated. Therefore one's ability to re-create an event is not simply a function of the "meaning similarity" between a probe and a trace component (note that the probe "boy" is very similar to all "boy" traces). Furthermore, the ability to remember should not always be a simple linear function of the *number* of connections between a "stimulus" and "response" item. For example, a simile such as *A whale is like a rabbit* could permit a *large number* of connections (both breathe, eat, move, live, exist, etc.), whereas a simile such as *A whale is like a skyscraper* may permit only a *single* "connection." Despite this, the latter simile may be more effectively cued recalled (given the subject noun) as a function of the degree to which a certain relationship permits one to differentiate among other items experienced on the acquisition list.

One advantage of emphasizing a differentiation–re-creation view of remembering is that it stresses how one's ability to remember a particular input will depend on the context of other items in which it was originally embedded. For example, consider once again the two different lists of animal similes. In these lists, similes such as *A whale is like a rabbit* were much more difficult to remember than were similes such as *A whale is like an elephant.* Similes such as the latter presumably allowed subjects to articulate unique, well-differentiated relationships between both members of each pair. But it is important to note that certain well-differentiated resemblances (for example, between a whale and an elephant) are unique *only in relation to a total set of acquisition experiences.* The same argument holds for the unique relationship between whales and skyscrapers as well. It seems clear that "uniqueness" is a relational "property," and cue effectiveness should therefore vary as a function of the total set of acquisition experiences. For example, we have presented the subjects with a set of similes like *A whale is like a skyscraper, An elephant is like a redwood, A moose is like a giant,* etc. Under these conditions subjects begin to have trouble accurately connecting each "stimulus" with each "response." Similarly, we find that a sentence like *A sparrow is like a rocket* is accurately cued recalled under some list conditions. But if this sentence is embedded with others like *A hawk is like an airplane, A robin is like a kite,* etc., frequent mistakes and mispairings arise once again.

The problems herein encountered are intuitively obvious. It is well known that "similarity" among items can cause "interference." But the fact that such problems seem obvious should not detract from considerations of their importance. In fact, any framework would be inadequate if it did not readily expect such "obvious facts." Note that the present framework emphasizes that interference is not simply due to normative "stimulus" or "response" similarity. Instead, interference is due to the uniqueness of acquisition *events.* For example, a robin and a hawk are understood in a similar manner when embedded in similes such as *A robin is like an airplane; A hawk is like a kite.* But if one hears *A robin is like a stoplight, A hawk is like a kite,* etc., we find that there is less confusion among the "stimulus" items and their respective "responses."

One way to view these problems of interference is to note that it is impossible to adequately predict remembering by considering only the *local* properties of individual "traces" of inputs. The *global* properties of a total set of experiences play an important role in determining subjects' abilities to adequately re-create previous events. Indeed, even a simile like *A whale is like a rabbit* can be well remembered (for example, given the cue "whale") if it is embedded in a set of totally unrelated (for example, nonanimal) similes. *Remembering is a function of the total set of experiences to which an input belongs* (see Garner, 1974). From the present perspective, the problem of re-creating an experience is therefore a function of the degree to which probes help to differentiate among or uniquely specify one of a set of previous experiences. We assume that some degree of differentiation or focusing is a prerequisite for achieving sufficient resolution, and that probe effectiveness therefore depends on the relationship between probes and the total set of acquisition experiences one has had.[7]

Recognition as a Function of the Set to Which Items Belong

Global aspects of the total set of acquisition experiences have powerful affects on recognition as well as cued recall performance. For example, assume that the subjects hear a sentence like *The rock crushed the hut* embedded in a set of 23 additional acquisition sentences. It is obvious that subjects will be excellent at recognizing this sentence if it is semantically unrelated to the other acquisition sentences (e.g., see Peterson & McIntyre, 1973; Shepard, 1967). But if the same sentence is embedded among a set of semantically related sentences as in the Bransford and Franks experiments (e.g., Bransford & Franks, 1971, 1973), only a small percentage of subjects will think that they heard that particular sentence before.

Of course, it is easy to dismiss the Bransford–Franks type of results as simply due to "confusion" or "interference." But the subjects are not confused about the global information derived from the total set of acquisition experiences. They know the overall events that were communicated. They do, however, have trouble distinguishing between information that was actually presented and information consistent with the overall, invariant events that were described. This problem can be seen as analogous to one in which a blindfolded person is presented with a number of successive "touches" in order to identify an object. The structure that is ultimately apprehended will be specified by invariant information detected over time (e.g., see Gibson, 1966). If the person is later asked to distinguish the overall object from a set of additional objects, he will most likely perform accurately. But if the person's hand is placed on the object in various ways, and he is asked to distinguish between his exact acquisition touches and other possible touches of the object, his performance may be relatively poor.

This problem can also be viewed from a slightly different perspective. At Vanderbilt, Normand Benjamin is currently pursuing a project that involves the perception of a single object (that is, a black circle) moving across a stationary background grid. One group of subjects sees a series of slides that depict discrete snapshots of the circle tracing a continuous trajectory (e.g., like a falling ball

[7] Note that lists of highly similar items (all animals, all proper names, etc.) frequently result in many "errors" in remembering. It might be argued that such lists are unrepresentative, and overemphasize "errors." However, consider the fact that most classroom situations involve attempts to teach general ideas and concepts that are initially undifferentiated from one another. Students can frequently grasp abstract, global characteristics of the to-be-learned material, yet be unable to articulate precise examples and arguments that they experienced. This suggests that memory studies that use undifferentiated lists may be *more* representative of real-world situations than are studies that utilize initially highly differentiated lists.

that hits something and bounces back up). Following this acquisition sequence, a perceiver is aware of this continuous trajectory. Intuitively, one is more confident about the overall trajectory than about the discrete snapshots of the ball that were seen. In fact, preliminary results indicate that the subjects have difficulty differentiating between OLD and NEW static snapshots of the ball located on the acquired trajectory. But any snapshot that shows the ball at a position removed from the overall trajectory is easily recognized as something different from the acquisition set. Benjamin's study also includes a second group of subjects who see the same slides during acquisition, but the slides are randomized so that a continuous trajectory does not emerge. Preliminary results indicate that these subjects are less likely than Group 1 subjects to falsely recognize NEW snapshots if the latter were snapshots depicting the ball on the trajectory acquired by subjects in Group 1. Benjamin's results suggest that the invariant information detected as a function of the total set of acquisition experiences constitutes the most immediate and salient aspect of "what was learned."

Of course, the previously noted Bransford–Franks experiments might not be analogs to the "touching" example or to Benjamin's experiments. Other accounts of the Bransford–Franks experiments have been proposed. For example, Anderson and Bower (1973) assume that subjects count the number of "momentary context tags" associated with each proposition in a test sentence (e.g., see Anderson & Bower, 1973, pp. 347–352). The greater the number of tags associated with the propositions in each test sentence, the greater the probability that the subjects will say that they heard that sentence before. But assume that one presents subjects with a 24-sentence acquisition list structured like those in the Bransford–Franks experiments and includes one additional, single proposition sentence that is semantically *unrelated* to the other sentences. The subjects will be excellent at recognizing this sentence despite the fact that there is only one "momentary context tag" to count.[8] According to Anderson and Bower (1973) recognition performance given unrelated sentences involves the use of different decision strategies (e.g., see Anderson & Bower, 1973, p. 348). But in a mixed experiment, what tells the subjects which strategy to use? That is, in order to use different decision strategies, one must differentiate between related and unrelated sentences. Hypotheses that different strategies are used for related and unrelated items merely begs the question of how the initial differentiation occurs.

The problem of "specific remembering" of unique events can also be viewed from a different perspective. In general, subjects in the Bransford–Franks paradigm have difficulty distinguishing between OLD and NEW sentences. Yet there

[8]We ran this experiment just to be safe. All subjects recognized the ONE *The cat was scared* when it was unrelated to other acquisition sentences. Less than 40% of the subjects recognized the same sentence when it was included with five additional sentences (some ONES, TWOS, and THREES) about a cat (as in the Bransford–Franks paradigm).

is some ability to differentiate among these items; especially at the level of ONES (e.g., see Anderson & Bower, 1973, pp. 350–351; Bransford & Franks, 1971). However, a reanalysis of the OLD–NEW data from Bransford and Franks (1971, Experiment III) indicates that only certain ONES contribute to this difference. The reanalysis was motived by Singer and Rosenberg's (1973) findings that the subjects' "yes" responses to test sentences were strongly affected by the presence or absence of the main clause of the overall events (and see Franks & Bransford, 1974).

The ONE sentences from Bransford and Franks (1971, Experiment III) were partitioned into those that did versus did not contain the main clause of the events acquired during acquisition. For example, the ONE *The rock crushed the hut* was assumed to express the main clause of the FOUR *The rock which rolled down the mountain crushed the tiny hut at the edge of the woods.* Results indicated that there was no difference between OLD and NEW ONES that contained the main clause (for example, percent yes ratings were 37.3% and 34.6% for OLDS and NEWS, respectively). There was, however, a marked difference between ratings for OLD versus NEW ONES that *did not* contain the main clause (that is, percent yes ratings were 36.4% and 17.7% for OLDS and NEWS, respectively).

Consider these results in connection with the fact that a completely unique sentence embedded in a Bransford–Franks paradigm is extremely well recognized. If the subjects are listening to a set of semantically related acquisition sentences and hear a ONE like *The hut was tiny,* at least *some* of them may perceive it as unrelated to any previous experiences. Lack of information about the main clause may prompt the subjects to perceive such ONE's as unique. During recognition, these subjects should therefore recognize such paticular utterances, hence there should be overall recognition differences depending on whether such ONES were OLD or NEW. On the other hand, ONES with main clauses should be less likely to be perceived as unique during acquisition. Therefore, ONES with main clauses would be expected to receive equivalent ratings irrespective of whether they were OLD versus NEW. Considerations such as these may help clarify why researchers such as Reitman and Bower (1973) found such high degrees of specific "memory." They presented subjects with inputs such as 12, 14, 134, 1, etc., and assumed that subjects would use these to form an "overall idea" such as 1234. But why should subjects perceive inputs such as *twelve, fourteen,* etc. as subparts of an "idea" like 1234?

From the present perspective, the important issue is not whether people are always accurate versus inaccurate in their abilities to *remember.* Instead, the issue involves *the conditions under which subjects* can re-create previous experiences they have had. One can, of course, concentrate on accuracies and assume that inaccuracies are due to "errors," "confusion," "interference," etc. On the other hand, one can focus on the acquisition of global, invariant information as a function of a total set of acquisition experiences. In Benjamin's study with the moving dot, for example, it seems clear that the continuous trajectory (for Group 1 subjects) is the most salient aspect of what was learned. The information derived from the total set of acquisition experiences sets constraints on one's abilities to re-create previous acquisition experiences (i.e., remember). In short, it appears that what is learned cannot simply be equated with a list of previous memories. In fact, it would appear to be the global nature of what was learned that sets constraints on one's abilities to re-create (i.e., remember) those inputs experienced during the acquisition task.[9]

Further Constraints on Recognition

An emphasis on the total set of acquisition events also highlights another problem: Given a recognition test, how do subjects know that they have *not* experienced a particular item during acquisition? Do they have to search through all their stored traces in order to realize that a foil does not "match" any of these traces? Do subjects know "where to look" for a foil and then check to see if it has an appropriate context tag?

There are conditions under which subjects do *appear* to "search the acquisition set" in order to reject items (e.g., Sternberg, 1966). In these studies, the larger the size of the acquisition set the greater time it takes to say "no" (as well as "yes"). But even under these very short-term memory conditions, decisions are affected by the global structure of the set of acquisition items. For example, Morin, De Rosa, and Stultz (1967) presented the subjects with acquisition sets like 3456. They found that the subjects' responses were a function of the "distance" between probes and the list boundary. For example, subjects were faster at rejecting 9 than 7.

Results such as those of Morin *et al.* (1967) are not gracefully incorporated into "exhaustive search" models nor "look for a context tag" models. Yet it is easy to believe that such results occur only under special circumstances and with special kinds of materials. Perhaps they represent the exception rather than the rule. But assume that subjects hear a list of nonsense syllables and later are presented with foils–one of which is a picture of a red triangle. Such a foil will be so readily rejected that it's presentation would seem ridiculous from the subjects' (and experimenter's) point of view. Or assume that the subjects hear a list of words that all have some invariant semantic structure (for example, all are examples of fruits), and are later presented with foils like *truck* or *rock*. Once again, the subjects should be able to reject these with ease.

Of course, the preceding examples are obvious. And there are a number of ways to conceptualize such results. For example, one could assume that subjects

[9] Problems of re-creating previous experiences become even more extreme when one attempts to remember things like "how I used to think about a particular problem," (say as a graduate student) etc. In these situations, one's present perspective seems to play an important role in determining the nature of the "memories" he re-creates.

"store" a proposition like "all inputs are nonsense syllables," "all inputs are fruits," etc. One could then readily reject foils that did not "fit" the constraints that the proposition expressed. But would this approach illuminate the problem or bury it? For example, how does one know that a foil is not a nonsense syllable, or not a fruit? Does one first find this type of information in "semantic memory" and then use it to "cut off" a search of "episodic memory"? If so, then how does semantic memory operate? For example, if one is asked "Do you know the meaning of *salakan*?," does he have to search the entire contents of his memory in order to arrive at a negative answer? Similarly, does one have to search all possible information in order to reject a statement like *Some chairs are people*? Such decisions are made very quickly (Meyer, 1970); and the further apart the conceptual boundaries, the easier the negative decisions are to make (e.g., Moyer, 1973).

It seems clear that the "rejection" problem occurs in "semantic" as well as "episodic" memory. To ignore it in accounts of "memory" may be to ignore one of the most important sources of constraint on adequate theories of remembering. From the present perspective, work on this problem may help illuminate how resonance operates as a function of one's level of attunement, and how one's current level of attunement can be changed and focused in response to a particular probe. With respect to "episodic memory," the subjects seem to reject items which afford no re-creation of a previous experience. Some of our investigations into the problem reveal statements such as "I'm positive I didn't experience that during acquisition because I know that I would have especially noted it if I did." The problem of rejecting items may therefore be intimately related to the problem of why we are not constantly deluged by the re-creation of previous, personal experiences with familiar inputs. Problems of resonance are inextricably bound to characterizations of one's present level of attunement. We know very little about these attunement processes, but it seems reasonable to assume that in a typical memory experiment one's level of attunement will be a function of abstract characteristics of the total set of acquisition experiences. The ease with which subjects can reject items should therefore be a function of a foil's relationship to the set of acquisition experiences as a whole.

SUMMARY AND CONCLUSION

We have questioned some of the assumptions underlying the prevailing memory metaphor. Spatial components of the metaphor include assumptions such as "traces are stored in certain locations" and "certain traces are stored together in episodic memory" (for example, as in hierarchical organization). Similar assumptions are frequently made about "semantic memory;" for example, that "ideas" are stored at greater or lesser distances from one another and that this affects the time to get from one place to another, the speed of "spreading activation" (cf. Meyer, Schvaneveldt, & Ruddy, 1972), etc. These spatial assumptions strongly affect conceptualizations of the nature of search and retrieval processes; for example, that one must know *where* to look to find a stored trace (plus its appropriate context tag).

The metaphorical status of these assumptions is not the problematic issue. Indeed, some theorists (e.g., Hesse, 1966) have argued that all explanations are of the nature of metaphoric redescriptions. The issue, then, concerns the *fruitfulness* of one's metaphors. The issue concerns the tradeoff between the memory metaphor's ability to help conceptualize certain phenomena and its tendency to foster neglect of other problems that might otherwise stimulate theoretical growth in a number of areas.

Consider the assumption that certain "ideas" are stored at certain "distances" from one another in "semantic memory." Such conceptualizations convey the impression of some static form of storage invariably accessed when making decisions. For example, the "distance metaphor" might capture the notion that given a triad like *shirt–shoe–rock, shirt* and *shoe* seem to be "closer together" than *rock* and *shoe.* But assume that one is looking for objects that could be used to pound a nail into the wall. Now *shoe* and *rock* seem to be "closer together" than *shoe* and *shirt.* In short, static conceptualizations of semantic memory fail to orient one toward the flexibility of understood relationships as a function of the context or setting in which events occur (e.g., see Anderson & Ortony, 1976; Barclay, Bransford, Franks, McCarrell, & Nitsch, 1974; Barclay & Jahn, in press; Bransford, McCarrell, & Nitsch, 1976).

This chapter has also questioned the fruitfulness of assuming the episodic events are "stored together." Assumptions about spatially organized structures may "explain" some aspects of free recall performance (for example, clustering). Yet it was also argued that the explicit presentation of retrieval probes allows the subjects to "bypass" such hypothesized structures. That is, if the subjects had to "search through" such structures in order to "find" traces containing the information specified by a retrieval probe (for example, a "trace" containing the word *violin*) then it is not clear why they could not simply have searched and found that trace under nonprobe conditions. We therefore suggested that phenomena such as clustering in free recall may reflect more about the nature of the cues implicitly accessible to the subjects than the "spatially organized storage" of the inputs per se.

The preceding arguments make certain assumptions about the processes by which probes help one remember previous experiences. If the presentation of a probe simply tells one "where to look" to "find" a certain item then the spatial components of the memory metaphor are still reasonable. But how could a probe tell one "where to look"? If probes somehow "specify the addresses" of certain stored items, then why is the effectiveness of probes limited? For example, why are some components of an event more effective than others for "retrieving" the total event (e.g., see Peterson, 1974). Or why does the same cue for 28 different sentences fail to facilitate recall? Because of a limit on the number of "addresses" that can be attached to a particular item (for example, "boy")? Because of a cut-off on search? In our opinion, it is unfruitful to assume that probes tell one "where to look" for previously stored traces. It may be as unfruitful to assume that cues retrieve "idea traces" as it is to assume that a sunny day acts as a cue to help one retrieve "happiness traces" or "spring fever traces." It seems more fruitful to ask how cues help one *re-create* previous experiences.

Following Bartlett (1932), we suggested that remembering involves processes similar to thinking. Both processes frequently begin with an abstract "attitude" (cf. Bartlett, 1932) or "level of attunement" that needs to be further articulated or focused. The "retrieval" problem underlying remembering was assumed to be analogous to a process of helping one further focus or articulate his thoughts. The most powerful variable affecting cued recall as well as recognition seems to be *the relationship between the probe and the total set of acquisition experiences.* A probe must allow one to further focus his thought processes by permitting a sufficient degree of differentiation among previous experiences. And the degree of differentiation is relative to the subjects current level of "attunement" resulting from the set of acquisition experiences as a whole.

Of course, problems of differentiation are one of the most widely known "facts" in psychology. Everyone realizes the importance of constructing experimental lists so as to avoid unnecessarily "confusing" the subjects. And it hardly seems surprising that given a "confusable" list, the subjects *do* make "mistakes." But what do these obvious facts indicate about the nature of remembering? In particular, what do they indicate about the notion that an input results in a relatively independent, stored trace?

Assume that the subjects are presented with discrete, unrelated inputs (e.g., Shepard, 1967). Under these conditions, the subjects look like "exact copy" mechanisms that simply store traces. Yet one can radically change the probability that particular inputs are remembered by manipulating the acquisition set in which they are embedded. For example, Bransford, Franks, and Nitsch (in preparation) find that the same schematic face may be either poorly or well recognized depending on its relationship to the other faces shown during acquisition. And when the subjects are provided with inputs that allow the specification of certain wholistic, invariant structures (e.g., Benjamin's on going work; Bransford & Franks, 1971), their "memories" are more related to these wholistic structures than to "copies" of the exact inputs per se. Similar variables appear to affect the "strength of connections" between traces or trace components. For example, a simile like *A sparrow is like a rocket* appears to result in the formation of a "strong" sparrow–rocket "connection" when it occurs in some acquisition contexts. Yet in other acquisition contexts, the "connection" appears to be weak.

The preceding arguments illustrate some of the challenges of contextualism (see Jenkins, this volume). From this perspective, "context" is not simply a variable to be manipulated. Instead, contextualism suggests an orientation toward problems that questions many prevailing assumptions; for example, the assumption that the problem of remembering is equivalent to the problem of "finding" discrete traces and "following the connections" from one element of a trace to the next. And a contextualist orientation suggests methodological caveats. For example, remembering is assumed to be a function of the total set of acquisition experiences (that is, of the global context in which inputs are embedded). Memory performance is therefore not simply a function of local properties of individual traces, but is rather a function of the global characteristics of the set of acquisition experiences as a whole. It follows that certain variables may or may not be important depending on the acquisition context. For example, it seems clear that one could set up conditions in which subject nouns are better retrieval cues than object nouns. Yet one can also do the reverse. If one's theoretical purpose is to make general statements about particular populations of entities (for example, about the retrieval effectiveness of subject nouns versus object nouns; about recognition accuracies for four proposition versus one proposition acquisition sentences) then he can quickly run into difficulty. The effectiveness of such variables will be a function of the relationship between inputs and the acquisition set as a whole.

We close by noting that a basic reason for interest in the problem of "memory" involves a concern with the processes by which past experiences affect one's subsequent interactions with the environment. For example, it is frequently assumed that such interactions depend on the nature of one's knowledge stored in "long-term memory." From this perspective, one's actions and interpretations are therefore assumed to be mediated by "contact" with previous "memories" that were stored. Yet we have suggested that "what is learned" cannot be reduced to the problem of how one forms and stores "memories." In fact, we have argued that learning involves the detection of invariant information from a set of acquisition experiences, and that one's ability to accurately *remember* depends on "what was learned." If the problem of remembering is assumed to depend on the organism's state of attunement following acquisition, and if learning is viewed as the problem of how organisms become attuned to perceive situations, then Gibson's (see Section 1) claim that perception does not depend on memory (that is, on contact with previously stored memories) becomes an extremely important idea to pursue.

ACKNOWLEDGMENTS

This chapter was supported in part by grant number NE-6-00-3-0026 to John D. Bransford and Jeffery J. Franks. We are extremely grateful to Keith Clayton for his helpful comments and advice.

REFERENCES

Anderson, J. R. Item-specific and relation-specific interference in sentence memory. *Journal of Experimental Psychology: Human Learning and Memory.* 1975, **104**, 249–260.

Anderson, J. R., & Bower, G. H. Recognition and retrieval processes in free recall. *Psychological Review,* 1972, **79**, 97–123.

Anderson, J. R., & Bower, G. H. *Human associative memory.* Washington, D.C.: Winston, 1973.

Anderson, R., & Ortony, A. On putting apples into bottles–a problem of polysemy. *Cognitive Psychology,* 1975, **7**, 167–180.

Barclay, J. R., Bransford, J. D., Franks, J. J., McCarrell, N. S., & Nitsch, K. Comprehension and semantic flexibility. *Journal of Verbal Learning and Verbal Behavior,* 1974, **13**, 471–481.

Barclay, J. R., & Jahn, G. Distance semantique variable et "La" structure de la memoire semantique. In S. Erlich & E. Tulving (Eds.), *Lau memoire semantique.* Paris: Bulletin de Psychologie, 1976.

Bartlett, F. C. *Remembering: A study in experimental and social psychology.* Cambridge, England: Cambridge University Press, 1932.

Bergson, H. *Creative evolution.* (Translated by A. Mitchell) New York: Henry Holt & Co. 1911.

Bernstein, L. *The co-ordination and regulation of movements.* London: Pergamon Press, 1967.

Bower, G. H. Stimulus-sampling theory of encoding variability. In A. W. Melton & E. Martin (Eds.), *Coding processes in human memory.* Washington, D. C.: V. H. Winston & Sons, 1972. Pp. 85–123.

Bransford, J. D., & Franks, J. J. The abstraction of linguistic ideas. *Cognitive Psychology,* 1971, **2**, 331–350.

Bransford, J. D., & Franks, J. J. The abstraction of linguistic ideas: A review. *Cognition: International Journal of Cognitive Psychology,* 1973, 211–249.

Bransford, J. D., Franks, J. J., & Nitsch, K. E. Schematic faces: The abstraction of prototypic forms. Manuscript in preparation.

Bransford, J. D., & Johnson, M. K. Consideration of some problems of comprehension. In W. Chase (Ed.), *Visual information processing.* New York: Academic Press, 1973. Pp. 383–438.

Bransford, J. D., & McCarrell, N. S. A sketch of a cognitive approach to comprehension. In W. Weimer & D. Palermo (Eds.), *Cognition and the symbolic processes.* Hillsdale, New Jersey: Lawrence Erlbaum Assoc., 1974.

Bransford, J. D., McCarrell, N. S., & Nitsch, K. E. Contexte, comprehension et flexibilité semantique: Quelques implications theoriques et methodologiques. In S. Erlich & E. Tulving (Eds.), *La Memoire Semantique.* Paris: Bulletin de Psychologie, 1976.

Bransford, J. D., & Nitsch, K. E. Investigations of some constraints on the effectiveness of intra- list retrieval cues. Manuscript in preparation.

Chomsky, N. *Aspects of a theory of syntax.* Cambridge, Massachusetts: MIT Press, 1965.

Craik, F. I. M., & Lockhart, R. S. Levels of processing: A framework for memory research. *Journal of Verbal Learning and Verbal Behavior,* 1972, **11**, 671–684.

De Groot, A. B. *Thought and choice in chess.* The Hague: Mouton, 1965.

Ebbinghaus, H. *Memory: A contribution to experimental psychology,* 1885. (Translated by H. A. Roger and C. E. Bussenius.) New York: Columbia University Press, 1913.

Franks, J. J. Toward understanding understanding. In W. Weimer & D. Palermo (Eds.), *Cognition and the symbolic processes.* Hillsdale, New Jersey: Lawrence Erlbaum Assoc., 1974. Pp. 231–261.

Franks, J. J., & Bransford, J. D. A brief note on linguistic integration. *Journal of Verbal Learning and Verbal Behavior*, 1974, **13**, 217–219.

Garner, W. R. *The processing of information and structure*. Hillsdale, New Jersey: Lawrence Erlbaum Assoc., 1974.

Gibson, E. J. *Principles of perceptual learning and development*. New York: Appleton-Century-Crofts, 1969.

Gibson, J. J. *The senses considered as perceptual systems*. Boston: Houghton-Mifflin, 1966.

Gibson, J. J., & Gibson, E. J. Perceptual learning: Differentiation or enrichment. *Psychological Review*, 1955, **62**, 32–41.

Greene, P. H. Problems of organization of motor systems. *Quarterly Report No. 29*, Institute for Computer Research, University of Chicago, 1971.

Gregory, R. L. Seeing as thinking: An active theory of perception. *The Times Literary Supplement*, June 23, 1972, 707–708.

Hart, J. T. Memory and the feeling-of-knowing experience. *Journal of Educational Psychology*, 1965, **56**, 208–216.

Hayek, F. A. *The sensory order*. Chicago: The University of Chicago Press, 1952.

Hayek, F. A. The primacy of the abstract. In A. Koestler & J. R. Smythies (Eds.), *Beyond reductionism*. Boston: Beacon Press, 1969.

Hesse, M. B. *Models and analogies in science*. Notre Dame: University of Notre Dame Press, 1966.

Katona, G. *Organizing and memorizing*. New York: Columbia University Press, 1940.

Katz, J. J., & Fodor, J. The structure of a semantic theory. *Language*, 1963, **39**, 170–210.

Köhler, W. *Gestalt psychology: An introduction to new concepts in modern psychology*. New York: Liverwright, 1947.

Light, L. L., & Carter-Sobell, L. Effects of changed semantic context on recognition memory. *Journal of Verbal Learning and Verbal Behavior*, 1970, **9**, 1–11.

Mandler, G. Organization and memory. In K. W. Spence & J. T. Spence (Eds.), *The psychology of learning and motivation*. Vol. 1. New York: Academic Press, 1967. Pp. 328–371.

Meyer, D. E. On the representation and retrieval of stored semantic information. *Cognitive Psychology*, 1970, **1**, 242–299.

Meyer, D. E., Schvaneveldt, R. W., & Ruddy, M. G. Activation of lexical memory. Paper presented at the meeting of the Psychonomic Society, St. Louis, Missouri, November, 1972.

Mohs, R. C., Wescourt, K. T., & Atkinson, R. C. Search processes for associative structures in long-term memory. *Journal of Experimental Psychology: General*, 1975, **104**, 103–121.

Morin, R. E., DeRosa, D. V., & Stultz, V. Recognition memory and reaction time. *Acta Psychologica*, 1967, **27**, 298–305.

Moyer, R. S. Comparing objects in memory: Evidence suggesting an internal psychophysics. *Perception & Psychophysics*, 1973, **13**, 180–184.

Neisser, U. *Cognitive psychology*. New York: Appleton-Century-Crofts, 1967.

Nesbitt, J. G. Memory for nouns from similes as a function of ease of comprehension: An investigation of some interactions among memory measures. Unpublished doctoral dissertation, Vanderbilt University, 1974.

Norman, D. A. *Memory and attention*. New York: Wiley, 1969.

Peterson, R. G. Imagery and cued recall: Concreteness or context? *Journal of Experimental Psychology*, 1974, **102**, 841–844.

Peterson, R. G., & McIntyre, C. W. The influence of semantic 'relatedness' on linguistic integration and retention. *American Journal of Psychology*, 1973, **86**, 697–706.

Reder, L. M., Anderson, J. R., & Bjork, R. A. A semantic interpretation of encoding specificity. *Journal of Experimental Psychology*, 1974, **102**, 648–656.

Reitman, J. S., & Bower, G. H. Storage and later recognition of exemplars of concepts. *Cognitive Psychology,* 1973, **4,** 194–206.

Saltz, E. *The cognitive bases of human learning.* Homewood, Illinois: The Dorsey Press, 1971.

Shepard, R. N. Recognition memory for words, sentences, and pictures. *Journal of Verbal Learning and Verbal Behavior,* 1967, **6,** 156–163.

Singer, M., & Rosenberg, S. T. The role of grammatical relations in the abstraction of linguistic ideas, *Journal of Verbal Learning and Verbal Behavior,* 1973, **12,** 273–284.

Staudenmayer, H. Understanding conditional reasoning with meaningful propositions. In R. J. Falmagne (Ed.), *Reasoning: Representation and process in children and adults.* Hillsdale, New Jersey: Lawrence Erlbaum Assoc., 1975.

Sternberg, S. High-speed scanning in human memory. *Science,* 1966, **153,** 652–654.

Tulving, E. Cue dependent forgetting. *American Scientist,* **62,** Jan.–Feb., 1974, 74–82.

Watkins, M. J., & Tulving, E. Episodic memory: When recognition fails. *Journal of Experimental Psychology: General,* 1975, **104,** 5–29.

Author Index

The numbers in *italics* refer to pages on which the complete references are listed.

T

U

V

Subject Index

B

D

E

N

For Product Safety Concerns and Information please contact our EU
representative GPSR@taylorandfrancis.com
Taylor & Francis Verlag GmbH, Kaufingerstraße 24, 80331 München, Germany

www.ingramcontent.com/pod-product-compliance
Ingram Content Group UK Ltd.
Pitfield, Milton Keynes, MK11 3LW, UK
UKHW020024200926
475702UK00014B/2053
9781138205055

Contributors

Simon Batterbury is Lecturer in the School of Anthropology, Geography and Environmental Studies at the University of Melbourne, Australia, and has taught geography and development studies at the University of Arizona, the LSE, Brunel University, the University of Colorado and Roskilde University (Denmark). He has worked on the political ecology of dryland agriculture and rural development in West Africa for a decade, particularly in Burkina Faso and Niger.

Reginald Cline-Cole is Senior Lecturer in Geography at the Centre of West African Studies, University of Birmingham, UK. His research and teaching interests focus on rural change, with emphasis on development issues at the people–environment interface, and on indigenous perceptions and valuations of environmental resources. He recently co-edited *Contesting Forestry in West Africa* (2000, Ashgate, Aldershot, with Clare Madge) and *ICTs, 'Virtual Colonisation' and Political Economy*, Special Issue of the *Review of African Political Economy* (with Mike Powell. 2004, ROAPE Publications, London).

David J. Francis is Director of the Africa Centre for Peace and Conflict Studies at the University of Bradford, UK. His recent publications include *The Politics of Economic Regionalism: Sierra Leone in ECOWAS*, (2001, Ashgate, Aldershot) and 'Nigeria and West Africa,' in Darryl Howlett and John Glen (eds), *Realism and Culture: A Strategic Debate* (2002, Ashgate, Aldershot). His forthcoming book, *Uniting Africa: Building Regional Security Systems*, is being published by Lynne Rienner.

Bara Guèye is a socio-economist with long established training skills in participatory research and planning methods. He currently co-ordinates IIED's PRA/MARP training programme in the West African Sahel.

Jimmy Kandeh is Associate Professor in the Department of Political Science at Richmond University, USA. He specialises in the areas of comparative and African politics, and is the author of numerous articles on West African politics and recipient of a US Institute of Peace Grant. He has just finished a book on West African politics.

Joyce Kannan is Assistant Professor of History at Wright State University, Dayton, Ohio, USA, where her areas of specialisation include East Africa, gender, development and Christianity.

Fergus Lyon is with the Centre for Enterprise and Economic Development Research at Middlesex University, where he is an applied researcher on economic development policy. He is currently taking part in a joint study of market institutions and urban food supplies for the urban poor in Nigeria and Zambia. He has written a book on participatory social research methodologies and published several articles on agricultural marketing, urban food systems, micro-enterprises and trader associations in Ghana (which was also the subject of his PhD). His research interests lie in social relations of markets, regional policy and Third World development.

Adebayo Olukoshi is Executive Secretary of CODESRIA (Council for the Development of Social Science Research in Africa) in Dakar, Senegal. He is also Research Professor at the Nigerian Institute for International Affairs, and was previously Senior Research Fellow/Research Programme Coordinator at the Nordic Africa Institute in Sweden.

Abioseh Michael Porter is Professor of English and Department Head at Drexel University, Philadelphia, USA. His areas of specialisation include the African novel in French and English, and Comparative Black Literary Relations.

Gina Porter is Senior Research Fellow in Anthropology at the University of Durham. She studied Geography at Liverpool University before spending ten years teaching in several Nigerian universities. She has been based at Durham University since 1986, first in the Geography Department and, since 2001, in the Anthropology Department. She has undertaken field research, which combines ethnographic approaches with a strong interest in spatial perspectives, in Nigeria, Ghana, South Africa, Kenya, Brazil, Papua New Guinea and India. Her recent publications include the jointly edited (with P. Fernando) *Balancing the Load: Women, Gender and Transport* (2002, Zed, London) and *Knowledge, Power and Development Agendas: NGOs North and South* (with Mawdsley, E., Townsend, J. and Oakley, P.) (2002, Intrac, Oxford).

J. Barry Riddell is Professor of Geography at Queen's University, Kingston, Ontario, Canada. The focus of his research has been on the experience of change and development in the Third World, including the diffusion of change, transportation evolution, population migration, periodic markets, the role of the state, urban bias, the food crisis, themes in literature, structural adjustment, globalisation, landscapes of coping, and the nature of geographical investigation in the Third World.

Elsbeth Robson lectures in Development Studies at Keele University, UK. Her research interests, which are wide and varied, include children's geographies and geographies of young people; geographies of caring and reproductive work; geography and gender; and gender and development geographies of HIV-AIDS, disability, impairment and health. She has edited (with Katie Willis) *Postgraduate Fieldwork in Developing Areas: A Rough Guide* for the Developing Areas Research Group of the Royal Geographical Society – Institute of British Geographers, and published numerous journal articles.

Ken Swindell is Honorary Senior Research Fellow at the Centre of West African Studies, University of Birmingham, UK, where he taught for many years until his retirement. His recent publications include *Participation in Practice: Case Studies from the Gambia* (with David Brown *et al.*, ODI, 2002, London) and *Rural Change and Development in Tropical Africa* (with David Siddle) (1990, Basil Blackwell, Oxford).

Camilla Toulmin, a socio-economist, is currently Director of the International Institute for Environment and Development, London, where she previously managed the Drylands Programme, which she set up on joining the organisation. She has worked for many years on dryland and resource management and governance issues in the Sahel, and was a member of the expert panel for the United Nations Desertification Convention. Her recent work includes research on changing rights to land in West Africa, livelihoods and poverty in Mali, challenges and opportunities relating to decentralisation, and collective management of common resources. Her publications include *Cattle, Women and Wells* (1992, OUP, Oxford), *Sustaining the Soil. Indigenous Soil and Water Conservation in Africa* (co-edited with Chris Reij and Ian Scoones) (1996, Earthscan, London), *Evolving Land Rights, Policy and Tenure in Africa* (with Julian Quan) (2000, DFID/IIED/NRI, London) and *Negotiating Access to Land in West Africa: A Synthesis of Findings from Research on Derived Rights to Land* (with Philippe Lavigne Delville) (2001, IIED, London).

Series Preface

In the late 1980s, the Developing Areas Research Group (DARG) of the then Institute of British Geographers produced a series of three edited student texts under the general editorship of Prof. Denis Dwyer (University of Keele). These volumes, focusing on Latin America, Asia and Tropical Africa respectively, were published by Longman and achieved wide circulation, thereby also contributing to the financial security of DARG and enabling it to expand its range of activities. These are now out of print. The Latin American volume was revised and published in a second edition in 1996.

However, there have been dramatic changes in the global political economy, in the nature of development challenges facing individual developing countries and regions, and in debates on development theory over the last decade or so. In a review of the situation in 1997/8, the DARG Committee and Matthew Smith, the former Geography Editor at Addison Wesley Longman (now Pearson Education) therefore felt that mere updating of the existing texts would not do these circumstances justice or catch the imagination of a new generation of students. Accordingly, we have launched an entirely new series.

This is both different in conception and larger, enabling us to address smaller, more coherent continental or subcontinental regions in greater depth. The organising principles of the current series are that the volumes should be thematic and issue-based rather than having a traditional sectoral focus, and that each volume should integrate perspectives on development theory and practice. The objective is to ensure topicality and clear coherence of the series, while permitting sufficient flexibility for the editors and contributors to each volume to highlight regional specificities and their own interests. Another important innovation is that the series was launched in January 1999 by a book devoted entirely to provocative contemporary analyses of *Development as Theory and Practice; current perspectives on development and development co-operation*. Edited by David Simon and Anders Närman, this provides a unifying foundation for the regionally focused texts and is designed for use in conjunction with one or more of the regional volumes.

The complete series is expected to include titles on Central America and the Caribbean, Southern and East Africa, West Africa, South Asia, Pacific

Asia, the transitional economies of central Asia, and Latin America. While the editors and many contributors are DARG members, other expertise – not least from within the respective regions – is being specifically included to provide more diverse perspectives and representativeness. Once again, DARG is benefiting substantially from the royalties. In addition, a generous number of copies of each volume will be supplied to impoverished higher education institutions in developing countries in exchange for their departmental publications, thereby contributing in a small way to overcoming one pernicious effect of the debt crisis, namely the dearth of new imported literature available to staff and students in those countries.

David Simon
Royal Holloway, University of London

Series Editor
(Chair of DARG 1996–8)

Acknowledgements

This book has been long in the making. Along the way, we have become indebted to friends and colleagues on three continents for their help and encouragement, not least the chapter authors who have been, for the most part, understanding and professional. David Simon, the series editor, deserves a special note of thanks for his patience, encouragement and, above all, his mediation skills!

We would also like to thank the various editors with whom we have liaised during the long gestation period of this book, most recently Andrew Taylor, for not *quite* giving up on us and the project. Harry Buglass of the Institute of Archaeology and Antiquities at the University of Birmingham prepared the accompanying map and figure.

Chapter 2 was originally published by the Council for the Development of Social Science Research in Africa (CODESRIA), BP 3304, Dakar, Senegal. (website: http://www.codesria.org).

Finally, we cannot thank our respective families enough for their unflinching support and forbearance.

Reginald Cline-Cole and Elsbeth Robson
April 2004

CHAPTER 1

Paths through socio-economic change, livelihoods and development in West African worlds

Reginald Cline-Cole

1 A 'natural' West African region?

References to either 'West Africa' or a 'West African Region' raise important questions relating as much to geographic space as to self-identification within such space. For, contrary to the claims of early regional geographers like Harrison-Church (1957) who, in his time, spoke of 'a real physical separateness' characterising a West African region, there exists no 'organic' delimitation of such a region. In fact, the notion of a 'West Africa' has always been understood in a number of different ways throughout history. Thus, rather than referring to a territory fixed in either time or space, imagined geographies of West Africa are characterised by shifting 'boundaries', 'limits' and 'understandings'. In part, of course, this is due to the fact that the concept and label of a 'West Africa' are both relatively recent and European, rather than (West) African in origin. In part, too, this is due to the fact that there was never any consensus over European understandings of the concept, with early British delineations, for instance, differing from contemporaneous French imaginings, sometimes significantly (Morgan and Pugh 1969).

Nor do contemporary regional (boundary) geographies of exclusion/inclusion demonstrate any greater consensus, derived as they are from these contested historical geographies, in addition to being based on national territories, whose political or international boundaries date only to the period of colonial rule and after, and were 'carved out without much care for underlying social, cultural and economic dimensions' (Toulmin and Guèye 2003) (Figure 1.1). In both academic and popular usage, then, the label has been used variously to refer to:

- the area south of the Sahara Desert and west of the Nigeria–Cameroon border, covering both the mainland area and the Atlantic Ocean islands of Fernando Po, Sâo Tome and Principe, and Cape Verde, and representing between two-thirds and four-fifths the size of the United States of America or a somewhat greater proportion of Eastern and Western Europe combined (Morgan and Pugh 1969; Raynaut 1997);
- the territory identified above, but with the addition of Chad, to give a region which occupies slightly less than a third of the land area of sub-Saharan Africa (Aryeetey-Attoh 1997, 2001);

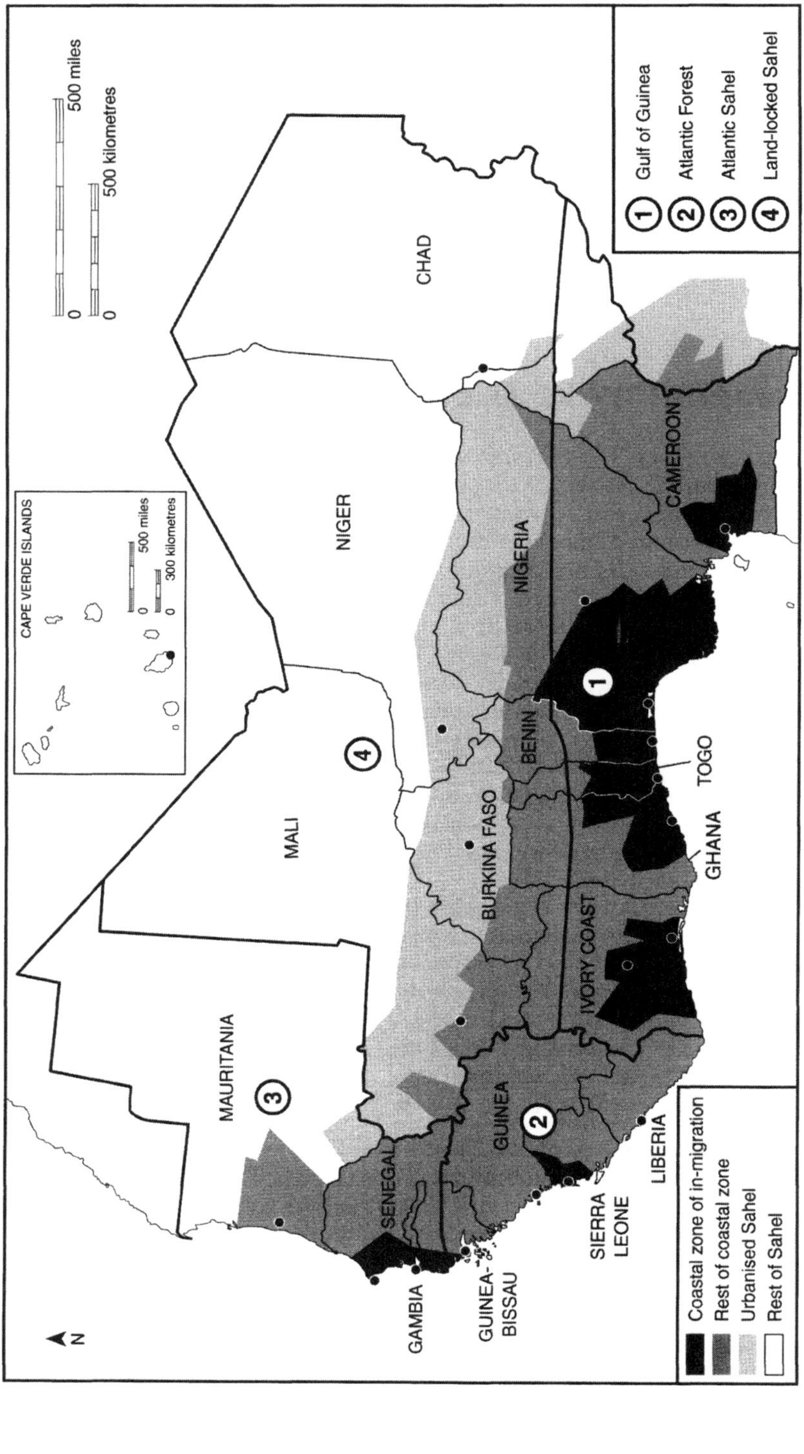

Figure 1.1 West African worlds. *Source:* adapted from Cour and Snrech (1998).

- an even more extensive region which includes, not just Chad, but also Cameroon and, more rarely, the Central African Republic (Baker 1992; Cour and Snrech 1998; Toulmin and Guèye 2003); and
- the 15 member countries (Benin, Burkina Faso, Cape Verde, Côte d'Ivoire, Gambia, Ghana, Guinea, Guinea-Bissau, Liberia, Mali, Niger, Nigeria, Senegal, Sierra Leone and Togo) making up the Economic Community of West African States (ECOWAS) which was formed in 1975.

Regardless of whether we are dealing with a 'lesser' (first and fourth delimitations above) or 'greater' (second and third 'definitions') West Africa, it is largely, in many cases, only (western-) educated indigenes and, increasingly in recent years, regional politicians and policy makers, who describe themselves as West African, and their region as West Africa (although, even here, as both Olukoshi and Francis show in Chapters 2 and 6, respectively, francophones and anglophones use different, frequently conflicting, pan-West African referents). However, as these groups constitute a distinct minority, we are thus left with the intriguing thought that the vast majority of 'West Africans' rarely, if ever, think of themselves as such. Rather, the inhabitants of this part of Africa routinely identify themselves via membership of (frequently more than one) ethnic group(s)/ 'nation(s)', which are not always sub-national in nature or extent; and/or as citizens of individual countries (or as people with claims to multiple citizenship); and/or through allegiance to wider transnational religious communities (Islam, say, or, increasingly, Pentecostalism).[1] There are, in West Africa as elsewhere, several layers to the politics of belonging, including the very real possibility of the politicisation of ethnicity, with serious implications for national cohesion and political stability (see Chapter 10).[2]

It is significant, therefore, that although ethnic identities frequently represent more tangible and more immediate realities than notions of the 'nation-state' or the 'West African region', they are neither static nor unchanging; are far from being entirely parochial in outlook; are internally diverse rather than homogeneous; are subject to transformation in some respects, even while maintaining continuity in others; are capable of absorbing 'outsiders' or 'strangers' who may not (to start with at least) speak the host group's language, share the same ancestry, or even inhabit the same territory; and, finally, are dependent on interaction with other ethnicities/identities. In particular, it is vital to recognise that, given the long and complex history of regional population movement and interaction, meanings and definitions of ethnicities have changed over time, and continue to do so in complex and fascinating ways. Indeed, the notion of assuming an identity, of acquiring the trappings of a given ethnicity, is as widespread as the idea of inheriting a given ethnic identity at birth; dense webs of origins and complex mixes of imposed and assumed identities are far from being exceptional, making it extremely difficult, as many West Africans put it, 'to tell what nation somebody is from, or belongs to'. Ethnic identity is real and contestable but, even if only partly so, also negotiable. Furthermore, as a form of social or cultural capital, it is integral to the negotiation of access to, and rights and privileges in, productive and other resources, and the constitution of livelihoods; it is just as capable of *ex*-cluding as of *in*-cluding (see, for example, Watts 2003).

Furthermore, located in large numbers outside their countries of origin, West Africans are reputed to be some of the most mobile people in all of Africa, with a diaspora of considerable size living outside the region in other parts of Africa, Europe, North America and elsewhere (see also Chapter 3). Significantly, as continuing internal and cross-border migration accelerate the creation of multi-ethnic, multi-religious settlements and communities of all kinds (see below), the links between identity, citizenship rights and access to livelihood capital/resources, commonly defined by, and currently closely tied to ancestry and birth, will need to be redefined and/or renegotiated, leading, in some cases, to an inevitable hardening of identities (see Chapters 2 and 7).[3] Through political advocacy and networking, for instance, West Africans in the wider diaspora can influence the nature and outcome of such localised/regional rethinking of regional communities, flows, boundaries and identities, in the same way that they have succeeded, thanks largely to their economic strength, in imposing the question of dual nationality/citizenship on the political agenda in countries like Ghana (where annual remittances from émigrés totalled more than foreign investment flows throughout the 1980s and remained substantial during the 1990s) and, to a lesser extent, Sierra Leone, where a wide-ranging public debate on the rights and privileges of citizenship is underway as part of post-war reconstruction (Akyeampong 2000; Henry and Mohan 2003; Mohan and Zack-Williams 2002; Zack-Williams and Mohan 2002; http://www.sierraleonehomecoming.com/program.htm#).

Indeed, an increasing number of these diaspora groups are now actively exploring means and methods for supporting development in Africa, as much through capacity building as through fund-raising and advocacy. Thus, in addition to contributing to consultations on Britain's international development policy and canvassing the opinion of young diasporan Africans in relation to Africa's development, the London-based NGO, African Foundation for Development (AFFORD), for example, organises a periodic eight-week course, in collaboration with Birkbeck College, University of London, on 'Africans Without Borders: Development from a Distance', which has the following stated aims, to: 'critically examine and debate the contribution of the African diaspora to Africa's development'; 'consider the role of African diaspora organisations in terms of influencing development and practice in ways that advance the interests of African development'; and 'critically examine contemporary issues including advocacy, sustaining small and community development groups, future strategies and development policy processes' (http://www.afford-uk.org/). As with their other activities, which include operating a 'job shop' designed to match diasporan Africans with employment opportunities in the development sector in, or for Africa, this capacity-building initiative targets a range of locally based and active development organisations and institutions, including hometown/ethnic associations, national development groups and NGOs, religious associations, investment groups, etc. (cf. Ndofor-Tah 2000).[4]

Undoubtedly, such a 'forging of ties is both *in place* and *across space* and clearly links the developmental fortunes of Africans living at home and abroad' (Mohan and Zack-Williams 2002: 224; emphasis added), a realisation that some West African governments, no less astutely than potential business investors, have been quick to try and turn to their (and the wider public's) advantage. Thus the Sierra Leone Government, for instance, in collaboration with diasporan business interests, organises an annual Homecoming Summit over the Christmas period – when diasporan Sierra Leoneans visit 'home' in large numbers – with the aim of providing a forum for constructive debate about the country's future, including key processes and critical resource areas for redevelopment, as well as programmes and initiatives for facilitating diasporan participation in such redevelopment (Sierra Leone Homecoming Summit 2003).

Sometimes, of course, these diasporan linkages and networks have been adopted by, and adapted to, the service of less-desirable pursuits like drug smuggling, people trafficking and money laundering, both within and between countries in West Africa, as well as between this region and countries in southern Africa, the EU and North America, and they have thus fed into complex imagined geographies of globalisation, immigration, asylum, crime and – in the wake of 9/11 – terrorism; and this to the extent that G8 crime, intelligence and security agencies have been co-ordinating their attempts to fashion responses to what is a perceived 'West African' variant of transnational organised crime (http://www.wjin.net/Pubs/2243.PDF; http://www.wjin.net/Pubs/2017.PDF).[5] It is fortunate, then, that Robson reminds us in Chapter 3, with reference to child trafficking, of the need to 'untangle, make sense of, and look beyond these contemporary moral panics ["terror talk"] and imagined geographies', and to ask what is really known of the emergence and dynamics of the phenomena in question, particularly within the broader context of global–local economic restructuring and all that it entails.[6] I turn now to these contexts.

2 *'Regionalising' overlapping contexts of livelihood and development*

The relevance of the foregoing for this book – part of a series of thematic and issue-based *regional* volumes devoted, in the words of the Series Editor, to the study of 'changes in the global political economy, in the nature of development challenges facing individual . . . countries and regions, and in debates on development theory' – should by now be evident. First, a recognition of the complex and dynamic nature of regional specificities is reflected in the 'fluid' way West Africa is understood and used in this book: sometimes as a 'greater' region, other times as a 'lesser' territory, but mostly as the nascent economic community of regional states, ECOWAS. Second, and relatedly, the book's title, *West African Worlds*, represents explicit acknowledgement that, however defined, the area in question is a 'large and complex mosaic of cultures and ecologies [whose] boundaries are not water-tight' (Toulmin and Guèye 2003); and which, in an era of globalisation, cannot justifiably be defined solely with reference to the locally resident population (given, as we have seen, the financial power, and institutional and other linkages at the disposal of diasporan West Africans, and attempts by regional governments to court this constituency: Zack-Williams 1995).

Both of the above have important implications for a consideration of development (understood in the general sense of planned socio-economic and environmental change) and livelihoods (the sum of individual and collective activities undertaken by individuals and groups to ensure production and reproduction) at the full range of geographic scales. To begin with, the territory in question is, after all, Africa's most balkanised region, as well as one of its most populous sub-regions. It is divided into some 15–18 ethnically plural and religiously diverse nation states, with populations ranging in size from more than 100 million in Nigeria to less than half a million in Cape Verde, and is inhabited by maybe up to half of sub-Saharan Africa's occupants (see Chapter 2). Furthermore, since the beginning of the colonial period, the size and geographical distribution of population has changed considerably, with overall totals growing at an annual rate of 2.7 per cent between 1960 and 1990, during which time the urban share of overall population increased from 13 per cent to 40 per cent, while coastal and more southerly populations have grown faster than those in the Sahelian interior, as greater economic opportunities along the coast have attracted both local and international migrants from further inland, and contributed, along with the other elements of population growth and redistribution, to a significant rise in the overall population: land ratio (Cour and Snrech 1998; Toulmin and Guèye 2003). Furthermore, as Toulmin and Guèye show, in Chapter 7, such diversity and dynamism pose a major challenge for understanding socio-economic evolution and change, leading to attempts to regionalise the territory into either extensive geographical zones of broadly homogeneous ecology, demography and economy (Cour and Snrech 1998), or more micro-scale socio-geographic zones unified by shared agro-ecological and market constraints, demography, state interventions and peasant strategies, and centred on well-defined local settlements (Raynaut 1997) (Box 1.1; Figure 1.1).

The regional context for the pursuit of individual and household livelihoods, then, is a combination of, on the one hand, enormous diversity (in population size, composition and distribution, as well as economic strength and prospects) and sometimes striking contrasts (in areal extent and physical features or 'natural' endowments); and, on the other, a unity deriving from, among other things, a very long and complex history of mobility and interaction pre-dating European contact; a short and varied but long-lasting experience of European colonialism (excepting Liberia); a recent history of sometimes acute economic and political difficulties (ECOWAS 2000a, 2000b); and, with three exceptions (Cameroon, Chad and Mauritania), membership of ECOWAS (Aryeetey-Attoh 2001; Baker 2000; Cour and Snrech 1998; Morgan and Pugh 1969). Given such a context, regionalisation of the kinds described in Box 1.1 and mapped in Figure 1.1, is useful in both livelihood and development policy and practice terms, for example in showing the nested and interlinked nature of both the resulting sub-regions, and the broad patterns and processes of economic production and

Box 1.1 (Sub-)regions within a region

Geo-demographic Settlement Zones	Economic/Production/Livelihood Zones
• **Zone of coastal in-migration** occupying only 8 per cent of regional territory but supporting 41 per cent of region's population, which is centred on rapidly-growing main coastal urban centres and their densely-populated immediate hinterland;	• **Gulf of Guinea** or economic engine of West Africa, which is the main producer of regional exports of crops, timber and petroleum, with Côte d'Ivoire and Nigeria accounting for two-thirds of total regional production; densely-populated urban system;
• **The rest of the coastal zone**, currently a relatively underpopulated and under-urbanised area of emigration (but a zone of future immigration), which supports 28 per cent of regional population on a quarter of regional land;	• **Atlantic Forest** with favourable natural resource endowment; low population densities and population growth; average rates of urbanisation; endemic conflict; and largely unfulfilled economic potential;
• **An urbanised Sahelian zone** of dense settlement clusters and intense economic activity experiencing serious natural constraints and characterised by net emigration, which supports a quarter of regional population on 13 per cent of the region's territory; and	• **Atlantic Sahel** which is heavily urbanised but with limited agrarian resource base and, consequently, high emigration rates to Europe and North America; and
• **The rest of the Sahel**, with its low demographic and economic potential and resulting high rates of emigration.	• **Land-locked Sahel** representing the poorest and least urbanised zone, which is economically dependent on the Gulf of Guinea, but which is an important agro-pastoral and cotton/groundnut zone in its own right.

Source: Cour and Snrech (1998).

social reproduction – livelihood pursuits, in other words – within and across them. In some ways, too, such regionalisation might help in addressing the difficulty of mapping diasporic linkages, networks and dynamics at different geographic scales, at least up to the scale of the West African region as a whole (cf. Guèye 2003; Mohan and Zack-Williams 2002; Zack-Williams and Mohan 2002), a task which has been underway for a considerable period of time (Adepoju 2002; Beauchemin and Bocquier 2003; Cordell, Gregory and Piché 1996; Morgan and Pugh 1969; Swindell 1978,

1985), but which is rendered difficult by periodic interruptions to, and redirection of, population flows by social (civil disturbance, war, state policy, etc.) and natural (drought, flood, etc.) factors and processes (see Chapters 3, 5, 7 and 11).

More generally, such regionalisations are useful for thinking, in ways reminiscent of early attempts by Morgan and Pugh (1969), say, about how demographic and other variables come together in time and space, and impact on regional landscape, society and economy, in addition to emphasising the enormous degree of flexibility and adaptability (which has always been) required to ensure individual, family and community production and reproduction, particularly in a context of (increasing) multitasking, usually in more than one locality (see Chapter 11). Clearly, too, this needs to be seen as an extension of the mutual constitution of work–space–time resulting from the continuing contact between (different categories of) Africans, Europeans and others, which Swindell and Batterbury explore in depth in Chapters 9 and 11, and whose material expressions are observable on regional landscapes in a diversity of ways (Batterbury 2001, 2004; Cline-Cole 1998; Mortimore 1998; Mortimore and Adams 1999).[7] Indeed, de Haan and Zoomers (2003) have argued forcefully for a more critical awareness of the role of scale when considering livelihood diversity and change, notably the need for multi-level (rather than simply micro-scale) analysis and for differentiating between individual and household livelihoods; this, they argue, 'help[s] us to better understand local development by analysing how people . . . respond to global challenges' (p. 359).

Consequently, all the chapters in this book, including the one devoted to an exploration of (under-)development in fictional writing, attempt multi-level analyses of the kind advocated, albeit from a range of disciplinary perspectives, while also paying heed to the need to consider 'internal' aspects of their chosen topics along with larger 'external' questions (cf. Dickenson 1996). Indeed, while Porter and Lyon's (Chapter 8) discussion of social capital argues for precisely this kind of flexible 'scaling' in the study/analysis of socio-economic network relations, Batterbury highlights, in Chapter 11, the latter's pervasiveness in the complex processes of negotiating socio-economic and environmental change, in a context in which development interventions of a range of kinds influence daily life and individual decision-making.

Significantly, too, in facilitating the identification of areas with social, economic or environmental characteristics that are of importance to human welfare and development – vulnerability to drought/flood; rapid population growth/decline; a depleted natural resource base; etc. – trends and shocks, in other words, which impact on livelihood opportunities (Henninger 1998; see also Chapter 11), such geographies serve a number of purposes:

- first, as an illustration of the integrative role of regional and other migration which, for many, is a means for seeking out a better life, with people often ignoring frontiers and formalities during seasonal and longer-term migration in search of employment or land for settlement, or as they flee conflict and/or penury (Adepoju 2002; Beauchemin and Bocquier 2003; Cordell *et al.* 1996; Rain 1999; Toulmin and Guèye 2003);

- second, as reminders of the dangers of exclusivist ethnoregionalism and/or nationalism, and of the need for socio-economic initiatives at the national level (e.g. Nigeria's National Youth Service programme; holistic resource management initiatives in a number of Sahelian countries) and broader regional level (e.g. the West African Economic and Monetary Union and ECOWAS) to counter their more retrograde manifestations (Bruce and Mearns 2002; Toulmin and Guèye 2003; see Chapter 2); and
- third, to reiterate the state's indispensable role in carefully targeted development planning/co-ordination, mediation and intervention (Aryeetey-Attoh 2001; Baker 2000; Morgan and Pugh 1969; see Chapters 10 and 11).

In particular, the last of the roles identified in the preceding paragraph raises potentially awkward questions for planned socio-economic change and poverty reduction, especially in a context of market-led economic restructuring involving state withdrawal from the sectors of productive activity, as well as social welfare and service provision, which are addressed, briefly in the following two sections, but in considerably more detail in Chapter 2. At least as important, however, must be the question of how and to what extent a combined focus on livelihoods and development, and a rejuvenated role for the State, can inform 'desirable' interventions while hopefully helping to avoid 'damaging' mediation (Mortimore 1998; Mortimore and Adams 1999). Clearly, as several of the contributions to this volume suggest, while 'a limited, non-interventionist state may be conducive to mature democracies [it] is incompatible with the needs of emerging democracies in regions like West Africa' (Chapter 10). Significantly, however, as with eastern and southern African countries (Potts 2004), some of West Africa's most influential development partners do not, contrary to their public declarations, demonstrate the same enthusiasm for this viewpoint (Cline-Cole 2003; see also Chapters 2, 5, 7 and 9), despite the fact that, as Olukoshi (2002b) perceptively observes, the alternative to a 'bad' state is a 'better' state, and not no state at all, or, possibly even worse, one which merely fulfils IFI prescriptions for creating an 'enabling environment'. I return to this question in Section 4.

3 'Development' and livelihoods: indices, trends and dynamics

Although it has very few landlocked countries, boasts relief which is generally conducive to rail and road construction/development (regional relief is made up almost entirely of low-lying plateaux, plains and alluvial basins, and isolated highlands), and demonstrates a seeming capacity for change and adaptation (Aryeetey-Attoh 1997, 2001; Morgan and Pugh 1969), West Africa also contains some of the world's poorest populations, as well as national economies which are, for the most part, growing too slowly to reduce such poverty significantly in the short-to-medium term (ECA

Box 1.2 Characteristics of contemporary regional political-economic peripheralism

- Generally small, weak, low-income economies which are heavily dependent on primary production, with insufficient diversification and minimal value added by manufacturing;
- Predominantly extra-regional trade links, which are subject to market vagaries/uncertainty (terms-of-trade movement, price and currency volatility, protectionism by core economies, etc.);
- Short-term fluctuating but limited long-term economic growth, even stagnation, during the post-independence period;
- Inadequate and unreliable road, telecommunications and energy infrastructure;
- Limited capital/financial flows (aid/FDI/savings);
- Generally unsustainable levels of indebtedness;
- Low human and social development indices (HDI);
- Political instability and bad/poor governance;
- Unbalanced development (economic cores and peripheries);

Sources: Baker (1992); ECOWAS (2000a, 2000b, 2002); Stock (1995).

2002, 2003; ECOWAS 2000a, 2000b). It is little wonder that the ECOWAS Executive Secretary recently spoke of the urgent need to 'catalyse' development and poverty reduction in the region (World Bank 2004b). In reality, West African socio-economic systems and economies owe their characteristics which, as Box 1.2 details, are suggestive of contemporary global peripheralism, to their historical (pre-colonial, colonial and post-colonial) experience. In turn, this is inextricably linked to the region's position within a global/ising world economy, as annual (inter)national economic and development reports, along with several of the chapters which follow, make clear.

Several of the characteristics in Box 1.2 are taken up at some length later in the book. Here, I will only mention in passing that, by and large, countries in the region have made little progress in diversifying their 'traditional' production base away from an inordinate dependence on relatively unprocessed low-value primary mineral and/or agricultural produce, even if levels and patterns of dependence differ in detail (Stock 1995; World Bank 2004b; see Chapter 2).[8] However, with reference to non-traditional exports (NTEs), tourism is increasing in importance in countries like Burkina Faso, Côte d'Ivoire, the Gambia, Mali, Senegal and, particularly, Ghana, where tourism currently represents the third most important foreign exchange earner, with the potential for expanding even further, and where tourism is only a single strand in a complex panoply of measures being pursued to promote export-led growth fuelled by the diversification of, and expansion in NTEs (ECA 2003; ECOWAS 2000b).[9] It is also worth mentioning the Gambia's current drive to market itself, through its (World

Bank-funded) Investment Promotion and Free Zones Agency, as an attractive investment destination and Export Processing Zone in close proximity to EU and USA markets (both of which give preferential access to goods from the Gambia), as well as ready access to the ECOWAS market (GIFZA 2003). President Olusegun Obasanjo has also offered government support for exiled white Zimbabwean farmers who are willing to consider settling in Nigeria and to undertake commercial farming, in a move which has not won universal local approval, but which is justified by official government sources as a sound development initiative designed to both attract private foreign investment and expertise, and help to rejuvenate the country's moribund large-scale commercial farming sector (http://www.smh.com.au/articles/2004/03/24/1079939716909.html?from=storyrhs) (see also Chapter 7).

Nonetheless, if individual countries all 'diversified' into the same range of 'non-traditional' export activities (horticultural produce for the European market, for instance), this would merely increase supply/competition, while lowering prices/profits (given, that is, that countries in the region both export and import the same range of goods/commodities/services). The EU's chocolate law, which became effective in August 2003, following an extended period of negotiation, is instructive in this regard. This ruling – which allows chocolate makers to use up to 5 per cent (cheaper) vegetable fats in place of (more expensive) cocoa butter in their products, while still being able legally to describe these as 'chocolate' – could see Côte d'Ivoire (the world's biggest cocoa producer) and Ghana (whose economy is based largely on cocoa production) suffering heavy losses in export income as a result, despite the optimism expressed by Ivorian farmer representatives (EU Business 2003). Paradoxically, however, Sahelian countries like Burkina Faso and Mali, which export shea butter, a substitute for cocoa butter, could conceivably benefit, by breaking into the lucrative chocolate market, as could regional producers of palm oil, another acceptable vegetable fat substitute (BBC 1999).[10]

Furthermore, in addition to being dependent for its export income on a restricted range of commodities, West Africa's strongest trade ties are predominantly extra-regional rather than intra-regional, with the EU supplying more than half (56 per cent) of regional imports and absorbing close to two-thirds of exports, while recorded inter-state trade in the region is estimated at only 10–11 per cent of total trade (Cour and Snrech 1998; ECOWAS 2000b). Significantly, as Box 1.3 reminds us, such outward-orientation in trade relations raises important questions regarding vulnerability to world market demand and price fluctuations, protectionism, unfavourable terms-of-trade, purchasing power of exports, etc., particularly in the light of fluctuations in the structure, volume and direction of capital inflows.[11] By the turn of the millennium the massive capital flight which characterised the 1980s and early 1990s appeared to be in the process of being reversed, with domestic investment rates increasing and, in the process, reflecting, perhaps, the continued significance of remittances from West Africans in the diaspora,[12] although the larger share of such investment probably travels via the intermediary of merchants or informal foreign exchange bureaux like Kara International – to take two of

Box 1.3 Risks and realities of outward orientation

The external balance of ECOWAS countries was affected by the generally poor economic situation, by the manner in which monetary and budgetary policies were implemented, and by fluctuations in the value of local currencies against the American dollar, the main currency in which external trade is expressed.

The prices of the major commodity exports (coffee, cocoa, cotton, rubber, groundnut) fell in 1999, with the average prices of these products reaching their lowest levels in ten years in August 2000.

The price of oil tripled, from US$10/barrel in February 1999 to US$35 in the third quarter of 2000, with higher prices boosting the budget revenue of exporting countries like Nigeria, while threatening serious macroeconomic imbalances in most of the oil-importing countries, where there is a widespread feeling that increases of between 10 per cent and 60 per cent in the pump price of petrol will fuel widespread inflation and further slow down economic activities.

In 1999, the Ghanaian cedi, the CFA franc, the Nigerian naira and the Guinean franc lost 49 per cent, 16 per cent, 15 per cent and 29 per cent, respectively, of their value against the dollar, a situation the countries could have exploited to boost their exports and improve their current account balances, but were however unable to do due to structural problems which affected production, and because they generally pay for their imports in dollars.

Twelve of the ECOWAS countries are highly indebted countries, with debt servicing expected to gulp, on average, about 30 per cent of regional export earnings, while the already high external debt stock further worsened the balance of payments of countries in the region.

Debt cancellations announced by some bilateral creditors are not what they are made out to be, with some creditors insisting, for example, that the local currency equivalent of cancelled debts should go to NGOs, to enable them to execute their projects, in what would amount to the debt being paid in full to NGOs rather than to the governments of creditor countries. Similarly, cancellations sometimes take complicated forms, involving debtor countries being required to pay the debt service that is due before being compensated with grants, ostensibly to be used to purchase imported goods, in a convoluted arrangement which involves no new allocation of funds, and cannot in actual fact be taken as further debt alleviation.

Growth and development in ECOWAS countries will require outright cancellation of their debts, without which there can be no reduction in regional poverty.

Source: ECOWAS (2000a, 2000b, 2002).

the channels favoured by Senegalese émigrés, for example – and which are already supplanting postal and money orders, and bank transfers, across large parts of their home country (Tall 2004).[13]

Nonetheless, according to the ECOWAS Executive Secretary's 2000 Report (ECOWAS 2000b), many development problems persisted, linked in direct and indirect ways to high regional population growth rates combined with lower rates of economic growth:

> The need to build schools, hospitals, roads, hydroelectric dams, and water pipes and to create enough jobs to accommodate this rapid population growth – these are the challenges that our countries have had to face since independence, and which they will have to face for many more years. A demographic growth rate which doubles the population every 25 to 30 years is a shock that only a few other regions of the world have experienced. The shock is all the more violent in that it is accompanied by a deterioration in the region's economic conditions, at a time when the needs of the population are immense.
>
> (ECOWAS 2000b)

Not surprisingly, the report continues, despite remarkable early post-independence progress achieved in health, nutrition and education improvements, as well as in other areas of human capital development (see Section 4 below), infant mortality rates at the turn of the new millennium were much higher than in other developing world regions, while primary school enrolment rates were unacceptably low, secondary enrolment even lower, and enrolment into tertiary institutions in decline. Furthermore, diseases like HIV-AIDS, malaria and tuberculosis continued to pose a major threat to health, life expectancy and, ultimately, economic production and social reproduction. Taken together, the Executive Secretary concludes, these factors have combined with low per capita incomes to give rise to some of the lowest human development indices (HDI) in the world, a perspective which finds plenty of support in the data summarised in Table 1.1, which suggests that some 14–15 of the region's 17–18 countries are classified as LDCs (Less-Developed Countries), with inadequate access to, poor levels of provision of, and slow rates of growth in health services, education and water; and that 10–11 of the lowest 16 rankings of the UNDP's Human Development Index are accounted for by West African countries (Toulmin and Guèye 2003). Nor is this all; for despite various structural adjustment programmes,

> development [has] fall[en] far short of expectations, [with] published statistics . . . giv[ing] a false picture of the economic situation, masking the fact that the vast majority of the West African population was slowly but inexorably becoming poorer.
>
> (ECOWAS 2000b)

Significantly, this *fin-de-siècle* assessment coincides with Baker's (1992) much earlier description of West African states as 'nations caught in economic traps [in which] poverty and low living standards are as widespread now as they were at independence [because] there has been little improvement in social and economic conditions over the past twenty-five to thirty years'.

Table 1.1 West Africa, socio-economic data, 2001/2002

Country	*Area 000km²*	*Pop (mill)*	*Life Expectancy (years at birth)*	*Adult Literacy (% rate)*	*Net Primary enrolment (%)*	*GDP per Capita (US$)*	*HDI rank (1–175)*	*LDC*[1]	*LIC*[2]
Benin	113	6.4	50.9	38.6	na	368	159	Yes	Yes
Burkina Faso	274	12.3	45.8	24.8	36	215	173	Yes	Yes
Cameroon	475	15	49	na	na	580	135	Yes	Yes
Cape Verde	8	0.4	69.7	74.9	99	1317	103	Yes	LMC[3]
Chad	1284	8.1	44.6	44.2	58	202	165	Yes	Yes
Côte d'Ivoire	322	16.1	41.7	49.7	64	634	161	No	Yes
Gambia	10	1.4	53.7	37.8	69	291	151	Yes	Yes
Ghana	239	20.0	57.7	72.7	58	269	129	No	Yes
Guinea	246	8.2	48.5	41.0	47	394	157	Yes	Yes
Guinea-Bissau	28	1.4	45.0	39.6	54	162	166	Yes	Yes
Liberia	99	3.1	41.4	54.8	50	170	na	Yes	Yes
Mali	1240	12.3	48.4	26.4	43	239	172	Yes	Yes
Mauritania	1023	2.7	51.9	40.7	64	366	154	Yes	Yes
Niger	1267	11.1	45.6	16.5	30	175	174	Yes	Yes
Nigeria	924	117.8	51.8	65.4	na	319	152	No	Yes
Senegal	197	9.6	52.3	38.3	63	476	156	Yes	Yes
Sierra Leone	72	4.6	34.5	36.0	na	146	175	Yes	Yes
Togo	57	4.7	50.3	58.4	92	270	141	Yes	Yes

[1]Least Developed Country; [2]Low Income Country; [3]Middle Income Country
Source: Toulmin and Guèye (2003); UNDP (2003); World Bank (2004a); UNAIDS (http://www.onusida-aoc.org/Eng/Poverty,%20debt%20and%20AIDS.htm); World Bank (http://www.worldbank.org/data/countrydata/countrydata.html).

Toulmin and Guèye's (2003) recent evaluation of regional progress towards, and prospects for, the achievement of the Millennium Development Goals (MDGs) of improving access to water, reducing maternal and infant deaths, improving school enrolment and halving the number of people suffering hunger and poverty by 2015 concludes that much greater international, regional and national commitment and focus would be required if these goals are to be achieved (see also ECA 2002, 2003). ECOWAS's (2000b) assessment is even less sanguine; in order to cut acute poverty by half by 2015, it notes, West Africa must *both* record an unrealistically high annual economic growth rate *and* ensure a more equitable distribution of income in a region with some of the most pronounced rural and urban inequality income measures in Africa (see also Ali and Thorbecke 1998).[14]

While it is worth pointing out that there are important intra- and inter-country disparities, as well as gender, class, age, ethnic, religious, spatial, structural, etc. dimensions, to much of the foregoing,[15] it is equally important to recognise, as Cour and Naudet (1996) recommend, that 'Western' data collection paradigms and methods 'paint a bleak but inaccurate picture of the continent', largely by ignoring, or, probably more accurately, misunderstanding the 'vibrancy of the real African economy' (what Olukoshi describes as the 'informalisation' of the regional economy in Chapter 2). Toulmin and Guèye (2003) also contend that such misunderstanding derives from weaknesses in the nature of the surveys (size, representativeness, periodicity), the difficulty of collecting culturally- and/or politically-sensitive data on production, reproduction and exchange, and assumptions regarding the nature and sources of individual, household and community income. Cour and Naudet thus argue for new criteria for judging West Africa which accurately reflect the key role of the informal/non-modern sectors in national and regional economies and acknowledge the high levels of unrecorded regional trade (estimated at 20–25 per cent of total regional trade by the ECA). In response, Cour and Snrech's (1998: 6) social accounting matrices (SAM) approach sought to 'construct a view of the economy based on the major social groups that contribute to it, rather than on the different economic sectors'. It concludes that, compared to public sector accounting methods, SAM 'is more complete for the relationship between domestic supply and demand, the contribution of urban and rural communities to the economy, the production and consumption of non-tradeable goods and services, and the contribution of the informal sector to the economy'.

This is hardly surprising, for as Barber (1997: 4) has observed of popular cultural forms of production, in what is undoubtedly of much wider socio-economic significance, '[m]uch of what is consumed by "the people" in Africa is also produced by them, according to the small-scale methods of the modern informal sector'. Put differently, SAM does not just permit the exploration of livelihood needs, dynamics and diversity, while recognising the close links between rural and urban spaces, places and inhabitants, it also provides the basis for the upward re-evaluation of domestic investment in regional economic performance over the final third of the last century, and leads to the conclusion, *contra* ECOWAS, that 'despite [its] mediocre economic performance, the region was able to cope with massive growth in its population . . . without disasters or increased poverty [which] in itself is a remarkable achievement' (Cour and Snrech 1998: 6). While this probably overstates the case somewhat (poverty *was* widespread and *did* increase, in some cases prior to, but in practically all cases, during the SAPping years of adjustment and economic reform, although the impacts were highly differentiated both spatially and over time; see Chapter 7 and Section 4 below), it does have the merit, albeit not entirely intentionally, of indirectly underscoring the vital role of women, who dominate informal sector activity in regional production (see Chapter 2 for a discussion of this role, which is also alluded to by Porter in Chapter 4 and Kandeh and Kannan in Chapter 10). In turn, this raises the thorny issue of whether, and to what extent, governments and administrators of regional economic institutions like ECOWAS, may have been tempted to underestimate incomes and 'talk down' economic performance 'in order to ensure their countries remain within the UN category of "Least-Developed Country", and [thereby] qualify for poverty-focussed aid funds' (Toulmin and Guèye 2003).[16]

Take the case of HIV-AIDS, mentioned subsequently by a couple of chapter authors in this book, and considered by the ECOWAS Executive Secretary in his 2000 Report as 'the greatest threat to the health of the peoples of West Africa today [which] has led to a reduction in the demographic growth rate and life expectancy in several countries'. While there is little question about the threat that the epidemic poses to countries and populations in the region (Box 1.4), this is highly differentiated both in incidence and impact, and there is no consensus that regional population growth rates are expected to be too adversely affected by HIV-AIDS in the short-to-medium term (Cour and Snrech 1998). Nonetheless, regional countries have wisely responded to the threat by developing national AIDS-control programmes, which have been designed with due recognition of the regional context of inter-country dynamics,[17] and, just as importantly, have been funded by 'development partners' (http://www.onusida-aoc.org/Eng/Publications/West%20African%20Initiative.htm). One of these partners, the UN, through its Joint Programme on HIV-AIDS (UNAIDS), and in collaboration with other key partners like the World Bank and IMF, among others, has subsequently gone much further, and designed the Debt Initiative against HIV-AIDS, which seeks to integrate HIV-AIDS control with poverty reduction, by encouraging regional governments to allocate a portion of debt reduction to finance HIV-AIDS control and, thereby, to 'stimulat[e] the productivity of countries even in situations of low HIV prevalence' (http://www.onusida-aoc.org/Eng/Poverty,%20debt%20and%20AIDS.htm).

In this, as in other regions of Africa, then, HIV-AIDS reduction and control has been incorporated into the core global development preoccupations of debt reduction, economic growth and poverty reduction (with OXFAM (2002), for instance, identifying HIV-AIDS as the greatest threat to the attainment of the Millennium Development Goals), thereby creating new 'development opportunities' which eligible Heavily Indebted Poor Countries, estimated to contain more than one-third of sufferers, have attempted

Box 1.4 HIV-AIDS in West Africa

While the epidemic is more developed in Southern and Eastern Africa, it is no less true that in West Africa, hitherto considered a low prevalence region, the epidemic is gaining ground. Historically, of course, population movements and economic co-operation are factors that have created the interdependence between coastal and Sahelian countries. West Africa is the scene of intense migratory movements influenced by the level of economic development of the countries that make it up. The flow of immigrants is from the Sahel to coastal countries. With relative economic prosperity, the latter attract other countries' nationals in search of salaried work or lucrative activities. These men and women often live in precarious conditions that make them vulnerable to STIs and HIV infection. On their return to their countries of origin, information and disease management become burning issues, especially in the rural environment where the knowledge of the epidemic and the quality of care are low. (http://www.onusida-aoc.org/Eng/Publications/West%20African%20Initiative.htm)

- The geographical distribution of the epidemic in the countries of the Lake Chad Basin is varied, with four of the five (CAR, Cameroon, Nigeria, and Chad) presenting a generalised epidemic with a prevalence rate of more than 5 per cent, with only Niger recording a prevalence of about 3 per cent; some regions and towns have a HIV prevalence rate often above 10 per cent.
- In the Mano River area, prevalence rates range from 1.5–2.2 per cent in Guinea, through 4.9–6.1 in Sierra Leone to 8.29 per cent in Liberia.
- The pandemic is well established in Ghana and Togo with 3 per cent of pregnant women infected, and in Mali, where 6 per cent of sexually-active patients in the border area near Côte d'Ivoire are affected;
- It is estimated that in Côte d'Ivoire, 10 per cent of the sexually-active population are infected and that about 2.2 million people are HIV-positive in Nigeria.
- In contrast to the foregoing, countries like Senegal, Guinea Bissau, Mali and Benin still record relatively low rates.
- The HIV epidemic is having a particularly devastating impact on the young adult population which thus deprives the society of a great part of its most productive labour.
- The impact on the social sector and on the affected countries' economic sectors is being felt at the individual, family and community and national levels, with the health sector being especially affected, as in Abidjan, Côte d'Ivoire, where 80 per cent of the hospital beds at the infectious diseases unit are occupied by people living with HIV, and in Burkina Faso, where the HIV-related occupation rate is about 50 per cent.

Sources: http://www.onusida-aoc.org/Eng/Lake%20Chad%20Basin.htm; http://www.onusida-aoc.org/Eng/Abidjan%20Lagos%20Corridor.htm

to exploit with varying degrees of success, as the example of Cameroon, considered one of the two countries under greatest threat in the region, shows (http://www.onusida-aoc.org/Eng/Poverty,%20debt%20and%20AIDS.htm).

The post-independence period, then, needs to be seen, at least in development terms, as a period during which the West African region has had to contend with the combined challenges of a rapidly growing and constantly redistributing population, a frequently hostile but always evolving global economy and, across the Sahel, an unpredictable and variable climate (see Chapter 11).[18] The effects of these challenges have been experienced to varying degrees, within and between localities and nation states, leading to a diversity of landscapes, societies, economies, polities, etc. And while several of the latter are taken up in later chapters, it is worth reiterating here that an important geographic effect has been the emergence, on the one hand, of combined identities; composite nationalities and multiple ethnicities; and, on the other, multiple modes of livelihood, almost invariably gendered, involving varying degrees of mobility, as well as investment in social, cultural, physical and other capitals.

Thus, at the regional scale, as Toulmin and Guèye (2003) observe, '[s]uccessful West African households may have family members stretched all over the region, as well as other parts of the world, in education, and business, as farmers and wage labourers. Remittances from such activities provide an important source of income to those back home.' On a more local scale, in a resource-poor area like the 'post-development' village of Fandou Beri in southwestern Niger, for instance, which lost its schoolteacher, urban jobs, market revenue and extension agents during the crisis years of the 1990s, Batterbury (2004) describes a similar scenario:

> A continuous series of efforts to ensure basic subsistence and household needs (human, as well as material) [being] enlisted at various times [with] these consist[ing] of an increase in male out-migration to northern Ivory Coast (where men work selling cloth), increased livestock ownership by settled . . . farmers, and business activities like trading in the local region or selling fuelwood to Niamey, labouring for cash, and so on.

Nor are pastoral livelihoods devoid of such multi-local strategies, as the case of migrant Fulbe in the Bandiagara area of southern Mali shows (de Bruijn and van Dijk 2003: 301):

> They are extremely mobile, changing village once every year or so, until they find a place to settle. Sometimes they split up the family. We found an example of a family with one brother with his children taking care of the family herd, a second brother looking after the herd of a Dogon cultivator, and a third brother who had remained on the Seeno plain to cultivate the family field. Such families exploit resources over an area 100–200 kilometres wide. This strategy is designed to maximise the growth of the family herd by minimising the burden on it from the consumption demands of the family.

A good many, though by no means all, of the West Africans implicated here do, like Porter's fictional characters in Chapter 4, 'exist at subsistence level', although not necessarily independently of the market, as both the descriptions above and the enormous unofficial movement of commodities (petrol, grains, tubers, livestock products, etc.) and currencies within and between states in the region constantly remind us (see Chapters 2, 3, 6, 8 and 10).[19] Indeed, such movement, often not unrestricted, and frequently clandestine,[20] is currently being 'talked up' as a potential security risk demanding coordinated action between regional governments, as well as with locally-stationed UN peacekeeping forces, in an era of heightened regional security concerns fuelled by a combination of both wider post-11 September concerns, and the more immediate lessons of (threatened) insurrection, *coup* plots/rumours and state collapse (UN 2004).[21]

In truth, however, many of these features have roots deep in the region's past, although they are continuously (re-)made under constantly changing conditions of existence.[22] Tall's (2004) study of the role of Information and Communication Technologies (ICTs, cable, satellite, Internet, mobile phone, camcorder) in maintaining links between long-distance Senegalese émigrés and their rural home communities highlights this particularly well, in addition to being a good example of the popular appropriation of ICTs, and the highly personalised and unexpected ways in which these can be, and are, adapted. In particular, the study shows how both émigrés and their families are served by these tools, and how, in turn, these tools influence their lifestyles, by facilitating private financial transfers; connecting villages to the wider world via the cellular telephone; allowing émigrés to participate indirectly in the cultural life of their villages of origin through the use of the camcorder and video cassette recorder, etc. Tall concludes, first, that 'the emergence of the new technologies and their appropriation by émigrés creates new social configurations both in the new home and in the community of origin, and contributes to the emergence of new spatial understandings'; and, second, that 'ICTs are . . . instrumental in social integration, powerful levers for social rebalancing and for strengthening local spaces within a globalized system'. His description of global–local interaction and interdependence is, I think, no less instructive than Batterbury's earlier effort (see note 5): when the Northern Italian region of Lombardy sneezes, Tall notes, the village of Ndiambour in central-northern Senegal catches cold. It is little wonder, then, that the ECOWAS 1999 Report lamented the fact that the region was at risk of being by-passed by the information revolution, 'this dynamic sector of the world economy', and warned against the dangers of such an eventuality, particularly when accompanied by capital flight and the brain drain.[23]

The lesson, it seems, is clear: a focus on broader-scale political economy should not mean the neglect of individual, household and group livelihood concerns. It is a lesson, Batterbury argues most directly in Chapter 11, which should inform development planning and intervention. It should also inform perceptions of the nature of the challenges for a combined development and livelihood study, posed by the varied worlds which make up West Africa. As Turner (1999: 212) has observed with reference to regional pastoral systems, 'regional analysts should think of regionally-scaled land-use [and other] change as resulting from regionally scaled factors as mediated by *local* social relations' (emphasis in original).

4 Development and livelihood debates

Partitioned, as Toulmin and Guèye (2003), among others, have noted, with little concern for underlying social, cultural and economic dimensions, post-independence West African states 'have faced great difficulties in attaining political consensus regarding how they are to be managed, and the distribution of power and wealth'. Indeed, although '[m]uch of the first post-independence decade was marked by efforts to give meaning to the social bargain that underpinned the nationalist anti-colonial struggle' (Olukoshi 2002a: 6; Box 1.5), the patterns of 'unbalanced' development which resulted (illustrated in Figure 1.1), with their inequalities and disparities ('cores' and 'peripheries', privileged and marginalised, favoured and ostracised) within and between countries, economies and populations, often overlain by regional/ethnic overtones, did not prevent the emergence of sometimes prolonged political tensions and conflicts and, on occasion, even civil war (see Chapters 2 and 5). Clearly, as Olukoshi concludes

Box 1.5 Early post-independence development

1. Aided by reasonably high levels of economic growth during the first decade of independence which, with few exceptions, were higher than population growth rates, most countries adopted development planning with the aim of improving the foundations of their economies and increasing access to opportunities in a context of huge, pent-up demand.
2. For much of the first post-independence decade, then, and irrespective of whether regimes were socialist, free market, or mixed-economy in orientation, governments invested, without exception, in the expansion of the social and physical infrastructure of their countries in a manner which widened access to:

   - education;
   - modern health facilities;
   - transportation;
   - housing; and
   - skills development.

3. Also, irrespective of the ideological leanings which they professed, all independent governments reserved an important role for the state in the development process.
4. When the growth rates recorded by African countries during the 1960s and early 1970s are compared with those recorded during the structural adjustment years of the 1980s and 1990s, the immediate post-independence years, for all their shortcomings, seem to have been golden years of some sort, in spite of the best efforts of the Berg Report (World Bank 1981), used by the International Financial Institutions to justify imposition of Structural Adjustment, to falsify the history of that period.

Source: Olukoshi (2002a).

in somewhat understated terms, 'the effort to give content and meaning to th[is] post-colonial social contract was not without its internal contradictions and limitations', as evidenced by diminishing state/government legitimacy, increased political authoritarianism, the erosion of citizenship rights and a downturn in economic growth (ibid.).

And yet, such contradictions and limitations did not lie in state interventionism, *per se*, but in the nature of the West African state's interventions, as Kandeh and Kannan note in Chapter 10, which 'have systematically benefited the few while disadvantaging and impoverishing the majority'. In part, too, they were the product, Toulmin and Guèye (2003) would no doubt argue, of regional governments being 'subject to the latest donor fads for new plans and strategies, [and of having to] master . . . new initiatives from the development community, in order to comply with ever-changing conditions for accessing aid'. Of these, Economic Stabilisation and Structural Adjustment Programmes (SAPs) have proven to be both highly contentious and considerably more than passing donor fads. They are also the intellectual and ideological forebears of the Poverty Reduction Strategy Process (PRSP), which currently represents the 'central plank in donor relations with many developing countries [and] main framework for discussion of aid priorities and national budgetary allocations [in addition to being] the . . . requirement for all countries seeking HIPC funding for debt relief' (Toulmin and Guèye 2003).

SAP-related questions are many and varied, and receive continual mention throughout this book. It is, therefore, on SAP's links to livelihoods and development thinking, links which I consider fundamental to an understanding of the recent trajectories of West African worlds, that I concentrate here. In particular, I am interested in the fact that two decades of neo-liberal hegemony, notably its mantra, There Is No Alternative (TINA), and its single-minded anti-statism, served to constrain meaningful debates on, and the effective pursuit of, 'alternative' development futures, which did not subscribe to the so-called Washington consensus, its obsession with the market, and its determination to distance the state from the practice of development.[24] And yet, as Olukoshi (2002b) reminds us, rather than the self-serving end it did become, 'structural adjustment was intended to be a temporary diversion from development, offering crisis-ridden economies a chance to "stabilise" themselves before returning to the medium- and long-term tasks of employment-generation, income enhancement, resource distribution and equity, investment etc.' Consequently, he argues, the rebirth of interest in development thinking is, first, a direct reflection of the failure of structural adjustment to live up to its promise, not only to reverse the decline in the fortunes of crisis-ridden economies, but also to ensure a more equitable distribution of the benefits of adjustment; and, second, a product of the gradual transformation, under the pressures of increased democratisation, of the environment of authoritarianism and repression which had accompanied the implementation of unpopular market reforms, and which was far from conducive to the promotion of an agenda of accountable and participatory development (ibid.).

There does appear to be plenty of evidence from West Africa in support of this viewpoint. To start with, World Bank, ECOWAS and ECA Annual

Reports agree on the extensive and long-running, albeit varied, histories of far-reaching economic and public sector reforms undertaken by regional economies, involving liberalised markets and trade; increased private-sector participation in national economies; reduced budget deficits; limiting Central Bank financing of public debt; etc. At the heart of these reforms were, first, the desire to co-ordinate national macroeconomic policies, mitigate macroeconomic imbalances, improve the efficiency of the public sector and the management of public affairs (including, in some cases, establishment of anti-corruption committees); and, second, the hope/expectation that obstacles to development would be removed and, in the process, boost economic growth, generate increased income, reduce poverty levels and, above all, attract vastly increased overseas investor interest and resources. And yet, the two most recent ECA Reports (2002, 2003) indicate that not a single West African country is currently rated among the leaders in macroeconomic performance terms. Indeed, Nigeria, Guinea and Chad are located near the bottom of the ranking, which is associated with economies characterised by considerable levels of accumulated debt, high budget deficits, limited liberalisation with frequent policy reversals, ineffective pro-poor efforts, and poor access to, and reliability of telecommunications, transport and electricity.

But while the reservations expressed with respect to Nigeria's immediate prospects in the 2002 report are perfectly understandable, given that country's recent political history, the suggestion, contained in the following year's report, that continued growth in Ghana's economy was not assured in either the medium or long term, comes as more of a surprise. Thus '[t]he medium-term outlook is cautiously optimistic', while 'long-term growth rates suggest that Ghana is locked into a low-growth trap'. However, 'of greater concern is that growth has not transformed the structure of the economy or delivered significant improvements in the quality of life'. And this about a country long considered a model adjustment economy! I cannot think of better support for Olukoshi's (2002b) observation, that 'such [economic] growth as has occurred [in a few adjusting countries] has been too low and episodic as to make a difference and has not necessarily led to a more equitable distribution of benefits'; or for his reminder of how processes of adjustment and reform themselves become integral components of the dynamics of stagnation and/or decline, prompting not entirely unjustified references to the political economy of *mal*adjustment (cf. also Stoneman 2004).

Certainly, by the turn of the new millennium, criticism of orthodox adjustment by regional policy makers had become sufficiently insistent for ECOWAS Report 2000 to openly acknowledge the worst-kept secret in all of Africa, that development-as-adjustment had 'fallen far short of expectations', and exhort the region's leaders to 'act to reverse this situation', on the grounds that:

> For a long time, the debate around this issue has focused on the choice that must be made between growth and social development, between stringent management and economic recovery. The Bretton Woods institutions have been the greatest proponents of this theory which has

> now received short shrift. Yet, if the new pet theory – poverty reduction – were to be taken as being in opposition to growth, and the rigour which that implies, the issues involved would still not be any clearer. The fact is, one must not preclude the other. That is why West African countries must avoid such clear-cut choices and the many attendant pitfalls, failing which they will remain locked in a vicious cycle of underdevelopment – impoverishment – armed conflict, while all efforts to curtail these phenomena will continue to fail.

In this, the report appears to come close to a call for a vision of development built on democracy, increased equity and policy heterodoxy (cf. Olukoshi 2002a). In any case, the report justified this rethink on the grounds that, although countries in the region were still confronted by many and varied development problems,

> th[e] new century affords a golden opportunity to end the region's marginalisation. The last decade was one of rapid political change and the result has been the advent of more responsible governments following multi-party elections. Also, there is now a broader consensus on the need to move away from the defective economic models of yesteryear. There is now talk of development underpinned by economic reforms, improved management of public affairs, human resource development and infrastructural growth. In addition, there is a much clearer awareness of the crucial role that regional integration can play in promoting the economic growth and development of the countries in the region.

The theme of regional integration, which feeds into current preoccupations within the development literature with notions of 'imagining' regional development communities (Power 2004; Watts 2003), is taken up at length in the 2002 report, *Fostering Regional Integration through NEPAD Implementation*, which envisions West Africa's future as an 'integrated' and 'united' region, a 'viable space within which small economies can better organise themselves to survive economically and politically in a highly competitive world'. However, the vision is of a region–space which will, significantly, be mediated through the prisms of both NEPAD (the New Partnership for Africa's development), and the African Union (AU, the successor to the Organisation of African Unity), whose members adopted NEPAD in 2001 as their preferred strategy for both achieving sustainable development in the twenty-first century and integrating the continent (Figure 1.2). The NEPAD/AU combination, then, is seen as the main tool for creating an 'enabling environment' conducive to the 'smooth [and] rapid' insertion of an integrated ECOWAS region into a global/ising world economy; indeed it could be argued that ECOWAS sees this as *the only meaningful* way forward for the region's countries, whose markets it considers too small, and economies too weak, to weather the storm of globalisation successfully as individual/istic entities (in the way that Ghana and The Gambia, among others, have been trying to do; see Section 3 above). Viewed in this way, ECOWAS can be considered, like its opposite number SADC in southern Africa, to exist partly to demonstrate the sovereignty

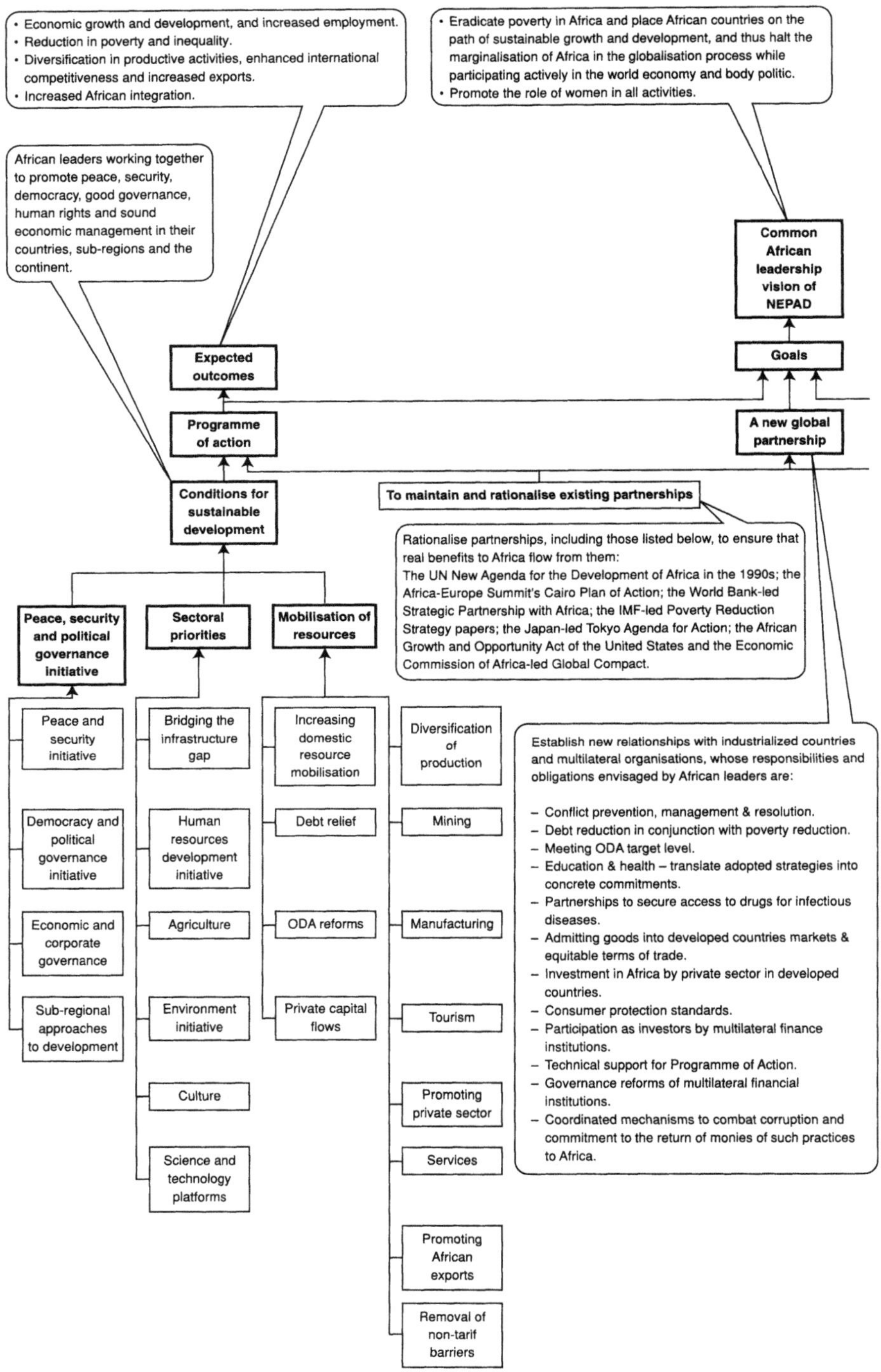

• Economic growth and development, and increased employment.
• Reduction in poverty and inequality.
• Diversification in productive activities, enhanced international competitiveness and increased exports.
• Increased African integration.
• Eradicate poverty in Africa and place African countries on the path of sustainable growth and development, and thus halt the marginalisation of Africa in the globalisation process while participating actively in the world economy and body politic.
• Promote the role of women in all activities.
African leaders working together to promote peace, security, democracy, good governance, human rights and sound economic management in their countries, sub-regions and the continent.
Common African leadership vision of NEPAD
Goals
Expected outcomes
Programme of action
A new global partnership
Conditions for sustainable development
To maintain and rationalise existing partnerships
Rationalise partnerships, including those listed below, to ensure that real benefits to Africa flow from them:
The UN New Agenda for the Development of Africa in the 1990s; the Africa-Europe Summit's Cairo Plan of Action; the World Bank-led Strategic Partnership with Africa; the IMF-led Poverty Reduction Strategy papers; the Japan-led Tokyo Agenda for Action; the African Growth and Opportunity Act of the United States and the Economic Commission of Africa-led Global Compact.
Peace, security and political governance initiative
Sectoral priorities
Mobilisation of resources
Peace and security initiative
Democracy and political governance initiative
Economic and corporate governance
Sub-regional approaches to development
Bridging the infrastructure gap
Human resources development initiative
Agriculture
Environment initiative
Culture
Science and technology platforms
Increasing domestic resource mobilisation
Debt relief
ODA reforms
Private capital flows
Diversification of production
Mining
Manufacturing
Tourism
Promoting private sector
Services
Promoting African exports
Removal of non-tarif barriers
Establish new relationships with industrialized countries and multilateral organisations, whose responsibilities and obligations envisaged by African leaders are:
– Conflict prevention, management & resolution.
– Debt reduction in conjunction with poverty reduction.
– Meeting ODA target level.
– Education & health – translate adopted strategies into concrete commitments.
– Partnerships to secure access to drugs for infectious diseases.
– Admitting goods into developed countries markets & equitable terms of trade.
– Investment in Africa by private sector in developed countries.
– Consumer protection standards.
– Participation as investors by multilateral finance institutions.
– Technical support for Programme of Action.
– Governance reforms of multilateral financial institutions.
– Coordinated mechanisms to combat corruption and commitment to the return of monies of such practices to Africa.

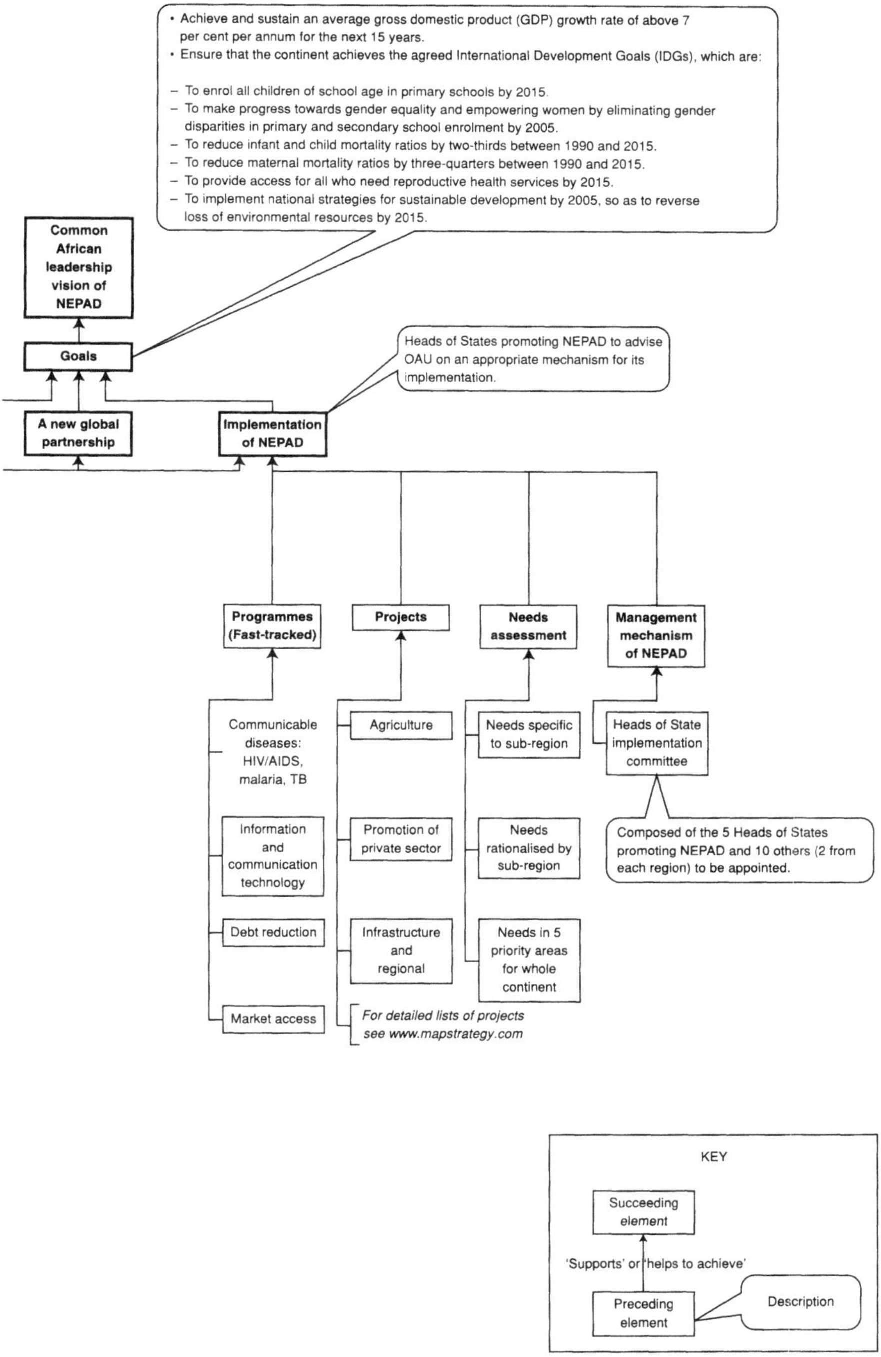

Figure 1.2 Mapping NEPAD. *Source*: adapted from Lamba (2002).

of member states and partly to prepare them to respond to the challenges of globalisation (Power 2004; see also Chapter 6).

Significantly, however, just as in the case of adjustment, the conceptual basis of the AU–NEPAD–ECOWAS triumvirate is neo-liberalism (see the preferred methods for mobilising resources in Figure 1.2), a fact which explains both its widespread acceptance among development partners, including, crucially, the IFIs (ECOWAS 2002),[25] on the one hand, and its alienating effect on several of the best-known African intellectuals and activists, on the other.[26] Among the latter, this neo-liberal 'connection' raises important questions regarding the true nature of the post-Washington consensus envisioned, as well as the extent to which NEPAD is truly anchored in regional development realities and specificities, despite its declared commitment to regional needs assessment and rationalisation (see Figure 1.2). With reference to the first of these queries, Adebayo Adedeji, retired Executive Director of the Economic Commission for Africa, is seriously concerned about NEPAD's dependence on freer trade and increased aid; the questions these raise about dependence/dominance and policy autonomy; and the fact that both the AU and NEPAD are top-down rather than bottom-up (development) initiatives, which need to be democratised and imbued with principles of popular participation and good governance (Adedeji 2002).

These are concerns shared by Adebayo Olukoshi, Executive Director of the Council for the Development of Social Science Research in Africa (CODESRIA), who calls attention to the coincidence between NEPAD diagnoses and prescriptions (including its self-prescribed conditionalities), on the one hand, and the central tenets of neo-liberalism, on the other. His critique also encompasses the extent to which NEPAD/ECOWAS is truly anchored in regional development realities and specificities. In particular, he suggests, NEPAD appears to be designed more to pander to a donor audience than to respond to, or represent the concerns of, a domestic constituency, which was not consulted prior to its adoption (Olukoshi 2002a). Furthermore, given that ECOWAS citizens, as several chapters in this book make abundantly clear, practise a brand of mostly informal/ised integration which, ironically, ECOWAS hopes to intensify, expand and formalise (Cour and Snrech 1998), Olukoshi is concerned that so much of ECOWAS's focus amounts to the creation of an environment favourable to the local operation of private international capital and thus 'to the detriment of the kinds of long-term investment which the region should be aiming to attract, and for which a role for the state is indispensable' (Chapter 2). Furthermore, he argues, as ECOWAS is the only regional cooperation organisation whose membership cuts across the region's linguistic divide, its vision of a development community is one which is only partly shared by linguistically-exclusive organisations like the francophone Union Économique et Monétaire Ouest Africaine (UEMOA), which are also devoted to regional cooperation (ibid.).

To be sure, the post-Washington consensus represented by NEPAD/ECOWAS does offer, superficially at least, a more nuanced version of neo-liberalism than the orthodox adjustment of the Washington consensus, allowing, for instance, an increased (but still limited) role for a renascent (developmental?) state (Potts 2004). However, PRSPs, the current vehicle for neo-liberalism and democratisation of the policy process, demonstrate only a partial understanding of the heterogeneity of poverty and poor people; provide little information on the factors underlying rural poverty (e.g. access to land, ethnicity and gender); pay little attention to productive sectors of the economy; and neglect international and global constraints which hinder more productive and sustainable livelihoods for poor people (Toulmin and Guèye 2003). And yet, as SAM (see Section 3), among other indices suggests, underneath all the seeming disorder, livelihoods are pursued with vigour, imagination and varying degrees of diversity, security and sustainability (see Chapters 4, 5, 7, 8 and 11). Recalling Turner's (1999) earlier observation of the need to recognise regional change as resulting from regional-scale factors mediated by local social relations, it is possible to see here the intersection of the regional- and national-scale development concerns of ECOWAS and the governments of its member states with the multi-scale livelihood preoccupations of regional inhabitants (see also Toulmin and Guèye 2003).

Such an intersection connects the state, via its governance framework, to the management of relations of access to, and use of resources, and thereby to the structure of local, regional and global power relations (Olukoshi 2002a). It is precisely these resources which people use to shape their lives and thus local development, and thereby to ground or localise globalisation in space and place (Bebbington 2003; de Haan and Zoomers 2003). The needs assessment identified in Figure 1.2, then, needs to be based as much on a recognition of the role of agency in livelihoods as on the structural and geographical constraints which influence such agency. And this is as relevant when referring to individual and household livelihoods, as when the focus is on community or regional livelihood, or indeed livelihoods at the national scale (see Chapter 7). In this connection Bryceson's (2002) recent policy proposals, based on a detailed analysis of the changing contexts and dynamics of rural livelihoods in Africa, in particular their support for 'food first' agricultural policies; initiatives to better understand livelihood structure/functioning in order to ensure livelihood security and diversity; and capacity-building and infrastructural provision/improvement merit close attention in national and regional policy-making circles. Her mention of the need for governments at all levels 'to engage people in assessments of their geographical comparative advantage in search for local specialisations', and of the wisdom in '[c]onsortia of government, non-government organisations (NGOs), private businesses and local people becom[ing] involved in a common vision of regional potential' (ibid., p. 737), returns us to the theme of regionalisation and, by extension, questions of scale and interdependence, which Toulmin and Guèye, for example, take up in their chapter.

Above all, however, they take us back to considerations of the nature of the state and its role in the restoration of what Olukoshi (2002a) describes as a 'developmentalist agenda', although he warns that this should not be interpreted as a call, either to recreate the pre-adjustment state with all its limitations (including the assumption that development was the exclusive domain of the state) or to replicate the errors of pre-adjustment developmentalism; what he advocates is a developmental democracy which:

> whilst addressing key concerns in the areas of economic growth, employment, equity, and investment would also be participatory and accountable to the popularly-elected structures of government. In addition, it would be a state that invests in the development of the capacity of its personnel, not just with regard to policy-making for which technical and politico-administrative skills are required, but also in the area of negotiations for the advancement of the interests of the citizenry [with]in the existing global system.

Clearly, as Box 1.6 shows, this is a vision which goes much further than recent support for, and promotion of, participatory development, decentralisation of local government, and an increased role for civil society (cf. Toulmin and Guèye 2003).

Put differently, this agenda is one which is synonymous with the search for paths through socio-economic change, livelihoods and development in West Africa, the task which chapter authors approach from a diverse range of disciplinary perspectives in the pages which follow.

5 *Paths through* West African Worlds

Including this chapter, and a short conclusion, the book is made up of a total of 12 chapters, which are organised loosely into five unequal sections or parts. Following this opening synthesis, Olukoshi provides a wide-ranging overview of regional political economy. Significantly, he adopts a combined retrospective and prospective approach to his task, and highlights both historical continuities and discontinuities. His thoughts on potential (mostly (geo-)political) obstacles in the way of regional integration, and the risks inherent in the uncritical negotiation of the complex processes of globalisation serve as particularly useful reminders of the region's peripheral location within the contemporary global economy, and the need for meaningful local debates about the long overdue reassertion of a revivified and redefined 'developmentalism' within policy processes. Along with the present chapter, Olukoshi's contribution provides a general context for subsequent contributions, which combine theory and practice to varying degrees, in addition to evincing an interest in gender, class, ethnicity, etc., as part of the development of chapter themes.

This is illustrated particularly well by the following two chapters by Robson and Porter, respectively, which make the point, albeit in different ways, of the need to look beyond the physical confines of West Africa in order to better define the region and highlight the complex and dynamic ties which bind this geographical entity and its populations, both to itself as well as to a globalising world economy. Thus Robson focuses her chapter on the confusing and increasingly 'globalised', but very real, world of child exploitation and trafficking, through an examination of children in, and of, West Africa. She roots the chapter geographically, while allowing the exploration of global/local links between the countries in the region and the large populations of West African origin and descent in Europe and elsewhere. The challenge, as she sees it, is to distinguish between

Box 1.6 An agenda for economic and developmental transformation

1. An agenda for economic transformation will pose a variety of governance challenges, including the following:

   (a) The integration of social policy into economic policy (rather than simply treating the former as an add-on to the latter following the latter's design and implementation) to respond to the need to go beyond notions of social safety nets and poverty reduction, for the simple reason that poverty is sufficiently widespread across Africa to make nonsense of ideas about 'targeting', for example, which are integral to schemes and programmes for the mitigation of the social costs of adjustment favoured by the IFIs;
   (b) The subordination of economics to politics and popularly-elected institutions of government, and a move away from a narrowly-defined economic orthodoxy centred on an equally narrow notion of the market;
   (c) The embrace and institutionalisation of economic heterodoxy in place of the narrow orthodoxy fostered by the IFIs, such heterodoxy being much more attuned to democratic economic governance than orthodoxy which, in the African context at least, produces or reinforces repressive governance structures;
   (d) The recapturing of the economic policy terrain by Africans and, in so doing, the reversing of the usurpation of structures and processes of domestic policy-making and implementation by the IFIs;
   (e) The restoration of a long-term perspective in economic policy-making to mark a break from speculative growth and finance, and to promote a focus on the 'real sectors' of the economy which are capable of making a difference in the lives of the vast majority of the citizenry; and
   (f) The 'de-donorisation' of the entire policy apparatus and process as part of a wider effort to ensure that:

      (i) identified priorities are rooted in local understandings and realities; and
      (ii) that solutions which are fashioned are sustainable and involve groups which bear the brunt of the reform agenda.

2. In turn, a renewed developmentalist agenda would entail at least the following:

   (a) The need for the restoration of the state as a legitimate player in the development process;
   (b) The re-kitting of the state in order to imbue it with the capacity for playing a developmental role, including the capacity for strategic interventions and effective bargaining;
   (c) The integration of a structure of accountability into the political process in order that the state and its managers are brought under popular democratic scrutiny; and
   (d) The greater harmonisation of the structures of elected government with the policy process, with a view to ensuring that technocracy is subordinated to democracy in the development process.

Source: Olukoshi (2002b).

healthy cultural practices of (transnational) fostering, on the one hand, and the exploitation or abuse of children, on the other. In contrast, Porter explores the fictional world of resource conflicts, civil war, colonialism, the Cold War and the difficulties of mediating the tensions of newly-acquired political or flag independence in Nigeria. Through a study of Kolawale Omotoso's *The Combat*, Porter highlights the dangers, paradoxes and realities of contemporary warfare in West Africa, and conveys the message that 'wars of underdevelopment' (including civil strife and disruptive state collapse) merely serve to stunt economic progress and to delay the effective pursuit, and eventual achievement of development, however defined. It does of course also, as it is threatening to do in Côte d'Ivoire, possess a real potential for *un*-developing economies. It is worth mentioning, if only in passing, how these chapters access radically different kinds of geographical imaginaries to interrogate the highly contested nature of socio-economic change at the individual and/or collective levels.

The four chapters which constitute Part 2 of the book tackle themes related broadly to the functioning of regional economies and polities, starting with Riddell's implication of urban and elite bias policies, and their associated redistribution of wealth/resources from rural-to-urban and peasant-to-elite, in state collapse in Sierra Leone. In some ways this chapter represents a continuation of Porter's preoccupations in Chapter 4, given that Riddell appears to be arguing that contested 'imaginings' of a post-colonial Sierra Leone impeded 'the forging of nationhood in the pursuit of betterment', leading, paradoxically, to the 'unimagining' of the polity – at least in its guise as a development community. In both cases, of course, civil war ensued. The post-crisis need in Sierra Leone (as elsewhere) is clearly for a more inclusive and more equitable imagined community of the kind Olukoshi advocates in Box 1.6, notably with the transparently democratic and participatory structures and processes which Riddell spells out in his chapter. Riddell also draws out the wider lessons of the Sierra Leone experience for its regional neighbours and other African countries, although the chapter is careful to establish that these should not be interpreted as rules.

Confirmation that the lessons of Sierra Leone (or indeed the linked case of Liberia) were not lost on regional policy makers is provided by Francis's description, in Chapter 6, of how the systemic regional crisis of which state collapse in Sierra Leone was a part, prompted the redefinition of the parameters of regional co-operation and integration to include security concerns and, eventually, the formation and deployment of ECOMOG, the ECOWAS Cease-fire Monitoring Group. As Francis makes clear, the hand of regional leaders was effectively forced by the threat to national and regional security, as well as regime survival, posed by violent civil wars in Liberia, Mali, Sierra Leone and Guinea Bissau; their contagion effect and associated small arms and refugee movements and flows; and, particularly, the disruption of the pursuit of the objectives of economic integration by political instability and societal conflicts. For Francis, therefore,

> [t]he recognition of the nexus between economic integration, regional security and regional stability means that ECOWAS should henceforth

prioritise human and social security, democratic governance, and promote respect for human rights as the enabling environment within which the objectives of ECOWAS integration and regional economic development can be achieved.

In addition, ECOMOG emerges from the study as the unlikely means via which ECOWAS was forced to extend its traditional state-centric focus to encompass a more pluralistic conception of politics as well as regional integration and development.

Toulmin and Guèye (Chapter 7), and Lyon and Porter (Chapter 8), shift the focus of attention away from policy preoccupations and on to livelihood concerns in their respective chapters in Part 3. In their wide-ranging and copiously documented review of regional agriculture, Toulmin and Guèye establish the continuing importance of agriculture to regional economy and society, and highlight the central place of family farms and farming within rural livelihoods. They also describe the broad transformations underway in the agricultural sector, and argue that further agricultural growth is essential if significant poverty reduction is to be achieved, although they also recognise that in a global economy, policy and other improvements which would make a major contribution to the improved welfare and livelihoods of large numbers of regional producers, may well be beyond the power of local, national and regional individuals and groups to initiate. In their view, the future of the family farm is far from being assured, particularly in the light of fierce and unfair competition within a global economy, with the result that 'rural incomes have become increasingly diverse', as producers attempt to minimise risk 'by growing a range of different crops, raising different species of livestock, or investing in a broad set of assets and social networks'. They conclude with a reminder of the impacts of OECD government policies on local farming and other livelihoods in West Africa, and the need to counter the worst of these through effective mobilisation and advocacy at all levels.

It is at the lowest of these levels, the local, that Lyon and Porter concentrate their efforts at demonstrating 'how an understanding of collective action and institutions of civil society (commonly described as social capital in the literature) can relate to policy-making, especially the process of targeting interventions for local economic development'. They focus on how social institutions shape economic life, primarily with reference to production and marketing systems in urban and rural areas of southern Ghana, and covering bilateral relationships as well as group activities of a range of kinds, ranging from small groups of farmers to nation-wide organisations. In a socio-economic and natural environment as risky and as vulnerable as the one under review, social capital becomes an indispensable livelihood resource, particularly where so much business is transacted 'on trust', and where the networks of interaction are constantly reshaped in response to changing social and economic conditions and opportunities. Like Toulmin and Guèye, Lyon and Porter provide a timely reminder of the fact that livelihoods are anchored in place even as they range across space, are mediated via variables such as gender, ethnicity, age, class, etc., and that development interventions should be both broad-based, and integral parts of initiatives aimed at creating an enabling environment 'for groups, reducing their barriers, mediating conflict and finding ways for people to come together and start their own activities'. They also, again like Toulmin and Guèye, but also like Olukoshi (Chapter 2) as well as Kandeh and Kannan (Chapter 10), emphasise the need to, first, target interventions, privilege locally-meaningful policies, rather than the common usage of blueprint policies transferred from one location to another; and, second, provide support for initiatives which enhance livelihood sustainability and security, where necessary through encouraging their expansion 'beyond their geographical and regional limits, connecting people with similar interests and concerns'.

The final three chapters are devoted to research on and in West Africa which allow a rethinking of the contribution of local/ised or regional insights to broader intellectual debates about socio-economic change and development. Ken Swindell's reflections compare concepts of time and space as they developed under industrial capitalism, with those which shape working practices in West African rural agrarian systems, before reviewing regional West African development and change in the context of European contact. He shows how time and timing are 'reflected in agricultural, pastoral and industrial practices, which are performed within specific spaces'; and notes that time and space are inseparable, although different cultures measure and evaluate these differently. Against this background, the chapter goes on to highlight how African livelihoods and lifestyles were modified by contact with Europeans to create 'new social and economic contexts and notions of the state and modernity', and discusses the nuanced outcomes of what were complicated and sometimes prolonged exchanges. The implications for livelihood and development are explored in some detail, as are 'differences in understandings and attitudes towards working practices and lifestyles, which are integral to the trajectories of industrial capitalism and the intertwined development pathways of the North and South'.

Kandeh and Kannan also address the question of intertwined development pathways, in their case, those which link 'democracy, development, gender, nation-building and state formation'. To this end they provide an overview of past and current regional West African attempts at state-building, national integration, and gender and broader economic development; explore the links between democratic institutions, women's position and market economies; and propose methods for tackling the crisis of governance, fragmented societies, gender bias and inequality, and widespread poverty. They conclude that to consolidate fragile regional democratic systems, regional governments should reject orthodox adjustment and governance reforms, and opt for more heterodox reforms which improve the conditions of existence of regional inhabitants.

Finally, Batterbury offers a thought-provoking piece on efforts by farmers on the Central Plateau of Burkina Faso to plan their own agricultural systems, and the role of development in this process, in an area which boasts persistent development interventions. He concludes that while 'low-level, flexible support' is vital in the marginal environment in question, 'the challenge is to allow farmers to identify and create space for their own interests'. However, arguably of greatest significance in livelihood/development terms, is his observation that 'while recognizing the value of indigenous local knowledge as a basis for carrying out agricultural tasks and making a living, it is also vital to acknowledge that dryland farmers in West Africa are equally capable of designing a plan of action and sticking to it, and of assimilating and valorizing new knowledge from external sources.'

Taken together, the contributions making up *West African Worlds* bridge the region's linguistic divides in their coverage, with contributors representing a good mix of West African and West Africanist voices from a broad range of geographical locations and disciplinary backgrounds or traditions. The collection is linked together, less by a rigid, organising thematic structure, than by its issues-based approach, and its underlying belief that a collection of this kind can, at best, only indicate a selection of possible paths through the complex of realities making up society and nature in the area under review.

Notes

1. With reference to Pentecostalism see van Dijk (2000).
2. As van Dijk (2002) has recently observed, '[e]merging states in Africa have been dealing with a situation where, in some domains of social and political life, the inhabitant may be considered the quintessential citizen (inclusive of perhaps all the connotations of nationalism and xenophobia this entails) whereas in other domains an ethnic subjectivity has emerged as the most relevant identity marker . . . [T]hese uncertainties about status and identity are produced by the fact that citizens are subjects and that contradictions arise precisely because of the fact that there is unequal access to power, political participation and presence because of a subjective identity.'
3. van Dijk's (2002) observation as part of his study of tensions/anxieties between Ghanaian migrants and locals in Botswana highlights maybe *the* key issue at play: 'the crucial point to be made here is that in the case of foreigners and aliens, uncertainties may arise because of them being neither the one nor the other; of being neither a citizen in a given country, nor of being a subject in an ethnicized meaning of the word'. See also the papers presented to the Workshop on Landrights and the politics of belonging in West Africa, Frankfurt/Mainz, 3–5 October 2002 (http://www.uni-mainz.de/~ifeas/Land/Abstracts.html; accessed on 12/4/2004).
4. Activities of the kind described represent a return of sorts to the spirit of much earlier diasporan initiatives associated with the UK-based West African Students' Union during the 1930s and 1940s (for example, Adi 2002).
5. The UK National Criminal Intelligence Service, for example, has a West African Organised Crime Section ('West African organised crime has a big impact on the economy of the UK and other major industrialised countries, [with] the main activities [being] fraud, personal identity theft and corporate impersonation, with strong intelligence to suggest that funds obtained through fraud fund drug trafficking and other major crime'; http://www.ncis.co.uk/waocu.asp), while the Metropolitan Police has issued a West African fraud alert (http://www.met.police.uk/fraudalert/419.htm). In reality, they are both devoted entirely to Nigerian so-called '419' or advanced fee fraud, which 'involves the creation of bogus business proposals which promise the recipients

substantial financial reward for participating. Once the victim agrees to be involved in the deal, the initiating party requests the payment of various "advance fees" (for example, for banking charges or as a bribe to "smooth the way"). The collection of these fees is the object of the scam – once a victim is "hooked", further requests for payment are made' (Shaw 2001). See the Nigeria–419 Coalition Website (http://home.rica.net/alphae/419coal/), which is devoted to countering this scam through educating the (global) public (as, indeed, is the Metropolitan Police's fraud alert referred to above).

6. Shaw (2001), for example, attempts an analysis of this kind in his review of the emergence and spread of West African (overwhelmingly Nigerian) criminal networks in southern Africa, although the use of the descriptor 'West African' rather than 'Nigerian', both here and in the sources sited in note 3, raises interesting questions regarding representations of West Africa(ns) in both the popular and official imaginations, which are, unfortunately, outside the scope of this introduction. However, such concerns need to be borne in mind, in the light of passages, such as the following, taken from an international expert group report on West African Organised Crime, which appear to exceptionalise the criminals in question: 'West African crime groups generally consist of flexible networks rather than closely structured organisations' and 'The speed and adaptability with which West African criminals operate means that existing mechanisms can be ineffective in both preventing the crimes being committed, and in identifying those involved' (http://www.wjin.net/Pubs/2243.PDF).
7. Batterbury's evocative imagery is worth recalling in this respect. 'The Sahel', he notes, in his chapter in this volume, 'is one of the best places in Africa to observe the particular forms of modernity and tradition that occur at the periphery of the world system: where Toyota Landcruisers bearing highly paid development experts meet chiefs, farmers, livestock herders, and a cast of rural characters in sometimes uneasy circumstances, laden with possibility and concealed intention.'
8. At a recent summit of ECOWAS Heads of State with World Bank President James D. Wolfensohn, the Executive Secretary of ECOWAS reiterated that countries in the region remain fragmented, with small, undiversified economies (World Bank 2004b).
9. The Ghanaian Government has been providing support for non-traditional exports through its Export Promotion Council, which has targeted the garments and textiles sector, and cassava starch, salt and palm oil production, among other things, in the hope of attracting $3 billion of investment into the country, creating 90,000 full-time jobs for local people, and increasing the estimated $42 million earned from nontraditional exports to the US in 2002 (ECA 2003).
10. Similarly, the recent political troubles in Côte d'Ivoire have proved a boon for cocoa farmers in Cameroon, for example, who have reported increased sales, and are responding by expanding their farms (Foster 2002).
11. Net private capital totalled about a fifth more than foreign direct investment by the late 1990s, with an increase in private investments contrasting with a stagnation in public spending; ODA represented roughly the same percentage of GNP throughout the 1990s, despite its decrease in per capita terms; and Nigeria's petroleum and gas sector was by far the overwhelmingly favoured destination for incoming investment capital, with the secondary sectors in Côte d'Ivoire, Ghana and Senegal attracting much smaller volumes of these flows (ECOWAS 2000b; 2002; Cour and Snrech 1998; Stock 1995; World Bank 2001).
12. Remittances from Cape Verdeans reportedly represent some 17 per cent of GDP, while Ghanaian remittances outstripped Foreign Direct Investment (FDI)

for most of the 1980s and totalled, annually, $US250–350 million from US sources alone (Mohan and Zack-Williams 2002). In 2002, remittances from Ghanaians abroad totalled $1.2 billion (ECA 2003).

13. It is worth pointing out that while Briggs and Yeboah (2001) note, with reference to (urban) Ghana and Tanzania, that a significant share of these private remittance flows goes toward consumption rather than production, Tall (2004) highlights the investment element of such resources in (rural) Senegal alongside evidence of consumption.
14. It is worth observing that West Africa contained both the country with the least (Côte d'Ivoire) and most (Sierra Leone) unequal income distribution in sub-Saharan Africa. Riddell shows in Chapter 5 how a perceived historical bias against rural populations, places and spaces in Sierra Leone was implicated in that country's slide into civil war.
15. For instance, UNCTAD (2000) categorises SSA countries into 'good performers', 'potentially emerging countries' and 'others', with reference to their potential for meeting the MDGs by 2015, with Benin, Burkina Faso, Côte d'Ivoire, Mali, Senegal, Togo, Ghana and Mauritania being considered potentially emerging economies.
16. For example, ECOWAS itself notes that some countries recorded remarkable economic performances (albeit for short rather than sustained periods of time) during the late-1990s, even in comparison with the rest of the world (see also ECA 2000).
17. UNAIDS notes, for example, that 'the intense mobility of populations resulting from socio-political, ethnic or religious instability; cross-border migrations, the vulnerability of women infected by HIV-AIDS, linked to socio-cultural factors and poverty, are the factors which influenced and continue to influence the spread of the epidemic and the response thereto'.
18. While, as Kathy Baker (2000) has recently demonstrated at length, the climate of West Africa as a whole is now recognised to be disequilibrial, the sahelian drylands are subject to some of the most variable rainfall totals and patterns anywhere in the world with major implications for livelihoods and development: thus flooding killed hundreds of thousands of livestock, destroyed tens of thousands of homes and damaged 2500 hectares of crops in 2002, in the same year that drought and poor rainfall reduced agricultural production in Mauritania and Niger (ECA 2003; see also Chapter 11). In short, this '*condition sahelienne* [is] characterised by unstable climatic circumstances, irregular rainfall patterns and periods of drought' (Turner 1999: 285). It is also worth mentioning the enormous influence which climate, particularly rainfall, wields over Ghana's economic fortunes via river flow into, and lake level fluctuations of, the Volta lake, and, therefore, of the country's capacity for hydro-electric power generation (ECA 2003).
19. Unrecorded trade between Togo and Ghana, for example, is believed to total several times the volume/value of official trade (ECA 2003).
20. Clandestine border crossing is partly the result of people's experiences with officialdom in a context in which (un)official roadblocks on inter-city and inter-state roads, and the imposition of illegal 'levies' on users by state security agents, remain commonplace, while immigration and customs officials continue to demand or accept bribes at border crossing points, etc. In a recent address to the Commonwealth Business Forum on the theme 'Combating Corruption', Sierra Leone's President Kabbah describes corruption as 'an enemy of the state' and 'a security threat to a democratic state [which] delegitimizes th[at] state', and refers to negative public perceptions of customs officers and the police: 'how often are we not told, that public workers such as customs and police officers are prone to solicit or even demand bribes because they are

poorly paid [as if] this is an excuse for soliciting and demanding bribes?' (http://www.statehouse-sl.org/speeches/he-com-bus-dec4.html; accessed on 20/4/2004).

21. The measures under consideration by the UN Security Council, in consultation with regional governments, include 'the possibility of "hot pursuit" operations, joint air patrolling, shared border responsibility, the establishment of a sub-regional reserve force, the possible reinforcement of airspace monitoring and joint planning for the repatriation of foreign combatants' (UN 2004). Although the key areas of concern will be arms, mercenaries and child labour, there is always the possibility that increased regulation will be seized on as an opportunity for perpetuating graft.
22. For instance, for Batterbury (2004), 'two processes have had a particular effect on rural peoples in the West African Sahel over the last thirty years: the arrival of significant rural development schemes and projects initiated by the state and by donors (following the droughts of the 1970s), and the concomitant "loss" of these same initiatives at certain times and in certain countries, impelled by state failures, the withdrawal of aid, conflict, or economic collapse. In response to both scenarios, local people have proven adept in their responses' (see also his Burkinabe case study in Chapter 11).
23. It is worth reminding ourselves that the processes and outcomes which Tall describes are hardly those which formal/state e-strategies would have recommended/promoted or predicted, and were certainly not those the writers of the ECOWAS report would have had in mind (see Cline-Cole and Powell 2004).
24. While NGOs may not have shared IFI enthusiasm for the market, they did benefit, as a category of development agents, directly from IFI determination to restrict the state's role in the development process.
25. The report lists the following supportive ECOWAS partners: European Commission, EU, World Bank, IMF, UN Secretariat and specialised agencies and bilateral donors (including USAID).
26. See, for example, the papers presented to the African Forum for Envisioning Africa, 26–29 April, Nairobi, Kenya (http://www.hbfha.com/nepad.htm).

References

Adedeji, A. (2002), 'From the Lagos Plan of Action to NEPAD and from the Final Act of Lagos to the Constitutive Act: Whither Africa?' Keynote address to the African Forum for Envisioning Africa, 26–29 April, Nairobi, Kenya. (http://www.worldsummit2002.org/texts/AdebayoAdedeji2.pdf; accessed on 21/4/2004.)

Adepoju, A. (2002), 'Fostering free movement of persons in West Africa: achievements, constraints, and prospects for intraregional migration', *International Migration Review* **40(2)**, 3–28.

Adi, H. (2002), 'The African Diaspora, "development" and modern African political theory', *Review of African Political Economy* **29(92)**, 237–51.

Akyeampong, E. (2000), 'Africans in the Diaspora: the Diaspora and Africa', *African Affairs* **99**, 183–215.

Ali, A. and **Thorbecke, C.** (1998), *Poverty in Sub-Saharan Africa: Magnitude and Characteristics*. AERC, Nairobi.

Aryeetey-Attoh, S. (ed.) (1997), *Geography of Sub-Saharan Africa*. Prentice Hall, Upper Saddle River, New Jersey.

Aryeetey-Attoh, S. (2001), 'West, Central, East Africa: diversity in development' in Clawson, D. (ed.), *World Regional Geography: A Development Approach*. Prentice Hall, Englewood Cliffs, New Jersey.

Baker, K. (1992), 'The changing geography of West Africa' in Chapman, G. and Baker, K. (eds), *The Changing Geography of Africa and the Middle East*. Routledge, London.

Baker, K. (2000), *Indigenous Land Management in West Africa. An Environmental Balancing Act*. Oxford University Press, Oxford.

Barber, K. (1997), 'Views of the field' in Barber, K. (ed.), *Readings in African Popular Culture*. International African Institute in association with James Currey and Indiana University Press, Oxford and Indiana.

Batterbury, S. (2001), 'Landscapes of diversity: a local political ecology of livelihood diversification in south-western Niger', *Ecumene* **8(4)**, 437–64.

Batterbury, S. (2004), 'Within, and beyond, territories: a comparison of village land use management and livelihood diversification in Burkina Faso and southwest Niger' in Gausset, Q., Birch-Thomsen, T. and Whyte, M.A. (eds), *Beyond Territory and Scarcity: Social, Cultural and Political Aspects of Natural Resource Management Conflicts*. Nordic African Institute, Uppsala.

Beauchemin, C. and **Bocquier, P.** (2003), *Migration and Urbanisation in Francophone West Africa: A Review of the Recent Empirical Evidence*, Document de travail DIAL DT/2003/09, DIAL, Paris. (http://www.dial.prd.fr/dial_publications/PDF/Doc_travail/2003-09.pdf; accessed on 4/4/2004.)

Bebbington, A. (2003), 'Global networks and local developments: agendas for development geography', *Tijdschrift voor Economische en Sociale Geografie* **94(3)**, 297–309.

Briggs, J. and **Yeboah, I.** (2001), 'Structural adjustment and the contemporary sub-Saharan African City', *Area* **33(1)**, 18–26.

British Broadcasting Corporation (BBC) (1999), *Economies Threatened by Chocolate Compromise*, BBC News Online, October 29. (http://news.bbc.co.uk/low/english/world/africa/newsid_492000/492460.stm; accessed 12/2/2001.)

Bruce, J.W. and **Mearns, R.** (2002), *Natural Resource Management and Land Policy in Developing Countries: Lessons Learned and New Challenges for the World Bank*. International Institute for Environment and Development Issue Paper No. 115. IIED, London.

Bryceson, D. (2002), 'The scramble in Africa: reorienting rural livelihoods', *World Development* **30(5)**, 725–39.

Cline-Cole, R. (1998), 'Knowledge claims and landscape: alternative views of the fuelwood-degradation nexus in Northern Nigeria', *Environment and Planning D: Society and Space* **16**, 311–46.

Cline-Cole, R. (2003), 'Perspectives from yet *other* places, spaces and voices: a commentary on Michael Watts's "Development and Governmentality"', *Singapore Journal of Tropical Geography* **24(1)**, 34–48.

Cline-Cole, R. and **Powell, M.** (2004), 'Editorial: ICTs, "virtual colonisation" and political economy', *Review of African Political Economy* **31(99)**, 5–9.

Cordell, D., Gregory, J.W. and **Piché, V.** (1996), *Hoe and Wage: A Social History of a Circular Migration System in West Africa*. Westview Press, Boulder, Colorado.

Cour, J.-M. and **Naudet, D.** (1996), 'West Africa in 2020', *OECD Observer* **200**, June/July, 20–6.

Cour, J.-M. and **Snrech, S.** (eds) (1998), *Preparing for the future. A Vision of West African Long-Term Prospective Study* (*WALTPS*). OECD/Club du Sahel, Paris.

Dickenson, J. (ed.) (1996), *Geography of the Third World*. Routledge, London.

ECA (2000), *Economic Report on Africa 2000: Transforming Africa's Economies*. ECA, Addis Ababa.

ECA (2002), *Economic Report on Africa 2002: Tracking Performance and Progress*. ECA, Addis Ababa.

ECA (2003), *Economic Report on Africa 2003: Accelerating the Pace of Development*. ECA, Addis Ababa.

ECOWAS (1999), *Executive Secretary's Report 1999*. ECOWAS, Abuja.

ECOWAS (2000a), *Executive Secretary's Twenty-fifth Anniversary Report*. ECOWAS, Abuja.

ECOWAS (2000b), *Executive Secretary's Report 2000*. ECOWAS, Abuja.

ECOWAS (2002), *Executive Secretary's Report 2002*. ECOWAS, Abuja.

European Union (EU) Business (2003), *Ivorian Cocoa Farmers Unfazed by New EU Chocolate Directive*, 5 November. (http://www.eubusiness.com/afp/031105200150.ub6lk0cc; accessed 18/4/2004.)

de Bruijn, M. and **van Dijk, H.** (2003), 'Changing population mobility in West Africa: Fulbe pastoralists in central and south Mali', *African Affairs* **102**, 285–307.

de Haan, L. and **Zoomers, A.** (2003), 'Development geography at the crossroads of livelihood and globalisation', *Tijdschrift voor economische en sociale geografie* **94(3)**, 350–62.

Foster, J. (2002), 'Cameroon cocoa farmers' sweet profits', BBC News 25 October. (http://news.bbc.co.uk/1/hi/business/2360345.stm; accessed on 12/3/2003.)

The Gambia Investment Promotion and Free Zones Agency (GIFZA) (2003), *Invest in The Gambia. Doing Business in Peace*. (www.investinginthegambia.gm; accessed on 6/4/2004.)

Guèye, S. (2003), 'New information and communication technology use by Muslim Mourides in Senegal', *Review of African Political Economy* **30(98)**, 609–25.

Harrison-Church, R.J. (1957) *West Africa. A Study of the Environment and of Man's Use of it*. Longmans, Green and Co., London.

Henninger, N. (1998), *Mapping And Geographic Analysis Of Human Welfare And Poverty: Review And Assessment*. World Resources Institute, Washington, DC. (http://www.povertymap.net/publications/doc/henninger/index.htm; accessed on 6/4/2004.)

Henry, L. and **Mohan, G.** (2003), 'Making homes: the Ghanaian Diaspora, institutions and development', *Journal of International Development* **15(5)**, 611–22.

Lamba, D. (2002), *An Intent Structure Map of NEPAD*. (http://www.worldsummit2002.org/texts/structureNEPAD.pdf)

Mohan, G. and **Zack-Williams, A.B.** (2002), 'Globalisation from below: conceptualising the role of the African Diasporas in Africa's development', *Review of African Political Economy* **29(92)**, 211–36.

Morgan, W.B. and **Pugh, J.C.** (1969), *West Africa*. Methuen, London.

Mortimore, M.J. (1998), *Roots in the African Dust: Sustaining the Drylands*. Cambridge University Press, Cambridge.

Mortimore, M.J. and **Adams, W.M.** (1999), *Working the Sahel: Environment and Society in Northern Nigeria*. Routledge, London and New York.

Ndofor-Tah, C. (2000), *Diaspora and Development: Contributions by African Organisations in the UK to Africa's Development*, Report to AFFORD. AFFORD, London.

Olukoshi, A. (2002a), 'Governing the African political space for sustainable development: a reflection on NEPAD', Paper presented at the African Forum for Envisioning Africa, 26–29 April, Nairobi, Kenya. (http://www.hbfha.com/nepad.htm; accessed on 10/4/2004.)

Olukoshi, A. (2002b), *Governance and Sustainable Development: Some Notes*. CODESRIA, Dakar. (http://www.worldsummit2002.org/texts/Olukoshi.rtf; accessed 2/3/2004.)

OXFAM (2002), *Debt Relief and the HIV/AIDS Crisis in Africa: Does the Heavily Indebted Poor Country Initiative (HIPC) Go Far Enough*? Briefing Paper No. 25. OXFAM, Oxford. (http://www.oxfam.org/eng/pdfs/pp0206_no25_debt_relief_and_the_HIV_crisis.pdf; accessed on 13/4/2004.)

Potts, D. (2004), 'Development challenges and debates in eastern and southern Africa' in Potts, D. and Bowyer-Bower, T. (eds), *Eastern and Southern Africa. Development Challenges in a Volatile Region*. Pearson Education, Harlow.

Power, M. (2004), 'Geographies of governance and regional politics' in Potts, D. and Bowyer-Bower, T. (eds), *Eastern and Southern Africa. Development Challenges in a Volatile Region*. Pearson Education, Harlow.

Raynaut, C. (ed.) (1997), *Societies and Nature in the Sahel*. Routledge, London and New York.

Rain, D. (1999), *Eaters of the Dry Season: Circular Labour Migration in the West African Sahel*. Westview Press, Boulder, Colorado.

Shaw, M. (2001), 'Regional traffick: towards an understanding of West African criminal networks in southern Africa', *African Security Review* **10(4)**, 75–94. (http://www.iss.co.za/Pubs/ASR/10No4/Shaw.html; accessed on 18/4/2004.)

Sierra Leone Homecoming Summit (2003), (http://www.sierraleonehomecoming.com/program.htm#).

Stock, R. (1995), *Africa South of the Sahara: A Geographical Interpretation*. The Guilford Press, New York.

Stoneman, C. (2004), 'Structural adjustment in eastern and southern Africa: the tragedy of development' in Potts, D. and Bowyer-Bower, T. (eds), *Eastern and Southern Africa. Development Challenges in a Volatile Region*. Pearson Education, Harlow.

Swindell, K. (1978), 'Family farms and migrant labour: the strange farmers of the Gambia', *Canadian Journal of African Studies* **12(1)**, 3–17.

Swindell, K. (1985), *Farm Labour*. Cambridge University Press, Cambridge.

Tall, S.M. (2004), 'Senegalese émigrés and new information and communication technologies', *Review of African Political Economy* **31(99)**, 31–48.

Toulmin, C. and **Guèye, B.** (2003), 'How will West African countries meet the MDGs?' in Satterthwaite, D. (ed.), *The MDG and Local Processes: Hitting the Target or Missing the Point?* IIED, London. (http://www.meetingthemdgs.org/pubs.html; accessed on 2/2/2004.)

Turner, M. (1999), 'Merging local and regional analyses of land-use change: the case of livestock in the Sahel', *Annals of the Association of American Geographers* **89(2)**, 191–219.

United Nations (2004), *Security Council Reviews Steps to Facilitate Cross-Border Operations in West Africa*. UN News Service, Washington (http://allafrica.com/stories/200403260965.html; accessed on 19/4/2004).

UNCTAD (2000), *Capital Flows and Growth in Africa*. UNCTAD, Geneva.

UNDP (2003), *Human Development Report 2003. Millennium Development Goals: A Compact Among Nations to End Human Poverty*. Oxford University Press, Oxford.

van Dijk, R. (2000), *Christian Fundamentalism in Sub-Saharan Africa: The Case of Pentecostalism*, Occasional Paper. Centre of African Studies, University of Copenhagen.

van Dijk, R. (2002), 'Localisation anxieties: Ghanaian Pentecostalism and issues of strangerhood in Botswana', Paper presented to conference on 'Postcolonialism Today: Theoretical Challenges and Pragmatic Issues', University of Toronto, 26–29 September, Toronto, Canada.

Watts, M. (2003), 'Development and Governmentality', *Singapore Journal of Tropical Geography* **24(1)**, 6–34.

World Bank (1981), *Accelerated Development in Sub-Saharan Africa*. World Bank, Washington.

World Bank (2000), *Entering the Twenty-first Century: World Development Report 1999/2000*. The World Bank, Washington.

World Bank (2001), *Attacking Poverty: World Development Report 2000/2001*. The World Bank, Washington.

World Bank (2004a), *World Development Report 2004: Making Services Work for People*. The World Bank, Washington.

World Bank (2004b), *Ecowas Leaders, World Bank Head Push Regional Approaches On Trade, Infrastructure And Peace*, News Release No:2004/280/AFR, DevNews Media Centre. (http://web.worldbank.org/WBSITE/EXTERNAL/NEWS/0,contentMDK:20182937~menuPK:34466~pagePK:64003015~piPK:64003012~theSitePK:4607,00.html; accessed on 15/4/2004.)

Zack-Williams, A.B. (1995), 'Development and Diaspora: Separate Concerns?', *Review of African Political Economy* **22(65)**, 349–58.

Zack-Williams, A.B. and **Mohan, G.** (2002), 'Africa, the African Diaspora and development', *Review of African Political Economy* **29(92)**, 205–10.

CHAPTER 2*

Regional political economy: retrospect and prospect

Adebayo Olukoshi[1]

1 Introduction

This chapter examines a selection of trends and structural factors in the contemporary political economy of West Africa with a view to assessing their likely effect on the needs and capabilities of the countries of the region in the new millennium. This assessment is carried out, not only in the context of demands within the region for achieving a more rapid system of democratic development, but also in relation to the ways in which West Africa might more fully respond to the demands of globalisation. The chapter presents a selective overview, which is intended to be both retrospective and prospective. It is argued that in this age of intensifying globalisation, West Africa's future centres around a choice between closer regional co-operation, on the one hand, and the continued pursuit of individual national strategies, which are often not co-ordinated on a regional basis, on the other (Lavergne 1997; Olukoshi 2000). The key question is whether the necessary political will can be found to make the choices that will help unlock the full potential of the region's economies and polities.

2 A Political-economic history

The West African sub-region is unique in many important respects. Home to Nigeria, the world's most populous black country, and Liberia, Africa's oldest republic, it is also the region which produced the first black African country (Ghana in 1957) to win independence from European colonial rule. Ghana's example of radical nationalist agitation served as a source of inspiration for Sékou Touré who, in mobilising opposition to Charles de Gaulle's offer of independence within the French Community, ushered Guinea-Conakry into independence as the first francophone African country to jettison colonial rule. Guinea-Conakry's defiance was to rapidly pave the way for the formal independence of the rest of the countries of francophone Africa.

* This chapter was originally published by the Council for the Development of Social Science Research in Africa (CODESRIA), BP 3304, Dakar, Senegal (website: http://www.codesria.org).

Additionally, one of the first military coups d'état in post-independence Africa took place in the region when members of the Togolese armed forces toppled and murdered Sylvanus Olympio in January 1963. Since then, West Africa has developed a reputation as the coup d'état belt of the African continent, with only two of the countries in the sub-region, Senegal and Côte d'Ivoire, having managed to escape direct military rule until the latter was eventually overcome by its crises, succumbing to a coup in December 1999. Each of the other West African countries has experienced an average of about three coups d'état since the early 1960s; the number of attempted coups in the region is countless.

Prolonged military rule in West Africa has not only generated deep-seated political instability, it has also fanned a growing culture of militarism which has combined with other factors, not least deep-seated economic decline and widespread youth disaffection, to propel several countries into full-scale war. Thus, Liberia was led into a lengthy and ruinous war following the outbreak of an armed rebellion against the military dictatorship of Samuel Doe; Sierra Leone soon followed as a section of the armed forces joined rebels of the Revolutionary United Front (RUF) to plunder the country and wreak havoc on the populace. Guinea-Bissau too was to slide into civil war in 1998 that culminated in the overthrow of Joào Nino Vieira from power in May 1999. In Niger and Mali, two francophone countries that have been exposed to some of the harshest forms of military authoritarianism, repeated armed clashes between the army and Touareg rebels fighting for greater autonomy occurred during the late 1980s and in the 1990s. Countries such as Nigeria (which had a civil war from 1967 to 1970), Guinea-Conakry, and Ghana have on occasion tottered on the brink of outright war and a breakdown of civil order. The two countries that have not had a history of direct military rule have also had their share of authoritarian, even personal rule (see Chapter 5).

Yet, in spite of the experience of prolonged military rule, West Africa has a thriving civil society of long standing, and was in the forefront of the movement, in the late 1980s and early 1990s, for political liberalisation. Indeed, the innovative and popular sovereign national conferences that were held in several francophone and lusophone African countries were first convened in West Africa, beginning with Bénin Republic. Associational life also has a long history in the region, and although the most authoritarian regional regimes did attempt to stifle the development of different civic associations, especially those organised by students and various urban-based interest groups, these associations proved remarkably resilient. Indeed, they were in the vanguard of the resistance to continued colonial domination and the growth of post-colonial authoritarian rule, in addition to playing a leading role in the quest for political reforms in the late 1980s and early 1990s. This long history of civil society activism in West Africa was underpinned by a lively intellectual and political environment associated with the Négritude of Léopold Sedar Senghor, the Egyptology of Cheikh Anta Diop, and the radical Pan-Africanism of Kwame Nkrumah (M'bunyinga 1982). So strong were these politico-intellectual strands that during the 1945–mid-1970s period, West Africa became, at various times, a credible base for a variety of black philosophers and activists, ranging from long-term residents like George Padmore and Frantz Fanon to short-term visitors like C.L.R. James and Abdurahman Babu.

Unlike other regions of the continent, West Africa did not experience settler forms of colonialism of the kind associated with places like South Africa, Namibia, Zimbabwe, Mozambique, Kenya, Algeria, and the Democratic Republic of the Congo (formerly Zaire). The general explanation for this absence of settler colonial rule has centred on the prevalence of malaria in the mosquito-infested rain forest and savannah belts of the region. The deadly toll in lives which the mosquito exacted on early European explorers, missionaries and colonial officials was a key factor which deterred white settler colonial rule. It is, however, also possible that the widespread influence of Islam in the savannah belts also played a part, especially as a number of the pre-colonial political formations in the area, not least the Sokoto Caliphate, the Kanem-Bornu Empire, the Bambara states, and the various Senegambian states, were already built along theocratic lines. Partly on account of the absence of settler colonialism, regional independence struggles, though intense and vigorous, did not, in most cases, result in the kinds of sustained and prolonged armed struggles that characterised the experiences of most of the settler colonies of East, Southern, and North Africa. Only in the Portuguese colonies of Guinea Bissau and Cape Verde were armed struggles fought to wrest independence from the colonising power, a fact that was reflective, in part at least, of the particularly onerous nature of Portuguese colonial rule.

That armed liberation wars were not fought to usher most of the countries of West Africa into independence was, taken in a historical context, ironic. For it was in West Africa that some of the stiffest wars of resistance to colonial rule were encountered by the forces of European imperialism. In effect, as regional pre-colonial political formations represented some of the most advanced efforts at nation-state building in Africa, it was not surprising that a host of vested interests developed around these polities to make resistance to the colonial incursion almost inevitable. Once armed resistance to European invasion was defeated, colonial powers proceeded to introduce measures aimed at facilitating their rule. In the francophone and, to a lesser extent, lusophone colonies, the main mode of control that was developed centred around the policy of assimilation and the goal of obliterating local cultures and creating black French/Portuguese men and women. In anglophone Africa, 'indirect rule', which entailed reliance on existing, if re-oriented, 'traditional' structures of governance, tended to be the norm. Irrespective of the mode of colonial governance that emerged, West Africa was to become the region where the earliest intellectual and political currents against colonial rule developed most fully. In many cases, these currents fed into a wider pan-Africanist agenda, which was aimed at recapturing the history and identity of the black race. Not surprisingly, it was also in West Africa, specifically in Accra, that the first Pan-African congress to be held on African soil took place, attracting the participation of the key nationalist and intellectual leaders of Africa and the Diaspora (M'bunyinga 1982).

3 Some key socio-economic trends

3.1 Ethno-religious pluralism

Inhabiting one of Africa's most populous regions, West Africans constitute a steadily growing population, which is both rapidly urbanising and extremely mobile. Population is becoming increasingly concentrated in the southerly coastal parts of the region, where continuing internal and cross-border migration is accelerating (region-wide) processes of creation/maintenance of multi-ethnic, multi-religious (urban, semi-urban and rural) settlements. Policy and political challenges flowing from regional demographic dynamics in the next few decades will include, first, how a steadily growing population will be fed and provisioned; and, second, how to (re-) define citizenship rights and responsibilities within increasingly complex regional societies. The first of these challenges has direct implications for agricultural development generally, and a regional food security strategy in particular, and raises questions about the capacity of both governments and non-governmental organisations to provide the infrastructural support essential to the pursuit of an adequately broad range of sustainable livelihoods. Relatedly, the second challenge concerns the key question of how to ensure widespread access to livelihood capital/resources (which are historically mediated largely by birth and ancestry) within an increasingly multi-religious and multi-ethnic context (with more people living in settlements other than their places of origin or birth).

Put differently, the management of the affairs of regional ethnic, religious and other minorities has direct implications for the conduct of governance and the prospects for national stability, particularly against a post-1970 background of ethnic and religious revivalism and economic decline, and the challenges they pose to secular nation-state projects. Already, in response to the diminution of the capacity of the state to meet its social responsibilities to its citizenry, religious and ethnic associations have been revived or established to play a role in social provisioning; and although this could be converted into a useful instrument in the renewal of civic culture, it could also result in the heightening of exclusivist forms of ethnic consciousness. Clearly, West African countries need to reform their economies and political systems, conscious of the need to better accommodate and benefit from their ethnic and religious plurality.

3.2 The agrarian basis of economies

National economies in the region are predominantly rural and agricultural, although minerals feature prominently in the export profiles of countries alongside agricultural commodities. In the years following independence, most countries witnessed a narrowing of their export base in a seemingly inexorable march towards monoculturalism; economies came to depend increasingly on the export of one or two commodities. Indeed, countries like Nigeria and Sierra Leone took on a decisively *rentier* character, as they depended almost exclusively on mineral rents for their revenues (Bach *et al.* 1988).

As settler colonialism did not take root in the region, large-scale land alienation of the kind that was witnessed in parts of Eastern and Southern Africa did not occur. Thus smallholder peasant households account for most agricultural output, even though large-scale plantation agriculture has long been practised in localised areas, particularly in Côte d'Ivoire, but has also gained ground more recently in Nigeria, Ghana, and Senegal, as corporate and non-corporate interests take to large-scale farming in the context of the region's prolonged economic crises (see Chapter 7). Peasant agriculture has been accompanied by considerable rural–rural and rural–urban migration; peri-urban farming, mostly on the outskirts of cities and towns, is also commonplace in the sub-region, sometimes tied to the livelihood strategies of urban workers and professionals, who supplement their diminishing real wages and salaries with income generated from part-time farming. As in other parts of Africa, women are vital members of the farming population, who participate in planting, harvesting, processing and marketing activities (e.g. Spiro 1987; see Chapter 7).

The rapid expansion of West Africa's population, coupled with the difficulties associated with raising peasant productivity, poses a major question with regard to food security. Against the background of a decline in both per capita agricultural output and the regional commodity market share, almost all governments attempted to improve agricultural output through, first, 'Green Revolution' programmes that amounted to little and, second, through market-led macro-economic reform efforts associated with International Monetary Fund (IMF)/World Bank-sponsored structural adjustment programmes (Gibbon *et al.* 1993). Indeed, structural adjustment was initially legitimised as a pro-rural programme that was allegedly aimed at shifting the domestic terms of trade in favour of the farming populace and, in so doing, revive regional (and continental) agricultural fortunes. Thus, currency devaluation, trade liberalisation, and the commercialisation/privatisation/liquidation of agricultural parastatals was undertaken as part of the effort to promote market-based incentives for the farming population. Yet, the programmes have, on the whole, not resulted in any dramatic increases in agricultural output or productivity, although increases, in absolute terms, may have been recorded for some of the region's food and cash crops (de Haan *et al.* 1995; see Chapter 7). The reasons for the lacklustre performance of adjustment programmes have been extensively analysed (Brydon and Legge 1996; Mkandawire and Soludo 2002; Mohan *et al.* 2000; Olukoshi 2003; Olukoshi *et al.* 1994). Suffice it to note that key elements in the market reform programmes tended to cancel one another out, with the consequence that they did not produce the envisaged results. The situation was not helped by the indiscriminate removal of input subsidies, the lack of attention to the infrastructure needs of the farming communities, the inadequacy of marketing and financing institutions, and the difficulties posed by the increasingly unfavourable international terms of trade for primary commodity exporters. The quest for an improvement in agricultural output and productivity, therefore, seems to be one area that will continue to attract a great deal of policy attention (see Chapter 7).

3.3 The travails of industry

At independence, most countries hoped to promote rapid industrialisation as an integral part of their quest for economic development. Without exception, they articulated policy measures aimed at promoting import-substitution industrialisation. Apart from the macro-economic policies which they adopted, various governments also articulated a host of incentive measures aimed at attracting foreign investment, and encouraging the participation of local capital, in manufacturing. In cases where the local private sector was still weak, as in instances where a sizable indigenous capitalist class had been created, the state played a direct role in the promotion of the industrial development process, by entering into joint venture arrangements with multinational enterprises and local investors to undertake manufacturing. The results were mixed, both at the national and regional levels. Nigeria, Côte d'Ivoire, Ghana, and Senegal emerged easily as the four most industrially advanced countries, both in terms of the size of their manufacturing sectors and in the number of people employed in these sectors. To varying degrees, all countries were able to satisfy a portion of their consumer goods needs through local production. A growing cross-border trade in goods produced within the sub-region also emerged.

However, although the 1960s and 1970s recorded significant increases in the level of local manufacturing activity, particularly in Nigeria and Côte d'Ivoire, industrial development was fraught with difficulties:

- the entire import substitution strategy was dependent for its success on the continued capacity of the state to finance the import requirements of the manufacturing sector. These requirements included not only raw material inputs, but also intermediate and capital goods. The implication was that any serious crisis in the capacity of the state to earn the foreign exchange with which to pay for the import needs of industry would immediately translate into a crisis for industry. This was all the more so as the manufacturing sector was mostly geared towards serving the domestic market; not being export-oriented, it contributed little to the balance of payments viability of the state, thereby becoming a source of pressure on available foreign exchange resources. Thus, when in the second half of the 1970s and in the early 1980s, West African countries experienced serious balance-of-payment problems, many manufacturers were immediately affected, with some factories collapsing outright, and others retrenching workers and scaling back their capacity utilisation levels.
- manufacturing in the period to 1980 was too heavily concentrated in the production of light consumer goods, with insufficient attention to intermediate and capital goods production. This imbalance in the region's manufacturing structure was reinforced by the fact that, on the whole, local value-added in the manufacturing sector was generally very low. Furthermore, there was very little internal linkage between agriculture and industry.

These and other shortcomings ranked among the issues which the IMF/World Bank adjustment policies promised to redress; in fact, these market-based policies simply reinforced the crisis in the manufacturing sector, setting countries in the region on the path to de-industrialisation. The devaluation of local currencies in Ghana and Nigeria, for example, significantly increased the cost of imported inputs for use in industry; this experience would be replicated in francophone West Africa, following the devaluation of the CFA franc in 1994. Unable to meet the increased costs of inputs, many factories simply resorted to curbing their capacity utilisation levels further and rationalising their workforce. This trend was further intensified by the adverse effects on local manufacturing of the implementation of trade liberalisation measures, which resulted in the flooding of the regional market with cheaper imports. Also, the deregulation of interest rates resulted in astronomical borrowing costs which manufacturers were unable to cope with.

There is a distinct possibility, given the difficulties facing manufacturers, that West Africa risks reverting to a simple role as producer of primary commodities and importer of consumer goods. This prospect is made all the more likely, given that the new industries that were supposed to emerge from the ashes of the collapsed import substitution factories have failed to materialise. The difficulty of undertaking local manufacturing under conditions of structural adjustment has meant that not many new factories have been established in place of those that have collapsed or are collapsing. Yet, it is inconceivable that West Africa could ever hope to develop without industrialising. This is a challenge which the countries of the subregion would need to address through the articulation of policies aimed at stemming the tide of de-industrialisation. Such policies would necessarily have to overcome the weaknesses of earlier attempts at import-substitution industrialisation. They would also have to take account of the World Trade Organisation's tariff and other trade-related regimes, with a view to devising strategies for ensuring that their development needs are catered for. For it is difficult to imagine that industrial development can occur on a sustained basis without some measure of state protection; similarly, opportunities that could be derived from the exploitation of regional economies of scale would have to be closely explored.

3.4 The external debt burden

The severe economic strains which West African countries have been under date back, in some cases, to the early 1970s, when the Organisation of Petroleum Exporting Countries (OPEC) quadrupled oil prices and, in so doing, created severe balance-of-payments problems for most of the states in the region. With the exception of Nigeria, which is Africa's biggest oil exporter and a member of OPEC, all other West African countries were, and still are, net importers of oil (Bach *et al.* 1988). Combined with diminishing terms of trade for their agricultural exports, their growing budgetary problems, and the inflationary consequences of their fiscal policies, the problems which the majority of West Africa states suffered as a result of the OPEC oil price increases of the 1970s translated into a domestic and external debt crisis in the early 1980s. As far as external debt problems were concerned, these were mainly the result of the bilateral, multilateral, and private trade loans which countries accumulated during the course of the 1970s, but which they became increasingly unable to service by the early 1980s. Nigeria, which was a big winner from the OPEC oil price increases, was itself to join the bandwagon of economic crisis and external indebtedness following the collapse, in the early 1980s, of the world oil market.

Although Nigeria is, by far, the single biggest debtor nation in the region, the majority of countries have had to contend with unsustainable levels of debt; and, as servicing external debt became one of the greatest economic challenges facing West African countries for much of the 1980s and 1990s, the entire region suffered net resource transfers. Not surprisingly, West Africa earned the dubious distinction of being home to some of the very poorest nations on earth, at least according to human development surveys carried out by the United Nations Development Programme (UNDP), at a time when per capita aid was low and declining for the majority of countries in the region. Clearly, the magnitude of the debt problem, and its toll on social service provision (especially health and education), as well as on physical infrastructure, is such that, if not contained, threatens to completely undermine 'development' in the area. Indeed, it is partly in response to the decline of formal social institutions and physical infrastructure, that regional production and economies have become increasingly informalised (see Section 3.5). Containing the debt crisis beyond the traditional resort to rescheduling and token gestures of cancellation (such as those that have been implemented within the ambit of the *Francophonie*, by the Group of Eight (G8) countries, and the so-called Heavily Indebted Poor Countries [HIPC] Initiative) will be one of the key economic policy challenges facing the region and the donor community in the years ahead. Prospects for economic recovery, and a return to the path of growth, will be considerably enhanced by a substantial reduction in the debt service obligations of debtor countries.

3.5 The widening frontiers of informalisation

West Africa is an area where informal economic activities are both widespread and have an extremely long history (Igué and Soulé 1992). These activities span virtually all economic sectors and cover both domestic retailing and cross-border trading activities (Meagher 2003). Informal sector operations are evident in the financial sector through the activities of parallel market currency dealers, local-level money lenders, and community-based savings clubs, while informal production structures mostly take the form of cottage-type manufacturing. But it is in the commercial sector, and the financial processes associated with it, that informal sector structures and processes have been most fully developed. Women play a very prominent role in informal commercial operations, not just as retailers at the domestic level (e.g. Coles 1991), but also in transborder transactions. Indeed, so central are women to West Africa's informal trade that myths about the ubiquitous 'market mammies' and the vast resources which they control are widespread (Grandmaison 1969). Yet, not all women have managed to transform their informal sector activities into sites of accumulation; a majority remain at the level of subsistence in a market which caters largely to low-income households, and is characterised by intense competition. It is possible that up to half of the entire regional population may be involved in informal sector activities of one kind or another (CILSS/ Club du Sahel/CINERGIE 1995).

Much regional inter-state trade is accounted for by this informal sector. Indeed, while formal commercial exchange between the countries amounts to just over 5 per cent of total exports, informal sector flows are considerably more significant and increasing. Small-scale traders shift resources between places as far apart as Nigeria and Senegal, as well as between localities in West and Central Africa, in their search for markets. In this they were aided by the convertibility of the CFA franc. Significantly, the suspension, in August 1993, of the CFA franc's convertibility outside the West and Central African franc zones does not appear to have deterred these informal sector operators. Commodities traded by the informal sector operators across boundaries consist of goods from Europe, North America, and the Far East imported into one or more of the countries in the area, and then re-exported to other parts of the region. Bénin Republic is, by far, one of the most important re-export centres in West Africa, although Niger and Senegal are also significant players in this regard. Not surprisingly, the view that informal sector commercial flows are destined to inherit a greater share of sub-regional trade, in spite (perhaps even *because*) of the many obstacles that stand in the way of formal trade flows, is a widely-held one. This way, it is thought, regional economies will become increasingly integrated, even if formal regional co-operation efforts, such as those represented by ECOWAS, continue to be plagued by problems (Ubogu and Orimolade 1984) (see below and Chapter 6).

The former colonial powers, especially Britain and France, remain the main formal trading partners of West African countries; they are also the leading sources of foreign investment in the region. However, commodities produced by locally established factories are also widely circulated by informal sector operators. A key issue which has arisen concerns the impact of informally traded manufactured goods on local industrial production, particularly in a context where a growing proportion of such goods consists of cheap imports from the Far East. From a policy point of view, a widening disconnection between goods that are traded informally and local manufacturing structures is feeding into the dynamics of de-industrialisation. Indeed, it is doubtful that regional integration could ever be sustained over the long term, as long as local structures of production are undermined by regional patterns of informal commerce (CINERGIE 1993; Egg and Igué 1993).

4 Structural factors and processes

4.1 An inherited 'language divide' and regional geo-politics

With the exception of Mauritania, all the countries in the region are members of the Economic Community of West African States (ECOWAS), which was founded in 1975 as a joint Togolese–Nigerian initiative, although each country also belongs to one or another of a number of smaller sub-regional groupings. Even though all countries signed the ECOWAS treaty and its protocols, several lines of division continue to undermine efforts at meaningful regional co-operation (Mahamane *et al.* 1993). Perhaps the most important of these is that corresponding to the linguistic legacy of colonial partition. The 'language divide', and the political load which it both carries and symbolises, has often militated against closer interaction among the countries of the sub-region, with matters not being helped by the massive influence which France continues to exert over its former colonies (Osterdahl 1997). Indeed, international Franco-British geo-political contests are all too often refracted through a West African prism, with consequences for the scope and intensity of regional co-operation.

As France's geo-political and commercial interests in francophone West Africa have fed into the language divide and have, therefore, constrained the scope for fully-fledged integration across linguistic lines, France's own commitment to an expanding European Union raises the legitimate question, and one which has generated debate and anxiety in francophone West Africa, of the future of the 'special' links between Paris and its ex-colonies (CILSS/Club du Sahel/CINERGIE 1995). For the moment there is talk in Paris of establishing a link between the CFA franc and the euro, even as France continues to play a pivotal role in encouraging greater co-ordination among the francophone West African states within the Union Économique et Monétaire Ouest Africaine (UEMOA). It is, however, still possible that in the years ahead, as they cease to be 'special' to Paris, the francophone countries will themselves seek to diversify their relations more aggressively and, in so doing, probably engage other West African states more intimately than is currently the case. Similarly, Nigeria, as West Africa's biggest economy (Ate and Akinterinwa 1992), might also attempt to project itself much more fully, both in the fallout from the resolution of its deep-seated problems of internal governance, and as part of its own attempt at strengthening the ECOWAS framework for regional co-operation (see Chapter 6).

4.1.1 France in West Africa: does the CFA Franc Zone have a future?

Through the legacy of its colonial policy of assimilation (a systematic attempt at the denial and negation of their indigenous cultures) and a host of neo-colonial instruments and mechanisms, France's relations with its former colonies have remained very close, with Paris having a direct say in the internal political and economic affairs of the majority of these countries. Indeed, France maintains a military presence in several and has defence/security co-operation pacts with practically all of them. As members of *la Francophonie*, their alliance with France was and, to a great extent, still remains central to Paris's claim to 'big power status' in world affairs. French commercial interests spanning practically all economic sectors not only dominate the economies of the francophone countries, but also enjoy privileged access through a combination of political, economic and cultural factors.

Perhaps the most important instrument through which France has developed its politico-economic grip on the francophone countries is the CFA franc. This is the common currency of all of the francophone West African countries, with the exception of Guinea, which had much earlier said *'Non'* to Charles De Gaulle's neo-colonial project in Africa, and opted for an autonomous path of its own with its own national currency. Guinea maintained this course until Sékou Touré, its independence leader, died in office. The CFA was, from the outset, connected to the French franc in a fixed parity relationship. It was also convertible, with convertibility guaranteed by the French Central Bank, but fully backed by the foreign exchange earnings of the francophone countries lodged with the Bank in Paris. Each of the francophone countries maintained an account with the Bank of France and with the Banque Centrale des Etats de l'Afrique de l'Ouest (BCEAO), which serves as their common central bank. From 1948 to January 1994, the fixed parity remained unchanged at 50 FCFA to 1 FF. In January 1994, the parity was changed to 100 FCFA. That devaluation was preceded by the restriction of the convertibility of the CFA to its West African francophone zone (Olukoshi 1995a).

It is worth noting that the arrangement which linked the CFA franc to the French franc played an important part in bolstering the French currency as an international, freely convertible medium of exchange. But more than that, it conferred numerous advantages on French businesses by way of preferential access to the markets of the francophone countries. For the leaders of the francophone countries, in addition to the convertibility of their currency, which they seemed to cherish, the arrangement was perhaps the greatest symbol of the 'special' relations that they believed they enjoyed with France and its leaders. The devaluation of the CFA franc was, therefore, an important matter laden with great symbolism for them. Did it, for example, mean the devaluation of France's relations with them? Beyond this, France's own increasing engagement with Germany and the wider European Union project has also raised questions about the future of the link between the French franc and the CFA franc. What does the abandonment of the franc and the adoption by Paris and other key European players of a common currency (the euro) mean for the CFA? Will the European Union be prepared to inherit France's commitments to the francophone countries, including the guarantee of the convertibility of the CFA franc?

The questions are many and will increase as the European economic and political integration project gathers pace, however unevenly or unsteadily, in the years ahead. In a bid to reassure local political and policy opinion across francophone Africa, French officials have taken to suggesting that the relationship between the CFA franc and the French franc will be transferred to the euro. This has, however, fuelled a discussion of the appropriate rate of exchange at which the CFA franc would be pegged to the euro, and the role which the new European Central Bank (ECB) might have in managing the hardness and convertibility of the CFA. Anxiety is widespread that further devaluation of the CFA is perhaps inevitable. Hopefully, continued uncertainty of this kind will concentrate the minds of regional policy makers sufficiently for meaningful means of progressing plans for regional monetary union, either allied to, or independently of the euro, to be explored and, eventually, adopted.

4.2 The political framework for governance

The majority of countries in the region attained independence as multi-party systems, at least nominally. However, in many cases, multi-partyism soon gave way to single party or military rule. In countries like Côte d'Ivoire and Senegal, where the multi-party framework was maintained, one party, the party of the independence struggle, was overwhelmingly dominant. The rapidity with which military rule spread from Togo to encompass all the other countries of the sub-region, with the exception of Côte d'Ivoire and Senegal, and the rapid, often violent regime turnover that the region witnessed in the period up to the late 1990s, is symptomatic of the crisis of governance that continues to afflict the area. In the overwhelming majority of countries, political succession was, until the onset of multi-party political reforms, unpredictable, achieved by unconstitutional means (mainly coups d'état), and accompanied by violence. Indeed, even as most of Africa moved decisively during the late 1980s and early 1990s to embrace electoral pluralism, Nigeria, Sierra Leone, and the Gambia slid into military rule before massive local and international pressure compelled their military rulers to embrace programmes of transition to elected government. Not surprisingly, many commentators consider West Africa to be one of Africa's most volatile regions. Clearly, a key test of recent political reforms, which many countries have embraced under local popular and donor pressure, will be their capacity to deliver orderly, constitutional succession on a sustained basis in the years ahead.

Most of the countries in the region convened and held multi-party elections as part of the political reform process that swept through much of Africa during the late 1980s. All the elections were bitterly contested, and in the cases of Ghana, Guinea, and Côte d'Ivoire, sections of the opposition boycotted the polls altogether. In Senegal, violence associated with the contest between the incumbent regime and its opponents resulted in a number of key opposition leaders being arrested; in Togo, assassinations and attempted killings were rife and marred the entire electoral process. Only Mali, Bénin, Cape Verde, and Niger had fairly open elections that were not too bitterly contested. And only in Cape Verde, Niger, Bénin, and Mali did the electoral outcome result in the removal of incumbents from power. In Cape Verde, the incumbent government was beaten outright by the opposition; in Mali and Niger, the heads of the incumbent regimes that presided over national conferences were not eligible to contest the elections that took place; in Bénin Republic, Mathieu Kérékou was already too weakened and discredited by the processes that led to the convening of that country's sovereign national conference to mount a serious challenge to the main opposition coalition. Nonetheless, in the face of an impasse between the president and parliament, Niger was to slide back to military rule before the late General Barre Mainasara transformed himself into an elected civilian president through an electoral process that was marked by fraud. The bitter aftermath of that process was to stalk Niger's political landscape until May 1999 when Mainasara was assassinated by his bodyguards and Niger was brought back to full military rule. In Bénin, after a period in opposition, Kérékou was returned to power, adding to the number of West African countries – Ghana, Mali, Burkina Faso, etc. – where second elections, characterised by widely varying degrees of success, had been held as part of the renewed drive towards multi-party politics.

It seems clear, then, that the task of national reconciliation is still a major one in the region, and that the quest for democratisation remains fragile and may not necessarily deliver sustained political stability (see Chapter 11). In particular, the bitterness between the opposition and incumbent government/party remains very strong in several countries, notably in the absence of acceptable power-sharing mechanisms in hotly contested terrains like Côte d'Ivoire, Ghana, Burkina Faso and, to a lesser extent, Senegal and Togo. Matters have not been helped by the fact that across the region, elected governments have had to stick to the implementation of unpopular International Monetary Fund (IMF)/World Bank structural adjustment programmes, which have fed into pre-existing economic difficulties, to take a severe toll on the working and living conditions of the majority of the regional populace, albeit to different degrees and in different ways. It would seem, then, that a key theme likely to dominate internal political debate in the years ahead is that which revolves around questions of how to create the best electoral strategies and institutional approaches for reconciling competing domestic political interests. Evolving a framework for reconciliation will not be easy given the numerous vested interests that have developed in support of competing claims for power. But it is clear that the evolution of such a framework will be indispensable to the quest for a return to the path of economic growth and development.

An important feature of politics in West Africa which is not sufficiently frequently remarked upon, but which will be central to the future of the region's countries, centres on the mode of organisation of government in multi-ethnic, multi-religious societies. This is a question which is made all the more pressing by the fact that armed intra-state conflicts have increased in frequency. With one exception, countries in the region inherited centralised state systems in which central government wielded a great deal of power at independence. But even in Nigeria, which had a fairly loose federal system in the immediate post-independence years, the years during and since the civil war have seen a rapid erosion of the basis of the country's federal system of government, and an increased concentration of power in the central government (partly as a result of prolonged military rule) (Ibrahim 1995). Thus all of West Africa was, in the period up to the 1990s, governed under highly centralised systems of government which were commonly underpinned by varying degrees of political authoritarianism.

The unitarist state project which countries embraced was supposed to feed into strategies for promoting national unity, integration and economic development. However, the legitimacy crisis of the state, created/exacerbated by prolonged economic crises and the revival of ethnic and religious identities, has posed direct challenges to this unitary, centralised state project. It would seem therefore that another dimension of the governance question in West Africa in the years ahead will centre on the most appropriate system of government necessary for the pursuit of the goals of national cohesion and rapid economic development. Would, for example, centralised/unitarist arrangements be more or less appropriate than decentralised/federalist/confederalist systems? This concern also touches directly on the choice between presidential and parliamentary systems, on the one hand, and majoritarian and coalition-based governments underpinned by one or another proportional representation arrangement, on the other. In any case, the increasing restlessness of minorities in Niger, Mali and Burkina Faso (with their Touareg problem), Côte d'Ivoire (with increasing friction between the so-called autochthons, migrants, and Muslims in the north), Senegal (with its long-standing Casamance problem), Nigeria (with its deepening ethnic, religious and regional crises most sharply expressed in the oil-rich delta), Guinea (with the contest pitching Mandingos, Sousous, and Foullahs against each other), and Ghana (Nanumbas vs. Konkonbas, for example), among others, suggests that the question of how best to administer countries will remain a key issue in the years ahead.

4.3 Political conflict, civil disorder and state failure/collapse

For all the volatility and instability that have characterised politics in West Africa, it is amazing that, with the exception of Nigeria which slid into a civil war between 1967 and 1970, and, discounting the on-off conflict in Senegal's Casamance province, the region knew no major systemic breakdowns until the late 1980s/early 1990s when Liberia slid into a prolonged and devastating civil war. This war was to spread to Sierra Leone, with the consequence that the Mano River basin tri-state area (which, in addition to Liberia and Sierra Leone, also includes Guinea-Conakry) became engulfed in war and disorder. Certainly, the crisis in the Mano River basin tri-state area was the most serious systemic breakdown witnessed in the region since the end of the Nigerian civil war. Indeed, Liberia became West Africa's first truly 'collapsed' or 'failed' state in the Somalia mould.

Elsewhere, in the sahelian states of Mali, Burkina Faso, and Niger, central government authorities were, from the late 1980s, locked in conflict with their Touareg populations, resulting in skirmishes between government troops and rebel fighters, although these were far less serious than the Liberian and Sierra Leonean civil wars. Guinea-Bissau, too, was to slide into a civil war pitching rival sections of the army against each other in 1999. For the majority of the francophone countries, however, a strong French presence, not just in terms of investments but also in terms of military posts and personnel, may have played a role in reducing the pressures towards separatism and internal civil war. Still, it is clear that for the foreseeable future, the promotion of reconciliation and reconstruction in war-torn societies, and the prevention of systemic break down in other countries will remain key features of politics and governance.

Projects of reconciliation and reconstruction would, inevitably, involve close attention to the establishment of a new social contract between the state and society; the reconstruction of the state to redress the unidirectional retrenchment which it suffered during years of economic reform; and the provision of a new set of principles around which national energies could be mobilised, and which could endow the state with a sense of purpose and coherence. Also, the issue of the type of economic policies which may be best attuned to the goal of national reconciliation and reconstruction would have to be addressed. Clearly, the trend whereby societies emerging from conflict are made to adopt neo-liberal economic measures that are deflationary in thrust is one which would need to be re-thought and balanced against the need for the promotion of job-creating, infrastructure-renewing and production-enhancing economic growth and development. Furthermore, the question of how to make the political system more representative of, and responsive to, the interests and concerns of the citizenry beyond periodic elections will need to be tackled.

Finally, state capacity and legitimacy in curbing the traffic in light weapons that have flowed into West Africa in greater quantities than before, and which have helped to fuel many an intra-state, inter-communual conflict, will need to be addressed. As part of this process, a co-ordinated regional strategy might need to be considered for checking the activities of both international mercenaries and mercenary organisations, as well as transnational mining interests engaged in illicit commercial transactions in regional conflict zones. This suggests a need to transcend narrow sectionalism and nationalism, particularly of the kind associated with the legacies of colonial rule.

4.4 Boundaries that unite or borders which divide?

The colonial partition of Africa, arbitrary and shoddy as it was, left most of the continent with 'artificial' boundaries that were bound to be sources of conflict. Members of some ethnic groups found themselves divided between two or three states, while the lifestyles of nomadic groups like the Fulani and the Touareg were insufficiently catered for. In a bid to minimise the potential for conflict which the arbitrariness of the boundaries could generate, the Organisation of African Unity (OAU) decided that all inherited boundaries should be accepted and respected as demarcated by the forces of colonialism. It is, however, in West Africa that most of the (often violent) boundary disputes that have been witnessed on the continent have unfolded: Nigeria vs. Cameroon; Nigeria vs. Bénin; Nigeria vs. Chad; Ghana vs. Togo; Mali vs. Burkina Faso; Burkina Faso vs. Côte d'Ivoire; Senegal vs. Mauritania; Guinea vs. Sierra Leone etc. In several cases, the disputes have degenerated into recurrent, if often short-lived armed conflicts, which have often been fuelled by struggles over the control of human, mineral, or land resources.

Existing attempts at managing inter-state boundary disputes have mostly centred on the establishment of bilateral joint commissions or bilateral boundary commissions to map out areas of disagreement between the countries involved. These commissions have, however, not been successful at preventing the periodic outbreak of armed hostilities between neighbours in the sub-region (e.g. Nwokedi 1985). Beyond *ad hoc* mediation efforts put in place after border wars have started, there is no effective multilateral mechanism for preventing the outbreak of violent border disputes in the first place. The platform provided by ECOWAS has never been used for tackling boundary disputes, in spite of the rhetoric in the late 1970s and early 1980s about an ECOWAS defence and security pact. Clearly, then, boundary disputes will continue to constitute a significant element of the politico-security problems afflicting the region in the years ahead, making the search for more creative approaches to managing borders for the mutual benefit of the countries a pressing policy and politico-diplomatic concern. At issue is the need to ensure that borders unite rather than divide the peoples of West Africa, both in *de facto* and *de jure* terms. The issues raised by shared water resources illustrate this particularly well.

4.4.1 Shared water resources

West Africa's Niger and Senegal rivers are two of the seven most important water bodies in all of Africa. From a regional point of view, however, by far the most important waterway is the Niger (other important waterways are the rivers Mano, Volta and Benue). Emerging from the Futa Djallon mountains in Sierra Leone, it traverses several African countries eastwards before emptying itself into the Atlantic Ocean through the coastal Niger delta. In addition to its huge hydro-electric potential, the Niger is also a source of water for both household and industrial use, as well as for farming, livestock and fishing. Given its strategic importance to the socio-economic development strategies of the countries of the region, it is clear that it can be both a stimulus for tremendous levels of co-operation and a source of dispute between the countries that have a shared interest in its use.

Given a long-run decline in regional rainfall totals, particularly in the semi-arid areas, and the sometimes striking variability which characterises rainfall totals and distribution, the strategic significance of the Niger, Senegal, Volta, Mano and Benue rivers to the water resource and agricultural development objectives of various countries is bound to grow. So too will the potential for conflict. It is perhaps a foretaste of the kinds of dispute which shared water resources have a potential for generating, that in the period since the 1960s, growing concern has been expressed about the use to which individual countries have sought to put the sections of regional rivers that traverse their territories. Nigeria, for example, had to address the concerns of some of its neighbours (especially Niger) when it embarked on the construction of the gigantic Kainji dam on the Niger; it has also had cause to express its anxiety to Mali over attempts to extract water from the same river for rice irrigation and other agricultural purposes. Clearly, the easiest way to avert the possible outbreak of 'water wars' in the future will be to devise strategies for developing the full potential of the rivers within the wider framework of regional co-operation/integration (Obiozor *et al.* 1994). This was attempted, for example, through the Mano River Union and the Niger Basin Authority (successor to the Niger River Commission), whose mandate was to 'promote and co-ordinate the studies and programmes dealing with the projects for development of the water resources of the Niger basin' (http://www.abn.ne/webeng/nbainfo/nbainfo1/intro.html); both agencies are, however, moribund as they were never really well-funded, and were unable to attract sufficient international support for their operations.

In addition to the rivers that serve as a common resource, the area also has two important lakes, Volta (Ghana) and Chad (Nigeria–Chad border). The former is one of the biggest artificial lakes in the world and is a legacy of Nkrumah's grand vision for the agro-industrial transformation of Ghana. It is a source of water, not only for domestic, agricultural and industrial use, but also for hydro-electric power for Ghana itself and its immediate neighbours like Mali, Burkina Faso and Côte d'Ivoire. As any interference with the Volta River, the main source of water flowing into the lake, will have far-reaching consequences, Ghana has always closely monitored the use to which the authorities in Burkina Faso have put the section of the Volta River that traverses their territory. So far, open hostilities over the management of the Volta River and Lake have been avoided, although there was tension between Ghana and Burkina Faso in 1998 over the latter's decision to build a dam on the river, which was blamed for subsequent low water levels at Akosombo and the disruption to electricity generation and supply in Ghana which resulted from this.

Also, Nigerian and Chadian soldiers have, on occasion, engaged in hostilities over rights to, and the use of Lake Chad, notably by inhabitants of settlements located near or around the lake. These hostilities have taken place in spite of the existence of both the Nigeria–Chad Joint Commission, which is supposed to harmonise the interests of both countries in the development and use of the resources of the lake, and the Lake Chad Basin Commission, which also includes Niger and Cameroon, and which had been set up 'to encourage cooperation in developing the Lake Chad region' (http://www.focusintl.com/whos0022.htm). Nonetheless, it is worth recognising the recent mediation efforts of the latter (http://www.unwire.org/UNWire/20031205/44911060.asp), following a build-up of tension in the area, in the wake of an International Court of Justice adjudication designed to ensure the long-term resolution of boundary disputes in the lacustrine zone between Nigeria and Cameroon, and involving territorial and population transfers between the two countries (http://allafrica.com/stories/200310310814.html). Interest in both the lake and the territory around it has been heightened by suspicion that the area may be rich in hydrocarbons, even as tension within and between local populations has intensified over the last three decades or so, as lake levels have fluctuated wildly and, in the process, threatened local and regional livelihoods, thereby necessitating new and increased patterns of mobility in the pursuit of livelihood diversification and sustainability (see Chapter 7).

5 *Between functional regionalism and regional economic integration*

Although West Africa is home to a large number of cross-national organisations (Soderbaum 1996) which are, nominally at least, interested in the promotion of regional co-operation, only one of these, ECOWAS, boasts a membership that cuts across the region's linguistic divide. The existence of a large number of regional co-operation organisations is not, by itself, necessarily a bad thing, even if many of these organisations have parallel mandates and, unlike ECOWAS, tend to be linguistically exclusive. However, several of these organisations compete with ECOWAS and duplicate its functions. Perhaps the most prominent of these is the francophone Communauté Économique des États de l'Afrique de l'Ouest (CEAO), which was set up soon after the founding of ECOWAS, to perform broadly similar functions as the latter in relation to the francophone countries. The Union Économique et Monétaire Ouest Africaine (UEMOA), formed in January 1994 as a successor to the CEAO, also stands in direct competition with ECOWAS; and this at a time when the latter's persistent funding difficulties continue unabated. As elsewhere on the continent, West Africa therefore boasts regional co-operation and integration initiatives, whose record leaves much room for improvement, partly because of destructive competition, but partly also because of a lack of co-ordination of effort (Ezenwa 1992).

Similarly, numerous functional organisations, which could carry out specific tasks, have also been plagued with operational and financial difficulties. CILSS (the Permanent Inter-State Committee for Drought Control in the Sahel), for example, which was set up with the assistance of the European Commission following the droughts of the late 1960s and early 1970s, has not been able to support an adequate number or spread of projects to either minimise the worst effects of drought or stem the advance of desertification processes. Similarly, the problems of the West African Clearing House (WACH), which was transformed into WAMA (the West African Monetary Agency) in 1996, are even worse. Although it was set up by regional central banks to promote greater formal regional commercial and financial interaction and pave the way for the eventual emergence of a single monetary zone, most countries do not use its services, thereby frustrating the institution in the pursuit of its goal. Several other examples of stalled, failed, or moribund efforts at functional co-operation can be cited, leading to the conclusion that West Africa might well be lost between functionalism and integration (Ezenwa 1992). Significantly, neither functionalism nor integration has been able to attract sufficient political/policy commitment (and finance) to make a significant difference in the levels of co-operation among the countries of the region, although this is not to suggest that the two are necessarily incompatible. Policy-makers and donors will, however, have to decide which area to give greater priority in order to improve the livelihood chances of the majority of the region's people.

With France's active support, UEMOA has attempted to take a higher profile in the promotion of policy co-ordination among the francophone countries, culminating in the creation of a common francophone West African stock exchange based in Abidjan, and poised to rival the existing stock exchanges in Nigeria and Ghana. Also, the francophone countries are taking steps, within the framework of the treaty of the Organisation for the Harmonisation of African Business Law (OHADA), to streamline their commercial law, partly in order to enhance the smooth functioning of the Abidjan stock exchange (http://www.jurisint.org/pub/ohada/text/text.01.en.htm). This is a significant development, even if there is plenty of room to doubt the efficacy of the promotion of stock market capitalism as a path in (West) Africa's quest for economic development. Of equal significance, perhaps, is the fact that the francophone West African stock exchange is being promoted independently of those in Nigeria and Ghana, where the authorities have also adopted policy options which make little or no reference to a wider regional context. Nor is this all. For ECOWAS is pursuing its own measures aimed at increasing formal financial transactions within the region, the most significant of which include the launch of the ECOWAS traveller's cheque and the establishment of the ECOWAS exchange rate mechanism.

Clearly, considerable scope for greater policy harmonisation and co-ordination exists, and ought to be exploited much more, particularly, although not exclusively, in the area of infrastructural development, one of the cardinal objectives of ECOWAS since its founding. Indeed, a great deal of emphasis was placed on the development of a trans-ECOWAS highway from Lagos (Nigeria) to Nouakchott (Mauritania), and the promotion of a cross-border telecommunications system to ease contact between the region's people. Although some 83 per cent and 70 per cent, respectively, of the trans-coastal and trans-sahelian components of the highway are reportedly complete (http://www.sec.ecowas.int/), progress has been highly uneven, with some quite good sectors which are motorable all year round, and others which are still undeveloped and only properly motorable during the dry season. The same is true for the telecommunications project, where the goals achieved have been given a recent fillip by progress with circum-African optical fibre ocean cable (the region's capital cities are now connected by microwave links) (http://www.sec.ecowas.int/). Although the days are gone when a telephone user in an anglophone country wishing to communicate with somebody in a francophone one had to have the call routed through exchanges in Paris and London, direct telephone contact remains frequently tedious and sometimes highly inefficient. As the highway and telecommunications projects are areas where some donor support might be helpful, it is worth noting that the African Development Bank has taken an active interest in both projects. Success in the area of transport and communication development must be central to any effort at promoting greater socio-economic and cultural interaction among the peoples of the region, and in equipping the region and its peoples for confronting globalisation.

6 Preparing West Africa for the challenges of globalisation

Across West Africa there is widespread policy recognition of the challenges of globalisation. Unfortunately, many of the scholarly and policy discourses are cast in terms of the need to avoid 'marginalisation' by increasing West African exports to the world market, attracting greater direct and portfolio foreign investment inflows, and promoting a generalised policy of market liberalisation, public enterprise privatisation, and capital account deregulation. In all of this, the accent is placed on the creation of an environment 'conducive' to the local operation of private international capital (Olukoshi 2000).

However, it is not at all certain that such a response to globalisation will necessarily launch West Africa on the path of sustained economic development, which has been the object of policy-making since independence. Apart from the fact that no region of the world has ever developed on the basis of an unregulated market, there is a danger in focusing excessively on incentives that are geared towards the narrow interests of portfolio investors, to the detriment of the kinds of long-term investment which the region should be aiming to attract, and for which a role for the state is indispensable. Furthermore, West Africa's capacity to respond to the forces of globalisation will be enhanced by a more systematic effort at promoting the investment activities of local entrepreneurs, especially those which enhance the regional productive base in agriculture and industry. In part, this calls for a more concerted attempt at removing administrative and other barriers, including security and gender barriers, to intra-regional trade and investment in West Africa (see for example Meagher 1997).

6.1 Regional peace-keeping

Following the onset of the Liberian civil war in the early 1990s, attempts were made to shore up the ECOWAS security and defence pact in order to stem the descent into anarchy in that country. The issue was, however, a highly divisive one since several countries, especially those supporting rebel leader Charles Taylor, were suspicious of Nigeria's intentions, given that it had initially openly supported the dictatorship of Samuel Doe. The Nigeria-led ECOWAS Monitoring Group (ECOMOG), which was eventually formed to serve as a peace-keeping force in Liberia, was controversial from the outset, and was openly opposed by Côte d'Ivoire, Burkina Faso and several other francophone countries (Vogt 1992). This, and the indiscipline of the ECOMOG force, contributed a great deal to the prolongation of the intervention, and raised serious questions about the efficacy of the initiative (see Chapter 5).

However, hailed as a major initiative in regional peace-keeping and conflict resolution at a time when the leading world powers were unwilling to commit troops and resources to peace-keeping in Africa, and in spite of the numerous (military, politico-diplomatic, and financial) difficulties which it encountered, ECOMOG was to have its mandate extended to Sierra Leone, where, with Nigerian troops at its core, it helped to restore the elected civilian government of Ahmad Tejan Kabbah which had been toppled by a combined group of rebel insurgents and renegade government soldiers. Similarly, following the outbreak of fighting in Guinea-Bissau, ECOMOG was also to establish a presence there in a bid to restore some order ahead of fresh elections (see also Chapter 6).

6.2 Organising civil society for development and (gender) equality

A final issue relates to the nature of regional civil society. At one level, given the region's early engagement with anti-colonial nationalism and radical as well as moderate forms of Pan-Africanism, it is not surprising that several countries hosted civil society associations, including youth organisations like the West African Students Union (WASU), which served as platforms, in the post-1945 period, for opposition to colonial rule. The rapid spread of Western education in the region acted as a catalyst in the formation and proliferation of civil society organisations such as the professional associations of lawyers, doctors, journalists, and teachers. The development of the colonial economy itself spawned a number of local interest groups associated with the emergence and spread of capitalist relations. Perhaps the most prominent of these were the trade unions of workers, the associations of farmers set up to promote their case for better produce prices, and the chambers of commerce that brought various categories of business people together. Added to these are the innumerable town/community development associations/unions for which the region, especially its anglophone countries, is famed.

Athough set up to serve a development purpose, these associations/unions fed into the process of the 'thickening' of civil society, as did the establishment, by the 'educated elites', of independent newspapers. Indeed, sectors of this 'thick' civil society, often involving women's and children's groups, were to play a key role in the movement for political liberalisation in the late 1980s and early 1990s. Some, with women's groups in the forefront, continue to work towards greater equity in society, frequently starting with challenges to entrenched patterns of patriarchy and gender inequality, which reinforce a situation whereby, even in 'matrilineal' societies, women are generally subordinated to men, while bearing a disproportionate proportion of the burden for reproducing society (e.g. WIN 1992). Indeed, in a bid to strengthen the prospects for greater equality for women in the development process, various women's organisations from both sides of the anglophone–francophone divide came together to found in 1983, with the support of the ECOWAS, the West African Women's Association (WAWA), one in a series of efforts at organising women in the sub-region for the collective promotion and defence of their interests (http://www.fasngo.org/en/network/ngos/text/wawa.htm).

WAWA's work is an admixture of advocacy, awareness-building, and project support (especially of the income-generating type relevant to women). As an umbrella organisation, it encourages all women's associations at both the domestic and local or national levels to work cooperatively under its ambit. Its success will depend on its ability to establish itself as a credible body worthy of the support of both West African women and interested overseas or international donors (see, for example, Fonjong 2001). Certainly, its interest in promoting women's income-generating activities fits in well with projects already being promoted by local citizens' groups and NGOs. Significantly, WAWA advocates the total involvement of women in *all* aspects of processes of regional development (http://www.alliancesforafrica.org/news.asp?news=163) (see Chapter 11).

7 Conclusion

In seeking to come to terms with the West African scene in all its complexity, variety and dynamism, scholars engaged in overview analyses of a retrospective/prospective kind have tended either to project extreme pessimism (e.g. Kaplan 1994) or radiate wild optimism (see Chapter 6). So what future awaits West Africa in the years ahead? On the whole, it would seem that the options open to the countries of the region will centre around a straight choice between a greater effort at promoting regional co-operation or persisting with individual national efforts with little or no cross-country co-ordination. Most West African policy-makers are aware of the similarity of the problems that confront their countries; they are equally aware that they have to dialogue with one another more seriously. Yet, the impediments that stand in their way are many, not least among them the French factor, and Nigeria's lingering crisis of governance, as well as political difficulties in several other West African countries.

On the evidence that is currently available, it seems likely that most countries will continue to try to develop individual national strategies while paying comparatively less attention to regional integration (Bossard 1994). Perhaps the best that can be hoped for is that governments will be inclined to integrate *some* regional perspective into their national strategies. Most of the governments themselves will have more than their fair share of internal political problems to worry about in the years ahead, and since politics dictates a lot of what happens in the area, it can be expected that a great deal of policy attention and political energy will be devoted to managing domestic affairs. Unfortunately, popular, civil-society pressures for concerted regional co-operation remain relatively underdeveloped in West Africa; also, continuing economic crisis in the area will limit the scope for functional forms of co-operation. The expansion of cross-border informal sector exchanges will, however, ensure that the boundaries of interaction among the peoples of the region are widened (Meagher 1997).

In sum, it would seem that the future of the region will lie somewhere between extreme pessimism and wild optimism. Several factors, including economic performance, the quality of governance, the capacity of civil society to organise and assert itself, and the long-term global strategy of France, could act to sway the balance in one direction or the other. The remarkable adaptability and innovativeness of the region's people, including their capacity to devise multiple livelihood strategies and popular alternative forms of provisioning should, however, mean that many will manage to live at, or just above, subsistence, in spite of all indicators that point to a continuing crisis in the formal economy (see, for example, Chapters 1 and 8). It is such resilience and adaptability that explain why the region has not previously been engulfed in widespread, all-encompassing anarchy; and although these attributes should not be taken for granted, they probably will continue to ensure that economy and society somehow manage to function, albeit to varying degrees of effectiveness. The creative harnessing of these resources should go a long way to improving the conditions of existence in the region. Perhaps it is to the means for harnessing these human resources on a regional scale that political and policy attention needs to be directed. For it is, ultimately, only through successful regionalism that West Africa's full potential is likely to be realised, at the local, national and regional levels.

Note

1. This is a substantially revised, updated and reduced version of my *West Africa's Political Economy in the Next Millennium: Retrospect and Prospect*, which was initially published as Monograph 2/2001 in the CODESRIA Monograph Series. I am grateful for copyright permission for publication of this version, and would like to thank the editors for their invaluable assistance in preparing the manuscript for this volume.

References

Ate, B. and **Akinterinwa, B.** (1992), *Nigeria and its Immediate Neighbours*. NIIA, Lagos.

Bach, D., Egg, J. and **Philippe, J.** (eds) (1988), *Le Nigeria: Un pouvoir en puissance*. Karthala, Paris.

Bossard, L. (1994), *Nigeria and the Perspectives for Regional Integration in West Africa*. Club du Sahel/CINERGIE, Paris.

Brydon, L. and **Legge, K.** (1996), *Adjusting Africa: IMF, World Bank the IMF and Ghana*. I.B. Tauris and British Academic Press, London and New York.

CILSS/Club du Sahel/CINERGIE (1995), *Preparing for the Future: A Vision of West Africa in the Year 2020*. CILSS/Club du Sahel/CINERGIE, Paris.

CINERGIE (1993), *Regional Economic Integration Issues Between Nigeria, Bénin, Cameroun, Niger and Chad*. Cotonou Meeting, 6–8 May 1993, Mimeograph.

Coles, C.M. (1991), 'Hausa women's work in a declining urban economy: Kaduna, Nigeria, 1980–1985' in Coles, C. and Mack, B. (eds), *Hausa Women in the Twentieth Century*. University of Wisconsin Press, Madison, Wisconsin.

de Haan, L. *et al.* (1995), in Simon, D., Van Spengen, W.V., Dixon, C. and Naerman, A. (eds), *Structurally Adjusted Africa: Poverty, Debt and Basic Needs*. Pluto Press, London.

Egg, J. and **Igué, J.** (1993), *L'Intégration par les marchés dans le sous-espace 'Est': L'Impact du Nigeria sur ses voisins immédiats*. INRA/UNB/IRAM, Club du Sahel, CILSS, Paris.

Ezenwa, U. (1992), *Assessment of the Impact of Selected Economic Integration Instruments: Sectoral Transformation and Restructuring in West Africa*. ECA, Addis Ababa.

Fonjong, L. (2001), 'Fostering women's participation in development through non-governmental efforts in Cameroon', *The Geographical Journal* **167(3)**, 223–34.

Gibbon, P. *et al.* (1993), *A Blighted Harvest: The World Bank and African Agriculture in the 1980s*. Africa World Press, New Jersey.

Grandmaison, Le Cour (1969), 'Activités économiques des femmes Dakaroises', *Africa* **39**, 138–52.

Ibrahim, J. (1995), *West Africa and the Federal Question: Nigeria's Bad Example*. Mimeo, Zaria.

Igué, J. and **Soulé, B.** (1992), *L'Etat entrepôt au Bénin: Commerce informel ou solution à la crise*. Karthala, Paris.

Kaplan, R. (1994), 'The coming anarchy', *Atlantic Monthly* **273(2)**, 44–76.

Lavergne, R. (ed.) (1997), *Regional Integration and Co-operation in West Africa: A Multidimensional Perspective*. Africa World Press, Lawrenceville, New Jersey.

Mahamane, B. *et al.* (1993), *Regional Co-operation and Integration in West Africa*. OECD/CINERGIE/ADB, Paris and Abidjan.

M'bunyinga, E. (1982), *Pan-Africanism or Neo-Colonialism*? Zed Books, London.

Meagher, K. (1997), 'Informal integration or economic subversion? Parallel trade in West Africa' in Lavergne, R. (ed.), *Regional Integration and Co-operation in West Africa, A Multidimensional Perspective*. Africa World Press and IDRC, Lawrenceville, New Jersey and Ottawa.

Meagher, K. (2003), 'A back door to globalisation? Structural adjustment, globalisation and transborder trade in West Africa', *Review of African Political Economy* **30(95)**, 57–75.

Mkandawire, T. and **Soludo, C.** (eds) (2002), *African Voices on Structural Adjustment. A Companion to Our Continent, Our Future*. IDRC/CODESRIA/Africa World Press, Ottawa, Canada and Lawrenceville, New Jersey.

Mohan, G., Brown, E., Milward, B. and **Zack-Williams, A.B.** (2000), *Structural Adjustment: Theory, Practice and Impacts*. Routledge, London.

Nwokedi, E. (1985), 'Strands and strains of good neighbourliness: the case of Nigeria and its francophone neighbours', *Genève-Afrique* Vol. XXIII(1).

Obiozor, G., Olukoshi, A. and **Obi, C.** (eds) (1994), *West African Regional Economic Integration: Nigerian Policy Perspectives for the 1990s*. NIIA, Lagos.

Olukoshi, A., Olaniyan, R.O. and **Aribisala, F.** (eds) (1994), *Structural Adjustment in West Africa*. Pumark/NIIA, Lagos.

Olukoshi, A. (1995a), 'The CFAF devaluation revisited', *SAPEM* **8(7)**. (http://csf.colorado.edu/ipe/sapem/sapem8.7.html; accessed on 5/2/2004.)

Olukoshi, A. (1995b), 'Understanding the basis for the reversal of Nigeria's economic policy Direction', *SAPEM* **8**.

Olukoshi, A. (2000), *Democratisation, Globalisation and Effective Policy Making in Africa* (www.idrc.ca/tec/workingpaper_ehtml; accessed on 12/1/2004).

Olukoshi, A. (2003), 'Globalisation, equity and development: some reflections on the African experience'. Paper presented at the GDN Annual Conference, 19–21 January 2003, Cairo, Egypt.

Osterdahl, I. (1997), *La France dans l'Afrique de l'après Guerre froide: Interventions et justifications Document de Recherche* 2. NAI, Uppsala.

Soderbaum, F. (1996), *Handbook of Regional Organizations in Africa*. NAI, Uppsala.

Spiro, H.M. (1987), 'Women farmers and traders in Oyo State, Nigeria' in Momsen, J.H. and Townsend, J.G. (eds), *Geography of Gender in the Third World*. Hutchinson, London.

Ubogu, R.E. and **Orimolade, W.A.** (eds) (1984), *Trade and Development in ECOWAS*. Vikas Publishing House, New Delhi.

Vogt, M.A. (ed.) (1992), *The Liberian Crisis and ECOMOG: A Bold Attempt at Regional Peace Keeping*. Gabumo, Lagos.

WIN (Women in Nigeria) (1992), *The WIN Document: Conditions of Women in Nigeria and Policy Recommendations to 2000 AD*. Ahmadu Bello University Press, Zaria, Nigeria.

CHAPTER 3

Portraying West Africa's children: moral panics, imagined geographies and globalisation

Elsbeth Robson

1 *Introduction*

As portrayed by the global news media, children in and of West Africa appear to suffer a steady stream of exploitation as child slaves, prostitutes, soldiers, plantation workers and domestic servants. The 'terror talk' (Katz 2001: 717) which characterises these negative discourses of crisis, would appear to be supported by a body of reports, statements and claims from UNICEF, the International Labour Office (ILO), Save the Children and other international NGOs (non-governmental organisations) engaged in earnest debates around children's rights, modernity and development. This chapter explores, attempts to untangle, make sense of, and look beyond these contemporary moral panics and imagined geographies of West Africa's children to ask what we really know of these youngsters' work and migration in the context of globalisation. In particular, the chapter asks whether forces of economic restructuring are to blame for the alleged recent explosion in child labour, child migration and trafficking. Focussing on children in, and of, the specific region of West Africa roots the chapter geographically, while allowing exploration of global/local links – especially between the countries of West Africa and the large populations of West African origin and descent (including many privately fostered children) in the UK. The focus on children is a deliberate choice of a visible subject which has major implications for the way West (and other) Africans are perceived, but a subject which has so far not benefited from sufficient critical scholarship.

2 *Moral panics and West Africa's children*

As global citizens we all live in a cosmopolitan world, in a time that has been labelled as an age of anxiety and conspiracy theory (Parish 2001). Today is an uncertain world for everyone, including populations in West Africa and those who make up the West African diaspora (Box 3.1). This uncertainty impacts not least upon children, whether they know it or not. This chapter begins by considering representations in the global news media, of young people in and of West Africa and how they are frequently

Box 3.1 The West African diaspora

The West African diaspora includes considerable populations of West Africans and many people of West African descent living outside the West African region elsewhere in Africa, in Europe, in North America and throughout the world. See for example Uduku (2002) on the extent of the Igbo diaspora as demonstrated through the World Igbo Congress; Reynolds (2002) on Nigerians in Chicago; and Frost (2002) on Kru of Liberia in Freetown and Liverpool. Similarly, Henry and Mohan (2003) document the institutions and organisations of Ghanaians in the UK which support development of ancestral homes in Ghana.

portrayed as victims of endless abuse. This section draws together media reportage and secondary material from NGO and other sources to present, examine and comment on some of the prevalent discourses of crisis surrounding West African children.

2.1 Media portrayals of childhoods in crisis

In various recent news items child slaves are reportedly being trafficked between the countries of West Africa, and from West Africa to Europe. Reputable media such as the BBC report from places such as Benin City in Nigeria, that children are being sold by their parents and then trafficked to neighbouring countries where they are sold again (BBC 2001b). The BBC publish maps showing suspected routes of child trafficking (e.g. from Benin to Togo, to Côte d'Ivoire) and report that children from Mali also work as 'slaves' on the cocoa farms of Côte d'Ivoire (BBC 1999, 2002b). Local and national news media in the UK report threatened closure of a social services-provided safe house – a secure environment for unaccompanied trafficked youngsters arriving at an international London airport to prevent them being sold into prostitution in Europe (BBC 2003; UK Newsquest 2003). A national UK radio station features a report of orphan girls from Sierra Leone, found working in a brothel in a city in the south of England. Their traffickers had told them they were bringing them to Europe to work as maids (BBC Radio 4 2003). The *Independent* (UK) newspaper claims that child servants are often sent from West Africa to work for professional African families in Europe (Hickman 2003). An investigative journalism team from the UK in West Africa were reputedly offered a child for $5 and the paperwork for $500 (Baker 2002). A bibliography of UK media reports of children trafficked into and through the UK for sexual purposes is provided by Somerset (2001) for the period 1996–2001. Several of the reports identified highlight Nigeria as a source of child prostitutes brought to the UK. News sources also report on child soldiers, specifically in Sierra Leone (BBC 2002a) and children trafficked from poor rural Benin to work as domestic maids and marketplace hawkers in richer Gabon (BBC 2001a).

Box 3.2 Muti killings

'Muti' is a South African term associated with herbal medicine and traditional healers, or herbalists. '[*M*]*uti* (magical) murders, [are those] in which body parts – especially skulls, hearts, eyes, and genitals – are removed and used or sold by deviant traditional practitioners to increase the wealth, influence, health, or fertility of a paying client' (Scheper-Hughes 2000: 204). In a single region of South Africa alone it is estimated there are about 300 muti murders each year (Baker 2002). Ritual murders have been recorded by an official commission to be on the increase in South Africa (Comaroff and Comaroff 1999).

In the UK at least, the media picture of children in and of West Africa includes in recent times extensive coverage of the death of eight-year-old Victoria Adjo 'Anna' Climbié. This little girl died in February 2000 from hypothermia precipitated by neglect, malnutrition and physical abuse inflicted by her great aunt and her boyfriend. Victoria was informally fostered by her great aunt and had come from Côte d'Ivoire, where she was born, to London less than a year previously. The parents and family of Victoria back 'home' in Côte d'Ivoire believed she was enjoying a better life in Europe. Given the cultural values of much of West Africa, where child rearing is seen as a responsibility of the extended family, the great aunt's offer to educate Victoria in Europe was welcomed unproblematically as an honour for the family (Quansah 2002: 12). The aftermath of Victoria's death has seen a public enquiry and much scrutiny of the social services, as well as soul searching by the 'African community' in the UK, which is most numerous in London (Demuren *et al.* 2002).

Another horrific death in London of a child of West African origin, has also provoked similar responses and has been the focus of much media and public attention. The unknown boy who has been named 'Adam' (identified as Nigerian[1]) was ritually murdered and on 21 September 2001 his headless and limbless torso was found floating in the River Thames in central London (Baker 2002; BBC Channel 4 2003). This as yet unsolved murder case has brought much public consternation that not just belief in the power of human sacrifice, but its actual practice, is present in one of the most modern capital cities of the developed world. In contrast such 'muti' murders are frequent in many parts of Africa, believed by their perpetrators to be powerful sacrifices, or carried out as a source of body parts for use by those who believe in the power of concoctions made with human remains (Box 3.2). Many 'ordinary' Africans undoubtedly abhor such practices. However, the universally most abhorrent aspects of magic, superstition and the supernatural, including ritual child sacrifice, might appear to be alive and well in an (albeit deviant) minority of the West African diasporic community in London. This perhaps reveals part of the 'darker side of modernity' (Giddens 1990: 7) and a particularly grisly commodification of body parts. Reputedly, children regularly disappear in parts of West Africa, believed to have been abducted for ritual killings and/or the acquisition of body parts for magical purposes as reported by the international news media (BBC Channel 4 2003) and scholars (Bastian 2001: 81) alike.[2]

Furthermore, occult cosmologies are prevalent throughout the world – no less in Africa (Moore and Sanders 2001) than in North America, Europe and elsewhere. In the USA, for example, polls show that the percentage of adults believing in paranormal phenomena (including the devil, ghosts, and communication with the dead) increased in the decades towards the end of the twentieth century (Vyse 1997: 16–17). It should not then be a surprise that belief in the power of child sacrifice is undefeated by modernisation, development, rationalisation and technology.

2.2 *NGO portrayals of children as abused victims*

Such 'terror talk' (Katz 2001: 717) in the media concerning children both in and of West Africa would appear to be part of more widespread hyper-vigilance and moral panics about children's vulnerability. The 'terror talk' which characterises the negative media discourses of childhoods in crisis (as illustrated and examined above) would appear to be supported by a stream of reports, statements and claims from UNICEF (e.g. Salah 2001), the ILO (International Labour Organisation), Save the Children, Anti-Slavery International and other smaller NGOs like AFRUCA (Africans Unite Against Child Abuse) in the earnest debates around children's rights, modernity and development.[3] Taking the issue of child slavery, for example, Anti-Slavery International highlight the plight of children like Aminata (Box 3.3).

Anti-Slavery International (2003a) document many more cases of child slaves in West Africa. There are numerous further cases documented elsewhere. For example, the cases of two girls trafficked from Nigeria to the

Box 3.3 Aminata: a child slave in Gabon

'Aminata is ten years old. In March 2000 she was found under a public bench in Libreville, Gabon's capital. Her legs showed fresh scars from a recent beating. Thousands of miles from her home in Togo, she was clearly terrified and bewildered. She was taken to Centre d'Accueil, run by volunteers, and slowly her story began to unfold.

Aminata had been living with her family when a woman called Fatima visited their home. Arrangements were made and Aminata left with the woman. It was the start of a long journey, first by car and then by boat. Once in Libreville she was forced to sell cakes on the street. Her 'employer' took all her earnings and left her with nothing.

After Aminata had been rescued and brought to the Centre, she was visibly traumatised.'

Source: Anti-Slavery International (2003b).

Box 3.4 Child trafficking

Trafficking is defined as the 'illicit and clandestine movement of persons across national and international borders, largely from developing countries and some countries in transition with the end goal of forcing women, girls and children into sexually or economically oppressive and exploitative situations for the profit of recruiters, traffickers, crime syndicates, as well as other illegal activities related to trafficking, such as forced domestic labour'.

Source: UN General Assembly 1994, cited in Salah (2001: 2).

UK and through the UK on to Belgium and Italy are detailed by Somerset (2001: 39–43). Anti-Slavery International, ECPAT UK (End Child Prostitution, Pornography and Trafficking), UNICEF, ILO and the World Bank[3] have all undertaken studies and expressed concern at the increased number of children being trafficked (Box 3.4) within and out of West Africa (Salah 2001; Ouattara 2002). Efforts are being made to rehabilitate and repatriate trafficked children within West Africa via NGOs, transit camps and the efforts of embassies. Beyond the West African region children are trafficked to several European countries via various routes. Trafficking of children is of course illegal, and can be read as a darker side of the strong diasporic links between West Africa and Europe. Many children also move legally between West Africa and Europe within the context of families – both real and fictitious.

Informal and private child fostering practices play a large role in these complex webs. According to various sources it is estimated there are 10–12,000 African children in private foster care in the UK alone (Ariyo 2003a; Utting *et al.* 1997).[4] About 65 per cent of these foster children are thought to be from West Africa. Fostering of children within kinship networks is a common practice in West Africa (Box 3.5). While most of these fostered children are not strictly trafficked, in some cases the claims of kinship between children and their carers may be somewhat spurious.[5] Mubanga (2002) identifies some of the reasons why parents in West Africa send their children to Europe to live, sometimes with complete strangers. These reasons include (false) images of the 'good life' in Europe, displacement of children due to armed conflicts in West Africa leading to asylum seeking in Europe, poverty, globalisation and ease of international travel. It is recognised by concerned welfare organisations and others (e.g. Utting *et al.* 1997: 44–5) that once in Europe these children (like Victoria Climbié) are especially vulnerable to abuse because they are often poor, isolated, socially excluded, and living in the most deprived social groups and areas. Furthermore, private foster care, in the UK at least, remains as yet unmonitored by government social services. Private fostering appears more prevalent among (West) Africans than among other ethnic groups, except the Chinese, in the UK (Utting *et al.* 1997: 44). We cannot be sure whether all, or even most, fostered children of (West) African origin in the UK are

Box 3.5 Child fostering in West Africa

Informal fostering, especially within extended kin, is a common traditional practice among many African ethnic groups, not least in West Africa. Parents often send children to live with grandparents, aunts, uncles, or other relatives variously to benefit from better schooling opportunities, to enable parents to work or study (perhaps away from home), to learn their mother tongue, to receive discipline and so on. Childless women foster their nieces and nephews, bringing them up as their own. In some cases children are also fostered by people who are not blood relations. Fostering of a child from low status parents to a household or guardian of higher socio-economic status is common. This is a way of improving that child's future life chances and the security of its natal household members. Fostering is frequent among societies with high infant mortality and is also an indigenous coping method for caring for orphans created by war, famine or disease. The majority of social caring mechanisms in West Africa are brought about through institutions such as these indigenous fostering practices, rather than by 'social services' of the kind known in Europe and other parts of the global North. Some studies (e.g. Bledsoe 1990, in Sierra Leone) have shown that foster children in some West African communities are treated more harshly by their guardians than children living with their biological parents.

foreign-born. According to the government report of Lord Utting (1997: 44–5), West African children in foster care may have parents who are students, working, or travelling to and from West Africa, or who are permanently in West Africa but want their children to benefit from UK healthcare, education and other facilities. Most foster placements of these children are transracial; so some black West African children are being brought up by white carers in predominantly white rural areas.

It is a challenge to distinguish between healthy cultural practices and exploitation, or abuse, of children. Cultural practices of transnational fostering of 'nieces' and 'nephews' within extended kin of West African families linked across West Africa, Europe and elsewhere, reflect broadly African beliefs that a child belongs not just to his or her parents, but to the whole family and community. Such practices represent a valuable heritage and traditional ways of educating a child, but they can be abused by commercial exploitation and by deviant individuals.[6] Transnational fostering can also make it difficult for social services, say in the UK, to trace and protect children who may move frequently and who may not be fluent in the language of their host country.[7]

Unaccompanied children arriving as asylum seekers from West Africa (especially Nigeria, Liberia, Sierra Leone and Ghana) are known to disappear into the UK or elsewhere in Europe, even if taken into local authority care. Much of what we know about child trafficking comes from investigative journalism and from trafficking intercepted by immigration officials at points of entry and exit, when visas are applied for with false papers, when children escape and turn to churches, welfare organisations or the police, for help. The case of more than sixty-six disappeared youngsters thought to be aged 13–22 years is under police investigation in West Sussex (Somerset 2001: 13, 26). This case includes boys as well as girls trafficked from West Africa, although girls are in the majority (Somerset 2001: 13). Ariyo (2003b) has suggested that an increasing number of children from West Africa are being exploited for domestic labour and possibly also being brought into the UK for welfare benefit fraud and/or prostitution. Some are believed to be *en route* through the UK to prostitution elsewhere, with Italy a frequently cited destination.

Such children may have been abducted from their homes. Others may be tricked into huge personal debt (even as much as £25,000) to the traffickers for their passage and then coerced into exploitative (especially sexual) labour. Also the threat of violence or death to them and their families and the use of terrifying witchcraft ('voodoo' or 'juju') force them not to reveal their traffickers (Somerset 2001: 14, 26). It is commonly suggested by commentators that the families of trafficked children may have willingly paid for them to go overseas for a 'better life', or that their parents may have been forced by poverty to 'sell' their child to earn money for them overseas. Some children, however, themselves become directly involved with traffickers and may voluntarily approach them in efforts to escape situations of poverty and little hope for a better future. Not all the girls trafficked from West Africa to Europe for prostitution were unaware that the sex trade was their destination, but in other cases children were duped into being trafficked with false promises of educational opportunities, easy work, extravagant earnings and suchlike (Somerset 2001: 22).

It is estimated that there are 5–10,000 unaccompanied children in the UK (Somerset 2001: 44) which includes trafficked children, asylum seekers and some privately fostered children. Obviously not all unaccompanied children are from West Africa and not all are the victims of traffickers, but nonetheless they are all potentially vulnerable individuals. Children trafficked to the UK from West Africa may enter the country with adults pretending to be their parents, be smuggled in or even brought in under sponsorship schemes (Somerset 2001: 44). There are increasing reports of unaccompanied children from Africa arriving in Britain and then disappearing out of local authority care into exploitative labour (especially the sex trade; but also welfare and benefit fraud, domestic servitude, market trading, farming and begging) in the UK, or elsewhere in Europe – especially Italy (Mullenger 2000). It is difficult, if not impossible, to estimate the numbers involved but there is 'enough evidence to show that the UK has a trafficking problem' (Somerset 2001: 44).

It is possible that 'Adam' was trafficked to the UK for ritual murder. 'Adam' may have come from Africa to the UK through Germany because when found he was wearing a pair of shorts which were sold only in Germany. His parents may not know he is dead. A clearer example of child trafficking involves two dead children who were found in Brussels hidden on a plane which had arrived from West Africa (Ouattara 2002). Children are also crossing borders to work within West Africa, especially given the permeable nature of borders within ECOWAS (see Chapter 1), and widespread perceptions of attractive well paid jobs in foreign countries of West Africa and Europe. For example, Malian children are found working in the coffee estates of Côte d'Ivoire (Ouattara 2002) although under conditions described as near-slavery. NGOs widely claim that child trafficking is on the increase globally (ILO 2003) involving increased numbers of children trafficked to the UK and through the UK including children from various African countries (Kanu 2002).

UNICEF estimates at least some 200,000[8] children are trafficked every year in West and Central Africa to work on fishing vessels, farms, in the sex trade, in sweatshops or in homes as domestic labourers (UNICEF 2003). A UNICEF, ILO and International Institute for Tropical Agriculture study found rampant use of child labour in cocoa-growing communities in Cameroon, Côte d'Ivoire, Ghana and Nigeria. Many children (more boys than girls) under 14 years old were found to be using pesticides, machetes and engaged in other hazardous work often without pay (allafrica.com 2003).

I have so far briefly examined some of the powerful discourses presented by the media and NGOs of West African children in crisis. In the remainder of the chapter I attempt to make better sense, untangle, and theorise the mass of different forms of evidence about the nature of childhood for children in and of West Africa. This starts with questions of who constructs these discourses, how exactly are these constructed and to what end? To begin to answer these challenging questions it can be asserted that in part these discourses are constructed and perpetuated by a global news media which thrives on tales of disaster and scandal. In addition to investigative journalists sniffing out stories about the betrayal of childhood innocence, NGOs construct similar stories of the abuse of children's rights.

However, in order to avoid inaccurate caricatures it is useful to note that NGOs are very diverse and complex organisations. Some of them are also very active in problematising and critiquing aspects of globalisation, structural adjustment and so on, by engaging in political criticism and not just taking moralistic stands on issues like child abuse.

The discourses of child abuse promulgated by NGOs can be read in different ways. In part the driving force may not always be simply sincere altruism, moral disapproval, or ethical drive, but an imperative to stay in business. In other words, certain representations of abused children are perpetuated in order to sustain the corporate business interests of the NGOs and the media. At a deeper level it is certainly possible to read the anxieties expressed in the media and official reports about trafficking of West African children as slaves, servants, drug mules, workers, beggars, prostitutes, sources of body parts and even for sacrificial murders as a form of conspiracy theory. To a certain extent, some of the occurrences reported really take place; but perhaps we should question the degrees of exaggeration, spin, and hype involved. An alternative reading would suggest that high profile, heavy media coverage of isolated (albeit horrific) cases of child abuse have sparked off a moral panic of global dimensions.

Another reading, drawing on the perspectives of Castañeda (2000), would see stories of child disappearances, abductions, abuse and sacrifices as rumours or modern urban legends which may, or may not, be strictly true. Given the difficulties of disentangling fact from fiction, this perspective sees compelling 'fables' of children's maltreatment being perpetuated by the global media as powerful tales that resonate with fears of modern (especially urban) existence globally (see Chapter 4 for one such fictional representation). These 'stories' are embodied with mythological power so their consumers can never be entirely sure if they are valid, hence their promulgation by concerned NGOs and the like as 'pseudo-fact'. Such theorisations and analysis are explored later in this chapter.

3 *Beyond the media hype and moral panics*

With respect to trafficking of children within and beyond West Africa this section attempts to look beyond the Western media hype and to contextualise global panics of NGOs and others to see what is known, understood and theorised about the phenomenon more analytically. The intention is not to cast doubt on, or deny, the existence of the various forms of exploitation reported by the media.

To begin with it is clear that child trafficking is not a new phenomenon, but one that has changed with globalisation. We know from the intergovernmental body, the International Organization for Migration (IOM), that reliable and accurate statistics on the trafficking of children simply do not exist, and that available solid empirical research is sparse (IOM 2000: 98). Although the mechanisms through which child trafficking occurs are understood and recognised in international legal instruments and conventions, the phenomenon of child trafficking has not yet been fully understood (IOM 2000: 105).

The notion of push and pull factors used in migration studies can be helpfully applied to the analysis of child trafficking. IOM recognises that pull factors include market demands of the sex trade and the commodification of body parts (IOM 2000: 105–6), but fails to highlight the demand for domestic and other labour, as well as welfare fraud. A document agreed by regional governments, UNICEF, employers' and employees' associations, ILO and other NGOs identifies eleven factors which particularly contribute to the prevalence of child trafficking in West Africa:

- poverty
- cultural values and practices
- unawareness of the risks involved
- insufficient training and educational opportunities
- the desire of children to migrate in search of economic and social wellbeing
- high demand for cheap and submissive child labour
- traditional migration of adults within the framework of economic activities
- inadequate or non-existent national legislation on child trafficking
- inadequate border controls
- weak institutional mechanisms
- preponderance of informal economy (CPA 2000: 1–2).

Further 'push factors' in child trafficking include large families, natural disasters and unemployment. Children are recruited into trafficking by abduction, sale by family, false promises of work and bogus adoption agencies (IOM 2000: 105). Parents in West Africa want a better life for their children, while young people want opportunities to improve their circumstances. These understandable desires for betterment may lead to such outcomes as girls ending up working in the sex trade in Europe. Unscrupulous operators supposedly take advantage of others' poor circumstances and their (at times mistaken) belief that their children can have better lives in Europe and then be able to help their parents. Furthermore, in addition to existing poverty, instability and disruption due to conflict, militia-initiated abduction, and the widespread corruption prevalent in much of West Africa are among the numerous reasons why children are trafficked (ILO 2003; Somerset 2001: 22, 38).

While certainly identifying valid factors contributing to child trafficking, such analyses as the CPA report (2000) do not look further for explanations, towards for example, the development of neo-liberal economic policies (such as structural adjustment programmes – see Chapter 2) which have exacerbated poverty and further encouraged coffee, cocoa, cotton and other plantations to demand cheaper labour.[9] There is no acknowledgement of the 'dark side of modernity' which separates producers and consumers. Coverage by the media and NGO reports rarely focus on the consumers of children's labour such as chocolate buyers in the global North, or Western males with sexual appetites for young West African prostitutes.[10]

Present-day criminal trafficking has some kind of roots in various 'traditional' migrant and other labour practices. For example, one such particular dimension of migration of child workers in various parts of West Africa involves girls (who often marry young) travelling to work elsewhere to earn money for their trousseau (wedding goods). Indeed there is a well-established practice of girls from Northern Ghana working as headloaders in the markets of Accra for six months to a year to accumulate capital to start trading in their home area and to collect goods for their marriage (Asomaning *et al.* 1996). Such so-called 'traditional' or 'indigenous' practices of girls moving (being sent?) away to earn money before marriage can easily involve crossing borders and hence become transnational migration.[11]

Another traditional practice of migration of young men and boys within West Africa involves *almajarai* who are Islamic pupils who move from their parental homes to live with an Islamic teacher or Imam for extended periods, commonly several years, as part of indigenous religious education systems. It is a practice with a long history, particularly among the Hausa and other Muslim ethnic groups and one that frequently involves cross-border migration. In complex ways *almajarai* are engaged in 'working' their way through their studies by begging for alms and doing manual labour in return for food from households in the community. During this period of work and study they are given shelter by the Imam's household and farm for him.

4 Children's rights

A children's rights approach is founded on the United Nations Convention on the Rights of the Child (UNCRC) (Unicef 2004) and various related legislation such as that outlawing child labour enacted by the International Labour Office and its International Programme on the Elimination of Child Labour (IPEC) (ILO 2003). Such an approach considers children's rights to be enshrined in legal tools that define them in 'universal' transnational spaces. The definition and defence of children's rights in national bodies of law (such as the UK Children's Act) are part of a wider global human rights movement. This movement, which advocates the universal rights of children, faces clashes with the cultural and international variations in attitudes to issues like physical punishment of young people,[12] parental control vs. children's rights to privacy or freedom of choice of religion, and young people and work. The recent debates over a child rights bill in the Nigeria National Assembly exemplify such cultural clashes (Israel-Abdulai 2003). The bill was derived from the Organisation of African Unity (OAU) charter on the rights and welfare of the child, which itself is a by-product of the UNCRC. It is being hotly debated in Nigeria and so far has been rejected on several grounds. These include arguments that its implementation would make illegal such practices as child hawkers. Given the prevalence of poverty and the importance of informal sector trading, hawking and street or market selling by children is key to the daily survival of millions of low income households. More fundamentally, different ethnic groups within Nigeria define the age at which a child reaches adulthood and may legally marry, quite differently. These differences could not be accommodated by a bill that proposed a single age of majority of 18 years. Overall the bill was accused of being part of long-standing western imperialism aiming for global uniformity of culture and government while seeking to annihilate indigenous cultural and religious practices.

There are also other problems of definition in trying to understand the 'real' state of children in and of West Africa. For example, even where it does not involve migration, the line between child fostering and child (domestic) labour is a fine one (Turner 1996: 144). Similarly, it is not a new phenomenon that African girls and young women are engaged in unpaid domestic work in their own and other households. Thus, in Ghana and elsewhere girl maidservants in many urban households are 'fostered' from rural relatives, even in relatively low income households. From a study of fifty-four poor urban households in Accra, Turner (1996) established that girl maidservants act as domestic anchors by staying in the home to ensure security while other adults and child members of the household are out at work or school. The girl maids undertake many domestic tasks involving waste disposal, collecting water, washing clothes and utensils, minding infants, food preparation and assisting in trade. They are generally unpaid but their board and lodging is provided (as they live in) and they receive occasional gifts such as clothes and shoes. Such housegirls make other household members much more flexible in their income earning and other activities (Turner ibid.). These arrangements often mean that the young women in question have little or no opportunity to acquire formal educational qualifications or other employment-related skills.

5 Globalisation, peripheral capitalism and development

This section explores whether the concepts of globalisation and peripheral capitalism can help in understanding and explaining the apparent rise in the type of child abuse and exploitation detailed above. Globalisation is characterised by some commentators as a unique global era we all currently inhabit with high levels of connectivity between people, places and things; free flows of capital, commodities and individuals around the world and a new world order involving massive shifts of capital and technology and compression of time-space.[13] Thus, it is clear that the ease of modern international travel facilitates the movement of children (whether legally or illegally) between West Africa and Europe. In addition, economic restructuring contributes to the wealth disparities between global North and South, providing some of the push factors for child labour and trafficking within and beyond the West African region.

But how can we really theorise the work and migration of West African children in the context of globalisation? We might argue it is simply part of globalisation that human beings, including children from poorer parts of the global economic periphery, have become mere goods traded as commodities (slaves, sacrifices, body parts). Furthermore, it could be argued that this trafficking is simply enabled by global transport and communications, and pushed by structural economic inequalities. Changes, shifts and insecurities of the global economy certainly mean increased uncertainty in everyday life and a lack of control for many of the world's citizens over their everyday lives. We all have to ride the 'juggernaut' of modernity (Giddens 1990: 139). Complexities of the socio-economic political world today mean we all live in a state of perpetual nervousness. All of us, not only children in and of West Africa, live in a disordered world, victims of the 'elusive effects of transnational forces' (Comaroff and Comaroff 1993: xxv). The 'malcontents of modernity' (Comaroff and Comaroff 1993) include the rhetoric and risks of the global market and large-scale economic restructuring which mean some individuals, like certain West African children, become its unfortunate victims. This can be read as an aspect of the uncertainties of late capitalism, in a big and untidy world which no longer has a centre.

It is perhaps no surprise that child abduction (for sacrifice, body parts, or other abuses) does not seem to disappear with the rise of modernisation, rationalisation, technological change, and so-called economic development.[14] Rather, it reappears despite scientific progress and thrives in what can be read as kinds of moral commentaries on the global economy. Such abuse of children appears to be especially prevalent among social groups (like West Africans) who are experiencing rapid economic and social change giving rise to tension and strains in their social fabric. Specific exacerbating factors can be identified as widening gaps between rich and poor, widespread corruption of officials, and undermined respect for politicians and others in authority.

In the first era of globalisation in the eighteenth to late nineteenth century there was a huge movement of human beings, including children, as commodities in the trans-Atlantic slave trade. In this second era of globalisation, we should not be surprised to find children still being traded as slaves,[15] albeit with some differences from the earlier era.

The economy of the West African region can be described as having made a rapid transition to peripheral capitalism. Furthermore, much of West Africa has been experiencing ongoing economic and political crises in recent decades. This has led to much disintegration of the social fabric including transformation of family forms, loosening ties of kinship and weakening control of children (Zack-Williams 2001). With kinship structures undermined children have been left with little security and hence have turned to surrogate families among street children or militia and rebel forces by becoming child soldiers (ibid.). Zack-Williams describes these circumstances creating alienated and marginalised children as 'a rupture in the intergenerational bargain' (2001: 73). He maintains that traditional social relations within West African families have been ruptured, destroying the coping capacities of the extended family with its strong reciprocal bonds of kinship:

> The super-exploitative nature of imperialism, imposed via the collusion of a local kleptocratic elite, has led to capital flight, uneven development and the inability of local social institutions such as the family to cope with the exigencies of life within peripheral capitalist formations. The result is an additional burden on the family, in contrast to capitalism of the centre where state sponsored institutions have increasingly encroached on and substituted for 'traditional' functions of the family.
> (Zack-Williams 2001: 76)

As elsewhere in West Africa fostering children to more affluent families, friends or relations, known as the *mehn pikin* (wardship) system in Sierra Leone, was a way for families to try to cope with crises such as those elaborated above. But under the extreme economic crises of recent times, exacerbated by intensive structural adjustment policies which have adversely affected marginalised social groups such as women, children and the poor (Dennis 1991; Sparr 1994), many foster children finding themselves exploited have exerted their agency and taken to the streets of cities becoming street children or child-soldier recruits.

6 Globalisation and the occult

Everywhere it seems 'child abuse has become the quintessential crime . . . it condenses a multitude of anxieties [about risk]' (Castañeda 2000: 149). Anxieties about the abuse of children's bodies appear to circulate in the global economy (Parish 2001: 4). Comaroff and Comaroff (1999) use the phrase 'the occult economies' to convey the preoccupation in Africa with sexual abuse and slavery of children which comes to symbolise an endemic malaise in which the rich and powerful strengthen themselves by appropriation of the poorer, weaker members of society who struggle to survive. In other words, children's bodies are focus for contemporary anxieties about the manifestations of global capital in everyday life. Rumours of child abduction, trafficking and sacrifice are stories about global fears of the risks of a globalised world and its North–South economic inequalities (Castañeda 2000).

A different take on the multiple modernities of globalisation and a way of problematising wealth, power and commodities in the post-colonial world inhabited by children would suggest that, alongside globalisation, there is a growth in the occult economy and occult discourses such as witchcraft (see Moore and Sanders 2001; Scheper-Hughes 2000: 204). So, for example, in the Democratic Republic of Congo (DRC) a recent rise in children being accused of witchcraft and sorcery has been reported (Anon. 2003). Some would argue it is not mere coincidence that while the economy and infrastructure of the DRC collapsed in the past decade due to war and government corruption, it was children who were blamed when households experienced personal tragedies such as sickness, unemployment or bereavement. Given their relative lack of agency, children become scapegoats. It is related that within occult discourses some individuals will go to any lengths for greed in a kind of 'gourmet capitalism' that involves ritual mutilation, human (even child) sacrifice and human cannibalism by modern African elites (Parish 2003). These practices reflect widespread discourses of children as innocent victims at the hands of elites.

We should not be surprised that in post-colonial Africa and its global diasporic communities witchcraft is alive and well – as much among the poor, as educated elites. Indeed, the general sentiment on the continent and among scholarly commentators is that witchcraft is being experienced as on the increase and this increase at a period of globalisation is no coincidence (Moore and Sanders 2001: 2–3). Witchcraft in Africa has been and continues to be associated with the tensions connected with new forms of production, consumption and political control, social insecurity and differentiation (Moore and Sanders 2001: 9–10). According to current thinking in anthropology and related disciplines, witchcraft operates as part of modernity, or rather the multiple modernities which comprise globalisation (Moore and Sanders 2001: 11–12).

Following the explanations of anthropologists (Moore and Sanders 2001), children's bodies, within the terms of exchange characteristic of globalisation, become equated with commodities. Stories and rumours of child abduction, cannibalism, ritual murder, teenage witches, trade in children and their body parts can be read as imaginative moral frameworks for making sense of the contemporary conditions of wage labour, consumption, migration, regimes of production, economic liberalisation, development programmes and the functioning of markets. In other words, frameworks for making sense of modernity in which many people experience themselves as lacking or excluded, but a few are seen to have enriched themselves greatly, with the implications of corruption and exercise of legitimate, or illegitimate, power. Thus, moral panics perpetuated by the global media, fuelled by the concerns of NGOs and others represent real moral geographies in which the anxieties expressed about witchcraft and so on are real and are expressions of the tensions of modernity.

7 *Daily life: reality check*

Despite the grim toll of abuse meted out to children in and of West Africa that has been related thus far in this chapter, we need to pause at this stage to take a check on the reality of the daily lives of the majority of youngsters of the region. Certainly, most children in and of West Africa are not abducted as slaves, or sold by their parents into exploitation, or taken for sacrifice. As seen earlier in this chapter the media, NGO and other agency claims and portrayals of abused children are often biased towards the worst cases of maltreatment and even guilty of misrepresentation by implying that such phenomena are generalised, when in reality they apply to relatively small numbers of children.

Despite some variations within the region, and fewer educational opportunities extended to girls than boys, the majority of West Africa's children are well nourished and go to school (Table 3.1). In circumstances broadly characterised by the perpetuation of tradition and culture they grow up learning, working and playing. Like the girls trading for their mothers in Northern Nigeria (Schildkrout 1980), or boys working as apprentices in metal-working enterprises in Senegal (Morice 1982), or foster

Table 3.1 Indicators of children's well-being for selected West African countries

	Child malnutrition	*Gross primary school enrolment (%)*		
	(% under 5)	*(% of school-age population)*	*male*	*female*
Benin	23	95	113	78
Burkina Faso	34	44	52	37
Cameroon	22	108	115	100
Ivory Coast	24	71	78	65
Gambia	17	82	86	78
Ghana	25	80	84	76
Mali	27	61	71	51
Niger	40	35	42	29
Nigeria	31	82	89	74
Senegal	18	75	79	70
Togo	25	124	138	110
Average	**26**	**78**	**86**	**70**

Source: World Bank, http://www.worldbank.org/data/countrydata/countrydata.html
(Accessed 2/02/04).

children labouring on the farms of their guardians in Sierra Leone (Bledsoe 1990), most children in West Africa are working children, and hence largely invisible contributors to global production and reproduction (Robson 1996). Relatively few urban children of wealthy families have Western-style childhoods from which work (whether paid or unpaid) is largely absent.

Many, many children, in and of West Africa, are safe, well and happy, working, playing and going to school. Such images can be considered to challenge and contextualise the generalised negative discourses perpetuated by the Northern media and NGOs which in reality apply only to a small number of abused children. Finally, even if the number of West African children in slavery and so on has been grossly exaggerated by the media and NGOs it still remains a very real problem that deserves analysis and explanation. Furthermore, as Manzo (2004) argues, abused African children are a telling symbol of African marginality, not just a figment of overheated Western imaginations.

8 Conclusions

With respect to children and young people, this chapter has focused on, and elaborated, some aspects of the global–local links between the countries of West Africa and the large populations of West African origin and descent (including many privately fostered children) in the UK. Media portrayals of children in and of West Africa are found to be dominated by moral panic and discourses recounting the abuse of innocents. While it is difficult to separate fact from fiction, these imagined geographies and negative portrayals are supported by the output of international non-governmental bodies, often working within a children's rights framework. The chapter has examined above some of the factors behind the complexity of child trafficking within and beyond the West African region, highlighting the roles of globalisation and the occult in processes of rapid change, disintegration and rupture. While documenting some notable and abhorrent abuses of children within these complex networks, it is noted that despite the impacts of globalisation these experiences are the exception, rather than the norm for children in and of West Africa. However, it is noted that exploitation of such young people is reported too often. In seeking to understand why these would appear to be a particular 'West African' set of problems, it is concluded that child abduction, slavery and so on thrive as a kind of moral commentary on corruption and inequality in the regional and global economy, and a signifier of a wider African condition.

Acknowledgements

I would like to thank Reg Cline-Cole, Jane Parish, David Simon and Kate Manzo for critically reading earlier versions of this chapter and making helpful comments and suggestions to improve it. Thanks are also due to Mike Moore for helping to obtain references from a distant library.

Notes

1. Analyses of Adam's bone DNA have identified matches with areas of south-west Nigeria suggesting he grew up there (BBC Channel 4 2003).
2. Comaroff and Comaroff (1999) have written thoughtfully about the phenomenon (real or imagined) of ritual murder in South Africa, said to have become 'big business' and to target young people under 12 especially (p. 290). They also remark how these narratives of 'the brutalization of children' are not unique to South Africa (p. 281).
3. A quick glance at the websites of these, and similar organisations, reveals a common discourse of crisis, abuse of childhood and neglect of children's rights.
4. Utting (1997: 43) reports that in 1991 the African Family Advisory Service in the UK estimated there were 6000 West African children in private foster care in England.
5. In a recent case the Nigerian *Guardian* newspaper reported that in Manchester, UK a Nigerian couple claimed six children living with them were their biological offspring. In addition to finding them guilty of neglect of the children, the courts also found all the children to be unrelated biologically to their so-called 'parents' and only two of them to have been formally adopted by the couple (Uwaleke 2003).
6. Indigenous cultural ideas about the necessity of discipline and hard work for fostered children (cf. Bledsoe 1990) can be at odds with Western notions of appropriate ways of child rearing and children's rights.
7. More cynically some may say this is an excuse that social services use when statutory child protection fails; as in the spectacularly tragic example of Victoria Climbié cited above.
8. Due to the illegal nature of the trade in children, corruption and absence of central data collection systems, there are no wholly accurate statistics available, only estimates.
9. It should be acknowledged that the use of 'apprentice' plantation labour in the shape of children predates the era of SAPs.
10. Interviews with immigration officers, police, social service workers, lawyers, researchers and journalists in the UK suggest that men create the market for young prostitutes and that Italian men in particular prefer black women who are considered 'rare' and 'exotic', but also inferior to Italian women (Somerset 2001: 37).
11. Within West Africa trans-border trade of a shady nature is not new and has been in existence since pre-colonial times, and, rather than being eliminated (as intended) by economic reforms since the 1980s, the context of structural adjustment has led to a boom in trans-border trade and its globalisation (Meagher 2003).
12. Ogunsola (2002: 22–3) outlines the debates about physical punishment of children with respect to 'traditional' African culture.
13. See Johnston *et al.* (2000: 315–16) for a good overview of these concepts associated with theorising globalisation.
14. The commodification of the human body and its parts is certainly not new and occurs in many forms in different cultural settings (Sharp 2000). For example, in her investigation of the shady world of organ procurement and transplantation, the anthropologist Scheper-Hughes (2000) shows clearly how body parts have become commodities on the world market with the advance of medical transplant techniques.
15. A UK Chief Immigration Officer maintains that child trafficking from West Africa in its current form has been going on for about 30 years (Somerset 2001: 22). The likelihood is that it has a much longer historical trajectory.

References

allafrica.com (2003), 'Child labour rampant in cocoa sector, new study says'. (http://allafrica.com/stories/200207300581.html; accessed 28/02/03.)

Anon. (2003), 'DR Congo's Child "Witches"' (email to AFRUCA list@yahoogroups.com 19/1/03).

Anti-Slavery International (2003a), 'Anti-Slavery International Home Page'. (http://www.anti-slavery.org; accessed 28/02/03.)

Anti-Slavery International (2003b), 'Human traffic – Aminata'. (http://www.antislavery.org/homepage/resources/africagallery/gallery.htm; accessed 28/02/03.)

Ariyo, D. (2003a), 'Safeguarding African children in the UK' (email to AFRUCA list@yahoogroups.com 17/01/03).

Ariyo, D. (2003b), 'New dimensions in the trafficking of children to the UK' (email to AFRUCAlist@yahoogroups.com).

Asomaning, V., Amponsah, F., Attah, M., Apt, N. and **Grieco, M.** (1996), 'Bearing the weight: the centrality of head loading in a petty trading structure' in Grieco, M., Apt, N. and Turner, J., *At Christmas and on Rainy Days: Transport, Travel and the Female Traders of Accra*. Avebury, Aldershot.

Baker, A. (2002), 'The case of "Adam": was he trafficked for ritual killing?'. Paper presented at the AFRUCA seminar on the Trafficking of African Children to the UK, School of Oriental and African Studies, University of London, 20 November 2002.

Bastian, M. (2001), 'Vulture men, campus cultists and teenaged witches: modern magics in Nigerian popular media' in Moore, H. and Sanders, T. (eds), *Magical Interpretations, Material Realities: Modernity, Witchcraft and the Occult in Postcolonial Africa*. London, Routledge.

BBC (1999), 'Child traffickers arrested in Togo', BBC online network 27 July 1999, London. (http://news.bbc.co.uk/1/hi/world/africa/404342.stm; accessed 28/02/03.)

BBC (2001a), 'The slave children', BBC news online, 5 Oct. 2001, London. (http://news.bbc.co/uk/1/hi/programmes/correspondent/1519144.stm; accessed 9/01/04.)

BBC (2001b), 'Trafficking nightmare for Nigerian children', BBB news online, 10 Jan. 2001, London. (http://news.bbc.co.uk/1/hi/world/africa/841928.stm; accessed 29/01/04.)

BBC (2002a), 'UN names sides using child soldiers', BBC news online, 17 December 2002, London. (http://news.bbc.co.uk/1/hi/world/africa/2582095.stm; accessed 09/01/04.)

BBC (2002b), 'Meeting the "chocolate slaves"', BBC news online, 13 June 2002, London. (http://news.bbc.co.uk/1/hi/world/africa/2042474.stm; accessed 9/01/04.)

BBC (2003), 'Child safe house "may close"', BBC news UK edition online, 27 May 2003, London. (http://news.bbc.co.uk/1/hi/england/southern_counties/2938994.stm; accessed 9/01/04.)

BBC Channel 4 (2003), *Torso in the Thames*, TV documentary (60 minutes) broadcast 27 November 2003.

BBC Radio 4 (2003), 'Woman's Hour' – item on child trafficking broadcast 24 February 2003.

Bledsoe, C. (1990), '"No success without struggle": social mobility and hardship for foster children in Sierra Leone', *Man* (new series) **25(1)**, 7–88.

Castañeda, C. (2000), 'Child organ stealing stories: risk, rumour and reproductive technologies' in Adam, B., Beck, U. and Van Loon, J. (eds), *The Risk Society and Beyond: Critical Issues for Social Theory*. Sage, London.

Comaroff, J. (1997), 'Consuming passions: child abuse, fetishism, and "The new world order"', *Culture* **17(1–2)**, 7–19.

Comaroff, J. and **Comaroff, J.** (eds) (1993), *Modernity and Its Malcontents: Ritual and Power in Postcolonial Africa*. University of Chicago Press, Illinois Chicago.

Comaroff, J. and **Comaroff, J.** (1999), 'Occult economies and the violence of abstraction: notes from the South African postcolony', *American Ethnologist* **26(2)**, 279–303.

CPA (2000), 'Common platform for action of the sub-regional consultation on the development of strategies to fight child trafficking for exploitative labour purposes in West and Central Africa' (www.unicef.org/media/nesnotes/platform.pdf; accessed 28/02/03).

Demuren, L., Oludipe, O., Cobbina, C. and **Twum-Danso, A.** (2002), Conference Report, *The Challenges of Migration: The Experiences of the African Child in the UK*. AFRUCA, London.

Dennis, C. (1991), 'Constructing a "career" under conditions of economic crisis and structural adjustment: the survival strategies of Nigerian women' in Afshar, H. (ed.), *Women, Development and Survival in the Third World*. Zed Press, London.

Frost, D. (2002), 'Diasporan West African communities: the Kru in Freetown and Liverpool', *Review of African Political Economy* **29(92)**, 285–300.

Giddens, A. (1990), *The Consequences of Modernity*. Polity, Oxford.

Henry, L. and **Mohan, G.** (2003), 'Making homes: the Ghanaian Diaspora, institutions and development', *Journal of International Development* **15(5)**, 611–22.

Hickman, M. (2003), 'Eight children destined for sex trade taken into care', *The Independent* 21/7/03.

International Labour Organisation (ILO) (2003), 'Stop child trafficking', *World of Work: The Magazine of the ILO* **47**, 4–6.

IOM (2000), *Migrant Trafficking and Human Smuggling in Europe*. International Organization for Migration, Geneva.

Israel-Abdulai, T. (2003), Situation of children's rights in Nigeria. (For special issue committee email posting to AFRUCA list@yahoogroups.com 6/3/2003.)

Johnston, R.J., Gregory, D., Pratt, G. and **Watts, M.** (eds) (2000), *The Dictionary of Human Geography*, 4th edn. Blackwell, Oxford.

Kanu, M. (2002), Opening address at AFRUCA seminar on the Trafficking of African Children to the UK, School of Oriental and African Studies, University of London, 20 November 2002.

Katz, C. (2001), 'Vagabond capitalism and the necessity of social reproduction', *Antipode* **33(4)**, 709–28.

Manzo, K. (2004), 'On the backs of children: marginality and modern enslavement in West Africa', unpublished working paper.

Meagher, K. (2003), 'A back door to globalisation? structural adjustment, globalisation and transborder trade in West Africa', *Review of African Political Economy,* **30(95)**, 57–75.

Moore, H.L. and **Sanders, T.** (2001), *Magical Interpretations, Material Realities: Modernity, Witchcraft and the Occult in Postcolonial Africa.* Routledge, London.

Morice, A. (1982), 'Underpaid child labour and social reproduction: apprenticeship in Kaolack, Senegal', *Development and Change* **13(4)**, 515–26.

Mubanga, A. (2002), 'African children and migration: the causative factors' in *The Challenges of Migration: The experiences of the African child in the UK,* Report of AFRUCA Conference, 23 January 2002.

Mullenger, N. (2000), 'Immigrant and illegal youth sex workers in Italy' in Barrett, D. (ed.), *Youth Prostitution in the New Europe: The Growth in Sex Work.* Russell House, Lyme Regis.

Ogunsola, A. (2002), 'The challenges facing African children in the UK' in Demuran, L., Oludipe, O., Cobbina, C. and Twum-Danso, A. (eds), *The Challenges of Migration: The Experiences of the African Child in the UK,* Conference Report. AFRUCA, London, pp. 22–5.

Ouattara, M. (2002), 'Trafficking of African children: the causative factor'. Paper presented at the AFRUCA seminar on the Trafficking of African Children to the UK, School of Oriental and African Studies, University of London, 20 November 2002.

Parish, J. (2001), 'The age of anxiety' in Parish, J. and Parker, M. (eds), *The Age of Anxiety: Conspiracy Theory and the Human Sciences.* Blackwell/Sociological Review, Oxford.

Parish, J. (2003), 'Infant body parts and moral panics: mistrust and social obligations amongst West Africans in Britain'. Paper presented at Keele Youth Research Network workshop, Keele University, 26 March 2003.

Quansah, G.A. (2002), 'The effects of living with the death of a child victim of abuse and bullying – I' in Demuren, L., Oludipe, O., Cobbina, C. and Twum-Danso, A. (eds), *The Challenges of Migration: The Experiences of the African Child in the UK,* Conference Report. AFRUCA, London.

Reynolds, R.R. (2002), 'An African brain drain: Igbo decisions to immigrate to the US', *Review of African Political Economy* **29(92)**, 273–84.

Robson, E. (1996), 'Working girls and boys: children's contributions to household survival in West Africa', *Geography* **81(353)**, 403–7.

Salah, R. (2001), 'Child trafficking in West and Central Africa: An overview'. Paper presented at the First Pan-African conference on Human Trafficking, Abuja, February 2001. (Paper available on www.unicef.org/media/newsnotes/africchildtraffick.pdf.)

Scheper-Hughes, N. (2000), 'The global traffic in human organs', *Current Anthropology* **41(2)**, 191–224.

Schildkrout, E. (1980), 'Children's work reconsidered', *International Social Science Journal* **32(3)**, 479–89.

Sharp, L.A. (2000), 'The commodification of the body and its parts', *Annual Review of Anthropology* **29**, 287–328.

Somerset, C. (2001), 'What the professionals know: the trafficking of children into, and through, the UK for sexual purposes', Report for ECPAT UK, London.

Sparr, P. (ed.) (1994), *Mortgaging Women's Lives: Feminist Critiques of Structural Adjustment*. Zed Press, London.

Turner, J. (1996), 'Female domestic financial responsibilities and household survival: travel strategies in a developing country' in Grieco, M., Apt, N. and Turner, J. (eds), *At Christmas and on Rainy Days: Transport, Travel and the Female Traders of Accra*. Avebury, Aldershot.

Uduku, O. (2002), 'The socio-economic basis of a diaspora community: *Igbo bu ike*', *Review of African Political Economy* **29(92)**, 301–11.

UK Newsquest (2003), 'Sex slavery safe house is threatened', *UK Newsquest Regional Press – This is Mid Sussex*, 8 May 2003 (email to AFRUCA list@yahoogroups.com 11/05/03).

UNICEF (2003), 'News note: background on child trafficking'. (http://www.unicef.org/media/newsnotes/01nn01.htm; accessed 28/02/03.)

UNICEF (2004), 'Convention on the rights of the child: Full text of the convention'. (http://www.unicef.org/crc/fulltext.htm; accessed 29/01/04.)

Utting, W., Baines, C., Stuart, M. *et al.* (1997), *People Like Us: The Report of the Review of the Safeguards for Children Living Away from Home*. HMSO, London.

Uwaleke, I. (2003), 'British Court seeks true identity of six Nigerian kids', *Guardian* (Nigeria) (posted to AFRUCA list@yahoogroups.com 29/05/03).

Vyse, S.A. (1997), *Believing in Magic: The Psychology of Superstition*. Oxford University Press, Oxford.

Zack-Williams, A.B. (2001), 'Child soldiers in the civil war in Sierra Leone', *Review of African Political Economy* **28(87)**, 73–82.

CHAPTER 4

Fictional worlds in struggles over West African (under-)development? Kolawole Omotoso's **The Combat**

Abioseh Michael Porter

1 Introduction

what paranoiac wrath drove us thus far
what rain storms shall come to wash this stream of blood away
what riverfloods shall dampen this jungle floor and wipe our guilt away
make liquid this plastered blood and purge our lives again
what avatar shall be to lead us to other beginnings?
(Omotoso 1972: 83)[1]

As the rhetorical questions in the quote which opens this chapter imply, Kolawole Omotoso's *The Combat,* like most fictional writing with the Nigerian civil war as the theme, is loaded with questions concerning the motivations behind, and consequences of that war. But, unlike a good number of these (and other African) 'civil war novels', Omotoso's work raised these questions long before they became fashionable. Should this war have been fought in the first place? How could it have been avoided? Who benefited most from the war? As such questions are raised quite early, and addressed in a sustained manner throughout the novel, this chapter aims to examine both the fictional world Omotoso creates in *The Combat,* and the internal logic which appears to drive events in this world. In particular, I am interested in Omotoso's use of symbolism in creating literary myths regarding the dangers, paradoxes and realities of contemporary warfare in West Africa. *The Combat*'s message is, in the light of recent events in Guinea Bissau, Liberia, Sierra Leone and Côte d'Ivoire, as relevant today as when the book was first published in 1972 (see Chapters 2, 5, 6 and 10).[2]

2 Writing the (Nigeria–Biafra) war

The civil war was, without doubt, the single most traumatic national or even regional event to take place in independent West Africa (see Chapter 2). It is estimated that more than a million people died, while hundreds of thousands of others were either injured or displaced as a direct result of the war, with probably more people dying of starvation and disease than were actually killed during the fighting. Not surprisingly, there is a wide and diverse body of writing devoted to the war, including fiction, drama, poetry and song, which exist alongside (auto-)biographies, academic histories, etc. And even though this chapter concentrates on the literary rather than the historical, it is worth starting with historical representations of the war before moving on to fictional accounts of the war. This is for two reasons. First, much fictional writing on the war assumes familiarity with the background to, and actual history of, the war. Second, and deriving from this, several writers incorporate thinly-disguised historical events and episodes from the war in their fiction. A historical context is thus invaluable for a finely-textured understanding of the fictional worlds which inhabit the pages of novels devoted to the civil war.

2.1 Historical background to the war

Box 4.1 summarises a selection of written histories of the causes of, and run-up to the war, focusing on events which occupy a prominent place in the fiction which this chapter discusses. The key role played by ethnic and regional rivalry in the construction of imaginary (war) geographies is evident (see also Chapters 2 and 10).

2.2 Fiction as history and history as fiction

A tragedy of such proportions was bound to capture the imagination of both Nigerian and non-Nigerian writers and artists. Thus writers as varied as Chinua Achebe, Elechi Amadi, Buchi Emecheta, Frederick Forsythe, Festus Ijayi, Chukwuemeka Ike, Eddie Iroh, Ali Mazrui, Flora Nwapa and Wole Soyinka, in addition to Kole Omotoso, have, with varying degrees of artistic skill, adopted the war as a major theme in their creative writing. Indeed, as Chidi Amuta (1983: 84) noted, the 'civil war constitute[d] the most important theme in Nigerian literature (in English) in the 1970s'. Given this chapter's literary focus, I use Buchi Emecheta's (1982) *Destination Biafra* to highlight fictional accounts of the causes which may have contributed to the war.[3]

Destination Biafra is a powerful novel which incorporates some thinly disguised historical events from the war (Porter 1995).[4] A major point Emecheta makes throughout the novel is that the political legacy that was bequeathed to Nigeria by the British at independence was not only doomed to fail, but it also contained within it the potential for degenerating into complete chaos. For the novel's narrator, as well as some of the British characters (and, I suspect, for Emecheta herself), the kind of 'democracy by proportional representation' which Nigerians inherited at independence had very little to do with genuine concern on the part of the British for either democratic principles or the potential for promoting post-independence development. 'Democracy' in this fictional world was based primarily, if not solely, on ensuring that political power at the federal level was in the hands of the Hausa, the largest ethnic or regional group. In so doing, the British sidelined the Yoruba and Igbo, denying them any real political control; and assumed that their economic interests would thereby

Box 4.1 'Actual' histories: motivations for, and implications of, the war?

1. The Nigerian civil war, also known as the Biafran War, was fought from July 1967 to January 1970 between the then Eastern Region, which declared itself an independent state, Biafra, and the rest of the Federation, led by the Federal Military Government of Nigeria, which regarded this as an illegal act of secession. The war was fought to reunify the country and avoid its disintegration. While the immediate causes of the war were the coup and counter-coup of 1966, which altered the political equation in the country, and destroyed the fragile trust and/or uneasy truce that had obtained among the major ethnic groups since independence in 1960, the genesis of the war lay in the country's geography, history, culture and demography.
   Source: Atofarati (1992).
2. Nigeria obtained independence from British rule on 1 October 1960, leading to the formation of a Federal Government based on the parliamentary system. Elections held in 1959 had led to the emergence of a number of ruling parties:

   - the National Council of Nigeria and the Cameroons (NCNC), led by Nnamdi Azikiwe, in the Eastern region;
   - the Northern People's Congress (NPC), led by Ahmadu Bello, Sardauna of Sokoto, in the Northern Region; and
   - the Action Group (AG), led by Obafemi Awolowo, in the Western region.

   With no party winning an outright majority during the elections, the NPC joined with the NCNC to form the government. At independence in 1960, therefore, Abubakar Tafawa Balewa became Prime Minister and Nnamdi Azikiwe, Governor General.

'In 1962, part of the Action Group split off to form the Nigerian National Democratic Party (NNDP), led by S.I. Akintola. In 1963, the Mid-Western Region was formed from part of the Western Region. In the same year, Nigeria became a Federal Republic with Nnamdi Azikiwe as President. A great deal of controversy followed the 1963 population census, which the NCNC felt overestimated the number of people in the Northern Region, giving them a greater representation in the federal parliament. In January 1966, a group of Igbo army officials staged a coup d'etat to overthrow the government, killing Balewa, Bello and Akintola and placing General Johnson Aguiyi-Ironsi in charge of the new military government. He suspended the regional constitution, dissolved all legislative bodies, banned political parties and formed a Federal Military Government that was more central in nature. There were strong suspicions that Aguiyi-Ironsi favoured the Igbo (Ibo) over other ethnic groups, fuelled by the fact that the military government did not prosecute the army officers responsible for killing the northern leaders. Many northerners saw the coup as a plot to make the Igbo dominant in Nigeria, and there was hostility from the Muslim population. Fighting broke out between the northerners and the Igbo, and in July 1966 a group of northern army officers revolted against the government, killed General Johnson Aguiyi-Ironsi, and appointed the army

Chief of Staff, General Yakubu Gowon, as head of the new military government. In 1967, Gowon moved to split the existing 4 regions of Nigeria into 12 states. The military governor of the Eastern Region, Colonel Chukwuemeka Odumegwu Ojukwu, refused to accept the division of the Eastern Region and declared that this region would become an independent republic, named Biafra. This led to a civil war between Biafra and the remainder of Nigeria. The war began in June 1967 and continued until Biafra surrendered on 15 January 1970. Over 1 million people died during the conflict.'

Source: *Nigerian Civil War Collection*, School of Oriental and African Studies, University of London http://www.aim25.ac.uk/cgi-bin/search2?coll_id=93&inst_id=19 (accessed on 30 March 2004).

3. The Republic of Biafra was a 'secessionist state . . . in existence from May 30, 1967, to Jan. 15, 1970. At the outset Biafra comprised, roughly, the East-Central, South-Eastern, and Rivers states of the Federation of Nigeria, where the Igbo people predominated. The country, which took its name from the Bight of Biafra (an arm of the Atlantic Ocean), was established by Igbos who felt they could not develop – or even survive – within Nigeria. In September 1966, numerous Igbos had been killed in Northern Nigeria, where they had migrated in order to engage in commerce. The secessionist state was led by Lt. Col. Chukwuemeka Odumegwu Ojukwu and included some non-Igbo persons. Biafra's original capital was Enugu; Aba, Umuahia, and Owerri served successively as provisional capitals after Enugu was captured (October, 1967) by Nigerian forces. Seeking to maintain national unity, Nigeria imposed economic sanctions on Biafra from the start of the secession, and fighting between Nigeria and Biafra broke out in July, 1967. After initial Biafran advances, Nigeria attacked Biafra by air, land, and sea and gradually reduced the territory under its control. The breakaway state had insufficient resources at the start of the war – it was a net importer of food and had little industry – and depended heavily on its control of petroleum fields for funds to make purchases abroad. It lost the oil fields in the war, and more than one million of its civilian population are thought to have died as a result of severe malnutrition. At the time of its surrender on January 15, 1970, Biafra was greatly reduced in size, its inhabitants were starving, and its leader, Ojukwu, had fled the country. During its existence Biafra was recognized by only five nations, although other countries gave moral or material support. Civilian groups were organized in a number of countries to publicize the case for Biafra and to raise funds for the secessionist state.'

Source: *The Columbia Encyclopedia* (1993) http://biafra.info/biafra/nigeria-biafra-civil-war-republic-of-biafra.html (accessed on 2 April 2004).

be safeguarded. Emecheta represents the Igbo and Yoruba as more ambitious and more 'radical' than the Hausa, who are attributed characteristics associated with feudalism, political naivete and a lack of 'radicalism'.

This is why in the opening pages of *Destination Biafra*, Governor Macdonald, the last Governor of colonial Nigeria, is both worried and upset by the refusal of the Sardauna of Sokoto 'to leave his palace to come and live with the "Kaferis" [non-believers] in the South [read: Lagos]' (p. 3). For the British in this novel, therefore, the criteria for selecting Nigerian successors to the colonial administration did not appear to include attributes such as capability, dedication, ability or loyalty to one's country; all that seemed to matter was that British economic interests were safe and secure. Thus Macdonald concludes, in a discussion with some of his friends, that 'the thing is to back the Hausas with everything we have' (p. 9). It is for the same reason that Macdonald's friends, the former Governor, Sir Fergus Grey, and, especially, his son Alan (a military training officer with the Nigerian government and an embodiment of the Cold War), are so desperate to ensure that Nigeria does not fall into the 'wrong' Nigerian hands. Alan, the stereotypical 'friend of Africa', a point highlighted by the fact that he is in a relationship with the Nigerian finance minister's daughter, provides what seems like the perfect Cold War justification for the British position:

> These vast areas are full of oil, pure crude oil, which is untouched and still needs thorough prospecting. Now we are to hand it over to these people, who've had all these minerals since Adam and had not known what to do with them. Now they are beginning to be aware of their monetary value. And after independence they may sign it all over to the Soviets for all we know.
>
> (p. 6)

It comes as no surprise, then, that even after the Sardauna refuses to become Prime Minister of Nigeria, the British authorities (especially Governor Macdonald and Alan Grey) do everything in their power – including broadcasting a premature gubernatorial announcement declaring Nguru Kano, the British-supported candidate, victorious in the general elections – to have a Hausa elected as Prime Minister, while an Ibo is named President, a largely ceremonial post. Emecheta thereby makes the point that outside interference in Nigeria's affairs, which became particularly noticeable during the civil war, actually had its origins in pre-colonial times. Indeed, Emecheta suggests that the pervasive but unspoken cause of the war was British selfishness and short-sightedness, which led to a flawed transition to independence.

The novelist is, of course, aware that the civil war did not take place only because of foreign interference. She therefore demonstrates how some of the causes of the war were also directly attributable to the actions of Nigerian politicians themselves. She points out, for example, that in addition to the British manipulation of events, there were Nigerian politicians who used tribalism as a way of convincing their constituents to vote for them: 'They [the Tetekus and Ogedemgbes] were from the same minority tribe, and people knew that if all went well for the[m] in the general election their relations and tribesmen would not be forgotten' (p. 16). We are also told that during the election campaign, one candidate

> to the accompaniment of talking drums, told his constituents that if they voted for a person from another tribe they would be selling their own soul to the devil: If you offend a man from your own tribe you can beg him through the gods of the family. But if you offend a man who does not even understand your language, how can you tell which is his god?
>
> (p. 16)

Emecheta suggests, perhaps with some exaggeration, that such appeals to group identity and tribal loyalty, as well as to the kind of ethnic 'solidarity' that encourages voters to vote only for members of their own ethnic group (regardless of qualifications and ability), were partly responsible for the subsequent breakdown of the country's political structures (see also Chapter 10).

In several episodes, Emecheta indicates how, in spite of partly idealistic and partly pragmatic efforts at genuine national reconciliation by a few politicians, voting patterns reflected ethnic/regional affiliation or allegiance. Such crass and unprogressive tribalism – and I use this term wilfully and deliberately – is captured most tellingly by Emecheta in her depiction of the *bakodaya* episodes in a number of constituencies in Northern Nigeria, where several candidates who were indigenes garnered several hundred thousand votes each, while their non-local and non-northern opponents received *bakodaya* or no votes at all.

Emecheta also highlights the role of less-than-desirable behaviour of politicians, including some 'elder statesmen', in the breakdown of law and order and the eventual outbreak of war. Thus, when Chief Oluremi Odumosu, who had given up his position as leader of the Yoruba-dominated Action Group to contest the federal elections, is appointed leader of the relatively powerless federal opposition party, he engages in a very bitter and, ultimately, infantile struggle with his former deputy and friend, Chief Durosaro, to regain the position of leader of the more powerful regional Action Group. Emecheta's description of the 'squabble' between the two chiefs leaves no doubt that their actions contributed directly to the initial wave of killings in the Western Region:

> At home, the Ogedemgbes switched on the television, and it was then that they heard what at the time sounded comical and childish, as the squabbles of the two Western chiefs were reported. But then the horrific news started to come. Over thirty people had been killed . . . thugs had been employed by both sides and innocent people were being killed in the streets . . . many market places had been emptied as rival thugs looked for their opponents.
>
> 'Honestly, could not Chief Odumosu have given in gracefully? Whose fault was it that he didn't become a minister in the Federal House? And after all, five years isn't forever!' Stella Ogedemgbe spat in anger.
>
> 'All those innocent people killed for nothing,' observed Debbie mournfully.

> 'That's politics, my dear. I only hope our Prime Minister acts in time to stop more atrocities . . .'
>
> 'Power, just greed for power,' his wife started again, her anger mounting.
>
> (pp. 48–9)

Emecheta uses passages such as this one to make one of her major points: a good number of politicians in post-independence Nigeria were interested only in gaining power by any and all means, rather than in providing public service to both their country and compatriots. This, she suggests, contributed significantly to the war.

Emecheta points too to the indecisiveness of the fictional Prime Minister, Nguru Kano, as another reason for the political turmoil. Instead of taking effective and preventative action against rabble rousers, Kano is portrayed as 'going up and down, consulting first of all with the now redundant governor-general and then, on Macdonald's advice, his master the Sardauna in the North' (p. 56). This provokes one of the ringleaders of the first coup, the first military Head of State, Brigadier Onyemere, to comment: 'I wish we had a Prime Minister who would act quickly. It's all very well for him to be dignified, but we need someone quick-thinking to deal with this kind of situation. Let's hope it will be the last' (p. 56). As it turns out, Onyemere's fears are not completely unfounded, for very soon people begin to demonstrate and riot in various cities, actions which finally force the Prime Minister to declare a state of emergency in the riot-torn Western Region.

In the meantime, however, the Ibos in Northern Nigeria, reeling from the 'majority tribe takes it all' approach of the elections, feel increasingly betrayed and insecure, while those in the East become more and more resentful and apprehensive of suggestions by the federal government that they should be prepared to share revenues from the newly-discovered oil in their region with the rest of the country. They regard such a suggestion as unfair because '[d]uring the cocoa and timber days of the West, they reasoned, all the money went to the Yorubas there; and the revenue from the groundnuts went to the North. So why should the East now be deprived of oil revenue?' (p. 59).

2.3 Fictionalised causes, courses and curses of war?

According to Emecheta, then, the causes of the war were multifarious and complex, and included, but were not limited to:

- the imposition of an ineffective and nominally independent administration by a greedy foreign power (Britain);
- the desperate desire for, and manipulation of power by local politicians who were interested only in the trappings of government and the material advantages that come with it;
- tribal and regional chauvinism; and, of course,
- political corruption and economic exploitation (both internal as well as external).

But while the novelist goes back to the pre-independence period to provide us with some context and perspective for the behaviour of some of the actors in the novel, it is in her narration of events just before and, especially, after the first coup that we see even more reasons for the war. We learn, for example, that while northerners, particularly the revered Sardauna and the Prime Minister, are killed, and while the non-Ibo Federal Minister of Finance is summarily executed during the coup, 'not a single top Ibo politician had been killed' (p. 66). To make matters worse, Ibos living in northern Nigeria openly rejoice at the outcome of the coup; with inconceivable stupidity and lack of sensitivity, 'banners, placards and slogans thrust up where Ibos lived in Hausaland jeered at the death of the Sardauna' (p. 69). We also read of provocative, Ibo-inspired graffiti and placards mocking the death of the Sardauna, 'the anointed King's son' (p. 70).

It is no surprise, then, that the situation in Emecheta's fictional world after the first coup is one that is rife with mutual suspicion, insecurity and even fear, both among civilians and soldiers. Initially, the coup-plotters try to establish control by appointing the most senior officer as Head of State, and by selecting other senior officers as commissioners in charge of the regions. The Head of State does his best to reduce the tensions and inter-ethnic and religious rivalry that seemed to prevail in the country, apologising, for example, to the Northerners for the suffering and losses they had incurred during the first coup, while also attempting to appease other angry factions. When, in response to a statement by Alan Grey, he says '[b]ut I want to make them [the people] understand that the old politicians will not even smell the lucrative posts they had before. I want to hand power back to the people' (p. 74) we, like the narrator, feel that he is genuine. But all this lasts for only a short time; after a triumphant visit to the North, the Head of State and Yoruba Commisioner for the Western Region are murdered during a counter-coup. And, very soon, events in the country degenerate into near anarchy.

3 A combat different from many others: locating **The Combat** *within Nigerian civil war fiction*

To return to Omotoso, *The Combat* is the second of more than seven works of fiction to his name. It is significantly different from most Nigerian war novels, including Emecheta's, because of the author's style and presentation. Matched in its symbolism perhaps only by Soyinka's (1973) *Season of Anomy, The Combat* is so distinct from other Nigerian civil war novels that Ofeimun (1988: 185) has paid the author the following underhand compliment: 'Because of its deliberate fantasy, we cannot say that Omotoso has written a novel of the Nigerian civil war. Yet, we cannot argue that he has not.' Similarly, another critic has suggested that,

> [w]ith the oil boom and aggressive competition, Nigerians have since found too much to live for simply to dream and despair. Against this

Box 4.2 Metaphor

1. A metaphor is a rhetorical trope or a figure of speech making a comparison between two seemingly unrelated objects without using 'like' or 'as';
2. A transference of one object's characteristics onto another. http://www.lcc.gatech.edu/gallery/rhetoric/terms/metaphor.html (accessed on 31 March 2004).

> background, the absurdity of Omotoso's *The Combat*, in particular, is hard to accept as a logical response; hence his disciples have been few compared to the now thriving 'industry' of Nigerian detective fiction, of which Omotoso himself is one of the best practitioners.
>
> (Amuta 1983: 92)

It seems clear, however, that these scholars are chastising Omotoso, not so much because he has not written a civil war novel, but because he has not written it in the mimetic or imitative mode that is prevalent in Nigerian war fiction. He deliberately, for example, and in contrast to, say, Eddie Iroh, leaves out specific references to location and graphic descriptions of exploitation and poverty brought about by the war. Thus, whereas Iroh uses a very mimetic technique to discuss invented, though largely convincing scenarios concerning the war, and, following the tradition of other Nigerian writers, uses historical events and characters, as well as specific place names, to examine the roles of both indigenous and foreign participants in the war in his trilogy (*Forty Eight Guns for the General* (1976), *Toads of War* (1979) and *The Siren in the Night* (1982)), Omotoso intentionally avoids such a mimetic strategy. What we see in Omotoso's text is an artistic modification of the genre rather than its poor representation. Ironically, the very elements for which some readers might criticize Omotoso – his calculated use of the fantastic and the absurd – are the very ones that have not only helped to introduce a new dimension to war fiction in West Africa, but have also rendered the fundamental connections between senseless wars and underdevelopment first identified by the author some thirty years ago as relevant now as they were then.

The rest of this chapter examines how Omotoso's use of commanding metaphors (Box 4.2), indeed searing images, suggests a world that seems not only to be severing itself from its recent and distant past, but also continuing to deprive itself of meaningful development if it proceeds along the path of self-destruction and civil warfare. In other words, long before major writers such as the Ivorian, Ahmadou Kourouma, in his *Allah n'est pas obligé* (2000), for example, decided to show warfare as a cruel machine that crushes everyone – including the young – in its path, Omotoso had been at the vanguard of the creation of new literary myths on the dangers, paradoxes and realities of contemporary warfare in Africa.

4 Two siblings in foolish but mortal combat

The plot of *The Combat*, in brief, is as follows. Two ordinary, in fact very poor men, who are also best friends and housemates, Ojo Dada and Chuku Debe (identifiably Yoruba and Ibo names, respectively), lock themselves in an absurd combat for reasons they themselves do not seem to understand. The events leading to this senseless fight begin after Chuku accidentally runs a boy over at his motor mechanic friend's repair yard. Unbeknown to Chuku, the boy had been playing behind the taxi-cab he drives for a living; Dada had been repairing one of the taxi's tyres when the accident occurred. As soon as Dada realizes what his 'friend and brother' (as the narrator constantly refers to each of the protagonists) has done, he chases after him and, after finally catching up with him, insists that Chuku should apologize for the harm he has done to the boy. The barely literate Chuku, still ignorant of what happened, initially interprets Dada's actions as the whims of his cerebral, bibliophilic friend. When it becomes apparent to Chuku that his friend is serious in his demand for an acknowledgement of guilt, as well as an apology, he refuses to accede to his friend's demands, convinced that what happened was a genuine accident, and that he had not been guilty of any malicious intent.

The two friends finally decide to engage in a duel as a way of resolving what they obviously have allowed to become a very serious problem. But the dilemma is complicated even further by another entanglement. Sometime previously, Chuku and Dada's closeness and almost identical nature had attracted them both to a young woman, Moni, who later had a son, who each man claimed as his offspring. Paternity of this boy thus becomes an additional bone of contention between the two friends. These rather domestic, even if seemingly extraordinary, events soon assume international proportions, when the potential combatants go to the South African and Russian ambassadors – perfect embodiments of the Cold War – to seek military assistance for their impending combat. The preparations for the battles in both the civil court (where a judge has to settle the paternity issue) and the school yard battlefield (where the duel is to be fought) take on an increasingly bizarre twist as the opponents lose sight of what had pitted them in combat against each other in the first place, and now become mere pawns in the hands of their external sponsors. After some hollow and abortive attempts at peace-making, the civil courts render a judgement which pleases neither the principal combatants nor Moni, the now-rich 'Dee Madam'. The narrator then concludes the novel by introducing a related theme, that is, that Moni's parents, the boy's guardians, show themselves to be totally selfish grandparents with little or no concern for the boy's welfare.

4.1 Narrative technique in The Combat

Although the structure, maybe even the story line of *The Combat* might be unacceptable to some, I believe that Omotoso's narrative technique – a fine blend of the parabolic with elements of the burlesque (Box 4.3) – makes *The Combat* both interesting and important for our purposes. And,

Box 4.3 Parable and burlesque

Parable:

1. From Greek *parabole* 'comparison' or 'similitude'.
2. Short fictitious narrative that illustrates a moral attitude, a doctrine, a standard of conduct, or a religious principle.
3. The term originally referred to a Greek rhetorical figure, a kind of extended simile, involving the use of a literary illustration.

Source: *Encyclopœdia Britannica*, 2004. http://www.britannica.com/eb/article?eu=59821 (accessed on 30 March 2004).

Burlesque:

1. From French, *comical*, from Italian *burlesco*, from *burla*, 'joke', probably from Spanish, from Vulgar Latin *burrula*, diminutive of Late Latin *burrae*, 'nonsense', from *burra*, 'wool'.
2. A literary or dramatic work that ridicules a subject either by presenting a solemn subject in an undignified style or an inconsequential subject in a dignified style.
3. A ludicrous or mocking imitation; a travesty.
4. A variety show characterized by broad ribald comedy, dancing, and striptease.

Source: *The American Heritage Dictionary of the English Language*, Fourth Edition http://www.exoticworldusa.org/frame_whatis.html (accessed on 30 March 2004).

as with all parables, this novel is short, the story being told in only eighty-eight pages. Furthermore, its combination of highly realistic and fantastic events also makes for intriguing reading.

As if to draw a parallel with the pre-war links between Eastern Nigeria and the rest of the country, Omotoso begins his novel by establishing the long-standing links between Ojo Dada and Chuku Debe. Their lives are inextricably linked; indeed, it is their friendship, above all else, which has made their lives of abject poverty bearable. Even though they live in this state of almost total poverty – their bedrooms are part of a crowded shack; their bathroom is built from bamboo and has no doors; and Chuku can afford only a pair of 'tyre-soled slippers' (pp. 2–3) – the most fascinating thing about their relationship, in the beginning at least, is their friendship with, and support for one another. Thus when Chuku goes to have a bath he finds that Ojo has left some water for him to use; they treat each other with consideration and mutual respect, leaving their toiletries in neat and tidy piles in opposite corners of their tiny, shared bathroom, for instance. Nor is this all, for they had invested jointly in a rediffusion box (an early form of transistor radio) when they first moved in (p. 3). In sum, then,

Omotoso suggests that these friends had coexisted peacefully, even communally, prior to the incident with the boy, even though their shared existence had been neither easy nor comfortable.

In a clear reversal of Nigerian stereotypes, it is Chuku, the Ibo, who is 'the brawn' and his Yoruba friend, Ojo, whose character is 'the brain'. It is thus Ojo who loves reading (including Shakespeare in abridged form), and who often reminds Chuku that the latter is 'stark illiterate' (p. 7); Chuku, for his part, treats his friend with gentle derision. The most important point, however, is that before the quarrel and the decision to engage in combat, the relationship between the two men was mutually dependent. Thus Chuku does not even think twice about dumping his 'much patched inner tube' and 'threadbare tyre on a mud-caked tyre rim' (p. 7) at Ojo's for repair; and Ojo not only carries out the repairs, but does so, as far as we can tell, for free.

4.1.1 Separating two peas in a pod?

According to Omotoso, it is precisely this kind of symbiosis – of being stuck with each other – that should have served as a check on the hostilities which developed. Significantly, the novelist does not take sides. Rather, he uses his fiction to stress at least some of the following:

- the Nigeria–Biafra war is a war which should never have been fought in the first place;
- the ties that bound, and could have continued to bind the warring sides together, were much more than anything that could or should have separated them;
- the war was fought for the most bizarre and inexplicable of reasons;
- the major combatants very quickly allowed themselves to be manipulated by outside forces with little genuine interest in the well-being of the warring factions;
- in the final analysis, the combatants gained nothing for their efforts.

In pursuing these themes, Omotoso uses specific historical events such as the first military coup which resulted in the deaths of the Sardauna and the Western Region Premier (p. 5); the talk of a return to peace in Nigeria (p. 19); and prayer services for peace during the war (p. 53). Furthermore, as McLuckie (1987) has pointed out, he also uses the physical attributes of the protagonists to lend an atmosphere of reality to the novel.

It is instructive, too, to observe Omotoso's use of symbolism, for it is through this that we come to understand his presentation of the ideas outlined above. In almost every conceivable way, the characters, especially Ojo and Chuku, become metonymic representations of 'postcolonial' African countries, and, especially Nigeria, the homeland of both characters.[5] Their extreme poverty – emphasized by their surroundings and conditions of existence – helps to underscore the reasons why they could not have afforded the luxury of fighting one another. Like most 'developing' countries, these individuals exist at subsistence level (see Chapter 1). Chuku cannot even afford to buy himself a new rag to clean his cab ('He took out a rag formerly of a yellow colour now almost completely covered with black filth', p. 4); and when he is able to pay for an extremely modest breakfast at a roadside stall, he does not even have enough money left over to buy a daily newspaper. Similarly, the former gas station where Ojo repairs cars and tyres is indicative of his social status ('The small glass office was now empty except for a few jerry cans belonging to Ojo Dada. The window-glass had been smashed', p. 6). With a masterstroke of irony, the novelist also introduces the boy, Isaac (the correctly-named sacrificial lamb for whom most of the parties are vying, but who is not identified initially to the reader as such), as an extremely poor, starving and abandoned urchin. It is no accident that in a work that is very sparse on details, Omotoso devotes almost three full pages to Isaac's attempts at scrounging a decent meal for himself (pp. 9–12).

4.1.2 Common bonds: poverty and friendship, disunity and stupidity

But poverty is not all that brings the two leading characters together. Their friendship and common predicament are the things, Omotoso suggests, that should have kept them together. Aside from the constant references to, and demonstrations of their friendship (we see on p. 13, for example, that the word 'friend' is used five times in describing one or the other), we also notice how their separate/individual lives are almost indistinguishable. Here is the narrator's description of their journey from Akure to Lagos for the settlement of the paternity suit:

> So the decision of the court in this dispute was the other matter which brought Ojo and Chuku to Lagos that day.
>
> When they had finished reading the paper, they went down to a buka [kiosk] and had a big breakfast of eko [fermented maize/corn meal] and akara [bean cake]. Then instead of taking tea – lemon tea it is called in Lagos, but it is the same concoction made out of some grass as in the up-country area from which Ojo and Chuku came – instead of drinking lemon tea, they each had a bottle of Star beer. At about 7.30 they went to St Anna magistrate's court, a matter of yards from Tinubu Square. There was nobody when they arrived. They had been lucky to get a lift in a car – they paid a shilling each – and thus had been able to avoid the rush at the bus stop and the crowds and the jostling and pulling and pocket-picking.
>
> (p. 23)

Even though the actions and behaviour here are supposed to have been performed by two individuals, one notices constant references to the third person plural. The combined actions of the characters are so identical that they could easily have been performed by a single individual; indeed, it is difficult to distinguish one from the other. What Omotoso stresses, in other words, is that Nigeria and Biafra had too much at stake in each other's survival to be engaged in war. Ultimately, he finds both the reasons for the war, and the war itself, absurd. He hints at *The Combat*'s grotesque side by his sarcastic use of an episode from Philip Rush's (1964) *The Book of Duels* as his preface:

St. Foix asked the gentleman next to him to sit farther away.
'Why so, sir?' the gentleman asked.
'Because, sir, you smell.'
'That sir, is an insult. My seconds will wait on you, and you must fight me.'
'I will fight if you insist, but I don't see how that will mend the matter,' St. Foix answered. 'If you kill me I shall smell too. If I kill you you will smell, if possible, worse than you do at present.'

4.1.3 Mock-heroism and bathos[6]

The mock-heroic tone of this passage obviously allows the statements and actions of the characters to degenerate into bathos while reprising the need for good sense. This is indeed an integral part of Omotoso's narrative technique. He makes it quite clear from the outset that even though *The Combat* contains references to actual historical events and people, it also deliberately distances itself from history by collapsing actual events which occurred over a period of several years into a few days. Indeed, everything in *The Combat* is compressed into a six-day period (perhaps symbolic of the six-year period of post-independence civilian rule which preceded military intervention and civil war): the first military coup; the failed peace talks at Aburi, Ghana; the actual commencement of hostilities – these all occur during this six-day period in Omotoso's fictional world.

It is after Chuku accidentally runs Isaac (the proverbial sacrificial lamb) over, however, that the novel's strange, even surrealistic qualities begin to emerge. As Omotoso demonstrates in the passage where the accident takes place – the passage, incidentally, where we find the most frequent use of the word 'friend' – Chuku is totally unaware of what has happened. But as soon as Ojo, his close friend, becomes aware of the accident, he chases after Chuku and, after a heated argument (which turns out to be a small crowd-pleaser), they resolve things thus:

Both of them kept silent for a few minutes like actors who had forgotten their lines. Ojo at last broke the silence:

'You might think it is annoying that I don't wait until we get home before I tell you this, but you did it outside, not inside our house. You must apologize for it or else I am not going to live in the same house with you. The alternative is . . .'

Chuku Debe looked at his friend and frowned. What was the alternative? He was still convinced that his friend must be mad, but he was getting angry now. He did not like being held up so early in the week. And by his friend, too, the man with whom he shared so much. With impatience, he asked:

'Enh-en, go on. Wetin? . . . [What?]'

He remembered now that something had held him up for a fraction of a second as he was leaving Ojo Dada's place of work. But he was not ready to accept that he had run over anybody, or even if he had, to apologise for it.

'So you must either come and apologise or else . . .'

'Or else wetin? . . . [Or else, what?]'

'Or else you must accept my challenge to a single combat. If you beat and kill me, then you are in the right and you have not done anything wrong. God would have vindicated your cause . . .' At last Chuku spoke, he spoke with the sense of occasion and the solemnity demanded of such issues.

'I gree. I go fight you. Make God helep man wey lose [I agree. I will fight you. May God help the loser].'

(pp. 15–16)

4.1.4 Sacrificing all for nothing?

There are two very significant points about this passage. The first is the way in which the two friends, quite unthinkingly, are prepared to sacrifice their friendship and everything that it implies by assuming only absolute and extreme positions in their attempts to settle the dispute. They show no desire to use common sense and good judgement, and appear ready to sacrifice the friendship they have invested so much time and effort in cultivating. The second point is even more disturbing. Chuku and Ojo decide on their line of action without even thinking of the victim. At no time does either man think of providing much-needed assistance to the injured boy. They allow their egotism and self-righteousness to cloud their reasoning to such an extent that, unlike the Abraham and Isaac story in the Old Testament, where good sense ultimately prevails, they literally and metaphorically transform the boy, Isaac, into a sacrificial lamb (see Chapter 3 for moral panics in representations of West African children). The relevance of this episode to the Nigeria–Biafra situation is clear. For Omotoso, the events leading up to the civil war were complex, making the apportionment of guilt and blame difficult. Nonetheless, there is little doubt, he appears to be saying, that behaviour which could not have been considered wholly acceptable or even tolerable was implicated in the outbreak of war. He suggests, moreover, that such conduct may not always have been malicious in intent, and could have been addressed by means other than warfare and bloodshed.

4.1.5 Cold War pawns in a macabre fight

This, then, is why Omotoso deliberately trivializes both the idea of this kind of war, and the actual combat itself, by using language that suggests the mock-epic. As soon as Dada and Chuku decide to have their fratricidal battle, they begin to make highly ridiculous but deadly serious plans, including enlisting military assistance from the South African and Russian embassies, respectively. But even before we get to this stage of this macabre farce, Omotoso complicates matters some more by creating a parallel combat between the two men. This time, though, the battle is for a child of dubious paternity, who later turns out to be Isaac, and who both men claim as their son. It is significant that as the men fight for the boy in court, they show, just as they do after the accident, no interest at all in either his existence or welfare: 'But the courts could not decide. The case went on from year to year. The two friends came and went from the court to their house. It had gone on for nine years . . . But the evidence for the case – the child – had not been seen for many years' (pp. 22–3).

The discrepancy between the platitudes, exhausting litigation and combat preparations, on the one hand, and the absolute lack of interest in the boy, the object of the combat, on the other, is astonishing; indeed, this mismatch would be funny if its implications were not so grave. Omotoso thus uses the discrepancy as a major weapon to show that the combat(s) for the boy (Nigeria) had less to do with stated reasons – love, altruism and so forth – than with greed, vanity, egotism, self-righteousness and misplaced hostilities. This is why the narrator comments, soon after the initial adjournment of the court case, that '[t]his was the last time that Chuku Debe and his friend Ojo Dada were to stand together and look at somebody, something, they had once shared. For the rest of the week they began to see everything in fragments only – even when they stood together in the same court to hear the decision – they all stood there, but not together any longer; the three of them. Ojo, Chuku and Dee Madam [Isaac's mother]' (pp. 23–4).

It is not surprising then that Ojo and Chuku rush off to foreign embassies to seek help for arms for what will soon develop into a full-blown war. The ludicrousness of their intent and actions is underscored by what must have seemed then like an impossible scenario: a black African going to the (pre-majority rule) South African embassy for help to fight another black African. This is given even sharper focus by the 'reception' accorded the arms-seekers. At the South African embassy, Ojo is treated with mock respect and extreme condescension (at one point the ambassador says to Ojo: 'Yes, of course, you people . . . I mean we Africans, are always such musical people. We've got rhythm in our veins', p. 27) while he is served South African sherry from a bottle with a label proclaiming that the sherry was from Cyprus. But Omotoso's contempt for the whole exercise is highlighted when, in exchange for South African 'assistance', Ojo agrees, as a *quid pro quo*, to give up the boy (over whom they are to engage in combat) and his mother to South Africa. In like manner, Chuku Debe is treated with complete contempt and disrespect for his mental abilities at the Soviet Embassy. After getting more than an earful on the virtues and vices of almost all the 'isms', he cheers when some embassy workers shout '[w]e have nothing to lose but our gains' (p. 36). Of course, he is also asked for the boy – this time just the boy's mind, since he is asked to send the boy to Russia to study. Like Ojo, he dutifully agrees to the request.

4.1.6 An overstocked armoury and a cemetery

Having secured the promises of military assistance from their 'foreign sponsors', the two friends make elaborate preparations for the fight. Fittingly, they get their respective military training in places that would be associated with death – the overstocked armoury of the South African embassy and a cemetery. Their 'friends' not only encourage them to go out there and hurt each other, but they also make it clear to Chuku and Ojo that this battle is going to be for entertainment. In the words of the South African ambassador, 'You will have to provide entertainment for the people who come to watch, you see' (p. 46). Indeed, this sets the tone for the rest of the novel; this unnecessary, but now very serious, conflict is trivialized on every possible occasion. Thus when arrangements for 'peace talks' are made, they become mere circuses:

> For the rest of the day, and working through interpreters (for they no longer understood each other), Ojo Dada and Chuku Debe negotiated. The meetings took place at Glover Memorial Hall. The two teams of negotiators sat face to face. But they could not come to an agreement. They thought it was because they did not understand one another's languages. However, the reason was that neither Dee Madam nor the child was there. There was hardly anything concrete on which to base their negotiations.
>
> (p. 49)

Similarly, the religious service for peace sees the church transformed from a place of worship into a fashion bazaar and a centre for exchanging hot gossip, while the combat itself is reduced to a television event involving negotiation with television companies for screening rights. And, like characters in some of the more 'realistic' war novels, the leading opponents in this war engage in serious propaganda battles. They both have grandiose-sounding public relations documents, make overblown speeches and hold press conferences, even though these activities are all devoid of any serious discussion of the real causes and potential consequences of the impending combat. No serious reference is made to the child (country) or its welfare. Instead, hackneyed phrases abound amid scenes of breath-taking absurdity. Omotoso uses Chuku Debe's press conference, for example, to lampoon these characters to the extent where this almost degenerates into direct abuse:

> The first question came from an American journalist:
>
> 'How could H.E. (His Excellency) always be friends with H.O.E. (His Other Excellency) if they were going to fight to the death on Saturday?' Chuku Debe smiled when this question was translated into Pidgin English for him. His answer, which has been translated into grammatical English here, was as follows:
>
> 'We can always be friends even if he dies. You see, we don't believe that people die; only ideas die. There will always be other Ojo Dadas. Only their ideas will be different. I will always love them all.'
>
> A British journalist wanted to know what brand of cigarettes H.E. smoked . . .
>
> 'What make?' the British journalist asked. 'Is it British or American?' Chuku Debe consulted with one of the men behind him. Then he said:
>
> 'It comes from Cuba.'
>
> All the journalists wrote that down. The Tanzanian journalist present was already thinking of an article to be entitled 'Recent Trade Movements between Latin America and Mainland Africa.' He would quote H.E . . . The French journalist from *Le Monde* wanted to know what H.E.'s opinion was about Women's Lib. 'Would H.E. liberate his wife if he had one?'

> 'Such things as Women's Lib,' Chuku Debe began to answer, 'take place only in the decadent West. There is no room for Women's Lib in Nigeria. Women here know their places. We all know our places here. . . .'
>
> 'What does H.E. think of men sharing their wives? Is this another facet of the decadent West?'
>
> Chuku Debe was angry – but only for a fraction of a minute.
>
> He said: 'No comment.'
>
> (pp. 59–60)

Ojo Dada's rendezvous with the press is not any different from the parody above. Here is how he addresses the press:

> 'It surprises me no end that you have been taken for a ride. I had expected far more intelligent reporting from you all, especially the British, than you have shown yourselves capable of giving. Did you believe all that load of rubbish H.E. told you . . . ? So he told you that he was telling you the truth? Well, I am going to tell you the real truth. There are eggs and eggs: so also with truths . . . Now listen to this: Some time ago my friend was driving a car, and as a result of his driving he ran over a human being . . . H.E. ran over him and ran away. I tried to talk to him as my friend and brother to go back and apologize for this life so wantonly mutilated. What did he do? I ask you, do you know what he did? I will tell you: he spat into my face. Do you know what it is like to be spat on? He did it to me . . . like this . . . just like this! What should I have done in such circumstances? Kiss him and say what a great guy he was? No! No man is given such generosity of heart . . .'
>
> (p. 69)

Omotoso resorts to such outright mockery because of his contempt for a war that, in his view, should never have been fought. He suggests quite strongly – through both Chuku's buffoonish performance and Ojo's lies – that those who had the biggest stake in the war were neither involved in, nor informed about, its planning; and that some of those who actually planned the war made a big and sorry joke out of the whole thing. In fact, at the end of his press conference, Ojo acknowledges as much when he fails to refute the allegation implied in the following question asked by a reporter: 'Is there any truth in the rumour circulating that neither of you is going to fight, but that you will choose some unfortunate men to fight for you?' (p. 71). Ojo knew only too well that there was more than a germ of truth in the rumour.

4.1.6 Exploiting the vulnerable in society

The subject of the exploitation of vulnerable people in society is successfully combined with, and highlighted in, the story of Isaac and his grandparents towards the end of the novel. Isaac is depicted as the embodiment of the young people of Biafra and the rest of Nigeria, who were manipulated and then sent to their deaths by their 'grandparents' (selfish members of the older generation interested only in their own self-gratification). Isaac's grandparents take advantage of him and use him as a weapon against one another, to the extent that the boy has to run away from home for good (see the discussion in Chapter 4 of child abuse and neglect of chidren's rights). And, as if she does not want to be outdone by the others in their sheer exploitation of Isaac, his mother, Dee Madam, decides, after years of absolute neglect, to organise a lavish tenth birthday party for him. The symbolic links between Isaac and Nigeria can be seen in this very intense description of Dee Madam's discovery of her now-dying boy (a child previously abandoned by his feuding parents and other 'loved ones'):

> Meanwhile Dee Madam drove around the streets looking for her son. Eventually, she came to the drive of the Texaco petrol station. She saw the body lying there. She shooed off dogs and pigs, which were hovering around ready to tear the body apart among themselves. Having shooed off the dogs and the pigs she was able to approach. She beat the flies off the body, using her *ibori*. The flies buzzed angrily away. Dee Madam knelt down and pushed the body over; beneath it were crawling ants of many races. She gave the body another push – by now it was a couple of feet away from the ants which had begun to nibble at it. She put her ear to the heart of the body and concluded that life was still there.
>
> (p. 86)

Still self-serving and totally oblivious to the boy's needs, Dee Madam and her 'guests' continue with both the macabre birthday party and plans for the combat of death before the guests are forced out by the stench of Isaac's body. In the end, Dee Madam is left, all alone, with her son's rotten body on this his tenth birthday – a period that coincides with both the tenth anniversary of Nigeria's 'independence' and the end of the civil war.

5 Conclusion: irony in/of (Nigeria's) 'civil' conflict(s)?

Omotoso's hard-hitting irony is sustained to the very end. Unlike some other writers, he does not see the harm that was ultimately inflicted on the 'young' (read 'newly independent') Nigeria as something that was unavoidable, or that could be reduced simply to the inexplicable/inexcusable actions of one hateful ethnic group against another or others. The novel's structure and symbols seriously question the motivations and plans of the principal proponents of the war. And while Omotoso obviously shows that mistakes (some of them fatal) were made, he also makes it clear that, in the words of Chidi Amuta (1983: 92), 'the love of life, the survivalist instinct which hastened the end of the Nigerian civil war' should have been the most compelling reason for the fighters to try to solve whatever problems they may have had by means other than fighting. He emphasizes this point further by dedicating the book to Christopher Okigbo, the fine poet who died fighting on behalf of Biafra. The novelist's anti-war stance is not directed at all wars; he is against *this* war, he suggests, because the motivations of the war's main supporters were, at best, dubious.

A major conclusion which can be drawn from this novel, then, is that while Nigeria as a nation did have (and Africa as a continent does have) some very serious developmental issues and other problems, the proponents of war and instigators of civil conflicts often neglect the most pressing of such problems, while concentrating on others that do not perhaps merit either the attention or effort spent in trying to resolve them. In other words, if Omotoso's tone and attitude throughout the text are decidedly negative, it is because he wants to convey to the reader the totally negative impression that such wars leave on him.

Thus my goal in this chapter has not been to verify the authenticity (or lack thereof) of actual historical events in *The Combat.* Instead, I have focused on the fictional world created by Omotoso and looked at the internal logic that governed this world. Avoiding the beauty and the pitfalls of mimesis, Omotoso uses symbolism, not so much as a screen for a panoramic sweep of society, or for illuminating the causes of the Nigeria–Biafra civil war, but to highlight some of the seemingly ineluctable but frequently avoidable reasons for loss of human life and economic destruction. The world Omotoso has created, then, is one in which cultural, socio-economic and environmental development is unlikely to be achieved if unnecessary wars, avoidable civil strife and disruptive state collapse continue; it is reminiscent of the potential pitfalls identified in both Olukoshi's overview of regional political economy (Chapter 2) and Kandeh and Kannan's (Chapter 10) caution about the risks to state-building and national integration in emergent West African democracies. As Ayi Kwei Armah, another African writer who often tries to highlight the root causes of development's perceived failures in Africa, perceptively observes in *Two Thousand Seasons* (cited in Boehmer 1995: 199), 'the search is for paths to a "necessary beginning", the start of a different history, "to work out better directions, to follow better visions in our salvaged lives"'. In Omotoso's fictional world as in real West African worlds, then, such better or improved visions must, of necessity, directly address problems of development (poverty, hunger, disease, etc.) as an integral part of processes of nation-building and democratic renewal. The consequences of failure can, as Riddell's (Chapter 5) analysis of state collapse in Sierra Leone reminds us, be too horrible but all too real to contemplate.

Notes

1. All page references are to this 1972 edition, which is listed in the references.
2. Nigerian-born Kolawole Omotoso holds degrees from the Universities of Ibadan and Edinburgh (PhD in Arabic literature). He is currently professor in the Department of Drama at Stellenbosch University, South Africa, having previously taught at the Universities of Ibadan, Ife/Obafemi Awolowo, Western Cape, Stirling and Lesotho. His other fictional works include *The Edifice* (1971), *Season of Migration to the South* (1994), *Just Before Dawn* (1998), and the autobiographical novel, *Memories of a Recent Boom* (1982).
3. All page references are to this 1982 edition, which is listed in the references.
4. This section draws on Porter (1995).
5. Metonymy refers to the substitution for, or use of, an arbitrary or suggestive word in place of what is actually meant (http://www.lcc.gatechedu/gallery/rhetoric/terms/tropes.html, accessed on 30/3/04).

6. Bathos refers to a 'change in mood from the important and serious to the trivial or ridiculous' (http://www.askoxford.com/concise_oed/bathos?view=uk; accessed on 28/03/04).

References

American Heritage Dictionary of the English Language, 4th edn (2000), Houghton Mifflin, Boston, Massachusetts (http://www.yahooligans.yahoo.com/reference/dictionary).

Amuta, C. (1983), 'The Nigerian civil war and the evolution of Nigerian literature', in Wylie, H., Julien, J. and Russell, J.L. (eds), *Contemporary African Literature*. Three Continents Press, Washington, DC.

Atofarati, Major A.A. (1992), *The Nigerian Civil War: Causes, Strategies, And Lessons Learnt*, US Marine and Command Staff College history paper. (http://www.globalsecurity.org/military/library/report/1992/AAA.htm; accessed 1/4/04.)

Boehmer, E. (1995), *Colonial and Postcolonial Literature: Migrant Metaphors*. Oxford University Press, New York.

The Columbia Electronic Encyclopedia, 6th edn (2003), Columbia University Press, New York (http://www.infoplease.com/encyclopedia.html).

Emecheta, B. (1982), *Destination Biafra*. Fontana, London.

Encyclopædia Britannica Online (2004), (http://www.britannica.com/).

Iroh, E. (1976), *Forty Eight Guns for the General*. Heinemann, London.

Iroh, E. (1979), *Toads of War*. Heinemann, London.

Iroh, E. (1982), *The Siren in the Night*. Heinemann, London.

Kourouma, A. (2000), *Allah n'est pas obligé*. Éditions du Seuil, Paris.

McLuckie, C. (1987), 'The Nigeria-Biafra Civil War in Fiction', unpublished MA Thesis, University of Alberta, Canada.

Ofeimun, O. (1988), 'Kole Omotosho', in Ogunbiyi, Y. (ed.), *Perspectives on Nigerian Literature*, Vol 2. Guardian Books, Lagos.

Omotoso, K. (1971), *The Edifice*. Heinemann Educational Books, London.

Omotoso, K. (1972), *The Combat*. Heinemann, London.

Omotoso, K. (1982), *Memories of a Recent Boom*. Longman, London.

Omotoso, K. (1988), *Just Before Dawn*. Spectrum Books, Ibadan.

Omotoso, K. (1994), *Season of Migration to the South*. Tafelberg, South Africa.

Porter, A.M. (1995), 'They were there too: women and the civil war(s) in Emecheta's *Destination Biafra*', in Umeh, M. (ed.), *Emerging Perspectives on Buchi Emecheta*. Africa World Press, Trenton, New Jersey.

Rush, P. (1964), *The Book of Duels*. Harrap, London.

School of Oriental and African Studies (1958–1971), *Nigerian Civil War Collection*, archives, University of London (http://www.aim25.ac.uk/cgi-bin/search2?collid=93&instid=19).

Soyinka, W. (1973), *Season of Anomy*. Rex Collings, London.

CHAPTER 5

Urban bias, redistribution, and state collapse: the lessons of Sierra Leone

J. Barry Riddell

1 Introduction

Sierra Leone was devastated by the actions of the Revolutionary United Front (RUF) for a lengthy ten years. The members of this gang, whose declared aim was to overthrow a thoroughly discredited All People's Congress (APC) government, were seemingly ordinary people from the countryside, along with some semi-organized instigators. They wreaked havoc and destruction: killed peasant farmers and their families; burned whole villages; raped women; chopped off arms and legs; pillaged the countryside; looted entire communities; destroyed crops; and eliminated the country's limited infrastructure of roads, schools, and healthcare. The result was a people living in fear, with millions having fled their homes; a nation destroyed; a society that knew only chaos, murder, and death; a legacy of destruction; and a government that was in control of only the capital city and a few surrounding areas (Abdullah 1998; Bah 2000; Bangura 2000; Kandeh 2002; PAC 2000a, 2000b; Reno 1995b, 1996, 1998a, 2000, 2001; Richards 1996; Riley 1997; Zack-Williams and Riley 1993; Zack-Williams 1990, 1997b, 1999, 2001). The tragedy was exacerbated by the famine and disease (especially AIDS, malaria, and Lassa fever) it also caused. Why this horror and devastation? And, why did this movement's attack on the nation, its government, its elite, and its urban focus bring death and chaos to millions of ordinary citizens?

The horror of this period was heightened because many of the rebel soldiers were children, often drugged on alcohol and amphetamines, among other things (Richards 1996, 2001; Riley 1996; Zack-Williams 2001). They witnessed, or were forced to take part in, killings and destruction – including that of their own families, kin, farms, villages, and homes. Why was a generation destroyed and why did young people act as agents of murder, chaos, and devastation? Was it a matter of leadership and greed? It was certainly not because of the character of the people of Sierra Leone, their cultures, and their civil society. And why did the chaos continue over such a long time? There must be an explanation. People did not just kill, maim, and destroy for no reason. Why did the horror go on and on? Are its roots still in the country?

2 Toward an understanding of the horror

The explanation of these events (and those of the recent past) resides both in space and time, and its exegesis is also conditioned by certain factors – the setting or context. In spatial terms the 'heart of the matter' resided in the failure of the Sierra Leone state to integrate the new nation in the post-independence years: a fundamental aspect of national development is not only economic growth, but also the forging of nationhood in the pursuit of betterment (see also Chapter 10). Equally important is the fact that the people residing in the countryside were extremely unhappy that their resource base was exploited by the elite of the country to support their more-favoured lives. Furthermore, Sierra Leone was for long sheltered from the global influences of the IMF, which have largely removed what have been termed 'urban bias' policies elsewhere in Africa.

This urban bias system was employed in a rural-to-urban redistribution system in Sierra Leone by the government of the country since its Independence in 1961, but especially by the APC and its friends in the army, business, and bureaucracy over the 1968–91 period. This tool of development, which was intended to assist in the generation of national economic growth, was gradually converted to 'elite bias', as the redistribution was converted from rural-to-urban to peasant-to-elite. Such a distortion was exacerbated in the minds of rural citizens, who had been exploited since before the declaration of the British Protectorate in 1896, particularly as this continued into the post-independence decades. In effect, colonialism with a new face, internal colonialism (exploitation of the countryside and its people), was perpetuated.

The context within which bias and horror have been played out has three dimensions. First, the country is extremely wealthy because of its resources, especially diamonds, and their exploitation is fundamental to understanding daily events. Second, the African continent is dominated by a war pathology – as a playground of international machinations – and this is evident in mercenary forces; arms sales; child soldiers; the ubiquitous use of stimulants; military takeovers and other coups d'état; 'peace-keeping' forces and accords; warlordism, etc. Third, the country's people live in dire poverty and a state of underdevelopment. These are the keys to understanding the chaos, destruction and murder which racked the nation, starting in 1991, but whose root causes reside in the political economy of Sierra Leone's post-colonial geography and economy, especially as they were conditioned during the APC years, in that they relate to the quite disparate living standards between Freetown, the country's capital, and the countryside.

Much of this has been exacerbated by the actions of the leaders of countries such as Liberia, Burkina Faso, and Libya, and the personalities of local politicians and soldiers such as Foday Sankoh, Joseph Momoh, Valentine Strasser, Maada Bio, Charles Taylor, Johnny Paul Koroma, Tejan Kabbah which, together, contributed significantly to the story of state collapse (Bah 2000; Hirsch 2001; Reno 1995a; Richards 1996; Riley 1996; 1997; Zack-Williams and Riley 1993; Zack-Williams 1997a, 1999). Neither can issues such as international finance, the IMF and the World Bank, the country's economic decline, its poverty, its high rates of unemployment, currency devaluation, and the smuggling of its resources be ignored; nor can corruption, nepotism, patronage, ethnicity and party politics. However, the basic understanding of the origins of the horror is founded on the exploitation of the peasant – why s/he is agitated: this is, indeed, the 'heart of the matter'.

2.1 *Peasant disquiet*

In order to understand the rural discontent which pervaded Sierra Leone over the last century, it is vital to comprehend the peasantry and its feelings. The situation of a peasant farmer living in a village in the country's southeast illustrates the disquiet felt throughout the countryside. The context is that the dirt road which connects the peasant's village to the world beyond (and to produce markets which provide the sole source of income) is a sea of mud for much of the year, and is rutted and pitted during the remainder. The primitive state of the transport link extends back in time, for it was originally built as a feeder road connected to the colonial railway back in the 1920s; neither its function nor its condition has changed. The government closed the nearby railway about three decades ago, but the tracks remain in people's thoughts because the railway was a vital part of the peasant's economic life for years, from its opening in this area in 1908, to its final closure in the early 1970s. Good transport (mileage or maintenance) enabled the peasant to use such links to sell the cash crops produced, while poor transport rendered travelling very expensive, time-consuming, or impossible.

There is more to this disquiet of the countryside. Food is in short supply, or, when available, is expensive.[1] People live in poverty; their homes are made of mud, with straw roofs (corrugated tin for those who are relatively prosperous). There are few services (clean water, waste disposal, electricity, schools, and healthcare), and infant mortality rates are high. Life expectancy is about 30 years (if death does not occur in childhood).[2]

This has been the situation for generations. Either conditions have been difficult, or they have worsened during recent years. Despite all the government rhetoric in announcements and publications, conditions have not improved.[3] No wonder the rural youth are extremely vexed and troubled (Richards 2001), particularly when they compare their deprivation with the relative spendour in which the nation's 'leaders', the elite, live. Also, when the peasant's children attempt to improve their lives by moving into towns they find few jobs while having to contend with a high cost of living.

The mindset of the young peasant is especially important to consider for it essentially indicates that 'we have been ripped off for years and are fed up with it'. The history of the peasant's disadvantage extends back to the colonial period. They were first exploited by the British when the country was a colony (1896–1961). Then in 1961, Independence from the colonial yoke arrived, and hopes were raised that the path to betterment and development would be followed. However, prosperity did not follow. Conditions did not change; the peasant experienced continuing poverty.

The new Sierra Leone state replaced the colonial power as the peasant's enemy. Contact with the government meant regulation and taxation, but it also meant that there were few benefits, such as schools or healthcare, to improve life in the countryside. The people's reaction to the state's internal colonialism was to 'exit' from it or to avoid it at all costs (Hyden 1980) – and the peasant reacted by smuggling goods across the country's borders; moving or migrating elsewhere, especially to the city or the diamond mining areas; or avoiding the prices, supply, and demand of the market and reverting to the subsistence economy, where at least food was available. In effect, the post-colonial state operated much like the former colonial 'mother' country. The countryside and the people residing there were treated like a colony to be exploited. The situation was exacerbated because the government was corrupt, violent, and inept; it did not express the interests of the rural peasant, nor in fact those of Sierra Leone. In effect, the state comprised a bunch of thugs who lived well because of the efforts of peasants.

The extreme vexation of the peasantry is made even more pronounced by the sheer size of both the rural area and population. These rural dwellers are far more numerous than the single example of the village in the southeast. The rural population counts in excess of four million souls, belongs to 17 separate ethnic groups, and lives in an area of over 73,000 square kilometres. Nonetheless, peasant disquiet was quelled by the repressive activities of the state for a period of 30 years (1961–91). However, even this smothering state could not continue its system of plunder, for rural disquiet was like a cooking pot at the boil – the actions of the RUF removed the lid, and the pot boiled over.

Thus, the lives of peasants are in marked contrast to those of the Freetown elite. What made rural poverty especially maddening to the peasantry was the great difference between their lives of misery and those of the 'big people' in Freetown (especially as revealed during eponymous national corruption scandals), particularly as peasant suffering paid for the high living of this elite. While the people of the countryside suffered, these few privileged urban dwellers lived in big houses, ate well, had servants, attended schools, accessed healthcare, travelled abroad and, in many cases, drove luxury cars. A 'developmental state' (a growing Sierra Leone in which the lives of all citizens improved) was not what these so-called national leaders envisaged. No, the national scenario which they envisioned was one characterized by corruption, ineptitude, and kleptocracy. It was a world of uncaring leadership, of patronage, and of rent-seeking, which was dominated by a bunch of politicians, army officers, top bureaucrats and businesspeople (mostly foreign) who had grown fat by consuming the rewards of office, which were mostly paid for by peasants. They employed the tools of nepotism, violence, bribery, intimidation, and even murder, to maintain and cement their positions. The frequent changes of leadership (through coups or elections) did not mean any fundamental change for the countryside and its people. The faces and names might change, but the exploitation did not. As in other parts of Africa and elsewhere, these people treated what was public and belonged to the country as their own private reward (Bayart 1993; Chabal and Daloz 1999).

Thus, Sierra Leone was a kleptocracy. It was not betterment for all the country that the elite sought; rather, what took place was that the rewards of development and economic growth accrued to them, while the peasants bore the costs. In effect, as peasants attempted to survive in the countryside (or city/diamond mines when they migrated), they created a second, underground (informal or grey) economy of trading and smuggling. Meanwhile, the formal government structure which guided Sierra Leone (and was dominated by revenue from mining, especially diamonds) weakened and came under the control of a 'shadow state', with its patron–client networks (Reno 1995a).

Although the words of those opposed to the government – the RUF – differ greatly from their actions (the rhetoric is moral-sounding, but the reality is murder and chaos), their document, *Footpaths to Democracy* (1995), a rare attempt to outline its ideology, is telling. It indicates the strength of feeling behind peasant disquiet, and suggests that the system employed by this 'shadow state' and its entourage was one of the driving forces behind the chaos and murder. The foreward reads, in part, '[w]e can no longer leave the destiny of our country in the hands of a generation of crooked politicians and military adventurists . . . It is our right and duty to change the present political system in the name of national salvation and liberation' (sierra-leone.org/footpaths.html). Later, the document states that:

> [n]o more shall the rural countryside be reduced to hewers of wood and drawers of water for urban Freetown. That pattern of exploitation, degradation and denial is gone forever . . . of raping the countryside to feed the greed and caprice of the Freetown elite and their masters abroad . . . use state power to enrich themselves [,] intimidate the people [,] extract taxes and custom duties in Freetown [and] We are tired of our children dying of preventable diseases. We are tired of drinking muddy water. We are tired of our rural folks being exploited day in and day out . . . remove the rotten APC system.
>
> (sierra-leone.org/footpaths.html)[4]

The method by which this elite operated was 'urban bias'. Throughout Africa, and the entire Third World, it was a method of assisting economic development and growth whereby there would be a concentration of infrastructure and investment in 'growth centres' or 'growth poles', especially in (a) major city(ies). In turn, these would eventually lead to increased economic growth for the benefit of the entire country (Becker *et al.* 1994; Lofchie 1997). Resources were thereby removed from the rural areas in order to foster development and growth in the city – and it was always implied that the rewards of this betterment would eventually spread or 'trickle down' to the countryside, to the rest of the people of the country. The government conducted this differential development by its operation as a redistribution system.[5] The state, or the government and its agencies, could move resources from rural areas through tools such as taxation, and then locate them in Freetown, by allocating them, by spending them on budget items intended for national economic betterment, but which favoured the city and the elite (Riddell 1985a). The system was masked in the sense that taxes and budgets were like 'black boxes' to most people.

The outcome of the redistribution was geographical unevenness – a relatively poor countryside and a more privileged city; a deprived peasantry and a privileged elite.

Prior to depicting the tools of this urban bias or redistribution, and thus to begin to make sense of the decade-long violence, we must consider the events of the recent past, of the 1968–85 period. The roots of the corrupt system reside in the years of the post-Independence period, in the political career of one man and the surrounding political machinery which he established. The especially sad thing about his rule was that the primary force behind the construction of this undemocratic, one-party dictatorship was a former labour union organizer – Siaka Stevens.[6] There were others involved – his colleagues, competitors, and inheritors – but he set the style and is at the centre of the villainy. He eventually departed and later died, but he left behind a legacy of destruction, murder, and chaos to haunt the country. Foday Sankoh and the RUF were the visible cause, but Stevens began things, and was the root cause. He removed resources from the countryside and its people with the use of budgets, taxation, and spending. He eliminated opposition by violence and intimidation, by secret police, and by forming a one-party state in 1978. His was an extreme form of patrimonial rule (Boas 2001). He muzzled the media, labour organizations, and the armed forces. Any hindrances were removed; he and his associates ran the country and consumed its rewards.[7] Meanwhile the country spiralled into economic decline (Luke and Riley 1989; PAC 2000a; Reno 1995a, 1995b, 1996; Riley 1997; Riley and Sesay 1995; Weeks 1992; World Bank 1994; Zack-Williams 1990, 1992, 1997b, 1999).

He practised such 'urban bias'-type policies in Sierra Leone; effectively, they came to be translated into 'elite bias' policies in the post-Independence period, especially in the years of his political power, 1968–85. The resources derived from the rural areas and people to foster increased economic development were diverted into providing for the inflated and expensive lifestyles of himself and the other elite. Because the country's economy was supported by revenue from diamonds the stakes were high. This conversion of 'urban bias' into 'elite bias' is at the heart of the disquiet which pervaded the country, its poor, and its peasants. Stevens was able to carry this out because he was able to employ the financial rewards of his 'shadow state', especially from diamonds, to avoid the hand of international finance and its elimination of such 'urban bias' through the conditions normally attached to the Structural Adjustment Programmes (SAPs) of the International Monetary Fund (IMF) (Becker *et al.* 1994; Riddell 1997).

2.2 Diamonds

Prior to investigating how such 'urban bias' was conducted, it is necessary to follow briefly a seeming tangent to the argument of the chapter by considering diamond resources. Diamonds have been both a blessing and a curse to Sierra Leone in that they either provide state revenue or they pay for guns and dope. Above all, however, diamonds allowed the Sierra

Leone state to ignore the stringency of global finance, and the programmes of the International Monetary Fund (IMF) and the World Bank (WB). At Independence, diamonds (along with other less important minerals) provided the bulk of government revenues through sales, rentals, taxation, etc. – they were the country's economic engine (Bah 2000; PAC 2000a; Reno 1995a). However, over the period of Stevens's rule (1968–85), these monies were removed from formal government control and were gradually usurped by Stevens's 'shadow state' – in effect, removed from public hands to be placed into private ones (Reno 1995a, 1998b). Such a system was continued later by Joseph Momoh, Stevens's successor. However, Momoh's control of the diamond resources weakened and gradually the funds were pre-empted by the RUF – to finance their chaos, and purchase guns and landmines – and also by Taylor's Liberia.

Control of diamond production is financially and politically vital; it is the key to comprehending the longevity of Stevens's 'shadow state' and the RUF. Behind the horror in Sierra Leone, providing the context, is a complex story about rebels, mercenaries,[8] the armed forces, 'sobels' (soldiers by day and rebels by night), civil militias, and the machinations of business firms. The tale is like a combination of the Wild West, African political economy, and multinational business operations. However, the essential component of the story is how the country's resource base came to be in rebel hands – and was employed to fund the chaos, which made government unworkable.

In most other parts of Africa such a system of disparate rural-urban development was a common undertaking, but was removed by the Structural Adjustment Programmes of the WB and IMF. The effects of these SAPs are pronounced in the realms of service provision, employment, the cost of living, and the protection of local businesses. Currencies have been devalued, trade has been liberalized, state influence in the economy greatly reduced, subsidies eliminated, and the export of resources and 'cash crops' encouraged (Riddell 1997). However, in Sierra Leone, the hand of the international financial institutions was 'light', with the result that the system of urban bias remained intact and the country was able to avoid the devastation associated with such programmes.

In practical terms in Sierra Leone, the effect of such programmes has been relatively minimal. The World Bank has prepared reports, provided funds for certain limited projects (i.e. the Integrated Agricultural Development Projects (IADPs) of the late 1970s–early 1980s),[9] and has held discussions; however, no formal programmes have been implemented. IMF programmes were introduced in the 1960s and 1970s – too early to affect urban bias policies – and the programmes of the 1980s were all terminated or abandoned.[10] The result was that these IFIs were not instrumental in the removal of, or reduction in 'urban bias' policies.[11] In other words, the 'shadow state' operated freely. Only in 1994–97 was an IMF programme firmly implemented – however, by then, it was too late as the rural peasants had been exploited for generations. By the time that the IMF programme was underway, and conditions such as trade liberalization could take effect, the RUF action had been ongoing for three years, and peasant disquiet had boiled over.

In effect, government budget deficits (resulting from the elite expenditure and shortfalls in export revenues) of the 1980s were offset by exploiting peasants, by taxing diamond production, and by printing money (thus effectively devaluing the leone). No wonder that peasants were extremely vexed. Not only were the elite–peasant disparities pronounced, but also the operations of the 'shadow state' were obvious and the purchasing power of their limited currency was dramatically reduced as the exchange rate fell. The country's progress was in reverse and it was becoming underdeveloped. For example, the formal economic system was devastated, so that by the mid-1980s 70 per cent of exports were estimated to have left through non-formal channels (Reno, 1995a). Healthcare was largely unavailable and mortality rates had risen to the sad levels that obtained at Independence. The education system was in chaos and no longer was Sierra Leone known as the 'Athens of West Africa': after slow improvement in the early post-colonial years, development indices declined from about the late 1970s. Petroleum products were either unavailable or priced so high as to be unaffordable for the peasantry. Electricity supply was no longer available, nor was clean water. Not only were conditions difficult and deteriorating, there was also an historical dimension which underlined the plight of rural peasants. As well as the past and the present, the future was also bleak – for the children of peasants knew that only misery, poverty, sickness, and unemployment lay ahead. The future of the status quo held nothing for them. Conditions could not be worse. No wonder the RUF, despite the horror, was seen as offering possible betterment in some quarters.

2.3 *Redistribution*

Government redistribution is the method by which resources were drawn from the countryside into government coffers and then into the hands of the elite. Recall that in theory, the money was intended to concentrate the country's resources into a 'growth pole' or 'growth centre', which would stimulate the nation's economic development. However, these public resources were soon turned into private hands. The tools of such 'urban bias', which became 'elite bias', are depicted in Table 5.1. Here, the operations of the major instruments are briefly explained. However, these major tools can be thought of as 'the tip of the iceberg' for such bias was pervasive elsewhere in government policies and programmes (Riddell 1985a, 1985b, 1985c).

2.3.1 The Purchase of Cash Crops by a Monopoly Marketing Board

Peasants do not pay income taxes, and so the government of Sierra Leone employed a tool which had been used during the Second World War by the colonial power, Britain, to ensure the delivery of raw materials to the mother country – a produce marketing board which, in Sierra Leone, was the SLPMB (Sierra Leone Produce Marketing Board). The SLPMB purchased palm kernels, coffee, cocoa, and ginger from the many farmers living in the country's rural areas, then transported and bulked them, and eventually sold them on the world market. They paid peasant farmers

Table 5.1 Tools employed to create urban-elite bias

Major

1. The purchase of agricultural products (cash crops) by a monopoly marketing board, the Sierra Leone Produce Marketing Board. The SLPMB paid farmers approximately 45 per cent of world prices and the funds were transferred to the state via bonds, overstaffing, contracts, 'fellowships'. [The SLPMB was privatized in 1986, but by then it was too late.]
2. Currency overvaluation, which translates into relatively cheaper imports (mainly destined for urban consumers) and more expensive exports (mainly rural cash crops).
3. Urban employment growth by enlarging the bureaucracy or government-controlled parastatals. Also included is spending on security (police and military), partly to help in enforcing other urban bias policies, partly to provide patronage appointments, but especially to create urban employment.
4. Set a maximum price on urban rice sales and thus 'subsidize' urban dwellers while lowering the returns of rural producers (though rice moved through many informal channels as well).

Other

1. The taxing of international trade – so as to favour urban goods and disbenefit rural cash crops.
2. Invest in commercial agricultural development schemes which provide subsidies and positions to favoured people/areas (for example, the Integrated Agricultural Development Projects of the 1970–80s fostered commercial agriculture, while suggesting that peasant agriculture was experiencing improvement).
3. Urban industry protected by tariffs, duties, and regulation. Most of the articles produced were consumer items (mainly urban) – cigarettes, beer, matches, soft drinks, and textiles.
4. Locate most social services and utilities (health care, education, clean water, electricity, and paved roads) in urban places.
5. The selling of import licences and foreign exchange allocations.
6. Individualizing (from communal) land tenure and thus removing peasant access to land while stimulating production for the urban market and allowing land agglomeration.
7. National spending with an urban bias.
8. The movement of money abroad – capital flight – to avoid devaluation, inflation, and a weak economy.
9. Further examples include the hosting of the meetings of the Organization of African Unity in 1980 with its spending on items such as housing and cars, turned over to the urban elite afterwards; the urban and elite bias of the spending under the National Development Plan of the late 1970s (Riddell 1985b); the management of foreign aid projects; and minimum wage legislation positively affecting urban standards.

All of the above were not only masked by rhetoric, but such disparities reflected class bias, ethnicity, regionalism, environmental differences, historical inertia, economies of scale, personal attributes, and training, as well as urban bias – thus, the lack of clarity.

only a proportion of the world price: the value varied from year to year and from crop to crop, but is estimated to have been 45 per cent of the world price. Officially, their role was to dampen the wild fluctuations in the prices paid to producers in order to maintain production and farm income. In reality, while some of the residual funds (profits) went toward the SLPMB's operating expenses, millions of leones were amassed, and then transferred into government hands in rent-seeking behaviour. Meanwhile, the government spent this money largely on the elite and in the capital city.[12]

Rural life was thereby made poorer by the SLPMB because much peasant income was removed.[13] The schools and health facilities that were paid for out of their revenues tended to be found in cities and not in the countryside. This 'urban bias', was expressed by spending on urban infrastructure (electricity and paved roads were most evident), colour televisions, urban schooling, healthcare and barracks for the army and police (in order to keep them satisfied with the status quo).[14] The children of rural peasants died, or could not attend school, while the elite in Freetown lived in relative luxury – the big Sport Utility Vans (SUVs) were an obscene sign often mentioned in media reports.

2.3.2 Currency overvaluation

The manipulation of the exchange rate of the national currency is a major tool employed in the transfer of resources from rural to urban locations.[15] As long as the government 'overvalues' the currency, imported goods (mainly urban consumer and industrial goods) are relatively 'cheap', while exports (mainly rural cash crops) are relatively 'dear' (Lofchie 1997). In this sense, there is not an explicit and visible movement of resources; however, the result is the same. This overvaluation occurred from 1961 to 1985, while the currency was 'pegged' to the British pound. By the time it began to 'float' or 'devalue' from 1985 onwards, rural–urban transfer had been carried out; the taxing of agricultural exports was lessened – but it was too late. Besides, the cost of imports mounted markedly.[16]

2.3.3 Employment Growth

The government employs national revenue in order to create jobs in a growing bureaucracy and in parastatal (state-controlled) organizations involved in production, service provision, or infrastructure. As well as creating such patronage positions, urban unemployment could also be addressed and urban disquiet dampened. In fact, such employment was the country's sole growth industry, and it was a major issue of contention in the aborted IMF programmes of the 1980s.

2.3.4 Rice Prices

The government has subsidized the price of rice paid by Freetown residents for over half a century (Riddell 1985a). By setting a maximum level on the price of this basic commodity, they were in effect reducing living costs in the city. This price ceiling on rice was felt by peasants in the countryside in terms of the reduced producer price of rice – thus a reduced income level. The result of this has been a further subtle element of the rural-to-urban transfer. The resulting supply deficit was made up by the import of rice, paid out of national revenues.

Table 5.1 indicates many other methods of urban bias by which this rural–urban transfer was conducted. The 'rip off' was evident in the lives of the peasant, when compared to the city dweller – houses, services, infrastructure, standard of living, and health.[17] Such exploitation of the peasants had deep historical roots.[18]

The answer to why urban bias occurred is easy if you are like Robert Kaplan, who wrote about the chaos in Sierra Leone in *The Coming Anarchy* (2000). He seems to say that it was in the genes of Sierra Leoneans to behave violently, or that it was a matter of Third World people being unable to cope with modernization (Kaplan 1994). Actually, his argument is a bit more subtle, even if it does not address the 'why?' question, speaking instead to the issue of what is happening. It depicts the chaos and horror but lacks a realistic explanation. However, a more concrete explanation resides in understanding the 'why' issue – the answer is that the state acts as a redistribution mechanism. It is to consider how national economic development became perverted and transformed into a patronage system, with the tool of 'urban bias' becoming converted into 'elite bias'. The economic engine behind this was provided by the revenue which the country's mineral resources, especially diamonds, supplied.[19]

3 Conclusion: lessons of the Sierra Leone experience

The 'heart of the matter', therefore, is about political economy, policy and inequality, and it has deep historical roots and geographical expression. It includes a portable resource base (diamonds), disenchanted youth, and rent-seeking behaviour. Below are six lessons which can be drawn from the country's disaster. I am hesitant to generalize from one case and indicate the causes of conflict throughout the continent. There is much in Sierra Leone which is unique – the RUF, the personalities, the political context, the diamonds, and the colonial legacy. However, certain lessons (not rules!) can be drawn from this experience:[20]

1. A major implication of the events in Sierra Leone is that an integral element of development, betterment, or economic growth is national integration. All people and all ethnic groups must feel and act as if they are part of the nation-state. They bear the costs of this new entity and they must also share in the rewards. Too often reference is made to divisive factors such as ethnicity, locality, religion, and urbanization.[21] However, these issues must disappear and be replaced by national feeling, or they can continue as elements of self-identification, but must be secondary to national affiliation (see Chapter 10). The lesson is that no matter how difficult development is, all people, in all ethnic groups, in all parts of the country must be committed to the nation and its

development. For example, even with the return to multi-party politics in 1991, the peasant continued to have little voice, as party politics were dominated by the wealthy and powerful – i.e. not everyone was an equal shareholder in Sierra Leone. A tying together of the country and its people is made difficult because of the recency of Independence – and the fact that African states are 'artificial' creations of colonialism, and different ethnic or religious groups were melded together in the past in order to meet the needs of a distant colonial power. But national unity is also hampered by poverty, which means that the state is unable to provide social services everywhere and does not foster economic development evenly throughout the country. Also, the national economy largely obeys a global and neoliberal economy, policed by the WB and IMF. The lack of national integration in Sierra Leone was directly related to the rise of the RUF. The destruction and chaos that the movement caused unfortunately contained ways of earning a living, finding employment, and providing resources for the country's youth – ways of being integrated into this developing nation in a perverse manner.

2. The domination of state, government and economy by a predatory elite must be curbed. The care and feeding of such an elite has unfortunately dominated the political economy of Sierra Leone in the four decades since independence from colonialism. The accompanying exploitation of some people or areas has been very common throughout the African continent, and this neopatrimonial rule finds expression in descriptive phrases used to depict politics there such as 'the vampire state', 'the rentier state', 'kleptocracy', 'burden of the state' and 'politics of the belly' (Bayart 1993; Davidson 1992; Frimpong-Ansah 1991; Kandeh 2002; Leys 1996; Martinussen 1997). However, the indication of political manipulation goes only part of the way towards an explanation as lesson 3 below indicates. The winner is identified, but not the loser, nor the process of allotment.
3. The government's ability to act as a redistribution system via taxation and allocation must be ended, as well as the legacy of peasant exploitation. There would appear to be three components to such a remedy. First, peasant life could be improved by providing higher prices for the goods which they sell (Bates 1981, 1983, 1988; Mosley 2002). Second, a link must be made between urban demand for consumer items such as food and the countryside. Third, there is a need for the alteration of the extant political system from the present 'winner takes all' system. This fits in with lesson 2 – the removal of the elite – in the sense that they should not be allowed to use politics to tilt the commanding heights of the economy in their favour.
4. SAPs lead to a 'hollowing out' of the state – the removal of its regulatory authority. Because Stevens and the APC were able to avoid the hegemonic neoliberal agenda of the Washington Consensus with the use of revenue from minerals, they were able to practise their nefarious policies of urban-elite bias. When the mineral revenue was drastically reduced as was pre-empted by the 'shadow state', the RUF, and Taylor's Liberia, SAPs became the order of the day. During Stevens's years in power only one minor programme of the IMF was implemented (Weeks 1992),

and thus the hand of international finance was 'light' and didn't interfere with Stevens's patronage politics.[22] Because it was light the urban-elite system continued unchecked throughout the APC–Stevens reign and beyond. Thus the source of peasant disquiet was not addressed either by local (Sierra Leone government) or global (IMF/WB) forces. However, the fact that neither chose to address peasant disquiet is not propitious. The IMF loaned 'Emergency Post-Conflict Assistance' in both 1998 and 1999, and provided a team which investigated the country's economic circumstances in 2001.[23] In addition, the Government of Sierra Leone wrote 'Letters of Intent' to the organization in both 1999 and 2000. These five documents are complex economic planning instruments. They address items such as the national budget, export revenue, and indices of poverty. However, they do not address urban/elite bias. They are quiet about the causes of peasant unrest. Because they do not speak to them, the issues of peasant disquiet and government redistribution remain. I would not praise such SAPs. They do not result in the recovery and growth that their proponents indicate. Their devastation of the Third World has been pronounced (Glassman and Carmody 2001; Mohan *et al.* 2000; Riddell 1992) and they simply seem to ignore both capital flight and terms of trade, while making everyone pay the debts which have benefited the few. However, they do begin to remove one of the sources of peasant disquiet – urban bias policies and the disparities between peasants and the elite – even while exacerbating poverty by lessening the budgetary ability of the government to provide social services.

5. In Africa many conflicts revolve around resource extraction – diamonds in Sierra Leone, minerals in the Congo, oil and diamonds in Angola, oil in Sudan, etc. There are two sets of actors entangled in the process. On the one hand, there are multinational firms involved in oil extraction, gold mining, and diamond production. Their ethical concerns are not those of the African people or the betterment of African countries. These are side issues to the search for earnings or profits. On the other hand are the local organizations, such as the RUF in Sierra Leone. These are the agents of local warlords (Reno 1998b). They are not interested in victory; rather, the strife acts as a cover to their activities. The goal is not the winning of hearts and minds, but profit. The lesson is that in the quest for such profits by global firms and local actors, the latter's activities undermine and weaken the nations in which they occur.
6. Neither Sierra Leone nor the other countries of the region can look to the international community for a solution. One only needs to contrast the greater level of funding provided after Kosovo with the meagre funds provided for recovery in Sierra Leone to point to the fact that, British and UN (United Nations Mission in Sierra Leone) intervention notwithstanding, Africa is of only passing interest to the world, at its margins. Similarly, the heavy involvement of ECOMOG was an expression of Nigerian regional aspirations (see Chapter 6), while the IMF and WB were not represented on the ground at the time, although the Bank has since made its presence felt locally (Hirsch 2001). Significantly, too, international diamond marketing remains an enigma.

Events in Sierra Leone underline the vital importance of certain issues. First, there needs to be a method for controlling multinational companies involved in resource extraction throughout the Third World; 'blood diamonds' have funded the disaster, funded the RUF, led to great profits for the likes of Taylor in Liberia, and provided the context for Sierra Leone's horror.[24] Resource exploitation has become the fate of many African nations as the continent has unfortunately become the periphery of the world's periphery.

As well as the external context, which has resulted in poverty for most people and great wealth for a few, internal factors within African countries are also vital considerations. With diminishing revenue, the struggle for access to a diminishing economic pie becomes more intense within the political arena which controls economic access. Such political-economic power underlies peasant disquiet which, when combined with the corrupt, unethical, and public–private conversion behaviour of the national elite, goes far in accounting for the chaos.

The country must have foreign support to overcome the past decade. Sierra Leone's cupboard is bare! Government offices and records were destroyed. Funds were looted. The country and its people, its economy, and its infrastructure lie in ruins. The leaders of post-conflict Sierra Leone need support. The World Bank and other 'development partners' possess much-needed resources, and talk the talk of development. Most of the Third World continues in poverty, despite decades and volumes of rhetoric. Now is the time for the Bank to walk the walk and recognize that underdevelopment reflects both internal and external forces.

Notes

1. Rice, the basic foodstuff, has become a luxury because of its high cost – and this is vital, given rice's symbolic value.
2. For example, a health survey conducted in the 1970s indicates infant mortality rates in rural areas to be much higher than those for Freetown –33 per cent vs. 20 per cent (cited in Riddell, 1985a: 531).
3. On each of my four research visits in Sierra Leone, I have been inundated by media reports and official government documents – the worst such expression was the spending priority reported in the budget, which was incorrect and acted as a method of hiding reality. These masking instruments were part of an array of tools employed to hide the exploitation taking place. Indeed, this rhetoric is but a mellow expression, for violence, intimidation, murder, disappearance, bribery, and political manipulation were also employed. Siaka Stevens's operations were confusing and obfuscating because he effectively combined being a friendly father figure with an authoritarian iron fist.
4. The document contrasts the country's wealth of natural resources and how most people live in 'state sponsored squalor', and depicts the elite as 'an organized bunch of criminals', 'inefficient, irresponsible and corrupt.' In essence, it explains why it feels that the Sierra Leone state had to be destroyed. In reality, however, the RUF was an intellectual void, for this statement is partly plagiarized and partly penned by outsiders. Abdullah and Muana (1998) have observed that '[t]he RUF . . . defied all available typologies on guerilla movements. It [was] neither a separatist uprising rooted in a specific demand, as in

the case of Eritrea, nor a reformist movement with a radical agenda superior to the regime it sought to overthrow. Nor d[id] it possess the kind of leadership that would be necessary to designate it as [a] warlord insurgency. The RUF . . . made history; it [wa]s a peculiar guerilla movement without any significant national following or ethnic support. Perhaps because of its lumpen social base and its lack of an emancipatory programme to garner support from other social groups, it . . . remained a bandit organization solely driven by the survivalist needs of its predominantly uneducated and alienated battle front and battle group commanders. Neither the peasantry, the natual ally of most revolutionary movements, nor the students, amongst whose ranks the RUF-to-be originated, lent any support to the organization during its . . . years of fighting'.

5. There are several 'objective' explanations as to why such redistribution takes place: these include the colonial legacy which tended in the past to use the city as a control point and focus, the fear of the urban mob who tend to riot or revolt if lifestyles deteriorate, the fact that textbooks on development and histories of now-developed countries told of urban concentration, and also self-interest – i.e. the fact that the government personnel and supporters tended to reside there.
6. Stevens inherited a legacy of British colonial command, which was characterized by authoritarian rule and plunder, while the Independent government of Albert Margai certainly established the beginnings of a corrupt state. However, Stevens's kleptocracy should not be excused. He wrote a highly biased version of his tenure (see Stevens 1984).
7. Reno (1998b) estimated that he amassed some $500M, while Boas (2001: 708) characterizes him as a 'perfect form of neopatrimonial ruler'; and Kandeh (2002, 180) depicts his rule as that which 'transformed Sierra Leone into one of the world's leading producers of human misery', and goes on to characterize his period of rule: 'He envisioned himself as the head of the extended Sierra Leonean family and claimed roots in all major ethnic groups. He cultivated the picture of himself as "Pa Siakie", the father of the nation'.
8. There were many organizations acting as 'dogs of war', 'corporate troubleshooters', or 'soldiers of fortune'; some were clandestine, but the major armies for hire included Gurkha Security Guards, Executive Outcomes, and Sandline International. The paymasters are not known.
9. World Bank sponsorship of such projects in 1972, 1975, 1981, and again in 1981 amounted to $34.8 million. They were a vital part of the government's image of concern for rural areas, though the main focus of these was upon marketed production and not upon improving the lives of most peasants.
10. The vocabulary employed varied from 'declared ineligible' to 'cancelled after the first tranche' but in reality the international organizations backed away because of corruption and ineffective economic policies. For example, the 1986 Programme of the IMF and the reason for its suspension can be found in Longhurst *et al.* (1988).
11. Two examples of the usual set of conditions partly illustrate what would have happened: 'trade liberalization' removes the protection which sheltered urban enterprise in business and production; and 'downsizing bureaucracy' lessens the government's ability to employ patronage, while also leading to urban unemployment and unrest.
12. One index was the allocation (spending) under the country's National Development Plan of 1974/5–1978/9 (i.e. during Stevens's rule). At that time the peasant population included approximately 75 per cent of the population, but agricultural spending totalled only 17.1 per cent of the allocations for development during the five-year period. Further, these funds were employed in an

attempt to stimulate cash-crop production on commercial ventures, not to assist peasant subsistence production (Riddell 1985b).
13. The World Bank (1994) indicates that over the 1981–3 to 1989–91 period producer prices fell by 62 per cent. Mosely (2002: 178) indicates that such a 'Bates wedge' (the difference between export and producer prices) was a common strategy in 18 'peasant export economies' of Sub-Saharan Africa (see Bates 1981, 1983, 1988).
14. As well, funds went toward items such as a sports complex, foreign embassies, tourist hotels, and preparations for the then forthcoming Organization of African Unity (OAU) meetings to be held in Freetown in 1981 (Riddell 1985b).
15. In fact, the World Bank indicated that over the period between 1981/3 and 1989/91 agricultural 'taxation' increased by 33.4 per cent, largely due to exchange rate manipulation (World Bank 1994: 245).
16. For example, according to the exchange rate in effect on 30 April 2001, an item purchased abroad and imported to Freetown which had cost one leone in December 1967, would have cost 1695 leones on 30 April 2001. (Exchange rates as recorded in the magazine, *West Africa* (2001), **4273**.) 'Black market' exchange rates differ; however, the dimensions of the cost differential are evident.
17. For example, a health survey published in 1978 indicated the following urban–rural differences (figures are percentages):

    1. infant mortality rates, in Freetown = 20.0, in Rural = 33.3;
    2. significantly underweight children, in Freetown = 18.3, in Rural = 32.4;
    3. malaria parasites in blood, in Freetown = 4.0, in Rural = 36.2; and
    4. chronically undernourished children, in Freetown = 10.3, in Rural = 26.6

    (Government of Sierra Leone and the United States Agency for International Development, 1978).
18. In fact, the Sierra Leone Peoples' Party (SLPP), the political party which formed the first post-independence government, was founded in 1951 in order to give voice to the rural people who had felt such deprivation. The colonial treatment of the urban (Freetown) and rural areas differed, and was solidified in the Colony–Protectorate dichotomy of the years of British colonial rule.
19. Diamond production began in 1935 and has provided an annual export averaging 1 million carats (reaching 2 million in 1970). However, this national economic engine which at Independence provided most of the government's revenue was reduced by the 1980s to a mere trickle – for example, by 1988 official exports were reduced to a mere 48,000 carats.
20. Cramer (2002) indicates the commonalities and uniquenesses of the armed conflicts that occurred in Sub-Saharan Africa in the decades of the 1980s and 90s; he indicates that causal generalities are 'fuzzy' and indicates (p. 72) 'the single greatest need here is for further individual and comparative case-study research.'
21. A distressing fact is that when political/military appointments are discussed in Sierra Leone, reference is made to ethnic origins. Even most national political parties are regarded as having an ethnic base.
22. Stevens avoided IMF programmes in that they have been associated with coups, demonstrations, and riots as the cost of living mounts, services are reduced, and employment is cut.
23. As well, the World Bank has invested $65m in three rehabilitation projects since December 1999 and also provided $100m in emergency aid in 1998.
24. As the following quote indicates, the conflict diamonds initiative was designed to tackle this problem: 'On 1 December 2000, the United Nations General Assembly adopted, unanimously, a resolution on the role of diamonds in fuelling conflict, breaking the link between the illicit transaction of rough dia-

monds and armed conflict, as a contribution to prevention and settlement of conflicts (A/RES/55/56). In taking up this agenda item, the General Assembly recognized that conflict diamonds are a crucial factor in prolonging brutal wars in parts of Africa, and underscored that legitimate diamonds contribute to prosperity and development elsewhere on the continent. In Angola and Sierra Leone, conflict diamonds continue to fund the rebel groups, the National Union for the Total Independence of Angola (UNITA) and the Revolutionary United Front (RUF), both of which are acting in contravention of the international community's objectives of restoring peace in the two countries' (http://www.un.org/peace/africa/Diamond. html).

References

Abdullah, I. (1998), 'Bush path to destruction: The origin and character of the Revolutionary United Front/Sierra Leone', *Journal of Modern African Studies* **36,** 203–36.

Abdullah, I. and **Muana, P.** (1998), 'The Revolutionary United Front: a revolt of the lumpenproletariat', in Clapham, C. (ed.), *African Guerillas*. James Currey, Oxford.

Bah, A.M.S. (2000), 'Diamonds and mercenaries: exploring the dynamics of the Sierra Leone conflict', *Peacekeeping and International Relations* **29(1)**, 1–6.

Bangura, Y. (2000), 'Strategic policy failure and governance in Sierra Leone', *Journal of Modern African Studies* **38(4)**, 551–77.

Bates, R.H. (1981), *Markets and States in Tropical Africa*. University of California Press, Berkeley, California.

Bates, R.H. (1983), 'The nature and origins of agricultural policies in Africa' in Bates, R. (ed.), *Essays on the Political Economy of Rural Africa*. Cambridge University Press, Cambridge.

Bates, R.H. (1988), 'Governments and agricultural markets in Africa' in Bates, R. (ed.), *Toward a Political Economy of Development*. University of California Press, Berkeley, California.

Bayart, J. (1993), *The State in Africa: The Politics of the Belly*. Longman, London.

Becker, C.M., Hamer, A.M. and **Morrison, A.R.** (1994), *Beyond Urban Bias in Africa: Urbanization in an Era of Structural Adjustment*. James Currey and Heinemann, London and Portsmouth, New Hampshire.

Boas, M. (2001), 'Liberia and Sierra Leone – dead ringers? The logic of neopatrimonial rule', *Third World Quarterly* **22(5)**, 697–723.

Chabal, P. and **Daloz, J.-P.** (1999), *Africa Works: Disorder as Political Instrument*. James Currey and Indiana University Press, Oxford and Bloomington, Indiana.

Cramer, C. (2002), 'The economics and political economy of conflict in sub-Saharan Africa' in Belshaw, D. and Livingstone, I. (eds), *Renewing Development in Sub-Saharan Africa*. Routledge, London and New York.

Davidson, B. (1992), *The Black Man's Burden: Africa and the Curse of the Nation-State*. Times Books, New York.

Frimpong-Ansah, J.H. (1991), *The Vampire State: The Political Economy of Decline in Ghana*. James Currey, Oxford.

Glassman, J. and **Carmody, P.** (2001), 'Structural adjustment in east and southeast Asia: lessons from Latin America', *Geoforum* **32(1)**, 77–90.

Government of Sierra Leone and the United States Agency for International Development (1978), *Sierra Leone: National Nutrition Survey*. Nutrition Assessment Unit, Division of Population, Family and International Health, School of Public Health, University of California, Los Angeles, California.

Hirsch, J.L. (2001), *Sierra Leone: Diamonds and the Struggle for Democracy*. Lynne Rienner, Boulder, Colorado and London.

Hyden, G. (1980), *Beyond Ujamaa in Tanzania*. Heinemann, London.

Kandeh, J.D. (2002), 'Subaltern terror in Sierra Leone' in Zack-Willliams, T., Frost D. and Thomson, A. (eds), *Africa in Crisis: New challenges and possibilities*. Pluto Press, London and Sterling, Vancouver.

Kaplan, R.D. (1994), 'The coming anarchy: How scarcity, crime, overpopulation, tribalism and disease are rapidly destroying the social fabric of our planet', *The Atlantic Monthly*, February, 44–76.

Kaplan, R.D. (2000), *The Coming Anarchy: Shattering the Dreams of the Post-Cold War*. Random House, New York.

Leys, C. (1996), *The Rise and Fall of Development Theory*. Indiana University Press and EAEP and James Currey, Bloomington, Indiana, Nairobi and London.

Lofchie, M. (1997), 'The Rise and demise of urban-biased development policies in Africa' in Gugler, J. (ed.), *Cities in the Developing World: Issues, Theory, and Policy*. Oxford University Press, Oxford.

Longhurst, R., Kamara, S. and **Mensurah, J.** (1988), 'Structural adjustment and vulnerable groups in Sierra Leone', *Institute of Development Studies Bulletin* **19(1)**, 25–30.

Luke, D.F. and **Riley, S.P.** (1989), 'The politics of economic decline in Sierra Leone', *Journal of Modern African Studies* **27(1)**, 133–41.

Martinussen, J. (1997), *Society, State and Market: A Guide to the Competing Theories of Development*. Zed Books, London and Atlantic Highlands, New Jersey.

Mohan, G., Brown, E., Milward, B. and **Zack-Williams, A.B.** (2000), *Structural Adjustment: Theory, Practice and Impacts*. Routledge, London and New York.

Mosley, P. (2002), 'Agricultural marketing in Africa since Berg and Bates' in Belshaw, D. and Livingstone, I. (eds), *Renewing Development in Sub-Saharan Africa: Policy, Performance and Prospects*. Routledge, London and New York.

Partnership Africa Canada (PAC) (2000a), *The Heart of the Matter: Sierra Leone, Diamonds and Human Security*. Partnership Africa Canada, Ottawa, Ontario.

Partnership Africa Canada (PAC) (2000b), *Sierra Leone One Year After the Peace Accord: The Search for Peace, Justice and Sustainable Development*. Partnership Africa Canada, Ottawa, Ontario.

Reno, W. (1995a), *Corruption and State Politics in Sierra Leone*. Cambridge University Press, Cambridge.

Reno, W. (1995b), 'Markets, war, and the reconfiguration of political authority in Sierra Leone', *Canadian Journal of African Studies* **29(2)**, 203–21.

Reno, W. (1996), 'Ironies of post-Cold War structural adjustment in Sierra Leone', *Review of African Political Economy* **67**, 7–18.

Reno, W. (1998a), 'Sierra Leone: weak states and the new sovereignty game' in Villalon, L.A. and Huxtable, P.A. (eds), *The African State at a Critical Juncture: Between Disintegration and Reconfiguration.* Lynne Rienner, Boulder, Colorado and London.

Reno, W. (1998b), *Warlord Politics and African States.* Lynne Rienner, Boulder, Colorado and London.

Reno, W. (2000), 'No Peace for Sierra Leone', *Review of African Political Economy* **84**, 325–9.

Reno, W. (2001), 'The failure of peacekeeping in Sierra Leone', *Current History* **100(5)**, 219–55.

Richards, P. (1996), *Fighting for the Rain Forest: War, Youth and Resources in Sierra Leone.* James Currey and Heinemann, Oxford and Portsmouth, New Hampshire.

Richards, P. (2001), 'Youth, food and peace: a reflection on some African security issues at the millennium' in Zack-Williams, T., Frost, D. and Thomson, A. (eds), *Africa in Crisis.* Pluto Press, London and Sterling, Vancouver.

Riddell, J.B. (1985a), 'Beyond the geography of modernization: The state as a redistribution mechanism in independent Sierra Leone', *Canadian Journal of African Studies* **19(3)**, 529–45.

Riddell, J.B. (1985b), 'Internal and external forces acting upon disparities in Sierra Leone', *The Journal of Modern African Studies* **23(3)**, 389–406.

Riddell, J.B. (1985c), 'Urban bias in underdevelopment: appropriation from the countryside in post-colonial Sierra Leone', *Tijdschrift voor Economische En Sociale Geografie* **76(5)**, 374–82.

Riddell, J.B. (1992), 'Things fall apart again: structural adjustment programmes in sub-Saharan Africa', *The Journal of Modern African Studies* **30(1)**, 53–68.

Riddell, B. (1997), 'Structural adjustment programmes and the city in tropical Africa', *Urban Studies* **34(8)**, 1297–307.

Riley, S.P. (1996), *Liberia and Sierra Leone: Anarchy or Peace in West Africa?* Conflict Studies 287 Research Institute for the Study of Conflict and Terrorism (RISCT), London.

Riley, S.P. (1997), 'Sierra Leone: the militariat strikes again', *Review of African Political Economy* **72**, 287–92.

Riley, S.P. and **Sesay, M.** (1995), 'Sierra Leone: the coming anarchy?', *Review of African Political Economy* **63**, 121–6.

Stevens, S. (1984), *What Life has Taught Me.* Kensal House, London.

Weeks, J. (1992), *Development Strategy and the Economy of Sierra Leone.* Macmillan and St. Martin's, Houndsmills and New York.

World Bank (1994), *Adjustment in Africa: Reforms, Results, and the Road Ahead.* Oxford University Press, New York.

Zack-Williams, A.B. and **Riley, S.** (1993), 'Sierra Leone: the coup and its consequences', *Review of African Political Economy* **56**, 91–8.

Zack-Williams, A.B. (1990), 'Sierra Leone: crisis and despair', *Review of African Political Economy* **49**, 22–33.

Zack-Williams, A.B. (1992), 'Sierra Leone: the deepening crisis and survival strategies' in Nyang'oro, J.E. and Shaw, T.M. (eds), *Beyond Structural Adjustment in Africa*. Praeger, New York, Westport, Connecticut and London.

Zack-Williams, A.B. (1997a), '"Kamajors", "Sobel" and the militariat: the return of the military in Sierra Leone politics', *Review of African Political Economy* **73**, 373–80.

Zack-Williams, A.B. (1997b), 'Labor, structural adjustment, and democracy in Sierra Leone and Ghana' in Siddiqui, R.A. (ed.), *Subsaharan Africa in the 1990s: Challenges to Democracy and Development*. Praeger, London and Westport, Connecticut.

Zack-Williams, A.B. (1999), 'Sierra Leone: the political economy of civil war, 1991–98', *Third World Quarterly* **20(1)**, 143–62.

Zack-Williams, A.B. (2001), 'Child soldiers in the civil war in Sierra Leone', *Review of African Political Economy* **87**, 73–82.

Websites

Information on Sierra Leone can be found at <www.sierra-leone.org>.
PAC maintains the website www.partnershipafricacanada.org.

CHAPTER 6

Expanding the frontiers of integration: regional economic and security dynamics

David J. Francis

1 Introduction

This chapter explores the evolution and transformation of regional economic co-operation and integration, in particular the expansion of the frontiers of economic integration into security regionalism.[1] The transformation of contemporary world politics since the early 1990s, allied with the effects of globalisation, have converted West Africa into the new theatre of violent intra-state conflicts, with devastating consequences for regional peace, security, economic development and social progress. Civil wars and conflicts have reversed the developmental and economic gains of decades of regional integration and co-operation (Sahel and West Africa Club 2002). These have not only stretched the capacity of the 15-member Economic Community of West African States (ECOWAS) (the region's foremost institution for economic integration) in managing and resolving these intra-state conflicts, but have also undermined the possibility of achieving the common market objectives of the regional organisation.

Arguably, the pursuit of economic integration and regional co-operation cannot be divorced from the wider context of peace and security; there can be no long-term development, sustained economic growth and lasting peace in the face of war and protracted socio-political conflict. Indeed, the achievement of the ECOWAS objectives of integration and co-operation, as well as the establishment of the foundations for long-term economic growth and sustainable development, are only possible under conditions of regional peace and stability. As the Sahel and West Africa Club (2002: 3–4) has recently noted, '[v]iolent conflict constitutes one of the most severe threats to development and, indeed, existence. It compromises governance systems, threatens people's lives and health, limits their livelihoods and economic activities, makes more uncertain . . . agricultural production, and severely undermines market access and economic competitiveness.' Herein lies the nexus between economic and security regionalism in West Africa. This chapter examines this link through the prism of ECOWAS regionalism, and the latter's expansion into conflict intervention and management, on the one hand, and the ECOWAS Cease-fire Monitoring Group (ECOMOG), on the other.

2 Regional political economy[2]

The 'geographical expression' that is West Africa is a 'region' which exhibits a diverse range of historical, ethnic, cultural, political, economic, religious, ecological, and linguistic characteristics, and has a trilingual European cultural heritage (anglophone, francophone and lusophone), itself a product of colonialism (Ajibewa 2002). Modern state power in these countries is, to a very large extent, a reflection of colonial power, and is based on bureaucratic control and exploitation of trading and production relations by the ruling and governing classes. In the majority of cases, ethnicity continues to play a significant role in the nature of domestic politics and in the struggle for control of state power. With the notable exception of Guinea Bissau, where an armed struggle, led by the PAIGC (Partido Africano da Independência da Guiné e Cabo Verde) against Portuguese colonialism, was necessary to achieve independence, West African countries achieved political independence in a relatively peaceful manner, through political agitation and the mobilisation of nationalist fervour against colonial rule.

Contact with European imperialism incorporated West African economies into the capitalist world system, primarily as producers of raw materials. Thus 'cash crop' economies are organised around products like coffee, palm oil, cassava, cocoa, groundnuts and pineapples, while 'extractive' (mineral) economies depend on strategic resources such as oil, diamonds, bauxite, iron ore, tin, zinc, copper, uranium, gold, rutile and manganese. As export economies, countries in the region do not have control over externally-determined market prices for their products. This partly explains their peripheral status in the world economy. It also partly accounts for the limitations on independent socio-economic development in these countries. Uneven regional economic development is reflected in the urban and coastal focus of the majority of these economies, as well as accounting for intra-regional patterns of migration, and contributing to regional conflicts of economic interest within and amongst these states (Ajibewa 2002; Dunn 1978).

Efforts at industrialisation should have been a means of diversifying the economic base of the sub-region, but have been hindered by poor or inadequate infrastructure, as well as a lack of technological development and manufacturing expertise, on the one hand, and inordinately heavy reliance on multinational corporations (MNCs) and bilateral economic co-operation with Western governments, on the other. Arguably just as important, countries do not only 'produce the same things', which compete with each other in national markets within the region, but there is also 'little or no linkage between the manufacturing sector and other sectors such as agriculture' (Ajibewa 2002: 5). Furthermore, with less than 10 per cent of official trade being intra-regional, national economies are often in competition with each other for external trading partners, markets, foreign capital and technology.

Although West African economies, like others in the global South, experienced healthy economic growth during the 1960s and 1970s, a combination of external and domestic factors produced unfavourable economic conditions and promoted underdevelopment during the 1980s and 1990s. This forced most governments to implement IMF/World Bank Structural Adjustment Programmes (SAPs), with specific economic objectives and stringent conditionalities. The experiment with SAPs has not generated widespread or sustained economic growth and development, has not reduced gender and spatial inequalities, and has not led to an improvement in the material conditions of existence of the majority of West Africa's peoples, some of whom number among the world's poorest (Brydon and Legge 2000; Olukoshi 1998; 2003).

In political terms, the immediate post-independence experiment with democratic pluralism, based largely on the political systems of former colonial powers was replaced, for the most part, by centralised and undemocratic regimes and dictatorships, leading to a succession of military coups. The tidal wave of political liberalisation in post-Cold War West Africa, supported by Western governments and international financial institutions such as the IMF and World Bank, swept away one-partyism and some of the autocratic regimes. In states like Liberia, Mali, Sierra Leone and Guinea Bissau, this led in part to political instability, civil war and state collapse. Indeed, state implosion and its effects on regional peace and security have led writers such as Robert Kaplan (1994: 46) to paint a rather pessimistic vision of post-Cold War West Africa, which is reportedly:

> becoming the symbol of world wide democratic, environmental and societal stress, in which criminal anarchy emerges as the real 'strategic' danger. Disease, overpopulation, unprovoked crime, scarcity of resources, refugee migrations, the increasing erosion of nation-states and international borders, and the empowerment of private armies, security firms, and international drug cartels are now most tellingly demonstrated through a West Africa prism.

Although Kaplan's 'The Coming Anarchy' (1994) raised some serious security issues facing West Africa, it is, however, an exaggerated account. What is indisputable is that post-Cold War West Africa exhibits contradictory elements of reversal (civil wars, poverty, economic underdevelopment, etc.) and renewal. Far from 'reverting to the Africa of the Victorian atlas' portrayed by Kaplan, West Africa has re-invented itself by taking responsibility for solving some of its regional problems, albeit with qualified success.

In political economic terms, West African countries are marginalised in both the international divisions of labour and power; as developing, or least developed states, they operate within a set of international rules and regulations fashioned by the dominant capitalist economies (Dickson 1997). The economic and political vulnerabilities of West African states explain their propensity for external dependence. These states have therefore had to devise strategies for coping in an unfavourable international economic and political system, and, since the 1990s, have had to face the complex challenges of intra-state wars and conflicts, and regional instability. Not surprisingly, even though none of the articles in its founding Treaty mentions sub-regional defence and security, ECOWAS has become much more effective at managing regional conflicts than at progressing economic integration (Frempong 2003; Uche 2001).

3 Background to ECOWAS (Economic Community of West African States) integration

In general, a variety of factors, both external and domestic, were responsible for the initiation of a West African integration project (Frempong 2003). Economic imperatives were a driving force in the creation of a West Africa-wide community, as regional states perceived the formation of an economic community as a strategy for national and regional development. Economic integration was seen as a means of overcoming the disadvantage of small size and, through the benefit of economies of scale associated with a large regional consumer market of over 200 million people, providing opportunities for enhanced economic growth and development. Region-wide economic integration was seen as the best means of maximising the economic advantages to be derived from economies of scale, comparative advantage and complementarity of goods. A further economic motivation stemmed from the desire to industrialise and advance technological progress that would generate trade expansion and stimulate economic growth and the productive capacity of the region. The idea of a regional economic bloc that would serve as a collective bargaining platform alongside other economic blocs in the world, within the context of the New International Economic Order (NIEO) of the 1970s, also provided a powerful motivation. These are economic motivations which are generally shared by regional integration projects in other world regions.

Political motivations were also crucial in the creation of a West African economic community. Economic regionalism was perceived as a route to the creation of a political bloc that would enhance the political leverage of regional states *as a group*. It was generally acknowledged that the formation of a West African economic community would provide a political platform for the sub-region to play an influential role in continental politics and broader Cold War power politics. It was assumed, not only that a West African community would provide the institutional political framework to conduct the international relations of the sub-region, but also that a regional community would provide a forum to pursue independent foreign policy strategies under the umbrella of a regional bloc, while at the same time sourcing foreign aid resources.

Pan-West African solidarity also served as a motivating factor. The ideology of Pan-Africanism served as an attractive political motivation for West African leaders, who proposed the formation of regional economic and technical co-operation schemes as the basis for a gradual movement towards African political unity. Concerns for national and regional security, political leverage derived from collective bargaining, and the domestic political considerations of all the member states played a significant part in the evolution of West African economic regionalism.

The motivation behind the formation of a West African economic community needs to be situated within the wider context of the ideology of South–South co-operation, which had its roots in the dissatisfaction with North–South relations and the perception of Southern marginalisation within the international division of labour and of power. As the Third World perceived the structure of international economic relations, designed and maintained by the North, as responsible for their marginalisation and permanent peripheral status in the global economy, member-countries demanded a New International Economic Order (NIEO) that would serve as an alternative to the liberal international economic order that was advantageous to the North. The Arab–Israeli war in 1973, and subsequent OPEC price rises, provided political and economic leverage for the main oil producers in the South. The OPEC action provided a political forum for united action, where the countries of the South 'could exercise commodity power over the North' (Dickson 1997: 25).

The NIEO debate thus became crystallised in the Third World ideology of empowering the South in the international system. The demonstration effects of OPEC's political power provided a rallying point for regional economic blocs in the South. In particular, the failure of the NIEO to bring about any significant transformation in the structure of international economic relations between the North and the South, motivated Third World countries, including those in West Africa, to focus on bilateral and regional co-operation arrangements for economic development and progress. South–South co-operation was therefore seen as a viable collective strategy based on self-reliance, and a means to surmount the imbalance of the North–South divide, whilst at the same time making the international system more responsive to the needs of the South. West African states, like the majority of Third World countries, therefore clung to the ideology of Third World or Southern empowerment, admittedly mostly half-heartedly, as an alternative form of political and economic expression.

Significantly, too, West African states have a long tradition of functional co-operation which dates back to the pre-colonial period. Historical evidence points to the fact that there existed an 'integrative habit' in pre-colonial West Africa, with co-operative efforts between regional kingdoms and city-states, involving economic and commercial ventures, and encompassing the watersheds of the Senegal and Mano rivers, as well as the Lake Chad basin. Indeed, Walraven (1991: 111), for example, speaks of widely-developed trade networks spanning a region which boasted 'one of the most advanced trade- and agriculture-based economies on the continent'. The tradition of functional co-operation was further strengthened during the colonial era when administrative, economic and political expediencies forced colonial governments to establish inter-territorial and intra-regional politico-administrative and economic structures.[3] In 1946, for instance, the French created a government of the Federation of French West Africa (AOF), and a francophone West African Customs Union, with a centralised common currency, the CFA franc zone, the convertibility of which was guaranteed by France in 1962. The British, for their part, organised common services in anglophone West Africa, and created the West African Currency Board, as well as the West African Produce Board, to handle the marketing and management of agricultural products.

A number of these arrangements, such as the monetary union between francophone West African countries and France, extended into the post-colonial era. French West Africa, drawing on a common history of functional co-operation, was instrumental in the establishment of several economic unions, including: the Niger River Commission (RNC); the Chad Basin Commission (CBC); the Union Monétaire de l'Ouest Africain (UMOA); the Union Douanière de l'Afrique de l'Ouest (UDEAO); the Organisation of Senegal River States (OERS); the Senegambia Confederation, and the Communauté de l'Afrique de l'Ouest (CEAO). It can be argued that the habit of co-operation, established during the pre-colonial and colonial periods, laid the foundation for economic regionalism in post-independence West Africa.

Nigeria, the driving force behind the creation of a West Africa-wide economic community, was motivated by a variety of domestic, regional and international considerations, the majority of which were economic, political and strategic in nature. The influence of a combination of rich strategic resources and numerical strength (it is Africa's most populous nation) apart, two events shaped Nigeria's leadership role in the formation of a West African regional economic community in an area which it regards as its 'natural' sphere of political and economic influence. First, the Biafran civil war of 1967–1970 established the link between national security and regional security. The war was a turning point in Nigeria's history in that it shifted the country's foreign and security policy orientation from 'isolationism' to 'interventionism' in regional affairs. Second, the oil crisis of 1973 brought Nigeria into the international limelight because of its strategic oil resources. Nigeria became an indispensable oil producer for the West, and used the forum provided by OPEC to flex its political muscle in African and international affairs. Oil diplomacy became a major instrument of Nigerian foreign policy, with the country's civil war history and strategic oil resources strengthening its leadership ambitions in West Africa. This reinforced Nigeria's self-image as the country with a 'manifest destiny' to lead the region.

Nigeria's leadership role in the formation of ECOWAS was therefore in pursuit of the traditional ends of politics: power, prestige and political influence. West African economic regionalism was to provide Nigeria with a platform for a more activist diplomacy in African affairs. Furthermore, Nigeria's West African leadership role was geared towards limiting French influence (which rivals Nigeria's for leadership) in the sub-region. As Nigeria has always regarded French influence in West Africa as a threat to its own national security and political independence, an economic integration project under its leadership was perceived as a counter-weight to French influence (see also Chapter 2).

Given its considerable economic, military and political involvement in the sub-region which dates back to the colonial period, France is the most influential extra-regional actor in West African integration. Indeed, France has consistently discouraged *effective* socio-economic and political co-operation between francophone and anglophone West Africa in the post-Independence era, largely because it considers francophone West Africa as the centrepiece of its African foreign policy. Thus for Olatunde Ojo (1980), France has been overtly anti-integration. Not surprisingly, regional francophone states have maintained a series of interlocking post-colonial relationships in the form of economic and technical co-operation, all of which have been largely dependent on France. However, France's anti-integration stance appeared to have strengthened the resolve of anglophone West Africa in bringing about the formation of a region-wide economic community.

4 The formation of ECOWAS (1972–1975)

The formation of ECOWAS was the result of a complex combination of regional factors and initiatives. The late President Tubman of Liberia can be credited with leading the diplomatic and political initiative for the creation of an economic community. In a speech on 7 January 1964 he introduced the idea of a free trade area in West Africa, and, subsequently, organised a series of bilateral and multilateral consultations with other West African governments to discuss the possibility of creating a free trade zone. The Liberian initiative encouraged the United Nations Economic Commission for Africa (UN-ECA) to organise a West African free trade summit in Monrovia in 1968. The francophone states did not attend the summit. Between 1965 and 1972, all attempts to create a regional economic community were unsuccessful, as the political divide between the francophone and anglophone West African states, a clash of national interests, and complex geopolitics hindered the formation of ECOWAS, despite the institutional support of the UN-ECA for the project.

General Gowon of Nigeria and President Eyadema of Togo could be credited with spearheading the campaign for the formation of ECOWAS. The creation of the CEAO in 1972, which excluded anglophone countries and gave observer status to Togo, brought a new diplomatic impetus from the two leaders. In the post-civil war era, the Gowon government made a determined effort to win over francophone interests that had supported the Biafra secessionists. To counter the political influence of the francophone grouping, Gowon proposed an all-West African economic community and, in collaboration with Togo, formed the Nigeria–Togo embryonic West African Economic Community (WAEC) in 1972; membership was open to all countries in the region. This led effectively to the emergence of two rival economic groupings in the region: the CEAO, whose membership was exclusively francophone; and the Nigeria–Togo union, which was to serve as the basis for a more inclusive West African community. In the interim, in 1973, the Mano River Union (MRU), linking the anglophone states of Liberia and Sierra Leone, was established (Guinea would join the union in 1980).

A series of meetings of West African states from 1964 to 1975 led directly to the establishment of ECOWAS, with the support for an all-West African economic community generated by Togo, Dahomey (Benin) and Niger creating the momentum for other francophone states, particularly Senegal and Côte d'Ivoire, to join the organisation. The ECOWAS Treaty was signed in Lagos on 28 May 1975 by the original fifteen member states. Cape Verde, the sixteenth member, joined in 1977, following independence from Portugal.[4] The realist political pursuits of West African states are reflected in their political gains from the formation of ECOWAS: 'Big brother' Nigeria and Togo secured the rights to host the ECOWAS

Secretariat and Fund, respectively, while Côte d'Ivoire provided the new organisation's first Executive Secretary. This set the stage for the future politics of regionalism in West Africa, and ECOWAS's domination by the 'big' countries like Nigeria, Côte d'Ivoire, Ghana and Senegal. The formation of ECOWAS provided a major organisational framework for regional economic integration and political co-operation (Asante 1986; Francis 2001).[5]

5 The main features of the ECOWAS Treaty: aims, objectives and institutional framework

The primary objective was to establish a common market with a focus on trade liberalisation, harmonisation of economic policies and the removal of barriers to the free movement of factors of production, i.e. people, goods and services. It proposed to achieve this in 'stages', through the establishment of a:

- free trade area with no tariff (quantitative and qualitative restrictions) on intra-regional trade
- customs union with no intra-regional tariff, but a common external tariff towards third countries
- common market allowing free movement of the factors of production; and
- economic integration that would harmonise the economic, monetary, fiscal, and agricultural policies of the community.

The aims of the Community outlined in Article 2 of the 1975 Treaty also proposed to undertake sectoral development programmes in areas such as industry, transport and communication, energy and infrastructural development (ECOWAS 1975).[6] To achieve the objective of monetary integration and equitable distribution of the benefits of economic integration and co-operation, the Treaty proposed to establish a fund for co-operation, compensation and development. Clearly, like the majority of economic integration schemes, ECOWAS's economic objectives are protectionist and exclusionary.

The institutional mechanisms charged with administering and directing the affairs of the ECOWAS Community include: the authority of Heads of State and Government; Council of Ministers, Executive Secretary; Fund for Co-operation and Development; Tribunal of the Community; and the ECOWAS Parliament. A variety of specialised commissions have been established, including: the Trade, Customs, Taxation Statistics, Monetary and Payments Commission; the Industry, Agriculture and National Resources Commission; the Transport, Telecommunications and Energy Commission; the Social and Cultural Affairs Commission; and the Security and Mediation Council. An additional technical commission is that of the Community Computer Centre (CCC), with responsibility for computerising the collection, acquisition and management of Community customs and external trade statistical data. The Revised Treaty of 1993 made important changes to the 1975 Treaty to reflect the changed international political and economic environment. The Revised Treaty added an Economic and Social Council; a Community Parliament; and a Community Court of Justice. It also established a specialised technical Commission for Political, Judicial, Regional Security and Immigration (ECOWAS 1993).

The common market objectives of trade liberalisation and free movement of persons are at the heart of ECOWAS integration. A 'borderless' West Africa, which facilitates the free mobility of the factors of production, has been created, at least in principle. Free movement continues to generate support and commitment from ECOWAS countries, in spite of a general reluctance on their part to open up their economies to regional competition. The freedom to move without visa restrictions within the community is regarded as the most important symbol of the existence of ECOWAS. However, community citizens still have to contend with illegal barriers such as road blocks and attempts at extortion by customs and immigration officers. These limitations have not detracted from the relatively successful achievement of the free movement protocol, when compared with other regional integration projects in Africa (SADC is a case in point; see Gibb 2004).

6 Expanding the security frontiers of ECOWAS integration

The political and security dimensions of ECOWAS regionalism have, until recently, been fairly muted. This is understandable given the Community's economic origins. But the phenomenon of violent intra-state conflicts in West Africa has brought home the realisation that the objectives of economic integration are unattainable in an environment of political instability and societal conflicts. In the 1990s West Africa became a theatre of violent civil wars in Liberia, Mali, Sierra Leone and Guinea Bissau. These domestic conflicts did not only threaten regional and international peace and security, but also challenged the capacity of the United Nations and regional organisations to manage and resolve these conflicts. Though these civil wars were domestic in nature, they had regional and international ramifications. Indeed, the most serious threat to regional peace and security is the 'contagion effect' of such civil wars. These domestic conflicts are thus perceived with apprehension as the 'fire next door', a bush fire with little or no respect for national boundaries, with consequences which are felt far beyond state borders (Francis 2000a). These brutal intra-state conflicts have led to state collapse, with contagion effects which threaten national and regional security, due mainly to the influx of refugees and the proliferation of small arms.

It is therefore a concern for regime survival, and national and regional security, that has forced West African leaders to take an active role in managing and resolving these regional conflagrations. In particular, as the Mano River states of Liberia, Sierra Leone and Guinea have been locked in a vicious cycle of civil war and sub-regional insecurity, ECOWAS leaders have assumed collective responsibility for intervening in, and 'extinguishing' these threatening regional 'fires'. Clearly, the imperative for regional peace and security, as a precondition for achieving economic integration objectives, has imposed itself on the consciousness of regional political leaders, who created a home-grown regional security and conflict management mechanism in 1990. The formation of the ECOWAS Cease-fire Monitoring Group, ECOMOG, and the experiment with ECOMOG security regionalism, suggests that political and security issues have come to dominate the ECOWAS economic integration agenda. The transformation of ECOWAS, that is its assumption of the mantle of security regionalism, is part of the wider response of regional groupings to the challenges of economic globalisation and the changed international conflict environment of the 1990s and after (Frempong 2003; Uche 2001).

7 The creation of ECOMOG: the Liberian civil war and the international neglect of Africa

The outbreak of the Liberian civil war and the (lack of) response on the part of the international community led to new thinking in West Africa on how to address regional security and economic crises. The immediate cause of the Liberian civil war was the rebel invasion led by Charles Taylor of the National Patriotic Front of Liberia (NPFL) on Christmas Eve in 1989. The insurgency was against nearly ten years of tyrannical rule by President Samuel Doe who, in 1980, as a Master-Sergeant, had led a bloody military coup (in which Charles Taylor also participated) against President William Tolbert. Due to the level of state weakness and economic impoverishment, Taylor's invasion, which was supported by Burkina Faso and Côte d'Ivoire (both ECOWAS members), and Colonel Muammar Qaddafi's Libya, succeeded, in less than a year, in controlling 90 per cent of the country (i.e. twelve out of the country's thirteen counties), which he later called 'Greater Liberia', and over which he proclaimed himself president. During this period, Liberia effectively degenerated into chaos and anarchy. The authority of President Doe did not extend beyond the Executive Mansion in Monrovia. He was subsequently captured and killed by fighters of the Independent National Patriotic Front of Liberia (INPFL), led by 'General' Prince Yormie Johnson, whilst on an 'official mission' to the ECOMOG headquarters (Francis 2000b).

The level of human carnage and destruction during the civil war led to massive population displacement and refugee flows, and created a humanitarian catastrophe. According to a US State Department Report (1990), '[a]ll combatants routinely engage[d] in indiscriminate killing and abuse of civilians, looting and ethnically based executions, with one of the worst single episodes occurring in July when . . . soldiers killed approximately 600 persons taking refuge in the courtyard of St. Peter's Church'. West African nationals were also targeted for brutal reprisals by all parties to the conflict for allegedly supporting rival insurgents. This brutal civil war and humanitarian catastrophe directly threatened wider regional peace and security.

The Liberian civil war had important implications for the response of the international community to violent intra-state conflicts in Africa. When the war broke out, numerous calls for the United States and the UN to intervene went unheeded, even though the USA had a special relationship with Liberia, both because of the country's history (it was founded by freed slaves from America) and its strategic and economic value during the Cold War. The changed international environment of the post-Cold War era meant that foreign intervention was limited to the protective evacuation of Western nationals by US marines.

The international response to the Liberian civil war, which coincided with the end of the Cold War and the outbreak of the Gulf War, was to set the pattern of international neglect of African conflicts in the post-Cold War period. The end of the Cold War adversely affected Africa in that there developed a general reluctance amongst major international powers to continue the traditional practice of unilateral intervention in African conflicts. Also, Africa was of limited strategic, political and economic relevance to the major powers during this period. The UN, in addition to its preoccupation with the Gulf War, was vastly over-burdened with new post-Cold War responsibilities. Thus the so-called new world order, and the post-Cold War peace dividend, did not considerably impact on international response to African conflicts such as the Liberian civil war. The international neglect, and differential treatment of African conflicts created space for West African leaders to develop new ideas and home-grown approaches to regional security and conflict management, which were devoid of Cold War ideological considerations.

7.1 The birth of ECOMOG

The expansion of ECOWAS's security frontiers happened by default. Spreading sub-regional conflict and instability, coupled with the international neglect of Africa, foisted on West African leaders the pragmatic political necessity for expanding into security, an expansion that incorporated the new and vexing challenges of the region's security landscape. The then Nigerian president, General Ibrahim Babangida, in an impromptu briefing on the Liberian crisis in 1990, stated that '[w]hen certain events occur in the sub-region depending on their intensity and magnitude, which are bound to affect Nigeria's politico-military and socio-economic environment, we should not stand by as helpless and hapless spectators' (Nwachukwu *et al.* 1991: 104).[7] Nigeria thus took the political and diplomatic initiative in convening the ECOWAS Standing Mediation Committee (SMC) because it perceived the Liberian crisis as a threat to national and regional security. An ECOWAS peace plan for Liberia was designed as a framework to resolve the country's civil war. It provided for an immediate cease-fire; and the establishment and deployment of ECOWAS Cease-fire Monitoring Group (ECOMOG) troops as a multinational intervention force to monitor the observance of the cease-fire; and the establishment of an interim government of national unity as a prelude to holding democratic elections under international supervision.

The ECOWAS peace plan for Liberia was supported by both the OAU and the UN. ECOWAS therefore had to adapt its traditional economic integration institutions to play a conflict management and resolution role. ECOMOG's mandate embraced elements of peacekeeping and enforcement, hence the justification for military intervention. However, when ECOMOG's 'Operation Liberty' landed in Monrovia on 24 August 1990, it was without the consent of one of the main parties to the conflict, the NPFL. With no peace to keep, or cease-fire to observe, and with little or no previous experience in peacekeeping, the ECOMOG intervention force inevitably got embroiled in the Liberian crisis. This was to have serious implications for the peacekeeping force, and particularly for its role as a neutral inter-positionary force in the conflict. Arguably, the Liberian civil war was a 'clear and present' danger to regimes in West Africa, several of which were of dubious legitimacy. West African leaders were therefore not ready to risk the possibility of the Liberian crisis initiating a regional domino effect. Indeed, political realists would argue that the struggle for regime survival was the primary motive for the rather unusual regional military initiative to respond to this particular 'regional' security threat (Adebajo 2002; Alao 1998; Francis 2001).

8 The regional economic and security nexus

The politics of economic regionalism ensured an ECOWAS preoccupation with regional political co-operation and confidence building, especially in such areas as the peaceful resolution of inter-state disputes and in forging common positions on international affairs. ECOWAS foreign policy responses to inter-state disputes and other threats to regional security have been based on mobilising regional solidarity in dispute/conflict mediation, and in forging common ECOWAS positions on controversial global issues. The pursuit of national interest in the guise of regional co-operation provides the opportunity for ECOWAS members to articulate common foreign policy positions when deemed necessary. However, such willingness to pool sovereignty goes beyond simple realist interpretations; it is an acknowledgement of the driving force of political, economic and security interdependence (and shared vulnerability) for collective action (Keohane and Nye 1989).

Thus the ECOWAS experiment with security regionalism provided a platform for the regional organisation to formulate and articulate a common foreign policy on security and conflict management issues. To this end, two important instruments relating to regional security were adopted at the December 1999 ECOWAS summit in Togo:

- a protocol establishing a permanent mechanism for conflict prevention, management and resolution, peace and security; and,
- a regional moratorium on the importation, export and manufacture of light weapons.[8]

Regionalism has therefore provided a framework for institutionalised co-operation at the political, economic, security and diplomatic levels. Thus while ECOWAS has historically been preoccupied with economic regionalism, the significance of regional peace and security has never been lost on member states. The 1975 Treaty did not make any provision for political and security co-operation. To fill this vacuum, a 1978 Protocol on Non-Aggression and a Protocol on Mutual Assistance in Defence (1981) were signed by Community members. These defence protocols were confidence-building mechanisms for peaceful co-existence, which reflected the recognition that regional peace and security were a necessary prerequisite for economic development and socio-political progress. In particular, the 1981 Defence Pact provided for permissible armed intervention by ECOWAS, even if only in defence of member states against external aggression. In the event, this represented an unprecedented provision for legitimate intervention in the internal affairs of member states, a 'co-operative protection' mechanism against civil strife, which *could* also be used to counter 'proxy' wars and/or externally-orchestrated civil wars (Okolo and Wright 1990). Significantly, however, the principle of non-intervention in domestic affairs of member states, which is enshrined in both the UN and OAU Charters, barred ECOWAS member states from intervening militarily in such conflicts.

Effectively, therefore, the Liberian civil war highlighted the need for a regional policy approach to the propriety of military intervention in domestic conflicts of ECOWAS leaders. The ECOWAS extraordinary summit in Mali in 1990 thus established the rules of engagement for the threat, and use of force by the regional community. Subsequently, the 1993 Revised ECOWAS Treaty, in an attempt to respond to the imperatives of regional security, specifically provided for regional political and security co-operation (ECOWAS 1993).[9] Additionally, the 1977 francophone Mutual Defence Pact (ANAD or Accord de Non-Agression et d'Assistance en Matière de Defence) was integrated into the new ECOWAS security mechanism in 1999.

Civil wars in West Africa, and their threat to regional peace and security, have led to the need to redefine the notion of security. With the end of the Cold War, Africa was 'on fire', racked by a multiplicity of intra-state conflicts. Furthermore, domestic conflicts easily become 'regionalised' or 'scaled up' because the majority of West Africa's 'fragile polities, by definition, are easily permeable. Therefore, internal issues . . . get transformed into inter-state issues quite readily' (Deng *et al.* 1996: 146). In the post-Cold War period, political instabilities and state implosion have become a prominent feature of Africa's political landscape. The lid placed on Africa's simmering conflicts during the Cold War era was now removed, as support for client states was no longer forthcoming. Insurgents therefore took up arms to contest state hegemony or the dominance of a small ruling and governing class. The result has been catastrophic state collapse and societal fragmentation, for example, in Somalia, Democratic Republic of Congo, Liberia, Sierra Leone and Rwanda.

In West Africa, emerging non-military security threats range from crime, drugs, HIV-AIDS, small arms proliferation, poverty, resource scarcity, religious and environmental problems to ethnic oppression. These have instigated conflicts. The state can no longer continue to be the single referent of security, and traditional responses for solving security threats are grossly inadequate to deal with the multiplicity of security threats in the changed conflict environment of the 1990s and after. The Liberian conflict impacted on the redefinition of security in the West African sub-region. The OAU, for its part, and after decades of perceiving security in traditional military and external terms, finally acknowledged at its Dakar, Senegal, summit in 1992, that 'there is a link between security, stability, development and co-operation in Africa' (Keller and Rothchild 1996: 33).

Insecurity in West Africa has been the product of both internal fissures and fission, as well as external factors. Therefore, the formation of ECOMOG was a manifestation of the interplay between 'economic development, regional security, democratization and conflict management in Africa as a whole' (Inegbedion 1994: 219). However, the changing focus of the security problematic in the West African region is part of the wider concern with rethinking security, that is with broadening and deepening the conception of security (Baldwin 1999). Although military security remains important, human, environmental, economic, societal and food security represent more serious threats for the majority of West Africa's peoples than traditional inter-state wars.

9 *ECOMOG: peacekeeping, peace enforcement and conflict management in West Africa*

The West African experiment with security regionalism has led to involvement in peace support and conflict management operations in Liberia (1990–97); Sierra Leone (1997–2000) and Guinea Bissau (1999). The expansion of ECOWAS regionalism into the security domain was an *ad hoc* coalition to respond to regional security threats posed by the Liberian conflict. However, 'ad hocery' characterises all coalitions that have come together to conduct complex emergency operations (Taw and Grant-Thomas 1999). For example, the first UN peacekeeping operation was formulated on an *ad hoc* basis in response to the Suez crisis in 1956, although the United Nations Emergency Force (UNEF) would become a model for subsequent UN peacekeeping forces.

It could be argued that the contagion effects streaming from the influx of refugees, the spread of national dissidents, arms proliferation and a militarised West Africa were enough to force member states to band together to prevent the spread of instability. The ECOMOG coalition was therefore a rational approach to serve the national interests of Community members. The incentives were enough to coerce ECOWAS leaders to overcome their differences and political rivalries and, under the banner of ECOWAS, to address regional security issues collectively, while at the same time securing the fragile stability of some illegitimate governments and weak states.

ECOMOG's interventions have generally been cast in humanitarian terms. These complex emergency operations have ranged from peacekeeping and peace-enforcement, through democratic intervention and humanitarian relief assistance, to helping to restore collapsed states. The ECOMOG experiment reflects the emerging phenomenon of intervention in domestic conflicts by intergovernmental collective security arrangements. The American-led UN intervention in Haiti, UNPROFOR in Bosnia, UNOMSOM I & II in Somalia and KFOR in Kosovo represent other examples of this trend.

9.1 Peacekeeping and Conflict Management in Liberia

ECOMOG intervened in Liberia without a formal peace agreement or cease-fire. A United Nations Observer Mission (UNOMIL) was sent to Liberia under a UN-ECOWAS co-operative security arrangement to legitimise and facilitate the ECOMOG mandate. The ECOWAS and ECOMOG twin-track conflict management strategy of political negotiation and military pressure led to peace talks in Banjul, Bamako, Geneva, Lomé, Yamoussoukro, Cotonou, Akosombo and Abuja. The coercive diplomacy adopted by ECOMOG led to the signing of a series of cease-fire agreements and the eventual commencement of disarmament and demobilisation of warring factions. Through diplomacy backed by force, the ECOWAS peace plan for Liberia, which was also supported politically and diplomatically by the UN, OAU and key Western governments and institutions, succeeded in its primary objective of ensuring that democratic elections were held. The elections, held under the supervision of ECOWAS and other international observers in July 1997, were won by Charles Taylor, with the tacit support of the regional hegemon, Nigeria.

Though ECOMOG's intervention did not solve the underlying root causes of the conflict, or eliminate the potential for relapse into further conflict, it nevertheless brought a deadly civil war to an end, and not only helped to stabilise war-torn Liberia, but also stopped a humanitarian disaster, assisted with engineering the restoration of the collapsed state, and ensured democratic governance based on respect for the rule of law (in place of the law of the gun).

9.2 Democratic Intervention and Peace Enforcement in Sierra Leone

The contagion effect of the Liberian civil war was felt in Sierra Leone, when Corporal Foday Sankoh's Revolutionary United Front (RUF), supported by Charles Taylor, invaded the eastern border areas of the country in March 1991. The Taylor-sponsored RUF insurgency eventually led to the overthrow, in 1992, of the All Peoples Congress Party (APC) regime by a military junta, the National Provisional Ruling Council (NPRC). The re-introduction of democratic governance in 1996 was aborted by the intervention of the military in May 1997. ECOWAS mediation led to the signing of the Conakry Peace Accord for Sierra Leone in late 1997. Failure to implement the peace agreement provided the opportunity for ECOMOG to intervene militarily, in action which led to the overthrow of the Armed Forces Revolutionary Council (AFRC) military junta, and the eventual restoration of constitutional order in Sierra Leone. This was unprecedented in the political history of West Africa. In the event, ECOMOG intervention not only helped to restore constitutional order, it was also instrumental in mediating a negotiated political settlement to the brutal nine-year civil war, in addition to providing security for the state.

9.3 *Co-operative peace brokerage in Guinea Bissau*

The insurgency led by General Ansumana Mane against the authoritarian regime of President Bernado Nino Vieira was largely the product of the politics of underdevelopment in Guinea Bissau. The sacking of General Mane as head of the army by President Vieira following allegations that the former had sold arms to the Senegalese separatist movement in Casamance, led to armed revolt by soldiers loyal to Mane in June 1998. This led to intervention by neighbouring Senegal and Guinea, under the auspices of ECOWAS, in support of the beleaguered President Vieira. Senegal's participation in this intervention was considered to be in its national interest, because of the impact of the Casamance separatist rebellion in southern Senegal.

In response to an appeal from President Vieira, an ECOWAS Committee of seven was formed to facilitate a negotiated settlement to the conflict. Furthermore, ECOMOG's security mandate was expanded to include Guinea Bissau. A cease-fire, brokered jointly by ECOWAS and the Community of Lusophone Countries (CPLP), was signed in Praia, Cape Verde, by the two factions in August 1998; a peace accord was signed later that year, in November, in Abuja. Although a Senegalese-led ECOMOG observer mission was entrusted with the responsibility for monitoring the cease-fire agreement, rebel soldiers eventually overthrew the Vieira government, and set up a government of national unity in 1999. The military returned to its barracks, after organising domestic elections, but staged another (this time bloodless) coup in September 2003, forcing the incumbent president to resign and replacing him with an interim government of national unity, pending new elections.

ECOWAS diplomacy contributed to ending the fierce fighting in what was an internal conflict in Guinea Bissau and, through co-operation with the CPLP and the UN, contributed also to post-war peace-building and reconstruction.

10 Strengthening conflict management capacity: establishment of an early warning system

In recognition of the nexus between peace, security, conflict management and ECOWAS integration, an Early Warning System has been established with regional observation networks. These regional observatories are responsible for conflict tracking; as well as for observing, analysing and reporting on socio-political, economic and security situations in the region with the potential for escalating into armed conflict. Four regional zones for conflict tracking and mapping have been established (Adibe 2002).[10] A Security and Mediation Council (SMC) formulates strategies for responding to conflicts and instability, or for diffusing potentially violent conflict in the sub-region.[11] Strategies include setting up fact-finding missions; using the good offices of the Executive Secretary for dialogue, intervention and mediation; utilising the services of the Council of Elders;[12] and, as a last resort, the deployment of military force.

However, what is noticeably absent from the ECOWAS Early Warning Response mechanism is a framework for early response. The examples of the Rwandan genocide in 1994, and the violent and bloody conflict in Sierra Leone in 1991, demonstrate the limitations of early warning response mechanisms. These examples show that the problem is not one of early warning, but of the failure or lack of early response to conflicts that exhibit all the indications of degenerating into armed violence. It is therefore argued that it will serve the ECOWAS security framework particularly well to develop a twin-track mechanism of early warning *and* early response mechanisms.

11 Blurring the frontiers of economic and security regionalism: implications for African international relations

ECOWAS expansion into the security frontier has relevant implications for African and international politics. When its *ad hoc* multinational intervention force, ECOMOG, was created, it was criticised by political analysts and media commentators as an example of how not to conduct peacekeeping operations outside the traditional UN framework (Shaw and Okolo 1994). ECOWAS security regionalism has shown relative success in peace support operations and conflict management. As a regional intergovernmental collective security organisation, it has assumed a dynamic of its own, and has therefore affected the nature of African international relations. The ECOMOG conflict management experiment has major implications for the understanding of post-Cold War African politics. It has moved the regional community beyond its primary state-centric focus to a pluralistic conception of domestic and international politics. In its management of West African crises, ECOWAS has had to deal, not only with collapsed states, but also civil society organisations, warlords and extra-regional actors.

Civil wars in West Africa have undermined the traditional norms of international society, in that ECOMOG interventions contravened OAU/AU and UN principles of non-intervention and political sovereignty. These principles have historically constrained the effectiveness of these organisations in the management and resolution of domestic conflicts. However, the threats posed by civil wars in West Africa have led to a fundamental rethink of the norms of international society within the ECOWAS region. This appears to have influenced the organising or constitutional principles of the new African Union, which recognises the collective right of African states to intervene in situations of state collapse, gross violations of human rights and war crimes. West African leaders, like the majority of those in the rest of Africa, now recognise that non-intervention and political sovereignty are no longer sacrosanct when it comes to deadly internal conflicts.

A fundamental shift in the international relations of African states is their recognition that 'internal human rights violations (and civil wars) are a threat to international peace and security warranting the attention of outside states' (Damrosch *et al.* 1993: 160). Thus the OAU, which has spent decades hiding behind the protection offered by the norms of international society, had to endorse ECOMOG intervention in the West African conflicts. This paradigm shift in African inter-state relations means that states now have the responsibility to demonstrate, not only the 'legal fiction' of juridical sovereignty, but also domestic sovereignty. ECOWAS interventions have been concerned not only with managing and resolving armed conflicts, but also with the reconstruction of collapsed states and halting humanitarian catastrophes. These kinds of 'reconstitutive interventions' have been regarded as permissible breaches of international law (Zartman 1995).

The ECOWAS experiment in security regionalism has influenced other regional and sub-regional organisations. The West African example in Liberia served as the basis for the OAU's adoption of a security agenda, in 1992, as a mechanism for the management of continental conflicts. It was followed by the adoption of the Mechanism for Conflict Prevention, Management and Resolution in 1993. The ECOMOG peacekeeping and peace enforcement operations have established a new co-operative security norm, for example in terms of task-sharing between the UN and ECOWAS in the maintenance of international peace and security. ECOWAS security regionalism is emerging, albeit partially, as the practical realisation of the OAU's 'try Africa first' approach to conflict management and resolution.

12 Conclusion

ECOWAS expansion into the frontier of security regionalism is a novel initiative, but the experience shows that developing a multinational force is the easiest part; sustaining the intervention and implementing an exit strategy are frequently considerably more difficult. ECOMOG interventions are also very expensive operations for the largely underdeveloped economies in the region; indeed, ECOMOG operations have been funded by resources from Denmark, the EU, Japan, Sweden, the UK, the USA and the Netherlands, among other sources, in addition to the newly-established ECOWAS peace fund. However, the ECOMOG experience demonstrates the need for the regional security organ to move beyond the traditional neutral inter-positionary approach to peacekeeping, and to adopt a more comprehensive approach to regional security that embraces peacemaking, peacekeeping, peace enforcement, conflict management and conflict prevention.

The recognition of the nexus between economic integration, regional security and regional stability means that ECOWAS should henceforth prioritise human and social security, democratic governance, and respect for human rights as the enabling environment within which the objectives of ECOWAS integration and regional economic development can be achieved. Peace, security and development are a necessary prerequisite for West African integration. However, the salient point is that the ECOWAS institutional and military approach to security is insufficient to respond to the myriad of non-military regional security threats such as increasing poverty, depressing social and development indicators, intra-communal violence and ethno-religious strife. According to the ECOWAS/ International Peace Academy Conference held in Abuja in 2001, 'ECOWAS's capacity to tackle the nexus between good governance and security will be key to any attempt to build peace in West Africa, *and hence achieve the economic integration objectives* [*sic*]' (Ero *et al.* 2001: 4).

Notes

1. Frempong (2003: 7) defines regionalism as 'attempts by neighbouring nation-states, reinforced by a sense of common purpose or predicament within a definite region or defined area, to foster economic or political co-operation among themselves in order to lessen their dependence on others outside the region'.
2. The analysis presented here draws extensively from Francis (2001, pp. 8–12).
3. Functional co-operation refers to co-operation in pursuit of common interests around a shared geographic space, frequently independently of a free trade agenda, either in a specific sector such as security or health, or across a wide range of sectors of common interest including regional security, transport, culture, science and technology, and the environment (http://www.acs-aec.org/column/index 16.htm).
4. Mauritania withdrew from ECOWAS in December 2000, ostensibly because it was opposed to plans for the establishment of a single monetary zone and currency, 'which it insist[ed] . . . would undermine its sovereignty and local currency, the Ouguiya' (http://www.arabicnews.com/ansub/Daily/Day/991228/1999122860.html).
5. The Lagos Plan of Action, which was adopted by the OAU in 1980, and which promoted self-reliance and self-sustenance through regional economic and social integration of African economies, also provided stimulus to the then nascent ECOWAS.
6. *Treaty of the Economic Community of West African States (ECOWAS) 1975*, Lagos: ECOWAS Secretariat, 1975.
7. It is possible that such external neglect was part of a broader Western project to pressure Africans into policing their own conflicts, rather than having the United States, in particular, acting as global policeman.
8. This moratorium was almost certainly linked to international efforts to control light weapons proliferation at the time.
9. Chapter X, Articles 56 and 58 addressed the issues of both inter-state and intra-state conflicts, and recognised the need to 'establish a regional peace and security observation system and peacekeeping forces'. *ECOWAS Revised Treaty*, Abuja: ECOWAS Secretariat, 1993, pp. 35–6.
10. The four zones include: 1. Cape Verde, Guinea Bissau, Mauritania, with Banjul, The Gambia as the zonal HQ, 2. Côte d'Ivoire, Mali, Niger and Ouagadougou, Burkina Faso as the HQ, 3. Ghana, Guinea, Sierra Leone and Monrovia, Liberia as the HQ, 4. Nigeria, Togo and Cotonou, Benin as the HQ. For a more detailed analysis see Adibe (2002).

11. SMC comprises Heads of States and Governments, Foreign Affairs Ministers and Ambassadors, and is responsible for taking important decisions relating to peace, security and the deployment of any peacekeeping and enforcement troops. It has established a Defence and Security Commission constituting defence chiefs and security experts.
12. The Council of Elders, comprising 32 eminent persons, is charged with the task of facilitating negotiation, mediation and reconciliation in potential conflict situations. This is a recognition of the relevance of traditional African conflict management and resolution mechanisms and the utility of regional societal resources for conflict prevention and resolution.

References

Adebajo, A. (2002), *Building Peace in West Africa: Liberia, Sierra Leone and Guinea Bissau*. Lynne Rienner, Boulder, Colorado and London.

Adibe, C. (2002), 'Muddling through: an analysis of the ECOWAS experience in conflict management in West Africa' in Laakso, L. (ed.), *Regional Integration for Conflict Prevention and Peace Building in Africa*. Department of Political Science, University of Helsinki, Helsinki.

Ajibewa, A. (2002), *From Regional Security to Regional Integration in West Africa: Lessons from the ASEAN Experience*. Centre for Democracy and Development Working Paper No. 5. London: CDD. (http://www.cdd.org.uk/pdf/ECOWASworkingpaper.pdf; accessed on 27/12/2003.)

Alao, A. (1998), *The Burden in the Liberian Civil War*. Ashgate, Aldershot.

Asante, S.K.B. (1986), *The Political Economy of Regionalism in Africa: A Decade of the Economic Community of West African States (ECOWAS)*. Praeger Publishers, New York.

Baldwin, D. (1999), 'The concept of security', *Review of International Studies* **23(1)**, 5–26.

Brydon, L. and **Legge, K.** (2000), *Adjusting Society: The World Bank, the IMF and Ghana*. Lynne Rienner, Boulder, Colorado.

Buzan, B. (1991), *People, States and Fear: An Agenda for International Security in the Post-Cold War Era*. Harvester Wheatsheaf, New York.

Damrosch, L., Clark, J. and **Steinberg, J.C.** (ed.) (1993), *Enforcing Restraint: Collective Intervention in Internal Conflicts*. Council on Foreign Relations Press, New York.

Deng, F., Kamaro, S., Lyons, T., Rothchild, D. and **Zartman, I.W.** (1996), *Sovereignty as Responsibility: Conflict Management in Africa*. The Brookings Institution, Washington, DC.

Dickson, A. (1997), *Development and International Relations: A Critical Introduction*. Polity, Cambridge.

Dunn, J. (ed.) (1978), *West African States: Failure and Promise: A Study in Comparative Politics*. Cambridge University Press, Cambridge.

ECOWAS (1975), *Treaty of the Economic Community of West African States*. ECOWAS Secretariat, Abuja, Nigeria.

ECOWAS (1993), *Revised Treaty*. ECOWAS Secretariat, Abuja, Nigeria.

Ellis, S. (1999), *The Mask of Anarchy: The Destruction of Liberia and the Religious Dimension of an African Civil War*. Hurst, London.

Ero, C., Waheguru, P.S.S. and **Toure, A.** (2001), *Toward a Pax West Africana: Building Peace in a Troubled Sub-region*. Report, International Peace Academy/ECOWAS Conference, September, Abuja, Nigeria. (http://www.ipacademy.org/PDF_Reports/PDF_REPORT_PAX_W_%20AFRICANA.pdf; accessed 1/1/2004.)

Francis, D. (2000a), 'ECOMOG: a new security agenda in world politics' in Bakut, T.B. and Dutt, S. (eds), *Africa at the Millennium. An Agenda for Mature Development*. Palgrave, London.

Francis, D. (2000b), 'The fire next door: regional diplomacy and conflict management in West Africa', *African Review of Foreign Policy* **2(2)**.

Francis, D. (2001), *The Politics of Economic Regionalism: Sierra Leone in ECOWAS*. Ashgate, Aldershot.

Frempong, A.K.D. (2003), 'Trajectories of sub-regional conflict management: an assessment of ECOWAS'. Paper presented at CODESRIA's thirtieth anniversary celebration grand conference, Dakar, Senegal, 8–11 September 2003. (http://www.codesria.org/Links/conferences/dakar/frempong.pdf; accessed 29/12/2003.)

Gibb, R. (2004), 'International and regional trade in eastern and southern Africa' in Potts, D. and Bowyer-Bower, T. (eds), *Eastern and Southern Africa: Development Challenges in a Volatile Region*. Pearson/Prentice Hall, Harlow.

Inegbedion, E.J. (1994), 'ECOMOG in comparative perspective' in Shaw, T. and Okolo, J. (eds), *The Political Economy of Foreign Policy in ECOWAS*. St. Martin's Press, New York.

Kaplan, R. (1994), 'The Coming Anarchy', *Atlantic Monthly* **273(2)**, 44–76.

Keller, E. and **Rothchild, D.** (eds) (1996), *Africa in the New International Order: Rethinking State Sovereignty and Regional Security*. Lynne Rienner, London.

Keohane, R. and **Nye, J.** (1989), *Power and Interdependency*. Harper Collins, New York.

Nwachukwu, I. and **Obiozor, G.A.** (1991), *Nigeria and the ECOWAS Since 1985: Towards A Dynamic Regional Integration*. Fourth Dimension Publishing Company, Lagos, Nigeria.

Ojo, O. (1980), 'Nigeria and the Formation of ECOWAS', *International Organization* **34(4)**, 571–604.

Okolo, J. and **Wright, S.** (eds) (1990), *West African Regional Co-operation and Development*. Westview Press, Boulder, Colorado.

Olukoshi, A. (1998), *The Elusive Prince of Denmark: Structural Adjustment and the Crisis of Governance in Africa*. Nordiska Afrikainstitutet, Uppsala.

Olukoshi, A. (2003), 'Neoliberalism on Trial: The Nationalist and Pan-Africanist Case for a Prosecution'. Paper presented at CODESRIA thirtieth anniversary grand finale conference. Dakar, 10–12 December 2003.

Sahel and West Africa Club (2002), *The Impact of Violent Conflict on Structural Stability in West Africa: Developing Medium-Term Scenarios for the Prospective Study Process*. Preliminary consultation document for the Strategy and Policy Group Meeting, Paris October 2002. OECD, Paris. (http://www.oecd.org/dataoecd/18/59/1838651.pdf; accessed on 27/12/2003.)

Shaw, T.M. and **Okolo, J.E.** (eds) (1994), *The Political Economy of Foreign Policy in ECOWAS*. Macmillan, Basingstoke.

Taw, J.M. and **Grant-Thomas, A.** (1999), 'US support for regional complex contingency operations: lessons from ECOMOG', *Studies in Conflict and Terrorism* **22(1)**, 53–78.

Uche, C.U. (2001), *The Politics of Monetary Sector Cooperation Among the Economic Community of West African States Members*. World Bank Policy Research Working Paper No. 2647. World Bank, Washington, DC.

United States State Department (1990), *Report on Human Rights in Liberia*. US State Department, Washington, DC.

Vogt, M. (ed.) (1992), *The Liberian Crisis and ECOMOG: A Bold Attempt at Regional Peacekeeping*. Gabumo Publishing Co., Lagos, Nigeria.

Walraven, K. (1991), 'Some Aspects of Regional Economic Integration in Africa' in *Hague Yearbook of International Law*, Vol. 4. Martinus Nijhoff Publishers, Dordrecht.

Zartman, I.W. (ed.) (1995), *Collapsed States: The Disintegration and Restoration of Legitimate Authority*. Lynne Rienner, London.

CHAPTER 7

Transformations in regional agriculture and family farming

Camilla Toulmin and Bara Guèye[1]

1 Introduction

Agriculture remains a centrally important part of the West African economy. It provides food supplies for local consumption and revenue from the export of cash crops; accounts for 30–50 per cent of GDP in most countries; and represents the major source of income and livelihoods for 70–80 per cent of West Africa's population. Although the economies and peoples of the region are diversifying into a range of other activities, farming is likely to remain of central significance to incomes and livelihoods for the foreseeable future (Fafchamps *et al.* 2001). In the early years following independence, most countries followed state-led policies aimed at rapid economic growth, based on industrialisation and taxation of the agricultural sector. Such approaches brought disappointment and led to great structural changes in the 1980s, with the introduction of Structural Adjustment Programmes (SAPs) and greater attention to the importance of agriculture as the basis for economic growth. Current donor and government focus on meeting the Millennium Development Goals (MDGs) has refocused attention on the rural economy, given that it is estimated that 70 per cent of the world's poorest people are rural dwellers. Improvements to returns gained from, and the productivity of, agriculture have been identified as a key means to reach the poverty reduction targets. Governments in the region are therefore interested in seeing how agriculture might be 'modernised' to better meet the many demands made of it.

This raises important questions regarding the meaning of 'modernisation'; whether agriculture can 'modernise' on the basis of the smallholder family farm sector; and what the consequences for meeting poverty reduction targets might be if governments favoured large-scale farms over smallholder farms (Toulmin and Guèye 2003). Equally, agricultural policy has multiple linkages with other government strategies and associated measures. For example, new land tenure legislation will affect the structure and performance of the farming sector. There are also important tradeoffs to consider between support for large-scale commercial farms and commitment to broader objectives such as increased productivity and greater equity. Furthermore, access to land and natural resources has increasingly become a political issue, with the rise in multiparty activity. The association of different parties with ethnic or economic interests, and their relations with customary leaders, have served to politicise land questions, adding further tensions to local land conflicts. Competition over land and its associated resources has thus become a major source of conflict.

This chapter describes the remarkable strength and adaptive capacity of smallholder farmers in West Africa. It highlights the continued existence of worrying levels of poverty and food insecurity, and argues that the continuing sustainability of the family farming sector is by no means assured. It demonstrates how low returns to farming limit the capacity and interest of farmers to invest in their land, and discourage younger family members from staying in the sector. This is significant, as low and uncertain farm incomes provide a weak foundation on which to build more diverse local economies in rural areas. Indeed, increased agricultural yields and output represent an essential precondition for broader growth, in addition to benefiting poorer groups in society. Apart from exceptional cases where access to a specific resource has allowed the conventional model of economic growth to be by-passed (such as Hong Kong and oil-rich states), economic development seems to depend on the prior strengthening and intensification of agriculture, which provides food supply for the cities and inputs for domestic processing and export production, as a means for broader diversification.

Yet this model of economic development, diversification and growth has run up against serious barriers in the case of many (West) African countries, which have been forced to liberalise their economies within a global economy in which they face fierce and unfair competition. As Mazoyer (2001) argues, a combination of mechanisation, input use and agricultural support measures in richer parts of the OECD, mean that staple crops can be produced in great quantity and sold around the world at prices which beggar developing country farmers. Such conditions have led to calls for developing countries to re-establish tariff barriers for agricultural commodities, creating a more favourable environment in which their farming sector can develop, and setting up barriers against dumping of farm produce from other parts of the world (Koning 2002). Without such protection, it is argued, the virtuous circle – of rising demand and prices for food, increased investment and intensification of farming, increased incomes and investment of surplus in economic diversification, leading to further growth in food demand – cannot be expected to occur. Improved producer prices constitute the *sine qua non* for addressing poverty in poor countries like those in West Africa, while revenue generated by tariffs on agricultural imports would provide a significant source of income for governments. It remains to be seen whether West African governments have sufficient room for manoeuvre in the World Trade Organisation (WTO) and other negotiating arenas, to argue successfully for getting such measures accepted as essential for longer-term growth and poverty reduction (Koning 2002).

Table 7.1 Change in per capita production of major food crops, 1961–63 to 1997–99 (per cent)

Country	*Cereal crops*	*Root and forest crops*	*Change*
Ghana	Rice, maize, millet, sorghum		**+59.8**
		Cassava, yams, plantains	**+66.3**
Nigeria	Rice, maize, millet, sorghum		**–1.2**
		Cassava, yams, plantains	**+76.3**
Mali	Rice, maize, millet, sorghum		**–2.6**
Niger	Rice, millet		**–24.2**
	Cowpeas		**+131.2**
Côte d'Ivoire	Rice, maize, millet		**+30.5**
		Cassava, yams, bananas, plantains	**–28.5**
Senegal	Rice, maize, millet, sorghum		**–41.2**
	Cowpeas		**+33.3**

Source: Mortimore (2003).

2 *Agricultural production*

2.1 *Food crops*

Table 7.1 presents data for six West African countries on per capita production of major food crops for the period 1961–63 to 1997–99, derived from FAO statistics (Mortimore 2003). The table demonstrates the diversity between country experiences, with the case of Senegal and Niger sharing a marked negative trend for major cereals (rice, millet, maize, sorghum) over the period, but much more positive trends in cereal production for Ghana, Nigeria, Mali and Côte d'Ivoire. For Ghana and Nigeria, there was a deep trough in farm production in the early 1980s and growing dependence on imported food. Subsequent policy shifts in favour of domestic agriculture helped provide greater incentives to farmers and a recovery in production levels.

In the case of Niger, lying almost entirely in the Sahelian and Saharan zone, the agricultural sector is particularly vulnerable to drought. As a consequence, cereal production was badly hit by the rainfall failures of 1973–75 and 1983–84. Nevertheless, evidence from Maradi Department in southern Niger shows increasing output per capita and rising yields (Hamadou 2000). Growth in cowpea production was strongly positive, due in large part to high levels of demand from neighbouring Nigeria. In Mali, all four cereals recovered strongly from a trough in 1981, this upward trend continuing for rice and maize, while faltering for millet and sorghum. In Côte d'Ivoire, per capita production of rice, maize, and millet rose by 30 per cent over the period, although root and forest crop production declined by a similar percentage.

Comparable evidence is provided by a recent study of Burkina Faso (Mazzucato and Neimeijer 2000). Here, taking data from FAO for the period

1961–98, they show that yields of the most important crops have increased considerably over the last forty years, despite a 20 per cent decline in rainfall. Rice and maize yields increased threefold while those for sorghum, millet and groundnuts doubled (Mazzucato *et al.* 2001). They go on to argue that 'while increased mechanisation, migration and fertiliser use have contributed to some degree to the increase in rice and maize yields, those are unlikely to be significant factors in the case of the other crops . . . Farmers seem to have been able to even increase output without relying on external inputs to replenish soil fertility' (Mazzucato *et al.* 2001: 6).

Thus the overall trends for food crop production show a remarkable degree of stability for some crops, and increases for others, despite often adverse climate, economic and policy environments. Such performance is particularly striking when combined with data on export crops, which show very large rates of growth in many cases, such growth having been achieved against a background of substantial decline in prices for the major commodities produced by West African farmers over the 1970–98 period (Kherallah *et al.* 2002).

2.2 Export crops

2.2.1 Cotton

Cotton has been a major export commodity from West Africa for the last 50 years, with current estimates showing that some 6 million farming households, perhaps as many as 18–20 million people, rely on cotton production in the region. It is produced entirely by smallholders, on farms varying from 3–20 hectares in size. West Africa produces an estimated two million tons of seed cotton, 80 per cent of which comes from French-speaking countries, particularly Mali, Côte d'Ivoire, Benin and Burkina Faso. Growth in output has been substantial over the last decade, with a doubling in area cultivated between 1978/9 and 1988/9, and a further doubling to 1998/9 (Ton 2001).

The expansion in cotton production has arguably accelerated differentiation within the agricultural sector, with households equipped with animal traction being able to do well and expand production, while the 30 per cent or so of households with only manual tools have been unable to participate effectively in this source of income (Ton 2001). Being reliant on access to plough equipment once everyone else's fields have been prepared means that crops are sown late, with adverse impacts on yield. Similarly, critics of Mali's Compagnie pour le Développement des Textiles (CMDT) argue that existing policies for agricultural intensification lack a poverty focus, and have increased the technical options available to middling and wealthier households, while providing little opportunity for those with limited capacity to invest. Given the intensive labour, credit and management inputs required for cotton production, the crop may well not be the most appropriate for small, poor farmers to adopt. Analysis of income sources for farm households in the village of Zaradougou, southern Mali, identified cotton as the major source of income for households in the wealthier and middling income classes, while several households in the poorest group (which included households already indebted to the CMDT), did not cultivate cotton at all (Brock and Coulibaly 1999). Women rarely benefited from direct access to the credit, inputs and extension advice provided by the CMDT.

Cotton farmers are strongly affected by world market prices which, at half the long-term average, are currently (2002/2003) at their lowest levels for thirty years. This is the result of a large global harvest, generated in part by high subsidies paid to farmers in rich countries, combined with low levels of demand. Farmers in the US and EU are protected from this price slump by high levels of producer support in the form of subsidies. By contrast, major losses in incomes and revenues have been felt by many developing country farmers, including West African producers, since there is no system of subsidies to protect farmers from such an adverse shift in world market prices. Given that all regional cotton production relies on smallholders, one can reasonably assume that they have all been damaged to some extent by the recent fall in world market prices.

2.2.2 Cocoa

Cocoa production is concentrated mainly in Côte d'Ivoire and Ghana, with smaller quantities being produced by Nigeria and Cameroon. With new sources of global supply entering the market from Latin America and East Asia (especially Vietnam, Indonesia), West African farmers no longer play a dominant role in global supply of cocoa. The current conflict in Côte d'Ivoire, which in 2000 provided more than 40 per cent of world market supply, has provoked a substantial hike in prices, of considerable benefit to neighbouring Ghana, as well as more distant producers. Cocoa is produced principally by smallholders in West Africa. There are a few large-scale plantations in both Ghana and Côte d'Ivoire but, overall, they represent a small percentage of both output and cropped area. It is estimated, for example, that there are one million smallholdings producing cocoa in Côte d'Ivoire and 800,000 in Ghana. Thus, improved trade opportunities and prices for cocoa have the potential to benefit a large number of small farmers in the region.

Cocoa production involves a very labour-intensive process to clear land, plant and maintain cocoa trees and harvest the crop, and has always relied heavily on access to labour, both family and hired. In Ghana and Côte d'Ivoire, much of this labour has come from both local sources as well as neighbouring countries. Prospective labourers offer to work in exchange for access to land through various sharecropping arrangements, thereby enabling migrants to acquire their own farms. Over the last 40–50 years, such opportunities have attracted several million Sahelians from Burkina Faso and Mali seeking to acquire land holdings of their own in Côte d'Ivoire. While land reserves were still substantial, and cocoa prices good, this policy of expansion based on in-migration could be maintained. But, with the downturn of the 1980s, and a growing perception that land reserves were being exhausted, conflicts between local people and incomers have grown, with rising levels of contest regarding 'rights' and claims to land. In Ghana, the Aliens Act of 1969 resulted in the expulsion of hundreds of thousands of Sahelians who had come to make a living from cocoa, many of whom subsequently moved to Côte d'Ivoire. Migrant labour remains important in western Ghana, but this is principally provided by people from other parts of the country who, as citizens, can claim firmer rights than non-nationals.

Thus, cocoa production has, in the past, been an important channel through which poorer farmers with labour to invest could acquire land and earn a living. However, this option has now disappeared as far as most Sahelians are concerned. With the current conflict in Côte d'Ivoire, it remains to be seen how the cocoa sector will re-establish itself there, and the nature of rights and opportunities available to non-indigenous groups which will emerge.

There is limited evidence for the distributional impacts of recent trends on different parts of the cocoa farming sector. In the case of Ghana, the liberalisation of cocoa marketing has been at best partial, with some part of the export market opened to private licensed exporters, while the Ghana Cocoa Board (COCOBOD) retains its dominant role. Konadu-Agyemang (2000) notes that, while Structural Adjustment has brought improved incomes for some cocoa producers, it is principally the large-scale farmers who have gained the lion's share. In the case of Côte d'Ivoire, the impacts of liberalisation of the cocoa sector, combined with growing political tension, have generated deep and damaging cuts in income, and a rapid rise in poverty in many parts of the country (Losch *et al.* 2003).

3 Agricultural performance

3.1 Crop cultivation

Available evidence suggests that when food and export crops are taken together, many West African countries have been remarkably successful in generating rising levels of output in response to market demand at national, regional and global levels, with the farming sector appearing to have great capacity to increase production when conditions are right. This is even more marked when account is taken of the growth in many lesser crops (e.g. sheanut, sesame, fruit and vegetables) for which data are not collected on a systematic basis (Wiggins, 2000). Thus Mortimore (2003) argues that, far from facing 'crisis', regional agriculture has been remarkably successful and responsive to new markets and opportunities, with smallholders in most countries increasing substantially their levels of output and productivity, despite often adverse conditions (Box 7.1). Similarly, Guyer (1997: 4–5) notes for Nigeria:

> Production and distribution systems have grown over the past several decades, and possibly at a rate which compares favourably with other historical cases even if not with the great spurt achieved in Asia through green revolution technologies. The food system has responded to demand despite difficulties of transport, no refrigeration, a narrow range of storage techniques and no commodity futures market. So even if up

Box 7.1 Accounting for trends in regional food crop production (1960–2000)

- Four of the six countries (the exceptions being Senegal and, to a lesser extent, Niger; see Table 7.1 for the list of countries) have maintained food production per capita in terms of a 'basket' of staple food commodities, or improved it, and some have recovered from deep crises in the early 1980s, to levels comparable to, or better than those of the early 1960s. Only in Senegal did the indices decline from the beginning to the end of this 40-year period; in Niger decline was arrested (though not reversed) after 1985.
- The performance of major crops, or of groups of crops, has often differed within the same country. An overall 'food sufficiency index' takes account of grain-tuber energy equivalents, allowing room for adaptive swings in crop preferences, both of consumers and of producers.
- Fluctuations, clearly attributable to rainfall variability (especially in Niger, Mali and Senegal), translate in per capita terms to a threat to food sufficiency at a national level, which increases the likelihood that food security comes under threat in poorer households, including those of many producers, who may sell productive assets afterwards.
- There appear to be many adaptive strategies at work as producers shift among crops and diversify in response to food marketing opportunities. This process has been noted in Senegal where the traditional crops are most under threat.
- Since the production of food per capita only rarely correlates either with the growth of the total population or with the growth of the agricultural population, a simple demographic mechanism must be discounted in the food equation.
- Much more important are policy and the global economic environment, which better explain the widespread decline in food sufficiency that occurred in many countries during the 1980s, and the subsequent recovery in most of them.

Source: Mortimore (2003).

to 20 per cent of food has been imported at certain moments, even if some of the urban poor fail to meet nutritional standards, and even if many urban inhabitants also farm, in comparative and historical terms the feeding of Nigerian towns across the great waves of macro-economic and political fluctuation has been an impressive achievement of productive technique and social achievement.

3.2 Livestock rearing

Although statistics on livestock numbers remain unreliable, the FAO suggests that livestock populations have grown throughout the region over the last 30–40 years (Mortimore 2003). While individual countries have experienced major fluctuations during periods of drought in the 1970s and 1980s, the index of livestock units per head of human population has remained broadly constant, implying a level of growth of 2–3 per cent per year. There have nevertheless been major changes in terms of the distribution of livestock numbers within the region, as well as the make-up of herds. In general, livestock have shifted southwards into higher rainfall areas, with a larger proportion held by settled farming groups. In addition, many former mobile herders are now becoming more sedentarised. Thus, for example, the major part of the national herd in Mali is now found in the Sikasso region, where cattle provide valuable inputs into the local cotton farming system (traction, manure, assets). Equally, Côte d'Ivoire has pursued a strong pro-livestock policy in the northern part of the country, attracting herders from neighbouring Mali and Burkina Faso, as well as encouraging investment in cattle amongst Ivorian farmers and traders. The proportion of the national herd made up by sheep and goats has risen, these animals conferring greater flexibility and resilience in the face of risk than cattle and camels, and offering prospects for lucrative fattening activities, especially in the neighbourhood of major towns. Such fattening is of especial interest in the weeks before major festivals. Intensive milk and dairy production around major cities is also gradually being established.

There is little or no data regarding the structure of livestock ownership in different parts of West Africa. During the droughts of the 1970s and 1980s, concern was raised regarding the impoverishment of many pastoral herders, forced to sell remaining breeding stock. While there was evidence for acquisition of herds during the drought by urban investors and farming populations able to benefit from falling animal prices and the desperate situation faced by pastoral households seeking food, there are no data to show whether such a shift in ownership has been maintained. Local level studies in farming areas tend to show that a few households own the major share of village-held animals. Economies of scale make it easy to maintain a large herd, but difficult and slow to build up from a small base. Thus, for example, data from village studies in Mali show that many households own one or two pairs of oxen, while large herds are restricted to a small number of households (Brock and Coulibaly 1999; Toulmin 1992).

3.3 Overall

Description and analysis of the agricultural sector and processes of transformation depend on a limited and unreliable body of data. There is particular difficulty with information regarding land use changes, the distribution of holdings, access to land and levels of productivity. National level data suffer serious weaknesses due to the limited capacity of many governments to maintain effective statistical coverage of agricultural production throughout the country. Some countries are now strengthening such systems of data collection, which are essential to understanding the dynamics of change within different farming systems, as well as pointing to areas of food deficit or falling productivity. Given the weak statistical base, analysis of changes to West African farming requires the combination of different sources and forms of evidence. These include local level studies, aerial photographs and satellite imagery, focused household surveys, poverty studies, and national level data.

If this absence of good quality data partly explains the contrasting interpretations of observable trends in regional agriculture in the literature, a further explanation is to be found in the diversity of country experiences over the past forty or so years. Thus, for Ghana, Côte d'Ivoire, Nigeria, Niger, Senegal, Burkina Faso and Mali, the last 30–40 years have shown much more positive experience with agricultural growth than is usually admitted by those asserting Africa's agriculture to be in crisis (Mortimore 2003). Despite periodic drought, switches in policy, devaluations and cutbacks in state support, farmers have managed to maintain growth in food production and kept pace with population growth, while at the same time expanding exports of key commodities. Furthermore, cropping patterns have shifted towards a more diverse range of commodities, from basic grains to maize, cowpeas, sesame and market gardening, in response to growing urban demand generated from expanding urban centres (OECD 1998). Livestock numbers have also been maintained, with a growing level of integration between animal and crop production in many areas.

The widely experienced trough in agricultural productivity which characterised the years between the late-1970s and mid-1980s was corrected through changes in government policy toward the agricultural sector, such as liberalisation of markets for key commodities and abandonment of price controls on basic grains. Equally, tight controls over choice of crops within state-managed irrigation have been lifted, freeing farmers to take advantage of new markets, such as fruit and vegetables within the Office du Niger in Mali. Where, as in the cotton zone of Mali, consistent support (such as technical assistance, credit, access to inputs, marketing) has been provided to farmers, performance has often been remarkable, with increases in both overall output and unit yield being recorded.

However, a continued ability to adapt and respond to new opportunities, and to the challenges of globalisation, are by no means assured. Farmers will continue to invest effort and capital in improving farm production where a reasonable return can be assured. But such returns are threatened by cheap imports, falling world market prices, and difficulties in accessing credit and inputs. At the same time, policies in favour of agricultural modernisation would appear to favour large-scale producers at the expense of the millions of family farms, which make up the majority of the agricultural sector. Such favouritism is justified by policy-makers on the grounds that family farms are unable to deliver a 'modern' agricultural economy. Yet this position is based on a highly partial interpretation of the evidence available, one which ignores the invaluable contribution of the region's millions of small farmers to domestic food supplies and commodity exports, as well as the broader multi-functionality arguments in favour of promoting smallholder agriculture.

Box 7.2 Family or household?

Family farm, or farm household? What is the difference between the two? Which term should be used?

Farm household is the term usually employed to describe the unit of production which farms a common field and eats from a common granary.

In practice, farm households usually operate in more complex ways. For example, individuals within the household may have their own private fields and granaries. Some livestock are owned individually, while others are the joint property of the household as a whole. Off-farm income earned by some members can also be shared or retained by the individual earners.

Several farm households may make up a *larger family group*, which no longer functions as a single production unit. Nevertheless, there may be some residual functions which are carried out by this larger family group, such as the management of lineage land, the planning and negotiation of matrimonial alliances and certain religious ceremonies.

Here, we use the term 'family farm' or 'farm household' interchangeably to mean the domestic group which works a common field and eats together, while recognising that in reality, family life is always more complex than this.

4 'Family farm' or 'farm household'?

Although widely used in a self-explanatory way, the term 'family farming' or *agriculture familiale* covers a broad range of often very different situations. Thus, some French authors strongly advise the use of the term in its plural form, *agricultures familiales*, to demonstrate the diversity of systems and contexts under discussion (Belières *et al.* 2002). The organisation and practice of farming systems vary greatly between agro-ecological zones, from one country to another, and between different socio-cultural groups. Within such diversity, however, there are certain key features which characterise family farming, relating to the particular connection between the structure and composition of the household and its associated farm assets and activities (Box 7.2). This relationship has important implications for how decisions are made regarding the choice of crops; the organisation of family labour and its allocation to different tasks; management of farm land and other assets; and questions of inheritance (CIRAD-TERA 2002, cited in Belières *et al.* 2002). In most parts of West Africa, farm production is based on family labour which, while often unpaid, is assured a return in the form of longer-term rights and expectations. Thus, family farms rely on labour contributions from their various members who, in return, will receive food and shelter, support in times of illness and old age, and help with costs of marriage, tax payments, and so on. Equally, commitment of labour to the family farm enterprise ensures its members maintain their rights to family property when a division of the estate takes place. This web of mutual obligations and rights is under strain in many areas, as a result of economic pressures, shifts in religious and cultural values, and the breakdown of large domestic groups into smaller nuclear units.

While much agricultural production relies heavily on family labour, non-household workers often represent a significant source of additional labour. Partly because of insufficient labour within the family resulting from illness or out-migration, and partly resulting from the pursuit of a strategy of agricultural expansion, many farmers rely on hiring labour from other families in the village, or on seasonal farm workers, for land preparation, cultivation, harvesting and crop processing (see Chapter 9). Thus, it is important to avoid seeing the family farm as an isolated economic unit focused entirely on agriculture and reliant exclusively on its own resources. Further characteristics of family farms typically include a diverse set of activities and outputs involving a range of crop and livestock production, fishing, hunting and gathering, trade and craftwork, as well as seasonal or longer-term migration (Zoundi 2003). Family farms often rely on a set of social networks linking relatives and neighbours in near and more distant locations, through which mutual support is provided. Maintenance and investment in these networks constitute an important element in the household's strategy, since they can provide an essential safety net in times of crisis (see Chapter 8). Within the family farm, access to land and farm assets tends to be acquired through inheritance or other social arrangements, such as loans.

The family farm, its land and associated assets (equipment, livestock, trees etc.) are under the authority of the household head, who is responsible for the collective management of these assets, the allocation of labour between different activities, management of grain stores, and decisions on new strategies and directions to be pursued. In practice, the household head will often delegate day-to-day management of fields and animals to a younger brother, while monitoring activities closely. The principal objective of the family farm is, first, to provide its members with food and shelter; and, second, to sell whatever is needed to obtain cash to meet household needs like clothing, medicines, school fees, investment in new equipment, and tax payments. Surplus crops may be stored to protect against future harvest failure, or sold and re-invested in livestock, other assets or social capital.

Family farms thus have three broad dimensions:

- A socio-cultural dimension, since this form of agriculture is mainly reliant on the human resource base of the family, strongly anchored in a particular community, through a web of relationships and strategies, both individual and collective, and reinforced by values of solidarity and long-term commitment.
- An economic dimension, characterised by an integration of diverse activities in household production, given the various opportunities available in immediate and more distant areas, and operating according to the following priorities – consume, store, sell.
- A technical dimension characterised by a desire to maintain and improve the land and resources on which they rely, and combining activities in ways which reduce exposure to risk.

In contrast to commercial enterprises, family farms tend to work relatively small areas of land. The prioritisation of consumption over commercialisation is, however, undergoing change in many areas, given the growing need for cash, leading to important shifts in how land and labour are allocated between food and cash crops. Equally, grain is an important cash crop for some farmers, as well as providing for the household's food needs. Nevertheless, family farms face distinct problems, which include:

- A growing shortage of land and its rapid increase in value, especially in peri-urban areas. Most West African smallholders claim rights over land through customary procedures and do not hold formal paper title. As a result, these land claims may be vulnerable to stronger interest groups who are seeking land and can get governments to back their claims through formal procedures.
- Illiteracy and poor access to schooling for many rural people, so that they have limited power to engage with the formal sector, whether in marketing, producer organisations, or contacts with government. Low levels of literacy may also hinder easy access to new technologies and innovative practices, as well as achieving more effective management of the farm enterprise.
- The low value accorded to the status of an agricultural smallholder, with the sons and daughters of farming households doing their best to escape a life of hard labour for little return. This low status also translates into little respect being given to local knowledge and ways of life, such as traditional medicine, skills in local craftwork, or systems for classifying grasses, soils and trees.
- The poorly developed organisation of smallholder agricultural producers constitutes a serious problem in a context of rapid integration of marketing and production systems. While government parastatals used to play an important role as providers of inputs and credit, and buyers of certain crops, most governments have been forced to disband these organisations and privatise these functions. In the absence of a well-developed co-operative movement, small farmers have very little organised marketing power or negotiating ability with input suppliers and crop buyers.
- The question of inheritance and fragmentation of land holdings is a serious problem for the viability of the family farm, which benefits from certain economies of scale when able to combine the labour and assets of several family members, rather than being limited to a nuclear family or single individual. While it is not always the rule, the death of the household head often leads to the break-up of the family into two or more separate units, with a division of the land and other assets. This fragmentation can lead to them becoming more vulnerable to risk and less able to maintain the livestock and equipment needed to run the farm.

As Box 7.3 shows, however, farming households are complex and dynamic institutions, which evolve over time.

Box 7.3 Dynamics, diversity and differentiation in family farms

Farm households in West Africa are highly diverse in size and structure. In any rural setting, there is usually a wide range of farm households, varying in size from small nuclear groups, comprising a married couple and young children, to larger complex domestic units in which there are several married couples, their children and aged parents. The size and structure of farm households are partly determined by cultural values, but are also the consequence of demographic processes, the skill exercised by the household head, and responses to economic opportunities.

The large, extended farm household traditionally associated with West African agricultural society has undergone major changes in recent generations. In some places, these large groups have broken up into smaller, nuclear families. Such a break-up may be a response by younger men seeking greater autonomy from their elders and no longer being willing to submit to their authority. Thus, Amanor (1999) describes the dissolution of forms of mutual obligations between fathers and sons – the former to provide land, pay tax, and contribute marriage expenses for the latter, who in return are expected to work for the family estate. Similar contests between senior and junior family members are described for Côte d'Ivoire (Chauveau 2002) and Nigeria (Smith 1966).

In other contexts, the large extended household remains of great significance. In the village of Zaradougou in southern Mali, for example, 85 per cent of the population lives in large complex households, ranging from 10–90 people in size. These domestic groups combine cotton and maize farms with cocoa and coffee plantations in Côte d'Ivoire as well as livestock, orchards and trading activities. Large size enables a diverse portfolio of incomes and assets (Brock and Coulibaly 1999). Within these large households, there is commonly a distinction maintained between collective and individual economic activity. Thus, household members are expected to work on the joint family field for a certain part of their time, being free to pursue their own interests in the remaining period. Maintaining a balance between collective and individual economic activity is a key management skill which some family heads master well. Where they fail, large households usually break up into their component units.

In risk prone environments, there are considerable advantages to living in large domestic units. For example, in the village of Kala in central Mali, larger households were associated with higher levels of livestock wealth (cattle/person) and access to farm equipment (plough teams/person), as well as greater food security (harvest/person). Benefits from shared production and investment in large households (averaging 24 people in size) were substantial. Nuclear families (averaging 8 people) were much more vulnerable to risk and were not able to benefit from economies of scale in production, investment and income diversification (Toulmin 1992). Differentiation between farm households takes place over time as some families do better than others and can increase their control over key assets (land, livestock, labour, capital). Others suffer impoverishment, due to harvest failure, family illness, sale of assets and the need to work for others. Such processes of social differentiation have always existed to some extent. But it is important to ask: are such processes now becoming more significant? Is socio-economic differentiation linked to increased integration with the market economy? How might poorer farm households be enabled to protect their assets at times of crisis, and reduce vulnerability to impoverishment?

5 *Towards a typology of farm households*

West Africa exhibits a very diverse array of family farms, in terms of factors such as size, assets, market orientation, income, diversification of activities, reliance on migrants' earnings and vulnerability to risk. A typology of farm households within such diversity depends, as with all classification systems, on the objectives sought. For example, in the cotton-growing region of Southern Mali, the CMDT, the parastatal body responsible for cotton production and marketing, uses a fourfold classification of farm households based on a combination of farm size and type of equipment used, which enables the CMDT to target different kinds of technical advice.

A recent review of family farms in a global setting proposes a three-way classification of rural producers (Box 7.4a). The resulting typology, whose main aim is to examine levels of market involvement, access to technology and exposure to risk within processes of rural differentiation, suggests that family farms in West Africa are to be found largely in the second and third categories. These farming enterprises, which have been able to survive until now, may face a more challenging future as local markets and food systems become increasingly globalised. Zoundi (2003) presents a three-fold classification of family farms, which echoes the categories outlined in Box 7.4. The first category comprises those with a strong involvement in crop production for the market, and where this guides very substantially the choices made regarding resource allocation. The second category is made up of those farm households largely focused on production for satisfying their own needs. A third, intermediary, category can be identified for which some balance is maintained between market and subsistence activities. As Zoundi (2003) notes, such intermediate households are often those who, while formerly focused on subsistence production, are now allocating more time and resources to market production, as a result of the rising need for cash to satisfy diverse household needs.

A three-fold classification of this sort, which builds on the insights of Vorley (2002) and Zoundi (2003), while corresponding with the range of situations found across West Africa, would have the characteristics identified in Box 7.4. However, it should be recognised that a wide range of households in terms of size, activities, reliance on off-farm sources of income, land tenure situation and so on, is to be found within each of these broad categories. Equally, it should be remembered that these are not mutually-exclusive categories; there is likely to be mobility between them

Box 7.4 Three rural worlds, and three types of family farm

(a) Three rural worlds . . .
Rural world 1: Globally competitive, embedded in agri-business, commodity producers and processors, politically well-connected, export-driven, adopters of Green Revolution and transgenic technologies.
Rural world 2: Locally-oriented, with access to and control over land, multiple and diverse enterprises, undercapitalised, declining terms of trade and at serious risk of future impoverishment.
Rural world 3: Fragile livelihoods, limited access to productive resources, multi-occupational migrants straddling rural and urban life, unskilled and uneducated, dependent on low wage labour, redundant to global food and fibre production systems.

Source: Vorley (2002: 9).

(b) . . . And three types of family farm
Type 1: Farmers oriented towards the market, organised around one of the major cash crops, such as cotton, cocoa, coffee, fruit and vegetables. Often highly specialised, they are exposed to significant risks from fluctuations of, or in, global market prices. Within this group can also be found farms in the urban and peri-urban zone, specialising in producing for the market.
Type 2: Farms in which cereal production and cash crop activity are more or less balanced in terms of their relative importance. Such farm households often pursue considerable diversification, as a means to protect themselves from climatic and market risks, the level of diversification depending on local conditions, access to land and the size of household.
Type 3: Farms oriented towards grain production for subsistence needs, some part of the harvest being sold to raise cash. They constitute the poorer households with limited access to inputs and markets, with little equipment and few livestock. In many places, these households are finding it particularly difficult to make ends meet and undergoing a process of de-capitalisation which will lead eventually to their disappearance.

from year to year, and over longer time periods. For example, a farm household which suffers the loss of a key family member, through out-migration or death, may be forced to re-orient its pattern of production from a market focus, to the satisfaction of food needs. Conversely, a very good harvest in one year may provide the means for a household to invest in new equipment and pursue a more market-oriented cropping pattern in future.

It is this diversity of farm households, and their differential ability to respond to market opportunities, invest in productive assets, and meet their needs, that has led some observers to pronounce the end of the family farm. Those in favour of promoting investment in large-scale commercial agri-business can always find examples of impoverished, subsistence-based families, unable to cope with the multiple challenges of prices, climate and risk. Those seeking to demonstrate the dynamism and viability of family farms can point to a very different set of smallholders, who have clearly demonstrated their ability to address new markets and adopt new technologies. Policy measures need to consider how best to address the very different needs and pathways associated with each kind of producer.

6 Mapping agrarian change in West Africa

West Africa is a highly complex and diverse region, whose diversity of setting presents a major challenge for understanding change and the

Box 7.5 Mapping the Sahel

Raynaut *et al.* (1997) use 14 geographical territories, which often have a particular identity, associated with an ancient pattern of land use surrounding a long-settled market town or administrative centre (such as around the Hausa cities of Maradi, and Kano), a geographical coherence in terms of soils, farming practice and commercial crop development. These areas include: the Senegalese groundnut basin, the inner Niger Delta, the Senegalese river valley, the pioneer farming zones of southern Mali and south-west Burkina Faso, the Sahelian belt of agro-pastoral systems, the Casamance, the Ader massif, and extensive pastoral rangelands. While recognising the risks of an over-simple characterisation of these major types of situation, this approach does allow for a means to understand the different patterns of economic and social change which can be discerned between settings, and to highlight the importance of certain factors underlying trends and evolutions in different places. Raynaut *et al.* identify four main processes which help explain change – agro-ecological constraints, demography, market constraints and state interventions, and peasant strategies in response to the diverse opportunities available.

Similar approaches have been taken by other writers to identify areas which have a certain meaning in social, economic, political or ecological terms. Thus, for example, the Adja Plateau in southern Benin or the *terres de barre* have long symbolised a particular socio-economic pattern. Equally, writers have talked of the pioneer farming areas of central Benin, the densely populated Upper East region of Ghana, the current cocoa frontier of western Côte d'Ivoire, or the abandoned cocoa-lands of Eastern Ghana. While to some extent this attempt to create a series of socio-geographic regions is an artificial device, it helps in understanding the different dynamics and pathways of change being followed, as well as the inter-connections between these areas. The massive inflows of migrant farmers into the south west of Burkina Faso cannot be understood without knowing the difficult circumstances faced on the drought-prone Mossi Plateau further north, and by Burkinabé migrants in Côte d'Ivoire.

Box 7.6 Capitalising on new opportunities in dryland Mali

The Sourou Valley in southern Mali was, until recently, a dryland forest area used for grazing. As a result of dam construction downstream in Burkina Faso in 1988, the river level has risen and extended upstream, allowing Malian cultivators to farm rice as well as their traditional millet crop. This has led to the rapid clearance of forest in the floodplain of the Sourou valley, in a process without any specific government or other project intervention. An estimated 6000 ha have been brought under cultivation as a result. There has been a substantial inflow of people seeking land, as well as herds in search of rice stubble as dry season grazing. This new cropping activity is said to have greatly reduced food insecurity in a formerly very vulnerable area, with many individuals and households reporting increasing incomes and levels of consumption, as well as falling rates of out-migration. Evidence of increasing differentiation between households is emerging: better-off households own oxen and other cattle, as well as large and well-flooded rice fields, and report higher yields per ha.

Source: Woodhouse *et al.* (2000).

evolution of farming and socio-economic systems. The approach taken by the West Africa Long-Term Prospective Study (WALTPS) (OECD 1998) and other such surveys has been to identify several large geographical regions within each of which there exists some homogeneity. Thus, WALTPS identifies three zones: the Gulf of Guinea, Atlantic Sahel and Forest areas, and the landlocked Sahel. This choice of regions combined issues of ecology, demographic pressure, and the role of economic poles or growth centres that attract resources and act as regional markets. In contrast, Raynaut *et al.* (1997) draw on a range of case studies and insights from across the Sahelian region, to identify a series of more micro-focused territories or geographical areas with certain characteristics, and focused around a well-defined local centre (Box 7.5).

The evolution of rural areas is the result of a combination of several factors, amongst which the strategies employed by peasant farmers themselves constitute a central component. In cases such as the Sourou Valley, Mali, farmers have worked on their own initiative to seize new opportunities for irrigated agriculture in a dry zone (Box 7.6).

In more marginal regions, the joint effects of environmental change, demographic growth and structural adjustment have led to farming becoming less central to household livelihoods, as in south-west Niger (Box 7.7).

In areas where cash crops used to be dominant, farmers are learning new ways of making ends meet (Faye *et al.* 2001). Senegal has witnessed a steep fall in groundnut production since the 1960s, when this crop was the major source of export earnings and farm income. Conventional explanations have

Box 7.7 Adapting to increased risk and withdrawal of services in Niger

The Zarma farmers of Fandou Beri, south-west Niger, practise an extensive form of agriculture, mainly producing millet for household consumption. Reduced fallows and changes in rainfall, combined with structural adjustment measures, have led to increased reliance on seasonal migration and petty trading. Over the period 1952–92, the area of the village territory under cultivation increased from 11 to 23 per cent. Good quality soils within the village territory have disappeared and yields have declined. However, little intensification of production has occurred. Fertilisers were used for a period in the 1980s, but after project support and subsidies were withdrawn, their use dwindled. Zarma farmers do not routinely apply manure to their fields. Their limited livestock holdings are entrusted to Peul families and there is little integration between crops and livestock on Zarma farms. Cropping appears to have become less diverse as a result of changing environmental conditions, such that sorghum is no longer cultivated in significant quantities and cash crops such as cotton and groundnuts are rare. Short-cycle millet varieties have been adopted by farmers. Livestock ownership is becoming more attractive to Zarma farmers as a result of favourable animal prices, but there is little indication of any trend towards more integrated animal and crop production. Compared to the 1980s, sales of crop surpluses are now rare because of very low yields. Almost all young men leave the village by harvest time to earn cash elsewhere. Women derive income from selling a variety of items, such as prepared food and sauce ingredients, and from petty trading. Other home-based activities include mat making and raising animals.

Source: Batterbury *et al.* (1996).

blamed population growth for causing land scarcity and a reduction in fallow lengths, with the latter being seen in turn as the cause of falling yields and, together with a reduction in woodland, as evidence of environment degradation. Only gradually was it realised that economic factors were also at work, particularly a price and marketing system that forced farmers in a risky environment to rely on credit for access to inputs, and which deprived them of much of the benefit of world prices (Box 7.8).

7 Key drivers and challenges of change in agriculture

7.1 Land use change

Patterns of land use have undergone enormous change in the last 30–40 years with a large and continuous expansion in the area under cultivation.

Box 7.8 Diversifying away from agriculture in Senegal

In Diourbel Region, a new dynamic is observable, particularly since the change in agricultural and pricing policy which began in the 1980s. People in the area have always responded to different market opportunities for their produce and labour. Despite a decline in rainfall, farmers have maintained or raised yields per unit of rainfall, selectively using technologies introduced by the extension service. Rising meat prices have led to a massive swing to livestock production, using new fattening methods. Farm trees have been conserved, and crops diversified in favour of cowpeas and hibiscus. However, despite Senegal's heavy imports of rice, millet production has been limited to rural consumption needs, since there is no urban market for this crop.

Low agricultural incomes due to falling output prices and rising input prices have encouraged such substantial diversification into non-farm activities and urban out-migration that the proportion of land farmed may have declined despite population growth. The headquarters of the Mouride brotherhood, Touba, is the largest town in the Region, despite officially still being regarded as 'rural'. Touba, Dakar and overseas destinations have all attracted migrants, and many rural families have an urban branch. Remittances are not used for farm investments, but for consumption needs, and the little farm investment that takes place is livestock-oriented.

Source: Faye *et al.* (2001).

This has led to clearance of much forested land in coastal and savannah regions, and a large number of farmers moving from high to less densely settled areas, seeking land. Thus, for example, it is estimated that in Ghana cropland occupied only 14.5 per cent of national space in 1961 but 25.5 per cent in 1995; equally, in Côte d'Ivoire, cropland increased from 8.5 per cent to 23.5 per cent over the same period (Mortimore 2003). Similar rates of growth can be found in much of the region, though the paucity and quality of data remains a problem.

Such a large increase in cultivated area stems from various sources. Demographic growth is clearly an important driver with natural growth in the farm population of 2–3 per cent per annum producing equivalent growth in the area farmed, where land is still reasonably abundant. Migration flows into a particular area can generate very rapid rates of land use change, such as has happened in west and south-western Burkina Faso, where more than 80 per cent of the land is farmed by people who have come from elsewhere, especially the drought-prone Mossi plateau, where land is scarce. Large-scale programmes to clear onchocerchiasis (River Blindness) have helped open up broad areas for settlement that were formerly very lightly used. The widespread adoption of animal traction and, in some places, tractors has also led to very large increases in farmland. Many pastoral groups have adopted a much more settled pattern of life, given livestock losses during previous droughts and their increasing desire to establish firmer rights to land. National land tenure policy has also prompted greater land clearance in some areas where, for example, rights to land are conferred through its *mise en valeur* ('being put to good use' – evidence for this usually being taken as making a physical investment, such as digging a well, constructing a building or soil conservation structures). This has encouraged strategic behaviour by some to cut and clear land in excess of what is actually needed, as a means of demonstrating use and consequent land rights.

Expansion of land for cultivation is likely to continue in those areas where resources are available, since this provides the best return on scarce supplies of labour. This massive investment of labour in clearing new land has often been portrayed in negative terms and described as 'deforestation' and 'land degradation'. Yet, in many cases, it constitutes a landscape transformation bringing higher returns to the land user than semi-natural vegetation. As noted by Mortimore (2003) 'such a landscape transformation represents an immense investment of effort in clearance . . . The value and achievements of private investments in African agrarian landscapes have been consistently underestimated by outsiders.' This is not to deny that removal of the vegetation for farming will likely render land more vulnerable to erosion, or that reducing the availability of fallow land also cuts back on pasture and wild produce. As land becomes scarcer, and more valuable, farmers are likely to make greater investment in ways of intensifying land use which should address some of these concerns. Such intensification will be more probable where agricultural prices bring a reasonable return, and land users have reasonably secure rights over the land they farm.

7.2 Environmental change

Environmentally, over the last 30 years, there have been major changes in patterns of rainfall, land cover and vegetation throughout West Africa. The dry Sahelian region has been most affected by rainfall changes, having experienced a decrease of 20–30 per cent in expected rainfall between the periods 1931–60 and 1961–90 (Hulme 1996). Not only has rainfall declined substantially, but its distribution within the farming season has become more unpredictable. The major droughts of the 1970s and 1980s prompted a substantial shift southwards by farmers and herders in search of better watered areas, bringing major increases in population pressure in southern areas and the coastal region. Future trends in climate for the region as a whole are still unclear (IPCC 2001).

Despite such adverse climatic conditions, many farming communities have managed to cope by changing their practices, diversifying incomes, and adopting new crops and forms of land use that bring reasonable returns. The Mossi Plateau in central Burkina Faso demonstrates such adaptation and the important role of simple technical improvements in strengthening farmer response to climate change (Box 7.9).

Box 7.9 Investing in soil conservation brings results in Burkina Faso

The Central Plateau of Burkina Faso has undergone many changes over the last 20 years. With 500–700 mm rainfall, it is characterised by marginal soils and high population densities (up to 100 persons/km^2). In 1980 this was considered the most degraded region of Burkina Faso. The vegetation was rapidly disappearing, cereal yields were on average 400–500 kg/ha, groundwater levels were falling rapidly and between 1975 and 1985 up to 25 per cent of families left the villages to settle in regions of higher potential. Improved methods of soil and water conservation (SWC), introduced over the last 15–20 years, have helped address some of these difficulties and led to major benefits, which include:

- Yields of sorghum and millet have increased substantially, and household food security has improved.
- The process of vegetation degradation has been reversed on cultivated fields treated with soil and water conservation (over 100,000 ha).
- Increased investment in livestock by both men and women, and more intensive animal management mean that more manure is available for improving soil fertility.
- More forage is available for livestock due to regeneration of vegetation.
- Many villages have seen rising water tables (+ 5 m or more) due to increased infiltration of rainfall and runoff.
- Rural-to-rural and rural-to-urban migration has decreased since the start of SWC programmes.
- Organisational capacity of villagers has improved.
- Local people reckon there has been a substantial reduction of rural poverty (up to 50 per cent) between 1980 and 2002.
- The cumulative impact of SWC can also be found in agro-statistical data at provincial level. For instance, in Bam province the cultivated area did not increase as expected, but decreased slightly since 1989, while cereal yields increased by 50 per cent.

Comparing villages with and without SWC projects, it is clear that the introduction of low-cost, risk-reducing and productivity-enhancing SWC has played a key role in triggering agricultural intensification and environmental improvement. Other factors have also played a role. For instance, the devaluation of the West African currency in early 1994 stimulated investment in livestock, and the improvement of major roads between Ouagadougou and two regional capitals reduced transaction costs and allowed traders from Côte d'Ivoire, Ghana and even Nigeria to send their lorries to Yatenga province to buy sesame, cowpea and vegetables.

One interesting farmer-innovator on the Mossi plateau is Ali Ouédraogo, now around 70 years old, who started to rehabilitate degraded land in 1983. Living on the edge of the small town of Gourcy, Zondoma province, he was trained by the Oxfam PAF project to lay out and construct stone bunds. He has now treated many hectares of formerly barren land with a mix of bunds and planting pits, or *zaï*, creating a much better environment for his sorghum crop. At the same time, he has encouraged regeneration of trees through planting indigenous tree seeds along the contour lines and preserving those seedlings that sprout in his field. In this way he can combine cereal cultivation with availability of perennial forage for his animals, the dung from which then returns to the soil via a large compost and manure pit he has established.

Sources: Chris Reij (personal communication); Reij and Waters-Bayer (2001).

7.3 Increasing land scarcity and value

The last thirty years have witnessed a very rapid growth of population, expanding urban centres and major migratory flows throughout the region, although the impact of such processes has been uneven. Having once seemed in ever abundant supply, in many areas good land is now becoming relatively scarce, due to a variety of factors. Such scarcity brings rising market values, and greater difficulties for poorer groups seeking access to this resource.

Gaining secure access to land is of particular importance to poorer people, whose livelihoods depend on balancing a range of different activities, including negotiating access to a plot of land and being able to use the local commons. These rights are often not full property rights but various forms of secondary access. Yet such rights are increasingly subject to threat, as land values rise and new interests enter the land arena. There is growing competition for high productivity land, particularly where a reliable water supply will permit irrigation. The poor tend to be particularly vulnerable in areas undergoing rapid change, such as on the peri-urban fringe and in cash-crop producing zones. While in past decades, local land users were vulnerable to the state alienating their resources, the last few years have seen the emergence of private sector investors in much of West Africa, seeking land for farming.

The price of land is rising as it becomes scarcer. In Côte d'Ivoire, 30 years ago, incoming farmers could gain large areas of land in the forest zone in exchange for customary payments of kolanuts and a chicken, and a small cash sum (Koné 2002). Now, in many places, it is impossible to access land except through major cash payments to land rights holders, either in terms of annual rents, or through mortgaging arrangements. Equally, in western Burkina Faso, arrangements for accessing land have shifted substantially from long-term loans, to shorter-term rental, with payments either in cash or through provision of services (for example, labour, ploughing) (Paré 2001).

7.4 Structural adjustment, devaluation and liberalisation

From the 1980s onwards, all countries in the region have been through a process of structural adjustment, involving liberalisation of the economy, devaluation of the currency and a range of associated measures. The effects of such liberalisation have been mixed and difficult to evaluate, given partial adherence to structural adjustment policies in some cases, a great diversity of settings, and a lack of good time series data. In general, where liberalisation helped remove tax and levies; on agriculture, this brought benefits to the farming sector and provided a boost to the millions of smallholders making up this sector (Kherallah *et al.* 2002). One major consequence of this has been the near-total disappearance of state and parastatal marketing structures involved in marketing of agricultural produce. A few such organisations still exist (such as the CMDT in Mali) but, even where they have survived, their power and functions have been greatly slimmed down. The purpose of liberalisation has been in part to promote the free play of market forces, but also to relieve the state of a financial burden which was, in many cases, draining away central government resources. Liberalisation has certainly created space for the multiplication of economic actors (input suppliers, traders) in those places where their operations are profitable, but with the abandonment of pan-territorial pricing, poorer farmers in more marginal areas have faced difficulties since the services provided by a parastatal structure have not been replaced by the private sector. Elsewhere, the removal of tight production and marketing controls has helped open up many new possibilities to farmers, as can be seen by the rapid expansion in off-season fruit and vegetable production in Mali's Office du Niger (Dembélé *et al.* 2001).

For export crops, such as cotton, groundnuts, and cocoa, the impact of withdrawal of agricultural subsidies and cheap fertiliser was offset for a period by a combination of better world market prices and gains associated with devaluation. Thus, for cotton production in Mali, the combination of higher producer prices due to devaluation and rising world market prices in the mid-1990s more than outweighed the extra costs of buying the inputs needed to guarantee a good harvest. However, current world market prices are at their lowest level for thirty years, due to overproduction at the global level, fuelled by agricultural subsidies in the US and EU. In the case of livestock, the higher returns from animal sales, post-devaluation, much more than compensated producers for any input costs.

However, liberalisation also brought multiple and damaging impacts where it overturned the established systems for input supply, marketing, and provision of credit. A recent assessment of the effect of such policies in Côte d'Ivoire clearly points out their contribution to the current political and economic crisis, by accelerating the tearing up of the economic and social fabric which had provided the basis for some level of political consensus between competing groups (Losch *et al.* 2003). One consequence has been the rapid descent of much of the population into poverty, with income per head falling by half, further aggravating the social and ethnic tensions between groups (see Chapter 10). In the case of Côte d'Ivoire, it is estimated that the proportion of those in poverty tripled from 10 per cent to 31 per cent of the population over the period 1987–2002 (Losch *et al.* 2003). Measures to liberalise the economy were particularly damaging because of their simplicity, and dogmatic quality, based on short-term perspectives and a lack of proper preparation and supportive measures.

Box 7.10 Kano, a long-established city state in northern Nigeria

The Kano Close Settled Zone is well-known for the long-established system of farming which it has supported for several centuries. It provides 'an example of a farming system which has reached the point in the intensification process at which all land is under cultivation, all palatable crop residues are used as fodder, and trees are conserved' (Harris 1996: 13). Soil fertility is maintained by labour-intensive management involving the close integration of livestock and crops. Long before inorganic fertilisers became available, and even now for those who cannot afford them, animal manure with bedding and compound sweepings are vital components in maintaining the physical and chemical properties of the soil. Hence, every household aspires to own as many sheep and goats as possible. The crops are weeded very regularly and the plant biomass fed to animals. Trees are browsed and their fodder used as forage. Fuel wood is harvested from dead wood, and cut branches. All trees are privately owned so they are protected for the future. The resulting landscape is one of 'farmed parkland', similar to that found in the forest transition zone of Guinea (Fairhead and Leach 1996) and in the long established areas to the south of Ségou in Mali. However, even in the lower density, drier landscapes further to the north and east of Kano city, the landscape is one created and maintained by farmers and their livestock to generate a sustainable set of crops, forage and bush materials.

Source: Mortimore and Adams (1999).

Thus, the old state monopolies were merely replaced by private oligopolies, very often foreign owned, which eliminated the role of, and possibilities for, Ivorian enterprise. The downturn in world market prices for cocoa and coffee further damaged incomes and prospects.

7.5 Increased linkages into markets: the role of urban centres

While the rate of overall population growth and urbanisation rates have both been high over the last half century or so, bringing about a significant rise in the overall population:land ratio, urbanisation has been noticeably rapid (see Chapter 1). Urban and peri-urban areas in West Africa have long exercised a very powerful influence over the neighbouring hinterlands, spreading economic development through market relations, and political and administrative control through the imposition of taxation and military levies (Box 7.10).

Yet this beneficial impact from improved access to markets is matched by a growing level of land insecurity, as Box 7.11 shows.

Urban growth and rising demand for food, fibre and other farm products provide a valuable motor for agricultural intensification, and

Box 7.11 Uncertain land rights for peri-urban farmers in Ghana and Nigeria

Change and development in the peri-urban region of Kumasi have followed a pattern of intensification and increasing returns over the last 30–40 years. While in the 1960s, forest cover and fertile soils were still supporting cocoa production in the 10–20 km belt around the city, by the 1970s production had shifted to cassava, maize and okra, with a rapid rise in production for the city's market in the 1980s and 1990s. Cassava has now become the most important crop, associated with tomatoes and other vegetables. Declining soil fertility and farm size have brought about increased use of fertilisers and agro-chemicals and growing interest from amongst younger farmers to engage in farm production. Often migrants renting land, they constitute a more entrepreneurial class of younger male farmers. The rapid growth in Kumasi is provoking considerable uncertainty amongst farmers close to the city who see much cultivated land being converted to building plots. As a consequence, many land users feel increasingly insecure regarding their usufruct rights, and vulnerable to finding themselves landless, the chief selling the land over their heads for building plots and paying the land-user no compensation. As a result, there is a growing reluctance amongst farmers to invest in improving soil fertility and applying other agricultural inputs since they risk losing all benefits from this. By contrast in the more distant areas some 20 km or more from Kumasi, farmers are intensifying production with greater assurance that they will benefit from such investments.

Even those with land feel the need to pursue more promising livelihood options, given the threats to land holdings. Kasanga (1998) notes that many people consider urbanisation to have generated rising poverty and insecurity (52 per cent) with only 2 per cent considering urbanisation to have brought increased incomes. The rising cost of living from increased rents has pushed some people into more distant areas, with many people no longer being able to gain access to land through traditional channels, given its appropriation and conversion to house-building.

In peri-urban Port Harcourt, insecure and uncertain rights over land provide a similar disincentive for land users to invest in higher levels of productivity. Despite a very large urban market on their doorstep, many land users are part-time farmers, seeking to supplement their incomes with a little extra food but hoping to find a paid job in the city rather than concentrating on market gardening, given the risks associated with land.

Sources: Brook and Dávila (2000); Anikpo (2000).

transform property rights. The key questions concern how best to manage the scramble for land rights in peri-urban areas where land values are rapidly escalating, to ensure that land users retain a strong incentive further to invest in the productivity of their plots and feel assured of their longer-terms claims.

7.6 Social change

In social terms, much of West African rural society is experiencing the fragmentation of large domestic groups into smaller family units with principles of long-term reciprocity being replaced by shorter-term calculation of economic advantage (Amanor 1999). This means that elders can no longer assume the free provision of labour services from their sons, since the latter have equally had to abandon their expectations of gaining land from their fathers, due to land shortages and sales of land outside the lineage (Chauveau 1997; Paré 2001). Equally, relations between women and men have undergone significant change, with women increasingly demanding that they be paid for work done for their husband's estate.

Such transformations to the social structures and institutions within which people plan their lives are widespread. As Guyer (1997: 206) has observed for south west Nigeria:

> the 'household' of man, wife (or wives) and dependent children is even less of a production unit in 1988 than it was in 1968. Young people work for wages, even from their senior kin. Wives farm on their own account, and husbands hardly intervene in any way with their wives' farms . . . the work that kinsmen used to carry out for each other under the rubric of long term cash reciprocity, such as porterage by wives in return for ceremonial contributions and labour by juniors in return for bridewealth, have been obviated by changes in social life and translated into much more short-run forms.

These changes to social structures, expectations, values and domestic institutions will have major consequences for patterns of economic development, especially in the agricultural sector, protection of more vulnerable groups from diverse sources of risk, and levels of poverty. The shift from collective to individual forms of activity and wealth creation, and breakdown of large into small domestic units seem inevitable results from the process of social modernisation. Government rarely, if ever, explicitly considers the potential damage to social well-being and loss of social capital which these changes bring with them.

7.7 Diversification of agriculture and livelihoods

Throughout West Africa rural incomes have become increasingly diverse, with farming accounting in many cases for only 30–40 per cent of total revenue (cash and kind combined). Diversifying to protect against risk has long been part of household strategies for survival and growth, whether it be by growing a range of different crops, raising different species of livestock, or investing in a broad set of assets and social networks. The last 30–40 years have witnessed substantial shifts in patterns of consumption and potential markets. While rising incomes and urban development have provided new market opportunities for certain skills, some traditional crafts have been forced out of business, with the arrival of cheaper substitutes. Thus, today, rural women rarely wear homespun cotton cloth, given the wide range of cheap, machine-woven cotton fabrics now available. Equally, the makers of clay pots, and menders of calabash bowls, find far less demand for their skills now, given the availability of light and strong plastic and galvanised iron vessels.

Adverse circumstances have forced some people to develop new sources of revenue, as when herders have lost so many animals they can no longer maintain a pastoral existence and must start to farm. At the same time, some people have turned to a new livelihood in town due to a collapse in their former way of making a living. But in many cases, livelihood diversification has been a positive, conscious choice, with people seeking out new opportunities that provide a better return on their effort. Examples include the large number of farmers from Burkina Faso and Mali seeking land to farm in Côte d'Ivoire, and the widespread adoption of fishing as an additional source of activity throughout the region (Morand *et al.* forthcoming). Equally, while some traditional crafts have suffered a loss of markets, others continue to thrive, while the increase in consumer goods and equipment has generated many additional sources of activity (such as bicycle and mobylette/scooter repairs, sewing machines, construction work in town, loading and unloading lorries, and so on). Migration, whether to town or to another farming area, is often portrayed as a response to desperation. But this paints too negative a picture of what, for many of those involved, constitutes an opening up of many new opportunities, bringing a significant cash income.

Patterns of diversification tend to be associated with location and the kind of household (size, wealth, etc.). Wiggins (2000) argues that there is likely to be more diversification taking place in higher potential, more ecologically varied farming areas, as the local economy provides a greater range of options for people to pursue *in situ*. However, there is also strong evidence for households in low rainfall, higher risk settings developing more diverse income sources, though this frequently involves migration away from home (Reardon 1997) (Box 7.12). Larger and wealthier households also tend to diversify more successfully than small, poor households, the former being able to take risks as they have both the labour available and the assets to invest in new activities.

As in other fields, it is often the early innovator who faces the highest risks but is also likely to reap the higher rewards. Diversification of income and assets in the form of a broad household portfolio provides greater protection against the multiple hazards faced by farm households everywhere, as shown by recent thinking on rural livelihoods (Ellis 2001; Hussein and Nelson 1998; Scoones 1998). Maintaining and expanding the large domestic unit is an integral component in such a diversification strategy.

7.8 *Agro-industry and* 'nouveaux acteurs'

While the vast majority of West African agriculture and land remain in the hands of smallholders, there has been a significant interest in farming from the industrial sector, though this has ebbed and flowed depending on circumstances. Thus, in Nigeria in the 1970s and 1980s, government aimed to encourage large-scale, private investment in agriculture, and backed up such an approach with changes to land tenure laws (Olofin

Box 7.12 Patterns of diversification shift over time, Mali

In Dalonguebougou, central Mali, eight broad categories of livelihood diversification were being followed by different groups, including trade (at both individual and household level), agricultural wage labour, small stock rearing, cotton weaving and spinning, granary making, fortune telling, and a range of other skills (carpenter, tailor, bicycle mechanic). Successful farming households have pursued a series of investments bringing good returns over the last 50 years, as can be seen below.

Date/period	Form of diversification
1950s/60s	Expansion of groundnut cultivation, first by hand and then through the purchase of ox-drawn ploughs
1970s	Purchase of cattle herds, particularly during drought years, when grain and livestock prices favourable
1980s	Purchase of cattle herds, particularly during drought years, when grain and livestock prices favourable
mid-1990s	Enlargement of bush fields using plough teams, expansion of trade into shop-keeping

Sources: Toulmin (1992); Brock and Coulibaly (1999).

and Patrick 1989). In more recent times, a number of West African governments have opted for policies in favour of the 'modernisation of agriculture'. One central element has been to promote more secure forms of land tenure to allow for privately owned land as a means to encourage long-term investment in land improvement. Another element has comprised positive measures to encourage the establishment of agricultural entrepreneurs in rural areas, by ensuring access to land and preferential access to key inputs. Thus, for example, Senegal has just approved a project 'Sénégal Agricole' which plans to put in place 25 large-scale agricultural schemes and half a dozen agropoles. Together, these are hoped to provide an additional 30,000 hectares of irrigated land over the next five years (Walfadjri 2002).

Some governments espouse policies aimed at 'agricultural modernisation' which assert the need to do away with many small-scale peasant farms, on the grounds that they can no longer cope with competition and technological change (Observatoire Paalga 2001). Others, such as Senegal, explicitly commit themselves to support for family farms, while seeking to complement their presence with large-scale agro-industrial developments (Government of Senegal 2003). However, in the West African context, there is no evidence for the superiority of large-scale commercial agriculture, which has performed very poorly over recent decades (Belières *et al.* 2002). The global evidence on farm size and productivity also shows small farms generate higher yields than large-scale enterprises (Box 7.13).

Box 7.13 Farm size and productivity

Are small farms more or less productive than large farms? A substantial body of research shows that productivity, taken as output per hectare, is higher on small than large farms (Deininger and Squire, 1998; Netting 1993). The data stem mainly from Asia and Latin America, with little work done on farm size issues in sub-Saharan Africa. This inverse relationship between farm size and productivity is the result of several factors. Small farms rely much more on family labour which tends to require much less supervision than hired workers. Given differences in land area available, it is rational for small farmers to maximise returns to their scarce factor, land.

A recent survey of 'new agriculturalists' in Burkina Faso suggests that the large farms being established have low yields and poor performance in comparison with neighbouring peasant farms. However, many of these new farms have only very recently been established, and may therefore record improved productivity over the longer term (Ouédraogo 2002).

Work amongst West African farmers suggests that there may be some economies of scale in farming, such that farm households with 10–20 people and one or two plough teams do better than nuclear families containing couples and young children which are reliant on hand tools (Belières *et al.* 2002; Toulmin 1992). However, moving beyond this size not only appears not to bring additional benefits, but is also associated with lower returns and greater vulnerability to market price variability, access to cheap credit, etc.

Current debate regarding the future of agriculture in West Africa has focused on the choice between family farming and agri-business. The first is often presented as backward, inefficient and subsistence-oriented, while the second is attributed the virtues of being modern and forward-looking, efficient and market-oriented. Yet, in practice, such distinctions are false, with levels of performance largely the product of external conditions and incentives. Large-scale commercial farming is itself highly differentiated, with a range of strategies being pursued. Some large farmers are seriously engaged in running a profitable business, while for others, the receipt of preferential inputs and access to credit may be a prime motive. Equally, some 'large farmers' are more interested in acquiring claims over land for speculative, rather than productive purposes. Many examples show that these farms have suffered damaging reversals when government preferences are withdrawn, and access to inputs and foreign exchange becomes harder. By contrast, small-scale family farms maintain a degree of autonomy which allows them to cope with adverse circumstances, while family labour enables a rapid and flexible response to emerging economic opportunities. There are also distinct differences within the family farm sector between large, adaptable farm households, and small, highly vulnerable groups with few assets or capacities to cope with change.

During the 1970s, the governments of Ghana and Nigeria tried to encourage foreign firms to invest in agriculture (Box 7.14). The Nigeria

Box 7.14 Private sector investment in large farms: a dismal story

Many transnational companies with operations in Ghana had accumulated profits from their activities but were unable to transfer them abroad due to shortages of foreign exchange. It was hoped that their investment in joint private–state farming enterprises would increase agro-industrial activity. The government guaranteed access to land, social infrastructure and tax exemptions for equipment and other inputs. However, only 12 companies were in fact willing to take up these schemes, with 4 of these still in business in the late 1980s, failures having been due to litigation relating to land, and poor access to foreign exchange for imports of inputs. Nevertheless, the scale of land appropriation for some of these schemes was very considerable, with the Benso Oil Palm Plantation taking 27 square miles of land, and displacing 3000 peasant farmers. The expansion of oil palm production and expropriation of land for the Ghana Oil Palm Development Corporation (GOPDC) has resulted in a scarcity of land for many farmers and for food production. With few opportunities in agriculture, many youths are moving into informal sectors that are being criminalised by the state, such as chainsaw timber production and small-scale mining, and engaging in activities which involve pilfering, such as night-time harvesting from the GOPDC oil palm plantations. These activities reflect the recognition amongst rural dwellers that state policies are not in their interests or administered on their behalf.

Sources: Amanor (1999) and Guyer (1997).

indigenisation decrees passed in the 1970s obliged foreign firms to re-invest profits in the Nigerian economy. The Land Use Act of 1978 was also designed as a means to free up land from customary claims for allocation to modern agribusiness. Land was nationalised and long-term leases put into place, with customary owners ceding rights for up to 99 years. Numerous individuals and interest groups started looking for land: the Boy Scouts of Nigeria, General Obasanjo, the United Africa Company (UAC), civil servants, various churches, etc. Structural adjustment in 1985 brought a ban on imports of wheat, barley and other ingredients for brewing and animal feed, so companies sought regular sources of supply through developing their own farms. For example, UAC and Leventis set up their own farming ventures for sourcing needed inputs. The Texaco farm in Ogun State covered a total of 3,886 acres, having been set up in 1975 as a means of using oil profits. However, it closed in 1987, due to economic difficulties and financial irregularities. It focused on cassava production and also provided a site for experimentation with new varieties generated by the neighbouring International Institute of Tropical Agriculture (IITA) research centre. A factory was built on site to process cassava into flour, using mainly women workers. But it was very difficult to run the business at a profit, due to strong competition for wage labour from local farmers, and volatile prices for the processed *gari*. The devaluation of the currency took a further turn in 1986, making imported inputs prohibitively expensive. Vertical integration of these farms means they operate as enclaves within rural areas, and have few linkages to the local economy, apart from employing a certain number of workers, and land acquisition.

Such examples tend to confirm the evidence presented by Belières *et al.* (2002) regarding the difficulties faced by large commercial farm enterprises in Senegal. Here, considerable areas of land were allocated to applicants seeking big holdings, who relied on access to cheap credit to develop and work the land. The devaluation of the CFA franc in 1994, combined with market liberalisation and restrictions on credit, led to the collapse of many commercial farms, which proved unable to compete with smallholders and imports of cheap rice. By contrast, family farms have been able to adapt and intensify, using cheap labour in preference to costly credit and machinery.

7.9 Producer organisations and institutional change

For a decade or more, throughout West Africa, a range of producer organisations (POs) have established themselves and strengthened their position, at local, national and sub-regional levels. These organisations are in part the result of government withdrawal from important areas of economic activity, including agricultural input supply and marketing. They have also emerged in a context of greater political liberalisation, and now represent a political force to which governments must listen. This became clear from the strike by Mali's cotton farmers in the 2001 season, due to low prices and continued waste and corruption within the CMDT. The strike cut output by half, with many cotton farmers switching to maize and other cash crops for that season.

Producer organisations cover a wide range of activities, from management of a common woodland or pasture resource, water user associations, collection and sale of a particular crop, to providing access to fertiliser, seed and credit (Bosc *et al.* 2001). Grouping together through collective action enables producers to take advantage of economies of scale, as well as making their voices heard in government policy and decision-making circles. Additionally, producers hope to increase their negotiating power with companies buying their crop, all the more necessary as globalisation is bringing an increased concentration and integration of agro-business throughout the world. In some cases, producer organisations have also provided a valuable bridging function between farmers and sources of technical expertise, such as research and extension structures. Foreign aid funds have often been instrumental in strengthening the role that POs can play, with associated risks of the leadership becoming increasingly distant from the interests and needs of the membership.

Examples of producer organisations operating at national level include the *Comité National de Concertation des Ruraux* (CNCR) in Senegal, the *Fédération des Unions des Producteurs* (FUPRO) in Benin, and the *Syndicat des Exploitants Agricoles à l'Office du Niger* (SEXAGON) in Mali (GRAF/GRET/IIED 2003). The CNCR provides an interesting case, which brings together a series of PO federations in Senegal, and has become a central actor in dialogue between government, donors, and producers on agricultural strategy and related issues, such as land tenure. Such POs have the advantage of providing a channel to make the case for greater support to agriculture in general, as well as to take account of the particular constraints faced by smallholders. Policy- and decision-making in government tend to follow both formal and informal procedures. Smallholders have less easy access to informal mechanisms that operate via old boy networks, and lobbying through high level political contacts, which are usually the preserve of powerful economic actors, such as large commercial farmers and agribusiness. Thus, POs need to make best use of official channels and opportunities to give voice to the needs of less powerful actors.

At sub-regional level, there has been increased interest in generating pressure on governments and regional institutions to ensure producer interests are better taken into account in negotiation processes relating to the World Trade Organisation (WTO), the European Union's Common Agricultural Policy (CAP) reform, and Cotonou negotiations [which aim to increase long-term foreign investment with the potential for supporting sustainable development into African, Caribbean and Pacific countries; eds]. Examples include the *Réseau des Organisations Paysannes de l'Afrique de l'Ouest* (ROPPA), the *Association Cotonnière Africaine* and the Union of Chambers of Agriculture for West Africa. ROPPA, which was established in 2000 as a West African network, with members initially in Benin, Burkina Faso, Côte d'Ivoire, the Gambia, Mali, Niger, Senegal and Togo, has been particularly vocal in support of family farming, and opposed to the agribusiness model being promoted by some as the means to 'modernise' agriculture. 'This vision (in support of family farming) has been inspired by a global perception of the role of agriculture in society, not only for producing food and fibre but also performing many other economic, social and environmental functions' (Belières *et al.* 2002). Thus, the argument being made by ROPPA and others supports broader debates regarding the 'multi-functionality' of agriculture and consequent need to avoid a purely economic or market-based approach.

7.10 Agricultural policy and modernisation of agriculture

Agricultural policy aims to address a broad range of objectives, such as increasing agricultural productivity and contributing to food security, reducing poverty and improving the livelihoods of rural producers, increasing capacity to compete with imported agricultural products, diversifying agricultural exports, managing the sustainable use of natural resources – soils, water, forests, grazing – on which agriculture relies, as well as ensuring a balanced pattern of development within the overall territory of the country (Government of Senegal 2003). Much recent debate on agricultural strategy within a number of West African countries has emphasised the need for 'modernisation', a term which has been interpreted in diverse ways, depending on context, but which tends to translate into:

- establishment of land tenure legislation to support private property, through titling of land, and associated measures to increase the volume and security of transactions in land;
- increase in the size of agricultural land holdings through the allocation of concessions to large-scale commercial farmers, and associated preferential access to inputs, credit, equipment, etc., and
- decrease in the number of very small farm holdings and associated population, as the modernisation process develops.

Questions of agricultural policy and strategy are currently being debated at three different levels: the place of agriculture within the context of national Poverty Reduction Strategy Processes (PRSPs); the common agricultural policy being developed for the UEMOA (the francophone West African Economic and Monetary Union) sub-region; and the New Programme for African Development (NEPAD) framework, being discussed by the G8 and other global fora. Together these different levels of strategic thinking should lead to a clearer focus on the choices faced at national and global levels, and the extent to which there are major tradeoffs between:

- reducing poverty and improving economic opportunities for West African farmers versus continuing the funding of enormous farm subsidies in OECD member states (currently at $350 billion per year);
- small-scale family farms and large scale commercial agriculture;
- securing the rights of customary land users and providing private title to land for inward investors.

In some cases, these tradeoffs may be less clear-cut, with possibilities of 'win-win' situations, and complementarities between, say, promotion of agri-business and creation of widespread benefits to local communities. In other cases, these tradeoffs involve clear political choices regarding the distribution of benefits to different groups, both at national and global levels.

8 Prospects for agriculture and family farms: the next 10–20 years

Looking forward, can family farms feed West African nations and compete on global markets? Based on past experience, the answer is a qualified 'Yes'. The future structure and performance of West Africa's farming sector will be the result of a number of factors, some of which are outside the control of national decision-makers.

1. ***Demand for staple food commodities is unlikely to decline, given current rates of population growth and food preferences determined by both culture and poverty.*** Rising incomes will provide a more diversified market for a broader range of grains, fruit and vegetables, livestock produce and other higher value products. The strongest evidence that family farms will continue to satisfy these markets is the strength of recovery from stagnating food production in the 1980s. Economic incentives rather than capacity are the chief constraint, hence the

importance of increasing the competitiveness of West African agriculture within the sub-region and ensuring protection from cheap imports.

2. ***National agricultural policy and strategy are important factors affecting the direction and form taken by the farming sector.*** Governments face choices between the kinds of agriculture they wish to promote. Design of agricultural strategy does not take place in a vacuum, but is subject to lobbying and pressures from a range of internal and external actors. If the family farm is to continue as a central component of the agricultural sector, national farmer federations and producer organisations will need to argue the case in their favour and challenge alternative visions which see 'modernisation' as needing to follow a route favouring large commercial farms. With the growing importance of sub-regional policy debate and decision-making, such lobbying also needs a sub-regional dimension.
3. ***Other national policy measures have important linkages to the future performance of the farm sector, most particularly reforms to land tenure legislation and administration.*** Tenure reform is under discussion in many West African countries, with a focus on ways to increase levels of agricultural productivity, reduce conflicts, ensure equitable access, and promote sustainable land use. Changes in the law and administration of land tenure inevitably have distributional consequences. Many governments have sought to assert their underlying rights to manage land and allocate it to those they choose, by wresting control from customary structures. In some cases, this can open up opportunities to acquire land for groups with weak rights under customary systems but, most often, this assertion of control by government becomes a means to disempower ordinary farmers in favour of the elite. If smallholder agriculture is to have a secure future, it needs an appropriate system of tenure legislation and administration which firmly supports the rights of the small farmer against land-grabbing.
4. ***Environmental challenges constitute a potential threat to continued growth in agricultural output.*** Future trends in rainfall are unknown, and global climate models are not able to predict with any confidence the likely change to weather patterns in the West African region. However, rising global temperatures seem certain, and these will bring increasing levels of evaporation. This means that the value of any given level of rainfall will lessen in terms of its contribution to primary production. For this reason, all farmers will need to pay greater attention to more intensive management of water and soils.
5. ***Rising levels of demographic pressure, especially around major towns, will increase the scarcity and value of land.*** In many peri-urban areas, these processes are leading to high levels of insecurity for rural dwellers, whose rights as long-term occupants of the land are ignored by the powerful in the rush to grab a precious asset. Governments must find ways to provide greater security over land, to encourage investment, ensure equitable access and reduce risks of conflict, especially in these high risk zones. Farmers have shown themselves ready to invest substantial amounts of effort in land improvement where they face promising markets for their crops, and are confident of their land

rights. Security does not necessarily stem from issue of paper land titles, but is the consequence of the state recognising the legality of local processes for managing land.

6. ***The composition of West African farm production must continue to evolve in response to emerging markets for some products, and falling returns for others.*** For example, there are serious questions about the viability of rice farming in the Senegal River Valley, given the availability of cheap rice from SE Asia. A better strategy might be for Senegal's irrigated agriculture to focus on higher value commodities which can better offset the costs of pump irrigation. Crop diversification in this direction has been apparent for some years, such as into okra for Dakar's markets. Rice growing in the Office du Niger, Mali, faces a more promising option for the future in part due to some natural protection from imports as a result of the country being landlocked, as well as reliance on gravity irrigation rather than diesel-fuelled pumps. The future of the West African oil seed sector needs thought, given its need to compete in an over-supplied global market. Establishing a quality product for domestic and foreign markets will be important, as well as ensuring compliance with stringent new phytosanitary controls, especially for groundnuts, which face particular challenges to demonstrate no trace of aflatoxin.
7. ***New niche markets may offer promising alternatives, through fair trade, organic or ethical trade initiatives.*** While currently only a tiny proportion of the market for most products (the exception being coffee), there is a rapid growth of interest amongst western consumers in the sources/origins of the food they eat. However, such interest is a two-edged sword, with part of the environmental movement keen to promote local food systems above all else, a move which could shut off opportunities for many southern farmers. Niche markets need good transport and infrastructural connections if they are to offer a significant outlet for farmers. Currently, many fair trade and organic schemes present serious obstacles to smaller producers because of the transaction costs associated with being part of such a scheme. Evidence shows that if smallholders are to benefit as a group, the standards or certification scheme must have promotion of 'small farmers' as an explicit objective. If this is not the case, then the tendency will be for them to be squeezed out by larger, better organised producers.
8. ***The future impact of global markets on economic incentives in West African agriculture will depend on successful negotiations at the WTO and attention to improving farmgate prices, including measures to protect the agricultural sector, where necessary.*** The end of surplus dumping by the USA and the EU is a precondition for improved market incentives for family farms and large-scale commercial farms alike. If West African farmers continue to face falling world market prices for their principal exports abroad, and fierce competition from OECD farm surpluses in their home markets, the future of the rural population will be greatly damaged. The farming sector has managed remarkably well over the last 20–30 years in the face of serious difficulties, but there are limits below which rural life becomes insupportable.

9. ***There is a stark mismatch between commitment from OECD nations to meeting the MDGs, especially making a serious reduction in global poverty levels, and current policy towards their own farming sector, and trade measures.*** This provides a valuable lobbying and advocacy opportunity for informing the OECD public and working with a range of groups able to exert pressure on current processes of negotiation. Such pressure will be more effective where backed by good material which underlines the links between OECD farm and trade measures and the prospects for a sustainable livelihood for farmers in West Africa.
10. ***Export agriculture has been promoted as the obvious escape route from economic stagnation in African countries. But does this strategy make sense in the context of a long-term decline in the terms of trade for tropical commodities? And is a downward pressure on world market prices not inevitable if all countries pursue the same policy of expanding agricultural exports?*** Increased processing of primary commodities is a key means to add value to exports as well as food into sub-regional markets (such as instant coffee produced in Côte d'Ivoire). Continued pressure is needed for change to tariffs imposed by OECD nations for processed commodities which would otherwise offer an important means of generating increased incomes and employment in poor countries.

9 Conclusion

This chapter has sought to describe the broad transformations underway in West Africa's agricultural sector. Agriculture is central to the West African region and will remain so for the foreseeable future. Further agricultural growth is essential if poverty reduction goals are to be realised. Family farms, in all their diversity, remain by far the most dominant component of the agricultural sector. Improvements to national, regional and global marketing opportunities would therefore make a major contribution to the welfare and livelihoods of many millions of people.

Family farms have been remarkably successful in generating increased food and export crop production for domestic and foreign markets. The category 'family farming' covers a wide range of agricultural operations from highly market-oriented farms closely linked into global markets, through mixed market and subsistence-based farm households, to those which barely scrape a living from the land. Key characteristics of family farming include the close link between the structure and composition of the household and its associated farm assets and activities. These links have important implications for the choice of crop, organisation of family labour, management of investment and assets, and questions of marriage and inheritance. The typology of family farms discussed brings a more explicit recognition of the great diversity within the sector, which needs to be factored into any design of agricultural policy and support measures. An understanding of the family farm and its various components should help governments to better understand regional agrarian structures and the multiple values they represent. While this threefold typology is valuable in distinguishing different kinds of farm household, it should be remembered that these are not water-tight categories; there may be considerable movement between categories. Such mobility is the consequence of the interplay between economic and social dimensions, especially the tensions between younger and older household members, and between those of different parentage. These frictions can lead to cleavages within the household, and the break-up of large extended domestic groups, leading to reduced resilience in the face of risks.

The weak statistical data base makes it hard to assess in detail the distributional impact of recent transformations on different kinds of farm household. However, taking cotton, which is grown by some ten million households in West Africa, as an example, it is reasonable to assume that they have all suffered the consequences of recent falls in world market prices, given the liberalisation of marketing systems and the abandonment of price stabilisation by parastatal bodies. Equally, fluctuations in cocoa prices will have been felt by the two million or more smallholders in Ghana and Côte d'Ivoire, who provide the bulk of West Africa's harvest. When devaluation of the CFA franc and anti-dumping measures led to improved market conditions for West African livestock production, animal owners throughout the region responded by investing further in this sector and intensifying production through stall-feeding and fattening activities.

There is growing understanding and concern amongst rural producers, producer organisations, national governments, NGO networks, and some donors, about the very damaging effects of OECD trade and agricultural policy on the prospects of farmers in the developing world. The ongoing WTO negotiations provide the main forum for inter-governmental discussion of, and pressure group lobbying on future agreements on agricultural trade and domestic policy. Major imbalances in global power limit the room for serious gains by West African countries within such negotiations. The only means to achieve significant improvement in the opportunities open to West Africa's farmers will be through strengthening domestic pressures in OECD member states to curb agricultural handouts, cut export subsidies and address the need for policy coherence. Long-term security and self-interest concerns make the wisdom of such a policy shift somewhat more 'saleable' today than in the past. Nonetheless, the adoption of such a strategy would require the development of multiple partnerships with a wide range of groups, both in West Africa and the OECD, and the marshalling of clear evidence of the impacts caused by OECD government policies on local farming and other livelihoods in the West African region.

Note

1. This is an extended extract from *Transformations in West African Agriculture and the Role of Family Farms*, our joint report to the Sahel and West Africa Club, as part of its programme on the Transformation of West African Agriculture. We are grateful for permission to publish this version, which has been selected and arranged by the volume editors.

References

Amanor, K. (1999), *Global Restructuring and Land Rights in Ghana* Research Report No. 108. Nordiska Afrikainstitutet, Uppsala.

Anikpo, M. (2000), *Derived Rights and the Security of Tenure in Oyigbo Local Government Area, Rivers State.* IIED/GRET, London.

Batterbury, S.P.J., Warren, A. and **Waughray, D.** (1996), *Social and Environmental Relationships, Land Use and Land Degradation in Southwestern Niger.* Final report to the ESCR Global Environment Change Programme. Department of Geography and Earth Sciences, Brunel University, Uxbridge.

Belières, J.-F., Bosc, P.-M., Faure, G., Fourniers, S. and **Losch, B.** (2002), *What Future for West Africa's Family Farms in a World Market Economy?* IIED Drylands Programme Issue Paper No. 113. IIED, London.

Bosc, P., Eychenne, D., Hussein, K., Mercoiret, M.-R., Rondot, P. and **Mackintosh-Walker, S.** (2001), *The Role of Rural Producers' Organisations in the World Bank Rural Development Strategy,* World Bank Rural Strategy Background Paper No. 8. World Bank, Washington, DC.

Brock, K. and **Coulibaly, N.** (1999), *Sustainable Rural Livelihoods in Mali.* Institute of Development Studies Research Report No. 35. Institute of Development Studies, Brighton.

Brook, R. and **Dávila, J.** (2000), *The Peri-Urban Interface.* University of Wales, Bangor.

Chauveau, J.-P. (1997), 'Jeu foncier, institutions d'accès à la ressource et usage de la ressource', in Contamin, B. and Memel-Foté, H. (eds), *Le modèle ivorien en crise.* Karthala, Paris.

Chauveau, Jean-Pierre (2002), 'The institution of the "tutorat" between autochthones and migrants, and its evolution'. Paper presented at the workshop 'Land rights and the politics of belonging in West Africa', Frankfurt, 3–5 October 2002.

CIRAD-TERA (2002), *Programme Agricultures Familiales et Mondialisation.* CIRAD, Montpellier.

Deininger, K. and **Squire, L.** (1998), 'New ways of looking at old issues: inequality and growth', *Journal of Development Economics* **57(2)**, 257–85.

Dembélé, I., Kater, L., Koné, D., Koné, Y., Ly, B. and **Macinanke, A.** (2001), 'Seizing new opportunities: soil fertility management and diverse livelihoods in Mali', in Scoones, I. (ed.), *Dynamics and Diversity.* Earthscan Publications Ltd, London and Sterling, Vancouver.

Ellis, F. (2001), *Rural Livelihoods and Diversity in Developing Countries.* Oxford University Press, Oxford.

Fafchamps, M., Teal, F. and **Toye, J.** (2001), *Towards a Growth Strategy for Africa.* Centre for the Study of African Economics, Oxford.

Fairhead, J. and **Leach, M.** (1996), *Misreading the African Landscape.* Cambridge University Press, Cambridge.

Faye, A., Mortimore, M., Tiffen, M. and **Nelson, J.** (2001), *Région de Diourbel: Synthèse.* Drylands Research Working Paper 23e. Drylands Research, Crewkerne, Somerset.

Government of Senegal (2003), *Projet de loi d'orientation agricole.* Government of Senegal, Dakar.

GRAF/GRET/IIED (2003), *Making Land Rights More Secure*: Proceedings of an International Workshop, Ouagadougou, 19–21 March 2002. IIED, London.

Guyer, J. (1997), *An African Niche Economy: Farming to Feed Ibadan 1968–88*. Edinburgh University Press, Edinburgh.

Hamadou, S. (2000), *Evolution à longue terme des productions agricoles du système de commercialisation et des prix des produits dans la zone de Maradi.* Drylands Research Working Paper No. 32. Drylands Research, Crewkerne, Somerset.

Harris, F. (1996), *Intensification of Agriculture in Semi-arid Areas; Lessons from the Kano Close Settled Zone.* Gatekeeper series No. 59. IIED, London.

Hulme, M. (1996), 'Rainfall changes in Africa: 1931–1960 to 1961–1990', *International Journal of Climatology* **12**, 685–99.

Hussein, K. and **Nelson, J.** (1998), *Sustainable Livelihoods and Livelihood Diversification.* IDS Working Paper No. 69. Institute of Development Studies, Brighton.

IPCC (2001), *Climate Change 2001. Impacts, Adaptation, and Vulnerability. Contribution of Working Group II to the Third Assessment Report of the Intergovernmental Panel on Climate Change.* Cambridge University Press, Cambridge.

Kasanga, K. (1998), *Rapid Urbanisation, Land Markets and Gender Insecurity in Peri-urban Kumasi, Ghana.* Final Research Report to the Mazingira Institute, Nairobi.

Kherallah, M., Delgado, C., Gabre-Madhin, E., Minot, N. and **Johnson, M.** (2002), *Reforming Agricultural Markets in Africa.* IFPRI and John Hopkins University Press, Baltimore, Maryland.

Konadu-Agyemang, K. (2000), 'The best and the worst of times: structural adjustment programs and uneven development in Africa. The case of Ghana', *Professional Geographer* **52(3)**, 469–83.

Koné, M. (2002), *Gaining Rights of Access to Land in West-Central Côte d'Ivoire.* GRET/IIED, London.

Koning, N. (2002), *Should Africa Protect its Farmers to Revitalise its Economy?* Gatekeeper Series No. 105. IIED, London.

Losch, B. (2002), *La Multifunctionnalité face aux défis des agricultures des Suds: une perspective de refondation des politiques publiques?* SFER, Paris.

Losch, B. and **Chauveau, J.-P.** (2003), *Le processus de libéralisation et la crise ivoirienne.* CIRAD/DIAL, Montpellier.

Mazoyer, M. (2001), *Protecting Small Farmers and the Rural Poor in the Context of Globalization.* Food and Agriculture Organization of the United Nations, Rome.

Mazzucato, V. and **Niemeijer, D.** (2000), *Rethinking Soil and Water Conservation in a Changing Society: A Case Study in Eastern Burkina Faso.* Tropical Resource Management Papers No. 32. Wageningen University, Wageningen, The Netherlands.

Mazzucato, V. and **Niemeijer, D.** (2001), *Social Networks and the Dynamics of Soil and Water Conservation in the Sahel.* Gatekeeper Series No. 101. IIED, London.

Morand, P., Sy, O.I. and **Breuil, C.** (forthcoming), 'Millions of West Africans rely on the fisheries sector: is their canoe taking them towards increasing poverty or more sustainable livelihoods?' in Toulmin, C. and Wisner, B. (eds), *Towards a New Map of Africa.* Earthscan, London.

Mortimore, M. (2003), *The Future of Family Farms in West Africa : What Can We Learn From Long-term Data?* Paper commissioned by IIED for the OECD, London.

Mortimore, M. and **Adams, W.M.** (1999), *Working the Sahel.* Routledge, London and New York.

Netting, R. (1993), *Smallholders, Householders.* Stanford University Press, Stanford, California.

L'Observatoire Paalga (2001), Newspaper, Burkina Faso.

OECD (1998), *Preparing for the Future. A Vision of West Africa in the Year 2020. West Africa: Long-Term Perspective Study,* Cour, J.-M. and Snrech, S. (eds), Club du Sahel, Paris.

Olofin, E. and **Patrick, S.** (eds) (1989), *Land Administration and Development in Northern Nigeria: Case Studies.* Bayero University, Kano, Nigeria.

Ouédraogo, M. (2002), *Les Nouveaux Acteurs et la Promotion des Activités Agro-Sylvo-Pastorales dans le sud du Burkina Faso.* IIED, London.

Paré, L. (2001), *Negotiating Rights: Access to Land in the Cotton Zone, Burkina Faso.* IIED/GRET, London.

Raynaut, C. (ed.) (1997), *Societies and Nature in the Sahel.* Routledge, London and New York.

Reardon, T. (1997), 'Using evidence of household income diversification to inform study of the rural non-farm labour market in Africa', *World Development* **25(5)**, 735–47.

Reij, C. and **Waters-Bayer, A.** (2001), *Farmer Innovation in Africa.* Earthscan Publications Ltd, London.

Scoones, I. (1998), *Sustainable Rural Livelihoods: A Framework for Analysis,* IDS Working Paper No. 72. Institute of Development Studies, Brighton.

Smith, M.G. (1966), 'Hausa inheritance and succession', in Derrett, J. (ed.), *Studies in Laws of Succession in Nigeria.* Oxford University Press, London.

Ton, P. (2001), *Cotton Production and Rural Livelihoods in West Africa.* Oxfam, Oxford.

Toulmin, C. (1992), *Cattle, Women and Wells. Managing Household Survival in the Sahel.* Clarendon Press, Oxford.

Toulmin, C. and **Guèye, B.** (2003), 'How will West African Countries meet the MDGs?', in Satterthwaite, D. (ed.), *The MDG and Local Processes: Hitting the Target or Missing the Point?* IIED, London. (http://www.meetingthemdgs.org/pubs.html; accessed on 2/2/2004.)

Vorley, B. (2002), *Sustaining Agriculture: Policy, Governance, and the Future of Family-based Farming.* IIED, London.

Walfadjri (2002), 'Stabilité régionale. Les raisons d'être d'un désastre ivoirien', *Walfadjri* **3245 (6 Janvier)**.

Wiggins, S. (2000), 'Interpreting changes from the 1970s to the 1990s in African agriculture through village studies', *World Development* **28(4)**, 631–62.

Woodhouse, P., Bernstein, H. and **Hulme, D.** (2000), *African Enclosures.* James Currey, Oxford.

Zoundi, J. (2003), *L'innovation technologique dans le processus de changement structurel de l'agriculture familiale en Afrique de l'Ouest.* CSAO, Paris.

CHAPTER 8

The social relations of economic life and networks of civic engagement: 'Social Capital' and targeted development

Fergus Lyon and Gina Porter

1 Introduction

Over the past two decades there has been growing interest amongst donors and NGOs working in West Africa in the developmental potential of a strong civil society:

> Social Capital is seen by some as a necessary ingredient for civil society to function effectively. In the economic sphere social capital is seen to have much potential to reduce the transaction costs associated with formal co-ordination mechanisms like contracts and bureaucratic rules and thus improve efficiency, while in the political sphere it promotes the kind of associational life which is necessary for the success of limited government and modern democracy.
>
> (Fukuyama 2001: 131)

There is a broad view that interventions can be made which will harness underlying social forces and energy in society (World Bank 2000) to expand current social capital in the region and thus produce a dense and robust civil society.

In this chapter we focus on a range of different forms of social institutions that commonly shape economic life in West Africa. Taking southern Ghana as a case study area, we aim to address a number of issues. First, we review some of the forms of collective action that are characteristically found in the region today. Drawing on detailed studies we explore how these forms of collective action sustain themselves. We then consider how forms of collective action can be conceptualised and examine the usefulness of the term 'social capital' in this context. Finally we examine how an understanding of collective action and institutions of civil society can relate to policy making, especially the process of targeting interventions for local economic development.

2 Social relations and institutions in southern Ghana's agricultural production and trading networks

In contexts like southern Ghana, where people have to survive in highly risky and vulnerable environments, it is important to understand how they can improve their economic well-being through stabilising or increasing their income and increasing their access to key resources. The forms of civil society that have impact on people's lives range from forms of bilateral linkages, through community groups, to larger scale organisations. They can range from informal networks without rules or regular interaction, through to formalised organisations with clear hierarchies and associated bureaucracies. In this section we present empirical material related predominantly to production and marketing systems of urban and rural areas in southern Ghana. Since a majority of people live in rural areas and engage to varying degrees in agricultural production and trade, these institutions have a huge impact on the livelihoods of Ghanaian people and especially the poorer groups in society. We first consider some of the institutions that shape bilateral relationships (i.e. interaction between individuals and their supporting networks and norms) and then move on to review organisational forms that are made up of group activities, ranging from the community to the national level.

2.1 Bilateral relationships in production and trading networks

Ghanaian small-scale farmers and traders work in a highly unpredictable and uncertain environment. In addition to the vagaries of the weather and seasonal shifts in trade, they have little recourse to legal redress as they carry out their business. This is not an issue when dealing with 'cash in hand' transactions, but throughout the production and marketing chain both farmers and sellers have to rely on other parties to honour verbal agreements that are based on trust.

At the production stage there are a number of different forms of agreement in operation that allow farmers faced with a shortage of capital to gain access to labour and pay at the end of the season when crops have been marketed. Some of these are based on payment of wages at the end of the season, while others relate to a wide range of sharecropping arrangements, with the labourers paid a proportion of the harvest.[1] Both systems depend on a degree of trust between participants, since hired hands must be trusted to work as hard as expected, while sharecropping arrangements rely on the grower telling the land owner about the full extent of the harvest to be shared.

Many farmers have to rely on informal means of finance as banks are unwilling to lend to their ventures (Nikoi 1996). A survey of 160 vegetable farmers in Brong Ahafo Region (Lyon 1999, 2000) found that a majority obtained loans from other villagers and also relied on forms of trade credit: 27 per cent obtained credit from input suppliers and 11 per cent received credit from traders. This credit flowed around the system with 39 per cent of farmers lending to other farmers at different times of the year.

Two-way flows of credit were found to occur between farmers and traders. Sixty-eight per cent of traders interviewed in Brong Ahafo received harvested produce from farmers on credit and 78 per cent of itinerant or wholesale traders sold on credit to retailers. The traders are predominantly women, working alone or with daughters and nieces (Clark 1994; Gore 1978; Schwimmer 1976). In addition to the flow of credit, traders and farmers develop 'customer relationships' in order to acquire information and to ensure they have a guaranteed demand or supply. The credit provision by traders carries an implicit rate of interest as they pay the farmers lower prices for their produce. This 'interest' ranged from six per cent to 220 per cent for a three-month period, with a majority of the estimates in the 20–25 per cent range. No farmers were found to be tied into debt for many years and forced to take out consumption loans repeatedly. Farmers receiving credit appeared to be less critical of traders than those without credit as they recognised that they would not have been able to grow vegetables at all without the traders' support (Lyon 2000).

Each of these agreements is based on relationships of trust: written agreements or collateral are rarely employed. The flexibility of the arrangements is an important attraction to farmers as their production is risky and those lending allow them to repay their debt in following seasons. The renegotiation of contracts is found in a number of other studies of Ghanaian trade and business (Fafchamps 1996). Relationships are built up over periods of working together, through reciprocity such as giving credit to each other and social activities. They may also rely on pre-existing networks since actors will have information on each other already.

Examples of such pre-existing networks include families, churches and people of the same ethnic group. The ability to build up interpersonal trust depends on the 'density' of networks that individuals can draw on. In Ghana, as throughout West Africa, small but dense and cohesive networks are crucial to the survival of small businesses (Barr 2000). It is this 'institutional thickness' (Amin 1996) that is the basis for civil society. Some examples of networks in the region extend for generations (Lovejoy 1973, 1986). In the case of produce trade, networks may extend over long distances and are usually based on the landlord system, which may draw on both broad ethnic and closer family ties (Hill 1971). Such ties are crucial in a situation of imperfect markets where information is essential as a means of minimising search costs and operating more efficiently. Wherever trust is present, 'agents can lower their guard and economise on transaction costs such as the need to inspect quality before buying or the need to organise payment in cash at the time of delivery' (Fafchamps and Minten 1998). However, networks are constantly being reshaped and new networks formed as a result of changing social and economic conditions and opportunities (Lovejoy 1986). Mortimore (1989), for example, describes a Manga network in Nigeria extending between a village in the far north of the country and Lagos in the south. This started in the early 1970s when two Manga migrants set themselves up as trading landlords dealing in goats in Lagos. A more recent example from Nigeria is the development of the irrigated vegetable trade in the 1990s between farmers on the Jos Plateau and landlords based in southern market centres (Porter 2001).

Many farmers also used intermediaries or guarantors who are trusted by the lender and who know the receiver. The basis of these relationships is therefore the trust that allows individuals to lend or share information while there is a risk of the other party acting opportunistically. Relationships of trust are also underpinned by the sanctions that one party can exert over the other. Traders want to know where farmers live and will ask to meet their relatives before they lend them money, so that they can return to exert moral pressure on the individual if there is a risk of not being repaid. Loans extended between wholesale and retail traders are given in similar manner: in Kumasi market traders 'try to learn the buyer's hometown or place of business before extending credit' (Clark 1994: 175). The moral pressure used demonstrates the importance of 'norms of behaviour' that are accepted in a community. These include customs of co-operation, reciprocity, avoiding deception, keeping verbal contracts and deciding on acceptable sanctions. Where cash loans are concerned in Kumasi market, 'only traders disqualified from both commercial and family assistance, presumably for misbehaviour, would resort to moneylenders' (Clark 1994: 180).

2.2 *Group activity related to production and trading networks*

Farmers, traders and others involved in trading networks in southern Ghana were found to have a number of different types of collective action that allowed them to negotiate the complex and uncertain economic environment. These forms of co-operation allow them to have access to resources they could not otherwise obtain, to increase their bargaining power, and shape the economic context in which they work. They range from small groups of farmers labouring on each others' farms, to nation-wide organisations with hundreds of thousands of members and considerable political power.

Many farmers in southern Ghana participate in co-operative labour systems with groups of other farmers, called *nnoboa*. In such cases there is a risk that some members of the group will not work as hard as others, or leave the group once their farm has received input from the group. This is avoided by working with people who are known already and from the same community. Farmers may also come together for co-operative marketing and price bargaining. This is common in Brong Ahafo Region where farmers in a single community select a representative – generally male – who is known to be good at bargaining and trustworthy. The representative will then negotiate with traders on behalf of the farmers in the community and hold out for higher prices. This form of bargaining can only function during periods of scarcity in the markets when farmers are not desperate to sell their perishable crops. The success of these associations depends on the ability of the group to stop individuals selling to traders at lower prices. On the one hand there is peer pressure from other farmers, and on the other the power exerted by community leaders, especially the chief. Significantly, in communities where there has been a chieftaincy dispute – not uncommon in Ghana – the powers of these associations are severely limited.

There are even limited examples of farmers selling as a single entity in Brong Ahafo. Such co-operatives are rarely sustainable, however, as those responsible for selling are not trusted by the other members and the informal nature of the marketing system results in a lack of transparency for farmers. In the 1960s and 1970s there was considerable investment in co-operatives for Ghanaian cocoa farmers. Prices were fixed and publicised and the co-operatives were also involved in marketing of agricultural inputs. Unfortunately, they became increasingly politicised, a problem that has affected co-operatives in many low income countries (Attwood and Baviskar 1988).

Road and path maintenance is another area of collective action essential to the pursuit of agricultural production and trade. Most village paths in Ghana's Central Region are maintained only by that group of farmers whose farms are located along the path in question; more important paths, tracks and minor unpaved roads which lead to other settlements will be maintained by the whole village. The village 'alarm' or *gong-gong* is beaten when such a path (or other communal work such as school construction) needs attention and the whole village, including older children, will be expected to participate. Those who refuse are fined the equivalent of a day's labour. The power to fine is vested in the chief and his authority is based on the respect for the concept of chieftaincy, and the acceptance of certain 'traditional behaviour' as the norm. Similar patterns of communal village path and road maintenance, and the accompanying sanctions of non-compliance, are common across West Africa. Indeed, on Nigeria's Jos Plateau such communal work extends beyond local paths to culvert repair and even bridge construction on inter-village roads (Porter 2002).

Moving along the marketing chain from the rural producers to the urban markets, other forms of association can be observed. In urban economic spaces there are complex forms of trader association that play crucial roles in organising the market, ensuring traders' welfare, and assisting the traders in building bargaining power. These associations are also the vehicle for negotiation with local authorities. The ability of the traders to exert power depends on their control of key spaces, notably the land allocated for markets. The ability to sustain this control depends on the unity of the association and the ability of the leaders to ensure that non-members are restricted. This control is only possible with the tacit or explicit approval of local authorities. The associations will select leaders with the skills to enrol politicians and persuade civil servants. Clark (1994) provides fascinating insights into the operations of women traders in Kumasi Central Market, and how they work to gain access to credit and other resources, manage information and pursue power along the commercial axis. Leaders of the women's commodity groups – *ahemma* – wield substantial power through their authority based on rendering services in dispute settlement and negotiations (ibid.), and, in some commodity groups, there are formal or informal alliances with traders of the same commodity in other markets. In the case of yam, there is a formal network extending across the whole of Ghana which is headed by the Kumasi head of the yam traders who, in the late 1980s, was also elected a member of the Kumasi City Council (ibid.). Nonetheless, women are ultimately subordinate to men in the market: commodities permitted or reserved for men provide higher levels of average income and capital accumulation, while loans, gifts and inheritance, though reportedly generally following same-sex lines, encompass more female to male transfers than the opposite, thus further accumulating advantages to men (ibid.).

Similar associations are used by truck and taxi drivers. They are a vital cog in the marketing system, and play key roles in supporting the traders who buy from rural areas. There are a number of associations in Ghana but the transport system is dominated by one, the Ghana Private Road Transport Union (GPRTU). Each town has at least one branch that is semi-autonomous and is responsible for members' welfare, dispute settling, station building and lobbying on behalf of members (membership is open to owners and drivers of vehicles, lorry park guards and transport porters: almost all members are men). The associations are organised in clear hierarchies, resembling military organisational forms. The union controls the main stations/ranks and levies a charge on all vehicles. Those refusing to pay may be 'arrested' by the union guards. The dominant union is able to maintain its position by having loyal members who will intimidate any driver who does not join their ranks. Thus although GPRTU provides positive benefits for its members, negative impacts are felt by passengers who pay higher prices because of limited competition from those competitors who choose not to join and face intimidation. The monopolistic position of the union is ensured through lobbying local and national government (Fouracre *et al.* 1994).

3 Social capital as an explanatory tool for collective action institutions in West African civil society

The preceding section provided a glimpse of the diversity and density of social institutions which commonly play a part in the promotion and regulation of economic life in West Africa. Such institutions are perceived to be a significant component of existing social capital in the region. In order to further explore the role of social capital and the potential for donor and NGO interventions aimed at building social capital for targeted development in West Africa we must now ponder the origin and meanings of the term 'social capital'.

The term social capital came to prominence with the publication of Robert Putnam's seminal book *Making Democracy Work*, based on an analysis of institutions in Italy, although he was drawing on earlier work in sociology by James Coleman (1990). The popularity and wide-ranging academic roots of the concept of social capital has led to a number of definitions but the most common themes used by the authors above and others are 'networks, norms and trust that facilitate co-ordination and co-operation': in essence, social capital brings voluntary co-operation which leads to performance. However, Fukuyama (2001) argues that trust, networks and civil society, which have been associated with social capital are 'epiphenomenal', i.e. secondary phenomena, arising out of social capital 'but not constituting social capital itself'. Fukuyama's preferred definition of social capital is as 'an instantiated informal norm that promotes co-operation between two or more individuals'. He sees it as a by-product of religion, tradition, shared historical experience and other types of cultural norms.

The concept of social capital attempts to bridge a number of different social science paradigms, from neo-classical economics, through to political economy. Consequently, it suffers from a lack of clear conceptual basis and historical/academic background. Furthermore, the lack of rigorous definition has opened up the term to attack from economists who are still uncomfortable with the lack of quantifiable measurements and difficulties encountered in using it in modelling, although some attempts are now being made by economists to tackle social capital analytically, focusing on links between social capital, welfare and performance (Barr and Toye 2000). Meanwhile, amongst those who take a non-positivist approach to social science, it is perceived as a route whereby economistic interpretations can colonise the social sciences and reduce attention to political economy (Fine 2001). Nonetheless, the term 'social capital' has struck a chord with policy makers, arguably precisely because it cuts across debates in the social sciences.

Putnam's work in Italy focuses on quantifiable indicators such as membership of formal groups (such as literary societies and political clubs), voting turnouts, etc. The cases shown in this chapter demonstrate that there is much more to the 'social' than these crude quantitative aspects and formal groups. In particular, we need to know a great deal about internal group cohesion and about the external relationships of individual groups (the negative or positive externalities) in order to assess their actual and potential impact. While, in theory, Putnam takes a broad definition, he closes it down when he comes to empirical work. In the next section we explore the different aspects of social capital encapsulated in 'trust', 'networks' and 'norms'. Drawing on the case study material, we provide examples of collective action and social relationships which are the day-to-day manifestations of 'social capital'.

Networks refer to the inter-personal linkages that make up social life. There are many cases of networks, both bilateral and multilateral, which impinge on and help to shape the economic sphere in West Africa. The mapping and study of the number and extent of networks has generated considerable interest in sociology over the last 30 years. However, to understand how these networks impact on social and economic life, it is necessary to examine the qualitative nature and the strength of the ties that hold networks together. Networks can range from weak ties of acquaintances who can move between groups carrying both ideas and information, to the strong ties of families where in-group solidarity may actually militate against multiple identities and co-operation with outsiders (Granovetter 1973). This leads us on to the discussions of trust and norms.

Trust has been examined in a variety of different social science contexts and defined in a number of different ways (Misztal 1996). A dictionary definition of trust is 'a firm belief in the reliability, truth or strength of a person: a confident expectation and a reliance on the truth of a statement without examination' (OED 1995). Empirical studies of the concept of trust always come up against linguistic difficulties and a lack of a single word that has the same meaning as the English word 'trust'. In the Ghanaian Twi language, used by the majority of people interviewed for the case studies in Brong Ahafo, the word *gyedi* means confidence, knowledge of a person's ability or reliability, as well as belief and faith.

Trust is vital in all market transactions when those involved are unwilling to rely on institutional arrangements or cultural norms alone (Granovetter 1985). It is based on a perception of the probability that other agents will behave in a way that is expected (Gambetta 1988). It is therefore a calculation, although the means by which an individual makes such a calculation are shaped in part by the social forces affecting them. This is evident throughout the case studies, whether it is trust between individuals, trust through intermediaries, or trust in the actions of other members of groups. Individuals will weigh up the risk and act according to their perceptions. They will draw on information on the reputations of other members and also evaluate the extent to which sanctions can be applied. The sanctions may be peer pressure, exclusion from future benefit, recourse to authority or, in a small number of cases, threats of violence. Thus, as explained above, knowing where a creditor lives is often a crucial factor in the decision to build a 'customer' relationship.

However, trust can come about without calculating, such as when someone acts out of habit. Habits are drawn on by us all in order that we can assume away some risks and make other calculations possible (Hodgson 1988). This was evident in cases where people were asked why they co-operated when there was a risk that others would default. A common response was for people to laugh at this question because it was not something they had considered explicitly before. A similar response from respondents came when asked why they feared certain forms of authority.

Norms define what actions are deemed acceptable and are the foundation on which trust is constructed, hence their prioritisation in Fukuyama's definition of social capital. Norms also relate to the types of sanctions that can be used to ensure other individuals co-operate. There has been considerable debate over the role of norms in economic development (Moore 1994; Platteau 1994) although the intangible nature of norms makes them difficult to observe empirically. Most studies of norms rely on game theory modelling or historical studies with only limited attempts to draw on ethnographic studies that have illuminated the subject within the context of their wider objectives (Granovetter 1993). The cases shown above are based on a wide range of norms that shape how people behave, the nature of the co-operation, and how they reciprocate. The sanctions applied to people are also shaped by the moral values and the sanctions exerted through 'shame'. This form of peer pressure is greater when people live in close proximity to each other. Where people do not live near each other, they were found to be looking for commonalities or shared values such as the same religion or church, or the same ethnic group.

This suggests that norms cannot be created at will, but can be seen as 'historically rooted cultural endowments' (Platteau 1994). They are learnt through socialisation, especially during childhood, through families, schools and religious organisations. The strengthening and sustaining of norms depends on the extent to which civil society as a whole, or particular groups within it, are willing to take action and sanction norm breakers (Platteau 1994). While the market can erode norms of society, by breaking down social relations, it also creates a new set of social relations and moral values that are common to those working in markets together (Hirschman 1982; Moore 1994). The new forms of group activities, especially those found in urban areas, demonstrate this.

4 *Social capital as a policy tool*

Social capital is a useful term because it brings the social context into view: an awareness of social capital can be critical for understanding development (Fukuyama 2001). However, there are debates over the extent to which there can be a policy to increase or build social capital. Social capital is perceived by donors as encompassing the features of social organisation (trust, norms, networks) that can improve the *efficiency* of society by facilitating co-ordinated networks. Thus, a large proportion of donor programmes attempt to promote group activities as a way of delivering services and/or strengthening civil society. In many cases there has been an uncritical promotion of all types of group activity, whether they be localised forms of collaboration or nation-wide organisations.

However, an assessment of different types of group activity in southern Ghana suggests that successful groups are usually those which have not received direct support. Social capital has often been built in this case over a long period through repeated community interaction. Those groups that do receive external support tend to become reliant on the aid and fail to grow once the support is removed (Lyon 1999). Nonetheless, policy makers may be able to encourage group activities and their associated social capital by creating an enabling environment for groups, reducing their barriers, mediating conflict and finding ways for people to come together and start their own activities. There are also opportunities to train people in how to build groups and manage collective action. Unfortunately, donor programmes tend to be uncomfortable with the long time frames required to have an impact, and the lack of hard quantifiable indicators.

Support for social institutions needs to recognise the less formal linkages and relationships as well as formal networks. There is also a need to understand how collective action is built up in different contexts. This requires policy to be culturally appropriate rather than attempting to replicate models perceived to be successful elsewhere. The 'micro-finance revolution' is a good example of the unquestioning replication approach. Group-based programmes have been popular for almost a decade as a means of reducing the costs of micro-finance delivery to poor people across low income countries in Asia and Africa, following the success of the Grameen Bank in Bangladesh. Social capital, in the form of networks and norms of association, is perceived as a substitute for financial collatoral in loan disbursal and recovery in these programmes, but this can have complex and adverse implications as a study by Mayoux (2001) in Cameroon effectively illustrates.

Mayoux considers the case of women and micro-finance programmes in Cameroon, where she has examined seven programmes, all of which put considerable reliance on women's existing client networks (i.e. kinship, neighbourhood and market networks). Women's participation in groups has been promoted there as a key to increasing financial sustainability through drawing on social capital which is seen as one of the few resources which poor women possess. At the same time participation in the group is assumed to empower women, and build social capital through automatically strengthening their economic and social networks. Thus there is an assumption that outcomes will be uncontentiously beneficial, but this view ignores the potential negative dimensions of social capital.

Mayoux finds the interrelationships between social capital, empowerment and sustainability extremely complex, but argues that there is no consideration of the ways that gender inequality structures how the different types of social capital can operate negatively for women. Men's 'social capital' (formalised in macro-level discriminatory institutional relationships and structures, such as physical gender segregation in urban markets where men dominate cash crop sales) reinforces gender subordination, both in the household and in relation to access to community resources and markets. This blocks women's attempts to expand their businesses.

Mayoux also draws attention to the complex power relations between women: the social capital of some women may, she argues, operate to the serious detriment of others. This finding is supported by our case studies of trader associations in Ghana. Women who gain power sometimes support gender subordination. Mayoux cites cases of programmes which have increased community inequalities by excluding the poorest women. She thus concludes that inequalities in existing organisations, networks and rules of association may be exacerbated by micro-finance programmes, but suggests there are possibilities for building on existing social capital more successfully, through building on existing networks for mutual support, and developing new networks whilst working towards altering the nature of rules and norms which are unequal. She also argues that there is a need for change at the macro-level, including federations to lobby for benefits to poor informal sector traders, and a broad-based movement for gender advocacy: 'The current preoccupation with social capital and its lack of analytical rigour risks further marginalizing attention to the underlying and critically important issues of gender inequality in resources, rights and power' (Mayoux 2001: 462). Furthermore, inequalities based on ethnicity, age and class also shape the relationships within civil society (Lyon forthcoming).

Micro-finance provides a good illustration of the fact that some institutions simply cannot be readily transferred between societies. Targeted support needs to recognise spatial differences in the formation of social relations which are related to variations in culture and history, and the fact that social relations are easier to build up with physical proximity, or the ability to meet people with whom trust can be built up. This is easier in tight communities, but also needs inter-community ties for opportunities to develop. Remote rural communities, such as those resident away from good motorable roads, are therefore likely to be at a considerable disadvantage when it comes to extending networks (Porter 2002). Monga (1995) argues that while there is no lack of social capital in most African countries, 'the problem is its limited scope in the absence of formal or informal links between the various components of civil society'. From a francophone African perspective, he sees the challenge as one of expanding the networks of existing groups beyond their geographical and regional limits, connecting people with similar interests and concerns. Although his work emphasises the political sphere, it has some resonance with our conclusions about economic life in southern Ghana. It emphasises the need for a particular type of social capital, the linking social capital consisting of vertical ties between ordinary poor people and those in positions of influence in formal organisations. These linkages can be crucial to economic improvement, because of the influence they may bring to bear on official decisions on resource allocation such as new roads, provision of health and educational facilities and a myriad of other issues. Entrepreneurs need assistance with improving the institutional environment (and their linkages to formal organisations), rather than with their networking activities *per se* (Barr 2000). Unfortunately, creation of such linkages is beset with pitfalls, given the fact that the boundaries between state and society, public and private, are neither clear nor consistent in West Africa (Berman 1998), and that personal ties of ethnicity and kinship often tend to distort networking and create negative externalities.

5 Conclusions

Existing research and conceptualisations of social capital suffer from a number of weaknesses. Of particular concern is the fact that greater attention has been given to formal networks that are observable and quantifiable. These are only one part of what can be defined as social capital. Concentration on these aspects can result in the 'softer' aspects, such as trust and norms, being ignored. A drive for quantification has come from the need to prove how social capital is related to economic growth. The World Bank put considerable effort into such studies in an attempt to prove to economists that the concept was important (Narayan and Pritchett 1997). Such studies are forced to make assumptions about causality, i.e. what causes social capital and what does it cause? Our case studies show that social capital can lead to a range of different forms of civil society institutions, which in turn add to the stock of social capital, i.e. that there is no simple or linear relationship.

Functionalist approaches have tended to dominate studies which take a social capital perspective. There are assumptions that social relations may raise efficiency by reducing transaction costs. However, in many cases, people do not act only to reduce their transaction costs. There is also a need to understand the processes that people go through to build social relations. This involves a detailed study of trust and power, and has serious ramifications for policy-makers who often make false assumptions about how individuals act in 'the market', by implying that individuals will always act to meet the wider social objectives of society.

Social capital studies have often made the assumption that all social capital is beneficial for the whole of society. However, there are many cases of collective action which impose negative externalities, a point which is receiving growing recognition, for example through Mayoux's work on gender reviewed above. The World Bank *World Development Report 2000/2001* (2000) reflects this in that it presents a somewhat more nuanced view of social capital, which includes distinguishing (following Putnam) a range of types of social capital: bonding, bridging and linking. Nonetheless, defining what is 'good' or 'bad' social capital still raises serious difficulties as what is good for some may affect others adversely. The example of driver unions presented in this chapter is a good illustration of the potentially negative component of social capital, in that the unions benefit their members at the price of excluding non-members. Trader associations in Ghana provide another example of groups (in this case groups of women) working together to survive in a highly risk-prone and fluctuating market. They are regularly accused of excluding farmers and non-members and, at times, of using threats to ensure this exclusion (Clark 1994). Their ability to exclude allows them to reduce dramatic price fluctuations, thereby reducing their risk of losing capital, and, therefore, increasing the amount of capital in the food marketing system. The evaluation of the welfare benefits of a group using social capital therefore becomes a political decision. A rather different Ghanaian example (Collier and Garg 1999; cited in the World Bank *World Development Report* 2000), is the case of locally dominant (ethnic) groups who receive a 25 per cent premium over the wages of other groups in the public sector, with consequent negative impact on overall performance in the sector. As Berman (1998) observes, civil service departments and public enterprises constitute virtually bottomless financial reservoirs for those who manage them and the political authorities which head them, with the consequence that ethnically based patron–client networks are able to reach to the very centre of the state apparatus. Social capital interacts with political institutions in complex ways which are not always recognised in social capital studies.

To conclude, this chapter has illustrated the wide range of forms of social institutions that help to shape the economic life of rural and urban people in West Africa. It has documented a selection of forms of collective action that are found in food systems, with particular reference to southern Ghana and, from this, examined a number of issues relating to how to conceptualise social institutions and their impact on civil society. It points to the huge number of groups and other networks to which individuals belong. Social capital has been presented as a way of conceptualising these relationships. Despite the fact that the concept is difficult to define and operationalise, it has the advantage of attracting a wide range of academic disciplines and policy makers to discuss the issues of social relations and cultural norms. This opens up debates and allows the cultural differences between places to be recognised. However, this recognition now needs to be reflected in far greater specificity or targeting of policies by donors,

NGOs and governments, rather than the common usage of blueprint policies transferred from one location to another.

Acknowledgement

This chapter draws on research funded by the Department for International Development of the United Kingdom (DFID Crop Post Harvest Research Programme Projects R7149, R7575 and R7924). However, the Department for International Development can accept no responsibility for any information provided or views expressed. We wish to acknowledge the assistance of Frank Owusu Acheampong who contributed to our research in southern Ghana.

Note

1. Similar types of relationship were used to gain access to land by those who were landless or did not have land near roads or water sources.

References

Amin, A. (1996), 'Beyond associative democracy', *New Political Economy* **1(3)**, 309–33.

Attwood, D.W. and **Baviskar, B.S.** (eds) (1988), *Who Shares? Co-operatives and Rural Development*. Oxford University Press, Delhi.

Barr, A. (2000), 'Networking for success and survival in Ghana: does size matter?', *Development Research Insights* **34(9)**. (http://www.id21.org/insights/insights34/insights-iss34-art06.html)

Barr, A. and **Toye, J.** (2000), 'It's not what you know – it's who you know: economic analysis of social capital', *Development Research Insights* **34(9)**. (http://www.id21.org/insights/insights34/insights-iss34-art02.html)

Berman, B.J. (1998), 'Ethnicity, patronage and the African state: the politics of uncivil nationalism', *African Affairs* **97**, 305–41.

Clark, G. (1994), *Onions Are My Husband: Survival and Accumulation by West African Market Women*. University of Chicago Press, Chicago, Illinois and London.

Coleman, J. (1990), *Foundations of Social Theory*. Harvard University Press, Cambridge, Massachusetts.

Collier, P. and **Garg, A.** (1999), 'On kin groups and wages in the Ghanaian labour market', *Oxford Bulletin of Economics and Statistics* **61**, 133–52.

Fafchamps, M. (1996), 'The enforcement of commercial contracts in Ghana', *World Development* **24(3)**, 427–48.

Fafchamps, M. and **Minten, B.** (1998), *Returns to Social Capital Among Traders*, IFPRI, MSSD Discussion Paper No. 23. IFPRI, Washington, DC.

Fine, B. (2001), *Social Capital Versus Social Theory: Political Economy and Social Science at the Turn of the Millennium*. Routledge, London.

Fouracre, P.R. *et al.* (1994), 'Public transport in Ghanaian cities: a case of union power', *Transport Reviews* **14(1)**, 45–61.

Fukuyama, F. (2001), 'Social capital, civil society and development', *Third World Quarterly* **22(1)**, 7–20.

Gambetta, D. (1988), 'Can we trust trust?', in Gambetta, D. (ed.), *Trust: Making and Breaking Cooperative Relations*. Blackwell, Oxford.

Gore, C. (1978), 'Food Marketing and Rural Development: A Study of an Urban Supply System in Ghana'. Unpublished PhD dissertation, Pennsylvania State University, Philadelphia, Pennsylvania.

Granovetter, M. (1973), 'The strength of weak ties', *American Journal of Sociology* **78(1)**, 360–80.

Granovetter, M. (1985), 'Economic action and social structure: the problem of embeddedness', *American Journal of Sociology* **91(3)**, 481–510.

Granovetter, M. (1993), 'The nature of economic relations' in Swedberg, R. (ed.), *Explorations in Economic Sociology*. Sage, New York.

Hill, P. (1971), 'Two types of West African house trade' in Meillassoux, C. (ed.), *The Development of Indigenous Trade and Markets in West Africa*. Oxford University Press, Oxford.

Hirschman, A.O. (1982), 'Rival interpretations of market society: civilizing, destructive, or feeble?', *Journal of Economic Literature* **20**, 1463–84.

Hodgson, G.M. (1988), *Economics and Institutions: A Manifesto for a Modern Institutional Economics*. Polity Press, Cambridge.

Lovejoy, P.E. (1973), 'The Kambarin Beriberi: the formation of a specialised group of Hausa kola traders in the nineteenth century', *Journal of African History* **14(4)**, 1014–27.

Lovejoy, P.E. (1986), *Salt of the Desert Sun: A History of Salt Production and Trade in the Central Sudan*. Cambridge University Press, Cambridge.

Lyon, F. (1999), 'Cooperation and Group Formation'. Report to the UK Department for International Development submitted under the Crop Post Harvest Programme, Project R7149, 'Access to market opportunities in Ghana's off-road communities.'

Lyon, F. (2000), 'Trust, networks and norms: the creation of social capital in agricultural economies in Ghana', *World Development* **28(4)**, 663–82.

Lyon, F. (forthcoming), 'The relations of cooperation in group enterprises and associations in Ghana: exploration of issues of trust and power', in Amin, A. *et al.* (eds), *Institutions of Local Economic Development*.

Mayoux, L. (2001), 'Tackling the down side: social capital, women's empowerment and microfinance in Cameroon', *Development and Change* **32**, 435–64.

Misztal, B.A. (1996), *Trust*. Polity Press, Cambridge.

Monga, C. (1995), 'Civil society and democratisation in francophone Africa', *Journal of Modern African Studies* **33(3)**, 359–79.

Moore, M. (1994), 'How difficult is it to construct market relations? A commentary on Platteau', *Journal of Development Studies* **30(4)**, 818–30.

Mortimore, M.J. (1989), *Adapting to Drought: Farmers, Famine and Desertification in West Africa.* Cambridge University Press, Cambridge.

Narayan, D. and **Pritchett, L.** (1997), *Cents and Sociability: Household Income and Social Capital in Rural Tanzania,* Policy Research Working Paper No. 1796. The World Bank Social Development and Development Research Group, Washington, DC.

Nikoi, G. (1996), 'The experiences of rural banks in enterprise credit: Akuapem rural bank case study' in Aryeetey, E. (ed.), *Small Enterprise Credit in West Africa.* The British Council/ISSER, Accra.

OED (1995), *Concise Oxford Dictionary of Current English,* 9th edn. Oxford University Press, Oxford.

Platteau, J.-P. (1994), 'Behind the market stage where real societies exist. Part II: The role of moral norms', *Journal of Development Studies* **30(4)**, 753–817.

Porter, G. (1999), 'Access to market opportunities in Ghana's off-road communities: crop post-harvest programme', Project R7149, Final Technical Report to the UK Department for International Development.

Porter, G. (2001), 'Rural access issues and the supply of urban food markets in Nigeria', crop post-harvest programme, Project R7924, Final Technical Report to the UK Department for International Development.

Porter, G. (2002), 'Living in a walking world: rural mobility and social equity issues in sub-Saharan Africa', *World Development* **30(2)**, 285–300.

Putnam, R. (1993), *Making Democracy Work: Civil Traditions in Modern Italy.* Princeton University Press, Princeton, New Jersey.

Schwimmer, B.E. (1976), 'The Social Organization of a Southern Ghanaian Town'. Unpublished PhD dissertation, Department of Anthropology, University of Stanford, Stanford, California.

World Bank (2000/2001), *World Development Report. Attacking poverty.* World Bank, Washington, DC.

CHAPTER 9

Work, time and space: Britain and West Africa in the nineteenth and twentieth centuries

Ken Swindell

1 Introduction

Recording the passage of time, marking the remembrance of things past and the celebration of individual and collective events, constitute a basic preoccupation of humankind. Such activities are the cornerstone of religious practice, and underpin the social cohesion of family, community and nation; and while time can be understood as long-term secular shifts, or as shorter term seasonal periodicities, all human situations are subject to everyday routines, which may comprise the symbolic, the social or economically necessary. Time and timing are integral to basic economic activities, reflected in agricultural, pastoral and industrial practices, which are performed within specific spaces. And there is a sense in which time and space are inseparable. But the manner in which time and space are measured and evaluated is embedded within different technologies and cultures. Thus profound economic and social changes are usually accompanied by new patterns and perceptions of time and space in the home and workplace, as well as shaping leisure. Arguably agricultural and industrial revolutions, and their economic and social transformations can be viewed through changing paradigms of time. In a 1967 essay, E.P. Thompson explored the shift from task-orientated time to waged-labour time in Britain, where time once 'passed' became 'spent', and time-disciplined factory work became the subject of worker–employer struggles as hours lengthened (Thompson 1967). The internalisation of these new concepts of time and labour was achieved by imposition and assumption, and their spread was neither sudden, nor universal.

The mechanisation of British industry in the late eighteenth century owed a good deal to the existence of a range of engineering skills, not least clock-making, but the mechanised factory required new concepts of time and its measurement. Factory systems created new patterns of work which altered people's daily lives, giving rise to new social milieux and political values. The control and management of labour in factories and offices demanded new daily routines, which also invaded domestic life. Concepts of time, space and work were altered and have been subject to continuous adjustment through new technologies, with late industrial capitalism demanding further compression of time-space, and requiring workers and consumers to adopt new regimes of work and leisure. Yet even within the North, access to information technologies is by no means universal, while the discrepancy between Africa and the North is huge. But the differences are also manifest in understandings of time, work and space, which this essay argues are fundamental to issues of development and underdevelopment in the widest sense.

In Africa, despite many changes in livelihoods and lifestyles, especially in urban and industrial enclaves, economy and society are still heavily influenced by rural and agrarian practices, and how time and work are personally and collectively measured, managed and valued. And if Africans have clung to these values, it is not surprising, given the frequent shifts in direction of 'development' initiatives and failed transformations, and the vicissitudes of world markets on which they are heavily dependent (see Chapters 1 and 7). A major problem for development programmes, such as educational schemes, financial reform, political reform and especially agricultural development, is that they are premised on values and managerial capacities embedded in industrial – and now late industrial – societies in Europe and America (see Chapter 2). There is resistance to the North's expectations about how people's time-space referents operate, how they should behave in the workplace, and their concepts of land tenure. Misunderstandings about the culture of work and the control of labour and land in Africa persist, and may be a major stumbling block to the transfer of technical practices, political agendas and programmes of change. There is a strong argument for understanding how under industrial, or agrarian conditions of existence, domestic routines, work routines and patterns of public and family life are stretched across time and space, and become powerful elements in the reproduction and transformation of societies. The North–South gap is not just about economic performance and life expectancy, it is also about differences in understandings and attitudes towards working practices and lifestyles, which are integral to the trajectories of industrial capitalism and the intertwined development pathways of the North and South. Yet many analyses and theories of change and development in Africa seem marginally, if at all, concerned with the implications of different concepts of time and space, and their measurement, although there is a considerable body of anthropological literature which addresses the timing of agricultural and pastoral practices.

This chapter comprises two sections. The first reflects on concepts of time and space as they developed in Britain under industrial capitalism, compared with West African rural agrarian systems, and how they shape work and working practices. The second half takes up this slant on work, time and space to review aspects of development and change in West Africa, broadly in the context of European contact. Hopefully, it provides another means of understanding what has become known as the North – South gap. At the outset it should be stated that this does not comprise a hidden agenda which suggests a pre-ordained model of change and development, nor a celebration of the Weberian Protestant work ethic. Rather it suggests that values and attitudes forged in industrial Europe (and America) have influenced the actions and reactions of both Europeans and

Africans right up to the present, especially with respect to social and economic development.

From a theoretical point of view the following account has some resonance with Bourdieu's Theory of Practice, as well as Structuration Theory (Bourdieu 1977). Both are concerned with reconciling objectivity and subjectivity in social science; the first based on work in agrarian and pastoral societies, the second on urban industrial milieux. Both explore concepts of time, space and daily routines, which are also issues for studies in time-geography (the exploration of 'time-geography' has been associated with a number of Swedish geographers, especially Hägerstrand (1975, 1978); but see also Pred (1977) and Parkes and Thrift (1980)). Time-geography is concerned with the location of individuals in time-space, and the environmental constraints on movement. Structuration Theory expands this with concepts of co-presence, and the positioning of actors and their interactions, and the interlacing of social contexts. And, importantly, the 'situatedness' of interactions in time and space. 'Structuration' considers how daily routines are part of the constitution of society; in Giddens' words, 'practices biting into space and time are at the root of the constitution of both subject and social object' (Giddens 1986). However, these constructs pay less attention to 'empty', or ambiguous spaces, which may be symbolically charged and often important in African societies (Sobel 1998). In conclusion, this paper explores how concepts of time, space and work are embedded in development policies.

2 *Factories, offices and industrial time*

The proliferation of new technologies and sources of power was an integral part of the Industrial Revolution in Britain, but there were already important ones in place, which were evident in rural as well as urban Britain. For example, significant developments in mechanical clockmaking occurred in the late Middle Ages in Western Europe, when the construction of accurate mechanical clocks measuring hours and minutes was achieved by using a falling weight and a system of gears, which required precision engineering and careful regulation. Perhaps the peak of clockmaking activity was the search for the construction of a chronometer which could be used at sea to measure longitude. The longitude problem was of such importance that the British parliament passed the Longitude Act in 1714, which offered a huge sum of money by contemporary standards (£20,000) for the solution to this navigational problem (Sobel 1998). Both the naval authorities and mercantile interests lobbied parliament, as the security of the realm, political success and the wealth of nations floated upon the oceans. While it was perfectly easy to measure latitude accurately by reference to the sun, moon and stars using sextants, it was less easy to determine longitude in movements paralleling the equator either westwards or eastwards. As a result of the longitude problem, thousands died, and many cargoes were lost, even in home waters. The solution was provided by a village carpenter, John Harrison, whose chronometer proved invaluable to European seafaring nations both in war and peace, and facilitated the mercantile hegemony of Western Europe, and the expansion of Imperial ambitions, culminating in a far-flung British Empire (Sobel 1998).

These clock-making skills were of crucial importance to the Industrial Revolution which began to take hold in Britain in the late eighteenth century, and were part of a repertoire of skills and a long established pool of technical knowledge, which prefigure what has become known as the Industial Revolution. Medieval villages had water-powered cornmills and windmills, which required gearing systems, while church organs were probably one of the most complex machines used in the eighteenth century. Indeed, there are those who believe the Industrial Revolution was less revolutionary than often imagined, and was part of an ongoing process of technological innovation (Clarkson 1985; Crafts 1985). It can be argued that contemporary African cities and villages contain not inconsiderable pools of skill and innovative practice; the problem is how to organise and channel these reserves to maximum economic and social effect. In Britain there was a convergence of technology (old and new), with rising population levels, lowered factor costs, expanding markets and financial and political structures. And there was a concomitant agricultural revolution, with new technologies, land enclosures and land–labour ratios.

The innovations in eighteenth- and nineteenth-century British industry were as much social as technical, and required new concepts of workplace and home, together with changing time–space relationships, as the factory became the locus of production. The first successful factory system was set up at Cromford in Derbyshire by Richard Arkwright in 1771. Arkwright's spinning mule, powered by water, was set in a purpose-built factory, which initiated similar factories along the River Derwent, using Arkwright's patented machine (Swindell 1965). But how were the first machines and factories built? Arkwright's solution was to advertise locally for clock-makers to build the machines, while his only source of architects and masons was found among those who built large country houses for the gentry, such as nearby Chatsworth, the seat of the Dukes of Devonshire (Fitton and Wadsworth 1951). The early factories along the Derwent have a resemblance to the large country house, and like thousands of factories which were to follow, especially in the textile industry, they were all topped by a bell or clock tower.

Clock-making and time-keeping were reciprocals. It was essential to use clock-makers' skills, but also necessary that the new labour force be at work on time, as with the advent of new work patterns, time was of the essence. Ackroyd (2001) describes London after the 1850s as a 'city of clock time' and a centre of mass production, which was more closely controlled and carefully organised, with 'business and government supervised by a vast army of book keepers who customarily wore uniform dark costumes' (pp. 661–5). Competitive and profitable unit costs of mass produced goods not only depended on mechanisation, but also on the vertical division of labour and piecework, which used shift systems and time-controlled applications of labour, to ensure a steady flow of finished goods. New supervisory jobs appeared, such as those of the 'time-setter' and 'progress-chaser', together with accounting and office systems, while planned maintenance work was crucial.[1] Of especial importance was the shift system; labour was stretched across twenty-four hours, radically altering personal movements and interactions, which ultimately spread into a wide variety of 24-hour service systems. This was essential for the efficient extraction of surplus value.

In general, factories and offices required a more sophisticated calibration of machines, standardised production processes, as well as standardised modularised products to serve mass markets with cheap goods. Therefore, labour had not only to be mobilised, but efficiently managed, effectively controlled and trained. This led to the 'watched workplace', where human capital was monitored to increase productivity and profit. By the end of the eighteenth century, the workers at Robert Owen's New Lanark mills had their productivity and behaviour recorded in supervisors' day books. He also developed a model industrial community, where supervisors also moved into workers' homes to ensure adequate standards of hygiene: thus there was surveillance at work and at home. An organised productive labour force emerged, as a majority gradually internalised new values of time, work discipline and cleanliness. Factory production and factory labour created new physical and social spaces, especially the differentiation between work and home, as well as having widespread effects on social and political organisation.[2] Factories created new 'locales' or bounded spaces for social interactions within specific contexts, while locales were 'regionalised' as time–space zones related to routinised practices, which ordered clusters of social interactions. Thus factories and offices, like schools, have specialised places related to divisions of labour, with varying degrees of surveillance, which have been termed 'front' and 'back' regions (Giddens 1986; Goffman 1959; Hall 1966).

Industrial change was part of an ongoing process of economic development in Britain. It brought about a significant redistribution of population with increased urbanism. Factories not only created new spaces which separated work from the home, but new settlements and modular housing, which led to some appalling conditions until better standards were achieved through Public Health and Housing Acts in the late nineteenth century. New housing created new locales and internal spaces, which led to new routines of movement, behaviour and interaction. The concentration of production increased the general mobility of the population, both for work and leisure. New systems of point production demanded new systems of transport, for the distribution of goods and raw materials, and, eventually, a commuting workforce.

Railways were an integral part of British industrialisation, but, importantly, timetabling was essential if the service was to work. Thus time became standardised across the country: the railway and its timetable restructured and compressed time and space, and created new geographical and social mappings. The railways also allowed new forms of leisure for the mass of the population, with annual migrations to the seaside, together with day trips. By the mid-twentieth century the advent of motor transport further accelerated population movements and their co-ordination, and virtually created a 'geography of Sunday', when industrial and urban populations reversed their daily routinised flow into cities and workplaces, as they moved *en masse* into the countryside.

3 African systems of time, space and work

The establishment of the factory system in Britain was paralleled by agricultural innovation, such as new cropping systems, and importantly by the Parliamentary Enclosures. But agricultural and pastoral practices were still regulated by the movement of the seasons. Almanacs were especially important as they were a cheap source of knowledge and included a calendar; apart from the Bible they were the most widely read and influential form of literature until the early nineteenth century (Capp 1979). Most almanacs had information on farming, such as the best times to plough, sow, fell timber and manure crops, while they also contained information about new crops and their cultivation. They contained predictions of weather, and although weather prophets were socially marginalised by the nineteenth century, they had not disappeared; recently, the notion of propitious moments in the agricultural cycle has reappeared under the guise of 'biodynamics'. Almanacs were rooted in astrology and astronomy, two sciences which, until the Enlightenment, were inseparable, forming the basis of science, and the foundation of medicine, physiology, botany and metallurgy.

3.1 Calendrical systems

Astronomical observations have historically provided systems of time-keeping; for example, they formed the basis of a calendrical system used by the Ancient Egyptians and Aztecs of Mexico, while the Muslim world pioneered astronomical and mathematical techniques, which influenced medieval Europe, as well as spreading into Africa. In non-Muslim areas Africans also had calendrical and time-keeping systems of some sophistication. The Asante calendrical system was not only used to keep time; it also influenced political and social decisions of the individual and the state. The Asante were, until the 1880s, a pre-literate people, but as McCaskie (1980) has demonstrated, there was a calendrical and daily time system which was exact and often symbolically charged, even if it was not committed to paper. The calendar operated on a repeated 42-day cycle, which was mechanically recorded by placing stones in pots. However, there was no standardisation, as the commencing days varied among groups and across states. There were also concepts of good days and bad days, with the latter outnumbering the former, which constrained individual and collective action. The system of counting propitious and non-propitious days is essential to understanding Asante history, as it influenced political and social actions and materially affected the outcome of the Asante wars of the late nineteenth century. By comparison, Eurocentric models of time–space accept clock time as an unquestioned dimension of the constraints in topological models, whereas time in some societies is itself fluid, and socially and economically conditioned.

In Islamic societies, calendrical systems based upon precise observations of sun, moon and stars are part of a long and well-established tradition, while the daily sequence of prayers still creates a web of movements and specialised places. Apart from the importance of calculating the major festivals of Islam, the use of solar and astral observations related to the zodiac was – and is – most commonly found in juridical astrology, which attempts to evaluate and condition human behaviour. Although the prediction of personal fortunes is a contentious area in Islamic practice (like Christianity), its incorporation and acceptance rests on the premise of an interlinked cosmos which manifests God's purpose, wherein God uses stars to communicate with his creation. Religious teachers devise almanacs and calendars, as well as providing a wide range of personal advice and talismans. In northern Nigeria imported almanacs are used in the towns and larger villages by malams or Islamic scholars, who are in the business of giving advice to clients who include both the very rich and the poor. Advice on marriage, migration, how to achieve a successful business and political career – all find a steady stream of clients. During military ruler Sani Abacha's regime in Nigeria, he was reportedly attended by 300 malams, and, before the presidential elections (he died before they took place), another 1000 were believed to have been scattered throughout the country. Recourse to astrology is by no means limited to African politicians; for example, late president De Gaulle of France and ex-US President Ronald Reagan, and his wife Nancy, consulted astrologers.

In parallel with juridical astrology, there is natural astrology and Arab scholars adopted the Greek model of the four seasons as agricultural templates, according to the entry of the sun into the first zodiacal constellations of each season, the year commencing with the Spring equinox. Alternatively, Arabs of the Yemen Peninsula had systems of reckoning based on observations of stars which correlated with meteorological phenomena, such as rainfall regimes (Varisco 1985). However, Islamic scholars have constructed more complex calandars based on the rising and setting of selected stars and constellations, to define the seasons and the timing of agricultural activities. These are referred to as 'agricultural marker stars' using 28 marker stars, 27 of which rise or set each 13 days, with an additional star with a 14-day interval, to give the 365 days of the solar calendar. Some markers are part of zodiacal constellations, others not; some are observed at rising, others at setting, so there is no internal consistency. Varisco (1985) believes that in Yemen, each local community devised its own practical system of seasonal reckoning, which means a general system of observation was 'localised' and adapted to offset latitudinal variations in sighting the relevant phenomena.

Agricultural star calendars, imported from Yemen and Saudi Arabia, are widely available in northern Nigeria, with farmers consulting local malams about the timing of farming activities, especially about the beginning of the rains, as well as at moments of crisis. Such consultations, together with local knowledge of vegetation and weather patterns, are an integral part of farmer preparation for the growing season, rather than a desire for predictions regarding specific commencement dates for the annual rains. Malams can also adapt general star calendars to fit local situations. For example, I recall seeing a system of marker stars in northern Nigeria identifiable with the Yemeni system, which had been latitudinally adjusted, so the planting times for early millet in Sokoto occur at different astral points than at Zaria, some 160 miles south, where the rains begin much earlier (personal interview Malam X: Sokoto, 1979). Compared with European calendars, which are also locally available, star calendars and their use by malams are seen as allowing for the most propitious moments for a whole range of actions, while remaining within the practice and precepts of Islam. In general, the reference to the supernatural, the religious and astrological are part of a deep-seated cautiousness shared by many farmers and herders – and not just in (West) Africa – as they confront the natural world in pursuit of a living.

While Africans often had elaborate time-keeping systems, Bourdieu (1977) has chosen to describe the written calendar as a 'synoptic illusion' in the context of practice. In his studies of the Berber of North Africa, he uses the calendar as a means of demonstrating the errors which can arise from intellectualist theories of social systems and classifications (Bourdieu 1977). One of the most powerful functions of timing and time-keeping lies in the realm of agricultural practice, which overtly relies on specific injunctions, rituals, taboos and sayings, or semi-codified objectifications. Bourdieu (1977) argues that once the observer begins to collect informants' knowledge of ordered practices and transforms them into a synoptic calendar, then there are problems. For example, identical periods are given different names, and identical names may cover different periods of differing length, all of which may vary according to ethnicity, region and village. In Islamic areas, as noted above, terms may or may not cover the same moment, depending on location, while there can be wide variations in the rate of farming, or pastoral activity, within specific 13-day periods as defined by marker stars. For rural communities, the farming year is built around wet and dry seasons, but may begin at different times according to geographical location, or a culturally significant crop; for example, the beginning of the year for the pastoral Fulani of northern Nigeria does not coincide with that of their agricultural neighbours, the Hausa.[3] Among the Berber Bourdieu studied, rites and taboos emphasise different moments, while there are 'good nights' and 'lesser nights', rather similar to Asante good and bad days. There are times of waiting and activity, as well as ambiguous times of passage between wet and dry season.

There is a temptation to collate amassed information and initiate a homogenisation process, and to some extent this does occur with the imposition of religious codes. Within Islam the emergence of written calendars was probably an attempt to harmonise astronomical systems used by scholars and clerics with local observations and practice, thus creating a universal system of star sightings, which could still be adjusted to local conditions. In addition to the intellectual ordering of these calendars, they were probably devised to co-ordinate taxation. But calendars turn events into a linear narrative, whereas agricultural practice is far from linear and continuous, and may more aptly be decribed as intermittent and circular. As Bourdieu (1977) points out, just as genealogy substitutes unequivocal homogenous relationships established once and for all, for a temporally disconnected set of islands of kinship, and just as maps replace patchy experiential space of practical paths by homogenous continuous geometry, so a calendar substitutes a linear homogenous continuous time for practical time. For the agriculturalist and pastoralist, whatever the calendrical system employed, there are incommensurable islands of duration, each with its own rhythm: time flies or drags according to the task. The guide-marks of the agricultural year are ceremonies, specific tasks, observations of season and weather, but once these are placed on a continuous line, it creates questions about the intervals, which are no longer topologically or metrically equivalent. Thus agrarian and pastoral time is less mechanistic, and lacks close continuous calibration; it is looser and less compressed.

3.2 Concepts of land and space

Cognate to the concepts of time are those of space, which for agriculturalists and pastoralists may be patchy and discontinuous, and measured 'loosely' in diverse ways. Degrees of boundedness, contiguity and closure can differ from one society to another, or between agriculturalists and pastoralists, which may reflect population levels, cultivation and herding techniques, as well as cultural practices. Europeans frequently find it difficult to understand rights and access to land, while Africans may experience problems with each other's land systems. Rotational fallow has not entirely disappeared from the forests and savannas of West Africa, and when Europeans have tried to map bush farms in differing states of use, they have found formal topographic survey methods less than satisfactory. Even more difficult is the mapping of intercropping, which may include trees, and the absence of pure stands within the farms (Norman *et al.* 1965). Europeans brought their own cultural baggage with them to Africa, and when faced with 'deconstructed' systems of land use and farming, they were unsure of whether they were facing 'un peu de tout' [a little of everything], or 'beaucoup de rien' [a lot of nothing]. Relatively extensive cultivation systems have rights to land vested in communities, and rights are part of the membership of social and political groupings, and most frequently the link is between land and lineage. But importantly, security to land does not have to be a particular piece of land; access for use and need might be the criteria, and may vary according to changes in family size and composition. There are three possible ways in which land and tenure may be conceptualised and perceived (Bohannan 1963). First, people have some kind of representational map of their country. Second, they have sets of concepts for speaking and dealing with relationships between themselves and 'things'. Third, the spatial aspect of their social organisation has some expression in word and deed. Westerners easily correlate (1) and (2), especially through sets of legal mechanisms relating to specific pieces of land. On the other hand, many Africans more easily correlate (1) and (3). Their map was, and still may be, one of a spatial and economic organisation which is fluid, and literally stretched and restretched over time and space. There are different geographies of person–thing and person–person relationships (see Chapter 1).

Concepts of land and space extend beyond technical classifications, and must be viewed as part of a whole spectrum of environmental understandings and interpretations; environment and people are part of each other, and inscribed in cosmological ideas and understandings. Bush farmers have an ambiguous perception of the boundary between forest and farmland, or the wilderness and the tamed. Although forest landscapes over the years may have been transformed by burning and farming, symbolically and historically the forest is held at bay, and is not necessarily a permanent condition. In Asante culture, trees and forest, which are endowed with power, and traditionally surround society's transformative actions, keeping the latter in check, create ambiguous or liminal spaces when felled or converted to farmland (McCaskie 1980, 2000). Land, and the symbolic and social space it occupies, can be surrounded by ambiguities. And not only where Animistic beliefs prevail; in Islamic societies, land may be circumscribed by Islamic law, although at the same time it may still be the subject of pre-Islamic cultural understandings.

But rising population pressure, the farming of export crops, and new political structures such as the nation state, have meant changes in the 'meanings' and use of land (see Chapter 7). Family lands tend to become demarcated, parcellised and sometimes registered, and there occurs a conjunction of traditional and modern meanings. Land markets develop, especially around urban areas and along arterial roads, although there may still be communal or family constraints on land sales. Also, land may be bought and sold, but this does not necessarily imply loss and accumulation and a 'market'; it may be redistribution according to need with a corresponding cash payment. Sales, purchases, borrowing and loaning may occur even within a single household; the situation is not clearcut, and categories are not mutually exclusive. And when demarcation has occurred, farms may still lack consolidation, comprising scattered plots derived from historic allocation, which gave a variety of good and poor land (Siddle and Swindell 1990). Such situations are at some remove from eighteenth- and nineteenth-century rural Britain, which experienced widespread pulses of enclosure, with processes of individualisation and exclusion, together with new land markets, leading in some cases to the wholesale removal of farmers. The persistence of communal tenure in Africa led the World Bank and IMF to press for individual tenures, in the belief that this would promote greater efficiency of land use (Bassett and Crummey 1993). This view tended to overlook the flexibility and potential efficiency of 'communal tenures' in certain situations, as well as the emergence of demarcation and land sales. However, the development of clear-cut land markets in rural West Africa is relatively slow and patchy, and compounded by problems of inheritance, subdivision, risk and credit.

The issue of land is a particularly difficult one for development agencies, because it resists meaningful collation and cadastral mapping. Cadastral mapping and contiguity are aspects of an agrarian capitalism, which facilitate formal land registration, and a definitive title to ownership. As noted above, such a one-to-one correspondence, even of demarcated plots, is not prevalent, and reflects the complex system of a spectrum of rights of ownership and use, which ebbs and flows over time, with limited states of permanence and clear titles. Such are the rocks of demarcation and 'ownership' on which many of the development initiatives of outsiders have foundered. On the other hand, in more commercially developed areas, such as around towns and along major routeways, where the competition for land is greatest, one finds more formal demarcation and ownership, often enmeshed in a morass of intrigue and corruption (Swindell and Ilya 1992).

3.3 Concepts of work

The flexible spatial and temporal arrangements of land, situated within varying social and economic contexts, also has implications for work. Land allocation gives rise to particular routines of work and social interaction, described by the pathways of daily movements from the village and among scattered plots. The field and village provided different locales. The fields, at least for the young and hired workers, may be analogous to 'back regions', with less surveillance and disclosure, compared with the communal life of the village and compound. Certainly, the supervision of field labour is a common problem for farmers, which is why labourers are paid by the piece and not the hour. Also, fields may be precisely gendered places (Leach 1992). Overall, there is a daily round of common tasks and practicalities involved in sustaining livelihoods, and household reproduction, as well as regular visits to market places, all of which are shaped by seasonal rhythms. These are the recursive actions of daily life, which 'go without saying', because they 'come without saying'. The concept of work for many rural Africans is different from that in industrial societies; it is less clearly segmented and comprises a *bricolage* of productive activity, which expands and contracts seasonally. Dichotomies of work and non-work, work and leisure are difficult to sustain, other than when engaged in commercial agriculture, or paid off-farm employment.

But it would be wrong to regard African livelihoods, lifestyles and understandings of work as ending at the edge of the village; historically they encompassed larger segments of space and time, while West Africa has long been part of the global economy through the Saharan and Atlantic slave trade, and then legitimate trade, which eventually replaced it (Lovejoy 1991) (see Chapter 1). West Africa was, and is, famous for its trading networks, which took goods over vast distances and linked forest, savanna and deserts, and produced ethnic and cultural diasporas. The Sudan-Sahel had a notable string of entrepots such as Kano and Djenni, while caravans were sites of complex organisation and division of labour, with settlements of migrants, known as *zongos*, appearing from the thirteenth century onwards. This merchant trade relied on elaborate credit and underwriting systems, as well as a generalised currency using cowrie shells (Hopkins, 1973). Trading for the Hausa and Dyula was both professional and casual, permanent and seasonal. Labour migration and trading were also *rites de passage* for many men, which in Hausa was referred to as 'yauwon dandi' – the walk of the world (Olofson 1976). But it was predominantly long distance travel during the dry season, when the movement of goods and personnel was easier, which was the opposite of the factory workplace, with its hourly and weekly time frames, and a stabilised workforce separated from the land and an agrarian culture.

4 European contact and the world economy

The presence and economic power of Europeans changed African livelihoods and lifestyles, creating new social and economic contexts and notions of the state and modernity. The question is by how much and with what consequences? And, in the long run, has there been more divergence than convergence in the conditions of existence and well-being between Europe and Africa?

Colonialism introduced (or re-inforced) alien systems of time and space, which brought new constraints on the organisation of life and labour, especially in administrative and industrial contexts. This was particularly evident in white settler areas. Europeans were intent on creating order out of apparent chaos, often unaware, or unconcerned, that Africans had their own modes of ordering lives and cosmological understandings. Not that Africans wholly embraced these new European systems; they managed (and still do) to achieve a parallelism, or co-existence of different cultural conceptualisations of time and space. But arguably the most definitive act by Europeans was a geographical one – the partition of Africa and creation of colonial boundaries. New spatialities were imposed on existing ones, with a new political map where contiguity was arbitrary and complete, as Europeans attempted to capture the unknown, delineate it, and define it through linguistic and legal systems. This geographical act of partition and naming created 'Africa', comprising a set of territories and boundaries, which progressively translated into new sets of social and economic conditions and interactions (see Chapter 2). At first, colonial provinces were grouped – for example, French West Africa – with Africans viewing these boundaries as a means of keeping Europeans rather than Africans apart; Africans frequently ignored these boundaries. Indeed, the colonial powers generally recognised their permeability as necessary for the flow of migratory labour, despite occasional attempts to control movements (Mabogunje 1972; Stichter 1986).

In post-colonial Africa the emergence of nation states built on European partition has created important boundary locales, where the co-presence of specific sets of social agents, and webs of interaction, have given rise to zones of intense activity, creating points of friction and contestation. Surprisingly, these have attracted less attention from researchers and observers than might be expected, despite the insights they give on the many strands in the fabric of African societies and political economies. The legacy of partition is the contemporary rag-bag of disparate-sized territories, many with limited resources, some landlocked, and most with small populations and limited internal markets, which pose severe problems for development. Despite attempts to correct these effects in the post-Independence period through various kinds of union, the arbitrary imposition of political boundaries remains the most enduring act of colonialism, which has also proved the most problematic.

4.1 The diversification and re-ordering of West African economies

As the nineteenth century progressed, the economy of West Africa was increasingly organised by European interests around legitimate commerce, that is the collection and shipping of agricultural produce. Unlike slaving, which was the preserve of rulers and merchants, the development of an agricultural export trade enabled thousands of small household producers to become involved in a wider cash economy. And, gradually, African producers became subject to the vagaries of the world markets, especially after 1870, when the terms of trade shifted against them and mercantile competition intensified (Hopkins 1973). It was a seasonal collecting economy, based on credit, which over time became more reliant on labour migration. While at first African merchant interest was involved, the larger foreign trading houses gradually assumed more control and, among them, there was a slow concentration of businesses and commercial capital, *vide* the Royal Niger company. On the other hand, production was diffused and atomised within myriad households, who integrated commercial export crops within their existing cropping systems. The merchant houses and shipping companies were quite happy with indigenous production; risks were spread through a hierarchy of traders and sub-traders, and profits were especially good on the importation of trade and wage goods, which were used as part of the credit system for producers of groundnuts, cocoa and cotton (Shenton 1986; Swindell 1992a). What happened here was, in a sense, the very opposite of industrialising Europe, where point production processes in factories led to stronger vertical divisions of labour and the emergence of a large controlled wage paid labour force, increasingly concentrated in towns. Furthermore, the African export economies were essentially labour intensive ones; the production of export crops was seasonal and integrated into existing farming schedules, albeit with some modification. In West Africa, there was very limited land alienation, few agrarian enclosures, although tracts of land were designated as forest reserves. Also, there were virtually no plantations with heavily constrained labour forces devoted to a single staple, which had most of the conditions of control and surveillance of factory regimes. Instead, the domestic unit was the core of production, with farmers being *in* the market, while not fully *of* the market, and being in the global economy, without their lives being fully globalised.

There were significant differences for those who went to work in the mines and towns, which developed in the late nineteenth and early twentieth centuries under colonial rule. Mining was limited to enclaves in West Africa, but was of much greater significance in eastern and southern Africa. Here, new labour regimes were harsh, and the level of control and management of labour more akin to Europe. As the mining economies flourished and urbanism increased, there was much talk of de-tribalisation; a whole literature was spawned on the making of industrial workers and townsfolk, especially in such locations as the copperbelt in Zambia (Ferguson 1999). By the 1980s, the process of modernisation and new urban lifestyles allied to mineral exports had hit the buffers, and, as one author has suggested, the widespread sale of second-hand Western clothing is now a current metaphor of modernity and the urban condition (Hansen 1999).

The degree of disconnection from rural roots across Africa was always variable, and labour compounds and urban lodging houses for migrant workers were pervasive, while 'urbane', rather than 'urbanised', may have been more appropriate for many town dwellers. In many instances families remained back home, work contracts were limited, turnover could be high and, for economic and political reasons, workers were not wholly uprooted from their rural environments, with many returning there on retirement. This was a process of 'straddling' different economies, societies and cultures – and, as suggested earlier, different work regimes; on the one hand, the wage and labour lines, on the other, the family farm producing food and, in some instances, cash crops (see Chapter 7). The household was reproduced by a combination of wage labour and family farm labour. This 'straddling' was sharpest in the case of mine, railway or port labour. But if mining accounted for a significant proportion of export earnings in some West African countries, such as Sierra Leone and Ghana, the number of short and long distance migrants involved in commercial cash crops was huge (Kitching 1980).

4.2 Migration, livelihoods and lifestyles

Periodic labour migration has not produced a fully 'proletarianised' labour force, subject to the kind of labour disciplines encountered in factories. The high turnover in the lower paid jobs, although allowing many rural and urban Africans to experience waged employment with wider social and economic horizons, has not meant that they have fully absorbed the labour practices of factory workers. Once again, it has been partial change. New lifestyles have been acquired by means of new consumer and wage goods, such as radios, watches and imported foodstuffs, but wages were (and still are) often used to provide food back home. Family tensions may be increased by absence, as a significant number of men experience parallel or bi-modal lifestyles, stretched over time and space. Migrant workers shuttle between different locales, which have very different social structures and sets of interactions, as well as routines evidenced in their space-time geographies. This represents a departure from the traditional combination of non-farm occupations located within the household and village, either concurrently, or seasonally (Swindell and Iliya 1992; Swindell and Mamman 1990). Cyclical and periodic employment has not produced a labour force comparable with European factory employment located close to home, which drew into its grasp whole communities, often employing children, as well as large numbers of women in one place.

Where there has been permanent migration into towns, many urban households find employment in what has become known as the informal sector. This may comprise small businesses, petty trading, ephemeral wage employment, whose chief characteristics include their atomisation, lack of formal controls and structures. And, there is often a connectivity with rural homelands, through transfers of goods and money – in both directions.

In essence, the informal sector is characterised by the social, rather than the industrial division of labour, and it can be viewed either as a symptom of innovative vitality, or one of pervasive poverty. Both the urban and rural poor are not so much unemployed, as having too much to do; they engage in a *bricolage* of jobs, situated in a multiplicity of social and economic locales, requiring high levels of geographical mobility. Informal sector employment and small businesses have much in common with the flexible farming systems used by many West Africans and, like farming, many sucessful businesses fail to survive the founder because of inheritance laws. In industrial capitalist societies, primogeniture and credit facilities have been powerful structures in the maintenance and growth of firms and farms.

The access to small farms by a generality of African people is a problem for the management and control of permanent labour forces in both government and private sectors. In 1902, Watts, the first Agent General of the Niger Company, identified the problem succinctly when commenting on Lugard's attempt to reduce government carrier and soldiers' wages; he opined that 'if he (Lugard) wants them to work for threepence per day he will have to return them to slavery, as long as they can go back to their farms'.[4] In the boom years of the 1970s, many expatriate companies in Nigeria preferred expatriate Ghanaian labour because it was much more difficult and expensive for workers to return home for occasional visits connected with harvesting and ceremonies.

The labour question dogged most colonial administrations in West Africa, and it was related to the persistence of slavery. Apart from any moral considerations, Europeans faced a pervasive and, in their eyes, an anachronistic system of labour control and organisation, deeply rooted in the African political economy, which they were trying to change and develop. Slavery frequently took the form of agricultural servitude where slaves might work on small farms of their owners, or on larger farms if they belonged to aristocratic households. In general slavery was part of a spectrum of social and economic control and dependency and although domestic slavery was widespread, West Africa did not experience the plantation slavery of the Americas and Caribbean. However, there were significant regions, usually associated with the historic centralised states, such as Mali, Songhai and Hausaland where a substantial proportion of the population were slaves (Lovejoy 1991). Here was a large potential labour force, although Lugard feared that sudden emancipation might risk civil disruption. In the end slavery was drastically reduced by outlawing the legal status, if not the condition, of slavery, which precipitated its slow death (Lovejoy 1991). The available labour force was increased, but it did not produce the factory-bound worker; instead it created more small household producers, together with seasonal or periodic migrant workers who met the demands of an economy geared to seasonal agricultural exports, as well as the labour needs of transporters and the ports. Much as administrators wanted a disciplined workforce, seasonal export economies – frequently migrant-driven – did not create the necessary social and economic conditions. Nor did the mining and urban industrial enclaves succeed in entirely breaking the ties with the countryside.

4.3 The reforming impulse

Nineteenth-century Christianity was also concerned with the ending of slavery in Africa, and there were great hopes for the 'civilisation' of Africans expressed through education and missionary work, which would produce a literate piety with new value systems, including a new work ethic. It was possible, even in 1956, to read a popular history of the British in Nigeria, whose author's leitmotif was: 'Let not England forget her precedence in teaching nations how to live' (Thorp 1956). Such views translated into the imposition of peace and justice, the opening of roads into the interior, the suppression of slavery and human sacrifice: the missionary pursuing the works of Christian mercy, evangelising as he educates, and the trader bringing his wares across the seas. A God-fearing, clean and hardworking literate African was the goal, and arguably was one of the first 'technical fixes' popular with subsequent developers. The colonial enterprise was marked by cheapness, and the missionaries provided education on the cheap, as well as hopefully inculcating new lifestyles and literacy. But in West Africa, at the end of the day, the Church's main contribution was relatively modest and limited to the provision of government clerks and clergy (Twells 1996). It was, however, important in promoting the use of English, as the language of a developing African elite, who could be co-opted into systems of indirect rule.

The hopes for education have continued to be promoted up to the present by external agencies, as well as African governments, but in a secular form. In the post-colonial period, education was given a much higher profile, but it has tended to be top-down, concentrating on new universities and, although the provision of primary school has been greatly expanded, their material situation is often dire, especially after the introduction of Structural Adjustment Programmes (SAPs). In contrast, primary education in nineteenth-century Britain was substantially developed, not through pedagogic and philanthropic initiatives (although these were useful), but through legislation and the development of industry. The Factory Acts in Britain in the 1860s limiting child employment meant that children were increasingly available for school, while industry and the service sector raised the demand for literate clerks and factory workers, who could read simple instructions and were numerate and literate enough to operate simple accounting and warehousing procedures. A mixture of social conscience and enlightened self-interest led Robert Owen to set up one of the earliest infant schools in Britain in 1816. In contrast, in African agrarian societies, public universal education systems are at odds with production systems centred on the household. Marginal inputs of labour at times of clearing, weeding and harvesting are not consonant with regular timetabled schooling.[5] Yet it is true that education may be an investment for rural people, if it secures a family member a good job in the city, with a chance of making remittances back to the farm. But education and off-farm employment can be disjunctive as well as conjunctive categories: there is often a delicate trade-off situation. On the one hand, they remove potentially the best farm workers, who may become detached socially and economically if they marry and raise families in the city. On the other hand, the maintenance of rural links is important for remittances, and in the face of poorly paid or insecure city jobs. The education-off-farm job scenario is, for many middle and lower grade workers, the epitome of 'straddling' and flexible diversification, rather than specialisation.

5 *Twentieth-century development initiatives*

The aims and impact of British imperialism were complex, but metropolitian economic and political interests were not geared towards the creation of industries, especially manufacturing, in overseas possessions. Capital flows were directed less to industry (other than mining) and more towards agriculture which, only in White settler areas, or Dominions, allowed for capitalised agriculture. The main thrust of colonial development in West Africa in the early twentieth century was the provision of infrastructure, especially transport. But after the 1914–18 war there were new initiatives, as the post-war economic boom in agricultural exports was followed by a slump and the Depression of the 1920s. During these post-war years agricultural departments were set up to improve the quantity and quality of export produce, which would compete better internationally, while competition *among* the colonies also sharpened (Shenton, 1986). But the social impact of export crops went beyond prices and incomes: the organisation of exports by colonial administrations introduced new time frames for the production and marketing of crops, with declared buying seasons, more standardised products, and specific spaces for the dissemination of inputs and the buying of produce, all of which re-orientated the ebb and flow of population and social interactions, especially during the buying season. But in West Africa, it was the standardisation and regularisation of the *product*, which concerned the administration, not the daily organisation of labour, which rested either on the decision of households, or of constituent individuals.

After the Second World War, colonial attitudes began to change as African political resistance accelerated and a wave of new development initiatives was launched which, in Britain, was assisted by the new Socialist Government. But the emergence of America and Russia as the two new superpowers altered the political and economic map of the world. The United States, which nursed a desire to establish its supremacy over world trading networks, doubted that the European colonial systems could stave off a communist threat. The West was in need of a new non-communist manifesto, which was enunciated in Rostow's staged take-off into sustained growth (Rostow 1960). But integral to both Western and Soviet manifestos was a belief in the power of transferred technology. In the spirit of the age a swathe of large-scale agriculture projects was launched by Britain, most famously the groundnut scheme in Tanganyika, the poultry scheme in the Gambia, as well as the Gambian and Sierra Leonean rice schemes. France expanded the middle Niger rice scheme in Mali, and developed the Richard Toll irrigation project in Senegal. The large irrigation projects and agricultural schemes in various guises and sizes have continued up to the present; the most notable being the irrigation and river valley development schemes across northern Nigeria in the 1970s and 1980s (Adams 1992).

A huge amount has been written about the economic and social trajectories of these schemes, which are found in neo-Marxist analyses, as well as liberal concerns about viability and appropriateness. Explanations of failures include the power of international capital, economic and political dependence, inappropriate technology and size, corruption, poor management, planners' ignorance of local farming practice and the concerns of farmers, together with a lack of training and education. Both capitalist- and socialist-inspired schemes have met similar fates: disappointing results and failure to meet objectives. And both were premised on similar assumptions about the power of new technologies to instantly transform existing practice, while harbouring misconceptions about local farmers and their understanding of the environment, and their tried and tested methods of farming. New technologies, including fertilizers, seeds and irrigation technology, come from industrialised societies and cultures and are premised on a wide spectrum of cultural and social practices and understandings. For example, modern irrigation schemes based on barrages and canal systems need precise crop regimes based on meticulous canal and pump maintenence, requiring strict watering schedules, and a rigorous programme of management. The breakdowns in communication about water release after heavy rains have led to some disastrous consequences. In other words, they are 'industrial' schemes, which depend on the involvement of a relatively stable set of producers who are culturally aware of regular time-based practices such as obtain in factories, in specific locations.

But many producers integrated into large, or small, rural schemes rely on livelihood strategies embracing several jobs, requiring mobility over sometimes quite large geographical spaces, sometimes referred to as 'action space' (Painter *et al.* 1994) (see Chapter 1). As noted earlier, there is a long history of job mobility and petty trading, especially in the Sudan-Sahel. The sedentary villager is something of a myth and there are adverse opportunity costs for farmers asked to commit themselves to the job- and location-specificity of an irrigation scheme, given the returns to their labour on the scheme. In the face of a string of failures, there has been the shift to IMF fiscal solutions to improve the lot of rural Africans, although the push for 'market principles' and 'globalisation' are scarcely new concepts to West Africa. These new objectives may stabilise and give some correction to African economies and polities, but there is little evidence of them promoting deep-seated change and development: development is as much about a clash of cultures and associated conceptions of work, time and space, as it is about technology and financial structures and strictures.

In terms of social and cultural practice in the agricultural realm, we are looking at time which tends to be circular, not linear, not continuous, but patchy, with rhythms integral to specific activities. Group solidarity is often reinforced by routines and daily rhythms, whereas those who 'race with time' are perceived as those who threaten to turn circular time into linear time, and simple reproduction into indefinite accumulation. Bourdieu (1977) has used the term *doxa* to represent self-evident truths about the social and natural world, compared with orthodoxy and heterodoxy, which embody an awareness and recognition of different and antagonistic beliefs. In Bourdieu's terms, as science and technology developed in Europe, understandings of nature and science became 'a long labour of disenchantment' or testing, in a world of liberal opinion and scepticism. Although clearly *doxa* are challenged by cultural contact and face moments of political and economic crisis, this does not necessarily produce critical discourse. On the other hand, class struggles are about dominant systems and classification – and the latter preoccupation was very much part of the cultural impact of colonialism (and thereafter). The naming of plants and trees and their classification by agriculturalists and foresters, the naming of places on maps, which turned patchy space into continuous space, and the boundary which created new areas of tension were a product of European intervention (Madge and Cline-Cole 1996). As Sartre opined, 'words wreak havoc, because they find names for what has been lived namelessly' (Sartre; cited in Bourdieu 1977: 170). Also, the introduction of languages associated with conquest can command attention and authorise and legitimate physical, social and political domains and institutions, hence the importance of education for many Africans, and the former's use by colonial and post-colonial governments. Under well-stratified or class-based social systems the orthodox becomes the given and the norm, yet its existence depends on the opposite, heterodoxy, which articulates heresy and competing opinion. Such an antithesis is also an essential part of democratic systems of governance.

In the post-colonial world, American, European and international attempts to re-shape and re-organise African livelihoods and lifestyles have continued, through a succession of discourses about development and change, using a language legitimised and empowered by Western orthodoxy (see Chapters 1 and 2). This has produced a trajectory of development models and schemes, subject to continuous change and challenge (Crush 1995). But as the earlier arguments have indicated, the cultural and social nexus of much so-called development is couched in a discourse which is at odds with the thinking of rural people about what they are doing, and what is going on. This is not to say that there has been no agrarian change; introduced cash crops, for example, were adopted by West Africans through a mixture of indirect force and self-interest. However, it is arguable whether change wrought by merchant capital and trading has led to significant changes to agricultural life, and concepts of time and space. New practices have been welded onto old ones, as farmers perceive the benefits. Since the 1970s more successful economic change in West Africa has probably come in response to the process of urbanisation, the rising importance of urban food markets and the rise of peri-urban commercial food farming (Swindell and Iliya 1992). But this is still at some remove from the controlled commercial contract farming practised in Europe, or in some parts of Africa, for example Kenya. In Europe, producer prices are either underwritten or subsidised, whereas in Africa this is rarely the case, although inputs are frequently provided at subsidised prices.

The resistance of farmers to foreign transformations and innovations spurred further interest in African farming systems in the 1980s, to create what has become known as Indigenous Technical Knowledge (ITK), ethnoscience and the 'grass-roots upward approach' (Richards 1985). The failure of large-scale improvement schemes, sometimes allied to resettlement, highlighted managers' ignorance of the knowledge of local farmers, whose resistance to new methods and their faith in tried and tested methods was often vindicated. Anthropologists, geographers and some economists began to explore, or extend exploration of farming systems and farming practices in West Africa, with the object of using this knowledge as the possible basis for an indigenous agricultural revolution. The emphasis was on farmers' innovative capacities, and use and knowledge of local ecologies. Farming became likened to 'performance', with repertoires of skills and variations on themes, not dissimilar to the extemporisation of the jazz musician. And part of the performance was the power negotiations among the performers. The idea was that development agencies should fully take account of existing methods, and there should be a cross-fertilisation of new and old. Certainly, there was plenty of evidence that the 'flexibility and coping strategies' of indigenous farmers was better than most of the schemes which had been thrust upon them. The exploration of ITK highlighted local innovative farming practices and, as with concepts of land, this has been extended to situate farming within a wider set of cultural understandings of nature, environment and cosmos (Croll and Parkin 1992). But there has been a corresponding lack of analysis of the more difficult problems of consumption and levels of nutrition. Also, there is limited information on post-harvest losses through debt repayment, bad storage and even theft. Faced with difficult environmental circumstances and rising population levels, farmers have shown remarkable resilience and innovation, for example through intensification of land use, but what has happened to levels of consumption and nutrition is less clear. In the North, long-run improvements in levels of well-being and lowered mortality have usually been associated with regular rather than seasonal food supply, as well as increased production and consumption associated with changing factor relationships of land, labour and capital, together with growing industrial and urban markets.

6 Some conclusions

The direct commercial and political involvement of Europeans in the nineteenth and early twentieth centuries left their mark on African societies and polities, but their impact was in many ways marginal: there was limited convergence with the developing economies of Western Europe and America in terms of economic performance and changing livelihoods and lifestyles. Economic influence was mostly through international markets and credit, while the cultural hegemony exercised by Europeans, although important, has been patchy or superficial. Much the same can be said of development programmes and trade initiatives in the late twentieth century. Reluctantly one is left with the view that, compared with their European counterparts, African workers were 'exploited', but not exploited enough (Kay 1975). Surpluses were extracted by foreign capital, but through the prices that Africans received for their produce. Attempts to transform West African societies created neither disciplined workers, nor effective consumers, nor was there an adequate development of civil and political society, reaching down to the grassroots. One of the inherent failings of imperial rule was the imposition of political and administrative systems from on high; thus at Independence, administrations contained few adequately trained civil servants and managers. In the period after Independence waves of foreigners appeared with their own development models and political agendas for the transformation of African political economies. Planned interventions included large-scale rural development schemes, Basic Needs Programmes, Green Revolutions, and Structural Adjustment Programmes. Now the North seems to think that a demand for 'fair' elections – if necessary backed by force or sanctions – will somehow create democracies, and sufficiently 'enable' local development.

There is a sense in which Africa was and remains a European construct: as Africans have frequently remarked, 'You came and told us we were Africans'. There is also a sense in which Africa in the mind of the North is more of an idea than a place, a view enhanced by nineteenth-century European explorers, traders, missionaries and writers, whose readers delighted in the exotica of the 'Dark Continent', and the mirror image it presented of European enlightenment and progress. And it would be hard to deny the continuation of these images in the contemporary media and perceptions of Northern politicians, and their universal application to a huge geographical area. On the one hand, it is characterised by famine, plague, warfare and corruption; on the other, it embraces exotic locations and the environmental sanctity of nature reserves, guarded as much by Europeans as Africans.

On balance it looks as though a convergence between the livelihoods and lifestyles of Africa and the 'North' is as distant as it was after the Second World War. After 50 years of development initiatives from major political blocs and international institutions, the socio-economic gap has widened between the North and Africa. There are also significant gaps developing in the areas of information technology and the further compression of time and space. The situation was deemed so bad in the 1990s that critics talked of the 'end of development', and the 'disconnection of Africa from the world economy', or at least of the continent remaining a permanent periphery (Sachs 1997). This is a view which points to the failure of the modernisation project, and one which eschews linear development models and teleologies. There is also the prospect of the (re)invention of a geographical determinism, which puts tropical Africa within some kind of physical limbo, where climate and natural hazards seriously impede, or slow economic progress. In short, the end of development and the abandonment of progress is a bleak outlook for Africans.

So can partially transformed agricultural societies with little influence on the behaviour of world markets, make significant progress, not only towards better social and economic conditions, and better governance, without some kind of industrialisation? Can atomised agricultural societies create civil societies conducive to the emergence of democratic-style polities? But this, as they say, is another story, which requires much more analysis, together with an evaluation of the state of industry in Africa. An analysis by Sachs (1997) suggests that nowhere has tropical agriculture led the escape from poverty, although it could be argued that fluctuating world markets, together with continuing subsidies to Northern farmers, hardly assist Africans. Africa may 'develop' but not at the risk of Northern agricultural and political interests. To some it may appear that the North has moved from top-down economic interventions back to political ones, or what has been referred to as 'benign imperialism' and a New World Order. In some quarters development thinking has come full circle: the 1980s model of Africa exploiting its comparative advantage for the supply of tropical produce, together with integrated development projects to improve local food supply, leads to the possibility of an African future as a supplier of cheap, manufactured goods and services, and as an importer of food. Thus the industrial scenario of the 1950s, so long rejected, has partially re-appeared, suggesting there may be ways forward for some sub-Saharan countries. There is an argument that African countries without some industrialisation, or rather that culture of work, politics and civil society which is embedded in industrial societies, will have some difficulty in engaging successfully with capitalist economies which, for better or worse, dominate the international economy. And, while a celebration of 'otherness' and populist scenarios of African agriculture and informal industry are important in the short run, unless they significantly improve levels of well-being, there is the danger that they are more about survival than development. Sustainable development is more than environmental prudence; it is also about the social, economic and political milieux which are necessary for better livelihoods and lifestyles.

Notes

1. The training of the workforce in the regular daily maintenance of machines, and of their performance was important, together with associated punishment for neglect. Similarly, the planning and recording of periodic maintenance and overhauls was something which was especially incumbent on supervisors.
2. Industrialisation and urbanisation broadened political and civil society during the nineteenth century. The Trades Union Council was established in 1868, although it was not until after 1900 that unskilled workers dominated trade unions. Friendly Societies of working men flourished, and weekly contributions took care of sickness and funeral expenses. By the 1840s, the Foresters, Druids, Buffaloes and Rechabites had become national organisations, embracing a multitude of local branches, each with its committees and officers. By 1872 Friendly Societies had 4 million members and, as social organisations, were only exceeded in importance by the churches
3. Among the Hausa the farming year begins in the middle of the late dry season, *bazara*, while among the Fulani it is the end of the rainy season, *kaka*. The former is marked by the star *budaina* and the latter by *sarfa*. Among the Avatime in southeastern Ghana, the calendar for rice cultivation sets the pattern for the agricultural year, with the rice cycle beginning in June with the appearance of a constellation, and initiates the ritual 'new year'. See Brydon (1981).
4. Ms. Rhodes House: Scarborough papers, vol. 10 ff, 91.W.Watts to J.E. Flint, 4 April 1902. See also Swindell (1992b).
5. Something of this conflict of interest is expressed through the ambiguity of the Hausa phrase *kudin makaranta* – school fees, which can mean the 'fee' paid to the headteacher for recording the presence of an absent child.

References

Ackroyd, P. (2001), *London: The Biography*. Vintage, London.

Adams, W.M. (1992), *Wasting the Rain*. Earthscan, London.

Bassett, T.J. and **Crummey, D.E.** (1993), *Land in African Agrarian Systems*. University of Wisconsin Press, Madison, Wisconsin.

Bohannan, P. (1963), '"Land", "tenure" and "land tenure"' in Biebuyk, D. (ed.), *African Agrarian Systems*. Oxford University Press, London.

Bourdieu, P. (1977), *Outline of a Theory of Practice* transl. by R. Nice. Cambridge University Press, Cambridge.

Brydon, L. (1981), 'Rice, yams and chiefs in Avatime: Speculations on the development of a social order', *Africa* **51(2)**, 659–77.

Carlstein, T., Parkes, D. and **Thrift, N.** (eds) (1978), *Timing Space and Spacing Time*, Vol. 1 of *Making Sense of Time*. Arnold, London.

Capp, B. (1979), *Astrology and the Popular Press*. Faber and Faber, London.

Clarkson, L.A. (1985), *Proto-Industrialization; The First Phase of Industrialization*. Macmillan, Basingstoke.

Cohen, A. (1965), 'The social organization of credit in a West African cattle market', *Africa* **35(1)**, 8–20.

Crafts, N.F.R. (1985), *British Economic Growth During the Industrial Revolution*. Oxford University Press, Oxford.

Croll, E. and **Parkin, D.** (1992), *Bush Base: Forest Farm. Culture, Environment and Development*. Routledge, London.

Crush, J. (ed.) (1995), *The Power of Development*. Routledge, London.

Ferguson, J. (1999), *Expectations of Modernity. Myths and Meanings of Urban Life on the Zambian Copperbelt*. University of California Press, Berkeley, California.

Fitton, R.S. and **Wadsworth, A.P.** (1951), *The Strutts and the Arkwrights*. Manchester University Press, Manchester.

Giddens, A. (1986), *The Constitution of Society: Outline of the Theory of Structuration*. Polity Press, Cambridge.

Goffman, E. (1959), *The Presentation of Self in Everyday Life*. Doubleday, New York.

Guyer, J. (ed.) (1987), *Feeding African Cities: Studies in Regional Social History*. Manchester University Press for IAI, Manchester.

Hägerstrand, T. (1975), 'Space, time and human conditions' in Karlqvist, A. and Lundqvist, L. (eds), *Dynamic Allocation of Urban Space*. Saxon House, Farnborough.

Hägerstrand, T. (1978), 'Survival and arena: on the life history of individuals in relation to their geographical environment', in Carlstein, T., Parkes, D. and Thrift, N. (eds), *Timing Space and Spacing Time*, Vol. 2: *Human Activity and Time Geography*. Edward Arnold, London.

Hall, E.J. (1966), *The Hidden Dimension*. Bodley Head, London.

Hansen, K.T. (1999), 'What style on the cheap means in Zambia', *Africa* **69(3)**, 343–65.

Hopkins, A.G. (1973), *An Economic History of West Africa*. Longman, London.

Kay, G. (1975), *Development and Underdevelopment*. Macmillan, London.

Kitching, G. (1980), *Class and Economic Change in Kenya: The Making of a Petite Bourgeoisie, 1905–1970*. Yale University Press and London and New Haven, Connecticut.

Leach, M. (1992), 'Women's crops in women's spaces: gender relations in Mende rice farming' in Croll, E. and Parkin, D. (eds), *Bush Base: Forest Farm*. Routledge, London.

Lovejoy, P. (1991), *Transformations in Slavery: A History of Slavery in Africa*. Cambridge University Press, Cambridge.

Mabogunje, A.L. (1972), *Regional Mobility and Resource Development in West Africa*. MacGill/Queen's University Press, Montreal, Quebec and London.

Madge, C. and **Cline-Cole, R.** (1996), 'The West African Forest Zone in the European Geographical Imagination', *Geography* **81**, 24–31.

McCaskie, T. (1980), 'Time and the calendar in nineteenth-century Asante; an exploratory essay', *History in Africa* **7**, 179–200.

McCaskie, T. (2000), 'Trees and the domestication of power in Asante thought' in Cline-Cole, R. and Madge, C. (eds), *Contesting Forestry in West Africa*. Ashgate, Aldershot, and Burlington, Vermont.

Norman, D.W., Fine, J.C., Goddard, A., Pryor, B., Hays, H.M. and **Huizanga, B.** (1965), *A Socio-Economic Survey of Three Villages in the Sokoto Close-Settled Zone*, Samaru Miscellaneous Papers No. 34. Institute for Agricultural Research, Samaru, Ahmadu Bello University, Zaria, Nigeria.

Olofson, H. (1976), 'Yauwon Dandi: A Hausa category of migration', *Africa* **46(1)**, 66–79.

Painter, T., Sumberg, J. and **Price, T.** (1994), 'Your *terroir* and my "action space": implications of differentiation, mobility and diversification for the *approche terroir* in sahelian West Africa', *Africa* **64(4)**, 447–64.

Parkes, D. and **Thrift, N.** (1980), *Times Spaces and Places: A Chronogeographic Perspective*. Wiley, Chichester.

Pred, A. (1977), 'The choreography of existence: thoughts on Hagerstrand's time geography', *Economic Geography* **53**, 207–21.

Richards, P. (1985), *Indigenous Agricultural Revolution*. Hutchinson, London.

Rostow, W.W. (1960), *The Stages of Economic Growth: A Non-Communist Manifesto*. Cambridge University Press, Cambridge.

Sachs, J. (1997), 'The limits of convergence: nature, nurture and growth', *The Economist*, 14 January, 19–21.

Sartre, J.-P. (1971), *L'Idiot de la famille*, Vol. 1. Gallimard, Paris.

Shenton, R.W. (1986), *The Development of Capitalism in Northern Nigeria*. James Currey, London.

Siddle, D. and **Swindell, K.** (1990), *Rural Change in Tropical Africa*. Blackwell, Oxford.

Sobel, D. (1998), *Longitude: The True Story of a Lone Genius Who Solved the Greatest Problem of his Time*. Fourth Estate, London.

Stichter, S. (1986), *Labour Migration in Topical Africa*. Cambridge University Press, Cambridge.

Swindell, K. (1965), 'The Cromford cotton mills: their site and location', *East Midland Geographer* **3(8)**, 461–69.

Swindell, K. (1992a), 'African food imports: peanuts and ricebowls in the Gambia, 1843–1934' in Hoggart, K. (ed.), *Agricultural Change, Environment and Economy*. Mansell, London.

Swindell, K. (1992b), 'The struggle for transport labour in northern Nigeria, 1900–1912: a conflict of interests', *African Economic History*, **20**, 137–59.

Swindell, K. and **Iliya, M.A.** (1992), *Accumulation, Consolidation and Survival: Non-farm Incomes and Agrarian Change in Northwest Nigeria*. Working paper 6, Joint Committee on African Studies: African Agriculture, Crisis and Transformation Social Science Research Council, American Council for Learned Societies, New York.

Swindell, K. and **Mamman, A.B.** (1990), 'Land expropriation and accumulation in the Sokoto periphery, northwest Nigeria', *Africa* **60(2)**, 73–187.

Thompson, E.P. (1967), 'Time, work discipline and industrial capitalism', *Past and Present* **38**, 56–97.

Thorp, E. (1956), *Ladder of Bones*. Jonathon Cape, London.

Twells, A. (1996), 'A state of infancy: West Africa and British missionaries in the 1820s', *Wasifiri* **23**, 19–30.

Varisco, D.M. (1985), *Medieval Agriculture and Islamic Society*. University of Washington Press, Seattle, Washington.

CHAPTER 10

State-building, national integration, gender and economic development in emergent regional democracies

Jimmy D. Kandeh and Joyce A. Kannan

1 Introduction

Democracy has perennially taken a backseat to the imperatives of economic development, national cohesion and political stability in post-independence West Africa. Political incumbents routinely dismissed multi-party democracy as a Western invention that was more likely to retard development, undermine national unity and threaten stability than improve the lot of impoverished populations. Post-colonial democratic institutions and processes were hurriedly cast aside and replaced by single-party and military dictatorships that pledged to maintain political stability, foster national integration and promote economic development. But developmental or benevolent dictatorships turned out to be rare occurrences. What emerged instead were predatory regimes that deflated state capacities, privatised violence, informalised economies and sowed seeds of discord and rebellion. The failure of authoritarian regimes to deliver on their developmental promises led to renewed public demands across Africa for a more representative and transparent system of governance. Democracy, however, has to do better than authoritarianism in fostering economic development and national cohesion or risk rejection and replacement by demagogic alternatives (Sklar 1986).

The potential role of the state in building support for democracy, promoting economic development and fostering national unity cannot be overstated. Democracies cannot thrive when states falter or abdicate responsibility for protecting citizens and providing basic amenities; nor can there be any socio-economic development and national integration without the active intervention of the state. As Adam Przeworski reminds us, 'the successful cases of democratisation were precisely those where the state expanded its role as a provider of social protection and . . . education' (Przeworski *et al.* 1995: 37). A limited, non-interventionist state may be conducive to mature democracies but is incompatible with the needs of emerging democracies in regions like West Africa. The problem is not that the state in West Africa is interventionist but that its interventions have systematically benefited the few while disadvantaging and impoverishing the majority. Reconfiguring such a state so that it embodies and promotes universal concepts and interests requires the adoption of basic democratic tenets, norms and principles. How effectively and impartially state institutions perform their tasks has a direct bearing on the degree of national cohesion and public support for democratic institutions. The performance of democratically elected governments is, therefore, critical to prospects for democratic consolidation. Positive performance by the government can empower individuals, make them effective citizens and lay the groundwork for democratic growth and maturation. Rather than being antithetical to economic development and national unity, democracy is part of the solution to the problems of underdevelopment, disunity and chronic political instability.

This chapter provides an overview of past and current attempts at state-building, national integration, gender and economic development in West Africa. It explores the links between democratic institutions, women's position and market economies and proposes a holistic approach to tackling the problems of weak institutions, fragmented societies, gender oppression and mass impoverishment. While democracy may provide a better means for tackling the basic challenges facing African societies than its alternatives, the sustainability of democratic rule begins with the type of democracy adopted or the degree to which democratic institutions and procedures accommodate existing cultures and social conditions. It is necessary, if democratic growth and maturation are to be achieved, to adopt only those economic reforms that consolidate democracy by improving the lives of citizens, while rejecting those that impoverish popular sectors, exacerbate social tensions and undermine sovereignty. Put another way,

> If democracy is to be sustained, the state must guarantee territorial integrity and physical security, it must maintain the conditions necessary for an effective exercise of citizenship, it must mobilize public savings, coordinate resource allocation, and correct income distribution. And if state institutions are to be capable of performing these tasks, they must be reorganized rather than simply reduced.
>
> (Przeworski *et al.* 1995: 12)

This is particularly significant in light of the failure of peripheral capitalism to generate prosperity, gender equality and democracy in Africa.

2 *Regional democracy: a balance sheet*

Democracy can be defined as a representative system of government characterised by competitive elections, citizen participation and political accountability of leaders, civil and political rights, and an independent judiciary. Mainstream liberal democratic theory places a high premium on vibrant associational life and a culture of tolerance, accommodation, bargaining and compromise, as essential ingredients of a democratic polity. But democracies do not emerge nor are they sustained in a vacuum; rather they are the products of historical forces and social conditions that differ among countries. Ever since Aristotle, and while democracy has been predicted for societies where the middle strata are large, corresponding predictions for societies with overwhelmingly poor populations have been tyranny and oligarchy. Rousseau maintained that the social state is advantageous to all when none is too rich or too poor, thus linking democratic prospects to reduction in social disparities. Socio-economic equality was also cited by Alexis de Tocqueville as one of the factors that explained the success of democracy in America while Adam Smith and neoclassical economic theory identified the middle class as the most important social force in democratic emergence and consolidation. Seymour Martin Lipset's social requisites of democracy (education, large middle class, economic prosperity) also emphasised the relevance of social structure in nurturing and improving democratic prospects (Lipset 1959).

Democracy, in short, is related to social structure and is the product of historical circumstances. But while both liberal-pluralist democracy and capitalism grew out of historical conditions that were internal to Europe, they were, in contrast, superimposed on (West) Africa from outside in complete disregard for local traditions and conditions. Any discussion of regional democracy must, therefore, separate the factors that gave rise to it from those required for its consolidation. Indeed, the absence, in areas like West Africa, of most of the conditions that allow democracy to thrive and mature, explain the large number of failed regional democratic experiments.

There have been at least two waves of democratic experimentation in Africa since independence. The first coincided with the dawn of independence when colonial powers bequeathed democratic institutions to their former colonies before granting them freedom. Inspired by nationalism and the principle of self-determination, this phase, which started during the late colonial period, was short-lived. The Westminster model of parliamentary government, with a prime minister and loyal opposition, failed to constrain political incumbents who were far more interested in consolidating power than nurturing and preserving democracy. The French presidential model, with its preference for a directly elected executive president, fared no better. One after the other, countries that were once considered promising democracies fell by the wayside as one-party despots and military tyrants took over the reins of government. But while authoritarian regimes were justified as necessary to bring people together and mobilise scarce human resources for development, the vast majority of single-party systems were self-serving and rapacious.

Democratisation of the 1960s unravelled for a variety of reasons.

- Colonialism had subverted and destroyed many of the indigenous democratic practices of Africa, leaving behind a statist, authoritarian legacy that could not be reconciled with the democratic aspirations of popular sectors.
- Democratic experiments were entered into without adequate preparation (the Congo serves as perfect example) and acculturation to democratic governance.
- The first wave of democratic experiments was led by elites whose interests were at odds with those of popular sectors.
- The absence of procedural consensus or agreement on democratic rules and procedures among political elites doomed early democratic experiments.

- Africa lacks hegemonic ruling classes which can rise above their immediate interests and pursue policies that benefit society as a whole. Democracy and development require a political leadership that can minimally identify with the needs, interests and aspirations of society.
- Low levels of political institutionalisation rendered state institutions malleable and amenable to the interests of political incumbents.
- A weak, uninformed and fragmented civil society lacked the resources and autonomy to contest and resist attempts by political incumbents to subvert nascent democratic processes.
- The politicisation of ethnicity transformed elite and factional conflicts into communal face-offs that undermined national cohesion and political stability. Politicisation of cultural differences, as Robert Dahl notes, can in turn limit the possibility of polyarchy or pluralist democracy (Dahl 1971).
- The external environment during the Cold War did not augur well for democratic experiments as a preoccupation with communist containment allowed despots such as Samuel Doe of Liberia to stay in power. Halting the spread of communism was considered more important than promoting democracy, with some even going so far as to argue that authoritarian governments may be better suited to instituting market reforms than democratically elected governments.
- Perhaps the most important reason for the democratic breakdown of the 1960s was the performance of democratically elected governments, especially their failure to respect democratic norms and procedures, tackle the problem of official corruption and promote economic development. These failures delegitimised democratic experiments and provided pretexts for authoritarian alternatives.

Brief interludes of democratic flirtation occurred even as most leaders became venal despots. Unsuccessful re-democratisation was attempted in Ghana (1969, 1979) and Nigeria, for instance, with failure casting renewed doubt on Africa's democratic prospects. In Ghana, where the 1966 overthrow of Kwame Nkrumah's one-party dictatorship was followed by three years of military rule, the return of constitutional democratic rule under Kofi Busia lasted less than three years before the government was ousted in yet another military coup. The new military junta under the leadership of General Ignatius Acheampong adopted a populist stance in its first year in power but rapidly 'degenerated into unrestrained predation' (Young 1999: 20). Acheampong was later ousted in a palace coup that installed General Fred Akuffo as head of state, but both men, along with another former military dictator, General Akwasi Afrifa, were executed by firing squad in the days following the coup of 4 June 1979. The new junta, which was led by Flight Lieutenant Jerry Rawlings, proceeded with planned elections, after which power was transferred to the duly elected government of Dr Hilla Limann, which was in power for only two years, before it was overthrown in another coup led by Rawlings, who complained of continued corruption and official harassment, among other things.

In the case of Nigeria, preparations for a transition to civilian democratic rule began after the end of the civil war in 1970 but General Yakubu Gowon's foot-dragging on the issue of military disengagement led to his removal in a 1975 palace coup. The man who replaced him, General Murtala Mohammed, jumpstarted a transition process that had stalled under Gowon, and although Mohammed was later assassinated, his successor, General Olusegun Obasanjo, dutifully executed the transition plan. But democratisation in Nigeria, as in Ghana, failed because while

> Constitutional engineering could manage cultural pluralism . . . institutional ingenuity was no match for corruption. The colossal scale of venality, along with the equally stupendous rigging of the 1983 elections, destroyed the legitimacy of the second republic. The popular welcome accorded the renewed military intervention at the end of 1983 seemed to serve as a requiem for African democracy.
>
> (Young 1999: 21)

Africa's second democratic wave started with Benin's national conference, which resulted in the effective seizure of power by civil society as intellectuals, students, teachers and unions took the lead in voicing opposition to the government of Mathew Kerekou (see Chapter 2). State failures, especially the inability to pay its workers, sparked the confrontation between Kerekou's fledgling government and civil society. Events in Benin were to reverberate throughout francophone Africa, where the national conference became the preferred mode of transition from authoritarian dictatorship to constitutional democracy, although the Togolese president, Gnassingbe Eyadema, remained unmoved despite being forced to convene a national conference.

The release of Nelson Mandela in 1991, and his election as President of South Africa in 1994, gave a huge boost to democratic forces on the continent. In addition, several transition elections of the second wave saw the exit of post-colonial dictators in, among others, Mali, Cape Verde and Sâo Tome et Principé. Elections in Ghana, Gambia and Burkina Faso were self-succession affairs, while Sierra Leone's elections of 1996 led to the temporary transfer of power from a military junta to elected civilians. Nigeria, Africa's most populous country, was another story altogether. What started as a seemingly credible attempt to democratise under General Ibrahim Babangida was brazenly aborted by the annulment of the results of the 1993 elections. This plunged the country into a protracted crisis that forced Babangida from power, creating a void that allowed General Sani Abacha to seize power in 1994. Abacha's democratic transition programme was a sham, with all five political parties naming him as their presidential candidate. Abacha's sudden death in mysterious circumstances in 1998 put Nigeria back on the transition track to democracy, with the election of Olusegun Obasanjo as President in 1999.

Democratisation in the form of multi-party elections also gained momentum in war-torn countries, although these elections often brought neither peace nor democracy. Elections in Sierra Leone (1996) and Liberia (1997) were held without first disarming combatants, which made it easier for warring factions to resort to war after losing elections. In Sierra Leone, rebels of the Revolutionary United Front (RUF) and the bulk of the national army were opposed to the 1996 elections that ended four years of military rule (see Chapter 5). It therefore came as no surprise that both armed factions came together in 1997 to overthrow the democratically elected government and establish a ten-month reign of terror. This usurpation was undone by regional military intervention but not before the country was laid to waste by criminal insurgents (see Chapters 5 and 6). Unless combatants are disarmed and demobilised, as in Sierra Leone (2002), elections in war-torn states are not likely to yield peace or further the cause of democracy.

Given the persistence of many of the conditions that derailed democratic experiments in the 1960s, there is no compelling reason to believe that maintaining democratic institutions will be any easier the second time around. The end of the Cold War may have improved the external environment for democratisation but the internal obstacles to democratic consolidation are no less formidable and intractable today than in the 1960s. The adoption by the International Monetary Fund (IMF), World Bank, regional banks and other donor agencies of political liberalisation as a conditionality for financial assistance may have improved the international climate for democratisation in Africa but African states are generally poorer today than in the 1960s, and the gap between political classes and the masses continues to widen. In contrast to the 1960s, however, authoritarian alternatives have been discredited and the internal impetus for democratisation is far stronger today than at independence. But while mass pressures can usher in democratic experiments, fragile democracies cannot be consolidated without the commitment of ruling sectors to democratic norms and procedures. Since elite commitment to democracy continues to lag behind the democratic aspirations of the masses, the problem of democratic consolidation in Africa may have less to do with the masses than with political classes who stand to lose the most from the institutionalisation of democratic governance.

Although the democratic renewal of the 1990s swept aside many long-standing African despots, there have been very few cases of consolidation in West Africa. Signs of progress in consolidating democracy are evident in Senegal, Benin and Ghana, although there has been alternation in power – a key indicator of democratic maturation – only in Benin and Senegal. In many cases, incumbents adroitly manipulated and hijacked the transition process to ensure their continued hold on power. The determination of entrenched elites to hang on to power resulted in the liberalisation of corrupt regimes throughout the continent, a development that is unlikely to inspire confidence in democratic rule. These ruptureless transitions once again highlight basic facts of contemporary political life in Africa – that what governments do in office is more important than whether or not they are elected, and that democracy in Africa should be seen less as an end in itself than as a means to peace, stability, development and a better life for all. Regime change, or a fundamental transformation of the norms and principles of governance, is, from this perspective, more critical to democratic consolidation than alternation in power of political parties.

The issue of what form of democracy is most appropriate cannot be glossed over, especially in light of neo-liberal prescriptions that undercut the role of the state in welfare provisioning. Liberal-pluralist democracy, with its emphasis on individual rights and a limited state, cannot be expected to take root in Africa until the social conditions that make this possible are established. This requires a more interventionist role by the state in providing social amenities, eradicating mass poverty and combating corruption than the IMF is prepared to accept. The anti-statist bias of current economic reforms has been dictated not by local or historical conditions but by a neo-liberal ideology that takes issue with state welfarism. The absence of freedom from want threatens democracy no less today than in the 1960s and a non-existent local bourgeoisie cannot be expected to pick up the slack created by dysfunctional states. Ambivalent middle-class support for democracy, the anti-democratic interests of political classes and demobilisation and marginalisation of peasants continue to pose formidable obstacles to democratic consolidation in Africa.

Local power is also in dire need of popularisation and transformation. Since the colonial era, the exercise of local power by traditional authorities has been divorced from the interests of their subjects; this has been the consequence of what Mahmood Mamdani (1999) refers to as 'decentralized despotism'. Abuse of power, especially its transformation into a means of accumulation, is not the sole preserve of national politicians; it is widespread at all levels of political authority and is as commonplace at the local level as at the national level. Traditional authorities have, since the colonial era, parlayed their positions into sources of personal aggrandisement, much in the same way that national politicians have converted public offices into sources of personal wealth. Selection of candidates for leadership positions at the local level is usually based on membership in ruling houses, which in many cases comprise the descendants of the local collaborators of colonial administrations. Not only does the concept of ruling houses lack legitimacy (chiefs wield real local power and are not mere political mannequins), the practice of making members of such houses the only eligible candidates for local offices severely limits the pool of leadership material at the local level. Most of the combatants in recent insurrections in Africa have been rural youth, and their participation in these wars has dispelled images of rural dwellers as demobilised, conservative and less threatening to national authorities. Given the depth of rural poverty and alienation, coupled with the progressive disqualification of the state as provider of security and basic amenities, it is not surprising that the threat to national authority comes as much from rural as from urban residents. Abuses of power at the national level are duplicated and multiplied at local levels, resulting in the alienation of urban and rural publics from processes that reproduce impoverishment and prolong despair.

The effect of democratisation on economic development is critical to gauging the prospects for democratic consolidation. Democracy cannot succeed unless it translates into better lives for average citizens and better prospects for social emancipation and development. In the context of societies blighted by widespread poverty, democracy without development is a recipe for failure. Development gives meaning and relevance to democracy, making it easier to legitimise its institutions, processes and norms. While economic development is not a sufficient condition for the emergence and consolidation of democracies, it is doubtful whether democracies can be sustained and consolidated in the absence of meaningful socio-economic advance. Popular struggles for democracy are, after all, struggles for a better life; they are not simply struggles for an expansion of political space or for procedural rights. As Catherine Newbury (1994: 2) points out,

> The . . . issue of redistribution in the economic sphere and responsiveness to the needs of disenfranchised social classes is not part of the definition of democracy as procedure. But rural dwellers in Africa and the urban classes want more than social peace, due process in the judicial system and political accountability. They hope for justice as well as legal order; they want improved opportunities to feed their families and educate their children . . . Authoritarian regimes are being rejected because for the most part they have failed to meet these needs; democratic regimes will be judged (in the popular mind) on their ability to respond to such concerns.

The capacity to respond to such concerns and needs is invariably diminished by the untrammelled rapacity of political classes.

3 A development impasse?

The rhetoric of development continues to ring hollow in many parts of Africa, where physical survival has practically replaced progress as both mass aspiration and leadership achievement. Most of the world's failed states are in Africa, making the continent a major recipient of relief aid and donor handouts. Africa is more marginal to the global economy even as it becomes more dependent on it. The annual World Development Reports suggest that the continent's share of world output, trade and investment has declined over the long term, as have economic growth rates and per capita income levels, even taking into account a modest and partial turnaround in trade in the mid-1990s. Increased involvement by the international financial institutions (IFIs) in African economies and the spiralling debt burden of the continent serve as reminders of the extent of the continent's dependency on external sources of financing. No longer, however, is it fashionable to posit the incompatibility of democracy and development, given the twinning of the two concepts in the post-Cold War policy prescriptions of IFIs.

Development is not only compatible with democracy, it is perhaps the best safeguard against insecurity. Realist approaches to the study of national security reduce the concept to defence of a state's territorial boundaries and protection of its basic values. Security, from this standpoint, is the pre-eminent but not the only national interest of states. National interests encompass what states need (security, economic well-being) and what they aspire to do or become (promote capitalism, become developed, etc.). Both need and aspirational dimensions of national security are closely intertwined. For instance, by promoting capitalism and liberal-pluralist democracy, Western countries are not only shaping world processes to conform to their values and preferences; the belief is that they would be safer as a result, assuming democracies do not fight each other. In a similar vein, it can be argued that by promoting development African states would not only be improving the well-being of their citizens, but they would also be enhancing their security. Development provides people with the opportunity to defend a system that is worth having; on the other hand, 'where people have difficulty knowing what benefits they derive from belonging to a system, they will have little incentive to fight for its survival' (Ochoche 1998: 123).

Security can, therefore, be equated with development because 'without development, there can be no security' (McNamara 1968: 149). Underdevelopment poses the greatest threat to security and it is a threat against which guns are useless. Africa is awash with arms but armaments have failed to make West African states more secure, not because of some security dilemma, according to which states become less secure as they try to become more secure, but because the military approach to security has been geared toward providing regime security rather than national security. Although more Africans suffer from food insecurity than from military insecurity, more money is spent on the latter than on the former. In many instances, food insecurity is the result of armed conflicts involving security forces. Demilitarising security and linking it to development is just as important as coupling development with democracy.

The obstacles to economic development are as daunting today as they were at the time of independence. Africa remains the poorest and least industrialised continent in the world, with the highest illiteracy and infant mortality rates and the lowest average life expectancy. Constraints on development have been both internal and external, with the internal impediments becoming more salient with the passage of time (see Chapter 6). Among the internal constraints, the following are noteworthy: poverty, illiteracy, disease, monoculture, dual economy, low per capita income, poor infrastructure, capital shortage, low skill levels, small market and a kleptocratic political class. External constraints to development include structural dependency, declining terms of trade, lack of currency convertibility, inaccessibility of First World markets, exchange rate uncertainties, deflationary bias of the world economy, high debt repayments, global recession and IMF conditionalities. Notwithstanding the contributions of underdevelopment and dependency theories to our understanding of the development process in Africa, it is official corruption or predatory accumulation that poses the greatest threat (internal or external) to development and social progress in Africa.

West African states have embraced a variety of development strategies at one time or the other. Most of these approaches have failed to yield significant results. Perhaps the most disastrous has been import-substitution industrialisation (ISI), especially with local products failing to be price and quality competitive (see Chapter 2). Self-reliance had a promising start but could not overcome its inherent limitations as a development strategy; indeed, self-reliance is better seen as a strategy for survival rather than development. Economic regionalism seems to be the wave of the future but efforts at regional integration in West Africa lag behind those in other parts of the world (see Chapter 2). Export promotion is another promising development strategy, as it exposes locally-produced products to external competition, but its success largely depends upon attracting foreign investment and accessing foreign markets. The recent transition from the Organisation of African Unity (OAU) to the African Union (AU) was accompanied by plans to create an African Common Market that is supposed to be modelled after the European Union's (EU) evolutionary experience. Overcoming the obstacles to the creation of an African Common Market would not be easy and it remains to be seen whether this goal can be realised in the foreseeable future. The New Partnership for Africa's Development (NEPAD), an initiative by industrialised democracies to provide development funds for Africa while promoting democracy and tackling corruption, remains under-funded but has the potential for establishing a linkage between good governance and development. Missing in much of the discourse on strategies of development is the issue of women and their centrality to the development process. Unless this issue is satisfactorily resolved, it will continue to frustrate development efforts in a region and continent where women are the most disadvantaged, exploited and repressed.

4 Gender and development

Obviously the condition of women in sub-Saharan Africa is indicative of the havoc and devastation wrought on society by the economic and political trends of the past thirty or so years. According to the latest development indicators published by UNIFEM, poverty, disease, and illiteracy continue to impede women's life opportunities on the continent, not least in West Africa. In fact since 1990, when the first comprehensive study on the state of the world's women was published by the UN the AIDS pandemic, civil wars, and genocide have all had an impact in reinforcing traditional ideologies about gender and production that have in turn made failures in experiments in democratic transitioning and market liberalisation particularly burdensome to women. The reasons for the decline in Africa's economic fortunes in the post-independence period are well documented although the dichotomy that some scholars still want to insist exists between 'internal' (state failure, corruption) and 'external' (colonial legacy, continued subordination of African economies to Western markets) causes of underdevelopment is now increasingly being shown to be false and clearly an oversimplification of what is a very complicated problem for African governments to resolve.

Questions of state failure aside, most recent scholarship in the women in development (WID) paradigm emphasises the persistence of patriarchal gender ideologies in defining women's participation in society, the dominance of Western development ideology in development planning, as well as appropriation by Western feminists of the WID agenda in Africa, as equally important factors influencing the promotion of sustainable development continent-wide. The question of women in development (WID), or gender and development (GAD) as it is now more commonly referred to, makes apparent the particularly difficult task facing African governments in trying to resolve the development impasse.

The endless catalogue of disasters which have befallen the continent since independence has made most countries in Africa almost totally dependent on assistance from the West in some form or other in order to pursue development objectives. From the provision of extension healthcare services, the financing of experiments in sustainable agriculture, and support for community-based business initiatives, to promoting programmes against domestic violence and female circumcision, Western agencies and development workers are everywhere in evidence on the continent dispensing advice and planning solutions. Nonetheless dependency on assistance from the West has meant the imposition on Africa of Western-inspired development models, which a number of scholars have contended, compounds the problems of underdevelopment in certain communities rather than easing them. The emphasis on gender mainstreaming in development discourse since the 1970s is a particular case in point.

In the late 1970s and 1980s a new wave in development economics and social science scholarship began to challenge liberal-modernist thinking on, and Western prescriptions for, Africa's economic ills. Goran Hyden's (1983) revival of Myrdal's (1968) concept of the soft state in the 1980s, which parodied the failure of African governments to create the supportive infrastructure considered necessary to both enable market liberalisation and encourage industrialisation and foreign capital investment, was perhaps most typical of the latter approach. Africa's dependence on earnings from agricultural exports made deficiencies in state provision of economic infrastructure seem somewhat self-defeating, particularly when, as was so often the case, it was a matter of ensuring that basic efforts were made to maintain or improve communications linking rural producers with urban and international markets. In most cases post-independence development has meant little more than the reproduction of pre-existing rural and urban hierarchies. But where scholarship in the modernist paradigm sees this as the outcome of the African state's failure to properly define itself independently of the functions of non-state institutions, arguments presented by Boserup and others suggest that the problem actually lay in Western expectations of the state in Africa.

By the 1980s development practitioners had found that modernisation theory's insistence on separation between state and traditional institutions often limited the state's capacity to support traditionally marginalised groups such as women. The shift from modernisation to the more dynamic theories of the Latin American dependency school, which focused not so much upon providing models for development, as on explaining the causes of stagnation in Latin America's economies, had the most significant impact on defining later gender and development discourse. Dependency theory argued broadly from the perspective that capitalist transformation of Europe occurred within a historical continuum in which European nations were able to industrialise and then expand via colonisation of other territories. Having borne the brunt of European expansionism, it continued, economies like those of Latin America could not therefore be expected to perform like those of Western Europe or North America, because the latter's political and economic domination of the region had to be taken into account. Where growth of western economies was organic and reflected internal dynamics and processes, the Third World had experienced inorganic and distorted growth as a result of its relationship with

Europe, dependency theorists argued. The theory was easily applied to other regions of the world, and of the many monographs published during the 1970s and 1980s on Africa that borrowed from the school, Walter Rodney's seminal treatise on the causes of African underdevelopment stands out as perhaps one of the most thoroughly argued and compelling presentations (Rodney 1972).

In the theory of underdevelopment offered by Rodney it is the historical relationship between the industrialised North and the underindustrialised South that explains the rate of economic development in the latter, and not the internal failures of state structure or elected governments to devise policies and provide the infrastructure to facilitate national growth. With its heavy reliance on Marxist materialism, dependency theory was more useful to an emerging gender and development discourse; in seeking to examine people in their 'actual historical situation', it gave a more accurate portrayal of the conflicting dichotomies of interests, internal as well as external, that promoted uneven distribution of resources between states and individuals within those states. Applied to macro-level economic interactions within Africa and other Third World countries, the argument exposed gender as a crucial factor in development.

Nonetheless, as Scott (1995), Bessis (2001), Simon (1999), and others interested in the impact of development on women have argued, both modernisation and dependency theory are largely hegemonic 'in that many fundamental questions, particularly about the gendered meaning of development, require no elaboration; they constitute the "common sense" about political development and dependence in the Third World' (Scott 1995: 6). Modernisation theory, grounded in masculine notions of what it means to be modern, embraces a formal conception of equality and a view of women as closer to nature that reproduces liberal ideology, and justifies a sexual division of labour between mental (male) and physical (female) labour. Dependency theory, focusing on 'systemic and structural characteristics' – the kind of labour people perform, the ways they organise this labour, and the social relations that individuals form with each other as a result of their labour and its mode of organisation – tended, like Marx, to view women's labour as 'natural and bound to the household' (Scott 1995: 6). Gender and development discourse, as it emerged out of the debates between the international women's movement, development practitioners, activists and scholars in the 1970s, was a departure from the past, in that it placed women at the centre of discussion.

Still, it was not so much the arguments presented by underdevelopment theorists, or gender and development advocates that transformed international development discourse, as the conjunction of these intellectual developments with a period of financial crisis in third world countries that highlighted the importance of women in economic development. Environmental disaster and political unrest, starting in the 1970s, severely weakened Africa's economies, and increased dependence on foreign aid. By the 1980s political disorder, rising food costs, inflation, and poverty, threatened to plunge many countries into civil unrest. Through all of this women were able to maintain productive activity, expanding their repertoire of income-generating skills to meet the needs of household reproduction, even during the difficult years of the Structural Adjustment Programmes (SAPs). Not only were donors finally forced to acknowledge women's role in economic production, the importance of women's unpaid household work in supporting greater male engagement in the economy finally became visible, and, accordingly, women were elevated in international development discourse to the status of heroines. Donor agencies were suddenly encouraged to establish structures and programmes within their organisations to enable them to better serve women's potential to contribute to national development.

The inauguration, at the 1975 International Women's Conference in Mexico City, of the United Nations (UN) International Decade for Women (1975–85) marked international recognition of the need for changes in existing development policy and practice, and initiated discussion in the West on gender-sensitive economic planning as a solution to the problems of economic development in the Third World. Over the course of the Decade for Women, attitudes within the international development community seemed to change radically, reflected in reports, resolutions, and programmes that articulated a broader appreciation of the rights of women everywhere to equitable access to economic resources, as well as the significance of women's contribution to the promotion of a humane and sustainable future. The Third UN Women's Conference in Nairobi in 1985 focused partly on challenging pre-existing development frameworks employed by governments and institutions, and proposing new ones that placed gender at the centre of development. Much of the debate at the meeting addressed the ways in which policy could be used to ensure that gender equity as a general principle in planning for economic development is applied to, and remains a key consideration in, devising sustainable solutions to the environmental, technological, and human resource needs of the Third World. In particular, attention was given to outlining the type and form of structural changes required within organisations, institutions and government departments to assure adequate representation of women's voices and interests in economic development policy.

Out of the Nairobi conference came the *Nairobi Forward-Looking Strategies for the Advancement of Women*, a set of proposals that set forth the precise changes necessary for creating conditions that will enable women to attain empowerment. They call for promotion of sexual equality; increased autonomy and power of women; recognition of women's unpaid work; advances in women's paid work; improvements in quality and access to health services and family planning; better educational opportunities, and the inclusion of women 'in promoting peace and disarmament' (UN 1991: 113). The minimum targets to be achieved by the year 2000 were: enforcement of laws guaranteeing implementation of women's equality; increase in the life expectancy of women to at least 65 years in all countries; reduction of maternal mortality; elimination of women's illiteracy; and the expansion of employment opportunities (UN 1991).

Targets, however, are only useful in telling us where society should be as far as the development of certain groups is concerned, and not how to get there. If we look at the impact that the proliferation of gender and development policies has had on women's lives in West Africa, it is clear that since the adoption of the *Nairobi Forward-Looking Strategies*, conditions for many women have actually become worse. According to recent UN statistics, only 46 per cent of women and 40 per cent of men reach the age of 65, the lowest proportion in the world. In fact where average life expectancy in 1985 was 53 years, it was estimated that children born in 29 countries in sub-Saharan Africa would face life expectancies of just 47 years by 2003 (UNICEF 2001). Regional variations in women's life expectancy obviously reflect the impact of civil conflicts and economic decline on population growth. The AIDS pandemic, as well as reducing life expectancy, is having, and is predicted to continue to have, an impact on population growth rates, albeit mainly slowing the rate of population increase. There are also continuing disparities in male and female literacy rates, which limit women's opportunities for employment outside the household. Indeed much of the criticism of gender in development planning is that it has done very little to challenge prevailing ideologies regarding gender which have in essence been underscored by the liberal modernisation emphasis in development planning. Therefore, while the profile of women in national and international development has been raised, and gender-sensitive planning acknowledged by all major development agencies as the cornerstone of economic development, the practical benefits to women of all this attention have not been immediately apparent.

Accompanying the rise in 'gender-mainstreaming' in international development discourse, then, has been a scholarly debate on gender in development that, until most recently, appeared mainly to reinforce the hegemony of Western development theory. However, frustration with multilateral agencies that profess commitment to promoting gender-sensitive development, while at the same time imposing conditions on borrowers that can be seen to exacerbate women's poverty (such as Structural Adjustment Programmes), has led scholars and grassroots activists to begin to reconsider accepted development paradigms. The history of gender in development as an operational model indeed exposes the existence of ideological assumptions within donor agencies regarding modernisation and development that serve to reinforce Western paradigms rather than recognise African realities. Scholars argue that the assistance programmes to Third World countries promoted by the World Bank and other Bretton Woods institutions have relied on a false and dichotomous juxtaposition of traditional and modern practices. According to Vandana Shiva (1988: 12):

> Poverty, as the denial of basic needs, is not necessarily associated with [the] existence of traditional technologies, and its removal is not necessarily the outcome of the growth of modern ones. On the contrary, the destruction of ecologically sound traditional technologies, often created and used by women, along with the destruction of their material base is generally believed to be responsible for the 'feminisation' of poverty in societies which have to bear the cost of resource destruction.

Failure to acknowledge the patriarchal bias in capitalist modernisation theory has tended to reinforce the 'feminisation' of poverty by reproducing and entrenching attitudes that limit women's access to economic resources, as well as their participation in decision making. Modernisation theory, as noted above, is premised on particular meanings of development, which Eisenstein (1981: 22) and others have argued rely on durable notions of a 'hierarchical sexual organization of society'. In Africa the persistence of patriarchal gender ideology in ordering society and influencing the organisation of labour has entrenched gender inequality such as to make the goals of sustainable economic development almost impossible to reach. However African women are doubly affected by the limitations of patriarchy, for not only are they subjugated under the traditionalism of African kinship and social ideologies, but also, and more significantly, as many development activists argue, their interests are marginalised under the patriarchal bias of capitalist-inspired modernisation theory.

As Gordon observes (1996: 17), patriarchal gender ideology has developed in various forms over time to encompass the 'sexual division of labour, the division of public and private life, and the motherhood ideologies, which define women as emotional and dependent', allowing for women's sexuality, reproduction and labour to be appropriated by individual men and society as a whole. Capitalism not only benefits from this social subordination of women, but also, according to Marxist–socialist scholars, has to reproduce it in order to ensure profits. 'In other words', Mies (1986: 171) suggests, 'capitalism has to use, to strengthen, or even to invent, patriarchal man–woman relations if it wants to maintain its accumulation model.' Exploitation of hierarchical divisions in labour based on patriarchal notions of women's proper gender roles allows for the unambiguous extraction of male wage labour and surplus by capital. This enables capital to benefit through women working for subsistence, or lower wages in factories, and as unpaid agricultural labour, as well as providing a pretext for employers to underpay male wageworkers. Scott's (1995) discussion of modernisation and dependency in development planning is indeed premised on a theoretical construction of Western development theory as inherently capitalist, masculinist and patriarchal, and thus antithetical to the interests of African women.

Faced with this charge, the tendency has been for donors to blame the failure of programmes to increase women's participation in formal market production on governments and traditional institutions that discriminate against women. The unwillingness of governments to intervene in the private affairs of citizens to enforce women's human rights is said to compound the difficulties donors face in overcoming cultural and religious ideologies that restrict women's control of property, freedom of movement and autonomy outside patriarchally defined institutions. In pointing to the persistence of gender stereotyping, and its effect over the past three decades in preventing West African women from accessing and benefiting from education and other opportunities for self-improvement, therefore, we highlight what we consider to be the greatest development challenge facing the region. This is important because a key effort in the bid to transform African economies into free-market democracies over the past three decades has been the greater interest shown in addressing the issue of gender in national development planning.

Yet while women in the West have been successful by and large in challenging the more blatant manifestations of gender discrimination in their societies and have won political concessions and legal changes that have dramatically transformed their position in society, African women have not been able to achieve the unity of action necessary to induce change. Ideologies of ethnic and corporate group organisation entrench patriarchal gender ideology and tie the interests of individual women to the development of kin and ethnic group interests in a way that makes it difficult for women to organise as a pressure group to pursue their specific concerns. This is perhaps the greater development challenge facing Africa, shifting the consciousness of individuals from an emphasis on ethnic loyalties and kin ties toward a consciousness that embraces ideologies of nationhood, civic responsibility and gender equality.

5 *National imaginaries*

A nation is a people united by a sense of common history, culture and destiny. Ernest Renan (1990) defined nation as a 'spiritual principle' that emphasises a common past, present and future. Historical memory of past endeavours, sacrifices, defeats and triumphs are the building blocks of nations. This sense of solidarity may require forgetting elements of the past that are too painful to form part of an inclusionary nationalist narrative. Thus nationalist discourse in Nigeria is tempered and arrested by the north–south divide, which may be more threatening to the future unity of Nigeria today than at any other time, especially with the introduction of Sharia law in northern states of the federation. A similar North–South divide, albeit with a strong dose of anti-foreigner xenophobia, threatens the future of Ivory Coast as a viable state and a potential nation.

There is a sentimental side to nationality, which develops through myths, symbols and folklore. For Eric Hobsbawm, the most important components of nationhood are invented and these include myths, symbols, traditions and public monuments, especially the cult of the founding fathers (Hobsbawm and Ranger 1983). Anthony Smith (1989), who also draws attention to the role of human will and effort in the construction of nations, makes the important distinction between 'lateral' and 'vertical' ethnicities (Smith uses the term *ethnies*). Nations formed on the basis of lateral ethnicities privileged an aristocratic core whose culture was bureaucratically diffused to outlying areas. By contrast, nations constituted on the basis of vertical ethnicities required a redefinition of common culture and were the products of anti-colonial nationalism whose prime movers included historicist intellectuals, cultural entrepreneurs and secular nationalists. Given the multi-ethnic character of West African states, Smith's concept of vertical *ethnies* comes closest to helping us understand processes of ethnic mobilisation and nation-building in these societies.

Nationalism is the ideology of the nation. It expresses loyalty to the nation that transcends or supersedes other forms of group loyalties. This implies positive orientation toward the national entity, over and above sub-national identities. An individual may be a Nigerian or Senegalese and may be adapted or accustomed to living within the territorial confines of their respective country, but unless their orientation toward the national imaginary is positive and stronger than their ethnic loyalties, their country would continue to lack nationhood (see Chapter 4). As an attitudinal index, orientation is more critical to national integration than adaptation, which is a behavioural index.

The national landscape in West Africa very much resembles that of the Balkans and, to a lesser extent, the former Soviet Union. References to Africa as the most Balkanised continent are obviously rooted in the Balkan imagery. West African states are the products of European colonialism, with their territorial borders delimited by European powers. Like their Balkan counterparts, the states of Africa enclose a multiplicity of ethnic groups, many of whom did not share a common political system prior to colonial subjugation. Colonialism brought together groups that never had a history of living together and divided groups that had lived together. Since the territorial states are not contiguous with ethnic boundaries, a national imaginary constructed by the state cannot be ethnic-specific if it is to succeed in constituting a new nation. Such nationalisms must at once transcend ethnic, religious and linguistic divisions; they must be secular and multi-ethnic, otherwise the alternative of ethnic selectivity/exclusion can neither legitimate state institutions nor build a cohesive nation. For the vast majority of West African states, only an amalgamated national identity makes sense and is likely to succeed (see Chapter 2).

Two models of national integration, pluralist and assimilationist, are relevant to the African context. The pluralist model emphasises constructing a new national identity without eliminating sub-national loyalties, while the assimilationist model favours the construction of a homogeneous identity. The pluralist model celebrates difference; the assimilationist model promotes sameness. But an assimilationist, national imaginary can be amalgamative as opposed to incorporative. In the case of assimilation through amalgamation, no single group identity is privileged; rather, two or more groups are united to form a new identity that is irreducible to any single group. Incorporation refers to a process whereby one or more groups lose their identity by merging into another group, which retains its identity (Young 1977). Given the multicultural composition of West African states, amalgamation would seem to be preferable to incorporation as a mode of transforming culturally disparate *ethnies* into new nations. The pluralist mode of integration also has potential in the African context, assuming loyalty to sub-national identities does not continue to trump allegiance to the nation-state.

At least four main competitors of post-colonial nationalist discourse can be identified – secessionist (Eritrea, Biafra), irredentist (Somalia, Morocco, the Touareg in several sahelian countries, the Jola in Senegal's Casamance region), autonomist (Caprivi Strip) and hegemonist (Ashantis in Ghana, Kabre in Togo and Hausa/Fulani in Nigeria). Secessionism has greater legitimacy under international law than irredentism, but the charter of the African Union (AU) explicitly prohibits any redrawing of colonial boundaries (see Chapters 2 and 6). This legal prohibition did not prevent the impulse to secede among the Igbos of Nigeria. Some hegemonic ethnic projects were either derailed before independence, as was the case of the Krios of Sierra Leone, or were swept away by the contradictions of post-colonial society, as in the case of Liberia's Americo-Liberians. Historically disadvantaged groups have also sought to be hegemonic when in power – Krahns in Samuel Doe's Liberia, Limbas under Momoh (Sierra Leone) and Jolas in Yaya Jammeh's Gambia serve as perfect examples of groups that were once marginalised but that later became relatively advantaged under governments led by ethnic compatriots.

There are many pitfalls of nationalism in Africa, starting with those identified by Fanon – chauvinism, jingoism, xenophobia and anti-class bias. Fanon's (1963) contention, which seems to have been validated by Africa's post-colonial experience, was that nationalism would lead African states down a 'blind alley' unless national consciousness is transformed into political and social consciousness. This calls for tackling the problems of poverty, hunger, disease and ignorance head-on but the 'spiritual penury' of Africa's political classes and their inability to articulate ideologies around which the masses can unite has forced a retreat from nationalist to ethnic discourses, not to mention opportunistic and xenophobic redefinitions of nationals as foreigners. Alassan Quattara, a former Vice-President of Ivory Coast, was declared a foreigner so as to make him ineligible to contest elections for the Ivorian presidency. Efforts to scuttle Quattara's presidential bid have plunged Ivory Coast into an ethnoregional crisis from which it is yet to recover. What Fanon had to say about the Ivory Coast in the 1960s could just as well have been said of the country today. Consider, for example, the following passage from *The Wretched of the Earth*:

> In the Ivory Coast . . . the anti-Voltaic troubles are in fact racial riots. The Dahoman and Voltaic peoples, who control the greater part of the petty trade, are, once independence is declared, the object of hostile manifestations on the part of the people of the Ivory Coast. From nationalism we have passed to ultra-nationalism, to chauvinism and finally to racism. These foreigners are called on to leave; their shops are burned, their street stalls are wrecked, and in fact the government of the Ivory Coast commands them to go, thus giving their nationals satisfaction.
>
> (Fanon 1963: 156)

The contemporary emphasis on *Ivoirité* effectively excludes northerners from membership in the Ivorian nation, a development that has not only led to civil war but to the partitioning of the Ivory Coast on the basis of ethnoregionalism.

The nation as gendered imaginary constitutes another major blind spot in nationalist discourses. Women, as Anne McClintock (1991) observes, have been lavishly metaphorised (motherland, mother of the nation) in nationalist narratives but their representation as symbols of the nation has been incommensurate with their marginalised voices. McClintock (1991) identifies five ways women are implicated in nationalism – reproduction of community (biological role); boundary reproduction, which involves control of female sexuality and sexual/marital restrictions; symbols of national difference; cultural carriers – politics of honour, dress and demeanour; participants in national struggles. The failure of nationalist discourses to incorporate the concerns of women, coupled with the under-representation of women in state institutions and political processes, cannot but limit the transformative potential of national imaginaries.

Nationalism and ethnic mobilisation both tend to vitiate class conflict. National and ethnic consciousness can undermine and stifle the development of solidarities based on class. Nationalism, however, has been less effective than ethnic mobilisation as an antidote to class conflict. The linkage between competitive politics and the politicisation of ethnic identities highlights the class dimension of ethnic conflicts, which are less about ethnicity than about the interests of elements of political classes. Ethnic mobilisation is in this regard a double-edged sword that works against the elaboration of an inclusionary nationalism and the development of subordinate class solidarities. It can be argued that politicised ethnicity serves the project of class domination by stifling the development of class consciousness, thereby helping to reproduce class domination. However, this is rather simplistic since classes exist within, as well as across ethnic groups. Elites may be less nationalistic than the masses but they are the primary beneficiaries of both nationalism and ethnic mobilisation.

The collapse of the state in Somalia has demonstrated that being a nation does not in and of itself guarantee continued national cohesion, nor does it make it any easier to construct durable and effective state institutions. Failure to construct legitimate and effective state institutions can undermine nationalist projects and imaginaries. If the nation cannot create the state in Somalia, one can only wonder how the state can create the nation in much of the rest of Africa. Lack of state effectiveness is one of the main reasons African states are not nations. Effective states control their borders, protect citizens, regulate societies and routinely extract and allocate resources. State failures in Africa have had far-reaching implications, not only for security and development but also for nation building. When all is said and done, ethnic mobilisation and nationalist revivals 'are not caused by democratisation but by institutional decline and state failures' (Gourevitch 1979).

6 *The crisis of the state*

As the locus of power and, under normal circumstances, as the most superordinate institution of domination in society, the State is to be distinguished from regime and government. 'Regime' refers to the principles and norms of a political system while 'government' describes the occupants of public office who serve as agents of the state. Historically constituted on the basis of territoriality, sovereignty and a functioning government, all states seek security, revenue, hegemony, legitimation and autonomy (Young and Turner 1985). States differ, however, not only in the degree of national cohesion and sovereignty but in their capacity to provide security, regulate society, raise revenue and allocate resources. The extent, for example, to which states are relatively autonomous of social forces, varies from case to case and across historical periods (Skocpol 1979). States, for the most part, 'are almost never autonomous from social forces', but whereas 'a state's apparent disconnectedness from social groups turns out to be associated in some cases with strength (as in some rapidly industrializing countries)', it is, in the case of Africa, associated with weakness (Migdal 1994: 3).

The specificity of African states derives historically from the fact that:

> . . . the State . . . develops in a different set of conditions than those faced by the advanced industrial economies, largely because of the historical role of foreign capital in the periphery and the resultant weakness of local bourgeoisies. This weakness, in turn, makes the establishment of local hegemony difficult and creates the conditions for highly coercive . . . regimes.
>
> (Carnoy 1984: 7)

Sub-Saharan African states have been 'especially vulnerable to collapse because the principles of governmental legitimacy have yet to be fully espoused or understood' (Schutz 1995: 109). It can be argued that lacking effectiveness, most African states have failed to 'establish institutions that are capable of constraining and outlasting the individuals who occupy their offices' (Jackson 1990: 22). And because state institutions are weak, they are amenable to the interests of those who control political power.

If the State is the locus of political power, the regime is the form of rule or the manner in which power is organised and exercised. Regimes, according to Stephanie Lawson (1993: 187), 'embody the norms and principles of the political organization of the state, which are set out in the rules and procedures within which governments operate'. In Stephen Krasner's formulation:

> Principles and norms provide the basic defining characteristics of a regime. There may be many rules and decision-making procedures that are consistent with the same principles and norms. Changes in rules and decision-making procedures are changes within regimes, provided that principles and norms are unaltered.
>
> (1984: 3)

Regime determines how state power is organised and exercised, rather than who exercises power or runs the government. A regime change heralds a break from the institutional norms and practices of the past and marks a new beginning in the life of a state. Persistence, on the other hand, of a widely discredited and loathed regime invites political unrest and rebellion.

Government, as agent of the State, refers to 'the specific occupants of public office who are in a position to make binding decisions at any given time' (Chazan *et al.* 1992: 39). In contrast to the view of Jackson (see above) that African states lack institutions which outlast the individuals occupying government office, others suggest that governments are more ephemeral than regimes and 'a state may remain in place even when regimes come and go' (Fishman 1990: 428). Regimes can both outlast governments and survive state collapse but governments that devour their states cannot be expected to restore them. When states collapse, regime and governmental survival are more likely to impede than facilitate processes of state reconstruction. When governments survive the collapse of their states, it is often because the interests of political incumbents shape the nature of the regime, and it is this absence of regime autonomy that obfuscates the distinction between state and government in Africa. In the many instances where governments collapse without taking their states down with them, either the institutions of rule are relatively autonomous of the government or countervailing societal forces are stronger than the government. Relative autonomy allows the state to operate independently of any particular government, while subjecting the latter to its regime (principles and norms). Sometimes, armed oppositional forces may bring down governments but may rescue the state in the process. When state and government collapse simultaneously, as in Samuel Doe's Liberia, it means the State can only be put back together, if at all, from scratch.

To the degree that the State has functioned in a manner that obstructs democracy and development, reforming the State has to begin with the transformation of its regime. The prevalent regime type that needs to be transformed is essentially predatory. The hallmark of predatory regimes is the unfettered conversion of public offices and resources into personal wealth by the political class. As Sara Berry writes:

> class relations are based partly, but not exclusively, on differential access to the state. Politicians, senior civil servants and military officers exercise a great deal of power over access to foreign and domestic capital and markets, and they have used this power both to accumulate large fortunes and to consolidate their control of the economy. Exploitation occurs not so much through the labour market . . . as through a burgeoning de facto market in government contracts, licenses and offices. Corruption is not a matter of personal ethics but a central mechanism of resource allocation and control.
>
> (1985: 13)

Control and access to public offices and resources determine the social location of predatory elites. Predatory accumulation has impoverished societies, delegitimised political institutions and alienated popular sectors from the state. State power has facilitated the material formation of political classes but the corruption and repression that define its exercise preclude the construction of legitimate political institutions. The prolonged absence of a legitimate political order can in turn generate widespread discontent, social disorder, armed insurrections and, in some cases, state collapse.

The key attributes of predatory regimes in Africa include the primacy of domination over legitimation, debureaucratisation of the state, privatisation of violence, informalisation of the economy and ethnoclientelism. The exercise of power, under such conditions, is dissociated from the interests, needs and aspirations of mass publics. Not only is the state's resort to violence delegitimised as a consequence; the absence of autonomous rules of contestation allows political competitors to resort to the same coercive means of ousting governments that incumbents rely on to stay in power. Re-feudalised apparatuses of domination may be consistent with predatory forms of accumulation but they are certainly incompatible with the promotion of democracy, nation-building and development.

Deflation of state capacities has been one of the direct outcomes of decades of predatory domination in West Africa (see Chapter 5). The state was debureaucratised so as to expedite the conversion of public resources into private wealth and transform it into an instrument of private accumulation. The protective, extractive, allocative and regulative capabilities of the state were, in the process, severely eroded and in some cases obliterated. Informalisation of the state's extractive functions shrank its revenue base, making it increasingly difficult to allocate resources, deliver public goods and pay state employees. This allocative retreat in turn undermined the state's ability to regulate society and maintain law and order. In effect, while the weakness or fragility of the State may favour political classes, it is at odds with the aspirations for development of the masses.

Collapsed or not, the State is in dire need of reconstruction in West Africa. Decoupling state and government is key to state reconstitution in Africa. Authoritarian restitution of the state by a strongman or warlord is problematic because if warlords are allowed to form the new State, as was the case in Charles Taylor's Liberia, 'they assure the return of the system that brought about its own collapse' (Zartman 1995: 269). Regarding alternative models of state restoration, Marina Ottaway (1995: 235) has noted that:

> The authoritarian solution – perhaps more promising in the short run – in the long run is very likely to lead to a new cycle of discontent and collapse. The democratic solution is certainly the most desirable and probably the only viable one in the long run, but it is unfortunately the most difficult to implement in the short run.

Democracy may be the only viable route to legitimising the state and restoring its effectiveness but the hijack of contemporary democratic experiments by anti-democratic forces does not bode well for the future. A democratic reconstitution of the state is quite possible in West Africa but only if political power is legitimised, government is subordinated to the State, processes of accumulation are distanced from the exercise of power, and the relationship between state and society is transformed. Regime transformation, however, is unlikely in the absence of hegemonic ruling classes whose interests are not fundamentally opposed to popular sectors.

Regime transformation is key to restoring the effectiveness of the state in Africa. State construction involves the enlargement and refinement of state capacities, the legitimation of political institutions and processes and the institutionalisation of political power. Political institutionalisation, according to Samuel Huntington (1968: 19), is the process by which political arrangements and procedures achieve value and stability. Popularising political power through regular and free elections represents a start but so are mechanisms designed to foster transparency in government transactions. It is not only the effectiveness of the State that has to be restored; its battered image is also in need of an overhaul. The best way to address the image problem is by improving the probity and effectiveness of state institutions in the performance of its basic tasks. This is an issue less for the masses than for political leaders entrusted with the responsibility of running the State.

The State cannot be effective, however, in building support for democracy and promoting development if it retreats from social provisioning or the performance of its welfare functions. While the emphases on fiscal responsibility and transparency in public affairs are broadly supportive of democratisation, the same cannot be said for some of the privatisation schemes and anti-subsidy recommendations of the IFIs. While it is true that governments in Africa have generally failed to build support for state institutions, this is not because the state has been interventionist but because the interventions of the state have done less to promote mass welfare than to enrich political incumbents and their associates. An interventionist state that is ineffective cannot be rendered effective by simply making it less interventionist. The relevant issue is not whether the state is interventionist but who benefits from its interventions. Ensuring that state interventions do not privilege the affluent few or disadvantage the impoverished majority is a more promising approach to restoring state effectiveness than downsizing its involvement in the provision of basic amenities and social goods.

Clearly, a limited, facilitative state is not suited to meeting the challenges of societies that are seeking to democratise and develop simultaneously. Industrialised democracies can afford a limited state because of a high level of material and human development, not to mention the existence of hegemonic ruling classes and large middle sectors. Before these societies arrived at where they are today, however, and before they became mature democracies, the State was interventionist and protectionist. Even in the sumptuous comforts of contemporary Western society, governments still bail out and provide subsidies for declining sectors and endangered private businesses. Corporate welfare may be suited to the needs of advanced capitalism in Western democracies but for African states, it is mass welfare that is more likely to build support for democracy and the State.

7 *Conclusion*

The problems of democracy, development, gender, nation-building and state formation in Africa are inextricably intertwined. Weak states are corollaries of weak economies but even weak, peripheral economies require effective states for their development. The democratic reconstruction of the State incorporating greater gender equity is vital to both the legitimation of its institutions and the effectiveness with which it carries out its functions. Legitimation can enhance the regulative capacity of African states and a significant enhancement in a state's extractive and allocative capacities can also help build support for state institutions. Ultimately, it is how African men and women are governed, rather than who governs them, that would have the most bearing on development, nation-building and prospects for democratic consolidation alongside eradication of gender oppression. Building support for democratic governance requires rehabilitating the State by first transforming its regime. Put differently: African states are not likely to consolidate fragile democratic systems, promote economic development, enhance gender equality and foster national cohesion unless there is a decisive break from the spoils regime practices of the past.

References

Berry, S. (1985), *Fathers Work For Their Sons: Accumulation, Mobility and Class Formation in an Extended Yoruba Community*. University of California Press, Berkeley, California.

Bessis, S. (2001), 'The World Bank and women: instrumental feminism', in Perry, S. and Schenck, C. (eds), *Eye to Eye: Women Practising Development Across Cultures*. Zed Books, London and New York.

Boserup, E. (1970), *Women's Role in Economic Development*. Earthscan Publications, London.

Carnoy, M. (1984), *The State and Political Theory*. Princeton University Press, Princeton, New Jersey.

Chazan, N., Mortimer, R., Ravenhill, J. and **Rothchild, D.** (1992), *Politics and Society in Contemporary Africa*, 2nd edn. Lynne Rienner, Boulder, Colorado.

Dahl, R. (1971), *Polyarchy*. Yale University Press, New Haven, Connecticut.

Eisenstein, Z. (1981), *The Radical Future of Liberal Feminism*. Longman, London and New York.

Fanon, F. (1963), *The Wretched of the Earth*. Grove Press, New York.

Fishman, R. (1990), 'Rethinking state and regimes: Southern Europe's transition to democracy', *World Politics* **42**, 422–40.

Gordon, A. (1996), *Transforming Capitalism and Patriarchy: Gender and Development in Africa*. Lynne Rienner Publishers, Boulder, Colorado and London.

Gourevitch, P. (1979), 'The re-emergence of peripheral nationalisms: some comparative speculations on the spatial distribution of political leadership and economic growth', *Comparative Studies in Society and History* **21**, 303–22.

Hobsbawm, E. and **Ranger, T.** (eds) (1983), *The Invention of Tradition*. Cambridge University Press, Cambridge.

Huntington, S. (1968), *Political Order in Changing Societies*. Harvard University Press, Cambridge, Massachusetts.

Hyden, G. (1983), *No Shortcut to Progress: African Development Management in Perspective*. University of California Press, Berkeley, California.

Jackson, R. (1990), *Quasi-States: Sovereignty, International Relations and the Third World*. Cambridge University Press, New York.

Krasner, E. (ed.) (1984), *International Regimes*. Cornell University Press, Ithaca, New York.

Lawson, S. (1993), 'Conceptual issues in the comparative study of regime change and democratization', *Comparative Politics* **25(2)**, 183–205.

Lipset, S.M. (1959), 'Some social requisites of democracy', *American Political Science Review* **53**, 69–105.

Mamdani, M. (1999), *Citizen and Subject: Contemporary Africa and the Legacy of Late Colonialism*. Princeton University Press, Princeton, New Jersey.

McClintock, A. (1991), 'No longer in a future heaven: women and nationalism in South Africa', *Transition* **51**, 104–23.

McNamara, R. (1968), *The Essence of Security: Reflections in Office*. Harper and Row, New York.

Mies, M. (1986), *Patriarchy and Accumulation on a World Scale: Women in the International Division of Labour*. Zed Books, London.

Migdal, J. (1994), *State Power and Social Forces*. Cambridge University Press, Cambridge.

Myrdal, G. (1968), *Asian Drama* (3 Vols). Twentieth Century Fund, New York.

Newbury, C. (1994), 'Paradoxes of democratization in Africa', *African Studies Review* **37(1)**, 1–8.

Ochoche, S. (1998), 'The military and national security in Africa' in Barthily, A. and Hutchful, E. (eds), *The Military and Militarism in Africa*, CODESRIA, Dakar.

Ottaway, M. (1995), 'Democratization in collapsed states' in Zartman, I.W. (ed.), *Collapsed States*. Lynne Rienner, Boulder, Colorado.

Przeworski, A. *et al.* (1995), *Sustainable Democracy*. Cambridge University Press, Cambridge.

Renan, E. (1990), 'What is a nation?' in Bhabha, H. (ed.), *Nation and Narration*. Routledge, London.

Rodney, W. (1972), [1989] *How Europe Underdeveloped Africa*. East African Educational Publishers, Nairobi.

Schutz, B. (1995), 'The heritage of revolution and the struggle for governmental legitimacy in Mozambique' in Zartman, I.W. (ed.), *Collapsed States*. Lynne Rienner, Boulder, Colorado.

Scott, C. (1995), *Gender and Development, Rethinking Modernization and Dependency Theory*. Lynne Rienner, Boulder, Colorado.

Shiva, V. (1988), *Staying Alive: Women, Ecology, and Development in India*. Zed Books, London.

Simon, D. (1999), 'Development revisited: thinking about, practising and teaching development after the Cold War' in Simon, D. and Närman, A. (eds), *Development as Theory and Practice*. Pearson, Harlow.

Skocpol, T. (1979), *States and Social Revolutions*. Cambridge University Press, Cambridge.

Sklar, R. (1986), 'Democracy in Africa' in Chabal, P. (ed.), *Political Domination in Africa*. Cambridge University Press, London.

Smith, A. (1989), 'The origins of nations', *Ethnic and Racial Studies* **12(3)**, 340–67.

United Nations Population Fund (UNFPA) (2000a), *The State of World Population 2000: Monitoring ICPD Goals: Selected Indicators*. (http://www.unfpa.org/swp/2000/english/indicators/indicators1.html; accessed on 22/1/2004.)

United Nations Population Fund (UNFPA) (2000b), *The State of World Population 2000: Overview of Adolescent Life*. United Nations Publications, New York.

United Nations (1991), *The World's Women 1970–1990: Trends and Statistics*. United Nations Publications, New York.

UNICEF (2001), *Early Marriage: Child Spouses*, Innocenti Digest No. 7. Florence, Italy. (UNICEF Innocenti Research Centre Web site: www.unicef-icdc.org/publications/pdf/digest7e.pdf; accessed on 18/01/2004.)

Young, C. (1977), *The Politics of Cultural Pluralism*. University of Wisconsin Press, Madison, Wisconsin.

Young, C. (1999), 'The third wave of democratization in Africa: ambiguities and contradictions' in Joseph, R. (ed.), *State, Conflict and Democracy in Africa*. Lynne Rienner, Boulder, Colorado.

Young, C. and **Turner, T.** (1985), *The Rise and Decline of the Zairian State*. University of Wisconsin Press, Madison, Wisconsin.

Zartman, I.W. (ed.) (1995), *Collapsed States*. Lynne Rienner, Boulder, Colorado.

CHAPTER 11

Development, planning, and agricultural knowledge on the Central Plateau of Burkina Faso

Simon P.J. Batterbury

1 Introduction

Efforts to plan, shape, and organize dryland West Africa's vast rural hinterlands and its diverse peoples date back to the early days of its political and administrative control by the European powers. The semi-arid Sahel region, bordering the Sahara desert and stretching westward from Chad to the West African coastline, fell under the sway of France from the earliest establishment of trading posts in modern-day Senegal in the 1600s, through to the establishment of unbroken French administration by the 1890s. Britain extended into northern Nigeria and retained its colony in the Gambia, despite French efforts to secure it. Although formal colonial administration was a major political rupture for the region's numerous ethnic groups and kingdoms, the numbers of European settlers, soldiers and administrators in the landlocked colonial territories were never great. Their direct influence was confined to emerging colonial capitals, major towns, and the more promising locations for agriculture and resource extraction. There were, however, very major indirect influences through the imposition of a monetary economy and taxation, the heavy-handed use of labour for colonial projects, the cultivation of a new French-speaking elite administrative class, and a tide of Christian missionary activity. Yet even trade in commodities like groundnuts involved just a few selected locations.

The Sahel maintained a peripheral place in the twentieth-century European imagination, even as its mysteries were better understood by successive travellers, settlers and scholars (Cline-Cole 1998; Madge and Cline-Cole 1996). Playing only a small part in the two world wars, it was the major, punitive droughts of the 1970s that refocused global attention on this region. The image of a 'dying Sahel' provoked an international response. 'Development' and external aid flows established themselves in earnest. A combination of international donors, governments, and an increasing number of non-governmental organisations – with their diverse aims varying from humanitarian assistance to overt political influence on public policy – were initially concerned with emergency relief, and secondarily with the long-term, sustainable transformation of food production and distribution systems. Technical interventions were designed to boost agricultural and rangeland productivity and to usher in 'modern' resource-use techniques. These included the expansion of research into Green Revolution-style higher yielding food grains and pulses, improvements in infrastructure and distribution, and major funding for 'natural resource management' (Sanders *et al.* 1996; see also Chapters 7 and 9). The latter, the focus of this chapter, was driven by genuine concern about ecological degradation – all too evident to observers of the drought-prone regions in the 1970s, and during a second run of drought years and hardship in the 1980s – and the recognition of the vital role that natural resources play in rural livelihood systems (see Chapters 1 and 2). The tide of development projects, their technical apparatus, and their ideas and vision, washed up on an unrelenting but not impervious shore of time-honoured beliefs, political hierarchies, and livelihood systems. Its waves have never receded, except briefly in nations experiencing political instability and violence, or where outright anti-Western sentiment prevailed.

By the 1990s development thinking in the Sahel had evolved further. At the national level, debate has been dominated by the fate of the major loans proffered to the Sahelian states by the World Bank and other institutions demanding economic 'structural adjustment' and severe loan conditionalities like reduced public spending and the curtailment of agricultural subsidies. Sahelian nations have been poor at repaying these loans, and in several countries, including Niger, the relationship with the Bank has been severely strained at times. At the local scale, the effects of new fashions in development thinking impelled a greater willingness to fund locally managed schemes for income generation and environmental rehabilitation, following the failure of many large 'top–down' initiatives. Land tenure security has been a persistent concern, and the fight to get communal land tenure recognised as a vital part of rural systems has now been achieved in several countries (see Chapter 7). There is a better understanding that variances will always exist in resource entitlements by gender and status, and that more complex and more nuanced measures of poverty and wealth are needed (Batterbury and Forsyth 1999; Carney 1998; see also Chapter 1). Led by Senegal and, notably, by Mali, there is increasing devolution of political powers away from central line-ministries and government bodies, to local institutions and elected officials. The Sahel, therefore, is one of the best places in Africa to observe the particular forms of modernity and tradition that occur at the periphery of the world system: where Toyota Landcruisers bearing highly paid development experts meet chiefs, farmers, livestock herders, and a cast of rural characters in sometimes uneasy circumstances, laden with possibility and concealed intention. The Central Plateau of Burkina Faso is one of the largest rockpools of persistent development interventions, and I discuss two major features of its experience in this chapter: efforts by the region's farmers to plan their own agricultural systems, and the role of development in this process. The latter involves the symbolic enlistment of development in new power dynamics and material aspirations at the community scale.

2 Development: planned and performed

The Sahel has often been heavily scrutinised by theorists of international development, given the large numbers of projects in operation there, and their pervasive influence on everyday life and individual decision-making (Batterbury and Warren 2001). Two critical perspectives dominate. For some, the last thirty years of improved planning and the provision of basic skills and services to the Sahelian rural poor is a normal feature of the modernist drive to improve food security and to address poverty in the postcolonial period. It is, therefore, rational, and its success may be gauged by an assessment of poverty and income trends. As a direct counter to this, is the view that development support is little more than an unhealthy perpetuation of inappropriate colonial links, and now forms part of the aggressive globalisation of cultural norms and economic linkages in the region. It serves pre-established external interests, and does not sufficiently involve local people, nor really address their needs (cf. Escobar 1995). A side-debate here is the important claim by some agrarian populist thinkers who argue that, regardless of one's ideological stance on the merits of development aid, substantial donor support is not really required in much of rural Africa anyway, except *in extremis*. Africans, this argument runs, are quite capable of solving their own technical and economic challenges. This perspective certainly has its supporters in West Africa (Mortimore 1989; Richards 1985).

The middle ground between these positions is, I think, one of healthy cynicism towards development; it clearly has an impact for good or ill, but the nature of these impacts is highly nuanced and differentiated since development sets up new power dynamics between actors, and these dynamics can be both destructive and creative (Long 1992; Olivier de Sardan 1995; see also Chapters 5 and 7). Most importantly, a discrete development project with limited objectives and timeframe may try to ameliorate living conditions and poverty in its zone of operations, but – following the populist argument – it is highly likely that local people are fully cognisant of its limits and possibilities, and are busy 'detouring' aid, employing it in their own struggles to achieve more security or status, and thus using it for unintended purposes. Such is my argument below.

Paul Richards's ideas have been highly influential in these critiques, since they have worked as a launch-pad for challenges to dominant ideas about modernity and economic development backstopped by aid and donors.[1] Richards, a geographer-cum-anthropologist based at Wageningen University in the Netherlands, has worked for decades on the rice-farming agricultural systems of Sierra Leone, beginning fieldwork long before the major political conflicts of the last few years. In his early work on indigenous agricultural systems he illustrates how an astounding range of innovations was taking place in West Africa's rice-farming systems, much of this occurring behind the backs of Western scientists and development workers (1985; 1986). His major contribution was to suggest that rice farmers obtained decent crop yields and insured their subsistence by a highly reflexive and locally appropriate set of agricultural 'performances' that had everything to do with locally appropriate knowledge but bore little relation to the formal goals of modern development planning, and that permitted them to remain highly responsive to ecological change and to new ideas.

Richards's critique suggests that significant problems will accrue from externally-planned development interventions. Development projects have beginnings and endings, and their personnel have to assure that budgets are spent and goals are met. Development agents (and international agricultural research centres producing new crop varieties), miss the 'performances' of flexible traditional farming systems, unless they are highly skilled and anthropologically aware. It is hard for them to permit indigenous agricultural knowledge to unfold organically, in the same manner that an interpretive musical performance floats free of a prepared score, since the effects on poverty and welfare would be far from certain, targets would be impossible to set, and the majority of foreign donors would be displeased. Rather, development is almost always 'planned', and is overseen by professionals with an eye to expediency, rather than by farmers with intense local knowledge of what works best for them.

This critique is valid, but I think there is perhaps more synergy between the goals and means of international development projects and local agricultural performance than is acknowledged. To argue my point requires an engagement with some of Richards's original claims, with reference to the dryland farming systems of the Central Plateau of Burkina Faso. One can find some interesting synergies between the new breed of natural resource management projects in this part of the Sahel, and local interests. My argument is that dryland agriculture, devoid of external development assistance, actually contains the seeds of 'planning' practices and outlook, such that both 'planning' and 'performance' coexist in these semi-indigenous dryland farming systems, and continue to do so when development projects enter the scene. Rather than reacting solely and spontaneously to changing farming conditions, I argue that producers are also deliberately and conspicuously planning ahead: 'building' their production systems, rather than 'treading lightly' in bush areas where fallowing is possible. An analysis of real development impacts, combined with a sustained interrogation of local and regional knowledge systems and livelihoods, provides the best way to understand many contemporary realities in the parts of the Sahel that are now experiencing the sustained and deep impacts of development projects (Batterbury 2004; Batterbury and Warren 2001).

3 The Central Plateau of Burkina Faso

The Plateau (latitude 11° to 14° N, longitude 3° W to 1° E) is a Sahelian region of low hills and gentle slopes falling to valley bottoms or *bas-fonds*. Annual rainfall has most recently fluctuated between 450 and 800 mm per year, but rainfall events can be extremely localized, and seasonal rainfall distribution is highly erratic. The most commonly farmed soils are ferruginous, often with a hard pan at depth, and are poor in nitrogen and phosphorus. Sensitivity to erosion is high. Strong overland flow from summer storms can strip unprotected topsoil leaving a characteristic patchwork of bare, hardened soil between 'hummocks' of vegetation. These *zipelle* areas are infertile and can spread to form wide unproductive areas. Dramatic ravines and gullies can form, dependent on soil type and slope (Roose and Piot 1984). Contour stone bunds (*diguettes*) consisting of lines of stones and rocks placed across the land contour are cheap and popular erosion control methods, and are much publicised by development projects (Atampugre 1993).

Moderately impacted by French colonial authority from the last decade of the nineteenth century, the region failed to yield sufficient revenues for France, and so its labour force, predominantly Mossi farmers, were heavily taxed; they were also employed in the richer and more commercial colonies, frequently along the West African coast. The Mossi ethnic group are believed to have conquered the region in the 1400s or earlier, and retained political dominance through the colonial period into independence from France in 1960. Decision-making still falls to local chiefs, combined with a hierarchical francophone government system. Population has grown since the early twentieth century, although this was strongly checked by labour extraction by the French colonial authorities (Gervais 1987) and by more recent voluntary outmigration to seek paid work along the Atlantic coast. Remittances from migrants in Côte d'Ivoire, to which there has been a large migration stream (checked only by widespread xenophobic reactions and civil war from 2001), and major cities like the Burkinabe capital, Ouagadougou, are significant in the local economy, and are used mainly to meet customary obligations and immediate cash needs. Fulani herders also traverse the area; they are less numerous than the Mossi, and compete with them for agricultural land in some areas.

Every household cultivates millet or sorghum on extensive bush fields, weeded by *daba* hoe and usually without the benefit of organic residues or fertiliser. Cowpeas and okra are intercropped with millet with some peanuts, Bambara groundnut and other minor crops, sometimes on separate plots. The in-fields close to dwellings are also farmed, often put to early maize, using animal residues and household sweepings where available. Married women may have separate fields, but lack security of use rights over these. Labour shortages can exist at periods of peak demand in the agricultural cycle (see Chapters 7 and 10). *Sosoaga*, or work groups, are engaged by a few richer cultivators to prepare and weed their fields. All other labour is carried out by household members, or by exchange arrangements between neighbours.

Mossi agriculturalists now deal with a diversity of institutional actors involved in natural resource management interventions (Moore 2001). Aside from agricultural extension services and community forestry projects run by the state, there are externally-funded projects concerned with soil and water conservation which promote low-cost techniques for land rehabilitation that have been developed over the last twenty years. These techniques have been disseminated thanks to the work of European volunteer services, NGOs and various government and bilateral programmes (Reij *et al.* forthcoming). Key techniques, notably *diguettes* on shallow mid-slope soils, have now been widely adopted by local communities and individuals.

Projects promoting *Gestion des Terroirs Villageois* (village land use management, or GTV) often involve both NGOs and government services. GTV projects have assisted village organisations to take control of, and oversee the territory over which they enjoy traditional land rights, and helped them to undertake soil and water conservation and other improvements on this land (Batterbury 1998). The intervention of these outside agencies has been problematic, since GTV is based on delineated territories and is reliant in part on consensual village politics (Engberg-Pedersen 2003; Gray 2002).

In this chapter, I focus on the particular technological changes set in motion by GTV initiatives, in particular PATECORE, one of the largest such projects in Bam Province. Like other projects which are part of the PNGT, the national GTV programme which is supported by both bilateral donors and the World Bank, PATECORE has received funding from bilateral sources, in its case, German aid since the late 1980s.

4 The construction and management of dryland farming systems

Richards' studies on the rice-growing zones of Sierra Leone suggested that shifting rice cultivators attempt to 'hitch a ride upon, rather than to override and forcibly control, processes observed in "nature"' (1989: 51). In carving out a farm from the forest, Mende farmers employ their detailed agro-ecological knowledge, seldom needing to create enduring and managed landscapes in order to grow their crops. They work with, and help preserve, ecological diversity. This has become a common image of West African farmers, and has been taken up and extended in other studies of West African farming systems which stress improvisational skill, and the success of local agricultural techniques (Fairhead and Leach 1996; Leach 1992; Simpson 1999).

Richards' suggestion that this process of 'hitching a ride' on ecological systems, and the improvisation in this and other aspects of farming, can best be compared to that of a freely interpreted musical performance, emerges from these observations (Richards 1987, 1993). Little of such a 'performance' is preplanned – rather, crop mixes and farming operations are strung together and modified with inventiveness and opportunism. Richards constantly stresses the practical, everyday problem-solving abilities of rice cultivators, and his work is regarded as a benchmark in the recovery of an overdue assertion of the populist argument that directly challenges 'top–down' models of agricultural research and extension (Bebbington 1994; Scoones and Thompson 1994; Watts 1989). The implication is that successive attempts by colonial regimes and agricultural research organisations to 'improve' African agriculture have failed to appreciate how farmer performances are adapted to environmental and labour constraints.

I am not convinced, however, that further north in regions like the Central Plateau, the dryland regions of the sub-continent, 'hitching a ride' in the less diverse agro-ecologies which prevail there will achieve similarly positive outcomes. Forms of indigenous knowledge, technologies, institutions and ecological characteristics are different in the Sahel and Sudano-Sahel belt of West Africa. The farming enterprise in regions of poor soil quality or low soil fertility in the Sahel demands different labour inputs and techniques than the short-fallow shifting or rotational cultivation widely used in the humid tropics of Sierra Leone. In northern Burkina Faso and southwestern Niger, it has become less and less common to see traditional long-fallow agriculture, even where population densities are relatively modest; the availability of good quality land for farming is declining (Marchal 1983). By contrast, dryland farming in the Sudano-Sahelian belt requires land users to marshal considerable labour and apply it to often limited land, and to invest scarce capital, to obtain what are sometimes meagre harvests from unyielding or exhausted soil. For example, a young male farmer in the Mossi regions of Burkina Faso must 'build' his farm, from the moment he leaves the family plot and commences cultivation on his own account, in order to meet regular subsistence needs through the years. As Chris Reij (1994a) has suggested for the Yatenga Mossi region in Burkina Faso, it appears that, where fertile land is scarce, young men lacking private land access and income may choose to 'carve out' a farm from the barren, crusted soils of marginal *zipelle* land previously abandoned to agriculture. Similar processes can be observed elsewhere on the Plateau, for example in the close-settled zone around Kongoussi in Bam Province. These actions require not the clearing of vegetation from rich soils before cultivation, as in the Sierra Leone case, but the painstaking construction of planting pits (*zaï*) by men and women, and the collection and transport of manure to the site; compost, manure or local rock phosphate is thrown into the pits in order to restore some basic fertility to the rooting zone and to encourage termite activity. Reij suggests the treatment of one hectare of land – barely enough to nourish a farmer and a small family for a season – may take up to 100 person-days of backbreaking labour. Similar examples of highly intensive regenerative schemes can be found in southwest and central Niger, where degraded land is now being traded for its unrealised productive potential and considerable investments are being made in reclamation by various conservation techniques (Reij 1994b). Frequently, planting pits are supplemented by *diguettes*, to aid the infiltration of scarce runoff and brake the erosion of topsoil (Batterbury 1994; Reij 1994a, 1994b; Reij *et al.* forthcoming).

This process of land rehabilitation – increasingly common, as it is now encouraged by some of the numerous extension services and development projects mentioned in Section 1 – has much in common with the laborious process of building a house for one's own occupation. The metaphor is an interesting one, although we should be wary of overextending it; as Salmond (1982) and Porter (1995) note, explanatory metaphors also have power to generate a certain form of thinking and to exclude or marginalise others. They do, however, allow us to 'ground' our analyses in the real world. A family wishing to build a home must make many hard decisions about its location, its cost, its dimensions, and its design. Many possible variables, from personal preferences to financial constraints and difficulties encountered over land rights and access, may influence the final outcome of such an endeavour. Like the farmer, the builder must assemble scarce resources, call in favours, and set aside time. A farm, as Richards points out, is never 'finished' (1987). But the actions required to farm in dryland regions are much like those involved in the process of local house construction. The house builder must undertake a certain amount of initial work to raise the roof of a house; equally, the farmer will never obtain his or her first harvest from a formerly unproductive or low-yielding plot without sizeable initial investments of time and labour. This metaphor of 'building' is not designed to usurp a visualisation of dryland farming as rich in the 'performance elements' noted by Richards. Rather, my intention is to highlight the need to consider the structured and planned elements of dryland farming alongside the myriad performances, and processes of experimentation, enacted by farmers. It is this revised perspective, not the abstract metaphor itself, which matters (cf. Richards 1993; Salmond 1982).

Once constructed, a dwelling benefits its inhabitants in two distinct ways, which can be referred to as material and symbolic.

- *The Material: satisfaction and basic needs.* A home offers security; a base where the regular activities of the day are performed and where one can both work and relax. It is tinkered with, adapted, repaired and maintained not just to please neighbourhood gossips and busybodies, but to maintain the household's own needs for warmth (or shade), protection from the elements and shelter. It is a lived environment which slips into unconscious acceptance, like a favourite pair of well-worn shoes. A 'home-builder' is someone who creates a home for the pleasure of doing so, using skills learned through trial, error and experience, and reaps his/her rewards through the pleasure of living within this personally structured environment. He/she feels pride.
- *The Symbolic: status and appearance.* A dwelling is an expression of one's persona: it says who the owner is, as well as telling the observer something about the social and economic status of its occupiers. It is filled with personal objects and embellishments, and decorated in a style which sets it apart from one's neighbours. It is 'lived in'. It is a place to offer hospitality, to teach offspring the basics of household management and how they themselves must behave when they set up home on their own. Over the year, specific tasks must be carried out both to maintain appearances and to prepare for seasonal weather conditions. Leaving the compound unswept, or a hole in the roof unrepaired after a storm, invites neighbourly censure.

Mossi efforts to reclaim degraded or less fertile land can be likened to a builder preparing a site, staking boundaries, wheeling and dealing to procure the necessary materials, and then keeping costs down by doing the bulk of the work him/herself. Tapping affective kin networks or friendships, he/she might perhaps borrow or rent a donkey cart, picks and shovels from a friend. Unlike the case of the shifting cultivator in the Sierra Leone rice-farming zone, this young Mossi farmer's goal is not to steal a living on a plot destined to return to the natural forest from which it came – rather, the savings that went into his (or her) initial investment demand that the farmer secure a return from his/her labour in terms of adequate food crop yields for several seasons. In so doing, a successfully reclaimed and productive field may inspire admiration and, perhaps, jealousy from his/her peers. This could apply equally to the main millet plots of the household, as it could to the smaller and less-permanent personal fields of Mossi women (Compaore 1993). Those who 'build' their own habitats in this way will tailor them to their own requirements and generally wish to stay put for quite a while. The builder's knowledge comes from multiple sources (including development projects and extension workers), and it is impossible to freeze such knowledge in time or space for documentation and classification (Salmond 1982). My own fieldwork in a region of the Central Plateau (Department de Rollo, Bam Province), revealed a staggering range of traditional agricultural practices and erosion control techniques among Mossi, Yarsé and Peulh/Fulani cultivators. These include the construction of bunds and barriers from sticks, andropogon grasses and stones; micro-variations in planting densities and spacing, taking into account soil fertility and water supply; use of millet-stalk or straw mulches to encourage termite activity in hardened soils; and selective cutting of forest areas to encourage natural regeneration of certain woody species (Batterbury 1994; Reij 1994b).

Larger-scale, labour-intensive practices such as the digging of *zai*, the construction of extensive *diguettes* (more appropriate for the reclamation of very unproductive land), and growing use of compost pits, are techniques promoted by project and extension services, and were rarely practised in their present form before the arrival of volunteer services and NGOs in the late 1970s. Reij (1994a) dates the first improved *zai* techniques to the late 1970s; the first *'digue filtrante'* (permeable rock dam) on the Central Plateau is thought to date from 1981/2, and was initiated by a French volunteer in Rissiam, Bam Province in the early 1980s (Reij *et al.* forthcoming; Vlaar and Wessenlink 1990). Today, such techniques are widespread. Some farmers had learned of these techniques from neighbouring villages, not from project personnel, and adapted them to their own individual requirements. Traditional agricultural practices have been supplemented by introduced (but locally developed) soil and water conservation techniques, the latter being more appropriate where *in-situ* degradation is well advanced, and where the farmer is forced to consciously build up a functioning and sustainable production system (for example on severely indurated *zipelle* soils). Mossi farmers are engaged in carving out new agro-ecologies necessary to coax tired soils back into productive use; they are building for the future with new materials.

5 Choice and learning in Mossi communities

This use of ideas and techniques from external agents is itself an instance of a far more general phenomenon: the continuing incorporation of new ideas from a range of sources in the process of farm planning and management. This incorporation of new ideas occurs within certain constraints, but still demonstrates much diversity reflecting individual farmers' choices and world-views. This can be illustrated by looking at the varying ways in which farmers piece together livelihood strategies incorporating natural resource management. Like a house, a Mossi farm must be built to withstand all weather. It must be resilient to extremes of rainfall and wind, yet versatile enough to provide for changing family needs over a period of years. Historically, the Mossi have assured the resilience of their farms in several ways:

- By exploiting micro-environments, notably soil type differences. Soil characteristics are broadly correlated with position on a catenary sequence running from eroded, iron-rich escarpments (*tanga*) to clay-rich valley bottoms (*baogho*), and each is farmed with a varying crop mix and seasonal calendar. Where two or more plots are cultivated, these are commonly dispersed spatially across different ecological zones.
- By varying planting and weeding dates to balance labour availability and to reflect uncertainty over rainfall regimes.
- By increasing efficiency of rainwater use and runoff collection, as described above; since the 1980s, mainly through the use of stone and earth bunds, built across the land contours.
- By increasing livestock ownership. While not a major part of traditional Mossi farming systems, cattle, sheep and goats provide saleable assets yielding cash income when required. The devaluation of the West African franc in January 1994 provided a market incentive to farmers to trade more in livestock. Great attention is also given to the collection and dispersal of animal manure and compound sweepings (Reij 1994b).
- By diversifying the production base, through off-farm activities, and so increasing the household's ability to absorb the costs of a poor farming year. The production of coarse-weave cloth, panniers and roofing materials is common (Fiske 1990).
- By using donkey ploughs (but not ox-ploughs), appropriate only to certain soil types and field locations. Around 30 per cent of households in the two villages studied by the author operated ploughs in 1992, and others had access to ploughs through village associations.

The list could be greatly extended and compared with those from similar ecological zones elsewhere in West Africa (Ford 1982). For example, many Mossi practices mirror those identified in detail by Watts (1983) and Mortimore and Adams (1999) for the Hausa on the Nigeria–Niger border; by Netting (1993) for Kofyar farmers in central Nigeria; and by Mazzucato and Niemeijer (2000) in eastern Burkina Faso. The end result of farmers' efforts is a working farm modified to the flux of the seasons (alongside the means to provide small amounts of cash income). The farm may never be 'finished', as a house can be, but it provides for basic needs. These and other practices and design criteria form the architecture – the shape, the form, or design – of a farming system. Local ecology and environment – temperature and precipitation regimes, for example, and soil types – limit the design possibilities, as do community sanctions, land tenure rules, labour availability, and the competing demands of non-farm activities (see Chapter 9). They do not, however, disturb individual choice and creativity of the cultivator or the household.

If the aim of farming is to ensure basic subsistence needs, this can still be done in a staggering multitude of ways, even in remote Mossi villages in areas marginal for rainfed agriculture (cf. Netting 1993). Around Rollo in northern Bam Province, communities of Peulh pastoralists coexist with both Mossi agriculturalists and settled traders known as Yarsé; each group shows a tendency to adopt a favoured livelihood strategy biased towards agriculture, herding or commerce, and each group 'makes a living' more or less successfully. Nonetheless, individuals within these communities sometimes diverge widely from the 'cultural norms' of the group. Some of the most successful farmers are Yarsé, not Mossi, for example, and of these some are relatively new to farming or even recently-settled returnee migrants. A Yarsé ex-migrant farmer interviewed in 1993 near Rollo, Bam Province, had adapted techniques he had seen in plantation agriculture and on research stations in Côte d'Ivoire; these include surrounding 'squares' of perhaps one hundred maize plants with concentric ridged lines of sorghum and beans. This planting design, unique in the region, was efficient at encouraging maize cross-pollination and limiting species-specific pests, and may have had other benefits for soil fertility and moisture retention since it heeded contours and micro-topography. If the primary aim of a farm is to meet family needs and objectives, this can equally be achieved by any number of designs: the possibilities are numerous. The reason underlying this architectural (or agricultural) diversity is not just individual whim or personal aesthetics; today, a farmer in northern Burkina Faso can design his/her farming system based on multiple networks of information about practices, tools and techniques.

Knowledge, then, 'is built upon the accumulated social experience, commitments and culturally-acquired dispositions of the actors involved', is 'fragmentary and diffuse' and, of course, 'differentiated' (Long and Villareal 1994: 42–3). Important sources of knowledge are other family members and neighbours; to see what they have done, learn from their experiences, and adapt their strengths to one's own situation and needs. Secondly, as explained above, government extension workers and rural development projects have achieved almost complete coverage on the Central Plateau; most communities, should they choose, can participate in some programme of field visits from agriculture and forestry extension workers. Furthermore, if they demonstrate sufficient cohesion, community spirit and capacity for hard work, they may also tap into project funds for environmental protection, health or maternity care, water supply or primary schooling. Regrettably, women's cropping practices are less frequently addressed by these services (Compaore 1993). Travel and migration provides a third route to new ideas; see what other villages have done, what crop varieties they use, how their stone lines are constructed or what tree species thrive and protect fragile soils. Exploration of the 'interfaces' – the points at which different life worlds and social fields intersect – tells us much about how knowledge is transmitted and transformed by the different actors in this process (Long and Villareal 1994). As Norgaard (1994) and Long and Villareal (1994) point out, this process of knowledge acquisition is not one-way, but restructures the world-views and practices of the disseminators, producers and users of ideas and techniques. Sitting amidst the actors in the Burkina countryside today are a new class of educated cultural brokers who retain one foot in the villages: they are able to interpret development project requirements, write proposals to donors on behalf of village groups, and act as intermediaries between the worlds of oral and written tradition (Bierschenk *et al.* 2000).

It should again be stressed that none of these information channels can determine the design of an individual farm; they are a contingent set of factors influencing farming practice, and deeply embedded in the rhythm and flow of personal and local social relations (Bourdieu 1990). For example, adapting a 'foreign' technique, even the relatively accepted *diguettes* (contour stone bunds) for local use can be a hazardous business, not one to be accepted without question. Upon questioning farmers in one Mossi community, I was told that they did not care for one farmer's efforts at constructing such bunds across his fields because the 'shape was not right' – an act of critique, but also of learning, because this set of bunds was washed out at the onset of heavy rains and later had to be rebuilt. Here, the use of bunds can be explained by reference to the farmer's perceptions of erosion and its possible treatment (a 'plan'); but the way in which this technique is used or 'performed' (and especially understanding why it might fail) requires deeper analysis of personal world-views and local power relations.

6 Planned performances and social status

The use of the farm as a symbol of social status and power is an important factor influencing the outcome of the design process. Attachment to the land is strong for Mossi farmers, and they are connected to it by ritual and tradition (Fiske 1990). We have to ask, therefore, what local farming represents, in addition to whether it works. Mossi cosmology is strongly linked into the cycle of the seasons, the power of the earth-chiefs, and the ancestors. Farming has meaning and it serves symbolic ends, just like homes, churches, and monuments do in a city. Farmers sharing a common knowledge base and a history of sequential occupation admire a good design. A design, in the Mossi case, is a one-off; there are no identical plots. It will incorporate millet or white sorghum somewhere, but there may also be various cash crops, experiments with garden crops, fruit trees and plantations as well. The farm is indeed a 'performance' to be appreciated by others as well as an object of personal accomplishment and satisfaction. It has both temporal and spatial components: the fluctuations in millet vigour during the growing season, as well as the size and shape of the fields themselves. While performance elements are certainly present in Mossi cultivation systems, working newly reclaimed plots in dryland systems requires that there most certainly is a plan involved and, moreover, an entirely conscious one. The plan is to achieve a subsistence base by overcoming the soil fertility constraints of bare and hardened earth. But it is also a plan to convey a particular message about the farmer to the rest of the community (Fiske 1990).

Conscious farmer efforts at land improvement and rehabilitation, while being instrumental, are also symbolic. The suite of performances embedded in a farm signals something about its owner to a wider audience, in the same way a dwelling does. It may say 'I am rich, and have money for ploughs and fertiliser' or 'I can do all this, on my own', or 'I have perseverance – my crops, through careful planting, survived the drought'. Equally, a field of withered plants may broadcast a message of despair and failure, or simply a confirmation of a 'bad year' for all. Stunted millet plants, yielding less than 200–250 kilograms per hectare, indicate low levels of available nitrogen and phosphorus, and may provoke the comment from neighbours that it is 'about time he/she moved' to land fallowed and richer in nutrients. Farmers exhibit considerable curiousity about each other's abilities, notably about the extent to which an individual is able to second-guess rainfall patterns and manage planting, weeding and harvest operations successfully. In 1992, freak late rains ruined unharvested millet plants in the Bam region; those fortunate enough to have harvested early were viewed with a mixture of jealousy and appreciation by others. The messages sent out by farming practice and by fortune inscribe the individual or household in particular cultural networks, and can therefore be viewed as forms of symbolic capital (Bourdieu 1990). The everyday farming space also provides clues as to the character, status, wealth and labour power of its creator because messages are embedded in the events, actions and temporal and spatial elements of agriculture (Leach 1992).

Agricultural and technical diversity also provokes discussion about the successes and misfortunes of others (Fairhead and Leach 1994). The Mossi are no exception, and farms inspire great comment, derision and sometimes jealousy. Some planting strategies or farm designs run directly counter to prevailing practice, cutting across status roles and expectations, and are intended by the farmer as deliberate 'passive resistance' to norms and expectations (Scott 1985). For example, one of the most successful farmers in a village just south of Rollo, Bam Province lives in a traditional, near-subsistence Mossi community. When I first met him in 1992 he was young, recently married, well liked by his own age-set but – due to basic schooling and time spent in Côte d'Ivoire – a little stifled by the hierarchical and deferential Mossi social structure of his village. Wishing, however, to remain in the community and to farm, he signals to the elders his sense of difference and individuality. First, he built a rectangular house – a different but not startling departure from the norm. Second, his main field is split equally between groundnuts and short-variety millet – the only farm in the village to deliberately place reliance on cash income from groundnuts in this way, and to de-emphasise the ubiquitous subsistence crop (which he sometimes sells – a very rare practice). Brush, *pitta* grass (andropogon) and stone lines protect the crop from overland flow and aid moisture infiltration; aubergines and tobacco are grown under shady hangars. These individualistic practices – which seem to work – set him aside from his neighbours and especially from the zero-input millet stands of bush fields farmed by elders. He has, nonetheless, presented the community with a new technical option and resisted local norms.

Agricultural symbolism also operates at the level of the community. The participation of villagers in externally-funded natural resource management had major *symbolic* value – it created 'symbolic capital' for a community (Bourdieu 1990). After a few years of pilot operations, the PATECORE Gestion des Terroirs project had become, by the mid-1990s, a showpiece for the German Agency for Technical Cooperation (GTZ), since it had supported the construction of many kilometers of *diguettes* on the Central Plateau (Kahrmann 1997; Moore 2001). In the village of Toessin an extensive network of *diguettes*, built with the assistance of the PATECORE project, now criss-cross the relatively small area of agricultural land over which villagers held long-term rights (Figure 11.1). The work required the marshalling of work parties and communal labour during the dry season, sometimes involving up to 130 individuals. Agricultural extension agents and project staff assisted in the design and construction process, which was directed by a village committee. Participation in the hard work of building these structures was far from unwilling. In subsequent years, participation in resource conservation was deployed as symbolic capital – it was put on display to the local state, visiting officials, the extension services, and donors. Village farms, and areas of uncultivated *zipelle*, have been restored to productivity. But here is the twist: land rehabilitation gains further material rewards because it showed that this community – as opposed to neighbouring villages, some of whom were not on good terms with Toessin – could work together; design, construct, and participate according to the norms of development practice preferred in PATECORE and in many other natural resource management projects. In constructing *diguettes*, visiting development workers were treated with respect; meetings were usually well attended (although patriarchal in their management); and the village was, as a result, frequently visited by study teams from the NGO and the government.

Symbolic capital was, literally, transformed into concrete (Batterbury 2004) because by 2001, the village had a new primary school, to add to its artesian well that had been drilled earlier with Saudi aid. Several NGOs had become active in the village. Visiting the nearby small hamlet of Ibi Palaga eight years after the first *diguettes* had been constructed there by PATECORE, I also found a new well, costing thousands of dollars. These were some of the material gains from a socially constructed vision of harmony, participation, and hard work that the villagers had been able to maintain in earlier years. Toessin villagers had successfully created the image of a hard-working, and unified village, ready and willing to work with outside agencies and projects (Batterbury 1998). Primary schools cost more than *diguettes* and they need staffing; and teachers need houses and food. Because Toessin was very widely praised for its natural resource management work, this image stood them in good stead when convincing the local government that they, not neighbouring communities, should receive a new school. The conflicts and consuming jealousies that exist in Toessin were not made visible, and Toessin got the school – nearby villages, which built no *diguettes*, and had few links to external projects, did not. Attracting development, therefore, requires a sales job (Bierschenk *et al.* 2000; Laurent 1996). And the first material outcome – the *diguettes* – also allow symbolic capital to grow in productive and potentially lucrative ways.

Figure 11.1 Ten-year-old *diguettes* in the village of Toessin, 2001. *Source*: photo by author.

7 Discussion

Agricultural knowledge and rural development in West Africa are constantly reworked by farmers, and analysed by officials, extension workers and the occasional social scientist. Agricultural support and resource management has become more effective, locally based and 'participatory'. The major mistakes of the past are repeated less often these days. Richards's pioneering critique – that agricultural research and extension has largely misread the map of peasant agriculture and promoted inflexible and inappropriate packages of marginal value to farmers – has been widely acknowledged and partially accepted in the resource management sector. Rural development is more cognisant of ecological and social diversity than in the past, and frequently involves local land users and their organisations in setting research and programme agendas, at least in part.

I have argued that dryland farming can be planned, similar to the way in which a house is planned, built, and maintained. Building, and farming, require conscious, sustained and physically strenuous effort over long time periods, with heavy initial investments. No farmer in northern Burkina is able to justify a labour investment in bush-clearing and rehabilitation of a plot which is destined to be abandoned in the short term; many do not have the luxury of access to land suitable for traditional fallow-based cultivation, and thus their work must count towards meeting future needs. The sort of 'planning' involved in technical assistance to these farmers may have begun as mechanistic and top-down in the early days of the independence period: but the new breed of GTV projects, and efforts to empower local communities, are at least heading in the right direction. Dryland agriculture, where devoid of external development assistance, contains the seeds of 'planning', such that the presence of a development project is rarely alien and incomprehensible. Farmers are accustomed to forward thinking, the marshalling of resources, and the overcoming of – not just the working with – natural ecological constraints (Netting 1993).

If we see farmers as 'performers', sequentially adjusting their agriculture and their livelihood systems to the changing environmental circumstances and political economy, there is little need for development interventions other than to speed the process and to allow them to do what they are doing a little better (Mortimore 1989). This is, essentially, the populist argument. Help could be offered for micro credit schemes, assistance with grain storage, and even the provision of climate forecasts (Ingram *et al.* 2002). But if we see farmers as planners and builders of their community lands, farming systems, and livelihoods, then a different set of values begins to enter into development policy. People often know what they would like to have, because they do think ahead and have goals they want to attain. The new sort of development assistance in the Sahel, like funding for land rehabilitation and *diguette* construction, addresses some of these demands, and farmers are well aware of this – hence their careful and strategic participation in these initiatives. This participation has not meant weakened traditional agricultural systems: far from it. Planning, therefore, involves meeting material, symbolic and social goals. Building anything – including *diguettes*, new dwellings and communal buildings – can elevate community status.

Projects involved in environmental improvements and basic rural development activities need to recognise that such activities are undertaken for this reason, as well as for their more obvious benefits to crops and material welfare. A well-managed village centre shows superiority to neighbouring communities and to local government officials, as does a tidy woodlot or a new well built with external assistance. Perversely, the act of working together in order to present this image to outsiders can lead to internal village conflict and power struggles being downplayed or at least temporarily set aside. Completed 'works' can be consciously undertaken to present a particular image of diligence to potential donors and projects. It is important not to minimise this aspect of conscious, goal-oriented forward planning, and it is particularly important that development projects and extension agents probe deep enough to uncover its workings. Indigenous knowledge is instrumental as well as improvisational – it is put to work in personal and community activities, not left in the bank to accumulate interest.

8 Conclusions

To conclude, while recognising the value of indigenous local knowledge as a basis for carrying out agricultural tasks and making a living, it is also vital to acknowledge that dryland farmers in West Africa are equally capable of designing a plan of action and sticking to it, and of assimilating and valorising new knowledge from external sources. I have argued that we cannot afford to dismiss externally funded development projects as irrelevant or wholly destructive to local interests on the rural Sahel; but neither can we say that the encounter between the occupants of Toyota Landcruisers and local people has been unproblematic, or free of the clientilism and self-interest which mar many efforts at rural development in Africa. Even as they can empower, *diguettes* can also be used as weapons in land rights disputes and in community conflicts (Gray 2002). The actions of projects like PATECORE do have some positive effects for agricultural productivity and, importantly, in broadening the reach and range of symbolic capital. Mossi farmer engagement with development requires deadlines and forward thinking. On the Central Plateau, it is clear that farmers have mastered the process of negotiating development and benefiting from it in ways that the originators of evaluations and impact assessments may be slow to recognise (Laurent 1996).

The outsider's role may ultimately be to step back and provide a level of support necessary to allow the combined process of planning and inventiveness to take place, not to introduce inappropriate or dogmatic blueprints (Richards 1985). If states and donors are really serious about turning over environmental management to local institutions and recognising local differences and complexity, we need to recognise farmers as planners, not simply performers acting out their repertoire of indigenous technical skills. The final issue, then, is what building materials, and what tools, and what outside help, will be needed to build up and maintain the new agro-ecologies which the Mossi, and farmers in other dryland situations, are slowly developing? A role does exist for modest external support to village organisations, in the form of both technical assistance and practical help and advice (Dumont 1986). Low-level, flexible support is even more urgent in marginal farming environments like the Central Plateau, where intensive and permanent cropping systems are still rare. But the challenge is to allow farmers to identify and create space for their own interests (Long and Villareal 1994), and to leave decision-making where it really belongs – firmly in the village.

Note

1. Richards is not keen to generalise the results of local studies to other times and places. But his work does make claims of wider currency, because it suggests ways to think about agriculture and farming life.

References

Atampugre, N. (1993), *Behind the Lines of Stone: The Social Impact of a Soil and Water Conservation Project in the Sahel*. Oxfam Publications, Oxford.

Batterbury, S.P.J. (1994), 'Conservation and community: local organisations and environmental management in Burkina Faso', *West London Papers in Environmental Studies* **2**, 13–26.

Batterbury, S.P.J. (1996), 'Planners or performers? Reflections on indigenous dryland farming in Northern Burkina Faso', *Agriculture and Human Values* **13**, 12–22.

Batterbury, S.P.J. (1998), 'Local environmental management, land degradation and the "Gestion des Terroirs" approach in West Africa: policies and pitfalls', *Journal of International Development* **10**, 871–98.

Batterbury, S.P.J. (2004), 'Within, and beyond, territories: a comparison of village land use management and livelihood diversification in Burkina Faso and southwest Niger', in Gausset, Q., Birch-Thomsen, T. and Whyte, M.A. (eds), *Beyond Territory and Scarcity: Social, Cultural and Political Aspects of Natural Resource Management Conflicts*. Nordic African Institute, Uppsala.

Batterbury, S.P.J. and **Forsyth, T.J.** (1999), 'Fighting back: human adaptations in marginal environments', *Environment* **41(6)**, 25–30.

Batterbury, S.P.J. and **Warren, A.** (eds) (2001), 'The African Sahel 25 years after the Great Drought', *Global Environmental Change* **11(1)**, 1–96.

Bebbington, A.J. (1994), 'Theory and relevance in indigenous agriculture: knowledge, agency and organization', in Booth, D. (ed.), *Rethinking Social Development: Theory, Research and Practice*. Longman, Harlow.

Bierschenk, T., Chauveau, J.-P. and **Olivier de Sardan, J.-P.** (eds) (2000), *Courtiers en développement: Les villages africains en quête de projets*. Editions Karthala, Paris.

Birba, T.A. (1993), *Le Droit foncier traditionnel: Evolution et impact sur les mesures CES/AGF. Etude de cas dans trois villages: (Malfoulou, Sourayalla, Tang-pella) de la Province de Bam, Burkina Faso*. Report to PATECORE Comité Interafricain d'Etudes Hydrauliques, Ouagadougou, Burkina Faso.

Bourdieu, P. (1990), *The Logic of Practice*. Polity Press, Oxford.

Busch, L. (1978), 'On understanding understanding: two views of communication', *Rural Sociology* **43(3)**, 458–73.

Carney, D. (ed.) (1998), *Sustainable Rural Livelihoods: What Contribution Can We Make?*, Department for International Development, London.

Cline-Cole, R. (1998), 'Knowledge claims and landscape: alternative views of the fuelwood–degradation nexus in northern Nigeria', *Environment and Planning D: Society and Space* **16**, 311–46.

Compaore, N. (1993), *L'Organisation de la production sur les champs personnels des femmes et sa destination: Etude de cas de quatre villages de la Province de Bam, Burkina Faso*. Report to PATECORE. Ouagadougou, Burkina Faso. Comité Interafricain d'Etudes Hydrauliques (CIEH), Ouagadougou.

Dumont, R. (1986), 'Lettre au Dr Kouchner' in Dumont, R., *Pour l'Afrique, j'accuse. Le journal d'un agronome au Sahel en voie de destruction*. Librairie Plon/Presses Pocket, Paris.

Engberg-Pedersen, L. (2003), *Endangering Development: Politics, Projects and Environment in Burkina Faso*. Praeger, Westport, Connecticut.

Escobar, A. (1995), *Encountering Development: The Making and Unmaking of the Third World*. Princeton University Press, Princeton, New Jersey.

Fairhead, J. and **Leach, M.** (1994), 'Declarations of difference', in Scoones, I. and Thompson, J.T. (eds), *Beyond Farmer First: Rural People's Knowledge, Agricultural Research and Extension Practice*. Intermediate Technology Publications, London.

Fairhead, J. and **Leach, M.** (1996), *Misreading the African Landscape: Society and Ecology in a Forest-Savanna Mosaic*. Cambridge University Press, Cambridge.

Fiske, A.P. (1990), *Structures of Social Life: The Four Elementary Forms of Human Relations*. The Free Press, New York.

Ford, R.E. (1982), 'Subsistence farming systems in semi-arid northern Yatenga, Upper Volta', unpublished PhD thesis, University of California, Riverside, California.

Gervais, R. (1987), 'Creating hunger: labour and agricultural policies in southern Mossi, 1919–1940', in Cordell, D. (ed.), *African Population and Capitalism: Historical Perspectives*. Westview, Boulder, Colorado.

Gray, L.C. (2002), 'Environmental policy, land rights, and conflict: rethinking community natural resource management programs in Burkina Faso', *Environment and Planning D: Society and Space* **20**, 167–82.

Ingram, K.T.M., Roncoli, M.C. and **Kirshen, P.H.** (2002), 'Opportunities and constraints for farmers of west Africa to use seasonal precipitation forecasts with Burkina Faso as a case study', *Agricultural Systems* **74(3)**, 331–49.

Kahrmann, C. (1997), 'Survival in the Sahel: problems with applying participatory methods', *D+C Development and Cooperation* **5**, 22–4.

Laurent, P.-J. (1996), *Le don comme ruse. Anthropologie de la coopération au développement chez les Mossi du Burkina Faso*. Karthala, Paris.

Leach, M. (1992), 'Women's crops in women's spaces: gender relations in Mende rice farming', in Croll, E. and Parkin, D. (eds), *Bush Base, Forest Farm: Culture, Environment, Development*. Routledge, London.

Long, N. (1992), 'Introduction', in Long, N. and Long, A. (eds), *The Battlefields of Knowledge: The Interlocking of Theory and Practice in Social Research and Development*. Routledge, London.

Long, N. and **Villareal, M.** (1994), 'The interweaving of knowledge and power in development interfaces', in Scoones, I. and Thompson, J.T. (eds), *Beyond Farmer First: Rural People's Knowledge, Agricultural Research and Extension Practice*. Intermediate Technology Publications, London.

Madge, C. and **Cline-Cole, R.** (1996), 'The West African forest zone in the European geographical imagination', *Geography* **353(81)**, 24–31.

Marchal, J.-Y. (1983), *Yatenga, Nord Haute-Volta: la dynamique d'un espace rurale soudano-sahélien*, Travaux et Documents de l'ORSTOM, no. 167. ORSTOM, Paris.

Mazzucato, V. and **Niemeijer, D.** (2000), 'The cultural economy of soil and water conservation: market principles and social networks in eastern Burkina Faso', *Development and Change* **31(3)**, 831–55.

Moore, S.F. (2001), 'The international production of authoritative knowledge: the case of drought-stricken West Africa', *Ethnography* **2(2)**, 161–90.

Mortimore, M. (1989), *Adapting to Drought: Farmers, Famines and Desertification in West Africa*. Cambridge University Press, Cambridge.

Mortimore, M.J. and **Adams, W.M.** (1999), *Working the Sahel: Environment and Society in Northern Nigeria*. Routledge, London.

Netting, R.M. (1993), *Smallholders, Householders: Farm Families and the Ecology of Intensive, Sustainable Agriculture*. Stanford University Press, Stanford, California.

Norgaard, R.B. (1994), *Development Betrayed: The End of Progress and a Coevolutionary View of the Future*. Routledge, London.

Olivier de Sardan, J.-P. (1995), *Anthropologie et développement, essai en socio-anthropologie du changement social*. Karthala, Paris.

Porter, D.J. (1995), 'Scenes from childhood: the homesickness of development discourses', in Crush, J. (ed.), *Power of Development*. Routledge, London.

Reij, C. (1994a), 'Building on traditions: the improvement of indigenous soil and water conservation techniques in the West African Sahel', in Napier, T.L., Camboni, S.M. and El-Swaify, S.A. (eds), *Adopting Conservation on the Farm: An International Perspective on the Socioeconomics of Soil and Water Conservation*. USA Soil and Water Conservation Society, Ankeby, Iowa.

Reij, C. (1994b), 'Soil and water conservation brings results', *Haramata* **25(9)**, 11–13.

Reij, C., **Tappan, G.** and **Belemvire, A.** (forthcoming), 'Changing land management practices and vegetation on the central plateau of Burkina Faso (1968–2002)', *Journal of Arid Environments*.

Richards, P. (1985), *Indigenous Agricultural Revolution: Ecology and Food Production in West Africa*. Hutchinson, London.

Richards, P. (1986), *Coping with Hunger: Hazard and Experiment in an African Rice Farming System*. Allen & Unwin, London.

Richards, P. (1987), 'Agriculture as a performance', Paper presented at 'Farmers and Agricultural Research: Complementary Methods', IDS, University of Sussex, 26–31 July (shorter version published in Chambers, R., Pacey, A. and

Thrupp, L.A. (eds) (1989), *Farmer First: Farmer Innovation and Agricultural Research*. Intermediate Technology Publications, London).

Richards, P. (1989), 'Doing what comes naturally: ecological inventiveness in African rice farming', in Johannes, R.E. (ed.), *Traditional Ecological Knowledge: a Collection of Essays*. IUCN, Gland.

Richards, P. (1993), 'Cultivation: knowledge or performance?', in Hobart, M. (ed.), *An Anthropological Critique of Development: The Growth of Ignorance*. Routledge, London.

Roose, E. and **Piot, J.** (1984), 'Runoff, erosion and soil fertility restoration on the Mossi Plateau (central Upper Volta)', in Walling, D.E., Foster, S.S.D. and Wurzel, P. (eds), *Challenges in African Hydrology and Water Resources*. IAHS Publication No. 144. IAHS Press, Wallingford.

Salmond, A. (1982), 'Theoretical landscapes: on a cross-cultural conception of knowledge', in Parkin, D.J. (ed.), *Semantic Anthropology*. ASA Monographs in Social Anthropology No. 22. Academic Press, London.

Sanders, J.H., Shapiro, B.I. and **Ramaswamy, S.** (1996), *The Economics of Agricultural Technology in Semi-arid Sub-Saharan Africa*. Johns Hopkins University Press, Baltimore, Maryland.

Scoones, I. and **Thompson, J.T.** (1994), 'Knowledge, power and agriculture: towards a theoretical understanding', in Scoones, I. and Thompson, J.T. (eds), *Beyond Farmer First: Rural People's Knowledge, Agricultural Research and Extension Practice*. Intermediate Technology Publications, London.

Scott, J.C. (1985), *Weapons of the Weak: Everyday Forms of Peasant Resistance*. Yale University Press, New Haven, Connecticut.

Simpson, B.M. (1999), *The Roots of Change: Human Behaviour and Agricultural Evolution in Mali*. Intermediate Technology Publications, London.

Toulmin, C. (1992), *Cattle, Women and Wells: Managing Household Survival in the Sahel*. Clarendon Press, Oxford.

Vlaar, J.C.J. and **Wessenlink, A.J.** (1990), *Aménagement de conservation des eaux et des sols par digues filtrantes: Expériments dans la Région de Rissiam, Burkina Faso, 1986–1989*, Bound Report, AFVP/Wageningen University/Comité Interafricain 1986–1990 d'Etudes Hydrauliques, Ouagadougou. Association Française des Volontaires du Progrès.

Watts, M.J. (1983), *Silent Violence: Food and Famine in Northern Nigeria*. University of California Press, Berkeley, California.

Watts, M.J. (1989), 'The Agrarian question in Africa: debating the crisis', *Progress in Human Geography* **13(1)**, 1–41.

CHAPTER 12

Conclusion: West African futures?

Reginald Cline-Cole and Elsbeth Robson

1 Introduction

The chapters making up this book have examined regional continuity and change at a range of scales and from a diverse range of perspectives: they have effectively explored various West African worlds and, more importantly, offered these for our scrutiny. In the process, authors have attempted to highlight recent and longer-term change and development, while interrogating contemporary debates on the transformations and evolutions underway. In West Africa, as elsewhere on the continent, the key challenge confronting the development planner or policy maker, or, indeed, the urban inhabitant or rural producer, is the basic one related to securing and sustaining a livelihood within the context of dynamic change, usually involving but not restricted to, globalisation and neo-liberalism. Ironically, this is precisely the case that regional policy makers, and their development partners, have *always* made, even if not necessarily in the same language, to justify development intervention in regional society and nature. It is the case, too, given the region's continued dependence on a bewildering array of natural resource-based livelihoods, and the myriad and complex links between rural and urban 'fields' of livelihood activity spheres or spaces, that environmental modification and change remain integral components of the regional livelihood context.

Whether we are talking about individual, household, community, national or regional livelihood, what emerges from the preceding pages, as from the wider literature, is the need to recognise the diversity of existing livelihood pathways. Just as important is the necessity to protect, even promote, the flexibility which allows, for example, a national economy to attempt to protect and improve its 'traditional' production base, even while investing in non-traditional export activity; or individuals to 'straddle' rural and urban existences or, alternatively, formal and informal sector lives. Looking back over the last five or so decades, the suggestion is that national economies have been subject to enormous stresses and strains from a range of sources, both internal and external, and that these peculiar forms of group or collective livelihoods have proved barely sustainable, although individual trajectories have differed somewhat in detail. Significantly, too, it is now widely accepted that a focus on the *formal* economy does not come anywhere near close enough to capturing or reflecting the diversity and overwhelming *in*formality which characterises much economic production and social reproduction. Similarly, in response to their own recent question 'have rural people become better-off over the last 20–30 years?', Toulmin and Guèye (2003) respond, of necessity, with nuanced answers: against the background of a long-term historical process of increasing economic and social differentiation, they note, 'there exists a diverse set of pathways, only some of which imply greater impoverishment [for] while some farm households have been getting better-off, others have not been so successful'. The situation is no less nuanced in urban West Africa. In rural, peri-urban and urban areas, of course, some social groups, for structural or conjunctural reasons, have been (or can be) particularly vulnerable to impoverishment. The same holds true, as we have seen in the preceding pages, for countries or national economies.

So what are the prospects for the sustainable development of West African livelihoods and economies?

2 *West African futures?*

In the inaugural volume in this series, Simon and Närman shied away from 'the temptation to indulge in crystal gazing in the name of some profound fiftieth anniversary, end-of-century or millennial insight' (1999: 273). And with good reason; such exercises are always fraught with untold risks, particularly in the rapidly changing livelihood context of a region like West Africa. We do feel, however, that it would be remiss of us not to offer a rapid review of the various 'future(s) scenarios', some of which have already been mentioned by chapter authors, that can be gleaned from the existing literature. These can be grouped into the following 'vision-types':

- gradual or incremental medium-term change;
- renascent (West) Africa or emerging regional market; and
- West Africa as anarchic/chaotic global future.

2.1 Gradual or incremental change scenarios

We owe this particular vision (or, more accurately, set of three visions) to the West African Long Term Perspectives Study (WALTPS) (OECD/CILSS 1998). The WALTPS view of West Africa's future is informed by the assumptions that the context for regional livelihoods will continue to be influenced by both rapid population growth and redistribution and exposure to fierce, sometimes unfair, economic competition in the world economy. Significantly, too, WALTPS sees the crisis of the post-colonial state as an opportunity for 'a new, specifically African type of political system . . . to see the light of day' (1998: 19); and argues that external competition encouraged by Adjustment and globalisation could well have positive local consequences, such as an expansion in food production and the diversification and 'professionalisation' of the private sector. On the strength of the foregoing, WALTPS identifies three possible 'scenarios' of West African futures in the medium term, but cautions that these are only possible paths, and that the list is not necessarily exhaustive.

2.1.1 Path 1: 'Business-as-usual' scenario

This first scenario posits a livelihood/development context of continuing heavy dependence on a little diversified overseas or export trade; urban bias leading to rapid urban growth and significant rural–urban (and coastwise) migratory movements and flows; increased illicit trade in drugs, counterfeit currency and money laundering which gradually replaces dwindling supplies of traditional export agriculture and mineral commodities; and aid agencies which restrict themselves largely to dire emergencies, while playing only a minimal development role.

Crudely put, it is a vision of the future which is based on 'principles' of uncontrolled free-marketeering, and which represents a poorly disguised stereotype of pre-Adjustment regional economies, and one which clearly raises the spectre of social unrest and economic and political breakdown. It is thus a scenario which makes an unashamed case for regional self-reliance built on the complementarity between coastal regions developing at a rapid rate and their neglected sahelian counterparts who find it increasingly difficult to generate export earnings.

2.1.2 Path 2: Combined free enterprise, good governance and strategic growth scenario

In contrast to that above, this is a vision of the future which represents a stereotype of successful Adjusting (or SAPping) regional economies characterised by:

- rational exploitation of comparative advantage;
- formation of new competitive non-traditional sectors outside the primary commodity sector;
- an improved business climate to be rewarded by an increase in domestic and foreign private investment;
- separation of the state from the market;
- reform of the state; and
- greater (re-)integration into the global economy and international community.

Not surprisingly, this is a vision which sees good and conscientious adjusters as the potential 'economic poles' which will drive the regional economy as a whole, while poorly adjusting or non-adjusting economies will be doomed to economic stagnation and relative marginalisation. It is to the vision's credit, however, that it recognises that the increased polarisation of wealth and economic activity which such a scenario implies could lead to increased discontent among marginalised individuals and groups and, ultimately, civil unrest and regional destabilisation.

2.1.3 Path 3: Regional integration and sustainable growth scenario

This, the third and final, scenario which WALTPS conjures up, is one in which 'deliberate, radical reform' is attempted and inward-orientation encouraged; it is a vision free from autarchic sentiments. It is a pro-globalisation future, which envisages the creation of 'a wide regional entity' for the express purpose of enabling 'small and medium-sized agricultural and handicraft enterprises . . . to compete in a regional market managed collectively by member countries' (p. 32). This scenario is reminiscent, both of a 'borderless' region in economic terms (with the enterprises identified operating across the region as a whole), and of a region in which 'internationalisation' will be given preference over narrow national concerns in political terms; and is seen by WALTPS as representing a 'rupture with the past', but one which could create tension in the short term as economic activity will initially contract before eventually expanding, and because living standards will not only improve over the long term, but will be experienced initially in the economic poles. This scenario 'is the only one that suggests a truly regional pattern of growth and seeks to avoid excessive tensions within the region that could become violent' (p. 33).

Overall, it is a set of really nuanced viewpoints of regional dynamics and change which WALTPS brings to bear on the task of 'foretelling or predicting the region's future'. Thus although there are the inevitable generalisations and simplifications, one gets the impression that the task is approached with a lot of seriousness. Furthermore, WALTPS bases its projections on a wide-ranging assessment – and interpretation – of change and dynamics already underway, as well as on a recognition of the possibility/probability of multiple outcomes.

2.2 African renaissance/emerging market futures

The idea of an African renaissance or rebirth is one which is probably most readily associated with Nelson Mandela and his successor Thabo Mbeki, although an increasing number of African and non-African leaders and institutions did also adopt or invoke the notion. Visions of a renascent (West) African future start with a frank acknowledgement of the region's troubled post-colonial past, before going on to argue that these experiences can be considered to have laid the foundation for a bright(er) future of peace, prosperity and development: that in a number of significant ways (West) Africa's fortunes may well have 'turned the corner' or 'bottomed-out', and were finally on the road to improvement. It is this, the feeling/belief that the long years of stagnation and crisis were to be replaced by a period of progress and growth/expansion, which gives the vision its distinctiveness.

In particular, this vision of a renascent or reborn (West) Africa sees major advances in the areas of democratisation/conflict resolution and economic reform as laying the foundations for the region's re-integration into a globalising world economy. Thus the second wave of democratisation, as well as the success of regional conflict resolution (both of which have been discussed by authors in this volume) can be cited here as evidence of this rebirth (Raheem 1998); as could the argument, advanced by adjustment proponents, that countries which both avoided conflict and pursued institutional and economic reforms recommended by the IFIs, grew much faster than those which did not. The reinstatement of peace and a return to democracy in Nigeria was also considered to augur well for the region as a whole.

Within this wider context, a group of some 300 West African entrepreneurs have been 'selling' their region and its future to potential investors and partners in development as sub-Saharan Africa's 'newest emerging market' and 'largest trading bloc' (Enterprise Network, undated). The future this network of entrepreneurs paints is of a region ready, able and willing to participate in a meaningful way in a brave new neo-liberal and rapidly globalising world. It is a future which is bright and rosy, one which highlights the region's potential for profit-generation and emphasises the existence of regional stock markets and stock exchanges; and plans to establish a single West African currency and monetary zone. It is also a vision which foregrounds an assumed common approach to fighting crime such as drug trafficking and money laundering within the region, as it does progress in the areas of democracy and economic liberalisation.

2.3 *Anarchic, chaotic global future*

The third and final futures scenario is an apocalyptic one, which is probably best represented by Robert Kaplan's 'The Coming Anarchy', a vision which has already been subjected to critical review in Chapters 5 and 6, and which elicits a scenario similar to, but considerably worse than the WALTPS business-as-usual scenario above in its unremitting pessimism (Kaplan 1994). It is a scenario which Olukoshi, for example (see Chapter 2) has interpreted as a thinly-disguised invitation for the re-colonisation of the region, and one which, unlike the WALTPS scenarios, makes no allowance for multiple outcomes and strips regional inhabitants of all agency in reversing the trend of economic decline and social fragmentation which represent such serious threats to regional livelihoods and development.

3 *Conclusions*

Bearing in mind our earlier reference to the wisdom of exercising reticence when it comes to 'crystal gazing', we would like, at this point, to take the coward's way out and ask readers to reflect on these various versions of West Africa's future, and to decide for themselves which they consider most likely to materialise; which scenario they consider most plausible or realistic. We would point out, however, that many of the chapter authors, and we ourselves, would recommend a healthy scepticism about discourses of crisis which appear to have the sole or primary purpose of justifying unreconstructed neo-liberalism. In reality, as several of the chapters show, a variety of outcomes, rather than a single vision, are likely to unfold in the future, in much the same way that they have always done.

To borrow from Bradnock and Williams (2002: 272), in a sister volume in this series, '[i]n highlighting the dynamism of . . . [West Africa's] contemporary patterns of socio-economic change and development, their interleaving with global development issues as well as their rootedness in local societies, we hope that this book will be of relevance beyond the . . . [West African] region with which it is primarily concerned'.

References

Bradnock, R. and **Williams, G.** (2002), 'Conclusion: Development in South Asia, Ground-truthing constructions of regional change', in Bradnock, R. and Williams, G. (eds), *South Asia in a Globalising World.* Prentice Hall, Harlow.

Department for International Development (DFID) (2000), *Making Globalisation Work for the World's Poor: An Introduction to the UK Government's Paper on International Development.* DFID, London.

Enterprise Network (n.d.)

Kaplan, R. (1994), 'The coming anarchy: a premonition of the future', *Atlantic Monthly* **273(2)**, 44–76.

CILSS/OECD (1998), *Preparing for the Future. A Vision of West Africa in the Year 2020. West Africa Long-Term Perspective Study,* Cour, J.-M. and Snrech, S. (eds), Club du Sahel, Paris.

Raheem, T.A. (1998), 'Renascent West Africa', *Democracy and Development* **1**, 36.

Simon, D. and **Närman, A.** (1999), 'Conclusions and prospects', in Simon, D. and Närman, A. (eds), *Development as Theory and Practice.* Longman, Harlow.

Toulmin, C. and **Guèye, B.** (2003), 'How will West African countries meet the MDGs?', in Satterthwaite, D. (ed.), *The MDG and Local Processes: Hitting the Target or Missing the Point*? IIED, London.

Index

For Product Safety Concerns and Information please contact our EU representative GPSR@taylorandfrancis.com
Taylor & Francis Verlag GmbH, Kaufingerstraße 24, 80331 München, Germany

www.ingramcontent.com/pod-product-compliance
Ingram Content Group UK Ltd.
Pitfield, Milton Keynes, MK11 3LW, UK
UKHW020017200926
475702UK00014B/1929
* 9 7 8 0 1 3 0 2 5 9 4 9 3 *